February 11–15, 2012
Seattle, WA, USA

Association for
Computing Machinery

Advancing Computing as a Science & Profession

CSCW'12

Proceedings of the ACM 2012 Conference on

Computer Supported Cooperative Work

Sponsored by:

SIGCHI

Supported by:

IBM Research and Google

Volume 1

Association for
Computing Machinery

Advancing Computing as a Science & Profession

The Association for Computing Machinery
2 Penn Plaza, Suite 701
New York, New York 10121-0701

ISBN: 978-1-4503-1086-4 (Digital)

ISBN: 978-1-4503-1936-2 (Print Vol. 1)

Additional copies may be ordered prepaid from:

ACM Order Department
PO Box 30777
New York, NY 10087-0777, USA

Phone: 1-800-342-6626 (USA and Canada)
+1-212-626-0500 (Global)
Fax: +1-212-944-1318
E-mail: acmhelp@acm.org
Hours of Operation: 8:30 am – 4:30 pm ET

ACM Order Number: 612121

Printed in the USA

From the Conference Co-Chairs

We welcome you to the ACM 2012 Conference on Computer Supported Cooperative Work!

CSCW 2012 offers the opportunity to hear talks about the latest research results in the field of collaboration and collaborative technologies and to meet researchers and practitioners working on these topics from around the world.

The conference program embraces a variety of perspectives, reflecting how collaboration permeates different aspects of people's work, social, and (increasingly) political lives. This diversity of perspectives is mirrored by geographic diversity among contributors. Following the conference last year in China, CSCW 2012 witnesses an increase in the number of researchers from outside North America contributing to the technical program.

The CSCW 2012 program retains the richly articulated structure of previous conferences in this series. This program of workshops, papers, notes, panels, demonstrations, videos, interactive posters, and forward-looking horizon papers captures both the breadth and depth of the research in this field. At the same time the program offers an opportunity to reflect on the past; a special session discusses the two most-cited papers from CSCW 1992 and CSCW 2002 and the influence of this research on the development of our field.

This is the largest CSCW conference ever. More papers, notes, and interactive posters were submitted and more were accepted. The percentage of accepted papers and notes was also higher, but we believe the conference has retained the exceptionally high quality for which these conferences are known. CSCW 2012 introduces an innovative review process for papers and notes that includes two review phases intended to improve the quality of the contributions. This experiment was successful, and this review process is likely to be adopted in future conferences.

A conference the size of CSCW requires a huge amount of planning. There is a large team behind the scenes carrying out this work: chairs with different responsibilities have been organizing venues, deadlines, reviews, and logistics for more than a year. The success of the CSCW 2012 is due to the tireless efforts of the chairs, the associate chairs and paper reviewers, and the student volunteers: we deeply appreciate their commitment and dedication. It is also dependent on the financial support we received from our generous sponsors, and we all owe them our gratitude.

We hope you enjoy CSCW 2012 and its technical program.

Steven Poltrock
CSCW 2012 Conference Co-chair

Carla Simone
CSCW 2012 Conference Co-chair
University of Milano-Biccoca

From the Program Chairs

Constraint can spur creativity. Approaching the 26th anniversary of the CSCW conference, we were asked to move the submission deadline two months earlier to reduce the reviewing conflict with CHI 2012. In response, we used the additional time to innovate and to increase participation while maintaining or increasing quality, by allowing authors to revise and resubmit their papers and notes. Conference attendees and proceedings readers will ultimately assess the outcome, but overall the feedback from associate chairs, reviewers and authors has been very positive.

Submissions increased 57% from CSCW 2011 to a record 290 papers and 125 notes. We increased the program committee to 67 associate chairs (ACs) to handle them; 21 were women and 20 were from outside North America. They comprised representatives from computer science, social media and social networks, psychology, anthropology, software engineering, management, and design. Fifty were from universities.

Our process most resembled a journal special issue, with a submission deadline, a team of four reviewers, and one revision cycle under a firm time constraint (in this case five weeks). Each submission was assigned to two committee members, designated AC-Coordinator and AC-Reviewer. Each AC assigned one external reviewer. In the first round, each paper or note was blind-reviewed by the AC-Reviewer and the two external reviewers. Reviewers assessed the likelihood that it could be revised within one month to be acceptable. Based on the outcomes, submissions were considered 'conditional accept' (CA, 8.7%), 'revise-resubmit' (RR, 46.5%) or 'reject' (44.8%). In general, papers that received one or more positive assessments were offered the opportunity to revise.

Papers that had no positive assessment in the first round were rejected. We based this decision on an analysis of CSCW 2011 data, which revealed that submissions that did not get an advocate in the initial reviewing had 0% chance of acceptance. Sixty percent of CSCW 2011 submissions had no advocate, compared to 45% of CSCW 2012 submissions. The difference is that the CSCW 2012 submissions had a month in which they could be improved. By immediately rejecting the 45% that had no chance, we streamlined and focused the process, and reduced the number of reviews per submission despite the revision cycle.

The AC Coordinator relied on the reviews in providing written guidance to authors on how to revise RRs. Authors of RR and CA submissions had five weeks to prepare a revision and an explanation of how they had addressed reviewer concerns. Resubmissions of RRs underwent a full second review from the same four-reviewer team; most CAs were checked by just one AC. Reviewing teams were strongly encouraged to resolve decisions prior to the program committee meeting and indeed, only 6% of initial submissions had to be discussed in the meeting.

The program committee split into two subgroups followed by a plenary session to make the final decisions. 127 papers and 37 notes, 39.5% of initial submissions, reached acceptable quality through revision. This is almost twice the number presented in any previous CSCW, in part due to record submissions. ACs and reviewers nominated papers and notes for consideration for Best Paper awards; 4 were selected, with 17 awarded Honorable Mention.

The accepted work represents diverse topics. Relatively new topics for CSCW include crowdsourcing, civic engagement, and social media; more traditional CSCW topics include distributed work, coordination, ethnography, and collaborative software development.

This collaborative effort was an example of computer supported cooperative work. The entire CSCW community provided input throughout the process—many ideas and changes came from outside of the committee. Committee members had to adapt to new ways of working. Our analysis indicates that the work required of reviewers and associate chairs did not exceed that of past years, and authors benefited from two rounds of feedback from committed ACs and reviewers.

Our goal was to maintain a high quality threshold while enabling more papers to reach that threshold. We believe there are many benefits to a review process with more opportunity for constructive interaction between reviewers and authors. Authors benefit by learning more about the CSCW culture, and by producing papers that are better than they could have produced on their own. Reviewers benefit by seeing their work lead to improved papers. The community benefits, because more of its members are successful at producing high quality research each year.

As a community, we must consider new ways to assess conference quality—when a larger volume of high quality work is produced, older metrics no longer hold. Considering the fraction of submitted work that is of low quality to be a measure of conference quality is backwards. We need new measures of process quality and the resulting quality of accepted work. Through continued innovation, CSCW will remain the top venue for leading edge research on collaboration and technology. As with any new process, mistakes were made and much was learned. We look forward to participating as community members in ongoing innovation.

The other technical tracks contribute immeasurably to the program. A record number of interactive posters will be presented. The 14 workshops drew a remarkable number of submissions. With demos, horizon, panels, videos, special sessions, and three plenary keynotes, CSCW 2012 is a great start to the second quarter-century of the CSCW conference.

Jonathan Grudin
Program Co-Chair
Microsoft Research

Gloria Mark
Program Co-Chair
University of California, Irvine

John Riedl
Program Co-Chair
University of Minnesota

CSCW 2012 Table of Contents

CSCW 2012 Table of Contents

CSCW 2012 Table of Contents

CSCW 2012 Table of Contents

CSCW 2012 Table of Contents

CSCW 2012 Table of Contents

CSCW 2012 Table of Contents

CSCW 2012 Table of Contents

CSCW 2012 Table of Contents

CSCW 2012 Table of Contents

CSCW 2012 Table of Contents

CSCW 2012 Conference Organization

Conference Co-chairs	Steve Poltrock Carla Simone *(University of Milano-Bicocca)*
Treasurer	Stephen Hayne *(Colorado State University)*
Papers & Notes Co-chairs	John Riedl *(University of Minnesota)* Gloria Mark *(University of California, Irvine)* Jonathan Grudin *(Microsoft Research)*
Panels Co-chairs	Myriam Lewkowicz *(University of Technology of Troyes)* Michael Twidale *(University of Illinois)*
Videos Co-chairs	Pernille Bjorn *(IT University of Copenhagen)* Matthew Bietz *(University of Washington)*
CSCW Horizon Co-chairs	Gilly Leshed *(Cornell University)* Monica Divitini *(Norwegian University of Science and Technology)*
Workshops Co-chairs	Darren Gergle *(Northwestern University)* M. Antonietta Grasso *(Xerox Research Centre Europe)*
Posters Co-chairs	Cecilia Aragon *(University of Washington)* Hilda Tellioglu *(Vienna University of Technology)*
Demonstrations Co-chairs	Danyel Fisher *(Microsoft Research)* Luigina Ciolfi *(University of Limerick)*
Doctoral Colloquium Co-chairs	Leysia Palen *(University of Colorado)* Dave Randall *(University of Siegen)*
Madness Co-chairs	Sadat Shami *(IBM Research)* Jeff Nichols *(IBM Research)*
Publications Co-chairs	Taemie Kim *(Accenture Technology Labs)* Wendy Ju *(California College of Arts and Stanford University)*
Proceedings Co-chairs	Stacey Scott *(University of Waterloo)* Gina Venolia *(Microsoft Research)*
Publicity Co-chairs	Hideaki Kuzuoka *(University of Tsukuba)* Volker Wulf *(University of Siegen and Fraunhofer FIT)* Bin Hu *(Lanzhou University and Birmingham City University)* Joe McCarthy *(University of Washington, Bothell)*
Industry Liaison Co-chairs	Pamela Hinds *(Stanford University)* John Tang *(Microsoft Research)* Jeremy Birnholtz *(Cornell University)*
A/V Computing Co-chairs	Brian Meyers *(Microsoft)* Steve Abrams *(University of California, Irvine)*
Webmasters and Graphic Design Co-chairs	Victoria Schwanda Sosik *(Cornell University)* Dan Cosley *(Cornell University)*
Social Interaction Co-chairs	Sean Goggins *(Drexel University)* Elizabeth Churchill *(Yahoo!)*

Student Volunteers Co-chairs Norman Makoto Su *(University College Dublin)*
Alex Thayer *(University of Washington)*

Local Arrangements Co-chairs Mark Handel *(Boeing Research & Technology)*
Charlotte Lee *(University of Washington)*

Conference Managers John Lateulere *(IMS-Solutions)*
Joanne Lateulere *(IMS-Solutions)*

Associate Chairs Mark Ackerman *(University of Michigan)*
Daniel Avrahami *(Intel Research)*
Jakob Bardram *(IT University of Copenhagen)*
Jeffrey Bardzell *(Indiana University)*
Shaowen Bardzell *(Indiana University)*
Tora Bikson *(Rand Corporation)*
Jeanette Blomberg *(IBM Research)*
Geoff Bowker *(University of Pittsburgh)*
Barry Brown *(University of California, San Diego)*
Amy Bruckman *(Georgia Institute of Technology)*
Sheelagh Carpendale *(University of Calgary)*
Ed Chi *(Google)*
Luigina Ciolfi *(University of Limerick)*
Noshir Contractor *(Northwestern University)*
Gregorio Convertino *(PARC)*
Dan Cosley *(Cornell University)*
Scott Counts *(Microsoft Research)*
Ed Cutrell *(Microsoft Research)*
Giorgio De Michelis *(University of Milano-Bicocca)*
Alan Dennis *(Indiana University)*
Nicolas Ducheneaut *(PARC)*
Tom Finholt *(University of Michigan)*
Danyel Fisher *(Microsoft Research)*
Andrea Forte *(Drexel University)*
Darren Gergle *(Northwestern University)*
Carl Gutwin *(University of Saskatchewan)*
Tomoo Inoue *(University of Tsukuba)*
Steve Jackson *(University of Michigan)*
Wendy Ju *(California College of the Arts)*
Jofish Kaye *(Nokia)*
John King *(University of Michigan)*
Michael Koch *(Bundeswehr University Munich)*
Bob Kraut *(Carnegie Mellon University)*
Kari Kuutti *(University of Oulo)*
Hideaki Kuzuoka *(University of Tsukuba)*
Cliff Lampe *(Michigan State University)*
Elizabeth Lawley *(Rochester Institute of Technology)*
Charlotte Lee *(University of Washington)*
Catherine C. Marshall *(Microsoft Research)*
Joe McCarthy *(University of Washington, Bothell)*
David McDonald *(University of Washington)*
Hideyuki Nakanishi *(Osaka University)*
Bonnie Nardi *(University of California, Irvine)*
Les Nelson *(PARC)*
Christine Neuwirth *(Carnegie Mellon University)*

Associate Chairs (continued)

Jeff Nichols *(IBM Research)*
Sergio Ochoa *(University of Chile)*
Gary Olson *(University of California, Irvine)*
Judy Olson *(University of California, Irvine)*
Leysia Palen *(University of Colorado)*
Volkmar Pipek *(University of Kaiserslautern)*
Dave Randall *(Manchester Metropolitan University)*
Madhu Reddy *(The Pennsylvania State University)*
mc schraefel *(University of Southampton)*
Frank Shipman *(Texas A&M University)*
Chengzheng Sun *(Nanyang Technical University)*
Stephanie Teasley *(University of Michigan)*
Hilda Tellioglu *(Vienna University of Technology)*
Loren Terveen *(University of Minnesota)*
John Thomas *(IBM Research)*
Michael Twidale *(University of Illinois)*
Doug Vogel *(City University of Hong Kong)*
Dennis Wixon *(Microsoft)*
Volker Wulf *(University of Siegen)*
Naomi Yamashita *(NTT)*
Chen Zhao *(Microsoft Research)*

CSCW 2012 Reviewers

Jose Abdelnour Nocera
Joanna Abraham
Steve Abrams
Lada Adamic
Eytan Adar
Ana Afonso
Agustina Agustina
Ban Al-Ani
Morgan Ames
Margarita Anastassova
Tariq Andersen
Paul André
Judd Antin
Pedro Antunes
Cecilia Aragon
Mark Ashdown
Gabriela Avram
Maribeth Back
Brian Bailey
Aruna Balakrishnan
Elizabeth Bales
Rafael Ballagas
Nelson Baloian
Christoph Bartneck
Maria Cecilia Bastarrica
Scott Bateman
Eric Baumer
Jessica Bayliss
Richard Beckwith
Andrew Begel
Bo Begole
Marek Bell
Steve Benford
Hrvoje Benko
Nicholas Berente
Mark Bergman
Tony Bergstrom
Michael Bernstein
Qingqing Bi
Matthew Bietz
Christian Bird
Jeremy Birnholtz
Konina Biswas
Pernille Bjorn
Mark Blythe
Alexander Boden
Susanne Bødker
Ross Bohner
Alan Borning
Nathan Bos
Claus Bossen
Paolo Bottoni
Erin Bradner
Susan Brennan
Sue Brown
Jed Brubaker
A.J. Brush
Nick Bryan-Kinns
Simon Buckingham Shum
Moira Burke
Georg Buscher
Monika Buscher
Brian Butler
Keith Butler
Ayse Buyuktur
Dara Byrne
Pedro Campos
Matthew Canton
Xiang Cao
Erin Carroll
John Carroll
Julia Cassim
Marcelo Cataldo
Melissa Cefkin
Jilin Chen
Yunan Chen
Zebin Chen
Coye Cheshire
Marshini Chetty
Alvin Chin
Yoram Chisik
Elizabeth Churchill
Luigina Ciolfi
Torkil Clemmensen
Deborah Coleman
Kay Connelly
Eric Cook
Michael Cooke
Lisa Cowan
Lorrie Cranor
Justin Cranshaw
Jeff Cummings
Aaron Curtis
Laura Dabbish
Laurie Damianos
Catalina Danis
Scott Davidoff
Munmun De Choudhury
Anna De Liddo
David De Roure
Cleidson de Souza
David Dearman
Katie Derthick
Sebastian Deterding
Prasun Dewan
Nicholas Diakopoulos
Margaret Dickey-Kurdziolek
Xianghua Ding
Betsy DiSalvo
Alan Dix
Jonathan Donner
Matthew Easterday
Christopher Egert
Hironori Egi
Kate Ehrlich
Margaret Elliott
Nicole Ellison
David England
Ingrid Erickson
Thomas Erickson
JD Eveland
Shelly Farnham
Jesus Favela
Andrew Fiore
Jerry Fjermestad
Kristin Fontichiaro
Jodi Forlizzi
Luis Francisco-Revilla
Christopher Frauenberger
Jeana Frost
Susan Fussell
Jolene Galegher
Alex Games
Monica Garfield
Mike Gartrell
William Gaver
Werner Geyer
Eric Gilbert
Sean Goggins
Jennifer Golbeck
Gene Golovchinsky

Amy Gonzales
Victor Gonzalez
Sam Gosling
Nicholas Graham
Saul Greenberg
Christian Greiffenhagen
Andrea Grimes Parker
Martin Groen
Mark Gross
Tovi Grossman
Ning Gu
Luis Guerrero
Xitong Guo
David Gurzick
Zoltan Gyongyi
Malcolm Hall
Joachim Halse
Christine Halverson
Keith Hampton
Mark Handel
Sean Hannan
Benjamin Hanrahan
Franklin Harper
richard harper
W. Michelle Harris
Chris Harrison
Steve Harrison
Drew Harry
Björn Hartmann
Andrea Hartzler
Kirstie Hawkey
Gillian Hayes
William Hazlewood
Brent Hecht
Libby Hemphill
Valeria Herskovic
Morten Hertzum
Jan Hess
Clint Heyer
Pamela Hinds
Graeme Hirst
Bernie Hogan
Lichan Hong
Gary Hsieh
Hao-Wei Hsieh
David Huffaker
Jina Huh
Susanne Hupfer
Amy Hurst
Claudia-Lavinia Ignat
Michita Imai
Kori Inkpen
Rachael Ip
Lilly Irani
Ellen Isaacs
Petra Isenberg
Brian Jackson
Stephen Jacobs
Sarah Javanmardi
Aditya Johri
M. Cameron Jones
Sasa Junuzovic
Yoram Kalman
Ece Kamar
Anne Marie Kanstrup
Victor Kaptelinin
Karrie Karahalios
Jonas Karlsson
Kostas Karpouzis
Arvind Karunakaran
Andrea Kavanaugh
Michelle Kazmer
Wendy Kellogg
Crowston Kevin
Vijay Khatri
Julie Kientz
Sara Kiesler
Juho Kim
Matthew King
David Kirk
Lorraine Kisselburgh
Aniket Kittur
Cory Knobel
Gwendolyn Kolfschoten
Shin'ichi Konomi
Joseph Konstan
Timothy Koschmann
Gueorgi Kossinets
Adam Kramer
Travis Kriplean
Steinar Kristoffersen
Haewoon Kwak
Peter Lachenmaier
Carl Lagoze
Shyong Lam
Anthony LaMarca
Kristin Lamberty
Brian Landry
Tessa Lau
Christopher Le Dantec
Yoon Suk Lee
Julio Cesar Leite
Thomas Lento
Paul Leonardi
Gilly Leshed
Jim Levin
Sarah Lewis
Brian Lim
Jason Linder
Siân Lindley
Janne Lindqvist
Silvia Lindtner
Heather Lipford
Greg Little
Sophia Liu
Nicholas Lockwood
Danielle Lottridge
Stephan Lukosch
Kurt Luther
Wolfram Luther
Wayne Lutters
Leilah Lyons
Allan MacLean
Anmol Madan
Rui Madeira
Scott Mainwaring
Julie Maitland
Janet Malkovich
Lena Mamykina
Osama Mansour
Wendy March
Adam Marcus
Kai Pan Mark
Paul Marshall
David Martin
Maria Antonia Martínez-Carreras
Paul Marty
Alice Marwick
Tara Matthews
Tom Mattson
David McArthur
David McDonald
Indrani Medhi
Qiaozhu Mei
Helena Mentis
Vera Michalchik
David Millen
Rob Miller
Zara Mirmalek
Jonas Moll

Pascal Molli
Andres Monroy-Hernandez
Troels Mønsted
Alberto Moran
Jonathan Morgan
Daniel Morris
Christian Mueller-Tomfelde
Claudia Müller
Sean Munson
Brad Myers
Mor Naaman
Carman Neustaedter
Mark Newman
Jeffrey Nickerson
Kazushi Nishimoto
Sylvie Noël
Leena Norros
Chris North
Nora O Murchu
Hiroaki Ogata
Corinna Ogonowski
Kenton O'Hara
Masaya Okada
Jacki O'Neill
Michael Oren
Felipe Ortega
Babajide Osatuyi
Florian Ott
Antti Oulasvirta
Tyler Pace
Leysia Palen
Katherine Panciera
Tapan Parikh
Sameer Patil
Sharoda Paul
Thomas Pederson
Samuli Pekkola
Jorge Peña
James Pennebaker
Alex Pentland
Manuel Perez-Quinones
Daniel Perry
Mark Perry
Bruce Phillips
Jeffrey Pierce
Emmanuel Pietriga
Niels Pinkwart
José Pino
Volkmar Pipek
Steven Poltrock
Scott Poole
Sarah Poon
Michael Pope
Vitaliy Popov
Tom Postmes
Wanda Pratt
Reid Priedhorsky
Michael Prilla
Yan Qu
Emilee Rader
Andrew Raij
David Randall
Rebecca Randell
Yolanda Rankin
Rabindra Ratan
Janet Read
Stuart Reeves
Tim Reichling
Yuqing Ren
Paul Resnick
David Ribes
Alexander Richter
Julie Rico
Romain Robbes
Lionel Robert
Toni Robertson
Jennifer Rode
Steven Rohall
Betsy Rolland
John Rooksby
Daniela Rosner
Mary Beth Rosson
Dana Rotman
Mark Rouncefield
Evelyn Rozanski
Karen Ruhleder
Daisuke Sakamoto
Rahul Sami
Aleksandra Sarcevic
Anita Sarma
Steve Sawyer
Karen Schneider
Douglas Schuler
Till Schümmer
Stacey Scott
Taylor Scott
Shilad Sen
Burr Settles
Chirag Shah
N. Sadat Shami
David Shamma
Bin Shao
Patrick Shih
Katie Shilton
Irina Shklovski
David Sirkin
Marc Smith
Timothy Sohn
Diane Sonnenwald
Carsten Sorensen
Patricia Spence
Saurabh Srivastava
Kate Starbird
Charles Steinfield
Igor Steinmacher
Gunnar Stevens
Cristiano Storni
Susan Straus
Simone Stumpf
Fred Stutzman
Bongwon Suh
David Sun
Ja-Young Sung
Elisabeth Sylvan
Leila Takayama
Anthony Tang
Charlotte Tang
John Tang
Alex Taylor
Jaime Teevan
Hilda Tellioglu
Monica Tentori
Alexander Thayer
Jennifer Thom-Santelli
Stella Tian
Marianne Tolar
Catalina Toma
Bill Tomlinson
Michael Toomim
Cristen Torrey
Quan Tran
Manfred Tscheligi
Manas Tungare
Heli Väätäjä
Giuseppe Valetto
Tiffany Veinot
Theresa Velden
Gina Venolia
Janet Vertesi
Iris Vessey

Sarah Vieweg
Jesse Vig
Juergen Vogel
Stephen Voida
Mihaela Vorvoreanu
Ina Wagner
Patrick Wagstrom
Bruce Walker
Jing Wang
Peter Wardrip
Rick Wash
Mark Weal
Anne Weibert
Suzanne Weisband
Taylor Wells
Chunhua Weng
Linda Werner
Torben Wiedenhoefer
Andrea Wiggins
Uffe Wiil
Amanda Williams
Dmitri Williams
Megan Winget
Jill Woelfer
Allison Woodruff
Susan Wyche
Tina Yan
Sarita Yardi
Nick Yee
Jude Yew
Y. Connie Yuan
Masahide Yuasa
Mark Zachry
Massimo Zancanaro
Jun Zhang
Qiping Zhang
Xi Zhang
Shengdong Zhao
Phil Zhou
Xiaomu Zhou
John Zimmerman
Alejandro Zunino

CSCW 2012 Sponsor & Supporters

Sponsor: SIGCHI

Hero: NSF

Champion: Microsoft Research

Benefactors: SMART™

Contributors: GRAND — Graphisme, animation et nouveaux médias / Graphics, Animation and New Media; HUAWEI; NOKIA

Supporters: IBM Research; Google

Keynote Talk

The Penguin and the Leviathan: Towards Cooperative Human Systems Design

Yochai Benkler
Harvard Law School & Berkman Center for Internet and Society
Cambridge, MA, USA
yochai_benkler@harvard.edu

Abstract

A decade ago, Wikipedia burst into a world not ready to comprehend it. Thousands of people cooperating effectively, without price signals to offer "incentives" or managerial hierarchy to direct efforts, was an impossibility. And yet, it moves. And as it moved it combined with a deep shift across many disciplines, from biology and neuroscience to organizational sociology, experimental economics, and social psychology to paint a very different view of who we are as human beings. Slowly pushing back against decades of ever-refined analyses based on self-interested rationality, we begin to see that we are diverse beings; that a majority of us responds cooperatively to cooperative settings—we tend to treat well those who have treated us well, rather than take advantage of them; we tend to do what we think is right and fair, when it is clear in the setting what that is; we experience empathy, and it makes us more generous and trustworthy; we experience solidarity with others, and that makes us contributed more willingly to the group's goals. Moreover, explicit payments, the touchstone of mechanism design under universal self-interested rationality, turns out to have a much more complex relationship with motivation than simple addition. All this work in basic behavioral sciences combines with observations from organizational sociology, political science, and management studies combines with social software to provide an increasingly better articulated basis on which to develop a field of cooperative human systems design.

Categories & Subject Descriptors: H.5.3. [**Information Interfaces and Presentation**]: Group and Organization Interfaces – *collaborative computing, web-based interaction*, K.4.1 [**Computers and Society**]: Public Policy Issues, K.4.2 [**Computers and Society**]: Social Issues.

General Terms: Design, Economics, Human Factors.

Bio

Yochai Benkler is the Berkman Professor of Entrepreneurial Legal Studies at Harvard, and faculty co-director of the Berkman Center for Internet and Society. Since the 1990s he has played a part in characterizing the role of information commons and decentralized collaboration to innovation, information production, and freedom in the networked economy and society. His books include The Wealth of Networks: How social production transforms markets and freedom (Yale University Press 2006), which won academic awards from the American Political Science Association, the American Sociological Association, and the McGannon award for social and ethical relevance in communications. His work is socially engaged, winning him the Electronic Frontier Foundation's Pioneer Award (2007), Public Knowledge's IP3 Award (2006), and the Ford Foundation Visionaries Award (2011). It is also anchored in the realities of markets, having been cited as "perhaps the best work yet about the fast moving, enthusiast-driven Internet" by the Financial Times and named best business book about the future by Strategy and Business (2006). Benkler has served in an advisory capacity for a range of communications and intellectual property regulators and policy makers at the national and international levels. His work is freely available at benkler.org.

CSCW'12, February 11–15, 2012, Seattle, Washington, USA.
ACM 978-1-4503-1086-4/12/02.

Keynote Talk

Broader Impacts: Research You Can Use

Judith Olson
Don Bren School of Information and Computer Sciences
University of California, Irvine
Irvine, CA, USA
jsolson@uci.edu

Abstract
A number of threads of thought have come together recently having to do with how we make our research useable and useful to the world. One thread is inspired by a movement in medicine called Clinical Translational Science in which funding is given to researchers to translate basic research into guidelines, treatments, and regimens that clinicians can use. A second thread arose in reflecting about our own recent work in which we translated a theory about what makes for good distance collaboration into an online assessment tool and administered it to hundreds of people involved in remote collaboration. Upon completion of the assessment, each participant immediately gets a personalized report on the strengths of their collaboration, the challenges, and what to do about it. We get the data, and they get the help. These two threads point to making a difference, having broader impact.

In this talk I will review some ways we can have an impact, both directly to people, through design practice (our clinicians), and via a myriad of other tools while doing good research. I encourage us all to spend more energy on having more direct effects on the world in which we live.

Categories & Subject Descriptors: H.1.2 [**Models and Principles**]: User/Machine Systems – *human factors;* H.5.3. [**Information Interfaces and Presentation**]: Group and Organization Interfaces – *asynchronous interaction, collaborative computing*; K.4.3. [**Computers and Society**]: Organizational Impacts - *computer-supported cooperative work*

General Terms: Design, Experimentation, Human Factors.

Bio
Judith Olson is the Bren Professor of Information and Computer Sciences in the Informatics Department at the UC Irvine, with courtesy appointments in the School of Social Ecology and the Merage School of Business. For 20 years, she has focused on distributed teams, summaries of which are found in her most cited paper, "Distance Matters," (Olson & Olson, 2000), in her key theoretical contribution in the book *Scientific Collaboration on the Internet*, and her upcoming book, *Working Together Apart*. She has studied distributed teams both in the field and in the laboratory, finding the myriad of communication hurdles distributed teams have, the consequent underutilization of remote team members' skills and reduction in trust. Her current work includes studying two of the most difficult aspects of long distance collaboration: Crossing cultures and having no overlap in workdays. She is an ACM Fellow, was in the first class of inductees in CHI's Academy, holds a Lifetime Achievement award from SIGCHI, and was awarded the 2011 ACM Athena Award, translating to "woman of the year in computing."

CSCW'12, February 11–15, 2012, Seattle, Washington, USA.
ACM 978-1-4503-1086-4/12/02.

Keynote Talk

Science, Technology and Society Revisited: What Is Happening to Anthropology and Ethnography?

Marietta Baba
Organizational and Institutional Anthropology, College of Social Science
Michigan State University
East Lansing, MI, USA
mbaba@msu.edu

Abstract
Anthropologists and ethnographers have been important contributors to the field of computer-supported cooperative work, with many insights and attendant innovations derived from this partnership. More recently, the discipline of anthropology has taken a critical turn, one of the consequences being doubts regarding anthropology's relationship with science (as in "...the most humanistic of the sciences and the most scientific of the humanities.") A shift in stance from one that sought the classical position of the empirical scientist and/or the humanistic interpreter ("verstehen") to another that is more deliberately and self-consciously critical has potential implications for the position of technology in ethnographic field studies, both as a human tool and as a subject of inquiry. The evolution of the social sciences increasingly will be influenced by the availability of and access to massive amounts of digital information, and new types of technology for its collection and analysis. How anthropology and ethnography engage with this new world of digital information remains an open question. Regardless, they will face competitive challenges in the marketplace. The shifting currents that surround changes we are witnessing in anthropology and ethnography will be placed in a historical and social context, and implications for their future prospects will be explored.

Categories & Subject Descriptors: H.1.2 [**Models and Principles**]: User/Machine Systems – *human factors;* K.4 [**Computers and Society**]; K.4.3. [**Computers and Society**]: Organizational Impacts - *computer-supported cooperative work*; K.7.1. [**The Computing Profession**]: Occupations

General Terms: Human Factors

Bio
Marietta Baba is Dean of the College of Social Science, Professor of Anthropology, and Professor of Human Resources and Labor Relations, at Michigan State University. Previously, Dr. Baba was Professor and Chair of the Department of Anthropology, and founding director of the Business and Industrial Anthropology program at Wayne State University in Detroit, MI. From 1994-1996, Dr. Baba was Program Director of the National Science Foundation's industry-funded research program Transformations to Quality Organizations. Dr. Baba is the author of more than 75 scholarly and technical publications in the fields of organizational culture, technological change, and evolutionary processes. In 1998, she was appointed to serve on Motorola's global advisory Board of Anthropologists, the first of its kind in the U.S. Dr. Baba was a founding member and past president of the National Association for the Practice of Anthropology (NAPA, 1986-1988), a section of the American Anthropological Association (AAA). Currently, she is a member of the Editorial Board of the new Journal of Business Anthropology. In 2008, Dr. Baba was honored with the Conrad Arensberg Award for her contributions to the anthropology of work by the Society for the Anthropology of Work, a section of the American Anthropological Association.

CSCW'12, February 11–15, 2012, Seattle, Washington, USA.
ACM 978-1-4503-1086-4/12/02.

(How) Will the Revolution be Retweeted? Information Diffusion and the 2011 Egyptian Uprising

Kate Starbird
ATLAS Institute, Technology, Media & Society
University of Colorado, Boulder
Boulder, CO 80309-0430
starbird@colorado.edu

Leysia Palen
Department of Computer Science
University of Colorado, Boulder
Boulder, CO 80309-0430
palen@colorado.edu

ABSTRACT
This paper examines microblogging information diffusion activity during the 2011 Egyptian political uprisings. Specifically, we examine the use of the retweet mechanism on Twitter, using empirical evidence of information propagation to reveal aspects of *work* that the crowd conducts. Analysis of the widespread contagion of a popular meme reveals interaction between those who were "on the ground" in Cairo and those who were not. However, differences between information that appeals to the larger crowd and those who were doing on-the-ground work reveal important interplay between the two realms. Through both qualitative and statistical description, we show how the crowd expresses solidarity and does the work of information processing through recommendation and filtering. We discuss how these aspects of work mutually sustain crowd interaction in a politically sensitive context. In addition, we show how features of this retweet-recommendation behavior could be used in combination with other indicators to identify information that is new and likely coming from the ground.

Author Keywords
Crisis informatics, information contagion, information diffusion, microblogging, political disruption, Twitter

ACM Classification Keywords
H.5.3 Groups & Organization Interfaces—collaborative computing, computer-supported cooperative work, K.4.2 Social Issues

General Terms
Design; Human Factors

INTRODUCTION
Microblogging tools have been appropriated for a wide range of applications, including, but certainly not limited to, the networking and socializing we have come to associate with social media. Several research studies have documented the use of platforms like Twitter (the most popular microblogging tool, which has global reach) and Sino-Weibo (primarily used in China) during mass emergencies and large-scale crises [12,18,20,22,27]. Messages about the use of microblogging, specifically Twitter, during political protests conflict. Though celebrated by the Western media as a force for good during the Iran Election protests in June 2009 [7], follow-up research suggests the role of Twitter had been over-stated, noting that the social media revolution failed to affect the change it intended, and that the service may have been used by the government to crush opposition protests and identify protesters, whose lives were put in immediate danger [4].

During the "Arab Spring"—a string of political uprisings that took place in the winter and spring of 2011 across the Arab world—attention was again paid to the emerging role of social media. Following Tunisia's successful demonstrations, protesters took to the streets of Egypt to demand reform [15]. As had happened during the Iranian Election protests, people across the world tuned into the event via social media; there again mainstream media described a significant role being played by platforms like Facebook and Twitter [16].

In his attention-grabbing editorial about the difficulties of using social media to affect revolutionary change—change he claimed required high-risk activism—Gladwell wrote that the "revolution will not be tweeted" [6]. Our empirical consideration of the events in Egypt calls this claim into question.

Here, we report on this research, finding—to foreshadow a small bit of it—that 30% of the 1000 mostly highly retweeted Twitterers who were using popular hashtags related to the protests *were in Cairo* during the event, and that many of these were "on the ground" in street protests. Tweets from these users contained information about meeting times, injuries, violence, supplies needed, etc. Revolutionaries were clearly using social media services to coordinate their actions and garner support. While we will not confront head-on Gladwell's argument that social media fail as organizing tools for high-risk activism, this paper will address a piece of that argument, asserting that the low-risk "activism" enabled by social media (what others have termed "slacktivism" [13]) may indeed have been a productive component of this recent revolution.

In this paper, we examine the use of one Twitter feature—the retweet, a mechanism by which Twitter users pass on or forward information to other users. We use the retweet mechanism as a means to understand broader Twitter behavior around these protests, and to demonstrate how remote individuals participated in Egypt's 2011 revolution through low-risk, social media-enabled activities. To be clear about aims, we neither present a full description of Twitter activity during the protests, nor an analysis of the role that social media played (or didn't play) in *orchestrating* this event. Rather we show how consideration of the retweet mechanism reveals a good deal about information contagion across a large number of people and how this behavior figures into social movements.

To that end, we theorize that "the crowd" participated in at least two ways. By uncovering interaction via information propagation between those on the ground and those in the broader Twitterverse, we first demonstrate how the crowd, through a show of interest, expressed solidarity with the cause. We then show how some protesters embraced this show of interest and aligned with it, giving credibility to the idea of solidarity through social media. Second, we show how the crowd did the "work" of information processing (through retweeting), and discuss how we might be able to leverage that recommendation process to increase situational awareness during events.

BACKGROUND

Twitter and Mass Disruption

Twitter is a popular microblogging service with global reach, boasting well over 100 million registered users worldwide [25]. Although considerable attention has been paid by the media to the use of Twitter during political protests after the Iran Election and again during the Egyptian protests, few empirical studies have been done on the use of microblogging during political disruption. There is some literature that addresses this issue from a political perspective. Mungiu-Pippidi and Munteanu give an accounting of the role of microblogging during the failed "Twitter Revolution" in Moldova in 2009 [14]. Burns and Eltham warn that the hype around the role of Twitter during the Iran Election protests has been overblown and blinded to the negative consequences of the service's use [4].

A growing body of research in the area of crisis informatics, including several studies on the use of microblogging during mass emergencies and disasters, helps elaborate the topic of civil disruption and ICT. Though obvious disparities exist between these types of social convergence events—not least of which are the special brand of concerns about privacy and security that arise during planned internal protests—the behavior of the attendant audience as mediated by social media likely has some similarities by virtue of the disruptive nature of either kind of event.

Microblogging has been used during crisis events all over the world, including the 2007 San Diego Wildfires [12], the Oklahoma wildfires and Red River floods of 2009 [20,27], the 2010 Haiti earthquake [22], the 2010 Yushu earthquake in China [18], and other more recent earthquakes in Christchurch New Zealand [11] and Japan [17]. Research indicates that Twitter has been employed to seek information [27], solicit donations [18], organize volunteers [22], publicize the names of missing persons [11], and broadcast immediate needs [18], among other uses.

Information Propagation and Twitter

This paper focuses specifically on how information spreads through Twitter during political protests by way of the retweet mechanism. The retweet is a user-driven convention—now formally supported by one-click functionality on the Twitter platform—that acts to forward tweets, giving attribution to the original (or another upstream) author. Boyd et al. [3] found that retweets are used both for information diffusion and for engaging others. That study also noted the difficulty of identifying retweets and traces due to different syntaxes, user truncation, and added commentary across the tweet propagation. In the data collected for this study, we found four forms of the retweet convention in use: the most popular is `RT @username`. Also used at high volumes are `via @username` and `R @username` followed by the message, as well as `"@username:`, where the entire tweet is quoted.

Several studies have described dynamics of the retweet across large, random samples of tweets. Examining features that lead to increased retweetability, Suh et al. [24] found that tweets with URLs and hashtags were more likely to be retweeted. They also noted a strong linear relationship between a user's number of followers and the likelihood that that user's tweet would be retweeted. They suggested that "social context"—information about the Twitter author including followers, following, account inception date, etc.—can help identify the "value" of information. Kwak et al. [8] observed that retweets spread quickly and broadly, noting that the speed of diffusion could be an indication of strength of influence of the Twitterer, and suggesting that the number of followers a user has and the number of times that user is retweeted are different measures of popularity. Comparing Twitter and Digg, Lerman and Ghosh [9] found that information diffuses faster on Twitter, and that initial number of followers is not as closely correlated with retweetability as it is on Digg. Van Liere [26] used retweets to study the distance that a tweet travels and identified a type of Twitterer—the "information broker"—who connects to others according to shared interest and who spreads information across geographic distance.

Others have addressed information diffusion through microblogging sites during crises. Looking specifically at the retweet mechanism during crises, Starbird and Palen [21] found that retweets with topical keywords were more likely to be on-topic related to the disaster than non-retweets, suggesting a role of information recommendation performed by the crowd. They also noted different retweet patterns between those local to a disaster—who preferred to retweet messages written by people who were also locals—over those who were remote—who retweeted almost exclusively messages that possessed "broad appeal." Vieweg et al. [27] noted that retweeted information is more likely to include information that contributes to situational awareness than non-retweeted information, and Qu et al. [18] also found that retweets were more likely to contribute to situational awareness as well as to contain "action-related" information.

Complex contagion, a concept from sociology related to information contagion [5], may be an important dynamic of social media use during political protest. Romera et al. [19] researched how socially sensitive topics, including political ones, propagated through Twitter. They identified two different properties of diffusion: *stickiness*, the likelihood of information being spread after one contact; and *persistence*, the likelihood of information being spread after repeated contacts. They found that complex contagion to be at work on Twitter, reporting that political hashtags were more persistent than other types of tags, meaning that they were more likely to be spread after multiple exposures. Twitterers who are initially unlikely to join a conversation on a sensitive topic become more likely to join as they see increasingly more people becoming involved.

METHOD

Event Description: The 2011 Political Uprising in Egypt

This paper investigates Twitter activity during the 2011 political uprising in Egypt, a "mass disruption" event with mass social and informational convergence properties. Mass protests of Egyptian autocratic governance began on 25 January 2011, and continued for eighteen days until Egyptian president Mubarak resigned on 11 February [15]. Early on, social media appeared to have an active presence. In reaction to the initial, mostly peaceful protests, the Egyptian authorities cut internet access to major providers on 25 January at 12:20am EET[1], with service largely resumed by 2 February. The government also moved to disband protesters using a security police force notorious for torture. By 28 January, hundreds of thousands of people had gathered in Tahrir Square [15]. An ad-hoc medical facility was set up near the square to tend those wounded in skirmishes that had broken out between security forces and the protesters [1]. 2 February marked a significant shift from relatively peaceful protests to violent clashes between pro-Mubarak groups and anti-Mubarak protesters. Several non-Egyptian reporters on the ground in Tahrir Square, a central location for the protests, and other parts of Cairo were reportedly attacked by pro-Mubarak "thugs," as they came to be called [15,23]. Protests continued and tensions increased over the following week, finally culminating on 11 February when Mubarak stepped down.

[1] All times in this paper in local Cairo time, GMT +02:00

Data Collection

This research is based on Twitter data collected between 2 February, hours before Internet access was restored in Egypt, and 15 February, four days after Mubarak stepped down. Using sophisticated search architecture that takes advantage of several Twitter APIs [2], we collected both tweet and Twitterer data. For tweet collection, we relied on Twitter's Streaming API to collect tweets in real-time, filtering on the following terms: `egypt`, `#egypt`, and `#jan25`.[2] This captured tweets in English, as well as a range of other languages, including tweets written in Arabic, which constitute 15% of the data. For each unique Twitterer who contributed a tweet to this collection, we also captured all of their Twitter profile information including follower count at the time of the first tweet grabbed by our collection. These data—2,229,129 tweets and 338,895 unique Twitterers—comprise the *Egypt Twitterverse Proxy* set. Due to technical issues with Twitter data collection, we were unable to collect data during the early stages of the event (between 25 January and 2 February) and lost data during three short windows within the collection period. However, the type of analysis conducted here does not depend on a full accounting of all possible tweets. Additionally, the delayed capture of profile data, which resulted in elevated initial follower counts for local Twitterers, likely weakened some of the effects we report on later in this paper.

Highly Retweeted Twitterers

Accepting the retweet feature to be a measure of popularity [8] and possibly a recommendation feature during mass disruption events [20], we then attempted to identify and examine the most highly retweeted Twitterers. Retweets (using `RT @` and `via @` conventions) make up 58.5% of the *Egypt Twitterverse Proxy* set (all languages combined). Furthermore, 56.3% of all tweets with non-English characters (which include Arabic language tweets) in that set are retweets, which suggests that the retweet conventions have been at least partially adopted by Arabic language tweeters, and indicates that retweeting continues to be an important behavior during mass disruptions.

Searching against the two retweet conventions mentioned above, we calculated how many times each Twitterer was retweeted within the *Egypt Twitterverse Proxy* set, and then identified the top 1000 most-retweeted accounts. We then cross-referenced these usernames against the usernames of the Twitterers whose profile information we had collected, and located the profile and follower data of 956 of the 1000 highly retweeted usernames. The 44 missing usernames are likely absent because users protected (or restricted access to) their accounts or because they untraceably changed their

[2] Collecting Twitter data during mass disruption events requires rapid selection of search terms in an evolving information space [19]. Arabic speakers in our research lab selected these terms as the most popular during the early days of this event, resulting in a large, low-noise sample.

account names within the data collection window. The 956 remaining users and all of their keyword tweets comprise the *Egypt Highly RTed Twitterers* set.

For further analysis, we randomly selected a one-quarter sample from these 956 Twitterers. This resulted in 254 initial Twitterers. We then removed six accounts: three were removed due to a zero following count, which indicates a problem with the account or an account suspension; two were removed because their account names had changed during the event, altering their retweet numbers; and a final account was removed because it was a bot with more than 10,000 automatically sent tweets during the time period. The remaining 248 Twitterers comprise the *Egypt Highly RTed Sample* set.

Measuring diffusion of individual tweets

To further understand information diffusion, we traced the propagation of all retweeted tweets that were originally authored or attributed to a Twitterer in the *Egypt Highly RTed Sample*. We were able to trace the history of 313,662 retweets back to 34,605 original tweets authored by a Twitterer in this sample. We calculated both how many times an author was retweeted, as well as how many different tweets of theirs were retweeted. We also captured how many times each tweet was retweeted.

DATA SET	# Twitterers	# Tweets
Egypt Twitterverse Proxy Tweets sent during Egyptian protests Identified using keyword search: #jan25 #egypt Egypt *Used to identify highly RTed & track tweet/meme diffusion.*	338,895	2,299,129
Egypt Highly RTed Subset of *Egypt Twitterverse Proxy* Top 1000 most RTed accounts, where profiles could be found.	956	282,010
Egypt Highly RTed Sample 25% sample from *Egypt Highly RTed* *Coded for Location of Author.*	248	69,461

Table 1. Egyptian Protest Data Set Statistics

Qualitative Coding

To understand the types of accounts that are most retweeted, we categorized the Twitterers in the *Egypt Highly RTed Sample* along several criteria, including their account affiliation and location during the event. Because users occasionally include locations in their profile that are not their actual locations, or because they move around during events, we do not accept the location character string in the user profile as the true location. Instead, we manually "code" users for location by reading through each user's entire collected twitter stream (which ranged from tens to thousands of tweets for each Twitterer) looking for assertions of or references to being in Cairo during the period of the protests. Because this study centers around the activities in Cairo's Tahrir square, we coded each account's location relative to Cairo, using the following categorizations: *In Cairo, In Egypt but not in Cairo* and *Not in Egypt*. Twitterers who were in Cairo at any time during the event were coded as being *In Cairo*.

Many of the top 1000 most retweeted accounts in the Egypt data set had Arabic language tweets in their user streams. To make determinations of location and affiliation for Arabic language Twitterers, we first analyzed the profiles and user streams using an English translation generated by Google Translate software. When coding determinations could not be made in this way, we asked a native Arabic speaker to translate the tweet and profile data. Ultimately, we could not confidently determine the locations for three of 248 Twitterers in the *Egypt Highly RTed Sample*.

FINDINGS

Using both qualitative and quantitative analyses, we examine how the retweet was used to diffuse information during the Egyptian protests. We begin at the tweet level, investigating the propagation and re-appropriation of a single tweet meme that spread widely in the set. We then use a measure of the number of times a tweet is retweeted to uncover distinctions in retweetability among different types of information. Next, we shift back to look at the retweet as a method of recommending Twitterers as well as tweets, and examine the features of Twitterers who were most highly retweeted in our data.

Propagation of a Metaphor for the Revolution

The most popular tweet in the *Egypt Twitterverse Proxy* set is a proclamation of support for the removal of Mubarak, represented by an ascii-created "progress bar" graphic:

```
@adelshehadeh (10 Feb, 18:37): Uninstalling
dictator ... 99% complete ▓▓▓▓▓▓▓▓▓▓▓▓▓▓▓▓▓▓
▓▓▓▓▓▓▓▓▓░ #egypt #jan25 #tahrir #mubarak
```

Variations of the "Uninstalling dictator" with progress bar tweet appear 19,836 times in the data set. With this finding, we further investigated the morphology of the progress bar text and graphic, discovering that its use was widespread, cutting across Twitterverse, and began much earlier, progressing to this most popular form. It appears more frequently among those who are not local, though those who were on the ground also propagated it—a point to which we return at the conclusion of this section.

Over 1% of our *Egypt Twitterverse Proxy* set (23,012 tweets) reference the progress bar theme, as determined by inclusion of the block characters as well as occurrence of the % character. In total, of 338,895 Twitterers in the entire set, we found 20,727 who tweeted at least one progress bar tweet. We examined these tweets by hand to identify the major forms of the progress bar tweet and how they shifted over time, as well as the smaller changes that Twitterers made as evidence of the "work" that was put to sustaining and adapting the *meme* over time.

Throughout the time period of the protests, variations on the progress bar meme appear, morphing into new forms, but in most cases, keeping to and elaborating on a common "computing" metaphor. The first occurrence happens the morning of 2 February, suggesting that the progress bar was already propagating, though in smaller numbers, prior to data collection start. The tweet is retweeted twice:

@NotNaif (2 Feb, 11:49): Hosni #Moubarak Escape loading...] 99% #alarabiya #egypt #cairo #jan25 #FREEEGYPT #Internet #25jan #Arab

The next form extends the computing metaphor that is implied by the progress bar. It is only retweeted once in this form, but introduces both the ideas of "installing" and "freedom" into the information space:

@AntiMubarak (3 Feb, 01:41): RT @thameralzaidy Installing Freedom in Egypt 99% #Jan25

The first Arabic language tweet with a progress bar appears almost two days later. Adjusting the sentiment of the tweet to reflect a slightly less positive outlook after the violent clashes that took place on 2 February in Tahrir Square, @almuraisy suggests that "some more patience" is needed. This tweet was retweeted 6 times.

@almuraisy (4 Feb, 14:26): 99% هانت يا جماعة #Egypt #Jan25 #Tahrir

Of note, only 52 instances of the progress bar tweet (much less than 1%) had Arabic characters in the text.

The next form expands upon the "freedom" idea, and makes a strong connection to the progress bar with "loading." This is the first progress bar to diffuse broadly in our set, appearing 5977 times in a similar format:

@fakroona (4 Feb, 14:39): FREEDOM LOADING 99% #Egypt #Jan25 #Tahrir #Cairo #mubarak #sidibouzid #fridayofdeparture #yemen #syria #jordan

Interestingly, even though the "FREEDOM LOADING" and progress bar text, as well as the attribution to @fakroona, diffuses widely, the #fridayofdeparture hashtag is dropped in about half of the retweets, like the one below.

@StephanJourdan (4 Feb, 15:00): RT @fakroona: FREEDOM LOADING 99% #Tahrir #egypt #jan25

All these major progress bar tweet forms include variations in hashtag listings, as well as attributions to the original and downstream Twitterers. Boyd et al. [3] report that text and attribution often change over the course of a retweet's life, an effect they attribute partly to character length limits of tweets and to added commentary by downstream Twitterers. We see evidence in this study of people in different locales trying to make the tweet their own by slightly adjusting the meaning to take into account the event progression, or contributing new tags or short comments.

In a move similar to @almuraisy's Arabic tweet above, @RuwaydaMustafah also adjusts the popular meme to acknowledge renewed uncertainly in the success of the protests, introducing an "error message" on 4 February:

@RuwaydaMustafah (4 Feb, 15:25): FREEDOM LOADING 99% [Error : Please remove Mubarak and try again!] #Jan25 #Egypt

This tweet results in 324 instances, but is distributed fairly steadily until Mubarak steps down on the 10th. Notice that this tweet drops attribution to the original "freedom loading" author. Other variants of the metaphor appear, but are not as frequently propagated. Their presence nevertheless suggests attention to a "collective riff," and includes "downloading freedom" and the "blue screen of death" which appear 3 and 9 times respectively in our set:

@JameedKaraky (4 Feb, 17:21): #Jan25 Downloading Freedom in #Egypt 99%

@BanglarPain (4 Feb, 14:50): @fakroona #Mubarak Overload 99% Blue screen of death! #Tahrir #jan25 #Egypt

The latter tweet is a direct reply to @fakroona, explicitly playing off of @fakroona's popular progress bar tweet. The investment into the collective riff continues with some attention to incrementing the percentage value associated with the progress bar by 0.1%:

@Ahmoooos (10 Feb, 17:57): FREEDOM LOADING 99.8% [removing mubarak in processing right now please wait !] #Jan25 #Egypt #Mubarak #tahrir #cairo

New forms continue with the addition of more, and shortened progress bars, here with attention to leaders. Another variation on this style appears in the form of other nation states in the Arab world where recent protests have taken place or future protests have been proposed:

@alihabibi1 (10 Feb, 18:21):
Ben Ali 100% Mubarak 99%
Qaddafi ______ 42% Boutaflika ________ 19% #Jan25 #SidiBouzid

It was @adelshehadeh's tweet (at the beginning of this section), however, that generated the most propagation, and it didn't appear until 10 February, when the resignation of Mubarak was appearing imminent. That tweet accounts for 78% of the "progress bar" tweets in the set, and introduces the morphological change of "uninstalling."

Still more extensions of the computing metaphor continue to appear after the first appearance of the most diffused form of the meme, with references to "Egypt 2.0," "Fatal error," "kernel error," and "install Democracy, Disk #1 into drive E: gypt."

In these extractions of the major forms of the meme morphology identified here, we see the evolution of a tweet meme. The progress bar ascii graphic is probably not something that everyone can easily create. Once someone introduced it to the public sphere, it got picked up and modified. Though these different forms comprised a fairly high absolute number, their totals paled in comparison to one particular form that did not appear until 10 February. In the time leading up to that date, however, variations on the first form transformed it into a meme, a widely understood idea. Centola and Macy [5] call this "complex contagion," where multiple exposures from multiple "long-tie" sources ignite and support diffusion. The remixing of elements, all keeping within a computing metaphor, shows some degree of shared understanding of its purpose, and kept the meme propagating. The variations show collective "work" happening on the meme to keep it relevant and interesting, until it reached the point of widespread coverage and possibly saturation with the 10th of February "uninstalling dictator" tweet.

We note that most progress bar tweets appeared in English, though a small number also appeared in Arabic, Japanese, Korean, Dutch, German and Spanish. We suspect that the number of tweets in Arabic was lower than expected, and that the overall distribution tended strongly toward English because of the desire for contributions to the collective meme to be widely understood. To this point, many of the authors who originated new versions of the progress bar were tweeting from other locations in the Middle East.

Propagation by Others v Locals

To the question of whether tweet propagations like this effectively contribute to the basic work of the revolution, we look to how much this meme appeared in the tweet streams of those who were on the ground in Cairo versus those who were not.

In the *Egypt Highly RTed Sample*, where we coded for location, Twitterers who were not in Cairo were considerably more likely (27.6%) to send a progress bar tweet than those who were in Cairo during the protesting (17.6%). This suggests that this "sticky" meme had broad appeal in the wider Twitterverse, offering a short abstract of the event [21]. Indeed, another interpretation of this finding might be that non-local Twitterers were boosted into highly retweeted status by the popularity of the progress bar meme. We will explore this further in the latter half of the Findings section.

Perhaps more interesting than the discrepancy here is that 13 of our sample's 74 highly retweeted Twitterers who were tweeting from Cairo *were* taking part in propagating the progress bar tweet, including @sandmonkey, one of the ten most retweeted accounts in our set. Tracing the origin of several of the most popular variations, we find little evidence that any began in the streams of Cairo Twitterers. This suggests that Twitterers on the ground were, to some extent, embracing external declarations of solidarity as legitimate messages and voices within their cause.

In sum, the propagation of the progress bar meme by both those on the "inside" as well as the large attendant audience suggests interplay between both realms. Though such a meme could be perceived as "silly" and incidental to the event—and indeed, some people publicly asked for its distribution to stop—such phenomena need attention to fully understand their impact on newsworthy and risky events like a political revolution. It could be that wide propagation of a tweet-idea helps cast a light on events happening in other parts of the world. Participation by those in the midst of the geographical event suggests active endorsement of the meme. In other words, if those on the ground find value in the propagation of a tweet, then—in contrast to Gladwell's point [6]—perhaps that is one of the real measures by which one decides how much a role social technology plays in revolutions.

Broad Appeal v Local Utility

By tracing the most popular (highly retweeted) tweets originated by authors in the *Egypt Highly RTed Sample,* we see a similar bias towards broad appeal tweets, messages of solidarity with the Egyptian cause, as well high-level news.

`@JoeUnfiltered:`The people of #Egypt have shown the world that youth activism can change ANYTHING. 18 days has ended 30 years of oppression ***[RT 3989x[3]]***

`@DominicKavakeb:` `Its so vital that world understands this is not a divided #Egypt. This is the state attacking the people. #jan25` ***[RT 2660x]***

`@HuffingtonPost:` `BREAKING: Mubarak will step down, hand power to military tonight - Reuters http://huff.to/egyptnews #Egypt #jan25` ***[RT 1233x]***

These were the three most highly retweeted tweets originated by any author in our sample. The top tweet was retweeted 3989 times, the second 2660 times and the final tweet 1233 times. As above, none of these tweets were originally authored by individuals who were in Cairo at the time of the protests.

Highly propagated tweets originated by locals often follow the broad appeal pattern as well. Tweets about violence, detained friends or colleagues, requests for solidarity, and humorous tweets are often the most retweeted messages authored by the group. The following tweet, retweeted 998 times, is the most popular tweet authored by a local.

`@sharifkouddous:` `A couple just got married in Tahrir in front of army tanks. A revolution wedding. #Egypt #Jan25` ***[RT 998x]***

While witty and humorous tweets experienced "sticky" retweetability, serious tweets remarking on violence, especially violence against the media, and asking for support were also among the most popular. These two tweets asking for support for the release of Ayman Mohyeldin, a reporter for Al Jazeera, were retweeted a total of 1386 times.

`@nolanjazeera:` `the hashtag is #freeayman please retweet as much as u can to get this trending. Attacks on media in #Egypt MUST end now` ***[RT 985x]***

`@AymanM:` `Ayman has been detained by #Egypt military. Will keep everyone posted on his status as things develop (tweeted by friend)` ***[RT 401x]***

Popular tweets from locals also included first hand reports of violence or tactical information. The following tweet, a real-time accounting of violence on the ground, written by an NBC news reporter, was retweeted 591 times. The two subsequent tweets, which received considerably fewer retweets relayed tactical information about the evolving protests.

[3] This notation indicates the number of retweets.

@richardengelnbc: #egypt.. Just saw a protester hit by a molotov .. Saw him catch on fire.. Other protesters managed to put him out.. ***[RT 519x]***

@alaa: Army gave up and let us control flow of ppl at tv building #Jan25 ***[RT 336x]***

@3arabawy: The army has allowed a group of 100 Mubaraks thugs into Qasr el-Nil bridge now. #Jan25 ***[RT 175x]***

Less "popular" tweets by locals, as measured by the breadth of their diffusion within the larger Twitterverse, often contained more detailed information from the ground. The following tweets were retweeted fewer than 20 times each, but offer very specific details about the situation in Cairo.

@wilyawil: Im hearing from friends inside Tahrir Sq that best entrance is from Falaki st. #jan25 #egypt ***[RT 18x]***

@mosaaberizing: Weve taken over Talaat Harb entrance as well. Just the musuems left now. #Jan25 ***[RT 14x]***

The popularity of individual tweets shows a bias towards English language tweets. Though 34% of tweets in the *Egypt Highly RTed Sample* contain Arabic characters, only 20% of tweets that were retweeted from these Twitterers had Arabic characters. Arabic language tweets that were retweeted at least once received an average of five retweets, while non-Arabic tweets were retweeted an average of eight times. The first Arabic tweet from the Twitterers in our highly retweeted sample, a tweet from the @nytimes requesting an interview with someone on the ground, appears as the 83rd most popular tweet, retweeted 242 times.

@nytimes: في القاهرة او في اسكندرية او في سويز و تحب ان تكلم عن ال ضع؟ كلم @Nadia8 في انجليزي او عربي. #Egypt #Jan25 ***[RT 242x]***

Analyzing the diffusion of popular tweets through retweeting suggests that actionable or action-related information [18], information coming from the ground and, perhaps, appearing in the information space for the first time, can be found in the streams of local Twitterers, but not necessarily in their most popular tweets. Tracing the most popular retweets, even those sent by locals, may result in broad appeal messages. But tweets like the following may be more valuable to those acting on the ground, and perhaps to others who are remote, trying to better understand and support the situation on the ground:

@occupiedcairo: Medical supplies needed at temp. hospital at tahrir: neck supports and stitching thread #jan25 ***[RT 39x]***

How might the noisy retweeting by the well-intentioned and easily entertained crowd be leveraged to home in on actionable information being tweeted from the ground?

Who Were the Most Retweeted Accounts

Possibly a more effective strategy than investigating the most popular tweets during the Egyptian protests is identifying the most popular Twitterers. The number of times that an account is retweeted can be used as a measure of popularity [8] or, during a specific, mass disruption event, an implicit recommendation by the crowd that an account is a useful source of information [21]. In this section, we will describe features of the most highly retweeted accounts, and investigate the utility of using the retweet mechanism, in concert with other aspects of an account's "social context" [24] to home in on accounts with "local authority" [21].

Research has shown that many features of information propagation through social media have power law or other heavy-tailed distributions [9,10]. For our *Egypt Highly RTed* set, the number of times that an account was retweeted has a heavy-tailed distribution. Figure 1 shows this distribution, the number of accounts with x number of tweets, in linear-linear and log-linear scale. Note that the first bar in this distribution is at 170 tweets, the cut-off point for inclusion in the top-1000 Twitterer sample. The mean number of times retweeted is 1089, and the most highly retweeted Twitterer, @ghonim, was retweeted over 35,000 times.

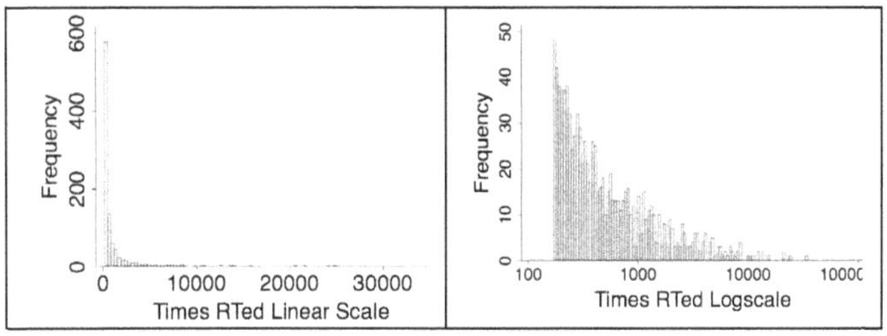

Figure 1. Times Retweeted, Linear-Linear & Log-Linear Scale

Top Ten Most Retweeted Accounts

Examining the top ten most retweeted accounts in the *Egypt Twitterverse Proxy* set (Table 2), we see the retweet acting to recommend Twitterers who, for the most part, were actively tweeting from Cairo. Many of these highly retweeted accounts were operated by journalists, or mainstream media with journalists on the ground. Others were popular Egyptian bloggers, and all have above average follower counts (see Figure 3).

Name	Times RTed	Followers	Affiliation	Location
@ghonim	35265	12491	individual	Cairo
@dima_khatib	25062	11320	journalist	Latin America
@bencnn	24066	21147	journalist	Cairo
@3arabawy	21607	9022	journalist	Cairo
@sandmonkey	20714	6943	blogger	Cairo
@alarabiya_ar	15681	14011	mainstream media	Arab World*
@monaeltahawy	14150	16048	journalist	Cairo
@ajenglish	13791	145246	mainstream media	Arab World*
@ajarabic	12687	30244	mainstream media	Arab World*
@monasosh	12609	2535	blogger	Alexandria

Table 2. Top 10 Most Retweeted Accounts (* denotes organizations with reporters on the ground.)

Top 1000 Most Retweeted: Location

Examining the location of the Twitterers in the *Egypt Highly RTed Sample* (Table 3), we see a relatively high number of local Twitterers. 89 of 248 Twitterers in the sample (36%) have evidence within their tweet streams of being in Egypt at some point between 2 February to 15 February. Of these, 74 (30% of the sample) were in Cairo during that time. 43 others were located elsewhere in the Middle East and the rest were spread across the globe, with the highest concentrations in Europe (27) and North America (54). Among the 248 there were three for whom we could not determine if they were in Egypt or not.

Location	# Twitterers	% of Sample
Egypt – Cairo	74	29.8%
Egypt – Other	15	6.0%
Unknown, possibly in Egypt	3	1.2%
Arab World	43	17.3%
Outside Arab World	113	45.6%

Table 3. Location for the *Egypt Highly RTed Sample*

Though we do not have the locations of the remaining 800,000 plus Twitterers who sent one or more tweets hashtagged with `#egypt` or `#jan25`, it is probable that nowhere near a third of them were on the ground in the protests in Egypt. Highly retweeted accounts appear to be more likely than other Twitterers to be local in this event. This finding suggests that during mass-participation events of global import, the retweet may serve as a mechanism through which the larger Twitterverse identifies and recommends local Twitterers.

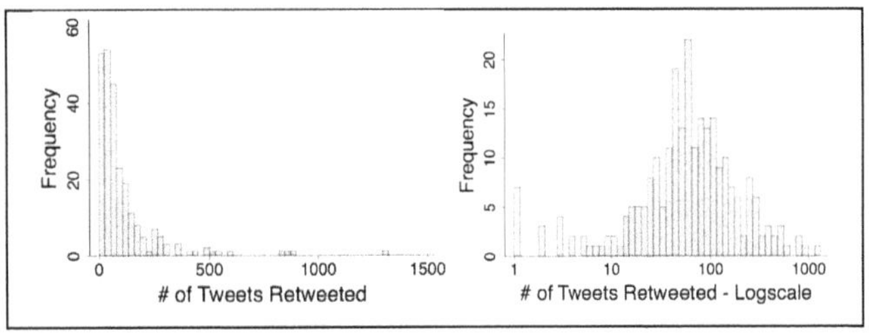

Figure 2. Number of Popular Tweets by Twitterer

Top 1000 Most Retweeted: Number of Retweets

As mentioned in the above section on Broad Appeal versus Local Utility, tracing the propagation of an individual tweet offers some insight into the value of that tweet measured by its contribution to situational awareness and newness in the information space. Similarly, the number of unique tweets, sent by the same author and propagated by the crowd, may be a measure of overall value of that user's tweet stream, in relation to a single event. In other words, though their overall number of times retweeted is the same, a Twitterer retweeted 500 times for a single tweet may be more likely to be a broad appeal Twitterer who is not on the ground, than a Twitterer retweeted 50 times for 10 different tweets.

Figure 2 shows the distribution of the numbers of individual popular tweets for each user in the *Egypt Highly RTed Sample* in linear-linear and log-linear scale. The number of popular tweets for highly retweeted Twitterers has a log-normal distribution. The mean is 108 retweeted tweets, with seven Twitterers in our sample having tweeted only one Egyptian protest tweet that was retweeted, albeit very broadly. Twitterers in Cairo were retweeted, on average, for a higher number of tweets (123), than those not in Cairo (102). Though this comparison of the number of retweeted tweets between locals and non-locals shows some difference, things become more interesting when we break down this effect in relation to different variables, below.

Top 1000 Most Retweeted: Followers

For Twitterers in the *Egypt Highly RTed Sample*, the number of followers has a log-normal distribution with a long tail. The mean number of followers is 116,318, with a high standard deviation of 500,000. The median is 1730. Comparing the count across Twitterer location shows a stark difference between the median number of followers for a highly retweeted local (790) and a highly retweeted non-local (2609).

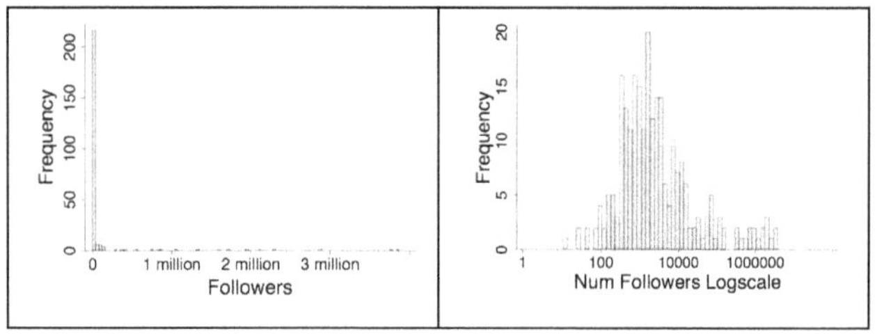

Figure 3. Number of Followers, *Highly RTed Sample*

Accounts with a higher number of followers get more exposure for their tweets, and therefore, each tweet they send has a proportionally higher chance of "infecting" the recipient or being passed on to others [18,24]. In our sample, the number of followers is positively correlated with the number of times a Twitterer is retweeted. However, the Pearson coefficient between the two variables is only 0.1306, indicating that follower number does not fully account for retweet popularity. While recognizing that retweets are one measure of popularity, Kwak at al. [8] noted this gap between the popularity measures of follower count and retweet count. The stark difference between average number of followers for highly retweeted locals and highly retweeted non-locals may suggest that during mass disruption events the follower-retweet gap is related to whether or not the Twitterer is in or near the affected area.

Using retweets and "social context" to identify locals

In the final section of this analysis, we will address the possibility of leveraging what we know about the retweet-follower popularity gap, as well as other measures of retweet behavior and social context to identify Twitterers and tweets from "the ground."

The preceding analysis suggests a relationship between different measures of tweet behavior, social context, and location. To evaluate these relationships we did a multinomial logistic regression, using location (*In Cairo, In*

Egypt, Not in Egypt, Unknown) as a polytomous (non-ordered) dependent variable. For our independent variables, we used follower count, number of times an individual is retweeted, number of different tweets authored by a Twitterer that are retweeted by the crowd, and the total number of total keyword tweets that each user sent during the collection window. To normalize the heavy-tailed distributions, we did natural log transformations on all of the independent variables.

Variable	Coef.	Std. Err	z	P>|z|
log_followers	-.691792	.1286891	-5.38	0.000
log_timesRTed	.5020533	.1802369	2.79	0.005
log_numtweets	-1.08295	.3713641	-2.92	0.004
log_uniques	1.18107	.4061834	2.91	0.004
_cons	1.716295	1.44004	1.19	0.233

Table 4. Multinomial Logistic Regression:
***In Cairo* case vs *Not in Egypt* base case**

Treating *Not in Egypt* as the base case for the analysis, we find statistically significant effects from all four independent variables, but only for those who were in Cairo during the event.[4]

Log number of followers and log number of tweets both have significant negative effects on a Twitterer's odds of being in Cairo during the event. The log number of times retweeted and the log number of different tweets that were retweeted were significantly, positively related to being in Cairo. These descriptive statistics suggest that a *highly retweeted* Twitterer is only more likely to be local when their initial follower count is low. Number of followers and total number of keyword tweets contributed raise a Twitterer's chance of being retweeted, but do not make them more likely to be local. These results also support the idea that a Twitterer with only one or only a few popular tweets related to an event is less likely to be local than a Twitterer with many different popular tweets.

CONCLUSION

Twitter content during mass emergencies consists of both "original" information—that coming into the information space for the first time—and "derivative" information which can be found elsewhere, as our previous research indicates [19]. Retweets, which constitute nearly 60% of tweets sent with tags referencing the Egyptian protests, are one form of derivative information. From this point of view, one could consider retweets as merely noisy output and members of the crowd only cheerleaders.

Another view that incorporates the ideas put forth in this paper is that retweets serve as a crowd-powered recommendation system. Plenty of Twitterers put thought into what they retweet [3]. This constitutes a form of work—and sometimes a form of collective work, as we saw in the propagation and morphing of a metaphor-driven tweet across the duration of the Egyptian protests.

We also demonstrate how considering the crowd from this angle of a working collective can help identify, among a vast number the tweeters, locals who may be introducing "original" information into the space. However, this process is not so straightforward such that finding the most popular tweets or most popular Twitterers will solve the "noisy crowd" problem. Instead, it is important to understand how and why people retweet what they do, including the distinction between broad appeal and local utility tweets, and leverage this understanding to home in on new, locally relevant information. This can be useful as state of the art moves forward toward more automatic forms of curation and collation of vast computer-mediated communication.

When we consider these tweet activities of the locals—who, in this case, were closest to the activist cause and performed some of the work of activism as represented by their tweets—in relation to the activities of the on-lookers, the interaction between them suggests a more integrated relationship than the "slacktavism/activism" [6,13] construct suggests. Here we see that parts of the crowd activity do more than create noise, and that the crowd's zealous but safe vicarious participation has perhaps a more meaningful and new connection to the hard work of the social movement than is readily visible.

This research on the use of the retweet mechanism shows the crowd doing work in two ways that make it a *functional*, if not necessarily central (and that debate needs to continue), aspect of social movements. First, expression of social solidarity is found through the collective, observable creation of a tweet-based, visual and metaphorical meme. This is a deliberate form of collective work. It is critical to recognize that the meme creation was also visibly acknowledged by local activists. These expressions of social solidarity, we propose, are the kinds of activities that draw and sustain attention on a cause, which in turn may sustain the cause itself. The second form of work happens individually but collectively has an effect—retweeting as information filtering and recommendation.

The behaviors of people both on the perceived "inside" and "outside" of the social movement show that responsibilities and weights of responsibility differ across the collective. However, the behaviors are interrelated, and as such, have elements of mutual benefit. Social movements indeed happened prior to social media, but we would be remiss to imagine social movements of the future not leveraging and adapting these tools to gather more to a cause.

ACKNOWLEDGMENTS

We thank our colleagues at Project EPIC, especially Aaron Schram and Kenneth Anderson, for their assistance. We thank anonymous reviewers for helpful critique. We are grateful to the US National Science Foundation, which

[4] One other statistically significant effect was found for log number of followers on the Unknown case, which had a slightly negative effect, with P = 0.025 significance.

funded this research through a Graduate Research Fellowship; grant IIS-0546315; and grant IIS-0910586.

REFERENCES

1. Al-Ghazawy, O. Tahrir field hospital saves hundreds of lives, Nature Middle East, 2011. Retrieved March 15, 2011. http://www.nature.com/nmiddleeast/2011/110214/full/ nmiddleeast.2011.18.html
2. Anderson, K. & Schram, A. Design and Implementation of a Data Analytics Infrastructure In Support of Crisis Informatics Research. In the *33rd International Conference on Software Engineering*, 21-28. (Honolulu, Hawaii, 2011)
3. boyd, d., Golder, S. & Lotan, G. Tweet, tweet, retweet: Conversational aspects of retweeting on Twitter, *Proc. of HCSS'10*, (Koloa, Hawaii, 2010), 1-10.
4. Burns, A. & Eltham, B. Twitter free Iran: An evaluation of Twitter's role in public diplomacy and information operations in Iran's 2009 Election Crisis. In Communications Policy & Research Forum, (2009).
5. Centola, D. & Macy, M. Complex contagion and the weakness of long ties. *American Journal of Sociology*, 113:702-734, 2007.
6. Gladwell, M. Why the revolution will not be tweeted. The New Yorker, 2010. Retrieved May 22, 2011. http://www.newyorker.com/reporting/2010/10/04/101004fa_fact_gladwell
7. Grossman, L. Iran's protests: Why Twitter is the medium of the movement. *Time,* 2009. Retrieved May 22, 2011. http:// www.time.com/time/world/article/0,8599,1905125,00.html
8. Kwak, H., Lee, C., Park, H. & Moon, S. What is Twitter, a social network or a news media? *Intl. WWW Conference,* (Raleigh, NC, 2010), ACM, 591-600.
9. Lerman, K. & Ghosh, R. Information contagion: An empirical study of the spread of news on Digg and Twitter social networks, in *4th Intl. AAAI Conference on Weblogs and Social Media*, (2010), AAAI, 90-97.
10. Leskovec, J., McGlohon, M., Faloutsos, C., Glance, N., & Hurst, M. Cascading behavior in large blog graphs, in *SIAM Intl Conference on Data Mining*, (2007).
11. Manhire, T. & Tran, M. Christchurch Earthquake: Hunt for survivors begins. *The Guardian*, 2011. Retrieved May 31, 2011. http://www.guardian.co.uk/world/2011/feb/22/christchurch-earthquake-hunt-for-survivors
12. Messina, C. Twitter hashtags for emergency coordination and disaster relief. *FactoryCity*, 2007. Retrieved May 31, 2011. http://factoryjoe.com/blog/2007/10/22/twitter-hashtags-for-emergency-coordination-and-disaster-relief/
13. Morozov, E. The brave new world of slacktivism. Net.Effect Foreign Policy, 2009. Retrieved: May 31, 2011. http://neteffect.foreignpolicy.com/posts/2009/05/19/the_brave_new_world_of_slacktivism
14. Mungiu-Pippidi, A., & Munteanu, I. Moldova's "Twitter Revolution" *Journal of Democracy 20*,3 (2009) 136-142
15. New York Times. Egypt News—Revolution and Aftermath. *New York Times*, 2011. Retrieved 31 May, 2011. http://topics.nytimes.com/top/news/international/countriesandterritories/egypt/index.html
16. New York Times. Times Topics – Wael Ghonim. *New York Times,* 2011. Retrieved 15 March 2011. URL: http://topics.nytimes.com/top/reference/timestopics/people/g/wael_ghonim/index.html
17. Neubig, G., Matsubayashi, Y., Hagiwara, M., & Murakami, K. Safety Information Mining – What Can NLP Do in a Disaster. *Proc of 5th Intl. Joint Conf. on Natural Language Processing*, (Chiang Mai, Thailand, 2011), 965-973.
18. Qu, Y., Huang, C., Zhang, P. & Zhang, J. Microblogging after a major disaster in China: A case study of the 2010 Yushu Earthquake, *Proc. of CSCW'11*, (Hangzhou, China, 2011), 25-34.
19. Romero, D., Meeder, B. & Kleinberg, J. Differences in the mechanics of information diffusion across topics: Idioms, political hashtags, and complex contagion on Twitter, in *Intl. WWW Conference*, (Hyderabad, India, 2011), ACM, 695-704.
20. Starbird, K, Palen, L, Hughes, A & Vieweg, S. Chatter on *The Red*: What hazards threat reveals about the social life of microblogged information, *Proc of CSCW* (2010), 241-250.
21. Starbird, K. & Palen, L. Pass it on? Retweeting in Mass Emerency, *Proc. of ISCRAM Conference*, (Seattle, WA, 2010).
22. Starbird, K. & Palen, L. "Voluntweeters": Self-organizing by digital volunteers in times of crisis, *Proc of CHI'11,* (Vancouver, CA, 2011), ACM.
23. Sweney, M. Al-Jazeera office attacked in Egypt protests. *guardian.co.uk,* 2011. Retrieved 15 March, 2011. http://www.guardian.co.uk/media/2011/feb/04/al-jazeera-office-attacked-egypt-protests
24. Suh, B., Hong, L., Pirolli, P. & Chi, E.H. Want to be retweeted? Large scale analytics on factors impacting retweet in Twitter network, in *IEEE Intl Conference on Social Computing*, (2010), IEEE, 177-184.
25. Twitter Blog. The evolving ecosystem. 2010. Retrieved May 30, 2011. http://blog.twitter.com/2010/09/evolving-ecosystem.html
26. van Liere, D. How far does a tweet travel? Information brokers in the Twitterverse, in *MSM'10*, (Toronto, 2010)
27. Vieweg, S., Hughes, A., Starbird, K., & Palen, L. Micro-blogging during two natural hazards events: What Twitter may contribute to situational awareness, *Proc of CHI'10*, (Atlanta, GA, 2010), ACM, 1079-88.

The Egyptian Blogosphere: A Counter-Narrative of the Revolution

Ban Al-Ani, Gloria Mark, Justin Chung, Jennifer Jones
Department of Informatics
Donald Bren School of Information and Computer Sciences
University of California, Irvine
{balani|gmark|juchung|jonesjj@uci.edu}

ABSTRACT
In this paper we investigate the role blogs played within the context of the Egyptian revolution of early 2011 using blog data authored between 2004-2011. We conducted topic modeling analysis to gain a longitudinal view of the interaction of societal, personal and revolutionary blog topics over this period. Furthermore, a qualitative analysis of blog posts during the period that bracketed the political uprising revealed Egyptian bloggers' concerns. Reporting events and supplying commentary provided bloggers with a means to voice dissent against institutionalized power represented by the government-controlled media. In short, blogs reveal a counter-narrative to the government-supplied version of events in Egypt during the 18-day uprising. These narratives offer rich documentation of how blogs, and perhaps social media more generally, can be utilized by individuals operating under repressive conditions.

Author Keywords
Blogs, topic modeling, counter-power, counter-narrative, socio-political uprising, empirical study, Middle-East and North Africa (MENA).

ACM Classification Keywords
H5.m. Information interfaces and presentation (e.g., HCI): Miscellaneous.

General Terms
Human Factors; Theory; Measurement.

INTRODUCTION
January 25, 2011 marked the first day in a series of protest demonstrations across Egypt that led to the resignation of then-president Hosni Mubarak on February 11, 2011. Many mainstream news outlets reported the use of Information and Communication Technologies (ICTs) by Egyptians [3]. Utilizing such technologies to support sociopolitical movements is not new; several movements have taken advantage of this means of disseminating information and gathering support from international observers [20].

Studies addressing the role of social media in sociopolitical movements have generally focused on cultures other than those of the Middle-East and North Africa (MENA) region where Egypt is located [3]. In fact, a decade ago scholars claimed that ICT would not be used with great success to challenge the government's power in the country or the region [cf 14]. Therefore, the Egyptian revolution provides an opportunity to study the use of social media as a means to challenge the power of an authoritative government.

As Faris [15] notes, organizing political opposition in Egypt was a difficult and formidable task. The Egyptian government routinely repressed participation in protest demonstrations through violence and intimidation. Protesters often suffered beatings, arrests, and other forms of rights abuse by authorities [15]. The Mubarak regime also constrained political dissent through the control of Egyptian media [14, 17].

Despite repression, Egyptians utilized blogs as platforms for free speech, in which opposition to Mubarak's authoritarian regime was gradually fostered, legitimized and organized. By adopting and combining various social media, political activists were able to circumvent traditional platforms of communication. In doing so, they were "*creating a kind of amorphous network that [would] be impervious to anything but an all-out assault by the state*" [15].

Under these circumstances, we believe blogs were valuable tools during the 2011 uprising. Our research was motivated by a desire to understand the revolution from the perspective reflected by Egyptian bloggers. We focused on how blogs were used by Egyptians in the context of the revolution, specifically analyzing content posted during the time frame of December 1, 2010 - February 28, 2011. We find that blogs were used to report and discuss the events that took place during the uprising and through this we discovered the construction of a *counter-narrative* that challenges the dominant, state-controlled narrative in Egypt.

RESEARCH CONTEXT: ICT, EGYPT AND THE UPRISING
Information and Communication Technologies (ICT) have been used to launch and conduct various sociopolitical movements that have had either a global (e.g. globalization) or local (e.g. against local government) focus e.g. [6]. Our

study of the use of blogs during the Egyptian uprising builds on these studies but focuses more on investigating its use by individuals during a period of unrest rather than its use by a group to launch or maintain a movement.

Previous research into Internet use has typically focused on women's movements, anti-World Trade Organization movements, and many others' use of ICT over time [19, 20]. The use of the Internet by the Zapatistas movement in the 1990's is perhaps the study most comparable to that of the Egyptian uprising and is considered the most widely reported [20, 12]. However, this movement occurred prior to the proliferation of several types of social media, including blogs. Furthermore, previous research of the use of ICTs typically did not include investigating individuals' use of such technology within the MENA region during a revolution.

Some have discredited the possibility that access to such technologies could play a role during an uprising in the MENA region [14]. Hosni Mubarak maintained firm control of the dissemination of information to Egyptians through state-run media. Even independent media publications—not permitted until 2000—were heavily censored by state authorities [17, 2]. The growing numbers of ICT users, however, were fundamentally changing how information was disseminated despite the Mubarak regime's harsh and sometimes violent repression of online communication. Egyptians connected by ever-growing networks became active participants in the creation, distribution, and consumption of information and ideas. Thus, political elites could no longer effectively control the supply of information that began to emerge from blogs of young (and often unemployed) Egyptians [13, 15].

The emergence of blogging in Egypt around 2004 i s considered closely linked with the Egyptian Movement for Change (often referred to by its slogan, *Kefaya*, meaning "enough" in Arabic) [1, 21]. The *Kefaya* members and supporters communicated information, publicized news, mobilized events and posted political platforms through ICTs, tactics never before seen in Egyptian politics [4]. Notably, the *Kefaya* movement utilized bloggers to spread its ideas of democratic political reform and contribute to its efforts of documenting human rights abuses by posting videos and photographs on their blogs [21].

Such activities were not limited to groups. For example, in 2006, a blogger posted an eyewitness account describing the sexual harassment of a group of women while police stood by and watched; another blogger backed up the account with photographs and video posted on his blog [1; 18]. As oppositional media intensified and became visible to an increasing number of citizens, Egyptian authorities reacted by attempting to repress its users and restricting media freedom [1, 9].

BLOGS AS A MEDIUM FOR COUNTER-POWER?

Led by international media, the Egyptian revolution sparked discussion about the power of social media and its utility as a catalyst for sociopolitical change [3]. Recognizing that social media have played a significant role in other political contexts, we chose to examine how blogs were used in particular during the 2011 revolution.

Manuel Castells has written extensively on the power of social media to affect society [7, 8]. According to Castells, networked communication and social media are fundamentally transforming relations of power. Castells suggests that dominant state actors, institutions and the power they exercise over the public sphere of communication are undergoing a "crisis of legitimacy." Castells observes that modern power relations, especially those linking governments and their citizens, are structured around control of the public sphere in part through control of vertical, broadcast-oriented communication mechanisms. He further argues that the failure of state institutions to evolve along with changing norms of civil society is resulting in the transformation of the public sphere by the masses. By adopting, aggregating and developing new forms of social media, individuals have greater ability to exert what Castells refers to as "counter-power", i.e. resistance to extant, institutionalized power relations.

Through self-generated, self-published content such as that enabled by social media, Castells maintains that citizens can challenge institutional power in two ways. First, political expression introduces modifications and new codes into established networks. A simple example is when YouTube videos capture politicians in "off-camera" moments in order to broadcast slander. This challenges the domination of formal political speeches broadcast by mass media. Second, power can be challenged by preventing communication networks from being controlled by institutions that support authority. This might include, for example, the posting of antigovernment sentiments on social media websites, which constitutes an expression of individual opinion that is often difficult or impossible through traditional broadcast media. As such, "mass self-communication" contributes to a new public space where social actors can exercise autonomy and promote change in ways that were previously impossible.

Others describe how ICT has dramatically reduced the costs and barriers to informational resources, altering the nature of power and increasing its diffusion [11, 15]. For example, female Internet café patrons in Cairo report feeling empowered by the ability to expand their social networks and increase awareness of sociopolitical realities outside of Egypt [24]. By facilitating cost-effective mobilization and secrecy to bypass the state, social media are counter-mediums to traditional media outlets [12].

How might blogs be a mechanism of wielding counter-power? As a mode of communication, blogs are neither dependent on nor necessarily obedient to public authorities like mainstream media. Prior to widespread use of social media, state-run media and a limited number of independent media controlled the dissemination and content of information in Egypt. However, with the emergence of social media, information and political speech are no longer confined to this narrow set of gatekeepers. Unlike micro-blogs, which impose length limitations, blogs allow for the construction of narratives. In this paper we investigate whether Egyptian blogs conveyed counter-power during the uprising, and, if so, what form that counter-power took.

METHOD

We use both quantitative and qualitative methods to gain insight into the role that the Egyptian blogs played during the revolution in 2011. As the revolution in early 2011 had origins that began years earlier, to track the relation of blogging with Egyptian political events would involve conducting a longitudinal analysis of blogs. To analyze such a huge volume of blogs using only qualitative methods would be a formidable task. However, quantitative methods can be used to provide an overview of blog trends. This approach is complemented by qualitative methods, which can provide rich descriptions of the data. We first describe our analysis using topic modeling, a text-based analysis method which enables us to analyze a large corpus of blog data longitudinally without a priori assumptions about the content. Topic modeling, in turn, reveals themes in blogs and their shifts over time. This enables us to then hone in on particular time points or topics and use qualitative methods for further analysis.

AN ANALYSIS OF THE EGYPTIAN BLOGOSPHERE

To collect our blog sample, we used an existing aggregator blog, *Omraneya*, which provides a curated index of more than one thousand Egyptian blogs. The aggregator indexes posts and enables readers to follow new posts minutes after they have been published [13]. A blog aggregator presents the most recently published items from several sources and automatically displays new posts as collective attention fades over time. The *Omraneya* site was cited as a reliable index of the Egyptian blogosphere by others in previous work. For example, Fahmi [13] utilized *Omraneya* and confirmed the authenticity of the indexed blogs. Authors of the *Omraneya* site reported that they provide "*free hosting space and free aid developing a website for any cause we find worthy or interesting and for any speech that is censored or prosecuted in Egypt.*"

We used a crawling application that collected each post in each blog hosted on Blogspot (a popular blogging service operated by Google) and indexed by the *Omraneya* Egyptian blog aggregator. We crawled all posts for each blog indexed by the aggregator, and the crawler application collected more than 18,000 individual posts spanning September 2004 to May 2011. To analyze the large corpus of text containing the indexed blog posts, we used topic modeling to generate insights about trends in the content of the Egyptian blogs over time.

Topic modeling, a form of natural language processing, is a generative probabilistic modeling technique that finds co-occurrences of words across a collection of documents [5]. These co-occurrences, referred to as topics, are generated without any a priori knowledge about the content of the documents. The topic modeling software is fed a collection of documents and generates two outputs: a distribution of words in each topic, and a distribution of topics in each document. These results can be used to visualize or otherwise describe the documents in the collection.

Although the results generated by topic modeling are statistical co-occurrences of words, a core assumption of topic models is that these groups of words generally relate to the semantic content of documents [10]. The formal, quantitative definition of topic that is employed in topic modeling allows the automation of quantitative analysis in substitution of other manual processes such as coding. This is particularly significant because the sheer quantity of material to be coded would make such a task nearly impossible by hand.

In our study, we used an individual blog "post" as a "document" for the purposes of topic modeling. Of the posts containing text, 9,597 were in Arabic, and 6,153 were in English. We could not assume that Arabic and English posts convey the same topics, so we treated them as separate corpuses for the purposes of topic modeling. As this method looks for statistical co-occurrences of words, both corpuses and topics, in Arabic and English, were disjoint sets, so while a single document can and often contains a distribution of topics rather than a single topic, posts containing English topics will only contain other English topics, and posts containing Arabic topics would contain only other Arabic topics, making a separate analysis more appropriate. Translation of both corpuses into a common language was not an option both due to the lack of acceptable automated tools and the editorial issues involved in the translation of foreign languages.

A subset of 1,026 blog posts was published between the dates of December 1, 2010 and February 28, 2011, dates that bracket the recent revolutionary activity in Egypt, which began in early January and culminated with the toppling of Hosni Mubarak's government on February 11, 2011. To focus our analysis on the Egyptian uprising, we selected these posts for further examination with topic modeling.

The Egyptian Blogosphere: years 2004-present

Arabic blog posts consist of blogs written with the formal Arabic language (Arabic is the official language of Egypt) and those written with the Egyptian dialect (spoken by Egyptians in their everyday life) [23]. As the Egyptian dialect is a variation of the formal Arabic and uses the Arabic characters in its written form, it is not possible to distinguish between the two using topic modeling.

Arabic Blogs

Our Arabic topic-modeling corpus contained 9,597 documents published between Sep 2004 and Aug 2011. The topic modeling software generated a l ist of topics, translated, and shown in Table 1.

As Table 1 indicates, topic modeling does not always generate sets of words that correspond clearly to analytically determined topics or subjects. However, a number of the topics did correspond to real-world topics. We read each grouping of words and hypothesized about possible thematic associations, and then cross-referenced these with a random selection of documents that the topic modeler indicated as containing the topic in question, empirically verifying the validity of the themes. We then associated the topics with the themes.

	Topics
T1	inside pass sex front husband man
T2	Politics Israel people America Arab Egypt regime Egyptian
T3	Land people generous knowledge Muslim Islam
T4	Distant little I-know yours moment speak heart something
T5	Year many talk print want maybe I-know
T6	Full crazy serve program Arab site Egypt share
T7	Game prince league overcome Mohammed Egypt Abu
T8	Speak truth more your think picture book person
T9	Correct seek small children illness way pictures big
T10	Mubarak security election group council constitution doctor

Table 1. List of translated Arabic blog topics, 2004-2011

Four coders identified topics 2 and 10 as being concerned with political issues, with topic 2 referring to foreign relations and 10 referring to domestic issues. The presence of the terms “constitution,” “election,” and “Mubarak” led us to identify the latter as most relevant to “revolution”. Topics 4 and 5 were associated with documents containing self-oriented language, such as “I know,” “I want,” and “I talk,” and so we labeled these “personal topics.” The coders could not identify a clear pattern in the content of the posts contained in the remaining topics and consequently, we did not assign them a label.

Topic modeling enabled us to look at the trends of topics over time. Figure 1 shows the percentage of blog posts in any given month that our software indicated as containing one of the topics we designated as pertaining to a political, personal or revolution theme. It is important to note that the topics were not mutually exclusive within a given post—each document could contain more than one topic. Dealing with this data in percentages enabled us to better see macro trends in topic prevalence, as the number of Egyptian blogs increased significantly in the period studied, corresponding with an increase in Internet usage in the country.

Using the topic modeling analysis on the Arabic blogs, we found a strong inverse relationship between the occurrence of personal, self-oriented posts, and posts about political issues. We also found that over time, Egyptian blogs became increasingly political in nature, suggesting an increasing use of this online medium for airing counter-governmental narratives.

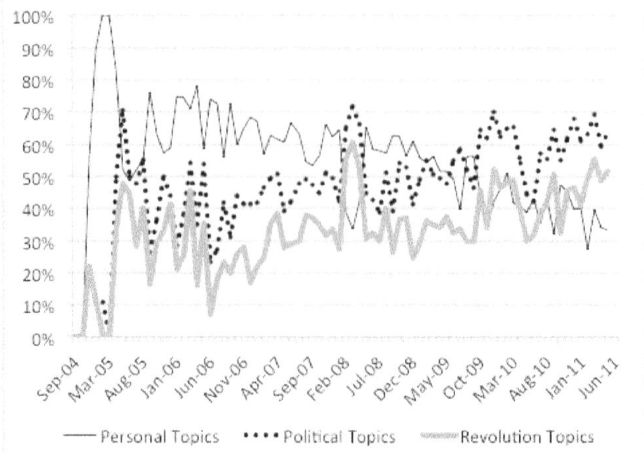

Figure 1: Percentage of Arabic posts containing topics by month

Fig. 1 shows that between 2006 and 2011, the percentage of posts containing personal topics steadily decreased from 65% to about 35%. During the same period, the percentage of posts containing revolution-relevant topics constantly increased, from about 15% to just over 50%, perhaps suggesting that politics and the regime were very (and increasingly) important topics in Egypt during these past seven years. Castells [8] notes that “most blogs are of personal character,” and that this type of mass-self communication is more akin to “electronic autism”—the exposition of personal experiences rather than attempts to galvanize others—than to the actual communication he identifies as integral to counter-power.

We found it particularly interesting that around the time of the uprising, there was an inverse relationship between posts that dealt more with revolutionary issues, and those that contained personal or self-oriented language. This is worthy of attention in light of the fact that the distribution of topics is not mutually exclusive—a given document often contains more than one topic. This trend also raises questions about the reasons for the decline in self-oriented language.

It is possible that Egyptian bloggers and perhaps even the Egyptian people writ large grew increasingly concerned with politics, or that politically-minded Egyptians increasingly used blogs as an outlet for expression. In addition, the prevalence of political speech in blogs stands in contrast with the observed suppression of political speech in the public arena in the years preceding and immediately prior to the revolution. In either case, there is an apparent change in the motivations of Egyptian bloggers over time. The blogs' shift from particularism and “autistic” narratives [8] towards universalism and more societally-oriented narratives seems to suggest that blogs increasingly served a counter-power role particularly during the time of the uprising.

	Topics
T1	egypt arabic islam riddler blog book muslim megabyte
T2	israel intelligence israeli cia war pakistan india military
T3	cairo dance food water night cup lovely add
T4	women human rights society law government country
T5	city house children street family left told gaza
T6	egypt egyptian political president mubarak elections regime democracy
T7	heart health body calories blood weight energy medical
T8	information chinese office service based system national group
T9	think love want things say feel friends thing
T10	egypt egyptian mubarak army revolution security police news

Table 2. List of English blog topics, 2004-2011

English Blogs

Our English corpus consisted of 6,153 documents for the data spanning Sep 2004 to May 2011. The topic modeling software revealed the topics shown in table 2.

Again, four coders identified topics broadly related to political and personal issues. Topic 4 dealt with issues of society, including human rights, women's rights, and law. We identified the content of posts containing topic 9 as personal or "self-oriented," similar to the Arabic. Topics 6 and 10 concerned Mubarak's regime, the goals of protest and uprising, and the events of the revolution; these were labeled as "revolution topics."

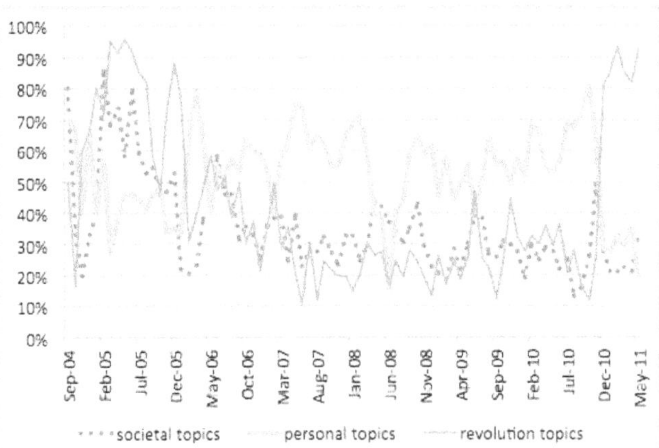

Figure 2: Percentage of English posts containing topics by month

In examining the English blogs, we found that, as with the Arabic blogs, an inverse relationship between the occurrence of personal and political topics existed. We also call attention to the dramatic reversal in quantity of revolution and personal topics in the months preceding and during the revolution.

A number of obvious patterns emerged. First, topics concerning 'revolution' have been discussed in the blogosphere as early as 2004. Though the discussion began to decline in 2006, it still was a constant presence in the blogosphere, constituting at least 20% of the discussion over the last eight years. The percentage of blog posts that concerned revolution experienced a significant upsurge in late 2010, increasing from just 11.9 percent in October of that year and 22.5 percent in November to 81.2 percent in December 2010. This increase bears a striking correspondence to the increasing amounts of protest activity in that month. However, while the Arabic blogs also saw an increase in occurrence of the revolution topic, the change was relatively minor—32.5% to 46.3%. While the surge in revolution-related posts seen in the English posts between October and December seems intuitive given the magnitude of the events occurring in the country, the lack of a corresponding surge in the Arabic blogs raises questions about what fundamental differences in purpose and audience might exist between the English and Arabic blogs, in addition to the possibility that posts written in English may predominately be authored by the Egyptian diaspora.

Though there was a great deal of variance in the number of posts that contained personal topics, it is notable that the number of blogs that used personal language dropped dramatically, from 81.0 percent in October 2010 to 21.3% in December of that year. This corresponds to our Arabic results.

In our analysis of the data, we discovered a number of interesting trends that merit further investigation: First, we found that the appearance of self-oriented language seemed to show a correlation with the appearance of topics about society. This suggests that, for Egyptian bloggers, issues like human rights could have been impacting their daily lives, and that these issues were important to a large proportion of bloggers from Egypt. This finding is consistent with the fact that bloggers often acted as citizen journalists, actively documenting their own experiences and observations of police torture, human rights abuses and the denial of civil liberties [1, 15].

Coders noted that increased posting about the regime was preceded by some months or days by topics concerning societal issues. If such a relationship exists, we might attribute a shift in attention to the regime to prior shifts in attention towards societal malaise—spikes in revolution topics in July 2008, July 2009, and December 2010 were all accompanied by significant spikes in societal topics in the preceding months. The most active time period for both revolutionary and societal topics occurred from April–September 2005, a period that marked an important presidential election in which substantive political reform was widely discussed both domestically and internationally. It also marks Kefaya at the height of its power. The results of the election were disappointing to many, and revolutionary topics dwindle and fall into a trough from 2007-09.

The differences between the results of our Arabic and English topic modeling were stronger than we had suspected they would be, and raise some interesting questions. The topics that were found in the English blogs seemed qualitatively different—more topics were found on the revolution and on human rights—notably, the issues that have been the focal point for Western attention on Egypt. These observed differences could be interpreted as English blogs being outward-facing instruments of communication to a foreign audience.

The upsurge of posts concerning revolution in December 2010 was of particular interest to us. We hypothesized that the use of English in blog posts was done to cater to an outside, non-Egyptian audience by both Egyptian residents and expatriates. Prior to late 2010, a majority of blog posts tended to concern various apolitical topics. However, as civil unrest in the bloggers' home country increased along with the prospects of revolution, many of these bloggers chose to report on or comment on the events taking place in Egypt at a time when the regime-controlled state media was squelching all reports of civil unrest. Despite the threat of retribution to those residing in Egypt, many bloggers chose to promulgate narratives of events in Egypt subverting those officially approved by the Mubarak regime, effectively enacting counter-power in an online space over which the regime could not exercise sufficient control.

Egyptian blogging bracketing the uprising

The period spanning early December and late February was of particular interest in our examination of the relationship between blogs and the Egyptian uprising. The key historical events of this period, such as the Tunisian uprising and the beginning of protests, and the changes to the blogging landscape we observed from the topic modeling led us to investigate more closely the blogging during this time. We qualitatively analyzed and coded blog posts authored between December 1, 2010 and February 28, 2011. Posts were written in English, formal Arabic, and the Egyptian dialect. In some rare instances more than one language was used in a s ingle post. Posts were analyzed by three researchers, one of whom is fluent in English, formal Arabic and the local Egyptian dialect. A total of 1,026 substantive blog posts (i.e. blank blogs and advertisements were removed) were collected by the aggregator during that period of time.

We found we were often unable to determine the demographics of the bloggers who were active during that period because some did not offer any profile information, or the information within the profiles was incomplete. Previous research suggests that such anonymity provides bloggers with a degree of security and consequent freedom to write about politics without fear of arrest [13].

Three researchers coded different parts of the data; one coder was fluent in Arabic and coded the Arabic blogs; two were fluent in English and coded the English blogs. A sub-set of the data was used to train the coders until all three agreed on the code meaning.

We found that posts fell into one of three types: *reporting* news, providing *commentary* and, *other*. Posts were coded as *reporting* when the blogger focused on reporting events objectively, similar to an article in a mainstream newspaper. Posts were coded as *commentary* when bloggers included personal opinions, personal accounts, or general observations regarding events in their posts. All other posts were coded as *other*, which discussed, for example, art, photography, crocheting, or TV programs.

We looked for evidence of mobilization efforts (in the protests) by bloggers to determine purpose. Blogs were coded as *action* blogs if the purpose of the post was either to urge participation in the uprising or to mobilize others by providing information to help coordinate or organize the uprising. Blogs that did not urge or mobilize action were coded as *non-action*.

A single post could be coded as both *commentary* and *action*, for example:

"*the light and at last the light and in the name of the martyrs call upon you to come to visit Tahrir square and home of the free but take with you an I D and let them search you at any entry way...*" [Translated from local Egyptian dialect]

The blogger encourages participation in the protests by "the light" of the martyrs, thereby supplying a narrative that legitimizes action against the government, what we consider a *counter-narrative*.

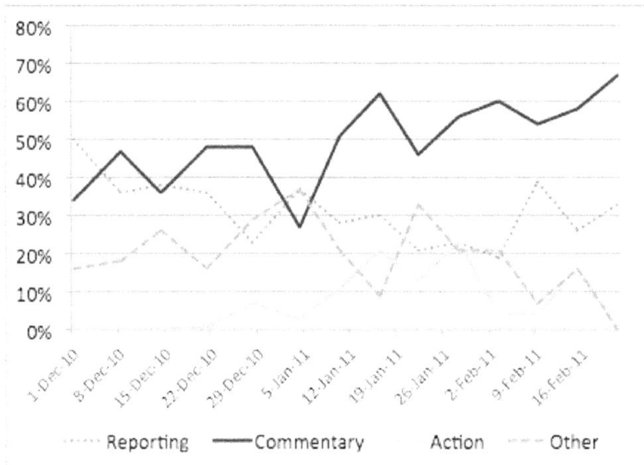

Figure 3: Percentage of blog types and purpose by month

Figure 3 illustrates the results of the manual coding for the December - February blog set. Contrary to our expectations, the number of action posts is surprisingly low, at most accounting for slightly more than 20% of all posts analyzed during that time period. Thus, roughly 80% of posts did *not* urge action or mobilization. We found that the majority of posts provided commentary, peaking at over 60% in January and close to 70% in February. Posts that reported news, however, maintained a relatively steady presence in the Egyptian blogosphere throughout this period.

In general, the blog posts reflected events occurring inside of Egypt. While action posts were non-existent prior to around mid-December, the frequency of their appearance gradually increased in tandem with the momentum of the uprising. On the other hand, the prevalence of commentary and reporting posts remained steady with that level prior to the onset of the uprising. Although we observe that the number of reporting posts was relatively consistent, they too increased slightly at certain points. We note, for example, the increase in reporting posts around the time when a car bomb exploded near a church which led to many casualties and damage to the church itself. Commentary posts began to increase after the bombing and the Tunisian uprising and then continued to increase during January. Thus, during this critical period of time in the MENA, blogs converged on discussion about the revolutionary events taking place.

The fact that commentary was the most prevalent type of post prior to and even more so during the uprising is an interesting finding worth exploring in more detail. During the period of time analyzed, we noticed blogs frequently referenced news stories from outside media sources in order to provide context for subsequent commentary on the issue or event. In doing so, they did not simply report news, they actively engaged in its content, made sense of it, and articulated an opinion that reflected their personal point of view. Unlike more objective, outside perspectives common in mainstream news journalism, commentary posts expressed the attitudes and the convictions of their authors.

For example, a post dated January 17 reacted to Egyptian mainstream news coverage of the Tunisian uprising:

"...The official media is reminding us over and over by all possible and provoking ways that what happened in Tunisia can't and will not happen to Egypt, the official media is speaking about pseudo achievements of Mubarak's economic policies living in their dream world that the people will buy their lies anymore. All these statements and all these denials are actually strong indicator on how scared and fragile the Egyptian regime is currently...."

The blogger recounts the government-sponsored narrative about the Tunisian uprising as being an isolated event that could not occur in Egypt referencing Mubarak's economic achievements. This post is an example of what we refer to as a counter-narrative, framing the official media coverage as an act of denial that proves the fragility of the regime.

THE SHAPE OF THE EGYPTIAN BLOGOSPHERE

Triangulating the results of both the topic modeling and the qualitative coding suggests that the blogs provided a narrative thread about the political uprising. While the qualitative coding revealed that most Egyptian posts consisted of commentary, the topic modeling further clarifies that the blogging of revolutionary topics increased and diminished in accord with the increasing and diminishing momentum of the uprising in Tahrir square.

Coders also noted the primary topic of each blog noting multiple topics when they were covered. We find several indications that the blog content is consistent with the notion of conveying counter-power.

Here we provide a general overview of the content. First, prior to the uprising, blog posts primarily consisted of reports and discussions about the November 29 - December five parliamentary elections and subsequent allegations of fraud and intimidation. This event, along with the car bomb attack near a church on January 1 dominated the Egyptian blogosphere during December and early January. The church bombing continued to emerge in posts the following month and led many bloggers in the Egyptian blogosphere to speculate about those responsible for the attack and the motives behind it. One such post is presented below (translated from Egyptian dialect):

"'religion is for God and the homeland is for everyone', they want a civil war they want sectarian conflict they want to distract people from their crimes they want to be outside the conflict zone and watch from afar..."

The blogger attributes the terrorist act to some unnamed third party that is taking advantage of a weak and corrupt government. The topic of the church bombing is discussed again in the weeks prior to and during January 25. One post written in Arabic reported that the Ministry of the Interior would announce the name of the perpetrator, and another blogger reported that a terrorist group was responsible. Both bloggers went on to discuss the implications of such news. Such posts provided updates to past news stories that motivate reexamination of the event and further interpretation of the underlying social and political forces perceived to contribute to the attack. They illustrate the impact of the event felt by many bloggers as well as their dissatisfaction with the government's response.

Second, blogging about the Tunisian uprising was prominent. The outward dissatisfaction of bloggers to the government's reaction to the church attack was amplified and propagated during the Tunisian uprising. We found reporting and commentary concerned with the topic of 'revolution' emerged shortly after the Tunisian uprising on January 14 2011, with several bloggers referring to it in their posts. Early posts provided emotional support to the Tunisian people, reported on their progress and commented on their courage. We found there was a gradual transition in this dialogue to include discussion of a revolution in Egypt. For example, one blogger questioned why the revolution had occurred in Tunisia rather than Egypt. An overt example of counter-power communication came when some began to refer to the demonstrations scheduled on January 25 as the beginning of the Egyptian revolution, e.g.:

"Will 25th of January 2011 be a remarkable Day in our history ??.. there is a big event organized by "We are all Khaled Said" group and supported by other opposition political parties and groups on that day and there are huge hopes that this event will change Egypt forever especially after what happened in Tunisia..."

Many blog posts provided constant updates on events occurring in Egypt from Jan. 25 onward. They reported diverse aspects of the uprising, e.g. police presence and government reaction. One Arabic post reports the arrest of journalists working for mainstream Egyptian media as they protested outside a media building. Others reported the increasing popularity of the movement and the difficulties that protestors encountered, for example:

"*There is a protest reportedly taking place in Ismailia Al Masry Al Youm is broadcasting a live stream from down town. Live Broadcasting by Ustream. The police has failed in attacking the protesters at Tahrir and the protest there is getting larger and larger. The protesters have managed to cross the security cordons and seemed to be heading to Kasr Al Nil bridge. The entrance and exists of Cairo are being locked.*"

Another post authored on the 25th, refers to pictures taken of the square, countering the videos shown on national TV:

"*... Protests began today for National Police Day (a national holiday that became effective only a year ago), but the voices were all the same: "Gamal, go back to your father (Hosni) and leave Egypt." ... I wanted to witness it, thus I set off on my journey to Tahrir Square around 1:15 pm. Roads were blocked off and I walked for about 25 minutes before reaching Tahrir.*"

The blogger provided a first-hand account through pictures and textual description of both the people who were participating in addition to the altercations between the police and the demonstrators. At times, an initial post was updated or followed up by later posts, connecting and creating a context for fragments of information. Thus, we find that bloggers countered the government-controlled narrative by posting and continually updating personal testimonies of the events taking place in the streets. By collectively contributing to an alternate narrative, Egyptian blogs became online communication mechanisms to counter and resist the power of the government.

The Egyptian government sought to repress communication through the Internet by ordering a "virtual curfew" (which lasted January 28–February 2) mandating that Internet service providers block all internet connections. Here we find a case of what Castells describes as blocking the mechanisms of control over the networks by the institutional power. Some bloggers were able to work around the curfew by corresponding through friends and family abroad and through other undetected means (e.g. phone, proxy-websites). One blogger continuously updated his post throughout the day on Jan 29 despite the curfew:

"*I woke up on my iPhone , the mobile phones are working while the internet is still not working. 10:25 AM Al Jazeera reporter in Alex : More than 20 bodies alone. 10:25 AM Arkadia mall was stolen yesterday. Some shops are stolen in Gamaat Al Doul. 11:15 AM Some mobile lines are working , some are not according to the the mobile phone operator and geography as far as I see.*"

The blogger provides a steady, almost hourly stream of information until midnight, with an intimate chronology of the blogger's experience during the revolution. Others provided links to blogs reporting the curfew, e.g.:

"*While the Egyptian government is now attempting desperately to crack down on all non-state-controlled media outlets, these activists have been using different forms of communications tools to build upon a message of nonviolent change they have been promoting...*"

These posts demonstrate how blogs were used to communicate the experiences of Egyptians during the revolution despite restrictive policies imposed by the Mubarak regime. Such posts illustrate how blogs were utilized to counter and (through the use of other media) circumvent the government's authoritative grip of power.

The utilization of blogs to counter institutionalized power continued even after Mubarak's resignation on February 11. We found many posts discussing the corruption of the Mubarak family and the newly empowered transitional government. Many doubted the transitional government's ability, competence and willingness to meet demonstrators' demands as this post authored on February 21 shows (translated from the Egyptian dialect):

"*We will remain standing to complete the revolution...we will go on strike again until our demands are met...*"

Here we see that even after the success of the revolution there is a precarious balance between institutionalized power and networked counter-power.

DISCUSSION AND CONCLUSIONS

Our investigation illustrates that the blog posts provided a consistent *narrative* often used to counter that provided by the authoritative power, the Egyptian government. Based on our results, we feel it is more accurate to interpret the Egyptian blogosphere during this period as providing counter-power through enabling the collective production of a *counter-narrative*.

First, in analyzing blogs, we noticed that the posts, through their commentary, together crafted a fluid, expressive narrative. Interestingly, while we initially anticipated finding more instances of organization and mobilization of protest movement (action posts), our findings detect subtler forces at play found in these commentaries.

Castells' argues that power is "the structural capacity of a social actor to impose its will over other social actor(s)" and that counter-power is "the capacity of a social actor to resist and challenge power relations that are institutionalized." Power, he argues, is based on the capacity to influence people's minds and as such, communication and communication infrastructures have always been important to issues of power. Prior to networked communication, this infrastructure was wholly under the control of the Egyptian government. As a result, information and communication control disseminated through the vertical, 'top-down' structure of broadcast-based media—television, newspaper, and radio—institutions of state power. On the other hand, networked communication defies such centralized control. The presence (and, according to the topic modeling, the increasing presence) of counter-narratives suggests that blogs served as an *alternative public space* in which sociopolitical issues and policies could be discussed, debated and disseminated. Social media can facilitate horizontal, many-to-many person communication, and, as our data demonstrate, allow the dissemination of these counter-narratives against power and domination.

As state media tried to downplay the size and strength of the uprising, first in Tunisia and then in Egypt, bloggers posted videos and first-hand accounts of what was actually happening in the streets. Counter-narratives broadcast on blogs were consumed and circulated by both domestic and international audiences. Egyptians blogging in English translated events and supplied counter-narratives for global audiences, contributing to the shape of debates that took place in the international public sphere. In this way, counter-narratives aimed to delegitimize the Mubarak regime's authority. By virtue of being social media, counter-narratives are broadcast into an online public sphere where discussion and linking are encouraged. This increases the chance that it will be shared by others. As the numbers grow, chances decrease that government authorities can contain it.

The results from topic modeling and qualitative coding together show that blogs converged on topics concerning the revolution during the December 1-February 28 time period. Reporting and commentary blog posts increased with the growing momentum of the Egyptian uprising, and the posts provided a narrative of the Egyptian uprising. The results illustrate the coalescence of blog post topics during critical periods of the uprising. The posts during that period transformed the shape of the Egyptian blogosphere from one that reflects the diverse interests of bloggers discussing personal and other topics into a cohesive thread, a counter-narrative to the government-controlled Egyptian media.

The communication we observed took place within a virtual public space where social actors can exercise autonomy and promote change in ways that were previously impossible. Such autonomy is typically attributed to western culture, as is the use of social media for mass-self communication [7]. Our results illustrate that such autonomy is not limited to a particular culture but can be enabled by access to these technologies.

The Egyptian government attempted to control the blog space by arresting several prominent bloggers. However as we found, they were unsuccessful, as the amount of blog posts about revolution and dissent against the government only increased with time. The Egyptian government also tried to control the public space by shutting down the Internet, imposing a "virtual curfew". However, Egyptians adapted to these restrictions and gained access to the Internet through other means -- an example of *counter-power* using social media.

Additionally, we argue that the malleability of the blog media enabled authors to adapt the tool to meet their needs. We found instances during the height of the protest activity where blog posts consisted of a series of updates as events unfolded, similar to the use of micro-blogs. We also found instances where media such as YouTube videos and photos were embedded into a blog, transforming the presentation of content from a single-media tool into multi-media. This hybrid presentation did not detract from the textual narrative but rather added to its complexity and enhanced its credibility. Also, bloggers linked their posts to other ICTs like the "We are all Khaled Said" and the "April 6th Youth" political groups referring to their websites and Facebook accounts. This suggests that users adapted tools to suit their emerging needs and in doing so showed their "adaptation adopting, aggregating and developing new forms of social media" [7]. Furthermore, such uses are an indication that these bloggers have greater ability to exert counter-power, as they confronted institutionalized power through their blog posts.

Castells describes one mechanism of counter-power as changing the codes of networks. The reports, commentary, pictures and videos posted by bloggers created a new norm of challenging official reporting of the events by mainstream Egyptian media (controlled by the government). The state-run media initially denied the spread of the movement (e.g. by showing video clips of empty streets) and later attributed the movement to some foreign power (e.g. Iran) [22].

In sum, we found that blogging gave Egyptians an opportunity to report and comment on the uprising by communicating information and opinions that were not generally available through state-run media. Both the topic modeling and our qualitative analysis showed a marked increase in blogs that focused on the revolution as it progressed. The communication reflected in blogs provided a narrative that countered the narrative controlled by the government. By contesting the dominant frame given by state-owned and controlled media, blogs provided a platform for what we characterize as a *counter-narrative*. We argue that the enablement of counter-narratives in a country where political speech in traditional venues was tightly controlled by the government is a convincing example of the enactment of counter-power through the use of contemporary social media. As more real-world examples of counter-power through social media appear in the coming years, we posit that the ability or inability of governments and other power-holding institutions to exercise control over the numerous forms of expression enabled by these technologies will become an issue of greater contention.

LIMITATIONS AND FUTURE WORK

We recognize that our study is limited to a particular population of literate individuals who have access to ICT. Our analysis of posts written using the English, Arabic, and Egyptian Arabic language provides some degree of representativeness to Egyptian society, English is typically considered to be preferred by the financially elite Egyptians, and Arabic is typically preferred by the educated, whereas the Egyptian dialect typically preferred by all other Egyptians [23]. Our analysis consisted of blogs using the popular Blogspot platform, which is not a fully comprehensive subset of the Egyptian blogosphere. However, given the size of the blogosphere we feel that we did generate a l arge enough sample that we could make inferences to some degree. Most research can only claim to analyze a cluster of posts within the blogosphere; we chose to focus on the Blogspot cluster.

Future work will involve further research into the Egyptian blogosphere to investigate differences between blogs written in English and non-English,, government blogs and other power frameworks (e.g. [16]).We also aim to study other areas of unrest within the region (e.g. Libya) to examine the shape of the blogosphere in different MENA countries and use those results for investigative comparison.

AKNOWLEDGEMENTS

This project was supported by NSF grant #0910640, #1128008, and through an NSF Graduate Research Fellowship awarded to Justin Chung. We also thank David Newman for his topic modeling expertise.

REFERENCES

1. Al Malky, R. (2007). Blogging for reform: the case of Egypt. *Arab media & society, (1),* 1-31. Retrieved from http://www.arabmediasociety.com/?article=12
2. Arvizu, S. (2009). Creating alternative visions of Arab society: emerging youth publics in Cairo. *Media, culture & society,* 31(3), 385-407.
3. Ashraf A. M.,, Nergis A., Friedman,B., & Mahdy E. F. (forthcoming). Commentary: The impact of social networking tools on political change in Egypt's 'Revolution 2.0', *Electronic commerce research and applications.*
4. Bechev, D. (Ed.), Schäfer, I. (Ed.), Boubekeur, A., Ezzeldeen, N., & Lahlou, M. (2010). Agents of change in the Mediterranean. Working paper: RAMSES2 consortium of Mediterranean studies (6th Framework Programme). Oxford.
5. Blei, D., Ng, A., & Jordan, M. (2003). Latent dirichlet allocation. *Journal of Machine Learning Research*, *3*, 993-1022.
6. Carroll, W., & Hackett, R. (2006). Democratic media activism through the lens of social movement theory, *Media, Culture & Society 28(1),* 83–104.
7. Castells, M. (2007). Communication, power and counter-power in the network society. *International Journal of Communication* [Online] 1:1.
8. Castells, M. (2009). *Communication power.* NY: Oxford University Press.
9. Committee to Protect Journalists. (2009, April 30). 10 worst countries to be a blogger. Retrieved from http://www.cpj.org/reports/2009/04/10-worst-countries-to-be-a-blogger.php.
10. Deerwester, S., Dumais, S. T., Furnas, G. W., Landauer, T. K. and Harshman, R. (1990) Indexing by latent semantic analysis. *JASIS*, *41*, 391–407.
11. Everard, J. (2000). *Virtual states: The Internet and the boundaries of the nation-stat*e. London: Taylor & Francis.
12. Earl, J. (2010). The dynamics of protest-related diffusion on the web." *information, communication & society*. 1*3(2),* 209-225.
13. Fahmi, S. W. (2009). "Bloggers' street movement and the right to the city: (Re)claiming Cairo's real and virtual "spaces of freedom." *Environment and urbanization 21(1),* 89-107.
14. Fandy, M., (2000). Information technology, trust, and social change in the Arab world, *Middle East journal (54)3*, 378-94.
15. Faris, D. (2008). Revolutions without revolutionaries? Network theory, Facebook, and the Egyptian blogosphere. *Arab media & society*, 6. Retrieved from http://www.arabmediasociety.com/topics/index.php?t_article=232.
16. Foucault, M. (1982). The subject and power, *Critical inquiry*, 8(4). 777-795.
17. Freedom House.(2010, May 3). *Freedom in the world 2010 – Egypt*. Retrieved from http://www.unhcr.org/refworld/docid/4c0ceaf5c.html.
18. Hamdy, N. (2009). Arab citizen journalism in action: Challenging mainstream media, authorities and media laws. *Westminster papers in comm. and culture, 6(1*), 365-72. doi: 10.3961/jpmph.2008.41.6.365.
19. Karatzogianni, A. (2004). The politics of 'cyberconflict', *Politics*, 24, (1), 46 – 55.
20. Lagman, L. (2005). From virtual public spheres to global justice: A critical theory of internet worked social movements. *Soc Theory*, *23, (1),* 42-74.
21. Oweidat, N., Benard, C., Stahl, D., Kildani, W., O'Connell, E., & Grant, A. K. (2008). *The Kefaya movement: a case study of a grassroots reform initiative.* Santa Monica, CA: RAND Corporation. Retrieved from http://www.rand.org/pubs/monographs/2008/RAND_MG778.sum.pdf.
22. Peterson, M., (2011). Egypt's media ecology in a time of revolution. *Arab media & society*, *13*. Retrieved from http://www.arabmediasociety.com/?article=770.
23. Warschauer, M., El Said, G., and Zohry, A. (2002) Language choice online: Globalization and identity in Egypt. *J of Computer-Mediated Communication*, 7(4).
24. Wheeler, D. (2007). Empowerment zones? Women, Internet cafes, and life transformations in Egypt, *Inf Technologies & Inter'l Development*, *4(2),* 89-104.

'Facebooking' Towards Crisis Recovery and Beyond: Disruption as an Opportunity

Bryan Semaan and Gloria Mark
Department of Informatics
Donald Bren School of Information and Computer Sciences
University of California, Irvine
{bsemaan, gmark@uci.edu}

ABSTRACT
This paper reports on an ethnographic study of Facebook use amongst a population living through ongoing disruption. We interviewed 45 Iraqi citizens, as well as received survey responses from 218 individuals, who have been experiencing the current Gulf War since March 2003. We show how people in a society experiencing conflict use Facebook in ways that are different to uses in non-war societies. We find that Facebook supports people living in crisis environments at two levels. First, Facebook aids people directly to recover from disruption. People used Facebook to create "safe lists", to seek help and provide assistance, and to re-construct their social scaffolding. But at a deeper level, citizens also used Facebook to maintain and develop new social norms, and to re-direct their country. We discuss how disruption can serve as an opportunity by which people can re-invent their societies and how our understandings of Facebook should evolve.

Author Keywords
Facebook, war, crisis, slippage, social-networking, recovery

ACM Classification Keywords
K.4.3 [Computers and Society]: Organizational Impacts – Computer-Supported cooperative work.

General Terms
Human Factors

INTRODUCTION
Information and Communication Technologies (ICTs) have become valuable tools for citizens during crisis events. A general finding is that with ICT use, a large number of people can coordinate efforts in providing aid for disaster victims. For example, ICTs have been found to be valuable for spreading community-relevant information [24] as well as locating information and finding victims [23]. With microblogging, people within and outside the disaster area have been found to gain situational awareness [31].

More specifically, Social Networking Sites (SNSs), such as Facebook and Orkut, hold promise as tools for supporting people in disasters, yet have been less studied in this domain [19, 27, 30]. SNSs have become popular online destinations in recent years. What makes these sites unique is that people can make their social networks visible to others. Unlike technologies such as Instant Messenger, people can make connections that they otherwise would not have made by traversing other people's networks; a search function is also available to search for friends, family, and even strangers [5].

Researchers have studied the use of SNSs from a variety of perspectives, e.g. "social searching" [15], social capital [7] and cultural differences [14]. As SNSs continue to be widely adopted, we believe that they could be valuable tools for supporting people during crises. They are malleable which enables them to adapt to a number of uses during disruption. People can form groups and can self-organize. Status update features can provide situational awareness of conditions in an area. People can find expertise through direct and second order connections. In fact SNSs might prove valuable in crisis situations far longer than the acute stages of a crisis. In this paper we focus on the SNS of Facebook. We are particularly interested in investigating the role of Facebook in supporting people not only during the acute crisis stage but also over the long-term, in enabling people to recover from ongoing disruption, and to maintain their daily lives. Our study is part of a larger research program where we are trying to better understand the role ICTs play in enabling resilience amongst populations disrupted by war [**Error! Reference source not found.**].

RECOVERING FROM ONGOING DISRUPTION
Disaster and crisis situations are non-routine events in societies that involve social disruption and physical harm [9]. Furthermore, such events can be conceptualized as the interrelationship between society (individuals, groups, communities and organizations), the physical environment (how social connections are affected), and culture (norms and values) [18].

In the aftermath of a crisis, the previous routines of daily life may no longer be viable as victims recover from the event. Researchers studying disasters have looked at this recovery process: how affected populations deal with, adapt to, and resume normal societal function following a crisis

CSCW'12, February 11–15, 2012, Seattle, Washington, USA.

event. The various activities associated with the process that lead to recovery [6, 12, 18, 21] have been modeled by Powell [6] as taking place in eight socio-temporal stages: pre-disaster, warning, threat, impact, inventory, rescue, remedy, and recovery.

The first four stages of Powell's model (pre-disaster, warning, threat, impact) include the time period from before a disaster is detected to when a disaster takes place. The pre-disaster phase is the period before a disaster strikes. The warning phase is where the potentially affected population is notified of the pending threat. During the threat phase, preventive measures are taken to mitigate potential effects. In the impact phase, the actual disaster takes place, and people begin to understand what changes may be necessary in order to lessen the effects of disruption.

The following three stages (inventory, rescue, remedy) describe the emergency related activities that people engage in that lead to the recovery phase. The first of these stages—inventory—is the period where people adjust to the crisis event and determine a course of action. It is marked by a sense of individualism where victims try to make sense of the event and take stock of their property and families [12]. One of the first activities people engage in following disaster is to try and determine the safety and location of family and friends [6]. For example, during Hurricane Katrina, "safe lists" were created where people could report their whereabouts, and using such lists it was possible for family and friends to locate one another.

The next stage, rescue, is a period where people engage in activities to aid in the relief effort. This phase can be marked by altruism, as often the public engages in pro-social behavior [6, 12]. The individuals and groups who emerge and lead the initial response effort are typically not from the formal authoritative groups that we associate with relief, such as the Red Cross, but rather citizens from the surrounding or local community who conduct search and rescue operations, distribute food and clothing, and make donations, in the aftermath of a disaster.

The stage before recovery, remedy, begins when formal organizing bodies, such as fire brigades and Red Cross personnel, provide relief. Hoffman [12] describes how, during this period, citizens begin to gather in a physical place and reconstruct their lives. People collocate and begin to re-establish their social networks: individuals forge new relationships, re-connect with others, and in some cases, relationships can deteriorate. People may also turn to close family members (i.e. parents and siblings) for support. During this phase, people often travel to the site of physical disruption to lend their loved ones a hand by helping them rebuild, or, by providing them with financial assistance.

The final stage, recovery, is characterized by a return to normalcy. Individuals have either returned to their homes or built homes in new locations, people continue to work and attend school regularly, and other societal activities resume.

In this paper we focus on recovery activities in a war environment. War environments are a special case of Powell's model as people are experiencing several stages concurrently. For example, people may be working on recovery from a recent attack while also experiencing new threats or warnings. While most disasters are small in scale, not catastrophic in extent, and take place over a small time interval [6], people who experience war can be subjected to prolonged disruption. Such events can cause people to live with and adapt to constant uncertainty in the environment, as they must deal with random events on a day-to-day basis. People living through ongoing crisis must develop continual situational awareness when enacting their daily routines, as disruptive forces, e.g. bombings, can randomly take place at any time.

Phase	Characteristics of Disaster	Characteristics of a War Zone	Facebook use and Recovery
Inventory	Citizens verify safety and well-being of family and friends (can be difficult)	Difficult to determine well-being of family and friends due to dangerous environment	Can search for family and friends
Rescue	Citizens engage in pro-social, altruistic behavior and lead the initial response effort	May not be able to trust strangers as they may be insurgents or members of a militia	Can connect with trusted contacts; Can connect with community
Remedy	Citizens try to meet physically; Citizens reconstruct social networks; Family and friends arrive to provide support	Unsafe to travel to meet others face-to-face; Difficult to collocate/ cannot trust strangers; Distance may separate support networks	Can re-construct social networks and reconnect with support networks
Recovery	Normal life resumes/new norms can emerge	Disruption becomes part of routine life/new norms can emerge	Some practices transfer to online interaction; Can develop/ maintain new practices

Table 1: Characteristics of war and Facebook use in relation to the latter four stages of Powell's disaster model

Table 1 contrasts how recovery activities differ during disaster and war environments vis-à-vis Powell's last four stages in his model. Table 1 shows our hypothesized view of how Facebook can be used, first, to support the activities that people engage in prior to recovery (inventory, rescue and remedy) and, second, to support the return to normalcy (the recovery stage) and the activities in the time beyond.

We expect that due to its malleability, Facebook can support a range of activities to help citizens recover in a war environment vis-à-vis Powell's model. During the inventory stage, citizens determine the safety and well being of family and friends. In disasters or war, people may be separated and it can be difficult to determine the whereabouts of others. Facebook can enable people to search for others via the built-in search function. During the rescue stage, citizens often engage in pro-social behavior and provide assistance and aid. In a war environment, however, people may not be able to rely on strangers as e.g., they may be members of a militia or insurgents—violent conflict can undermine interpersonal trust (trust between people) [1]. Facebook can enable people to connect with trusted contacts, such as family, friends, and community members, in order to request or provide assistance and aid. During the remedy stage, family and friends arrive to provide assistance and people meet together physically and reconstruct their social networks. In a war environment, since there is continual disruption, it may be difficult to collocate, as well as trust other citizens. Facebook provides citizens experiencing war with a safe online environment, where they can connect with trusted contacts, as well as reconstruct their social edifice.

Additionally, Facebook could support a return to normalcy, as well as new practices that go beyond the routine. During the recovery stage in Powell's model, citizens resume their normal lives. When a war is protracted, however, disruption becomes the routine. Routine practices may be difficult to maintain due to ongoing threats and an unsafe environment. For example, people may not be able to maintain social and religious obligations. Additionally, established norms may change. In normal environments people's interactions are governed by established rules and norms—where people interact in socially acceptable ways in public [10, 15]. In a war environment, however, new social norms may emerge with respect to how people view and treat others. For example, during World War II, it became acceptable for female African American nurses to tend to white male soldiers in the infirmary; it also became acceptable for women to assume many male-dominated societal roles in work. Barley [3] describes how external events can be so intense that they cause "slippages", or changes to a social system, to take place. When slippages persist, they become replicated patterns that people must adapt to on a continual basis. As a result, people must restructure their patterns of action in order to adapt to changing circumstances. Structural changes may emerge as a result. An environment disrupted by violent conflict may act as a catalyst whereby people must revise their daily practices in accordance with what is taking place in the environment.

Returning to Facebook, we expect that people might use it to maintain practices, as working online enables them to be independent of their physical environment. When slippages occur in the environment, Facebook may even support people in developing new practices through the affordances of meeting and coordinating with others.

Studies of crisis situations have found innovative behaviors associated with the recovery process in online settings [11, 19, 20]. ICTs (e.g. blogs and online forums) have enabled people from across the globe to participate in the crisis recovery process by providing assistance and aid, disseminating information, and providing social support [19]. These studies, however, concentrate on the acute phase of disaster—they do not examine prolonged disruption. Studies of the use of SNSs during disaster have looked at how people used Facebook to engage in distributed problem solving activities [30], to provide emotional support and guidance [19], to receive up-to-date information from peer-to-peer networks [27], and to determine the safety of friends through status message updates [19]. We are interested in how people use Facebook to engage in recovery activities in a war environment, where distance may separate family and friends, social norms may change, and trust may deteriorate.

METHODOLOGY

Our results are based on both interviews and a survey. We drew on cases from people living through ongoing disruption—Iraqis who have been living through war since March 2003. Beginning in September 2007, we have conducted interviews in both English and Arabic with 90 Iraqis who experienced the war. For this study we only analyzed our most recent set of 45 interviews (25 male, 20 female) beginning in April 2010, as these interviews focused on how our informants were using Facebook.

To recruit informants, we found individuals through various sources. First, one of the authors is an Iraqi-American who is part of a large Iraqi community in San Diego County, and we found informants for interviews through local contacts. Second, we recruited informants through several refugee groups and religious organizations (Christian and Muslim) in Southern California and abroad. Lastly, we also found informants through online sources. We only recruited informants who were no longer living in Iraq if they had recently left (less than 2 years abroad). After each interview we utilized a snowball sampling approach [4] where we asked our informants to recommend people that we could then recruit for our study. By finding informants through multiple sources our intent was to limit bias in our sample. Other CSCW studies have also utilized the snowball sampling approach, e.g. [11].

We asked people to compare their lives before and after the war. Disaster sociologists have used an interview methodology in the past and have found people's memories to be reliable long after an event [21]. It has also been found that people can correctly report typical, recurring activities they engage in over time [8]. We conducted interviews both in person (in Southern California), and across distance via mobile phone and Skype with people living in Iraq and other countries. Interviews lasted anywhere from two to six hours depending on technological conditions. At times the mobile and/or Internet networks in Iraq would become inoperable, and we had to switch to different communications technologies depending on what was available (i.e. switching from Skype to the mobile phone if the Internet went down). In some cases we would have to reschedule for a later time and date. We always exchanged multiple points of contact with our informants prior to an interview. All interviews were transcribed; Arabic interviews were first translated and then transcribed.

Additionally, in March 2011 we initiated an online survey based on interview responses that focused solely on Facebook use in Iraq. We received 218 responses. Prior to survey deployment, we read the survey to ten Iraqis to determine if the survey language was appropriate and made sense with respect to the Iraqi culture. From this feedback we revised some phrasing in the final survey design.

We recruited survey respondents using different threads. First, we provided key contacts in San Diego (i.e. family and friends, members of church and refugee groups) with recruitment flyers containing a web-link to the survey for distribution to Iraqi refugees who had recently arrived. Second, we sent a web-link with a description of the survey to key Iraqi contacts living in Iraq and abroad via e-mail and Facebook, asking them to distribute it to their local and global Iraqi friends and family members. If we had interviewed a contact, we asked him or her not to take the survey so as to limit redundancy in responses. Third, we posted an announcement in several Iraqi Facebook groups. Lastly, we distributed the survey using Twitter.

We developed an eligibility criteria for our survey. Respondents had to be either a native to Iraq or a current resident of Iraq; if not, they must have been living outside of Iraq for less than two years. We included a question to address this, and respondents who answered that they had been living outside of Iraq for over two years were sent to a page explaining they did not qualify for the survey. In order to further validate people's locations, we used an IP-to-Country service that allowed us to determine the location of all our respondents. We found that 73% of our respondents were living in Iraq, whereas the remaining lived in the U.S., Turkey, Germany, Sweden, the UK, Jordan, and Egypt. Considering that we have key contacts living in all of these locations that distributed the survey to members of their respective local Iraqi communities, we included these responses in our analysis. After removing survey responses that were completely blank, as well as responses from people who had been living outside of Iraq for over two years, we eliminated 39 responses. Out of our remaining total of 225 respondents (interviews and surveys), 218 (97.3%) reported regularly using Facebook.

Our respondents were diverse with respect to their gender (56.4% male, 44.6% female) as well as age (Table 2). They were also ethnically and religiously diverse. While the majority of our informants were from both the Shiite and Sunni sects of Islam, we were able to recruit individuals who were members of various ethnic and religious minorities in the country, such as the Assyrians (Christians), the Yazidis (a Kurdish religious minority) and Iraqi-Armenians. Our informants were also diverse with respect to their educational backgrounds and work roles. 85% of our respondents had either completed or were working on their Bachelor's degree. Students were studying biology, dentistry, medicine, journalism, political science, computer science, and engineering. Those who had completed college (53%) worked as doctors, journalists, professors, and in other fields. Our informants hailed from large urban cities in Iraq (Basra, Baghdad, Mosul, Arbil), as well as villages in the North of Iraq (Telkaif, Bashika).

Age Range	<18	18-21	22-25	26-30	31-40	41-50	51-60	>60
Percent	2.2	17.8	22.2	26.1	15	7.2	5.6	3.9

Table 2. Survey respondent age breakdown

We coded our documents using Atlas.ti. Guided by the research question of how Facebook was being used during the war, we utilized a grounded theory approach [26]. We first used open coding to identify general themes made explicit during interviews and free response sections in the survey, which we then reduced under axial coding.

RESEARCH SETTING

We have studied the use of Facebook in Iraq, a country that has been disrupted by war and violence since March 2003. Our informants are Iraqi civilians who lived in Iraq during the conflict. The current environment in Iraq is very unsafe for travel. Random bombings, kidnappings, roadblocks, fake checkpoints, and clashes among militias, insurgents, and the military—all contribute to making the country dangerous for travel [17]. The UN estimates that there are over 1.7 million displaced persons within Iraq [29].

Though Facebook penetration rate is officially listed as 2.69%[1], the actual usage rate may be higher; our informants reported that Iraqis frequent Internet cafes, as well as share computers and Internet connections. The majority of our informants used Facebook anywhere from one to five hours a day, and many claimed that they spent much time searching for people they had lost contact with, especially considering that more people are adopting the technology everyday.

'FACEBOOKING' DURING CRISIS

An important change that occurred in 2003 when the war began was the introduction and adoption of ICTs. The majority of our informants adopted Facebook at some point between 2006 and 2008, and they used the technology in a myriad of ways. After the initial setup and "friending", our respondents used Facebook in ways that were similar to those of U.S. college students [5]. They did social searching, identity management, coordination, and broadcasting. However, we discovered that there were also uses of Facebook that were unique to the physical world context (the war environment) and societal conditions (Iraqi traditions, social obligations and religion).

[1] http://www.socialbakers.com/facebook-statistics/

'Facebooking' towards recovery

Our data shows that the use of Facebook supported crisis recovery directly in multiple ways: by enabling people to determine the safety of family and friends, by providing a mechanism where people could provide as well as obtain assistance and aid, and by affording a safe environment where people could reconstruct their social networks.

Creating Facebook "safe lists"

In the inventory phase of Powell's model, people often determine the whereabouts of friends and family. For example, in the aftermath of Hurricane Katrina, "safe lists" were posted on various online websites such as one hosted by the local newspaper [23]. Similarly, one use of Facebook reported by our informants was the ability to establish "safe lists" by locating friends and family members with whom they had lost contact as a result of the war. When the disruption began in March 2003, the landline telephone infrastructure was severely damaged, impairing people's ability to locate others. Many of Iraq's citizens left the country and traveled to safe locations abroad without possessing the ability to contact other people to provide them with information regarding their personal welfare, while a large segment of the population became displaced within Iraq's borders. Many Iraqis (mostly in Baghdad) also moved to different neighborhoods as a result of the sectarian violence that emerged in the country causing Sunni's and Shiite's to move to segregated neighborhoods. While a main use of Facebook in the U.S. is to connect with people—weak ties where friendship once existed face-to-face but deteriorated across distance and time [14]—85% of the Facebook users in our sample reported using it to determine the well-being of strong ties (family members and close friends) as well as weak ties. Table 3 shows that the majority used Facebook as "safelists" for locating friends and colleagues. The reason that these categories may be higher than immediate family and relatives is that mobile phones may be used for locating the latter.

Safelist use	Immediate Family	Relative	Friend	Colleague	Neighbor
% Response	33.6%	60%	86.4%	75%	41.6%

Table 3. Percent of respondents who reconnected with others

Our informants have expressed that with the adoption of Facebook, the functionality has afforded them the ability to locate people at a much faster rate compared to other technologies like the mobile phone. Our informants reported that they spend an inordinate amount of time looking through their friend's lists perusing pictures in an effort to locate their loved ones. In this sense, when they discovered that a new strong or weak tie was on Facebook and added them to their friend's list, they were creating "safe lists." As described by one of our informants:

"...a lot of people left because of the security situation. On Facebook you can search for your friends and family... You will know where they are at, what they are doing. What has changed with them... So many of them that I could not find after 3 years or [more]... it was a wonderful thing"

Seeking help and providing assistance

In the rescue phase, citizens within as well as near the disaster zone often act as first responders [6]. Similarly, another use of Facebook reported by 23.2% of our informants was that they went online to seek help as well as to provide assistance during the war. Unlike other studies of ICT use during disaster, which have reported that pro-social behavior has been observed online [e.g. 28], in Iraq, citizens no longer trusted interacting with others in public settings [22]. After the conflict began, various militia and insurgent groups emerged and sectarian violence began to escalate in the country. Our informants reported they do not trust strangers in person because they may be sources of potential threats. Additionally, our informants believed the government to be incapable of providing support for a safe environment, the main necessity they reported they were lacking in their daily lives.

Our informants provided several accounts of how they and the people in their personal social networks used Facebook to seek and provide immediate help when kidnappings took place. It was important for them to be able to add people they trusted to their "Friend's lists" and have quick access to them. Our informants have been using Facebook to organize rescue attempts consisting of trust-based ties when family and friends were kidnapped or held hostage. More recently, people have used Facebook to obtain support from the police force—a departure from the norm, as our informants reported that the police were not performing the duties that Iraq's citizens expected of them. These reports were similar to the way in which the Tianya forum was used in China to request evacuation assistance from the government during the Sichuan Earthquake in 2008 [20].

One of our respondents, a journalist in Baghdad, described the details of a situation where he was personally kidnapped and how a combination of Facebook and his mobile phone proved to be invaluable in his eventual rescue. Like many Iraqis (especially those who worked for U.S.-based organizations), this individual carried multiple mobile phones at any given time—this particular informant carried three mobile phones from different carriers—in case of situations where they required immediate help or if they needed to switch to a different mobile network because of a lack of coverage. While traveling to work one morning, he was kidnapped and forced into the trunk of a car. His kidnapper, however, only confiscated two of his cell phones and failed to locate the third phone hidden on the inside of his jacket. Using his phone, he updated his Facebook status with a request for help designating his exact location when he was kidnapped, as well as the make and model of the automobile driven by his assailant. He sent the same message to all of his friends and family members via SMS as well in case they did not receive his Facebook update in time, and many of the people who received his message updated their Facebook statuses with a request for help. One of his family members' friends, after seeing the request for help, informed our informant's relative that the Iraqi police force has a Facebook page where a telephone number was available. After sending a message to the police on Facebook and making the required calls, the police received the request for help. Luckily, the street he was kidnapped on was a long one-way road littered with checkpoints and without outlet streets. When our informant (still locked in the trunk) arrived at the next major checkpoint, the police and a few of his family members were waiting to rescue him. Thus, Facebook enabled people to not only build a trusted citizen network on which they could rely for help, but it also provided them with a way in which they could gain access to official security forces.

During the remedy phase, it is often the case that family and friends arrive in a crisis zone to support their family members and friends as they reconstruct their lives [12]. Our informants reported that Iraqis now engage in a similar behavior using Facebook where they updated their status messages requesting financial assistance from family and friends because many of the people who they relied on could no longer be accessed easily in person.

Our informants also solicited financial assistance in a way similar to how blogs and online forums were used to obtain donations during Hurricane Katrina—what is known as "connected giving" [28]. Several new Facebook groups have emerged for the purpose of connecting people with other Iraqis so that they can request financial help when they are in trouble. Most of the Facebook groups were tied to very strong communities that existed from before the war. These communities were based on places that people once shared physically (i.e. neighborhoods, villages, social clubs). For example, we found Facebook groups that brought people together who once lived in the same neighborhoods in Baghdad, groups comprised of people from villages tied to certain religious or cultural minorities, such as the Yazidis and the Assyrians. These online groups provided our informants with the ability to connect with people they could rely on during financial crises.

The 'online Green Zone': Re-Constructing the Social Edifice

In the remedy stage, people often reformulate their social edifice [12]. It is during this time that family and friends begin to gather together in the physical space and socialize in an effort to restore old patterns; people also establish new relationships. Various obstacles existed making it difficult for people to reconstruct their social networks during the war: a lack of trust in strangers, difficulty traveling, and distance separating family and friends. Through Facebook, our informants could establish new relationships, as well as maintain their old social patterns in an online environment.

72% percent of our informants reported using Facebook to meet new people who they felt could not harm them physically due to their geographic separation. Though meeting new people is a widespread practice with Facebook, all of our respondents claimed that despite the security situation, Facebook also allowed them to re-construct their social edifice despite not being able to physical collocate easily. One informant, a female who once lived in Baghdad but subsequently moved to Sweden to escape the war, referred to Facebook as the "online Green Zone." Today, various parts of the country are designated as being green or red zones. Green zones are areas that are patrolled and protected by the U.S. armed forces, where various U.S. organizations operate, and are thus highly secure. Conversely, red zones are areas that are not safe. Our informants described how they were using the technology for several hours everyday—writing on people's walls, sending messages, as well as commenting and "liking" people's status updates and pictures. Thus, Facebook provided a safe place in which people could maintain their social lives without subjecting themselves to the dangerous physical environment.

'Facebooking' beyond recovery

Up to now, we have discussed how Facebook has been used in Powell's stages of inventory, rescue, remedy. Moreover, we discovered that Facebook not only supported the recovery phase, but also supported new practices beyond the formerly routine ones. We found that our informants used Facebook to maintain and develop new social norms, and to self-organize in an effort to redirect society. In some cases, structural changes emerged.

Maintaining and developing new social norms

In the recovery phase of Powell's model, people resume their normal lives. In Iraq, and other Middle Eastern countries, social duties are integrated into the fabric of Arab society where people are expected to adhere to well-defined social protocols. While it has been found that Facebook is used in countries such as South Korea to maintain social obligations in normal environments [13], in many cases technology was the only way that Iraqis could fulfill their social responsibilities.

As explained by our informants, Iraqi society revolves around the principle of "*uh-tee-rahm*". In its most essential form, the term can be defined as *respect*. People in Iraq adhere to various social rules that have developed over time that are based on respect for others, and showing this respect in socially acceptable ways. For example, during religious holidays, such as Ramadan and Christmas (known as "Eid" in Arabic), it is customary for Iraqis to visit their relatives and friends by traveling from home to home bearing gifts for each family they visit. When people in Iraq get married, tradition dictates that family and friends who are invited to the wedding attend and bring a "cash envelope" that they put in a money box that the groom and his new bride can use to start their new life. On a day-to-day basis, "*uh-tee-rahm*" also dictates that people visit as well as host family and friends for social engagements.

Our informants reported that they shifted to technology-enabled methods to continue these traditions. Using ICTs to maintain "uh-tee-rahm" has become an accepted practice because, according to our informants, people understand that it is difficult to maintain face-to-face practices in the country. One of our informants described that people possess a shared understanding of the way in which their social practices are evolving as a result:

"... everyone who lives in Iraq and who has left Iraq knows the situation here today... I live in Baghdad and I have a lot of relatives in Basra... They know I can't always come visit them... technology is the only way most of the time."

While people used an assemblage of technologies to engage in such practices, 89% of our respondents who adopted Facebook expressed how it was the most important factor in enabling them to maintain *uh-tee-rahm* when friends and family had children, for marriages, or even when people passed away. They used a variety of Facebook's features (i.e. wall posts) to maintain these practices.

In other cases, structural changes are beginning to emerge. 70% of our informants reported that they felt it was acceptable to use Facebook today even if they could travel to visit people. Thus, the war triggered a slippage where the expectations changed surrounding social obligations. In the most extreme case, people were using Facebook to evade social obligations in person by transferring them online. As explained by one informant, a 42-year-old college professor living in Northern Iraq:

"Before, I was obliged to go visit people. Let me give you an example. A friend of mine, well he's not a close friend, but he's someone I respect. This country is respect based. There's a kind of formality. And his father lately died, and I just gave my condolences via Facebook to him, which is something very bizarre...in this country, but this context called for it. [Facebook is] even replacing voice calls, which was at least recently...starting to be acceptable if you can't go physically somewhere. Phone calls would be OK if you couldn't go between two governorates. You could just do it by phone... but even this is fading..."

One important theme that arose in our interviews related to how people maintained *uh-tee-rahm* at the end of Ramadan. Ramadan is the ninth month of the Islamic calendar, where it is believed that the Quran (the Muslim religion's Holy Book) was sent down from heaven. Throughout the entire month, it is customary for people of the Islamic faith to adhere to certain rules, where they are to fast without food and water until sundown, as well as abstain from other practices. At the end of the month, Muslims celebrate for three days—the celebration is known as *Eid-ul-fitr*. During *Eid-ul-Fitr* it is customary for people to greet one another with the phrase "*Eid Mubarak*" (Happy Ramadan). Additionally, family and friends get together to observe the holiday, have dinner and share gifts. Our informants described how although they were unable to visit others and celebrate, they could greet friends and family with "*Eid Mubarak*" via Facebook. Some informants described how, by using Facebook, it was as if they were celebrating together with friends and family as if they were collocated:

"I'm used to staying up 'til 5 a.m. during Ramadan. But I am able to do that on Facebook now. Staying up all night, posting comments, laughing with others, posting videos, remembering many events that happened when we are together. And it made me sometimes not feel that time [pass], and I could not imagine that I was sitting using Facebook for 5 hours."

While people were maintaining the traditions surrounding Ramadan online, structural change emerged with respect to this practice. We have evidence (via analyzing Facebook wall posts) that people were celebrating with their friends and family across time zones. However, Eid-ul-fitr is to be celebrated at the conclusion of Ramadan. This suggests that some people were celebrating with others whose 30-day devotion period had concluded in other parts of the world, while Ramadan had not yet ended for them.

Our informants also described how Iraqis are now constrained by other social norms that emerged when the war commenced, a slippage created by the conditions of the war. Whereas before the war women held a relatively equal place in society to their male counterparts, our informants described newly emerging Sharia laws. In many locations women have been forced to adopt conservative Islamic dress, such as a "hijab" (head scarf). Also, in public it is difficult for individuals to converse with members of the opposite sex without risk. Similar to the way in which chat technologies reinforced or challenged Islamic relationship rules between long distance Arab couples [2], we found many instances in which our informants used Facebook to reinforce these new societal norms. For example, our male and female informants discussed how several of the women in their Facebook networks did not have a profile picture, as they wished to adhere to societal norms. As explained by one informant, a female college student in Baghdad:

"...most of the girls in Baghdad who use Facebook they do not put on their pictures... Even if I know one of them who uses a hijab, she does not put on her pictures...there is a lot of risks... in Iraq they still have this Middle Eastern mentality, especially the men, when they want to pick a girl to marry, if she's very traditional, or at least if her parents are, and comes from a well respected family... this girl if she wants to put this picture that's bad... [also] Islam does not support images of people..."]

We also found several examples where women challenged these new social norms using Facebook. As explained by an informant, a female medical student, women can now go online and socialize with whomever they want:

"When we go out it is so hard to be with boys... in Iraq there are these low level people and they want to hurt you if you are just girls going out by yourself, or if you are with boys who aren't from your family. They think this is haram [unacceptable]. When I'm online on Facebook I am safe and I can talk to whoever I want without worrying about..."

Thus, new Sharia laws led to structural changes in Iraqi society, yet some women are using Facebook as a means by which they can work around these new norms.

Self-organizing to improve Iraq

Our informants also used Facebook in ways that extended beyond restoring previous routines disrupted by the war. 33.1% of our informants described how they were using Facebook to self-organize to make improvements for the country. Our informants reported using Facebook to address several issues plaguing Iraqi society that they felt could be improved, and their efforts fell into several categories: infrastructure (i.e. education); women and minority rights; religious freedom; improving Iraq's relationship with the west; safety and security; and changing Iraq's image. We will focus on three of these efforts.

Following the war and the toppling of Saddam's regime, all of our informants described how they felt the current regime is unable to provide an adequate infrastructure for education. As a result, our informants have self-organized their own efforts via Facebook in order to generate additional resources. One informant, a male college professor, described how Iraq's educational system went from being one of the most universally recognized systems in the world to a system fighting for survival. In an effort to begin to improve education in the country, he created a Facebook group where he began to recruit other educated scholars. Together, with other Iraqis, he wished to connect with people who also felt the need to "*get Iraq back to where it was with respect to its educational superiority*". Here, he and other Iraqis have been discussing the current state of Iraq's educational system, as well as providing an online arena where Iraqis could come together from all over the world in order to obtain important resources in the form of grants, scholarships, and research opportunities.

Additionally, as previously described, new conditions have emerged concerning the role of women in Iraqi society. Our informants reported that today both males and females are using Facebook to self-organize women's rights movements. One informant, a female medical student in Baghdad, described how she felt compelled to educate people around the globe on what women living in the Iraqi war zone face on a day-to-day basis. Using Facebook, she sought to establish connections with people who could help her disseminate this information to a broader audience. After recruiting and meeting other like-minded people, one of the contacts she established happened to work for a British news agency. This individual sent our informant a camera where she then created a documentary about her life and the life of other Iraqi women, which was then posted on Facebook, and later aired on television. She received many positive responses and as a result of her efforts, she and other Iraqi women, as well as people all over the world, are trying to establish groups (i.e. Iraqis for Women's Rights) that can not only make people aware of how women are being treated in Iraq, but can also aim to provide Iraqi women with more equal rights.

Before the war, the Iraqi government's relationship with the West was tenuous at best, and Iraq's citizens were completely disconnected from people outside of their own country. Following the fall of Saddam's regime, different regions of the country were controlled by parties which adhere to their own set of ideologies. Iraqis today have mixed feelings about the west (especially the U.S.). Whereas before the war the average citizen did not possess the ability to connect with and learn about other cultures, today the landscape has changed drastically. Many of our informants have reported that they now use Facebook to connect with and learn about Americans, to educate people in the West about Iraq's culture, and, more importantly, to self-organize movements to help bolster the relationship between the two peoples. Many of our informants, especially those who were college students, established joint online projects via Facebook in order to promote cultural awareness. For example, a group of informants engaged in an art exchange between their university and a university in the United States. One informant, a male medical student in Baghdad, described the motivation behind this respective project:

"...we *wished to deepen the friendship bridge between Iraqis and Americans as a way to understand each other, so that we could co-exist peacefully in the future...*"

DISCUSSION AND CONCLUSIONS

Using a grounded theory approach, we found that Facebook aided people directly in their ability to recover from ongoing disruption in accordance with the latter stages of Powell's model [6] (inventory, rescue, remedy, recovery), despite the restrictions imposed on them by the physical war environment. Using Facebook, people determined the safety of family and friends, requested aid and assistance, and rebuilt their social scaffolding. The use of Facebook for direct assistance for recovery is similar to what recent studies have shown with respect to ICT use during disasters [e.g. 11, 19, 20, 27], as Facebook allowed people to engage in large-scale organizing. People could easily connect with a large number of people, and the barrier to entry is low. However, the use of Facebook can vary on an individual basis, or from situation to situation. People can decide whether they want their activities to be public, private, or somewhere in-between. For example, when requesting financial assistance, people could solicit only their trust-based networks by posting a status update that would be visible to the people in their Friend's lists. Conversely, people could request financial assistance through Facebook groups, which are typically public. This distinction is important. When using Facebook, people can *choose* which network (public or private) they want to use. In an environment where trust has deteriorated, the ability to make this choice can prove valuable.

Additionally, we found that people used Facebook to support the recovery phase as they maintained practices, but also modified practices, which led to structural changes in their society. We also found that our informants were using Facebook for activities that extended beyond the recovery phase of Powell's model, even while violence was still ongoing in the society. In the book *A Paradise Built in Hell*, Solnit [25] argues that people often use disaster situations to re-imagine their own societies. Crises possess disruptive power—old power structures and societal norms can be toppled—when this happens, new possibilities emerge for the citizens to redirect society.

We propose that Facebook became a medium through which citizens could "re-imagine" their society. On the surface, our informants used Facebook as a means through which they could *adapt* to the new environment. At first people were using Facebook to re-create the ways in which they would typically enact social obligations, as they were no longer able to maintain them in the traditional way, e.g. by maintaining *uh-tee-rahm* online. Over time, however, deep structural changes emerged. Our informants felt that the war context made it acceptable to use Facebook in cases where their traditions were not performed in a customary, face-to-face manner. In the most extreme cases, people used Facebook as a way out of their social obligations. Celebrating Eid-il-futr across time zones, "breaks the rules" in Islamic tradition. Thus, not only were people adapting to the situation at hand, but at a deeper level, they were also *re-inventing* how traditions should be enacted. Furthermore, women used Facebook to *re-invent* societal norms related to how they were treated in the public sphere by socializing with men, as well as putting up online pictures of themselves that cut across religious boundaries in the current environment. Within Facebook, people also created a new social infrastructure for education, women's rights, and Iraq's relationship with the west, in an effort to *re-direct* their society. However, it is important to consider that such practices may remain confined within the online environment of Facebook and it is not clear whether they have seeped out into the broader society.

Our findings demonstrate the malleability of ICTs like Facebook. The new Facebook-based practices were an adaptation to the war environment. By integrating Facebook into their daily repertoire, our informants were able to extend their physical capabilities despite the restrictions imposed on them in the physical world. People were able to create and experience the version of society that they wanted. Thus, Facebook served the needs of each individual, where it acted as an extension of "real life", an alternative to what was taking place in the physical world, and as a tool to support the recovery process.

We believe that in the field of crisis informatics, it is valuable to study prolonged disruption, and the ongoing use of ICTs during the recovery phase longitudinally. For the most part, disaster studies have focused on the emergency stages—thus, study findings are limited to those very specific periods of time following a disruption. Our findings suggest that environmental disruptions of war and disaster can be an opportunity by which people can rebuild and create new structures in their society. Social media is an important actor in this rebuilding process.

When environmental slippages take place, they can become triggers for new types of actions. In our study the war created slippages where, for example, societal norms changed with respect to women's rights. Our informants used Facebook to engage in new actions where they adapted to these new norms, as well as engaged in efforts to re-imagine their society. Other events, however, can cause slippages to take place—slippages are not unique to environments disrupted by violent conflict. For example, when new governments are elected, slippages may take place. The fall of the Tunisian government sparked a series of slippages throughout the Middle East (i.e. Egypt and Libya), where people began to engage their respective governments through protests, which was atypical in those societies. Using Facebook, people have been able to further their respective causes through the ability to mass organize.

Our findings raise interesting and important questions regarding the way in which technology is used to re-invent society. When ICT is used to maintain social obligations, how does this affect their religious practices and tradition? When examined more deeply, ICT is creating a conflict. For example, are the obligations surrounding Ramadan affected when people celebrate across time zones, enabled by ICT? In such cases, people must decide whether to adhere to certain rules (i.e. not celebrating until the correct time) or to appropriate ICT to celebrate with people across time zones irrespective of whether or not Ramadan is over. How can designers of technology take such potential conflicts into account?

Limitations and Concluding Remarks

We have several limitations to our study, most notably those which are associated with the snowball sampling technique we used to obtain informants. We do not know how representative our sample is of the Iraqi population, as our informants may have recommended people similar to them. By breaking down our sample, we find that nearly all of our informants were proactive in their adoption and use of technology. Thus, we cannot generalize our results to people who are not users of technology. Furthermore, the majority of our informants are either college graduates or college students. However, they come from different educational and professional backgrounds. They are also diverse with respect to age, gender, and ethnic identity. In an attempt to limit the issues associated with the snowball sampling method, we found informants through multiple seeds, which could help to diversify our sample.

Our goal in this research was not to generalize to the entire population of Iraq. Rather, our objective was to investigate how Facebook can be used as a tool to directly support the recovery process, as well as to support people's ability to re-imagine and rebuild their societies through new social structures. Our goal was to expand upon recent studies focusing on the use of ICTs, e.g. Twitter, following a disaster event [e.g. 19] to show how ICTs can aid people in recovery beyond the acute stage of a crisis.

ACKNOWLEDGMENTS

This project was supported by NSF grant #0910640.

REFERENCES

1. Abdul-Rahman, A. and Hailes, S. (2000). Supporting trust in virtual communities. *Proc. of HICSS*, 34, 1-9.
2. Alsheikh, T., Rode, J.A., and Lindley, E. (2011). (Whose) value-sensitive design: a study of long- distance relationships in an Arabic cultural context. *Proc. of CSCW'11,* 75-84.
3. Barley, S.R. (1986). Technology as an occasion for structuring: Evidence from observations of CT scanners and the social order of radiology departments. *Administrative Science Quarterly*, 31, 78-108.
4. Biernacki, P. (1981). Snowball sampling: Problems and techniques of chain referral sampling. *Soc. Methods and Research*, 10, 2, 141-163.
5. boyd, d., and Ellison, N. (2007). Social Network Sites: Definition, History, and Scholarship. *Journal of Computer-Mediated Communication*, 13, 1, 210-230.
6. Dynes, R. (1970). *Organized Behavior in Disaster*. Heath Lexington, Lexington, MA.
7. Ellison, N., Steinfield, C., and Lampe, C. (2007). The benefits of Facebook "friends:" Social capital and college students' use of online social network sites. *Journal of Computer-Mediated Communication, 12*, 4, 1143-1168.
8. Freeman, L. C., Romney, A. K. and Freeman, S. C. (1987). Cognitive structure and informant accuracy. *American Anthropologist*, 89, 2, 310-325.
9. Fritz, C. E. (1961). Disaster. In Merton and Nisbet (eds.), *Contemporary Social Problems*, NY: Brace and World.
10. Goffman, E. (1963). *Behavior in Public Places: Note on the Social Organization of Gatherings*. NY: Free Press.
11. Hagar, C., and Haythornthwaite, C. (2005). Crisis, farming and community. *Journ. of Comm. Inform.*, 1, 3, 41-52.
12. Hoffman, S. (1999). The worst of times, the best of times: Toward a model of cultural response to disaster. In Smith and Hoffman (eds.), *The Angry Earth*, NY: Rutledge.
13. Kim, K.H., and Yun, H. (2007). Cying for Me, Cying for Us: Relational Dialectics in a Korean Social Network Site. *J of Computer-Mediated Comm*, 13, 1, 298-318.
14. Lampe, C., Ellison, N., & Steinfield, C. (2006). A Face(book) in the crowd: Social searching vs. social browsing. *Proc. of CSCW'06*, 167-170.
15. Lofland, L. (1989). Social life in the public realm. *Journal of Contemporary Ethnography*, 17, 453-489.
16. Mark, G., and Semaan, B. (2008). Resilience in Collaboration: Technology as a Resource for New Patterns of Action. *Proc. of CSCW'08,* 137-146.
17. Oliker, O., Keith Crane, Audra K. Grant, Terrence K. Kelly, Andrew Rathmell, David Brannan. (2007). *U.S. Policy Options for Iraq: A Reassessment*. RAND corporation. 978-0-8330-4168-5, 102 pages.
18. Oliver-Smith, A., and Hoffman, S. (1999). *The Angry Earth: Disaster in Anthropological Perspective*. NY: Rutledge.
19. Palen, L. and Vieweg, S. (2008). The Emergence of Online Widescale Interaction: Assistance, Alliance and Retreat. *Proc, of CSCW'08*, 117-126.
20. Qu, Y., Wu, P.F., and Wang, X. (2009). Online Community Response to Major Disaster: A Study of Tianya Forum in the 2008 Sichuan Earthquake. *In Proceedings of HICSS'09*.
21. Rodriguez , H., Trainor, J., and Quarantelli, E.L. (2006). Rising to the Challenges of a Catastrophe: The Emergent and Prosocial Behavior following Hurricane Katrina. *Annals of Amer. Acad. of Pol. and Soc. Sci.*, 604, 82-101.
22. Semaan, B., and Mark, G. (2011). Creating a Context of Trust with ICTs: Restoring a Sense of Normalcy in the Environment. *Proc. of CSCW'11*, 255-264.
23. Shklovski, I., Burke, M., Kiesler, S., and Kraut, R. (2010). Technology Adoption and Use in the Aftermath of Hurricane Katrina in New Orleans. *American Behavioral Scientist*, 20, 10, 1-19.
24. Shklovski, I., Palen, L., and Sutton, J. (2008). Finding community through information and communication technology in disaster response. *Proc. of CSCW'08*, 127-136.
25. Solnit, Rebecca. (2009). *A Paradise Built in Hell: The Extraordinary Communities That Arise in Disaster*. NY: Viking.
26. Strauss, A. L. and Corbin, J. M. (1998). *Basics of Qualitative Research: Techniques and Procedures for Developing Grounded Theory*. Sage, California.
27. Sutton, J., Palen, L., and Shklovski, I. (2008). Back-Channels on the Front Lines: Emerging Use of Social Media in the 2007 Southern California Wildfires. *Proc. of ISCRAM'08*, 624-631.
28. Torrey, C., Lee, M., Burke, M. Dey, A., Fussell, S., and Kiesler, S. (2007). Connected Giving: Ordinary People Coordinating Disaster Relief on the Internet. *Proc. of HICSS'07*.
29. United Nations Refugee Agency (2011). 2011 UNHCR country operations profile - Iraq http://www.unhcr.org/cgi-bin/texis/vtx/page?page=49e486426
30. Vieweg, S., Palen, L., Liu, S.B., Hughes, A.L., and Sutton, J. (2008). Collective Intelligence in Disaster: Examination of the Phenomenon in the Aftermath of the 2007 Virginia Tech Shooting. *Proc. of ISCRAM '08.*
31. Vieweg, S., Hughes, A., Starbird, K., and Palen, L. (2010). Microblogging during two natural hazards events: What twitter may contribute to situational awareness. *Proc. of CHI'10*, 1079-1088.

Blogs as a Collective War Diary

Gloria Mark[1], Mossaab Bagdouri[2], Leysia Palen[2], James Martin[2], Ban Al-Ani[1], Kenneth Anderson[2]

[1]Dept. of Informatics
University of CA, Irvine
Irvine, CA 92697
{gmark, balani}@ics.uci.edu

[2] Dept. of Computer Science
University of Colorado
Boulder, CO 80309
{bagdouri, palen, martin, kena}@cs.colorado.edu

ABSTRACT

Disaster-related research in human-centered computing has typically focused on the shorter-term, emergency period of a disaster event, whereas effects of some crises are long-term, lasting years. Social media archived on the Internet provides researchers the opportunity to examine societal reactions to a disaster over time. In this paper we examine how blogs written during a protracted conflict might reflect a collective view of the event. The sheer amount of data originating from the Internet about a significant event poses a challenge to researchers; we employ topic modeling and pronoun analysis as methods to analyze such large-scale data. First, we discovered that blog war topics temporally tracked the actual, measurable violence in the society suggesting that blog content can be an indicator of the health or state of the affected population. We also found that people exhibited a collective identity when they blogged about war, as evidenced by a higher use of first-person plural pronouns compared to blogging on other topics. Blogging about daily life decreased as violence in the society increased; when violence waned, there was a resurgence of daily life topics, potentially illustrating how a society returns to normalcy.

Author Keywords

Blogs, collective identity, crisis, war, crisis informatics, longitudinal study, topic modeling

ACM Classification Keywords

K.4.3 [Computers and Society]: Organizational Impacts – Computer-supported cooperative work.

INTRODUCTION

Blogging is a global phenomenon. As of this writing, over 162 million blogs worldwide exist with over 800,000 blog posts indexed each hour [6]. Through blogs, people can express their views on local events as they unfold. This information is (mostly) accessible to a global audience, and often provides a range of viewpoints that traditional media do not cover. Blogs may collectively provide a public narrative about an event. In the case of a geographical region in conflict—as we focus on here—blogs provide reports, opinions, and other rich information to others outside the region that can be difficult to obtain, especially if the area is perceived as dangerous for travel.

There may be advantages to understanding the content of blogs when a society experiences a disruptive event. First, we expect that such an analysis of blogs can be used to assess the mood or "pulse" of the nation [cf 26]. Understanding how bloggers—as a subset of a population—respond to a disruption, for example in terms of recovery [24], can help researchers build theories about socio-psychological responses to disaster and crisis. A second reason is that the blog content of thousands of people written during a disruptive event can inform historical accounts about the time period. A third reason is that results can influence national or international policy decisions about the provision of humanitarian aid.

Though traditional media report selective excerpts about a disruption, they often do not adequately capture the response, mood, or opinions of affected residents. Though most wars and conflicts usually have extensive media coverage, such coverage is often influenced by factors such as the "creation" of news, profits, and rivalry, which can lead to media bias [4]. In contrast, bloggers might report on events that they feel are significant or of personal interest to them. Blogs provide an important perspective about a war that may differ from traditional media. For protracted crises like wars, blogs are the modern form of the war diary. In contrast to earlier times when a small number of war diaries took months or years to be published and thus reach a public audience, blogs can inform a global audience in near real-time on conditions of war, as well as on people's responses and adaptations to it.

We collected blog posts from the Iraqi blogosphere during eight years of the Iraqi war. Our broad research question is: what can the blogosphere reveal about how a society responds to war over time? We investigate how blogging about war differs from blogging about daily life, a focus of studies of blogs in non-war settings [22, 36]. However, a significant challenge for analysts using blogs as documentation of events is the sheer amount of material bloggers generate. Especially for emergent events such as disasters, disruptive political conflicts, or other mass emergencies, there may be millions of posts each day [3]. This leads to our concomitant research objective: to investigate how data analysis techniques yield insight into the collective expression of large numbers of people about a significant event over time.

LONGITUDINAL RESPONSES TO CRISES

In recent years, research in human-centered computing (HCC) has focused on how citizens coordinate and respond to crises [16, 38, 44, 46, 47] using personal information and communication technology. These studies have examined behavior during the emergency response period, which includes the phases of warning, impact and response, and then endures for about a two-week time frame post-impact.

Crises, however, do not occur as a snapshot in time; rather the experience and effects of a crisis unfold over a long period, sometimes lasting years. Oliver-Smith [37] discusses how responses to and effects of a crisis can last decades. The effects of September 11, 2011 and the 2005 Hurricane Katrina are still felt in the U.S.—as are disasters that have occurred decades before [31]—both by those directly affected as well as by a broader public.

It can be illuminating, then, to capture and analyze data written over the course of the event. Media such as Twitter and Facebook, which have been studied as communication channels during crises [39, 44, 46], do not as easily yield longitudinal data because of the difficulty in collecting the high volume in the brief time it is comprehensively available, or because of Terms of Use restrictions. On the other hand, blogs, unlike Twitter, have no character limit, which enables people to write about opinions, report news and personal experiences at length. Unlike ephemeral media such as mobile phone calls or short-lived data like microblog posts, blog posts are archived automatically (unless deleted by the blogger). Thus, years of reports by bloggers are available and archived chronologically, which makes it possible to understand how opinions, attitudes, and identity evolve in relation to the crisis effects. Further, blogs provide insight into how a group surrounding the blogger responds to events, because a larger public can comment on posts. For these reasons, blogs as data may reveal insights about citizen response to protracted crises.

Some researchers have studied the longitudinal aspects of reaction and recovery from crises. An anthropological study of the Oakland firestorm of 1991 [24] revealed how those affected first experienced a feeling of isolation as victims [15]. Those who lost their homes and belongings initially began to meet, and over time the meetings culminated in a disaster center. The role of place in disaster events has been researched as well by others. In earthquake events, it is not uncommon for places to emerge as public gathering spots to compensate for compromises to the telecommunications and road infrastructures. In the 1999 ChiChi, Taiwan earthquake, shrines became gathering places; during the 2004 Indian Ocean earthquake and tsunami, the UN Humanitarian Center in Sumatra became a public place to receive support from others experiencing the disaster [38].

Online Response in Dangerous, Protracted Events

In some crisis events and geographical areas, however, it is not possible for citizens to find others and meet physically. In Iraq the second Gulf War began in 2003, and is the subject of this investigation. The fall of the Iraqi government in 2003 heralded the beginning of widespread civil disorders and looting [23]. This violent disorder and disruption continued to escalate, heighten, and become more organized as the first free elections in Iraq drew near in 2005 resulting in an increase in the number of fatalities [19, 23]. The level of violence has continued to fluctuate, typically coinciding with political, religious and other events. Iraqis are routinely exposed to acts of violence such as random sniper fire and bombs exploding in public places. Recurring acts of violence lead to curfews, roadblocks and even battles within suburbs [1]. Such conditions have had a significant impact on everyday life [33].

In such an environment, we might expect citizens to experience a feeling of isolation. However, social media can afford residents under such circumstances the possibility to mitigate feelings of isolation by writing about experiences online to share them with a potential audience.

Blogging about war and daily life

Our first research question addresses the nature of blogs written during a war. Most studies of blogs have not addressed the nature of blog writing during a major disruption like war. Studies of blog genres in non-war environments consistently reveal that most blogs are classified as being of a "personal nature" [e.g. 22]. Nardi and colleagues [36] investigated why people write "personal diaries" in such a public forum as the Internet and discovered a range of motives: broadcasting their status, expressing their own views as well as seeking others' views, and articulating thoughts.

We consider that blogs written during wartime may be thought of as online war diaries. The war diary is a genre of writing that can be found as early as the Thirty Years War (1618-1648).[1] War diaries can be highly personal, as with the famous civil war diary of Mary Chesnut, deemed to be written "*for herself and for her eyes alone*" [11, p. 10]. The well-known diary of Anne Frank describes daily life events about her personal life and family in the context of a war.

However, unlike traditional war diaries, blogs during war are written in a highly public forum with the potential for citizens to share their experiences. How then might people express themselves about war in such a public forum? At what point would online blog accounts during this time reflect war in the forefront, and when would blogs rather address other subjects concerning daily life, as bloggers

[1] http://www.mdsz.thulb.uni-jena.de/sz/index.php

typically have been shown to write about [cf. 36]? From a macro-perspective, blog topics might reveal insight into the reactions or even the state of a population experiencing a crisis. Blogging about war might indicate for example, that a segment of society (as represented by the blogosphere) is under stress, whereas blogging about daily life might, for example, indicate that a society has adapted to the war setting. Our research question examines how blog topics change with the course of the war; can we find a pattern over time when citizens blog about daily life events other than war and when they focus on the war? How would such a pattern relate to external war events?

Identity in Wartime Blogs

Identity on the Internet has been a topic of interest since the Internet began to be widely adopted [48]. Our second research question addresses how identity is reflected when people blog during a war. Following the idea that blogs (in non-war environments) are generally found to be of a personal nature, how is identity expressed when people blog about an event that everyone in their region experiences? Is war reflected online more as a personal experience or as a collective experience? We might expect that people blog about war from a personal perspective, e.g. as war diarists such as Mary Chesnut had. We might expect that the reasons for bloggers to write in a self-referential voice include to serve as a catharsis, to relay their status of being safe, or to articulate their thoughts [36].

There are reasons, however, that we might expect citizens to blog about war using a collective voice. Individuals experiencing trauma have been found to use first person plural pronouns to refer to collective trauma [2]. Societies experiencing such trauma often expand "the circle of we," creating solidarity and a sense of collectivity, as have those that have experienced "collective abuse" [2]. Such trauma can lead to a collective identity that transcends the event [32]. In fact, war can even be a means for a group or society to build collective identity [12]. Thus, we may see the emergence of a collective identity in blog data where the topic of war is discussed.

In media written as narratives, psycholinguists explain that pronouns are markers of identity: the use of the personal pronoun "I" reflects self-identity whereas first person plural pronouns of "we" reflects group or collective identity [34, 41]. These markers thus reflect one's referential point: the self or others. Thus, pronouns can be considered to be not only simple descriptors, but also active assertions, with words that represent a specific choice of meaning [34]. In some cases, collective identity formation can also imply an identity-centric partnership of "us against them" [32]. Thus, analysis of pronoun markers is a means to assess the extent to which people focus on the self or others [41].

The Case of Iraq: The First Bloggers

The earliest known Iraqi blogger within Iraq began in 2003 [40]; many Iraqis living in Iraq and abroad began blogging soon after. Their blogs are diverse and express perspectives on a myriad of topics that include the war, daily life and personal interests. It is not possible to determine the total number of active Iraqi bloggers due to the size of the blogosphere. Previous studies (e.g. [1]) have sampled data based on an Iraqi blog that is dedicated to indexing all the blogs created by Iraqis within Iraq and the diaspora. It has been found that people used blogs to form communities of support, to garner emotional support, and to engage in dialogue about the conflict [1]. The current study instead takes a macro-perspective to track how perspectives learned from blogs unfold longitudinally vis-à-vis external events.

RESEARCH METHODS

Though qualitative research can provide a rich understanding of this type of data and domain, the large corpora of blog data can make extended manual analysis intractable. The scope of a qualitative analysis of blogs is limited by the sample size. We therefore employed automatic methods for exploring large-scale document collection content to study reaction to a crisis at the societal level. Specifically, we sought to explore the means by which the blogosphere can be considered more fully through natural language processing techniques.

Methods for analysis of large data sets

We first use topic models, an unsupervised approach to text analysis [5, 20], to reveal the set of underlying topics in the blog data. We then use select temporal and linguistic analyses of these clusters to gain insight into the nature of topics being discussed, their change over time, and what they reveal about collective expression during war.

Topic Modeling

Topic modeling is a computational approach based on generative probabilistic models, where no *a priori* information about the nature of the data is required [5, 20]. The history of these techniques can be traced back to vector-based methods such as Latent Semantic Indexing [12]. These techniques accept a collection of documents as input, and produce as output representations of the latent concepts (topics) that underlie the actual texts. In the case of topic modeling, these latent topics are represented by a probability distribution over terms (i.e. keywords) that are most characteristic of that topic. These distributions in turn can be used to compare the similarity of content of individual documents in the collection (in our case, individual blog posts) to each identified topic. We can then identify what topics appear in a given document at what relative concentrations, e.g. a post is mostly about daily life (75%) but also discusses the war (25%).

Since its introduction in 2003, topic modeling has been applied to a wide variety of domains and applications, many of which include correlations with, and in some cases predictions of, events external to the model. Yano et al. [49] used it to predict the users most likely to comment on a political post and to generate the content of these comments. Topic models have also been used to track the drift of topics over time in research fields [21] as well as in blogs about commercial products [28]. In a preliminary examination, Kireyev, et al. [27] applied topic models to crisis-related microblog posts. Work has also been done to validate the analysis of social media from external facts [7].

Pronoun Analysis

Word count techniques assume that the use of specific words, such as pronouns, reveal insight into meaning independent of the semantic content [41]. With respect to the use of pronouns, the analysis of the variation in use of referring expressions (noun phrases, names, pronouns, etc.) in spoken and written discourse has a long history in sociolinguistics and social psychology. Such analyses have been applied to collective identity [8], author and gender identification [29], cultural differences [17] and power and dominance relations [9]. Many of these studies have demonstrated the importance of differences in particular pronoun use as well as differences in the use of pronouns versus other referring expressions.

In this research, we first apply topic modeling to blog posts written during the Iraq War. We use the discovered topics to assign individual posts to particular topics (given the concentration of each topic in that post.) Having done this, we show how topics are correlated with external metrics and how the common themes in blogs changed over time in response to external events related to the war, thereby lending validity to the topic identification. We then examine in more detail the commonalities and differences among the clusters of posts by topic. We then apply pronoun analysis to clusters concerning war, comparing this to other clusters to infer personal or collective identity.

DATA COLLECTION AND PREPARATION

We developed an application to crawl a list of Iraqi blogs indexed at http://iraqblogcount.blogspot.com and http://iraqiblogindex.blogspot.com to create our dataset. These two indices contained 272 publicly available blogs, which we captured in their entirety. Since many authors write multiple blogs, a scan of the 272 publicly available blogs led to the discovery of 185 additional blogs written by the same authors. We captured these blogs as well, leading to a final data set of 457 blogs containing 46,828 individual posts and 188,011 comments covering the period 1 May 2002 to 3 February 2011. Our sample contains at least 236 unique blog authors. We cannot ascertain the exact number because the API did not return the ID of some profiles; thus we do not know the owners of 30 blogs. For each post, we extracted and stored the title, author, and publication date.

The posts were then preprocessed to detect the language used to enable comparison of Arabic versus English posts. We found that the actual language of the post did not always match the language indicated in the metadata of the post. In addition, we found that some bloggers tended to mix both languages in the same posts. These findings led us to base calculations on the number of Arabic versus English characters in a post's content to assign its language. A post that had more than 50% of the characters after excluding hyperlinks as Arabic letters was classified as an Arabic post and vice versa. This scheme resulted in 11,668 Arabic posts, 31,246 English posts and 3,914 undetermined. We analyzed only the English and Arabic datasets. We cannot ascertain if all the English bloggers lived in Iraq. Even so, though bloggers may not experience the violence of war directly, people outside of a war region can still experience its impact on the psyche and socio-cultural order [31].

Posts were then tokenized and stemmed. Stemming is an algorithm that aims to find the stem (i.e., the root) of a word by executing a set of operations such as the elimination of prefixes and suffixes. The Snowball stemmer [43] and Buckwalter morphological analyzer [10] were used respectively for English and Arabic posts. Our preliminary work showed that the use of stemming was of some benefit for English, and critical for Arabic posts.

APPLYING TOPIC MODELING

We then applied a widely used topic modeling toolkit [20] to our collection. For the English collection a model was trained on 31,246 posts containing a stemmed vocabulary of size 126,100; the Arabic model was trained on 11,668 posts with a stemmed vocabulary of size 73,250. The models presented here were trained with 10 topics for both English and Arabic.

The topics discovered by the English and Arabic models are illustrated in Tables 1 and 2. Each topic is illustrated with the top words that are most representative of it (the complete representation of each topic consists of a full distribution across all words in the vocabulary). The final column indicates each topic's percentage among all topics.

Topic modeling can enable identification of topics of primary interest, which helps analysts focus on posts predominately concerned with specific topics. For example, Table 2 shows how the model detected a set of posts that contribute to topic TE04, which include the words "Iraq Baghdad kill Iraqi force war attack, etc." Analysts interested in discussions of *country, politics, Iraq and Arabs* can locate those posts that contributed to this extracted topic.

To assess the accuracy of the models, a single researcher fluent in English and Arabic and familiar with this study domain analyzed random samples of Arabic and English posts. Four posts were randomly selected and manually analyzed for every month from 2003-2010 from the English data set, and from 2004-2010 from the Arabic data set (2003 was excluded because it only represented one blogger who posted about 4 posts per topic). The results of the manual analysis were consistent with the topic modeling categorizations.

ID	Topic	Percentage
TE01	People Iraqi Iraq Country American war Saddam live year kill America happen terrorist government	9.25%
TE02	year work company busy develop tea market project system service money provide case program	7.86%
TE03	day time t friend thing I'm feel start house talk go work good told car	9.44%
TE04	Iraq Baghdad kill Iraqi force war attack military police bomb report American soldier bush army	15.20%
TE05	Iraq al Iraqi govern politic elect Sunni party Iran Arab nation vote leader minister Kurdish	9.24%
TE06	god women Muslim love life man Islam men heart person religion woman Christian face eye	9.04%
TE07	oil de time receive model turn high t power radio la circuit set work point	10.51%
TE08	al news year day today call Baghdad ago Abu watch TV video family play story	7.78%
TE09	water picture city place black build white small food long game green open red photo	13.79%
TE10	post read blog write Arab book comment university time blogger music link interest student publish	7.89%

Table 1: Most frequent terms in the English posts by topic (TE = Topic in English)

ID	Topic	Percentage
TA01	one want elapse days same go people day man saying listen know	12.04%
TA02	life times poetry love amiability eye heart death night art soul beautiful spirit face sound	8.07%
TA03	Allah son say peace the Imam pray Islam Mohammed saying kin father worshipper Muslim prophet	12.12%
TA04	Iraq the force government president say council security governorate operation Baghdad visit America	16.58%
TA05	other many book enable write period something person same one do picture time site more	13.06%
TA06	the scholar religion history other Arab saying knowledge idea first origin culture earth own soul	9.24%
TA07	Iraq America Arab people occupation Saddam party war Ba'ath Iran nation force Israel resistant	7.13%
TA08	the Baghdad one expand day logic hour children poison ten three big kill car	7.39%
TA09	country politic operation united state no the government force meeting new other rights	7.44%
TA10	work year media company information office studying network university service program newspapers	6.94%

Table 2: Translations of the most frequent terms in the Arabic posts by topic. (TA = Topic in Arabic)

Blogging: a temporal mirror of war events

We first identified topics concerning war. Referring to Table 1, three independent coders interpreted topics TE01 and TE04 as topics concerning war. For example, included in TE01 were *American*, *war*, *Saddam*, *kill*, and *terrorist*. In TE04 were the words *kill*, *force*, *war*, *attack*, *military*, *bomb*, and *army*. These gave strong indication that the topics were about war. Figure 1a shows how the frequency of these war topics changed over time. War topics were considered *in proportion* to the overall topics discussed.

Next, we compared the blogged topics with external events related to the war to test whether the war topics corresponded with what was occurring in the world. We used the body counts index (number of civilian deaths) as a proxy for the level of magnitude or severity of the war. Data were collected from http://www.iraqbodycount.org, an independent nonprofit group that tracks the number of war-related civilian deaths in Iraq. According to the website, deaths are determined by cross-checking different news sources and reports from hospitals, morgues, and NGOs.

We correlated the body count with the proportion of war topics blogged (Figure 1a). We used one month as a time unit for conducting the correlation, a large enough unit to use to account for a lag in time from a war event (e.g. a bombing) to when the theme of war would surface in blog posts. Though we collected all posts from 2003 onwards, we only considered blogs and body counts starting from the year 2004, because very few blogs appeared prior. Keeping in mind that the Internet was not widely accessible in Iraq until after 2003, it took about a year for blogs to be written by enough people to enable study of thematic content.

Visually, the English blogs classified as containing war topics seems to mirror the magnitude of body count over the years of the war (Figure 1a and 1b) and indeed, we found a highly significant correlation of proportion of war topics in the English blogs, to body count: $R=.79$, $p<.0001$, $N=84$. This positive correlation reflects how, as the body count in Iraq rises, the proportion of war topics written in blogs about war also rises, and how as the body count drops, the number of war topics blogged also drops. Other topics rise as body count drops, such as topics concerning daily life. We consider the significant correlation we found to be an external validation of the topics identified as well as the use of the topic modeling technique.

A comparison of the English and Arabic blog war topics suggests that there is lag in Arabic posts (Figure 1a and 1c). Though we have no tangible explanation for this lag, we did note (during the manual analysis of posts) that Arabic posts tended to be more impersonal in nature and often relied on official reports of war events rather than personal accounts. Relying on official reports of events may mean that bloggers needed more time to find and synthesize appropriate reports. Other factors may have contributed to this lag. English posts may include those by Iraqi bloggers

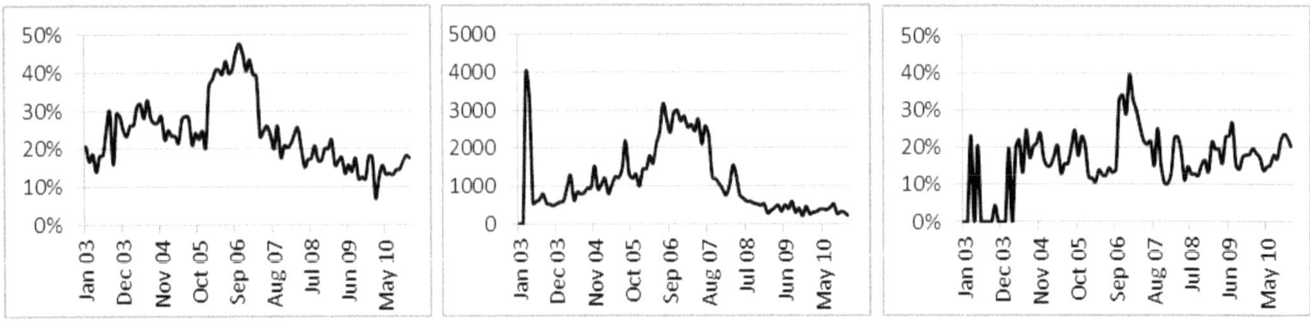

a. Timeline of war topics in English **b. Body count** **c. Timeline of war topics in Arabic**

Figure 1: Timeline of Iraqi blog posts discussing war topics and civilian deaths (body count)

living abroad who have better access to the Internet (i.e. they are not constrained by power outages as those living in Iraq are). Thus, they may be able to post responses to war events more quickly than those within Iraq. More research is needed to ascertain the reasons for the difference.

War vs. daily life topics over time

Our first research question asked how blog topics change over the course of the war. With topic modeling, particular themes can be selected, tracked and analyzed over time. Other studies of blogs [cf 22, 36], examined in non-war environments, revealed that most blogs concern accounts about daily life. (We refer to daily life topics as those that concern aspects of people's daily life not related to war.) We examined the topics to see which addressed daily life. In Table 2, topic TE06 contains the following string of words: "god women Muslim love life man Islam men heart person religion woman Christian face eye." One interpretation of this topic might be concerning religion, or relationships—or in short, themes about daily life. Three independent coders determined the following topics as those concerning daily life (see Table 2): TE3, TE6, TE8 and TE10. These topics all contained words that concerned daily life, such as *friend*, *family*, *music*, etc.

Figure 2 shows the relation of daily life topics in comparison to the war topics over time (shown in Figure 1a). Initially, as the Internet and blogs first started being adopted in 2003, the discussion of daily life topics were higher in proportion to the war topics. However, we see that

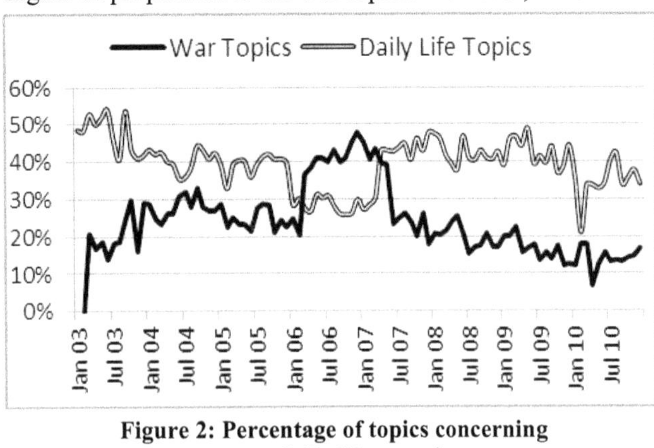

Figure 2: Percentage of topics concerning war vs. daily life over time

as the war progressed and as number of blogs increased, the discussion of daily life topics declined, especially as war topics increased as a proportion of all topics discussed in the blogs. The crossover point occurred just after December 2005, when the body count took a precipitous rise (see Fig. 1b), i.e. when violence of the war increased sharply. It was in December 2005 that the Iraq elections took place, with corresponding heightened violence.

A second crossover point occurred around April 2007. As the violence declined (see Fig. 1b), blogging of war topics decreased. However, what is especially interesting in Fig. 2 is the other perspective: blogging about daily life increased as the violence waned. This could reflect how when the crisis abates, people return to a sense of "normalcy," discussing topics about daily life.

Collective or personal expression of war?

Our second research question was to examine how identity is expressed in blog discussions about war. Following the idea that people form collective identity during trauma [2] combined with the idea that the use of first person plural pronouns ('we' and 'us') reflects the expression of a collective identity [34], we hypothesized that a collective identification with others about the war should be characterized by a high presence of first person plural pronouns in blogs.

We conducted an analysis of pronoun use in the Iraqi blogs as follows. We built a two-dimensional classifier of the posts. In the first dimension, a post can belong to one of three possible classes; (a) a war post if the sum of the distributions of war topics (TE01 and TE04) for that post exceeds 50%, (b) a daily life post if the sum of distributions of daily life topics (TE03, TE06, TE08 and TE10) for that post exceeds 50%, and (c) "other" if none of the previous two conditions is satisfied. In the second dimension, we defined an algorithm to distinguish 'I/me' from 'we/us' posts. A post was classified as an I/me post if the sum of the occurrences of the pronouns "I" and "me" in that post exceeds the sum of the occurrences of the pronouns 'we' and 'us', and vice-versa. We aggregated the posts by periods of equal lengths of one month.

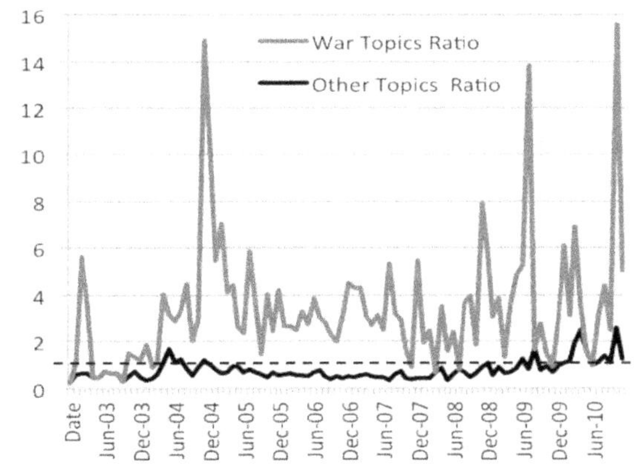

Fig. 3. Plot of ratios of 'We/Us' to 'I/Me' pronouns for War and all Other topics. Dotted line shows where ratio is equal.

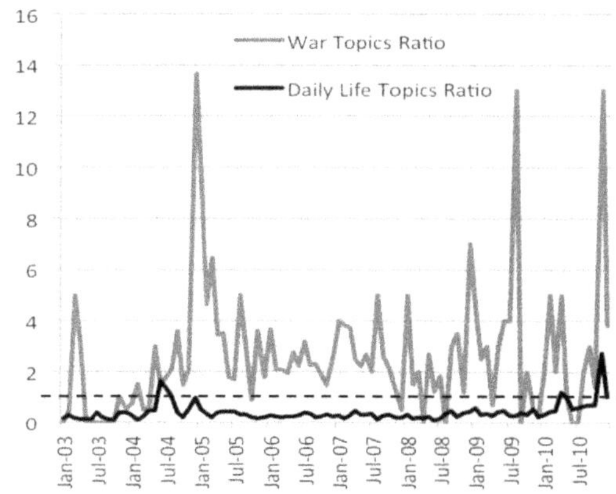

Fig. 4. Plot of ratios of 'We/Us' to 'I/Me' pronouns for War and Daily Life topics. Dotted line shows where ratio is equal.

We first examined first person plural pronoun use in the war topics compared to all other topics in our sample. We considered all the other topics as a "baseline" from which to compare the war topics. The dotted line in Figure 3 indicates where the ratio would be equal, i.e. where the first person plural and first-person singular pronouns would be used equally in the blogs. Figure 3 shows that the ratio of 'we/us' to 'I/me' pronouns exceeds a value of one for nearly all the blogs classified as war posts over the course of the war. This is consistent with the notion of reflecting a group or collective identity. What is interesting is that in the early war years, the ratio is less than one, which could indicate an individualistic reaction to a crisis, as Hoffman [24] found with victims in the Oakland firestorm.

However, it could be that blogging about any topic might reflect a collective identity. Figure 3 also shows that the war topics had far higher ratios of 'we/us' to 'I/me' pronoun use in relation to the rest of the blog sample, over nearly all the years of the war. A one-sample t-test of the difference of the ratios of war and all other topics over time (compared to a hypothesized mean of zero) shows that this difference is significantly greater than zero ($t(86)=8.23$, $p<.0001$). Thus, war blogs have a significantly higher use of first person plural pronouns compared to the rest of the blogs in the sample.

We then further contrasted the use of first person plural pronoun use for the war blogs compared to blogs about daily life. We cannot assume whether daily life topics would use a particular personal or collective voice, as the topics are so varied. Daily life topics may be written in a personal voice, as when one explains about their personal relationship or beliefs. On the other hand, daily life topics can also be about family, friends, or group activities, in which case they may use a collective, or group voice.

Figure 4 shows a plot of the ratios of 'we/us' to 'I/me' pronouns for the war blogs in relation to the daily life blogs. For daily life posts, the ratio is less than a value of one, over nearly all the years of the Iraq war. This ratio seems to trend towards a value higher than one in recent years, though research is needed to understand more fully why. A one-sample t-test of the difference of the war and daily life ratios over time shows that this difference is significantly greater than zero ($t(87)=9.7$, $p<.0001$). Thus, the use of first person plural pronouns is higher in war blog posts compared to the daily life posts, i.e. the type of posts consistent with those examined in previous studies of blogs in non-war environments.

DISCUSSION

Our goal was to examine a large corpus of archived blog data during a protracted crisis to try to gain a long term societal view of how people experience a war. We examined how blog topics changed over eight years of the war. We found an interesting relationship: as the war progressed over time, and as violent incidents increased, bloggers turned their attention to discussing the war. Even though there need not necessarily be an inverse relationship between blog topics of war and daily life, the proportion of blogging about daily life lowered as the war progressed. This suggests that when war is in the forefront of people's minds, especially when violent events occur, topics concerning daily life move to the background. During the height of crisis, bloggers discussed far more topics concerning the war, perhaps to make sense of the violence and uncertainty in the environment.

Theoretical models have been developed to describe the societal level processes that occur during one-time impact hazards; however, societal effects of long term crises have not been modeled. Powell [14] identifies eight sociotemporal stages ranging from predisaster to recovery. Closer to our work is that of Hoffman [24] who describes that people transition into recovery and adapt to the effects of a crisis in three stages: an individual stage where victims feel isolated, a collaborative stage where victims bond, and a third stage of return to normal life. Though Hoffman looked at a single disaster (the Oakland firestorm), our data could reveal stages of adaptation over a protracted crisis like war. We interpret the finding of the interaction of daily life and war topics, in relation to external war events, as follows. As violence erupts, people try to maintain daily life routines, as evidenced by a higher level of daily life topics in blogs. As a war progresses over time with increased violence, there is a gradual slipping away from normalcy, as measured by a decrease in discussion of daily life topics and increase in war topics blogged. War moves to the forefront of the blogosphere as the society copes with the violence; a collective identity in blogging about war is evident. As violence subsides, or perhaps as a society becomes adapted to the war environment, people try to recover behaviors experienced before the war. Topics concerning daily life begin to shift back into the blog discourse. Thus, we believe that these results have potential to be used to monitor the reaction to a protracted crisis such as war. This model could be tested and refined empirically, e.g. through interviews.

Why might blogging about daily life be interpreted as a return to normalcy for bloggers? Giddens [18] can provide one interpretation, as he has discussed how humans continually strive for normalcy:

Routine is integral both to the continuity of the personality of the agent, as he or she moves along the path of daily activities, and to the institutions of society, which are such only through their continued reproduction (pg. 60).

Thus, a means to regain normalcy is through the performance of routines; returning to a focus on daily life is a sign of reconstruction of the routine. As such, our analysis suggests that blog discussions of daily life in a crisis might be used as a gauge for a society's return to normalcy. This result suggests a future research direction to look more closely at the relationship of daily life blog topics to actual attitudes in the broader population.

The results also show how bloggers seem to reflect different types of identity for distinct topics through their use of language. They appear to reflect more of a collective identity when they discuss war, as evidenced by the higher use of first person plural pronouns. We did not find the same incidence of first person plural pronouns in the rest of the blog sample nor in the blog posts specific to topics of daily life. It is possible however that any topic about a public event might employ a collective voice. We were not able to test this as the topic modeling did not produce other topics that we could classify as "public" topics. However, even if other public topics did produce a higher incidence of first person plural pronouns, this does not discount our results concerning war. Finding a higher use of first person plural pronouns with war topics is consistent with the claim that trauma is associated with a collective identity [2, 34].

Collective identity is established through interactions [12]; thus, to establish a collective identity people must have a means for interaction. In war environments it can be dangerous to meet others in public. Blogging is done in an online public forum and affords bloggers the ability to share their perspectives with others who are also experiencing the war. Online interaction may provide the channel for a collective identity concerning a war or crisis to emerge. But whether this identity formation is directly bolstered by interaction with other bloggers in a public forum who feel the same or is rather a result of bloggers presuming that what they feel is a shared experience, is not possible to say with our data; nevertheless, there does appear to be a collective perspective regarding the blog discussion of common war events to a great degree.

War differs from other crises like an earthquake or flood that have a contained emergency period. War involves a pattern of continual emergencies and disruption. No sooner are people trying to recover from one crisis, e.g. a bombing, when they may be faced with renewed violence. By concentrating on smaller-scale individual events, such as with qualitative analysis, it might be difficult to identify recovery of a society from the effects of a war. However, by taking a macro and longitudinal perspective, we found that archived blog data could suggest evidence of a generalized recovery in terms of the pattern of topics blogged. This suggests further research to examine what insights archived data can yield about crisis recovery.

Methods for large-scale analysis

As the volume of data in blogs—and on the Internet in general—swells, we need to look toward methods to examine large-scale data. Analytically we found reassurance that topic modeling can sort content into meaningful topics; this was validated by a significant positive correlation of war topic blog entries with real-world war events. This suggests that blogs might be a good representation for monitoring the effects of external events in a society. Though hypotheses about the connections between current events and blogs seem plausible, what remained unclear about the topic model analysis alone was evidence of the degree of the connection and detection of shifts over time.

Topic models can provide several key types of information for researchers. First, they can provide an overview of what topics are "hot" in the blogging community at particular time points. In the case of crisis events, this can help researchers understand what topics are perceived as important from the perspective of the blogger (as opposed to the traditional news media). They can benefit researchers in a variety of fields. For example, policy experts can use the information to understand reactions to the implementation of a particular policy. Distilled topics may even have a predictive value of events that will transpire in a society, e.g. if bloggers discuss dissatisfaction with the current government. Evidence of this can be found in the 2011 uprising in Egypt [30].

Topic modeling also has the advantage of revealing rapid insights, in contrast to qualitative analysis of data. They enable us to deal with a volume of data that cannot be analyzed manually. Moreover, that volume allows us to discover low frequency topics that would certainly be missed in sampling. This is advantageous in the dynamic context of a conflict situation. Last, topic models can be used to understand the trajectory of different blogged topics over time and how they relate to external events. More research needs to be done to understand better how topic models can reflect broad views of a society over time.

Ideally, a researcher performing an ethnographic study of a conflict would want to travel to the location of the event. However, it is not always possible to travel to or stay in conflict zones because of the risk involved, the remoteness of the location, and/or the duration of the event. We believe that blog data provide an opportunity for researchers to understand from a distance the "mood" of a region that is experiencing a conflict over an extended or indefinite period of time.

Limitations

A limitation to the use of topic modeling is that the results (the topics) are subject to the interpretation of the analyst. For this reason we recommend having at least two independent coders to interpret the results and reconcile discrepancies in interpretation. We found it useful to have a researcher validate a sample of the topic results by hand.

A caveat in using blogs as a basis for generalizing to a broader society is that bloggers are not necessarily representative of the general population. As with users of any social media, they may have higher education and income. They are a self-selected group who may be more technically savvy than average. Therefore, our results must be used with caution in generalizing beyond the blogosphere. Also, we did sample some blogs by the same authors and this could have had resulted in a disproportionate representation by those authors. Yet most of the blogs in our sample had unique authors so this should not be such an uneven representation. Nevertheless, bloggers do provide a good sample of opinions about a region and event. That the topics correlated with an external societal event (body count) suggests that bloggers can represent a national discourse about a crisis to some degree.

CONCLUSION

War diaries have a long legacy. The translation of this practice to blogs by a large set of citizen writers affected by war opens up new opportunities to understand war, communication, and interaction. Challenges in analyzing such a large corpus of data require analysts to consider how to parse it in meaningful ways. Topic modeling offers promise, and the analysis offered here demonstrates that it maps to external indices that suggest validity. Furthermore, as would be expected, when wartime events are on the rise, written accounts of daily life move to the background. Finally, with the information topically parsed, linguistic analysis of pronoun use reveals an interesting finding that references to the collective 'we' also rise during wartime strife, suggesting fortification of a collective identity. These results stage the possibility for other analyses about the content of the writings of a society during life-changing periods in history.

ACKNOWLEDGMENTS

This project was supported by NSF grants #0910640 and #1128008.

REFERENCES

1. Al-Ani, B., Mark, G. and Semaan, B. (2010). Blogging in a region of conflict: Supporting transition to recovery. *Proc. of CHI'10*, ACM Press, 1069- 1078.
2. Alexander, J. C. (2004). Toward a theory of cultural trauma. In *Cultural trauma and collective identity*, in J. C. Alexander, R. Eyerman, B. Giesen, N. J. Smelser, and P. Sztompka. Berkeley: University of California Press.
3. Anderson, K. M. and Schram, A. (2011). Design and implementation of a data analytics infrastructure in support of crisis informatics research. Proc. *of the 33rd Intern'l Conf on Software Engineering (ICSE'11)*, 4 pp.
4. Baron, D. (2006). *Persistent media bias. Jour of Public Economics*, vol. 90, Issues 1-2, January 2006, 1-36.
5. Blei, D., Ng, A. and Jordan, M. (2003). Latent Dirichlet allocation. *J of Machine Learning Res*, 3:993–1022, 2003.
6. Blogpulse (2011). http://www.blogpulse.com
7. Bollen, J., Mao, H., and Zeng X.-J. (2010). Twitter mood predicts the stock market. arXiv:1010.3003v1.
8. Brewer, M. and Gardner, W. (1996). Who is this "We"? Levels of collective identity and self representations. *J of Personality and Social Psychology,* 71(1), 83-93.
9. Brown, R. and Gilman, A. (1960). The pronouns of power and solidarity. In Sebeok, T. A. (ed.) *Style in Language* Cambridge: MIT press. 253-76.
10. Buckwalter T. (2002). Buckwalter Arabic morphological analyzer Version 1.0. Linguistic Data Consortium, U of Pennsylvania. LDC Catalog No.: LDC2002L49.
11. Chesnut, M. (1981). *Mary Chesnut's Civil War.* C. Vann Woodward (ed.), New Haven: Yale Univ. Press.
12. Coles, Roberta L. (2002). War and the contest over national identity. *The Sociological Review* 28:586–609.
13. Deerwester, S., Dumais, S. T., Furnas, G. W., Landauer, T. K. and Harshman, R. (1990). Indexing by latent semantic analysis. *J of Amer Soc for Inf Sci*, 41: 391–407.
14. Dynes, R. (1970). *Organized Behavior in Disaster.* Heath Lexington, Lexington, MA.
15. Erickson, K. (1976). *Everything in Its Path.* New York: Simon and Schuster.
16. Foot, K. A, and Schneider, S. M (2004). Online structure for civic engagement in the September 11 web sphere, *Electronic J of Communication*, 14:3-4, 1-10
17. Gardner, W., Gabriel, S. and Lee, A. (1999). "I" value freedom, but "We" value relationships: Self-construal priming mirrors cultural differences in judgment. *Psychological Science,* 10(4), 321-326.

18.Giddens, A. (1984): *The Constitution of Society*, University of California Press, Berkeley, CA.

19.Green P,Ward T (2009). The transformation of violence in Iraq. *Brit J of Criminology,* 49:628–645.

20.Griffiths, T., and Steyvers, M. (2004). Finding scientific topics. *Proc of the Nat'l Acad of Sciences*, 5228-5235.

21.Hall D., Jurafsky D., and Manning, C. (2008). Studying the history of ideas using topic models. *Proc of the Conf on Empirical Methods in Natural Language Processing,* Assoc for Computational Linguistics, 363-371.

22.Herring, S. C, Scheidt, L. A., Wright, E., & Bonus, S. (2005). Weblogs as a bridging genre. *Information, Technology, & People*, 18(22), 142–171.

23.Hoffman, B. (2004), *Insurgency and Counterinsurgency in Iraq*, OP-127-IPC/CMEPP, Santa Monica: RAND.

24.Hoffman, S. (1999). The worst of times, the best of times: Toward a model of cultural response to disaster. In Smith and Hoffman (eds.), *The Angry Earth*, New York: Routledge.

25.Hoffman, T, (1999). Probabilistic Latent Semantic Indexing. *Proc of SIGIR'99,* 50-57.

26.Kamvar, S. and Harrison, J. (2009). *We Feel Fine: An Almanac of Human Emotion*. NY: Scribner.

27.Kireyev, Kirill, Palen, L. and Anderson, K.M. (2009). Applications of topics models to analysis of disaster-related Twitter data. *Neural Information Processing Systems Foundation Workshop*, Seattle, WA.

28.Knights, D., Mozer, M. and Nicolov, N. (2009). Detecting topic drift with compound topic models. *Proc of the 3rd Int'l Conf on Weblogs and Social Media.* AAAI Press.

29.Koppel, M., Argamon, S., and Shimoni, A. (2002). Automatically Categorizing Written Texts by Author Gender. *Literary and Linguistic Comp.,* 17(4), 401-412.

30.Lister T. and Smith E., 2011. http://articles.cnn.com/2011-01-27/world/egypt.protests.social.media_1_social-media-twitter-entry-muslim-brotherhood?_s=PM:WORLD.

31.Liu, S. B. (2011). *Grassroots Heritage: How Social Media Sustain the Living Heritage of Historic Crises.* Ph.D. Dissertation, University of Colorado at Boulder. Available at: http://sophiabliu.com/sophiabliu-dissertation.pdf.

32.Mardini, R. A., (2008). *Socializing Realism's Balance of Power: Collective Identity as Alliance Formation in Iraq.* Ph.D. Dissertation, Ohio State University.

33.Mark, G., Al-Ani, B., Semaan, B. (2009). Resilience through technology adoption: Merging the old and the new in Iraq, *Proc. of CHI'09*, ACM Press, 689-698.

34.Matthiesen, K. (2003). On collective identity. *Protosociology* 18, p. 66-88..

35.Mimno, D., Wallach, H. M., Naradowsky, J., Smith, D. A., & McCallum, A. (2009). Polylingual topic models. *Proceedings of the 14th Conference on Empirical Methods in Natural Language Processing*, pp. 880-889.

36.Nardi, B., Schiano, D., and Gumbrecht, M. (2006). Blogging as Social Activity, or, Would You Let 900 Million People Read Your Diary? *Proceedings of CSCW'04*, 222-231.

37.Oliver-Smith, A. (1996). Anthropological research on hazards and disaster. *Annual Review of Anthropology*, 1996, 25:303-28.

38.Palen, L & Liu, S. B. (2007). Citizen communications in crisis: Anticipating a future of ICT-supported participation, *Proc. of CHI* 2007, 727-736

39.Palen, L., Vieweg, S., Liu, S., Hughes, A. (2009). Crisis in a Networked World: Features of Computer-Mediated Communication in the April 16, 2007 Virginia Tech Event. *Social Science Computing Review*, Sage, 467-480.

40.Pax, S. (2003). *Salam Pax: The Baghdad Blog*, Grove Press.

41.Pennebaker, M. Mehl, R., and Niederhoffer, K. (2003). Psychological aspects of natural language use: Our words, our selves. *Annu. Rev. Psychol.* 2003. 54:547–77.

42.Polletta, F., and James, J. (2001). Collective identity and social movements. *Ann Rev of Sociology*. 27:283–305.

43.Porter M F (2001). Snowball: A language for stemming algorithms. http://snowball.tartarus.org/texts/introduction.html

44.Qu, Y., Huang, C., Zhang, P., & Zhang, J. (2011). Microblogging after a major disaster in China: A case study of the 2010 Yushu earthquake. *Proc of CSCW '11*, 25-34.

45.Ramage, D., Dumais, S., and Liebling, D. (2010). Characterizing microblogs with topic models. *Proc. of ICWSM'10*, 130-137.

46.Starbird, K. and Palen, L. (2011). "Voluntweeters:" Self-organizing by digital volunteers in times of crisis. *Proc of CHI 2011*, Vancouver, BC.

47.Torrey, C., Burke, M., Lee, M.L., Dey, A.K., Fussell, S.R., and Kiesler, S.B. (2007). Connected giving: Ordinary people coordinating disaster relief on the Internet. *Proceedings of HICSS'2007.*

48.Turkle, S. (1995). *Life on the Screen: Identity in the Age of the Internet*. New York, NY: Simon & Schuster.

49.Yano, T., Cohen, W., Smith, N. 2009. Predicting response to political blog posts with topic models. *Proc of the 2009 Annual Conf of the North American Chapter of the Assoc for Computational Linguistics,* 477–485.

"Beacons of Hope" in Decentralized Coordination: Learning from On-the-Ground Medical Twitterers During the 2010 Haiti Earthquake

Aleksandra Sarcevic[1], Leysia Palen[2], Joanne White[3], Kate Starbird[3], Mossaab Bagdouri[2] and Kenneth Anderson[2]

College of IST[1]
Drexel University
Philadelphia, PA 19104
aleksarc@drexel.edu

Department of Computer Science[2], ATLAS Institute[3]
University of Colorado
Boulder, CO 80309
{palen, joanne.white, starbird, bagdouri, kena}@colorado.edu

ABSTRACT

We examine the public, social media communications of 110 emergency medical response teams and organizations in the immediate aftermath of the January 12, 2010 Haiti earthquake. We found the teams through an inductive analysis of Twitter communications acquired over the three-week emergency period from 89,114 Twitterers. We then analyzed the teams' Twitter streams, as well as all digital media they generated and pointed to in their streams—blog posts, photographs, videos, status updates and field reports—to understand the medical coordination challenges they faced from pre-deployment readiness to on-the-ground action. Here we identify opportunities for improving coordination in a decentralized and distributed environment where staffing, disease trajectories, and other circumstances rapidly change. We extrapolate from these findings to theorize about how "beaconing" behavior is a sign of latent potential for coordination upon which mechanisms of coordination can capitalize.

Author Keywords

Computer-mediated communication; crisis informatics; disasters; field medicine; microblogging; social media.

ACM Classification Keywords

H.5.3 Groups & Organization Interfaces—collaborative computing, computer-supported cooperative work; K.4.2 Social Issues.

General Terms

Design; Human Factors.

INTRODUCTION

Age-old arguments continue about whether decentralization or centralization of functions is the optimal way for organizations to work and their members to cooperate, with fluctuations between these configurations marking each new age in modern business [2,5,14]. In disasters, however, there are no such options. For nearly all of its functions, disaster response is an inherently decentralized and distributed institution that is under continuous and unexpected change [28]. The more dramatic the catastrophe and the more difficult it is to converge onto a location, the more decentralized the response. Helpers new to disaster response—and there are always many of these—will ask, "Who is in charge?" and be shocked by the answer [17]. Coordination problems are prolific, with matters of medical response being especially critical because of the immediacy of needs [4,22,28]. The decentralization that characterizes field medicine results in a surplus of personnel in one area and a dearth in another, with loss of life as the consequence.

In the world of disaster management, the rise of social media has opened the space for aid organizations as well as members of the public to participate in generating, filtering and sharing real-time information during times of crisis [6,21,24,30]. A line of research inquiry as well as a line of methodological opportunity arise from such conditions, both of which we undertake in this paper. For the first—the line of research inquiry—we ask: What prospects and problems do social media create for the inherently decentralized coordination in disaster response? Unlike coordination of safety-critical systems, which is co-located and centralized [1,10], what are the features of decentralized work that need technological support? How are social media shaping that landscape of possibility now?

For the second, we aim to leverage the methodological opportunity that social media data provide for near real-time, situated, and often first-person accounts of events on the ground—situations for which field work would be limited and even at odds with the foremost aims of offering direct assistance. With the advent of social media use during post-impact disaster situations—even under the dire conditions of an event like the 2010 Haiti earthquake, the infrastructure was stabilized such that web access and social media use was possible by those who had the required hardware—we no longer need to rely on traditional post hoc written accounts of disaster field experience alone to obtain a rich accounting of the circumstances.

CSCW'12, February 11–15, 2012, Seattle, Washington, USA.

In short, this paper aims to study a large-scale, fast-paced, and stressful coordination activity that is highly distributed and decentralized—medical coordination during disaster response. We extend the methods of virtual ethnography [11] by systematically mining a comprehensive set of Haiti-related social media data to investigate the 2010 Haiti earthquake emergency medical response.

MEDICAL SITUATION AFTER THE HAITI EARTHQUAKE

On January 12, 2010, a massive earthquake struck Haiti near the city of Leogane, about 18 miles west of the capital Port-au-Prince. The severity and scope of impact of the earthquake was catastrophic. The Haitian government estimated that more than 222,000 people lost their lives and over 300,000 were injured [19]. The immediate medical needs were immense, requiring acute trauma care, orthopedic services and access to life-saving medications and equipment. The most common injuries included open and closed bone fractures, bone dislocations, complex open wounds, and head, face, and brain injuries. As one of the physicians noted in his dispatch from the field, "A city in need of hundreds of trauma centers had two or three" [20].

The earthquake damaged or destroyed much of the Haitian medical infrastructure, disrupting the healthcare system when it was most needed. Of the existing 49 hospitals, eight were totally destroyed, and 22 seriously damaged [19]. Those that remained functional were crowded with patients, forcing many people to be treated in temporary structures, such as inflatable hospitals and makeshift facilities. Many of the local healthcare workers were also killed or injured, or had lost family members. Medical facilities lacked essential medical staff, supplies, equipment and drugs.

A large-scale humanitarian response was launched in the immediate aftermath of the earthquake, with Pan American Health Organization and World Health Organization (PAHO/WHO) forming the Health Cluster (within the United Nations Cluster system) and leading the emergency medical response. Responsibilities of the Health Cluster included outlining medical relief priorities and coordinating support offered by over 400 health partners, non-governmental organizations (NGOs), and emergency relief agencies. According to PAHO/WHO reports, many of the responding agencies had no prior experience with Haiti, disasters, or the Health Cluster system [19].

Emergency medical response included rapid establishment of 17 field hospitals in the most devastated areas, two ship-based hospitals with hundreds of medical specialists and large capacities, distribution of emergency medical supplies, and provision of essential medications and medical equipment. Over 150 nations provided support by sending emergency medicine specialists, trauma and orthopedic surgeons, nurses and other medical personnel [9]. Humanitarian and medical aid agencies supplied food, water, hygiene kits, medical equipment and medications such as antibiotics, vaccines and anesthetics [19].

The Health Cluster, in collaboration with several other partners, established a Health Information Situation Room as the basis for coordinating medical response and collecting and managing health information. The goal was to have an overview of the needs, epidemic trends and services available on the ground [19]. Despite these efforts, emergency medical teams and organizations that responded to the earthquake faced great challenges in preparing for and providing medical care. Several physicians on the ground described the initial response as "ill-equipped, understaffed, poorly coordinated and delayed" [17]. Additionally, logistics of medical response were hampered by the destruction of infrastructure and transportation [31]. Importantly, telecommunications infrastructure was mostly restored to a workable degree. Though high rates of phone calls sometimes taxed the system, those on the ground who had access to data services could make use of them, including the use of microblogging services [8].

METHODS

To navigate the enormous social media-based information space and the online sources to which the social media communications pointed, we took Twitter communications as a starting point. Twitter is a popular microblogging platform that allows users to send 140 character messages to their followers, also captured in the public stream. In addition to reading posts, or "tweets," from their followers, people can search the public stream for keywords that would reveal topics of interest. As we know from prior research, tweet communications, which are increasingly used by professional groups and volunteers in disaster response, often contain pointers to other sources on the web [24]. By isolating "medical Twitterers" on the basis of words contained in their tweets—a significant methodological challenge on its own—we hypothesized that we would be pointed to other relevant online sources that could also be used for ethnographic investigation.

Immediately after the earthquake struck in Haiti, we started collecting tweets via Twitter's Search API using the keywords *earthquake*, *Port-au-Prince*, *Ouest*, *tsunami*, *Haiti*, and *tremblement*. Over the period of January 12 – March 10, 2010, the search generated 3.28M tweets contributed by 799,955 Twitter users. Our goal to identify medical tweets and on-the-ground Twitterers from this large dataset posed significant challenges, leading to a three-step process: (1) identifying tweets with medical information; (2) generating a sample of high-volume medical Twitterers and using the information in their tweets to identify emergency medical responders who tweeted from the ground; and (3) capturing Twitter streams of identified on-the-ground medical responders for further analysis. The detailed process is summarized in Figure 1.

Identification of Medical Tweets

Although the Government of Haiti called off the official search and rescue on January 23, 2010, some rescue efforts continued for another week [29]. We limited our collection

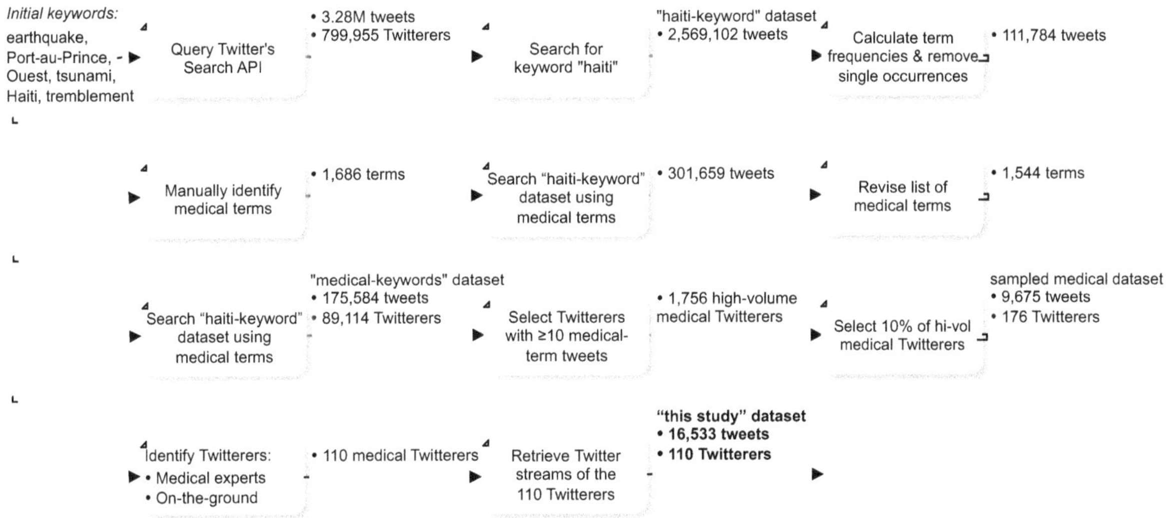

Figure 1. Summary of the procedures used to identify medical tweets and to reach the sample of 110 Twitterers.

of Twitter data to the three-week period—from January 12 to February 2, 2010. Using the 3.28M dataset, we selected all tweets that contained the term "haiti," which yielded 2,569,102 tweets (the *haiti-keyword* dataset). We then computed term-frequency counts for all words, including their misspellings and shortenings. We also removed links, email addresses, numbers, single letters, and punctuation and symbols, except hyphens and apostrophes. This process generated 211,047 terms, of which 99,263 occurred only once. Because single-occurrence terms carried little weight (e.g., they were not retweeted), they were excluded from analysis. This process yielded a list of 111,784 terms.

Two researchers, one with experience in ethnographic research on emergency medicine, manually reviewed the list and identified medical terms. Medical terms were defined as those that relate to medical conditions, interventions, treatments, professions, equipment, instruments, and supplies; medical institutions and healthcare companies; emergency response agencies and organizations; emergency medical transportation, public health issues, and anatomical parts. This broad search for medical terms resulted in 1,686 terms and 301,659 tweets. Through several iterations of the medical-terms list and analysis of the tweets retrieved by those terms, we converged on 1,544 terms that we hypothesized, based on experience with this dataset, would return authentic medical tweets. Using these terms, we again searched the haiti-keyword dataset, yielding 175,584 tweets that contained ≥1 authentic medical term (the *medical-keywords* dataset). Of these, 140,540 (80%) contained a URL or one of the common retweet conventions (RT @ or via @).

Identification of Medical Twitterers on the Ground

The medical-keywords dataset consisted of 89,114 Twitterers. We were specifically interested in identifying those on the ground to understand geographically constrained coordination. We used additional criteria to narrow the focus to either medical professionals or those affiliated with medical or aid organizations on the ground, including: 1) academic medical centers or hospitals from abroad that dispatched a field team; 2) temporary field hospitals or medical facilities on the ground; 3) medical aid or humanitarian organizations; 4) charitable or faith-based organizations specialized in providing healthcare; or 5) individuals with medical background and affiliated with a medical group on the ground.

To identify Twitterers who met this criteria, we selected a random sample of 10% who sent ≥10 tweets, resulting in 1,756 high-volume medical Twitterers. Because the volume of tweets per user falls in a heavy-tailed distribution [16], we applied a tweet-based, rather than Twitterer-based, sampling strategy. We randomly selected tweets from the medical-keywords dataset and then selected authors of those tweets, continuing the procedure until we reached a 10% (176) sample of high-volume Twitterers.

Next, we examined the tweets from the medical-keywords dataset of 176 high-volume users to identify on-the-ground medical responders. We studied the social networks for all Twitterers who were named or referenced in those tweets. This manual search required reading all the tweets for each high-volume user, identifying all the @<*name*> mentions, and investigating who the mentioned person is by reading their streams and exploring their Twitter profiles and personal or organizational websites. For most users, we were able to determine the deployment dates and locations based on the content of their tweets. Some users stated explicitly on their personal websites if they were in Haiti during the emergency response. The tweets also indicated if the user was a remote proxy tweeting on behalf of their medical team on the ground (e.g., "*Heard from David. Team is in the Dominican and will be heading to Haiti at 1:00am.*"). Once we reached the point of diminishing returns, meaning that we were not identifying new on-the-ground medical Twitterers, we stopped the search.

Medical Twitterer Category	%	Medical Twitterers
Academic medical centers and hospitals from abroad	5%	@BHWSurgery, @CRUDEM_Haiti, *@emoryhealthsci*, *@HopkinsMedNews*, *@MeridianNJ*, *@paloaltomedical*
Field hospitals	5%	@BHMhaiti, @CVN70, @IDFinHaiti, *@IDFspokesperson*, @USNSComfort
Medical aid and humanitarian organizations	49%	*@AAOS1*, *@AmeriCares*, *@ARCrelief*, *@Britishredcross*, *@CARE*, *@compassion*, *@crsnews*, *@directrelief*, @enochchoi, *@erlangerhealth*, *@federation*, *@HHI*, *@HHSGov*, *@HopeForHaitiFL*, *@icrcnews*, *@IMC_Worldwide*, @ISOHIMPACT, @itsChance, @Medishare4Haiti, *@medshare*, *@medteams*, *@merlinUK*, *@merlinUSA*, @mosctha, *@MSFAustralia*, *@MSF_canada*, *@msf_field*, *@MSF_ireland*, *@MSF_uk*, *@MSF_USA*, *@NavyMedicine*, *@NavyNews*, *@nphi*, *@operationbless*, *@oxfamamerica*, *@pahoeoc*, *@pahowho*, *@PIH_org*, *@projecthopeorg*, *@RedCross*, *@redcrosscanada*, *@savethechildren*, *@SSMHealthcare*, *@SurgeonsSOS*, @TeamRubicon, *@UNICEFLive*, *@unicefusa*, *@US_Air_Force*, *@usafpressdesk*, *@USAID_Haiti*, *@usaid_news*, *@uscoastguard*, *@USMC*, *@whonews*
Charity and faith-based organizations	13%	*@G2missions*, @haitihospitalap, *@hcjbglobal*, @LWCmissions, *@MeandMyHouse*, *@MercyShips*, *@missionMANNA*, @mohhaiti, *@One5Foundation*, *@operationsmile*, @Rockers4relief, @SAScharity, @SamaritansPurse, @thegreeneteam
Individuals affiliated with medical centers, teams or organizations	28%	@AlexforMerlin, @aokeke, @avrilbenoit, @bfrist, @blakecanterbury, @CarlosMiranda, @conneally, @craigkielburger, @DokteCoffee, @DrJimSears, *@drval*, @evanlyon, @francoordonez, @ijeanson, @johnpbuckner, @jonmartinlarsen, @lightxxx, @LucasCCarlson, @MartineATF, *@melindayiti* @MerlinChiefExec, @minhnguyenMD, @nateloucks, @nursetim, @Rich_UNICEFUSA, @rickperera, @shollingworth, @SanjayGuptaCNN, @spencenix, @TheDoctors, @troylivesay

Table 1. 110 medical Twitterers and their distribution across five categories. Italicized users represent remote proxies.

The result of this extensive analytical search was 110 found medical Twitterers who produced 16,533 tweets, a list that we believed was representative of major medical players on the ground (Table 1). Among these, 62 (56%) users represent remote proxies who tweeted on behalf of their medical teams on the ground (italicized users in Table 1). 21 (19%) users joined Twitter in the January 12-24, 2010 timeframe. Most of the new Twitterers were small NGOs, field hospitals and their affiliates.

Data Analysis: Extension to the CMC Information Space

Using Twitter's REST API, we obtained the entire Twitter streams for the three-week emergency period for 102 of the medical Twitterers. For the remaining eight, we used tweets from the medical-keywords dataset as their accounts had since closed.

As we hypothesized, Twitter streams pointed to other digital media that were published and broadcast through different computer-mediated communication (CMC) channels. A total of 6,210 (37%) tweets contained URLs, most of which led to official website communications, online field reports, blog posts, videos, Facebook posts, and photographs posted on sites such as Flickr or Twitpic (Table 2). We excluded news media reports because they do not necessarily contain first-hand information. Twitter streams of medical centers and physicians also pointed to their "dispatches from the field" and post hoc accounts published in medical journals. Two researchers on our team performed content analysis of this large information space using a dedicated room to display, examine and cross-reference data points across these many media. Over the period of two months, we inductively analyzed the data collected from Twitter and other CMC channels to identify themes related to coordination challenges and information sharing during the emergency response period.

To better understand the prospects and problems that social media create for the decentralized coordination in disaster response, we also analyzed social network graphs of the 110 medical Twitterers. Using their Twitter streams, we examined how they formed online relationships, whom they interacted with and whom they followed. To answer these questions, we identified the top 25 accounts that had the most mentions and retweets in our dataset. We also identified the accounts that our users mentioned or retweeted individually. Finally, we looked for the mechanisms by which medical Twitterers suggested other users to their followers.

EMERGENCY MEDICINE COORDINATION

We first describe the medical work coordination and use of social media during the preparation phase, followed by a description of coordination during field deployment.

Medical Coordination During the Preparation Phase

Our data analysis, complemented by the data from post hoc accounts published in medical journals, revealed three types of emergency medical responders to the Haiti earthquake based on their prior disaster experience and response time.

First, rapid deployment of emergency medical teams was accomplished by organizations with extensive experience in mass casualty response, such as military, disaster management agencies, government-sponsored organizations and other crisis-oriented entities. For example, the U.S.

Media Type	Number of Medical Twitterers
Photographs	93 (85%)
Websites	85 (77%)
Blogs	72 (65%)
Videos	69 (63%)
Facebook	65 (59%)

Table 2. Distribution of media use by type across medical Twitterers.

Navy aircraft carrier, USS Carl Vinson (@CVN70), arrived off Haiti on January 15. The Israeli Defense Forces Medical Corps field hospital (@IDFinHaiti), capable of providing sophisticated medical care, was fully operational on site only 89 hours after the earthquake struck [15].

Second, collaborative initiatives formed by U.S. medical centers, such as Project Medishare (@Medishare 4Haiti) [7] were also able to respond rapidly due to their preexisting relationships with established NGOs on the ground. Institutions worked with the implementing agencies on the ground to compose teams, create lists of medical supplies and equipment, and develop strategic plans.

Finally, those without preexisting relationships with NGOs on the ground or preexisting international disaster programs (e.g., ad hoc academic medical teams and self-deployed volunteers) responded later, faced significant preparation challenges, and were ill-prepared for the conditions on the ground [18]. As reported by physicians on the ground [17, 31], many donor countries sent emergency medicine teams to build field hospitals, but not all of them came prepared.

Two main coordination challenges emerged in the pre-deployment readiness based on the social media data and post hoc accounts: 1) information from partners on the ground was often incomplete and sporadic, and 2) needs on the ground changed throughout the response. Our analysis elaborated on these challenges and showed that social media were used not only for broadcasting information needs, but also for providing needed information.

Preparing for Conditions Based on Incomplete Information

Incomplete and sporadically available information about the conditions on the ground required preparation for a more universal medical response. For example, the location of team deployment and the actual team assignments were often not known until shortly before departure [18]. A team's preparation and needs assessment for necessary equipment and supplies were therefore in continuous flux.

Social media data showed that all three types of medical responders faced this problem. NGOs and individuals outside Haiti who organized teams of doctors for deployment requested information about site locations from those who were on the ground, regardless of whether or not they had previously established relationships. Consider for example a tweet directed by a leader of an NGO to Partners in Health (PIH), a non-profit organization:

```
@PIH_org this is Melinda Miles, I've worked with
PIH a lot and I have surgeons ready to go to
Haiti, who should I call?
(@melindayiti, Jan 16, 2010)
```

Larger medical and humanitarian aid organizations with an established presence in Haiti either contacted their staff on the ground or dispatched assessment teams immediately after the earthquake struck to obtain information on the most urgent needs. For example, Doctors Without Borders/Médecins Sans Frontières (MSF) had operated three medical facilities in Haiti since 1991 and had 800 medical staff on the ground. Although these facilities were badly damaged in the earthquake and many of the staff were injured, a few staff members were able to quickly assess the situation and share information through Twitter, Facebook and field reports posted on their website. Below is an excerpt from their January 13 field report:

> *"One of MSF's senior staff, [name], was out for most of the night, trying to assess the needs in the city and looking at the state of the medical facilities. 'The situation is chaotic,' he said. 'I visited five medical centers, including a major hospital, and most of them were not functioning.'"*

We observed many instances of individuals and organizations that responded immediately and operated at different locations on the ground using social media to disseminate information about needed medications, equipment and supplies. For example, @MartineATF, a self-deployed volunteer working at the Baptist Haiti Mission hospital (@BHMhaiti) in Port-au-Prince tweeted:

```
I've created a list of medical supplies in need
at BHM Hospital: @ me your email if you'd like me
to forward. (@MartineATF, Jan 16, 2010)
```

Similarly, International Medical Corps used both Twitter and Facebook to disseminate information about their needs:

```
Don't have enough of some basic wound care
supplies, nurses and those with basic first aid
experience. (@IMC_Worldwide, Jan 17, 2010)
```

These tweets and other social media posts contained important and useful information for those who were preparing for the deployment. Yet, publicly available social media communications do not provide any evidence that medical teams used such posts as an information source for their preparation. As reported in post hoc accounts, medical teams mostly relied on telephone and email to coordinate preparations [18]. After all, the above tweet from @MartineATF calls for email use as a means of communicating additional details. We observed, however, that social media like Twitter played a role in reaching potential helpers and providing contact information. As the above examples illustrate, most tweets from on-the-ground medical Twitterers were not directly addressed to anyone, nor were they passed on by these Twitterers from another source. Indeed, the 48 medical responders who tweeted from the ground produced a total 4,877 tweets, of which 3,335 (68%) contained no language indicating retweets or direct addressing to others (RT @, via @, or @<name>), with 27 of these Twitterers producing more than 75% of their tweets without addressing or redirection. Medical teams on the ground appeared to use social media to express their needs and report status, often without knowing who might be reading their messages or following their Twitter streams. We call this behavior *beaconing* to describe the regularly sent signals of information broadcast to the Twitterverse at large. As we explain later in the paper, beaconing is a precursor to coordination in a highly decentralized work environment.

Investigation of the teams' deployment dates and their Twitter interactions also revealed that relationships among some medical teams started to form *after* they deployed. We identified several clusters of medical responders who communicated with each other via Twitter during their deployment. To establish connections, teams made recommendations by relying on the #followfriday or #FF norm, by sending targeted follow requests, or simply by "recommending" accounts they trusted. For example, one such cluster formed among charity-based organizations, including @SamaritansPurse, @hcjbglobal, @MeandMy House and @ISOHIMPACT, whose medical teams deployed to the Baptist Haiti Mission hospital (@BHMhaiti). They connected with each other upon their arrival to Haiti, after @BHMHaiti sent a targeted request:

```
@MeandMyHouse @hcjbglobal Can you follow us so we
can send direct msgs? Thnx!"
(@BHMHaiti, Jan 18, 2010)
```

Based upon these findings, we hypothesize that medical teams did not use social media as an information source or even as a coordination mechanism during the pre-deployment readiness phase because they were not aware of streams or Twitterers on the ground who had the information they needed. In contrast, teams that were on the ground and in need of medical supplies and personnel did use social media to disseminate information about their needs, but did so broadly without directly addressing particular groups or individuals, hoping that someone would respond— this is, again, beaconing behavior.

We also noted that organizations—both large and small—and medical teams on the ground frequently posted photographs of medical facilities and physicians in action. In these photographs, one can see the severity of damage to the building or care facility, medical equipment in use, patient injuries, geographic location of the site, and even weather conditions. There is no explicit evidence that such photos were used for tactical planning. However, the availability of them in disaster response is a tremendous planning resource, if they could be readily available, consolidated and geo- and temporally-located.

Preparing for Conditions under Continuous Change

Medical needs were not only unknown, but were also changing on a daily and then weekly basis. This problem was most evident with medical personnel needs. In the immediate aftermath of the earthquake, the biggest demand was for orthopedic and trauma surgeons due to the traumatic nature of injuries sustained by victims. Many tweets and other online content reflected this need:

```
Haiti needs surgeons so I am going at 3 tomorrow-
desperate need for antibiotics, need in bulk
only-if you have extra: http://bit.ly/7bPOUh
(@bfrist, Jan 16, 2010, note: link is broken)
```

```
attention: no neurosurgeons in haiti that can be
found. needed, along with proper instruments.
please ensure uss comfort has one as well.
(@SanjayGuptaCNN, Jan 18, 2010)
```

Urgent demands for surgical care were also reflected through posts on the number of surgeries that field hospitals carried out daily. For example:

```
Update from #Haiti: We believe that 1,500
patients are inside and outside the hospital.
Approximately 70 to 80 percent need surgery.
(@IMC_Worldwide, Jan 17, 2010)
```

```
Doctors Without Borders surgical teams have been
carrying out an average of 130 operations/day in
#Haiti. http://bit.ly/5su7sF
(@MSF_USA, Jan 21, 2010)
```

A blog post from the Sutter Health medical team (@paloaltomedical) posted on January 25 further illustrates the need for acute surgical care:

"The Sutter Health team continues to treat patients and perform surgeries at St. Nicholas Hospital in St. Marc – working an average of 20 hours a day. Above [photo] Stephen Lockhart M.D., anesthesiologist and chief medical officer for Sutter Health's East Bay Region stands by the list of patients awaiting surgery. At 4:30 p.m. (Haiti time) there are 17 patients who still need treatment today."

About two weeks into the emergency response, calls for personnel needs shifted from surgeons to other medical specialists. Once the first wave of critically injured patients passed, a larger need for post-operative care specialists and rehabilitation medicine physicians emerged. In addition, less critically injured patients and those with chronic diseases started to seek help. Infectious diseases (ID) started to spread as well, resulting in a new call for ID physicians. This shift in personnel needs was also reflected through social media posts. Consider for example a tweet from @ISOHIMPACT, a charitable organization specializing in medical intervention and disaster relief:

```
Thinking of coming to Haiti? There will be a real
need for rehab medicine docs in ~1 month when
wounds healed and prosthetics available.
(@ISOHIMPACT, Jan 21, 2010)
```

On January 28, @IMC_Worldwide, the International Medical Corps, posted to their Facebook wall:

"noticed a dramatic change over the past 48 hours in the type of patients they [the doctors] are seeing. Instead of treating a constant stream of severe and urgent earthquake-related injuries, there are now patients coming to the hospital with less urgent medical needs, such as high blood pressure or minor skin growths."

Others provided similar status updates via Twitter:

```
Doctors Without Borders is now treating more
patients for pre-existing conditions & infections
in #Haiti http://bit.ly/4GffTl
(@MSF_USA, Jan 24, 2010)
```

```
Medical orgs in Haiti say surgical needs are
lessening & there will be greater need for
management of infections & mental health care.
(@HHI, Jan 27, 2010)
```

Several medical teams and individuals on the ground cautioned that even though surgical needs were lessening, there was still an overall demand for surgeons, especially in rural areas. In addition, many patients were being readmitted due to wound infections caused by inadequate initial care, requiring surgeries to be redone. Tweets below illustrate this continuous demand for surgical care:

```
Seeing a lot of patients with amputations that
were done poorly a week ago by other hospitals
with no follow up – many needing to be redone.
(@troylivesay, Jan 23, 2010)
```

```
There is still a need for docs and nurses in
Haiti. I hope people keep coming. #Haiti
(@DokteCoffee, Jan 29, 2010)
```

The shift in personnel needs affected not only those who were preparing for deployment, but also those who were already on the ground. @MissionMANNA, a non-profit organization providing medical care for malnourished children, reported via Twitter on January 29:

```
#Haiti #avlnews numerous teams of medics, nurses,
doctors, surgeons waiting in frustration outside
hospital, wanting desperately 2 be useful
(@MissionMANNA, Jan 29, 2010)
```

Sanjay Gupta, a neurosurgeon and medical correspondent for CNN, who was actively involved in providing medical care, blogged about a similar situation on January 25:

"...after a few days of limited help, there is now such a surge of surgeons, some medical personnel are being turned away from some of the big hospitals in Port-au-Prince. 'We appreciate your efforts, but we have more surgeons than we need,' is being repeated at the general hospital in downtown."

That some medical teams were still expressing the need for surgical care while others talked about a surplus of surgeons confirms the lack of coordination and information exchange among medical teams, but also demonstrates an opportunity for social media and other forms of ICT to aid in supporting the decentralized work conditions on the ground. Although medical teams expressed their needs and concerns through social media, there is no evidence in our data that they used social media for direct communications and coordination as they prepared for deployment.

Medical Coordination During the Deployment Phase

Upon their arrival, medical teams and groups faced different kinds of coordination challenges. One of the main problems often cited in post hoc accounts included the lack of organization on the ground [9, 31]. As several physicians reported from the field, "Doctors were coming to Haiti with no plan of what they were going to do and they received limited help and directions once they arrived" [17].

All disaster situations have spontaneous volunteers who converge onto the geographical arena [13]. It is also common for specialized groups to self-deploy, including engineering and medical teams, even if they have no prior disaster field experience [28]. In the 2010 Haiti earthquake disaster, emergency physicians and teams from university hospitals with experience in acute trauma care volunteered both their personal and institutional time to help a region in need. However, not all had disaster experience and were unprepared for the lack of coordination that characterizes disaster situations. These teams and NGOs that were coordinating their deployment often used social media to express concerns about the lack of centralized coordination. Consider a tweet from @melindayiti, a leader of the NGO called "Working together for Haiti":

```
Who is in charge of the response in Haiti? Where
is the national strategy?
(@melindayiti, Jan 16, 2010)
```

In contrast, teams and NGOs with more experience seemed to understand the reality of large-scale disasters and knew how to organize their activities:

```
Aid effort undeniably slower than we would want
but the reality is what it is. No infrastructure.
Little central control (govn. in a tent).
(@conneally from Red Cross, Jan 17, 2010)
```

```
In CARE's nightly coordination mtg, where team is
planning logistics, trucks, locations for
tomorrow's aid -- like a well-oiled machine!
(@rickperera from CARE, Jan 23, 2010)
```

We next describe three main coordination challenges in the deployment phase—coordination among hospitals, patient coordination, and medical supply coordination—and how these challenges materialized through social media.

Coordination among Hospitals on the Ground

Teams working in field hospitals reported difficulties in obtaining information about other field hospitals and makeshift facilities, and expressed the need for hourly updates on their capacities and capabilities [20]. As @lightxxx, a volunteer on a medical mission, reports:

```
Another thing there are no communications between
the hospitals # Haiti (@lightxxx, Jan 24, 2010)
```

Information about hospital capacities was needed for managing patient distribution, especially for patients needing specialized care. Analysis revealed that some field hospitals posted their status in real-time. Consider this Facebook post on January 17 by @CRUDEM_Haiti, the largest private hospital in North Haiti:

"A load of 6 patients was due to arrive yesterday evening but unfortunately on route the pilot was forced to turn back because of the terrible weather conditions. Our general surgery team arrived yesterday, an orthopedic team today. We need the patients to be brought to us in much greater numbers!!"

Or a tweet from the CARE organization, whose medical team operated in one of the hospitals in Port-au-Prince:

```
Hospital in Port-au-Prince #Haiti are full of
severely injured individuals; no room to accept
add'l wounded. (@CARE, Jan 14, 2010)
```

Here, too, we noticed medical teams exhibiting beaconing behavior—reporting their status and posting requests in hopes that someone would respond. During the preparation phase, no responses to such messages were discovered in the analysis. However, rèsponses to these requests were found to have occurred during the deployment phase. Interestingly, rather than coming from other medical responders on the ground, responses mostly came from digital volunteers, or "remote operators" of various backgrounds who were moving information between sources both on and off the ground, and were contributing to resolving the expressed problems [26]. Our analysis of social networks showed that many medical teams on the ground mentioned the following digital volunteers: @ShaunKing, @MelyMello, @SuziLeVeaux, @thehaitian, @Crimson_Cougar, @kiskeacity, @lorihcg, @VRWC Texan, and others. For instance, @mohhaiti, a non-profit Christian organization based in Port-au-Prince, posted an urgent need for food for their medical facility and almost immediately received help from several remote operators.

Patient Coordination and Transportation

Many patients required medical evacuation to the ship-based hospitals off the Haiti shore, while some patients required evacuation to hospitals in the U.S. Damaged infrastructure and scarce resources imposed multiple constraints on coordinating patient transfer.

In addition to using social media to express frustrations or discuss coordination problems, a few medical teams saw social media as a potential place for action and used it to coordinate patient care during their deployment. An instance comes from the IDF field hospital (@IDFinHaiti). On January 22, IDF doctors diagnosed a 4-year old Haitian with leukemia who needed urgent transfer to a U.S. hospital. @IDFinHaiti called for help via Twitter and blog:

`mike, 4, diagnosed w stage 5 leukemia 2day, trying to get him to US for treatment ASAP, ideas: idfinhaiti@gmail.com` **`(@IDFinHaiti, Jan 22, 2010)`**

`Mike, 4, stg 5 leukemia, we need someone to get him to the US for immediate care: http://is.gd/6OWBd` **`(@IDFinHaiti, Jan 22, 2010)`**

After 4.5 hours, their Twitter post announced that the patient was successfully transferred:

`Mike, 4, diagnosed with leukemia is being brought to Univ Miami Hosp for treatment by org 'God's Planet'!` **`(@IDFinHaiti, Jan 22, 2010)`**

Our data do not show any digital traces of the means by which this help was obtained; this likely happened privately via email, as indicated above. Nevertheless, we found a quote on IDF's blog that refers to "an overwhelming response" to their tweet, which in turn shows the promise of social media in supporting information exchange and work coordination during emergency medical response.

Medical Supplies Coordination

Obtaining essential supplies was difficult; medical teams complained about the overwhelming bureaucracy and delays in supply distribution. Reports via social media described supplies standing still on the tarmac:

`Witnessed all of the supplies stockpiled in the airport. So well protected that nothing gets out. Sad to see. #Haiti` **`(@ISOHIMPACT, Jan 26, 2010)`**

Problems were also reported with getting supplies to Haiti. The airport in Port-au-Prince reopened on January 13, with U.S. Airmen controlling the airport traffic. As reported on the U.S. Air Force website, the capacity was exceeded by more than 100 percent, increasing from 50 to 140 flights per day. Many planes wanted to land and many planes needed to depart because of evacuations.

Doctors Without Borders were incredulous that they could not land their planes with medical supplies and demanded the U.S. Air Force allow them to land, which created tensions and media outcry. Many MSF's tweets, field reports and blog posts discussed this problem:

`Total 5 #MSF planes w 85tonnes medical/relief supplies diverted from PaP to Dom.Rep. since Jan 14 http://bit.ly/7xheyT` **`(@MSF_canada, Jan 19, 2010)`**

"According to Dr. Greg Elder, deputy operations manager for MSF in Haiti, some sites are facing a 10 to 12 day backlog of patients due to the huge number of people who need treatment and ongoing delays in getting supplies into the country. Some victims are already dying of sepsis, an illness caused by infections that can affect people with untreated wounds." (Jan 20, 2010)

Twitterers around the world who followed the medical situation in Haiti massively retweeted MSF's complaints and directed them to the U.S. Air Force. In one of MSF's tweets, we see a positive outcome of such actions:

`Thanks for your RT's to the USAF – u helped land our diverted cargo plane in #Haiti yesterday! Good work everyone :) http://bit.ly/4Hhky6` **`(@MSF_canada, Jan 18, 2010)`**

Additionally, we observed a few instances of direct communications via Twitter between teams on the ground to coordinate medical supplies and equipment. As an example, @ISOHIMPACT expressed the need for a portable x-ray machine for one of their hospitals and @IDFinHaiti responded positively:

`Double Harvest (doubleharvest.org) has a real need for an X-ray machine. We are trying to find one stateside. Any ideas? Contact ISOH #Haiti` **`(@ISOHIMPACT, Jan 20, 2010)`**

`@VRWCTexan @isohimpact indeed we have a portable digital xray machine` **`(@IDFinHaiti, Jan 20, 2010)`**

`Looks like we have a port X-ray to pick up for hospital at Double Harvest. THANK YOU @IDFinHaiti and all who helped w this! #Haiti` **`(@ISOHIMPACT, Jan 20, 2010)`**

Though some communications between medical responders on the ground did occur, it seemed that remote operators (@VRWCTexan in the above case) played a critical role in establishing connections between the seekers and providers.

CONCLUSION

The nature of medical work in disaster response is a highly distributed and decentralized work activity, often ill-coordinated by virtue of the nature of the event itself. We have organized the discussion of coordination in this paper around coordination during preparation and field deployment, because much of a team's capacity on the ground rests on the appropriateness of the equipment and personnel they bring, advance knowledge of the circumstances of their deployment location, and advance knowledge of current medical needs on the ground.

Social Media and Coordination: Reality and Potential

Social media data as well as accounts in the published literature showed that pre-deployment preparation was hampered by teams not knowing the conditions they were about to face. We saw little evidence of social media being used for pre-deployment coordination. However, it is here where we saw the first round of opportunities for rapid and more comprehensive preparation through a network of those already on the ground or in a state of pre-deployment. Coordination among teams during preparation is important because of their potential to optimize resources and deployment sites while they still have flexibility to do so.

Once on the ground, the teams continued to perform their work under decentralized conditions, which was in part characterized by disparities between their capacities and the kind and number of patients who sought their services. In some cases, we saw too high a demand placed on medical teams and in other cases, too little. Uneven distribution of patient load is not uncommon in disasters, but this is a critical area of opportunity not only for optimal mobilization of patients but also for the optimal placement of field teams. A major lesson here is that if decentralization is the manner in which work is conducted, as it almost always will be in disasters, then offering decentralized solutions, which allow teams as a population to self-organize, is the best direction to take. Social media and other forms of ICT are a natural place to enable such decentralized coordination.

Beaconing Behavior as a Precursor to Coordination

The role of social media in the work of medical teams varied and, in general, had little use in the way of regular cross-collaboration. Naturally, one would expect that busy medical teams have little time to tweet or blog. Yet, we know that at least 110 medically-oriented groups *did* use social media to report on their on-the-ground relief efforts. It is from *how* they used social media that we can infer more about their situation, expand the potential for social media, and identify a new social media-abetted behavior that is characteristic of large-scale decentralized tasks.

Of the medical Twitterers we identified, it was the smaller organizations and NGOs that tweeted regularly, but without addressing a particular person. Furthermore, when they included URLs, those links led to identical content but posted in a different media, e.g., Facebook or website. The tweets provided valuable information about the teams' situation but were simply broadcasts, without specific interaction with others. This is what we call *beaconing behavior*. Beaconing suggests an intention to be heard and a desire to be found. It happens when Twitterers (in this case) do not know to whom to direct their communications. It happens when there are not enough resources to put into navigating the social media space to find people who can help. In a world where social media are a means into a common though massive information space [3], beaconing is one precondition for coordination in decentralized situations, where potential collaborators are unknown.

For larger organizations such as the Red Cross, UNICEF, and the military, beaconing does not describe tweet behavior. Such organizations have remote proxies and staff who can more adequately manage logistics. The smaller organizations seem to most benefit by the at-large digital volunteers who see the message beacons, and make the connections between potential partners, between requests and offers. It is in this "wired wilderness" [3] of massively distributed information spaces that well-attuned listeners detect and capitalize on the latent potential for coordination of teams on the ground.

Designing for the Decentralized Work of Disaster

Two implications for designing future ICT support during disaster response arise from this research. First, to enable efficient preparation and rapid response, it is important to connect teams on the ground (information providers) with teams preparing to deploy (information seekers). One way to support this need is to create an online destination where seekers and providers can find each other directly and exchange information. This method is being attempted by Sahana (sahanafoundation.org) and Ushahidi (ushahidi.com) though without particular attention to the details of medical response. Another way would be to augment the work of human agents with artificial agents to actively monitor social media statuses to find matches. Second, medical responders shared information about their needs but they were not the people to mediate between seekers and providers; this task was done by remote digital volunteers. This demonstrates a proof of concept that linking those on the ground with "connectors" who, as their primary task seek to make matches between needs and offers, can lead to a resolution of the problem. In other words, the already decentralized activity can become further decentralized by pushing some information functions to others outside harm's way. Instead of waiting for the crowd to surface its capacities in the moment, it is also possible to foster specific relationships during the pre-deployment phase with volunteers who can act as the remote proxies that large organizations formally employ.

Effective coordination is a critical but often elusive ally in disaster mitigation. The tragedy suffered by Haiti reveals opportunities for improving medical response. Though social media were in relatively little use for coordination of this scale in early 2010, we see proof of existence of new behaviors that could support medical teamwork and information sharing, with the points of improvement occurring not only in the field but also, critically, at the time of preparation and pre-deployment.

ACKNOWLEDGMENTS

We thank the U.S. National Science Foundation for funding this research through grants IIS-0910586 and IIS-0915871.

REFERENCES

1. Bentley, R. et al. Ethnographically-informed systems design for air traffic control. *Proc. CSCW 1992*, ACM Press (1992), 123-129.
2. Berman, P. Decentralized again. *Datanation 16*, 13 (1970), 141-142.
3. Bertelsen, O.W. and Bødker, S. Cooperation in massively distributed information spaces. *Proc. ECSCW 2001*, Kluwer Academic Publishers (2001), 1-17.
4. der Heide, A. *Disaster Response: Principles of Preparation and Coordination*. Mosby Inc., 1989.
5. Evaristo, J.R., Desouza, K.C., and Hollister, K. Centralization momentum: the pendulum swings back again. *CACM 48*, 2 (2005), 66-71.
6. FEMA. Use of social media tools at FEMA. *News Release FNF-09-040*, November 2, 2009.
7. Ginzburg, E. et al. Rapid medical relief—Project Medishare and the Haitian earthquake. *New England Journal of Medicine 362* (2010), e31.
8. Harvard Humanitarian Initiative. Disaster Relief 2.0: The Future of Information Sharing in Humanitarian Emergencies. Washington, D.C. and Berkshire, UK: UN Foundation & Vodafone Foundation Technology Partnership, 2011.
9. Hauswald, M., Richards, M.E., Kerr, N.L., Schmidt, T.A., and Helderman, T. The Haitian earthquake and academic emergency medicine. *Academic Emergency Medicine 17*, 2 (2010), 762–764.
10. Heath, C., and Luff, P. Collaboration and control: Crisis management and multimedia technology in London underground line control rooms. *Computer Supported Cooperative Work 11*, 1-2 (1992), 69-95.
11. Hine, C. *Virtual Ethnography*. SAGE, 2000.
12. Juhlin, O., and Weilenmann, A. Decentralizing the control room: mobile work and institutional order. *Proc. ECSCW 2001*, Kluwer Academic Publishers (2001), 379-397.
13. Kendra, J.M. and Wachtendorf, T. Reconsidering convergence and converger legitimacy in response to the World Trade Center disaster. *Research in Social Problems and Public Policy 11* (2003), 97-122.
14. King, J. Centralized vs. decentralized computing: Organizational considerations and management options. *ACM Computing Surveys 15*, 4 (1983), 319–349.
15. Kreiss et al. Early disaster response in Haiti: The Israeli field hospital experience. *Annals of Internal Medicine 153*, 1 (2010), 45-48.
16. Leskovec, J., McGlohon, M., Faloutsos, C., Glance, N.S., and Hurst, M. Patterns of cascading behavior in large blog graphs. *Proc. SIAM Conference on Data Mining*, 2007.
17. Lorich, D., Eachempati, S., and Helfet, D.L. Doctors: Haiti medical situation shameful. *Special report to CNN*, January 25, 2010.
18. McCunn, M. et al. An organized, comprehensive, and security-enabled strategic response to the Haiti earthquake: A description of pre-deployment readiness preparation and preliminary experience from an academic anesthesiology department with no preexisting international disaster response program. *Anesthesia & Analgesia 111*, 6 (2010), 1438-1444.
19. PAHO/WHO. Earthquake in Haiti—One year later. *Report on the Health Situation*, January 2011.
20. Pape, J.W., Johnson, W.D. and Fitzgerald, D.W. The earthquake in Haiti—Dispatch from Port-au-Prince. *New England Journal of Medicine 362* (2010), 575-577.
21. Qu, Y., Huang, C., Zhang, P., and Zhang, J. Microblogging after a major disaster in China: A case study of the 2010 Yushu earthquake. *Proc. CSCW 2011*, ACM Press (2011), 25-34.
22. Quarantelli, E.L., Taylor, V.A., and Tierney, K.J. Delivery of emergency medical services in disasters. *Preliminary paper # 46,* University of Delaware Disaster Research Center, 1977.
23. Schmidt, K. and Bannon, L. Taking CSCW seriously. *Computer Supported Cooperative Work 1* (1992), 7-40.
24. Starbird, K., Palen, L.A., Hughes, A., and Vieweg, S. Chatter on The Red: What hazards threat reveal about the social life of microblogged information. *Proc. CSCW 2010*, ACM Press (2010), 241-250.
25. Suchman, L.A. Office procedures as practical action: models of work and system design. *ACM Transactions on Office Information Systems 1*, 4 (1983), 320-328.
26. Starbird, K. and Palen, L.A. "Voluntweeters": Self-organizing by digital volunteers in times of crisis. *Proc CHI 2011*, ACM Press (2011), 1071-1080.
27. Tamura, Y. and Fukuda, K. Earthquake in Japan. *The Lancet 377*, 9778 (2011), 1652.
28. Tierney, K.J. Emergency medical preparedness and response in disasters: The need for interorganizational coordination. *Public Administration Review 45* (1985), 77-84.
29. United Nations. Situation report: Haiti Earthquake 2010, 1800 hrs 23 Jan 2010. http://reliefweb.int/node/342689
30. Vieweg, S., Hughes, A., Starbird, K., and Palen, L.A. Micro-blogging during the two natural hazards event: What Twitter may contribute to situational awareness. *Proc. CHI 2010*, ACM Press (2010), 1079-1088.
31. Zarocostas, J. Death toll in Haiti may reach 200,000. *BMJ 340* (2010), c331.

Relief Work after the 2010 Haiti Earthquake: Leadership in an Online Resource Coordination Network

Sean P. Goggins
Drexel University
outdoors@acm.org

Christopher Mascaro
Drexel University
cmascaro@gmail.com

Stephanie Mascaro
Atlas Research
shmascaro@gmail.com

ABSTRACT
The US Navy directed its vast resources at the relief effort following the Haiti Earthquake on January 12, 2010. To coordinate with non-governmental-organizations (NGOs) participating in the relief effort, the US Navy used an online discussion forum. What follows is an examination of the emergence, rise, on-the-ground utility and decline of this "walled-garden" style discussion forum. Our findings show that most site activity is broadcast oriented and does not result in discussion, but in the small percentage of cases where discussion emerges, participants are focused on the exchange of medical, Global Information Systems (GIS) and equipment on the ground oriented information. We show how activity on the discussion forum changes over time, and corresponds with events on the ground in Haiti. Four archetypical users are profiled to demonstrate how invisible brokerage style leadership, identified through grounded theory analysis of posts, can be made visible through network analysis of interaction traces. Our findings have implications for the use of forum style, "walled garden" technology for coordination and information sharing in future crises.

Author Keywords
Disaster Relief, Online Coordination, Government, NGO.

ACM Classification Keywords
H5.3. Collaborative Computing

INTRODUCTION
Effective coordination and information sharing in disaster situations is a matter of life and death. Social media, first responders, non-governmental organizations (NGOs) and both civil and military government organizations cooperate to respond to and manage the crisis that follows any disaster. Improving information sharing and coordination between government agencies with significant resources, NGOs and affected civilians will save lives by saving time and improving the information available for decision makers about resource distribution. The All-Partners Access Network (APAN) is a US Navy sponsored electronic forum that enables coordination between US government agencies – principally the Navy – and organizations that do not have access to government systems, such as NGOs. In this study we examine Government-NGO coordination in APAN[1] during the crisis that followed the January 12, 2010 7.0 earthquake disaster in Haiti.

Prior work in CSCW focuses on understanding and designing social and participatory media to help members of the public contribute to disaster response in a coordinated manner [32]. Similar coordination gaps exist between government resources like the US Navy and NGOs during a crisis. In the latter case, governments have logistical, medical and transportation resources that can both assist and be augmented by NGOs. Unlike current modes of citizen participation in relief efforts, Government-NGO coordination and information sharing relies on conventional, "walled garden" discussion forums like APAN. In a walled garden, access is vetted. In this way, information is at once more trustworthy and less available to those outside the network. This type of coordination and information sharing work is unexamined in prior CSCW studies of disaster relief.

Government-NGO crisis coordination through discussion forums centers on getting locally relevant information, responding to the need for information, connecting to others in crisis; and community computing [31]. The Haiti relief APAN forum is used for information-related discussions and coordination discussions, similar to the findings of Kodrich and Laituri [1]. This study examines how Government-NGO crisis coordination is facilitated by tools like APAN from three perspectives. First, we analyze and group topics of discussion to understand the most prominent types of interaction. Second, we relate activity in the forum to key government-NGO coordination events in the field. Third, we innovate methodologically to better understand participant behavior on the Forum.

In this paper we integrate grounded theory with network analysis of APAN page view (read) and forum contribution (post) data for two purposes. First, we identify interaction networks that emerge in the forums. Second, we also identify users who are not among the most active people in the forums, but who play key, "invisible broker" roles." An invisible broker is a leader who connects two networks of

[1] http://community.apan.org

activity within APAN, but is not identifiable from raw post activity. Our examination of the contributions of "invisible brokers" whom we identify through electronic trace data, shows that the substance of their post activity in the forums is focused on, literally, brokering and coordinating relief efforts on the ground.

Physical, Virtual and Technology Context of Study

The relief effort related to the Haiti earthquake has been examined from a number of other perspectives. For example, Mission 4536, a collaboration of private companies and emergency relief agencies, leveraged crowd sourced translation and geo-location with SMS-based reporting to collect and organize information from a distributed human network in Haiti [15]. The resulting system helped address immediate emergency needs, expanded employment opportunities during the disaster response and increased opportunities for participation in the disaster recovery period. Our work builds on these and other efforts by bringing focus to the role of government organized information and communications technologies (ICTs) designed to support information and coordination that leverages substantial government infrastructure; in this case, the US Navy's medical, equipment and GIS information capacity.

The 2010 Haiti Earthquake offers a unique context for analysis of government-NGO coordination because the destruction of the capital city of Port-Au-Prince, Haiti eliminated a significant portion of the telecommunications infrastructure, hampering coordination and rescue efforts. The analysis of information sharing and coordination through APAN during the Haiti crisis helps us to understand how individuals, representing NGOs and government agencies, participated in coordination of relief efforts *from a distance* and contributed to targeted action on the ground.

Given the scale of the Haiti disaster and the significant resources of the US Navy, it may be surprising that basic discussion forum technology is the center of coordination and information sharing [1]. Understanding the levels, types and leaders of interaction in this forum will inform future use of technology in disaster situations. For example, responsiveness to users, timeliness of information, ease of site navigation and information monitoring are key attributes in successful forum sites in disaster relief scenarios [27]. Here, we analyze a vivid, exemplar crisis.

CSCW AND DISASTER RELIEF

There are numerous systems in place to try to predict, prevent and respond to disasters; however the unique and chaotic nature of large disasters often means that standard procedures break down. The resulting confusion is compounded by the fact that despite the inferred meaning of the colloquialism "first responders," the first people on the scene of a disaster are usually the members of the local community and not professionals trained to respond to the emergency at hand [5]. In the past, these individuals would have affected the disaster locally (e.g., by providing disaster relief support to victims), but with recent innovations in ICTs, such as smart phones, camera phones, mobile texting, email, and GPS capability, they are able to communicate information more easily and are affecting the way people outside the disaster see and understand it as it is happening [24]. In fact, disasters often lead to innovative uses of ICTs [32]. Most prior CSCW research on disasters focuses on connecting the community with relief.

In time of disaster, information seems to flow in three directions – from authorities to the public [18; 19], from the public to authorities [10; 35; 38] and from peer-to-peer [24-26; 29; 31; 36]. For example, following the 2001 Gujarat Earthquake, the news media in India helped deliver key information using multiple lines of communication, including chat rooms, help lines and information dissemination. The electronic groups that emerged within these forums helped relief workers solicit donations for disaster relief [18]. Laituri and Kodrich [19] show that online news media does enable the public to be more involved in disaster relief through awareness and promotion of trusted charities. The public, in turn, seeks information verification to augment what they hear from official sources. They often do this using social connections both in their community and online [6; 12; 22; 35].

Through the use of ICTs and social media, the public is often able to contribute to the knowledge of the authorities in addition to communicating with their community [38]. For example, residents of the area affected by the 2007 wildfire in California reported about their experience and provided essential information about the crisis to people outside the area [10]. While looking at this disaster, Sutton et al. [35] learned that faced with disaster, the public seeks information from any available source "regardless of whether the source is considered authoritative or not." This idea of "citizen journalism" is relatively new, but has become commonplace in society [8].

The 2010 Haiti earthquake was the first time that social media was used as part of the US Government's formal response to a disaster [2]. Research into the role these online communities play suggests that when properly employed, they create "transformational knowledge sharing between communities", but when not properly employed are useless and distracting. The research also suggests that since timely information is of the essence during a disaster and it is often unclear who has the "best" information, in some cases more authoritative sources of information have an important, complementary role to play with social media. Connecting authoritative sources with social media then, is an area for future investigation that begins with our study of how more authoritative information sources, like APAN, function in a disaster.

Beyond communicating and sharing information with authorities, information in times of disaster often flows from peer-to-peer. For example, after Hurricane Katrina, people were able to connect with one another through social media and online neighborhood-based forums to locate missing family members, and organize relief efforts such as seeking and offering donations, shelter, and employment opportunities [24; 29; 31]. Websites were specifically created to facilitate "connected giving," providing a link between people who wanted to donate goods and services and people in need in the disaster area [36]. This peer-to-peer approach was efficient and bypassed the need to involve a third organization. Information and communication is also important while a crisis is occurring, and in the first hours of response. In the wake of the April 2007 shooting at Virginia Tech University, students were able to determine the welfare of their friends and fellow students through peer-to-peer communication across crisis stages [25] and generate an accurate list of the 32 victims using Wikipedia, Facebook and other social media before Virginia Tech released an official list [26].

Information communicated during disaster situations is diverse in its mode, nature and trustworthiness. Beyond simply sharing personal, situational or coordination information, people use online communities during disasters for interpersonal and emotional support. Torrey et al. [36] found that online communities are crucial for trust development in disaster relief efforts. For example, a computer network set up for people dealing with the foot and mouth disease crisis in the UK provided "a virtual space for interpersonal contact, community discussion, and mutual help among farmers at a critical time [13]."

Numerous schemas for categorizing and understanding the information communicated in the crises following a disaster have been discovered by prior research. Yan et al. [38] observed online discussions related to the 2008 Sichuan earthquake and identified four primary ways that the Tianya forum supported the community - information-related discussions, opinion-related discussions, emotion-related discussions, and action-related discussions. Similarly, Shklovski et al. [32] suggested that online disaster-related discussions fall into four main categories; getting locally relevant information, responding to information needs, connecting to others in crisis and community computing.

ICTs are crucial for bridging the gap between authority and information in a crisis. Garshnek and Burkle [7] articulated the importance of understanding the relative advantages and disadvantages of three basic pathways for communication: landlines, airwaves and satellite links. Social media and forums like APAN have altered this landscape. Now, disaster relief efforts rely on access to the Internet. Jaeger et al.'s [17] study of the Katrina Crisis found that Internet access was crucial for connecting members of a disaster struck community [17]. In a crisis, people, governments and NGOs rely on the Internet, including social networks, blogs and forums like APAN to share all types of information. Information sharing is a central issue in crisis management because those responding to the crisis seldom have both the best information and authority for making decisions [34].

Bui et al. [27] developed a framework for conceptualizing the types of issues that emergency relief workers must overcome, suggesting that the central issues in disaster relief management are information, coordination and the effects of disaster relief work on workers [3]. Information issues include information distortion and inconsistencies that must be reconciled. Coordination between governments and NGOs can be problematic because of government reluctance to release information with potential security implications and communication incompatibilities, including both language and technology. [3].

Most existing research on the use of ICTs in disaster relief is focused on how ICTs support emergency management [30] and the activities of disaster relief workers [20; 28]. But much of the research also attempts to develop a framework for understanding the issues or make suggestions for a future disaster relief model [29,37]. Haghani and Oh [14] developed a multi-commodity multi-modal model for logistics management in the time of disaster. Palen et al. [32] developed a vision for the future of disaster management, which leverages the use of ICTs by focusing on the potential of members of the public during disaster situations. They suggest that supporting the public and enhancing their ability to make good, timely decisions can reframe disaster relief as a socially distributed information system [23].

Many experts in the disaster relief field are advocating for the widespread adoption of a global information network like ReliefWeb[2], which was developed by the UN Department of Humanitarian Affairs in 1996. ReliefWeb is a central repository for maps, press releases, field reports, and important forms. Extending this idea, Okada recommends the implementation of a "one stop shop" that uses GIS technology and integrates with web-based groupware [33]. Similarly, Bui et al. [27] propose the development of a web-based global information network to link information, opportunities for collaboration and decision focus before, during and after a disaster [3].

This paper extends prior work through an analysis of how a walled garden, APAN, facilitates relief activities during the Haiti crisis. With the rest of this paper we present our research questions, methods and three main findings. Our discussion suggests future CSCW research on disaster relief integrates public, government and NGO coordination and information sharing.

RESEARCH QUESTIONS AND DATA

Our study is focused on understanding how government-sponsored coordination forums are utilized during disaster situations, how this use changes over time, and how

[2] http://www.reliefweb.int

leadership emerges in these forums. Our research questions are 1) What kinds of information and coordination occurred on the US Navy sponsored APAN site during the Haiti crisis; 2) How does coordination and information exchange change over time and 3) To what extent do mediation and coordination activities (invisible brokerage) by forum members become visible through electronic trace data.

We perform network analysis and grounded theory analysis of the electronic trace data from the APAN site and triangulate these activities with news reports of events on the ground to answer our research questions. Our analysis of the electronic trace data from the APAN Haiti Forum focuses on collaborative behavior within the forum, and use of the forum for information dissemination over time. There were 5,606 total discussion threads. To answer research question one (information and coordination behavior), we focus our content analysis of topics on the 228 (4%) initial posts that generated a response (threads). We chose to topically group threads because users did not focus on specific threads, they sought out multiple threads, often following a focus of interest discerned from our grounded theory analysis. Of the 5,378 posts without responses, 898 were image uploads and the remainder were standard format status updates.

Our network analysis, used to answer research questions two and three, incorporates read and post behavior across all threads. The posts on the APAN Haiti Forum began in the second week of 2010 and the *data are represented at the "week of the year 2010" unit of analysis*, not the week of the forum. The dataset incorporates all data on the forum from January 13, 2010 (Week 2) – June 3, 2010 (Week 24). We include all 23 weeks of data from the forum to demonstrate differences between read and post behavior.

METHODS

Our mixed-methods analysis follows our group informatics approach for building weighted social networks from electronic trace data [11; 21], which mitigates important theoretical and validity concerns previously identified [16]. Initially, the 228 threads where collaboration takes place were categorized based on salient themes that emerge through open coding [4; 9]. After open coding, the codes were grouped and then the authors performed axial coding on the 228 threads with responses until saturation of theme for each thread was obtained. The resulting codes and number of corresponding threads are provided in Table 1.

Table 1 - Top Five Discussion Topic Codes

Code	Count
GIS Information Need	26
Ground Status	26
Medical	25
Transportation Logistics	24
GIS Information Provision	18

Following the coding, the researchers constructed a weighted social network from the electronic trace data of post and read data independently. In our construction of the network, each comment in a thread has some relationship to all the comments before it, but the strength of that relationship decays along two dimensions. First, the strength of connection between a post and the posts immediately before it in the same thread, which are displayed while a comment is being added, are strongest. This strength is calculated using both time and proximity on a page. Comments that occur within one hour of each other have a more significant strength of connection (~50x at 1 hour as at 1 day, with a sloped decline) than comments that occur after a 1-hour window.

After constructing the network, we performed weighted network analysis on the trace data using two units of analysis: the week and the code of the discussion thread. We calculated network centralization for the entire network and weighted post and read betweenness for each actor within that network using the TNET package in the statistical software program, R. We also calculated weighted in and out degree centrality for each participant who posted or read data on the APAN discussion threads.

Betweenness is a social network measure that identifies actors who play a broker role between clusters of people. Betweenness in electronic trace data has two semantics: one related to the broker role, derived from post data, and another related to read behavior [11], sometimes referred to as lurking; though our content analysis suggests that in this case this behavior is more like information consumption than lurking. In social network analysis, degree centrality is a measure of a person's relative network participation. We use a weighted degree centrality measure that shows both in degree and out degree centrality separately. In our findings, the post "in degree" of user A is represented as user B responding to User A's post and post "out degree" is user A's response to user B's post. Similarly, read "in degree" of user A is an indication of user B reading user A's post and the read "out degree" of user A is calculated by analyzing the posts that user A is reading. Our combination of directed and weighted degree centrality analysis with betweenness centrality analysis of this electronic trace data enables us to discern the emergence of different types of leadership, information and coordination behavior. Degree centrality tells us about dominance; betweenness conveys two forms of brokerage behavior within topics and across forums and time.

FINDINGS

In total, 336 individuals posted information within the 228 discussion threads and 2,557 individuals read an item within those same threads. The individual with the most posts had 1,231 posts and the individual with the most reads had 3,093. These disparities between posters and readers are consistent across time and topic category.

Post and read frequency among participants varied over time. The drop off of posts was very steep. The number 11 poster had 112 posts after which there was a steep drop off and a long tail of individuals who had less than 10 posts (n=280). This is a classic power law distribution of activity by participants, which illustrates this forums similarity to other Internet forums. The read data illustrates a similar, but more gradual slope from the most active readers to those who rarely engaged in the forum. Read behavior continues months longer than post behavior (Figure 1). The top 16 posters all had more than 1,000 reads and the bottom 2,052 individuals all had less than 50 reads, illustrating a clustered group of active and inactive lurkers.

Topics Categorization

The 23 codes developed during our open coding (see methods) were applied during axial coding to each of the 228 discussion threads. Two of the most prevalent codes were those related to requesting GIS information (n=26) and those providing GIS information (n=18). Combined, these two areas of discussion reflect how information about the physical location of people, crisis events and resources can be coordinated from a distance during a crisis.

The other prevalent codes in the 228 discussion threads with responses were Ground Status (n=26), Medical (n=25) and Transportation Logistics (n=24). These topics reflect coordination efforts of individuals physically located in the United States and other countries attempting to provide assistance to Haiti. Much of the discussion related to finding out the status of relief and medical efforts in specific areas and coordination of transportation for supplies to and from areas within Haiti.

Table 2 - Relief Events Identified Through Forum Activity

Event	Date	Description
RE0	1/18/10	Major US Relief assets, including ships and supplies, begin arriving
RE1	1/19/10	Canadian relief forces install runway lighting to enable 24/7 arrival of aid
RE2	1/23/10	Haitian government declares an end to rescue efforts
RE3	1/25/10	Donors conference begins in attempt to develop ways to channel aid
RE4	2/1/10	USS Carl Vinson, USS Bunker Hill, USNS Henson leave Haiti
RE5	2/7/10	The USS Nassau ends its relief mission to assist world food program
RE6	2/9/10	The 22nd Marine Expeditionary Unit relieves the 24th Marine Expeditionary Unit in relief efforts
RE7	2/12/10	The US Relief force is reduced from 20,000 to 13,000 as other international aid arrives

Codes that received less activity represented niche information requests and the provision of specialized services. For example, the code Language Assistance (n=3) represented a set of three individuals who were interested in providing language support for individuals needing to communicate with those within Haiti. Codes such as Communication Infrastructure and Communication Status were two closely related categories that represented a set of discussions about the damage and rebuilding of the communication infrastructure and the status of communication mechanisms in certain parts of Haiti. These categories were used by individuals outside of Haiti to coordinate relief efforts and provided understanding of the parts of Haiti with limited capacity to communicate need. The most prevalent uses of the forum related to the unique resources available from the US Navy's extensive medical, transportation and GIS data related resources both at sea and on the ground.

Temporal Activity of the Network

The temporal nature of the network and its participants follow a definite ramp up and decrease of interactions that coincide with the events and stages that occur during the Haiti relief effort. Figure 1 illustrates post and read activity annotated with key events for the first 31 days of the relief effort. The specific events are enumerated in Table 2. Figure 1 and Table 2 illustrate the temporal rhythm of the network of participation in both posts and reads as it corresponds to important events on the ground. The most active posting and reading days on the forum correspond with events in the relief effort, coordinated through the site.

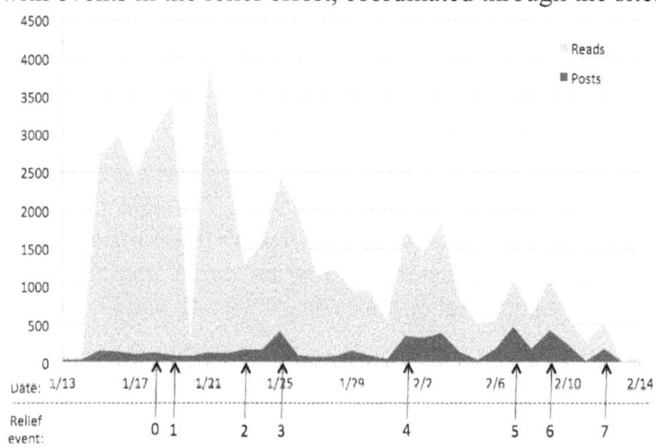

Figure 1 - Forum and Relief Event Timeline

On January 18, 2010, major United States relief assets began to arrive and foreign relief efforts ramped up. At this same time runway lighting was installed at an auxiliary airport to further assist in logistical transportation efforts. Five days later on January 23, the Haitian government declared rescue efforts over, shifting to a relief and recovery mission. Two days after the Haitian government declared rescue efforts over, Haitian Prime Minister Jean-Max Bellerive met with US Secretary of State Hillary Clinton and other world leaders in Montreal to determine how to best channel aid that was being collected to Haiti.

Two weeks later on February 7, US assets began to wind down immediate relief efforts with the departure of the USS

Nassau, which was responsible for coordinating with the United Nations World Food Program. As US assets were leaving Haiti, units that were on the ground were shifting purpose to help establish long-term relief. On February 10, electricity was restored to large portions of the capital city of Port Au Prince and two days after that the United States reduced its relief force from 20,000 to 13,000 troops.

Relating Forum Temporal Rhythm to Activity on the Ground

The posting behavior on the forum had a highly active period during the 31 days immediately following the Haiti Earthquake (an average of 167 posts per day). The three most active days were January 25 (n=408), February 7 (n=464) and February 9 (n=418). The number of posts quickly declined after February 13 to an average of 11 posts per day from February 14 to February 28. In March, there were just over 4 posts per day on average and in April an average of just over 2 posts per day. The number of posts became more sporadic in May. The last posts in the dataset occurred on June 3, 2010.

The read behavior within the network illustrates a similar ramp up and decline as the post behavior, but it is a more gradual decline and is sustained for much longer than the post behavior. This is likely due to the passive nature of reading as opposed to active nature of posting, and suggests that, while posting behavior diminished as the US Navy reduced its force, NGO users continued to access the forum for information. The most active days of read behavior were January 21 (n=3,813) and January 19 (n=3,290). These two days represent the second week of the forum's operation and followed a very active period of posting. It is likely that this activity represents individuals getting acquainted with activities on the ground. The highly active reading days were followed by highly active posting days as the five days including and following January 21st were some of the most active posting times on the forum (196 posts per day). This period immediately follows the arrival of substantial US and Canadian relief forces on January 18 and 19.

In the first 31 days of the forum there is an average of 1,277 reads per day, followed by an average of 127 reads per day from February 14 to February 28. The average reads per day declines from 58 in March to an average of 20 in April and 9 in May. This decline in number of reads per day, coupled with the decline in number of posts per day corresponds closely with relief events on the ground and relief force configuration changes.

Participant Behavior

We select four exemplar actors in order to provide a rich analysis of several actor types. For each specific actor we highlight, there are several actors who take on similar roles within the network, but would not surface through analysis of the forums that did not include thematic classification of topics and examination of electronic trace data across threads with the same topic category. Our coding enabled subsequent processing of the electronic trace data by category. Analysis of the temporal behavior of exemplar, high betweenness centrality actors in the network enables us to identify actors who play important, but invisible information brokering roles as discussion participants. We include a few representative quotations from the discussion board from our exemplar actors in order to establish the relationship between their network position (invisible brokers), derived from analysis of electronic trace data, and the nature of their contributions, derived from analysis of each discussion thread and post.

None of the four "invisible broker" actors that we use as exemplars of a set of similar users in our data set are in the top 10 of the individuals in post or read counts and none take any overt action to make their presence known. A table of these four individuals, their specific role and their background along with their raw activity count and rank are shown in Table 3.

Table 3 - Significant, Invisible Mediators

Position and ID	Post	Read
APAN RFI Manager (Lucy)	14	14
Government Contractor (Andrea)	15	38
Senior GIS Specialist (Mike)	35	58
NGO Executive Director (Ruth)	26	468

Lucy: APAN Request for Information Manager

Lucy is the Request for Information (RFI) Manager for APAN and her role was reflected in her network activity. Though Lucy's title indicates that she is an important part in the network, she is still outside of the top 10 in both read and post data. She had the highest participation rate of the users we chose as exemplars. In total, Lucy initiated 44 threads that received 267 responses, and contributed to an additional 59 threads with a total of 285 responses.

Lucy had the highest betweenness score in the categories of GIS Information Provision and Medical, and also placed high in betweenness in many other categories including Military Coordination, Request for Equipment and Security Information Request. For these topics, Lucy is an integrative information gatherer and provider. One example of this behavior is Lucy's use of information from one forum to assist a cruise line, asking in another forum where to send ships for temporary housing: *In another Forum, "Control of Vessel Traffic in and out of PaP", it is also stated that "the host nation has control of port traffic." Further it reports that the number that was good before the earthquake was* [ommitted]*"*.

In addition to placing high in those categories and actively participating in many other categories, Lucy had the highest overall post betweenness in week 2 and the second highest overall betweenness in weeks 3 and 4. These weeks correspond with the earthquake, the launch of the APAN site and the first arrival of US Aid to Haiti. Lucy's post betweenness dropped to the middle of the group in week 5, as the relief effort became established. After week 5, Lucy was non-existent in the post data. Additionally, Lucy had high post in degree and out degree in weeks 2-5 and more specifically had the highest post out degree in weeks 2-4. Lucy was a leader in the traditional sense, and an information broker during the first 3 weeks of relief.

Lucy established the purpose and activity of the forum in the early weeks; not surprising, given her title of APAN RFI Manager. Our analysis of the content of her posts consistently shows her in the middle of information flows. Her high post in and out degree during the first couple of weeks of the forum further confirm leadership role. Though Lucy did not post a lot after week 5, she did actively read. Lucy's transition from visible leader to invisible broker in the forum shows that changes in disaster relief missions are detectable from the analysis of forum trace data.

Measures of read in and out degree for Lucy illustrate that even though she was less active after week 7 in her read activity and after week 5 in her post activity, Lucy's posts were still being read throughout the course of the forum. This indicates that Lucy's posts were an integral part of the APAN Haiti Forum for those individuals participating in the later time periods, after the forum was initially established. The persistence of Lucy's importance in the network, independent of active posting or read behavior by her, illustrates a shift in her contributions from active collaboration to an information reference leader.

Andrea: Disaster Relief Consulting Firm Principal

Andrea is another important contributor to the forum as illustrated by her post and read ranks of 15 and 38. Her role as a principal of a disaster relief consulting firm helps to explain the difference between her activity and the activity of the APAN RFI Manager Lucy. Andrea, had the highest betweenness in the following categories: Communication Infrastructure, Communication Status, General Coordination Information, Ground Status, and Request for Equipment. Andrea also had high betweenness centrality in many other categories, including Coordination of Efforts, General Information Requests and Medical.

In addition to the high betweenness in posts based on categories, unlike Lucy, Andrea's "invisible broker" status, indicated by the betweenness measure, was consistent during the whole time period. Andrea had the highest post betweenness in weeks 3 and 4. Like Lucy, during this period Andrea had high in and out degree centrality as well; but unlike Lucy, Andrea's degree centrality was much lower after week 4. Additionally, Andrea had relatively high betweenness in weeks 2 and 7. This behavior, coupled with analysis of the text of Andrea's posts and her early high degree centrality, indicate initial efforts to build awareness of her firm on the forum, followed by more targeted participation in discussions where Andrea could offer her services. Though less central in her post behavior as time passed, forum users continued to pay attention to Andrea's posts throughout the relief period, as indicated by Andrea's in degree centrality during weeks 2-9.

Andrea's overall activity suggests a person who was trying to make herself known on the board by posting often to garner attention, but her betweenness centrality and analysis of her post content shows that she is more of an invisible broker than a leader. She initiates 51 threads that receive a total of 474 responses, placing her in the middle of much forum discussion. For example, as US Relief Forces begin arriving on January 18th, Andrea relays information about spotty and at risk cell phone infrastructure in Port au Prince in response to requests for information: *Yes - if you click on the link (title of the article) I posted it will direct you to digicel's website and map of coverage. ... fuel is a priority for the three cell towers that they have running. Coverage is not good in the PaP area.*

In the days after the US Navy relief effort began on January 18th, Andrea coordinated efforts to re-establish communication infrastructure in Haiti: *Update: The proposal is now at the stage where additional datasets will be required. a) Locations of Community WIFI network hubs desired by NGO; Command, and Haitian Government b) High resolution Imagery and GPS coordinates of said locations c) Priority of installation sites.* Her post in degree illustrates that she was not the most central poster, but that her high participation throughout the course of the forum increased her visibility to forum users. Andrea's high post in degree in the early and middle weeks illustrates that other forum participants paid more attention to her activity early in the time period but, unlike Lucy, did not revisit her topics later. This corresponds with the difference between Andrea, who participated in more transient topics, and Lucy, who coordinated topics that served as a foundation for the APAN forum. The contrast between Lucy and Andrea illustrates the difference in behavior between two very active individuals that are highly central and participate in many parts of the network. One is a government "connector", the other is an private sector or NGO "connector"; that is the meaning of high betweenness centrality.

Mike: GIS Specialist

Mike is in a different role than Lucy and Andrea. He receives many requests for new GIS information or clarification of previously supplied GIS information. His user profile indicates that he is a GIS Specialist at a disaster relief organization. His use of APAN is focused on GIS topics. Mike ranks number 35 in post data and 58 in read data. Fitting his title, Mike has the highest betweenness in the category, GIS Information Need and also places high in betweenness in General Information Requests. Mike *initiates no threads*, but responds to 16 threads that received a total of 100 responses; all categorized as GIS related.

The overall post and read betweenness measures for Mike also illustrate an interesting set of behaviors. In weeks 3-6, Mike appears in the top 10 each week for post betweenness, but is not present in post betweenness in any of the other weeks. This corresponds with the time period when US relief was initially arriving, and our analysis of the text of Mike's posts show that his work was facilitating the identification of specific locations for relief activity.

Mike has low (not top 15) in degree and out degree centrality in all weeks except week 6. It is during this time that he is very active in the forum responding to requests for information. Our analysis of Mike's post activity shows that during week 6 he is posting GIS information that can be consumed by NGOs and foreign government sources following the reduction in US Forces in Haiti.

The combination of the network measures with qualitative analysis of post content for Mike illustrates how somebody with specialized knowledge plays a vital role in maintaining relevance of the forum for NGOs. The high post betweenness in the early part of the forum's time period coincides with Mike's provision and clarification of GIS related questions and also points individuals to resources to help them better understand the situation in Haiti.

If we look only at the people who are "most active" in the forum, Mike does not appear. It is only through analysis of the data by specific categories that Mike's role as an invisible information broker becomes visible. The identification of individuals who play integral specialized roles is important in disaster relief efforts; and all information dissemination efforts, as they are important to ensure that decision makers also have the best information.

Ruth: NGO Executive Director

Ruth, like Mike, does not post a lot. Her rank in forum activity for posts (#26) and reads (#468) would not cause her to be noticed without the approach we use; but Ruth plays an important and central role in one niche aspect of the APAN forum supporting Haiti relief. Ruth is the Executive Director of an NGO that helps assist local community residents recover from disasters. Ruth has the highest betweenness in the category Orphanage Assistance and was the third highest betweenness actor in the category Coordination of Online Efforts. Ruth initiated 20 threads that received only 83 responses, and responded to 18 additional threads, with 83 total responses. The fact that Ruth was an invisible broker in those two categories surfaces her specialization. Her posts demonstrate that she focused on helping orphanages that were affected by the earthquake and coordinated online support for the relief efforts. This specialized activity is similar to Mike's participation in posts focused on GIS. For example, Ruth is active coordinating relief supply deliveries with a new person in the field via APAN on February 3, shortly after international forces grow in participation (i.e., new people on the ground): *Please let know when Susan returns from DR to PaP so that we may coordinate the kits to got to the clinics and orphanages we pre-designated.*

The post and read betweenness measures of Ruth illustrate the short and limited duration of Ruth's participation in the network. Ruth had the highest post betweenness in week 5, and was also relatively high in other weeks she participated: 3, 4, 8, and 9. Ruth's read data began in week 2, but her betweenness was very low at that point indicating limited participation. Ruth's read betweenness eventually climbed to be the second highest user in week 5. After week 5, Ruth had a read betweenness of zero, which indicates that she did not read other posts after week 5 and only contributed to the discussion at that point. This was likely the result of Ruth's ongoing, targeted efforts to help orphanages affected by the disaster. On the ground, week 5 is also when there is a transition in US forces, with three ships ending their missions. This led to coordination work for NGO experts with knowledge of the situation in Haiti to help transition the relief mission to international and local forces.

Ruth and Mike both illustrate different behaviors from Lucy and Andrea. Ruth and Mike are specialists involved in certain aspects of the coordination efforts online and thus only appear in specific parts of the network that become evident after qualitative analysis of the content. Lucy and Andrea are active in a broader scope of forum topics. These two different classes of invisible broker in the forum illustrate the importance of understanding the underlying activity and actions of users in a disaster relief network. They highlight the roles of specialized leadership and coordination for both governments and NGOs, made visible by the provision and discussion of information in forums like APAN during disaster scenarios. The identities of these information and coordination brokers are not evident without the mixed methods analysis we conducted.

DISCUSSION

This work has implications for future crisis informatics research. Here, we first analyzed how forum technology was used to help coordinate relief work in response to the earthquake in Haiti on January 12, 2010 by describing the kinds of information sharing and coordination that occurred. Second, we showed how the use of the forum changed over time and the extent to which people collaborated around specific topics. Lastly, we showed how certain types of individuals coordinated and brokered information in the forums, and how these behaviors are connected to relief activity on the ground and network patterns discernable from forum interactions.

Ours is the first study to look at Government-NGO information sharing and coordination behavior in an online forum. Though our topical categories of activity fit in the general categories found in earlier work looking at discussion forum use in disasters more broadly, the topics we find, like our study, are more specific. GIS information, transportation logistics, medical information and ground status information are dominant topics across many of the forums during the Haiti relief effort.

Several important questions are raised. How are the gaps in coordination and information sharing filled after the decline of government sponsored coordination sites for NGOs? Is it possible or advantageous to sustain coordination and communication through these sites during longer-term rebuilding projects? To what extent might communities be reinvigorated or reinvented following disaster scenarios if the role of such sites evolved, instead of ending with the end of US Government-NGO coordination?

The APAN site is a walled garden style forum, isolated from general citizen participation following disasters. Future designs that integrate closed, trusted communities like APAN with social media have the potential to increase direct support for the public during a crisis, as suggested by Palen [23]. Future CSCW research may consider the notion of a Government-NGO "aquarium" style discussion forum or coordinative tool. In this kind of forum the government and NGOs are able to share information with each other, and a central administrator decides what information can be distributed through social media, or made available through an APAN style forum.

Citizen contributions to government-NGO coordination forums through social media or direct access could be treated as annotations to verified information. To make a clear distinction between trusted and unverified information, citizen provided cell phone pictures, tweets or text messages could be represented in the style of Facebook comments or through the use of visually distinct text styles. Selectively sharing content from forums like APAN through social media could increase intrinsic motivation among both APAN participants and citizens to exchange information with each other. Such an exchange would increase perceived timeliness of information and responsiveness of site participants, which our work and prior work demonstrates are key dimensions of crisis response forum uptake and use. Citizen participation also has potential to help sustain crisis response forums and the resources of their members through the rebuilding phase.

Making invisible brokers visible is an important next step for CSCW work focused on crisis informatics. We triangulated coding of discussion boards with network analysis to surface a category of user we refer to as "invisible brokers". Many such brokers exist in the forum (~15% of users), but they are not visible through cursory examination of the forum itself. These are people who, in two cases (Lucy and Andrea) do make significant contributions to the forum at different times; and in two other cases (Mike and Ruth), are users who are generally not visible. In all four cases, we connect their high network betweenness centrality at different times with the content of their posts. Like all human relationships, the statistical measures and the coordinative behavior have an ambiguous relationship, but in this disaster relief data set, they clearly live together. The combination of a person's role, and events on the ground are connected to **when** different people are visible. This is also important, as NGOs focused on aid and GIS specialists are called for during different phases of a crisis.

Future CSCW research on crisis informatics should consider focusing on the use of our group informatics form of analysis, integrating electronic trace data with knowledge of the activities they correspond with to provide real time identification of invisible brokers. Unlike other forms of collaborative computing, where central project leaders sustain online community, in a crisis response situation there are a multitude of foci. Invisible brokers are vital to sustaining each of the key communication topics, and benefits to areas in crisis are likely to accrue if these key players are recognized for their important role, and identified to agencies responsible for crisis response and citizens.

Parts of this research were supported by the Office of Naval Research, Grant Number N000141110221.

REFERENCES

1. Baker, P. M. A. and Ward, A. C. 2002. Bridging Temporal and Spatial 'Gaps'. Information, Community & Society. 5, 2, 207-224.
2. Bedford, D. and Faust, L. 2010. Role of Online Communities in Recent Responses to Disasters: Tsunami, China, Katrina and Haiti. ASIST, 1-3.
3. Bui, T., Cho, S., Sankaran, S., and Sovereign, M. 2000. A Framework for Designing a Global Information Network for Multinational Humanitarian Assistance/Disaster Relief. Information Systems Frontiers. 1, 4.
4. Charmaz, K. 2006. Constructing Grounded Theory: A Practical Guide through Qualitative Analysis. Simon & Schuster.
5. Dynes, R. R. 1970. Organized Behavior in Disaster.
6. Fitzpatrick, C. and Mileti, D. S. 1994. Public Risk Communication. In Disasters, collective behavior and social organizaton, R. R. Dynes and K. J. Tierney,Eds University of Delaware Press.
7. Garshnek, V. and Burkle, F. M. J. 1999. Telecommunications Systems in Support of Disaster Medicine: Applications of Basic Information Pathways. Annals of Emergency Medicine. 34, 2, 213-218.
8. Gillmor, D. 2006. We the Media: Grassroots Journalism By the People, For People. O'Reilly Media.
9. Glaser, B. G. and Strauss, A. L. 1967. The discovery of grounded theory. Aldine.
10. Glaser, M. 2011. California Wildfire Coverage by Local Media, Blogs, Twitter, Maps and More. PBS Media Shift.
11. Goggins, S., Galyen, K., and Laffey, J. 2010. Network Analysis of Trace Data for the Support of Group Work: Activity Patterns in a Completely Online Course. ACM Group, 107-116.
12. Hagar, C. 2009. The Information and Social Needs of Cumbrian farmers during the UK 2001 foot and mouth disease outbreak and the role of information and

communication technologies. In The Socio-Cultural Impact of Foot and Mouth Disease in the UK in 2001: Experiences and Analyses, M. Doring and B. Nerlich,Eds Manchester University Press.

13. Hagar, C. and Haythornthwaite, C. 2005. Crisis, Farming & Community. The Journal of Community Informatics. 3, 2005, 41-52.
14. Haghani, A. and Oh, S.-C. 2010. Testing and evaluation of a multi-commodity multi-modal network flow model for disaster relief management. Journal of Advanced Transportation. 31, 3, 249-282.
15. Hester, V., Shaw, A., and Biewald, L. 2010. Scalable Crisis Relief: Crowdsourced SMS Translation and categorization with Mission 4636. ACM-DEV (15).
16. Howison, J., Wiggins, A., and Crowston, K. under review. Validity Issues in the Use of Social Network Analysis for the Study of Online Communities. Journal of the Association of Information Systems.
17. Jaeger, P. T., Langa, L. A., McClure, C. R., and Bertot, J. C. 2007. The 2004 and 2005 Gulf Coast Hurricanes: Evolving Roles and Lessons Learned for Public Libraries in Disaster Preparedness and Community Services. Public Library Quarterly. 25, 3/4, 199-214.
18. Kodrich, K. and Laituri, M. 2005. The Formation of a Disaster Community in Cyberspace: The Role of Online News Media after the 2001 Gujarat Earthquake. Convergence. 11, 3, 40-56.
19. Laituri, M. and Kodrich, K. 2008. On Line Disaster Response Community: People as Sensors of HIgh Magnitude Disasters Using Internet GIS. Sensors. 8, 3037-3055.
20. Landgren, J. 2006. Making Action Visible in time-critical work. Computer Human Interaction, 201-210.
21. Mascaro, C. and Goggins, S. 2011. Brewing Up Citizen Engagement: The Coffee Party on Facebook. Communities and Technologies.
22. Mileti, D. S. and Darlington, J. D. 1997. The Role of Searching in Shaping Reactions to Earthquake Risk Information. Social Problems. 44, 1, 89-103.
23. Palen, L., Anderson, K., Mark, G., Martin, J., Sicker, D., Palmer, M., and Grunwald, D. 2010. A Vision for Technology-Mediated Support for Public Participation & Assistance in Mass Emergencies and Disasters. ACM-BCS (8).
24. Palen, L., Hiltz, S. R., and Liu, S. B. 2007. Online Forums supporting grassroots participation in emergency preparedness and response. Communications of the ACM. 50, 3.
25. Palen, L. and Liu, S. B. 2007. Citizen Communications in Crisis: anticipating a future of ICT-supported public participation. Computer Human Interaction, 727-736.
26. Palen, L., Vieweg, S., Sutton, J., Liu, S., and Hughes, A. 2007. Crisis Informatics: Studying Crisis in a Networked World. International Conference on E-Social Science. 3, 1163-1167.
27. Paul, M. J. 2001. Interactive Disaster Communication on the Internet: A Content Analysis of Sixty-Four Disaster Relief Home Pages. Journalism and Mass Communication Quarterly. 78, 4, 739-753.
28. Reddy, M. C. and Dourish, P. 2002. A finger on the pulse: temporal rhythms and information seeking in medical work. Computer Supported Cooperative Work, 344-353.
29. Scaffidi, C., Myers, B., and Shaw, M. 2007. Trial By Water: Creating Hurricane Katrina "Person Locator" Web Sites. In Leadership at a Distance: Research in Technologically Supported Work, S. Weisband,Ed Lawrence Erlbaum.
30. Schafer, W. A., Ganoe, C. H., and Carroll, J. M. 2007. Supporting Community Emergency Management Planning through a Geocollaboration Software Architecture. Computer Supported Cooperative Work. 16, 4-5, 501-537.
31. Shklovski, I., Burke, M., Kiesler, S., and Kraut, R. 2008. Use of communication technologies in Hurricane Katrina Aftermath. HCI Emergencies workshop at Conference on Human Factors in Computing.
32. Shklovski, I., Palen, L., and Sutton, J. 2008. Finding Community Through Information and Communication Technology During Disaster Events. Computer Supported Cooperative Work.
33. Sovereign, M. 1997. Humanitarian Assistance and Disaster Relief in the next Century. Workshop Report Presented at the Institute for National Strategic Studies.
34. Suparamaniam, N. and Dekker, S. 2003. Paradoxes of power: the separation of knowledge and authority in international disaster relief work. Disaster Prevention and Management. 12, 4, 312-318.
35. Sutton, J., Palen, L., and Shklovski, I. 2008. Backchannels on the front lines: Emergent use of social media in the 2007 Southern California fire. ICSCRAM, .
36. Torrey, C., Burke, M., Lee, M., Dey, A., Fussel, S., and Kiesler, S. 2007. Connected Giving: Ordinary People Coordinating Disaster Relief on the Internet. Hawaii International Conference on System Sciences. 40.
37. Williams, C. and Gulati, G. J. 2007. Social Networks in Political Campaigns: Facebook and the 2006 Midterm Elections. American Political Science Association.
38. Yan, Q., Wu, P. F., and Wang, X. 2009. Online Community Reponse to Major Disaster: A Study of Tianya Forum in the 2008 Sichuan Earthquake. Hawaii International Conference on System Sciences. 42.

How and To Whom People Share: The Role of Culture in Self-Disclosure in Online Communities

Chen Zhao
Microsoft Research Asia
No. 5, Dan Ling Street,
Beijing, P.R. China
chzha@microsoft.com

Pamela Hinds
Management Science &
Engineering, Stanford University
Stanford, CA 94305-4026
phinds@stanford.eud

Ge Gao
Communication,
Cornell University
Ithaca, NY 14850
gg365@cornell.edu

ABSTRACT
The global expansion of the use of online communities, including social networking sites, necessitates a better understanding of how people self-disclose online, particularly in different cultures. In a scenario-based study of 1,064 respondents from the United States and China, we aimed to understand how self-disclosure is affected by communication mode (face-to-face vs. online), type of relationship and national culture. Our findings show that national culture interacts with communication mode and type of relationship to affect the extent of self-disclosure. Our analysis also suggests that peoples' disclosure depends on characteristics of the relationship, e.g., closeness and openness. Our results shed new light on how online communities might be designed for users in different cultures and for intercultural collaboration.

Author Keywords
Self-disclosure, communication mode, relationship, culture, social networking sites

ACM Classification Keywords
H5.m. Information interfaces and presentation (e.g., HCI): Miscellaneous.

INTRODUCTION
Self-disclosure is a process by which people deliberately share personal information with others [8] and is a key step in the development of interpersonal relationships [3]. Through disclosure, people achieve goals of social acceptance, relationship development, and relief of distress brought on by intense experiences [28]. Self-disclosure can also have a dark side, particularly if the recipient is unhelpful or rejecting [8]. Because of the importance of self-disclosure in interpersonal relationships, scholars, including those in psychology, communication and sociology, have examined this topic for decades. Despite extensive research on self-disclosure, however, there are several significant gaps in the literature. First, although self-disclosure occurs in a number of online contexts, including social networking systems, blogs and web forums, most CSCW and HCI research has focused on the role of anonymity [17], which may not be supported in most online communities. In online communities and social networking sites, people usually use their real identities and accurately present themselves [32]. Self-disclosure behavior, particularly using social software communication tools (e.g., online communities, blogs, social network sites, etc.) is not yet well understood. So, whether or not previous self-disclosure findings, which attribute self-disclosure to anonymity, also hold for online communities is unclear. Second, Green and her colleagues [8] call for more research on how culture and cultural norms affect disclosure, suggesting that individual differences, such as gender, have yielded valuable insights, but that we have little understanding of how different cultures conceptualize and express self-disclosure.

We are interested in the role of communication mode (e.g. face-to-face vs. online) in self-disclosure as a means of understanding relationship development via online communities. We also examine this question across cultures for two reasons. First, there has been a global expansion of the use of online communities, including social networking sites, and little is known about how these systems are or might be used in different cultures. Second, previous research shows that people from different cultures have different understandings of the meaning of self-disclosure and feelings about disclosing information [36].

In this study, we investigate 1) how self-disclosure is affected by communication mode and the closeness and openness of the relationship, and 2) if and how the patterns of self-disclosure vary across national culture. Through this research, we gain insight into how to design better online communities to support interpersonal relationship development. In particular, we aim to inform the design of online communities and social networking software to support diverse cultures and, to a lesser extent, intercultural interaction. To do so, we conducted a scenario-based study with a global IT company's employees in the U.S. and China to investigate how communication mode (face-to-face vs. online), type of relationship and national culture affect self-disclosure. A surprising finding in our study is that neither the U.S. nor the Chinese respondents disclosed more within the online community compared to face-to-face, which is contrary to previous Computer Mediated Communication (CMC) research. Our data suggest that one possible reason for this is that people have more concerns about controlling who has access to information within online communities than they do face-to-face. Our results also demonstrate that the extent of self-disclosure depends on the closeness of the relationship between communicators. Moreover, we find that respondents from the U.S. disclose more to coworkers compared to the Chinese and this may be because those in the U.S. have more openness in their relationships with coworkers. We discuss how these findings can help the CSCW community to design better software to support communication and social networking within and across national cultures.

BACKGROUND AND RELATED WORK

Self-disclosing communication occurs when people divulge personal information to others, particularly information that would otherwise remain private and that might expose vulnerabilities [8]. As a key step in the development of interpersonal relationships [8], self-disclosure has been an important concept for researchers over the past two decades. Disclosing increases the chances of the discloser liking the recipient and can strengthen ties that people develop online and face-to-face [3, 27]. Disclosure, however, has also been associated with stress for the discloser as he or she anticipates a negative event and for the recipient who may be burdened by the knowledge [8]. Further, in a work setting, disclosure can risk compromising co-workers' perceptions of the discloser as professional and competent [19].

Self-disclosure by Communication Mode

In recent years, there has been a surge of research interest in how self-disclosure varies by communication mode [15, 34]. Communicating through an online chat room or email, for example, can lead to more self-disclosure than interacting face-to-face [15, 34]. In a recent experiment, Schouten, Valkenburg, and Peter, for example, examined the influence of instant messaging on self-disclosure. They reported that self-disclosure was higher in instant messaging than face-to-face [29].

The mechanism driving the difference between self-disclosure online and face-to-face has been attributed to different perceptions of social cues and social norms under these two communication modes [18]. In a series of studies of online chat, for example, Joinson reported that visually anonymous chat, as compared with visually identifiable chat, lead to higher levels of self-disclosure [15]. Tidwell and Walther also proposed that heightened self-disclosure during online communication may be due to people's motivation to reduce uncertainty [34]. They found that students communicating over email displayed higher levels of self-disclosure compared with face-to-face, concluding that the limitations of email led subjects to be more direct in their questioning in order to achieve their uncertainty reduction goals. In a more recent study, undergraduate students' responding to an online survey reported that they disclosed more information about themselves on Facebook than outside of Facebook [2].

Numerous studies have reported increased disclosure online in the U.S. and also argued that anoymnity and reduced cues explain this behavior [15, 24]. In Joinson's book he discussed how being online increases self-disclosure and also attention to privacy, which seems contradictory. He concluded that self-disclosure depends on context and varies according to the target person, the process of interactions, and design of technology [16].

In our study, we were particularly concerned about online communities without anonymnity, e.g., where people interact using their real names and identities. We argue that computer mediated "identified" online communities do not lead to more disclosure than face-to-face for either U.S. or Chinese people. Regardless of anonymity, there may be other factors that affect disclosure online vs. offline. We predict, specifically, that control over third-party access to the disclosed information will be more important than anonymity in online communities because posts to online communities have the potential to be shared without the approval of the discloser. Recent research on privacy in online social networks has suggested that perception about control over who has access to information is a key element in decided whether to reveal private information [10]. Consistent with this, we hypothesize that people have more concerns about controlling third-party access to information within online communities compared to face-to-face, therefore people will disclose less in online communities.

H1a. People disclose less when communicating in an online community compared with face-to-face.

H1b. Lower self-disclosure within online communities compared to face-to-face will be mediated by concerns about control over information access.

Self-disclosure by Relationship

Key classes of information recipients (e.g., trusted colleagues, extended family, spouse, etc.) and type of information (e.g., failures, opinions, etc.) have also been identified as affecting with whom and what people are willing to share [26]. Consistent with social penetration theory, both anecdotal and empirical evidence has shown that the extent of self-disclosure depends on the relationship between communicators: The more intimate a relationship, the more in-depth the disclosure [3, 6]. We are interested in revisiting these findings, which have been tested in face-to-face contexts, in the online context. In line with previous research on face-to-face self-disclosure, we anticipate that people will disclose most with significant others and least with strangers. We also hypothesize that the intimacy, especially the closeness and openness of the relationship, will mediate between type of relationship and disclosure.

H2a. People will disclose most with significant others, such as close family members and close friends, and least with strangers.

H2b. The closeness and openness of the relationship will mediate between type of relationship (e.g., close family members, friends, strangers, etc.) and disclosure.

Self-disclosure in Different Cultures

Cultural comparisons examining self-disclosure in online media remain limited despite significant evidence demonstrating cultural differences in human behavior [23], in general, and in communication behavior specifically. Historically, many of these cultural differences have been identified between people from Western and Eastern countries [25]. Using this as a foundation, we compare disclosure behaviors between people from the U.S. and China. In the U.S., for example, people have been shown to talk more than Chinese in collaborative tasks [34], take more turns, and work harder toward consensus [30].

Despite the shortage of studies examining cultural differences in online self-disclosure, several studies are informative. First, significant evidence suggests that North Americans disclose more, in general, than do Asians. Based on a survey comparing U.S. and Chinese students, for example, Chen reported that U.S. students disclosed more than Chinese students on a variety of topics, including politics, religion, education, social problems and world affairs under face-to-face conditions [1]. Second, a handful of studies examining cultural differences in online disclosure suggest that Asians may disclose more online than face-to-face. Ma [22], for example, found that North American and East Asian college students displayed greater self-disclosure in computer mediated as compared to face-to-face interactions.

Although Chinese people may disclose more online than face-to-face, we further suggest that there will be an interaction between mode of communication and culture such that North Americans will disclose more face-to-face than will the Chinese, but that the difference will be eliminated when interacting online. In face-to-face interactions, the Chinese are likely to be more reserved than Americans to avoid disrupting interpersonal harmony and violating social norms [11]. As Ma argues, East Asians value indirect communication as a way of preventing embarrassment and threats to "face" and that online environments feel more indirect because they are perceived to be anonymous [22]. As we argued earlier, online communities, particularly social networking sites, tend to have less anonymity than assumed by previous studies, a feature which may reduce the "worry-free" advantage of anonymous online communication for Chinese. We therefore predict:

H3. U.S. compared with Chinese participants will disclose more when face-to-face, but have similar levels of disclosure online.

METHOD

To test our hypotheses, a scenario-based survey with a 2× 5×2 between-subject design was conducted, including three dimensions: communication mode (online vs. face-to-face), type of relationship between communicators (stranger, co-worker, co-worker who is also a good friend, close friend, close family member) and national culture (U.S. vs. Chinese).

Previous research in cultural psychology has established that a scenario-based approach is an effective way to understand cross-cultural differences (e.g., [37]). Given technology differences across the U.S. and China, scenarios are a good way to understand preferences independent of the technology participants currently have available or are using. This method is also well established within the HCI field with studies as diverse as understanding responses to breakdowns in robots [20] and examining information demands in context-aware applications [21]. In our study, we provided written scenarios describing a situation encountered by a discloser (to reduce social desirability effects of responding for oneself) and questions about whether and how this person would disclose the events of his day to a prospective recipient. The effectiveness of the scenario and some of the measures were pre-tested in a pilot study.

Pilot Study

Our pilot study was conducted to verify that the scenarios were understandable and sensitive enough to detect U.S. and Chinese respondents' disclosure preferences. We also evaluated whether or not U.S. and Chinese respondents could clearly distinguish the five levels of relationship.

The sample consisted of 13 U.S. (6 male, 7 female, M_{age}=41 years) and 13 Chinese respondents (7 male, 6 female, M_{age}=26 years) who were born, grew up and lived in the U.S. or China, respectively. All the respondents were asked to answer questions about their background to discern cultural identity (e.g., *countries in which they were raised, to what extent they identified with their own culture, etc.*), read two scenarios (see table 1), describe what they thought the person in the scenario would disclose about his day, and rate five interpersonal relationships (stranger, co-worker, co-worker who is also a good friend, close friend, close family member) on closeness and openness (7-point scales with 7 equal to more closeness and more openness). All materials were translated and back-translated by professional translators into English and Chinese.

Our pilot study results indicated that respondents in both cultures understood the scenarios and were able to answer questions about what the discloser might be expected to do in these scenarios. Moreover, the respondent's ratings on closeness and openness increased as the relationship moved from stranger to close friend and close family and showed clear distinctions between these five relationships in both cultures.

Main Study

The main study was a survey that presented demographic questions, personality scales, a scenario followed by questions pertaining to the scenario, and questions evaluating the effectiveness of our manipulations.

In cross-cultural experiments, one significant challenge is conducting controlled research with representative samples from the cultures of interest. Cross-cultural studies often rely on Chinese students who study in U.S. universities, though the limitations of this method are widely recognized. Limitations include a possible selection bias (e.g., Chinese who come to the U.S. may not be representative of the average Chinese) and adaptation issues (e.g., Chinese students attending U.S. universities may have adapted to the U.S. culture). To address these concerns, we conducted our experiment at a global company which has employees in both the U.S. and China. All materials were presented in English for the U.S. respondents and Mandarin Chinese for the Chinese respondents. Materials were first developed in English by the entire multi-cultural research team and then translated to Chinese by a professional translator who was blind to the experimental design. Finally, consistent with practices for cross-cultural research, the materials were "back translated" into English by two other professional translators to ensure no change in meaning.

Participants

The survey request was sent via email to a total of 12,000 employees from a global IT company who were randomly chosen based on their work locations (U.S. or China). The response rate was 11.58% (1,389). We further restricted our sample by two filter questions, including where the respondent was raised and what language(s) they spoke fluently before the age of 10, to make sure the cultural identity of each participant in this study was strictly either U.S. or Chinese. The final sample consisted of 1,064 respondents (496 U.S., 568 Chinese). There were 153 females and 343 males in the U.S. sample and 99 females and 469 males included in the Chinese sample. The mean ages of these two samples were 39.47 years (SD=9.63) for the U.S. and 30.77 years (SD=5.42) for the Chinese.

Manipulations

We have three primary independent variables in this study, including communication mode, relationship, and culture. Culture was not manipulated, but varied based on our sample of U.S. and Chinese. We then used the scenario for our remaining manipulations by changing the content of the scenario as depicted in table 1.

To evaluate the effectiveness of our manipulations, we conducted one-way ANOVAs including the control variables. To be specific, in evaluating our manipulation check for face-to-face vs. online, we found significant differences such that those in the face-to-face conditions recognized that the person in the scenario was face-to-face vs. online with the recipient of the disclosure (F[1,976]= 1397.69, p<.001). In our scenarios, we did not specify a particular online community because there is no single dominant online community that spans the U.S. and China. If we had referenced local social software in the study (e.g., Facebook in the U.S. and Renren in China), we would not have been able to determine whether the differences we found were caused by cultural differences or by different designs of the sites. This is an ongoing challenge for cross culture research on communication tools given that applications are often not designed the same way in different countries. Instead of choosing a particular online community application, we designed two questions to check if the U.S. and Chinese respondents had consistent understandings about the online community in terms of control over information access and anonymity. Our data show that there were no significant differences in perceptions of information access control (*what John chatted with this person about could be known to someone else*, F[1,526]=2.12, p=.15) or anonymity (*John's identity is*

Scenario: (1) is a project manager for a large company. He was recently put in charge of an important project. He worked extremely hard on the project. This morning, his boss called him into the office and **(2)**. That evening, he had an opportunity of chatting with a **(3)** and **(4)**.

Manipulations:

Cultural context	(1)	U.S.: John (then follows English version)	China: Zhang Min (then follows Chinese version)
Information valence	(2)	Positive: praised him for his good work. He received a promotion and a large pay raise	Negative: told him that his work on the project was unsatisfactory, He is being taken off the project and received a demotion and a large pay decrease
Relationship	(3)	stranger/co-worker/co-worker who is also a good friend/close friend/close family member	
Communication mode	(4)	Online: in an online community in which people register with nicknames	Face-to-face: at a gathering chatting

Table 1. Scenario (top) with the manipulations indicated by number.

	M	*SD*	1	2	3	4	5	6	7	8	9
1. Age	34.83	8.81	-								
2. Gender	-	-	-0.03	-							
3. Extroversion	25.19	5.44	0.08**	-0.12**	0.83						
4. Self-monitoring	10.95	4.20	-0.06*	-0.04	0.33**	0.72					
5. Net-behavior	13.37	5.25	-0.02	-0.03	0.10**	0.15**	0.71				
6. Information valence	-	-	-0.02	-0.00	0.04	0.05	0.02	-			
7. Communication mode	-	-	-0.03	0.03	-0.00	0.01	0.03	0.02	-		
8. Type of relationship	-	-	-0.01	-0.02	0.06	0.01	0.00	0.02	-0.01	-	
9. Culture	-	-	-0.49**	0.16**	-0.17**	-0.07*	-0.17**	0.01	-0.01	-0.03	-
10. Extent of disclosure	3.65	1.73	-0.08*	0.00	0.04	0.07*	0.10**	-0.03	0.06	0.32**	-0.02

*$p < .05$, **$p < .01$

Table 2. Full ANOVA analysis predicting the extent of disclosure.

known by the person with whom he was chatting, (F[1,526]=0.32, p=.57) between the U.S. and Chinese respondents.

Although we did not manipulate culture, we were able to use standard measures [5] to evaluate whether respondents' self-construals were different between cultures. Marcus and Kitayama describes Americans as having *independent* self-construals (a person who sees him/herself as unique with dispositional attributes that are independent of the relationships and contexts in which s/he is embedded) and Chinese as having *interdependent* self-construals (a person who sees him/herself as defined by the relationships and contexts s/he inhabits) [23]. Results show that the main effect of culture on self-construal was significant, (F[1,926]=22.75, p<.001), with the self-construal of the U.S. respondents (M=54.26, SD=10.31) being more independent than that of the Chinese (M=57.88, SD=9.66), as expected. All except our relationship variable were dichotomous. Relationship was treated as both a continuous variable, with 1=*stranger* and 5=*close family member*, and a nominal variable, with the same pattern of results. Unless otherwise indicated, we report the correlations and ANOVA tests for relationship as a continuous variable.

Dependent Variables

To test our hypotheses, we measured as our dependent variable the extent of disclosure that respondents predicted following the scenario. After presenting the scenario, we asked a question about the extent to which the discloser in the scenario would disclose to some specific others details about the events of his day (on a 7-point scale anchored by 1=*not at all* and 7=*very much*).

Control Variables

A consistent finding in the literature on self-disclosure is that females disclose more than males [4]. Dindia and Allen's study, for example, shows that the gender difference in self-disclosure varies when respondents disclose in different relationships (stranger, friend, parent or spouse). Females and males disclose similarly to a stranger whereas females disclose more in other relationships [7]. In our study we set gender as a control variable for all analysis.

According to previous work, the extent of self-disclosure is also influenced by whether the information is positive or negative, with people generally preferring positive self-disclosure to negative [33]. Not all evidence, however, favors positive disclosure. Pasupathi et al. [28], for example, studied the nature of what people disclose about their life experiences and found that respondents regularly disclose information about everyday negative events, although people were less likely to disclose negative events of more significance. In our study, we provide both positive and negative scenarios by manipulating the contents and set information valence as a control variable.

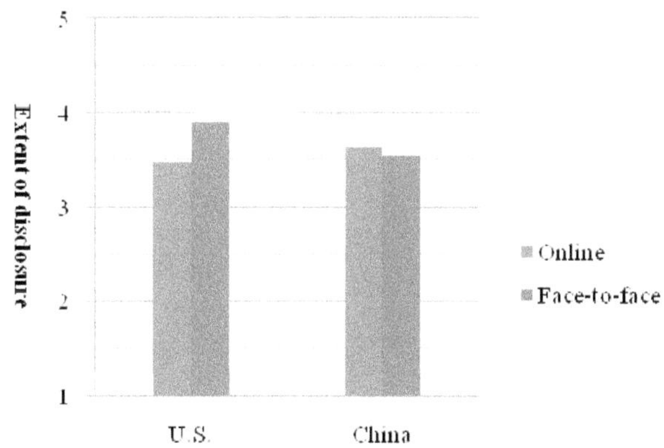

Figure 1. Extent of disclosure by communication mode and culture.

Previous studies of face-to-face disclosure indicate that the extent of disclosure may be sensitive to personal characteristics (e.g., extroversion or self-monitoring) (see [3]). We therefore measured these two factors as control variables in all of our analysis using the extroversion scale

[14] (α=0.83) and the self-monitoring scale [31] (α=0.72), respectively.

Considering the possible influence of one's current and past online experience on his/her online disclosure, we also measured respondents' online experience. We averaged across four items to create an online experience scale (α=0.71) and set it as a control variable in our analysis. Age is also set as a control variable in our analysis.

RESULTS

Table 2 shows the descriptive statistics and correlations between the primary variables in this study. To test our hypotheses, a 2×5×2 (communication mode [online, face-to-face] × relationship [stranger, co-worker, co-worker who is also a good friend, close friend, close family member] × 2 culture [U.S., Chinese]) ANOVA analysis was conducted to predict the extent of disclosure.

Self-disclosure by Communication Mode and Culture

Although the main effect of communication mode was not significant (F[1,979]=1.97, p=.16), the 2-way interaction between communication mode and culture was significant when predicting the extent of disclosure, F[1, 979]=5.64, p=.02 (see figure 1). The test of the simple main effect of communication mode shows that the U.S. respondents anticipated more disclosure when face-to-face compared to online (F[1,449]=5.97, p=.02), but there is no such difference for the Chinese (F[1,530]=0.49, p=.48). Thus, our findings provide partial support for hypothesis 1a in which we argued that people will disclose less when communicating in an online community as compared to face-to-face, but this result only held for US and not Chinese respondents. This analysis also provides insight into hypothesis 3a in which we argued and found that U.S. respondents would disclose more than Chinese respondents when face-to-face, but have similar levels of disclosure online. For online disclosure, there was no significant difference between the U.S. and Chinese respondents (F[1,509]=0.15, p=.70) whereas for face-to-face disclosure, the Americans disclosed significantly more compared to the Chinese (F[1,470]=5.18, p=.02).

These results are consistent with our predictions, but in contrast to previous research which shows that North Americans disclose more online compared to face-to-face no matter whether on CMC [15] or Facebook [2], and Chinese disclose more online compared to face-to-face [22]. We argued that previous research emphasizing anonymity would be overshadowed by current privacy concerns, particulary about having control over who has access to the information disclosed. Consistent with this, in our study context, anonymity did not explain disclosure behavior. Our respondents reported that neither online (M=4.85, SD=1.82) nor face-to-face (M=5.57, SD=1.72) was anonymous when asked the extent to which they thought that the discloser could be identified (1=*disagree strongly* and 7=*agree strongly*) although respondents perceived online to be more anonymous. There was no significant difference between the U.S. and the Chinese respondents in perceptions of anonymity (F[1, 977)=1.19, p=.28]. Further, in a mediation analysis, anonymity was not found to mediate the relationship between communication mode, culture, or the interaction between the two when predicting disclosure.

We hypothesized in H1b that concern over controlling access to information would have more explanatory power in determining disclosure in online communities. In support of H1b, we found that perceived control over information access mediated the relationship between communication mode by culture and the extent of disclosure. The U.S. respodents in our study had significantly more concerns about content being known to others when online compared to face-to-face (F[1,450]=7.46, p=.01), but this difference was not detected for the Chinese (F[14,530]=.02, p=.89). We tested the mediating effect of control over access to information and found that it was significant. That is, the interaction between communication mode and culture predicted the extent of disclosure, but when "control over access" was added to the model, control over access was significant and the relationship between communication mode/culture and disclosure became insignificant (see figure 2).

We therefore conclude that people have different levels of concern about others having access to information they disclose in online communities compared to face-to-face, which may lead to different levels of self-disclosure in these two modes. Our data suggest that the U.S. respondents had more concerns about what was said being known to others online compared to face-to-face and this was associated with predictions of less disclosure online. The Chinese did not show this difference and anticipated similar levels of disclosure when online and face-to-face, which supports our Hypothesis 1b.

Self-disclosure by Relationship and Culture

An ANOVA analysis reveals a significant main effect of relationship on self-disclosure, F[4, 979]=30.10, p<.001). That is, the extent of self-disclosure increases when people disclose in more intimate relationships, from strangers to co-workers, co-workers who are also good friends, close friends and close family members. Neither the main effect of communication mode nor national culture was significant, which shows that to whom people disclose is a key factor in determining self-disclosure in our sample.

This disclosure pattern holds across U.S. and Chinese respondents. So, our Hypothesis 2a, in which we argued that people will disclose more with more intimate others, is supported. We tested the extent to which closeness mediated between relationship type and disclosure and found that it did, thus also partially supporting Hypothesis 2b. The significance of the association between relationship and extent of disclosure diminishes once closeness is added to the model (from $F[4,979]=30.10$, $p<.001$ to $F[4,975]=1.23$, $p=.30$), suggesting that closeness may pay a significant role in explaining the association between relationship and extent of disclosure. The openness of the relationship, however, did not mediate between relationship intimacy and extent of disclosure.

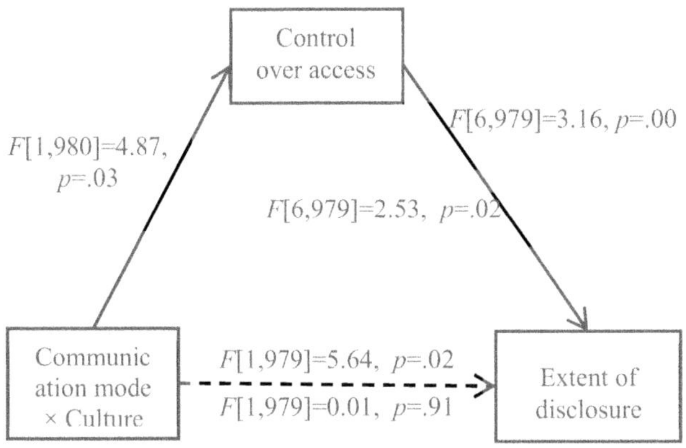

Figure 2. Control over access as a mediator between the interaction of communication mode and culture and extent of disclosure.

Given that we have five types of relationship, and ANOVA is often insufficient for full interpretation of the effects of independent variables on the dependent variable when there are more than three levels, we used orthogonal comparisons to explore the interaction between relationship and national culture.

For the U.S. respondents, the highest level of disclosure was with close family members, close friends and a coworker who is also a good friend ($M=4.26$, $SD=1.64$; $M=4.05$, $SD=1.75$; $M=3.90$, $SD=1.66$, respectively). U.S. respondents predicted the least disclosure with strangers

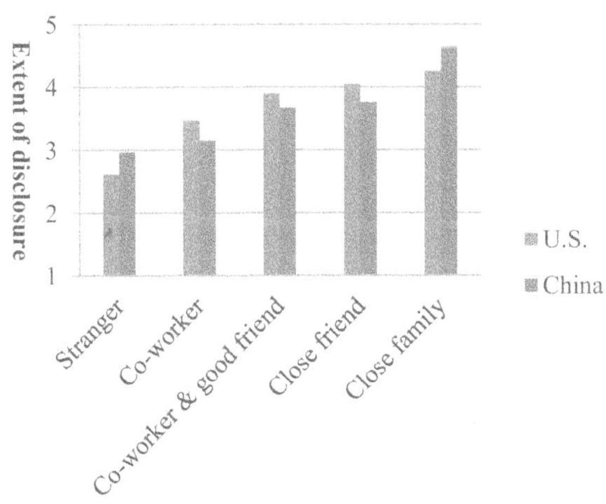

Figure 3. The influence of relationship on the extent of disclosure between cultures.

($M=2.62$, $SD=1.69$; $p=.00$). These four relationships were similar between the U.S. and Chinese respondents with Chinese respondents also predicting the highest levels of disclosure with close family members ($M=4.65$, $SD=1.61$), close friends ($M=3.76$, $SD=1.71$) and coworkers who are also good friends ($M=3.67$, $SD=1.61$; $p=.01$) and the least disclosure with coworkers and strangers ($M=2.97$, $SD=1.71$).

As can be seen from figure 3, there was some difference between U.S. and Chinese respondents' view of co-workers who were not good friends ($F[1, 204]=4.06$, $p=.05$). The Chinese treated these co-workers more as strangers whereas the US respondents predicted significantly more disclosure to co-workers than strangers. We conducted further analysis and found that the U.S. and Chinese respondents had similar perceptions of the co-worker relationship in terms of closeness, but that the U.S. respondents had significantly more openness to coworkers than did the Chinese ($F[1,211]=4.58$, $p=.03$). Openness, in fact, mediated the relationship between culture and disclosure in the co-worker relationship, suggesting that openness mediates the relationship between national culture and disclosure with co-workers, although not in other types of relationships.

DISCUSSION

Despite the global expansion in the use of social software, many applications are designed largely based on Western assumptions about social behavior [9, 12]. As online communities become increasingly important and social networking systems are rapidly adopted across the globe, research examining online self-disclosure in different cultures needs to keep pace. In our research, we strove to understand the role of culture in self-disclosure as a foundation for the future development of online communities, especially social networking sites. Our results demostrate that there are significant cultural differences in how and to whom people disclose and have implications for the design of social networking systems that will be used by people from different cultures.

Consistent with our predictions, but different from previous research, we found that U.S. respondents predicted more disclosure when face-to-face compared to online and Chinese predicted similar disclosure when comparing face-to-face vs. online. We hypothesized and found that peoples' concern about control of third-party access to information is a possible explanation for the extent of disclosure. The U.S. respondents had more concerns about content being known by others within online communities and this was associated with a decrease in online disclosure. Although the Chinese in our study exhibited the same concern, they showed more concern about third-party access to information when face-to-face than did the US participants. If concern about control over access to information explains differences in disclosure by mode, why then do the Chinese participants disclose equally over face-to-face and online?

Although speculative, we posit that that Chinese participants' experience with online media is different than U.S. participants' experience and, as a result, U.S. respondents have more privacy concerns. At the same time, Chinese may have more experience with privacy violations in face-to-face disclosures. Our research hypotheses are summarized in table 3.

In sum, our results clearly suggest a difference between U.S. and Chinese respondents' reaction to control over access to information, but additional research is needed to understand how this interacts with other factors and whether these differences are the result of cultural communication preferences (e.g. indirectness), participants' experience with local technology, or the local cultural (e.g. political) context.

Given these insights, we suggest that online communities should provide features to enable users to control third-party access to information. Facebook, Renren and Google Plus provide features for users to put different contacts into groups and customize privacy settings for each group. Users, however, have no control over whether the shared information can be disseminated further. We suggest social software provide users the option to define the parameters for sharing information with third parties. People, for example, could specify for a particular piece of information whether or not it could be passed on to others, to whom it could be shared, and how broadly. Users might be willing to disclose more if they are able to easiliy control whether or not the content can be shared further. Based on our findings, we anticipate that such features will reduce users' concerns and thus encourage more disclosure in both US and Chinese populations, although the effect may be strongest among US users.

Previous research on self-disclosure has primarily focused on the role of self-disclosure in relationship construction and development. As such, the recipient of disclosure and nature of the relationship has been identified as an important factor in the decision of how much to disclose. This factor, however, has not been included in most self-disclosure research examining communication over electronic media. One aim of our research was to understand self-disclosure by examining communication mode and relationship in a single study.

Looking at disclosure patterns across relationship types, we found that disclosure to co-workers was comparable to disclosure to strangers for the Chinese respondents. We also found that different disclosure levels for U.S. and Chinese respondents to coworkers were mediated by openness. There was a strong positive relationship between openness and disclosure with co-workers for U.S. respondents ($F[6, 96]=8.99$, $p=.00$), but not so with Chinese respondents ($F[6,115]=1.35$, $p=.24$). In fact, the relationship for Chinese respondents was, surprisingly, slightly negative such that

H1a.	*People disclose less when communicating in an online community compared with face-to-face. PARTIALLY SUPPORTED.*
H1b.	*Lower self-disclosure within online communities compared to face-to-face is mediated by concerns about control over information access. SUPPORTED.*
H2a.	*People will disclose most with significant others, such as close family members and close friends, and least with strangers. SUPPORTED.*
H2b.	*The closeness and openness of the relationship will mediate between type of relationship (e.g., close family members, friends, strangers, etc.) and disclosure. PARTIALLY SUPPORTED.*
H3.	*U.S. compared with Chinese participants will disclose more when face-to-face, but have similar levels of disclosure online. SUPPORTED.*

Table 3. Summary of research hypotheses

Chinese respondents predicted less disclosure with co-workers with whom they reported openness.

Our findings indicate that increasing openess may increase disclosure among American co-workers, but not among Chinese co-workers. How could an organization, if they so desired, enable more disclosure? Our results show that Chinese disclose significantly more to a co-worker who is also a good friend as compared with a co-workers who is not a good friend, which suggests that a friendship tie between co-workers may be instrumental in increasing sharing for Chinese. This insight echoes Yuki's work in which Americans trusted ingroup members (e.g. co-workers) more than outgroup members (e.g. strangers) but trust for the Japanese depended largely on friendship ties. [37]. We therefore suggest that social software could highlight shared personal interests, shared group memberships, and the longevity of the tie which could help increase the perception of friendship.

Our findings become particularly relevant when thinking about global teams and can inform the design of applications that support intercultural communications between global team members. For enterprise social networking systems, for example, in which self-disclosure may be desired for promoting collegial work relationships, systems could provide ways to create more of a sense of "interpersonal connection," especially for those who generally do not favor sharing with coworkers, such as the Chinese in our study. If social networking systems could make visible the group identities that are shared and/or the relational ties that bind workers, self-disclosure among coworkers may be enhanced. Of course, this suggestion should be taken with healthy skepticism because it assumes that disclosure is desireable and will facilitate collaboration across cultural groups.

Disclosure, for example, is not always preferred. Based on our results, an American might disclose things that make her Chinese co-worker feel uncomfortable due to asymmetric disclosure preferences between the U.S. vs. China. To facilitate more appropriate disclosure, enterprise social networking software could remind users of the disclosure norms when sharing information with co-workers from distant locations. For example, when an American discloses to a Chinese co-worker, the application could detect the extent of disclosure and automatically remind the American if the disclosure extent violates the norms for disclosure in China. Alternatively, to avoid cultural stereotypes, users could indicate the extent to which they are receptive to personal disclosure and the system could flag postings that cross over this line. Social networking systems could also learn about others' preferences based on their own disclosure behavior and their reactions to others' disclosure to set desired disclosure levels. These features are ambitious, but we hope are provocative and trigger ideas for short as well as long-term development. Leveraging technology to improve intercultural collaboration is a long journey and will likely require significantly more research and technology advances to achieve some of these goals.

Despite the advances made by this research, there are, as always, limitations. One limitation is that we used a scenario-based survey rather than observing actual self-disclosure behavior, so our data reflects the norms that people believe are followed, but we cannot guarantee that this matches behaviors. To validate the results of our study, it would be useful to collect behavioral data. One viable data collection approach might be to study an enterprise social networking system that is deployed in multiple countries as a means of keeping the technology constant and studying variations in behavior across cultures. Another limitation is that we sampled employees at a global company headquartered in the U.S. As such, the Chinese respondents undoubtedly have more exposure to U.S. culture compared to the average Chinese person. We believe that this is a conservative test of our hypotheses since Chinese with less exposure to U.S. culture are expected to differ even more from the U.S. sample. Still, it is critical to evaluate these findings with additional samples that are more reflective of the average Chinese (and the average person from the U.S.). Finally, our study focused on disclosers and recipients, but not on the social networks within which they were embedded, except to the extent that sharing with third-parties surfaced as a concern. To fully understand cultural differences in the use of social networking systems, further research that explores behaviors within the larger network is essential. Overall, we believe that these results advance our understanding of how online communities, including social networking systems, may be designed to faciliate or inhibit disclosure and, as a result, support relationship development. They also advance our understanding of how these systems might account for cultural differences.

ACKNOWLEDEMENTS

We thank the anonymous reviewers, Desney Tan, and James Landay for their insightful comments on earlier versions of this paper. We also thank Yurong He for her contributions to the research and the participants in our studies.

REFERENCES

1. Chen, G. Differences in self-disclosure patterns among Americans vs Chinese: A comparative study. *Journal of Cross-Cultural Psychology* 26, 1 (1995), 84-91.
2. Christofides, E., Muise, A., and Desmarais, S. Information disclosure and control on Facebook: are they two sides of the same coin or two different processes? *Cyber psychology and Behavior* 12, 3 (2009), 342-345.
3. Collins, N.L., Miller, L.C. Self-disclosure and liking: A meta-analytic review. *Psychological Bulletin* 116, 3 (1994), 457-475.
4. Cozby, P. C. Self-disclosure: A literature review. *Psychological Bulletin*, 79, 2 (1973), 73-91.
5. Cross, S. E., Bacon, P. L., and Morris, M. L. The relational-interdependent self-construal and relationships. *Journal of Personality and Social Psychology* 78, 4 (2000), 791-808.
6. Derlega, V. J., Wilson, M., and Chaikin, A. L. Friendship and disclosure reciprocity. *Journal of Personality and Social Psychology* 34, 4 (1976), 578-582.
7. Dindia, K., and Allen, M. Sex differences in self-disclosure: A meta-analysis. *Psychological Bulletin* 112, 1 (1992), 106-124.
8. Greene, K., Derlega, V., and Mathews A. Self-disclosure in personal relationships. In Vangelisti, A., Perlman, D. (Eds.), *Cambridge Handbook of Personal Relationships*. Cambridge University Press, UK, 2006.
9. Hinds, P., Liu, L, & Lyon, J. Putting the global in global work: An intercultural lens on the practice of cross-national collaboration. *Academy of Management annals, vol 5, no. 1, 2011*, 135-188.
10. Hoadley, C., Xu, H., Lee, J., & Rosson, M. Privacy as information access and illusory control: The case of the Facebook news feed privacy outcry. *Electronic Commerce Research and Applications*, 9 (2010), 50-60.
11. Hwang, K.. Face and Favor: The Chinese Power Game. *American Journal of Sociology* 92, 4 (1987), 944-974.
12. Irani, L., Vertesi, J., Dourish, P., Philip, K. & Grinter, R. (2010). Postcolonial computing: A lens on design and development. I*n Proc. of CHI 2010*, ACM Press (2010), 1311-1320.

13. Jones, E., and Gordon, E. M. Timing of self-disclosure and its effects on personal attraction. *Journal of Personality and Social Psychology* 24, (1972), 358-365.
14. John, O. P., Donahue, E. M., and Kentle, R. L. *The Big Five Inventory--Versions 4a and 54.* University of California, Berkeley, Institute of Personality and Social Research, Berkeley, CA, US, 1991.
15. Joinson, A.N. Self-disclosure in computer-mediated communication: The role of self-awareness and visual anonymity. *European Journal of Social Psychology* 31, 2 (2001), 177-192.
16. Joinson, A. N. *Understanding the Psychology of Internet Behaviour: Virtual Worlds, Real Lives.* Palgrave Macmillan Press, New York, US, 2003.
17. Joinson, A.N., Paine, C.B. Self-disclosure, privacy and the internet. In Joinson, A.N., McKenna, K., Postmes, T., and Reips, U. (Eds.) *Oxford Handbook of Internet Psychology.* Oxford University Press, Oxford, UK, 2007.
18. Kiesler, S., Siegel, J., and McGuire, T.W. Social psychological aspects of computer-mediated communication. *American Psychologist* 39, 10 (1984), 1123-1134.
19. Kreiner, G. E., Hollensbe, E. C., and Sheep, M. L. Where is the "me" among the "we"? Identity work and the search for optimal balance. *Academy of Management Journal*, 49 (2006), 1031–1057.
20. Lee, M. K., Kiesler, S., Forlizzi, J., Srinivasa, S. and Rybski, P. Gracefully Mitigating Breakdowns in Robotic Services. In *Proc. of HRI 2010*, 203-210.
21. Lim, B. Y., Dey, A. K. Assessing demand for intelligibility in context-aware applications. *In Proc. Of the 11th internal conference on Ubiquitous Computing*, ACM Press (2009), 195-204.
22. Ma, R. Computer-mediated conversation as a new dimension of intercultural communication between East Asian and North American college students. *Pragmatics and Beyond New Series* 39, (1996), 175-185.
23. Markus, H.R., Kitayama, S. Culture and the self: Implications for cognition, emotion, and motivation. *Psychological Review* 98, 2 (1991), 224-253.
24. McKenna, K., and Bargh, J. Coming out in the age of the Internet: Identity demarginalization through virtual group participation. *Journal of Personality and Social Psychology* 75, 3 (1998), 681-694.
25. Nisbett, R.E. *The Geography of Thought: How Asians and Westerners Think Differently and Why.* Free Press, New York, US, 2003.
26. Olson, J.S., Grudin, J., and Horvitz, E. A study of preferences for sharing and privacy. *Ext. Abstracts CHI 2005*, ACM Press (2005), 1985–1988.
27. Parks, M., Floyd, K. Making friends in cyberspace. *Journal of Computer-Mediated Commun.* 46, 1 (1996), 80-97.
28. Pasupathi, M., Mclean, K.C., and Weeks, T. To tell or not to tell: Disclosure and the narrative self. *Journal of Personality* 77, 1 (2009), 89-124.
29. Schouten, A.P., Valkenburg, P.M., and Peter, J. An Experimental test of processes underlying self-disclosure in computer-mediated communication. *Journal of Psychological Research on Cyberspace* 3, 2 (2009), 1-15.
30. Setlock, L.D., Fussell, S.R., and Neuwirth, C. Taking it out of context: Collaborating within and across cultures in face-to-face settings and via instant messaging. In *Proc. CSCW 2004*, ACM Press (2004), 604-613.
31. Snyder, M. Self-monitoring of expressive behavior. *Journal of Personality and Social Psychology* 30, 4 (1974), 526-537.
32. Stern, L. A., and Taylor, K. Social networking on Facebook. *Journal of the Communication, Speech & Theatre Association of North Dakota* 20 (2007), 9-20.
33. Taylor, D.A., Belgrave, F.Z. The effect of perceived intimacy and valence on self-disclosure *reciprocity. Personality and Social Psychology Bulletin* 12, 2 (1986), 247-255.
34. Tidwell, L., and Walther, J.. Computer-mediated communication effects on disclosure, impressions, and interpersonal evaluations: Getting to know one another a bit at a time. *Human Communication Research* 8, 3 (2002), 317–348.
35. Wang, H.C., Fussell, S.R., and Setlock, L.D. Cultural difference and adaptation of communication styles in computer-mediated group brainstorming. In *Proc. International Conference on Human Factors in Computing Systems 2009*, ACM Press (2009), 669-678.
36. Wolfson, K., Pearce, W.B. A cross-cultural comparison of the implications of self-disclosure on conversational logics. *Communication Quarterly* 31, 3 (1983), 249-256.Yuki, M., Maddux, W. W., Brewer, M. B., and Takemura, K. Cross-cultural differences in relationship- and group- based trust. *Personality and Social Psychology Bulletin* 31, 1 (2005), 48-62.
37. Yuki, M., Maddux, W. W., Brewer, M. B., and Takemura, K. Cross-cultural differences in relationship- and group- based trust. *Personality and Social Psychology Bulletin* 31, 1 (2005), 48-62.

Cultural Appropriation: Information Technologies as Sites of Transnational Imagination

Silvia Lindtner, Ken Anderson and Paul Dourish

Department of Informatics
University of California, Irvine
Irvine, CA 92767-3440 USA
{lindtner,jpd}@ics.uci.edu

People and Practices Research
Intel Corporation
20270 NW Amberglen Court, MS AG1-110
Beaverton, OR 97006
ken.anderson@intel.com

ABSTRACT
The diverse ways in which technologies are modified and appropriated into local contexts are an important theme in CSCW research. Today, translocal processes such as the formation of international corporations and the movement of people and ideas across nation states increasingly shape these local contexts of technology use and design. We draw from prior work on appropriation in CSCW and meld it with work from transnational studies to illustrate appropriation as a cultural phenomenon and as it unfolds in relation to emerging translocal processes. We ground our explorations in findings from ethnographic research on collaborations and exchange among IT professionals in urban China. This work makes two main contributions. First, it expands CSCW's focus on socio-technical systems by taking seriously socio-political and socio-economic processes. Second, it contributes to debates on cross-cultural and global technological development by employing transnational imagination as an analytical tool.

Keywords
Cultural appropriation, imagination, transnational, multi-sited ethnography, politics, globalization.

ACM Classification Keywords
K.4.0 Computers and Society: general

INTRODUCTION
Computer Supported Cooperative Work (CSCW) has a long tradition of detailed observational studies of particular settings in which information technologies are deployed. One reason for this form of investigation is the observation that technology use in practice is often much more varied than system designers might anticipate. Information systems are often put to novel and unexpected uses, and they may be tweaked and transformed to achieve goals never imagined by their designers. Accordingly, "appropriation" – the adaptation and transformation of information systems after they are deployed – has been a topic of investigation for researchers in the field.

Broadly, two aspects of appropriation have received empirical and analytic attention. The first is what has been called "unanticipated use," in which a system is used to do something that its designers did not expect, *e.g.* [13, 28]. The second is "customization" in which specific features of a system that allow for its adaptation or transformation are used to allow end-users or their proxies to change aspects of the system's behavior. Examples abound in the HCI and CSCW literature, *e.g.* [8, 15, 25, 33], illustrating that tweaks and appropriations by the user are key in making technologies work for different needs and settings.

In this paper, we take appropriation of technology as our topic and examine it as a cultural process. Cultural appropriation, like technology appropriation, refers to the ways that people adapt and "make the technology their own." By cultural appropriation, we introduce an analytical lens that highlights two new aspects of the same process: first, the ways in which people take up technologies into the social, economic and political spheres of their lives through processes of imagination. By including the work of imagination, this approach stresses that appropriation is not only a matter of unexpected reuse or of instrumental transformation, but is also a matter of re-encountering technologies – that is, of finding them meaningful in new ways. Second, cultural appropriation takes into account that appropriation of technology is increasingly taking place within translocal contexts. With the internationalization of corporations, for example, comes an increase in translocal collaborations and mediation of images and ideas. These ideas and values travel as much as our technologies themselves, shaping local appropriation. As such, it becomes increasingly important to revisit current frameworks towards appropriation in design and research to address the question of translocal mediation and cultural processes of technology appropriation [18].

We ground our analytical approach in findings from ethnographic research on the local and translocal collaborations and circulation of ideas among IT professionals in urban China. In our ethnographic research, we were struck by how digital technologies provided our study participants platforms for thinking about local politics and Chinese modernity, as well as transnational relations and social stature in international circles. Even those participants, who did not travel geographically between countries, still spoke of technologies in relation to global media images and ideals of a cosmopolitan lifestyle. Our data illustrates that this cultural appropriation of technology in contemporary global contexts means more than addressing the challenges of cross-cultural teams in international organizations or travel between global cities. It includes also how people imagine and articulate their participation across sites.

This paper makes the following two contributions: First, the focus on cultural appropriation allows us to account for the relationship between technical and non-technical practices such as articulation of collective belonging, economic interests and political discourse. This approach expands from CSCW's traditional focus on socio-technical systems theory and structuration theory [18, 25, 26] by taking seriously socio-political and socio-economic processes of appropriation. Second, this paper contributes to debates on cross-cultural engagement and global processes of technology development through the lens of transnational imagination.

Transnational Imagination

Faced with the complexity of contemporary global processes, what analytical tools can designers and researchers rely on? In this paper, we articulate how transnational studies, *e.g.* [3, 4, 24, 32, 35], provide an analytical sensitivity to help us better understand the role of appropriation in these contexts. Jones *et al.* suggest that future work on technology appropriation in a global context should expand from common analytical approaches such as structuration theory and socio-technical systems theory [18]. They stress the importance to further sociological debates in CSCW by drawing from global studies in order to develop new critical concepts [18]. It is exactly such an interdisciplinary analysis that we lay out in this paper. Our analytical frame of cultural appropriation, as such, melds core themes from globalization studies with prior research on appropriation in CSCW. We draw from two specific subsets of research in both disciplines:

From the CSCW and information studies tradition, we are building in particular on approaches such as socio-technical systems and interpretive flexibility by focusing attention on the creative aspects of technology appropriation, as well as on the material and historical boundedness of any technological innovation [18, 26]. From the global studies tradition, we propose transnational imagination to be a particularly fruitful starting point in approaching the challenges and complexities we face in the study of information technologies in relation to global phenomena.

Transnational imagination draws attention to the fact that global phenomena go beyond questions of travel and mobility [2, 20, 35]. It encompasses also movements of ideas, objects, and lifestyle choices, and works against reinforcing common binaries such as here versus there, developed versus non-developed. Prior research indicates that the work of imagination produces collectively-held notions about group identity, even if people have never met face-to-face or physically travelled, through the transnational circulation of ideas [2, 32]. Transnational imagination has found relevance broadly in anthropology, globalization studies, and also research in Human-Computer Interaction (HCI), *e.g.* [2, 3, 4, 20, 35]. For example, Arjun Appadurai, proposes transnational imagination as *"a faculty that informs the daily lives of ordinary people in myriad ways: it is the faculty which allows people to consider migration, to resist state violence, to seek social redress, and to design new forms of civic association and collaboration, often across national boundaries."* While Appadurai focuses on electronic media, Chris Kelty, in his study of the Free and Open Source Software movement between the U.S., India and Germany, examines how transnational imagination unfolds not only through technical, but also legal and social practices: *"free software is more than just the code..., it is also what is accomplished socially and culturally through sharing, coding and distributed collaboration."*

Building on this prior research, we illustrate how digital technologies are sites of expression for identity, social belonging and political alignment. Acknowledging the role of imagination allows us to see that appropriation includes not only the tweaking a system for one's own immediate needs, but includes arguing about the meaning of technologies, debating the nature of collaboration, and reflecting on one's social and cultural capital.

Cultural Appropriation

Our approach towards cultural appropriation is grounded in two fundamental ideas. First, appropriation may lie in how technology is framed and articulated, that is, transformed not as a technical artifact but as a cultural object. Consider, for instance, the different social meanings associated with a communication that happens via face-to-face interaction, via email, or via SMS text messaging. Which technologies are appropriate for scheduling a meeting? What if the meeting is a romantic encounter or a family event? Technology use takes on particular resonances and meanings in different settings, and this process of encountering technology as having specific meanings and values is a form of appropriation [12].

The second is that, while we study appropriation in particular locales, it often escapes those locales. Translocal movements of ideas, people and objects, have altered the ways in which we relate to one another, across diverse local contexts [2, 3, 23, 24, 32]. The ways in which we appropriate information systems reflects ideas about who we are and who we might be, about how we are connected to others, about our roles in relation to them, and about how the places we find ourselves in are connected to others. Social networking technologies, for example, provide sites for performing ideas of community and connection; user-contributed media shape ideas about participation, publics and audiences [17]. Information technologies are frequently used for communication, but information technologies also allow us to emulate others or to distinguish ourselves from them, or to enact ideas about who we are, not only locally, but also nationally and globally. Our approach stresses the importance of understanding technology appropriation as cultural encounter, rather than framing it as a linear model of knowledge transfer from West to East [4, 16, 30, 32]. Cultural appropriation, then, points not merely to the ways in which a technology is designed in Silicon Valley and then appropriated in China and "made Chinese," but to ways in which technology appropriation is always already a cultural process. Seeing culture as a process rather than as a pre-existing category taxonomized by regions, organizations or nation states allows us explore how technologies become meaningful as they are appropriated in everyday life and as social activity unfolds [16, 30, 32].

METHODS AND FIELD SITES

We ground our explorations through ethnographic research in urban China. We draw from three interrelated sets of data collected between 2007 and 2010: 1) interviews with IT policy makers and urban planners and analysis of public media discourse throughout the four years 2) a six month ethnographic study in 2008 and 2009 on the technology practices of Chinese professionals working at international IT corporations such as IBM, Intel and Lenovo in Beijing and Shanghai and 3) a six month ethnographic study in 2010 of a group of freelance designers, artists and IT entrepreneurs working out of a co-working space *c-work*[1] in Shanghai.

Taken together, these three data sets provide an illustrative case of the recent shifts in technology practice in relation to urban, social and political changes in China. Fieldwork was predominantly conducted by the first author, who has training in the Mandarin Chinese language, and with support of the second author and language interpreters for formal interviews and transcriptions. Research took place in Beijing and Shanghai. These cities were chosen because they are major hubs for both national and transnational migration, the stage for international events like the 2008 Olympic Games and the 2010 Expo, and are early adopters of digital technologies in China.

Throughout this research, we employed a multi-sited ethnographic approach [10, 22, 35] to trace the connections and frictions between our ethnographic sites and how broader political and economic developments manifested in specific practices. Multi-sited ethnography does not simply suggest that ethnography should be conducted in multiple places, or in different countries, in a comparative or holistic mode. Rather it begins with the assumption that local phenomena are in and of themselves inherently "multi-sited" through the kinds of global connections people make or imagine from within a single locale; it takes the relationship between sites as an object of ethnographic inquiry. Like previous work in CSCW and HCI that has adopted multi-sited ethnography, *e.g.* [4, 35], we trace the connections and distinctions that our participants made between their own technology practices and others.

Multi-sited ethnography is based on standard ethnographic methods such as participant observation, formal and informal interviews. An important aspect of multi-sited ethnography is to bring in those actors who are influential in shaping the structures of connectivity and transnational encounters [10]. As such, our ethnography also includes engagement with the site of policy and those state actors, who have a significant role in shaping technology appropriation in China. For this purpose, we conducted interviews with members from the Chinese Internet policy department and urban planning bureaus. We also carried out archival work of policy and state documents, as well as discourse analysis of local media coverage concerning the broader IT development in China.

Fieldwork was highly participatory in nature. For the second group, we conducted observations, interviews, and took part in the leisure practices at an urban entertainment site that attracted many of the IT professionals our research focused on. With the third group, we collaborated on art and design projects, observed and participated in interactions and collaborations at the co-working space, as well as at conferences and public art events that our participants attended. This form of ethnographic engagement allowed an in-depth understanding of daily work practices, the mechanics of the group's design and art practices, and changes in technology adoption over time. Interviews and participant observations were conducted both online and offline including offices, art galleries, homes, as well as social media that our participants used regularly, *e.g.* twitter, facebook, douban, sina weibo.

We now turn to our findings and trace material and semiotic linkages between these sites of technology appropriation. First, we begin by elaborating on the public moral and political debates about the appropriate use of technologies in China that shaped the collective understanding of technology among our participants. In particular, we focus on the appropriation of technologies for the expression of modernization discourse and national identity by Chinese state officials. We, then, continue by illustrating how Chinese professionals from international IT organizations and people at the co-working space appropriated technologies to express distinct lifestyles and ideas of cultural belonging. In the discussion, we analyze how, in each of these cases, technology appropriation brought people together through transnational imaginations and elaborate the implications of these findings for CSCW.

EXPRESSION OF NATIONAL VALUES

Information technologies broadly have become prominent subjects in debates over modernization in China [1, 24].

[1] c-work is a synonym for the co-working space used throughout this paper.

State media and government officials often portray Internet technology, and social media in particular, as an unsafe space that fosters crime and immorality. In calling the IT industry a "double-edged sword," the China Internet Network Information Center (CNNIC), China's central governmental station of Internet policy, for example, acknowledges the incredible economic potential of the IT industry at the same time as it cautions that many users have "submersed" themselves in a habit that is described as negatively impacting people's ability to function normally at work, school and in everyday life [6]. CNNIC considers online games and many social media, for example, as a "threat to a healthy development of China's youth" [6] and, by extension, the future of a harmonious society and China's modernization. The stipulation of unhealthy effects such as Internet addiction and social instability have become the main impetus behind the government's efforts to control the IT industry. This manifested in a series of interventions, ranging from the operation of the "great firewall of China," which blocks the access to certain websites and censors particular content, to the installation of control mechanism on computer terminals in Internet cafes [27].

What we wish to illustrate here is that state actors appropriate technologies to support broader ideological shifts in their discourse. Through the narrative of a harmonious society, Confucianist values such as a healthy and balanced life are re-invoked by state officials and in policy documents. These values are used to promote contemporary market reforms, globalization processes and technological developments while simultaneously rendering them as deeply intertwined with Chinese socio-cultural traditions. The social imaginary promoted has concrete effects on the urban and IT landscape of many Chinese cities: Internet cafés, which used to be prominent sites of Internet access among Chinese youth and migrants over the last ten years, have been subject to raids and mass closings, Internet companies have been encouraged to take a "public pledge of self-discipline" and are subject to "service standards" that stress the production of "healthy" products [9, 27]. With these expressions, state officials create a particular kind of national imaginary for Chinese citizens. For example, much of this recent re-design of Chinese cities is motivated by the desire to transcend a reliance on manufacturing to establish "world city" status in a global economy [19].

For example, in 2001, the 10th 5-year plan cites the establishment of a creative industry as a major project of cultural development in Chinese cities with the ultimate goal to grow China's soft power. [11] describe the origins of the creative industry policy discourse in the UK in the 1990s and how it has gained traction over the years in global debates and development strategies "*as a new engine of growth in developing countries…*" The import of the creative industry policy discourse into China corresponds with a broader ideological trend of appropriating foreign ideas and policies, while keeping in line with Chinese cultural values and belief systems [14, 19]. Terms employed by state officials such as "socialism with Chinese characteristics" reflect a post-Mao rhetoric of aligning modernization strategies such as the increase in foreign investment with the promotion of national autonomy – to modernize without being westernized [1, 24].

We see this again in recent narratives of re-designing Chinese cities to gain world-class cultural status. For example, in 2007, in his keynote speech to the 17th National Congress of the Communist Party, president Hu Jintao stressed the need to enhance Chinese culture as the country's "soft power": "*Culture has become… a factor of growing significance in the competition in overall national strength…* [we must] *enhance culture as a part of the soft power of our country to better guarantee the people's basic cultural rights and interests*." Creative industry clusters are seen to provide exactly such "cultural development centers." Our participants were by no means oblivious to discourses and policies surrounding their technology practice. On the contrary, many of them expressed discontent and distanced themselves from images of the Internet addict. Others attempted to leverage these changes for their businesses. In previous work, we have also shown how youths engage these state narratives in part shaping their ideas of selfhood and technology practice [21].

Although mobilizations of technological innovation in state discourse may have different consequences within the context of Chinese culture, politics and history, it is not a phenomenon unique to China. We stress here as a crucial take-away for CSCW to see appropriation of technologies in a locale like urban China not inherently and a-priori through a lens of othering. Indeed, fears about the negative impact of digital media use on youth also pervade public and media discourse in the United States and elsewhere. Subjects of common debate include the effects of video game violence, the dangers of online predators and access to pornography, and the impact of media multi-tasking on learning. Previous work addresses these various moral panics about the risks associated with the use of IT by children and youth [5].

Rather than ignoring value expressions of a "healthy" technological integration or treating them as a separate unit of analysis, we regard them as an important factor influencing identity formation and the appropriation of technology [12]. State actors deploy a range of strategies to proliferate a national imaginary of China's future as a global nation state. Imaginations for the Chinese nations such as the creation of a harmonious society and related policy change materially manifest in the redesign of Chinese cities.

IDENTIFICATONS WITH A COSMOPOLITAN LIFESTYLE

We now continue by illustrating how modernization discourses manifested in a series of popular entertainment clubs. We illustrate how the technological infrastructure in these clubs was designed to mark social differences and a cosmopolitan lifestyle.

The entertainment clubs that our participants regularly frequented offered a mixed media environment designed around a party game called the Killer Game, which became widely popular in China around 2006. The Killer Game is a role-playing murder mystery, a Chinese version of the Russian game Mafia or the American equivalent Werewolf. Succeeding in the game highly depends on players' skillful handling of argumentation and debate, observation and memorization. Before the game was taken up in the entertainment clubs, it was mostly played in people's homes and student dormitories. The entertainment clubs that offer Killer Game play in China today are exclusive urban spaces equipped with high-end interactive displays and sensor network technology. The first Killer Game club opened in Beijing in 2006, designed and built by one of our participants, Patrick[2], who had studied abroad for several years before he returned to China. By 2007, so Patrick told us, the franchise spread into other major cities in China and accumulated about 80.000 members. The clubs in Beijing and Shanghai, which we focused on in our research, mostly attracted young professionals from the IT and creative industry, who flexibly navigated China's urban hubs and also regularly travelled outside China for business, leisure and studies. Many of the people new to the clubs were returning after years abroad, often from the US or the wider Pacific Rim.

Upon arrival at a Killer Game club, one enters a main lobby with a reception and a lounge area for members to sit and chat. The walls of the lobby are equipped with high-resolution screens that display the list of members currently present in the club, their photos, nicknames and their in-game ranking. A quick glance onto one of the displays shows which of your acquaintances is on site. From the lobby, a series of gaming rooms can be accessed. The screens in the lobby and hallways display ongoing game sessions and distribution of players in the various rooms. The game rooms themselves are equipped with large displays and a computer terminal driven by the club's employees. The technology system in the rooms augments game play, triggers sound feedback based on actions in the game and records player activity. In addition, most of the clubs provide free WiFi access.

Our participants valued the social space and technical infrastructure of the clubs, because together they invoked an image distinct from the Internet café, which – as illustrated in the previous section - has the reputation of attracting the lower socio-economic class and to be a place where Internet addiction thrives [27]. Most of our participants owned mobile devices and stationary computers in their homes, and were thus not dependent on public Internet access as many people, who frequent Internet cafes. The Killer Game itself was rendered a particularly meaningful leisure practice, because it invoked for our participants an image of cultural competency in local and translocal social networking. For example, our study participants repeatedly told us that the game originated in Silicon Valley – not in Russia where it was actually invented – and was brought into China by a Chinese on his return to the homeland. When we asked if the Killer Game was, then, an American game, we repeatedly received answers like: *Of course not, this is a Chinese game*. Given that the Killer Game was invented in Russia yet imagined to originate from Silicon Valley, it is this underlying question of technology appropriation for the cultural expression of transnational identification that we set out to explore in this section.

[2] Synonyms are used for all participants. English synonyms are used for those who introduced themselves via English names.

Local Distinction & Transnational Connections

A pervasive phenomenon we observed in the entertainment clubs was that people rendered their practices as inherently distinct from other technologically mediated leisure activities in China. For example, our participants often described themselves and others who frequented the clubs as displaying a distinct quality, especially in contrast to Internet cafés, which they described as attracting members of the lower socio-economic class. Summer, a member of a club in Beijing, articulated this as follows: *...people who come here* [to the club] *are of high* suzhi [quality]*... this game provides opportunities for you to meet people, people of a certain circle. Not everyone likes this game... it is not like, how should I say, not very mixed, only people of certain levels will be here to play.*

Suzhi, here invoked by Summer in the first quote, is a common rendering of status and class in China. The notion of *suzhi* was used to describe human quality first at the time of the idea of population control in the 1980s where China's failure to modernize was attributed to low quality of its population [14]. As modernization projects increased privatization, [1] suggests, *suzhi* appears again in new practices of social distinction and expressions of middle classness, *e.g.* defining a "person of quality" in practices of consumption and social mobility. Our participants invoked *suzhi* not only on the level of human quality and socio-economic status, but also with reference to the technological infrastructure of the clubs and their members' ability to connect to an international scene of elite networking. We illustrate in more depth below.

When we asked the owner of the club in Shanghai why he would not provide computer stations similar to the Internet café in China, he told us that he only needed a wireless network to attract members, who would bring their own mobile devices. Through a wireless infrastructure, he explained, members could visit websites without the gaming club having to restrict their access and subject their online activities to screening. This is different from Internet cafés, where commonly a series of mechanisms is installed on the computer terminals to restrict access and record online traffic [27]. In the clubs, the preference for wireless infrastructures was crucial for the owners' and members' concerted efforts to create a local environment that was distinct from establishments such as the Internet café.

Our participants considered not only the technological infrastructure, but also the Killer Game itself as representing a distinct social status. Many considered the skills they acquired through playing the game crucial for their jobs in international companies or their own businesses in China and abroad. One of our participants, Zhen, left China 8 years ago to study and work in the U.S. Zhen described his experiences in the clubs as training him in the kind of "international thinking" he considers to be a necessary skill for employment in Chinese companies today: *I think this club really helps people to speak their opinion. In Chinese enterprise, people are more and more outgoing these days, this is a good thing... this game is training you for international thinking.*

What we illustrate here is that technologically-mediated experience was imbued with values of socio-economic class. Our participants drew upon the socio-technical space of the clubs to position themselves within a changing economic and social landscape in China that was portrayed as becoming increasingly international. In the beginning of this section, we alluded to how study participants perceived the game as inherently Chinese, despite it being invented in Russia, and imagined it as having originated from Silicon Valley. While the Killer Game was clearly being appropriated into Chinese culture, participating in it also entailed being able to relate to a world of transnational connections and an international lifestyle. This appropriation as a remixing of an existing game and cultural values of "international thinking," as one of our participants put it, lead to the design of a particular kind of transnational experience: a leisure practice that granted local distinction. People associated the game with international corporations and a cosmopolitan lifestyle that, once adopted, grants access to transnational networks of social relations.

In these processes of distinction making, technology was a site for people to situate themselves within broader social hierarchies. The appropriation of technology can function as a marker of cultural capital, socio-economic class identity and of belonging to a transnational elite.

THE CREATION OF A TRANSNATIONAL CLASS

We now turn to findings from ethnographic research at the co-working space c-work based out of Shanghai, which attracts an eclectic mix of technology designers, new media artists, bloggers, freelancers and young entrepreneurs. At the time of the research, c-space was located in an old factory that had been remodeled into a series of design studios as part of the larger urban re-design to stimulate creative production in China (described above). c-work provided desks for rent on an hourly, weekly or monthly basis, similar to co-working spaces in the U.S. and Europe. People who frequented the space were from abroad and China. At the physical site of c-work, on its website and across various social media that its members and visitors are using, people mostly communicated in Chinese and English. c-work's co-founders and people who frequented it regularly gave talks at international tech events such as the local TED (Technology Entertainment Design), at Chinese and international art & design festivals. c-space also regularly hosted events, including for example academic discussion forums, maker workshops, dorkbots and barcamps.

Across these activities, individuals associated with the space promoted collective ideas of technological innovation and digital creativity. In what follows, we illustrate how a transnational imaginary was produced through this collective appropriation of the notions "sharing" and "co-working" as a core work ethic.

Appropriating Usable Pasts to envision Global Futures

Daily work life in c-work comprised not only collaboration with others on technology design and art projects, or the production and sharing of code. Our participants also wrote about their work and reflected upon it. In these reflections on their work, they appropriated ideas and values from the past or from other places, and mixed them in order to give meaning to their technology practices. For example, the name that space chose for itself, makes this practice of remixing immediately visible. Translated into English the name stands for *new workunit,* an appropriation of the term *workunit,* which refers to state-owned institutions during the cultural revolution in China. The *workunit* constituted a core organizing principle of social transformation after 1949 [22], breaking up the large city population into smaller collectives that provided employment, housing and social benefits for workers and their families. It is this underlying practice of appropriating something so central to organizational life in China's past, and re-making it into something "new" that we set out to explore in this section.

The writings that members of the space produced had at the core two fundamental ideas: co-working and open sharing. Both were thought of as work ethics for the age of the Internet and as having originated in IT hot beds of the U.S. and Europe. The space coupled these concepts with themes relevant in the context of China. In mixing ideas about co-working and open sharing with ideas of creativity and innovation currently promoted in China, the space positioned its own designs, collaborations and texts in alignment with local and international values.

For example, co-working constituted not only a model to rent out space on an hourly, weekly or monthly basis. It was fundamentally deployed as a work ethic continuously promoted at international tech events hosted in China, *e.g.* TED, and in daily conversations with one another. Co-founders of the co-working space positioned co-working as a new form of organization that mixes the benefits of social media with those from the physical work space: *The nature of work is changing. So the nature of work space is changing. It has culture and is an environment that promises for the future. This is about combining elements of the physical workspace, of being productive, with social media, which means to be hybrid, to be efficient in real time.*

This practice is reminiscent of what Kelty [20] describes as the appropriation of "*usable pasts, [which are] less technical and more accessible narratives that make sense of the contemporary world by reflecting on the past and its difference from today... they are told not in order to remember the past, but in order to make sense of the present and of the future*" (p. 65). Across various talks, c-space's co-founders elaborated how co-working matters for a new form of creativity and innovation in China today. c-work drew its inspiration from a mix of resources, including the past, to make sense of China's presence and future. One of the co-founders, for example, frequented a co-working space during her time in Europe before she returned to China and ever since regularly accessed a Google group focused on co-working. She described both, the co-working space in Europe and the Google group, as *"inspiring and cool places that trigger my creative side."* Others drew inspiration from an array of websites on DIY or from texts on free and open source software such as Lessig's "Free Culture." Our study participants debated the role the past and new work ethics co-working play in China, both face-to-face and in online conversations. They reflected together on the meaning of these ideas for their own efforts and for social and economic change in China today.

In addition to co-working, another central work ethic that proliferated at c-space was the idea of open sharing. One of c-space's most active members, an acclaimed blogger, promoted sharing as a new creative force for China, which he entitled Sharism: *Sharism promises to be the politics of the next global superpower. It will not be a country, but a new human network joined by social software... new collaborative technologies will allow us to query, share and remix information for the public benefit... [it] is an ideology for our Internet Age. It is a philosophy piped through the human and technological networks of Free and Open Source software. It is the motivation behind every piece of User-Generated Content. It is the pledge of Creative Commons, to share, remix and give credit to the latest and greatest of our cultural creations.*

In and beyond the co-working space, Sharism was referred to as a symbol for Chinese creativity and innovation enabled by global and interdisciplinary collaboration. As visible in the quote above, Sharism was inspired by works like Creative Commons and by the Silicon Valley free culture movement. c-space not only promoted Sharism at tech talks and on the web, but also incorporated it into their material practices. For example, the interior design of c-space and its website were continuously re-designed to reflect a work ethic centered around open sharing. For example, opinions expressed by people who rented the space, or ideas that speakers at conferences put forward, found their way into the arrangements of furniture and computers and the ever changing visuals of the website.

What we observed across c-work's work ethics, its material manifestation in space and technology design was the inherent belief that a "better China" can be accomplished through a collective re-making of the past and the presence, performed with both local and international partners. It was through this circulation of ideas and their manifestation in material practices that brought together a set of people who identified themselves members of a larger, like-minded collective. The collective was in flux in terms of its members' transnational mobility, but stable through its shared ideas of building a new creative workforce.

DISCUSSION

In this paper, we return to a traditional topic for CSCW research, that of appropriation, and approach it via a non-traditional route. Our goal is to examine the cultural work of appropriation alongside the organizational and the technological. Two sets of contributions emerge from this work. First, we illustrate how appropriation as a cultural process is not necessarily geographically bound, but often evolves across multiple sites, through practices of imagination. If we take contemporary forms of mobility and transnational mediation seriously as important aspects of technology design, we need to explore the specificity of different technologies, their material and cultural forms as they span across diverse places, cultures and value systems [17]. Second, with cultural appropriation we suggest a widening notion of the socio-technical in CSCW in order to see material and social practices in relation to political and economic processes. Cultural appropriation does not constitute a subcategory of technology appropriation nor does it describe a process that comes after a technology is modified. Rather, it emphasizes appropriation as process of meaning making that can occur through both technical means and processes of imagination.

Transnational Imagination

The role of technology in global and cross-cultural processes has become a central debate in CSCW research [7, 16, 30, 31, 34]. Our approach contributes to these efforts by providing a new conceptual tool for understanding the circulation of technologies and their values. This approach resists common efforts in HCI that assume culture as a taxonomic category defined by geographically bounded spaces like the nation state to assess their different implications for design. Transnational imagination allows us to see a city like Shanghai, a site like the Killer Game Club or the co-working space as already in and of themselves heterogeneous nodes, rather than illustrative cases of a pre-assigned cultural category.

By highlighting the role of transnational imagination we draw from transnational studies, in particular Appadurai's seminal work [3]. Appadurai explores the confluences of modern travel and electronic media and their effects on the production of cultural identity, locality and belonging in a transnational era [3]. He investigates, for example, how people who have never met face-to-face come to think of themselves as Indonesian, Chinese or American. He suggests that the "mediascapes" produced by mass media offer new resources for the construction of identity and imagined selves across places, social and cultural practices and values. This approach leads to a broader understanding of "movements", one that does not just entail literal and physical travel, movement of people and goods and services, but also the movement of ideas, discourses and modes of thoughts. Our technological systems today are similarly part of these processes, shaping a collective imagination of "who we are." They are imbued with meanings and values that span across locales, along with the traditional media forms that Appadurai describes.

The work of imagination, especially when collective, Appadurai suggests, can become fuel for action in that it creates ideas of locales such as neighborhood and nationhood [3]. Imagination of who we are and where we belong, he suggests, are interwoven with transnational developments: such as the formation of international corporations, global markets and trading agreements, the movement of objects and ideas across national borders. For Appadurai, electronic media intensify these processes and make them available as part of everyday practice. This notion of imagination applies to our findings on digital technologies practices in urban China, wherein the technological systems we examined are sites of imagination in relation to both local and transnational developments.

Two important implications for CSCW arise. First, building on transnational studies, we begin to see appropriation of technology through processes of both connection and friction. Rather than assuming stable flows and connection across places and different value systems, transnational imagination focuses on the experiences of people and highlights how connections across places are continuously in the making through the economic, social and political struggles people face, as well as their aspirations and expressions of belonging [24]. The appropriation of technologies into local contexts can not be understood independently of political, historical and economic contingencies that both enable and control movements of people, things and ideas [3, 24].

Second, the lens of transnational imagination illuminates that appropriation is not a linear model of transfer of practices from West to East. In line with a recently emerging line of research in HCI, we contribute by providing a nuanced understanding of the role of technology in global processes that is not inherently about designing for the so-called developing world or the culturally "other" [16, 30]. We stress that much can be gained by an approach that considers technology appropriation in contemporary global processes not a-priori through distinctions such as how we "in here" versus others "out there" [30] use technologies and make sense of the world. Rather, we suggest seeing technology appropriation as a cultural encounter. For example, in this paper, we have highlighted how in particular locales cultural values, and economic political and social interests are negotiated as different actors come together. This view suggests understanding the design and use of technologies as sites of negotiations rather than through stable categories.

Collective Expression of Values

Our work shows that in appropriating technologies people produce not only content or tweak software code, but also create new meanings and values. These values are not determined by the technology, but evolve in relation to political alignments and economic interests. For example, the co-working space in Shanghai positioned its work in alignment with Chinese values of modernization as well as with international ideas of an open and free Internet. Ideas and work ethics from the past, from other places, from old and contemporary value systems, were appropriated in order to give meaning to technology practice today. In the Killer Game clubs, the mixed-reality space was the site for expressing *suzhi* differences to others in China, while also providing the opportunity to connect international network of IT professionals. And in the case of Internet addiction discourses mobilized by state actors, technologies are appropriated for the expression and production of national values such as harmonious development, which simultaneously function as images in transnational politics.

An area of consequence of this work for CSCW is the analysis of collaborative systems in terms of collective imagination. Many contemporary systems of interest to the CSCW community, including online games, user-generated content systems, and multimedia sharing systems, lie at the intersection of interactive systems, popular media and political discourse. In this paper, we elaborated how political discourse on IT development and its uptake in media is a pervasive phenomenon that shapes the meaning of technologies across local sites. We typically approach CSCW technologies from an interactive systems perspective, focusing on triggers and barriers to adoption and use and the emergence of forms of technologically-enabled practice. An interesting complementary approach is to see technologies as cultural forms, with an emphasis on cultural practice, ideology, communication, values and genre [12, 17].

We suggest that the lens of collective expression of values, allows us to see collaborative systems not only as socio-technical artifacts, but also as a cultural object. Approaching collaborative systems as a cultural object allows us understand the involvement of a range of actors in a given locale and how they collectively shape the meaning of technologies. For example, we show through our findings how state actors appropriate technologies for their own means: to further an agenda of modernization and to motivate a political project of a harmonious society.

Friedman and colleagues highlight the importance to include the values of a range of stakeholders into both the research and design process of a technological system [12]. We follow their approach by studying how values are being expressed and evolve through interaction, rather than seeing them as inherently inscribed into the technology [12]. We suggest it to be fruitful to merge these prior efforts in CSCW with Graeber's historically grounded anthropological theory of value [14]. While Friedman *et al.* focus on a specific list of human values with ethical import, Graeber more generally sees value as the way that actions become meaningful to the actor through incorporation into some larger, social whole, real or imagined [14].

In comparison to Friedman *et al.*, then, our approach is at once more specific and more general. It is more specific in that, rather than assuming a set of universal values, it considers values as they are enacted and/or imagined [32]. It is more general in that it traces how values are taken up as cultural reorientation across different sites and in relation to global processes. For example, we explore how values of open sharing and co-working, which have come to permeate debates in open-source communities and IT politics globally [20], are taken up in China and made meaningful in relation to both national policy and political debates as well as translocal processes of exchange and collaboration. The notion of appropriation can easily be read as empowerment of the user. By including the role of state actors into the analysis of technology appropriation, we elucidate how the politics of design and use unfold through contemporary socio-political processes and technological values. Our approach illuminates the creative ways in which people respond to political debates and decisions, but also how at the same time new distinctions and systems of power emerge.

One particularly important issue of relevance to CSCW that this perspective opens up is to see "collective" processes of technology appropriation as a site of analytic attention. When CSCW first emerged as a research topic, attention to "collaborative" aspects of technology use emphasized that the field of Human-Computer Interaction had typically focused on a single user and neglected the settings in which technologies were put to use amongst multiple people. It signaled, then, a move from one to many. An attentiveness to "collective" experience, by contrast, signals a move from many to one; that is, it attempts to understand how different people, with different, partially overlapping understandings of the world give rise to collective phenomena that transcend but shape individual experience. In our analysis, by focusing on information technologies as sites of imagination for a range of actors, we examine collective phenomena. Like ethnomethodological analyses in CSCW have drawn attention to intersubjective, more-or-less shared "knowledge in common," this perspective helps us to understand how collective interpretations of technology arise.

CONCLUSION

In this paper, we describe what we see as a shift from technical to cultural appropriation. Cultural appropriation provides a sensitizing concept for designers and researchers investigating interactions and collaborations across different sites, and translocal movements of ideas and technologies. It melds prior work on technology appropriation in CSCW with seminal work from transnational studies. To illustrate, we draw from ethnographic research on translocal collaboration and exchange of ideas among IT professions in urban China.

Cultural appropriation provides a constructive analytical lens for studying the role of technology in translocal processes. It resists the traps of more common models of linear transfer of knowledge from the West to the East. Our approach suggests that drawing from transnational studies allows us to engage socio-political and socio-economic processes such as the workings of systems of power, ruptures of flows, distinction making practices and how collective ideas of technological meanings and selfhood arise. At the heart of this exploration lies the role of transnational imagination which helps illustrate how particular locales are already in and of themselves culturally and socially diverse, rather than homogeneous entities that intersect through global flows.

ACKNOLWEDGEMENTS

We thank all our participants in this research as well as our colleagues Matthew Bietz, Marisa Cohn, Charlotte Lee, Katie Pine, Daniela Rosner and Janet Vertesi for their valuable input. This work was supported in part by Intel Research and the National Science Foundation under awards 091740, 0968608, 0968616, 1025761, and 1042678.

REFERENCES

1. Anagnost, A. *National Past-Times. Narrative, Representation, and Power in Modern China*. Duke University Press, 1997.
2. Appadurai, A. 1999. Globalization and the research imagination. Published by Blackwell Publishers.
3. Appadurai, A. *Modernity at Large: Cultural Dimensions of Globalization*. University of Minnesota Press, 1996.
4. Burrell, J. and Anderson, K. 2008. I have great desires to look beyond my world: trajectories of information and communication technology use among Ghanians living abroad. New Media Society, 10:203.
5. Cassell, J. and Kramer, M. 2008. High tech or high risk: Moral panics about girls online. In McPherson, (Ed.), *Digital youth, innovation, and the unexpected* (pp. 53-76). The John D. and Catherine T. MacArthur Foundation series on digital media and learning. Cambridge, MA: The MIT Press.
6. CNNIC 2009. *Statistical Survey on the Internet Development in China,* last accessed in Jan. 2010.

7. Diamant, E.I., Fussell, S.R., Lo, F-L. 2009. Collaborating across cultural and technological boundaries: Team culture and information use in a map navigation task. In Proc. of IWIC, 175-184.
8. Dourish, P., Adler, A., Bellotti, V. and Henderson, A. 1996. Your Place or Mine? Learning from Long-Term Use of Audio-Video Communication. Computer-Supported Cooperative Work, 5(1), 33-62.
9. Ernkvist, M., & Strom, P. 2008. Enmeshed in Games with the Government: Governmental Policies and the Development of the Chinese Online Game Industry. *Games and Culture, 3*(1), 98-126.
10. Falzon, M-A. (ed). 2009. Multi-sited Ethnography. Theory, Praxis and Locality in Contemporary Research. Ashgate.
11. Flew, T & Cunningham, S. 2010. Creative Industries after the First Decade of Debate, The Information Society, 26:2, 113-123.
12. Friedman, B., Kahn, P. H., Borning, A. Value Sensitive Design and Information Systems. 2006. In Zhang, P. and Galletta, D. (Eds). Human-Computer Interaction in Management Information Systems: Foundations. M.E. Sharpe, Inc: NY, pp. 348 – 372.
13. Fulton Suri, J. + IDEO. thoughtless acts? Chronicle Books LLC, 2004.
14. Graeber, D. Toward an Anthropological Theory of Value. The False Coin of our own dreams. Palgrave, 2001.
15. Heath, P. Hindmarsh, J. and Luff, C. *Workplace Studies. Recovering Work Practice and Informing System Design*. MA: Cambridge, 2000, University Press.
16. Irani, L., Vertesi, J., Dourish, P., Philips, K., Grinter, R. 2010. Postcolonial Computing: A lens on Design and Development. In Proc. of CHI'10, 1311-1320.
17. Ito, M. Engineering Play. A Cultural History of Children's Software. MIT Press, Cambridge, Massachusetts, 2009.
18. Jones, M. Orlikowski, W. and Munir, K. Structuration Theory and Information Systems: A Critical Reappraisal. In Mingers, J. and Willcocks, L. (eds). 2004. Social Theory and Philosophy for Information Systems. John Wiley & Sons, Ltd.
19. Keane, M. 2007. Created in China: The great new leap forward. London: Routledge.
20. Kelty, C. 2008. Two Bits: The Cultural Significance of Free Software and the Internet. Durham, NC: Duke University Press.
21. Lindtner, S., Nardi, B., Wang, Y., Mainwaring, S., Jing, H., Liang, W. 2008. A Hybrid Cultural Ecology: World of Warcraft in China. In Proc. of CSCW, November 2008, San Diego, California.
22. Lu, Xiaobo & Perry, E. 1997. Danwei. The changing Chinese workplace in historical and comparative perspective. Sharpe, New York.
23. Marcus, G. E. 1995. Ethnography in/of the World System: The Emergence of Multi-Sited Ethnography.*Annual Review of Anthropology, 24*(1), 95-117.
24. Ong, A. 1998. *Flexible Citizenship. The Cultural Logics of Transnationality*. Duke University Press.
25. Orlikowski, W. 1995 Evolving with Notes: Organizational Change around Groupware Technology. *Technical Report (IFSRC No. 314-95), MIT, Sloan School of Management*, Cambridge, MA.
26. Pinch, T.J. and Bijker, W.E. 1984. The Social Construction of facts and artefacts: or how the sociology of science and the sociology of technology might benefit each other, Social Studies of Science, 14: 399-441.
27. Qiu, J. L. 2009 *Working-Class Network Society. Communication Technology and the Information Have-Less in Urban China*. Cambridge, MA: The MIT Press.
28. Robinson, M. 1993. Design for unanticipated use.... *In Proc. of the third European Conference on Computer-Supported Cooperative Work*. pp. 187-202.
29. Star, S.L. and Strauss, A. 1999. Layers of Silence, Arenas of Voice: The ecology of visible and invisible work. *In Proc. of JCSCW, Journal of Computer Supported Cooperative Work*. Vol. 8, N. 1-2, pp. 9 – 30.
30. Taylor, A. 2011. Out There. In Proc. of CHI'11, 685-694.
31. Thom-Santelli, J. Millen, D., R., DiMicco, J., 2010. Characterizing global participation in an enterprise SNS. In Proc. of Conf. on Intercultural Collaboration, 251-254.
32. Tsing, A. 2004. Friction. An Ethnography of Global Connection. Princeton University Press.
33. Trigg, R. H. and Bodker, S. 1994. From Implementation to Design: Tailoring and the Emergence of Systematization in CSCW. In Proc. of CSCW 94, pp.45-54.
34. Weibert, A. & Wulf, V. 2010. "All of a sudden we had this dialogue...": Intercultural computer clubs' contribution to sustainable integration. In Proc. of Conf. on Intercultural Collaboration, 93-102
35. Williams, A., Anderson, K., Dourish, P. 2008. Anchored Mobilities: Mobile Technologies and Transnational Migration. *Proc. of DIS'08*, pp.323-332.

"This is How We Do it in My Country": A Study of Computer-Mediated Family Communication Among Kenyan Migrants in the United States

Susan P. Wyche
The Center for Human-Computer Interaction
Virginia Tech
Blacksburg, VA 24060 USA
spwyche@gmail.com

Rebecca E. Grinter
School of Interactive Computing
Georgia Institute of Technology
Atlanta, GA 30308 USA
beki@cc.gatech.edu

ABSTRACT
Although computer-mediated family communication remains a longstanding focus of study in Computer Supported Cooperative Work (CSCW), families who face challenges in communication due to differences in technology infrastructures remain understudied. To address this gap in the literature, we interviewed 39 Kenyan migrants living in Atlanta, Georgia, U.S. who regularly communicate with friends and family members living in their homeland. The contributions of this work are primarily empirical. Findings from our study reveal how high costs, identity management, and infrastructural differences between rural and urban areas in Kenya, impact decisions families and their extended members make when using information and communication technology (ICT). We present design implications and reflect on how understanding Kenyan migrants' ICT practices can positively influence design for the broader population.

Author Keywords
Family; Kenya; Connectedness; Transnational Communication; and Photosharing.

ACM Classification Keywords
H5.m. Information interfaces and presentation (e.g., HCI): Miscellaneous.

General Terms
Design and Human Factors

INTRODUCTION
A significant transnational practice affecting migrants' lives in the U.S. is their ability to use technology to connect with family members living in different countries. Not too long ago migrants made do with exorbitantly expensive calls, slow-paced post, or no contact at all. Today many rely on Information and Communication Technology (ICT) to regularly communicate with extended family members. Unfortunately, the benefits accompanying high-bandwidth Internet access and low costs phone calls are unevenly distributed and maintaining transnational ties remains difficult for individuals living in parts of the developing world. In rural parts of Kenya, the infrastructure necessary to support digital photo exchange and video-mediated communication (VMC) are scarce, consequently Kenyans living abroad can not use some ICT to connect with family members in their country of origin [11,42]. Further, despite the arrival of an undersea fiber-optic cable in Sub-Saharan Africa, lack of electricity and high costs suggest infrastructural differences and barriers to ICT access are likely to persist in parts of the developing world [1,18,28,42].

These obstacles pose challenges for African migrants wanting to communicate with friends and family living abroad, particularly those with members living rural parts of the continent. Yet, designers of collaborative systems often assume that communication occurs between families with similar Internet speeds and connectivity, thus overlooking ways families with extended members living in developing countries stay connected [13,42]. In this paper we argue that studying African migrants' ICT practices contributes to CSCW in two ways. First, studying these users highlights new factors to consider when developing ICT to support family communication. Second, our research reveals how studying computer-mediated communication between users in developed and developing countries challenges themes underlying domestic technology design.

We focus on Kenya because migrants from this East African country are part of a growing demographic in the U.S. and regularly communicate with people living in a country with a technology infrastructure that is less developed than those typically examined in CSCW studies (e.g., [20,23]). Over the last two decades, economic difficulties, increased poverty, and political instability have resulted in large-scale migration of Africans to the U.S. [25]. Census data indicate there are 1.4 million foreign-born Africans residing in the U.S. and that number is growing. More than two-thirds of these immigrants come from countries in sub-Saharan Africa, with the majority coming from Nigeria, Ghana, and Kenya [40].

We make two contributions with this work. First, we present findings from 39 (27 men and 12 women) Kenyan migrants residing in the metropolitan Atlanta-area, that reveal how they use ICT to stay connected with family members in their country of origin. Our research demonstrates how lack of Internet connectivity, infrastructural differences between rural and urban regions, and high costs affect decisions about communication in this transnational context. Second, we discuss how learning from Kenyan migrants' communication practices highlights alternative ways of imagining future computing design for families. We suggest designing systems that account for constraints users like those we studied encounter when communicating. For example, rather than developing applications that heighten expectations about communication, we imagine designing ones that encourage fewer exchanges. Systems that support occasional solitude, rather than constant connectivity, can make family communication less of an obligation for users in developed countries.

RELATED WORK: COMMUNICATION BETWEEN REMOTE FAMILY MEMBERS

Communication between remote family members continues to attract research interest within CSCW and related fields. Work in this area tends to focus on how ICT supports "connectedness," or the positive emotional sense that comes from feelings of staying in touch [33]. Researchers' early efforts explored how media space concepts could provide families with new computer-mediated ways to communicate. Hindus et al. [16] foreshadowed the increased pervasiveness of computing in North American and European domestic life. CSCW/HCI researchers have kept pace with these changes and empirically investigated computing and its changing role in family communication.

Tee and her colleagues explored how families living in the U.S. used ICT to stay connected with extended family members, or people who are related but do not live in the same household [36]. Findings from their research provide a detailed picture of how families use phone and email to communicate and share photos with distributed members. Results from these studies also suggest that families want additional ways to communicate with each other. Growing domestic Internet access and high-bandwidth connectivity provide families with these additional ways and have spurred research examining how families use VMC technologies to maintain feelings of connectedness. Commercial examples of these technologies include Google Talk, Skype and iChat.

Kirk, Sellen, and Cao, studied VMC in 12 British homes. Their findings reveal how these technologies make families "feel closer" with extended members, more than phone and email allow. VMC technologies enable family members to virtually share routines, feel involved, and for young children to interact with grandparents in ways that are difficult to achieve without video [23]. Judge and Neustaedter also found that families used video-conferencing to share immediate moments with extended members [20]. Ames and her colleagues uncovered additional ways extended families benefit from using VMC technologies to stay connected. These benefits include providing an engaging experience for young children and allowing families to communicate as a group [3].

In addition to providing rich descriptions of ICT use and family life this research also motivated novel systems such as the "The Family Window" [21] and "HomeNote" [34], that take advantage of the Internet's increased presence in some families' homes. These systems provide families with additional computer-mediated ways to stay connected with remote members such as exchanging images, notes, and written messages.

Our study extends this prior work in two ways. First, with some notable exceptions [2,6,7,39], there remain few detailed studies examining families with extended members living in developed and developing countries. In contrast, prior work tends to examine families living in developed countries (e.g., U.S. and U.K) who communicate with extended members in their countries or in other developed countries [20,23,36]. Yet, innovations in technology and globalization have resulted in new family structures with members living in developed and developing countries [6,25,38].

In terms of our methodological approach and topic of study our work is similar to Burrell and Anderson's research examining how Ghanaians living in London use ICT to support activities other than maintaining connections with their homeland [6]. Unlike their study, we focused on how Kenyans in the U.S. maintain associations with home because prior research suggests they may benefit from improved ways to connect with family members far away [29]. Kenyan migrants face challenges participants in prior CSCW studies are less likely to encounter. These include adapting to a new culture, locating affordable housing, and finding a job. Individuals like those we studied would likely welcome more computer-mediated opportunities to connect with family members abroad during this period of transition.

While CSCW researchers continue to explore geographically distributed work teams collaborating across countries with different infrastructures (e.g., [19,37]), families living in countries with low levels of personal computer ownership and limited Internet access receive less attention. Lack of electricity and high costs keep domestic Internet access out of reach for many in the Kenya and other developing countries [1,18,28,42]. Consequently, not all families rely on Internet and VMC technologies, but other forms of technology to stay connected. The second way our work contributes to CSCW studies of family communication is by broadening the community's understanding of how families with extended members living in countries with different technology infrastructures maintain feelings of connectedness.

OUR STUDY

We conducted semi-structured interviews with 39 individuals (27 men and 12 women) to understand how Kenyan migrants communicate with friends and family in their homeland. These interviews occurred over a three-month period during summer 2009 and took place at an "immigrant church" in Marietta, a suburb outside of Atlanta. Unlike prior experimental studies of individuals communicating between different countries [37], we wanted to learn from people who communicate with acquaintances living 8,000 miles away in a country with a less developed infrastructure than what exists in the metro-Atlanta area.

In the rest of this section we describe why our interviews took place in a church, provide details about our methods and participants. We also describe how the first author's race, gender, and national identity affected participant recruitment.

Site: The metro-Atlanta area provided us an excellent opportunity for studying Kenyan migrants because of the large number of native Kenyans living there. The city ranks in the top five metropolitan areas in terms of its African-born population and a significant number of those individuals are from Kenya [14,35]. Atlanta, GA, also has a high level of racial diversity and lower cost of living compared to other major U.S. cities; these factors make it an attractive location for African migrants to settle [5].

We conducted interviews in the church because our project was part of a long-term, multi-sited research project examining technology use in Christian churches [41]. Christianity has a remarkable strength in Kenyans' lives and churches tend to be "institutional isomorphic," or comprised of individuals who are similar to one another. It was unsurprising to find three predominately Kenyan congregations in the Atlanta area [30]. Our study took place at a mid-sized church (~500 attendees) because its minister was open to assisting us with our project. In addition to leading the church, he also taught Anthropology at an area college. His personal interest in our study helped us gain access to this site and its members. After meeting the church's minister (to obtain approval for our study) we made an announcement during a Sunday worship service and asked interested people to contact the first author to schedule an interview.

In addition to being accessible there were other reasons the immigrant church was an attractive site. First, there are few places in metro-Atlanta where we could readily find Kenyan migrants meeting on a weekly basis. Second, parishioners often stayed at the church for 1-4 hours following the morning worship service to engage in "fellowship," or informal conversations with other parishioners. This time provided us with opportunities to approach potential participants and ask them to engage in a 30-minute interview. Thirdly, prior studies suggest that immigrant churches remind migrants of their home country because they are settings where they can engage in familiar activities, such as communal worship [26]. This suggested the church was a place where participants felt comfortable reflecting on and discussing life in Kenya.

Participants: There were other reasons we focused on Kenyan-born individuals. The first author had prior experience conducting fieldwork in Kenya and believed this familiarity would help her build rapport and gain participants' trust during interviews. Further, unlike some African-migrants, Kenyans' migration to the U.S. is not typically driven by acute crisis (i.e., they were not forced to leave their country) [14]. This understanding paired with mainstream media reports indicating that technology use is on a significant upward trend throughout Kenya (e.g., [43]) motivated our choice. These factors meant our participants were likely to have friends and family members they wanted to communicate with and who were able to communicate with them. Thus, studying Kenyan migrants provided us with the most opportunities to study phenomena central to our research.

Study participants migrated to the U.S. for various reasons. Twenty-eight came to pursue educational and employment opportunities, while the remaining came to the country to attend family members' graduations or weddings and never returned home. Although the migration of most Kenyans comes from a desire to pursue a "better life," it is rarely the poorest who migrate. Instead it is those with a high socioeconomic status and with considerable financial resources who tend leave their country [14,29]. Our sample reflected this larger trend.

Interviewees differed along dimensions such as length of time in the U.S., educational background, and employment. Some individuals had lived in the U.S. for more than 40 years, while others had been in Atlanta for a few months. The average length of time in the U.S. within our sample was 9-10 years. All participants were adults and ranged in age from 18 to 57. Thirty-one interviewees reported having a college degree, or were working towards one, and five had advanced degrees (4 MBA's, 1 PhD). Participants held a variety of occupations, such as truck-drivers, nurses, accountants, teachers, employees at big-box retailers, and executives in multi-national corporations.

Despite this heterogeneity within our sample, there were characteristics shared among all participants. First, all were born in Kenya and had friends and relatives they regularly communicated with in the country. Second, in addition to speaking English, all but two participants spoke Swahili and their "mother tongue," which was typically Kikuyu. Kenya is comprised of at least forty-two different ethnic or tribal groups, each with a distinct cultural heritage. The majority of these we interviewed (n=28) identified as Kikuyu, Kenya's most populous ethnic group [25]. Finally, all but two participants expressed a desire to permanently return to Kenya in the future. Kenya remained "home" for these individuals.

Methods: We began interviews with questions about how long participants had lived in the U.S., about their motivations for coming to the country and to describe home. Following these initial questions we asked them about the technologies they regularly used. We intentionally used the term "technology" to understand how participants defined it, rather than us defining it for them. Then we shifted our focus to inquiring about how often participants communicated with friends, family members, and in some cases co-workers in Kenya. We asked them to describe the last time they communicated with someone in Kenya and to tell us what ICT they used and why. Interviews concluded with a series of questions about specific activities (e.g., photosharing) and specific practices (e.g., emailing and using Facebook).

We complemented our interviews with observations at 11 weekly worship services and social events at the church. These events included Mother's and Father's Day celebrations, Easter lunch and the church's annual "Cultural Show." Digital photographs were taken to document our observations. These occasions provided us with informal times to learn about how participants use ICT and talking about the events helped us build rapport with them during interviews. The first author generated field notes following each Sunday service to document her observations.

Reflexive Analysis: Recently, Rode has called for more "reflexivity" in CSCW/HCI research employing ethnographic methods [32]. In the context of social research, reflexivity refers to the ways in which the products of research are affected by the process of doing research [8]. It becomes more pressing for CSCW/HCI scholars to reflect on their relationships with individuals under study, particularly now that they are investigating users who are not necessarily members of these research communities. We briefly examine how the first author's presence as a non-Kenyan, white, and female researcher, affected participant recruitment. Given that she was often the only white-skinned and non-Kenyan individual at many of the services she attended, her presence drew attention. The first author asked a trusted informant to comment on her presence at the services and she replied:

> We spend Monday through Saturday in *your world* and Sunday is the only day of the week for us to be in *our world.*

"Your world" referred to settings where the majority of people were like the first author in terms of their nationality and skin color. Our informant implied that Sunday was different because it was the only day of the week when she was in an environment with other people "like her," or other native Kenyans. She added that members of the church were skeptical of "outsiders" and what they might want. This skepticism reflected a tension the first author felt when recruiting participants. On one hand, people welcomed her; indeed, churches are places where anyone can join in fellowship and worship with others. On the other hand, she was an outsider and her presence appeared to cause suspicion among some members. For example, some individuals appeared uneasy when she approached them to be interviewed. Thus, she decided to not interview them and instead focused her attention on those who were interested in the research.

Men were more willing than women to participate in our study. This difference is reflected in our skewed sample (27 men and 12 women) and could be attributed to the nature of our research. Participants often told us technology was a topic men knew more about than women.

Analysis: Our findings are based on 39 transcribed interviews, 58 photographs and 80 pages of field notes. We supplemented these data with memos documenting our thoughts and reflections about the themes emerging in our transcriptions. The constant comparative method guided our data analysis in conjunction with reading literature from CSCW, Human-Computer Interaction for Development (HCI4D) and transnational studies [15]. We also consulted with the minister of the church where our study took place on three occasions to discuss and verify themes appearing in our data. He recently completed a dissertation examining Kenyan immigrants in the U.S. [14]. Given that he was an insider and expert on Kenyans living in Atlanta his insights were invaluable during our data analysis process.

FINDINGS

The interviews with participants and our observations at the church revealed consistent patterns about Kenyan migrants ICT practices. In this section we describe these patterns and detail why participants preferred mobile phones to other technologies when communicating with people in Kenya. Then we shift our attention to specific ICT practices: photosharing, social networking and help-seeking (i.e., family members looking for assistance with how to use computer applications).

Our findings reveal how infrastructural differences between the U.S. and Kenya and high costs affect decisions families and their extended members make when using ICT. Further, as we elaborate on in our discussion, we contend that examining this transnational context reveals how some assumptions in CSCW work are not universal and highlights new design opportunities.

Overview of Participants' ICT Practices

All interviewees told us they used a variety of methods, such as mobile phone calls, email, social networking sites (SNS), mobile text messages, and sending packages to connect with friends and family in Kenya. Some forms of communication were more common than others and whether or not participants' family members lived in a rural or urban area affected their choices. Those with friends and family living in Kenya's capital, Nairobi, were more likely to use email and SNS, compared to those with family members living in rural "villages," where Internet access and electricity were often limited. There was significant diversity in terms of how often people communicated, how satisfied they were with their communications and how long or detailed each communication tended to be.

Communication Patterns: Despite these variations a typical routine of communication emerged among participants in which the migrant made weekly telephone calls to people in Kenya. Like prior studies indicate, due to the significant cost differences, calls nearly always originated from the U.S. [7,38]. At the time of our study, it was less expensive for migrants to call Kenya, than for their family members to call the U.S. Participants told us family members would "flash" them if they wanted them to call them in Kenya. Flashing is identical to "beeping," and it is when a person calls a mobile telephone number and then hangs up before the mobile's owner can pick up the call [9]. It is a free way to alert someone that you would like him or her to call you.

Participants most often described calling their mothers; indeed, in many cases it was the mother's responsibility to relay information from the family member living abroad to other family members in Kenya. If participants were not calling their mothers, they were likely calling their wives, siblings, friends from primary school, or in some cases business partners who oversaw participants' projects overseas. Examples of these projects include building a home or running a charitable organization. Participants' conversations typically centered on individual updates, changes in the weather, agriculture, politics, marriages, newborn babies and people who passed away.

Calls usually lasted no more than half an hour due to the cost of calling Kenya from the U.S. As one participant told us, it is "important not to get carried away when talking on the phone," because "the next thing you know $10 is gone." Pre-paid telephone cards and online services such as "VIP communications"[1] were significant parts of participants' strategies for maintaining contact while also monitoring the amount of money spent calling home.

ICT Preferences: Prior CSCW research examining communication between remote family members suggests VMC is "ubiquitous" and "mundane" [23]. We asked participants about their experiences with VMC technologies such as Skype. Three participants told us they used Skype to communicate with friends and family in Kenya. These individuals used the software application to talk with individuals who had access to higher bandwidth Internet. These exchanges often took place in their relatives' workplaces in Nairobi, rather than their homes. Domestic Internet access remains uncommon throughout Kenya [42]. Most people we interviewed did not use VMC technologies and many were unfamiliar with this ICT.

Like prior studies indicate, time zone differences and knowledge about peoples' daily routines abroad affected when participants called home [7,38]. It was cause for concern if these patterns were violated, or if participants called home at inappropriate times. For example:

> You have to know don't call them too late and don't expect them to call you, unless it is an emergency. So we have that understanding. When you get like a 3 o'clock call, you know it is a death and you really don't want that. When they call during the day you know things are good.

As noted earlier mobile telephone calls were the most common method participants used to connect with friends and family in Kenya. There were various reasons individuals preferred the mobile phone to email and SNS, but the real-time "direct" contact phones offered was the most common reason. A father and professional photographer told us about using his phone to supervise the construction of a house he was building in his home village:

> *Interviewer:* Do you go back to Kenya to supervise the construction?
>
> *Participant:* No, I have some dependable people doing the work. Email takes time for me, I don't like that, I would rather talk to you direct, so they call me during every step.

More than two-thirds of our participants preferred the phone because it was a more efficient way to communicate compared to email:

> I prefer the phone because some people might take some time before they go to check their emails. Like myself I take two to three days before I check the email so if it is something urgent then I wouldn't have been of any help to send email.

The "access, anywhere and anytime" usage style that shapes ICT use in the U.S. is not as widespread in Kenya where high-speed, easily accessible Internet access is not less common [42]. Many participants knew sending an email to someone in Kenya might mean waiting weeks for a response. Nearly every interviewee shared instances of sending emails and never receiving a reply. Reasons participants gave for slow response times centered on some family members' lack of domestic Internet access.

Others told us "email was not that important" to some of their friends and family abroad. When we asked them to elaborate on this, they consistently told us the urgency surrounding sending and replying to emails that many had become accustomed to in the U.S. was less common in Kenya. There were also fewer barriers for using the mobile phone compared to email. Sending and receiving email requires general computer literacy skills that some participants' friends and family members lacked.

We were struck by how our findings offered a counter narrative to some prevailing thinking in CSCW. Like Johri's research, our results suggest that email is not irreplaceable in communication and collaboration [19]. Our participants effectively maintained relationships with family members abroad without relying on email or VMC technologies. Some interviewees oversaw complex projects

[1] http://www.joinvip.com/

such as building a home or managing a charitable organization, solely relying on the mobile phone.

Cost is a significant factor for Kenyan migrants and their families. It affected the frequency and length of their conversations with family members. Further, costs indirectly affected other forms of communication, such as VMC, because high prices make domestic Internet access, personal computers, and "smartphones" out of reach for many Kenyans [42].

ICT Practices: Photosharing, Identity Management, and Transnational Help-Seeking

Here we elaborate on our previous findings by examining participants' specific ICT practices. In the process of uncovering how Kenya migrants used and *did not* use ICT to share photos, we learned how "living between" Kenya and the U.S. affected the content they shared with family members abroad.

Photosharing: Prior research examining communication between extended family members suggests that sharing photographs is useful for maintaining feelings of connectedness among extended family members [24,36]. We asked our participants about their media sharing practices and found that 28 exchanged photos and other forms of media with friends and family abroad. However, they did not always rely on ICT to support these interactions.

During our observations at worship services we repeatedly saw parishioners taking photographs with digital cameras. When special events, such as a guest singer or baptism took place, the sanctuary was full of flashing lights. We asked participants about what we saw and these responses were representative of many:

> It is important to send pictures home so they can see how you are changing, because it will be a long time before you go home, sometimes two years, three years.

Or

> I love taking pictures because a picture, that is a memory. I can track back my past and my progress.

Participants often used the term "progress" when talking about photographs. We learned that photos were used to document and communicate how migrants were acclimating to life in a new country. Photographs of significant events (e.g., weddings, baptisms, graduations and birthdays) were common and appeared especially useful for communicating that one was becoming "adjusted" to life in the U.S.

> That is the kind of pictures they would like to see. So, celebrations, weddings, and maybe if, for example, if I bought a new car, I would send them a picture of the new car. So all those that are celebration related are sent.

Studies examining digital photo sharing reveal that families exchange images through email because it is accessible and offers ongoing text conversation around shared photos [24].

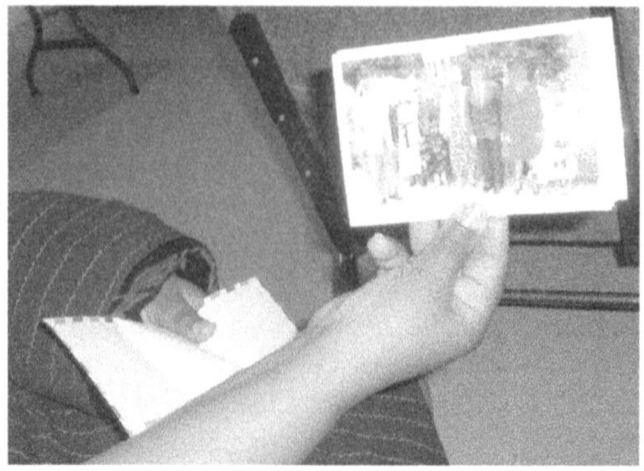

Figure 1. Participant showing us pictures she is sending home. Note the "airmail envelope" in her left hand.

We asked participants if they used the Internet to send digital pictures to Kenya. Those with family members living in Nairobi told us they used email and in some cases Facebook to share pictures. It was more common for participants to rely on non-digital forms of exchange (Fig. 1). For example, many interviewees asked a member of their church to carry paper photos or a CD with them when returning to Kenya:

> Mostly I give them to people who are going home, every time there is someone going home I give them photographs.

The church's minister estimated that during any given week at least one member of his congregation travelled to Kenya. Participants told us their family members would typically meet the person delivering the pictures in the Nairobi airport. Recipients would hold a sign indicating they were to receive the package coming from the U.S. Others relied on courier services to send packages to their relatives living outside of the capital. When we probed to understand why this form of exchange was used instead of email, we were consistently told it was "easier."

> This is how we do it—I can put those in the envelope and send. I find it much easier. You know why? In my country, the Internet is so expensive, even to receive and to send they pay.

Again cost was a factor that affected participants' interactions with friends and family abroad. Sending photo attachments via email often meant the recipient had to visit a cyber café and pay for using a computer with limited bandwidth. Downloading and uploading digital photos could take hours and result in the recipient spending more money.

Tee et al.'s research suggests the overhead associated with sharing photos is too high for some families [36]. In other words, the process of organizing, downloading, and uploading photos to send family members creates new demands on individuals' time. This did not appear to be a concern with our participants who engaged in additional forms of digital "photowork" such as packing pictures and determining who will transport them to Kenya [24].

Our findings reveal how the Internet has not completely displaced communication by exchanging material artifacts. They also highlight how non-digital forms of technology are used to maintain feelings of connectedness between extended families. There are daily flights between Atlanta and Nairobi and tese played an important role in facilitating photosharing among our participants.

Identity Management: Processes of immigration and globalization lead to new "third identities" that represent complex and shifting hybridizations of earlier cultures [10]. Our participants noted how living between two countries, or as one participant described it as "being a child of two worlds," affected their daily lives. It is now commonplace in the literature on globalization to observe that in a context of increasing cultural intermixing, individuals and cultures tend to hybridize, but it is less clear how this hybridization shapes ICT use [10]. When asking participants about photosharing we discovered how this hybridization affected their ICT practices.

During interviews we asked participants who used social networking sites to tell us about their experiences with them. Facebook was the most commonly mentioned site; indeed, as one young woman excitedly told us, "Facebook is becoming very big in Kenya!" Members of this online community reported having friends in the U.S. and in Kenya and that where their friends lived affected what information they shared online. For example:

> *Participant*: Like if it is my family photos, there are some photos that I can send to some people, and there are some photos that I can't send to some people.
>
> *Interviewer*: Can you give me an example?
>
> *Participant*: An example is like, you know, like when I take my family for swimming and they're in their swimming suit, we don't send those things back home.

This participant continued to tell us "things are more explicit in the U.S. than in Kenya," explaining that his parents would find pictures of his children in swimsuits "inappropriate."

Individuals acquire different cultural attitudes as they migrate, retaining parts of their culture of origin and adapting to their culture of adoption [10]. On one hand, this participant's decision to photograph his children swimming suggests he has adopted some aspects of the U.S.'s "more explicit" culture. On the other hand, his decision not to share the pictures with his family in Kenya reveals how he respects his parents' more conservative attitudes. These negotiations regarding photosharing manifested in other ways, for example:

> If I buy a new house I don't want to tell all my friends in Kenya I just got into my dream house. I would send a picture of it to my friends here, but not my friends in Kenya. Because you just want to be humble.

This 46-year old librarian, like other participants who experienced financial success in the U.S. was reluctant to discuss her prosperity with some family members in Kenya. This reluctance centered on two reasons. First, participants consistently described themselves as the "lucky ones," because they were able to come to the U.S. Many were able to achieve an income level that was out of reach to most people in Kenya. In turn, they did not want to appear boastful or not "humble." Second, many migrants were expected to send remittances to family members "back home. Although, participants described themselves as financially comfortable there were limits to the amount of support they could provide. Thus, they were guarded about displays of wealth because they might create unrealistic expectations about how much money they could send to family members in Kenya.

Within CSCW identity management remains a popular research topic [27]. Our findings point to opportunities to explore cultural norms affects computer-mediated communication within migrant communities, because it reveals additional negotiations users encounter online. Examining individuals whose social networks are comprised of people in the developed and developing worlds will also provide the CSCW researchers with a more holistic understanding of Facebook use. To date, prior studies tends take place with individuals who do not regularly communicate with friends and family in Africa.

Transnational Help-Seeking: Another finding from our research suggests that Kenyan migrants' interactions with family members in their home country include educating them about software applications and new ICT. Whether introducing them to SNS, or sending them money to purchase a mobile phone, participants introduced their family members in Kenya to technologies that are an integral part of their lives in U.S.

> I have a friend of mine, I talk to her on Facebook, I had to register her on Facebook and then, right now I am trying to get her to get Skype, but she is like 'oh, I can not do it, can you do it for me?'

Further, there were multiple instances of interviewees describing how they managed overseas family members' online accounts. This meant participants knew their family members' passwords. For example:

> Sometimes they will call me and ask, 'go to my inbox, and tell what is in my inbox,' so you have to go and check for them, and when you are talking to them on the phone you have to tell them.

American families frequently rely on extended member to help them with resolve domestic computer problems [31]. Our findings indicate this activity also occurs among families with members living overseas. In contrast to findings from other studies that suggest developing online applications for desktop or laptop computers, we propose the mobile phone as a platform for creating applications to assist computer support activities among families like those we studied. Exploring and developing such applications has the potential to broaden online participation among users in developing countries. Our finding also supports those from other studies suggesting attitudes about sharing passwords may be culturally specific and reveals the limitations of contemporary password policies [2].

DISCUSSION: SUPPORTING AND LEARNING FROM KENYAN MIGRANTS' ICT PRACTICES

Our findings point to factors designers should consider when developing computing applications that support communication between families. High-speed Internet access is not always available, digital forms of exchange have not replaced material forms, infrastructural differences between rural and urban parts of developing countries, and cost must be considered when designing systems for families in some transnational contexts. Here we elaborate on how these factors can shape design and the discourse surrounding technology development for family communication. We suggest ways to design (and not to design) for this context. Our discussion also describes what families living in countries where Internet access is easily available, fast, and relatively inexpensive can learn from Kenyan migrants.

Prior research examining communication between extended family members offers new ways for them to communicate that take advantage of the high bandwidth and faster Internet speeds available to many in North America and Europe [20,23].This research motivates new systems that allow distributed families to experience always-on video connection between their households [21,34]. In contrast, to these high-tech forms of exchange we found low-tech ways families maintained feelings of connectedness with family members who sometimes lacked electricity, personal computers, and Internet access. Participants in our study viewed keeping in touch with their family members as worthy of their time and money. It was an activity that required a level of dedication that becomes less necessary with the easily accessibly tools that some North American and European users increasingly rely on to communicate with extended family members.

It will be some time before a technology infrastructure exists throughout Kenya that supports effective VMC [1,18,28]. Large-scale formal rural electrification is unlikely to extend into the interior parts of Kenya, personal computers, and smart phones remain too costly for many [18]. Thus, migrants are likely to continue to rely on mobile phones, courier services, and in some cases use computers to connect with relatives. Many of these computers will be located in cyber cafés rather their relatives' homes. These constraints mean systems like the Family Window [21] are impossible for some of our participants to use with their family members.

Opportunities Not to Design: Our investigation prompted us to consider less tech-centric ways to address issues uncovered in our research [4]. Novel interfaces that provide users with greater privacy control or systems that require greater bandwidth were not applicable for participants with family members in rural Kenya. Instead, increasing family communication could be achieved through changing tariffs, subsidies for poor communities, special energy projects, improved access to computers and educating users about existing applications [22]. For example, we identified an opportunity to increase awareness among our participants and their family members in Kenya about the availability of VMC technologies such as Skype.

Cost was a consistent factor participants discussed. This finding suggests imagining systems that build on and improve users' current money exchange practices so those living in Kenya could have the resources to access the Internet at cyber cafés. To date, the popular mobile phone based money transfer service M-Pesa can not be used to exchange money between migrants living in the U.S. and their family members in Kenya [17]. Rather than designing new domestic communication technologies researchers may want to consider ways to make existing ones available to a wider number of users. In turn, this may promote more balanced development between developed and developing countries rather that continuing to perpetuate inequities between them [22].

Designing Within Constraints: Designing for constrained environments is more challenging than designing for ones where Internet access is always on and always accessible. Constraints force designers to think beyond developing applications and features that simply require more bandwidth and faster Internet connections.

An audio enhanced paper photograph is a simple and straightforward design example illustrating how technology can respond to participants with family members living in places with a technology infrastructure that differs from what exists in Atlanta [12]. One could imagine recording a message using a device embedded in a paper photograph or postcard to accompany a photo from a birthday or graduation and then sending it to Kenya. Listening to a family members' voices was another reason participants preferred mobile phone calls to email. These artifacts could also easily be included in packages and hand delivered home.

ICT for Other Families: Findings from our study also prompted us to reflect on what the families studied in prior CSCW/HCI research could learn from our participants. For example, Judge et al.'s work suggests families want more computer-mediated way to connect with extended family members [21]. In contrast, we imagine providing these families with less ways to use computing to connect. The introduction of more computing into families' lives brings with it new concerns and obligations families must negotiate. Examples include, demands on parents' time, concerns regarding privacy and anxieties around children having too much "screen time" [3,36].

Our participants appeared to be less concerned about these issues because costs and infrastructural issues sometimes restricted their interactions with family members they valued them in ways that have been overlooked in prior CSCW/HCI studies. Those we interviewed looked forward to their weekly conversations with family members in Kenya. Rather than developing new ways for families to communicate that rely on increased bandwidth, it may be worthwhile to understand how to make families' existing interactions with extended family members more valued.

For example, instead of developing applications that alert extended family members about each other's availability, we imagine creating systems that encourage chats on a weekly basis in hopes that doing so would make the activity seem like a special occasion. VMC could take place during ritualized family events such as Sunday dinners. This would mean communication would occur during a dedicated and scheduled time. Like those we interviewed, we hope this would appease family members' desires to stay connected and eliminate the need for always-on systems that support sharing impromptu moments. Thus, by making communication a weekly event rather than something that happens continually we hope to lessen the sense of obligations some families report having [3,36].

FUTURE WORK AND CONCLUSION

In this paper we describe how Kenyan migrants communicate with family members living in a country with a technology infrastructure that is less developed than those in the U.S. and U.K. Our findings reveal how inconsistent Internet access, limited bandwidth, high costs, and identity management affect transnational communication. We use these findings to suggest new research opportunities for the CSCW community, such as studying Facebook use within a transnational context. Such research would broaden the community's understanding of how SNS facilitate communication between users in developed and developing countries. We also propose alternative ways for technology developers to imagine systems designed to support family communication that do not require faster Internet connections and more bandwidth.

In our future work we will elaborate on another important issues noted in our paper—reflexivity in CSCW research using. The scope of this paper prevents us from providing more details about how our race, religious identity, and other factors affected our data collection and analysis. We conclude that reflexivity is a topic that merits further disussion in CSCW research. Our future research plans also include conducting fieldwork in urban and rural Kenya with the family members of those we interviewed in Atlanta to understand ICT use from their perspectives.

ACKNOWLEDGMENTS

We are grateful to Dr. G.G. Gitahi and members of his church for welcoming us into their congregation and for sharing their stories with us. Thank you to Morgan Ames, Jenna Burrell, Marshini Chetty, Aditya Johri, Erika Poole, Jennifer Rode, and anonymous reviewers for feedback on earlier drafts of this paper. Grants from the Intel Research Council and the NSF/CRA Computing Innovation Fellows program supported this research.

REFERENCES

1. "East Africa Gets Broadband: It May Make Life Easier and Cheaper," *The Economist*, June 20, 2009.
2. Alsheikh, T., Rode, J.A. and Lindley, S., "(Whose) Value-Sensitive Design: a Study of Long-Distance Relationships in an Arabic Cultural Context," *Proc. of CSCW'11*, ACM (2011), 75-84.
3. Ames, M.G., Go, J., Kaye, J. and Spasojevic, M., "Making Love in the Network Closet: The Benefits and Work of Family Videochat," *Proc. of CSCW'10*, ACM (2010), 145-154.
4. Baumer, E.P.S. and Silberman, M.S., "When the Implication is Not to Design (Technology)," *Proc. of CHI'11*, ACM (2011), 2271-2274.
5. Bodie, R., "Entrepreneurial Spirit Brings Africans here: Growth Points to Bright Future," *The Atlanta Journal Constitution*, Atlanta, 2003.
6. Burrell, J. and Anderson, K., "'I have great desires to look beyond my world': Trajectories of Information and Communication Technology use among Ghanaians Living Abroad," *New Media & Society 10*, 2 (2008), 203-224.
7. Cao, X., Sellen, A., Bernheim Brush, A.J., Kirk, D., Edge, D. and Ding, X., "Understanding Family Communication Across Time Zones," *Proc. of CSCW'10*, ACM (2010), 155-159.
8. Davies, C.A., *Reflexive Ethnography: A Guide to Researching Selves and Others*. Routledge, London, 2002.
9. Donner, J., "The Rules of Beeping: Exchanging messages via intentional "missed calls" on mobile phones," *Journal of Computer-Mediated Communication 13*, 1 (2008), 1-22.
10. Ess, C. and Sudweeks, F., "Culture and Computer-Mediated Communication: Toward New Understandings," *Journal of Computer-Mediated Communication 11*, 1 (2006), 179-191.
11. Ford, D.M., "Technologizing Africa: On the Bumpy Information Highway," *Computers & Composition 24* (2007), 302-316.
12. Frohlich, D.M., *Audiophotography: Bringing Photos to Life with Sounds*. Springer, 2004.
13. Gaver, W.W., "Affordances for Interaction: The Social is Material for Design," *Ecological Psychology 8*, 2 (1996), 111-129.
14. Gitahi, G.G. *Missiological and Cultural Implications For Kenyan Immigrants in the U.S.: A Case Study of Kenyan Immigrants in Metro Atlanta, Georgia*. PhD

dissertation, Reformed Theological Seminary, Jackson, Mississippi, 2005.

15. Glasser, B.G. and Strauss, A.L., *The Discovery of Grounded Theory: Strategies for Qualitative Research.* Aldine Publishing Company, Hawthorne, NY, 1967.

16. Hindus, D., Mainwaring, S.D., Leduc, N., Hagström, A.E. and Bayley, O., "Casablanca: Designing Social Communication Devices for the Home," *Proc. of CHI '01*, ACM (2001), 325-332.

17. Hughes, N. and Lonie, S., "M-PESA: Mobile Money for the 'Unbanked' Turning Cellphones into 24-Hour Tellers in Kenya," *Innovations, 2*, 1-2 (2007), 63-81.

18. Jacobson, A., "Connective Power: Solar Electrification and Social Change in Kenya," *World Development 35*, 1 (2007), 144-162.

19. Johri, A., "Look Ma, No Email! Blogs and IRC as Primary and Preferred Communication Tools in a Distributed Firm," *Proc. of CSCW'11*, ACM (2011), 305-308.

20. Judge, T.K. and Neustaedter, C., "Sharing Conversation and Sharing Life: Video Conferencing in the Home," *Proc. of CHI'10*, ACM (2010), 655-658.

21. Judge, T.K., Neustaedter, C. and Kurtz, A.F., "The Family Window: The Design and Evaluation of a Domestic Media Space," *Proc. of CHI'10*, ACM (2010), 2361-2370.

22. Kelly, T., "Beyond the three billion mark," *id21 insights*, 69 (2007).

23. Kirk, D., Sellen, A. and Cao, X., "Home Video Communication: Mediating 'Closeness'," *Proc. of CSCW '10*, ACM (2010), 135-144.

24. Kirk, D.S., Sellen, A.J., Rother, C. and Wood, K.R., "Understanding Photowork," *Proc. of CHI '06*, ACM (2006), 761-770.

25. Konado-Agyeman, K., Takyi, B.K. and Arthur, J.A. (eds.), *The New African Diaspora in North America: Trends, Community Building, and Adaptation.* Lexington Books, Latham, MD, 2006.

26. Kwakye-Nuako, K., "Still Praisin' God in a New Land: African Immigrant Christianity in North America," in Konado-Agyeman, K., Takyi, B.K. and Arthur, J.A. (eds.), *The New African Diaspora in North America: Trends, Community Building, and Adaptation*, Lexington Books, Latham, MD, 2006, 121-139.

27. Lampe, C., Ellison, N.B. and Steinfield, C., "Changes in Use and Perception of Facebook," *Proc. of CSCW'08*, ACM (2008), 721-730.

28. Mwiti, L., "Sea Cable Ushers in New Internet Era," *The Daily Nation,* July 23, 2009.

29. Odera, L., *Kenyan Immigrants in the United States: Acculturation, Coping Strategies, and Mental Health.* LFB Scholarly Publishing, 2010.

30. Pew Forum on Religion & Public Life, *Spirit and Power: A 10-Country Survey of Pentecostals*. Pew Research Center, Washington, DC, 2006.

31. Poole, E.S., Chetty, M., Morgan, T., Grinter, R.E. and Edwards, W.K., "Computer Help at Home: Methods and Motivations for Informal Technical Support," *Proc. of CHI'09*, ACM (2009), 1-10.

32. Rode, J., "Reflexivity in Digital Anthropology," *Proc. of CHI'11*, ACM (2011), 123-132.

33. Romero, N., Markopoulos, P., J., v.B., de Ruyter, B., Ijsselsteijn, W. and Farshchain, B., "Connecting the family with awareness systems," *Personal and Ubiquitous Computing 11*, 4 (2007), 299-312.

34. Sellen, A., Harper, R., Eardley, R., Izadi, S., Regan, T., Taylor, A.S. and Wood, K.R., "HomeNote: Supporting Situated Messaging in the Home," *Proc. of CSCW'06*, ACM (2006), 383-392.

35. Takougang, J., "Contemporary African Immigrants to The United States," *Irinkerindo: A Journal of African Migration, 2* (2009).

36. Tee, K., Brush, A.J.B. and Inkpen, K.M., "Exploring Communication and Sharing Between Extended Families," *International Journal of Human-Computer Studies 67*, 2 (2009), 128-138.

37. Wang, H.-C., Fussell, S.R. and Setlock, L.D., "Cultural Difference and Adaptation of Communication Styles in Computer-Mediated Group Brainstorming," *Proc. of CHI '09*, ACM (2009), 669-678.

38. Wilding, R., "'Virtual' intimacies? Families communicating across transnational contexts," *Global Networks 6*, 2 (2006), 125-142.

39. Williams, A., Dourish, P. and Anderson, K., "Anchored Mobilities: Mobile Technology and Transnational Migration," *Proc. of DIS '08*, ACM (2008), 323-332

40. Wilson, J., African-born Residents of the United States. Institute, *Migration Policy Institute,* 2003.

41. Wyche, S.P., Hayes, G.R., Harvel, L.D. and Grinter, R.E., "Technology in Spiritual Formation: An Exploratory Study of Computer Mediated Religious Communications," *Proc. CSCW'06*, ACM (2006), 199-208.

42. Wyche, S.P., Smyth, T.N., Chetty, M., Aoki, P.M. and Grinter, R.E., "Deliberate Interactions: Characterizing Technology Use in Nairobi, Kenya," *Proc. of CHI'10*, ACM (2010), 2593-2602.

43. Zachary, G.P. Inside Nairobi, the Next Palo Alto? *The New York Times*, 2008.

Adapting Collaborative Radiological Practice to Low-Resource Environments

Beth E. Kolko[1], Alexis Hope[1], Waylon Brunette[2], Karen Saville[1], Wayne Gerard[2], Rob Nathan[3]

[1]Dept. of Human Centered Design & Engineering
University of Washington
Seattle, WA USA 98195
{bkolko, alexishg, ksaville,}@uw.edu

[2]Dept. of Computer Science & Engineering
University of Washington
Seattle, WA USA 98195
{wrb, wayneg}@cse.uw.edu

[3]Dept. of Radiology
University of Washington
Seattle, WA USA 98195
ronathan@uw.edu

ABSTRACT

We describe how current radiological best practices are predicated on a sophisticated technological ecosystem usually comprised of multiple large-scale displays, and integrated record keeping and communication systems driven by high-speed networks. At the same time, current development of low-cost ultrasound (U/S) devices for low-resource settings trends towards small-scale, independent devices with palm-sized screens. We reviewed existing literature, analyzed findings from two years of fieldwork in Uganda, and conducted an interview study with clinicians about radiology work practices to determine which patterns and technologies contribute to the efficacy of ultrasound. We use these findings to inform how ultrasound technology in low-resource settings can most usefully be developed and deployed. In addition, findings are relevant for creating medical technologies for low-resource environments generally, as we make clear the importance of considering not just technology development aspects like power consumption and interface, but also larger technology and work ecosystems.

Author Keywords

ICTD, Radiology information systems, PACS, Professional practice, Teleradiology, Medicine, CSCW

ACM Classification Keywords

H5.m. Information interfaces and presentation (e.g., HCI): Miscellaneous.

General Terms

Human Factors; Design.

INTRODUCTION

There is a growing interest in how low-cost medical technologies can be developed and deployed in low-resource settings to improve global health indicators. Tools such as low-cost, point-of-care technologies (e.g. microfluidic diagnostic systems [35], mobile phone based microscopes [4], and phone-based cough detection [17]) have inspired new research approaches and interdisciplinary research communities. This global health research community shares many of its approaches with the information and communication technologies for development (ICTD) field, an emerging area of research focused on using computer-based solutions to address problems facing developing regions and underserved populations, including problems associated with collaborative practices in the workplace. In addition to healthcare applications, ICTD projects focus on a wide variety of problem spaces, such as education, agriculture, microfinance, and transportation [1, 11, 18, 24, 33]. Many lessons have been drawn from the successes and failures of ICTD research, most of which emphasize the importance of creating and deploying technologies that recognize the physical settings in which people live and work [2, 7, 20]. For example, ICTD researchers have identified a common set of design and computing constraints such as cost, low power, low connectivity, low literacy, multiple or marginalized languages, and accessibility challenges [12].

In addition to design issues focused on technological artifacts, researchers in the ICTD community have also learned to design with a focus on people and diverse usage contexts. Such work tends to be informed by social construction of technology and appropriate technology literature [26, 13]. Appropriate technology literature advocates for design that meets ethical, cultural, social, political and economic standards in the community for which it is intended. Leveraging existing systems, processes, and resources rather than trying to introduce radically new ones can help researchers design and deploy appropriate technology.

Our work builds on these foundations, in addition to central HCI literature and scholarship on design for resource-constrained environments [16, 19]. In addition, our work has been informed by the central concerns of the CSCW community, including work practices, place and space, and articulation work [34, 9, 29]. To this end, we have built our research with a focus on the differences in group work and socio-technological barriers that come to bear on ultrasound usage, and we expand upon notions of CSCW in Western-country contexts to users in developing regions.

For the past two years, informed by fieldwork in Uganda and the theoretical traditions mentioned above, we have been designing a portable maternal ultrasound (U/S) system for midwives in the developing world. Midwives—trusted and central figures within Uganda's existing healthcare system—are an appropriate audience for our system as they are the critical link between rural healthcare centers and referral hospitals that offer more comprehensive treatment options. It is our goal that this system (called the Ultrasound PLUS, — Portable, Learning- and User-centered System) will leverage Uganda's existing referral network and ensure that women with high-risk obstetrical (OB) conditions receive appropriate follow-up care. The Ultrasound PLUS also features an integrated Help system.

In our past work, we have tried to build technologies that adapt to existing patterns of trust and confidence, information-seeking practices, and technology usage within communities [27]. The consideration of workplace collaboration, however, is an additional constraint. Indeed, often missing from existing ICTD research and practice is an understanding of how technology-based work practices are affected when the technological ecology of those practices is changed. Collaboration that is not explicitly part of a job often provides a crucial means of domain learning, task efficiency, and general enculturation. Whether or not a technology supports these hidden work practices [30] can impact the success of an intervention.

U/S is widely used in the developed world. However, these contexts almost exclusively have multiple practitioners, technology-centric work practices, and multiple communication tools. Prior CSCW work in the medical domain speaks to such characteristics by exploring issues of information workflow and adapting interfaces, highlighting face-to-face communication, and the complexity of information needs as drivers of multi-layered collaboration [28]. Health specialists, operating under the strain of complex and ambiguous information flows, must continuously engage in group sense-making to collectively interpret and take action on patient data [25]. These teams utilize rapid feedback, shared context, and exposure to nuanced information for collective decision-making [23].

CSCW patterns, like those mentioned above, emerge in part from the interplay between technologies in place and work practices [8]. Our work with low-cost U/S recognizes that we cannot replicate all of the characteristics of work practice and space seen in developed world settings, and our design efforts must recognize and compensate for the changes in the larger technology ecology. Design in low-resource contexts poses unique challenges in assessing the patterns of relationships between a physical space and socio-technical conditions in which tools are used. In particular, new issues surrounding the role of mobile U/S technology arise; as circuits of mobility intersect and overlap in space [9], traditional midwifery work practices, patterns of trust, and power dynamics are altered.

In developing medical technologies for low-resource environments, the ICTD community has well-established techniques for adapting technologies. But less attention is paid to work context—how technical functionality actually scaffolds certain work practices, and this area is one we emphasize in our approach. To this end, our designs compensate for limited collaboration potential by building a novel medical help system within the U/S device and supporting existing work practices with minimal interference to the workflow.

BACKGROUND

The ecology and practice of midwifery in Uganda has provided substantial opportunities to rethink conventional workflow models and explore how to bypass resource constraints. Ultrasound—a medical imaging modality used in obstetric care—can be used to identify a variety of conditions that contribute to obstructed labor and hemorrhage at birth. However, we are trying to design a project that deploys ultrasound not just to generic best medical effect, but to best effect given the conditions of maternal care in Uganda.

The work presented in this paper reflects an ethnomethodological approach; researchers such as Brigitte Jordan have also investigated complex, non-Western obstetrics, unearthing the vastly different collaboration patterns that occur in developing-context medicine [14]. In stark contrast to institutionalized medical collaboration in Western medicine, maternal care decisions in developing contexts involve input from a wide spectrum of invested community and family members. These insights help us situate the process of building a technological artifact within those mapped cultural and theoretical concerns.

Our project is affiliated with a larger project within the University of Washington department of Radiology which has been training Ugandan midwives to perform diagnostic U/S exams using commercial stationary U/S devices and portable machines such as the GE LOGIQ Book XP (See Figure 1, Left). Initial work by researchers involved with this project suggests that current commercial devices may be inappropriate for widespread deployment in the developing world [5], and so we sought to design a more appropriate U/S machine (see Figure 1, Right). Our system is built from off-the-shelf technology using a USB probe and a convertible tablet PC.

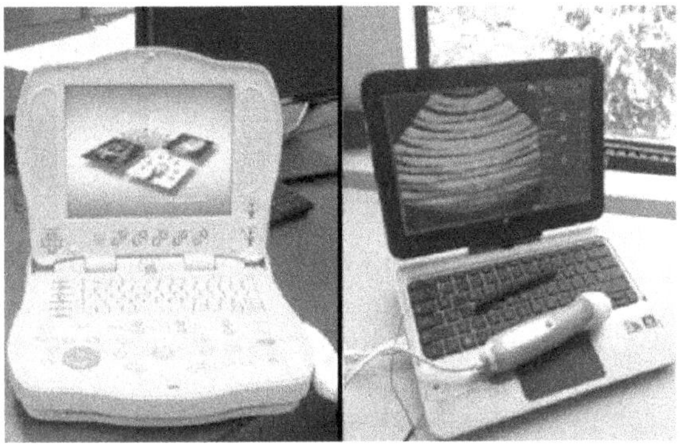

Figure 1. GE LOGIQ Book XP (left) and Ultrasound PLUS (right). The hardware and UIs differ.

Stationary ultrasound devices, used most commonly for obstetric care in the developed world, generally have advanced features that accommodate a variety of patients and medical conditions, but they are neither power- nor cost-efficient. Current low-cost U/S devices (e.g. GE V-Scan, Mobisante) tend to be small, independent devices with palm-sized screens. Additionally, most U/S devices are designed for advanced medical professionals in hospitals; these devices have complex user interfaces (UIs) and advanced features meant for expert users. They also lack robust help systems. In the United States, a typical U/S technician must undergo training for two years or more [6], which is not feasible for midwives in the developing world due to cost and mobility constraints.

Our design approach has been to reduce functionality to only that which is necessary to detect basic pregnancy complications: depth control, near- mid- and far-gain control, and contrast. Additionally, we have developed an integrated, contextual Help system that guides midwives through best practices in diagnostic U/S, and, through decision trees, assists them in making a diagnosis. The Help system also includes a built-in gallery of images taken by professional sonographers with which midwives can compare their current image. This portion of the design comes from the recognition, through fieldwork and observation, that work settings and training programs in Uganda differ from those in developed world settings.

In other words, our goal is to build an U/S machine that is not only an appropriate technology in terms of the physical design, but one that also matches the constraints on workplace collaboration and cooperation. Some of the questions we address in this paper include: How important is collaboration in the use of U/S? Are there diagnostic or treatment practices that are reliant on the technology ecosystem to the extent that we will not be able to replicate them with our U/S system? Where do radiologists compensate for technologies that don't do what they need? How would they adapt practice if they lost these tools? For more experienced radiologists/sonographers, etc, how does their memory of less technologized work environments compare to current practice?

To answer these questions, we draw on existing literature, two years of fieldwork in Uganda, and an interview study in Seattle to compare the U/S technology ecosystem in Uganda and in the United States. This knowledge will help us design a technology that accommodates differences in work practice and context, and that can be usefully deployed in low-resource settings.

UNDERSTANDING RADIOLOGICAL PRACTICE

Radiologists in the United States rely heavily on picture archiving and communication systems technologies (PACS), which allow them to store and retrieve images, communicate with other radiologists and clinicians, and display and process medical imaging data [11]. As images have transitioned from physical to digital artifacts, they have become distributed across invested medical personnel, allowing each of them greater understanding of how to interpret images. Three-dimensional imaging made it possible to bring multiple images into a single, online volume, simultaneously simplifying and allowing for more sophisticated analysis. The introduction of digital imaging allowed other members of the clinical team to cover traditional radiological tasks, enabling radiologists to invest more time in developing specialized radiological skills. PACS changed the collaboration patterns between radiologists and referring physicians, making that relationship more mediated technologically but also allowing for more collaborative interpretation of imagery.

Other researchers have performed ethnographic studies on the collaborative work practices surrounding PACS to understand the shaping effects of spatial arrangements on work practices. Much of this research focuses on spatial approaches to collaboration by studying work practice and work location, analysis of physical arrangement, and ordering of space in supportive of cooperative work [31]. Our work expands on this discussion by adding a comparison of cooperative work practices in a developed world context using PACS and remote clinics in rural Africa in non-PACS environments.

Teleradiology, a subset of a larger practice called telemedicine, involves the asynchronous transfer of digital images between two or more settings and builds on the premise of PACS. In a teleradiology scenario, local actors typically conduct image acquisition tasks, and remote actors provide interpretive services and/or consultation. Though most studies of teleradiology focus primarily on technical issues, usability issues, or clinical patient outcomes, the work practices surrounding teleradiology have also been the subject of previous CSCW analysis [15]. Karasti, for example, found that teleradiology increased the amount of articulation work done by radiologists as they had to ensure the teleradiology service ran smoothly. For instance, radiologists accustomed to traditional radiological models were used to receiving more contextual information about their patients than that which was typically part of a teleradiology system—including the patient's physical appearance and behavior—and sometimes had to request more information in order to make a confident diagnosis.

U/S—in part because of the ambiguity of the images—often requires more consultations between clinicians and radiologists than other imaging modalities. The need to collaboratively analyze, label and annotate U/S images means these teams rely heavily on robust interaction and consensus building. This two-way interaction ensures accurate image readings and provides the radiologist an opportunity to support the clinician in deciding which additional radiological tests are needed [36].

METHODOLOGY

Our methodology is composed of two pieces: 1) fieldwork in Uganda over the course of two years to understand the context of U/S use for midwives, and 2) interviews with sonographers, radiologists, and clinicians about their collaborative work practices and use of various technologies that enable collaboration. We combine these two approaches in order to demonstrate how the dramatic differences between the two work settings requires careful consideration of how to appropriately develop and deploy U/S technology for low-resource contexts.

Ugandan Fieldwork

Our work is affiliated with a larger project that began at the University of Washington department of Radiology in 2009. Team members from that project—including radiologists, radiology residents, and sonographers—have traveled frequently to Uganda to conduct program evaluations and field observations, including a November 2010 visit to six clinics which generated findings to inform our interview protocol for this study.

In early 2010, our design team surveyed midwives involved in an U/S training program taught by the Ernest Cook Ultrasound Research and Education Institute (ECUREI). Our surveys inquired about those midwives' experience and difficulty with learning current U/S technologies, what constitutes a typical U/S exam, and patient perceptions of healthcare in Ugandan communities [5]. The midwives' responses helped inform both the initial design choices for the U/S system, and the interview protocols we developed for future trips to the field.

In March and July of 2011, six members of our team traveled to Uganda to interview midwives involved in a pilot sonography training program, nursing and midwifery educators, maternal & child health advocates, a traditional birth attendant (TBA), and fifty-two rural mothers split across eight focus groups (results to be discussed in a future paper). Additionally, we visited 15 health centers (a mix of public, private, and private-not-for-profit models) in three districts in Western & Central Uganda to understand the variance in infrastructure, services offered, and patient load.

Below we discuss results from our interviews with midwives that focus on their current work practices and how the introduction of ultrasound is changing those work practices. We also observed the environment in which they conduct their exams and administrative duties, and we conducted usability tests with the current version of the Ultrasound PLUS prototype.

Interviews with Radiologists, Clinicians, and Sonographers

As part of our continuing efforts to understand the ways in which medical imaging supports clinical care, we conducted a total of seven semi-structured interviews with five doctors (three radiologists and two clinicians) and two sonographers in Seattle about their collaborative work practices and the various technologies that enable these collaborations. Participants' experience in the medical field ranged from 2 to 29 years. During some of the interviews we were able to conduct workplace observations of a trauma radiology center, and the U/S department of a large university hospital.

Doctors involved in our study have experience in public and private clinics, and urban and rural clinical settings. Three have experience in international settings. Medical specialties of our participants include trauma radiology, body imaging, family medicine, and high-risk OB. We chose to spread our interviews across the categories of radiologists, clinicians, and sonographers because the Ugandan midwives using U/S in our project act in all three of these roles when they use U/S with their patients.

FINDINGS

We have two groups of findings resulting from the Uganda and the United States fieldwork. This section discusses the themes that emerged from data-driven analyses of these two research activities, and it suggests opportunities for improving our current prototype system so that it better meets the needs of our target audience—midwives and other health workers in Uganda.

Clinical Sites in Uganda

Below is an aggregate example, based on our 2010-2011 interviews with midwives, that provides a scenario for radiological practice in a low-resource environment:

A midwife at a Level 3 Health Center (HC3) arrives in the morning to see women sitting on benches and on the grass surrounding the health clinics. Many women have brought pots of food and luggage with them, knowing that they may have to wait for care for several hours. Many also have small children sitting alongside. The midwife takes a few minutes to talk with all of the women about the benefits of prenatal care before taking one of them to an exam room for a clinical exam. The exam includes taking the patient's history, performing a palpation, and perhaps prescribing a prenatal malaria prophylaxis. Then, the woman is taken to a separate room (a smaller, darker room) for the ultrasound examination. The midwife uses ultrasound to determine the number of fetuses, the position of the fetuses (e.g. breech or heads-down), and the position of the placenta. She may also check for other anomalies and perform measurements. If she has questions, she can use one of her multiple cell-phones to attempt reach the experienced sonographer at the Level 4 Health Center (HC4); each cellphone holds a SIM card from a different provider, and no single provider has reliable coverage across the district. The midwife records the ultrasound findings in a patient history book that each patient carries with them to the health center. This information is also recorded in paper record books kept locally at the health center. If a pregnancy complication is found, or if the midwife has a question that she cannot resolve, the patient is referred to the HC4 for a follow-up ultrasound.

Solitary vs. Collaborative Practice

The majority of midwives interviewed (10 out of 12 participants) worked in clinics that employed two midwives and would have one midwife on duty per shift. At two of the five clinics we visited, we encountered other medical staff, including lab technicians and other nurses. The midwives, however, were the only health professionals trained to use the on-site portable U/S unit, meaning that midwives had few opportunities to ask anyone for help acquiring, optimizing, or interpreting U/S images. Midwives were only able to consult others with U/S expertise was the district's sonographic expert (charged with overseeing six clinics in total) dropped by to visit, or if the midwives' shifts overlapped. Occasionally, midwives were able to reach the sonographic expert by telephone. Despite these limited opportunities for communication, midwives often expressed that such communications were vital to their practice. One midwife stated that the two most important people for her in gaining expertise in U/S were the local sonographer and another midwife who worked at the clinic with her. As discussed below, however, consistent telephone connectivity is not a characteristic in most midwives' workplaces. The solitary nature of their work extends to in person as well as technologically mediated exchanges, either synchronous or asynchronous.

The Work Environment

All of the midwives interviewed worked long shifts at the clinics, frequently up to 12 hours. Over the course of a single week, we witnessed two different midwives work over 20 hours continuously. Each clinic we visited employed between one and six midwives, though midwives are often absent for a variety of reasons including illness or maternity leave. Examination rooms were consistently small, with few doors and limited privacy. Several ultrasound exam rooms (see Figure 2) have curtains to dim the room sufficiently to review ultrasound images.

In the clinics we visited, the clinical exam room (where intake and patient history occur) is separate from the scanning room, which may be on the other side of the clinic. The U/S device used by midwives is theoretically portable, but it is kept in a locked room for which only midwives determined to have U/S expertise have keys. Because the U/S machine is in a separate room, midwives are required to change locations halfway through a prenatal exam to use the device. When many patients are waiting and the current patient appears to have a normal pregnancy, moving locations to conduct the exam can be a disincentive to use U/S. Co-locating the device in the same room as other exam activities may encourage usage.

Midwives universally indicated that their patient load was consistently high, and highest on village market days; since patients would already be traveling that day, they often came to the clinic as well. At no time did midwives lack patients; one midwife reported that patients often slept outside the clinic to receive prenatal care. The number of babies delivered at the clinics ranged from 30 per month at the smallest clinic to 150 per month at the largest clinic.

Competing Responsibilities

One midwife, Sarah, considered herself a "small doctor," and actively encouraged her distributed midwife peers to do the same. Sarah endeavored to "stand on [her] own two feet" and have sufficient skills to provide each patient with coordinated, comprehensive care and treatment. In addition to using U/S to screen women for high-risk pregnancy conditions, midwives' other responsibilities include patient education and communication, delivering babies, and providing other types of care, including vaccination.

Midwives at clinics leverage the healthcare system's referral network, meaning more severe cases (e.g. high-risk pregnancies) are referred to higher-level health clinics equipped to deal with these contingencies. The referral system requires midwives to engage in articulation work to coordinate and monitor transfer of patients from one clinic to another. For example, midwives at clinics spend significant time reporting clinical findings and actions taken for each patient seen. If a case is particularly high-risk and urgent, they may call midwives at a higher-level clinic to alert them that the referred patient is on her way. Additional actors, such as ambulance drivers, also participate in coordinating and scheduling activities.

Technological Ecosystem

The technological ecosystem at each clinic varied, though there were common themes. Reliable power sources were mostly non-existent. Several clinics addressed the lack of infrastructure with solar panels. One clinic reported broken solar panels, and midwives told of delivering babies in the middle of the night by kerosene lamp.

Mobile devices were widespread. All midwives had basic cell phones; most had multiple phones for different providers with prepaid airtime. Throughout 2010-2011, our research team noted a lack of consistent cell service in the district. Clinics varied in the provider who had the most reliable service for that area, and even traveling 5-10 km could mean a new provider was needed in order to make a call. Functional Internet connectivity was non-existent in the clinics. GPRS modems provided some limited connectivity, though, as noted, cell service was sparse. In the villages, some residents had satellite televisions and would charge neighbors to watch programs on certain evenings. One midwife had a digital camera which she used to take photographs of us and mentioned that she would upload them to the Internet in Mbarara.

Remote Training Opportunities & Motivations

For all of the midwives interviewed, the only opportunities for continued education were in Mbarara, or Kampala, larger cities that are one and six hours away, respectively. For all midwives, it was difficult to travel to these cities for additional training, both because of the high cost of travel and because if they left, they would be leaving the only other midwife at the clinic alone for several weeks. One midwife, Faridah, said she only receives continuing education through the local sonographer when problems arise. Another midwife, Sarah, was much more proactive about receiving continuing education. She would often travel to Mbarara to access the Internet, which she used to keep abreast of best practices by emailing with various professionals she had met.

All midwives interviewed expressed a desire to learn more about midwifery, U/S, and medicine more generally. One midwife, Namutebi, expressed interest in our system's integrated help feature simply as an educational replacement for her textbooks, which she realized were extremely dated. When showed a prototype of our integrated help system, all midwives recognized in it the potential to assist with continuing education and help them remember what to do when faced with unusual medical conditions. One midwife stated, "if you are having trouble with the head circumference you can look at the text, and then you can measure the head circumference immediately." Another midwife asked if we could put our help system into the devices they are currently using, so they could begin accessing the information immediately.

Radiological Practice in the United States

Below is an aggregate example based on our interviews with sonographers, physicians, and radiologists in June 2011 that provides a scenario for radiological practice in a high resource environment:

A family practice doctor sees a patient, and, based on the initial exam, orders up an imaging test such as U/S. A radiologist receives what is known then as the referral. The radiologist may have questions for the family doctor, known as the referring doctor, based on the kind of imaging that was requested, in which case she or he will pick up the phone or walk down the hall, depending on the work setting. Once those issues have been clarified and the right tests decided on, the imaging is performed by a technician. The results are delivered electronically to the radiologist via PACS. At that point, the radiologist may have other questions about patient history and need more information in order to interpret the test results accurately. In order to do this, the radiologist will contact the referring physician (via phone, face-to-face, or e-mail), or even go visit the patient to acquire that information. In some cases, the radiologist will confer with other radiological colleagues for help making sense of an unusual test result. The family practice doctor receives the results and seeks out the radiologist for clarification or to discuss specific elements in the image. Both the family physician and the radiologist can look at the screen together, or they can talk on the phone while both look at the images using PACS. The referring physician makes patient care decisions based on the negotiated understanding of the test results.

This scenario demonstrates the intensely collaborative practice within which the clinical use of imaging technology is situated. This contrasts sharply with the picture of the remote practitioner that we see in Uganda. The technological infrastructure that supports this collaboration is also starkly different.

Solitary vs. Collaborative Practice

All radiologists, primary care physicians, and sonographers in Seattle reported that patient care is delivered by teams of practitioners, and that radiological practice, in particular, is performed and interpreted as part of a team process. As a reminder, we included these three types of U/S consumers because midwives in Uganda perform work that spans all three specialties, from selecting U/S as a diagnostic tool, to conducting the U/S exam, to interpreting the results.

Reliance on PACS

The collaboration described above predates computer technology; three decades ago radiologists and referring physicians would meet in the reading room and read films against a light wall. That collaborative practice today is mediated by PACS. All doctors interviewed indicated that they used PACS to read and annotate images, communicate diagnoses, and create an ongoing patient record. There are multiple versions of PACS, most are proprietary, and interoperability can be an issue across different systems. PACS was characterized by some respondents as complex and by others as intuitive; PACS systems are chosen by hospital administrations rather than individual practitioners, and they are adopted throughout the institution. PACS replaces darkened reading rooms where radiologists and other clinicians would consult while looking simultaneously at the films. PACS now allows for asynchronous collaboration, as radiologists and surgeons—or other clinicians—read, negotiate, and interpret U/S and other imaging test results. However, even though PACS seeks to make collaboration more efficient, it has not eliminated the need for synchronous consultations among radiologists and referring physicians, as described below.

The Work Environment

The work environment for all of our respondents—referring physicians, radiologists, and sonographers—is highly technological. They work with landlines, cellphones, pagers, networked computers, backup networks, automated voice recognition systems, multiple viewing stations, and email. Multiple screens are common (see Figure 2), as is computerized voice dictation that populates patient records. The reading room is still a dark place, primarily to improve image viewing on the screens.

Figure 2: Contrasting settings in which practitioners view ultrasound images: Ugandan Ultrasound Exam Room (left) and United States Radiological Viewing Room (right)

In the hospital setting where we conducted our research, which is a teaching hospital, the Fellow on shift reviews the work of the residents and consults with the attending physician as necessary. When attending physicians begin their shift, they start by reviewing the work done overnight by the residents, checking notes and diagnoses. When there are questions, the attending physician will walk over to discuss the images and interpretations with the Fellow or the residents. This teaching relationship provides realtime and ongoing learning opportunities, and later in this paper we discuss the importance this collaborative practice plays in the effective use of imaging.

Networked and In-Person Collaboration

Imaging reports stored in PACS can be used in both synchronous and asynchronous communicative contexts. In some clinical settings, clinicians are able to review images face-to-face with their radiology colleagues in viewing rooms. When this is not possible, reports serve as an asynchronous "shared text"—radiologists leave written or dictated notes and annotations alongside images which the clinician reviews and, based on that reading, then contacts the radiologist by phone for further consultation if necessary. The radiologists, in particular, reported using the phone heavily, with one doctor using the phone for 15 or 20 cases in a day when working an emergency room shift. The same doctor reported that when doing a significant amount of outpatient work—that is, reading the results of tests where the referral doctors are offsite, he used the phone up to a half dozen times a day. He said the phone was most often useful as a supplemental medium for complex cases, which generally meant more acute cases.

All of our interviewed physicians emphasized the importance of combining the knowledge and expertise of the radiologist and the referring physician, sometimes supplementing this information by walking over and observing the patient in order to help accurately interpret the films. As one interviewed physician stated, "I've been doing this a long time, and I know a lot of medicine, but I can only use that if I have a lot of history. So on complicated cases I want a lot of [patient] history."

In the United States, clinicians are able to consult with radiologists over the phone about images stored in networked PACS. Radiologists direct clinicians to various anatomical structures found within the images, and towards an ultimate diagnosis, using shared medical vocabulary. Although clinicians do not have the same depth of radiological vocabulary as radiologists, participants agreed there is sufficient shared medical vocabulary to explain findings. According to one primary care clinician, the purpose of reviewing the images with a radiologist—as opposed to the radiologist merely communicating the final diagnosis—was to continue to educate herself, and also to be able to describe findings to her patients.

Overall, substantial collaboration between the radiologist and the sonographer is necessary. As one radiologist reported, "U/S is [about] hands-on interaction, so you can look at images, and you can interpret [those images], but you have no idea what *wasn't* seen by the sonographer. There [can be] a loss of quality, because you can't look at the cases [when you don't do the scanning yourself]." Additionally, using collaborative, distributed practices with U/S can introduce complications that are specific to the technology. As one sonographer reported, U/S is different from other imaging modalities because the real time scan (with video) provides a "different scenario" than looking at still images after an exam. She "lose[s] a significant amount of understanding with still images," which makes it especially important that PACS allows upload of both images and video.

Opportunities for Consultation and Learning

All of the practitioners interviewed mentioned a variety of tools and methods they use to ensure ongoing medical learning and alliance with current best practices. These knowledge exchanges were both technologically mediated (e.g. through e-mail), mediated through more traditional mediums (e.g. handwritten notes), or unmediated (e.g. in-person communication or seminars).

Several participants mentioned reliance on medical information databases paid for by their respective hospitals, including UpToDate [32] and MD Consult [22]. Both services offer peer reviewed medical information and are available both online and offline. Participants mentioned that they use these resources to discover new treatment options and assist with patient education efforts.

One clinician with experience working in rural medicine mentioned reliance on MEDCON—a toll-free phone consultation and referral service for clinicians in Washington, Wyoming, Alaska, Montana and Idaho [21]. The participant described the importance of this service to remote referring physicians, who may not have a large network of colleagues to consult with in person. All of our participants emphasized the importance of being able to ask colleagues for help in person or over the phone. One sonographer mentioned that if she encountered something she was unsure of with a particular scan, she may ask a sonographer colleague to come into the exam room and scan the patient in order to provide a second opinion. This is not possible for remote practitioners, and in these cases, phone consultation would be even more important.

An additional challenge associated with networked collaboration for U/S relates to specific technical challenges. As one radiologist noted, "technical issues obviously [bear on the quality of test results]—speed, archiving, etc. In a practical sense, measurements you want but weren't taken are out. Brightness, contract, etc. adjustments are also out [when the scanning is done by a different person or at a different site]." While this radiologist said these were mostly solvable problems, in places with intermittent and unreliable connectivity where the sharing of images and information may be sporadic or expensive, such gaps can become especially important.

Also related to technical issues with U/S, "one other issue that is a big thing is that you're not involved in protocoling or [selecting] the type of equipment the case is done on. [It can be a problem] if you're not there to make sure things are done correctly. Lots of studies are not done quite right, so you need to repeat studies from a remote clinician." Such problems weren't as marked for imaging technologies like CT or MRIs, but for U/S these problems were notable. This is especially relevant for projects that seek to introduce U/S to remote or low-resource settings for local scans and depend on sending those images to developed world radiologists for interpretation.

Many of our participants described scenarios that highlighted the importance of trust in relationships between imaging specialists and referring physicians. As one sonographer mentioned, "Doctors like to get the feedback from the source. That's the importance of real time…Sonographers are there in the room with the images—they [referring physicians] trust us. Trust goes a long way." Because referring physicians are not in the room with patients during the scan and often lack the image interpretation skills required by U/S, they place their trust in radiologists and sonographers with whom they often have an established working relationship. One family medicine doctor with twelve years of experience said, "I trust the opinions of radiologists who are really good at clinical correlation…If I have worked with them for a long time, if they are usually right, I will ask 'By the literature, or by your experience, what's the prognosis?'"

DISCUSSION

Hidden Work Practices and Collaboration

A major difference between high-resource and low-resource radiological environment is the extent of collaboration. In high resource environments where health settings separate expertise into different practitioners, there also happens to be robust enough technological infrastructure to support collaboration. We would argue that coupling multiple practitioners with a sophisticated technological ecology is a pervasive expectation for U/S usage and constitutes an important hidden work practice.

Our interviews with practicing clinicians in the developed world indicate that much of the complexity surrounding radiological practice is managed through comprehensive and multi-layered collaboration. The efficiencies of PACS do not remove the necessity of ongoing cooperation among different clinicians. PACS also does not eliminate the need for strong trust relationships between clinicians.

Access to Expertise

Several US-based participants identified lack of either in person or technologically-mediated resources that can deliver best practices as the central challenge facing isolated/remote practitioners. As one doctor with rural medicine experience explained, "You're isolated in space, but you really do need access to experts." This finding is corroborated by the teaching relationship between radiologists and their residents; initially, radiologists guide the residents through past cases, primarily to ensure they understand why each study was requested. Over time, residents shift into a more autonomous role and radiologists spend less time checking for errors.

Importance of Technological Ecology

There are, in fact, an increasing number of commercial U/S systems targeted at the low-resource market. Small-scale and low-power devices are becoming common (e.g. GE V-Scan and Mobisante). However, as our research has shown, a smaller, cheaper, easier to use, or more portable U/S machine isn't all that is required for effective U/S implementation. Understanding the work context in which U/S is deployed makes it clear that the larger technology ecology has some bearing on the effectiveness of the device. Importantly, no low-cost U/S project to date has focused on how work practices interplay with technologies to create work outcomes.

As one of the radiologists we interviewed noted, missing context from an examination is one of the biggest obstacles in teleradiology. Video clips are one way to alleviate the problem of missing context, and many U/S systems provide a mechanism for recording video. Additionally, many commercial systems, which are comprised of integrated devices, offer a way to send images and video clips through the Internet. However, many areas in the developing world have limited (or no) Internet connectivity. Even GPRS for sending data over mobile networks can be severely limited or prohibitively expensive. Further, where Internet connectivity does exist, bandwidth is so limited that video clips cannot be sent in a reasonable time frame. Because our device is a simple tablet device, video clips and images can be transferred in a number of ways, including through saving files onto a USB drive.

Future Design Considerations

The findings from this study emphasize differences between work settings and practices across our research sites. For our work with the Ugandan midwives, we would hypothesize that U/S can work adequately in their clinics because their work practice currently requires them to be solitary practitioners who work alone and operate as sonographer, primary care physician, and radiologist all at once. Thus, there is no need for them to collaborate and share imaging results and interpretations with other practitioners, so the lack of robust technological infrastructure doesn't limit them. However, we foresee problems in a scenario when midwives send patients to referral hospitals and then introduce a collaborative work practice that spans rural clinic and hospital without a technological ecology to support collaboration between the sites. Additionally, we hypothesize that the introduction of U/S into more complex healthcare settings with specialized health practitioners but that lack technological infrastructure to support effective CSCW practices among those specialists would have difficulty effectively incorporating imaging technologies into their practice.

Indeed, our research indicates that U/S in single practitioner settings can work without a large technical infrastructure, in part because the real-time nature of the modality means that the sonographer has enough contextual information from being present at the time of scan in order to make her diagnosis. Despite the advantage of context provided by being present at the time of scan, however, U/S images are often ambiguous, and our design strategies need to address this issue. Our interviews with sonographers indicate that learning from other practitioners—both as a novice and an expert—is crucial, and our project needs to consider this in future work as we aim to better support remote practitioners. Our integrated Help system is an attempt at solving this problem. Additional design considerations for us, and the wider field, to consider include:

1) Imaging technologies designed for complex, cooperative health care in Western settings are unlikely to be successfully adapted for remote practitioners. Rural clinics do not have the resources or network infrastructure to collaborate through computer technologies. In addition, the resource-constrained health professional must assume multiple roles (e.g., patient consultation, performing scans, etc), reducing the need for a complex collaboration system.

2) Trust in the expertise of one's collaborators is important when scanning and reading are separated. If practitioners are separated geographically and/or culturally, how difficult will it be to establish trusted relationships between those who scan and those who read?

3) Because health practitioners in remote settings lack access to a variety of resources, system design must compensate for lack of infrastructure in natural and innovative ways. The Ultrasound PLUS help system enables midwives to access reference and support in lieu of in-person and technically supported collaborative networks.

4) While ICTD work has made great strides in understanding the interplay of technical and cultural issues, adding an understanding of CSCW issues and how work practices emerge out of available technical infrastructure will increase the likelihood that the rapidly growing field of low-cost healthcare technology development for low-resource settings will result in appropriate solutions. Even if it appears that minimal collaboration takes place (e.g. in the remote practitioner scenario), it still exists and, if recognized, can be better supported in the design of novel technologies.

CONCLUSION

The authors of this paper are a group of medical professionals, computer scientists, and social scientists committed to appropriate technology development that can solve problems in low-resource environments. This paper was motivated by an understanding that the field of CSCW provides insight into work practices, including hidden work and socio-organizational issues, that are crucial to any successful technology development project geared for professional settings. Our findings in this paper have provided a clear framework for moving forward in our design efforts for the Ultrasound PLUS, but they have also provided some beginning guidelines for technology development efforts for low-resource communities that hope to target collaborative workplace practices and creatively compensate for gaps in infrastructure.

ACKNOWLEDGMENTS

Thank you to Gaetano Borriello, Nicole Goldsmith, Leo Ham, Matthew Hicks, Pratik Prasad, Ginger Ruddy, Laura Schlenke. Also to William Richard and David Zar for their contributions to the ultrasound technology field. We thank Michael Kawooya and his colleagues at ECUREI. Finally, we thank our study participants. This work was supported by a grant from the Bill & Melinda Gates Foundation's Grand Challenges Explorations Initiative.

REFERENCES

1. Anderson, R. E. et al., "Building a Transportation Information System Using Only GPS and Basic SMS Infrastructure," ICTD 2009.
2. Anokwa, Y. et al (December 01, 2009). Stories from the Field: Reflections on HCI4D Experiences. *Information Technologies & International Development, 5,* 4.
3. Bardram, J. and Doryab, A. 2011. Activity analysis: applying activity theory to analyze complex work in hospitals. In *Proceedings of the ACM 2011 conference on Computer supported cooperative work* (CSCW '11).
4. Breslauer, D., et al 2009. "Mobile Phone Based Clinical Microscopy for Global Health Applications". *PLoS ONE.* 4 (7).
5. Brunette, W., Gerard, W., Hicks, M., Hope, A., et. al. 2010. Portable antenatal ultrasound platform for village midwives. In *Proceedings of the 1st Annual Symposium on Computing for Development* (London, United Kingdom, December 17-18, 2010). ACM DEV '10.
6. Bureau of Labor Statistics. (2011, June). Occupational Outlook Handbook. *Diagnostic Medical Sonographers* [Online]. Available: www.bls.gov/oco/ocos273.htm
7. Donner, J., et al (June 01, 2008). Stages of Design in Technology for Global Development. *Computer, 41,* 6.

8. Dourish, P. & Bellotti, V. 1992. Awareness and coordination in shared workspaces. In *Proceedings of the 1992 ACM conference on Computer-supported cooperative work* (CSCW '92).

9. Dourish, P. 2006. Re-space-ing place: "place" and "space" ten years on. In *Proceedings of the 2006 20th anniversary conference on Computer supported cooperative work* (CSCW '06).

10. Fridell, K., et al. "The Impact of PACS on Radiologists' Work Practice," Journal of Digital Imaging, Volume 20, No 4 (December), 2007: pp 411-421.

11. Gandhi, R., et al "Digital Green: Participatory Video for Agricultural Extension," ICTD 2007, pp.21-30.

12. Heeks, R. (June 01, 2008). ICT4D 2.0: The Next Phase of Applying ICT for International Development. *Computer, 41*,6.)

13. Herrera, A. (January 01, 1981). The generation of technologies in rural areas. *World Development, 9,* 1, 21-35.

14. Jordan, B. (1978). Birth in four cultures: A crosscultural investigation of childbirth in Yucatan, Holland, Sweden, and the United States. Montreal: Eden Press Women's Publications.

15. Karasti, K., et al "The Teleradiology System and Changes in Work Practices," Computer Methods and Programs in Biomedicine 57 (1998) 69 - 78.

16. Korpela, M., et al (August 01, 1998). Community Participation in Health Informatics in Africa: An Experiment in Tripartite Partnership in Ile-Ife, Nigeria. *Computer Supported Cooperative Work: the Journal of Collaborative Computing, 7.*

17. Larson, E., et al (2011). Accurate and Privacy Preserving Cough Sensing using Low-cost Microphone. To appear at the 13th International Conference on Ubiquitous Computing (UbiComp 2011), Beijing, China, Sep 17-21, 2011.

18. Leach, J., et al (January 01, 2004). Deep impact: a study of the use of hand-held computers for teacher professional development in primary schools in the Global South 1. *European Journal of Teacher Education, 27,* 1, 5-28

19. Le Dantec, C. and Edwards, W. 2008. The view from the trenches: organization, power, and technology at two nonprofit homeless outreach centers. In *Proceedings of the 2008 ACM conference on Computer supported cooperative work* (CSCW '08).

20. Malkin, R. A. (August 01, 2007). Design of Health Care Technologies for the Developing World. *Annual Review of Biomedical Engineering, 9,* 1.

21. MEDCON. (2011, June). [Online]. Available: http://uwmedicine.washington.edu/patient-care/referrals/pages/medcon.aspx

22. MD Consult. (2011, June). [Online]. Available: www.mdconsult.com/php/255837386-2/homepage

23. Olson, G. & Olson, J., 2000. Distance matters. *Human Comput. Interact.* 15, 2 (September 2000), 139-178

24. Parikh, T., et al "Mobile phones and paper documents: evaluating a new approach for capturing microfinance data in rural India," CHI 2006, pp. 551-560.

25. Paul, S.A., and Reddy, M. (2010). Understanding Together: Sensemaking in Collaborative Information Seeking. In Proceedings of the *ACM Conference on Computer Supported Cooperative Work (CSCW 2010).*

26. Pinch, T. and Bijker, W. The Social Construction of Facts and Artifacts: or How the Sociology of Science and the Sociology of Technology Might Benefit Each Other. *Social Studies of Science*, (1984), 399-441.

27. Putnam, C., Rose, E.,Walton, R. & Kolko, B. Mobile phone users in Kyrgyzstan: A case study of identifying user requirements for diverse users In *Proceedings of IPCC 2009* ,Honolulu, Hawaii, July 20-23, 2009.

28. Reddy, M., & Jansen, B. (2008) A Model for Understanding Collaborative Information Behavior in Context: A Study of Two Healthcare Teams. *Information Processing and Management.* 44(1): 256-273

29. Schmidt, K., and Bannon, L. 'Taking CSCW Seriously: Supporting Articulation Work', *Computer Supported Cooperative Work (CSCW): An International Journal*, vol. 1, 1992, no. 1-2, pp. 7-40.

30. Suchman, L. A. (1987). *Plans and situated actions: The problem of human-machine communication.* Cambridge: Cambridge University Press.

31. Tellioglu, H., & Wagner, I. (May 01, 2001). Work Practices Surrounding PACS: The Politics of Space in Hospitals.*Computer Supported Cooperative Work: the Journal of Collaborative Computing, 10,* 2.

32. UpToDate. (2011, June). [Online]. Available: www.uptodate.com/contents/search

33. Veeraraghavan, R., et al (March 01, 2009). Warana Unwired: Replacing PCs with Mobile Phones in a Rural Sugarcane Cooperative. *Information Technologies & International Development, 5,* 1.

34. Wagner, I. and Tellioglu, H. 2011. The multidisciplinary design group in Vienna. In *Proceedings of the ACM 2011 conference on Computer supported cooperative work* (CSCW '11).

35. Yager, P., et al (July 27, 2006). Microfluidic diagnostic technologies for global public health. *Nature, 442,* 7101.

36. Yakel, E., et al "Medicine in the Dark: Obtaining Design Requirements for a Medical Collaboratory from Observation of Radiologists at Work," CSCW (Computer Supported Cooperative Work) 96: Boston: November 16-20, 1996.

Repair Worlds: Maintenance, Repair, and ICT for Development in Rural Namibia

Steven J. Jackson
Department of Information Science
Cornell University
sjj54@umich.edu

Alex Pompe
School of Information
University of Michigan
pompe@umich.edu

Gabriel Krieshok
School of Information
University of Michigan
krieshok@umich.edu

ABSTRACT

This paper explores the nature and centrality of maintenance and repair ('M&R') work in the extension and sustainability of ICT infrastructure in the global South. Drawing from pragmatist traditions in CSCW and the social sciences at large, we develop a concept of 'repair worlds' intended to map the varieties and effects of such maintenance and repair activities. Empirically, our analysis builds on ethnographic fieldwork into local practices of maintenance and repair that have accompanied and supported the extension of mobile phone and computing infrastructure in the Kavango region of northeastern Namibia.

Author Keywords
Maintenance, repair, infrastructure, theory, ethnography, development, ICTD.

ACM Classification Keywords
H5.m. Information interfaces and presentation (e.g., HCI): Miscellaneous.

General Terms
Management, Theory.

1. INTRODUCTION

This paper explores the centrality of maintenance and repair work in the ongoing project of building robust, appropriate, and sustainable ICT systems in countries of the global south – a project to which CSCW has much to contribute. It also argues that CSCW has much to (re)learn in this process: about the nature and variability of socio-technical activity (especially as played out over cultural and infrastructural difference); the work required to sustain and adapt systems over time (including beyond initial moments of design and adoption); and the distinctively different worlds of design and practice that appear to us when we take erosion, breakdown, and decay ('broken world thinking') rather than novelty, growth, and progress as our starting point.

This perspective runs somewhat counter to the way we usually approach questions of design and development, in both CSCW and the ICT and development (ICTD) fields. Most accounts of ICT and development have emphasized encounters between organizations, communities and technologies at the front end, emphasizing pathways, patterns, and problems that accompany the introduction of (new) technological forms to (new) geographic and cultural communities. ICT-related development statistics and studies have long reflected this bent. We keep track of figures like ICT penetration, adoption, and diffusion, but rarely breakdown or abandonment. We capture statistics on cell phones purchased, but rarely cell phones discarded. We study how communities embrace or adapt to new technologies, but less often how they organize to sustain, manage, repurpose, or simply live with what they have. (As a thought experiment, consider how our statistical and design universes might shift if we imagined a fundamentally contracting technological world, and what we measured was technological breakdown, withdrawal and decline – a recessionary rather than a progressive, informatics?).

That we don't (usually) live in such a world may have less to do with any inner logic of economic or technological advance than with the remarkable and diverse human capacity for repair: the ability to make broken and breaking systems work, and to sustain what we have for at least a little while longer. This sensibility has long animated an important branch of American social thought, from John Dewey's insistence on disruption as site and instigation to thought [1], to the breaching experiments of ethnomethodologists like Garfinkel [2], to later Chicago School sociologists' concerns with infrastructure, articulation, and invisible work [3-5]. Social order, such work insists, is not the natural or inevitable outcome of 'structure,' but rather a remarkable and often fragile accomplishment. Social things, the pragmatists remind us, take work to maintain. And so, too, does technology.

In the paper that follows, we explore maintenance and repair as distinctive sites and categories of CSCW work, with particular focus on ICT and development efforts in the global South. Drawing on original ethnographic fieldwork conducted during summer 2010 in the Kavango region of Northeastern Namibia, we offer the beginnings of a thick description of the distinctive repair worlds that characterize, shape, and sustain the emerging ICT ecologies of the region. In the process, we open up new sites and themes for CSCW scholarship – many of which take us back to challenges and problems foundational to the field.

2. LITERATURE AND METHODS

CSCW has a rich albeit uneven history of attention to maintenance and repair concerns. In its design guise, such themes are often implicated in CSCW work attending to 'downstream' tensions in the relationship between design and use, leading to ethnographic descriptions and/or programmatic calls for tailoring, end user involvement, and more iterative or ecological approaches to the design problematic [6-8]. A related body of work has explored instances of breakdown and non-adoption confronting the deployment of CSCW artifacts and systems, including through contradictions embedded in the relationship between technical and organizational form [9-11].

Our own approach, building from pragmatist traditions, is to treat such instances of breakdown and failure as fully ordinary, and ask instead (with genuine curiosity and wonder) how it is that *any* sociotechnical arrangement can be made to work and persist through time. Here we connect to a third strain of CSCW work emphasizing the diverse and subtle forms of work that go into the ongoing operation of artifacts and systems as 'infrastructure' (vis-à-vis given forms of collective activity and variously situated social groups). Star and Strauss have analyzed forms of articulation work, much of it invisible, supporting the introduction and maintenance of collectively shared artifacts and systems [3]. In their 1994 CSCW study of the WORM community system, Star and Ruhleder advance an influential definition of infrastructure, emphasizing the embeddedness of infrastructure (in social arrangements and technical form); its tendency to remain invisible (except at moments of breakdown); its connection to membership in specific communities of practice; its relationship to an installed base (from which it inherits both strengths and limits); and its tendency to change in local and modular increments – in part through the resistances and breakdowns it occasions and encounters [4]. Subsequent CSCW scholarship has built on this definition, further developing the active [12-13], relational [14], agonistic, [15-16] and dynamic [16-17] dimensions of Star and Ruhleder's original formulation.

Our work brings a parallel sensibility to the analysis of ICT and development efforts in rural Namibia, with special attention to the distinctive problems and solutions surrounding sustainability in this space. The vehicle for our discussion is a distinctive notion of repair worlds, drawn from the same social worlds tradition (discussed below) that has informed and inspired much CSCW scholarship around infrastructure. We argue, in short, that ICT maintenance and repair activities in the Kavango region of Northeastern Namibia constitute a distinctive and complex kind of 'world,' whose function and variety is central to the nature and overall success of ICT development in the region.

To this end, we offer ethnographic data drawn from fieldwork conducted by two members of the project team between May and July 2010 around ICT and educational development efforts in the Kavango region of northeastern Namibia. This included 34 semi-structured interviews with regional technology providers, managers, technicians, and users, conducted in a combination of English and Rukwangali (the leading regional language) and focusing on patterns, practices, tensions, and barriers to effective and sustainable ICT adoption; and field observations at 14 different rural and urban sites in which primarily educational technologies (usually computer labs) were being deployed. Participants ranged in age from 20 to 55 years old, were evenly split between men and women, and were recruited according to their involvement as technology users, providers, or promoters in the region. Interviews and fieldnotes were translated (where necessary), transcribed, and coded by all three members of the project team according to the principles of grounded theory analysis [18-19]; early rounds of coding thus came to guide subsequent data collection efforts, including more focused attention (per grounded theory principles of theoretical sampling) to the dynamics of maintenance and repair that emerged as an early and central theme of the fieldwork. This initial fieldwork has since been supplemented through ongoing interactions with a team of local partners, who continue to conduct occasional interviews and supply materials relevant to the themes of the study. More broadly, our findings draw on one of the author's prior experience as an IT and education volunteer in the Kavango region between November 2006 and January 2009.

3. REPAIR WORLDS

For Strauss and fellow travelers in Chicago School sociology traditions, social worlds display a number of common properties. In each world, at least one primary *activity* (along with related clusters of activity) is strikingly evident: e.g., climbing mountains, researching, and collecting. There are *sites* where activities occur, implicating place, landscape, and a shared built environment. *Technology* (understood broadly as inherited or innovative modes of carrying out the social world's activities) is always involved. And while social worlds may begin from temporary and provisional divisions of labor, at some point *organizations* typically evolve to structure and manage key aspects of the world's activities [20].

Each of these broad categories can be further specified through a series of subprocesses, some of which may constitute distinctive and legitimate 'sub-worlds.' These may include partially autonomous activities dedicated to the finding, funding, protecting, and competition for sites; innovation, manufacturing, marketing, and training in technical skills; or the building, extending, defending, and repurposing of organizations. The discovery and study of such sub-processes and of their relationships, including conflictual ones, are essential features of social worlds research.

Social worlds are also subject to complex processes of boundary formation, both internal and external. Externally, relations and intersections between adjacent worlds may be sites of tension, innovation, and strategic action. Internally, social worlds may follow complex patterns of segmentation, giving rise to subworlds that will themselves exhibit some of the dynamics (including boundary dynamics) of worlds of a more general type. At such junctures, a number of crucial questions arise. Who has the power to speak, decide, claim membership, and represent on the part of that world and its inhabitants? How are newcomers socialized, and what is the range of allowable relationships (from core to more 'orbital' and overlapping memberships)? How do social worlds – and the more formalized instantiations like arenas and organizations that grow from them – form and change, and how do they relate to larger processes of social transformation (economic, cultural, political, etc.)?

A leading example of these ideas in action is provided by Howard Becker's Art Worlds [21], which approaches the making of art as a form of materially and collectively organized activity. To succeed as art, argues Becker, objects depend on a wide and heterogeneous list of components: ideas and possibly inspiration; but also forms of physical execution; materials (canvases and paint brushes, cameras, etc.); support work (from editing and ticket sales to the bringing of coffee); an audience, readership, or other network of response; a rationale or other (collective) justification of value; networks of training; and certain conditions of civic order which provide a stability of expectations against which the basic operations of the world can proceed. In stable and coherent worlds, these components will reinforce and overlap – for example, in the way aspiring artists and actors constitute a significant portion of the audience for experimental or emerging art forms. They also generate constraints and conventions that will shape and regulate the form and process of art – for example, conventions around symphony length and orchestra size, which shape and limit the nature of creative work in this space.

For IT and development scholars and the wider CSCW field, such perspectives carry important advantages. To begin, in contrast to structuralist traditions of social thought, social world analyses start from an explicit concern with social change – a significant advantage in the technology and development context – which nevertheless takes instances of stasis and consistency as equally central phenomena of interest (and requiring explanation in any careful analytic account). Second, in its gathering of 'human' and 'technical' elements under the undifferentiated notion of worlds, social world analyses offer us tools for thinking even-handedly across the interlinked worlds of people and things, opening up both dimensions of human signification embedded in the world of things, and the possibility of strategic 'switching' between human- and object-centered approaches to collective goals (this principle is nicely captured in Bruno Latour's example of the sleeping policeman [22], or Lawrence Lessig's principle of code [23]).

Finally, social world analyses have been historically good at calling attention to the kinds of support work, people, and artifacts that underlie the actual practice of distributed collective activity. From invisible work [3] to infrastructure [4,5], interactionist traditions have drawn new attention to people, practices, and artifacts operating beyond or beneath the margins of more formally recognized systems. In the process they have opened a space for precisely the sort of maintenance and repair concerns pursued here. In Star and Ruhleder's influential account cited above, for example, infrastructure is defined as a sort of social and material substrate or scaffolding to action that remains "invisible until breakdown" – at which point underlying processes are made visible, and new repertoires of action may kick in [4]. Ethnomethodologically inspired traditions of CSCW scholarship have relied on this same basic insight: for example, seminal studies by Lucy Suchman, Julian Orr and others which follow (not by accident) the experience of Xerox copier maintenance and repair workers to produce new insights around planning, design, and the nature of technically-mediated collective action [24, 25]. And growing efforts by CSCW and HCI researchers to foreground sustainability as a design value offer new opportunities to push questions of maintenance and repair back to the center of the field [26-27]. In the sections that follow we build from social world and interactionist principles to describe the repair worlds of the Kavango region in Northeastern Namibia.

4. ICT, MAINTENANCE AND REPAIR IN THE KAVANGO

In the past five years Namibia has seen an enormous growth of technological availability in both cellular technology and networked computing resources. Mobile phone ownership rates currently stand at over 50% of the population [28]. While low by global standards, Namibia's IT infrastructure remains among the most advanced in sub-Saharan Africa. And investment continues to grow. In 2008, Namibia's largest cellular provider, MTC, spent an additional NAD76 million (~US$10.1 million) in fiber optic backbone, bringing the company's total investments from 1995 through 2008 to NAD1.6 billion (~US$213 million) [29].

But such overall statistics mask significant regional variations. As with other national numbers, technology and wealth indicators in the country are dominated by the capital city of Windhoek, which continues to function as the reference point for questions of availability, pricing, and access. Because of this, nation-wide technology policies are often detached from the realities of the poorest regions, such as the Kavango, where development energy and dollars are most needed. Reflecting apartheid policies in place before national independence in the 1990s, Namibia is characterized by a Gini coefficient of 74.3, representing the largest national wealth disparity in the world [30]. This gap is largely reproduced in the balance of technology resources between Windhoek and the Kavango, and again between the regional capital of Rundu and the towns, villages, and rural homesteads that surround it.

To redress this gap, the Namibian government and foreign donors have begun heavy regional investments in computing infrastructure, centered primarily in schools. Since 2006, the national government's Tech/NA! program – an ambitious and country-wide school computerization initiative – has been operative in the Kavango. As of July 2010, Tech/NA! labs and training centers had been set up at the Rundu College of Education, two Teacher Resource Centers (TRCs), and several senior secondary schools. This has been accompanied by a series of parallel volunteer and donor-driven initiatives, including Computers for Kavango, a project started by U.S. Peace Corps volunteers that uses donations raised through Facebook to purchase rebuilt computer systems that are then shipped to Namibia and set up in smaller regional schools. The net result of these and other initiatives has been a steep increase in the number and availability of computers in the region: from an estimated fewer than 50 in 2006, to over 500 by May of 2010. Regional cell phone use and coverage has expanded even more dramatically, with population network coverage expanding from less than 50% to over 90%.

Nevertheless, as recently as 2007, there existed few formal operations in the Kavango region dedicated to ICT maintenance and repair. Users with broken mobile or computing devices faced the prospect of working with locally available parts recycled from old and broken machines; a trip to the national capital of Windhoek, ten hours away; or a visit to the town's informal repair market (described below). General computing equipment (memory sticks, printer cartridges, blank CDs, etc.) was available in limited and sporadic supply, and only in the regional capital of Rundu. In 2008, the two national cellular carriers, MTC and CellOne (now Leo), opened their first formal sales operations in Rundu; however, these remained focused on billing, phone, and SIM card sales, and offered no repair services beyond simple replacement.

4.1 Private Sector Sites

By 2009, the local repair ecology had begun to change. Three new 'tech shops' had opened, combining computer sales and repair operations. A representative example of this shop type was opened by 'Tom,' a hulking Afrikaaner from South Africa. To northern audiences, Tom's shop will look much like a family-owned small business: the shop occupies a permanent and prominent location at the center of town, the majority of the staffing is done by Tom's family, and the owner himself completes all repair tasks. Training is obtained by the owners outside of the Kavango region, and in many cases outside of Namibia (of the three formal technology repair businesses currently found in Rundu, two of the chief proprietors were educated in South Africa, and one in Egypt). The shops' supply chains follow similar lines: two receive their parts from South Africa and the third through an Egyptian supplier. Repairs at these shops usually consist of replacing failed hardware components, re-installing software, and removing computer viruses (a nearly universal feature of the Namibian computing landscape).

An even larger and more varied market has developed around cell phone repair. By 2010, no fewer than ten such shops had opened in Rundu, with an additional three to be found in the smaller regional towns of Nkurenkuru and Divundu. Most of these operate out of single room roadside stalls, in some cases converted shipping containers. Others have attached themselves to more established and apparently unrelated businesses, such as bars, clothing shops, or our favorite, Cell and Leather World. Shop owners are uniformly male but show a significant diversity of backgrounds. Many started as apprentices in other phone repair operations (often in the national capital of Windhoek) before opening their own businesses in the Kavango. Others were educated abroad, with one individual having obtained an MBA degree in his native Pakistan. While some have formal IT training (e.g. at universities and polytechnics in the capital), the vast majority – reflecting patterns in other local repair cultures (e.g. auto mechanics, tire repair shops) – have acquired their skills, networks, and reputations through apprentice relations. The most common activities engaged in by these workers are swapping batteries, unlocking phones, re-flashing operating systems, and replacing cracked screens.

At the opposite end of the spectrum from these semi-formalized operations lies the Rundu repair market. This open-air market is located at the center of town and houses a multitude of informal and small-scale enterprises grouped in a bazaar-like arrangement. While nominally a trading center, the open market functions as a defining social institution of the Kavango in general. It serves as a daily stop for many of Rundu's residents, whether to eat food, buy fabric, sell a chicken, or watch a soccer match. Over ten individual shops/stalls in the market deal in technology (both computer and cell phone); no fewer than five of these are dedicated to repair. The workers here offer skills and services built up over years of experience in this environment, dominated above all by an ad hoc capacity for tinkering. This tinkering culture is identifiable by three main characteristics. First, there is a tremendous amount of reuse and recycling of parts extracted from broken systems, rather than the purchase of new replacement components (it is hard indeed to find new parts in the Rundu market). Second, these repair shops operate largely beneath the expertise of a single person, occasionally supported by apprentices (usually family or at least ethnically related).

Lastly, the cost of procuring repairs at the market is lower than any other local option. This makes the open market notably cost-accessible, and thus the single busiest site by volume of maintenance and repair work in the region.

Figure 1: Repair worker in the Rundu open market, surrounded by discarded electronics to be salvaged for working parts.

4.2 Public Sector Operations

In addition to these private sites, a number of regional repair operations have grown up to serve the growing market in government or donor-supported computing initiatives. Reflecting the older but slower spread of computing infrastructure in the region, the vast majority of computers in the Kavango today remain the property of government ministries, and in particular the Ministry of Education. Official maintenance policies (explored in greater detail in [31]) state that all computers purchased by the government must be serviced by government-owned or approved operations. This poses significant challenges, for the projects themselves and for local repair worlds, as discussed below.

The primary regional computer repair center operated by the Namibian government is located in the Rundu Teacher Resource Center (TRC), a center administered jointly by the Ministry of Education and the National Institute for Education Development (NIED). Traditionally, the TRC was a place where teachers could make photocopies, attend workshops, and check out library books. However, in recent years the main resource utilized at the TRC has been its technology. Beyond its large and functional computer lab and reliable broadband connection, the TRC also houses two IT repair experts who serve as de-facto doctors for all school computer illnesses in the Kavango. Over our three months of observation, an average of three computers a day were brought in and repaired at the Rundu TRC.

The Rundu TRC's success as a repair center depends on the on-site knowledge of its staff and its regionally unique combination of resources. The TRC has become a drop-off point for old computers as the staff has the knowledge to extract working components from non-working systems. When this stockpile of parts does not fill the need for a given repair, the TRC staff act as liaisons to the private sector shops, such as Tom's. In addition, the TRC's generally solid broadband connection provides the rare ability for large software updates to be downloaded, in particular updates to operating systems and anti-virus software. The same Internet connection allows TRC staff to search for additional information when diagnosing and resolving unfamiliar maintenance and repair issues. As the typical computer lab in a Kavango classroom involves a wide array of hardware and software components, including sometimes spotty second-hand donations from the United States or Europe, such situations arise frequently.

4.3 Rundu Institute of Computing

A second quasi-public repair operation can be found in the Rundu Institute of Computing (RIC), located in a re-purposed concrete structure near the center of town between the new Chinese built shopping mall and a series of road-side stalls made from wood and discarded sheet metal. The center provides a variety of technology related services, but its most profitable are the repair of computers and cell phones. The shop and its owner, Andreas, enjoy a reputation as the best place to take any cell phone that is broken. Andreas performs most of the computer repairs himself; his former students turned employees perform the bulk of cell phone repairs. Like the stalls in the open market, the Rundu Institute offers prices lower than those at shops like Tom's. Also like the market, most components are repurposed or sourced locally (albeit with a higher reputation for quality and provenance: the RIC is not known to participate in the growing black market for stolen phones). In addition to the expertise of Andreas and his staff, the RIC depends on a now-considerable stockpile of components drawn from the dead and unfixable machines and handsets periodically brought to its door. The business has been in operation in one form or another for 7 years, and at its current location since 2005.

Figure 2: An apprentice at the Rundu Institute of Computing repairing a broken cell phone.

5. CHALLENGES AND INNOVATIONS

The variety of sites detailed above contributes to a significant range and heterogeneity in the repair worlds (and sub-worlds) of the Kavango region, each of which can be arrayed differently along axes of formality, quality, profitability, and institutional and social sectors served. This has produced a relatively varied and robust landscape of maintenance and repair in the region, with important (albeit overlooked) contributions to the spatial and social extension and sustainability of ICT infrastructure in the region. It has also produced some distinctive challenges and innovations, shared in story form below.

5.1 Cell Phone Hacking

One of the most common cell repairs performed at the Rundu Institute of Computing is the unlocking or re-flashing of cell phone operating systems. The institute's owner, Andreas, initially repaired only computers but quickly realized that the cell phone market was much larger and profitable. He used his knowledge of electronics and software systems to teach himself basic cell phone repairs. While he did not yet own a computer, he would visit Rundu's first dial-up Internet café in a local photocopy shop in order to research the subject. This allowed him to learn many aspects of cell phone hardware repair at a time coinciding with their mass adoption in the Kavango. Since 2008 Andreas has had access to a personal Internet connection and his cell phone repair abilities have grown enormously.

Andreas has used his Internet connection to circumvent a key problem of cell phone software repair: most phones do not allow easy access to manipulate or reset foundational software settings. The pervasive practice of SIM card swapping amongst members of families and social groups extends the use of a single handset (as widely celebrated in the IT and development literature), but also leads to the phone often becoming locked by mistake; for example, when SIM card passwords are entered incorrectly. However, with the use of special hardware components, the phone's software can be effectively hacked when connected to a PC. This solution depends on distinctly non-local ties, however; the necessary hardware components are not sold commercially in Namibia, and have been sourced (in this instance) from Russia. In the absence of local infrastructure, Andreas is similarly dependent on remote partners for learning and adaptation in the fast-moving phone market; as he explains,

"I am still learning many things, as the cell phones are changing quick. I meet partners on the Internet, on forums, who help me with my ideas... I have one partner from South Korea; (he) gives advice and has taught me many things. I tell my students that your partners are the most important thing in this business."

5.2 Disc Sharing

A second innovative practice uncovered in the course of our fieldwork applies to the maintenance and repair of computers in schools. Most computers arrive at schools as second hand donations without any software discs. Key barriers to on-site repair are limited repair knowledge of school staff, a lack of reliable Internet connections to diagnose problems, and the challenge of transporting broken machines over distance to the Rundu TRC. Thus, the most common software repair technique is to reinstall the computer's operating system. It is common for a computer to be given a fresh install, become infected with viruses (spread with USB memory sticks), and then be given a fresh OS installation within 2-3 months. Most repair staff are capable of starting from scratch with a system with the use of a system disc. This represents the most basic level of repair knowledge, but is also the practical reality for most computers in the region.

The lack of broadband connections limits the availability of large operating system updates. It is not uncommon to find multiple copies of the same out of date version of Linux or Windows being used at many schools in the region. These discs (and their pirated software keys) trace interesting resource-sharing routes amongst the Kavango's repair world. We found that discs follow the paths of students as they graduate, eventually reaching as many as five schools. One lab administrator near a border town with Angola recalls the following example:

"I was only taught how to install. I use this disc every week (copy of operating system disc). I copied it at my first school Himarwa when I was in grade 12 from a teacher there. I moved here and I knew that I would need it... Yes, I also share with others; other teachers at schools down the

road. They need it to fix their machines."

The adaptation and use of social networks is an innovative and prevalent tool used by actors in the Kavango's repair world. Just as traditional tools are often shared amongst an extended family, operating system discs find their usage multiplied through sharing.

5.3 Computer Labs as Business Models

A key challenge for the maintenance and repair of computers at schools in the Kavango is providing the upkeep costs for their labs. Few projects allocate any funds for ongoing maintenance or eventual upgrades of computers, instead defining success as the computers working when they were installed at the schools. This is especially negligent given that many computers are second hand or donations and are living a second life after having been discarded by their initial owners. The limited capital of schools is thus a major challenge for maintaining labs of aging hardware. The more rural a school, the less breathing room in its budget, and the more expensive it is to obtain and transport replacement components.

To deal with this problem, the Computers for Kavango initiative has introduced a model whereby unemployed youth in communities are trained in basic maintenance and repair of computers. In exchange for maintaining the labs, the youth are allowed to make use of the computers for income generating small to medium-sized business enterprises, ranging from photo printing to basic typing and document services (including personal resumes). Lab administrators are also allowed to offer basic computer classes to the community at large during school off-hours in exchange for a small tuition. Several of the youth administrators we interviewed had high enrollment in their courses and took great pride in their role as technology liaisons for the rest of the community.

5.4 Biography and Career Trajectories

To be robust and sustainable, social worlds must also: a) offer their members viable paths to learning and advancement; and b) provide mechanisms for the social reproduction of the world itself. This raises important questions of biography and career trajectory (and restores to individual actors a degree of specificity and agency lost under more structuralist analytic traditions). In the limited space available, we offer two brief biographical sketches of key roles and actors in our immediate study sites.

5.4.1 "Andreas"

A defining characteristic of the Rundu Institute of Computing is its use of teaching and apprentice style relationships. Andreas himself brings a formal education in computer and electronic technologies from the University of Namibia. Before opening the institute, he worked in the formal industry sector for Telecom Namibia, and then for three years as a school teacher of computer studies in the Rundu area. In his time as an educator, Andreas developed a strong relationship with several of his students who later joined him at the institute upon its formation seven years ago. Andreas teaches a year-long course in electronics and computer repair that he developed himself.

Typically two to three youth under the age of 25 will complete this training each year, and the majority of them then work at the Institute itself. After an average of two to three years, many of the apprentices will move on and start their own repair-centered business. (Several of the semi-formalized cell phone repair shops attached to local bars are former students of Andreas.) Beyond serving the cell phone maintenance and repair needs of the Kavango region, the Rundu Institute for Computing also serves as a transit point between formal expertise (as represented by Andreas' UNAM degree and experience at Telecom Namibia) and less formalized forms of work in the regional repair economy. But this between space also poses challenges. To begin, the semi-formal nature of the Institute limits Andreas' ability to attract outside lending, and thus to expand and upgrade his repair operations by hiring additional UNAM graduates. This prevents Andreas from off-loading some of his administrative responsibilities to others, as he'd like to do; as he explains,

"I prefer (to work) in the research, in development. The basement of this business is where I belong. I am not good at bringing in people and handling administration matters, but (my) time is spent there now."

The Institute has also struggled to build productive partnerships with the many formal volunteer and international development agency projects that have grown in the region in recent years. By overlooking repair operations such as Andreas', projects in effect lock them out (to the detriment of both parties). The reality of the repair and maintenance landscape currently found in the Kavango is that there is no shortage of broken computers in need of timely and cost effective repair. However, due to its insufficiently formalized status, one of the most skilled technology repair institutions in the region is unable to access this valuable market.

5.4.2 "Wesley"

Social reproduction through career evolution is also apparent in the following account of repair practice in the smaller town of Nkurenkuru, an hour to the west of Rundu. A teacher at a local high school was quick to tell us the repair work that his son Wesley performs while at home during school breaks. During most of the year Wesley studies computing technologies at the University of Namibia, the country's flagship institution located in the capital of Windhoek. Outside of school, he finds many informal maintenance and repair jobs at other informal businesses around Nkurenkuru. His father shared with us:

"My boy is coming here now to the market to work on two computers just there. They know and wait for him to return from school. They call him on his cell phone. I saw him the

other day with some very nice shoes and trousers I did not give to him. They came from money he earned finding work on these computers."

In dialogues with other community members, it became apparent that many technology users around Nkurenkuru knew and depended on Wesley, and planned their computer repairs around the school holidays when he would return home. While Wesley's formal expertise and standing is identifiable through his status as a student at university, the majority of his practical repair expertise has been developed in the informal setting. Wesley's experience while still a student not only augments his formal education; it provides him and his family a greater source of income to help absorb the costs of such an education. In addition, he provides a low-cost repair solution that maintains the technology landscape of a smaller town such as Nkurenkuru.

6. CHALLENGES

If the above stories offer evidence of promising and innovative workarounds to address the distinctive challenges of maintenance and repair in the Kavango, other problems have proven more intractable. Our fieldwork uncovered other instances in which the range and heterogeneity of repair worlds in the region and their interface with other institutional realities have constituted liabilities rather than assets.

6.1 Policy Barriers

In several instances, we found significant mismatches between the formal maintenance and repair policies of computers for education initiatives in the region and resources and realities of local repair worlds. The Tech/NA! program, for example, follows a centralized repair model in which all maintenance and repair operations are to be conducted at the newly created National Education Technology Service and Support Centre (NETSS Centre) located in Windhoek. Strictly followed (as it sometimes is), this policy requires all machines requiring attention (including for simple software upgrades and other routine maintenance) to undergo the expensive and somewhat risky trip to Windhoek via the national post system. Machines then join a repair queue stretching several weeks to several months before being returned (or not) to their original location. In the course of our fieldwork we encountered several labs that had been effectively shuttered by this process, with little immediate indication of restarting. This was despite the presence of a similarly government-owned resource in the Rundu TRC (to say nothing of the other sites noted above) fully capable of providing a large percentage of the necessary repairs.

This conflict brings a power dynamic embedded in infrastructure development to the forefront of repair practices in the Kavango Tech/Na! labs. The Tech/NA! systems have their software installed and configured in Windhoek prior to their deployment, with only staff in the capital given high-level administrative passwords and settings. In additional to the logistical logjams created, such excessively rigid repair policies marginalize local repair actors and prevent them from evolving new technical skills. To solve at least the first problem, the local TRC staff has hit upon the solution of simply re-flashing the client by booting with a USB memory stick, restoring all software settings to their initial state and usually correcting the problem (though at the sacrifice of all stored files). To avoid the loss of computers through trips to the capital, the TRC staff now distributes these USB sticks with usage instructions to all affected Tech/NA! labs.

6.2 Problems of Lockout and Control

When computers are brought to the TRC for repair, it is quite common for them to contain many files that have been copied to the machines by users. It is common practice for the staff to back up local files before the installation of a new hard drive or operating system. However, a large percentage of these files may consist of music collections or personal photographs, which the TRC staff deems non-educational. They thus do not back up these music files, and speak to the school staff on the dangers of spreading computer viruses through USB sticks by sharing music. In addition, the TRC may discourage "inappropriate" use by disabling the sound card and other system settings (which can only be restored through an administrator account, which teachers and students are forbidden from attaining).

On the surface this appears as a pragmatic response to the real problem of users inadvertently breaking and infecting computers. But such control mechanisms also shape and limit the adoption of computers in schools. While the use of computers for educational purposes is a worthy objective of computerization efforts in the Kavango, the most powerful local incentives to engage these efforts often lie in other interests and activities (e.g. music and entertainment). Our own fieldwork and experience suggests that the students and teachers leading adoption in the Tech/NA! and Computers for Kavango labs are precisely those who have become most proficient at using (and sometimes hacking) the systems for entertainment purposes. Along with the restrictive repair policies noted above, this tension between freedom, innovation, and control constitutes the single largest tension attending use of the labs today.

7. DISCUSSION: IMPLICATIONS FOR POLICY AND DESIGN

The concept of repair worlds advanced here and the more specific case of repair worlds in the Kavango region produce few immediate design implications of the sort common to CSCW scholarship (and questioned in [32]). But they do carry important lessons of both a practical and wider theoretical sort.

The first and most obvious of these concerns the need for better bridges between formal development project initiatives and the local repair worlds of the regions in which these projects are situated. The absence of this connection (as we see in each of the TechNA and Computers for Kavango cases above) represents a double loss: for the projects, which see efficacy severely undermined by the inability to effect timely and locally appropriate repairs; and for the repair worlds themselves, which lose an important chance for support, growth, and the upgrading of technological skills, which turn out once again under the old law of uneven development to be (re)centered on the capital [33].

Such efforts to lock out and control use through repair-unfriendly policies and design follows from a long and unfortunate history of control through design in the ICTD and wider international development context. From electric lighting kits [34] to telecenters [35] to hundred-dollar laptops, designers working in the development space have long shown a heightened concern with damaging or inappropriate use – and corresponding efforts to coax downstream users into 'proper' modes of engagement through design choices that lock out would-be tinkerers, modifiers, and adaptors. Sometimes this is for frankly paternalistic reasons – for example, perennial donor hand-wringing around the fact that development recipients may be using the resources of donor-supplied ICT resources for "trivial" reasons: checking football scores rather than crop prices; writing love notes rather than resumes. Regardless of inspiration, by limiting or short-circuiting the development of local repair worlds, such efforts to manage use through design and policy seem likely to undermine, rather than support, long-term goals of sustainability.

Our third and related point has to do with the distinctive opportunities for learning that breakdown, maintenance, and repair provide – within but also well beyond the international development context studied here. Our favorite example of this comes from parallel fieldwork in Madagascar, where we encountered Mr. Rakoto, a former electrician and now owner-proprietor of a phone and computing repair shop in the country's eastern Mananjary region. Here's how Rakoto describes his introduction to his current line of work:

"When cellphones first came to Madagascar, I was curious to see how they functioned, and how they might break. So I bought one, threw it into the river here and then took it apart to see how the water and soil damaged it, and how it might be fixed."

This represents, we think, a strikingly different way of approaching the problem of maintenance and repair than the one dominating northern imaginations of IT design and sustainability, in international development and possibly other CSCW contexts. It constitutes a local version of what we'd like to call "broken-world thinking": a gestalt shift in our ways of thinking about sociotechnical system development that moves moments of maintenance and repair, rather than just moments of design and adoption, to the heart of CSCW thinking and practice.

Finally, as alluded to above, the cases offered here challenge the presumed separation between the design of IT artifacts and the design of IT policies that has tended to limit CSCW work to date. In the repair worlds of the Kavango region, this line is difficult to draw. From the standpoint of programmatic interventions like TechNA! or Computers for Kavango, the design of artifacts and the design of policy are better imagined as an interrelated whole whose integration or appropriate relation will go a long way towards determining success of the larger enterprise. By holding too faithfully to this divide, CSCW may be neglecting important and necessary sites of intervention and thereby falling once again into what a respondent once identified to us as an "edifice complex" – the stubborn tendency to over-privilege artifacts or systems to the neglect of the supporting contexts in which their coherence and efficacy is sustained. This too is a basic lesson of social worlds scholarship.

8.CONCLUSION

As the sometimes rapid, sometimes halting spread of ICT networks, devices, and practices has unfolded over the past ten-plus years in Sub-Saharan Africa and elsewhere, the kinds of repair worlds described here have come to play an increasingly central role. Recognizing, analyzing and supporting this work promises important practical and theoretical gains. Repair worlds may constitute interesting and overlooked sites of local innovation and expertise. They may support important kinds of extension and tailoring, stretching and repurposing extant infrastructure to new geographic and social communities. They may remediate traditional relations of dependency and social exclusion, sometimes amplifying these and sometimes ameliorating them. And by supporting and augmenting locally appropriate infrastructures, they may support new forms of distributed collective work that can further broad developmental goals of economic, social, and environmental sustainability and justice.

Acknowledgements: The authors wish to acknowledge the support and contributions of Flay Julius, Disho Muruti, Benjamin Sigrin, and Alex Voltiviski; without their help this work would not have been possible.

9. REFERENCES

[1] Dewey, J. 1896. The Reflex Arc Concept in Psychology. *Psychological Review, 3.* 357-370.

[2] Garfinkel, H. 1967. *Studies in Ethnomethodology*, Prentice Hall, Englewood Cliffs, NJ.

[3] Star, S.L. and Strauss, A. 1999. Layers of Silence, Arenas of Voice: The Ecology of Visible and Invisible Work. *Computer-Supported Cooperative Work, 8.* 9-30.

[4] Star, S.L. and K. Ruhleder. 1994. Steps Towards and Ecology of Infrastructure: Complex Problems in Design and Access for Large-Scale Collaborative

Systems. *Proceedings CSCW 1994*. New York: ACM. 253-264.

[5] Star, S.L. 1999. The Ethnography of Infrastructure. *American Behavioral Scientist, 43*. 377-391.

[6] Trigg, R.H., Moran, T.P. and Halasz, F.G. 1987. Adaptability and Tailorability in NoteCards. *INTERACT*. Stuttgart. 723-728.

[7] Nardi, B.A. 1993. *A Small Matter of Programming: Perspectives on End-User Programming*. MIT Press, Boston.

[8] Dourish, P. and Edwards, W.K. 2000. A Tale of Two Toolkits: Relating Infrastructure and Use in Flexible CSCW Toolkits. *Computer-Supported Cooperative Work 9*(1). 33-51.

[9] Bowers, J. 1994. The Work to Make a Network Work: Studying CSCW in Action. *Proceedings of CSCW 1994*. Chapel Hill: ACM. 287-298.

[10] Grudin, J. 1988. Why CSCW Applications Fail: Problems in Design and Evaluation of Organization Interfaces. *Proceedings of CSCW 1988*. Portland: ACM. 85-93.

[11] Orlikowski, W. 1992. Learning from Notes: Organizational Issues in Groupware Implementation. *Proceedings of CSCW 1992*. Toronto:ACM. 362-369.

[12] Karasti, H. and Syrjanen, A-L. 2004. Artful Infrastructuring in Two Cases of Community PD. *Participatory Design Conference (PDC)*. Toronto: CPSR. 20-30.

[13] Pipek, V. and Wulf, V. 2009. Infrastructuring: Towards an Integrated Perspective on the Design and Use of Information Technology. *Journal of the Association of Information Systems (JAIS), 10* (5). 448-473.

[14] Star, S.L. and Lampland, M. Reckoning with Standards. In Lampland, M., and Star, S.L. ed. *Standards and Their Stories: How Quantifying, Classifying, and Formalizing Practices Shape Everyday Life*. Cornell University Press. 3-24.

[15] Ribes, D. and Finholt, T. 2009. The Long Now of Infrastructure: Articulating Tensions in Development. *Journal of the Association of Information Systems* 10 (5). 375-398.

[16] Jackson, S.J., et al. 2007. Understanding Infrastructure: History, Heuristics, and Cyberinfrastructure Policy. *First Monday, 12* (6).

[17] Edwards, P.N., Bowker, G.C., Jackson, S.J., and Williams, R. 2009. Introduction: Towards an Agenda for Infrastructure Studies. *Journal of the Association of Information Systems (JAIS), 10* (5). 364-374.

[18] Strauss, A. and Corbin, J. 1998. *Basics of Qualitative Research Techniques and Procedures for Developing Grounded Theory* (2nd ed.). Sage, London.

[19] Charmaz, K. 2006. *Constructing Grounded Theory: A Practical Guide Through Qualitative Analysis*. Sage, London.

[20] Strauss, A. 1978. A Social Worlds Perspective. *Studies in Symbolic Interaction, 1* (1). 119-128.

[21] Becker, H.S. 1982. *Art Worlds*. University of California Press, Berkeley.

[22] Latour, B. 2000. When things strike back: A possible contribution of 'science studies' to the social sciences. *British Journal of Sociology, 51* (1). 107-123.

[23] Lessig, L. 1999. *Code And Other Laws of Cyberspace*. Basic Books, New York.

[24] Suchman, L. 1987. *Plans and Situated Actions*. Cambridge University Press, Cambridge.

[25] Orr, J.E. 1996. *Talking About Machines: An Ethnography of a Modern Job*. Cornell University Press, Ithaca.

[26] DiSalvo, C., Sengers, P, and Brynjarsdottir, H. 2010. Mapping the Landscape of Sustainable HCI. *Computer-Human Interaction*. Atlanta: ACM. 1975-1984.

[27] Grinter, R., et al. 2010. *Computing at the Margins*. Georgia Institute of Technology, Atlanta.

[28] Dutta, S. and I. Mia. 2010. *The Global Information Technology Report 2009-2010: ICT for Sustainability*, International Telecommunications Union.

[29] Telegeography. 2008. MTC Namibia Invests USD40m, Ends Reliance on Incumbent's Transport Network, in *Telegeography Research*, PriMetrica.

[30] UNDP. 2010. Human Development Report 2010, *United Nations Development Program*. New York.

[31] Jackson, S.J., Pompe, A., and Krieshok, G. 2011. Things Fall Apart: Maintenance, Repair, and Technology for Education Initiatives in Rural Namibia. *Proceedings of the iConference 2011*. Seattle: ACM. 83-90.

[32] Dourish, P. 2006. Implications for Design. in *CHI 2006*. Montreal:ACM. 541-550.

[33] Smith, N. 2008. *Uneven Development: Nature, Capital, and the Production of Space* (3rd ed). University of Georgia Press, Athens.

[34] Akrich, M. 1992. The De-Scription of Technical Objects, W.E. Bijker and J. Law, ed. in *Shaping Technology/Building Society: Studies in Sociotechnical Change*. MIT Press: Cambridge. 205-224.

[35] McNamara, K. 2003. *Information and Communication Technologies, Poverty, and Development: Learning from Experience*. World Bank,Washington DC.

How Did You Feel During Our Conversation? Retrospective Analysis of Intercultural and Same-Culture Instant Messaging Conversations

Duyen T. Nguyen
Department of Communication
Cornell University
tn248@cornell.edu

Susan R. Fussell
Department of Communication
Cornell University
sfussell@cornell.edu

ABSTRACT
Research has shown that intercultural communication can be more problematic than same-culture communication. In this study we use a technique called retrospective analysis in order to examine these problems in greater detail. American and Chinese participants discussed a crime story with either an American or a Chinese partner using Instant Messaging (IM). After the session, each participant reviewed the IM conversation in two-minute segments and rated it on several dimensions. Chinese participants reported significantly more problems than American participants, and partner culture affected all participants' feelings of annoyance. An analysis of the communication problems participants reported showed four themes: mismatched communication styles, differences in conversational focus, relationship-building issues, and problems with the IM medium. The results show how differences in communication styles can affect intercultural conversations and provide design suggestions for new tools to improve intercultural collaboration.

Author Keywords
Cross-culture communication, CMC, retrospective analysis

ACM Classification Keywords
H5.3 Group and Organization Interfaces: Computer-supported cooperative work

General Terms
Experimentation, Human Factors

INTRODUCTION
Global virtual teams (teams consisting of members in different geographical locations collaborating via computer mediated communication) have been found to offer many benefits such as a broad variety of expertise to work on a task, the ability to leverage on local knowledge and the ability to work around the clock [22]. However, global virtual teams also face communication problems such as misunderstandings, negative impressions of members, lack of trust and mutual awareness of one another on the team, due to both the cultural differences among the team members and the dispersed, virtual nature of team communication [e.g., 32]

Previous work has shown that these communication problems can be attributed in part to cultural differences in communication styles [e.g., 12, 13]. For example, speakers who use a high-context speaking style, which relies on the situation to make meaning clear, may react negatively when interacting with a speaker who uses a more direct, low-context style. Similarly, speakers favoring a low-context, explicit style of speech may misinterpret the subtleties of more indirect high context speech. The picture is further complicated by the fact that prior studies of computer mediated intercultural communication show quite different patterns of results depending on the medium of communication [e.g. 26, 27], the type of task, and the cultural composition of the group [30].

In order to better prevent or correct the above problems in computer mediated intercultural communication, we need a better understanding of the various types of issues that may arise during the communication process of intercultural teams. While previous studies have pointed out problematic processes in intercultural communication such as grounding [e.g. 20], participants' reactions to the interaction were obtained in a single questionnaire or interview after the fact, these studies likewise can't pinpoint what is going wrong at the level of the moment-by-moment dynamics of the interaction. The goal of the current study is to provide a deeper understanding of the kinds of communication problems that arise in intercultural teams and the impact of these problems on team performance and members' liking for one another.

In the current study, we use a technique from psychology called retrospective analysis [11], in which participants review an interaction after the fact, privately, and indicate their affective and cognitive reactions to each snippet of the interaction on a moment-by-moment basis. Using this technique, we show how cultural differences in communication style can lead to more problems and annoyance in an interaction. We then use qualitative techniques to explore the nature of the reported problems.

In the remainder of this paper, we first review background literature on intercultural communication and outline our hypotheses. We then present a study in which American and Chinese participants first work with a partner from the same or the other culture to first solve a crime task and then retrospectively review their interaction and rate it on a variety of dimensions. After presenting our findings, we conclude with some design recommendations for tools to support intercultural communication as well as a discussion of future areas for research.

BACKGROUND

In this section we first describe some of the ways that cultures have been posited to vary in terms of their communication styles; then, we outline the specific hypotheses tested in our study.

Cultural Differences in Communication Styles

Research has shown that team members from different cultures frequently differ in their communication styles, which may then lead to collaboration problems [6, 17]. Several theories address these differences, from different approaches and foci. Hall [13] has identified two communication styles: *low context*, typically Western, communication that is verbally explicit and to the point, and *high context*, typically Eastern communication that is indirect, often ambiguous, and sensitive to the context in which it occurs (e.g., the relationship between speaker and addressee, nuances of facial expressions or tone of voice).

Both high and low context style may work well for collaboration among people who share the same style. However, in intercultural teams where members may have different styles, problem can arise [6]. For example, while low context communicators typically expect their partners to directly express their opinion, including disagreement, high context communicators tend to express disagreement indirectly though silence. In this scenario, a low context communicator may erroneously assume that his or her partner is in agreement. At the same time, a low context, direct, style of communication may be perceived by high context communicators as inconsiderate and dominating.

Other studies have found that members from more individualistic cultures, such as those of many Western countries, typically focus on getting work done efficiently. In contrast, members of more collectivistic cultures, such as many Asian countries, often focus on building good relationships and establishing rapport with one's partners in addition to task completion [30]. This may impact negotiation strategies [28], strategies for making requests [1], methods of interruption [25], and other communicative behaviors. Clashes in these communicative behaviors in intercultural communication may lead to communication problems.

Even though previous studies in intercultural communication have suggested that culture groups do differ in communication styles and that intercultural communication may be problematic [e.g 25], it is still not clear what kinds of problems may arise and what aspects of the communication process may be negatively affected. A handful of studies have examined particular communicative behaviors such as conversational grounding (the interactive process of making sense of a partner's utterances) which can be problematic in intercultural communication [20, 21]. However, in these studies participants' reactions to their partners' communication were inferred from team performance or assessed by survey after the fact, rather than assessed in the moment of the communication itself.

Culture Communication Styles and CMC

There is evidence that culturally-shaped communication styles affect computer-mediated communication (CMC) as well as face-to-face conversations between cultures, and that the pattern of the effect depends on the features of the particular CMC medium. Setlock et al. [27], for example, found that American participants were relatively terse regardless of what medium they were using, in keeping with the view that Americans favor a low-context, verbally explicit conversational style, whereas Chinese participants spoke much longer face-to-face than when using CMC, in keeping with the view that Chinese favor a high-context style that relies on contextual information.

While many studies have reported differences between how members of different cultures communicate in CMC, the pattern of results across the studies is not always clear. For example, while Chinese participants were more talkative than Americans in Setlock et al.'s study, which used a negotiation task [27], Wang et al. [30] found that Chinese pairs were *less* talkative in a brainstorming task unless they worked with an American partner. This and similar contradictions in the literature suggest that we need a more nuanced understanding of how the different culturally-shaped communication styles influence the communication process of intercultural teams, whether or not they create problems in the communication process, and what kinds of problems arise.

The Current Study

The goal of the current study is to look more closely at how participants experience the communication process with a partner from a different culture versus with a partner from the same culture. Specifically, we examine whether or not participants encounter more problems working with a partner from a different culture than with one from the same culture, what aspects of the communication process were (or were not) problematic, and how that affected the outcome of collaboration. We use a technique in psychology called retrospective analysis [11] to gain in-depth, moment-by-moment understanding of problems encountered in cross-cultural IM conversations.

We focus on IM conversations between Americans and Chinese as these two groups have been shown to prefer distinct styles of communication. American speakers tend to be direct and to the point, and willing to express emotions, whereas Chinese speakers tend to be more indirect, relying on context to make their messages clear.

We examine the total problems reported after the IM conversation and two specific aspects of the communication process that may be problematic in intercultural communication: involvement and negative emotion. In addition, we explore people's open-ended descriptions of the problems they encountered. We also analyzed the outcomes of collaboration. Below, we outline the hypotheses of our study.

Communication Problems

For the reasons we have discussed, differences in high and low context communication styles between two communication partners may lead to misunderstandings. The lack of social cues in a text-based medium such as IM may further complicate communication between partners who favor different styles [24]. Therefore, we propose that:

Hypothesis 1A: Chinese participants will report more problems communicating with an American partner than with a Chinese partner.

Hypothesis 1B: American participants will report more problems communicating with a Chinese partner than with an American partner.

Involvement in Conversation

Cegala and colleagues [2] conceptualize involvement in an interaction as, "the extent to which an individual participates with another in a conversation," (pp. 229) in terms of responsiveness to the situation, perceptivity about one's own and a partner's behavior, and attentiveness to the environment. Involvement also includes receptiveness, or a willingness to listen and offer feedback, for example through backchannel responses like *uh huh* or *yeah* or nonverbal behaviors such as head nods [8, 16]. Involvement increases affiliation, expression of intimacy, regulation of interaction and conversational cohesion, thereby fostering better understanding [29].

Previous studies have found that people from different cultures may differ in the way they express and interpret involvement cues such as back channel responses [4, 21]. For example a forward lean might indicate involvement for one culture and an attempt to dominate for another culture. Moreover, in text-based IM where non-verbal cues are not supported, it may even be more difficult to express and interpret involvement cues, especially when conversational partners have different expectations. Therefore, we hypothesize that:

Hypothesis 2A: Chinese participants will report less involvement communicating with an American partner than with a Chinese partner.

Hypothesis 2B: American participants will report less involvement communicating with a Chinese partner than with an American partner.

Negative emotions in communication

Moods and emotions have influences on team interaction and performance and effective team communication involves attention to members' affective states, emotions and feelings [18]. Although there has not been much research focused on finding the cause of negative emotions in intercultural interactions, studies within a single culture find that negative emotions result from different team processes. Cegala [3] suggested that that low involvement in interaction was highly related to negative affect, especially anxiety, tension and low self-esteem. Cramton [6] observed that when mutual knowledge and understanding were not established in geographically dispersed teams, feelings of anxiety and tension developed. Thus, we hypothesized:

Hypothesis 3A: Chinese participants will report more negative emotions communicating with an American partner than with a Chinese partner.

Hypothesis 3B: American participants will report more negative emotions communicating with a Chinese partner than with an American partner.

Outcomes of Intercultural Collaboration

As discussed above, the communication problems, level of involvement and negative emotions experienced during an interaction can influence how each participant feels about the team's performance. When the task involves information exchange, differences in communication styles can lead to inefficient grounding and lower perceived performance [20]. Moods and emotions also affect team interaction and performance [18]. Previous studies suggested that high understanding, high involvement and low negative emotions would lead to better subjective team performance. Based on Hypotheses 1-3 above, we hypothesize:

Hypothesis 4A: Chinese participants will report lower subjective performance collaborating with an American partner than with a Chinese partner.

Hypothesis 4B: American participants will report lower subjective performance collaborating with a Chinese partner than with an American partner.

It is still unclear from the literature how problems of understanding, involvement and negative emotions during a conversation may affect the objective final outcomes of intercultural collaboration. While Li [20] found that better grounding led to better performance, other studies did not find objective performance differences despite differences in communication styles [e.g., 27, 30]. Based on our previous hypotheses we suggest that:

Hypothesis 5A: Chinese participants will achieve lower objective performance collaborating with an American partner than with a Chinese partner.

Hypothesis 5B: American participants will achieve lower objective performance collaborating with a Chinese partner than with an American partner.

METHOD

In order to understand how cultural differences in communication styles affect intercultural interaction, we used a retrospective analysis technique developed in psychology [11]. Same-culture and cross-culture pairs first discussed and solved a crime case using a text-based IM program. Afterwards, they individually reviewed a recording of their interaction. At preset intervals, the recording was stopped and participants provided their feedback on the segment.

Participants

Participants consisted of 60 students (53% undergraduate, 65% female) studying at a large American university. Of these, 30 students were native Chinese speakers who had been born in the People's Republic of China (29) or Taiwan (1), and had spent less than 5 years in the United States or Canada. The Chinese participants spoke fluent or near-fluent English. The other 30 American participants were all born and raised in the United States or Canada and spoke English as their native language. Twenty-eight American were Caucasian and two were Asian.

Each participant was paired randomly with a partner from the same culture or from a different culture, resulting in three combinations: 10 Chinese-Chinese (CC) pairs, 10 American-American (AA) pairs, and 10 American-Chinese (AC) pairs. To control for age differences we paired graduate students with other graduate students and undergraduates with other undergraduates. Participants in a pair did not know each other prior to the experiment.

Materials

Task. The task consisted of discussing a crime story and identifying the culprit of the crime. The crime story, developed by the first author, involved a break in and a murder attempt on a victim named Alex. Alex is the leader of a rock band of four people. The other three members of the band were the three prime suspects, one of whom was the actual culprit.

Two different versions of the crime story were prepared, based on the reports of two witnesses. Each version contained 10 pieces of information important to solving the case. The two versions shared common information about the victim, crime location, and attack on the victim. They also included details complementing each other that needed to be combined to fully understand what happened, such as the time and location of each of the suspects before and after the crime. The two versions also contained three contradictory details about the crime: (a) the time of the attack, (b) the body builds of the culprit and (c) the color of the shirt the culprit was wearing as they were reported from the different perspectives of the two witnesses. These had to be resolved through discussion to identify the culprit. The details were presented on a single sheet of paper (622 words for version A; 644 words for version B).

Memory quiz. A paper and pencil *memory quiz* was created to test participants' understanding of the materials prior to discussion with their partner. The quiz consisted of 10 multiple choice questions on the key details of the crime (e.g., time, suspects).

Culprit identification form. Since every pair had to provide a common answer to the case, we created a shared Google document between the two participants in a pair, with two questions on it: one for indicating the culprit(s) of the crime, and another for the pairs' reasoning behind their identification of this culprit. Both participants in each pair were able to edit this shared document at the same time. At the end of the discussion they saved this document.

Post task survey. Participants completed an online survey asking about their reactions to the task and partner, their communication styles, and their basic demographic information. Task-related questions consisted of four 7-point scales adapted from the NASA TLX workload scale [15] to measure mental effort, temporal effort, overall effort, and frustration during the task, and two 7-point scales to measure participants' subjective evaluation of their team and individual performance on the task.

Partner-related questions consisted of four 7-point scale items measuring the participant's liking of his/her partner, the partner's liking of the participant, the participant's enjoyment and comfort in working with their partners.

We also included an exploratory measure to examine participants' perceptions of their communication strategies. Questions about communicative styles include a subset of 13 items from Gudykunst et al.'s [12] high and low context culture scale, selected from the three factors that have the highest loadings in this study: ability to infer meaning, interpersonal sensitivity and use of indirect communication.

Retrospective analysis survey. The online *retrospective analysis survey* consisted of 7 rating questions and an additional open response question that participants completed after each 2-minute video clip. The first three questions asked each participant to rate on 5-point Likert scales their level of tension (very tense-very relaxed), annoyance (very annoyed-not annoyed at all) and interest (not interested at all-very interested) in the conversation. The next two questions asked participants to rate how much their partners understood them and how much they understood their partners, respectively (1 = not understanding at all; 7 = very understanding). The remaining two questions asked the participants to rate how much their partners and they themselves felt involved with the conversation (1 = not involved at all; 7 = very involved). The final question asked whether the participant had noticed any problem with their interaction at the point of time shown in the video clip. If the answer was yes, we asked them to provide details about what went wrong and what they would have done to prevent/remedy the problem.

Equipment and Recording Processing

Participants in all pairs used identical Dell workstations running the same version of Gtalk for Window XP. We disabled the use of audio call in Gtalk. The Gtalk chat window of the two participants in each pair were recorded, synchronized and combined into a split screen video during their discussion using CamStudio 2.5 desktop capturing software and ShowMyPC 3011 remote desktop sharing software. The split screen video consisted of two frames, one for each participant's Gtalk chat window. During retrospective analysis, each participant was shown only the frame with his or her own chat window.

Two Dell workstations with Dell Ultrasharp 19 inch monitors (1140 x 900 resolution) were used to present the video clips during the retrospective analysis. The 20-minute video of the discussion was divided into 10 sequential clips of 2 minute each to be played one by one in chronological order to both participants using Quicktime Player.

Procedure

The experiment consisted of two phases: a discussion phase and a retrospective analysis phase. In the *Discussion Phase*, pairs of participants were brought into a room and assigned seats at two separated workstations with a divider in between. They signed consent forms and received task instructions. Each participant received one of the two versions of the crime story. They were given 10 minutes to read the story and learn the details of the crime, after which the hard copies were taken away and they were given the memory test. The experimenter then corrected the quiz and left the corrected quiz with the participants for the rest of the experiment. Participants were then instructed how to use the Gtalk text chat client.

Each pair then discussed the story via Gtalk for 20 minutes (Figure 1). In order to solve the crime, the pairs needed to gather all the information from both versions of the story, resolve conflicting details, and identify the culprit. At the end of their interaction, each pair submitted their conclusion about the culprit and the reasoning behind their decision in the culprit identification form. Each participant in the pair then separately filled out the post-task survey.

In the *Retrospective Analysis Phase*, the two participants were seated as in the previous phase. They were shown a series of 10 two-minute video clips of their conversation in Phase 1. After each clip, participants filled out the retrospective analysis survey. After the last clip, participants were debriefed, paid and dismissed.

Figure 1. Setting of the discussion phase.

Measures

The dependent variables were number of problems, levels of understanding, involvement and negative emotions, subjective outcomes and performance.

Problems. We collected a binary measure for whether or not problems were reported every two-minute segment of the 20-minute long interaction.

Involvement. Participants' ratings, on a 7-point scale, of how much they felt involved in the conversation (self's involvement) during each minute of their interaction were negatively skewed and recoded into three groups, representing the bottom, middle and top third of the responses (1 to 5=1 "low", 6=2 "middle", and 7=3 "high").

Interest. Participants indicated, on a 5-point scale, how much interest they felt in the conversation. This measure was also negatively skewed and recoded into three groups, representing the bottom, middle and top third of the responses (1 to 3 =1 "low", 4=2 "middle", and 5=3 "high").

Negative emotions. Participants' ratings on a 5-point scale of how tense and how annoyed they felt in the conversation were negatively skewed and recoded into three groups, representing the bottom, middle and top third of the responses (1=1 "low", 2 to 3=2 "middle", and 4 to 5=3 "high").

Subjective performance. The two questions measuring participants' subjective evaluation of team performance and individual performance were averaged to create a composite score (Cronbach's alpha = .54).

Liking of partner. The four questions measuring participants' liking and comfort while working with their partner were average to create a composite score about their emotional experience on the task (Cronbach's alpha= .81).

Perceptions of communication strategy. Responses to the 13 items were averaged (after inverting the low context items) to create a measure of self-reported high context communication style (Cronbach's alpha = .51). Since scale reliability was relatively low and a preliminary screening showed no differences between cultures ($F[1, 56]<1$, n.s), we do not discuss this measure further.

Objective performance. Pairs' answers to the crime task consisted of two parts: the name of the culprit(s) and an explanation for the solution. The identity of the culprit was scored 1 for correct or 0 for incorrect. The explanations were scored in terms of the presence of three key clues needed to prove the culprit guilty. Two research assistants blind to the conditions of the experiment coded responses for the presence of these clues (kappa= 90%).

RESULTS

We report the results in three parts: retrospective analysis, performance on the task. We follow these results with our qualitative analysis of the problems participants reported.

Retrospective Analysis of Pair Interaction

To test Hypotheses 1 to 4, we conducted mixed model

Analyses of Variance with self's culture, partner's culture and the interaction of these two as the fixed effects, and pairs, individual within pairs, and time within individual as random effects. Note that in mixed models, when tests of fixed effects involve a linear combination of variances at different levels of the model (e.g., group and individual), it is standard to estimate the degree of freedoms associated with the denominators by using Satterthwaite's approximation. Therefore, non-integer degree of freedoms may occur [23]. Because our hypotheses concern the fixed effects of culture, we present only these fixed effects below.

Problems in Collaboration. Hypotheses 1A and 1B predicted that participants would report more problems when working with a partner from another culture than when working with a partner from their own culture. To test these hypotheses, we conducted a mixed model analysis of the form outlined above, using the number of problems reported during the retrospective analysis as our dependent measure. We found a significant main effect of participants' culture (Figure 2). Chinese participants reported more problems than Americans, regardless of their partners' culture (for Chinese, M= .397, SEM= 0.05; for American, M= .167, SEM= 0.05; $F[1, 51.9]=13.46$, $p<0.01$). However, contrary to our hypotheses there were no effects of partner's culture and no interaction between participant and partner culture (both $F < 1$, n.s.).

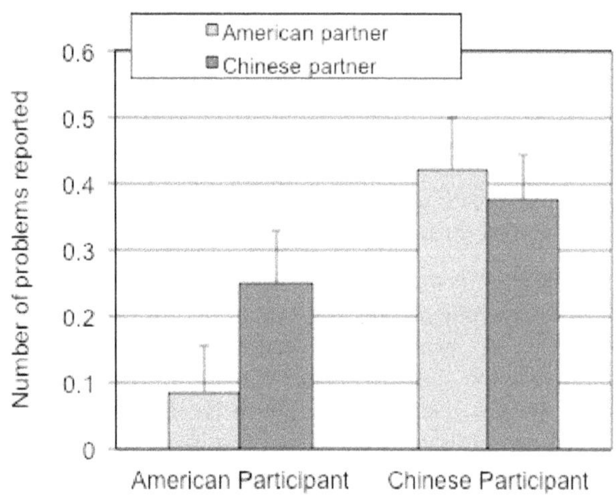

Figure 2. Mean number of problems reported per two-minute interval by participant culture and partner culture.

Involvement. Hypotheses 2A and 2B predicted that participants would report lower involvement when working with a partner from a different culture than when working with a partner of the same culture. Mixed model ANOVAS on the level of involvement and interest reported during the retrospective analysis showed no support for these hypotheses (all Fs<1, n.s).

Negative emotions. Hypotheses 3A and 3B predicted that participants would report more negative emotions when working with a partner from a different culture than when working with a partner from the same culture. A mixed model ANOVA on the level of annoyance reported during the retrospective analysis showed a significant main effect of partner culture ($F [1, 59.1]=7.7$, $p= .007$) (Figure 3). Both Chinese and American participants reported more annoyance working with a Chinese partner than with an American partner (for Chinese partner, M=1.84, SEM= .14; for American partner, M=1.47, SEM= .14). This contradicts Hypothesis 3A, while supporting Hypothesis 3B.

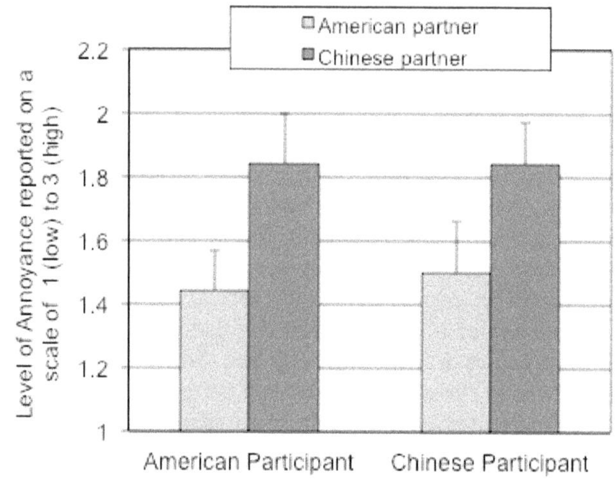

Figure 3. Mean level of annoyance reported per two-minute interval by participant culture and partner culture.

Outcome Measures

Subjective Outcomes. Hypotheses 4A and 4B predicted that participants would report lower subjective performance working with a partner from a different culture than when working with a partner from the same culture. These hypotheses were not confirmed. Two-way ANOVAs (self culture by partner culture) showed no effects of either factor on perceived performance ($F[1,56] <1$, n.s).

Performance. Hypotheses 5A and 5B predicted that participants would perform worse on the task when working with a partner from a different culture than when working with a partner from the same culture. These hypotheses were also not confirmed. A one-way ANOVA using culture combination (AA, AC, CC) as a between-pairs factor showed no significant effects for either the binary rating of the answers given by the pairs and or the total number of clues given in the explanations ($F [1,56] <1$, n.s).

Types of problems faced in collaboration

In the first part of the results, we found that participants encountered problems with intercultural communication and reported annoyance with their partners. In this part, we examine the kinds of problems participants faced, and some of the reasons why they were annoyed with their partners. We analyzed the comments participants gave for each problem they reported using a grounded theory approach [10]. Two coders, blind to experimental conditions, independently reviewed all the comments and came up with their own categorizations. They then discussed their schemes and identified four major categories of problems: mismatched communication styles, disagreement about the focus of the conversation, relationship-building issues, and problems with the use of IM.

Mismatched Communication Styles

Communication problems were related to aspects of the communication process between the two partners in a pair, such as understanding or involvement. For both American and Chinese participants, these comprised a large proportion of the total number of problems reported (over 25%). Participants noted problems understanding their partners, or making their partners understand them. Some participants attributed these problems to differences in communication styles.

"I guess it was more or less about the style of communication. I prefer direct communication but my partner seems to be more reserved, thinking through the things himself first. So I feel that in this period of the communication, he was involved in his own thinking instead of really getting the meaning of my message. And I was a bit annoyed that he did not really talk up. So I was not sure whether he understood me or not. To do it better, maybe he should talk more and I should have more patience to wait for his info." (Chinese in CC pair)

"I would expect my partner to give me feedback if she understood my explanation about why the two observers reported different colors of the t-shirt and the height later on. I remember I totally explained that for three times, as this was a key point, I need to know if she understood or not, agree or not. I became a little bit annoyed." (Chinese in CC pair)

We notice two conflicts in communication style. First, as illustrated in the comment above, some participants (both Chinese and American) preferred to communicate directly, even in potential disagreements, while their partners were more indirect and used silence to indicate disagreement or confusion. Second, there was a conflict in the speed of conversation. Some participants preferred a fast, back and forth conversation while their partner preferred to think through their response.

"Maybe I should have done it better, listening to him more carefully instead of always expressing my views all the time. But still, I personally prefer a faster conversation." (Chinese in CC pair)

They were also uncomfortable if their partners did not pay enough attention during the conversation, or diverged from the topic.

"I remember being very annoyed at this point, because we were finally comparing information, but then we were side-tracked." (American in AC pairs)

"I wanted to focus on the task 100%, but my partner talked about something irrelevant which did not help my understanding of his information. I believe we should have 100% focused on the task instead." (Chinese in CC pair)

Participants were also frustrated when their partner was not sufficiently responsive to them.

"I was slightly annoyed at this point because I had specifically asked about information regarding the suspect, Dave, and my partner seemed to ignore the question." (American in AC pair)

Some complained about how their partner were not talking enough, or responding fast enough and how they did not feel like having a back and forth conversation.

"Yes, we could have done it better if my partner could talk about things more quickly and directly. I was the one who did most of the talking which was not enough for me to understand what he thought." (Chinese in CC pair)

Disagreement about Conversational Focus

Additional problems pertained to the process the pairs went through to carry out the discussion task. For example, participants reported conflicts in the approach and process they and their partner used to discuss the task, for example, what to talk about first and last.

"I preferred to share our different information before analyzing it, but my partner was insistent on speculation without getting all the facts first." (American in AA pair)

Because of the difficulties they experienced exchanging information verbally, some participants felt they should have documented their information in a systematic and orderly fashion

"I think we should have actually created a table on the Google doc to share and combine information more quickly." (American in AA pair)

Others felt they should have focused their conversations differently. They were frustrated when their partners told them details they didn't expect and didn't know how make sense of such differences to come to a common conclusion.

"We didn't do right to convert our evidences together. We should consider why there are such a big difference in the words of those two witnesses and what makes the differences." (Chinese in AC pair)

"We should have talked about the evidence more. I think I was too quick to implicate Brian and she was not giving up the opposing information she had." (American in AC pair)

Relationship Building Issues

Consistent with previous research [e.g., 25] we found that Chinese participants mentioned problems with relationship building in addition to task-related conversation. These kinds of problems were never mentioned by American participants.

"I should have sent greeting sentence before directly entering the topic. It would be better for building good cooperation." (Chinese in AC pair)

"I should have expressed my appreciation for partner's agreeing on my opinion." (Chinese in AC pair)

Some participants complained about the dominating and judgmental manner of their partner during the conversation.

"I am a bit conservative. She is a bit judgmental." (Chinese in CC pair)

Trouble with the IM Communication Medium

Finally, having the conversation in a text-based instant messaging system created problems for some participants. Participants felt that the lack of visuals and the need to type out their opinions prevented them from fully and quickly expressing themselves.

"We felt that only chatting was not enough. We need to talk about the scenes mano a mano." (Chinese in CC pair)

"It just seems like a slow way to communicate, I would have put info together better had it been visual- which I did on my paper." (American in AA pair)

Moreover, since instant messaging allows two people to type simultaneously, a double-threaded conversation might happen that could be confusing

"We kind of had two conversations going on at the same time which probably made it hard for her to understand me, I probably should have written more complete sentences." (American in AA pair)

Chinese participants were particularly concerned about their written English in the chat medium. They were afraid that typos and unfamiliarity with chat language use on their part would confuse their partner. These problems however were not related to the level of fluency of English and in fact, no Chinese participant voiced any concern about their fluency of using English in a written chat environment.

"Another big problem for both of us, is we type in the whole spelling of the words all the time, we're not too familiar with the short forms of words used in online chatting by native speakers." (Chinese in CC pairs)

In some cases, this language barrier led to lack of trust in the partner.

"There seemed to be a language barrier, so I didn't fully trust what my partner was saying about the story." (American in AC pair)

DISCUSSION

This study aimed to examine the problems encountered in intercultural collaboration and their impact on people's affective responses and task performance. We found that Chinese participants reported more problems than Americans participants, regardless of the culture of their partners. Curiously, we found that participants, regardless of their own cultures, reported higher annoyance working with a Chinese partner. However, these communication problems and momentary annoyances had no long-term effect on task performance, nor did they affect how involved people felt in the conversations.

We had hypothesized that participants would report more problems working with a partner from a different culture than from the same culture. As shown in Figure 2, the means per condition were in the direction we predicted (Americans reported more problems with Chinese partners; Chinese reported more problems with American partners), but the differences were not statistically significant. Possibly, a future study with a larger sample would detect significant interactions between one's own and a partner's culture.

It is puzzling that participants of both cultures reported higher annoyance working with a Chinese partner. One explanation may be that the Chinese participants were speaking in a non-native language, leading to miscommunication. However our qualitative coding of the problems people reported also points to another factor: incompatibilities in communication styles among the Chinese participants. Some Chinese participants favored a direct low context style and, like American participants, had trouble communicating with Chinese who favored an indirect high context style. This variability in Chinese communication styles is consistent with other research showing that high context communicators (or those raised in that tradition) can adjust flexibly to match the styles of low context communicators [30], a process likely to occur when people are studying in the U.S. for an extended period of time. This too may explain the lack of significant differences between populations on the Gudykunst low vs. high context communication scales.

Our coding of the communication problems participants reported showed that a large proportion of them were related to communication styles, including a partner's "failure" to directly express his or her opinions, or a failure to engage in relationship-building behavior. It is also worth noting that in a written chat environment, our Chinese participants did not voice any concern over their English fluency. This is consistent with previous results that these environments were generally preferred by non-native English speakers to express themselves clearly [e.g. 24]. However, chatting also entails the use of some special English chat lingo that global team members may not be familiar with and should avoid in intercultural interactions.

The communication problems we discovered did not, in this study, have any impact on performance but it remains to be seen whether chronic patterns of misunderstandings and annoyance would affect team collaboration and team in real world global teams. It is also worth noting that participants in this experiment regarded the task of solving a crime story in 20 minutes a nontrivial task that required effort and time commitment, as evidenced by means on the NASA workload scale. Differences in involvement based on a partner's cultural background might arise when teams are engaged in tasks that demand less cognitive effort.

The different communication styles, and a lack of common ground were the often mentioned as reasons for a partner's "inappropriate" communicative behaviors. This echoed previous studies of how negative emotions may be linked to the communication process [3] and thus can provide a hint to how we could design technology to intervene the communication process to prevent negative emotions in intercultural interaction.

Design Implications

Our findings indirectly suggest some strategies for designing new tools to support intercultural communication. First, feedback displays and other interventions might improve intercultural teamwork by either making cultural differences more apparent to team members [e.g. 7] or by intervening automatically in problematic conversations [e.g. 31]. For example, participants reported that a lack of response from their partners made them frustrated and annoyed. To prevent this, a system might display feedback about each participant's contributions to the conversation, similar to the GroupMeter system [e.g. 19], making it obvious when one partner is providing less feedback than the other. In addition, Chinese participants reported negative emotions when the team did not pay attention to relationship building. A system might display feedback about the amount of social exchanges, such as greetings, to motivate intercultural teams to engage in team building activities.

Second, some of our participants mentioned that mere verbal exchange of information was insufficient for intercultural teams and that they needed other modalities, such as images or diagrams, to document their team activities in a more comprehensible way to all team members. This suggests that a combination of communication channels should be provided for efficient and effective intercultural team collaboration.

Third, our results indicate that negative emotions may be an important issue in intercultural collaboration. Therefore, tools might incorporate strategies to minimize the negative emotions that result when communication problems are encountered. We believe this is especially important given evidence that negative emotions can be contagious in CMC [14]. Significant progress has been made identifying emotions from CMC [e.g., 9], which could in turn drive interventions to increase positive mood (e.g. via pictures of positive events, color, music).

Limitations and Future Directions

There are several important limitations to the current study. First, we examined dyads, not larger groups of cross-culture members, which may be more typical of global teamwork. We also focused only on two out of the many cultures of the world. Furthermore, our Chinese participants were studying or working in the U.S and do not represent the larger population of Chinese people with whom Americans might collaborate. In the future, we plan to replicate the study using a more culturally diverse set of participants. We also did not control for participants' experience working in multicultural settings, which may have affected the experience of participants during the experiment.

Our next steps include a more detailed coding of the transcripts to further understand the dynamics of the dialogues at the time at which participants report a problem. We also plan to explore how our various measures of the communication process change over time during the interaction. With the findings from these analyses, we hope we can uncover the mechanism by which the communication process could lead to communication problems in intercultural collaboration. This in turn will help us characterize these problems at a deeper level, which hopefully will provide insights into how intercultural collaboration can be improved.

CONCLUSION

In this study we explored the problems that arise in intercultural communication in text-based Instant Messaging. We used retrospective analysis to examine three aspects of the communication process: number of problems, involvement and negative emotions, in 30 pairs of American and Chinese participants. We found that a person's own culture affected the number of problems reported whereas the partner's culture affected levels of annoyance during the interaction. However, we did not find an interaction between one's own culture and a partner's culture. We observed several themes in the kinds of problems participants reported facing during their interactions, including mismatching in conversational styles, task focus, emphasis on relationship-building, and use of the IM tool. Our findings help clarify when cultural can lead to problems in interactions and inform the design of new tools for intercultural communication.

ACKNOWLEDGMENTS

This work was funded in part by NSF grants #0803482 and #0942658. We thank Dan Cosley and Hao Chuan Wang for their thoughtful feedback on the experimental design, Stephanie Sanders, Kathryn Duerr, and Jin Liu for running participants and preparing data for analysis. We also thank Leslie Setlock and the anonymous reviewers for their feedback on past revisions of the paper. This material is based in part on work supported by the National Science Foundation, while Susan Fussell was working at the Foundation. Any opinion, findings, and conclusions or recommendations expressed in this material are those of the authors and do not necessarily reflect the views of the National Science Foundation.

REFERENCES

1. Ambady, N., Koo, J., Less, F., & Rosenthal, R. (1996). More than words: Linguistic and nonlinguistic politeness in two cultures. *Journal of Personality and Social Psychology,* 70, 996-1011.
2. Cegala, D. J., Savage, G. T., Brunner, C. C., & Conrad, A. (1982). An elaboration of the meaning of interaction involvement: Toward the development of a theoretical concept. *Communication Monograghs*, 49, 229-248.

3. Cegala, D.J. (1984). Affective and cognitive manifestations of interaction involvement during unstructured and competitive interactions. *Communication Monograph*, 51, 320-338.
4. Chen, L. (1995). Interaction involvement and patterns of topical talk: A comparison of intercultural and intracultural dyads. *International journal of Intercultural Relations*, 19, 463-482.
5. Clark, H. H., & Brennan, S. E. (1991). Grounding in communication. In L. B. Resnick, R. M. Levine & S. D. Teasley (Eds.), *Perspectives on socially shared cognition*. Washington DC: APA Press.
6. Cramton, C. D. (2001). The mutual knowledge problem and its consequences for dispersed collaboration. *Organization Science*, 12, 346-371.
7. Diamant, E. I., Fussell, S. R. & Lo, F. (2008). Where did we turn wrong?: unpacking the effect of culture and technology on attributions of team performance. *Proc. CSCW 2008,* 383-392.
8. Drummond, K. & Hopper, R. (1993a). Back channels revisited: acknowledgment tokens and speakership incipiency, 26, 2, 157–177.
9. Gill, A.J., French, R.M., Gergle, D., & Oberlander, J. (2008). The Language of Emotion in Short Blog Texts. *Proceedings of CSCW 2008.*
10. Glaser, B. G., & Strauss, A. L. (1967). *The Discovery of Grounded Theory: Strategies for Qualitative Research.* New York: Aldine de Gruyter.
11. Gottman, J.M. & Levenson, R.W. (1985). A valid procedure for obtaining self-report of affect in marital interaction. *Journal of Consulting and Clinical Psychology, 53*, 151-160.
12. Gudykunst, W. B., Matsumoto, Y., Ting-Toomey, S., Nishida, T., Kim, K., & Heyman, S. (1996). The influence of cultural individualism-collectivism, self construals, and individual values on communication styles across cultures. *Human Comm. Research*, 22, 510.
13. Hall, E. T. (1976). *Beyond culture*. Garden City, N.Y: Anchor Press.
14. Hancock, J. T., Gee, K., Ciaccio, K. & Mae-Hwah Lin, J. M.-H. (2008). I'm sad you're sad: emotional contagion in CMC. *Proceedings of CSCW '08.*
15. Hart, S. G., & Staveland, L. E. (1988). Development of a multi-dimensional workload rating scale: Results of empirical and theoretical research. In P. A. Hancock & N. Meshkati (Ed.), *Human mental workload* (pp. 139-183). Amsterdam: Elsevier.
16. Heinz, B. (2003). Backchannel responses as strategic responses in bilingual speakers' conversations. *Journal of Pragmatics*, 35, 1113-1142.
17. Hinds, P. & Kiesler, S. (2002). *Distributed work.* Cambridge, MA: MIT Press.
18. Kelly, J. R., & Barsade, S. (2001). Emotions in small groups and work teams. *Organizational Behavior and Human Decision Processes*, 86, 99-130.
19. Leshed, G., Hancock, J., Cosley, D., McLeod, P. & Gay, C. (2007). Feedback for guiding reflection on teamwork practices. *Proc. GROUP 2007.* 217-220.
20. Li, H. Z. (1999). Grounding and information communication in intercultural and intracultural dyadic discourse. *Discourse Processes*, *28*, 195.
21. Li, H. Z. (2006). Backchannel responses as misleading feedback in intercultural discourse. *Journal of Intercultural Communication Research*, 35, 2, 99-116.
22. Lipnack, J. & Stamp, J. (1997). *Virtual teams: Reaching Across Space, Time and Organizations with Technology.* NY: John Wiley & Sons.
23. Littell, R., Milliken, G. A., Stroup, W. W., & Wolfinger, R. D. (1996). *SAS system for mixed models*. Cary, NC: SAS Institute.
24. Massey A. P., Hung, Y. C, Montoya-Weiss, M. & Ramesh, V., 2001. When culture and style aren't about clothes: perceptions of task-technology "fit" in global virtual teams. *Procs. of GROUP '01*, 207-213.
25. Setlock, L. D. & Fussell, S. R. (2010). What's it worth to you? The costs and affordances of CMC tools to Asian and American users. *Proc. CSCW 2010*, 341-350.
26. Setlock, L. D., Quinones, P. & Fussell, S. R. (2007). Does culture interact with media richness? The effects of audio vs. video conferencing on Chinese and American dyads. *Proc. HICSS 2007*, 13.
27. Setlock, L. D., Fussell, S. R. & Neuwirth, C. (2004). Taking it out of context: collaborating within and across cultures in face-to-face settings and via instant messaging. *Proc. CSCW 2004*, 604-613.
28. Ting-Toomey, S. (1988). Intercultural conflict styles: A face-negotiation theory. In Y. Y. Kim & W. Gudykunst (Eds.), *Theories in intercultural communication* (pp. 213-235). Newbury Park, CA: Sage.
29. Villaume, W.A. & Cegala, D. J. (1988). Interaction involvement and discourse strategies: The patterned use of cohesive devices in conversation. Communication Monographs, 55, 20-40.
30. Wang, H., Fussell, S. F. & Setlock, L. D. (2009). Cultural difference and adaptation of communication styles in computer-mediated group brainstorming. *Proc. CHI 2009*, 669-678.
31. Wang, H. C., Rosé, C.P., et al. (2007). Thinking hard together: The long and short of collaborative idea generation for scientific inquiry. *Proc. CSCL 2007.*
32. Windsor, D. (2001). International virtual teams: Opportunities and issues. *Advances in Interdisciplinary Studies of Work Teams, 8*, 1-3.

Supporting Traditional Music-Making: Designing for Situated Discretion

Steve Benford, Peter Tolmie, Ahmed Y. Ahmed, Andy Crabtree, Tom Rodden
Mixed Reality Laboratory & Horizon Centre for Digital Economy Research
The University of Nottingham, Nottingham NG8 1BB, UK

ABSTRACT
An ethnographic study of Irish music sessions in pubs elaborates the collaborative work involved in making traditional music. Central to this distinctive achievement is the sequencing of tunes so that they hang together and combine to form discrete 'sets', which rely on a shared knowledge of musical repertoires. Our study shows how musicians develop this musical knowledge through the use of digital resources and social networks. It also reveals how musicians construct and make use of various paper props to help bring their knowledge to bear in the actual *in vivo* course of a session so as to maintain the moral order of making music together in a demonstrably traditional way. The social demands of musical 'etiquette' sensitise CSCW to the need to design technologies to support the 'situated discretion' that is essential to traditional practices. We elaborate this notion through a discussion of requirements for technologies that bridge between online resources and the collaborative sequencing of tunes during performance.

Author Keywords
Ethnography, traditional music, improvisation situated discretion, Irish music sessions.

ACM Classification Keywords
H.5.m. Information interfaces and presentation (e.g., HCI)

General terms
Human Factors

INTRODUCTION
Traditional Irish music sessions are to be found at venues around the globe, more often than not in a pub or a bar. At first glance they appear to be quite unstructured, with little attempt to 'stage' a performance as one might find in a theatre or concert hall. The music is fluid; played 'by ear'. It unfolds over the course of several hours and is punctuated by frequent breaks as participants peel off to chat and drink before they return to making music again. The music may appear loose and disorganised but a distinctive *moral order* or 'etiquette' shapes how a session is conducted, including what it is appropriate to play, when, how many times and with what instruments. Indeed, the subtle complexities of this etiquette have led to the publication of 'field guides' for beginners [13, 20].

A diverse range of interests in music, its practices, the collaboration that goes on between musicians, and the sharing of music itself has evolved in recent years. This includes work on the design of new instruments for both expert and non-expert musicians [e.g., 5, 6, 21]; support for musical coordination [e.g., 14, 23, 25] and improvisation [e.g., 7, 8, 9, 19, 29]; and for how people use, share, and synchronize music across a range of different social settings [e.g., 3, 4, 12, 16, 26, 33]. Set against these is the Irish music session, a vitally important feature of which is that it is *traditional* – electronic and digital instruments are consciously shunned: amplifiers are generally not welcome, let alone synthesizers or music software running on laptops. So given this apparent Luddite tendency, and that there are numerous avenues already being pursued, why are Irish music sessions of any relevance to CSCW?

The moral order of Irish music sessions is the key. It provides for the collaborative accomplishment *of tradition*, an accomplishment which seems to militate against technological intervention but in fact, only does so in the *in vivo* course of playing music together: *in making the tradition happen again.* Behind the scenes Irish session musicians are as technologically savvy and competent as the next man or woman in the street. Like anyone else they know how to make use of the Internet and they have been doing so for practical purposes of making traditional music for years. Specialized social networking sites support the community in transcribing, documenting and discussing the Irish repertoire, for example, and conventional social media are used to organise sessions and exchange materials.

The apparent dichotomy between traditional practice in actual sessions and the digital technologies that surround them is of interest to us, but also has broader salience for the wider CSCW community. Of particular relevance is the notion of 'situated discretion' which reflects the need to develop technology in ways that both respect tradition and yet enable traditional music-makers to continue to leverage the 'new world' into the 'old'. Below we elaborate the work involved in making traditional music, including the production and use of in-session resources and digital resources outside of sessions. In doing so, we uncover the distinctive problems and challenges that confront session musicians in accomplishing tradition and that in turn, inform this broader notion of situated discretion.

CSCW'12, February 11–15, 2012, Seattle, Washington, USA.

AN ETHNOGRAPHIC STUDY OF TRADITION

Our study of traditional Irish music sessions was conducted through an ethnomethodological approach [15], which has been widely practiced within CSCW as a way of sensitising designers to the social characteristics of particular settings and their work [11]. We visited various Irish music sessions, observing them as they unfolded, capturing video and photographs, and talking to participants. We also conducted informal interviews with some of the participants in their homes afterwards in order to explore how they prepared for sessions, including their use of online resources. Two researchers visited each session. One was an experienced ethnographer who observed and gathered data, while the other was a keen amateur Irish musician who joined in the sessions. Accompanying a player helped the ethnographer gain an inside perspective, enabling them to sit among the musicians rather than observing from the sidelines and facilitating discussions with them during the unfolding course of events.

We visited three different regular sessions in Nottingham in the UK, each informally named after its host pub. The 'King Billy' session meets every Thursday evening. It is a longstanding session, reputed to have been running for over thirty years, and is well known for a high standard of musicianship. The 'Vat and Fiddle' session meets on the second Sunday afternoon of every month, has been running for a few years, and is frequented by a wide range of players, including beginners, younger players, and relative experts. The 'Hop Pole' session is newer still, meets on a Tuesday evening in a suburban pub and is home to a wider variety of players in terms of experience and genre. Outside of these, we also visited the 'Elm Tree', a longstanding session that takes place in the city of Durham, providing an opportunity to observe what it's like to visit a hitherto unknown session as a nomadic outsider.

When we speak about an 'Irish session' we are not, of course, speaking of sessions that have to take place in Ireland; equally, many of the musicians playing at these sessions will not be Irish. Rather, we are talking of informal gatherings of local musicians in pubs and bars to play music whose dominant style and repertoire is drawn from the Irish tradition; a broadly recognisable form of music that has spread worldwide along with the Irish diaspora. The repertoire need not be exclusively Irish, and some sessions (more than others) are open to varied traditional styles including Scottish, English, Welsh, French, Scandinavian and American. Indeed, there is a deal of confusion as to the origin of many traditional tunes that have migrated between these various genres. Our sampling illustrated this diversity. The King Billy has a strong Irish focus, while the Vat and Fiddle and Hop Pole are more diverse, being open to a wide range of acoustic songs and tunes along with a good measure of 'Irish', and the Elm Tree reflected the influence of local Northumbrian music.

Given the relatively diversity of even this limited sample of sessions, we are careful not to claim too wide a generality for our findings; we cannot say that we would necessarily observe precisely the same practices in other sessions, especially in other regions or countries, though it is likely that at least some of the accountable features of the work involved in making this kind of music will hold because (as we shall elaborate shortly) they are embedded within common 'work practices' or methods of social interaction.

Elaborating the accountable character of social interaction is central to ethnomethodological studies [15]. In place of generalised versions of social order, ethnomethodology seeks to elaborate the social order in lived details of the incarnate organisation of social interaction – i.e., in details of its situated, embodied, and material character as it is made observable and reportable in local circumstances by the particular parties to it for the practical purposes of the work they are collaboratively engaged in 'here and now'. Our study focuses, then, on the interactional work the setting's members busied themselves with: the particular things they said, the particular things they did, the particular things they used and were visibly occupied with.

We present our findings in several parts, beginning with observations on the social organisation of sessions, including the organisation of the pub setting; how tunes are played; how they are sequenced together into sets; how this often relies on various paper props and cues; the notion of 'session etiquette'; and the use of online resources. Irish sessions, like any other live musical accomplishment, are complex phenomenon and so we restrict ourselves here to those features of our studies that speak most strongly to technology design and CSCW.

THE SOCIAL ORGANISATION OF IRISH SESSIONS

The pub or bar setting fundamentally shapes the nature of a traditional Irish music session. A session typically occurs within one area of a pub: side bars at the King Billy and Vat and Fiddle, in the centre of the back room at the Hop Pole, and in a larger bar at the Elm Tree, for example. All of these were connected to other areas in the pub, enabling the wider public to see into and pass through the space of the session. In spite of this, we saw no evidence of explicit attempts to reserve specific seating for the musicians. This distinguishes Irish sessions from other pub performances such as bands where there is a marked stage.

Another grossly observable feature of the social organisation of an Irish session is that the musicians try to sit in a circle if possible and will work hard to maintain the circle as other players arrive, facing inwards towards each rather than outwards towards spectators. This no doubt aids musical coordination as we discuss below, but it also adds to the sense of informal jamming rather than formal performance. Attendance at the sessions we observed ranged from a handful of musicians up to a maximum of about fifteen. Notably, the circle at the Hop Pole was bisected by a thoroughfare that led from the bar to outside the building where people go to smoke. The stream of people passing through at busy times clearly hindered the musicians' ability to see and hear one another, leading to coordination problems and fragmentation into sub-groups.

Figure 1. Playing in a circle at the Vat and Fiddle.

The temporal arrangement of the session is also significant. While there are generally understood start and end times, these are fluid, with the music beginning when enough musicians have assembled, settled down and had a drink, and ending as the last few drift away or the pub closes. There is no explicit public ritual to mark the beginning or end, the musicians just begin when they feel ready. A session usually lasts for several hours and musicians will come and go throughout just as they might for any other visit to the pub so that the line-up of players is constantly changing. New arrivals need not wait for a break in the music before entering the circle, greeting friends, finding space, unpacking instruments, buying drinks and settling down. Musicians often continue playing as this happens, although one or two may temporarily break off to greet a friend. To this we add the comings and goings of the musicians as they head to the bar or toilets, talk to each other, make phone calls, or go outside for a smoke, again often as the music plays.

Figure 2 (left) shows an example in which somebody passes among the musicians as they play to distribute leaflets, stopping to talk on the way.

Figure 2. Distributing leaflets (left) and 'clutter' (right).

There are many non-musicians present in the pub with varying relationships to a session. First are those who have consciously come along to the session, perhaps friends or family of the musicians, who are happy to sit amongst the musicians in the playing area, attending to the music and talking to them. These 'spectators' may have considerable expertise of the music and may be occasional players themselves. Second are those who do not appear to be directly known to the musicians, but who are evidently interested in the music. They may have heard of the session in advance, through posters in the pub or word of mouth, or just happen to be in the pub anyway. Our observations show them typically positioned in sight of, but probably not among, the musicians. They sometimes show their appreciation of the music through applause, although this is often not the case, and may depend upon the number of spectators, and maybe the quality and sense of performance of the playing. Last, are others who are present for other reasons and not necessarily interested in the music at all. They can usually be found in more distant areas of the pub and may well include pub staff.

Figure 3. Spectators sit among the musicians (left) while others watch from the back.

The pub setting is a bustling environment cluttered with people, musical instruments, cases and accessories (capos, picks and rosin) as well as general pub paraphernalia (drinks, snacks, beer-mats, menus). The result is a busy setting in which the music is intimately intermingled with other social activities, and in which it is perfectly acceptable to break off playing to engage in these before resuming. This informality is important to the musicians who have come along to socialise as well as to play – to enjoy the "craic" as they might say [20].

Playing tunes

Having set the scene, we now turn to the specifics of playing the music. The first question is how to begin a tune? The most common approach is for someone to 'self-select' [28], with one musician beginning playing in the hope that others will join in. Joining in is especially important and the expectation is that others will do so. It is therefore a problem when no one joins in, leaving the musician with the embarrassing options of petering out or continuing solo (solo performances do sometimes occur but are rare). Launching a tune is therefore a risky moment and not for the faint hearted. In some cases, most notably the Elm Tree, there is a more recognised leader who begins many of the tunes or explicitly invites others to do so. In others, such as the Vat and Fiddle, several musicians may be prepared, or even compete, to launch tunes. We witnessed examples of something akin to the turn-taking that takes place in everyday conversation [28] when musicians played short opening phrases of just a few bars backwards and forwards, before launching into the tune proper. These musical questions and answers seemed to be as much about eliciting and confirming support for joining in as about remembering how to play the tune, and were even seen to occur when those involved were sitting next to one another (and could have counted in). Interruptions are another recognisable aspect of turn taking, and it is not uncommon to see two or more musicians play across each other until one wins out and the other backs off.

Knowing when to join in is also a challenge, especially if the musician does not know the tune or has not played it for a while. Each tune is usually repeated several times so that fellow musicians can identify it and recall it to their fingers. Three repetitions is common, although two appeared to be the norm at the Elm Tree, while more were sometimes seen. Playing a tune just once is rare. The musical form of Irish tunes encourages joining in, typically consisting of several short parts that are themselves repeated (between 2 and 4 parts of 8 bars duration is common). This repetition supports improvisation by enabling players to introduce ornamentations around the basic melody, a key way of displaying virtuosity. Thus, in Irish music, players improvise simultaneously rather than taking turns as in Jazz or Blues. We also observed busking along, that is playing quietly or in a muted way when gradually recalling a tune or when learning it by ear (a valued part of the oral tradition). In general then, the structure of Irish tunes provides a framework that accommodates both beginners and experts simultaneously playing together.

Another question is which instrument to play? Irish tunes are typically played in unison on a range of melody instruments including fiddles, flutes, whistles, melodeons, and banjos. There are also accompanying instruments, most notably guitars and percussion, including the traditional drum (bodhrán). In general, we did not observe the use of amplified or digital instruments with the exception of a bass guitar at the Hop Pole. Some bring several instruments and swap so that the overall sound remains balanced, sometimes even swapping during an ongoing tune.

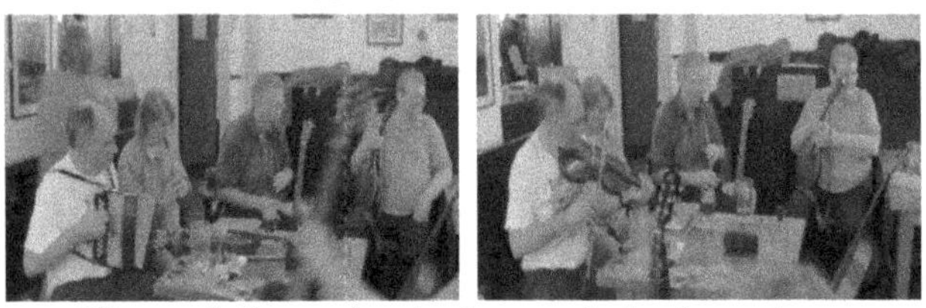

Figure 4. Swapping instruments during a tune

Choosing sets of tunes

It is typical to sequence several tunes together into a 'set'. An entire set may be planned in advance, although the choice of the next tune can also be made on the fly providing a further opportunity for improvisation. The 'right' to choose the next tune largely resides with the player who initiated the set, but not exclusively. It is not uncommon for others to take up the reins and extend an ongoing set with further tunes. Between two and four tunes per set are common, although longer sets occur, especially when multiple players are involved in choosing new tunes. While the sequencing of tunes does involve musical factors – it is more common to stay within one rhythmic style (e.g. Jig, Reel, Hornpipe), some key changes can sound effective (e.g., minor to major), and some tunes just fit well together – the choice of tunes is also very much a social issue involving several important non-musical factors:

What tunes do the other players know? This is perhaps the most critical issue – guessing which tunes another musician is likely to be able to play. Obviously, this is far easier when you know them well and much harder if you are a stranger. Our observations showed that players often come as subgroups of friends or family who share sets of tunes in common, while interviews revealed that some groups get together in advance of a session to prepare sets to play.

What is appropriate to this session? Individual sessions are more or less tolerant of varied musical styles (e.g., how narrowly focused on strictly 'Irish' music they are). Even if the genre is appropriate, there are clearly some sets that are common to a session and known to regular players. Indeed, a session often begins with these locally 'well-known' sets to warm everyone up before moving onto more adventurous and unusual choices. There are more or less 'standard' sets that are very widely known to go together, perhaps because they have appeared on popular recordings.

What has already been played today? The pattern of ongoing arrivals and departures of musicians that we noted earlier raises the further challenge of knowing which tunes have already been played as it is generally undesirable to repeat tunes within a session. We saw examples of players at the Hop Pole shouting out 'yellow card offense' (borrowing a disciplinary term from Football or Soccer) following a tune that was repeated from earlier on, a humorous but nevertheless clear warning. Even experienced musicians who are very familiar with a session may struggle with this aspect of choosing tunes if they arrive relatively late on.

Building a shared repertoire

In order to successfully negotiate these various social issues (on top of complex musical ones), musicians must build up repertoires of tunes that are shared by others at the session. Players may build up a repertoire over many years and in various ways, learning by ear, but also drawing on external resources such as books, recordings and the Internet as we discuss below. We saw players exchanging CDs and sheet music and recording tunes on phones and portable audio recorders. A common problem is learning the name of a tune and it is frequent to hear the question 'what was that?' The problem is that due to the oral tradition of learning the names of Irish tunes are often confused. The same tune can be handed on under different names in different places, while one name may map onto several different variants of a tune, or quite possibly different tunes. Tunes whose real name is unknown may be given temporary placeholder names – after the person who handed it on, for example, which may then be taken as their real names by future recipients. One player learned 'Dave and Rachel's Jig' from another who, it transpires, had learned it from Dave and Rachel. He then passed it on to others before eventually finding out that it is widely known as "McGuire's".

The use of Gaelic names can add a further set of difficulties and newcomers or visitors to a session need to tread warily, waiting to be invited to lead off a set, as was the case when we visited the Elm Tree. Here we were probed as to whether we know specific tunes and at one point were asked: "What tunes do you know?" with the addendum of "anything but The Kesh" (a standard tune at which the questioner clearly drew the line).

Paper props and cues

The challenges of building a shared repertoire, of having this to hand, and of figuring out how best to sequence tunes into sets in the heat of a live session, are reflected in the use of various paper props and cues. We observed examples of players discussing and choosing tunes from 'set lists' (lists of tunes pre-grouped into sets) and the organisation of these into more extensive personal folders. Moreover, many musicians carry a notebook for jotting down the names of tunes, contacts, dates and locations of sessions and gigs.

Figure 5. A set list (left) playing the dots (right)

We observed a few examples of musicians playing from 'the dots', i.e., from printed sheet music. However, our interviews revealed that players were aware that this could be controversial given the perceived importance of the oral tradition in Irish music. One volunteered that, as an accomplished player in a related genre and also a good sight-reader, he was aware of the issue but felt justified in using sheet music as a way of getting up to speed with this particular session. However, use of sheet music was relatively rare and certainly there was nothing like the routine setting up of music stands and use of scores that is commonplace in many other musical settings.

Figure 6. Set lists organised into a personal folder

More widely seen was the use of 'ABC notation', a bespoke lightweight notation for traditional music that uses alphabetic letters for note names and other symbols to show bar-lines, octave shifts and so on [1]. Variants of this (often further simplified) are used as a short hand to note down tunes and the notation is promoted by some tutors and Irish musical societies. While much less expressive than standard notation, it works well enough with the relatively standardised form of Irish tunes and is also highly compact and perhaps less distinguishable from other text and so less overtly visible as a musical score.

A compelling example of the utility of ABC notation was revealed in an interview with one player who described her personal folder of tunes. Her set lists comprised the names of the tunes along with just the first few bars of each in ABC notation: *"so I've got everything written down with just like the first couple of bars"*. It is especially significant here that she only requires the first few bars; the challenge is not to remember the whole tune, but just enough of the beginning to be able to segue into it from another tune, i.e., to remember how to bring it back to the fingers, given that another tune is already in her head. This, combined with the compact ABC notation, meant that she was able to distill the essential information that she required to execute a set of tunes into just a few short lines.

She also revealed the work involved in preparing this highly organised crib sheet and of rehearsing to it: *"so when I practice I tend to work off this .. and then I will only go back to the main notes to make sure I haven't introduced too many variations which sound OK but which aren't quite right"; "I tend to practice with this and I'll go through these tunes like these polkas and I'll mix them up"* and *"...then I've got um like sets of things that I think sounded quite good together"*. Finally, it was clear that this player attended several local sessions and maintained different crib sheets for each, reflecting their varying but overlapping local repertoires: *"so when I go down the Vat'n'Fiddle I will know the two tunes ... you know ... I'll have like ten sets of two tunes that I'm confident will go together and that I've practiced going from that into that so that I don't cock it up"*.

The moral order of session etiquette

Several of our discussions so far raise the topic of the moral ordering of music-making or 'session etiquette' – i.e., what social and musical behaviour is acceptable within an Irish session. We have seen that the kind of tunes and instruments that are welcome at a given session, the question of who begins a set of tunes, and the acceptability of playing to 'the dots' may be felt to be subject to a set of 'rules', at least by some participants. We directly observed examples of people calling others to account over matters of 'etiquette'. At one Vat and Fiddle session a group of visitors arrived and played a set of bluegrass tunes, which were politely listened to and greeted with applause, but followed by the question "but is it Irish?"

Our interviews uncovered more serious tales of 'calling to account' for using sheet music and playing inappropriate instruments (the use of amplified instruments being especially contentious). While such explicit calling to account may be rare, occurring only when participants feel that the moral order is breached and stands in need of repair [15], it is undoubtedly a serious matter when it does occur, and may lead people to permanently withdraw from a session. However, our study also suggests that there is significant *local variation* in etiquette. Certainly, the four sessions that we observed varied considerably as to how they were organised and what appeared to be musically and socially acceptable. It is also clear that each session gains a reputation for its flexibility or otherwise with regard to traditional etiquette. Finally, session etiquette is discussed in online fora [e.g., 32] as well as in more formal publications covering topics such as appropriate instruments, choosing tunes, joining in, and the importance of playing by ear [13].

In summary, there would appear to be a high degree of local variation and flexibility of session etiquette – perhaps much more so than books and online discussions would lead one to think – but that at the same time, participants are certainly aware of and influenced by it. Thus, while in practice it may be locally acceptable to get out the sheet music or perform a different style of tune, those doing so are probably aware that they are walking a line. This becomes particularly difficult for two classes of player. First, beginners may feel challenged by session etiquette, especially when they already feel exposed by being less skilful and experienced players. Conversely, it may be much easier to get away with local breaches of etiquette if one is demonstrably an excellent and experienced player, as the quality of one's playing may outweigh any number of lesser sins. The second challenging situation is when being a 'nomad', i.e., when visiting a foreign session, as was the case at the Elm Tree, as there are local variations in session etiquette to contend with and one's natural level in the musical pecking order is not immediately apparent. In this case even experienced players may feel the need to tread cautiously and there is a sense of gently probing the local rules and being tested out in return.

Online resources

There is a profound tension tucked away in the above observations. In the session itself there is an emphasis placed upon *appearing to be spontaneous*, with a dependence upon a minimal number of props. Yet accomplishing this apparent spontaneity involves a considerable amount of work. Our study revealed a whole constellation of activities that surround the sessions and that feed into the maintenance of this sense of spontaneity. Of particular note here is how Irish musicians have been turning to digital technologies, especially the Internet, as a means of building up their repertoire. Beyond the use of cameras and phones and exchange of CDs noted previously, we learned of a dedicated website for Irish musicians called 'The Session', established around 2002 to support the exchange of tunes and information about sessions. In its own words: *"The exchange of tunes is what keeps traditional Irish music alive. This website is one way of passing on jigs, reels and other dance tunes. Some of the tunes are well known, and some are more obscure. It's this mixture of the familiar and the new that makes for a good session."* [www.thesession.org, August 2010].

The core service provided by The Session is to enable its members to transcribe tunes into both standard and ABC notations and share them with others. Members can also comment on tunes, adding notes on tune names, variations, alternative keys, ways of playing, where the tune has been recorded, and other tunes that fit well with it. Tunes are searchable by name, type, key and who submitted the transcription, and members can bookmark their favourites to create personal and publicly visible tune lists. Members also upload information on recordings (album names, artists and track lists) which are cross linked to transcriptions where available. There is also a searchable database of sessions that includes name, location (country, city, map reference), day and time, organizer or venue contact details, and comments on style, skill level, and the quality of the beer. Three of the four sessions that we studied appeared on The Session as follows:

- **The King Billy (King Willian IV):** "This is the regular Thursday night session that has moved from the Mechanics. Good pub with wide selection of real ales. Parking OK and good bus connections."
- **The Vat and Fiddle:** "Session is every second Sunday of the month. Starts around 2.30 until about 6. Mostly traditional British Isles music with some American old time too." "Friendly pub just round the corner from the Railway Station." "New Musicians Welcome"
- **The Elm Tree:** "Very friendly session, with excellent musicians and a good choice of beer." "The Monday session is usually faster than the Tuesday one. The Monday session is actually the former Colpitts session."

The Session therefore offers an extensive, cross-indexed and evolving database of tunes, sessions and players that has been crowd-sourced from the community. The site currently claims over 63,000 members, a database of over 9,000 tunes, and information on over 3,000 recordings and 2,000 sessions worldwide.

Figure 7. A selection of notes on the tune "The Maid Behind the Bar" from thesession.org [August 2010]

Irish musicians have also been turning to more mainstream services. YouTube videos of tunes being played fast and slow were reported to be a useful resource for learning, and are also embedded into more specialist sites. Facebook hosts pages for sessions, and we observed people posting to indicate their plans to attend on a particular day. More recently, mobile applications have emerged to support Irish sessions including Tunepal, an iPhone app that maintains personal tune lists along with sheet music or ABC notation, connects to well known online repositories of tunes such as thesession.org, makes audio recordings, and contains tune-recognition software that attempts to recognize which tune is being played based on a musical analysis of the audio recording, although this is difficult to do reliably for some instruments and in the noisy environment of a live session.

BRIDGING PREPARATION AND PERFORMANCE

It seems then that Irish musicians are increasingly turning to digital resources to help them prepare for sessions, but that deploying these within the actual performance of a traditional session can be tricky due to the prevailing social and moral ordering of traditional music-making. Indeed, the effort put into carefully designing the current paper cues reveals some of the complexities inherent in this challenge. We might imagine several potential technologies to help with this bridging between preparation and performance, from extending emerging mobile phone apps with functionality for sharing repertoires, recommending tunes on the fly, or providing minimal cues to help musicians segue between tunes, to enhancing the physical objects that are already present at the session – instruments, musical accessories, pub paraphernalia, and paper – with digital resources. Ongoing work is exploring these various options through a participatory design process. What we *are* able to propose in this paper, based on our study, is something of the general design context for these new technologies. Specifically, we articulate a guiding design principle that we call 'situated discretion'.

Situated discretion

The success of any particular approach to design in this context, or indeed any combination of approaches, will largely depend on how well it respects the moral ordering of traditional Irish music sessions and the prevailing 'session etiquette'. This moral order is not an addition to the social organisation of music-making or any other activity. On the contrary, the social order *is* inseparably a moral order, the social organisation of interaction a moral organisation. The moral order constitutes the 'seen but unnoticed' foundation of interaction in real time [15]. While a great many novel solutions might be introduced into the setting, we need to be respectful of the moral character of traditional work practice then.

This means that technological interventions will only be realised if they can be appropriated in suitably *discrete* way with respect to 'session etiquette'. What makes the use of one technology more discreet than another? Is interacting with a phone in a session more discreet and therefore acceptable than using augmented paper or vice versa? Our study reveals that general mobile phone use appears to be acceptable within many sessions as a regular pub activity and so mobiles *might* prove to be a good option. However, might more musically oriented phone apps then come to be seen more like electronic instruments than social tools? We have seen that paper cues can be carefully constructed so as not to appear too much like musical scores. However, will further extending their functionality draw more attention to them to the point of breeching etiquette? Will extending the use of paper draw attention to what is already perhaps a somewhat risky practice?

The key to resolving such questions lies in understanding how the social accomplishment of a session is situated within the particular setting of a pub. As we have already pointed out, a session is a long way from being a concert. Instead at least as much of what's going on is about it being in a pub as anything else. There's drinking, chatting, clowning around, people turning up together and going together, disappearing off to order drinks, and so on. The use of mobile phones, or indeed paper, to support these everyday activities may well be acceptable and any new technology that could be interpreted in this way may prove to be sufficiently discrete. In short, what we are arguing for is not only discretion, but rather *situated discretion.*

This point about situated discretion is very much in line with the vision of ubiquitous computing in which digital technologies become embedded into the everyday physical world so as to better support people's practices and tacit knowledge, ultimately becoming unremarkable or even 'invisible in use' [34]. One common kind of vision for accomplishing the invisible in ubiquitous computing is to embed sensors and tags in the existing environment so that the technology is apparently hidden in what is already there. The difficulty is that invisibility is not something that just happens by virtue of hiding technology in existing materials. These materials still have to be situated *in accountable social interactions*. As we pointed out above, the problem with paper, for all its apparent diversity and pervasiveness of use [24], is that, in pub settings, musicians are already struggling to make the paper disappear. Thus, when one looks at the broader sets of practices surrounding pub-going and social 'get-togethers' there are numerous ways in which getting out a sheet of paper or opening up a notebook may be a *more visible* practice because it is out of the usual run of things for such settings.

What then of the alternative approach of developing mobile phone apps? Mobile phones were observed to be a natural part of the ecology of the pubs that we visited. Many musicians carry them and were observed breaking off and checking their phones during sessions in the same way that they broke off playing to talk to someone, head to the bar, or engage in any other normal pub activity. Might phone use in pubs, be seen as more unremarkable than using sheets of paper? The very multipurpose nature of the phone may lend to this. Someone using a phone could be engaged in many activities, checking for text messages for example, which is perfectly acceptable in the context of an Irish session. It may be difficult to tell what someone is doing when twiddling with their phone and generally not polite to look too closely. Thus, there is a degree of ambiguity about the use of a mobile phone in this context that may allow for multiple interpretations of what is going on, offsetting a 'calling to account' that would otherwise result in a 'loss of face' [2]. Of course, this depends upon whether new apps to support sequencing transform phone use into something that is visibly different from normal phone use and clearly concerned with supporting recall and improvisation, in which case situated discretion may be lost.

In short, being invisible is not an immutable property of a given technology but is fundamentally concerned with how the technology is situated by the people who use it, and how it is situated turns upon the social and moral ordering of the activities it will be embedded in. When we look to the social and moral ordering of Irish music sessions – when we look to see how they are *made* into traditional activities that technologies are situated in – we see elements of the 'making', of the interactional assembly and conduct of the music that are amenable to discrete interventions.

Support for sequencing tunes

Having said something of the general design approach, we are also able to comment on the requirements for future technologies to support Irish sessions; that is based on our study, we can recommend generally what they should do. While some challenges such as building a repertoire, becoming skilled on an instrument, and learning how to adjust one's playing to that of others, are common to many forms of music, others are more distinctive to this particular form. In particular, the challenge of sequencing tunes into sets lies at the heart of the Irish session and would appear to be especially tricky for some players. Sequencing is not only a musical challenge of knowing which tunes fit together; it is largely a social challenge of determining what others might know and what it is appropriate to play as a session unfolds. This brings it squarely into the focus of CSCW and it becomes interesting to ask what technologies might support Irish musicians in sequencing tunes? Based on our study, we suggest that the challenge of sequencing needs to address several more specific requirements:

- understanding which tunes might fit together musically
- providing sufficient cues that players can easily segue from one tune to the next when playing a set
- knowing who is present at the session
- knowing what tunes these others might know, including which are sufficiently rehearsed to be at their fingertips
- knowing which tunes have been played so far
- knowing which tunes are popular at this session;
- finding out what a particular tune is called

These problems are especially significant for two classes of participant: learners with relatively small repertoires who may be nervous about making gaffes, and newcomers to a given session who are unfamiliar with its shared repertoire, history and etiquette, including visiting nomads.

Earlier on, we suggested some general technological approaches to meeting these requirements and it is to these that we now return in order to conclude this current topic of discussion. In each case, the general aim is to better bridge between the work of preparing for a session, which is already relatively well supported by technology, and the actual situated practice of performing in the session which by and large, is not. We identify three broad approaches for achieving this bridging and in particular for supporting the sequencing of tunes.

Extending mobile services: while there are already 'apps' aimed at Irish musicians, these tend to focus on supporting the individual musician in managing their own tunebook, rather than supporting social aspects of sequencing. There would appear to be opportunities for extending such apps to enable attendees to locally broadcast their presence, exchange tunebooks, and compare repertoires, including rapidly highlighting tunes that they know in common. An further extension would be to support noting which tunes get played at the session, creating a record of what has already been played that day, and adding to longer term records of sets that have proved popular on previous occasions. These records might be shared among mobile apps or posted to current online social networking sites where they could be followed up after the session.

Integrating physical and digital. An alternative strategy would be to enhance the physical resources that musicians already employ, enabling them to be more closely and dynamically integrated with online resources. Ubicomp technologies might be used to tag notebooks, music cases and other paraphernalia with the identities of their owners, enabling them to easily 'sign in' to a session, identifying them to others and leaving a record that they were present. Similarly, tagging individual sheets of paper or pages in books with the names of tunes might help construct records of which tunes were played that day. Various tagging technologies could be relevant here from RFID to barcodes and glyphs that might be printed onto paper or even stickers to adorn and personalize instrument cases.

Involving spectators: A challenge for both of these approaches is that Irish musicians are already busy trying to manage the complexities of recalling and actually playing tunes in the moment of the session, which may restrict their ability or motivation to use mobile applications while they play. While tune recognition software may improve in the future, an interesting alternative would be to draw on knowledgeable spectators. Perhaps there is a role for those who are attending to listen to also help document the session and bring their interest and expertise to bear? Perhaps taking a more active role in this may even enhance their enjoyment of the session? We therefore propose exploring the potential for 'spectator interfaces' that are targeted at listeners rather than players and that engage them in documenting and discussing the activities of the session. These might even extend to other bystanders in the locality who are not familiar with the music but would like to learn more about what is happening.

SOME BROADER IMPLICATIONS FOR DESIGN

Beyond support for Irish music session, our study speaks to a wider and growing interest in collaborative music technology. One body of work has focused on the design of instruments, either enhancing traditional instruments (e.g., augmenting violin bows [5]) or employing emerging gesture recognition and tangible interface technologies to create new kinds of instruments, for professional musicians [21] or to support collaborative music making by non-experts [6]. Closer to our focus, a second body of work has considered technologies to enhance the coordination of musical performance ranging from augmenting conductor's batons [23] to attaching displays to instruments or stands so that performers can better follow dynamic scores [14]. This interest in coordination has also extended to studies of improvisation [7, 8, 10, 22, 30] and technology support for this [19, 29].

Like this previous work, our study has also considered the collaborative production of improvised music. However, in our study, the essence of improvising lies not in soloing or harmonizing on the fly, but rather in the act of sequencing – i.e., choosing and ordering sequences of tunes to be performed in a particular order. What is challenging here is that this is a distributed ad-hoc process that relies on tacit knowledge rather than explicit negotiation. Thus, we highlight the sequencing of music as an important aspect of collaborative improvisation and stress the need for new and distinctive kinds of collaborative musical interface to provide lightweight support for people to dynamically share repertoires and create sequences of tunes or songs. Our study also reveals how such technologies need to extend to support the work of preparing for a session as well as following up on new tunes and contacts afterwards. This requires bridging the dynamic aspects of sequencing within the session and online resources and social networks that support preparation and follow up.

We propose that there are opportunities for sequencing interfaces beyond our immediate focus on Irish sessions, for example in other kinds of jam sessions (folk and blues), karaoke, and also the sequencing of tracks by DJs. By highlighting sequencing, our study also relates to earlier studies of how consumers share and synchronize playlists of recorded music in social settings, for example at parties [12] or as part of everyday life [4, 26, 33]. It appears that sequencing playlists is an important way in which non-musicians can engage in a musical expression, suggesting further opportunities for interfaces to support improvised collaborative sequencing. Conversely, there is a sense that our Irish musicians are also sharing playlists, but in this case with a view to performing them live. It seems then that the socially negotiated act of sequencing may provide an interesting point of contact between the production and consumption of music, suggesting that technologies that support sequencing may ultimately have a wider appeal.

We have described how Irish musicians carefully design paper cues to enable them to bring the learning that they do outside of the session into the actual practice of the session without compromising the etiquette of 'playing by ear'. We have argued that new technologies need to be sensitive to etiquette and context while recognising that this may be an extremely subtle matter. Our final contribution in this paper is therefore to further emphasise the need for CSCW to look at traditional social practices as deserving of study and technology support while also raising important new challenges concerning etiquette, ubiquity, discretion and the complex boundary between the physical and the digital. Indeed, researchers have already begun to explore technology support for various other traditional social practices such as knitting [27], preparing food [18, 31], and religious observance [17, 35, 36], all of which may provide further opportunities for exploring the general approach of situated discretion.

CONCLUSIONS

We have documented key features of the traditional Irish session as a situated collaborative activity; sessions take place within pubs, they have fluid temporal arrangements, and they involve spectators in various ways. An especially salient feature is the way in which groups of musicians improvise together by sequencing known tunes into sets, a process that relies on tacit knowledge of which tunes others may know, which have already been played, and which are appropriate for this particular session. Underpinning this is a strong sense of etiquette which frowns upon the use of amplified instruments or the overt use of musical scores. At the same time, we have also seen how Irish musicians are turning to the Internet to support them in preparing for sessions, and how they carefully design paper props to help them bring this preparation to bear within the session itself without flouting etiquette.

An exploration of potential technologies to support collaborative sequencing stressed the importance of designing for 'situated discretion', that is for discreet use with respect to session etiquette within the context of a pub or bar. We conclude by suggesting that collaborative sequencing may be important for other forms of social music production and consumption and so warrants further attention within CSCW. Finally, we argue that CSCW should focus on supporting other kinds of traditional activity by bridging between burgeoning online resources and the subtleties of situated social practice.

ACKNOWLEDGEMENTS

We gratefully acknowledge the support of the Engineering and Physical Research Council (EPSRC) through the Widespread Adoption of Ubiquitous Computing platform grant (EP/F03038X/1) and the Horizon Centre for Doctoral Training (EP/G037574/1). Thanks also to the musicians who participated in this study.

REFERENCES

1. ABC Notation, http://abcnotation.com, August 2011
2. Aoki, P., Woodruff, A., Making space for stories: ambiguity in the design of personal communication systems, *Proc CHI 2005*, 181-190, ACM

3. Arrasvuori, J., Holm, J., Designing interactive music mixing applications for mobile devices, *Proc DIMEA '07*, 20-27, ACM
4. Baumann, S., Bassoli, A., Jung, B., Wisniowski, M., BlueTunA: Let You Neighbor Know What Music You Like, *Proc CHI 2007 (Interactivity)*, 1941-1946, ACM
5. Bevilacqua, F., Rasamimanana, N., Flety, E., Lemouton, S., Baschet, F., The Augmented Violin Project: Research, Composition and Performance Report, *Proc NIME 2006*, 402-406, IRCAM
6. Blaine, T., Fels, S., Collaborative Musical Interfaces for Novices, *New Music Research*, 32(4), 411–428, 2003
7. Bowers, J., Hellström, S-O., Simple interfaces to complex sound in improvised music, *CHI 2000*, ACM
8. Bowers, J., Improvising Machines: Ethnographically Informed Design for Improvised Electro-Acoustic Music, *ARiADATexts 4,* www.ariada.uea.ac.uk/ariadatexts/ariada4/ariada4_text.html
9. Bryan-Kinns, N., Daisyphone: the design and impact of a novel environment for remote group music improvisation *Proc DIS '04*, 135-144, ACM
10. Bryan-Kinns, N., Healey, P. G., Leach, J., Exploring mutual engagement in creative collaborations, Proc C&C '07, 223-232, ACM
11. Crabtree, A., *Designing Collaborative Systems: A Practical Guide to Ethnography*, Springer, 2003
12. Cunningham, S, Nichols, D., Exploring Social Music Behaviour: An Investigation of Music Selection at Parties, *Proc 10th International Society for Music Information Retrieval Conference*, 747-752, 2009
13. Foy, B., *Field Guide to the Irish Music Session,* Frogchart Press, August 2008
14. Freeman, J., Extreme Sight Reading, Mediating Expression and Audience Participation: Real-Time Music Notation in Live Performance, *Computer Music Journal*, 32 (3), 25-41, 2008. MIT
15. Garfinkel, H., *Studies in Ethnomethodology*, Prentice-Hall, 1967
16. Gates, C., Subramanian, S., and Gutwin, C., DJs' perspectives on interaction and awareness in nightclubs, *Proc DIS '06*, 70-79, ACM
17. Gaver, W., Blythe, M., Boucher, A., Jarvis, N., Bowers, J., Wright, P., The Prayer Companion: openness and specificity, materiality and spirituality, *Proc CHI 2010*, 2055-2064, ACM
18. Grimes, A., Harper, R., Celebratory Technology: New Directions or Food Research in HCI, *CHI 2008*, 467-476, ACM
19. Hoffman, G. and Weinberg, G., Shimon: an interactive improvisational robotic marimba player, Proc CHI 2010, 3097-3102, ACM
20. Irwin, C., *In Search of the Craic: One Man's Pub Crawl Through Irish Music*, Andre Deutsch Ltd, 2003
21. Jordà , S., G. Geiger, M. Alonso, and M. Kaltenbrunner, M., The ReacTable: Exploring the Synergy Between Live Music Performance and Tabletop Tangible Interfaces, *Proc TEI 2007*, 139– 146, ACM
22. Keegan-Phipps, S., Folk music and the pub session in Durham, MA thesis, Music Dept, Durham University.
23. Lee, E., Wolf, M., Borchers, J., Improving Orchestral Conducting Systems in Public Spaces: examining the temporal characteristics and conceptual models of conducting gestures, *Proc CHI 2005*, 731-740, ACM
24. Luff, P., Heath, C., Norrie, M., Singer, B., Herdman, P., Only Touching the Surface: Creating Affinities Between Digital Content and Paper, *CSCW 2004*, ACM
25. Miletto, E. M., Flores, L. V., Pimenta, M. S., Rutily, J., and Santagada, L., Interfaces for musical activities and interfaces for musicians are not the same, *Proc ICMI '07*, 201-207, ACM
26. O'Hara, K. Brown, B. *Consuming Music Together*. Springer-Verlag, 2005
27. Rosner, D., Ryokai, K., Reflections on Craft: Probing the Creative Process of Everyday Knitters, *Proc Creativity and Cognition 2009*, 195-204, ACM
28. Sacks, H., Jefferson, G., *Lectures on Conversation*, Blackwell Publishing, 1995
29. Snydal, J. and Hearst, M., ImproViz: visual explorations of jazz improvisations, *Proc CHI 2005*, 1805-1808, ACM
30. Sudnow, D., *Ways of the hand: the organization of improvised conduct*, Routledge & Kegan Paul, 1978
31. Terrenghi, L., Hilliges, O., Butz, A., Kitchen stories: sharing recipes with the Living Cookbook, *Personal and Ubiquitous Computing*, 11 (5), 409-414, 2007
32. http://www.thesession.org/discussions/display/10525
33. Voida, A., Grinter, G., Ducheneaut, N., Edwards, W. E., Newman, M., Listening In: Practices Surrounding iTunes Music Sharing, *Proc CHI 2005*, 191-200, ACM
34. Weiser, M., Ubiquitous Computing #1, www.ubiq.com/hypertext/weiser/UbiHome.html, 1988
35. Woodruff, A., Augustin, S, Focault, B., Sabbath Day Home Automation: "It's Like Mixing Technology and Religion", *Proc CHI 2007*, 527-536, ACM
36. Wyche, S, Hayes, G., Harvel, L., Grinter, R., Technology in Spiritual Formation: An Exploratory Study of Computer Mediated Religious Communications, *Proc CSCW 2006*, 199-208, ACM

A Gift from the City: Mobile Phones in Rural China

Elisa Oreglia
School of Information
University of California Berkeley, Berkeley, CA, USA
elisa@ischool.berkeley.edu

Joseph 'Jofish' Kaye
Nokia Research Center Palo Alto
955 Page Mill Road, Palo Alto, CA, USA
jofish.kaye@nokia.com

ABSTRACT
In rural Northern China, many people own a mobile phone without ever having purchased it: they received it as a gift from better off relatives, usually their migrant children. Drawing from ethnographic field work in three Chinese villages, we describe practices of mobile phone gifting and the social relations that underlie them, as well as the consequences of the circulation of mobile phones, from the change of use that happens when they move from an urban environment to the countryside, to the possibilities that they open up or close out for rural users. We conclude with implications for technology design that emphasize the situated nature of these experiences and thoughtful approaches to the design of 'traveling' mobiles.

Author Keywords
Mobile phones, gift, gifting practices, rural users, China.

ACM Classification Keywords
H5.m. Information interfaces and presentation (e.g., HCI): Miscellaneous.

General Terms
Human Factors; Design.

INTRODUCTION
Bing Long, a 16-year-old boy who lives in a small village in the province of Shandong in China, goes to junior high school in a nearby village. He has no money of his own aside from the occasional CNY50 (USD7.5) that he gets from his two older sisters, and owns four mobile phones.

"I use this a bit, that a bit, their functions are different, you see? For example, on this I can use QQ (an instant messaging program) but on this other I can't go online; then on this one I can read e-novels, and this I use to call."

He also owns a video game console, a DVD player, and, for part of the year, his sister's Sony PSP (Play Station Portable). All these devices are gifts from family members: mobile number one is his father's old one, number two, his mother's (which she herself received as a gift from her daughter, when her daughter bought herself a new one), number three, his middle sister's old one, and number four, the only new one, another gift from his middle sister, who works in a mobile phone factory. The other devices were all gifts from his eldest sister, who works in Beijing and is the family member with the highest income.

Not many people, in the countryside or elsewhere, own four mobile phones, but many rural residents own a mobile phone without ever having set foot in a mobile phone shop: someone gave it to them as a gift. These gifting practices enlarge the pool of mobile phone users well beyond what the current income and education levels of the Chinese countryside would predict. The ways people get their phones, the type of phones they have, and how they learn to use them, are an important space to explore in order to understand issues of ownership, access and use of ICT (Information and Communication Technologies) in emerging regions. A phone that is received as a gift is not chosen, and therefore might have functions that are inaccessible or irrelevant to the new owner. In addition, it may lack desired functionality. A phone received as a gift, as the vast literature on gift practices shows, comes with obligations that are sometimes welcome and sometimes felt like a burden. A phone received as a gift by someone who might not be able to afford one on her own can enhance the freedom of the receiver, or be perceived as a tool of control. Furthermore, while the gifting of phones is quite common, it is an area that is largely ignored by phone manufacturers, who instead emphasize the OOBE ("out of the box experience") of the first user of the new phone, rather than subsequent users.

This paper explores these themes as they play out in rural Northern China, a place of relatively low income, quite high mobile phone penetration, and a high rate of migration that creates a constant circulation of people, goods, and ideas from urban areas. The stories we tell, however, happen everywhere in the world – who hasn't gifted their old computer or mobile phone to a younger sibling or older relative? They are just more visible in places that are undergoing fast economic and social transformations, and where trends that exist elsewhere appear magnified, or happen on a bigger scale. Understanding better these phenomena, the kind of social relations they represent, the system of wealth redistribution they might support, and the

CSCW'12, February 11–15, 2012, Seattle, Washington, USA.

issues of usability they sometimes raise, can help understand better the life-cycle of ICT in all societies. The large body of literature on mobile phones that has emerged in recent years mostly does not focus on the *how* these objects end up in their owners' hands, and takes the possession of the devices as a given. We believe instead that understanding the circulation patterns of mobile phones, and the values embodied in both the devices and the path they take is necessary to understand the personal legacies that are built into gifted phones, as well as issues related the changing ownership.

We start our journey into the travels of mobile phones with a review of the literature related to gifting practices and a description of our field work details and methods. We discuss three findings: 1. how phones are gifted and circulate from urban to rural areas and within rural areas; 2. the social relationships that are sustained/reconfigured/ expanded or sometimes collapsed through these gifting practices and the obligations that are attached to it; 3. how mobile phone use changes with new owners. We will conclude with some remarks on the practical consequences of these findings.

RELATED LITERATURE

There is a rich vein of work in anthropology that frame gifts of material objects as ways of organizing and maintaining social order. One of the earliest and pivotal works in this area was *The Gift*, written in the 1920s by Marcel Mauss, who talks about *gifts* and the *economy of gift* as counterparts to the *market economy* [12]. Mauss states that for gifts to work as substitutes for or existing alongside a market economy, as well as legal and social organizers of societies, there needs to be a highly organized and widely accepted system of rules around them, i.e. "the gift cycle," which starts with the duty to give, is followed by the duty to receive, and is concluded by the duty to reciprocate.

Subsequent anthropologists have complicated and sometimes contested Mauss's view. [16] maintains that Mauss never actually defines what is a gift and what is not, and therefore conflates 'gift' and 'exchange;' [18] points out how the supposedly universal rules around gifting follow in fact localized rules in terms of who has the duty to give and who to receive, and whether reciprocation is required or, as in Indian contexts described by [13], forbidden. Looking at gifting practices in rural China, [18] describes gift giving practices where the prestige connected to the gift is accumulated by recipients who are higher in the social hierarchy than the gift givers, and who do not return the gift. He also highlights an aspect of gifts that is usually neglected in favor of economic or religious analyses: the emotions that are expressed by giving and receiving a gift. He ventures as an explanation the fact that sentiment might not be considered as other issues that highlight the uniqueness of various local systems of gift exchanges, 'sentiment' being too commonplace. And indeed, this seems confirmed by the little research there is on gift giving within families, an environment where sentiment is particularly relevant. [7] explores clothes gift among family members, and finds that resource distribution through gifts within households follows gendered lines, but the circulation of such gifts is quite complex, both following and challenging power structures. In his study of Christmas gifts given and received in Winnipeg, [5] confirms that the economic value of gifts seems less important than their symbolic value, and in [6] he confirms "How people act in their gift transactions is a result of how they think about relations between the sexes and between the generations."

In recent years, the digital world has been an interesting field to explore practices of gift giving and receiving. [15] and [10] consider SMS exchanges among youth as consistent with the gifting cycle proposed by Mauss, where sending and reciprocating text messages are essential activities to maintain one's role in a social network. [2] look at open source software projects as part of "gift giving in a digital world interconnected via global networks". Writing about the gift of mobile phones, [4] highlights how different ways of obtaining ownership or use of them entails different rights and different obligations for both givers and receivers. [1] mentions in passing the fact that many people, in particularly older people, in Asia seem to receive their phones as gifts, and hints that "this circulation of technology echoes older social, kin, political and geographic relationships," but does not elaborate on them.

This is the gap that our paper aims at filling: we discuss the gift of objects – mobile phones – and the practices, both older and new, that exist around these gifts in both the physical and the digital world. We observe that this type of gifting happens mostly within families, therefore in a context where rules on reciprocity and duties are different than those that regulate gifting outside the family. We finally suggest that this type of gifting follows specific directions that reflect the changing financial and power situation of the different members of the family.

METHODS

The roots of this research project lie in ethnographic field work on young rural-to-urban migrant women and their social use of information and communication technology (ICT) that author 1 did in China in summer 2007. The interviewees had owned several mobile phones in their years in the city, and while some had been stolen or broken, others had been given to relatives, usually back in their home villages. For example, Ms. Long, the sister of Bing Long we discussed above, gave her first mobile phone to her mother when she had enough money to buy a new model for herself; Ms. Song got her boyfriend's old mobile, and then gave her old one to a younger cousin who was about to leave their home village to come to Beijing.

Over the course of 2010, we traced the trajectories of a few of these mobile phones from Beijing to two villages in Shandong Province (which we refer to as 'A' and 'B') and one in Hebei Province ('C'), all between 3 and 10 hours travel by train and bus from Beijing. We started with three key interviewees in Beijing: Ms. Long, Ms. Gao and Ms. Yang. We then followed them back home when they went for Spring Festival or summer visits, and once in the villages we did semi-structured interviews, participatory observation, and casual conversations with their families, especially the members who had received the phones, and then with other people in the village, from neighbors, to shop keepers and traders, for a total of 45 rural interviewees. These conversations sometimes led us back to Beijing, to find and interview a relative who had gifted a mobile phone to a rural resident, usually children who had given mobiles to their parents. For example, Mr. Liu, a farmer in the second Shandong village we visited, had received his mobile phone from his daughter in Beijing, so after interviewing him in the village, we interviewed his daughter in the city, the fourth of our key informants. Interviews were conducted in Chinese and usually recorded, unless interviewees preferred us not to do so, and notes were taken during the interview and afterwards. They were then transcribed and coded.

The questions we asked had two themes. The first was exploring the ownership of mobile phones and computers and their use: how did people first learn to use their mobiles or computers, understanding details about favorite functions, contacts, and so. The second theme was understanding general issues of rural life, from education, to migration experiences, to farming and economic activities, and to the social life of the village. This research was part of a larger project, and not all the interviews were relevant to the issues we discuss in this paper. The names of the interviewees have all been changed.

The Villages

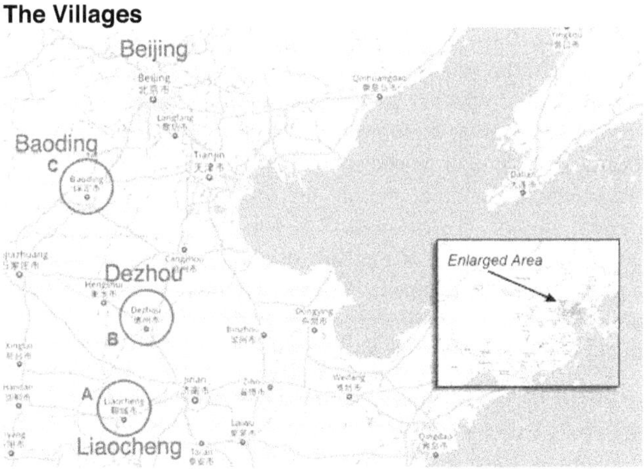

Figure 1: The nearest big towns to the villages studied

Village A is in western Shandong Province, about 2.5 hours from Liaocheng. Dirt roads lead to the village, and they are all in reasonable conditions and easily accessible for bicycles, motorcycles, and three-wheel scooters, although rather bumpy and narrow for cars. A bigger village with shops, paved roads and public transportation to the county is about half an hour walk away. Village A has about 60 permanent inhabitants, mostly older people and women with small children. As in the other two villages, houses are all traditional, single-family (although sometimes enlarged family) units, with a small courtyard closed by a wall. There is a mix of old-style, small brick houses, where older people typically live; restored houses, rebuilt in cement or enlarged, owned by families whose members include migrants, and who therefore have more disposable income; and abandoned houses that belong to families who have left and are unlikely to come back. En masse migration started about 10 years ago, and the main destinations are Shanghai, Qingdao and Beijing. Migrants work at a wide variety of urban jobs, typically assembly line manufacturing. They typically come back to visit during Spring Festival, but those who are not too far away come for shorter visits throughout the year. The village has no store, and itinerant traders stop by every day to sell daily necessities, or to buy agricultural products from the villagers.

Village B is also in western Shandong, but further north, close to the city of Dezhou, near the border with Hebei. The village is between the city and the county seat, and a one-lane paved road connects it easily to both. The village, of about 400 inhabitants, has well-kept dirt roads, an elementary school, a traditional doctor and a western-medicine one, and a few shops. Migration is widespread, but because there are many opportunities nearby, there is a mix of medium-long range migrants and short-range commuters (although interviewees used the same expression - 出去打工 *chūqu dǎgōng* - to describe any type of work outside the village).

Village C is in Hebei province, so close to the fast-growing county of Dingzhou, near the city of Baoding, that it is likely that it will be incorporated by it in the next five years. Seven to eight hundred people live in the village, and most of them both farm and work in Dingzhou, or have small manufacturing activities in their backyards. The age spread of residents is more balanced than in the Shandong villages, because long-range migration is not very common, so there are many more 'whole' families, where parents, children and often grandparents all live in the same compound.

All villages have electricity, telephone landlines, and good mobile phone coverage. In Village B and Village C there are also ADSL Internet connections, and Village A was scheduled to have one installed at the end of summer 2010.

A TRAVELING MOBILE PHONE: WHO MAKES A GIFT, WHO RECEIVES IT

The Long family and its many mobile phones are based in Village A, although only the mother, Mrs. Long, and the youngest son live there full-time.[1] The father, in his late

[1] The one-child policy, introduced in 1978, does not apply to several categories of people (e.g. minorities, couples who

40s, is a construction worker who used to have a full-time job in Beijing, but is now taking occasional, shorter-term jobs closer to home. The elder daughter, Ms. Long, was one of the interviewees from 2007. She had arrived in Beijing in 2004, and was working as a receptionist in a university in Beijing. At the time, she owned a Tianyu K-Touch candybar-style phone, a Chinese mid-market brand, with a camera and a radio function. In summer 2009, she wanted to upgrade to a better phone, because a lot of her friends had foreign-brand phones that she felt had more cachet than hers. She decided to buy a Samsung phone that cost about CNY1,200 (USD185), and to justify the expense she first said that her old phone did not work all that well, and needed to be changed before it broke. But since the phone did not break, she decided that her mother's phone was getting old and she could have used a newer one. She bought herself the Samsung phone, and on her next trip home gave her mother her old Tianyu.

On her visits home, Ms Long. usually brings gifts in the form of money, food, clothes, and ICT. There are rules, or perhaps rituals, around each type of gift. The money is separated from the money Ms. Long is supposed to send back to help with the family finances, as agreed with her parents when she first left. It is 'extra' money and is given to each family member separately, sometimes with specific instructions or wishes attached to it. For example, at Spring Festival she gave her brother CNY200 (USD30) to recharge his phone and to use the internet café; she gave her mother money in several separate occasions, from small sums of around CNY100 (USD15) to buy something specific, to more significant sums when they were discussing some house repairs that the mother wanted to make. Foodstuffs like oil, honey, and fruit, are brought back only at Spring Festival. The clothes Ms. Long brings back are a mixture of new items bought in Beijing specifically for her brother or her mother (which should not be given to other people) and Ms. Long's old clothes, which she gives to her mother with specific instructions regarding which ones she should keep for herself, and which ones she can give to other people as gifts. Her mother often uses these clothes as small gifts to give to her clients – she sells insurance part-time – when they make significant purchases. Ms. Long is also the major purveyor of new and used ICT in her household. To her mother, she gave her Tianyu phone, as well as her old digital camera, and, to her brother, her old MP3 player, and shared ownership of her PSP, which she keeps in Beijing for part of the year, and then leaves to his brother in the summer. She also bought the family's first television and DVD player one Spring Festival, as well as the video game console for her brother, much against her parents' wishes.

Figure 2: Mobile phones circulation in the Long family

Ms. Long's middle sister is 19 years old and works in a mobile phone factory in Yantai, a medium-size city on the coast, about 6 hours away from the village. The factory makes phones for a variety of Chinese brands, as well as copies of foreign brands. She bought her mother a new phone, out of sibling rivalry: the phone she bought was new, whereas Ms. Long gave her mother a used one. The new phone had a touch screen, something that she thought nobody else had in the village. Her mother was extremely pleased by this gift, which she felt would give her a lot of 'face,' that is, prestige, in the village and among her clients. As we will see below, she was never able to use it, and the phone ended back in its box, in a drawer of her bedroom, waiting to re-enter the gifting cycle.

Many families have similar, if not quite so complicated, stories of mobile phones as gifts. Typically, givers are migrant workers who have more disposable income, and more access to a wide variety of ICT, and recipients are people without much economic independence: older people, young people who are still in school, and women who don't have a job outside farming. Mr. Liu and Ms. Deng are both examples of people without much if any disposable income, who depend on other people for luxury purchases such as mobile phones. For example, Mr. Liu is a farmer in his mid-50s, lives in Village B and has three daughters, all married and living in urban areas. The daughter who lives in Beijing gave him a new mobile phone, and the daughter who lives in Dezhou gave his wife her old one.

A gifted phone is often a used phone, but sometimes it is a new one, usually chosen by the person buying it rather than the person using it. Ms. Deng, an 18 years-old from Village A about to go to university, owns a basic Nokia mobile phone. Before owning her own, she thought mobiles were a "very precious thing," and when people put theirs on the table, she didn't even dare to touch them for fear of causing damage. Her parents, both farmers, don't own a phone, and don't have much money to spare. A friend of the family, whose father does business in Guangdong and is well-off, wanted to make her a present, so when she was 16 they

are each themselves only children, and in some cases rural couples) and in rural areas is often enforced sporadically, which explains why all the families we interviewed had two or more children.

went together to a mobile phone shop in the county seat, where they chose together the Nokia, as she felt it was "good quality," and within her gift-giver's budget. She was hoping to buy a new phone when she moved to Jilin, Shandong's capital, to attend university, but was not sure that her parents were going to have the money for that, since the university fees and living expenses are high enough. Moreover, she says:

"especially at university, phones are all about status and face, so one needs to buy a good one, otherwise people will look down on you, just as they will if you're not wearing the right clothes, don't have the right computer..."

Sometimes, however, the dependence from other people is not financial, but is rather due to lack of education, and ignorance/distrust of technology. In other words, some people have the money to buy mobile phones, and might even be interested in owning one, but do not know how to choose it, and even less how to use it. In these cases, having an intermediary who provides 'guided access' is an essential step to fruitful ownership. Mrs. Gao used to live in a village in Dezhou that has since become part of the city and is a nurse in her mid-50s. She traces the origins of her two mobile phones and her desktop computer to the desire to stay in touch with her only daughter when she moved to another city to attend university, and to the very practical fact that her daughter gave her both mobile phones, and taught her how to use them as well as the computer. As we are seeing over and over again, she received her daughter's old mobile when she upgraded to a new one, and the daughter taught her the basics of operating the phone – how to make and how to receive a call, how to read a text message. The fact that she could ask her daughter for guidance if she forgot certain functions or could not do certain operations, gave her confidence to try out new functions such as text messaging or inputting names in the phone book, and made her less afraid of technology. When her daughter went abroad in 2007, she recruited the neighbor's son to help her buy and set up a computer with a camera to be able to video chat.

Mrs. Xing lives in Village C, and was introduced by her neighbors as 'the rich woman of the village,' because her husband has been working in Singapore as a scaffolding builder for many years. She owns a mobile phone and a laptop, and they are both gift from her husband – she says that he knows what she can use and what she needs, so he will give her a new one when something that is suitable for her comes out.

As these stories begin to show, there is a consistent pattern in the gifting of mobile phones in the three villages. A used mobile phone is gifted within the extended household, not outside it; it is of a lower value than the one owned by the gift-giver; it is typically not given for a specific formal occasion, such as Spring Festival, but it is rather an ad hoc gift that emphasizes informality and familiarity in the relationship between the gift giver and the receiver; it is given to a specific person, rather than to the family as a whole, but it can be re-gifted to another family member. The gifting and re-gifting changes the ownership of the mobile, which is always very specific: we did not see any instance of shared ownership, and very little shared use.

The direction in which gifts flow is determined by the economic position of the person who gives the gift in relation to the person who receives it, followed by their respective positions in the hierarchy of the household. In other words:

1. Urban dwellers (typically, migrant workers who have left the village but retain strong ties to it) give mobile phones to rural residents, never vice versa.

2. Male rural residents sometimes give mobiles to female rural residents. Ms. Hua, a mobile phone shop owner in Village B, says that the peak selling seasons are Spring Festival and after the harvests, when people have some disposable income, and men will come to buy a new mobile phone for themselves. In these occasions, they will give their old ones to their wives. Even when the family finances are held in common, as it is typical when most income comes from farming, husbands have more freedom to make a significant purchase like a mobile phone on their own. Mrs. Yang, in Village C, had long wanted a mobile phone of her own, and even though she was in charge of all the farming cycle including selling the crops, she would not spend the money for a phone without her husband's approval. Since he thought that she did not need one, she had to use the landline. Other women talked about using their husband's phones, but as a hardship to rectify as soon as possible. As Mrs. Xue, in Village C, put it:

"Now I have my own mobile. Earlier, I was sharing with my husband, but then when I started working again in (nearby village) I thought I should have mine, it was more convenient for work. I bought it myself, with my own money, three years ago. It was a basic phone. But now I use my husband's. We swapped because mine was better than his, so he took it."

3. Working age adults give mobile phones first to their parents, then to younger siblings, as in the Long and Liu family;

4. Working-age women give to older women or to younger siblings.

We are not claiming that these patterns of use are the generalized rule for mobile phone ownership and circulation in rural China, since we are drawing our data from ethnographic work that is limited in its geographical reach, and there are no surveys that focus on these specific issues, as also noticed by [4]. In the context of the Chinese countryside, Shandong and Hebei are relatively rich provinces, where the countryside is well connected to job- and opportunity-rich urban areas, and agriculture is profitable. In provinces that are more remote, less connected, less well-endowed in terms of land and industrial prospects, the situation might be very different, and the ownership of mobile phones, through purchase or gifting, much lower. However, these patterns are a useful starting point to understand how different circumstances influence ownership, use, and access to mobile phones.

MOBILE PHONES AND SOCIAL RELATIONSHIPS

What is the meaning of these gifts? Is there a "duty to give? Is there a "duty to reciprocate"? Can they be refused? This section aims at teasing apart the complex issue of what kind of relationships already exists or are created and how they might be modified by the gifting of mobile phones.

There's no free gift

Most of the literature related to gifting practices emphasizes the "duty to give" and the "duty to reciprocate," first theorized by [12] as the essential parts, together with the duty to accept a gift, of the gift cycle. Gifting practices *within and among* communities are interpreted as organized rituals that involve the functioning of social systems as whole entities. The much smaller body of literature that focuses specifically on gift giving *within* families, such as [6, 7], emphasize the symbolic and sentimental value of the gift, and the role it plays within the complex web of rituals, obligations, and ties building of family life[2]. In this context, gift giving is something that contributes to family relations, and therefore does not require the same "duty to return" that gifts within a wider community do require. Rather, it is a part of a relationship-building endeavor that lasts a lifetime and that is returned in different ways – with another gift, but also by a simple acknowledgment of the gift-giving gesture, or with the acceptance of the power relation that is created or underlined by the gift giving. The equivalent of the "duty to return" in a family context is incurred as a moral obligation towards the gift giver, which is fulfilled by accepting one's role in the gift-giving ritual (e.g. always have one's phone along, even if it is inconvenient) or by acknowledging the role of the giver in the receiver's life (e.g. a brother acknowledging that his sister cares about him, and the returning of the sentiment by doing her small favors when she visits).

Among our interviewees, mobile phone gifting is not perceived as something that is accompanied by the obligation to return the gift in kind. In fact, it is well understood that the gift is given to people without much income, so it is more part of a duty to care for weaker people within the family, or of what [4], in her description of the preference given to people in poor health in the sharing of mobile phones in rural Uganda, explains as a way to "promot(e) social cohesion within families and communities". The gift of a mobile is often described by interviewees as a way to be sure that older parents can be reached, as Mrs. Li from Village C describes:

"The first mobile I had was a Nokia, the basic one, which then I gave to my father in law. (Q: what does he use it for?) He doesn't really use it, it's more for us to find him."

This can be framed as a way to keep in touch with one's parents, and particularly one's mother, when far away, as explained by the young migrant women who had given their phones to their families, as well as a way to allow oneself to upgrade to a newer model without feeling guilty of wasting a working phone. Older parents, far from being a passive recipient of the gift, sometimes solicit it, explicitly pointing out that they are getting older and might need to be in contact:

"About three-four years ago (2006-07), that's when all the farmers started having mobile phones. That's because the people who migrated all had mobiles, so when they came back to visit, their old folks would say, that's a nice thing, give it to me, then we can connect - and so the migrant workers gave their old cell phones to their families." (Mr. Liu, Village B)

The fact that there is no duty to reciprocate the gift, however, does not mean that there are no obligations attached to it. In a very practical way, there are obligations both for givers and for receivers, and they tend to follow specific patterns. In the case of the givers, it is understood that if the receiver has very little or no disposable income, as it is typical for older parents living in rural areas and farming, the children also assume the duty to teach the basic skills to make and receive calls, to buy airtime and make sure that the phone always has credit, and to initiate calls. The receivers' 'duty' is to keep the phone in working conditions (e.g. functioning and charged) so that they can use it to make emergency calls or they can receive calls from their children, to learn how to use the phone from their children, and to have it always with them.

"My daughter taught me how to use (the mobile phone). I do not send SMS, the characters are too small and I can't see well. But I receive SMS and make and receive calls, and she showed me how to do that. The phone is a link with people who are away. For example I take it to the fields when I go to work. If they call at home and I'm in the field, then they can't reach me. But I take the phone with me, so they can reach me."(Mr. Liu, Village B)

School-age children are not expected to return a gift in any manner, since they are income-less, and in fact often depend on the mobile phone giver for money for airtime. They also tend to already know how to use the phone, sometimes better than the people who gave it to them, and are therefore outside the system of expectations and indirect

[2] In the Chinese case, gift giving within a community is part of the well-known and much studied phenomenon of *guanxi*, that is the art of building and sustaining relationships outside one's family. Gift-giving among close family members is not considered part of *guanxi*, so we don't refer to the extensive literature on the topic.[18] provides an excellent ethnography of this phenomenon in rural settings.

reciprocity around training, airtime purchase, making and receiving calls, etc that we described above. But, as [7] aptly notes, "even if it is true that the person giving has no expectation of return, this does not rule out the power dimension: dominance is all the greater when no return can come." (p530). For young adults receiving phones as well as money from older siblings or parents, these gifts are part of the many rewards/ punishments their life, and in particular their school life, is made of. Bing Long always receives phone/internet money from his elder sister accompanied by a stern reminder that he needs to do better in school. Mrs. Li confiscated her son's mobile phone during the school year, because the teachers said that he needed to concentrate on his university admission exam. His complaints that he might need to contact the parents for emergencies (he lived in the school dorm during semester) were quickly dismissed by both his mother and his teachers, and he was promised his phone back only if he did well in his exams.

Mobiles and freedom

We discussed above how for rural women who do not have their own income, it can be difficult to buy a phone autonomously, and ownership typically comes through a gift. As with the "duty to reciprocate," the "duty to receive" is also far from being universal, and it is subject to constant negotiations with the gift givers. For example, Mrs. Ouyang is a 55 year-old farmer in Village A, married with three adult children. When asked whether she had a mobile phone, she said no, that she did not own a phone and could not use one, but then went on to elaborate:

"*My children gave me a phone. They had one that they didn't use, so they gave it to me, but I don't use it, it's too much of a hassle. (Q: So you do have a mobile phone?) Yes, but I can't do much with it. I can receive calls. I also help my husband using his mobile phone, because his hearing is bad, so when someone calls him, he presses the key to answer, but then gives the phone to me and I talk. But I don't like talking on the mobile phone a lot, the reception is not clear, it's difficult to hear with clarity. But my husband can't hear at all, so I help him. Our friends say that we're "a deaf and a blind living together" because my eyesight is not good. But what are mobile phones for anyway? I think they're a hassle, like when I play cards with my friends, then the phone rings, and that's annoying, it interrupts what we are doing. (Q: So why do you have a mobile phone, if it's so annoying?) My husband needs it for business (he drives a tractor and rents it out occasionally), if you don't have a mobile, how do people find you? There's the landline, but then you're not at home and you might miss the call. But I don't like it. My son wanted to give me a cell phone, so that he can find me easily when I'm not at home and I'm out playing cards, but I don't want it! I'm afraid he'll find me too easily, and I don't want that. (Q: which one of your children gave you the old mobile?) Actually, I have a lot of old phones at home that our children gave us, they didn't use them anymore so they gave them to us. But I don't want to use any of them.*"

Mrs. Ouyang does not refuse the phones her children give her, and even remarked how they were trying to find a model that she would be able to use, and to teach her how to use the different functions – but she keeps on refusing to carry around her own phone, and uses one only to help her husband. The real value of these gifts lies in the reaffirming of the bond between her and the grown children, rather than in the objects themselves. She mentioned several times in the course of the interview that her son was extremely patient in teaching her all that is related to technology, and that her daughter who lives in Beijing always helps her in the fields when she comes back home, in addition to bringing gifts. The gifts are simply an articulation of family ties.

Some women, however, embrace these gifts as tools that allow them to carve out some independence from the occasionally constraining family life. Mrs. Yang, in Village C, had desired a mobile phone for a long time, but her husband did not think she needed one because all she did was farming. When she finally got a phone (in fact, author 1's old mobile) she was enthusiastic about the freedom it allowed her: *"I can do whatever I want to do! If I want to go somewhere to play cards or play mahjong, I just do it, they (her husband and live-in mother-in-law) can call me or I can call them if there's anything, they don't need to come looking for me. Definitively more freedom!"*.

In addition to meeting her friends to play cards, Mrs. Yang also wanted to be able to go and visit her own mother in another village whenever she wanted, which was something her mother-in-law disapproved of. Having a mobile phone allowed her to go for these visits without telling anyone, and still come back quickly if need be. Mrs. Long is also using her mobile as a way to increase her independence, in this case economic: a few years ago, she started selling insurance as a side-activity in addition to farming. At the time she had a landline, and used it to contact and follow-up with clients, all living in villages nearby. Although it was better than visiting them and finding that nobody was home, it was not very efficient. The mobile phone allows her to call them and be reachable herself at all times, and has helped her expand her business. Author 1 observed that several times, when visiting nearby villages to go to the market or run other errands, Mrs. Long would call clients living nearby, and if they were available she would stop and visit them. For school-age children too, owning their own phone can mean carving out some private space when their living conditions lack it (school dorms house 8 to 12 people or sometimes more per room, and private homes often do not have separate bedrooms). Ms. Deng remembers the great feeling of owning her very own mobile and being able to keep in touch, privately, with her classmates when she came home from school at weekends, *"although it can be embarrassing when one gets messages or calls very late at night and the parents wonder what it is..."*

Renewed social relationships

"Gift transactions confirm ties between individuals, and are thus a means of maintaining valued relationships." [5]. Gifts like clothes and mobiles can reaffirm a disinterested and non-utilitarian value in a relationship, but also be a relatively cheap way for the gift giver to increase their social status both within their family and in the village. In particular, for young women it can be a way to compensate for their absence and, sometimes, for their ignoring the duties connected with being good daughters, such as for example dating men they meet in the city rather than settling for arranged marriages in the village. Mobiles are particularly important in keeping the mother-to-daughter bond alive, - a significant change from Chinese traditions of women cutting the ties with their family of origin after marriage [20].

Figure 3: Mothers and grandmothers in Village C.

Changes in the economy and in society in the past twenty years have transformed this situation, and new ICT, in particular mobile phones, have allowed what [3] calls the "network of intimacy" between mothers and daughters to be reaffirmed independently of the ties with the rest of the family. This is something that several of our interviewees – both mothers and daughters – remarked upon. Although the conversations are often very short and utilitarian (as Mrs. Cai summarizes them, *"Did you eat? What did you eat?"*), they can happen whenever one of them wants to talk, and they require very little effort – a big change from previous times, when people in the city had to queue once a week to use public phones, or they had to write letters. Clearly these processes exist within a larger changing societal matrix of obligations, customs, traditions and relationships that go well beyond what is represented by conversations enabled by mobile phones, and that are beyond the scope of this paper.

NEW USER, DIFFERENT FUNCTIONS

These 'traveling' phones end up in a very different physical environment from the one where they started their lives, and are owned by users often with a different skill set, interests, and need than the original ones. In this section, we look at some of the challenges that this changes bring with them.

Physical Environment

A mobile phone in an urban environment is used mostly indoors, has its own charger, and has its back taken off only when the SIM card needs to be changed – a relatively infrequent event, as changing a SIM card means changing one's number, which is often considered not worthwhile even if there are better contracts on offer. In rural areas, all these conditions are reversed. Phones are used, and often charged, mostly outdoors, and in any case the distinction between indoor and outdoor is not as clean-cut as in urban areas, with courtyards being an extension of the indoor living spaces. All three villages have unpaved roads, and the rain season is short, so the environment can be extremely dusty. This represents a major challenge for mobiles and computers, as well as for televisions and other technologies, which is made worse by the fact that mobiles are often kept open, i.e. without their backs. Ms. Hua, the mobile phone shop owner, explained that many of her clients change their SIM card (and associated phone number) very often, to take advantage of special offers from the two main mobile phone operators, China Mobile and China Unicom. Nearly everyone uses pay-as-you-go SIMs without long-term commitments or even signed contracts, so many people buy a SIM card, which typically comes with some airtime, use up the airtime, and then change it to get a better offer. For example, one of our interviewees, Ms. Deng, changed her number four times in the course of a month, chasing better offers, or simply swapping cards to make different types of calls (long-distance versus local).

Figure 4: A wall-socket type mobile phone battery charger.

Moreover, phone chargers often got lost on the way, or people find them inconvenient, so many households use a phone battery charger like the one in the photo above. It is a very convenient way of charging all different types of phones, but it makes the problem of dust even worse, as phones are perpetually having their covers taken off. Indoor to outdoor use also means different ways of fulfilling the same need. For example, in urban environments, music listening tends to be a private activity, done with earbuds. In the villages, on the other hand, listening to the radio or to music is a social activity, and phones are often brought to the fields so that the radio can keep people company. Newer, urban phones often don't have speakers loud enough, nor a radio function, since people download MP3s and choose their own music. When phones like these arrive to the countryside, it is often a disappointment for the recipient as the supposed upgrade turns out to significantly less useful than the phone it is replacing.

Skill Levels and Interests

When phones are given to parents or other older relatives, the skill levels of the new users can be considerably lower than those of the original users. This problem is becoming worse as new models, including smart phones, reach the countryside. In fact, new, more sophisticated phones do not necessarily imply new, more sophisticated uses:

"I got my second phone in 2008, a bright pink Motorola with a camera,, that my son gave me. It had more functions (than my previous one), but I still used it like before, because I can't use all those functions. I brought it with me in the fields, and it fell, and it was completely smashed. So then my younger daughter bought me another Nokia like the one before. I always bring it with me when I go to the fields to work." (Mrs. Cai, Village C)

A similar thing happened to Mrs. Long: one summer evening in Village A, Mrs. Long showed author 1 the brand new mobile she had received from her middle daughter, the 19-year-old who works in a phone factory. It was a '*shanzhai*' copy of a Motorola smart phone, still in the box, and she carefully took it out and turned it on. The opening screen showed a small lock, a familiar sight for any smart phone owner, but completely opaque to Mrs. Long. She read carefully the instructions on the screen, "Slide your finger to unlock the screen," and after a few failed attempts due to her unfamiliarity with touch screens, poor instructions in Chinese, and a rather unintuitive interface, we finally managed to unlock it. Mrs. Long wanted to see where the radio was, and after pressing on the screen somewhat at random she located some music; once she had turned it on, however, she could not find a way to turn it off, or to lower the volume. When the screen went to sleep and she found that she could not unlock it again, she turned the phone off, put it back in the box, put the box away, and reverted to use her old phone.

Many older interviewees say that they use their mobiles as they use their landlines, that is they make and receive calls. Many people, again among older users, were aware of functions like text messages, and knew that people could sign up to receive daily news or the weather report, particularly appreciated by farmers. But not everybody interviewed could locate the text messages folder on their mobile. Even if they could read, many users did not have the skills required to input Chinese characters on mobile phones and computers, meaning even those who can locate and read text messages often cannot reply to them.

Despite the often minimal uptake of phone features, there is an increasing awareness of the connectivity it offers. A mobile phone opens up the possibility of communication channels between people in urban areas and those in the countryside, across places and across generations. The possibility is not always and not equally exploited, but when it is, it provides a way for people who have never migrated, or do not have much education, money, or social capital, to reach through their urbanized children some of the benefits of 'weak ties' – those relationships that [9] correlates positively with more opportunities. For example, Mr. Liu insists that the internet is for young people, or people who want to grow their business and find new opportunities, not for an old farmer like himself, who does not have many needs, and is not interested in making more money. However, when he needs to make important purchases, such as his last refrigerator, he calls his daughter in Beijing and asks her to check prices on the internet, so that he can find out whether he is getting a good deal at the county store. Or Mrs. Tao, who runs a small transportation company with her husband, and cannot use the internet herself, but often asks her daughter to research potential business contacts online. It's nothing that the landline cannot do, but mobile phones magnify the possibility.

Finally, gifted phones are rarely 'cleaned up' by their previous owners, so the new owners inherit music, photos, e-books and anything else that was loaded on the phone. The reaction to this inheritance depends very much by the age of the new owner. Young people like Bing Long can fully leverage both the content and the functions of old phones, and find them a window into what is fashionable in the city in terms of songs, games, etc. He uses each of his four mobiles in the way that maximizes its strengths: the one that used to belong to his sister has the best music, another one can go online, one has the best sound so he uses it to call, one has good novels, and his father's old one has good games. His primary phone is the one he uses to call, so when he goes around on his bike or to visit friends, that's the one he carries, but at home he uses each one according to its function. His mother's favorite function on her phone – her eldest daughter's old one – is the camera. She has never owned a camera, and the family has only a few photos taken by a photographer for special occasions. Since her daughter has shown her how to take pictures, she has used this function a lot, but she doesn't know how or where she can print out the photos, so every now and then she goes through her entire collection and deletes the older or less interesting ones. For a while she kept some of her daughter's old photos that had remained loaded on the phone, but then she deleted them to make space for her own. For owners who never go beyond the basic functions, existing content is neither a positive nor a negative aspect, because they cannot access it and often are not even aware it is there. Even something that is often taken as a basic function of a mobile phone, the address book, is usually ignored by older users: they keep an old-fashioned paper address book, and that is where they write their new contacts or look up numbers when they need to make calls. In many cases, there was no need for an address book altogether, because the only calls that were received were those of the children, and if the parents needed to make a call, they would do so from the landline and read the number off a piece of paper placed near the phone.

CONCLUSION

One of the implications of this work is the rethinking of what it means to design for multiple, sequential users of a technology. This is in line with a variety of research threads in HCI. For example, [8] have called for more sustainable HCI, and it is clear that there are opportunities to design for gifting and re-gifting of technology. One simple suggestion in line with designing for re-appropriation and gifting might be to include an accessible "reset system" command that allows the new user to set up the phone as they would like, and perhaps also provides a tutorial on features. However, this fieldwork suggests that such a feature may not support the rich experience of transferring both physical objects and its embedded digital contents. As physical phones are passed from one person to another, so too are the digital contents of these devices: ringtones, MP3s, photographs, books, movies, and address books. These ephemera are themselves part of the gift. As [6] points out, part of the processes of gift giving – wrapping paper, signed and personalized cards, and so on – provide a sense of decommodification, the removal of the gifted item from mundane and interchangeable processes of the market. The phone becomes not just "a phone," but rather "my phone;" not just "a Nokia 1280," but "the phone my eldest son brought back for me after his first year of work."

We became aware that there is a tension between the 'sanitizing' suggested by the first suggestion and the rich, situated nature of the digital heirlooms that become part of the experience of the gift. It is the awareness of these tensions and questions that we propose as lessons from this work. Much as Sengers writes in her recent discussion of her time in the Change Islands [14], we found that in understanding this technology use it is important not to import assumptions about efficiency as a metric for technology use, but rather to recognize the rich variety of ways in which people continue to acquire and experience technologies. As we saw in rural users' frustration with new phones that didn't include radios or loud speakers, assumptions about 'what makes a good phone' are drawn from a particular situation. There is no single solution, but we hope that drawing awareness to these transactions will encourage mobile manufacturers and service providers to be open to re-use, and not just use.

REFERENCES

1. Bell, G. The age of the thumb: A cultural reading of mobile technologies from Asia. *Knowledge Technology Policy* 19, 2 (2005), 67-88.
2. Bergquist, M. and Ljungberg, J. The power of gifts: organizing social relationships in open source communities. *Info. Sys. J.* 11, (2001), 305-320.
3. Bray, F. Constructing Intimacy: Technology, Family and Gender in East Asia. *East Asian Science, Technology and Society* 2, 2 (2008), 151-165.
4. Burrell, J. Evaluating shared access: social equality and the circulation of mobile phones in rural Uganda. *J. CMC* 15, (2010), 230-250.
5. Cheal, D.J. The Social Dimensions of Gift Behaviour. *J. Social and Personal Relationships* 3, (1986), 423-439.
6. Cheal, D.J. The Gift Economy. Routledge,.1988.
7. Corrigan, P. Gender and the Gift: The Case of the Family Clothing Economy. *Soc.* 23, 4 (1989), 513-534.
8. Disalvo, C., Sengers, P., and Brynjarsdóttir, H. Mapping the landscape of sustainable HCI. *Proc. CHI'10.* ACM Press (2010): 1975-1984.
9. Granovetter, M. The Strength of Weak Ties: A Network Theory Revisited. *Sociological Theory* 1, (1983), 201.
10. Johnsen, T.E. The Social Context of the Mobile Phone Use of Norwegian Teens. In J. Katz, ed., *Machines That Become Us*. Transaction Publishers, 2003, 161-169.
11. Katz, J. *Machines that become us*. Transaction Publishers, 2003.
12. Mauss, M. *The Gift: The Form and Reason for Exchange in Archaic Societies*. W.W. Norton, 1990.
13. Parry, J. The Gift , the Indian Gift and the 'Indian Gift.' *Man*, New Series 21, 3 (1986), 453-473.
14. Senger, P. What I Learned on Change Islands: Reflections on IT and Pace of Life. *Interactions*, (March-April 2011), 40-48.
15. Taylor, A.S. and Harper, R. The gift of the gab?: A design oriented sociology of young people's use of mobiles. *CSCW* 12, 3 (2003), 267–296.
16. Testart, A. Qu'est-ce qu'un don? In E. Magnani, ed., *Don et Sciences Sociales: Théories et pratiques croisées*. Editions Universitaires de Dijon, 2007.
17. Vargas, A.A. and Toro, M.S. Gift Giving and New Communication Technologies. In *Women and the Gift Economy: A Radically Different Worldview Is Possible*. 2007, 248-252.
18. Yan, Y. *The Flow of Gifts: Reciprocity and Social Networks in a Chinese Village*. Stanford, 1996.
19. Zhang, W. "A Married Out Daughter Is Like Spilt Water"?: Women's Increasing Contacts and Enhanced Ties with Their Natal Families in Post-Reform Rural North China. *Modern China* 35, 3 (2009), 256-2.

The Joy of Cheques: Trust, Paper and Eighty Somethings

John Vines[1], Paul Dunphy[2], Mark Blythe[1], Stephen Lindsay[2], Andrew Monk[3], Patrick Olivier[2]

[1]School of Design
Northumbria University
Newcastle upon Tyne, UK
{john.vines, mark.blythe}
@northumbria.ac.uk

[2]Culture Lab
School of Computing Science
Newcastle University
Newcastle upon Tyne, UK
{p.m.dunphy, s.c.lindsay,
p.l.olivier}@newcastle.ac.uk

[3]Department of Psychology
University of York
York, UK
a.monk@psych.york.ac.uk

ABSTRACT

A cheque is a paper document that orders the transfer of money between bank accounts. Whilst an eighty-year-old in the UK is predicted on average to live at least another ten years, cheques may not. Despite many older peoples extensive use of cheques, UK banks are eager to abolish them and design electronic alternatives that are less costly to process and less vulnerable to fraud. This paper reports on two qualitative studies that explored the banking experiences of 23 people over eighty years old. Cheques support financial collaboration with others in ways that digital payment systems do not. We argue that whilst it might be possible to improve the design of digital payment systems to better support financial collaboration, the case for retaining and enhancing cheques is stronger. Rather than replace cheques, we must design ways of making them less costly to process and better linked to electronic payment methods.

Author Keywords

Banking; trust; older old; cheques; paper.

ACM Classification Keywords

H.5.m. Information interfaces and presentation (e.g., HCI): Miscellaneous.

General Terms

Design; Human Factors.

INTRODUCTION

The banking industry has a long history of enthusiastically adopting new technology. Money has taken a variety of forms: stone, gold, silver, paper and, more recently, the airy nothingness of digital representation. Although the banks eagerly adopt new technologies, some of their customers remain more cautious. As new forms emerge, older financial instruments such as cheques (Figure 1) may seem outmoded, irrelevant to most people and too costly for businesses to administer. In 2009, the UK's Payments Council (a group of financial institutes who determine payment methods in the UK) announced the planned withdrawal of cheques from circulation in 2018 [30]. There followed such uproar that the Payments Council was forced into a "U turn" [13]. A Treasury Select Committee investigation concluded that the Payments Council was overly dominated by industry and did not adequately represent consumers. The Treasury report warns 'cheques have been saved, for the moment, but we need to remain vigilant. The incentives for the industry to get rid of cheques has not gone away' [13]. Older people in particular objected vociferously to the proposed abolition of cheques. People who are over eighty-years-old are the fastest growing demographic group in the world [33]. They are commonly referred to as the "older old" [9], but in this paper will use a more descriptive and neutral term, *eighty somethings* [34]. This paper reports findings from a study of the value of cheques to a group of eighty somethings in the North of England.

Cheques are still a popular payment method in many countries, including the United States (where they are known as checks), France (chèque), New Zealand, Australia and the UK [8]. These paper documents allow a bank account holder to write the name of a person or organisation they would like to pay, the sum they want to pay them, the date and their signature to authorise the transfer of funds.

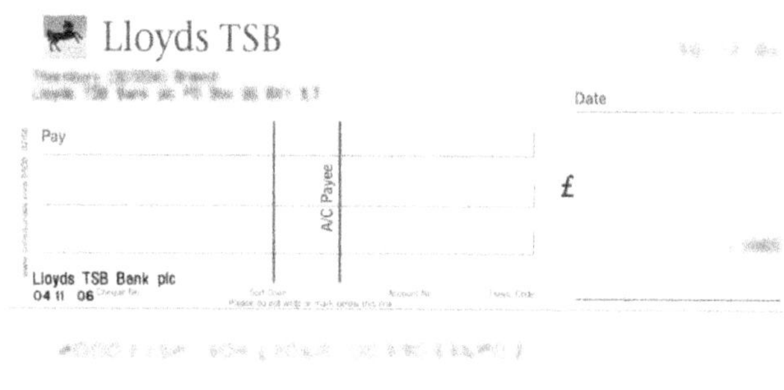

Figure 1. A cheque as typically used in the UK.

In the UK, the number of cheques used per annum peaked in 1990 and has declined steadily over the past five years [29]. Although the number of cheques being used each year is in decline, there are specific groups of people for whom they are highly desirable, such as charities, small businesses [32] and eighty somethings.

Throughout their lives the eighty somethings have had cheques available to them. An eighty-year-old today is predicted to live for another decade [9] and it remains a possibility that cheques will be discontinued in their lifetime. Any alternative financial instrument or service is likely to benefit from understanding what qualities of cheques make them particularly valued by older people.

We conducted two studies involving eighty somethings living in the North of England. The first study involved a series of in-depth, one-to-one interviews in which participants related their 'financial biographies' [34]. The second study involved group discussions centred on the theme of the future of banking and future banking services. Both studies indicated that for these eighty somethings the cheque is essential. The properties of cheques that we identified imply a number of requirements for the design of a future alternative that might bridge the divide between the needs of modern financial institutions and the needs of eighty somethings.

BACKGROUND

The beginning and end of cheques

The 1882 Bills of Exchange Act defines a '*bill of exchange [as] an unconditional order in writing, addressed by one person to another, signed by the person giving it, requiring the person to whom it is addressed to pay on demand or at a fixed or determinable future time a sum certain in money to or to the order of a specified person, or to bearer*' [5]. The current cheque is more uniform in appearance than early bills of exchange but still embodies these same principles. A cheque is used by a bank account holder to request the transfer of money from their account to the account of another person (or another account of their own). Banks typically supply cheques in the form of a book, in which each cheque is attached to a 'stub' where information can be recorded about the cheques that have been written and removed.

The cheque 'clearing' process in the UK is complex and resource intensive [28]. When a bank cashier receives a cheque from a customer she/he manually enters account details from the cheque into the bank's electronic database. The cheque is then sent off-site for a second processing stage where it is scanned. After this, a cheque is repacked and sent for physical storage – one UK bank has filled up a disused salt mine in the South of England with used paper cheques (anonymous pers comm.). The paper originals are kept for up to seven years for recording purposes and for validating transfers in the case of disputes.

The costs of processing cheques was the primary motivation for the unpopular proposal to withdraw cheques altogether in 2018 [29, 13]. For the banking industry cheques are difficult to process and used by only a small minority of customers. This small minority includes our group of eighty somethings.

Ageing, banking and paper

In 2007 a financial inclusion strategy was proposed in the UK that included accessibility guidelines for banking products and services for all [12]. The strategy was in part a response to studies and claims by advocacy groups that older people were at serious risk of exclusion from financial information, products and services provided by the retail banking sector [35]. AgeUK, the largest advocacy group for older people in Britain, has argued at length that older people are particularly vulnerable to the discontinuation of cheques [16] and are less familiar with alternatives such as telephone and internet banking [18]. Such concerns are also noted by the Payments Council who stated that 'the needs of harder-to-reach and vulnerable groups are identified and addressed in our work to develop a choice of alternatives to cheques' [31].

There has been a growing interest in recent years in developing novel payment methods, particularly on mobile platforms. Most UK retail banks, such as Barclays Bank PLC [2], offer smart phone applications that allow customers to make quick money transfers to pay bills and other people. PayPal's 'Bump' application [19] allows people in the same location to exchange money by knocking their smart phones against one another. SMS-based banking systems, such as Kenya's M-PESA [17], allow people to transfer money to others on basic mobile phones. Near Field Communication (NFC) technologies embedded in mobile phones and bankcards are being introduced by many banks, allowing customers to make payments by waving their device in front of a reader [22].

Crucially, all of these new payment mechanisms avoid the use of paper. As our study will highlight, the paper-based nature of the cheque is fundamental to how the eighty somethings and the carers in our study financially collaborate and form trust with others. Previous work in CSCW and HCI has identified the significance of paper in work environments [e.g. 20, 21, 25], with Sellen and Harper [24] providing a comprehensive overview of why attempts to replace paper with digital alternatives often fail. Likewise, our studies sought to go beyond a narrow exploration of functional qualities of cheques and contrast these with digital payment methods (although these are important). Instead, we were interested in the meanings and values associated with the paper cheque that are likely to be more difficult to achieve in any future remediation.

FIELD STUDIES

Methodology

Two data corpuses were drawn on for the analysis reported in the Findings section. The first corpus is a set of financial biographies from a study fully described and reported in [34]. Briefly, 12 eighty somethings provided in-depth interviews that formed a 'financial biography'. Participants were male and female and the majority described themselves as working class. All but one had little to no experience of computers. This first study also drew on interviews with 2 care home managers, a welfare benefits officer, representatives from older people advocacy groups and a representative of a leading British retail bank.

The results of this first study were used to inform discussions with a further 10 eighty somethings who took part in three separate participatory design workshops (6 participants in the first workshop, and 2 each in the second and third). Participants of this second study were all female and recruited from an established research panel of older people based at Northumbria University. Most of the quotes from older people in the *Findings* section come from these participants. In general, the participants of the second study described themselves as middle-socio-economic class. Three participants considered themselves computer literate and two others were attending computer literacy classes. Only one participant in the second study used online banking. Six participants reported having shared their finances with their husband during their lives, and one reported that she let her husband perform all of her banking on her behalf.

Each workshop began with an informal discussion of current financial practices. Participants were encouraged to question one another and the researchers on their behaviours and habits. This often led to useful exchanges between the older participants and younger researchers that highlighted generational differences in financial knowledge and experiences.

All of the sessions were recorded, transcribed and anonymised. A thematic analysis [6] was conducted on the transcripts, where data was summarised in open-ended codes and grouped together into four key themes. Findings from this second corpus have not been reported before. Whilst cheques were a topic of discussion in the earlier interviews—particularly by the care home professionals—we had not realised the significance of these instruments to the eighty somethings until our later workshops. Therefore, the initial study was revisited and previously unused items of data were incorporated into the thematic analysis.

FINDINGS

Four themes structure the following account: *signs; complexity; collaboration;* and *trust.*

Signs: control and events

Cheques often provide signs that are meaningful to the eighty somethings. Many of the eighty somethings emphasised how the physical form of a cheque book provides a space to document outgoing expenses. Rita prefers to use cheques for this reason, as often when using a credit or debit card she is not offered a receipt. *"Whereas a cheque, you fill in the stub ... you write your cheque, you fill in the stub, you've got your record of where it went, as long as you remember to fill the stub in."* She goes on to recall the one time in her life she did not completely fill the cheque book stub out. *"Ooh, it caused chaos that did."* She has always ensured that she fills in the stub ever since. When using a cheque the stub it is often the only easily accessible record she has about who and what she paid.

In the group discussions, participants talked about how many cheques or cheque books they would *"get through"*. Margaret uses them "*once every couple of months or something like that." "Oh I use them more often than that!"* replies Iris. Anna follows with *"about 4 or 5 a month."* A cheque book that lasts longer suggests fewer transactions, at least via cheques. Marjorie states *"we run through quite a few cheque books".* Betty, who reported having always been a heavy user of cheques, still uses them *"quite often."* At the same time, she reflects: *"the cheque book lasts longer than it used to though, doesn't it?"* The realisation that she uses fewer cheques than she used to appeared to sadden Betty. The cheque book itself acts as a physical reminder of the activity, or lack thereof, of a bank account over a period of time.

The writing down of transactions and the physical presence of the cheque book is also useful for those who care for eighty somethings. The care home managers would refer to times when they had to keep track of a resident's spending even if they are not legally authorised to do so. As a consequence, care home managers and staff spent a lot of time looking for indicators as to how well a resident is managing their finances. A dishonoured or 'bounced' cheque is one such indicator. Usually, a cheque is bounced when there are insufficient funds in the associated bank account, although a cheque might also be returned if the writing is illegible or it is dated incorrectly. A bounced cheque is usually posted back to the account holder. Unusual looking envelopes from the banks are often a warning sign of unusual activity occurring on a resident's account. The physicality of the cheque and how it is returned to account holder supports the subtle monitoring practices that are employed by care home staff.

The care home managers referred to how many of their residents find it difficult to access cash as a result of mobility or cognitive impairments. Consequently, some care homes hold a fund of cash on-site that the residents can withdraw from if they write out a cheque to the care home. This has a two-fold benefit: the resident has access to cash, and the care home is able to indirectly keep track of how much money that resident is spending. Care home manager Lynn described the situation of one resident, who they suspected was losing money. *"Because she comes to us to cash the cheques as she can't get to the bank, we can actually monitor how much she's taking and how often. We need to check that money is going somewhere safe, that somebody isn't walking with it."* Not only are the care home staff aware of how much is being spent through the amounts that residents withdraw from this on-site fund, but the cheque is marked with information that allows the ongoing tracking of a residents withdrawals over time.

As well as acting as signs of financial activity, cheques also act as signs of special events in peoples' lives. Agnes would send cheques to grandchildren for birthdays and special events. *"Usually for birthdays it is a cheque now they are older. If one of the grandchildren comes round and helps me, I will give them £1 cash when they are 6 and 7."* Cash would still be used for smaller 'gifts', especially when the children are younger. *"You wouldn't expect them to run to the bank with a couple of pounds, they would probably keep that in their room."* This choice of the cheque rather than cash often suggests a significant occasion rather than a spontaneous gift or gesture. Marjorie referred to how *"with the older ones, really £100 is possibly for a once a year or twice a year, Christmas and birthday, is what we would give to an 18 or 20 year old ... I wouldn't give that in cash."* This is not to say that cheques are the only method that the participants use to send money to their grandchildren. Agnes discussed how she and her husband are financially supporting one of their grandchildren during his time at university. *"We are helping the one at university and I think my husband pays a little something in each month and that's by direct credit banking."* Agnes and her husband do not send a cheque in this case, preferring to transfer money using telephone banking. Here, the functional basis of the 'gift' appears to be supported by what is perceived to be a more functional method of transferring money. For birthdays, Christmases and special events, however, they would always send a cheque: *"it's much more personal than a money transfer."*

Whilst, for our participants, the use of a cheque instead of cash is a sign of a large gift, it is also related to the age and maturity of the grandchild. Many of the eighty somethings said they would send a larger amount as their grandchild got older. Also, in order to send a cheque to their grandchild, said child must have a bank account into which it can be deposited. Marjorie observed that *"when they are young they don't have an account ... I think the younger pair give the cheque to their parents at Christmas and birthday, but the two older ones certainly have a bank account."* Many of the participants grew up in a period when it was particularly difficult to open a bank account—especially if you were female. Dorlores recalled that when opening an account in the 1970s she had to find a sponsor to *"vouch"* for her, despite her having a full-time job. *"I remember going down to the bank and being told this and I had to go back and find somebody who had an account at [bank]. [It] was always regarded as the people's bank ... it was the bank for the ordinary folk, but no, they were very strict. I had to find somebody who had an account to come down to the bank with me to say that I was a worthy person to have a bank account."* Whilst their grandchildren did not require a *"sponsor"* or full-time work to have a bank account, the opening of a bank account was still described as an important occasion in a child's life.

Cheques hold information that provides immediate access to the incomings and outgoings of a bank account and the state of a person's finances. But they also signify important moments in people's lives where large amounts of money have been received or spent. For some of the eighty somethings the cheque adds to the ceremony surrounding these special moments.

Complexity: distance and time

Whilst cheques are a paper document, its simplicity as a financial instrument disguises the complexity of some of the transactions performed with them. As described by the eighty somethings, payments are performed over large distances in space and time. As Betty reminds us, *"for years you've been told not to put actual cash in the post."* Cheques can be sent in the post because they are worthless to anybody other than the named payee. For the person who has written the cheque, there is some security in the knowledge that only the person named can bank it into an account under their name. When the possibility of cheques being withdrawn from use was brought up, many of the eighty somethings became deeply concerned about sending money over a distance.

Joyce: *"But if they do away with cheques, how do you send money, like if you've bought something and you want to pay by cheque?"*

Anna: *"If you want to give a present to somebody you send a cheque, like you do with the grandchildren. What do you do ... you want to send a cheque for their birthday."*

Harriet: *"Donations or anything, you know, charitable things."*

There are a number of alternatives to sending a cheque that can be used in these situations such as ordering a bank transfer using phone or internet banking. On a functional level, performing a transaction in this way would have the same end result as using a cheque. However, such alternatives did not appeal to our eighty something participants regardless of their level of computer literacy. Anna is computer literate and confident in browsing the Internet and sending/receiving emails. However, she does not like the idea of using a computer to perform banking *"Last week I had a plumber in. I had to pay him and I said will you take a credit card? He said, no I'll send you the bill online. So he sent it online. Well how am I going to pay, except by cheque?"* Many small traders such as plumbers, electricians and builders do not accept credit or debit card transactions as they often do not carry the required terminals or want to avoid the associated processing fees. Cheques therefore have traditionally been the dominant mode of payment in the UK for these types of tradesmen. The expectation in this scenario, however, is that in sending the bill over the internet, Anna will subsequently be able to pay the bill over the internet or request a transfer over the phone. *"No way, I'm not going to, I want my cheque."* It was not a case of Anna not feeling competent enough to make the payment over the internet but rather that she did not want to enter her account details into an unknown system.

Using cheques over a distance can cause uncertainty as to when the money will be received. In theory, UK first-class post should arrive within two days of being sent but this is not always the case. Added to this is the unpredictability of when the payee will take the cheque to the bank. Dolores wondered whether her grandchildren know what to do when they receive a cheque from her. *"Often I have to ring up and say "you haven't cashed that cheque." They say "oh I forgot.""*

Whilst geographical distance adds time to the completion of cheque transactions, delays in cashing and then clearing cheques also extends the time from the act of giving (or posting) and the transfer of funds. The timescales associated with processing a cheque are complex, as described by the Cheque and Credit Clearing Company (CCCC) in the following scenario.

'Daniel collects all cheques made out to his company from the previous week and takes them into his bank to pay in on Monday morning. His company account starts to earn interest on the money on Wednesday (+2 days), and by Friday morning (+4 days) his bank will enable him to withdraw the money from the deposited cheques from the account, even though the cheques could still bounce. By the end of the following Tuesday (+6 days), he can be certain that the cheques will not bounce, and the money from them cannot be reclaimed from the company account without his consent' [7].

In practice, it is difficult for an account holder to know when a cheque will be processed and the funds transferred. Doris considered it *"strange that it takes longer to clear a cheque in these days of instantaneous communication that it used to do."* However, these perceived irregularities do not bother most of the eighty somethings, as they reported mental strategies to simplify the process. Many of the participants referred to how once a cheque is written it is considered spent money. Iris states that *"once I've written a cheque it's gone out of the account as far as I'm concerned."* This is the same for Anna, who feels *"it's not my money anymore"* once a cheque is written and sent to the payee.

The complexity of the cheque clearing process means that the system is open to abuse and exploitation. Margaret recalled that she *"knew somebody who, when it was getting near the end of the month and she hadn't got much money, would put the wrong date on a cheque so they would send it back."* Such stories initiated responses of *"oh, gosh!"* and *"the cheek"*, signifying many of the participants abhorrence of such behaviour. Yet other exploits in the cheque clearing process – such as being able to cancel a cheque if it has not gone through the final stages of processing – are acceptable. Rita described the one time she cancelled a cheque and her bank still processed it. *"I subsequently played war that they hadn't done what I said and I got my money back."* In Rita's situation, the exploitation of the system was considered to be acceptable, to the point that the bank was to blame for not enacting her cancellation of the transaction. Whilst on the surface cheques appear to be mundane paper forms, the practices formed around them are complex and open to negotiation and exploitation. This is highly related to the theme of *collaboration*, as financial collaboration between people emerges from cheque use.

Collaboration: access and deviation

Cheques are not always used as a direct means of paying for a service or bill but are often used as a way of having others access cash, or for buying items on another's behalf. For example, cheques can be used not only as a formal alternative to cash but also as a way of gaining access to it. A bank account holder can write out a cheque to her own name (or to "CASH") and then use it to withdraw cash from that account. Cheques written to withdraw cash accounted for less than 6% of cheque transactions in the UK in 2009 [24] although this figure does not account for situations where people collaborate with one another through cheques to access cash. As previously noted, many residents in care homes find it difficult to visit their banks on a regular basis. Lynn, one of the care home managers, describes how her care home uses cheques as a way of giving the residents access to cash. *"We've got an amount of money in the bank. We draw from that and keep cash here that the residents can take cash from – with their cheques. The cheques then go back into the bank account."* Lynn describes how residents write out a cheque to the care home. This is then given to a member of the care home staff, who then deposits it in the care home's bank account. In the meantime, the resident is given cash to the amount on the cheque. For the care home, the collaborative cashing of cheques on-site provides one of the few ways of ensuring that residents can have ready access to cash. *"We're going to get problems because we're not going to be able to offer that service. It's – what can we put in its place and how are we going to manage... It's going to have a major impact here."* Lynn worries about how the residents will have access to cash if cheques cease to exist.

It is not just in care homes that cheque cashing is highly valued. For people that are housebound, either permanently or temporarily, writing cheques is a useful way to access cash. Doris recalled a recent situation where she helped a friend. *"During the snow, one of my neighbours who is housebound ... had no loose cash left to pay his cleaner or small things like that, so he gave me a cheque for £100 and I got £100 out of the hole in the wall."* In this case, it was not that large bills needed to be paid or that cash was their preferred mode of payment—it was that cash is still needed for small items. This necessity to continue having cash would prevail, even if her neighbour were able to manage their finances over the internet.

Cheques are also written collaboratively, that is, by people other than the account holder. Lynn discussed situations where they completed parts of cheques on behalf of the care home residents. *"You'd be surprised how many people we have come in the office, we give them a pen, put their hand on the book and say sign there. We've filled out the cheque."* Natalie, another care home manager, describes a similar situation with one of her residents. *"We fill it out, he signs it, we take it to Library Square to pay his charges and we've got receipts."* When discussing these situations there is an acceptance on the part the care home managers that these practices are not ideal. However, they feel obliged to help. If not, residents would be unable to pay bills or get access to cash. The nature of the cheque provides the opportunity for these collaborative practices to emerge.

In contrast, the dangers of the flexible nature of cheques are not lost on the eighty somethings. "*I only keep one cheque in my purse, not the book. I think the police are dead against you carrying a cheque book around.*" Many of the participants did not keep cheques on them when outside their house and only took their cheque books with them when absolutely necessary. Similarly, the potential for cheques to be completed by another person places care home residents at risk of financial abuse. *"We did have somebody here wrote themselves a cheque out, forged a signature."* In the case that Lynn here describes no money was lost as the account was long-closed. The physical design of the cheque is open to abuse, fraud and deviation from standard usage. At the same time, it is these very same properties of a cheque that make it useful as a collaborative instrument.

Trust: checking and security

The use of cheques, cards and cash involve different degrees of trust in institutions and people. This became particularly apparent when the participants reflected on their experiences of having cheques refused by trades-people.

Betty: *"The workman, say the plumber who just comes, "cash please, no I don't do cheques". And then of course it doesn't go through his books so he's not paying his income tax or whatever. But I find most of them do request ready cash.*

Doris: *"Well it has to go through his books."*

Anna: *"A cheque had to go through his accounts and he has to pay tax on it but if he's got cash in his hand it goes in his pocket."*

Betty, Doris and Anna discussed amongst themselves why they think such trades-people refuse cheques. Their understanding is that cash enables a tradesperson to avoid paying taxes. A cheque is a formalisation of the transaction between customer and seller. Not only does the cheque clearing process make the transaction accountable but it also means the money within the transaction is not immediately available to the tradesperson. The immediate access that cash provides to money compared to cheques can also be beneficial to payments between friends. Margaret noted how she *"wouldn't dream of giving a friend a cheque ... they would then have to go to the bank and pay it in ... if you've given them cash they've got it."* Cash is preferable in such a situation, as it requires less effort on the part of the person receiving it to access its value.

Many of the eighty somethings that used cheques also used bankcards. Most card transactions performed in the UK are authorised by entering a four-digit Personal Identification Number (PIN). Many were concerned with remembering this information. A number of the participants referred to ways in which they had concealed this information for future reference. In a group discussion, the participants responded to an anecdote by one of the researcher's of how his father wrote down his PIN:

Anna: *"I'd like to suggest ... that he gets a little address book and puts in a false name and false telephone number, with the last 4 digits being his pin.*

Iris: *"I do that, just in case I forget, yes, just as a reference."*

Anna: *"Yes, of course, nobody will know that it's a telephone number."*

Whilst the majority of the participants recorded their PINs by writing them down, many used strategies to ensure there was very little opportunity for another person to access them. Whilst recording PINs using an elaborate code was considered acceptable, sharing PINs with others was not. Margaret has never considered giving her PIN to anyone and said that she has never needed to. Reflecting upon a possible future scenario where she could no longer access the money in her bank account, she noted *"I suppose I'd give my son my pin number but he'd have to swear on a stack of bibles he wouldn't divulge it on pain of death and sign it in blood and things like that!"* Anna retorts *"Well you wouldn't give it to them unless you trusted them implicitly and that's the whole thing."* Joyce referred to the period immediately after she left hospital having had an operation. *"When I came out of hospital and was housebound for a few weeks, I gave my daughter my pin number. Let's hope she has forgotten."* Marjorie suggested whilst she would trust some people with her details, she would be hesitant to burden them. *"It's putting responsibility on them."*

Agnes was particularly against the sharing of this personal security information, exclaiming *"no, never ever. Never would I do that. It's not that I don't trust them, but you never know where it might end up."* She reflects on how this differs from cheques: *"I mean they know the numbers on the cheques, because if I've given them cheques, but they don't know the important numbers that only I know. There's only me that knows them."* Whilst Agnes would not ever use a bankcard in a collaborative manner, she has done so with cheques. *"We don't have a computer and sometimes I want to shop online, my friend does it for me, she pays it on the computer and then I give her a cheque. She pays it on her card and then I give her a cheque. ... They are friends that we've had years and years. We just trust each other, you've got to have some friends you trust."* In her own words, she trusts her friends with the numbers on a cheque but not with the *"important numbers"* that only she knows.

Iris referred to a situation a friend finds herself in. *"She is pretty well housebound and her son does her banking for her, he goes to visit every Sunday. He knows the pin number and he gets her card and he goes down to the bank and he draws out money for her ... [once] it swallowed the card and ... refused to give any money."* For some time, the lady was stuck without a bank card and now will not share the card again. *"She said, I don't really want to give the home help my card and pin number to go and do a bit of shopping. I need cash, how do I get it? Well actually, she writes a cheque and Tim cashes it at the bank."* Having come across difficulties with the sharing of the personal information related with collaboratively using bankcards, Iris' friend reverted to the cheque. Here, the cheque provided a way of accessing cash without having to share the sensitive information associated with bankcards.

For many of the eighty somethings, their friends, family and carers, the trust mechanisms associated with cheques stand in sharp contrast to those of cash and bankcards. Cheques engender trust between people. Cheques absorb some of the responsibility of a transaction, supporting collaboration between those who need access to cash or goods and those willing to go out of their way to help them achieve this.

DISCUSSION

Although the participants note that their own use of cheques is in decline, there are many circumstances where they envisage no other alternative to using them. In part, this may be related to unfamiliarity with electronic alternatives. Some of the situations of cheque use described by our participants have readily available electronic alternatives. Most financial service providers in the UK offer comprehensive internet banking services where money can be transferred quickly, and for free, from one bank account to another. The provision of such services, however, assumes a bank account holder with access to a suitable computer or mobile device to access them. Whilst it is no longer so unusual for an eighty-year-old to actively use computers and participate in online communities [10], older people are still far less likely than younger people to have access to the internet [18]. Indeed, with the exception of one of our participants, even those who used the internet from home did not use online banking services despite it being available to them.

The paper it's written on

As with much previous work within CSCW [e.g. 11, 15], our findings highlight the importance of the piece of paper a cheque is printed on. We have noted how the eighty somethings and care workers use the specific markings of individuals and the physicality of the paper cheque as denoting specific financial activities. As a cheque is written out, it is written to somebody or something. It is taken as a given that these markings are then checked by the bank when the cheque is paid in. The eighty somethings relate their signing of the cheque to giving a personal authorisation that the payment can be made – although, in reality, UK banks have no way of confirming the legitimacy of these signatures.

Electronic records are seen as ephemeral by the eighty somethings in our study, and while the record of electronic payments may in fact be much more secure and permanent than a paper cheque, its essential material qualities suggest otherwise. From the perspective of our participants a cheque is an enduring representation of a transaction from beginning to end.

In addition, although the information on the paper cheque is made into an electronic transaction at the bank, the physical record continues its journey to be scanned and then stored. If revoked by the bank or the account holder, this record is physically accessible and the same piece of paper is returned to the person who wrote it. Much like the records that many of the eighty somethings keep in their homes of the money that comes in and out of their accounts each month [34], this piece of paper outlasts the transaction it records and is available for checking if needed in the future.

Flexibility when needed

Cheques often come to the forefront when people have problems paying for bills or accessing money. The unused cheque affords being configured in a collaborative manner between people as a way of working around these difficulties. Someone who cannot physically access cash is able to write a cheque out to a friend, their caregiver, or another organisation and have them collect the money on their behalf. A person wanting to enjoy the benefits of shopping on the internet, but has neither the technical ability nor the equipment to do so, can write a personal cheque to a friend to do it on their behalf. Unlike bankcards, cheques do not require specialist terminals to perform transactions in-situ (as the processing is done elsewhere), and avoids the need to share sensitive information that people believe can be reused and abused. Unlike cash, they are valueless to anyone other than the named payee.

Part of the flexibility of a cheque comes from the requirement to only name a 'payee', and not a specific bank account number to which the amount will be transferred to. This has benefits for both the sender and receiver. The sender only needs to know the receiver's name in order to request the transfer—the receiver has the flexibility to choose what account they wish the money to be deposited into. The sense of giving money to others via cheques is highly valued by the eighty somethings, to the extent that they begin imagining the other receiving their gift.

Trust and openness

It has been documented in the past that younger people place more trust in online and mobile banking services than older people [26]. Our study reflects these findings. That the eighty somethings are more willing to trust a cheque than electronic transactions in certain contexts is interesting as, from a security perspective, cheques are a fundamentally insecure instrument. A stolen unused cheque is easily used in a deviant manner. A completed cheque can be physically adjusted to display a larger sum, or the payee can be changed given the right skill. Bauman [3] argues that the 'stranger shatters the security upon which daily life rests', in the sense that they bring values to a community that undermine the status quo and force reflection on norms. It is likely this happened as people first began receiving cheques from individuals outside the community and beyond the realm of social control. In 1965 the idea of a cheque guarantee scheme was introduced in the UK to retrospectively build trust into the cheque system.

Security through *openness* amongst close communities affords accountability but also enables members to develop a detailed picture of who can be *trusted* and *collaborated* with over time. Cheques are grounded in the expectation that the behaviour of members in the community can be influenced by social control. The fact that two individuals collaborate financially using a system that has widely known security loopholes while still arriving at a satisfactory outcome for both parties reflects strongly on their integrity. It is this model of security through *openness* that allowed one participant's friend to purchase items on their behalf, despite the cheque not yet being cleared. What is implicit in the sending and receiving of cheques is the ritual where parties probe the integrity of each other by turn-based exposure to risk. By accepting an unguaranteed cheque the recipient makes a gesture of trust towards the sender. Equally by sending a cheque the sender stakes a claim of being trustworthy. It is clear that the original trust-based model is the preferred mode of cheque usage: figures from 2007 show that of 1.4 billion cheques sent in the UK, only 7% were guaranteed [29].

DESIGNING FOR TRUST

Whilst cheques are still based on an eco-system of trust, current digital technologies are less so. Much like cheque use pre-1965, the user base of the Internet grew steadily and was mostly formed of people known to one-another. In 1988 Robert Morris Jnr released the Morris Worm which infected 10% of machines on the Internet. This breach destroyed the socially controlled security of the early Internet community and the focus changed to obtaining security via robust software mechanisms, removing the vulnerabilities that were once left open. In line with this, many modern payment methods, such as bankcards and phone/internet-based systems, are built upon traditional security features of authenticity, integrity and confidentiality.

Our study suggests that interpersonal trust cannot be explicitly designed into a payment system. The eighty somethings that would normally entrust friends and family with money are reluctant to do so with the *"important numbers"* that only they know. The explicit design of PINs and passwords into the system inhibits the financial collaboration between one another that is sometimes desired and, on occasions, a necessity. Partly, this is because PINs provide all or nothing access—if you share your PIN with someone to withdraw a specific amount of money or pay a particular bill on your behalf, then there is little to stop them using it for other payments or withdrawals if so inclined.

Cheque design supports the emergence of trust as they can be pre-configured by the account holder before being passed on. It is possible to configure the amount the transaction is for, the earliest date it should be performed, and who can deposit it. The possibility and extent of fraud is then limited. In the event that something does go wrong, a cheque can only be used once. It can also be revoked, and there is a permanent paper record to call upon. Whilst a cheque's security is 'open', there are clear aspects of its design that act as catalysts for trusting others.

There are design opportunities here to increase support for situations requiring shades of grey—for example, types of accounts and bank cards that are limited in the amounts of money, locations, and length of time they can be used for—so that trust is better enabled between individuals. However, in reference to designing a new cheque perhaps the strongest case is not to design a replacement at all.

IMPLICATIONS FOR NON-DESIGN

Baumer and Silberman [4] critique the tendency for HCI research to find applications of computational technologies where they might not be entirely appropriate. They argue that 'implications not to design' are a valuable part of a future, more critically aware and reflective, HCI discipline. Clearly, there is a substantial element of the cheque replacement discussion that fits well with this argument. Indeed, during later participatory design workshops with the eighty somethings this case was made quite explicit. When asked what "smart money" might look like Margaret replied "*Well I visualise it as a blank note with no sum on.*" Iris interjected "*Like a cheque in other words! You can...*"

Anna took up the thread "*Fill it in yourself!*" and Iris completed the thought: "*fill it in and validate with whatever amount you want.*" All of the workshop participants became animated and enthused during this exchange. Margaret smiled as she explained that a cheque was smart money: "*Because a cheque has all your details on.*" And Iris laughingly agreed "*It's only when it gets to the recipient that it's of any value!*" Doris offered her delighted conclusion: "*There's nothing new you know!*"

Doris' point here is not included simply to illustrate the eighty somethings attachment to the familiar or a reluctance to change. It is included to emphasise that, as GK Chesterton once remarked, progress is not always about leaving things behind. This is not to argue that the situation here requires no design intervention at all. It is clear that UK banks, and possibly those in other countries still using cheque-like payment systems, are intent on withdrawing them, if not sooner then later. Therefore, design and technological innovation is required to reduce the reasons why these paper instruments are so costly to the banks. In this context, rather than replace the paper cheque, it would be more appropriate to explore how it might be kept and better linked to the electronic payments systems banks use today. Previous work has explored the linking of paper documents to webspace via hyperlinks scanned from an OCR adapted pen [1], barcode scanners [27], and advanced computer vision and object recognition systems [23]. Anoto digital pen technology [14] has been established for a number of years, and could feasibly be integrated into the design of a typical cheque book so as to make electronic payments. These advances highlight the plausibility of not necessarily abolishing cheques, but rather finding novel ways of using the current paper cheque to make electronic transactions.

Innovations may also be found in approaches that support the continued existence of cheques without the banking industry's direct involvement. In Kenya, a lack of trust in large banking organisations and a need for accessing funds from a wide variety of locations has made the mobile payment system M-PESA highly popular [17]. Here money transfers are made via SMS on basic mobile phones and entirely administered by the mobile network. Similarly, in the UK there is a very real sense that large retailers such as Tesco, who have a stronger customer ethos and take more risks in the use of novel technologies, will begin taking significant custom from traditional banks [36]. Organisations such as ZOPA [37] make use of peer-to-peer platforms that brings lenders and borrowers together without the need of a bank. The design and technical challenge may be to establish non-banking sector organisations that accept and process cheques on behalf of customers—acting as an intermediary between account holder and the bank. Indeed, following the findings of this study the researchers are exploring how they can act as such an intermediary on behalf of the cheque-using participants.

Currently, the eighty somethings are performing small transactions to 'real' payees with a pre-paid cheque book, sending them to the first author who arranges the electronic transfer of funds on their behalf. Future work will explore in depth the uses that the participants made of these cheques, and how technology might better support the interactions between cheque user and intermediary.

CONCLUSION

This study has identified a number of concerns for the design of future payment methods that seek to replace the cheque. Whilst current electronic payment systems separate the recording of transactions from the payment method, cheques and the practices surrounding them make this connection transparent. As we have found, the model of cheque processing imagined by the eighty somethings is one where a piece of paper moves from place to place between people.

Digitising even small parts of cheque-based transactions might be detrimental to the models of collaboration, trust and security that the eighty somethings and their carers base their use of cheques on. Trust needs to be allowed to emerge in order to encourage financial collaboration between people. This is counter-intuitive to how contemporary digital payment systems are designed. People born before 1930 have built their attitudes and values to trust not through security protocols and authentication but by learning to keep track of where their money has gone and by knowing who to share it with. The security flaws of the cheque are what make it meaningful to this group of people and make them so useful in a care home setting.

Often, groups such as the eighty somethings are considered a special case to be catered for in the final years of their lives. Cheques appear to be a rare case where they are well catered for already—yet we (researchers, bankers, and younger people) are inclined to design them a replacement regardless. However, as we have argued in this paper, the implications for design are not always as strong as the implications for preserving much of what we already have. New services such as ZOPA [37] and M-PESA [17] indicate that future banking might involve not just new technologies but new institutions. When bankers next consider phasing out cheques it may be that their customers will consider phasing out banks.

ACKNOWLEDGEMENTS

We would like to thank our participants for their time, and Emma Jones and Lynn McInnes at Northumbria University for their support in organising the workshops. This research was performed as part of the New Approaches to Banking for the Older Old project and the Social Inclusion through the Digital Economy (SiDE) Research Hub, funded by Research Councils UK Digital Economy Theme.

REFERENCES

1. Arai, T., Aust, D. and Hudson, S., PaperLink: A technique for hyperlinking from real paper to electronic content. In *Proc. CHI '97*, (Atlanta, GA, 1997), ACM.
2. Barclays mobile banking services. http://www.barclays.co.uk/MobileBankingServices/
3. Bauman, Z. *Postmodernity and its discontents*. New York University Press, New York, 1997.
4. Baumer, E. And Silberman, M. When the implication is not to design (Technology). In *Proc. CHI '11*, ACM Press (2011), 2271-2274.
5. Bills of Exchange Act 1882. 1882.
6. Braun, V. And Clarke, V. Using thematic analysis in psychology. *Qualitative research in psychology*, 3 (77), (2006), 77-101.
7. Cheque and Credit Clearing Company. *2-4-6 timescales explained*. http://www.chequeandcredit.co.uk/246/
8. Cheque and Credit Clearing Company. *The Great British Cheque Report*, London, UK, 2009.
9. Dini, E. and Goldring, S. Estimating the changing population of the 'oldest old'. *ONS Population Trends*, 132. (2008) 7-16.
10. Harley, D. and Fitzpatrick, G. YouTube and intergenerational communication: The case of Geriatric1927. *Universal Access in the Information Society, 8* (1), 5-20.
11. Heath, C. and Luff, P., Documents and professional practice: 'Bad' organisational reasons for 'good' clinical records. In *Proc. CSCW 1996*, ACM Press (1996), 354-363.
12. HM Treasury *Financial Inclusion: An Action Plan for 2008-11*. HM Treasury, London, 2007.
13. King, M. Cheque Abolition Slammed by Treasury Select Committee. *The Guardian*, 24th August 2011.
14. Luff, P., Heath, C., Norrie, M., Signer, B. and Herdman, P., Only Touching the Surface: Creating Affinities Between Digital Content and Paper. In *Proc. CSCW '04*, ACM Press (2004), 523-532.
15. MacKay, W. Is paper safer? The role of paper flight strips in air traffic control. *Transactions on Computer-Human Interaction*, *6* (4), ACM (1999), 311-340.
16. Malenczuk, L. How will we pay? *Communique*, 1, UK Payments Council (2010), 4-6.
17. Mas, I. and Morawczynski, O. Designing mobile money services: Lessons from M-PESA. Innovations, 4 (2), Springer (2009), 77-91.
18. Office of Communications. *Accessing the internet at home*. OFCOM, London, 2009.
19. PayPal iPhone App. http://itunes.apple.com/us/app/paypal/
20. Piper, A., and Hollan, J. Tabletop displays for small group study: affordances of paper and digital materials. In *Proc. CHI '09*. ACM Press (2009), 1227-1236.
21. Plimmer, B., and Apperley, M. Making paperless work. In *Proc. CHINZ '07*. ACM Press (2007), 1-8.
22. QuickTap. http://shop.orange.co.uk/mobile-phones/contactless
23. Robertson, C. and Robinson, J., Live Paper: Video augmentation to simulate interactive paper. In *Proc. The Seventh ACM international Conference on Multimedia (Part 2)*, ACM Press (1999).
24. Sellen, A. and Harper, R. *The Myth of the Paperless Office*. The MIT Press, Cambridge, 2001.
25. Schilit, B., Golovchinsky G.,, and Price M. Beyond paper: supporting active reading with free form digital ink annotations. In *Proc. CHI '98*, ACM Press (1998), 249-256.
26. Singh, S. and Morley, C. Young Australians' privacy, security and trust in internet banking. In *Proc. OZCHI '09*, ACM Press (2009). 121-128.
27. Smith, J., Long, J., Lung, T. and Anwar, M., PaperSpace: A System for Managing Digital and Paper Documents. In *Proc. CHI 2006*, ACM Press (2006), 1343-1348.
28. Tripp, R. Current UK Cheque Clearing Process, 2007. http://www.howbankswork.com/15.1.html
29. UK Payments Administration. *Fact sheet for people who still write cheques backed by a guarantee card*. UK Payments Administration, London, 2008.
30. UK Payments Council. *The Future of Cheques in the UK*. UK Payments Council, London, 2009.
31. UK Payments Council. *Payments Council Cheque Replacement Programme 2010 – a progress report*. UK Payments Council, London, 2010.
32. UK Payments Council. *Cheque replacement programme: Commitments for consumers, small businesses and the charity and voluntary sector*. Payments Council, London, 2010.
33. United Nations. World population ageing: 1950-2050. (2002). http://www.un.org/esa/population/publications/worldageing19502050
34. Vines, J., Blythe, M., Dunphy, P., and Monk, A. Eighty Something: Banking for the older old. In *Proc. BCS-HCI 2011*, BCS (2011), 1-10.
35. Wells, J. *An inclusive approach to financial products*. Age Concern UK, London, 2008.
36. Worthington, S. And Welch, P. Banking without the banks. *International Journal of Bank Marketing*, 29 (2), Emerald (2011), 190-201.
37. ZOPA. http://uk.zopa.com/ZopaWeb/

Practices of Information and Secrecy in a Punk Rock Subculture

Jessa Lingel, Aaron Trammell, Joe Sanchez, Mor Naaman
Rutgers University, School of Communication and Information
jlingel@eden.rutgers.edu, aaront@eden.rutgers.edu, sanchezj@rutgers.edu, mor@rutgers.edu

ABSTRACT
By examining the information practices of a punk-rock subculture, we investigate the limits of social media systems, particularly limits exposed by practices of secrecy. Looking at the exchange of information about "underground" shows, we use qualitative interviews to examine uses of social media among fans. This initial analysis centers on understanding the tactical practices of information and technology to avoid police detection, particularly by comparing uses of more traditional online forums, such as message boards, with social network sites, such as Facebook. Understanding the uses and preferences for distinct technologies sheds light on how localized social context drives technological use. These findings are furthermore useful in their implications for design of applications sensitive to granular needs of users for secrecy.

Author Keywords
Information practices, subcultures, secrecy, social network sites.

ACM Classification Keywords
H1.2. User/Machine Systems, Human Factors.

INTRODUCTION
With the prevalent use of a technology comes a widening array of appropriations, adaptations and practices. In some contexts, uses of social network sites (SNS) may deviate from an otherwise mainstream set of technological practices to support a certain subculture and its activities. The research presented in this paper suggests that SNS form one part of a technological system of communication, where different applications are adopted in order to accommodate geographically-bounded (or localized) needs for secrecy within a subculture. In this project, we examine social norms of secrecy in the underground music scene ("the basement scene") in New Brunswick, New Jersey. We focus on the limitations and affordances of two distinct technologies: message boards and Facebook. Because communities engaged in quasi-legal activities have increased concerns of secrecy, understanding preferences for some technologies over others (such as message boards over SNS) offers insight into how localized needs can drive use of specific technologies even (and in this case, particularly) when those technologies are outdated. Using thick description of information practices within the basement scene, our investigation participates in human computing and interaction (HCI) scholarship that uses ethnography to address and complicate assumptions about the design of SNS [5], particularly in the context of secrecy.

CONTEXT: THE NEW BRUNSWICK MUSIC SCENE
There is a longstanding tradition in New Brunswick of do-it-yourself (DIY) music production. In the basement scene, shows are performed in basements of a DIY network of houses, typically occupied by students from the local university. Shows operate in a quasi-legal capacity on a number of fronts: As residences rather than venues, show houses do not possess licenses to host events that charge money for attendance. Alcohol often circulates at shows, which runs the risk of violating drinking age restrictions. Fans sometimes smoke inside, even when basements are crowded and the walls lined with material like mattresses or padded envelopes to provide sound insulation. All of these activities risk (and often result in) disapproval from neighbors, landlords, fire marshals and police. As a result, avoiding detection of shows from these groups has become a critical feature of the community's information practices. Within this context, SNS have been used both to promote shows and to maintain norms of secrecy. Given these conflicting objectives, the basement scene makes a superb case study for examining the subcultural use of particular technologies in the context of secrecy.

KEY TERMS AND PRIOR WORK
Before proceeding, we first define key concepts used throughout this work. We use the term "information practices" to refer to the ways that information is produced, used and disseminated in particular social settings [13], emphasizing the social and technological components associated with, and sometimes constitutive of, information. The term "technological protocols" [10] refers to practices that develop with the emergence of new technologies. "Social norms" are those rules within the scene related to keeping basement activities undetected by the local authorities. Finally, we use "tactics" to refer to specific practices and protocols used to conform to those norms.

Privacy, secrecy, security
Our engagement with existing literature on privacy and secrecy draws specifically from scholarship that addresses

these concepts in the context of community. In general, studies on privacy have tended towards the technological [1, 3, 7, 12], while studies of secrecy tend towards the psychological or sociological [6, 7, 8, 11].

Regarding privacy, to pick key examples, Ahern et al. [1] investigated factors affecting social media users in applying privacy policies in online photo sharing, revealing how people make decisions about every day privacy. Consolvo et al. [3] examined attitudes toward disclosure of location to one's social group. More broadly, Palin and Dourish [12] considered a number of technological developments (the family intercom, shared calendars, active badges, etc.) to develop a dynamic construction of privacy as shaped by social practice. These studies treat privacy practices as they relate to local norms, an approach that we share here.

Of the sociologically-oriented work on secrecy, Merten's ethnographic work [11] examined the role of secrets in the social worlds of adolescent girls, linking secret-keeping to a kind of social currency. Using qualitative interviews and participant observation, Fine and Holyfield [8] examined norms of trust and secrecy in a leisure organization of mushroom gatherers. Both studies use small, localized communities to identify participants' understandings of and uses for secrecy. Although we share an interest in understanding norms of secrecy in everyday life, this paper focuses on how those norms are operationalized through specific information practices and technological protocols. Along these lines, Barratt and Lenton [2] researched disclosures of drug use on a number of dance music message boards. We note similarities in the politics of discussing illicit activities online, but would add that in the basement community, there are geographic boundaries as well as cultural boundaries of shared (illegal) activities, both of which drive particular norms of secrecy.

Following Merten, [11] we use secrecy to refer to information tied to a group, in contrast to privacy, which refers to information grounded in the personal. Thus secrecy is used to refer to keeping what *we* do secret, whereas privacy refers to keeping what *I* do secret. In thinking about how social norms are constructed, looking at the level of community or subcultures allows for thicker descriptions of how these practices surface in response to particular political, legal and cultural factors [10].

METHODOLOGY

For this work, we conducted semi-structured interviews with ten members of the basement scene, most of them fans, but also band members and show promoters. Interviews, a focus group and dozens of hours of field observation of shows were conducted between the fall of 2009 and the spring of 2011 as part of an investigation into the social context of information in this community. These interviews and observations informed our understanding of the basement scene's history and some of the rules related to information sharing. Starting with contacts made through the course of field observations, we used snowball sampling to extend our interview pool. Participants were 19-28 years old (average age 23); six were male, four female. We use P1-10 in the discussion below as participant identifiers.

The interviews, conducted in the fall of 2010, were semi-structured and ranged from 45 to 90 minutes. Participants were asked to describe the most recent basement show they had attended, talking specifically about technologies and communication decisions used in the process of learning about and attending the concert. In addition, they were asked to describe how they keep abreast of upcoming shows, how and whom they inform about concerts, and about information practices in the basement scene. Interviews were then transcribed and coded using NVIVO software. Coding was guided by an interest in understanding sharing information in terms of secrecy and information control. At the same time, we allowed themes to emerge in the process of coding using a constant comparison method [4] (p. 73-74).

FINDINGS

In this section, we first outline the norms of secrecy related to information sharing in the basement. We then address the ways in which these norms have been described and observed among fans in the scene. In other words, which technologies are preferred for facilitating information sharing between fans, and why?

Basement Show Norms

The primary articulated driver of secrecy in the basement scene's information practices is avoiding detection of shows by the police. Scene members have developed a variety of tactics to avoid this kind of discovery. For example, some show houses have taken steps to insulate their basements with items like padded envelopes or moving boxes to reduce noise leakage and neighbor complaints. As well, through self-policing fans are asked not to congregate outside, where they might draw police attention. Finally, shows typically start and end early to avoid perturbing neighbors.

In terms of information practices, the most singular methods of avoiding police detection in the scene center on treating house addresses as secret. This custom of occluding addresses surfaced repeatedly in the course of interviews. As P5 described, "the information that's exchanged is basically when, how much, and who's playing. Never a where." Shows are publicized digitally (e.g. Facebook and message boards) as well as through word-of-mouth (e.g. flyers and text messages), but addresses are only exchanged in means deemed safe – face-to-face encounters and text messages being the most common. In the following section, we outline how practices of secrecy play out in online social environments, by comparing use of SNS and message boards.

Social network sites

For people new to the basement scene, SNS were often the initial introduction to subcultural practices of information control. P2 illustrated this mode of secrecy in his description of moving to New Brunswick: "when I first moved here I would go to Myspace and I would search the New Brunswick zip code to see if there was anything going on, and then there would be a struggle to find an address because I didn't know where anything was. I didn't know anyone really, I just tried to figure it out." This description demonstrates the extent to which social media sites enable outsiders to access some (but not all) of the information required for show attendance. Facebook and Myspace are used to publicize shows on pages for bands and show houses, and Facebook invites are used regularly by promoters, but addresses are never exchanged and communication is largely asymmetrical, from promoters to fans rather than between fans themselves.

Other interviews showed the extent to which social media is used "in suspicion." Many participants feared that the police were using various social media sites to obtain secret show information. As described by P5: "Somebody on the police force made a Myspace page ... and they wanted you to send them all the shows that were coming up ... kind of like posing as someone in the punk scene." Other participants have had a similar experience, as P7 described: "Cops have definitely contacted me before, trying to figure out where shows are ... If I get an email from someone, I always search their email on Facebook or Myspace." These and similar comments are indicative of the extent to which the (suspected) surveillance from police dominates discussions of SNS use in the basement scene.

Note that we did not witness shows being broken up in the course of research, although participants reported numerous accounts of this taking place, sometimes resulting in shows simply stopping, other times resulting in fines. We by no means dispute that police are a viable threat to the success of shows, however, we note that this threat serves an additional purpose, in that rhetoric surrounding police infiltration of SNS provides a remarkably effective justification for continued practices of secrecy. We hope to address this tension more thoroughly in subsequent work.

Message boards

In the course of interviews, participants referenced two message boards (which we do not name to provide confidentiality), one of which (recently discontinued) had been active for years, and the other having been created in the last year. Both were moderated by longtime scene members, and provided information on local shows. In asking participants to describe how shows are publicized on message boards, it was found that rules against listing show house addresses are maintained. As P1 stated, "I've never seen an address" on a basement-related message board.

Interestingly, although the more recent message board is technologically quite simple and its focus very narrow (New Jersey punk music), since its launch in late 2010, the site claims over 400 members, 2,100 threads and just under 38,000 total posts. The board was not used unanimously by participants, but it was referenced by P1, P2, P4, P5, P7 and P10, all of whom were longtime scene members. In contrast to concerns that police had infiltrated SNS, P4 expressed a feeling of safety talking about shows on message boards, because "we know that we can trust we're being read by thirty different people and none of them are cops." Thus, the smaller number of users and familiarity with handles allows for increased feeling of security on message boards. In sum, message boards were referenced as an opportunity for sustained discussions of bands, shows and albums in the local music scene, and these boards were furthermore valued by participants because the lower rate of adoption generated a sense of protection from unwanted attention of the authorities.

DISCUSSION

From these accounts, we see several themes related to technological protocols of secrecy: adherence to norms of secrecy as indicative of group membership, the use of SNS for purposes of inclusion as well as exclusion, and affordances of simplistic technologies over advanced ones when they parallel localized needs of secrecy.

The Politics of Technological Protocols

The use of sites like Facebook in subcultural environments exposes tensions of managing group boundaries. We found that SNS are used to test and confirm subcultural group membership. Adherence to various information practices and protocols that developed in the scene – such as verifying identities through Facebook – allowed members to judge inclusion in the basement community. Scene members were willing to undergo degrees of inconvenience, such as extra efforts to locate show addresses outside of Facebook, in order to comply with norms of secrecy. Gaining a sense of belonging through learning social norms is at the crux of membership for any group. In their research on risk in leisure groups, Fine and Holyfield [6] argued that obtaining information was one of the first goals of group membership (p. 28). In the basement scene, this objective could be altered such that fluency in information practices marked one of the first goals of subcultural membership. By adhering to community norms of secrecy, newcomers signal to other scene members their shared values. This cultural savvy often requires newcomers to acquire a base knowledge of acceptable technological protocols. Put simply, there is a highly-developed subcultural etiquette to practices of secrecy that play out across a network of technologies, including text messaging, SNS and message boards.

Community Sleuths and Hyper-secrecy

SNS are used for two seemingly conflicting purposes in the basement scene. On the one hand, SNS are used to bring people to shows, as in the near ubiquitous use of Facebook invites to publicize upcoming shows. At the same time, much of the "detective work" involved with distinguishing outsiders (police) from insiders (punks) took place using SNS. When unfamiliar names surface on message boards, or when e-mails from unknown senders arrive requesting information about shows, multiple participants reported using SNS to authenticate someone's inquiry. In some instances, participants questioned whether these norms of secrecy were in fact absolutely necessary. For example, P10 commented: "the change in technology has impacted things. I got a sense that with some people they do shows 'cause they feel like they are part of a secret something." As an old timer in the scene, P10 here provides a moment of thoughtful critique on the extent to which practices and protocols of secrecy are meant to avoid the police, versus being used to keep the scene exclusive.

Technology Hinders, Technology Helps

Given that message boards are older (as a technology), with less functionality and less powerful reach, one might ask why they would continue to be used, especially considering that SNS are an integrated part of everyday life for scene participants. Although the limited features and narrow pool of users might typically be viewed as drawbacks, from interviews, we surmise that message boards offer a number of advantages not afforded by SNS: Message boards have a long history in punk culture, whereas SNS are still relatively new; Message boards are created, moderated and used by known scene members, unlike SNS such as Facebook, which is owned by a for-profit company with millions of online users; Message boards are limited in content (in this case, topics of punk culture), while SNS offer an almost unlimited range of subject matter. Thus, even though message boards are far less sophisticated in terms of technology, they offer advantages of accommodating secrecy. For these reasons, longtime scene members continue to engage with each other using message boards because they do a better job of reflecting the punk values, DIY ethics, and localized norms of secrecy.

CONCLUSIONS

In this paper, we have argued that SNS operate as part of a complex web of technologies; even when technologies are ostensibly outdated and narrowly used, they can provide an online enclave appropriate for a subculture invested in maintaining practices of secrecy. We found that when motivated by social pressures (whether real or perceived), subcultures can develop very nuanced information practices that double as signals of inclusion and exclusion. Thus we see a kind of hacked symbiosis engineered by basement scene members in order to meet their localized needs. Further, this paper has offered an ethnographic explanation of the existence of and preference for non-dominant technologies, here brought into relief in the context of secrecy. One implication of these findings is a justification of the development of autonomous online communities, rather than, say, an emphasis on designing applications and add-ons for dominant sites. In the basement scene, Facebook and MySpace offer vital tools for promoting shows, but are insufficient for protecting community secrets, such as house addresses. The role of message boards is one of providing a means for in-depth communications about objects of shared interest, where SNS are viewed as inadequate for these discussions. In subsequent projects, we hope to extend the study of SNS serving a particular community or subculture towards contributing to designs that can reflect highly localized norms of secrecy and privacy.

ACKNOWLEDGMENTS

This work was partially supported by a Nokia University Collaboration Award, and the National Science Foundation under award IIS-1017845.

REFERENCES

1. Ahern, S., Eckles, D., Good, N., King, S., Naaman, M. and Nair, R. Over-exposed? Privacy patterns and considerations in online and mobile photo sharing. CHI 2007, April 28–May 3, 2007, San Jose, CA.
2. Barratt, M., and Lenten, S. Beyond recruitment? Participatory online research with people who use drugs. *International Journal of Internet Research 3* (2010), retrieved from http://ijire.net/issue_3.1/6_barratt _lenton.pdf.
3. Consolvo, S., Smith, I. E., Matthews, T., LaMarca, A., Tabert, J. and Powledge, P. Location disclosure to social relations: Why, when and what people want to share. CHI 2005, April 2-7, Portland, OR. Pp. 81-90.
4. Corbin, A., and Strauss, J. *Basics of Qualitative Research: Techniques and Procedures for Developing Grounded Theory*. Los Angeles: Sage.
5. Dourish, P. and Bell, G. *Divining a Digital Future: Mess and Mythology in Ubiquitous Computing*. Cambridge, MA: MIT Press.
6. Dourish, P., Grinter, R. E., Delgado de la Flor, J., and Joseph, M. Security in the wild: User strategies for managing security as an everyday, practical problem. *Personal Ubiquitous Computing 8* (2004), 391-401.
7. Erickson, B. H. Secret societies and social structure. *Social Forces 60* 1 (1981), 188-210.
8. Fine, G. A. and Holyfield, L. Secrecy, trust and dangerous leisure: Generating group cohesion in voluntary organizations. *Social Psychological Quarterly 59* 1 (1996), 22-38.
9. Goldstein, D. Towards a critical anthropology of security. *Current Anthropology 51* 4 (2010), 487-517.
10. Jenkins, H. *Convergence Culture*. 2006. New York: NYU Press.
11. Merten, D. Enculturation into secrecy among junior high school girls. *Journal of Contemporary Ethnography 28* 2 (1999), 107-137.
12. Palen, L. and Dourish, P. Unpacking "privacy" for a networked world. CHI 2003. April 5-10. Ft. Lauderdale, FL. Vol. 5, No. 1. 129-136.
13. Savolainen, R. Information behavior and information practice: reviewing the "umbrella concepts" of information-seeking studies. *Library Quarterly 77* 2 (2007), 109-13.

One Piece at a Time: Why Video-Based Communication is Better for Negotiation and Conflict Resolution

Wei Dong **Wai-Tat Fu**

Applied Cognitive Science Lab, Beckman Institute of Science and Technology and Computer Science
University of Illinois at Urbana-Champaign, 405 N Mathews Avenue, Urbana, IL, 61801, USA
wdong@illinois.edu, wd96@cornell.edu wfu@illinois.edu

ABSTRACT

We compared the effects of three computer mediated communication (CMC) channels (text, audio, and video) on how people performed an appointment-scheduling task. The task involved a grounding and a conflict resolution component. The results showed that video conferencing supported participant dyads in reaching a consensus that had better balanced performance between the dyads only when task difficulty was high and when there were more inherent conflicts in the task. Participants across the three CMC conditions also demonstrated different patterns of conversation dynamics during information exchange and negotiation. Mediation analysis showed that in video-based communication, strategies of exchanging less information at a time predicted higher levels of negotiation, which in turn predicted smaller performance differences in high conflict conditions. The results suggested that the design and use of communication technologies for remote conflict resolution should promote the strategy of exchanging information in small pieces, which could better support subsequent negotiation and foster a sense of fairness.

Author Keywords

Computer mediated communication, collaborative work, conflict resolution, negotiation, information exchange, communication strategy.

ACM Classification Keywords

H5.m. Information interfaces and presentation (e.g., HCI): Miscellaneous.

General Terms

Human Factors; Experimentation.

INTRODUCTION

There has been a long history of research on how features of different CMC channels could impact outcomes of different forms of remote collaborative work [3, 4, 6, 9, 14, 24, 31]. One common reason for collaborators to communicate is to come up with solutions or methods that are acceptable to both parties. More often than not, conflicts arise and it is critical for collaborators to communicate their needs and constraints to resolve these conflicts and reach agreement on certain tasks or problems. Conflict resolution usually demands collaborators to engage in negotiation and to obtain a mutual agreement, which may or may not be the best possible solution to both parties. In other words, one party may need to compromise and accept a solution that may not be optimal for a single party, but perceived to be optimal to both parties. Oftentimes, a sense of "fairness" is more emphasized in a successful negotiation that further facilitates subsequent collaboration. Given that the conflict resolution process often hinges on the effectiveness of communication between two parties, one may expect the communication channel to play a pivotal role in influencing the final outcome of conflict resolution via different communication strategies. A number of studies have been devoted to investigate this process [16, 21, 22, 26, 36]. Although video conferencing is found to be more supportive for conflict resolution in general, it is still unclear how video influences the negotiation and conflict resolution process [8]. To this end, we conducted detailed analysis on conversation dynamics to understand how exactly do patterns of negotiation and conflict resolution differ in different CMC channels.

The current study compared the effects of three common CMC channels (text, audio and video chatting) on an appointment-scheduling task. We were interested in understanding how the underlying variables in the conflict resolution process influence one another. Specifically, we focused on the two processes: *information exchange* to establish common ground and *negotiation* to resolve conflicts. We also examined the *final decision* focusing on the level of fairness in performance between collaborators.

Effects of CMC Channels on Conflict Resolution in Remote Collaborative Work

Although media richness has been identified as one of the most prominent antecedents of performance in distributed collaborative work via different CMC channels [12], the process is far more complicated and no single technology is perfect for conflict resolution in remote cooperative work [22]. A number of factors such as anonymity, uninhibited behavior, task types, culture and other contextual factors could play a role in moderating the effectiveness of CMC channels [1, 4, 6, 30]. Different frameworks have been established to understand the impact of CMC channels on the process of collaboration and conflict resolution.

Effectiveness of Information Exchange when Establishing Common Ground

A prerequisite of successful conflict resolution is to establish a mutual agreement of the possible solution space (i.e., grounding) [10, 11, 19] such that the potential cost-benefit comparison can be assessed among different solutions by each of the collaborators. Therefore, the process through which mutual ground was established during information exchange could have an impact on subsequent negotiation and conflict resolution. Communication methods may influence this process because the cost of information exchange may impact how likely people will exchange their needs and constraints and what strategies they will choose.

It has been found that information exchange can be suppressed and sometimes biased in computer-mediated group interactions compared to face-to-face groups [22, 23]. A fundamental difference between text and audio/video based channels is whether information exchange is done textually or verbally. Owing to the high cost of typing, the effectiveness of information exchange is much lower and the amount of information exchange is found to be much smaller in text-based channels such as emails [26, 34]. In addition, a large amount of non-textual information in both visual and acoustic format (e.g., speech tones, attention and facial expressions) cannot be directly conveyed by the text channel [31].

On the other hand, the existence of text history can serve as a compensation of low effectiveness in text communication because it is a quick reference for collaborators to easily retrieve previously conveyed information. This method of information retrieval is at relatively low cost compared to holding all the information in working memory when communicating through audio/video channels.

Because of these differences, collaborators may adopt different strategies after evaluating the cost and benefit of these CMC channels. These strategies might include the total amount of information they choose to exchange, the amount of information they bring up at each conversation turn, the choice of revealing certain information over another, and the way information is organized during the exchange process. For example, it is possible that collaborators using the text channel might choose a strategy of exchanging as much information as possible at each conversation turn to compensate for the low efficiency of typing. On the other hand, collaborators talking with each other would probably prefer bringing up small chunks of information in each conversation turn since it would be difficult for them to remember and consume a large amount of information all at once due to limitation in working memory capacity [2].

The way different pieces of information and different potential solutions are brought up will then influence how they are discussed during negotiation, which in turn would lead to different outcomes that are either optimal or suboptimal to one or both parties. When a large number of solution candidates are present, collaborators might find it hard to systematically compare and evaluate the pros and cons of every candidate. Whereas negotiation based on one or two solution candidates could be more thorough and efficient. However, this mechanism has not been directly examined as a potential pathway to explain how different CMC channels impact the communication process, which eventually influences the negotiation and final outcomes of conflict resolution.

Social Cognition in Effective Conflict Resolution

Conflict resolution is a demanding task in remote works. Several rounds of conversation exchanges are usually necessary during the negotiation process between the parties before a consensus can be reached. The negotiation process can be less effective due to a lack of social context and a reduced awareness of social presence [24].

Social cues in acoustic and visual format during conversation are also critical for collaborators to make inferences of other parties' preferences and characteristics (e.g., personality, mood and willingness to compromise). Then they can make adjustments to negotiation strategies to persuade other parties to compromise, and eventually maximize individual and/or group performance. Studies have shown that the ability of collaborators to pick up these social cues to achieve successful collaboration in general increases from text to audio and from audio to video channels. Visual cues such as facial expressions, gesture and focus of visual attention available in video conferencing was found to be especially important in complex social tasks [18, 20, 27, 35]. Quality and synchronicity of audio/video streams also play a crucial role in how easily the existing social cues can be picked up during audio/video conferencing [13, 17, 27].

The Current Study

The focus of the current study was to investigate how different CMC channels affect the process of information exchange and negotiation by analyzing collaborators' conversation dynamics during conflict resolution. The primary goal was to investigate some of the key processes as illustrated in Figure 1.

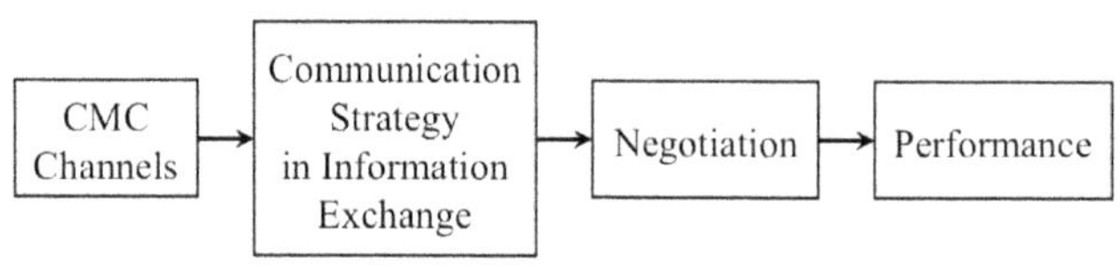

Figure1.The process of conflict resolution to be examined in the current study.

Specifically, we aimed at studying a) how different CMC channels would influence people's choice of different communication strategies when they exchange information to establish mutual ground, b) how the choice of communication strategies would influence subsequent negotiation for achieving mutual agreement on the final decision, and c) whether the negotiation process would affect the performance of collaborators. Mediation analysis, a statistical analysis method commonly used in social science studies to identify the effects that transmit along a chain of variables [25], was used to examine the effect of CMC channels in influencing the final performance of participant dyads on the task.

We chose the task of appointment scheduling in this study for two reasons. First, it is a very common subtask in most remote collaboration that people encounter in their daily lives, and they often play a pivotal role in the success of collaboration [33]. Second, it involves both the *information exchange* stage in which collaborators need to collectively find one or more time slot(s) that both parties are available, and the *negotiation* stage, in which potential solutions are proposed, evaluated, rejected or accepted, and preferences are expressed and perceived until one solution is eventually accepted by both parties. Although in real situations these two components could be intertwined, they are essential for successful conflict resolution and could be subject to changes in task difficulty (how easily the solution candidates can be found) and levels of conflicts (the amount of overlap between the needs and constraints of the two parties). Thus, we introduced these two independent variables to systematically examine the effect of CMC channels on the process of conflict resolution.

Based on previous studies and frameworks discussed above, we would expect that communication methods with a higher bandwidth (e.g., video condition) would be more supportive for reaching a consensus that optimized the performance of both parties and fostered a sense of fairness between them. Mediation analyses were conducted to reveal the mechanism of why the three CMC channels supported conflict resolution to a different extent. In particular, we would expect that participants using text-based communication would prefer the strategy of laying out a large amount of information at a time to compensate the low speed of typing, whereas participants using audio and video conferencing would prefer bringing up small pieces of information at each conversation turn. We also expect that smaller amount of information exchanged at each conversation turn would better support participants' subsequent negotiation, which in turn would predict the fairness of participant dyads' final performance.[1]

METHOD

A 2 (level of difficulty, within-subject) by 2 (level of conflict, within-subject) by 3 (CMC channels, between-subject) mixed design was employed in the current study. Participants were asked to work in pairs. Each person was given a 10-week calendar. Their task was to schedule 2 appointments for each week by communicating with each other via one of the three commonly used *CMC channels* (text, audio or video chatting). A scoring system was introduced to encourage participants to maximize personal scores by scheduling appointments on preferred time slots. We manipulated the *level of difficulty (easy vs. difficult*, as defined later) for each week by putting different score combinations in the solution space. A *level of conflict (low vs. high*, as defined later) was also introduced to further examine the process of negotiation.

Participants

One hundred and four people participated in the current study. Participants were scheduled in pairs and each pair was randomly assigned to one of the three CMC conditions. Participant pairs did not know each other before coming to the experiment. One pair of participants' responses in the text condition and one pair in the audio condition were excluded from the analysis due to technical problems, yielding the final sample size of 100 participants, 17, 16 and 17 pairs in text, audio and video condition, respectively. Participants in the 3 conditions were similar in age ($M = 23.90$, 22.97 and 24.13 years, $SD = 4.45$, 3.25 and 5.15 for text, audio and video condition, respectively, $F_{(2, 97)} = .64$, $p > .05$), gender (16, 13 and 15 males and 18, 19 and 19 females in text, audio and video condition, respectively), education level (college or higher), and their experience of using CMC tools in everyday life as measured in a questionnaire. All participants were daily users of email. In general, participants used Facebook most often for text chatting and Skype most often for audio and video chatting.

Materials

Forty pairs of weekly calendars were prepared. Each week contained a *problem space* of 40 hours (Monday-Friday, 9AM-5PM). Appointments can only be scheduled on whole hours. A scoring system was introduced in a way that participants could earn 0 to 3 points for each appointment depending on when it was scheduled. To help participants better comprehend the scoring system, time slots with higher points were explained as more desired for scheduling appointments in real life situations (see Table 1). Color-coding was also introduced when visualizing the calendars using Google Calendar (See Figure 2).

Time slot	Color	Points
Available, preferred	White	3
Available, but not preferred	Green	2
Not available, but event in this time slot can be rescheduled to make the slot available	Blue	1
Definitely not available, event in this slot cannot be rescheduled	Red	0
Not in the scope of the task	Grey	-

Table 1. Scoring system and color-coding of calendars.

[1] We also examined two other aspects in the process of conflict resolution in this study: how participant dyads a) allocated time differently in completing the tasks and b) cognitively navigated through the problem space in different ways when performing the tasks at different difficulty and conflict levels via different CMC channels. Results on these two aspects will not be reported here and can be found in our other article [15].

Figure 2. Example calendar of one week.

Level of Difficulty

Each week had a 12-hour *solution space.* Each appointment scheduled within the solution space would give both sides of the pair a non-zero score. The remaining 28 hours were non-solutions since at least one side of the pair would get 0 points if an appointment was scheduled in those time slots. The level of difficulty for each week was manipulated by varying the number of preferred time slots within the solution space (see Table 2). The 20 easy weeks contained more time slots with high point combinations, whereas the 20 difficult weeks contained more time slots with low point combinations. Thus, the chance of participants finding better potential solutions (with higher points earned by both parties) was higher for easy than difficult weeks.

Solution Space		# of Hours for Each Point Combination	
Point Combination (calendar 1 – calendar 2)		Easy	Difficult
Low	1-1, 1-2, 2-1	1	2
Medium	2-2, 1-3, 3-1	1	1
High	3-3, 3-2, 2-3	2	1

Table 2. Solution space for easy vs. difficult weeks.

Level of Conflict

In order to get participants more engaged and to increase the diversity of possible solutions, several bonus point conditions were introduced (e.g., earning an extra point by avoiding particular hours). After taking all bonus points into account, solutions that would yield the highest total score of the pair were identified. As a result of the introduction of bonus points, the 40 weeks could also be grouped into two groups. In *low-conflict weeks*, only one solution that yielded the highest total score could be identified, thus once such solution was found, neither side of the pair need to compromise. In *high-conflict weeks*, more than one solution that yielded the highest total score could be identified, and each side was able to earn different scores depending on which solution was chosen, thus a process of negotiation was necessary for either side to optimized his/her personal scores. One side of the dyad must compromise in order to reach a decision on high conflict weeks. The level of conflict was not directly manipulated, but identified during the process of examining the solution space of each week. However, the level of conflict was independent of the manipulated level of difficulty since roughly half of the easy weeks (12) and roughly half of the difficult weeks (11) were grouped into low-conflict weeks, and the rest into high-conflict weeks.

Procedure

Participants were seated at computers in different rooms. Due to limited room availability, several pairs in text condition were separated by large barriers that prevented them from seeing each other. Each pair received a 10-week calendar of 5 easy weeks and 5 difficult weeks randomly chosen from the calendar pool, in random order. Their task was to schedule two 1-hour appointments on two different days for each week; thus, each pair had 20 appointments for the whole experiment. It was emphasized to the participants that their goal was to get their individual score as high as possible, and the three who got the highest individual total scores in all participants would receive an extra $10 as a reward. Maximizing individual score was emphasized to elicit a higher level of conflict and a higher need for negotiation. Participants communicated with each other using Google talk through text, audio or video chatting and marked their scheduled appointments on a printed answer sheet. Participants in the text group could type in text in a box at the bottom of the interface and view the text history above the input box. Chat histories were saved. Participants in the audio and video groups were asked not to type in the chat box and the chat history area will be blank for audio group and replaced by a video stream with their partner's face centered for the video group. Conversations were recorded by screen activity recording software named *SnapzProX*. After scheduling all appointments, participants were asked to fill a short survey, in which they provided basic demographic information and answered questions about their experience of using CMC tools. Participants were then thanked and compensated for their time.

Measures

Performance

Participants' answer sheets were scored based on the scoring system in Table 1. A participant could earn up to 8 points for one week. Participant dyads' *overall performance* was measured by the sum of the scores of the pair averaged across 10 weeks.

Although it was possible that two participants could earn the same score, we did not get any tied pairs in the current experiment. Therefore, for all pairs in this experiment, there was always one person getting a higher total score than the other. We divided each pair into a high-performance side and a low-performance side. A *difference score* was calculated by subtracting the score of the low-performance person from the high-performance person for each week. This difference in performance within each dyad was used not only due to the interdependence in performance within each dyad, but also because this difference score would be more meaningful in measuring the result of negotiation than using individual scores. That is, more balanced scores would be expected as a result of thorough negotiation.

Conversation Dynamics

Participants' conversations during the task were recorded for the text condition and transcribed into text for audio and video conditions. Four coders read the conversations carefully and judged whether each sentence belonged to the following two categories: *time suggestion* and *negotiation*.

Time Suggestion: When a sentence was devoted to either revealing a person's own available time (e.g., I am available Monday afternoon), or asking partner's availability (e.g., would Friday 4 to 5 work for you?), it was categorized into the *time suggestion* category. This category was further divided into two sub-categories. When a person was listing all his/her available time, or asking partner's availability for the whole week, this sentence was categorized into the *condensed-format time suggestion* category. When a person was revealing his/her own or asking partner's availability for a single day or for no more than 2 time slots, this sentence was categorized into the *specific-format time suggestion* category.

Negotiation: When a sentence was devoted to evaluating (or comparing) potential points that could be earned for either or both sides of the dyad (e.g., if I take this green slot, I could also earn 2 bonus points, which is a better choice than taking that white one), or discussing the possibility that either side of the pair would (or would not) compromise by taking a less favored time slot (e.g., would you mind taking a green this time? I will do a green one next week), it was categorized into the *negotiation* category.

Sentences could be coded into both or neither of the two categories. Sentences that did not belong to the above two categories were also coded but were not in the scope of analyses for this article. Four native English speakers went through the training session, during which they were given feedback on their coding to ensure they achieved similar understanding of the coding scheme (inter-coder agreement was above 95% for all pairs of coders). Each coder then coded a quarter of the conversations independently. The number of sentences belonging to each category was counted within each week. Then the average number of sentences for each of the four week-types was calculated.

RESULTS

The effect of *CMC channels, level of difficulty* and *level of conflict* on participants' performance and conversation dynamics was examined. Mediation analyses were then performed to further reveal the process of how participants' communication strategies during information exchange predicted their involvement in negotiation, which in turn foreshadowed their performance.

Performance

Overall Performance

The *overall performance* did not differ between the three CMC groups (M = 13.58, 13.80 and 13.91, SD = .85, .41 and .49 for text, audio and video conditions, respectively, $F_{(2,47)} = 1.30$, $p > .10$). To further understand whether more balanced solutions were reached as a result of thorough negotiation, the *difference score* between each dyad was used as the dependent variable in the following analyses.

Level of Difficulty

Mixed-design analysis of variance (ANOVA) with *difficulty* as a repeated measure and CMC channels as between-subject variable yielded a significant interactive effect ($F_{(2,47)} = 4.78$, $p < .05$) on the difference scores of dyads, suggesting that different CMC groups performed differently on easy vs. difficult weeks. As illustrated in Figure 3a, the difference in participants' performances was comparable among three CMC groups for *easy* weeks ($F_{(2,47)} = 1.20$, $p > .10$). In contrast, difference in participants' performances on *difficult* weeks differed for the three CMC groups ($F_{(2,47)} = 3.60$, $p < .05$). Fisher's least significant difference (LSD) post-hoc comparison suggested that the difference in performance was higher for text and audio groups than video groups ($ps < .05$).

The results suggested that when the task became difficult, participants in video condition were able to reach a decision that better balanced the two sides' performance, as reflected in a smaller difference score, suggesting that they probably were able to get more involved in conflict resolution by negotiating with each other on difficult weeks.

Level of Conflict

Also taking participants' difference in performance as dependent variable, mixed-design ANOVA with *level of conflict* as a repeated measure and CMC channels as between-subject variable yielded a significant 2-way interactive effect ($F_{(2,47)} = 5.92$, $p < .01$), suggesting that different CMC groups also performed differently on weeks with low vs. high levels of potential conflict.

As shown in Figure 3b, for *low-conflict* weeks, CMC channels had a marginal effect on dyads' difference in performance ($F_{(2,47)} = 2.42$, $p = .10$). The effect of CMC channels was significant for *high conflict* weeks ($F_{(2,47)} = 4.40$, $p < .05$). Fisher's LSD post-hoc comparison suggested that the difference in performance was lowest for the video condition, which was lower than text condition ($p < .01$), and was marginally lower than audio condition ($p < .10$).

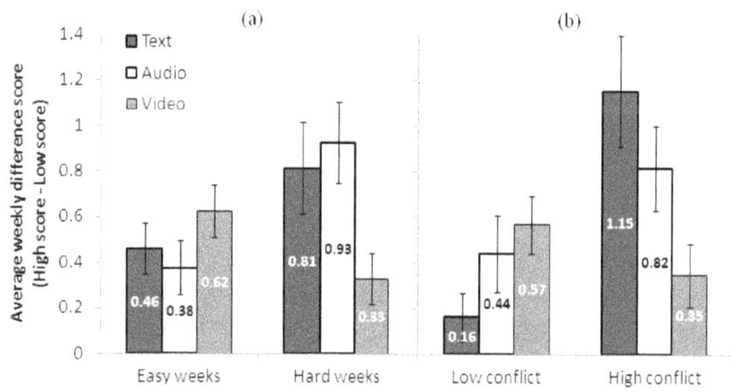

Figure 3. Difference score for easy vs. difficult weeks (a) and for low- vs. high-conflict weeks (b) in text, audio and video CMC groups

We can clearly see from Figure 3b that, as the bandwidth of CMC channels went higher from text to audio and from audio to video chatting, the difference score between dyads became smaller and smaller for high-conflict weeks, probably due to the fact that they were more and more likely to get engaged in negotiation and conflict resolutions when they need to. To further unpack the impact of CMC channels, we examined participants' conversation dynamics on how they exchanged availability information and the extent to which they got involved in negotiation.

Conversation Dynamics

Two aspects of participants' conversation were examined. First, at the stage of collaboratively identifying potential solutions, participants might use different *communication strategies* when exchanging information about their availability, which in turn might bring an effect on their subsequent negotiation and conflict resolution based on the identified solution candidates. Second, participants' involvement in *negotiation* was directly compared among different CMC groups for different week types.

Communication Strategies during Information Exchange

We examined the number of sentences participants used for suggesting times in *condensed* vs. *specific format*. Figure 4 clearly illustrated the different preferences participants have in choosing condensed vs. specific format to convey their own availability and to ask their partners' availability. Mixed-design ANOVA with information exchange format (condensed vs. specific) as repeated measures and CMC channels as between-subject variable yielded a significant 2-way interactive effect between the two variables ($F_{(2,47)} = 24.69$, $p < .001$). Although participants said more sentences in specific format than in condensed format in all three CMC groups (paired-sample $t_{(16)} = 2.26$, $p < .05$, $t_{(15)} = 9.74$, $p < .001$, and $t_{(16)} = 12.02$, $p < .001$ for text, audio and video conditions, respectively), the difference in video condition was the highest, followed by audio condition. This pattern of result was consistent across all week types.

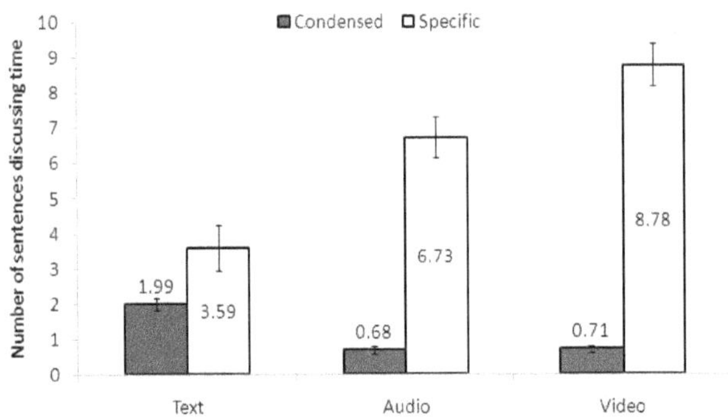

Figure 4. Number of sentences conveying availability in condensed vs. specific format.

The results clearly showed that participants in our study employed different strategies at the stage of information exchange to collaboratively find potential solutions. The choice of different strategies probably was due to the cost of different communication channels. Specifically, the high cost of typing and the easiness of retrieving information by looking back at the text history probably made the text group prefer laying out all their available times at once, whereas the low cost of talking and the difficulty of holding information in working memory probably made the audio and video groups prefer discussing a small number of possible time slots before moving onto other ones.

Since it would be very difficult to discuss a large amount of information conveyed in condensed format and compare a large number of solution candidates all at once, a prerequisite of sufficient negotiation would be discussing potential solutions in specific rather than condensed format, which happened more often in audio and video conditions. Therefore, we would expect that the different preferences on information exchange strategies would foster different levels of negotiation in the three CMC groups.

Negotiation

To control for the influence of overall talkativeness on participants' involvement in negotiation, we divided the number of sentences participants actually said (typed) on score-evaluation and negotiation for each week by the weekly average number of sentences said by the CMC group this dyad was from. We then used this *proportional score* to represent participants' involvement in negotiation.

Mixed-design ANOVA did not find a significant interactive effect between *difficulty* and CMC channels on the extent to which participants involved in negotiation ($F_{(2,47)} = .35$, $p > .10$, see Figure 5a). A main effect of week types ($F_{(1,47)} = 16.18$, $p < .01$) suggested that difficult weeks elicited more negotiation than easy weeks. The main effect of CMC channels was not significant ($F_{(2,47)} = 1.65$, $p > .10$).

In contrast, *conflict level* and CMC channels had a significant two-way interactive effect on involvement in negotiation ($F_{(2,47)} = 3.76$, $p < .05$, see Figure 5b). Paired-sample t-tests comparing low- vs. high-conflict weeks suggested that the proportion of sentences devoted to negotiation was similar for text condition ($t_{(16)} = .03$, $p > .10$), marginally different for audio condition ($t_{(15)} = 1.88$, $p = .08$), and significantly different for video condition ($t_{(16)} = 5.21$, $p < .001$). Thus, participants were more likely to get involved in negotiation for weeks involving higher levels of potential conflict in video condition, probably as an effort of resolving these conflicts.

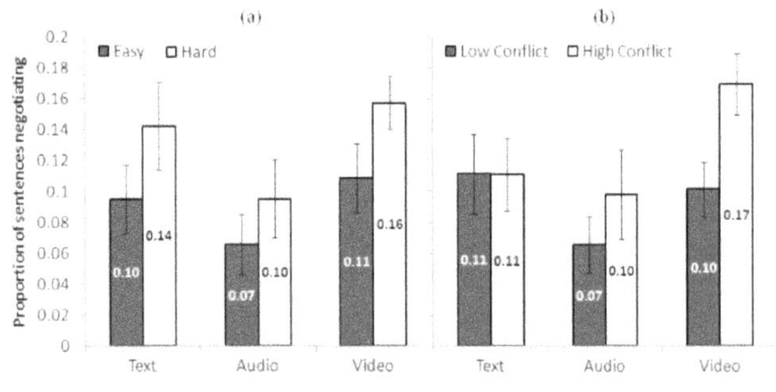

Figure 5. Involvement in negotiation for easy vs. difficult weeks (a) and low- vs. high conflict weeks (b).

The Mechanism of Why Video Chatting Better Supports Conflict Resolution

Recall that participants using video chatting were able to reach decisions that better balanced the performance of both sides when the tasks were difficult or involved higher levels of potential conflict. The goal of this section was to understand the underlying mechanisms of how participants' different conversation dynamics resulted in these performance patterns when using different CMC channels. Specifically, we hypothesized that communication strategies participants chose to exchange availability information established a common ground that influenced their involvement of subsequent negotiation, which in turn led to the different performance patterns. Mediation analysis was used to examine whether there was an effect flowing along this chain.

Mediation Analysis

Mediation analysis is commonly used in social science studies to identify the effects that transmit along a chain of variables [25]. The standard procedure of examining whether a mediation effect exists involves four steps of regression analyses [5] (see Figure 6).

Step1: Independent variable (X) has a significant effect (path c) on dependent variable (Y). Thus, there is an effect to be mediated.

Step2: X has a significant effect (path a) on mediator (M).

Step3: M has a significant effect (path b) on Y controlling for X (when X is taken into account). That is, both X and M should be entered in the regression equation to predict Y.

Step4: The effect of X on Y (path c') controlling for M is reduced compared to the original effect (path c). When c' is reduced to 0, it is a full mediation, otherwise a partial mediation. The indirect effect of X on Y through M (i.e., the reduction of effect from c to c') can be tested using the method promoted by Sobel [32].

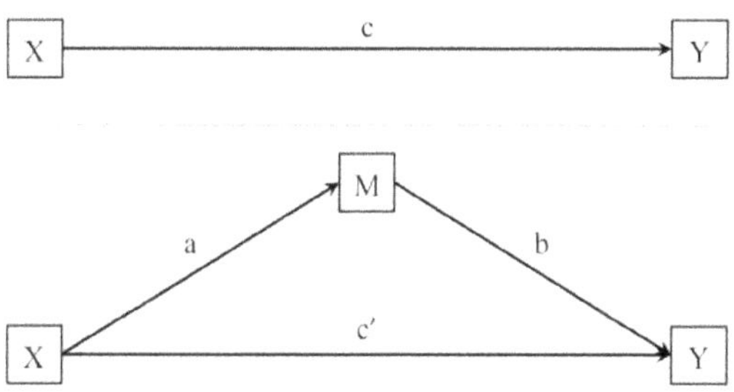

Figure 6. Conceptual Framework of Mediation Analysis

When a mediation effect is detected, one can conclude that M fully or partially mediated the effect from X to Y. That is, the antecedent variable X affects the mediating variable M, which in turn affects the outcome variable Y.

Negotiation Mediating the Effect of Communication Strategies during Information Exchange on Performance

Twelve sets of mediation analyses were conducted (4 week types X 3 CMC groups, one model each). In the analyses, the two communication strategies (condensed vs. specific) during information exchange were entered as independent variables (X), negotiation was entered as the mediator (M), and performance as measured in difference score for each dyad was entered as the outcome variable (Y). Mediation was detected only for high conflict weeks in the video group. Therefore, we will focus on this particular mediation model and the rest 11 models are not reported in detail in this article.

The whole mediation model is presented in Figure 7, with path coefficients (β) marked along each path. Exchanging information in condensed format did not have an effect on negotiation (β = .09), or on dyads' difference scores (β = -.24). However, exchanging information in specific format had a positive effect on negotiation (path a, β = .61, p < .05). That is, participants who exchanged availability information one or two small time slots at a time were more likely to get engaged in negotiation. Exchanging less information at a time had a negative effect on dyads' difference scores (path c, β = -.69, p < .01) before examining the mediation effect of negotiation. That is, exchanging availability information one or two small time slots at a time could also reduce the score difference between the two sides of each dyad, helping them reach a consensus that balanced the score each side could earn. Negotiation had a negative effect on the dyads' difference scores controlling for both condensed and specific format of information exchange (path b, β = -.52, p < .05). Thus, involvement in negotiation also helped getting the dyads reach better balanced decisions. Most importantly, when negotiation was taken into account in regression, the effect of exchanging less information at a time on performance was reduced to a non-significant effect (path c', β = -.37, p = .10). The reduction of effect was marginally significant (Δ = .32, p = .06) according to Sobel Test [28, 32]. Therefore, negotiation mediated the effect of exchanging a smaller amount of information at a time on reducing difference scores between the two sides of participant dyads in video condition when conflict level was high.

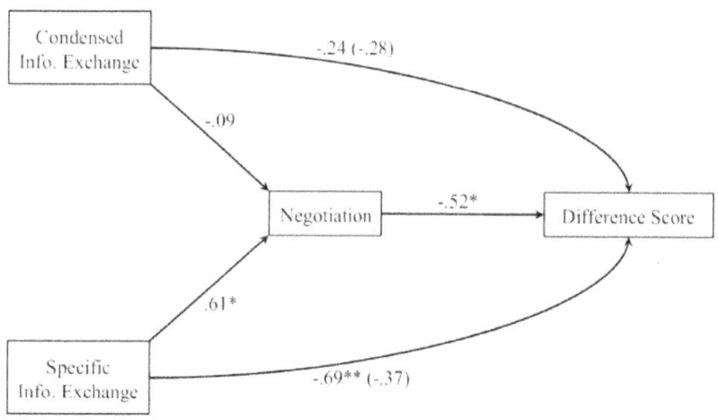

*: $p < .05$, **: $p < .01$

Figure 7.Negotiation mediating the effect of communication strategies on performance for high-conflict weeks in video condition. Note: numbers along the paths are standardized regression coefficients (β). The number in parentheses are regression coefficients when mediator (negotiation) was controlled for (i.e., path c').

The mediation analyses explained the mechanism of why participants in the video group were able to reach a well-balanced decision for this event-scheduling task when the level of potential conflict was high. Participants had a high tendency to exchange availability information in specific format (fewer than two 2 time slots at each conversation turn) when video chatting. This particular communication strategy established a common ground that better fostered negotiation, which was essential for conflict resolution. Thorough and in-depth negotiation then resulted in better-balanced performance for the dyads as reflected in smaller difference scores.

Table 3 illustrated example sections of conversation turns in text and video condition. We can see that in text condition, T2 mentioned 6 time slot candidates in one sentence. Although T1 compromised by taking one less preferred option, the pair reached a decision without in-depth discussion on all possible alternatives. Therefore, this decision might be sub-optimal. In comparison, the pair in video condition discussed one alternative at a time and was aware that both the available alternatives would require compromise from one side or the other before V2 compromised. V1 also offered to compromise in the future to ensure a feeling of fairness to V2.

Text	Video
T1: ok week 5, aug 30-sept 3 now? T2: yes, mon 2-3, tues 12-1, wed 11-12 4-5, fri 9-10 11-1, white T1: mon 2-3 works, and fri 11-12 is green for me, i will go with it, fine? T2: ok cool	V1: So 10 to 11 on Friday? V2: 10 to 11, you can't do 11 to 12? V1: Umm it's blue V2: Can you do 12 to 1? V1: It's green, would that work? V2: Ok so it's green one way or the other, so let's do 10 to 11 V1: Ok V2: 10 to 11 on Friday, and that way you get a white and I get a green V1: Ok that works, and we can compromise, I can do a green next, ok so now we're on week 3

Table 3. Example conversation exchanges in text and video condition.

A further look at the models for text and audio groups could reveal whether similar mechanisms also exist for these two communication channels. When conflict level was high, none of the paths in the mediation model was significant for the text group. Whereas for the high-conflict weeks in the audio group, information exchange in specific format had a positive effect on negotiation (path a), but negotiation was not predictive of the dyads' performance (path b). This result indicated that negotiation in audio condition was less effective in resolving conflicts than in video chatting, probably due to the lack of visual cues such as attentional focus, facial expressions and gestures.

CONCLUSION AND DISCUSSION

In the current study, we examined the effect of text-, audio- and video-based CMC channels on how people resolved conflicts and reached agreement in an appointment-scheduling task. Two within-subject variables (difficulty, level of conflict) were introduced to further decompose the dynamics of interaction within participant pairs throughout the conflict resolution process. In particular, we focused on the difference in performance between each participant dyad because this difference was a good indicator of how well conflicts were resolved, and reflected the effectiveness of communication and negotiation in each CMC method.

In general, our results were supportive of the idea that higher bandwidth could help with conflict resolution. First, participants who used the video-based communication method were more likely to agree on solutions that were equally good to both parties, especially in difficult and high conflict weeks, than participants who used the text- and audio-based channels. Second, analyses on conversation dynamics showed that participants using different CMC channels employed different strategies when exchanging information to establish common ground for the following stage of negotiation and conflict resolution. Specifically, we found that time information was exchanged in a more condensed format in text condition and smaller chunks of more specific time information was discussed in audio and video conditions. Third, we found that the extent to which participant dyads were engaged in negotiation was most sensitive to the level of conflict of a week when the video-based communication method was used.

Lastly but most importantly, mediation analyses revealed the underlying mechanism of why conflict resolution was better supported by the video channel. Because of the low cost of speaking than typing and the difficulty of holding too much information in working memory, participants tended to exchange less information at a time. They then began to discuss the information exchanged before moving onto exchanging the next piece of information. We found that this communication strategy fostered a thorough negotiation that was essential for conflict resolution, which in turn led to a better balance of performance between the collaborators.

This mediational mechanism explained why participants were less able to reach balanced performance when communicating through text and audio channels. High cost of typing and the easiness of looking for information from text history rather than retrieving from working memory probably made the participants prefer the choice of laying out all information at once when using the text channel. Although this strategy could be efficient in exchanging information as fast as possible, it would be hard to negotiate and compare among an overwhelmingly large number of solution candidates. When communicating through audio channel, participants also preferred the way of exchanging less information each time, similar to participants in the video group. This information exchange strategy supported a higher level of negotiation. But negotiation in the audio group seemed to be less efficient than the video group, as negotiation did not predict performance in the mediation model for the audio group. This was probably due to the fact that participants were less efficient in inferring their partner's goals, emotion, willingness to compromise, personality and other social cues that are essential for successful negotiation and conflict resolution. However, it is important to point out that the exact reasons of why participants chose different information exchange strategies when using different communication channels were not directly examined but speculated in the current study. Future studies need to identify possible antecedents of people's choice on information exchange strategies.

Further field studies are needed to verify the ecological validity and the generalizability of the findings from this study. However, it is highly probable that the same mechanism also arise in real-world negotiation scenarios as well as tasks that involve conflict resolution in a more complicated format. The strategy of exchanging information in small pieces at each time can be particularly helpful to establish common ground that better supports negotiation, especially when there is a large amount of information in the task space and a great proportion of it needs to be exchanged via communication among group members. Focusing on small chunks of information can help the collaborators stay synchronized in acknowledging and updating their status during the process of collaborative work. This strategy can also help reduce the chance of collaborators neglecting certain pieces of information that is particularly important due to the overwhelmingly large amount of information exchanged all at once.

Implications

The results of the current study provided insights on how the dynamics of interpersonal interaction induced by different CMC channels could influence the negotiation and conflict resolution processes. We believe that one important metric for successful conflict resolution is whether both parties can agree on a solution that is equally good for them. A high difference in performance or earned benefits in remote conflict resolution tasks can bring long-term detrimental effects on how collaborators judge the overall value of the collaboration, as well as their mutual trust [7]. In the long run, the trust and willingness to collaboration might diminish if either party perceives that there is an imbalance of benefits or costs in the collaboration, which apparently would result in an escalation of conflict level [29] and less efficient long-term effectiveness in the collaborative work. Therefore, special attention need to the paid to whether the interfaces of CMC tools could facilitate a feeling of "fairness" and trust among remote collaborators when they need to resolve conflicts through remote communication.

The results of the current study also brought important implications to the design of CMC tools to better support conflict resolution. Although increasing the bandwidth of the communication channel from text to audio, and from audio to video could be a solution to provide better support, sometimes this upgrading can be costly. According to our results, low bandwidth CMC tools can be designed to promote information exchange in small pieces at each conversation turn, so that users can be guided to thoroughly discuss information in small bits at a time before moving on to the next bit and to avoid getting lost and not knowing how to negotiate by laying out a large chunk of information all at once. In addition, new features can also be incorporated into low bandwidth CMC tools to help organize the exchanged information and related discussion. By grouping each piece of information together with corresponding discussion and negotiation, the tool could provide a structural help to the users on keeping track of the progress of conflict resolution. This could be especially helpful for tasks that are complex.

Future Directions

The process of conflict resolution could become even more complicated when other factors are taken into consideration in the dynamic process, such as collaborators' personality traits and sensitivity to others' emotions, intentions and needs, features in the communication tools such as time lag and quality of audio and video streams, translation of language and different group norms when multiple groups scattering all over the world are involved in the collaborative work. This may imply that there is no single best CMC method for all remote collaborative works. Perhaps it is more reasonable to choose different channels depending on the nature of the remote task, the individuals performing the task, and the individual and collective goal orientation of the team (e.g., competitive vs. collaborative goals). Future research should be focused on the complex interactions of these factors during remote collaborative work involving conflict resolution.

ACKNOWLEDGMENTS

We thank Susan Fussell for her helpful comments on previous versions of this article. We thank all the undergraduate research assistants (due to space limitation we cannot list their names here) for running the experiments, transcribing conversations and coding the data. This work was supported by the Office of Naval Research grant number N00014-07-1-0903, awarded to the second author.

REFERENCES

1. Anderson, A.H., McEwan, R., Bal, J., et al. Virtual team meetings: An analysis of communication and context. *Computers in Human Behavior*, 2007. 23: p. 2558-2580.
2. Baddeley, A. Working Memory. *Science*, 1992. 255(5044): p. 556-559.
3. Balakrishnan, A.D., Fussell, S.R., and Kiesler, S. Do visualizations improve synchronous remote collaboration?, in *Proceeding of the 26th annual SIGCHI conference on Human factors in computing systems*. 2008, ACM: Florence, Italy.

4. Baltes, B.B., Dickson, M.W., Sherman, M.P., et al. Computer-Mediated Communication and Group Decision Making: A Meta-Analysis. *Organizational Behavior and Human Decision Processes*, 2002. 87(1): p. 156-179.
5. Baron, R.M. and Kenny, D.A. The Moderator-Mediator Variable Distinction in Social Psychological Research: Conceptual, Strategic, and Statistical Considerations. *Journal of Personality & Social Psychology*, 1986. 51(6): p. 1173-1182.
6. Bordia, P. Face-to-Face Versus Computer-Mediated Communication: A Synthesis of the Experimental Literature. *Journal of Business Communication* 1997. 34(1): p. 99-118.
7. Bos, N., Olson, J., Gergle, D., et al. Effects of Four Computer-Mediated Communications Channels on Trust Development. in *ACM Conference on Human Factors in Computing Systems*. 2002. Minneapolis, MN. 4(1): p. 135-140.
8. Brett, J.M. *Negotiating Globally*. 2001, San Francisco, CA: Jossey-Bass.
9. Chapanis, A., Ochsman, R.B., Parrish, R.N., et al. Studies in Interactive Communication: I. The Effects of Four Communication Modes on the Behavior of Teams During Cooperative Problem-Solving. *Human Factors*, 1977. 14(6): p. 487-509.
10. Clark, H.H. and Brennan, S.A. Grounding in communication, in *Perspectives on socially shared cognition* L.B. Resnick, J.M. Levine, and S.D. Teasley, Editors. 1991, APA Books: Washington.
11. Cramton, C.D. The Mutual Knowledge Problem and Its Consequences for Dispersed Collaboration. *Organization Science*, 2001. 12(3): p. 346-371.
12. Daft, R.L. and Lengel, R.H. Information Richness. A New Approach to Managerial Behavior and Organization Design, in *Research in Organizational Behavior*, L.L. Cummings and B.M. Staw, Editors. 1984, JAI Press.: Homewood, IL. p. 191-233.
13. Daly-Jones, O., Monk, A., and Watts, L. Some advantages of video conferencing over high-quality audio conferencing: fluency and awareness of attentional focus. *International Journal of Human-Computer Studies*, 1998. 49(1): p. 21-58.
14. Diamant, E.I., Fussell, S.R., and Lo, F.-l. Where did we turn wrong?: unpacking the effect of culture and technology on attributions of team performance, in *Proceedings of the 2008 ACM Conference on Computer Supported Cooperative Work*. 2008, ACM: San Diego, CA, USA.
15. Dong, W. and Fu, W.T. Conflict Resolution in Remote Collaborative Problem Solving: A Comparison of Different Computer Mediated Communication Methods. in *The Annual Meeting of the Cognitive Science Society*. 2011. Boston, MA. p. 2142-2147.
16. Dorado, M.A., Medina, F.J., Munduate, L., et al. Computer-mediated negotiation of an escalated conflict. *Small Group Research*, 2002. 33(5): p. 509-524.
17. Firm, K., Sellen, A., and Wilbur, S. *Video-mediated communication*. 1997, Hillsdale, NJ: Lawrence Erlbaum Associates.
18. Fish, R.S., Kraut, R.E., Root, R.W., et al. Video as a technology for informal communication. *Commun. ACM*, 1993. 36(1): p. 48-61.
19. Fussell, S.R. and Krauss, R.M. Coordination of Knowledge in Communication: Effects of Speakers' Assumptions About What Others Know. *Journal of Personality & Social Psychology*, 1992. 62(3): p. 378-391.
20. Fussell, S.R., Kraut, R.E., Gergle, D., et al. Visual Cues as Evidence of Others' Minds in Collaborative Physical Tasks, in *Other Minds*, B. Malle and S. Hodges, Editors. 2005, The Guilford Press: New York. p. 91-105.
21. Goh, K.-Y., Teo, H.-H., Wu, H., et al. Computer-supported negotiations: an experimental study of bargaining in electronic commerce. in *7th International Conference on Electronic Commerce*. 2000. p. 104-116.
22. Hinds, P.J. and Bailey, D.E. Out of Sight, Out of Sync: Understanding Conflict in Distributed Teams. *Organization Science*, 2003. 14(6): p. 615-632.
23. Hollingshead, A.B. Information Suppression and Status Persistence in Group Decision Making The Effects of Communication Media. *Human Communication Research*, 1996. 23(2): p. 193-219.
24. Kiesler, S. and Sproull, L. Group decision making and communication technology. *Organizational Behavior and Human Decision Processes*, 1992. 52: p. 96-123.
25. MacKinnon, D.P., Fairchild, A.J., and Fritz, M.S. Mediation Analysis. *Annual Review of Psychology*, 2007. 58: p. 593-614.
26. Morris, M., Nadler, J., Kurtzberg, T., et al. Schmooze or lose: Social friction and lubrication in e-mail negotiations. *Group Dynamics: Theory, Research and Practice*, 2002. 6(1): p. 89-100.
27. Olson, J.S., Olson, G.M., and Meader, D.K. What mix of video and audio is useful for small groups doing remote real-time design work?, in *Proceedings of the CHI'95 conference on Human Factors in Computing Systems*. 1995, ACM Press: Denver, CO. p. 362-368.
28. Preacher, K.J. and Hayes, A.F. SPSS and SAS procedures for estimating indirect effects in simple mediation models. *Behavior Research Methods, Instruments, & Computers*, 2004. 36(4): p. 717-731.
29. Schoorman, F.D. and Holahan, P.J. Psychological antecedents of escalation behavior: Effects of choice, responsibility and decision consequences. *Journal of Applied Psychology*, 1996. 81: p. 786-794.
30. Setlock, L.D., Quinones, P.-A., and Fussell, S.R. Does Culture Interact with Media Richness? The Effects of Audio vs. Video Conferencing on Chinese and American Dyads. in *Hawaii International Conference on System Sciences*. 2007.
31. Siegel, J., Dubrovsky, V., Kiesler, S., et al. Group processes in computer-mediated communication. *Organizational Behavior and Human Decision Processes*, 1986. 37(2): p. 157-187.
32. Sobel, M.E. Asymptotic Confidence Intervals for Indirect Effects in Structural Equation Models. *Sociological Methodology*, 1982. 13: p. 290-312.
33. Tan, D.S., Gergle, D., Mandryk, R., et al. Using job-shop scheduling tasks for evaluating collocated collaboration. *Journal of Personal and Ubiquitous Computing*, 2008. 12: p. 255-267.
34. Thompson, L. and Nadler, J. Negotiating via information technology: Theory and application. *Journal of Social Issues*, 2002. 58(1): p. 109-124.
35. Veinott, E.S., Olson, J., Olson, G.M., et al. Video helps remote work: speakers who need to negotiate common ground benefit from seeing each other, in *Proceedings of the SIGCHI conference on human factors in computing systems: the CHI is the limit*. 1999, ACM: Pittsburgh, Pennsylvania, United States. p. 302-309.
36. Wee, H.-S.s., pirkul, H., Jacob, V., et al. Effects of Computer-Mediated Communication on Group Negotiation: An Empirical Study. in *28th Annual Hawaii Intenational Conference on System Sciences* 1995. p. 270-279.

Hospital Robot at Work: Something Alien or an Intelligent Colleague?

Sara Ljungblad[1,2], Jirina Kotrbova[3], Mattias Jacobsson[2], Henriette Cramer[2], Karol Niechwiadowicz[3]

[1] LOTS Design, Kastellgatan 1, 413 07 Göteborg, Sweden

[2] Mobile Life @ SICS, Kistagången 16, 164 40, Kista, Sweden

[3] Robcab AB, c/o Martins, S:ta Ursulas väg 21D, 722 18 Västerås, Sweden

sara@lotsdesign.se, jirina.kotrbova@gmail.com, majac@sics.se, henriette@mobilelifecentre.org, karol.niechwiadowicz@robcab.se

ABSTRACT

This paper describes a case study of the initial reactions to a transport robot running in a semi-public hospital environment. The robot was transporting goods and samples for an orthopedic department, moving within and between different departments for 13 days, and was used by the staff for five days. Based on this case, we discuss how the robot was perceived by staff and visitors and purpose an initial framework, a utopian model, describing four different perspectives; an alien, a machine, a worker and as a work partner. This has been derived from interviews, questionnaires and observation, and exemplifies different qualities that the robot was ascribed. We discuss how the perspectives may mutually co-exist and change, and are affected by time and familiarity with the robot at work.

Author Keywords

Courier robot; qualities; hospital; study; experience

ACM Classification Keywords

H5.3 Group and Organization Interfaces: Evaluation/methodology

General Terms

Human Factors; Design

INTRODUCTION

Hospitals have been studied extensively within the CSCW field (e.g. [45]), and a lot has happened since the late 60's when computer technology was first introduced in hospitals [7]. Many studies have revealed the complexity of workflows at hospitals where many different artifacts take part (e.g. [4], [45], [25]), and how tasks that are physically distributed are a challenge for the staff [5]. Studies of robots in hospital settings are an important emerging area for CSCW, to increase the understanding of robots in social practices and naturalistic settings. Today, robots are being designed to support staff in moving a person from one bed to another [11], take blood samples [50], support and perform surgery [35], and to be social companions and mediators for child patients [22]. Finally, there are courier robots for transporting goods, which may reduce the staffs' physically distributed tasks (e.g. [30], [44], [14]). However, much research is still needed to understand the emerging role, the acceptance, and use of different robots. This paper especially complements two previous studies that take emotional and social perspectives of how robots are perceived at hospitals ([39], [30]).

From a CSCW perspective, studies that emphasize the artifacts often focus on its function in a practice. For example, what role does a patient record play and for whom (e.g. [9], [25]), and how do different representations of computer technology affect coordination (e.g. [37], [8])? We contribute with a complementing perspective, by focusing primarily on how a robot in a hospital setting is experienced. We exemplify how it may give rise to certain kinds of associations, and the experienced qualities in this specific setting.

BACKGROUND

An increasing amount of research focuses on experience-related aspects in work settings, such as affective states [23]. For example, a study on how emotions affect work in a hospital context was conducted by [29]. However, we strive to understand the specific qualities that technology is associated with or ascribed, which is different from investigating affective states such as emotions or moods [23]. Models such as the Technology Acceptance Model (UTAUT, TAM [48]) attempt to describe factors expected to influence intent to use and actual usage of a system, such as expectations of effort needed on the user's part, performance of the system, facilitating conditions and social influence. Our perspective is more related to more dynamic *experiential qualities* that describe how something is experienced, and refers to specific qualities that emerge in interaction with a system [41]. However, we do not strive to create a universal design language of qualities, but rather aim to understand different perspectives that ascribed qualities may relate to. Our perspective is also different from work focusing on interaction design qualities that for example are categorized within practical, social, aesthetic, structural and ethical dimensions [3]. Rather, the qualities we are investigating are related to how people make sense of a system and what they attribute it when striving to address it as a meaningful experience [28]. Qualities are related to *affordances*. Affordances refer to the kind of use that artifacts invite, originally introduced as "action possibilities" in Gibson's ecological psychology [33]. Affordances were considered a relationship part of nature that may or may not be visible, known, and desirable. Norman [33] has previously argued that in a design context it is the perceived affordances that are interesting, taking the user's perspective and perceptions of the artifact. Achieving suitable affordances (or Norman's more recent perspective of adding suitable signifiers) in a design, can create a correct association or metaphor to a specific use. However, nor signifiers or affordances necessarily explain long-term relations or perspectives of an artifact, as they refer to the "surface" of a design. Thus, this does not fully represent our perspective of qualities, even if an unfamiliar robot may invite for a specific use and may be ascribed qualities due to specific added signifiers.

Ascribing qualities to robot technology

What qualities do people ascribe to things and why? Ascribing qualities to a robot (such as intelligence) is investigated in Taylor's [45] research on machine intelligence and exemplifies how people see machine behavior as intelligent. Forlizzi and DiSalvo [20] describe how people ascribed intelligence to vacuum robots, despite the fact that they had spent much effort preparing for the cleaning, because of the robot's limitations (e.g. moving furniture to accommodate the robot). Attributing intelligent behavior to a machine exemplifies how people create relationships with things [45]. Studies by Reeves and Nass for example have shown that people tend to respond to technology in ways that resemble social responses in interactions between humans [38]. Ascribing intelligence to 'things', is often referred to as a type of anthropomorphisation (e.g. [6], [47], [49]). Antrophomorphisation involves reading human characteristics into artifacts and treating them as such [16]. It exemplifies how people may attribute qualities to things, and also provides underlying reasons as to why. This supports our perspective that people have social relationships with artifacts, similar to how humans have relationships to humans and animals. From a psychological perspective, anthropomorphism is **not** a behavioral description of an observable action. Instead it *"requires going beyond what is directly observable to make inferences about unobservable humanlike characteristics"* [15]:144. The strength of anthropomorphic inferences will vary from one domain or context to another. Anthropomorphism is elicited from accessible agent knowledge, meaning that it is based on ones *self-knowledge* required earlier. Theories on social motivation also show that when people are dispositional lonely, they have a stronger tendency to anthropomorphize agents (ibid). Finally, anthropomorphisation is about effectance motivation, which is our desire to interact effectively with our environment, and being able to understand, predict and control it. Thus, it can be argued that antrophomorphism is a human strategy to *reduce uncertainties and unfamiliarity* in our environment [16]. Potentially, this could mean that people would ascribe qualities that they normally associate with other objects (or people) to a robot to make it more familiar. Anthropomorphisation has also been questioned as a concept, for example by Nass and Moon [29] who argue that people mindlessly apply social rules and expectations to computers, even if they "know" that the artifact lacks human capabilities. Mindless or not, anthropomorphisation brings forward the tendency to ascribe human qualities to technology, which is relevant for this paper.

A related perspective of people's tendency to ascribe specific social qualities is provided by Goffman [21] who discusses social *performances*. He states that when individuals are in a situation with others, they try to discover social data about the others in that situation. In the absence of full information, individuals use cues, tests, hints etc as predictive devices to understand 'who' the other is. Thus, performance, appearance, and social behavior play a key role in how we perceive others, even if the cues we act on might not be actually 'true'. We believe that it is possible that people also apply this when interacting with robots and other technology. For example, when trying to understand and express 'what' the robot is, they ground this on their own experience, that may be more or less frequent, or extended over time, have influence from media, and their experience of other machines, etc. [19].

Anthropological research exemplifies how things can be seen as *social creatures*, whose values and perceived *qualities* are constantly changing depending on context. This represents a somewhat different perspective, for example considering things as goods that are being traded (e.g. with an actor-network perspective [26] as taken in [1]).

From a human robot interaction perspective, the investigated robot lacks many human social characteristics, such as expressing and perceiving emotions, and communicating with a high level dialogue that *social interactive robots* have been classified with [20]. However, we are interested in how the studied robot may be *perceived* as having qualities that are considered social for example by; being *socially evocative* (object for anthropomorisation); embodying more or less human like *social cues*; and being *socially receptive*, such as being perceived to adapt to social behavior (ibid). Thus, the robot may affect its social setting and be interpreted to display social behavior simply by being and acting among people (e.g. [20], [30], [12]). We want to investigate what qualities people will ascribe to it, not only from a social perspective, but with a more holistic perspective on having the robot introduced into a work practice. Thus, we take the perspective that users define technology as active creators [42], and that the *coupling* of technology properties and their use (resulting in a specific experience) is done by users and not the designers [13]. Thus, our perspective is that designers can only aim to give raise to a specific kind of experience, but the actual experience and any attribution of qualities (whether human characteristics or not) is done by the users (ibid).

Studies of Transportation Robots at Hospitals

Several studies have investigated the need for transportation robots and the potential strategies for implementing them at hospitals. Evans et al. [14] and Rosetti et al. [39] present studies showing how automated delivery can improve the efficiency of hospital transportation, improve the overall organization, and reduce costs. Another related study looked at existing routines at the hospital and in particular what types of transportation tasks that could be improved by a robotic system [51].

A research study on Aethon's TUG robot especially brings forward organizational issues for robots in hospitals [30]. Aethon's TUG can deliver a variety of goods and has sound and voice effects. This study compared how hospital units at the hospital, such as postpartum units and medical units, experienced the same robot differently in workflow, political, social/emotional and environmental perspectives due to various toleration for interruption. The social/emotional results show that the staff at the medical units was irritated with the robot, especially when the robot interrupted their work. The staff at the post-partum units with a more relaxed work environment, lower traffic in the corridors and a different nature of social relationships, dealing with less life-and-death situations, felt less interrupted by the robot during their work. This study also found that the staff prioritized personal care relationships more than other tasks. The design implications suggest that robots for work environments should be designed to minimize interruptions and that social aspects should be integrated in the technology, such as allowing the robot to mediate communication between staff. Another study in a hospital environment used sensemaking theories and took a gender perspective when studying how a robot was perceived. While male hospital workers referred to the robot as a machine and consider it as a device that they can control, female hospital staff tended to see the robot as a freestanding human male. Nurses, mainly females, explained the robot as a novelty, mostly refusing it as a useless or frivolous item [40]. This is related to the alien perspective discussed in later sections of this paper. Our work is also related to robot studies outside the hospitals, such as a study of vacuum robots in households [20]. This study had the goal of understanding people's attitudes and experiences in order to create general design implications, and found that people ascribed qualities such as intelligence to robots.

THE STUDY

The study was setup at an orthopedic department, where the robot was running for 13 days. The staff was observed, and at the end of the study, they were interviewed or got questionnaires. Below we will describe the setup of the study in more detail.

The orthopedic department

The orthopedic department cares for patients with fractures, or even amputations, after surgery. There are about 20 staff working during the daytime, such as assistant nurses, nurses, doctors, and administrative staff. The corridors are busy. Apart from the staff moving in and out from rooms with blood tests, medicine and more, there are patients practicing to walk with or without walkers in the corridors, often getting assistance from one or several staff. Cleaners are coming with cleaning machines or garbage cans on wheels, and visitors are coming to see patients. Sometimes the staff uses a scooter to move inside and between departments. Specialized transportation staff is called in to move patients in beds or wheelchairs to surgery or back from other departments. Along the corridors are beds, medicine cabinets on wheels and other objects that are put aside. The department does not have any system to send samples to the lab (e.g. no pneumatic tube-mail, small freight elevators), so staff members need to leave their department and hand over samples in person. Staff also goes to the lab to collect blood plasma. The distance between the orthopedic department and the lab is about 200 meters, but as they are located on different floors, the walk between them necessitates use of elevators. It takes about 10 minutes to walk back and forth.

The robot system setup

Even though the robot was present and moving in the department for 13 days, the staff had in total five days to use it for transports. The remaining days had to be spent on making the robot create a map of the environment, technical support, and to set up the stations, etc.

The robot is designed to carry small goods, to drive with trailers, assist staff with bed transports and to guide people. This study focused on transportation of blood samples to the laboratory. The robot team who developed the robot has been in contact with some of the staff during the design process. Meetings have been held both at the hospital and the robot lab, to discuss potential robot support with staff.

The robot is 120 cm tall, 65 cm wide and 115 cm long. It has a safe (cabinet) that is opened and locked with an automatic latch using an RFID key card. Inside the safe is a forklift that the robot uses for automatic loading and unloading of goods. The robot design also has a big stop button on top. In this study this was removed to make space for a laptop. A technician would follow the robot around

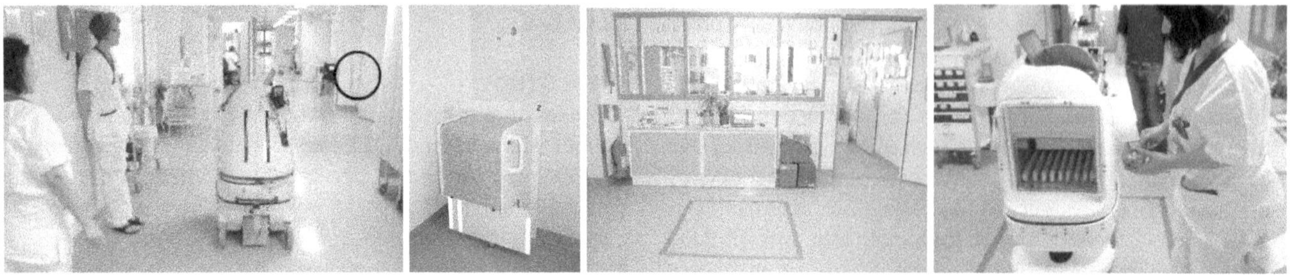

Figure 1. a) At department (box marked with ring). b.) Box close-up. c.) Station at the nurses' office. d.) Staff loading robot

with a wireless connection, prepared to support potential technical challenges.

The robot shape was initially inspired by the appearance of penguins and how they may be experienced; cute and not threatening, and the color is bright lime green. The robot moves in the middle of the corridors, and can speed up in some areas (for example in the hospital's basement where few people are walking). It uses natural landmark based localization. In the study, usage of the elevators by the robot was manually handled by the robot's technician, even though autonomous usage of the elevators was considered feasible to implement.

The orthopedic department was provided with two stations where samples could be sent or received, and one for charging. Firstly, the robot could be sent to be loaded and unloaded outside the nurses' office (see figure 1c). Secondly, a box at the department could be loaded or unloaded (see figure 1a,b). The box locked with a latch using an RFID key. The robot could automatically unlock it when docking or loading goods and then lock it again when leaving the station. A second box was placed outside the lab, a few floors down from the orthopedic department. The charging station was located in the patient cafeteria in the orthopedic department.

Ordering a transport

The staff had a computer at which they could place their orders, situated next to the nurses' office (See figure 1c). The staff would do a blood test, go to the computer and place an order, then typically wait for the robot to come to the marked spot, and load the goods directly into the robot.

Robot introduction

The robot team and the researchers held a general introduction to the robot with the staff during their daily coffee break. This included a presentation of the robot and its intended use, and of the team that would be present during the study. Two people from the staff were asked to test the robot by sending and receiving an order (box of chocolate). We also handed out and received consent forms for the study, and encouraged the staff to ask questions. Their questions included: Is it a he or she? How does it know its way? One person was worried about how to check ID if the robot would be used to collect blood from the lab. Information on how to conduct transportations with the robot was left in the coffee area.

Data collection

The study used a qualitative and ethnographic inspired methodology and research focus. We used several complementing methods to gather field-data. In total, 25 people shared their experience, either through an interview or a questionnaire. This was complemented with observations taken as notes. We focused especially on how the robot was perceived by the staff, its intended tasks and behavior in general. We also aimed to collect spontaneous comments about the robot, coming from staff, visitors and patients when meeting it in the corridor. One researcher from an independent research institute conducted the data collection, together with an assistant, who was hired by the robot team to support the study.

General interviews

During the last days of the study, we held general interviews with 12 people from the staff. Their names have been anonymized in the following text.

Seven of the interviews were held with the staff at the department, including a managing nurse (Kerstin), two nurses (Karl, Laura), and four assistant nurses (Peter, Emma, Sophia, Petra). The assistant nurses Sophia and Petra had only met the robot in the corridors, whereas all other interviews had also used it. The questions involved their current work practices, for example which type of errands they are doing, and how they felt about that. The questions also focused on the robot support, expectations and impressions of, for example, meeting it in the corridor and using it in their practice.

Three staff members from the lab were interviewed. One of the interviews included Anders, a biomedical analyst, and Elin, assistant nurse (responsible for the blood sample handling-in at the lab). They had collected blood samples from the box station together. The other interviewee, Anne, who was a biomedical analyst, had collected goods directly from the robot. The questions focused on their perspective to let a robot deliver blood samples, and how they felt about adapting their routines towards a potential robot system.

Two people from the cleaning staff, Johanna and Sonja, were interviewed together. Both had met the robot when cleaning the department. The questions focused on their overall experience of meeting the robot and potential concerns for their cleaning practice.

Four interviews were held with seven people visiting the hospital, found close to the entrance, when the robot was passing by. Four were women and three were men. One man and woman were approximately in their thirties, and the others were approximately between 60 to 75 years old.

Questionnaires

11 questionnaires were answered by four nurses and seven assistant nurses, who not had been interviewed. The questionnaires had similar questions as the interviews and were handed out after the robot had left the department. From the people who answered the questionnaires, five had used it once and six had met the robot in the corridor.

Observations

Overall, two people have conducted about 85 hours of observations, taking notes of peoples' reactions, for instance when meeting the robot in the corridor.

Analysis

We used an open coding qualitative analysis, using a bottom-up approach, starting from the data to find categorizations. The analysis covered transcribed interview data, observation notes, as well as questionnaires. Related quotations and observation notes were put in similar categories, and we went over the material several times during this process. The final categories are reflected in this paper, such as the staff's existing routines, expectations, using the robot to run errands, robotic support in development, and safety. Finally we have categorized perceived qualities into the different perspectives that are discussed in our model.

RESULTS

The results present the staff's perspective on running errands, their expectations of getting robot support, and their experience of the robot.

Perspectives of running errands between departments

All staff in the study confirmed that they carry out some kind of errands during their work. A majority of the staff carry out three or more different types of errands. The routine errands include transporting blood samples to the laboratory, beds, patients, trailers, medicine and food. In the case of blood samples, some are urgent and need to be analyzed by the lab immediately. Still, all are transported directly to the lab after being taken. The lab results are sent back to the nurses through the hospital's computer system.

The majority of the staff described that they run their errands 3-5 times per day, and others indicated that they usually run errands once per day or once almost every day. However, the number of the errands varies from day to day. Laura said the following about running errands in the department: "It is of course time-consuming, the time is taken from us." Assistant nurse Petra expressed that the errands cause some staff to "disappear from the department", so "if you can get help with it and avoid running, then it is good." Not all of the staff members were negative about running errands. Nurse Karl described them as a way to get some "breathing space" and that it's nice to "get a little rest from the department during those minutes."

Expectations of robot support

Early expectations about the robot's appearance may be inspired by science fiction or other prior media encounters with robots. Anne (at the lab) said: "if you think about robots, they are usually twitchy and edgy, with arms." Assistant nurse Peter said: "I thought.. it was not like that, I thought it was a small human [...] wheels and arms maybe, like the ones that you see the Japanese having".

During the first days, we held an introduction meeting, and some of the staff described the idea of getting help from a robot as something "new and exciting". Some considered the robot as "the future" and when fully developed as "a big help" to the department. However, in line with this, some also expressed their worries about reduction of staff.

Using the robot to run errands

Overall, the robot was used for about 20 transportations during the 5 days that it was available for the staff. Half of the transports were real blood samples and the rest were staged transportations, all done by 11 people in the staff. The nurses primarily took blood samples in the morning, and this was the most busy time at the department. This was also the time when the robot was used to send real blood samples. Some of the staff used the robot to send real blood samples several times, and one nurse even sent an urgent test on a busy morning. For technical reasons, we had to follow the robot on its transports. Some staff only sent staged goods once or twice, such as an empty blood sample. Whenever they used the system for the first time, we explained the procedure as they placed an order and used the RFID.

Most transports were ordered from the office station, putting the goods directly in the robot. In fact, we ran into technical difficulties unloading a box station with the robot, so the nurses were eventually asked to send their order from the robot instead of the box station. Several of the staff expressed that it felt inefficient to wait for the robot to come to the office station. Kerstin, the managing nurse, said: "It was slow before it got to the right place". Several described that in stressful moments they wouldn't use the robot in the future if they would have to stand and wait. The managing nurse also suggested that the robot should have a signal when it was ready, but also said that in fact it would have been easier to simply leave the tests at the box station, instead of in the robot.

Robotic support in development

Nine people from the questionnaires wanted a robot to conduct transportations for them, two did not. One wrote "Short distances. Big and clumsy robot" and the other gave no explanation.

According to a majority of the staff at the department, the robot could potentially help them to save time, unburden them, and give them more time for the patients. The majority of them were positive towards using the robot to run errands such as for blood samples, and transport of trailers or beds. All interviewed staff was positive about robot support to offload tasks, but also expressed that this was a system under development. Assistant nurse Peter said that "It's really good I think, but it needs more development". Manager nurse Kerstin expressed: "I'm more positive now, I really am. I believe in this, that it could offload somewhat for the staff, and that it is so easy to use with only one click on the computer and then order". However, she also said: I guess there's more to develop" and expressed the need for a prioritizing function, so that urgent transports could be prioritized; not having to wait for the robot; and to solve the technical issues such as opening the elevators (this would also be implemented in a fully working system). Several interviewees expressed that there is a limit for the kind of errands which the robot could support. For example, nurse Karl would never let the robot transport patients and was skeptical to let the robot guide visitors. "It would feel strange… (..) Maybe it turns out well the day it happens, but I'm skeptical about it."

Safety

Overall, the staff was concerned about the patients and their potential reaction to the robot. They stressed that the patients' wellbeing and safety should be prioritized. A common concern about getting the robot in the department turned out to be the doubt if the robot would really stop and "properly identify situations when someone is in the way?" or if it would drive into people. The department has patients with fractures, recent surgery and limited mobility, who need to move in the corridors. Peter commented: "There are several hip-surgery patients that do not know the machine". Thus, the staff was concerned if the robot would run into someone or would be in the way of their work, and some also expressed that the corridor was narrow.

Towards the end of the study, Nurse Karl said that: "If there is something in the way - he'll move, and he stops if someone is approaching fast. I think it seems safe. But I don't know if I would have trusted it as much if you weren't here and could stop him if needed." Managing nurse Kerstin said that: "I think it feels good. It stops when it feels an obstacle. […] that was a sort of a concern […]. You may be scared if patients would be there, and if it would react quickly enough. But, I think it feels good."

The staff was also concerned about issues such as if the goods were safe: "will it lay still and not break?" That would lead to "having to take an extra blood sample from a patient." When loading the robot, several would put very small goods between the forklift's rails, instead of on top of them as intended. It was suggested that the forklift would need a clear instruction describing the correct way of placing goods as well as a container.

Some routines rely on, for example, that patient IDs are double checked by staff that are handling out blood as well as with staff that are collecting blood at the lab. Thus, introducing a robot would require a change in those routines, which also was pointed out by Karl. Another issue is the RFID keys, which were pointed out as a safety risk, in case they would be misplaced.

ASCRIBING QUALITIES TO THE ROBOT

When analyzing our results we found that the robot was ascribed qualities which we found reflected different perspectives, viewing it as – an alien, a hospital worker, a colleague, a machine, or a mixture of these. These are not exclusive and can be overlapping, but supported our understanding of the experiences of the robot in this semi-public hospital environment. Thus, users or encounters could see the robot as an alien in certain aspects and as a worker at the hospital in other aspects. Also, this perspective is likely change over time, for example from alien to work-partner as the robot becomes more familiar. There is a difference in how something appears at first sight and how is may be perceived over time.

Despite of the penguin design inspiration, the robot was named "Kermit" by Karl, a name that quickly caught on. This was likely inspired by the green color. Almost all of the staff perceived the robot as being big, even at the end of the study. However, some also described the robot as "a little green pea", "a little guy" and as the French children's book character "Barbapapa". Several of the staff described that they like the robot's appearance because it feels "round, cute and human" and "not that edgy" as other equipment at the department. Karl pointed out that the staff had discussed their personal preferences between pink and green of the robot and that his own choice was green because: "It's a cool color". Kerstin expressed it as being a "lovely color."

An alien

How is the robot experienced for those who find it unfamiliar, for example for encounters? In our case, the overall design is intended to appear friendly but not invite explorative interaction. Still, this may be perceived as something alien for people who are unfamiliar with it. Apart from vacuum cleaners [43], and robot toys [18], there are few examples of robots in semipublic work environments such as offices, hospitals and schools. Thus, a science fiction inspired perspective of robots is prominent among many people [19]. Even informed staff might not know what to expect from an existing robotic product. Similar to findings by Siino and Hinds [40], the robot was described by several participants as a novelty and as being the future, inferring a sort of distance towards the robot.

Several staff were initially wondering: "Does it talk?". When we arrived at the hospital with the robot, and tried to find a space for the robot, someone in the staff was joking with the manager, saying "couldn't it be in your office?" Overall, people looked skeptical when they saw the robot, and some in the robot-team even felt that they were not welcome the first few days. The robot was commented on as being big and clumsy, before it had even been tested by the staff. The robot movement and behavior in the corridors was also unfamiliar for some. In the current design, people needed to get close to the robot before it changed paths. Moreover, the robot would move in the middle of the corridor in order to avoid doors that might be opened. Both of the cleaners, Johanna and Sonja, expressed that they would watch out when the robot was coming. Sonja said "You get unsure and you stand there and wonder where it is going".

The alien perspective was also found among visitors that did not know the robot and what to expect from it. Several visitors commented that it felt strange to meet the robot, even though they perceived it to move slowly. One visitor asked if it was intended for the moon, suggesting that it looked similar to something that is used in space. Overall, people appeared to be curious about the robot and asked: "What is it?", "What does it do?"

With an alien perspective, we believe that either people may lack a point of reference, or they may have very vague reference that does not support them in understanding how to interact with the robot or what to expect from it. It is likely that an alien perspective will keep occurring for those who are unfamiliar with the robot unless robots become more standardized everyday artifacts. In our case, people were wondering if the robot could talk, even though the design does not have any signifiers suggesting this (e.g. a mouth or face). Thus, it is especially important to consider how to support encounters to make correct first affordances, and eventually move beyond an alien perspective.

A machine

Another perspective that we found was to consider the robot as a (somewhat familiar) device or machine, instead of something alien. This perspective suggests that people describe the robot with a clear point of reference. For example, nurse Karl described it "like the cleaners' cleaning machine." Assistant nurse Sophia said that "it is small machine, an unburdening-machine", that has "no personality, it's a device", "like a small moving thing". Similar to a perspective of using a machine, Anne (a biomedical analyst at the lab) expressed the opinion that "robots are not personal". This machine perspective is different from the alien perspective, as it occurs when people use a machine as a reference point. Several visitors asked "Is it a cleaning machine?", and others suggested that it was "a cleaning robot" when being asked by the researchers about what "that thing" was. We characterized their perspective as a machine perspective, as this suggest that they have some sense of what to expect from the robot. This supports previous studies that describe how anthropomorphizing or even metaphors is a psychological mechanism to reduce the complexity that the unfamiliar results in [16]. In this case people who do not know what the robot is or does are still ascribing it qualities that they find familiar such as relating it to a cleaning machine.

The machine perspective raises questions about what metaphors potentially should be a part of a robotic design. Is it suitable to design the robot so that it appears similar to something people already are familiar with? In our study, Karl referred the robot to appear like the cleaners' cleaning machine and some visitors also referred it to this. As Norman and others have pointed out, metaphors are not always suitable to explain something unfamiliar [33]. If the metaphor is taken too literary, it can make the situation worse, by suggesting functionality or leading to a conceptual model that does not support a correct understanding of the system. If people would think that the cleaning machine has escaped from the cleaner when it is moving alone, this might not be a suitable metaphor. However, if people see this as a more futuristic cleaning machine that is cleaning autonomously, this may be an appropriate metaphor. In this specific case, personnel, visitors, staff, and patients that are not familiar with the robot, are not intended to interact with it either. Thus, the robot is intended to appear friendly and to be seen, but not provide affordances that invite people to interact and play with it. For example, there is no mouth (and the robot is not talking) and there is nothing in the design that is supposed to look like eyes.

A worker at the hospital

This perspective suggests that the robot takes a role as a worker at the hospital. From a perspective of looking upon the robot as a worker, it was clear that the robot should present itself as being part of the staff or the equipment at the hospital for visitors and patients. For example, the assistant nurse Peter suggested that, "It should be obvious that the robot works at the hospital. For example we have white coats." He even suggested that some kind of medical sign on the robot should show to which department it belonged. As a robot worker, it should also be seen clearly. Several in the staff pointed out that the current color was good "because you see it clearly", and "it should be green or orange or something like that. You see it [the color] well, clearly." Argyle [2] describes how both people and animals use appearance as means of communication, and at hospitals, it is usually quite clear who are the doctors, nurses, cleaners and patients (pajamas). Medical uniforms impress with medical expertise, through creating social distance (ibid). Similarly, a robot can indicate that it works at the hospital and reflect some competence.

A worker at the hospital also has to be credible, perform his/her tasks well, while not breaking social conventions or introduce new risks, such as running into people.

A work partner

For some, the robot was described almost as a work partner or something that you have a personal relation with. We believe that this is something that requires that the robot becomes familiar in one's practices, and also has proven that it is successful as a worker for an individual.

Meeting the robot in the corridor was for nurse Laura a thing that "feels good, almost like meeting a colleague." This is a very different perspective from for example assistant nurse Sophia, who only had met the robot in the corridor and saw no personality, but merely a moving machine.

Overall, the staff was first reluctant to find a space for the robot, and several expressed that they experienced the robot as being too big and clumsy. However, a few days later, we were observing a change in attitude. The robot had then been moving around in the department and shown that it did not bump into people, that it stayed out of the way, that the overall system was easy to use, and that the goods were delivered successfully. The nurse Karl said that he did not believe the robot could do all that: "First I hated it. It was big and ugly. Now it's not so much in the way anymore. It has a good place to be at". At the end of the study, Karl described it with qualities such as "cute" and "intelligent, discrete, because it is never in the way and it is reliable". He also said that "[the robot] is like a colleague who goes with samples, so I can skip going myself and can devote my time to something else instead. He is not just a machine. A couple of us admired him yesterday because he was so cute when he went away." Several of the other staff also described the robot using words as "cute", "cool", and "clever". From an "emerging intelligence" perspective, this reflects how people, when noticing that a machine manages changing conditions and work in their practice, may refer to it as being intelligent [45].

Some staff are only trusted for certain tasks, and this is also true with robots. Nurse Karl noted that the robot only should do "errand boy job". "I would never send a patient-transport with a robot," he said. Concerning the division of labor the managing nurse Kerstin said: "I don't think it should reduce our staff. ... It is a complement so we can avoid running around in the hospital. We do many things now that could be avoided." Lacking patient contact is one of the greatest frustrations when working as a nurse [34]. However, nurses do not only want to give practical care (e.g. give an injection), but need time for personal contact to get a good overview of the patient situation. This implies that design solutions that reduce routines and administrative work that takes time from patients, can make the overall work experience for the nurses more enjoyable. This may also affect the perception of the robot, if it is successful or not, to provide a more joyful work situation.

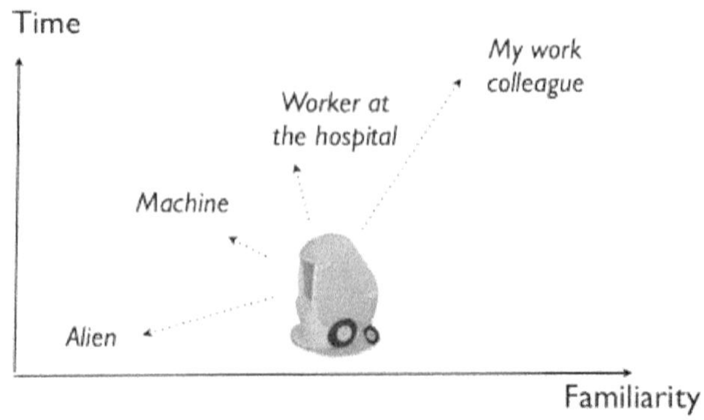

Figure 2: Utopian model over different user perspectives of robot qualities and how this may be affected by familiarity and time. Familiarity refers to if a robot successfully fits and contributes to the existing work practice.

DISCUSSION & FUTURE WORK

The theoretical outcome of this case study is presented as perspectives describing the robot as an alien, a machine, a hospital worker, and a work partner. This is a limited study, but the perspectives contribute to an increased understanding of robots in semi-public environments, reflecting on these as more general design challenges. The meaning of a technology "can only be described and its significance appreciated in the context of its uses and its users" ([10]:42). For Karl, the robot was both like a machine, and intelligent, and like a colleague. This exemplifies of how perspectives can mutually coexist, even for the same person. In some aspects or situations, it may be seen as a machine and in others, a kind of colleague.

The alien perspective suggests a design challenge when people do not have much experience with the robot, and do not feel comfortable or know what to expect, when they meet it. With more robots present in society, it is likely that the alien perspective will dissolve into the machine perspective and beyond, as people can get a better point of reference for robots due to a greater number of experiences with them. In the mean time, robots need to be designed with suitable signifiers and preferably provide references to machines that people are familiar with.

We exemplify the different perspectives in a model (See Figure 2). This could be read as a *utopia*, as many robotic designs (including the one presented here) may not be considered as a work colleague by most users. Only when a robot becomes familiar and proves to be successful, for example leading to more joyful work for the nurses overall, it may be perceived as somewhat intelligent or a kind of colleague. This also implies that even though a robot is designed with technically considered advanced 'social skills' (such as talking, understanding speech, face recognition etc), it may still not reach the level of being considered as a work colleague. Similarly, Groom and Nass discuss how design or research efforts that aims to position robots as human-like 'team-mates', rather than complements in specific situations and tasks, is unhelpful, and arguably an impossible goal to achieve [24].

Familiarity and *time* is required for people to consider that the robot is intelligent and may support them as some kind of colleague. The axis "familiarity" is a pre-condition for trust. We cannot trust something that is totally unknown, only gamble [25]. Our study was limited in duration, and even though staff became somewhat familiar with the robot, it is difficult to say if they have trust in the system. Familiarity is required in order to eventually start to trust that the robot will not run into people, make work more enjoyable etc. Karl expressed that he did not know if he would have trusted the robot moving about without the technicians. Kerstin instead said she felt good about it, as the robot had been stopping when it should. Time affects the possibility of interpretation [32], and more interactions over time will thus affect peoples' interpretation of the robot. Even if interpretations are constrained by the artifact, various groups' purposes, context, power, and knowledge base also affect interpretation [34].

This case study provides preliminary and limited findings of how robotic support can be perceived in a hospital setting. In a longer study, it would be interesting to investigate how the robot affect the staffs' collaborative activities such as coordination, and how it could be regarded by more people as "intelligent" in relation to their practice. Moreover it would be interesting to look into the aspect of trust as well as potential novelty-effects that only a larger long-term study can provide knowledge about.

CONCLUSION

We have conducted a case study of the initial reactions to a robot transporting blood samples at a hospital. Our contribution beyond the actual study, is a preliminary categorization of qualities that were ascribed to it, suggesting different perspectives that robot technology can be perceived as; an alien, a machine, a worker and a colleague. These may mutually coexist and are related to time and familiarity with the robot.

ACKNOWLEDGMENTS

This research has been funded by the LIREC project (FP7/2007-2013) and Riksbankens Jubileumsfond (Flexit).

REFERENCES

1. Appadurai, A. 1988. The Social Life of Things: Commodities in Cultural Perspective, Cambridge University Press, Reprint Edition
2. Argyle, M. 2007. Bodily Commmunication.. Great Britain, Norfolk. Routledge. Second Edition. First published 1975.
3. Arvola, M. 2008. Interaction design qualities: Theory and practice. In proc. of NordiCHI 2010. ACM.
4. Bardram, J. E. 2009. Activity-based computing for medical work in hospitals. ACM Trans. on computer-Human Interactions, 16(2): p. 1-36.
5. Bardram J. E. and Bossen. C. 2005. Mobility Work: The Spatial Dimension of Collaboration at a Hospital. Comput. Supported Coop. Work 14, 2 (April 2005), 131-160.
6. Barley, S. R. 1988. The social construction of a machine: Ritual, superstition, magical thinking and other pragmatic responses to running a CT Scanner. In M. Lock and D. Gordon (Eds.), Knowledge and practice in medicine: Social, cultural, and historical approaches (pp. 497-540). Boston: Kluwer Academic Publishers.
7. Bennett, W. L., Stroebel, C. F. and Glueck, B. C. 1969. Hospital automation: something more than a computer. In Proc.AFIPS '69 (Spring). ACM, New York, NY, 709-714.
8. Berg, M. 1999. Accumulating and Coordinating: Occasions for Information Technologies in Medical Work. CSCW 8, 4 (October 1999), 373-401
9. Berg, M. and Bowker, G. 1997. The multiple bodies of the medical record. The sociological Quarterly. 38, 3. pp. 513-537.
10. Blomberg, J. 1986. "The Variable Impact of Computer Technologies on the Organization of Work Activities". Proceedings of CSCW 86 (Austin, Texas), pp.35-42.
11. Chen, T. L. and Kemp, C. C. 2010. Lead me by the hand: evaluation of a direct physical interface for nursing assistant robots. In Proceedings HRI '10. ACM, New York, NY, 367-374.
12. Dietsch, J. 2010. People Meeting Robots in the Workplace. IEEE Robotics and Automation Magazine, June 2010.
13. Dourish, P. 2001. Where the Action is: The Foundations of Embodied Interaction. MIT Press, Cambridge, MA, USA.
14. Evans, J., Krishnamurthy, B., Barrows, B., Skewis, T. and Lumelsky, V. 1992. Handling real-world motion planning: a hospital transport robot. IEEE Control Systems Magazine,15 – 19.
15. Epley, N., Waytz, A., Akalis, S., and Cacioppo, J. T. 2008. When we need a human: Motivational determinants of anthropomorphism. Social Cognition, 26, 143-155.
16. Eyssel, F. Kuchenbrandt, D. and Bobinger, S. 2011. Effects of anticipated human-robot interaction and predictability of robot behavior on perceptions of anthropomorphism. In Proc. HRI'11: 61-68.
17. Fernaeus, Y., Håkansson, M., Jacobsson, M. and Ljungblad, S. 2010. How do you play with a robotic toy animal?: a long-term study of Pleo. In Proc. IDC '10. ACM, New York, NY, 39-48.
18. Fernaeus, Y., Jacobsson, M., Ljungblad, S. and Holmquist, L. E. 2009. Are we living in a robot cargo cult?. In Proc. HRI '09. ACM, New York, NY, 279-280

19. Fong, T., Nourbakhsh, I. and Dautenhahn, K. 2003. A Survey of socially interactive robots. Robotics and Autonomous Systems, 42(3-4). p143--166.
20. Forlizzi, J. and DiSalvo, C. 2006. Service robots in the domestic environment: a study of the roomba vacuum in the home. In Proc. HRI '06. ACM, New York, NY, 258-265.
21. Goffman, E. 1990. The presentation of self in everyday life, Penguin Group (First published 1959).
22. Goris, K. Saldien, J. and Lefeber. D. 2009. Probo: a testbed for human robot interaction. In Proceedings of the 4th ACM/IEEE international conference on Human robot interaction (HRI '09). ACM, New York, NY, USA, 253-254.
23. Grandey, A. 2008. Emotions at work: A review and research agenda. In C. Cooper & J. Barling (Eds.), The SAGE Handbook of Organizational Behavior (Vol. 1, pp. 234-261). Thousand Oaks, CA.
24. Groom, V. and Nass, C. 2007. Can robots be teammates? Benchmarks in human–robot teams. Interaction Studies 8:3 (2007), 483–500.
25. Heath, C. and Luff. P. 1996. Documents and Professional Practice: 'bad' organisational reasons for 'good' clinical records. In Proc. Computer-Supported Cooperative Work. Boston, MA USA. pp: 354-363.
26. Latour, B. 2005. Reassembling the Social - An Introduction to Actor-Network-Theory. Oxford University Press.
27. Lewis J. D. and Weigert, A. 1985. Trust as a social reality. Social Forces. Vol.63. No.4. pp. 967-985.
28. Ljungblad, S. 2008. Beyond users: Grounding technology in experience Doctoral thesis. Department of Computer and Systems Sciences. Stockholm University.
29. Mentis, H., Reddy, M. and Rosson, M. B. 2010. Invisible emotion: information and interaction in an emergency room. In Proc. CSCW '10. ACM, New York, NY, USA, pp. 311-320.
30. Mutlu, B. and Forlizzi, J. 2008. Robots in Organizations: The Role of Workflow, Social, and Environmental Factors in Human-Robot Interaction. In Proc. HRI'08, Amsterdam, pp. 287-294.
31. Nass, C. & Moon, Y. (2000). Machines and mindlessness: Social responses to computers. Journal of Social Issues, 56(1), pp. 81-103.
32. Norman. D. A. 1998. The Invisible Computer. MIT Press, Cambridge, MA, USA
33. Norman, D. A. 2011. Living with complexity. MIT Press, Cambridge, Massachusetts, USA
34. Orlikowski, W. J. and Gash, D. C. 1994. Technological frames: making sense of information technology in organizations. ACM Trans. Inf. Syst. 12, 2, pp. 174-207.
35. Passerotti, C.C. and Peters, C.A. 2006. Robotic-assisted laparoscopy applied to children. World J Urol. 2006 Jun;24(2):193-7.
36. Pingel, B. and Robertsson, H. 1998. Yrkesidentitet i sjukvård – position, person och kön. Arbete och hälsa 1998: 13 Vetenskaplig skriftserie. Arbetslivsinstitutet (In Swedish)
37. Reddy, M. P., Dourish, and W. Pratt. 2001. Coordinating Heterogeneous Work: Information and Representation in Medical Care. In Proc. of ECSCW'01 Bonn, Germany. 239-258
38. Reeves, B. and Nass, C. 1998. The Media Equation: How People Treat Computers, Television, and New Media Like Real People and Places. Cambridge University Press, New York, NY, USA.
39. Rossetti, M.D., Kumar, A. and Felder, R.A. 1998. Mobile robot simulation of clinical laboratory deliveries. In Proc.Winter Simulation, 1415 – 1422.
40. Siino, R. M. and Hinds, P. J. 2005. Robots, gender & sensemaking: Sex segregation's impact on workers' making sense of a mobile autonomous robot. In Proc. of ICRA'05, 2773-78.
41. Stolterman, E. and Löwgren, J. 2007. Thoughtful interaction design, MIT Press.
42. Suchman, L. 1987. Plans and Situated Actions. Cambridge University Press (1987).
43. Sung, J., Christensen, H. I. and Grinter, R. E. 2009. Robots in the wild: understanding long-term use. In Proc. HRI '09. ACM, New York, NY, 45-52.
44. Swisslog courier robots. Available at: http://www.swisslog.com/ Downloaded 2011-06-02
45. Symon, G., Long K. and Ellis, J. 1988. The coordination of work activities: Cooperation and conflict in a hospital context. In Proc. CSCW'88, 5,1,
46. Taylor, A. 2009. Machine Intelligence. In Proc. CHI'09. ACM, Boston, USA.
47. Turkle, S. (1984). The second self: Computers and the human spirit. New York: Simon and Schuster.
48. Venkatesh, M. Morris, G. Davis, and F. Davis. User acceptance of information technology. MIS Quarterly, 27(3):425–478, 2003.
49. Winograd, T. & Flores, C. 1987. Understanding computers and cognition: A new foundation for design. Reading, MA: Addison-Wesley.
50. Zivanovic, A. and Davies B. L. 2000. A robotic system for blood sampling. IEEE Trans Inf Technol Biomed. Mar 4(1): 8-14
51. Özkil, A.G., Zhun, F, Dawids, S., Aanes, H., Kristensen, J.K. and Christensen, K.H., 2009. Service robots for hospitals: A case study of transportation tasks in a hospital. IEEE Automation and Logistics, pp. 289-294.

Psychology of User Experience in a Collaborative Video-Conference System

Takashi Yamauchi
Texas A&M University
College Station, TX
takashi-yamauchi@tamu.edu

Takehiko Ohno, Momoko Nakatani, Yoichi Kato
NTT Cyber Solutions Laboratories
Yokosuka-shi, Japan
ohno.takehiko@lab.ntt.co.jp

Arthur B. Markman
University of Texas
Austin, TX
markman@psy.utexas.edu

ABSTRACT
The authors employ behavioral theories of human motivation and affect and present an explanation for why some CSCW experience is satisfying and engaging for a user. In a longitudinal experiment, participants were divided into four groups and solved two open-ended problems together using a video-conference system. Traditional metrics of usability and product acceptance were examined with respect to psychological variables such as personality, background knowledge, mindsets (i.e., implicit beliefs) and feelings toward group members. The results show that group-level mutual affect and implicit beliefs on one's ability (e.g., whether intelligence is fixed or malleable) are strong predictors of system usability and acceptability judgments. It is proposed that evaluating one's experience with a CSCW system is a meaning-making process and that the variables that modulate this process also influence subjective judgments of usability and acceptability of a complex collaborative system.

Author Keywords
User satisfaction; UX, psychology; affect; belief; usability

ACM Classification Keywords
H5.3. Group and Organization Interfaces: Theory and models; Computer-supported cooperative work

General Terms
Experimentation

INTRODUCTION
One reason why psychological theories can be useful for CSCW research is that they can provide a general explanation for why some computer-mediated experiences are satisfying and engaging for a user [8,19]. Conceptual frameworks such as information processing, affordance, and cognitive architecture have generated testable hypotheses and guidelines instrumental for single-user product design. However, these frameworks are not entirely feasible for CSCW interfaces because of added complexity inherent in group interaction [11]. What kind of conceptual fabric is needed to formulate theories of user experience in a CSCW environment?

To help improve group performance, CSCW researchers have identified important variables, such as group awareness, common ground, shared visual information and teamwork coordination, and have presented critical design principles and implementation procedures [1, 10, 16]. However, to make a "good" CSCW product, these pragmatic variables should be supplanted; the product should be not only useful but also *engaging* and *satisfying* for the users [13, 18]. But to make an engaging and satisfying product, it is crucial to know how users come to evaluate their experiences with a CSCW system.

Here, we propose a conjecture that psychological models of meaning-making (sensemaking) can provide useful frameworks for user experience in a CSCW setting much in the same way that affordance and cognitive architecture helped the evolution of single-user interfaces. We argue that the evaluation of one's experience in a collaborative setting is basically a meaning-making process, and the variables that intervene this process influence "user experience."

To test this idea, we developed an experimental study, where 29 college students were divided into four groups and solved two problems together in a 2-month period using a video-conference system. We examined subjective metrics of usability and product acceptance with respect to other psychological variables such as personality, background knowledge, implicit beliefs and feelings toward group members. Although improving the pragmatic properties of CSCW products is of prime importance, the focus of this paper is on the subjective side of user experience because this area has been relatively less explored in CSCW research.

In a nutshell, we show that group-level mutual affect and implicit beliefs (one's beliefs about intelligence and the world in general) influence participants' subjective judgments of system usability and acceptability. The influence of implicit beliefs becomes particularly strong when tasks are complex and demanding. A positive mutual affect among group members leads to increased product acceptance, and mutual affect is further reinforced by collective performance for problem solving.

In what follows, we first introduce the theoretical background on human motivation and affect, report one experimental study, and conclude with a discussion of theoretical implications of the results for CSCW research and practical implications for product design.

THEORETICAL BACKGROUND AND HYPOTHESES

Klein et al. [14] and Pirolli and Card [20] provide models of sensemaking [26]. The two models differ in specifics but share some basic properties. Sensemaking consists of dynamic processes of data selection and frame/schema revision. Relevant data are selected according to one's frame (prior knowledge/beliefs/mindsets), the data are interpreted and the frame is revised according to the interpretation. Sensemaking goes through cycles of this data selection/interpretation and frame/schema revision loop. Our central hypothesis is that user experience is a meaning-making (sensemaking) process. "Experience" does not come to people unambiguously. Experience is selected, sensed, represented, and interpreted by people [6]. In this process, beliefs and affects play critical roles. Beliefs guide what data to select and how to select them, and affect interferes with the evaluation of the data.

Group-level Mutual Affect

The importance of affect in product design is well known, but affect in HCI has pertained to a specific product. We think that group-level mutual affect (e.g., feeling of closeness of group members) can also be an important factor because affects are contagious and affects coming from unrelated sources can be easily fused into the evaluation of a product.

Much psychological research has shown that relatively simple manipulations of inducing a positive affect, such as viewing a comedy film for a few minutes or writing about happy events, influence subsequent decision making of unrelated objects. Surprisingly, affect influences judgments even when affective states elicited by an event are unrelated to the object of judgment [2].

Schwarz and Clore [22] present one of the most stunning demonstrations of affect contamination. In their experiment, the researchers interviewed subjects about their general happiness with their lives. Subjects were selected randomly and telephone-interviews were conducted on either a sunny day or a rainy day. Those who had an interview on a sunny day gave higher happiness ratings than those who had an interview on a rainy day. When the link between mood and weather was made clear to subjects, the ratings made on the rainy day went up, indicating that subjects' ratings about happiness were partly due to their erroneous generalization of their unhappy mood on the rainy day.

Affect misattribution occurs easily because of the tight neural connections between the limbic system and the prefrontal lobe, where evaluative information is weighted by emotions [3]. A similar misattribution is likely to happen in the judgment of usability and acceptability. Usability and acceptability of a product will be judged by pragmatic, hedonic, and aesthetic features of the product [13]. However, in making an actual judgment, a user will *interpret* his/her memories of experience. In this process, affective experience with group members can contaminate their evaluation [2].

Implicit Beliefs

Another important variable of a meaning-making process is people's mindsets (i.e., implicit beliefs) [6]. Collaborating with people to solve complex open-ended problems through a computer-mediated system requires sustained coordination [1]. In this context, belief about one's ability, such as whether one's intelligence is fixed or malleable, influences his/her experience.

Dweck [6] shows that people who assume that their intelligence is fixed and unchangeable (i.e., fixed intelligence belief) are likely to focus on performance-oriented goals (displaying one's own competence). In contrast, people who believe intelligence can be cultivated and is malleable (i.e., malleable intelligence belief) tend to focus on mastery-oriented goals (enhancing one's learning and understanding). These two types of goal-setting define people's experience particularly at the time of difficulties. People with a performance-oriented goal tend to give up easily, whereas people with a mastery-oriented goal tend to be more resilient at a time of setbacks because their goal is to improve their learning and understanding.

Implicit beliefs about intelligence (i.e., whether intelligence is fixed or malleable) have been shown to be one of the most reliable predictors of human performance, particularly when the task is challenging such as adolescents learning advanced mathematics, college students acquiring interpersonal skills, and company workers developing complex decision making skills [6].

Likewise, we postulate that people's implicit beliefs about intelligence influence their experience with a collaborative video-conferencing system. Those who think intelligence is malleable will have mastery-oriented proactive interactions with the product and their collaborators, and this proactive interaction will lead to a positive experience with the product. In the experiment described below, we tested the impact of mutual affect and implicit beliefs on usability and acceptability judgment of a video-conference system.

EXPERIMENT

In our 2-month-long experimental study, four groups of participants (seven to eight participants per group) met eight times using MeetingPlaza, a multi-party Web conferencing and collaboration system (http://www.meetingplaza.com); each group worked together to solve two different problems—one that was relatively easy and the other that was more challenging [15], and wrote two one-page white paper proposals together as a group using MeetingPlaza.

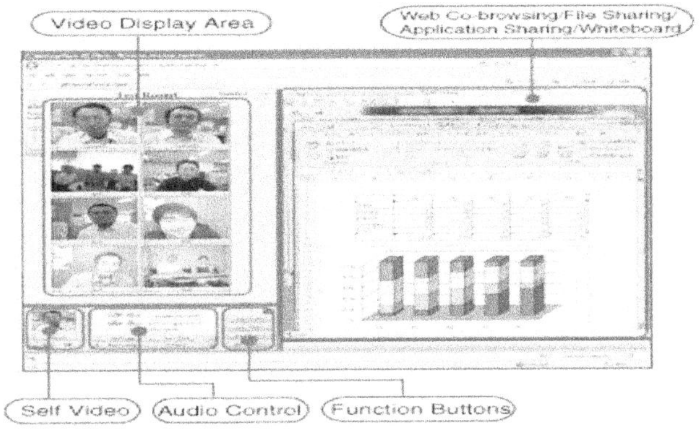

Figure 1. Screen shot of MeetingPlaza.

Participants interacted with each other under two different MeetingPlaza conditions—full and restricted. MeetingPlaza has web-, file-, whiteboard- and application-sharing functions that facilitate collaborative communication. For example, the web-share function allows participants in different locations to view the same web site on their own computers at the same time. The file-sharing and application-sharing functions help people in remote locations to view and manipulate the same file together (e.g., an MS Word file). In the full MeetingPlaza condition, all of these sharing functions were left intact. In the restricted MeetingPlaza condition, all of these sharing functions were disabled; thus, participants could communicate only with video and audio devices and had to write papers together without any file- or application-sharing functions. In this regard, the collaboration in the restricted MeetingPlaza condition was more difficult, while that in the full MeetingPlaza condition was relatively easy.

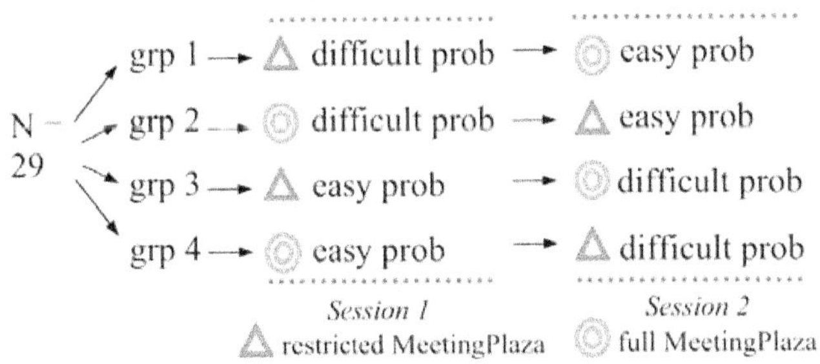

Figure 2.The design of the experiment.

In this manner, participants were divided into four groups, and solved two problems, difficult and easy, using restricted and full versions of MeetingPlaza.

Hypotheses and Predictions

On the basis of the theoretical background discussed previously, we formed the following hypotheses.

[H1] Group-level mutual affect (e.g., feelings of closeness toward group members) influences subjective judgments of system usability and acceptability. In particular, those who have high positive group-level affect should give high acceptability and usability ratings even when other psychological variables are controlled for.

[H2] Implicit beliefs of users influence usability and acceptability judgments. In particular, those who have a malleable intelligence belief should give favorable ratings.

[H3] The effect of implicit belief of intelligence is pronounced particularly when the problem is demanding and challenging, and collaboration is difficult and cumbersome. Specifically, it should be pronounced when participants are solving a difficult problem and when they are collaborating using restricted MeetingPlaza.

The rationales for these hypotheses are as follows. First, group-level mutual affect can be fused into the evaluation of the conference system, as a user makes a system evaluation based on his/her memory of the experience with a product. Thus, positive mutual affect will be translated into positive product evaluation [H1]. Next, users' implicit beliefs also influence system usability and acceptability judgments because users' beliefs determine how they interact with a product. Those who think intelligence is malleable will have mastery-oriented proactive interactions with the product, and this proactive interaction will lead to a positive experience with the product [H2].

Finally, people with a malleable intelligence belief tend to regard challenging situations as an opportunity for growth, whereas people with a fixed intelligence belief tend to regard challenging situations as a nuisance [6]. Thus, the same situation (e.g., solving a difficult problem) can be interpreted positively or negatively depending on their beliefs of intelligence. In this manner, the impact of implicit beliefs of intelligence will be magnified in difficult situations (e.g., solving the difficult problem or using restricted MeetingPlaza) [H3].

H1 and H2 were tested by applying regression analyses. H3 was tested by comparing the impact of intelligence beliefs under two conditions: the difficult and easy problem conditions, and the restricted and full MeetingPlaza conditions.

N=	29	Major: psychology = 16; public health = 2; political science, history, general studies, telecommunication, management, accounting, industrial engineering, electrical engineering, chemical engineering, nursing, nutrition = 1
(Male, Female)	(14, 15)	
Freshman	1	
Junior	5	
Sophomore	6	
Senior	12	
Graduate student	4	
Staff	1	
Average age (range)	21.1 (18~27)	

Table 1. Participant information

Participants. Thirty-two participants were recruited from the Texas A&M University community. They were assigned randomly to four groups. Three participants chose not to take part in the experiment after the first meeting. Thus, a total of 29 participants completed the two problem solving sessions (Table 1). Participants received a payment of $144 ($12 per hour for a total of 12 hours for their involvement). Bonus payments of $24~$48 were made to group members who produced the best and second-best white papers. In a separate experiment, 47 undergraduate students were recruited from the university psychology subject pool for the evaluation of the white papers submitted by the four groups.

Materials. We employed eight questionnaires to assess participants' implicit beliefs (beliefs about intelligence, morality and the world), personality (neuroticism, extraversion and psychoticism), technological literacy (computer-literacy and Internet-literacy), expectations (expected ease of use and expected usefulness of the product), perceived system usability, product acceptance and group-coherence (group-level affect, communication effectiveness and opinion convergence).

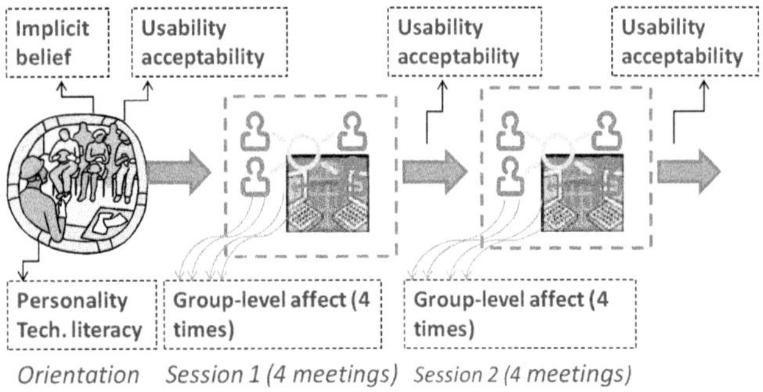

Figure 3.The logistics of the experiment.

Participants' implicit beliefs were assessed at the orientation meeting. Group-level coherence (affect, communication and opinion) was measured by electronic questionnaires given at the end of each meeting. Participants' subjective judgments of system usability and acceptability were collected three times in a two-month period, before using the system (at the orientation meeting), in the middle of using the system (after the fourth meeting), and at the end of the experiment (after the eighth meeting) (Figure 3). All the other questionnaires were given at the orientation meeting.

Implicit belief. The implicit belief questionnaire assesses the extent to which people conceptualize intelligence, morality, or the world as a dynamic or fixed construct (e.g., you can/cannot do much to change one's intelligence/morality/world; see Appendix) [6]. A factor analysis indicated that the three belief measures (intelligence, morality, and world) were not associated with respondents' gender, political attitudes, cognitive ability, confidence in intellectual ability, self-esteem, or morality. The questionnaire also had high internal reliability (α=0.84 – 0.96) and test-retest reliability of the measures over a 2-week period was 0.8 or higher [7].

Personality. Revised versions of the Eysenck personality questionnaire (EPQR) have been applied to predict people's job performance, religious beliefs, risk-taking behavior, and consumption behavior. Francis et al. [9] developed an abbreviated version of the EPQR that has four dimensions (extraversion, neuroticism, psychoticism, and lie scale) with six questions each. The questionnaire assesses personality of a person with three dimensions, extraversion (high-low tendency to seek external stimulation), neuroticism (high-low level of negative affect), and psychoticism (high-low level of impulsiveness). Following the suggestion in [9] we did not analyze lie-scale scores in the present experiment.

Technology literacy. The technology literacy questionnaire was developed for this experiment based on the digital literacy questionnaire by Hargittai [12]. Our questionnaire consists of two categories, computer literacy and Internet literacy, and a total of 10 questions. The computer literacy measure has four items related to knowledge about software (e.g., PowerPoint) and programming language (e.g., Java). Internet literacy consists of six items related to common Internet-based activities (e.g., tweeting or on-line shopping).

Expected ease of use and expected usefulness of the product. We modified Davis's Technology Acceptance Model (TAM) [4] and developed questionnaires assessing expected ease of use and expected usefulness of the product (six questions for each). We included the term "expected" because our questionnaires were given shortly after MeetingPlaza was introduced to the participants but before they actually used the system.

Usability. We employed Lewis's Computer System Usability Questionnaire (CSUQ; 19 questions) [17]. The CSUQ consists of three factors, system usefulness, information quality, and interface quality. The pre-usability questionnaire was given at the orientation meeting shortly after participants were introduced to the system but before using the system. The post-usability questionnaire was given twice at the end of session 1 and at the very end of the experiment.

Acceptability. To measure participants' behavioral intention of adopting the video-conference system, we created 10 acceptability questions based on [5, 25]. These questions assessed participants' intention to continue to use MeetingPlaza if the system were made available to them.

Group-level coherence. We measured group-level coherence of individual members with three dimensions, mutual affect (e.g., how close do you feel with each member of your group?), opinion convergence (e.g., how close was your opinion with that of each member of your group?), and communication effectiveness (e.g., how effectively did you communicate with each member of your group?). Every participant rated how he/she felt about each group member at the end of every group meeting (a total of eight meetings), the ratings he/she gave to all group members were averaged over affect, communication effectiveness and opinion convergence dimensions, and these average values were treated as his/her group-level affect, communication effectiveness and opinion convergence (see [23] for a similar measure).

Procedure. The experiment consisted of four segments: orientation, session 1, session 2, and paper evaluation. Below, we describe the segments in chronological order (Figure 4).

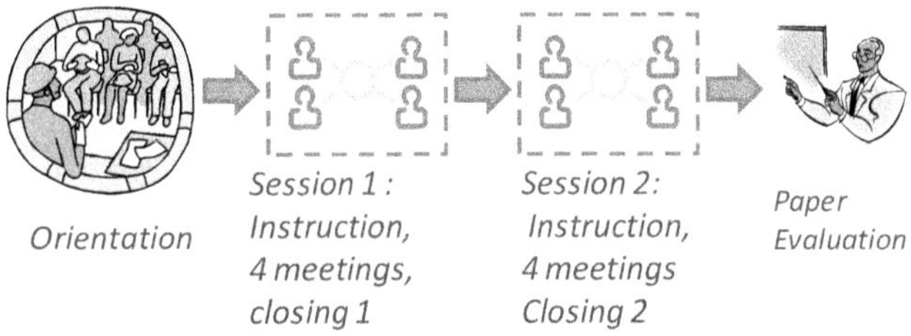

Figure 4. Four sections of the experiment

Orientation. The orientation meeting was held in a large classroom. First, participants indicated their implicit belief, personality and technology literacy, and then the experimenter introduced MeetingPlaza. At this stage, participants were allowed to view MeetingPlaza, but they were not allowed to use the system. After this brief instruction, participants indicated their expected ease of use and expected usefulness of MeetingPlaza, along with their expected usability of the product (pre-usability) and their intention of using the product in the future (acceptability).

Sessions 1 & 2. Approximately 1 week after the orientation meeting, participants were assigned to four groups, and each group had its first on-line meeting using MeetingPlaza. In this segment, participants received extended instruction and demonstrations of MeetingPlaza functions and tested MeetingPlaza by themselves. The groups that were assigned to the restricted version of MeetingPlaza were given instruction without any sharing functions. The groups that were assigned to the full version of MeetingPlaza were given full instruction of all sharing functions. Each group met twice a week, and discussed solutions for the assigned problems using MeetingPlaza. Each meeting lasted about 1 hour. Participants were discouraged from discussing the problems outside the problem-solving sessions. Although we had no mechanism to enforce this rule, we assumed that outside interactions were relatively rare because many of the participants did not know each other before the experiment.

Session 2 was given 1 week after the end of session 1. The procedure of session 2 was identical to that described in session 1.

Closings 1 & 2. Two closing meetings, closing 1 and closing 2, were held at the end of sessions 1 and 2, respectively. In closings 1 and 2, participants filled out the usability and product acceptance questionnaires. Closing 2 was the final meeting.

Paper evaluation. In a separate experiment, 47 undergraduate students participated in the paper evaluation experiment (male=23, female=23, unknown=1) and rated the eight papers written by the four groups in six categories (creativity, implementation, coherence, effectiveness, cost, and communication) on a 0–100 scale. They were encouraged to rate the papers in the same way a professor grades their papers in a classroom.

Design The problem-solving experiment was designed with a 2 (problems: difficult, easy) x 2 (sharing functions: restricted, full) x 2 (order: restricted-first, full-first) factorial. In the difficult problem condition, the difficult problem was given (i.e., how to improve the university), and in the easy problem condition, the easy problem was given (i.e., recommendations for freshman job search). In the restricted condition, all the sharing functions of MeetingPlaza were disabled. In the full condition, these sharing functions were made available to participants. In the restricted-first condition, restricted MeetingPlaza was given in session 1 and full MeetingPlaza was given in session 2. This order was reversed in the full-first condition. The four groups solved the two problems and used both the restricted and full versions of MeetingPlaza.

Results

All questionnaire responses were converted to a 0-1 scale such that the direction of the observed scores corresponded to the direction of the psychological dimensions in question. Thus, a high score corresponded to a high degree of the given dimension (e.g., extraversion in the personality questionnaire). In the implicit belief questionnaire, a high score corresponded to a high degree of malleable belief. This section summarizes the white paper evaluation, user profiles, acceptability and usability scores obtained in the orientation and closings 1 and 2, and evaluation of the three hypotheses.

White paper evaluation. Overall, white papers addressing the difficult problem (i.e., how to improve the university) received significantly lower evaluation scores (M=84.7, SD=6.9) than those addressing the easy problem (i.e., recommendations for freshman job search) (M=88.3, SD=5.3); $t(46)=4.75$, $p<0.01$. Given the difficult problem, there was a significant difference in group performance: $F(3, 136)= 9.1$, $MSE = 69.54$, $p<0.01$. Given the easy problem, no statistical difference was observed in group performance: $F(3, 138)=1.03$, $MSE = 24.75$, $p=0.38$. These results suggest that, as expected, the difficult problem was indeed more challenging and the difference in problem solving was pronounced in the difficult problem.

User profiles. The responses on the 10 questionnaires (Figure 5) show that there were no ceiling or floor effects, except for the responses regarding expected ease of use and expected usefulness. This problem will be discussed in the next paragraph and later in the Results section. ANOVAs (analysis of variance) comparing the four groups in each of the ten user profile dimensions showed that the mean profile scores of the four groups were not statistically different: F's(3, 25)<2.2, p's>0.11.

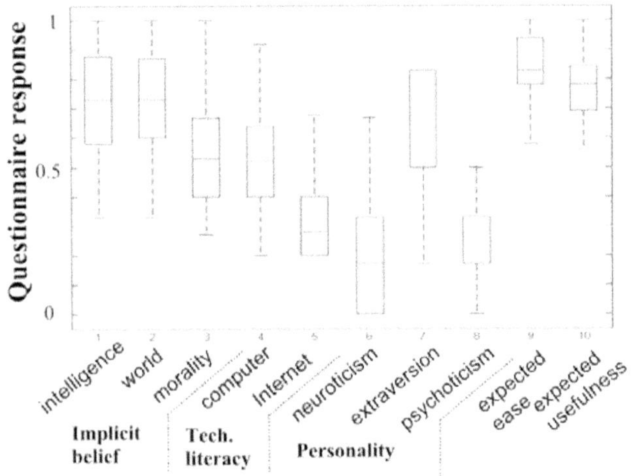

Note. The central mark and the edges of a box are the median and the 25th and 75th percentiles, respectively. The whiskers are the most extreme data points

Figure 5. Boxplots for questionnaire responses.

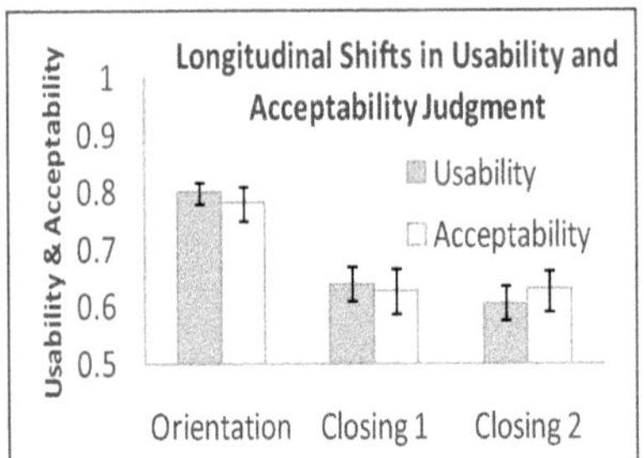

Figure 6. Usability/acceptability change

Acceptability and usability. Participants' initial reactions to MeetingPlaza were overwhelmingly positive. At the end of the orientation session, MeetingPlaza was regarded very favorably (usability, M=0.80, SD=0.11; acceptability, M=0.78, SD=0.17; Figure 6). However, the ratings of MeetingPlaza dropped significantly at closing 1 (usability, M=0.64, SD=0.64; acceptability, M=0.63, SD=0.21) and closing 2 (usability, M=0.61, SD=0.18; acceptability, M=0.63, SD=0.22). Two 3 (sequence: orientation, closing 1, closing 2) x 4 (group: 1, 2, 3, 4) ANOVAs revealed that this drop occurred uniformly in all groups: usability, F(2, 50)=18.61, MSE=0.02, p<0.01; acceptability, F(2, 50)=9.70, MSE=0.02, p<0.01. Neither the main effect of group nor the interaction between sequence and group was observed in both usability and acceptability measures: F's<1.5, p>0.24. These results suggest that MeetingPlaza created a positive impression on the college-age participants but the excitement dropped considerably once the participants used the product for problem solving, indicating that using the collaborative video-conferencing system was much more challenging than anticipated.

Evaluation of H1 & H2. The two hypotheses were evaluated by multiple regression analyses. To facilitate comparisons of coefficients, standardized coefficients (β) were reported, and to ameliorate the problem of multicollinearity, step-wise regression and regular multiple regression were employed together. In the step-wise regression procedure, the forward selection method was adopted with the entry criterion of 0.1 to ensure that all relevant predictors were included in the regression models. To control for the impact of group-specific properties (e.g., female-male ratios of individual groups), hierarchical linear regression was applied.

Independent variables were personality (psychoticism, extraversion, neuroticism), expected ease of use, expected usefulness, technology literacy (computer, Internet), implicit beliefs (intelligence, morality, world), and group-level coherence (mutual affect, communication effectiveness, opinion convergence). The group-level coherence variables were included in the models assessing closings 1 and 2 only. The values of independent variables and the dependent variables—usability and acceptability scores—were calculated by taking the mean of questionnaire scores of each participant.

Our step-wise regression analyses showed that there is a clear shift of predictors explaining system usability and acceptability. When usability and acceptability were measured at the orientation meeting, expected ease of use (usability, β=0.59, p<0.001), expected usefulness (acceptability, β=0.54, p<0.001) and Internet literacy (acceptability, β=-0.27, p=0.09) accounted for the dependent measures. However, once participants had used the system, the impacts of these predictors disappeared.

	Orientation		Closing 1		Closing 2	
	U	A	U	A	U	A
Neuroticism			*-.34**			
Usefulness		.54**				
Ease	.59**					
Internet literacy		*-.27*^{m}				
Group affect			.28^{m}	.29^{m}		**.35***
IB world				*-.45**	*-.41**	*-.38**
IB morality			*-.50***			
IB intelligence			.36*	.30^{m}	**.50****	.38*
R^2	.35	.45	.48	.39	.31	.40

*Note. U: usability; A: acceptability; IB: implicit belief. The numbers are standardized β coefficients. p**<0.01, 0.01≤p*<0.05, 0.05≤p^m<0.1. The numbers with bold face were analyzed with their cohort effect (see the main text).*

Table 2. Results of stepwise regression analyses

At closing 2, only group-level mutual affect (acceptability, β=0.35, p<0.05), implicit belief of intelligence (usability, β=0.50, p<0.01; acceptability, β=0.38, p<0.05) and of world (usability, β=-0.41, p<0.05; acceptability, β=-0.38, p<0.05) were significant predictors.

The results from multiple regression analyses were analogous to those described above. At the orientation session, the important predictors were expected ease of use (usability, β=0.52, p=0.09) and expected usefulness (acceptability, β=0.49, p=0.08). At closing 2, the most important predictors were implicit belief of intelligence (usability, β=0.45, p=0.08) and world (usability, β=-0.42, p=0.08), and group-level mutual affect (acceptability, β=0.47, p=0.09). These results suggest that implicit beliefs of intelligence and world and group-level affect were important predictors of usability and acceptability judgment at closings 1 and 2 even after other psychological variables, such as personality trait and technology literacy were controlled for.

Cohort effects: hierarchical linear regression. The two predictors, group-level mutual affect and implicit belief of intelligence, were evaluated with the data obtained from individual participants. Because MeetingPlaza is a collaboration tool, the impact of these variables should be scrutinized with respect to the properties obtained from each group. For this reason, we employed hierarchical linear regression models [21] and examined two questions: (1) whether the effects of the predictors—mutual affect and implicit belief of intelligence—would remain strong even after the variability of the four groups was taken into account (Model 1 in Table 3); and (2) whether group-specific properties—the ratio of female and male participants in each group and the white paper evaluation score that each group received—modulated the impact of the predictors (Model 2 in Table 3).

Here, we focused on the implicit belief of intelligence and group-level mutual affect at closing 2 (the bold faced numbers in Table 2) because the judgment scores obtained at closing 2 represent participants' final evaluations of MeetingPlaza and these two variables are our main theoretical concern.

Model 1	Individual layer: $Y_{ij} = \beta_{0j} + \beta_{1j}X_{ij} + u_{ij}$; Group layer: $\beta_{0j} = \gamma_{00} + u_{0j}$; $\beta_{1j} = \gamma_{10} + u_{1j}$
Model 2	Individual layer: $Y_{ij} = \beta_{0j} + \beta_{1j}X_{ij} + u_{ij}$; Group layer: $\beta_{0j} = \gamma_{00} + u_{0j}$; $\beta_{1j} = \gamma_{10} + \gamma_{11}W_j + u_{1j}$

Note. Subscript j denotes group ID and Y_{ij} represents the usability or acceptability score obtained from participant i of group j. β_{0j} and β_{1j} are intercepts and slopes of the regression line of group j, respectively. u's are error terms. γ_{00} is the overall mean of the usability/acceptability scores and γ_{10} is the mean of the slopes of the four groups. W_j represents group-specific values (e.g., either the female-male ratio of group j or the problem solving score of group j) and γ_{11} is the coefficient for predictor W_j.

Table 3. Hierarchical linear regression models

Our hierarchical models had two layers, individual and group (Table 3). Model 1 assumed that the intercepts and slopes of the regression lines (β_{0j} and β_{1j}) varied among the four groups; Model 2 further assumed that the slopes of individual-layer predictor β_{1j} (e.g., mutual affect) were modulated by a group-specific variable (problem-solving scores or female-male ratios). Note that the "group-level mutual affect" variable was included in the individual layer (i.e., X_{ij}), because the values of this variable were calculated for individual participants. The values of group-specific variable W_j (e.g., problem-solving scores or female-male ratios) were calculated for each group, not for each participant.

Our first question, whether the two predictors influenced the usability/acceptability scores beyond the variability of individual groups, was tested with the null hypothesis $\gamma_{10}=0$ in Model 1. This null hypothesis was rejected with t-ratio (3)=3.16, p=0.05 (implicit belief of intelligence) and t-ratio(3)=5.67, p=0.01 (group-level mutual affect), indicating that the impacts of the two predictors were significant even after considering the variability of the four groups.

Our second question, whether the group-specific properties (female-male ratios and problem-solving scores) influenced the impact of the two predictors, was tested with the null hypothesis of $\gamma_{11} = 0$ in Model 2. In the case of the implicit belief variable, this null hypothesis was *not* rejected in both the female-male ratio variable (t-ratio(2)=2.49, p=0.13) and the problem-solving score variable (t-ratio(2)=-1.49, p=0.28), suggesting that the effect of the implicit belief of intelligence was unlikely to be influenced by the group-specific properties. In the case of mutual affect, the female-male ratios did not influence the slopes of the mutual affect variable (t-ratio(2)=-2.68, p=0.12). However, the group-specific problem-solving scores were statistically related to the impact of mutual affect: t-ratio(2)=7.16, p=0.02. This result suggests that the association between mutual affect and product acceptance scores was particularly strong in the groups that earned high problem solving scores.

Evaluation of H3. In H3, we predicted that the impact of the implicit belief of intelligence would be pronounced particularly when the collaborative situation was difficult and cumbersome (e.g., the difficult problem condition and the restricted MeetingPlaza condition). The rationale of this prediction was that implicit beliefs of intelligence influence users' goal-setting behavior. Those who believe intelligence is fixed tend to regard challenging situations as setbacks, whereas those who believe intelligence is malleable tend to regard challenging situations as an opportunity for growth. Thus, depending on people's beliefs of the malleability of intelligence, the same situation can be interpreted positively or negatively [6]. If our hypothesis that user experience is a meaning-making process is plausible, the impact of implicit beliefs of intelligence should be pronounced in the difficult problem condition and in the restricted MeetingPlaza condition. To test this prediction, we applied regression analysis separately to the difficult / easy problem conditions and restricted / full MeetingPlaza conditions.

As predicted, our step-wise regression analyses showed that implicit belief of intelligence was a very strong predictor of usability and acceptability ratings in the difficult problem condition (usability, β=0.75, p<0.001; acceptability, β=0.54, p<0.01) but not in the easy problem condition (partial correlation between implicit belief of intelligence and usability, r=0.11, p=0.68; partial correlation between implicit belief of intelligence and acceptability, r=0.06, p=0.83), supporting the prediction that the implicit belief of intelligence would be particularly strong when participants were solving the difficult problem.

To further examine this idea, we separated participants into two groups—those who had a high intelligence malleability belief and a low intelligence malleability belief (median split)—and applied ANOVAs. A 2 (implicit belief of intelligence, high vs. low) x 2 (problem, easy vs. difficult) ANOVA revealed that the interaction between the two factors was significant for the usability measure: F(1, 27)=4.29, MSE=0.016, p<0.05, and the acceptability measure to some extent, F(1, 27) = 4.19, MSE = 0.17, p=0.05 (Figure 7), suggesting that the implicit belief of intelligence was positively correlated with usability and acceptability judgments particularly when participants were solving the difficult problem.

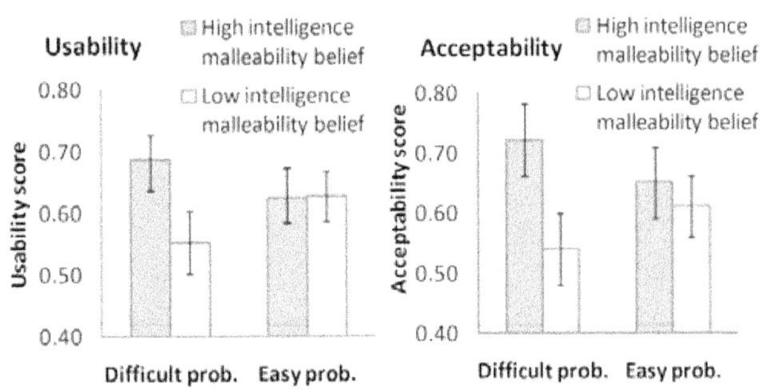

Figure 7. High/low intelligence malleability belief and usability/acceptability judgment

Implicit belief of intelligence was a strong predictor in the restricted MeetingPlaza condition (usability, β=0.40, p<0.05; acceptability, β=0.56, p<0.01). However, the impact of this variable was still present in the full MeetingPlaza condition (partial correlation with usability, r=0.53, p<0.05, and acceptability, r=0.44, p=0.08). It is likely that the full MeetingPlaza was equally cumbersome as the restricted MeetingPlaza was for some users. This interpretation is discussed in the next subsection.

Interpretations

The results of the step-wise regression analyses suggest that both group-level mutual affect and implicit beliefs of intelligence and world were strong predictors of usability and acceptability judgments once users actually had used the system. Overall, these variables accounted for 30–50 % of the variance of the dependent measures.

Group-level mutual affect was stronger in acceptability judgment but not in usability judgment. Usability judgments involve cognitive and pragmatic elements more, and the influence of affect may be limited in these pragmatic variables. Our acceptability questionnaire had questions addressing attitudes toward the product (e.g., "working with this tool was fun") as well as usefulness ("I could communicate with my group members easily") and intention ("I would continue to use this tool"). Mutual affect was correlated with all the constructs of the acceptability measure (for all cases, r's>0.38, p<0.05) but the correlation was particularly high with the attitude construct (r=0.44, p=0.02). Furthermore, the correlation between group-level affect and acceptability was strong even after the effects of communication effectiveness and opinion convergence were partialed out (r=0.45, p<0.05), suggesting that group-level affect influenced system acceptability independently of effective communication or opinion convergence of group members. This suggests that the influence of group-level affect was most likely due to misattribution.

There was a link between group-level mutual affect and group-specific problem solving performance, indicating the possibility that positive problem-solving activities reinforced positive mutual affect, which in turn resulted in favorable assessments of the product. However, the interpretation of this result should be made with care because of the small sample size (n=4) in the present study. The relationship between mutual affect, problem-solving performance and product acceptance should be scrutinized further in future studies with a larger sample size (at least 10).

As expected, the effect of implicit beliefs was strong particularly in the difficult problem condition, supporting the view that one's beliefs influence the interpretation of challenging situations. The impact of implicit belief was present in both the restricted MeetingPlaza condition and the full MeetingPlaza condition. This result was unexpected. Our post-hoc examination revealed that the full MeetingPlaza condition was as cumbersome as the restricted MeetingPlaza condition. Because MeetingPlaza's sharing functions require a high level of broadband connection, many of our participants experienced serious technical problems in the full MeetingPlaza condition. There were 35 occasions of technical problems in the full MeetingPlaza condition while there were only 10 occasions of technical problems in the restricted MeetingPlaza condition. This suggests that the technical problems associated with the sharing functions probably made the full MeetingPlaza condition unexpectedly cumbersome for collaboration.

Another unexpected result was the impact of implicit belief of world. This variable had negative correlation with system usability and acceptability. Those who believed that the world is dynamic and transient were less likely to give high usability and acceptability ratings. This result was unexpected. Implicit belief of world was probably related to the fixed and malleable nature of technologies in general. It is possible that participants who considered the world to be dynamic and fluid also regarded new technologies as dynamic and fluid. As a result, those who had a malleable belief of world might have given lower acceptance scores to the product, as they expected new technologies would replace existing technologies quickly.

In summary, implicit beliefs of intelligence and world were strong predictors of usability and acceptability judgments once users actually had used the system. The effect of the implicit belief of intelligence remained strong even after the variability of the four groups was taken into account and was pronounced in the difficult problem. Group-level mutual affect was a strong predictor of product acceptance but not usability judgments. The impact of group-level affect was most likely due to misattribution, and there was an indication that the influence of mutual affect was reinforced by effective group interactions during problem solving sessions.

DISCUSSION

The two psychological variables—affect and implicit beliefs of intelligence—are both well known in psychological research. Given the generality and robustness of these variables, we think that they could influence people's experience with a wide range of collaborative communication systems. Communicative factors, such as common ground and group coordination, are important to establish successful group collaboration. The present study suggests that by improving mutual affect and mindsets, these communicative factors can be enhanced. Because the group-level communicative factors are strengthened by sustained group awareness [1], mindsets (e.g., implicit beliefs of intelligence) are likely to play a critical role as they influence people's goal-setting behavior. Future studies need to investigate this possibility.

We suggest that psychological models of meaning-making can provide conceptual frameworks for CSCW research much in the same way that affordance and cognitive architecture helped the evolution of single-user interfaces. Along with other communicative variables, mindsets and mutual affects help elevate subjective assessments of system usability and acceptability of groupware.

Design Implications

On the basis of the results discussed above, we propose the following design implications.

- Affect can be easily misattributed.

Positive affects can be generated by interactions of people. The idea that affect can be easily misattributed suggests that affects originated from unrelated sources can still influence user experience. Once a user gets a smile, the source of the smile can be easily fused with the actual experience of the product itself.

Positive emotions can be generated in package design, website presentations, words used for a menu, the day and the time a product is shown, or the room in which an experiment is conducted. Note that recent success of the social discount website, Groupon, is attributed not so much to the discounts that Groupon users can get but more so to the short witty sentences Groupon writers (mostly amateur poets, actors and writers) create for the product introduction (*New York Times*, May 28 2011). Product designers need to think about affect in a much broader sense.

- People's general beliefs define how they interact with complex systems.

The implicit belief variables are interactive variables. They did not influence participants' usability and acceptability judgments when the video-conference system was introduced to them. The impact came after participants actually used the product together with other group members.

Belief is not an entirely static construct. One's malleable belief about intelligence can be induced at least temporally [6]. Product designers are accustomed to thinking about how to make a product easy, fun, and pleasant to use. One neglected area is how people learn to use the product. It is customary to separate the development of a user manual from product development. Because learning experience can influence how the product is viewed, the development of a user manual should be made concurrently with the development of the product [24]. By cultivating a sense of step-by-step learning accomplishment, self-control and self-efficacy can be cultivated in users, which in turn influences the way users judge the product.

Limitations and Future Directions

We used open-ended problems for collaborative problem solving. The psychological variables identified in the current study may be subject to this type of ill-defined problems. The generality of the current findings and the link between user experience and user performance should be tested further with different problems (e.g., referential communication tasks), different CSCW systems, and different populations of subjects. It is particularly important to examine the extent to which the psychological variables influence actual performance of group members using groupware.

APPENDIX

Implicit belief questionnaire [6]. 1-3: intelligence, 4-6: morality, 7-9: world. The questionnaire employs a 1- 6 Likert scale.

1. You have a certain amount of intelligence, and you can't really do much to change it.

2. Your intelligence is something about you that you can't change very much.

3. You can learn new things, but you can't really change your basic intelligence.

4. A person's moral character is something very basic about them and it can't be changed much.

5. Whether a person is responsible and sincere or not is deeply ingrained in their personality. It cannot be changed very much.

6. There is not much that can be done to change a person's moral traits (e.g., consciousness, uprightness, and honesty).
7. Though we can change some phenomena, it is unlikely that we can alter the core dispositions of our world.
8. Our world has its basic or ingrained dispositions, and you really can't do much.
9. Some societal trends may dominate for while, but the fundamental nature of our world is something that cannot be changed much.

ACKNOWLEDGMENT

We thank Na-Yung Yu and Amanda Hahn for their support. The authors acknowledge the grant from NTT Corporation.

REFERENCES

1. Carroll, J. M., Rosson, M. B., Convertino, G., & Ganoe, C. H. Awareness and teamwork in computer-supported collaborations. *Interacting with Computers 18*, (2006), 21-46.
2. Clore, G.L. and Huntsinger, J.R. How emotions inform judgment and regulate thought. *Trends in Cognitive Sciences 11*, (2007), 393-399.
3. Damasio, A.R., Descartes' Error: emotion, reason, and the human brain. Putnam, New York, NY, USA, 1994.
4. Davis, F.D. Perceived usefulness, perceived ease of use, and user acceptance of information technology. *MIS Quarterly 13*, (1989), 319-340.
5. Davis, F.D., Bagozzi, R.P. and Warshaw, P.R. User acceptance of computer technology: A comparison of two theoretical models. *Management Science 35*, 8 (1989), 982-1003.
6. Dweck, C.S., *Self-theories: Their role in motivation, personality and development.* Psychology Press, Ann Arbor, MI, USA, 1999.
7. Dweck, C.S., Chiu, C. and Hong, Y. Implicit theories and their role in judgments and reactions: A world from two perspectives. *Psychological Inquiry 6*, 4(1995), 267-285.
8. Finholt, T. A.. and Teasley, S. D. Psychology: The need for psychology in research on computer-supported cooperative work. *Social Science Computer Review 16*, 1 (1998), 40-52.
9. Francis, L.J., Brown, L.B. and Philipchalk, R. The development of an abbreviated form of the revised Eysenck Personality Questionnaire (EPQR-A): Its use among students in England, Canada, the U.S.A. and Australia. *Personality and Individual Differences 13*, 4(1992), 443-449.
10. Gergle, D., Kraut, R. E., and Fussell, S. R. (2004). Action as language in a shared visual space. In *Proc. CSCW 2004,* ACM Press (2004), 487-496.
11. Grudin, J. Groupware and social dynamics: Eight challenges for developers. *Communication of the ACM 37*, 1 (1994), 92-105.
12. Hargittai, E., An update on survey measures of web-oriented digital literacy. *Social Science Computer Review, 27,* 1 (2009), 130-137.
13. Hassenzahl, M. and Tractinsky, N. User experience – research agenda. *Behaviour & Information Technology 25*, (2006), 91-97.
14. Klein, G., Moon, B. and Hoffman, R.R. Making sense of sensemaking 2: A macrocognitive model. *IEEE Intelligent Systems 21*, 5 (2006), 88–92.
15. Kohn, N.W. and Smith, S.M. Collaborative fixation: Effects of others' ideas on brainstorming. *Journal of Applied Cognitive Psychology 25*, 3 (2011), 359-371.
16. Leshed, G., Perez, D., Hanock, J. T., Cosley, D., Birnholtz, J., Lee, S., McLeod, P. L., and Gay, G. Visualizing real-time language-based feedback on teamwork behavior in computer-mediated groups. *In Proc. CHI 2009*, ACM Press (2009), 4567-4582.
17. Lewis, J.R., IBM computer usability satisfaction questionnaire: psychometric evaluation and instructions for use. *International Journal of Human-Computer Interaction 7*, 1 (1995), 57-78.
18. Norman, D. A. Introduction to this special section on beauty, goodness, and usability. *Human-Computer Interaction 19*, (2004), 311-318.
19. Olson, J. S., Card, S. K., Landauer, T. K., Olson, G. M., Malone, T., and Leggett, J. Computer-supported co-operative work: research issues for the 90s. *Behaviour & Information Technology 12*, 2 (1993), 115-129.
20. Pirolli, P. and Card, S.K. The sensemaking and leverage points for analyst technology as identified through cognitive task analysis. In *Paper presented at the International Conference on Intelligence Analysis.* (2005), May. McLean, VA.
21. Raudenbush, S. W. and Bryk, A. S. Hierarchical Linear Models: Application and Data Analysis Methods. Sage, Thousand Oaks, CA, USA 2002.
22. Schwarz, N. and Clore, G.L. Mood, misattribution, and judgments of well-being: informative and directive functions of affective states. *Journal of Personality and Social Psychology 45*, (1983), 513–523.
23. Straus, S.G., Technology, group process, and group outcomes: Testing the connections in computer-mediated and face-to-face groups. *Human-Computer Interaction 12*, (1997), 227-266.
24. Thimbleby, H. Creating user manuals for use in collaborative design. In *Proc. CHI 1996*, ACM Press (1996), 279-280.
25. Venkatesh, V. and Morris, M.G. User acceptance of information technology: Toward a unified view. *MIS Quarterly 27*, (2003), 425-478.
26. Weick, K. *Sensemaking in organizations.* Sage, Thousand Oaks, CA, USA.

Recognizing Team Context during Simulated Missions

Steven E. Poltrock, Mark Handel, Stephen Poteet, Paul Murray
Boeing Research & Technology
Seattle, WA 98124 USA
spoltrock@gmail.com; {mark.j.handel, stephen.r.poteet, paul.murray}@boeing.com

ABSTRACT
We investigated ways to automatically analyze movement and verbal behavior of teams of soldiers engaged in simulated military missions. Analysis of location data revealed that soldiers' locations were consistent with 3 stationary patterns and 2 movement patterns. Analysis of their dialogue detected statistical regularities. An automated text classifier was developed that employed these regularities to code dialogue utterances. These analyses demonstrate the feasibility of interpreting collaborative activity automatically and constructing models of team context for teams of soldiers engaged in trained activities.

Author Keywords
Context, teamwork, dialog analysis, location analysis.

ACM Classification Keywords
H.5. 3. Information interfaces and presentation (e.g., HCI): Group and Organization Interfaces: Computer-supported cooperative work.

General Terms
Experimentation.

INTRODUCTION
Team collaboration and decision making are extremely challenging when teams are under high stress in dangerous physical environments. Firefighters, police special weapons and tactics teams, and military sections or squads are faced with situations that involve challenging cognitive demands. They must understand their mission and their plan for accomplishing it. They must know the roles that each team member will perform, and their ability to work together depends on their trust in each other to perform these roles reliably [28]. During the mission they must acquire, interpret, and share information about the environment and its risks [19, 24]. They must maintain awareness of the team's location with respect to threats in the environment and with respect to resources such as other teams or equipment. Each individual must also maintain awareness of his/her position with respect to other team members [6]. Finally, they must take actions to affect the environment, monitor the results of these actions, and compare the results with the plan and mission.

Providing technological support to teams in dangerous environments is both important and challenging. Technology may be able to provide critical and timely information, but determining criticality and timeliness requires some understanding of team context. This paper reports research exploring the feasibility of automatically modeling elements of a team's context, providing a foundation for recognizing and satisfying the team's information needs.

Research in multi-agent systems suggests that agents can help individuals and teams meet cognitive demands under time stress [15, 44]. Software agents can reason about elements of a team's context including the mission and plans, the roles of team members, geographic information, and the locations of resources and identified threats. To provide timely and useful advice, agents must also know other elements of context such as the status of the team with respect to the mission and plan, the locations of team members, and their current activities. Agent research often involves analyzing specific team tasks (such as search) to determine opportunities for assistance and the context information required to provide that assistance [e.g., 20, 43, 44]. Because teamwork in dangerous environments includes many tasks and is situationally dependent, we adopted a different approach: our research explored potential ways to automatically collect information about team context from behaviors (movements and speech) that are made observable as a consequence of team interaction.

We empirically investigated how team context could be recognized by analyzing the behaviors of a team of soldiers performing three simulated missions. Video games are commonly used for military training [17, 42] and provided the simulated environment, with each soldier represented by an avatar. The game continuously recorded the position and orientation of each avatar and when weapons were fired, providing information that could be obtained in the field from GPS devices and weapon sensors. We also recorded and transcribed each soldier's utterances, which could be obtained from trained speech recognition systems.

We explored several ways to recognize the team's context in these three missions using only information that could be available to software agents. We analyzed soldiers' relative locations and developed algorithms for recognizing both stationary and movement configurations that military teams are trained to adopt. We also manually coded the utterances and explored ways to code them automatically. In this paper we review related work, summarize the data collection, and describe the movement analysis and the dialogue coding. We conclude by noting both the potential and limitations of this approach.

RELATED RESEARCH

Our research has drawn on work in a variety of fields, and we limit our review here to the work most closely related to CSCW. The closest research is investigations of emergency response behavior, especially firefighting, and methods for supporting it. Landgren [24] observed fire crews and noted that their behaviors were temporally structured and verbal communication was important in supporting sensemaking and collaboration. Patterns in fire fighting behavior have been identified that involve strikingly different activities· [10]. Technological support for fire fighters has included communication networks [5, 24] and a combination of ubiquitous computing devices carried by fire fighters and displays viewed by incident commanders. Other research has focused on training fire fighters using simulation games [46, 47].

Field studies of military activity are dangerous, of course, and rarely appear in academic publications. The Command Post of the Future [9] is a research program investigating command in battlefield situations. Its focus is on developing technologies for mobility and better decision making, including multimodal interaction, information visualization, and knowledge-based reasoning. This program, like some of the fire fighting research, focuses on the information needs of commanders and the sensors needed to collect this information.

The objective of our research is to recognize critical elements of context automatically from sensors that soldiers could wear. Context has a rich history [11], but efforts to define the requirements for context models and operationalize and refine these models began in the field of ubiquitous computing. Schilit and Theimer [38] were among the earliest to elaborate context, defining it as locations ("where"), identities ("who"), and changes ("when" and "what") to nearby people and objects. Dey and Abowd [11, 12] extend this to define context as "*any information that can be used to characterize the situation of an entity.*" This is a broad definition, and requires some understanding of the application domain. Petrelli emphasizes the need of any model to reduce complexity, because not everything can be included [34]. However, Bolchini, et al. [3] survey a number of different context models, reinforcing the basic dimensions of who/what/when/where, but also emphasizing the process nature of context: the "why" and "how" of the user's activities.

The definition of Dey and Abowd [11, 12, 32] reflects the concerns of a single entity or person, a primarily egocentric view of context. However, military missions are rarely executed by a single warfighter; rather there are fire teams, squads, platoons, companies and larger units that all must be aware of each other's actions and intentions. One approach to understanding context in a team situation has been to focus on common ground [22]. For example, Jones and Hinds [20] studied how a SWAT team established and maintained common ground, and applied this understanding to robot teams. Other research has studied context in high-stress situations such as disaster recovery [48] and more informal environments such as design teams [35]. The artificial intelligence community has also studied context [30], emphasizing formal representations of context [14, 37] and formal manipulation of these models [1].

Connected mobile devices are increasingly ubiquitous, and can provide raw context data, such as when, where, and who else is in the same area [27]. Eagle and Pentland [13] report results from using mobile phones, gathering information about individual's location and proximity to other people, and showing that they can detect activity, relationships, and organizational rhythms. Other work has extracted higher-level contextual information from low-level data [45], evaluating how to share [26, 43] and present this information to users effectively [50]. Agent-based approaches incorporating context have supported awareness [2] and distributed teams [36].

Within mobile computing research, location and proximity have been the easiest data to obtain. In addition, team members' communication can support dialog analysis, which has long been used to understand work context and teams' activities. Early work, such as McGrath [31] and Olson et al. [33] coded conversations in meetings to understand the activities and goals of teams. More recent work has analyzed instant messaging conversations to understand uses of the technology [18]. Research in speaker-dependent speech recognition in noisy environments shows promise of achieving performance levels adequate to support automated dialog analysis.

METHOD

Instead of observing actual battles or live battle simulations, data were collected using computer-based battlefield simulations. Many military services use similar simulations today to train their personnel [42]. The simulation engine was a modified version of the Battlefield 2 computer game as described in [29, 4]. Participants perceived, moved, and acted in a virtual world in which they were represented by avatars. Each participant had his own display and used a keyboard and mouse to interact with the environment. Teams of participants were seated in the same room but distributed so that they could not communicate verbally or see each other's displays. Instead, participants communicated over a full-duplex audio channel. Each wore a headphone with a microphone, and all their communication was recorded. We also recorded their position every 5 secs to the nearest meter. Although this is more precise than commercial GPS systems, it is much less precise than augmented military systems [40].

The participants of interest were trained, experienced soldiers. In the first experiment they were an eight-man section of United Kingdom (UK) solders led by a UK officer. In the second experiment they were a nine-man section of United States soldiers led by a soldier who was coached by a US officer. Their enemy (located in another room with similar equipment) were not military personnel but were coached, before and during the experiment, by military officers to behave as an insurgent force.

A UK officer designed the three missions conducted in these experiments with slight modifications for the second experiment. The first mission required clearing a route following the main road through a village, and they expected to encounter insurgents who would try to prevent them from securing this route. The second mission required assaulting and clearing an enemy position in a partially wooded rural terrain. The third mission required crossing a bridge, taking defensive positions on the opposite side, and holding this position while another fictional platoon advances.

Soldiers were first trained in the use of the simulation environment. Before each mission they gathered together for a mission briefing delivered by their commanding officer, which concluded with the section leader devising and explaining his plan for accomplishing the mission. The soldiers returned to their stations and began the mission. During each mission the officer acted as platoon leader, communicating with the section leader. Each simulated mission continued until the mission was accomplished or the team concluded that their situation was hopeless and requested evacuation. Finally, the team gathered together for an after-action review.

MOVEMENT ANALYSIS

Analyses have been completed only for the three missions completed by UK soldiers. The soldiers exhibited clear patterns both when moving and when stationary. Sometimes soldiers explicitly referred to these patterns by name, such as herringbone and bounded overwatch, which are described below. Section movements were governed by team structure. Each fire team generally moved as a unit as directed by the fire team leads, with the section lead coordinating movements of the two fire teams. Sometimes the fire teams divided themselves into two 2-man units that moved separately and were coordinated by their fire team lead. Sometimes each member of a 2-man unit moved separately, but again these movements were coordinated, as described below.

Stationary and Movement Patterns

We discovered five location-related patterns adopted by these soldiers and learned that these patterns are well known among military personnel and are described in a US Field Manual [49]. It should be noted that although these are classical formations, the specific details and their applications vary widely among forces, depending on their particular tactics, techniques and practices. Each force, such as US or UK soldiers, or SWAT teams would need to be independently analyzed for their particular formations.

The three stationary formations are Herringbone, Coil, and Line. In the Herringbone formation the two fire teams were stationary alongside one another, with the team on the left facing left and the team on the right facing right. From above, the pattern resembles herringbone twill or a zipper. According to [49], this is a mounted formation that provides all around security, but here the soldiers used it while dismounted. In the Coil formation, the team was arranged in a stationary circular pattern looking outward. The soldiers at the front watch forward, those at the back watch behind the team, and those on the left and right sides guard the flanks. Fire teams were often deployed in a Stationary Line formation when firing at a known enemy location. In this formation the soldiers are side by side facing the same direction.

The two moving formations are File and Bounding Overwatch. In the File Formation, fire teams often advanced in a single file with the last man in the file looking rearward. The Bounding Overwatch is used when advancing across an exposed area toward an enemy position. Half the soldiers in an advancing formation lay prone firing at the enemy position while the other half ran forward a short distance, threw themselves to the ground, and took up firing. The first half then ran forward beyond the positions of the second half, took cover, and began firing. They repeated this technique until they reached the enemy position

Automatic Pattern Recognition

We observed that these patterns described the way soldiers moved or positioned themselves about 90% of the time. Recorded locations were analyzed to explore the feasibility of implementing heuristics for recognizing stationary and movement patterns. Three statistics – speed, dispersion and linearity – were calculated for each of the two fire teams at about 10 second intervals. Speed is the rate of change in virtual meters per second of the fire team's centroid. Dispersion is the standard deviation of their locations. Linearity is measured by finding the first moment of the fire team's locations, rotating the coordinate system so that the first moment is along a 45-degree axis, and then computing the correlation of soldiers' x and y coordinates [41].

These three measures provide a foundation for discriminating between the location-related patterns. These heuristics were developed from an analysis of idealized formations, then applied to the observed data from the missions. Stationary and movement patterns are easily discriminated by comparing speed to a criterion. When stationary, a team with high linearity is in either a herringbone or line formation, and these two can be discriminated by analyzing the orientations of the soldiers. When moving, a team with high linearity and relatively constant dispersion is in the file formation, and a team with oscillating dispersion is performing a bounding overwatch movement. Based on these criteria, we did exploratory analyses which suggested that these simple heuristics will reliably discriminate among most of the observed movement patterns. However, because of the continuous nature of movement, we are unable to use standard measures of reliability such as Kappa metrics.

These movement patterns contain important information about the team's context. A team in a line formation is generally observing or firing at a known enemy location. Teams in coil or herringbone formations are guarding against enemy attacks. Teams in file formation are moving in an area without enemy contact, and teams performing a bounding overwatch maneuver are assaulting an enemy position.

DIALOGUE ANALYSIS

When people collaborate they communicate with one another to ensure that everyone understands the team goal, their role in achieving it, the progress the team is making, and any external events that influence the team. A human observer listening to a team's communication may learn much about their context. The research question we address is whether software agents, lacking natural language understanding, can extract useful information about context from the team's dialogue.

Our analysis was based on transcripts generated manually from recordings of each team member. The transcript was prepared by a professional who made initial decisions about the beginning and end of the utterances. However, we found it necessary to go through and split some utterances into two separate utterances. As will be discussed, the choice of utterance boundaries is a non-trivial concern in the dialog analysis. We developed a scheme for coding utterances, analyzed the structure of the dialogue, and began investigating ways to automate the coding. Software agents would require automated speech recognition, and commercially available products claim they achieve 99% accuracy in real time. Future dialogue analyses could also include prosody.

Roles

In military missions the command structure is important, and it was well understood by both teams of soldiers although there were some differences between the US and UK team structure. For the UK, there were eight men in the section, divided into two four-person fire teams. The section lead also led fire team 1, while another solider led fire team 2. Generally, fire team 1 had a leading role, and fire team 2 had a supporting role. For the US, there was a nine man squad; one soldier was the squad lead, and each four-person fire team had a team lead. In some analyses we compare utterances of leads (squad, section, and fire team leads) and soldiers (members of the fire teams).

The Coding Scheme

Analysts observed that communications followed some consistent patterns. For example, leaders explained the immediate planned steps, and then issued orders to execute this plan. Other soldiers responded by asking questions for clarification, acknowledging their understanding of the plan, and acknowledging the orders. Dialogue structure seemed much more consistent than the communication observed during pilot research with non-military participants. An initial coding scheme was developed by selecting elements from schemes for coding dialogues of teams of astronauts [16] and search teams [43]. This initial coding scheme consisted of the dialogue acts *statement, intentions, order, question, response, request,* and *confirmation.* Three additional dialogue acts (*greeting, report,* and *ignore)* were added to code utterances that were not adequately described by the initial set. Task codes were also added during the coding process to capture the main topic of each dialogue act. The resulting coding scheme is summarized in Table 1 and described in detail below.

The greeting code was assigned to utterances in which soldiers greeted other soldiers who arrived late to a mission. This code was also used for utterances that appeared to serve a politeness function.

The statement code was assigned to utterances in which a soldier conveyed information to the team. This is similar to the *Information Sharing and Meta-cognition* codes of [16]. Statements conveyed information about the speaker's personal status, such as a statement about location or an expression of surprise. Statements conveyed information about their mission progress or plan status, such as "Smoke's done" to convey that smoke grenades had been thrown. Statements conveyed information about the presence or movement of enemy forces, such as "Enemy in and around that area." Statements conveyed orienting information, such as "You see the obvious tree line, left-hand edge..." Statements conveyed other information, such as "I take it we've got a Bedford moving along the road to the rear." Rhetorical questions were coded as statements.

The intentions code was assigned to utterances in which a soldier described what he expected or planned would happen in the near or far future. This is similar to the *Problem solving* codes of [16]. Leaders often stated their intentions prior to ordering an action or asked soldiers to prepare for an action. The task code captured the topic of the intention, including movement ("We'll move along the right-hand edge of this road"), guarding ("...secure the right side of the bridge"), firing ("...individual fire from the right-hand side"), diverting the enemy's attention ("Heave a couple of smokes along the left-hand side..."), and suppressing an enemy location ("...you're fire support into the enemy position").

The order code was assigned to utterances in which a soldier directs one or more soldiers to do something immediately. This is similar to the *Directing the actions of others* code of [16]. The task codes for orders were similar to those for intentions. Orders were only given down the chain of command; when two persons of equal status made

Dialogue Act	Task Code	UK Frequency			US Frequency		
		All (n=675)	Leads (n = 477)	Soldiers (n=198)	All (n=736)	Leads (n=461)	Soldiers (n=275)
Greeting		.3%	.2%	.5%	0%	0%	0%
Statement	Personal status, plan status, enemy, orienting, other	19.7%	14.9%	31.3%	21.6%	11.9%	37.8%
Intentions	Move, guard, fire, divert, suppress	5.5%	7.7	0%	1.2%	2.0%	0%
Order	Attend, move, guard, fire, divert, suppress, report, other	21.4%	29.9	1.0%	22.4%	35.4%	.7%
Question	Location, identity, status, seen, other	12.4%	15.1	6.1%	13.3%	10.4%	18.2%
Response	Location, identity, status, seen	10.4%	5.6	21.7%	8.0%	7.4%	9.1%
Request	Confirmation, permission, help, repeat	2.5%	2.7	2.0%	8.6%	4.8%	14.9%
Confirmation	Understood, confirm, seen, yes, no	13.8%	11.7	18.7%	9.1%	8.9%	9.5%
Report	PC channel	5.6%	7.9	0%	9.5%	15.2%	0%
Ignore	Joking, nonverbal, unknown	8.3%	4.0	18.7%	6.3%	4.1%	9.8%

Table 1: Dialog and task codes with their frequencies for leads and soldiers from the US and UK.

a request of each other it was coded as a request or question. Orders were broadly similar to intentions, with the addition of three more task codes: to attend ("Lads, all of you, this is the crack"), to report ("Make sure you do a head check that everyone's there"), and a catch-all for other topics ("Don't breathe down the microphone"). Notice that the orders to attend and to report were both implicit commands, requiring the behavior without explicitly stating it.

The question code was assigned to utterances in which a soldier asked one or more other soldiers for information. Questions and answers were part of the codes used to capture interactive patterns in [16]. Questions were about location ("Where are you?"), identity ("Who's that?"), status ("You ready with that smoke?"), whether something was visible or seen ("Look, see me?"), or about other topics, such as the keyboard controls used to accomplish some action.

The response code was assigned to utterances intended to answer a question, and as noted above questions and answers were used to capture interactive patterns in [16]. The response task code was always the same as the question to which it was a response. Answers to a question sometimes came from someone other than to whom the question was directed.

The request code was assigned to utterances that asked for something other than information. There does not appear to be any equivalent code in [16]. Soldiers requested confirmation, which constitutes agreement or acceptance of an order or instruction. These requests were often short queries at the end of an order, such as, "Happy?" Soldiers requested permission to do something or requested help, such as, "Can someone give him a first aid kit?" Soldiers also requested that someone repeat what they had said, such as, "What was that?"

The confirmation code was assigned to utterances that acknowledged or confirmed something. These were subtly different than responses. A confirmation could be a simple yes, such as "Aye," to express agreement with a previous positive response. A confirmation could be no when it confirmed that a response was negative. A confirmation could indicate that utterances were understood, and these were typically short statements such as "Yeah" or repetition of the key part of the statement to show that it was comprehended. Confirmations could truly confirm agreement and commitment, such as a soldier's statement, "Yeah, roger," when the soldier was asked whether he was happy with the plan. Confirmations stated that some object under discussion had been seen. Note that if a soldier asked whether an object had been seen, then the reply was coded as a response. But interjections such as "yep" during a discussion of objects in view were confirmations that the objects had been seen.

The report code was assigned to utterances made by the team leader to the team's platoon commander. Other members of the team could not hear these utterances. They were transmitted via another communication channel called the PC Channel.

The ignore code was assigned to utterances that were unrelated to the mission. These utterances were generally attempts to be amusing. The ignore code was also assigned to nonverbal utterances (e.g., coughs) and when the utterance's intended purpose was unknown. The ignore code was also used for utterances specifically about the simulation environment, such as "What's the key to crouch?"

The utterances were coded by carefully reading the transcript, listening to the recorded dialog, and deciding what the speaker intended. The initial coding was done by one coder, who wrote the initial coding scheme. Then, two more coders independently coded one US and one UK mission transcript. Agreement between the set of two coders for dialog acts using Cohen's Kappa was $\kappa = .79$ for all transcripts, indicating substantial agreement [25]. The two coders then met, reconciled the differences and updated the coding key based on areas of ambiguity. These reconciled coded transcripts, where disagreements had been resolved, serve as the basis for all the subsequent analysis in this paper.

One persistent problem in the coding reconciliation was observed when an utterance in the transcript spanned multiple sentences. Our initial approaches, such as "code the first sentence" or "code the longest sentence" lacked theoretical support. We developed a set of heuristics to split a single transcribed phrase into multiple utterances.

There was much less agreement on task codes. When the two raters agreed on the dialog act, agreement on the task code was $\kappa = .46$, "moderate agreement" [25]. This lower level of agreement is probably due to the substantially larger number of task codes (nearly 30 versus 10 dialog acts); these is a significantly smaller sample of each of the tasks codes, so a single disagreement between coders has a much greater impact on the reliability. This is supported by looking at only the three most frequent dialog acts. We find that task code agreement was often better: Order, $\kappa = .73$, Statement, $\kappa = .11$, and Question, $\kappa = .62$. Further work on revising the coding key for greater clarity and/or removing some of the lesser-used task codes should help increase inter-rater reliability[8].

Dialogue Act Frequency

The frequency of utterances and the type of utterance is strongly dependent on the role of the speaker within the team (see Table 1). The leads spoke far more frequently than the other soldiers, and the squad/section lead spoke more than the other fire team lead. For instance, in the UK mission, the section lead, who also led FT1, made 41% of all utterances and the leader of FT2 made 26%. The other six soldiers individually made an average of 5.5% of the utterances. The US mission was similar: the squad lead made 39% of all the utterances and the two fire team leads made 24% of the utterances. The remaining six US soldiers individually made an average of 6.2% of the utterances.

Dialog Act	Team Leads	Other Soldiers
Greeting	.01	.02
Statement	.13	.35
Intentions	.05	.00
Order	.33	.01
Question	.13	.13
Response	.06	.14
Request	.04	.09
Confirmation	.10	.13
Report	.11	.00
Ignore	.04	.13

Table 2. Dialog act proportions for team leaders and all other soldiers.

The total number of utterances varied across missions, corresponding to differences in their durations. The relative frequencies of dialogue acts were strikingly similar across the three UK missions despite substantial differences in the mission objectives. Similar patterns were found for the two of three US missions that have been coded. As Table 1 shows, only rarely did non-leads ever state their intentions, give an order, or report anything. Although the leader of the second UK fire team spoke less frequently, the distributions of dialogue acts are similar for the two leaders. The other six soldiers appear strikingly different from the two leaders but similar to one another. All eight soldiers made statements, asked questions, responded to questions, and gave confirmations. Interestingly, US soldiers were much more likely to make requests and ask questions than UK soldiers.

Table 2 presents the mean proportions of the two (UK) or three (US) leaders' utterances assigned to each dialogue act and the mean proportions of the six other soldiers' utterances assigned to each dialogue act. These means are estimates of the conditional probabilities of these dialogue acts given that the speaker is known to be a leader or a follower. When a team leader speaks, the most likely dialogue act is an order and the second most likely is a statement. When a soldier speaks, the most likely dialogue act is a statement and the second most likely is a confirmation. Such conditional probabilities are useful when constructing automated statistical coders.

Distributions of Task Codes

The task codes provide additional detail about the intended purpose of each utterance. Different dialog acts have different sets of task codes. Because team leaders and other soldiers had different distributions of dialog acts, we examined their task codes separately.

Unlike the dialog acts, the task codes for team leaders varied greatly from one mission to another (the data are not included because of space limitations). These differences in the task codes reflected differences in the tactics and the landscape that required different conversational content. For example, the section attempted to divert attention from their planned assault route in a mission requiring an assault in wooded terrain by throwing smoke grenades, and this tactic was reflected in the task codes for utterances describing the fire team leaders' intentions and orders.

Because of this variability in task codes, it would not be useful to estimate task code probabilities for team leaders by averaging over different kinds of missions. Probability estimates of task codes could be obtained by conducting a much larger study with a wide range of missions. Task code probabilities could be determined for missions with similar parameters.

The soldiers' task codes were much less variable across missions than the team leaders' task codes. Most questions and responses were about locations. Most confirmations indicated that a statement had been understood. Most soldiers' statements were about personal status or about the enemy. Apparently the soldiers' utterances are much less influenced by the mission and by tactics. Consequently, frequency distributions could be used to estimate the probability of each task code, providing the prior odds needed in Bayesian decision making.

Sequential Dialogue Acts

The temporal relationships of utterances are crucially important in a dialogue. Table 3 shows the estimated probability of the dialogue act in a column following immediately after the dialogue act in a row. These are estimated conditional probabilities; if a soldier asks a question, for example, then the probability is 0.40 that the next utterance is a response.

Some dialogue acts appear to be highly dependent on the dialogue act that precedes it. Some dialogue acts are frequently repeated. Intentions frequently follow intentions, orders follow orders, reports follow reports, and statements follow statements. Intentions, orders, reports and statements are generally long and require multiple utterances to complete, explaining this dependency.

Looking at the columns, we see that intentions and reports rarely follow any other dialog act, whereas orders follow nearly all the other dialog acts (except for questions and requests) about equally often. Requests nearly always occur after an intention. The leaders often explained their intentions and then requested confirmation that the intentions were understood. As noted above, these requests for confirmation are often followed by a confirmation. Thus the pattern *Intentions ... Intentions, Request, Confirmation* is common.

Dialogue Act	State-ment	Inten-tion	Order	Question
Statement	.32	.02	.15	.12
Intention	.11	.39	.15	.02
Order	.22	.01	.38	.09
Question	.13	.01	.12	.21
Response	.19	.04	.19	.17
Request	.11	.05	.18	.09
Confirm	.21	.03	.29	.15
Report	.14	.00	.20	.08
	Response	Request	Confirm	Report
Statement	.03	.07	.13	.07
Intention	.00	.15	.11	.04
Order	.02	.05	.13	.04
Question	.40	.03	.04	.01
Response	.19	.05	.12	.00
Request	.05	.11	.28	.09
Confirm	.03	.05	.16	.03
Report	.01	.04	.02	.48

Table 3. Estimated conditional probabilities of sequential dialogue acts. (Note: Greeting and Ignore omitted)

Automated Dialogue Coding

The statistical regularities found in the dialogue of this team suggest that statistical classifiers are a promising approach to code soldiers' communication automatically (see [21] for a review of this approach). Statistical classifiers are trained on part of a manually coded corpus and tested on the remainder of the corpus. Our explorations of this approach, still at an early phase of investigation, employed automatic text categorization [39], which automatically assigns one (or more) of a set of predetermined categories to a piece of text based on features of the text. We analyzed only the dialogue of the first of the three missions. We simply defined the features as the words in the text, without any pre-processing such as combining words into common phrases, unifying word variants or synonyms, or expanding acronyms or abbreviations. The categories were the manually coded dialogue acts for this mission.

We divided the utterances into a training set (75% of the utterances) and test set (the remaining 25%) using stratified random sampling, ensuring that the training and test set each had approximately the same proportion of utterances of each class as the original set. We trained a Naïve Bayes classifier, and used the resulting classifier on the test set. Excluding the rare *Greeting* class, the classifier's precision ranged from 27% (Response) to 100% (Report) and recall ranged from 19% (Response) to 85% (Confirmation). We compared the classifier with the manual coding using the Kappa statistic, obtaining $\kappa = .43$, indicating moderate agreement between what humans assigned and the dialog acts assigned by the classifier. These preliminary results suggest that automated categorization of the utterances may prove a successful means for coding soldiers' dialogue acts in real time.

CONCLUSION

The objective of this research was to begin laying the groundwork for a system that would provide real-time assistance to team's of soldiers engaged in missions. The software agents of such a system could provide timely information to soldiers about threats and resources and help the team coordinate their activities. This research focuses on understanding the team's context, which is essential to recognizing which information would be useful to the team and how it should be delivered. The results suggest that wearable sensors could provide data sufficient to recognize elements of context in real time. We assumed that the only sensors were a GPS device and a trained speech recognition system. Future sensors may detect weapon use, and smart clothing [27] may support recognition of body positions and gestures, but these context elements were not considered in our research.

When reviewing recorded simulations, analysts noted repeated patterns in the soldiers' speech, movement, and weapons firing, patterns that were not evident in pilot research with teams composed of researchers who lacked military training. These patterns were most evident in their location data, which closely corresponded to formations described in military field manuals. Whether moving or stationary, soldiers were arranged in a recognizable formation about 90% of the time. Preliminary analyses suggest that these formations can be automatically discriminated by simple heuristics. These heuristics require comparisons with empirically determined criteria, and larger data samples may be required to develop and validate these heuristics.

The soldiers' dialogue also followed consistent patterns, although national differences still emerged. Team leaders were most likely to give orders or make statements. Other soldiers were most likely to make statements or give confirmations. There were also patterns in the sequences of responses; leaders often stated their intentions, then gave orders, and these orders were confirmed by the other soldiers.

Teams' movements and speech behaviors provide clues about context that could not be obtained by observing a single person engaging in comparable missions. Location sensors directly provide *who*, *where*, and *when* dimensions of context. Their movement patterns provide evidence for *what* and *how* dimensions, suggesting whether they are attacking (bounding overwatch), suppressing (line formation), or defending (e.g., coil formation). Soldiers learn these patterns through repeated training, and we anticipate that soldiers from different forces will employ different patterns, requiring different recognition techniques. This research demonstrates that movement pattern recognition is possible and informative, and much more research will be needed to develop libraries of recognition algorithms and pattern interpretations.

Team speech also followed patterns that were informative about context. Leaders prepared their team for action by stating their intentions, making explanatory statements, and requesting acknowledgment that intentions were understood. Leaders initiated action with orders. These patterns are revealing about who is involved in an action and when it is about to occur. In engagements soldiers made statements about enemy sightings and positions. These statements are informative about *what* and *where* dimensions of context. Again, however, these patterns are likely to vary across forces with different training and areas of specialization, requiring the eventual development of libraries of analytic methods for recognition and interpretation.

This research has employed relatively simple methods of speech analysis, and more sophisticated methods may yield more accurate recognition. Automated text categorization technology learns statistical patterns to associate features of the text with the dialogue act codes. The classifier we developed was not capable of using all the statistical patterns we had observed. This Naïve Bayesian classifier had no information about the speaker or sequential properties of the dialogue but, nonetheless, achieved surprisingly good agreement with the manual coding. We anticipate that automated text categorization could achieve much better performance with three enhancements. First, pre-processing the text will reduce variability in the text features. This processing could unify variant word forms by stemming or lemmatization. The text included many contractions such as "who's" and "where's" that were treated as separate features from "who" and "where". Second, the role or identity of the speaker can be a feature, allowing the classifier to learn that different roles are more likely to utter different dialogue acts. Third, we can use a categorization algorithm that is sensitive to the sequential properties of the dialogue observed in Table 3 such as Hidden Markov Models [21] or Conditional Random Fields [23].

The long-term objectives of this research are ambitious; the realization of an automated military support system would require many years of research and development. Even as an exploratory study this research has limitations of sample size and validity. The movement analysis is based on data from only a single team of 8 UK soldiers and the dialogue analysis is based on only two teams, one US and one UK. Furthermore the teams engaged in simulated missions, not actual combat. Simulations provide a convenient environment for observing behavior in situations that would be very dangerous in real life, but eventually observations and any algorithms that result from this research must be validated in live training exercises and actual combat situations. Of course, the results of both training exercises and combat situations in the military are often classified, which limits the ability to publish the results. Nonetheless, this research suggests that the collaborative activity (movements and dialog) of teams engaged in military missions provide cues regarding team context. There are patterns in these activities, and these patterns can be recognized and interpreted, contributing to dynamic models of team context.

ACKNOWLEDGMENTS

Research was sponsored by the U.S. Army Research Laboratory and the U.K. Ministry of Defence and was accomplished under Agreement Number W911NF-06-3-0001. The views and conclusions contained in this document are those of the author(s) and should not be interpreted as representing the official policies, either expressed or implied, of the U.S. Army Research Laboratory, the U.S. Government, the U.K. Ministry of Defence or the U.K. Government. The U.S. and U.K. Governments are authorized to reproduce and distribute reprints for Government purposes notwithstanding any copyright notation hereon.

REFERENCES

1. Jie Bao, Paul R. Smart, David Mott, Dave Braines. A Formal Context Representation Framework for Network-Enabled Recognition, *Proc. International Technology Alliance*, (2010).
2. Bardram, J.E., Hansen, T.R. The AWARE architecture: supporting context-mediated social awareness in mobile cooperation. *Proc. CSCW 2004*, ACM Press (2004), 192-201.
3. Bolchini, C., Curino, C.A., Quintarelli, E., Schreiber, F.A. and Tanca, L. A data-oriented survey of context models. *SIGMOD Record, 36*, 4 (2007), 19-26.
4. Bowyer, H., Waggett, P., Poltrock, S., and Handel, M. Using commercial PC games in defense research, *Proc. 9th International Animation, Games & SFX Conference*, (2008), Swansea, UK.
5. Camp, P.J., Hudson, J.M., Keldorph, R.B., Lewis, S., Mynatt, E.D. Supporting communication and collaboration practices in safety-critical situations. *Ext. Abstracts CHI 2000*, ACM Press (2000), 251-252.
6. Carroll, J.M., Rosson, M.B., Convertino, G., and Ganoe, C.H. Awareness and teamwork in computer-supported collaborations. *Interacting with Computers, 18*, 1 (2006), 21-46.
7. Chalmers, M. A historical view of context. *Computer Supported Cooperative Work, 13*, 3 (2004), 223-247.
8. Craggs, R., and Wood, M.M. Evaluating discourse and dialogue coding schemes, *Computational Linguistics, 31*, 1 (2006), 289-296.
9. DARPA Information Exploitation Office, *Command Post of the Future*. http://dtsn.darpa.mil/ixo/programdetail.asp?progid=18
10. Denef, S., Keyson, D.V., and Oppermann, R. Rigid structures, independent units, monitoring: Organizing patterns in frontline firefighting. *Proc. CHI 2011*, ACM Press (2011), 1949-1958.
11. Dey AK, Abowd GD. Towards a better understanding of context and context-awareness. *CHI'2000 Workshop on the What, Who, Where, When, and How of Context-Awareness*, (2000), ftp://ftp.cc.gatech.edu/pub/gvu/tr/1999/99-22.pdf
12. Dey, A. 2001. Understanding and Using Context. Personal Ubiquitous *Comput. 5*, 1 (2001), 4-7.
13. Eagle, N. and (Sandy) Pentland, A. Reality mining: sensing complex social systems. *Personal Ubiquitous Comput. 10*, 4 (2006), 255-268.
14. Edmonds, B. Learning and exploiting context in agents. *Proc. AAMAS 2002*. ACM Press (2002), 1231-1238.
15. Fan, X., Sun, B., Sun, S., McNeese, M., and Yen, J. RPD-enabled agents teaming with humans for multi-context decision making. *Proc. AAMAS 2006*, ACM Press (2006), 34-41.
16. Fischer, U., L. McDonnell, and J. Orasanu, Linguistic correlates of team performance: Toward a tool for monitoring team functioning during space missions, *Aviation, Space, and Environmental Medicine, 78*, 5, (2007), 86-95.
17. Ford, M., Barlow, M., and Lewis, E. An initial analysis of the military potential of COTS games. *Proc. SimTecT2003*, Australia, (2003).
18. Handel, M. and Herbsleb, J. D. What is chat doing in the workplace? *Proc. CSCW 2002*, ACM Press (2002), 1-10.
19. Hollan, J., Hutchins, E., and Kirsh, D. Distributed cognition: Toward a new foundation for human-computer interaction research. *ACM Trans. on Computer-Human Interaction, 7*, 2 (2000), 174-196.
20. Jones, H. and Hinds, P. 2002. Extreme work teams: using SWAT teams as a model for coordinating distributed robots. *Proc. CSCW 2002*, ACM Press (2002), 372-381.
21. Jurafsky, D. Pragmatics and computational linguistics. In L. R. Horn & G. Ward (eds.), *Handbook of Pragmatics*, Wiley-Blackwell, (2006), 578-606.
22. Kraut, R.E., Fussell, S. R., Brennan, S. E., & Siegel, J. Understanding the effects of proximity on collaboration: Implications for technologies to support remote collaborative work. In P. J. Hinds & S. Kiesler (eds.), *Distributed work*. MIT Press, (2002), 137-164.
23. Lafferty, J., McCallum, A., and Pereira F. Conditional random fields: probabilistic models for segmenting and labeling sequence data. *Proc. ICML 2001*, (2001).

24. Landgren, J. Making action visible in time-critical work. *Proc. CHI 2006,* ACM Press (2006), 201-210.

25. Landis, J.R., & Koch, G.G. The measurement of observer agreement for categorical data. *Biometrics, 33,* (1977), 159—174.

26. Ludford, P. J., Priedhorsky, R., Reily, K., and Terveen, L. Capturing, sharing, and using local place information. *Proc. of CHI '07,* ACM Press, (2007), 1235-1244.

27. Mann, S. Smart clothing: the shift to wearable computing. *Communications of the ACM, 39,* 8 (1996), 23-24.

28. Manoj, B.S., Baker, A. H. Communication challenges in emergency response. *Comm. of the ACM, 50,* 3 (2007), 51-53.

29. Masato, D., Norman, T.J., Poltrock, S.E., Bowyer, H., and Waggett, P. Adaptive military behaviour in a collaborative simulation. *Proc. of the SISO European Simulation Interoperability Workshop* (2008).

30. McCarthy, J. Notes on formalizing context. *IJCAI,* (1993), 555–562.

31. McGrath, Joseph, Time Matters in Groups. In *Intellectual teamwork: social and technological foundations of cooperative work*, Lawrence Erlbaum Associates, (1990).

32. Morse, D.R., Armstrong, S., and Dey, A.K. The what, who, where, when, why and how of context-awareness. *Ext. Abstracts CHI 2000*, ACM Press (2000), 371-371.

33. Olson, J.S., Olson, G.M., Storrøsten, M., & Carter, M. Groupwork up close: A comparison of the group design process with and without a simple group editor ACM *Trans. on Information Systems, 11*, 4 (1993), 321-348.

34. Petrelli, D., Not, E., Strapparava, C., Stock, O., and Zancanaro, M. Modeling context is like taking pictures. *CHI 2000Workshop on The What, Who, Where, When, Why and How of Context-Awareness* (2000).

35. Poltrock, S., Grudin, J., Dumais, S., Fidel, R., Bruce, H., and Pejtersen, A.M. Information seeking and sharing in design teams. *Proc. GROUP 2003,* ACM Press (2003), 239-247.

36. Poon, S.S., Thomas, R.C., Aragon, C.R., and Lee, B. Context-linked virtual assistants for distributed teams: An astrophysics case study. *Proc. CSCW 2008*, ACM Press (2008), 361-370.

37. *Proc. of the Second International and Interdisciplinary Conference on Modeling and Using Context* (1999).

38. Schilit, B., Theimer, M. Disseminating Active Map Information to Mobile Hosts. *IEEE Network, 8*, 5 (1994) 22-32.

39. Sebastiani, F. Machine learning in automated text categorization. *ACM Computing Surveys, 34*, 1 (2002), 1-47.

40. Space-based Positioning Navigation & Timing National Executive Committee, http://www.pnt.gov/public/faq.shtml

41. Stojmenovic, M., Nayak, A., and Zunic, J. Measuring linearity of a finite set of points. *Proc. IEEE Conference on Cybernetics and Intelligent Systems (2006).*

42. Stone, R. Serious games: virtual reality's second coming? *Virtual Reality, 13*, 1 (2009), 1-2.

43. G. Sukthankar, K. Sycara, J. Giampapa, and C. Burnett, Communications for Agent-Based Team Support. In V. Dignum (Ed.), *Multi Agent Systems: Semantics and Dynamics of Organizational Models IGI*, ISBN: 1-60566-256-9 (2009).

44. Sycara, K., Norman, T.J., Giampapa, J.A., Kollingbaum, M.J., Burnett, C., Masato, D., McCallum, M., and Strub, M.H. Agent support for policy-driven collaborative mission planning. *The Computer Journal, 53*, 5 (2010), 528-540.

45. Terry, M., Mynatt, E. D., Ryall, K., and Leigh, D. Social net: using patterns of physical proximity over time to infer shared interests. *Ext. Abstracts CHI 2002*, ACM Press (2002), 816-817.

46. Toups, Z.O., Kerne, A., Hamilton, W., Blevins, A. Emergent team coordination: From fire emergency response practice to a non-mimetic simulation game. *Proc. Group'09,* ACM Press (2009), 341-350.

47. Toups, Z.O., Kerne, A., Hamilton, W.A., and Shahzad, N. Zero-fidelity simulation of fire emergency response: Improving team coordination learning. *Proc. CHI 2011,* ACM Press (2011), 1959-1968.

48. Truong, H-L., Manzoor, A., Dustdar, S. On modeling, collecting and utilizing context information for disaster responses in pervasive environments. *Proc. CASTA 2009,* ACM Press (2009), 25-28.

49. US Army, FM 3-21.71 *Mechanized Infantry Platoon and Squad (Bradley)* (2002).

50. Winterboer, A., Cramer, H. S., Pavlin, G., Groen, F. C., and Evers, V. 2009. 'Do you smell rotten eggs?': evaluating interactions with mobile agents in crisis response situations. *Proc. Human-Computer Interaction with Mobile Devices and Services*, ACM Press (2009), 1-2.

Participation in an Online Mathematics Community: Differentiating Motivations to Add

Yla R. Tausczik, James W. Pennebaker
Department of Psychology
The University of Texas at Austin
{tausczik, pennebaker}@mail.utexas.edu

ABSTRACT
Why do people contribute content to communities of question-answering, such as Yahoo! Answers? We investigated this issue on MathOverflow, a site dedicated to research-level mathematics, in which users ask and answer questions. MathOverflow is the first in a growing number of specialized Q&A sites using the Stack Exchange platform for scientific collaboration. In this study we combine responses to a survey with collected data on posting behavior on the site. User behavior suggests that building reputation is an important incentive, even though users do not report this in the survey. Level of expertise affects users' reported motivation to help others, but does not affect the importance of reputation building. We discuss the implications for the design of communities to target and encourage more contributions.

Author Keywords
question-answering, online communities, scientific collaboration, motivation

ACM Classification Keywords
H.5.3 Information Interfaces and Presentation: Group and Organization Interfaces—*Computer-supported cooperative work*

INTRODUCTION
Communities of user-generated content, such as Wikipedia, Flickr, and Yahoo! Answers, rely on their users to make contributions. Therefore an important and well-researched question is: What motivates users to contribute? We investigate motivation in a specialized question answering site, MathOverflow (mathoverflow.net) in which users ask and answer research-level mathematics questions.

Many previous studies have looked at cooperation in communities of user-generated content in which contributions are low-cost and in which ties between users are loose. In this paper we describe the motivations to contribute in a community in which participation has greater costs and benefits.

RELATED WORK

Self-reported Motivations to Contribute
Many studies have investigated the reasons people give for why individuals contribute to communities of user-generated content (e.g. [18, 23, 24, 25, 19]). These studies have identified a wide range of motivations, ranging from fun to helping to reputation building. Dholakia and colleagues [9] with slight modifications by Lampe and colleagues [19] find evidence for six categories of benefits of participating: getting information, giving information, reputation building, relationship development, recreation, and self discovery.

Motivations vary based on the community type [21]. Building reputation and self-development may be especially important in career oriented communities. Contributors to open-source software were found to be more motivated by gaining reputation and self-development compared to contributors to Wikipedia, who were more motivated by altruistic reasons [25].

Two qualitative studies identify motivations that may be especially important to those users answering questions. Five major themes were identified in interviews of contributors to Knowledge-iN, a large South Korean Q&A site [22]. The themes were helping others, learning, promoting their business, recreation and accumulating points [22]. Contributors to Yahoo! Answers explained that they only answered questions when they thought their question would be well received by the question asker and would not get lost in the crowd [8].

In this study we describe motivations to participate on MathOverflow (MO) using the categorization developed by Dholakia and colleagues. We compare the relative importance of the motivations on MO to motivations analyzed in the studies described above.

Inferring Motivations to Contribute
One of the common problems with self-reports is that they are subject to response biases. In particular, individuals are likely to inflate reports of socially desirable items and deflate reports of undesirable ones [26]. This may be especially true when individuals are selecting between items such as helping others and enhancing ones reputation. An alternative to

self-reports is to measure behaviors that can be used to infer attitudes or motivations (e.g. [11]).

Gaining recognition is one benefit that users are likely to under-report, but has been inferred to encourage participation by observing individuals' behavior. Measures of recognition, such as the number of comments in response to a submission, have been shown to be related to participation level; those that receive more recognition participate more [28]. Furthermore, individuals have been shown to change their participation in relation to the amount of recognition they receive. For example, during the time period when Chinese Wikipedia was blocked on mainland China, thereby reducing readership, unblocked contributors dramatically reduced their contributions [34]. Not only are individuals sensitive to the amount of recognition they receive, in addition recognition may consistently reinforce participation. Huberman and colleagues [14] found a consistent pattern over time in which YouTube contributors posted more videos if two weeks earlier the videos they had contributed had received more views. In fact, recognition may be so reinforcing that it can create a positive feedback loop accounting for large discrepancies that are seen between users who contribute at high rates and those that contribute at low rates [33].

Other studies have used this same technique of detecting the kinds of social feedback that encourages participation (eg [15, 4]). These studies have mostly focused on predicting whether first time contributors continue to participate or not.

Reputation Systems

Authors have argued that one of the reasons the Stack Exchange platform is successful is because it is designed to make use of a reputation system [20]. In the platform questions and answers are rated by community members. The ratings that authors receive for their work contributes to a reputation score that is listed on their user page and next to their name whenever posting.

One of the advantages of an explicit reputation system is that it may increase participation on the site. Content ratings can encourage users who post highly appreciated content to contribute more because they have received positive feedback from other users [17]. Qualitative descriptions of two Q&A platforms with explicit reputation systems support this prediction. Contributors to Knowledge-iN in interviews both suggested and disputed that the game like aspect of earning points from answering questions motivated them to contribute more answers [22]. An analysis of StackOverflow users suggested two kinds of users, those who are motivated to answer questions by achieving high reputations and earning privileges and those that are motivated by answering the questions in themselves [20].

Theoretical Context

In this paper we explain motivations to contribute by describing the specific benefits that drive users to participate. This perspective has the potential to explain why certain kinds of feedback reinforce participation. The perspective comes from a long history of theories of motivation. It would be considered a functionalist perspective in psychology, meaning that individuals engage in behavior for specific functions. It is best exemplified in the explanations for participation in social movements [16]. According to this theory, motivation is understood at the individual level, and social rewards such as gaining reputation, or individual rewards such as developing knowledge, must outweigh the costs of participating in order to motivate users. In addition, social and individual rewards must go beyond collective rewards, such as a useful encyclopedia, because these are available to everyone whether or not they participate. This theory has been shown to be useful for describing motivations to participate in online communities [13].

Benefits can go beyond what we might think of as traditional rewards, such as monetary compensation. Social exchange theory has described what might normally be identified as a social process, such as relationship formation, as an exchange of social benefits. For example, both building reputation and helping others can be thought of as social benefits that motivate users to share more knowledge in an online community [32].

It is more fruitful to think of the benefits that we discuss as intrinsically motivating users. This is because voluntary online participation is more likely to be driven by intrinsic motivation [18] and those motivations which are extrinsic are likely to have the same advantages as intrinsic motivations, because they are self-directed [29].

MATHOVERFLOW

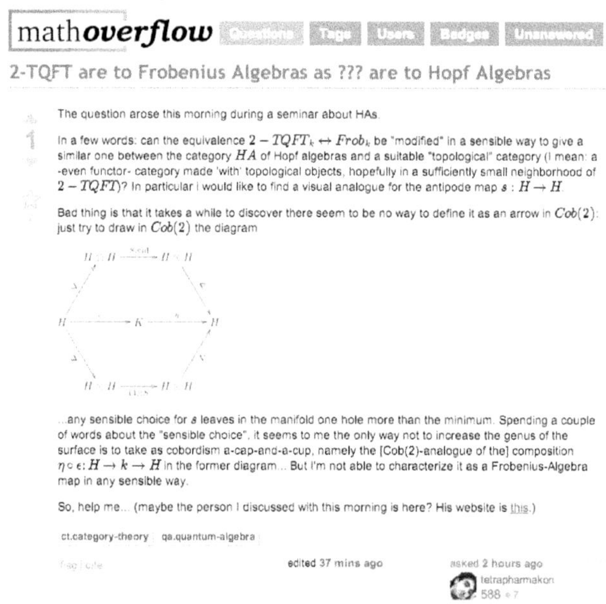

Figure 1. An Example Question

There is an expanding literature on large scale communities of question answering (e.g. [1, 22, 20]). MathOverflow is one of a new kind of community that lies at the intersection of participatory online communities and scientific collaboration. Two distinct features of MathOverflow, the higher costs and benefits of participation, make it an interesting community in which to investigate motivations.

There is a growing development of these specialized question answering communities. The Stack Exchange platform that was first developed for StackOverflow now hosts 51 other specialized Q&A sites. MathOveflow (MO), which was started in September of 2009, was the first to use the platform for scientific collaboration. News of MO spread through posts on popular math blogs, a notice in the American Mathematical Society publication, newspaper articles and by word of mouth and attracted large numbers of academic mathematicians.

Nearly a year later there were approximately 11,300 questions and 27,300 answers, contributed by 5,270 authors. In a survey conducted for this project we found that among more frequent users to the site 90.5% were in a mathematics degree program at some point. In this sample 96.6% were male and on average they were 32 years old (sd = 10.8). The site receives high traffic and regular users check the site frequently. The respondents reported, on average, visiting MO between every day and every two days. MO, like mathematics, draws users internationally although the content is in English and the site has the majority of individuals from English speaking countries.

One of the ways that the site is an interesting community to study is that many see it as an extension of the academic mathematics community. Users are encouraged to use their real names. Of those sampled 81.7% said they used their real name as their user name. It is difficult to quantify how many people on the site know each other offline, but individuals have the perception that behaviors on MathOverflow can affect their reputation in the larger mathematics community. One user stated that he used his real name because he was 'hoping a potential employer sees that I have interesting things to say'. Another user said even if he did not use his real name 'my research areas would narrow me down to one or two people anyway'. There are greater potential benefits of participating in MO. Developing professional ties and obtaining recognition are especially important for career development. Users may expect that by participating in MO they can develop professional relationships and gain recognition.

Expertise and career stage is an important individual difference in scientific collaboration and on MathOverflow. There was a wide range of the highest mathematics career stage that individuals had achieved or were working on: 14% Bachelors degree, 9% Masters degree, 34% PhD, 17% postdoctoral fellow or lecturer, and 26% professorship. Slightly more than 40.1% of users had published no math papers of those sampled, whereas at least one person reported publishing over 200 papers. The median number of papers published was 2 papers.

There are 9,536 registered users, and of those 5,268 have made at least one contributions. Contributions follow a power law distribution where the majority of the contributions are made by a small number of users. Fifty percent of the questions are contributed by 6.3% of the users and fifty percent of the answers are contributed by 2.4% of the users. Of those users who have made at least one contribution, the mean number of question per person is 2.14 (median = 1, sd = 5.39) and mean number of answers per person is 5.19 (median = 1, sd = 19.8). However the median number of days from when the person first logged into their account to the last time is long, 42 days (mean = 102, sd = 120).

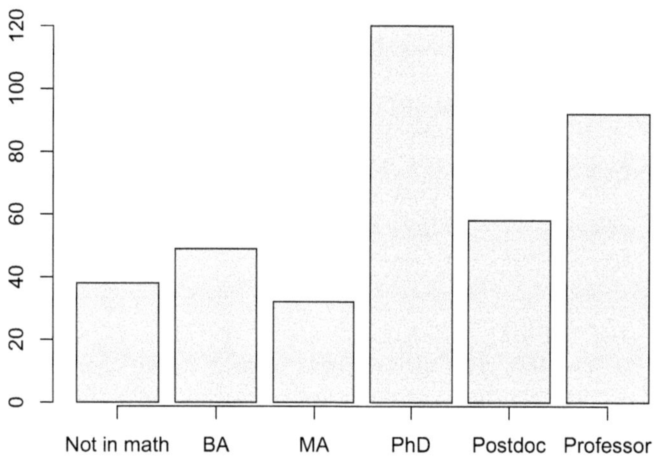

Figure 2. MathOverflow users' level of expertise. Shows the highest math degree that a user is working on or has obtained.

In order to keep the community limited to research level math questions there are extensive lists of the kinds of questions that are appropriate to MO and those that are not. Moderators and community members police questions and will downvote and close those questions below research level. For example an unidentified user posted a question:

> What are the applications of Postnikov approximation? As I understand it, it is dual to a cell decomposition and can, e.g. be used for computing some homotopy groups of spheres.

A commenter writes:

> Why not try reading any exposition of Postikov towers? The applications usually appear right after their definition. I've voted to close.

While some lower level questions like this one are made (often by newcomers) the site is mostly limited to very high level questions that have not been answered directly in other resources. Contributions on MO are not low-cost. Contributions often require original and new thinking which is effortful. Also, by contributing users potentially miss out on rewards from having published the same ideas in peer-reviewed journals. math.stackexchange.com was created for lower level math questions. Despite the high level, most questions on MO get answered, only 16.3% go unanswered and on average a question gets 2.42 answers.

There have been at least two other major online sites developed to aid research level mathematics through large scale online collaboration: polymath and Tricki. These other sites predate MO. While polymath1, the first and most successful of five projects had 39 contributors [7]; Tricki in September of 2010 had 100 users who have made at least one edit [10]; MathOverflow in October 2010 had 5,268 authors who had made at least one contribution. Already MO has a magnitude more contributors. We investigate the success of MO in gaining popularity.

THE CURRENT STUDY

In this study we undertake three major research objectives. We describe the motivations to contribute to MathOverflow; we compare the motivations of individuals with different levels of expertise; and we evaluate the importance of three kinds of social benefits in motivating contributions.

Objective 1: To describe the motivations for contributing to MathOverflow.

We investigate the reasons why users participate in MathOverflow. Other research has identified a variety of reasons why individuals contribute to communities of user-generated content, such as information seeking, entertainment, skill development, and altruism [19, 25]. We develop a full picture of the motivations to contribute by combining multiple sources. 1. Self reported motivations 2a. The kinds of participation that users undertake 2b. Which kinds of feedback encourage or discourage future participation.

Thus we combine two standard approaches to studying motivation in online communities. They each have their own advantages and disadvantages. The first method relies on gathering self-reported motivation from users (e.g. [23]). The second method relies on inferring user motivations from particular patterns of behavior, such as examining what feedback on past participation leads to future participation (e.g. [14]). The first method has the advantage of being able to describe user motivation in a deeper and more nuanced way through self-reports. The approach has the disadvantage of being susceptible to response biases. The second method has the advantage of being able to measure the motivations that drive actual behavior even if users are not consciously aware of them or do not report them. It has the disadvantage that it is more difficult to describe the true motivation behind the patterns in behavior. We combine both methods to make use of their complementary advantages.

Objective 2: To compare the motivations of individuals with different levels of expertise in mathematics.

One of the interesting aspects of MO being at the intersection of communities of user-generated content and scientific collaboration is the potential importance of expertise. The importance of level of expertise is something that is shared with software development and appears in the literature on contributions to open software. However expertise is more explicit and elevated within science. Level of expertise may influence the reasons for contributing to MO. Making helpful contributions will most likely be easier for individuals with more expertise [31]. Skill development may be less important to those with more expertise. Those with longer tenure in mathematics may have more organizational commitment that will translate into a stronger desire to benefit the community in MO [6]. We evaluate whether the motivations of senior professors differ or are similar to the motivations of undergraduate students. Findings about levels of expertise will likely generalize to other communities because expertise is an important part of knowledge sharing in general. The advantage of studying it in MO is that expertise is easier to measure.

Objective 3: To contrast the importance of three different kinds of social benefits.

Recognition has been identified as a potential motivator for contributions (e.g. [14]). We can be more specific in describing how recognition may matter. For example, recognition may be import because it is a proxy for social rewards. Social rewards may be especially important in motivating contributions. We investigate three possible kinds of rewards that may be motivating users to make contributions.

The first social motivation we investigate is ***reputation building***. Broadly our definition of reputation building also includes seeking social approval. Social exchange theory states that individuals choose to interact in order to receive specific social benefits [3]. If by contributing users can gain reputation in the community; building reputation can act as a social benefit that motivates contributions [32]. Related work has shown that social approval can also be an important motivator. When users are told that other community members like their past submissions they are more likely to make more contributions in the future [5].

The second motivation we investigate is ***relationship development***. The design of MO and other Q&A platforms creates an environment in which there is a direct recipient who benefits from the submission of an answer to a question. Sohn and Lekenby show that communities in which there is reciprocal exchange motivate more contributions [30]. One of the incentives of answering a question may be to help the question asker. By answering a question users build up social capital with the question asker in particular, this could be through impressing the asker or by inducing gratitude.

The third motivation we investigate is ***constructive feedback***. Constructive feedback is not a social benefit in of itself. Desire for constructive feedback is driven by a desire for skill development, however the process is social. Individuals may contribute to MO to obtain advice from a larger community on their ideas. The importance of whether the community critiques their answer may provide individuals with incentives to contribute. Skill development is an important motivation to contribute to other career focused communities [25].

We compare these motivations by examining user behaviors on MathOverflow. By using patterns of user behavior, Huberman and colleagues found that YouTube users' contributions were reinforced by getting recognition in the form of views [14]. We examine a broader set of community responses to assess which of these responses encourages participation. By looking at multiple kinds of community responses we can compare the importance of the three kinds of benefits that we have identified.

In this study we focus on answers. We record seven kinds of feedback authors can get on their answers and how many answers they later submit. There are two kinds of feedback that are important for reputation building. On MO community members can upvote or downvote answers to express their approval or disapproval of the answer. Ultimately the upvotes minus the downvotes make up the contribution's score. Together contribution scores make up the reputation score a user gets for the site. If higher scores on answers and fewer downvotes encourage more answers in the future we can infer that they are partially motivated by reputation building.

There are also two kinds of feedback that are important for relationship development. Question askers can select the answer that they like best, also question askers often directly comment on questions expressing interest or gratitude. If question answerers are encouraged by these two forms of response from question askers we can conclude that they are partially motivated by relationship development.

Finally community members leave comments on answers, in which we can measure whether individuals express either agreement or disagreement with the answer. If question answers are influenced by these comments we can infer that they are partially motivated by constructive feedback.

One possibility is that these three social benefits–reputation building, relationship development, and constructive feedback–may overlap conceptually. In terms of proximate motivations these social benefits are conceptually distinct. For example by receiving better scores users immediately get social approval and by receiving comments that agree or disagree with the answer users immediately get constructive advice on the content of their answer. These three social benefits may overlap in terms of deeper motivations. For example, if an individual is motivated by becoming higher status then they may be more inclined to being motivated by social approval or by constructive feedback. In this study we are only able to distinguish between proximate motivations. However, by distinguishing proximate motivations we have discovered something about the mechanisms through which motivations drive behavior.

METHOD

Information about users was collected by combining responses to a self-report survey with posting behavior on MO. Participants were recruited through two methods during September, 2010. All active participants (at least 30 reputation points) who included a personal website with a valid email address in their profile were contacted to take the web survey via email. The survey was also advertised on the main MO website (with a link to the survey) for four days. Posting behavior for users that completed the survey was compiled from publicly available dumps from MO servers. Posting behavior was collected for approximately one year from September 2009 (when the site began) to October 2010.

User Survey

A total of 401 participants completed the survey. A smaller sample of 217 users elected to give us their username on MO during the survey. This smaller sample was used in combined analyses of self-reports and user behavior. The users sampled contributed at the time about 27.5% of the posts on the site. This sample is most likely not representative of MO; it overrepresents the most frequent contributors to MO. However, we are most interested in what motivates the frequent contributors because their efforts result in the majority of content on the site.

Users were asked to report demographic information, including the highest mathematics degree they were working on or had obtained and to complete a motivations scale. **Level of expertise** was operationalized as the highest mathematics degree, which consisted of the levels: undergraduate, masters, PhD, post-doctoral fellow or lecturer, and professor. Masters students were classified as those in masters level programs; PhD students were classified as those in PhD programs even if they had not obtained a masters yet. To simplify figures, level of expertise was dichotomized based on whether a participant was above the PhD level. The motivations scale was adapted from a scale used on the online community of user-generated content, Everything2.com [19]. The questions were modified to be specific to the uses of MO and mathematics research in general. The self-discovery items were not included because they were not relevant to MO.

User Behavior

Survey data was matched with user behavior on the site. Two kinds of user behavior was recorded. First we recorded basic contribution information. For each user the **rate of questions** and the **rate of answers** was recorded; this was the total number of questions and answers divided by the time the user was active on the site. By looking at the rate of contributions we controlled for differences in when users discovered or left the site. We further broke down the contribution of answers into two kinds: answers to popular questions and answers to unpopular questions. Popular questions were defined as those that scored in the top 25% of all questions, unpopular questions were defined as those that scored in the bottom 25% of questions. The cutoffs were respectively greater or equal to 13 points and less than or equal to 3 points. For each user the **rate of answers to popular questions** and the **rate of answers to unpopular questions** was recorded.

Second we examined which kinds of community feedback encouraged or discouraged future contributions. We focused this analysis on the contribution of answers. We measured several feedback variables:

reputation building

score: The quality rating community members gave the answer (log transformed)

downvoted: Whether any user indicated that they disliked the answer

relationship development

accepted answer: Whether the question asker accepted the answer

question asker comment: Whether the question asker left a comment about the answer

constructive feedback

comments: The number of comments left by others about the answer (log transformed)

agreement: The amount of agreement expressed in the comments

disagreement: The amount of disagreement expressed in the comments

The comments were linguistically analyzed using Linguistic Inquiry and Word Count (LIWC), which measures categories of psychologically meaningful words [27]. The level of agreement was operationalized as the amount of positive emotion words (e.g. 'excellent') and assent (e.g. 'yes', 'agree'). The level of disagreement was operationalized as the amount of negative emotion words (e.g. 'difficult') and negations (e.g. 'no', 'not'). To create measures of agreement and disagreement z-scores of the two linguistic categories were taken and summed.

Using four distinct models we tested whether community feedback encouraged or discouraged the submission of answers. First we examined whether the feedback given to the first answer a user submitted predicted if the user would go on to post an answer again. Logistic regression was used with the posting of an answer again as the outcome variable and the feedback variables as predictors. The analysis was restricted to users who submitted an answer not a question first to avoid confounds related to contribution history. We report Nagelkerke pseudo R^2 for this model.

Next we examined which feedback encouraged submission of future answers for multiple periods of time. A method similar to the one established by Huberman and colleagues was used to determine which kinds of feedback encouraged or discouraged submission of answers [14]. Submissions were divided into two-week intervals. For each user, feedback variables were measured for periods in which there was at least one answer and were paired with the number of answers in the next two-week interval. Feedback variables were averaged across the two week period. This method allows observation of feedback for many time periods per user rather than focusing on a single contribution.

Multi-level models were used; two week time periods were nested within users. By using multi-level models we were able to control for individual differences in the rates of answers and quality of feedback. A two-step process was used to evaluate the significance of the feedback variables. All feedback variables except agreement and disagreement were included in the model. Then the model was restricted to those answers which received comments, the significant variables from the first model were included as well as agreement and disagreement. We report the percentage of variance explained when adding the predictor variables to the intercept only model; this is a common substitute for R^2.

This second method was used to examine feedback given to answers in general and to answers to popular and unpopular questions separately.

RESULTS

The results are grouped by the method used. The results relevant to the three objectives are intertwined and will be summarized in the discussion.

What reasons do users give for why they participate?

Confirmatory factor analysis (CFA) was performed with the same factor structure presented by Lampe and colleagues [19] excluding the omitted factor, self-discovery. CFA showed that this 5 factor model was a poor fit (RMSEA = 0.13). Exploratory factor analysis of the motivation scale was conducted. Observation of the scree plot revealed three factors. Oblique rotation was used; all items loaded above 0.30. The first factor, which we will refer to as recreation, included questions pertaining to entertainment and procrastination (α = 0.82, mean = 2.67, sd = 1.08). The second factor, which we will refer to as self advancement, included questions pertaining to information seeking, reputation building, generating ideas, and relationship development (α = 0.74, mean = 2.07, sd = 0.74). The third factor, which we will refer to as helping, included questions pertaining to providing information to others or contributing to a body of mathematics knowledge (α = 0.83, mean = 2.29, sd = 1.11). All three factors have alpha reliability above the 0.70 acceptability cutoff, indicating that they are internally consistent. Confirmatory factor analysis with the new 3 factor model was a better fit (RMSEA = 0.10).

The strongest reasons for participating in MO were in order: recreation, helping, and self advancement. Breaking down the motivation questions into subscales provides more detail on individuals motivations (see table 1). Both reputation building and relationship development scored very low. Getting information scored the highest.

Table 1. Means and standard deviations for motivation subscales.

Factor	Subscale	mean (sd)
Recreation	entertainment	2.63 (1.21)
	procrastination	2.72 (1.22)
Self advancement	getting information	3.01 (1.34)
	generating ideas	2.04 (1.01)
	reputation building	1.51 (0.75)
	relationship development	2.22 (1.16)
Helping	helping	2.30 (1.11)

Those with higher levels of expertise differed significantly in their self-reported motivations from those with lower levels of expertise. Repeated measures ANOVA with level of experience (e.g. undergrad, masters ... professor) as a between subjects variable and motivation type as a within subjects variable showed a significant interaction between level of experience and motivation type (F(2,385) = 17.5, p < 0.001). Figure 3 shows that individuals with more expertise rated that they participated in MO to help others more than individuals with less expertise. There was no difference for the other kinds of motivations.

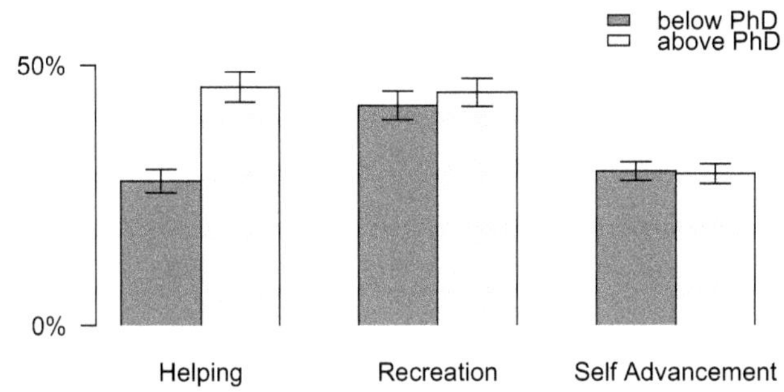

Figure 3. Self-reported reasons for participating in MathOverflow separated by level of expertise. Postdocs, lecturers and professors are grouped into 'above PhD'. Graduate students, terminating PhD students, and undergraduate students are grouped into 'below PhD'.

How do users participate?

The different ways that people participate in the site also give us insight into the reasons why they contribute. We found that users with higher levels of expertise answered more questions and asked fewer questions. Repeated measures ANOVA with level of expertise as a between subjects factor and participation type as a within subjects factor showed a significant interaction between level of expertise and participation type (F(1,194) = 22.7, p < 0.001). Figure 4 shows that those beyond the PhD level produced on average more answers (mean = 2.47, sd = 2.68) and fewer questions (mean = 0.40, sd = 0.48) than those at or below PhD level (answers: mean = 1.38, sd = 1.81; questions: mean = 0.62, sd = 0.85).

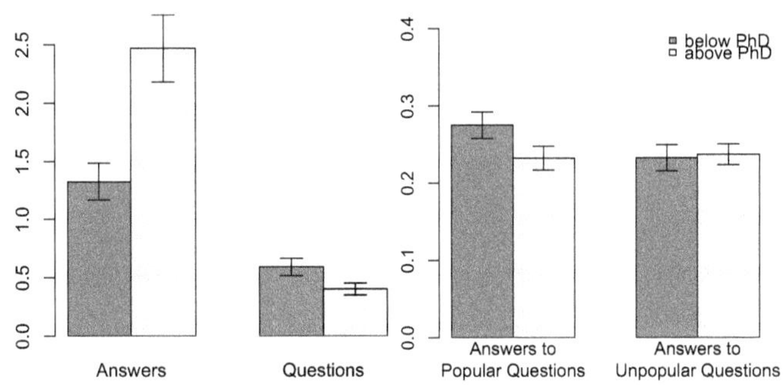

Figure 4. Patterns of participation separated by level of expertise. The left figure gives the rate of questions and answers per two weeks. The right figure gives the rate of answers to popular and unpopular questions controlling for overall rate of answering.

MO is limited to fact and advice oriented questions, so there are not distinct kinds of questions (unlike Yahoo! Answers which has both informational and conversational questions [12]). However there are differences in the popularity of questions. We found that level of experience predicted different rates of answering popular and unpopular questions.

Figure 4 shows that users with less expertise had a higher rate of answering popular questions compared to users with more expertise controlling for answering rate overall ($\beta = -0.03$, df = 178, p = 0.006, $R^2 = 0.04$). There was no difference based on level of expertise in the rate of answering unpopular questions ($\beta = 0.01$, df = 178, p = 0.16, $R^2 = 0.01$)

What feedback encourages participation?

The kinds of feedback that encourage participation can reveal the incentives that drive users to contribute (see table 2).

Table 2. Four models identifying the kinds of feedback that encourage or discourage submitting answers. Model 1: does feedback to a users' first answer predict answering again? Model 2: does feedback to answers predict future contributions over multiple timeperiods? Model 3/4: does feedback to answers to popular/unpopular questions predict future contributions over multiple timeperiods? Pseudo R^2 and degrees of freedom are given for the models with and without language predictors (models with language predictors in parentheses).

	Model 1: First Answer odds	Model 2: Answers Overall β	Model 3: Answers Popular Questions β	Model 4: Answers Unpopular Questions β
intercept	0.00	-0.63	-0.05	-1.07
score	9.73***	0.34***	0.21***	0.56***
downvoted	0.53***	-0.05 †	-0.07 †	-0.11 †
accepted answer	1.36*	0.04 †	0.14**	0.41
question asker comment	1.11	0.00	0.09*	-0.01
comments	0.93	-0.03*	-0.06**	-0.01
agreement	0.96	-0.00	0.01	-0.00
disagreement	1.08 †	0.02**	0.02*	0.02*
Pseudo R^2	6.4% (6.8%)	4.5% (8.6%)	5.0% (5.8%)	6.0% (5.9%)
df	2126 (1029)	6076 (4236)	2451 (1492)	2484 (1540)

Signif. codes: '†' 0.10, '' 0.05, '**' 0.01, '***' 0.001*

The results provide evidence that reputation building is an important incentive driving participation. In all four models, receiving a higher score on an answer was the strongest and most consistent predictor of future contributions. Users who received higher scores on the first answer they submitted were more likely to submit answers in the future. Users were more likely to submit more answers after periods in which they received higher scores. Receiving downvotes on one's first answer was strongly related to not answering another question. Periods in which a users' answers were downvoted was marginally related to making fewer future contributions for the other three models. The importance of answer scores and marginal effect of not being downvoted suggests reputation building is an important incentive.

Feedback related to relationship development was only partially related to encouraging future contributions. Of particular interest is the fact that this feedback mattered for answers to popular questions and not for answers to unpopular questions. Periods in which users' answers to popular questions were accepted by the question asker or in which the question asker commented on the answer encouraged future contributions. This was not true for answers to unpopular questions. Relationship development may be especially incentivizing when it is with high reputation individuals or when it occurs with a large audience.

Unexpected findings were found for community responses related to constructive feedback. Receiving comments discouraged participation in two of the models. When comments were given, three models showed that disagreement significantly encouraged participation and one showed it was marginally related to participation. Agreement in comments was not related to participation.

The direction of effects were consistent between what encouraged first answers and answers in general. Answer score was significant for both first answers and answers in general. Whether an answer was downvoted, accepted by the question asker or commenters expressed disagreement with it was marginally significant for one model and significant for the other. Many of the effects were consistent across all four models, which suggests there are consistent incentives to contribute. The largest differences were found between answers to popular and unpopular questions.

Finally, we tested whether level of expertise moderated the effect of answer score, the strongest predictor, on future contributions. Including an interaction effect between level of expertise and score was not significant ($\beta = 0.04$, $p = 0.73$); the main effect of score continued to be significant. There is no evidence that receiving higher answer scores is a larger incentive for those with lower levels of expertise.

DISCUSSION

In this study we described some of the motivations to participate in MO using a self-reported questionnaire and by inferring motivations from behavior on the site. Reputation building was found to encourage participation, although it was the lowest self-reported motivation. Other kinds of community responses also encouraged participation. Users with higher levels of expertise reported using MO to help others more frequently.

Motivations to use MathOverflow

Past work has categorized motivations to participate in online communities into six categories [9, 19]. On MO, three of these, getting information, reputation building, and relationship development were strongly correlated. Within MO these three factors are more strongly interrelated than in other communities. One explanation is that they are all necessary components of individual advancement as a mathematician. Moreover the self-discovery motivation was not relevant to this community. Thus, on MO these motivations factored into only three categories–recreation, helping, and self advancement. If however we examine the original categories, motivations on MO were similar to motivations on Everything2.com in that recreation was reported as most important and reputation building and relationship development were reported as the least important [19].

There was partial support from an analysis of user behavior on the site that reputation building, relationship development and constructive feedback motivated contributions. This will be explained in more detail in a later section.

Level of expertise

Level of expertise was related to only a few key differences in motivations. Users with higher math expertise reported that they use MO to help others more. These users also submitted answers at a faster rate. Users with higher levels of expertise may use MO to help others because they are better able to do so and/or because they feel a desire to share their expertise.

Despite the potential importance of informal recognition for users with lower expertise [2], we did not find that MO users with lower expertise valued reputation building more highly. Users with lower expertise did not report using MO for self advancement more frequently and moreover they did not contribute more in response to getting higher scores on answers. Although one should be cautious in interpreting null results, one explanation is that encouragement from gaining recognition may not plateau as users gain more expertise.

Reputation building, relationship development, and constructive feedback

User behavior was analyzed to complement findings from self-reports of motivations. We found evidence that reputation building did act as an incentive encouraging contributions. Partial support was found that other kinds of community responses also encouraged participation. All of these effects are weak; they explained 4% to 8% of the variance. However, even if these incentives are strong we would only expect to discover weak effects given the amount of error introduced by averaging feedback over time.

The strongest, most consistent evidence was found for the importance of reputation building in encouraging contributions. This is in contrast to self-reports which list it as the lowest rated motivation for participating in MO. The importance of reputation building is consistent with observations of other scientific collaboration. Reputation building on MO is a form of informal recognition and informal recognition can take the place of formal credit in large scale collaborations [2]. There is no formal credit (such as authorship on a paper) on MO, making informal recognition more important. In addition, MO provides the opportunity to gain interpersonal recognition that may not be as available through other means.

There was weak evidence that relationship development acted as an incentive to contribute. The evidence suggested that relationship development was more important when answering popular questions than unpopular questions. It may be of more value when the relationship is with high status question askers or when there is a large audience observing the connection. The fact that relationship development is more important for popular questions suggests it may be another form of reputation building.

There were mixed results for constructive feedback acting as an incentive. Looking first at all contributions, receiving constructive feedback (comments) acted as a disincentive. Second, when we restricted the analysis to those contributions which had comments, then comments that disagreed the most acted as an incentive. Disagreement shows that the commenters took the answer seriously. For example in the comments in response to an answer on MO the person who had asked the question first wrote: "Thanks. It will take some time to see if that's what I need, but it looks interesting." and then "No, this doesn't help. Thanks anyway."

It was this second comment that scored high for disagreement. This response was very polite, but it was critical of the answer which turned out not to be helpful. Even though the answer turned out to be a false lead, the response demonstrated that the questioner seriously considered the user's answer and in this case was glad they had contributed it. Users may be looking for more than simple approval from their audience. It may be important that their submissions were considered substantial contributions even if not ultimately helpful. Having one's answer accepted without comment is better still.

Limitations

The method of inferring motivations from user behavior has some limitations. Although we measure the effect of community response on subsequent contributions, we cannot be certain that it is the feedback that is causing the change in contributions. There are alternative explanations. For example, users may have had streaks in which they posted good answers that got positive responses and also answered many questions. Even if there is a causal relationship, there are multiple psychological reasons why community response might encourage participation. For example, receiving a high score on a question may be motivating because it increases a user's reputation score, or alternatively because it confirms that the user has expertise worth sharing.

Applications and future directions

Authors have argued that content ratings systems could encourage users who post highly appreciated content to contribute more [17, 20]. Our findings confirm that ratings can be used to encourage participation. Altruistic tasks, such as answering questions, have fewer direct benefits. Thus providing explicit social benefits may be important. 'Tricki', the wiki like project to create a repository of mathematics knowledge, was not as successful as MO. This may in part be because there were no social rewards for users who contributed knowledge. On MO users who write answers get credit both in terms of the rating they receive and comments from other users; on Tricki there was no direct credit or feedback from others.

Future work should investigate how to best design a content rating system to encourage participation. In the process of evaluating such a rating system, this work would further clarify the motivations to participate. There are a number of questions left to investigate. One, would answer ratings be more encouraging if they were more differentiated? For example, there could be separate ratings for quality, novelty, providing references, or being thought provoking. This would provide insight into whether users are rewarded by any kind of recognition or only specific kinds. Sites such as Slashdot already use ratings systems that have more clearly refined meanings. Two, would answer ratings be as encouraging if they did not contribute to a user's overall reputation score? Three, would quality ratings be more encouraging if individuals could tell who was rating their answer? If so, which raters (e.g. friends, popular users) would be the most encouraging? Sites such as Daily Kos have this design; content ratings also include a list of the users who cast the votes. The fact that a response from the question asker matters more for popular questions suggests that users may be encouraged by the approval of some MO users more than others.

CONCLUSION

MathOverflow is the first in what may become many participatory online communities of scientific collaboration. In this paper we described some of the motivations that encourage users to participate. We showed that users with more expertise report using MO to help more, but do not differ in using it for reputation building from those with less expertise. Multiple forms of community responses encourage participation, of these reputation building may be especially important.

REFERENCES

1. L. A. Adamic, J. Zhang, E. Bakshy, M. S. Ackerman, and A. Arbor. Knowledge sharing and Yahoo Answers: Everyone knows something. In *Proc. WWW 2008*, 665–674. ACM Press.
2. J. P. Birnholtz. What does it mean to be an author? The intersection of credit, contribution, and collaboration in science. *Journal of the American Society for Information Science*, 57:1758–1770, 2006.
3. P. M. Blau. *Exchange and Power in Social Life* Wiley, New York, 1964.
4. M. Burke, C. Marlow, and T. Lento. Feed me: Motivating newcomer contribution in social network sites. In *Proc. CHI 2009*, 945–954. ACM Press.
5. C. Cheshire. Selective incentives and generalized information exchange. *Social Psychology Quarterly*, 70:82–100, 2007.
6. D. Constant, L. Sproull, and S. Kiesler. The kindness of strangers: The usefulness of electronic weak ties for technical advice. *Organization Science*, 9:119–135, 1996.
7. J. Cranshaw and A. Kittur. The Polymath Project : Lessons from a successful online collaboration in mathematics. In *Proc. CHI 2011*, 1865–1874. ACM Press.

8. D. Dearman and K. N. Truong. Why users of Yahoo! Answers do not answer questions. In *Proc. CHI 2010*, 329–332. ACM Press, 2010.

9. U. M. Dholakia, R. P. Bagozzi, and L. K. Pearo. A social influence model of consumer participation in network- and small-group-based virtual communities. *International Journal of Research in Marketing*, 21:241–263, 2004.

10. T. Gowers. http://gowers.wordpress.com/2010/09/24/is-the-tricki-dead/, 2010.

11. A. G. Greenwald, T. A. Poehlman, E. L. Uhlmann, and M. R. Banaji. Understanding and using the Implicit Association Test: III. Meta-analysis of predictive validity. *Journal of Personality and Social Psychology*, 97:17–41, 2009.

12. F. M. Harper, D. Moy, and J. A. Konstan. Facts or friends? Distinguishing informational and conversational questions in social Q&A sites. In *Proc. CHI 2009*, 759–768. ACM Press.

13. G. Hertel, S. Niedner, and S. Herrmann. Motivation of software developers in Open Source projects: An internet-based survey of contributors to the Linux kernel. *Research Policy*, 32:1159–1177, 2003.

14. B. A. Huberman, D. M. Romero, and F. Wu. Crowdsourcing, attention and productivity. *Journal of Information Science*, 35:758–765, 2009.

15. E. Joyce and R. E. Kraut. Predicting continued participation in newsgroups. *Journal of Computer-Mediated Communication*, 11:723–747, 2006.

16. B. Klandermans and D. Oegema. Potentials, networks, motivations, and barriers: Steps toward participation in social movements. *American Sociological Review*, 52:519–531, 1987.

17. J. Koh, Y.-G. Kim, B. Butler, and G.-w. Bock. Encouraging participation in virtual communities. *Communications of the ACM*, 50:69–73, 2007.

18. K. R. Lakhani and R. G. Wolf. Why hackers do what they do: Understanding motivation and effort in Free/Open Source Software projects, In *Perspectives on Free and Open Source Software* J. Feller, B. Fitzgerald, S. Hissam, K. R. Lakhani, Editors, pp. 3–22. MIT Press, Cambridge, MA, 2005.

19. C. Lampe, R. Wash, A. Velasquez, and E. Ozkaya. Motivations to participate in online communities. In *Proc. CHI 2010*, 1927–1936. ACM Press.

20. L. Mamykina, B. Manoim, M. Mittal, G. Hripcsak, and B. Hartmann. Design lessons from the fastest Q&A site in the West. In *Proc. CHI 2011*, 2857–2866. ACM Press.

21. T. D. Moore and M. A. Serva. Understanding member motivation for contributing to different types of virtual communities: A proposed framework. In *Proc. SIGMIS-CPR 2007*, 153–158. ACM Press.

22. K. K. Nam, M. S. Ackerman, and L. A. Adamic. Questions in, knowledge iN? A study of Naver's question answering community. In *Proc. CHI 2009*, 779–788. ACM Press.

23. O. Nov. What motivates Wikipedians? *Communications of the ACM*, 50:60–64, 2007.

24. O. Nov, M. Naaman, and C. Ye. What drives content tagging: The case of photos on Flickr. In *Proc. CHI 2008*, 1097–1100. ACM Press.

25. S. Oreg and O. Nov. Exploring motivations for contributing to open source initiatives: The roles of contribution context and personal values. *Computers in Human Behavior*, 24:2055–2073, 2008.

26. D. L. Paulhus. Measurement and control of response bias In *Measures of Personality and Social Psychological Attitudes*, J. Robinson, P. Shaver, and L. Wrightsman, Editors, pp. 17–59. Academic Press, Inc., San Diego, CA, 1991.

27. J. W. Pennebaker, R. J. Booth, and M. E. Francis. Linguistic Inquiry and Word Count: LIWC, 2007.

28. P. Russo and O. Nov. Photo tagging over time: A longitudinal study of the role of attention, network density, and motivations. In *Proc. ICWSM 2010*, 146–153. AAAI.

29. R. M. Ryan and E. L. Deci. Intrinsic and extrinsic motivations: Classic definitions and new directions. *Contemporary Educational Psychology*, 25:54–67, 2000.

30. D. Sohn and J. D. Leckenby. A Structural Solution to Communication Dilemmas in a Virtual Community. *Journal of Communication*, 57:435–449, 2007.

31. M. M. Wasko and S. Faraj. It is what one does: Why people participate and help others in electronic communities of practice. *The Journal of Strategic Information Systems*, 9:155–173, 2000.

32. M. M. Wasko and S. Faraj. Why should I share? Examining social capital and knowledge contribution in electronic networks of practice. *MIS Quarterly*, 29:35–57, 2005.

33. F. Wu, D. M. Wilkinson, and B. A. Huberman. Feedback loops of attention in peer production. In *International Conference on Computational Science and Engineering*, 409–415, 2009.

34. X. Zhang and F. Zhu. Group size and incentives to contribute: A natural experiment at Chinese Wikipedia. *American Economic Review, Forthcoming*, 2010.

Dynamic Changes in Motivation in Collaborative Citizen-Science Projects

Dana Rotman[1], Jennifer Preece[1], Jennifer Hammock[2], Kezee Procita[1], Derek Hansen[1,3], Cynthia Parr[2], Darcy Lewis[1], David Jacobs[4]

[1]College of Information Studies, University of Maryland iSchool
[2]Smithsonian Institute
[3] Fulton College of Engineering and Technology, Brigham Young University
[4]Department of Computer Science, University of Maryland

drotman, preece, kprocita, djacobs @umd.edu, dlhansen @byu.edu, cparr, hammock @si.edu

ABSTRACT

Online citizen science projects engage volunteers in collecting, analyzing, and curating scientific data. Existing projects have demonstrated the value of using volunteers to collect data, but few projects have reached the full collaborative potential of scientists and volunteers. Understanding the shared and unique motivations of these two groups can help designers establish the technical and social infrastructures needed to promote effective partnerships. We present findings from a study of the motivational factors affecting participation in ecological citizen science projects. We show that volunteers are motivated by a complex framework of factors that dynamically change throughout their cycle of work on scientific projects; this motivational framework is strongly affected by personal interests as well as external factors such as attribution and acknowledgment. Identifying the pivotal points of motivational shift and addressing them in the design of citizen-science systems will facilitate improved collaboration between scientists and volunteers.

Author Keywords

Crowdsourcing, citizen science, scientists, volunteers, motivation, collaboration, ecology.

ACM Classification Keywords

H5.m. Information interfaces and presentation (e.g., HCI): Miscellaneous.

General Terms

Human Factors, Design

INTRODUCTION

Citizen science, or the collaboration between scientists and volunteers, has been well documented [1-2]. Traditional scientific inquiries are conducted by individuals with scientific education and qualifications, i.e., professional scientists. Collaborative citizen-science projects, on the other hand, include citizen scientists: individuals who typically lack formal credentials and do not hold professional positions in scientific institutions or projects, who participate in scientific endeavors related to their personal interests. Distributed technologies offer new opportunities for conducting scientific inquiries on a larger scale than ever before by extending beyond geographically collocated tasks and enabling distributed collaboration. Citizen science has found success in various ways, in multiple disciplines: from documenting observations (eBird), collecting and analyzing data (Galaxy Zoo), creating content (VitalSigns Gulf preservation initiative), to curating it (Encyclopedia of Life - EOL).

Bonney et al. [3] divided citizen science projects into three major categories: (1) Contributory projects, in which volunteers contribute data to projects designed by scientists; (2) Collaborative projects, designed by scientists, but where volunteers can not only contribute data but also aid in the project design; and (3) Co-created projects, where both scientists and volunteers are involved in all parts of the project. In most cases collaboration between scientists and volunteers does not amount to co-creation or collaboration, but is maintained in the contributory phase, as data collection and in some cases partial data analysis (e.g. classification, documentation) is done by the volunteers under scientists' supervision. The data is then delivered to scientists who use it in their research.

In order to facilitate broader, sustainable, and more inclusive collaboration between scientists and volunteers we must design environments that speak to the needs of both groups. To be able to do that, we first need to understand what motivates each group and how to structure activities that leverage these unique motivations.

In this paper, we explore these motivations. We present a complex framework of motivational factors that affect participation in citizen science projects. Two pivotal points in volunteers' participation are significantly affected by motivational factors: the initial decision to participate in a project and the ensuing decision to continue this engagement once the initial task is completed.

We situate our exploration in the design of a new tool for conservation-focused collaborative citizen science, named Biotracker (www.biotrackers.net). This paper's contribution is in identifying the points at which motivational interventions are crucial, as well as identifying the types of motivations that are pertinent at each point. These findings will be used in developing the Biotracker system. We also hope to inspire other novel system designs for citizen science projects.

PREVIOUS WORK

Citizen science

Citizen science is based on a longstanding tradition of assistive participation of volunteers in scientific endeavors, which predates the Internet [1-2]. Advances in communication technology, specifically online and mobile interaction, enable citizen science to become more distributed and more widely practiced than ever before. Citizen scientists make contributions to many disciplines where the collection of large-scale field data is crucial, including biology [4], environmental studies [5], astronomy [6], but also in other fields, such as chemistry, and mathematics [7].

Collaboration between scientists and volunteers

Citizen science is not without its problems. Jonas Salk succinctly put it: "Scientists often have an aversion to what nonscientists say about science" [8]. Scientists, educated, trained and placed within the hierarchal academic world, are sometimes wary of letting others, who do not have the same credentials as they do, into their labs and research. Citizen scientists, who are volunteers without formal training or credentials, challenge this pattern. In many cases, although volunteers are allowed to take part in scientific processes, they are limited to distributed data collection and limited analysis, and are excluded from later phases of the research, in a way that prevents complete collaboration [5].

Scientific collaboration is shaped by a variety of factors, ranging from the social norms of science and the structure of disciplinary knowledge, to the specific characteristics and idiosyncrasies of existing formal and informal research networks and alliances [9-10]. The scientific work is founded upon shared vocabulary, practices, and meanings, and is dependant among other things, on mutual recognition of prestige, knowledge and competency [8]. Prestige, for example, is critical to establishing collaborations [10]. Consequently, bridging between scientists and volunteers, whose prestige in the scientific community is inherently different, is difficult.

For all these reasons, and although the contribution of volunteers to the development of science has been well documented [11-14], their participation is often considered peripheral.

Motivational framework

Bos and his colleagues [15] defined one type of scientific collaboratory that supports collaboration between distributed scientists and volunteers as "open community contribution systems". A major issue for such communities is the need to motivate contributors while also ensuring the credibility and validity of the input data according to scientific standards. Indeed, one of the biggest challenges for community contribution systems, and communities of practice more generally, is to "allow participants at all levels to feel like full members" [16]. This is particularly challenging in boundary spanning communities where community members have different values, goals, and criteria for assessing the quality and merit of contributions.

Researchers have found a wide variety of reasons, at both the individual and group level, that explain why people participate in online collaborative activities [17]. Examples like Wikipedia, EOL, eBird and even geocaching games suggest that there are a wide variety of methods to motivate individuals to contribute to repositories [18-19], even if we do not fully understand these motivations. Social psychology theories have been harnessed to examine contributions to online repositories and recommender systems. These studies, which tested various social and technical interventions, found that emphasizing the uniqueness of an individual's contribution and setting group goals increased participation, as did expert and peer oversight [20-21]. Others [22] emphasized the significance of facilitating small scale contributions from larger pools of participants. However, none of these studies were conducted in a scientific context.

Batson et al. [23] identified four types of motivations for social participation towards common goals: egoism, altruism, collectivism, and principlism. *Egoism* occurs when the ultimate goal is to increase one's own welfare. *Altruism* has the goal of increasing the welfare of another individual or group of individuals. *Collectivism* has the goal of increasing the welfare of a specific group that one belongs to. *Principlism* has the goal of upholding one or more principles dear to one's heart (e.g., justice or equality). Batson's theory did not address collaborative science, but it is compelling in this context, as it emphasizes the role of motivation in building and sustaining community involvement, such as is needed for collaborative scientific projects. Therefore, we selected this theory as a general framework against which we will compare our findings.

METHOD

Our aim in this study was to gain an in-depth understanding of the various motivations that lead scientists and volunteers to engage in collaborative projects together. The research questions guiding this study were:

(1) What are the major motivational factors affecting volunteers and scientists engagement in citizen science projects?
(2) What are the major motivational barriers to such collaboration?

In January-April 2011 we deployed an online survey that assessed participants' views regarding the four motivational factors outlined by Batson et al. The survey was based on a pilot study that was tested in December 2010 with 20 participants. We administered both the pilot and the survey via SurveyMonkey and on paper. Snowball recruitment was done by publicizing a link to the survey on the Encyclopedia of Life newsletter, and by directly contacting various groups interested in biodiversity, conservation, or citizen science. Social media was also utilized for this purpose, as links to the survey were published on Biotracker's Facebook page and on Twitter.

In all, we collected 142 responses. While we couldn't calculate overall response rate, completion rate for participants who began filling out the survey was 54% (for the two groups combined). We provided participants with definitions of the terms "professional scientist" and "volunteer" and asked them to self-identify with either group (scientists n=62, 44%; volunteers n=80, 56%). The majority in each group had more than one year's experience engaging in citizen science projects (75% of scientists and 56% of volunteers). The level of expertise was determined for the scientists based on their position within the academic world (e.g., doctoral student, lab technician, tenured and tenure track researchers, etc.), and for volunteers, by years of participating in citizen science projects. The male to female ratio was similar in both groups (60% of scientists were male, while 57% of volunteers were male). There was no difference in age distribution between the two groups.

For statistical analysis, comparisons of motivational factors within groups were performed using Friedman's test (the non-parametric test for differences between groups across multiple conditions); comparisons of motivational factors between groups were performed using the Mann-Whitney test (the non-parametric test for two independent samples). For both tests the level of significance was set at 0.05, Bonferroni adjustment was used in both cases to account for multiple comparisons. Data from the survey was analyzed using SPSS v.18.

The survey respondents were asked to provide contact details if they would be willing to be interviewed for the study. Of the 46 respondents we contacted, 11 were interviewed. We also recruited 7 interviewees through the same social media outlets mentioned earlier. Interviews were semi-structured, conducted by two of the research team members via telephone or Skype, and were recorded and transcribed. Interviews were between 30 minutes and an hour long. The interviewers also took notes and, where appropriate, collected additional data (e.g., personal and organizational websites, reports of scientific projects, newspaper articles). Of the interviewees, 7 were professional scientists ranging from PhD students to senior faculty, and 11 were volunteers. Volunteers' experience ranged from several months and participation in a few projects to more than 10 years' experience and deep involvement with consecutive projects. Most participants (15) had more than 3 years' experience. One participant was a professional scientist who began his career as a volunteer, thus presenting both viewpoints. Eleven interviewees were female and seven were male. Their ages ranged from early twenties to late fifties, though most were in their thirties and forties. All engaged in conservation, ecology, and natural history related projects.

The interviews were analyzed using grounded theory [24]. Grounded theory allows for themes and concepts to arise from the data itself, in a way that portrays the actual sentiments and experiences perceived by the interviewees. To achieve that, the interviews were divided into two groups (scientists and volunteers), and each interview was coded manually to reveal emergent categories (e.g., "motivational factors", "initiating collaboration" "work patterns", etc.). These categories were later bundled into themes (e.g., "cycle of collaboration"), which were axially referenced within each group and across groups, to reveal higher-level concepts. Following the analysis, most interviewees were contacted again 10 weeks later and asked to review our findings. The vast majority of interviewees concurred with the findings. Where interviewees offered further insights, we've adjusted our findings accordingly.

FINDINGS

We first discuss the survey results. We then follow with an in-depth analysis of the qualitative findings emerging from the interviews.

Survey findings

Participants were asked to rank on a Likert scale (1-5, where 1 is strongly disagree and 5 is strongly agree) statements that reflected their views regarding collaboration between scientists and volunteers. The statements were inspired by Batson et al.'s [23] framework, and were similar for both populations, with the necessary adjustments made to address each population. A sample of the statements is presented in Table 1.

Egoism:
The data volunteers provide enhance my research (scientists)
Collaboration with scientists enables me to open my horizons to new ideas and knowledge (volunteers)
Collectivism:
Collaboration with volunteers can be helpful to others in the scientific community (scientists)
Collaboration between scientists and scientific volunteers is beneficial for the volunteers (volunteers)
Altruism:
Collaboration with volunteers helps educate them about scientific methods (scientists)
Collaboration between scientists and scientific volunteers is beneficial for scientists (volunteers)
Principlism:
Collaboration with volunteers is worthwhile because I believe that all scientific knowledge should be accessible to everyone, regardless of their expertise (scientists)
Collaboration with scientists is worthwhile for making scientific knowledge accessible to the public and outside the scientific community (volunteers)

Table 1. Sample survey items; target population is noted in parenthesis.

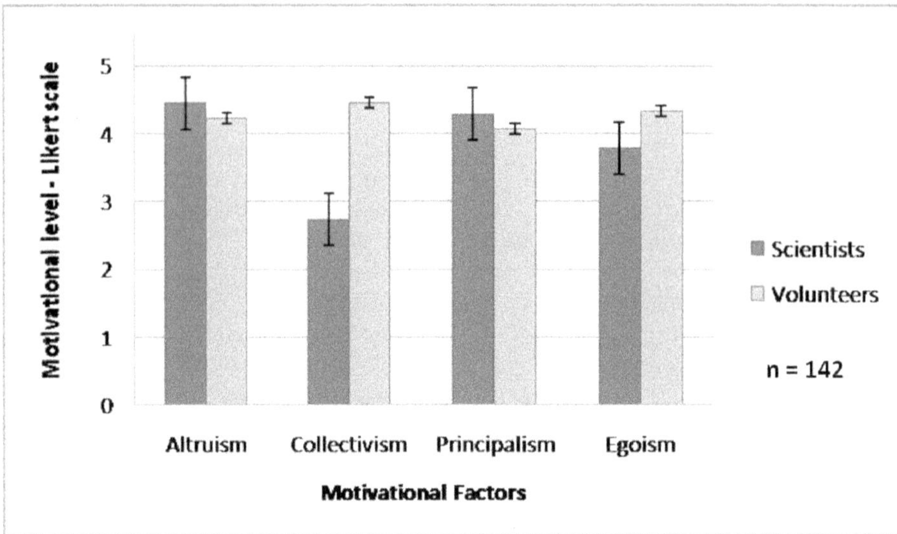

Figure 1. Scientists' and volunteers' attitudes towards motivational factors affecting their participation in scientific collaborations

Among volunteers, the average response rating to each of the categories was similar (average scores ranging between 4.08 and 4.46) (Figure 1). Scientists valued altruism (average score 4.45) and principlism similarly (4.29), but valued egoism (3.78) slightly less. Collectivism, or increasing the welfare of one's group, (2.73) was valued significantly less as a motivational factor by scientists (Friedman's test, with post hoc Wilcoxon Signed-Rank test, $df=3, p < 0.001$).

When comparing between groups (Mann-Whitney test), there was a small but statistically significant difference between scientists and volunteers in the way they valued *egoism* (mean response 3.8 for scientists vs. 4.2 for volunteers, U=250, $p < 0.001$) making egoism a slightly more salient motivator for volunteers; however, there was a marked difference in regards to another factor – *collectivism*. The mean response for scientists was lower than for volunteers (2.732 vs. 4.456, U=68.5, $p < 0.001$). The compilation of within groups and between groups differences in regards to collectivism suggests that volunteers believed collaboration with scientists would benefit the volunteer community more than scientists believed it would benefit themselves (i.e., the scientific community), but also that scientists valued collectivism less than other motivational factors. Specifically, altruism and principlism, were deemed most important by scientists, reflecting the notion that science is made to benefit the greater good. Age, gender, and level of expertise did not significantly influence the responses of volunteers or scientists (p value was found to be non-significant).

These findings were used as antecedents to the qualitative inquiry.

Qualitative interviews

In this section we discuss findings pertaining to (1) volunteers' motivations; (2) scientists' motivations; (3) motivational obstacles to collaboration.

Volunteers' motivations for collaborating with scientists

Based on the survey results, in which volunteers acknowledged the importance of four motivational factors laid out by Batson et al. as almost equal, our expectation was that volunteers will exhibit a comparable view in the interviews. A more fine-grained analysis of the interviews revealed that these motivations are not equally salient, and also do not occur at the same point in time. Volunteers by and large presented a range of egoism-related reasons as the initial and most substantial motivation for their engagement in citizen science projects. Other motivations – collectivism and altruism – were missing from the initial decision to participate in a scientific project, but surfaced at a later stage, effecting long-term engagement.

Initial interest – Volunteers' initial interest in citizen science projects stemmed from many elements, all related to egoism: (1) familiarity with- or personal curiosity about- a specific species (*"I'm one of those arachnoids geeks"*), a landscape, or environment, or a process (*"I see a lot of insects interacting with the plants and, to understand plants better, I need to know what those insects are"*); (2) previous engagement in scientific projects, in schools or as a hobby; (3) an existing hobby that is closely related to citizen science (e.g., photography); or (4) a career building step for aspiring scientists (e.g., *"[my motivation is] gaining the experience and seeing what it is, maybe having something for my resume"*).

Most volunteers saw participation in scientific projects as an opportunity to extend and expend their personal knowledge of specific domains and species. The role of this motivational factor was highly dependent on scientists' attitudes towards the volunteers – when scientists acknowledged the need to educate people and not *"treat them as dumb"*, as one volunteer put it, volunteers embraced the opportunity to learn more and widen their scientific horizons (*"we had a chance to sit down with a lot of the scientists who were in the field, and [we] could ask any question. You wanted to go down there with a magnet attached to your brain and try to absorb everything they had to say*").

Although the specific personal take on participation in scientific projects was different for each volunteer, in all cases, their initial interest originated from individual gain and personal interest, positioning **egoism** as the leading factor for initial involvement in citizen science projects. The following quotes from two different volunteers are indicative: *"I think personal interest comes first. Personal interest and personal gain, with information"; "I would be less inclined to participate in something I had little interest* [sic] *even if it was a worthy endeavor"*.

Following their initial engagement, volunteers presented secondary motivational factors, which although important, affected only their ongoing participation in citizen science projects, and not their initial decision to participate in these projects:

Recognition and attribution – all volunteers emphasized the power of being recognized for their individual contributions as a crucial motivational factor. Although volunteers clearly accepted the distinct roles of scientists and volunteers in scientific work ("*it's not always collaborative, it allows people to contribute their ideas to solve a problem, but it's usually the scientists that yank the problem and put them out there to their community*"), they nonetheless felt an intense need to be recognized and appreciated for their contributions, however big or small. Recognition happened when individual contributions were singled-out by scientists and explicit credit (through attribution) was given to the volunteers who collected, analyzed, or curated data. One volunteer articulated his expectation of attribution, which was echoed by many others, as a major motivational factor: "*I'm not really, obviously, objected to glory. I do expect attribution... I would like people to use it [the data he contributes] but I would like attribution...I would always like to be the first one to put a photo up there...it's got to count somehow*". This type of recognition was especially important where selected artifacts (e.g. photos, samples) or specific data contributed by volunteers was used by scientists in publications. For recognition purposes, volunteers did not differentiate between peer-reviewed and open-access publications, unlike scientists; both were valued uses of the data they contributed: *"if a name ends up in the acknowledgments, the name ends up in a poster, it's a measurable thing...I can show the family members and make it more of a positive experience"*.

An alternative type of recognition was mentioned by several volunteers; invitation to participate in scientific training organized by the scientists. While scientists saw training as an essential teaching process that ensured a minimal benchmark for data quality, volunteers viewed training as an opportunity to be initiated and accepted into the scientific world, and be recognized for the value of their contribution: "*from a volunteer standpoint there is a pretty big hurdle in getting through volunteer training... you have to go through all this extensive training. But, to be honest, I like it more than [another volunteer project] I looked into... because [the other project is] a lot less thorough and to me that makes it a lot less scientific... because people going through the thorough training feel like they're contributing a lot more because... I think they understand what the [scientists] are doing*". Repetitive training, such as annual reaccreditation, or seasonal meetings, was also seen as a ritual reinstating their commitment to the scientific project. Rigorous training needed for some projects was noted as more prestigious than "come as you wish" volunteer projects: *"our training is very extensive. It's a 2-3 years commitment, because of our short season. I haven't gotten certified yet but I went through partial training and so I'm proud to say I'm recognized by the local chapter of the [zoological] trust"*.

Feedback – feedback differed from recognition in that it was not associated with an individual contributor and particular contributions, but rather addressed the overall contribution of a volunteer, a group of volunteers, or the outcome of the entire project. Feedback mechanisms were expected to create a communication route between scientists and volunteers, but they also became prominent motivational factors. Volunteers sought feedback and were appreciative of those scientists and projects that have taken proactive steps to facilitate this: "*it's not about spending time or money. It's more about the constant feedback to the volunteers that what we're doing is useful and being used*". When scientists were not cognizant of providing periodic feedback to their volunteers, volunteers felt peripheral, became de-motivated, and tended to forgo future work on those projects: "*I've done other stuff and you know you don't get feedback, like 'here is what we did with the work you did', and so you don't feel like it's being used well and you don't feel like you want to continue to contribute*"

Feedback took many forms: impromptu updates about the research and its outcomes or pre-scheduled periodic meetings with groups of volunteers, intended to provide them with updates about their work, research procedures, and the way their work affected the scientific project. Alternatively, feedback was given personally, but unlike 'recognition' it did not focus on the individual contribution but more on how volunteers as a group contributed to the research and how the data they collected was used.

Community involvement – community involvement was not mentioned as a primary motivation for participation in scientific projects, even when the project had a substantial effect on the volunteer's local community. However, once volunteers were already involved in citizen science projects, the impact of their work on their local community became an influential motivating factor: "*it's the combination of being an effective citizen scientist and seeing the community thrive... people really care about their natural resources here*". Some volunteers stressed their continued commitment to scientific projects that were taking place in their area because of their potential effect on their community. One such example was a water contamination monitoring project, where citizens collected samples from streams and rivers which were previously deemed not fit for commercial harvesting. When the contamination level lowered and these areas reopened for commercial fishing, they boosted the local economy. Following that, participation in related citizen science projects rose steadily. Another aspect of community involvement was a social one, both within collocated communities - *"I've started conversations with people locally who are just very knowledgeable, it seems to easily slide into a community [involvement], though by community I mean more 'neighborhood'"*; and distant ones - *"I think it's the social support as well. I've got a lot of friends who are in various mammal groups across the country, and we give each other a lot of mutual support"*.

Advocacy – advocacy was seen as a collectivist motivation (unlike education, which emphasizes the personal gains volunteers get from their participation in citizen science projects). Advocacy was a motivational factor that did not influence the initial decision to participate in these projects, but became important as volunteers considered their ongoing participation. Most volunteers embraced the opportunity to understand better the issues pertaining to environmental policy that affected them and their communities through their participation in citizen science projects: *"I want to be kind of a liaison between the scientific field ... and the common person who has the questions and doesn't know how to ask"*. They saw this newfound understanding as an educational benefit from which they not only personally gained, but also an asset that they can later bring to their local or distributed communities. As one volunteer who worked at a nature center said: "*it's the perfect opportunity to help people understand their environment ... [I] hope that something that you say will make [a] dent and make them more curious and they'll go home and pick up a book or they'll call you back...it gives them a touch of what belongs to their environment*". A special emphasis was placed on children's learning: *"[small mammal walks are] a really good way to get kids engaged with the natural world. [it ends] their sort of disconnection with the earth which I think personally is what drives most of us"*.

However, one volunteer mentioned advocacy as being the exact opposite, or a "*big turn-off*" because "*the day we put an opinion or try to do advocacy our data becomes compromised...and that's something I think scientists need to be really careful of*".

Scientists' motivations for collaborating with volunteers

Unlike the numerous motivational factors affecting volunteers' participation, scientists exhibited a more limited motivational range. Echoing findings in previous studies [8, 25] scientists act within a well established tradition of "invisible colleges" [26] to which they are accountable. Within this tradition, scientists saw citizen science projects mainly as an opportunity to facilitate large-scale data collection. They then used the data in the common peer-reviewed publication process.

Scientists as leaders of the scientific process - according to scientists, the volunteers' role in citizen science projects ranged from data collection (e.g. photos, specimens, samples, and observations), to data analysis (e.g. classification of collected specimen, database management) and in several unique cases even included contributions to scientific or popular-science publications. However, in most cases scientists preferred to have volunteers remain within the ascribed role of field data collectors; cases where volunteers were engaged in other roles were few and exceptional: "*I see them as most helpful in making accurate observations... they are basically the field component*"; *"basic science is very under-funded, it's impossible to get out to the field these days so it [citizen science] saves a whole bunch of time and money"*. Although some scientists mentioned that if they found enough interested volunteers who would be willing to take upon themselves more complex roles that would contribute to data analysis "*that would be great and definitely useful*", they didn't "*see that as common or easily found [as field work]"*. In most cases, from the data collection onward, and more pointedly in the latter stages of the research, the scientists asserted themselves as leaders of the research and the ensuing publications; they did not see a place or a role for volunteers in these later stages, as "*there's just a few of us able to do that kind of thing [work]"*. Therefore the primary motivation for their collaboration with volunteers was to maximize the useful products they can gain from this collaboration; thus limiting it to what one of them termed "*valuable but limited*" volunteer contribution.

Education and policy – a secondary motivation was scientists' altruistic notion of contributing to the common good through educating the public. This finding was salient both in the survey results and in our interviews, as well as in previous studies of scientific culture [8]. Scientists not only wanted to introduce volunteers to their specific domains: "*I think that they are really learning about these specific pollinators... it's a small piece of information they can really use"*; *"I want to increase climate literacy*", but also wanted to educate them about the scientific method as a whole. For example, they commented: "*for volunteers in the field... even though they weren't doing the lab work... I wanted them to learn the entire process so that they understood how critical it is every step of the way to have a set technique*". Another educational aspect was engaging educated citizens in influencing the public's thinking about science, relevant fund appropriation, policy decision-making, and making them understand better the role of science for the greater good. One scientist voiced a sentiment echoed by several others: "*I don't think people can make good decisions, be it policy or environmental or anything else, unless they understand how things work. This provides the opportunity to educate people through a valid citizen science program. So when they go to the polls they can become active in their communities about something that they care about*".

Education had a flip side as well: by working with people coming from a different knowledge base the scientists gained a different perspective about their work: "*a lot of master gardeners know more than I do about certain aspects of plant phenology. I know pieces of it better than they do, but I can learn from them, too*"; and "*it is nicer to work with people in a different atmosphere than the research community...just getting out of the little bubble that we're in*".

Obstacles to collaboration

The findings from our interviews also pointed to de-motivating factors affecting collaboration. These factors were especially potent at two decision points: the entry point, or the decision to participate in a project, and the ensuing decision to participate in more tasks or continue participating in the project for an extended period of time after the initial task was completed. Both groups mentioned similar obstacles, coming from different perspectives:

Mutual apprehension and trust – some of the sentiments shared by most of the volunteers were: "*scientists are intimidating*", "*scientists speak a different jargon*", "*scientists have a reputation of being arrogant*", "*they are just so unfriendly*". Volunteers' initial hesitancy was grounded in the existing power balance between scientists and volunteers. While volunteers were eager to aid scientists they were also in awe of them, recognizing the fact that scientists were trained professionals, upholding rigid standards, and advancing the research for their own purposes as well as for the greater good. Overcoming this initial awe was difficult. Some volunteers felt that bringing their own ideas to the research table would not be positively accepted by scientists, but the few who reported that they have indeed broached the subject and offered input were pleasantly surprised when the scientists were cordial and even excited about these ideas.

From their perspective, scientists were wary of the volunteers' level of commitment and quality of work. In general they held positive views regarding collaboration, but the technicalities of obtaining high-quality data from volunteers was a reason for concern. "*Quality assurance*" and "*quality control*" were two of the most recurrent themes in scientists' accounts. They stressed the need to get as much information as possible about the volunteers' expertise, participation in previous projects, level of training, and level of commitment, as preliminary requirements in order to deflect unwanted volunteers from joining their projects. This was also their way of ensuring that only "good" data will be delivered by volunteers. Some scientists had mechanisms to support that, by requiring paid-for training, assuming that uncommitted volunteers will not bother to pay for participation; others administered online tests, assuring the knowledge base of the volunteers and predicting their success in collecting data. Others preferred to cast a wide net, but slowly "retire" volunteers who did not uphold rigid scientific standards: "*you train them, you observe them... and if they're not capable they have to get another job*"; "*you've got to go and train 100 people if you want 15 to show up on a regular basis*".

For both scientists and volunteers, creating a sustainable collaborative environment necessitated trust and credibility: "*people won't come back if there isn't that loop of credibility and things that they can see that are being accomplished as a result of the data that they are collecting*". Trust building was a long process that largely depended on both sides fulfilling each other's expectations and motivations. One problem with establishing this trust was the fact that the two groups did not always explicitly convey these expectations and motivations to each other.

Not addressing existing motivational factors – volunteers were familiar to some extent with scientists' work and motivations, but when scientists were asked about volunteers' motivations, most did not recognize volunteers' prevalent motivations. They mentioned motivations stemming from "*wanting to be outside*", "*wanting to do something meaningful*", and "*working with their friends or family [on scientific projects]*", but many scientists failed to recognize the initial interest volunteers had in scientific problems as their primary motivation. Attribution and recognition were identified as important to volunteers, but their importance was downplayed by several scientists despite the role they actually played in volunteers' engagement: "*I find that people don't want to stand out... people are put off by highlighting certain [contributions] we don't do it in a huge way... recognition can backfire*". This gap undermined the two groups' ability to reach the desired trust, and to attain a higher level of collaboration.

DISCUSSION

Community involvement motivational framework

Batson et al.'s [23] model identified four distinct factors affecting motivation to participate in activities that promote social benefit. Although this model can explain some of the motivational premises in which collaborative scientific work is grounded, our findings show that it does not translate well for collaborative citizen science projects. Such projects are inherently complex activities, spread over long periods of time, and spanning multiple tasks. In these projects motivations not only change over time, but are especially salient at particular intersections of activity and decision making.

This complexity can be seen in the way the four motivational factors identified by Batson et al. – egoism, collectivism, altruism and principlism – presented in the two groups we have studied. An in depth exploration of the motivational factors affecting participation of both groups in collaborative projects revealed that both scientists and volunteers presented egoism as the primary motivation for engagement in citizen science projects. However, they expected their goals to be different: volunteers wanted to do something that would satisfy their needs, would interest and educate them through their participation, while scientists wanted to promote their careers. Other motivational factors were less pronounced at the onset of collaboration, but appeared to have an influence on volunteers' ongoing participation. For volunteers, egoism, was satisfied through attaining attribution and recognition, particularly by scientists. Collectivism was accomplished by the scientists providing group feedback to the volunteers, and also through community involvement and advocacy, where collectivism emphasized locality. Altruism was achieved by aiding scientists in data collection (and, rarely, data analysis) processes. Scientists indicated that altruism (public education) was the second important motivational factor after egoism, which for them was tied to the need for scientific data and desire to publish. These results were also supported by survey findings. The one significant difference between the volunteers and scientists was in their perception of collectivism – volunteers saw it as being just as important as other motivational factors, while the scientists indicated that working with volunteers will not be greatly beneficial to the scientific community as a whole.

Interestingly, although in the survey both groups agreed as to the role of principlism in motivating collaborations, this factor did not come up in our interviews. One possible reason for that may be that during the interviews principlism was often "folded" into discussions of other factors such as collectivism and altruism – as one interviewee put it:*" initially, it was doing something for my own good, because I just wanted to know what those bugs were. But continued participation I would say is more a mix of that and doing something for the larger community"*.

Based on these findings, we see our major contribution as highlighting the temporal nature of motivation and identifying points in time in which motivational factors affect participation in ecological citizen science projects. We present a dynamic model for the engagement cycle of volunteers, where motivations facilitate engagement and come into fruition at different stages of the collaborative process.

Figure 2 illustrates this cycle of engagement and the related motivational pivotal points. Volunteers' initial interest leads them to seek opportunities that would broaden their horizons and allow them to engage in an enjoyable activity. Their interest may be only tangential to the scientific project, as was exemplified by the case of an avid photographer who finds interest in a project documenting insects although she is not be interested in insects *per se*. At this point in time the other motivational factors Batson et al. [23] identified do not come into play. For scientists egoism reflects the need for large scale, comprehensive data collection to benefit their studies. This need leads scientists to cooperate with volunteers who provide them with data that is difficult or costly to collect otherwise. It is the synergy between the two different forms of egoism that creates the initial collaboration between the two groups. At this point in time the initial interest is enough to warrant some level of volunteer participation, especially from people who are already attuned to the idea of citizen science.

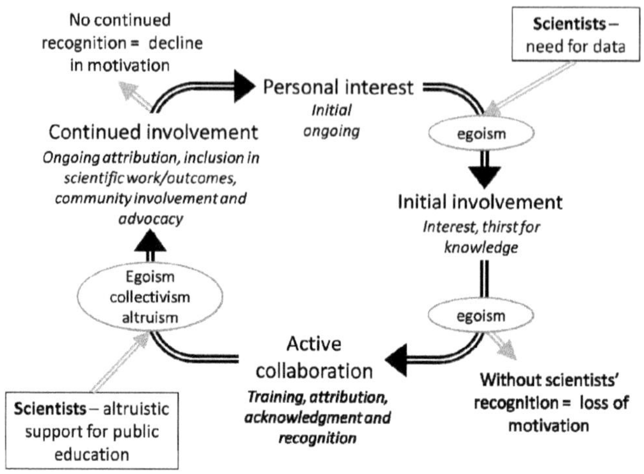

Figure 2. A process model of volunteers and scientists involvement in citizen science projects.

It is at this point that our model diverges from that presented by Batson et al [23]. Unlike their description of motivational factors as goal-directed, we propose that time has a significant effect on motivation: when volunteers' motivations are explicitly recognized they will engage further in active contribution to collaborative projects. Where these motivations are ignored (even if this is done inadvertently) volunteers' participation will decline. That is not to say that scientific projects that do not address such motivational factors will lack volunteers: if the project is interesting enough volunteers may be inclined to participate in it initially – yet, with time even avid participants will drift away,

The other formative point is at the end of a task or a project. This is when volunteers reassess their participation in the project. At this point other motivational factors - altruism and collectivism – come into play. Interestingly, what we have learned is that although this assessment is made at the end of a task or the beginning of a new one, it is mostly based on previous experiences and less on future expectations. When volunteers reflect on their previous experiences they look at the specific project, the ways in which various motivational factors were met and how they felt during the project. In this reflection an emphasis is placed on the secondary motivational factors, but also on recognition as a manifestation of egoism.

The model is cyclical, since many ecological scientific projects are lengthy and are designed in multiple stages, which can benefit from volunteer participation. In order to ensure long term, sustainable volunteer participation, their range of motivations should be repeatedly acknowledged and addressed throughout the project lifecycle. Although we highlighted the two pivotal points at which volunteers make an active decision regarding their participation, it is the ongoing appreciation and acknowledgment of volunteers that they remember and draw upon when making that decision.

As Bonney et al. [1] defined, citizen science projects can range from merely contributing data to collaborative and co-creative projects. In order to move from simple data collection to meaningful collaboration, scientists need to understand volunteers' motivations and accept them as being synergistic to theirs. This can be done through education, but it seems that an easier way would be to facilitate this change through design that will appeal to the two groups' unique motivations.

Designing for ongoing collaboration

When designing tools or communities for citizen science projects, the various motivational factors and the points in time in which they are crucial for sustaining participation should be addressed. The dynamic model we presented, allows us to suggest some implications for designing collaborative tools to support the volunteers' and scientists' participation in citizen science projects:

- *Timing* – to ensure that the proper motivational probes are emphasized at the right time, the design should enable identification of points in which participation declines (or can decline) such as the end of a task, and interject the proper motivational probes. For example, when a project is initiated, recruitment materials can emphasize the inherent interest of the topic and volunteers' chance to learn, but materials provided to recruited volunteers should emphasize opportunities for recognition, advanced training, and social engagement. Throughout the lifecycle of the project appropriate materials can accentuate volunteers' contribution to their community or to the greater good. Games, with their intrinsically rewarding mechanics, may be used to attract people who are not initially interested in a less appealing topic (i.e., bacteria; worms) or engage them further in a topic of their liking.
- *Highlighting data use* – the system needs to make available information about where, how and to what extent the data were used, in order to provide feedback to the volunteers. Collaborative citizen science projects can include an automated mechanism that tracks each time data is used and what it was used for (publication, online repositories, etc.), augmenting a notification mechanism which routinely highlights cases when volunteer-generated data is used, and notifies volunteers periodically. Similarly, attribution should be clear, accentuated and easily manageable.
- *Locality* – local interests were often mentioned as catalysts for continuous involvement. Designing tools that are grounded in the local flora and fauna, or associated with local groups, highlighting the most pressing needs for local conservation, will accentuate ways in which volunteers' contribution to their immediate community is crucial, and can help in maintaining their engagement for longer periods of time.
- *Synergy* – by setting common standards for collaborative science projects, small scale and local projects can be networked in a way that will leverage locality into mass endeavors (such as the yearly bird counts). Synergistic ties between smaller communities will enable the discovery of data, people and projects that may be of interest. Networked synergy can be created by providing open APIs to local databases, setting common standards for data entry, storage and publication.
- *Matching scientists, volunteers and tasks* – overcoming geographical barriers by creating a common infrastructure, or a "pool" for citizen science projects in various domains, where scientists can create missions, or ads, for volunteer services, based on their need for data, analysis or other services. Volunteers who will offer their services will be asked, at signup, to select their areas of interest, location, and expertise, and suggest potential roles in which they can contribute. At a later stage the system can be designed to automatically unearth secondary motivations (locality, desire to educate others) based on data derived from users and behavioral patterns that intervenes at pivotal times of participatory decline, and assign tasks appropriately.
- *Breaking tasks into smaller scale "building blocks"* – similar to locally based projects, smaller scale building blocks allow volunteers to easily find tasks that would appeal to their interest and anchor their engagement for a sustainable period of time. This approach will also aid in overcoming some of the initial awe of mass scientific projects, and enable volunteers to take control over their level of participation. For example, "Observing bugs in your backyard" may sound more feasible than "documenting the insects of the pacific north-west".

CONCLUSION

We conducted a mixed method study in which we have used an existing motivational model to examine the motivational frameworks of participants in ecological citizen science projects, with an emphasis on volunteers. We have shown that scientists and volunteers participate in scientific endeavors for different reasons. Professional scientists want to advance science and further their own professional career, while volunteers participate in scientific activities out of interest, curiosity and commitment to conservation and related educational efforts. Volunteers' motivations are temporal, dynamic and change even when the ultimate goal remains the same. Two significant points in time deserve special attention – the initial encounter between a volunteer and scientific projects and the point at which a project ends and the volunteer has to decide whether to continue contributing to other projects. It is at these points where motivational influences are most important. Identifying the right ones and nurturing them may result in stronger and more sustainable collaboration between citizens and scientists.

Our findings have important implications for designing tools to encourage volunteer participation and for facilitating collaboration between volunteers and scientists in ecological citizen science, and also for other types of citizen science projects. When building tools for citizen science projects, motivational factors have to be addressed and built into the tools, as contributors will be more inclined to participate in collaborative scientific projects when given the proper motivational impetus at the right time. Future studies that empirically evaluate design interventions, such as those we have proposed, will help to assess the usefulness of the proposed model in specific use-cases.

ACKNOWLEDGMENTS

We thank the NSF SoCS program for its support through grant # 0968546.

REFERENCES

1. Irwin, A. *Citizen science: a study of people, expertise, and sustainable development.* Burns & Oates, 1995.
2. Stewart, P. A. The value of the Christmas bird counts. *The Wilson Bulletin*, 66, 3 (1954), 184-195.
3. Bonney, R., Ballard, H., Jordan, R., McCallie, E., Phillips, T., Shirk, J. and Wilderman, C. C. *Public Participation in Scientific Research: Defining the Field and Assessing Its Potential for Informal Science Education - a CAISE Inquiry Group Report.*, Center for Advancement of Informal Science Education, Washington, DC, 2009.
4. Sullivan, B. L., Wood, C. L., Iliff, M. J., Bonney, R. E., Fink, D. and Kelling, S. eBird: A citizen-based bird observation network in the biological sciences. *Biological Conservation*, 142, 10 (2009), 2282-2292.
5. Kim, S., Robson, C., Zimmerman, T., Pierce, J. and Haber, E. M. Creek watch: pairing usefulness and usability for successful citizen science. In *Proc. CHI 2011*, ACM Press (2011), 2125-2134.
6. Raddick, M. J., Bracey, G., Gay, P. L., Lintott, C. J., Murray, P., Schawinski, K., Szalay, A. S. and Vandenberg, J. Galaxy zoo: Exploring the motivations of citizen science volunteers. *Astronomy Education Rev.*, 9 (2010), 010103.
7. Cranshaw, J. and Kittur, A. The polymath project: lessons from a successful online collaboration in mathematics. In *Proc. CHI 2011*. ACM Press (2011), 1865-1874.
8. Latour, B. and Woolgar, S. *Laboratory life: The construction of scientific facts*. Princeton Univ Press, 1979.
9. Bozeman, B. and Corley, E. Scientists' collaboration strategies: implications for scientific and technical human capital. *Research Policy*, 33, 4 (2004), 599-616.
10. Hara, N., Solomon, P., Kim, S. L. and Sonnenwald, D. H. An emerging view of scientific collaboration: Scientists' perspectives on collaboration and factors that impact collaboration. *Journal of the American Society for Information Science and Technology*, 54, 10 (2003), 952-965.
11. Van House, N. A. Digital libraries and practices of trust: networked biodiversity information. *Social Epistemology*, 16, 1 (2002), 99-114.
12. Van House, N. A. *Trust and epistemic communities in biodiversity data sharing*. JCDL' 02. ACM Press (2002), 231-239.
13. Ellis, R. and Waterton, C. Environmental citizenship in the making: the participation of volunteer naturalists in UK biological recording and biodiversity policy. *Science and public policy*, 31, 2 (2004), 95-105.
14. Wiggins, A. and Crowston, K. Conservation to Crowdsourcing: A Typology of Citizen Science. In *Proc. HICSS'44*. IEEE (2011), 1-10.
15. Bos, N., Zimmerman, A., Olson, J., Yew, J., Yerkie, J., Dahl, E. and Olson, G. From shared databases to communities of practice: A taxonomy of collaboratories. *Journal of Computer Mediated Communication*, 12, 2 (2007), 652-672.
16. Wenger, E. *Communities of practice: Learning, meaning, and identity*. Cambridge Univ Press, 1999.
17. Preece, J. and Shneiderman, B. The reader-to-leader framework: Motivating technology-mediated social participation. *AIS Transactions on Human-Computer Interaction*, 1, 1 (2009), 5.
18. Forte, A. and Bruckman, A. Why do people write for wikipedia? Incentives to contribute to open content publishing. *In Proc. of GROUP*' 05 (2005), 6-9.
19. Nov, O., Anderson, D. and Arazy, O. Volunteer computing: a model of the factors determining contribution to community-based scientific research. In *Proc. WWW* 2010. ACM Press (2010), 741-750.
20. Cosley, D., Frankowski, D., Kiesler, S., Terveen, L. and Riedl, J. *How oversight improves member-maintained communities*. In *Proc. CHI 2005*. ACM Press (2005) 11-20.
21. Kriplean, T., Beschastnikh, I. and McDonald, D. W. *Articulations of wikiwork: uncovering valued work in wikipedia through barnstars*. In *Proc. CSCW 2008*. ACM Press (2008), 47-56.
22. Benkler, Y. Coase's Penguin, or, Linux and" The Nature of the Firm". *The Yale Law Journal*, 112, 3 (2002), 369-446.
23. Batson, C. D., Ahmad, N. and Tsang, J. A. Four motives for community involvement. *Journal of Social Issues*, 58, 3 (2002), 429-445.
24. Strauss, A. and Corbin, J. M. *Basics of qualitative research: Grounded theory procedures and techniques*. Sage Publications, Inc, 1997.
25. Cohn, J. P. Citizen science: Can volunteers do real research? *BioScience*, 58, 3 (2008), 192-197.
26. Crane, D. Social structure in a group of scientists: A test of the" invisible college" hypothesis. *American Sociological Review*, 34, 3 (1969), 335-352.

Engaging New Digital Locals with Interactive Urban Screens to Collaboratively Improve the City

Ronald Schroeter
Urban Informatics Research Lab, Institute for Creative Industries and Innovation
Queensland University of Technology
r.schroeter@qut.edu.au

ABSTRACT
Local governments struggle to engage time poor and seemingly apathetic citizens, as well as the city's young digital natives, the digital locals. This project aims at providing a lightweight, technological contribution towards removing the hierarchy between those who build the city and those who use it. We aim to narrow this gap by enhancing people's experience of physical spaces with digital, civic technologies that are directly accessible within that space. This paper presents the findings of a design trial allowing users to interact with a public screen via their mobile phones. The screen facilitated a feedback platform about a concrete urban planning project by promoting specific questions and encouraging direct, in-situ, real-time responses via SMS and twitter. This new mechanism offers additional benefits for civic participation as it gives voice to residents who otherwise would not be heard. It also promotes a positive attitude towards local governments and gathers information different from more traditional public engagement tools.

Keywords
Public screens, mobile media, locative media, place-based community engagement, mobile interaction, urban informatics

ACM Classification Keywords
H5.m. Information interfaces and presentation: Miscellaneous.

General Terms: Design; Human Factors.

INTRODUCTION
We created *Discussions In Space* (DIS) [21] as a design experiment offering a novel and additional mechanism for residents in Brisbane, Australia, to engage in the consultation phase of an urban planning project conducted by Brisbane City Council (BCC).

The *DIS* project facilitates a public civic feedback, discussion and opinion platform by installing a large public screen, which passersby can interact with using their mobile phone's SMS and Twitter capabilities. By promoting civic topics, issues and questions, the installation invites citizens to submit their opinion to the publicly visible screen, hence providing a platform for collective expression and possibly public discourse amongst residents. This discourse may be carried out through the system itself, or extend into the realm of face-to-face interaction. Collaborative and distributed editing and censoring capabilities ensure that the content reflects the norms and values of the study's stakeholders, namely the university and the local government partner.

The study in this paper is specifically interested in system designs that effectively engage with a majority of residents, whom local governments generally have difficulties to engage with. Our pilot study involved interviewing four urban and neighbourhood planners of the BCC. They identified, categorized and labelled two significant demographics: "backyard buddies" (not interested or involved, often transient, younger residents) and "loyal locals" (e.g., time poor professionals or young families, new home owners). From the local governments perspective, key characteristics of these demographics are a) not caring enough to engage on their own accord and co-create their urban environment or, b) although interested, simply not finding the time in their busy lifestyles to visit time-consuming community consultation events or even online participation tools. Yet, urban planners perceive them as a demographic, which uses the city more than those demographics that generally have more of a say and provide more input in current urban planning decisions. Further, some planners see them as the "voice of reason" when changes need to happen in one way or another [22].

The research is situated to investigate forms of in-place digital augmentation, which seek to enhance the experiences of citizens in physical spaces with digital technologies that are directly accessible within that space, e.g., mobile phones and interactive public screens.

The departure point is that in-place digital augmentation may offer significant new opportunities in the context of civic participation, where citizens collaboratively aim at making their community or city a better place. The hypothesis is that it allows specifically those urban dwellers, who would not seek out online participation tools on their own accord, to serendipitously participate in a civic process where and when it is needed, in place.

We acknowledge that the underlying reasons for non-participation are more complex than simply a lack of time and interest [6]. However, this study does not claim to make engagement all-inclusive, nor does it aim for the holy grail of mass scale deliberative democracy. Rather, this paper focuses on engaging young university students in an innovative way, in particular by pushing civic issues to them and reducing the barriers for them to participate. Although students are an over-used population for technology evaluations, they are indeed often non-participants on local, civic issues because of their age, transience and self-perceived immaturity. Further, they are an interesting demographic to investigate from an urban planning perspective as mentioned above.

RESEARCH OBJECTIVES AND QUESTIONS

The following research question guided the design of *DIS*: How can interactions, applications and technologies be designed to allow new digital locals to take a more active role in making their community and city a better place? In this paper, the following two objectives are examined and evaluated:

Research Objective (RO) 1: Examine the **hypothesis** that bringing digitally augmented participation into places where people pause and congregate, offers new opportunities towards civic participation, e.g., reaching out to people who would not have their say otherwise (cf. section *Analysis RO1*).

Research Objective (RO) 2: Evaluate the **design implications** for digitally augmented participation from a human-computer interaction perspective: A. What are the nuances of use of such applications (cf. *Analysis RO 2A*), and B. what are the problems and implications of deploying them from the user's perspective (cf. *Analysis RO 2B*)?

RELATED WORK

The great potential of the location-centric media channels such as public screens and mobile phones have been widely recognized [7, 12, 15, 24] in order to achieve Jane Jacobs' premise: "Cities have the capability of providing something for everybody, only because, and only when, they are created by everybody" [10].

Lane et al. [12] see public authoring as a powerful force to enrich the public domain by sharing local information, knowledge and experiences by ordinary people about the places they live, work, and play in. Central online forums are often limited to the same core group of users [11]. Public displays are able to offer a convenient "push" mechanism of content to extend visibility of local issues beyond those groups. The mechanism is most effective in locations where people pause for a moment during their daily activities [15].

Interactive public screens have been used to increase social interactions within work places [5, 8] research environments [17] and work related social settings [3] amongst co-workers, as well as cafes [4, 18] and urban outdoor environments [19], where users can share and interact with user-generated content. Such systems often require users to access an advertised website and register [5, 17, 18]. However, a low barrier of entry is crucial to increase adoption of such systems [8]. Accessing a website presents a greater barrier than direct access/input [20], especially in less controlled public or urban environments. However, direct input via public input terminals [3] or rich (multi-) touch interfaces [4, 19] can present a barrier through the "social awkwardness" of performing the input in public [3]. Further, the novelty effect of rich multi-touch interfaces can distract from the actual content [19]. Multi-touch interfaces are also more expensive and more difficult to install in urban environments. Bluetooth based interfaces (such as SnapAndGrab [16] proved to be a barrier in our pilot study and statistics indicate low Bluetooth usage in Australia [2].

Only few works present a civic goal (rather than a social goal or none at all) using interactive public screens. Most closely aligned to this paper are CitySpeak [13] and TexTales [1]. Both allow SMS input. CitySpeak has only been trialled indoors and the display is not themed in any way, except through its contextual placement within the respective venue, e.g., a public lecture. TexTales presents civic topics, such as "smoking in public places", which users can comment on via an SMS. They found that the conversations were not only sustained within the system, but also carried on in the physical and social space around it. CitySpeak and TexTales require moderation at the location, causing a delay of 30-60 seconds for messages to appear. They did not investigate the motivation for users to interact (or not), and did not provide a detailed analysis of sent messages.

This project seeks to engage unengaged young residents, who do not seek out civic (online or face-to-face) platforms by themselves. It aims to achieve this goal by a) "advertising" civic issues ("push" via public screen), b) a low barrier of entry, c) allowing participation on a "low level" (cf. "consulting" within the public participation spectrum [9], e.g., giving feedback about an urban plan), and d) making it engaging and fun.

DISCUSSIONS IN SPACE

The situated screen application (Figure 1) includes the civic topic and sub-questions (top/left), instructions how to send a message via SMS or Twitter (bottom/left), the user-generated messages (right) and a footer (bottom/right) with links to a mobile website and the T&Cs. It invites users to provide their feedback right there and then.

Figure 1: Screenshot of the public screen application

User input: Allowing input through the user's ubiquitous personal mobile device provides a low barrier of entry, reduces social awkwardness and may distract less from the civic content. SMS is the lowest common denominator in terms of accessibility. It does not require smart phones, the installation of software, prior learning, or accessing or registering with a website. In addition, it allows input to any passive screen that a local government might own as part of their existing urban screen infrastructure (from bus stop screens to large event screens). Twitter growth is fast, but has not reached the mainstream yet. Hence, it serves only as an additional input channel.

Moderation: After the user sends a message, a push notification system notifies one or multiple distributed administrators to perform a moderation task. In an online type chat room, moderators a) accept new posts and label them as being "*on-topic*" (which means the post addresses the topic displayed on the public screen) or "*off-topic*" (post addresses another issue) or b) *decline* them.

It is envisaged that future deployments of the system by local governments hook into their existing resources to perform the moderation themselves, such as communications officers, forum administrators, call-centre staff or urban planners themselves, etc. Considering a local government's risk aversion, their careful approach to such new technologies, the users' behaviour to game the system and the near real-time requirement to enhance user-experience, it is highly unlikely that this task can be automated anytime soon. Wikipedia style crowd sourced moderation would have to be carefully sourced and managed, which a) was not within the scope of this project and b) would require even more work convincing the local government partner to give this a try.

Public screen application: Approved messages are immediately pushed to the public screen application, where the user-generated content is presented in a dynamic, visually appealing way (animated speech bubbles) to effectively engage the audience. Usernames are automatically generated for each SMS user (concatenating random word(s) from a dictionary plus the last three digits of the mobile phone number) to give messages a more personal touch (rather than 'anonymous'). Providing unique (but pseudonymous) names gave the option for more advanced users to refer to previous posters such as by the convention '@user 123' as used in Twitter. The system specifically does not propose a formal syntax for choosing a username or for addressing previous messages to the users in order to not raise the barrier of entry. The goal was to keep this first iteration as simple as possible.

The bubbles rotate through an array of posts in order to grab the attention of passersby. The parameters of the array are configurable as follows: overall number of messages; number of most recent posts; number of posts that must be on-topic; number of a random selection of older posts; number of admin posts (highlighted red and used to convey messages from the admin to the users via the screen, e.g., reminding users to not be offensive); frequency of shuffling the posts on screen; frequency of refreshing the array (only applies to older, random messages); time for recent off-topic posts to expire.

In this study, the array was set to the 4 most recent posts (on- or off-topic; off-topic posts were set to expire after 15min during the study) plus a random selection of 4 older on-topic posts, which were updated every 90 seconds. This allowed opinions to receive a fair hearing [6] and keep the application engaging if there are no new messages sent to the system.

STUDY DESIGN

As part of the bigger project, *[project name]* has been deployed within a wide range of *locations*. Each location offered either a highly mixed or very targeted audience (*people*). In addition, we also mixed the *content* between open questions and narrowly targeted ones about a particular theme, including political or local, civic issues.

This multiple-case study method (part of the larger program) allowed us to triangulate the impacts that variations within the *location* (incl. positioning, orientation, size, etc.), *people* (demographics) and *content* parameters have on how *[project name]* is used. Overall, the approach allowed for an isolated inquiry into the unit of analysis (the design of the application) and a holistic view about how these external factors influence the system in different ways.

The one case study presented in this paper is triangulated against two prior case studies in particular: One that took place at a similar location within the university, but with a more location-specific content about a planning related question regarding the university itself, and one that presented the same content to a similar demographic (people), but in an outdoor urban environment (location), a bus stop.

Location & People: The university campus borders on the Central Business District (CBD) of the inner-city, so staff and students are likely to be affected by and familiar with inner-city issues (see content below) as they commute to it on a regular basis. A foyer inside one of the campus' main buildings (see Figure 2) features two large projection screens and plenty of seating arrangements. Both screens are usually not interactive and show TV news, announcements, etc. *[project name]* ran on one of the screens. Several large lecture theatres connect to the foyer, and it gets particularly crowded with students waiting there before lectures start every full hour. Occasionally, university staff pass through the area as well.

Figure 2: *DIS* and BCC stand at the university

In addition, a Brisbane City Council (BCC) stand was set up in front of the screen. It featured an approximately 3x3m area of tiled flooring with a large printed map of the inner Brisbane area. One senior and one junior urban planner occupied the stand on weekdays between 10am and 2pm. During those times, passersby were able to ask the planners questions about the urban planning project, but more importantly present their "bright idea for Brisbane's future" by placing building blocks on the map, which planners would take notes of.

DIS provided an additional engagement tool to the stand, while the stand in turn provided additional context to *DIS*. The application ran while it was manned by BCC staff, as well as outside those hours. During manned hours, residents who had something to say could therefore opt between talking to the planners directly, sending in a message via the screen, or both.

Content: The topics and questions had to be formed considering a) the size limitation of possible replies limited to approx.160 characters; b) the time limitation (easy & fast to understand, and giving users enough time to think about a possible answer); c) the language of the target audience; d) the need to convey excitement and positivity (encouraging contributions about positive and constructive suggestions about the bigger picture and the future of the city); and e) a balance between all of the above and the urban planners' need to seek information to inherently complex problems.

In collaboration with the planners we arrived at the following three themes and sub-questions:

- Share your bright idea – How would you like to see the city grow? What would be the most positive change?
- Is Brisbane cool/uncool? – What's your favourite hang out spot with friends, and what makes it so special? What makes Brisbane a good place to live, work or use?
- Bus, cycling, train or car? – How did you get here today? How could your daily commute be improved? What would convince you to leave your car at home?

As a precaution and sign of risk aversion by BCC, the installation was branded solely as a university project rather than a local government initiative because of liability issues and because only the university team ultimately had technical control over the displayed, mostly user-generated content. The aspect of branding is relevant to consider in the light of the findings as it might have influenced the use of such an application.

Time: The system was deployed between 8am and 8pm every weekday for three weeks (15 days). Each of the three themes above was used for one week.

Moderation: The timeframe of the study posed a challenge for the moderation team, in this case consisting of three researchers and one university staff. All shared the moderation task during normal working hours by being logged into the online moderation room in the background, which would notify the moderators of a new post. Outside the working hours, moderation took place via a mobile phone, which was able to receive notifications via instant messages. The aim was to have at least one moderator on duty during operating hours. However, considering that all moderators had to go about their normal job duties, it was not always possible. As a consequence the moderators developed strategies, e.g., during busy times, one moderator volunteered to solely moderate so that incoming posts would not constantly distract others. The median response time between receiving an SMS or Twitter message and approving or declining a post was 22 seconds (min 5 seconds, maximum 3.7 hours) over the entire study. The push notifications proved extremely useful. The design implications of the moderation process will be discussed later.

METHODS

The nature of the system implies that it collects data itself, i.e., the messages that were sent to the screen via one of the input channels are stored in a SQL database, including the type of input channel, the participant's mobile phone number, twitter account or IP address, the time when the message was received and when it was handled by one of the moderators.

The labels used during the moderation process (on-topic, off-topic, declined) did not reflect the nature of each message in appropriate detail. In order to allow a more fine-grained overview, two researchers individually analysed a subset of the data borrowing from Grounded Theory [23] techniques, and then collaboratively discussed and agreed on one or more codes for each message (Table 1).

codes	description	#
random	unrelated to the topic	314
related	related to the topic	192
angry	a complaint, e.g., "Cramming people into the western suburbs without improving public transport infrastructure = typical stupidity. Build a busway before the problem gets worse!"	26
fun	a joke or users having fun with the application, which does not always have to be off-topic, like the following idea "Public fires for marshmellows"	172
egocentric	self promoting or posting a message about a personal problem, e.g., "Higher car parks so that my 4wd will fit! Atleast 2.2metres high"	27
test	testing the application or the moderation process, e.g., "Shamwow!"	46
thoughtful	valid, thoughtful contribution, e.g., "Make the ClimateSmart/WaterWise households initiatives complusory for all Brisbane residents."	60
group	message directed at a specific group of people or the people reading the screen, e.g., "This great! Everybody do it!"	16
personal	message directed as a specific person, e.g., "happy birthday for tomorrow MAGGIE"	100
previous	message was about a previous topic on the screen	10
repeat	same message has been sent before	39
reply	message is in reply to a previous post	12
unsuitable	message is unsuitable for display on the public screen	102

Table 1: Codes incl. description and number of occurrences

In addition, the qualitative data collection took place in three further stages:

Stage I – Covert observations of participants: The observer "blended in" to the environment easily without disturbing the normal characteristics of the space. One observer was present from approx. 9am to 6pm for the first 12 weekdays. Field notes were taken throughout this stage to document the observations. Furthermore, an agile approach allowed implementing little tweaks in response to the observations.

Stage II – Interviewing passive and non-users: This stage took place within the last few days of the deployment. 32 random people at the location were invited to a semi-structured interview about their general thoughts and initial reactions towards the application, as well as their general online presence, civic engagement behaviour and demographic. The number of passive users of such a system is much greater than the number of contributors, so the random selection in this stage resulted in interviewees who largely chose not to send a message to the screen. Note, however, that some were observed to send a message but misled the interviewer when asked if they had sent a message, possibly because they did not use the system as the design intended.

Stage III – Follow-up phone interviews with contributors: In order to address the research questions above, it was necessary to follow up with participants who *did* send a message. Therefore, the submitted posts were analysed after the installation and a cross-section of 20 contributors who a) sent their message via SMS, and b) submitted a post that was coded as being thoughtful, e.g.: *"Busway connecting royal brisbane hospital bus station 2 hawthorne via the valley and new farm with pedestrian access on the require bridge across the river"*; *"Brisbane needs to emphasize its fantastic geographical subcultures (eg West End) and whole range of restaurants and cocktail bars in suburbs outside of the city. Brisbane is a growing cultural hub!" (This SMS was sent as a concatenated multipart SMS, hence longer than 160 characters)*

The 20 contributors were invited to a follow-up interview over the phone. The invitation was sent over an SMS that asked them to agree to the interview and to specify a convenient time to call. 9 out of the 20 contributors replied with a positive response. The semi-structured interview followed similar questions to the ones carried out in stage two, with the additional focus on questions targeting the participants' motivation for sending in an on-topic message and whether they are the kind of residents who generally know how to have their say and take the time to make themselves heard.

THE DATA

The system received 656 posts from 225 distinct users over the 15 weekdays, approximately 44 per day. 26% were on-topic, 48% were off-topic, and 26% had to be declined, as they were offensive or otherwise inappropriate (Figure 3).

We received 607 SMS compared to 49 tweets (Figure 3), which clearly demonstrates the right design decision in emphasising SMS, a low-tech solution towards providing the lowest common denominator in terms of access, e.g., two of the nine SMS contributors also had a public Twitter account, but were not able to access it from their phone. In addition, the following themes emerged from the data:

How expressive were the messages? On-topic posts were consistently more elaborate than off-topic and declined

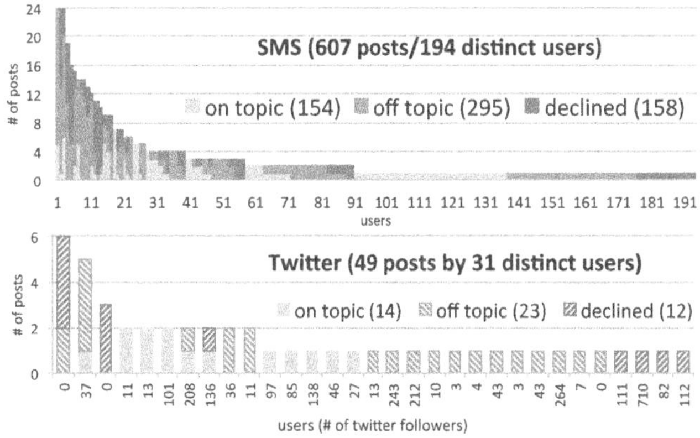

Figure 3: Numbers of SMSs and Tweets per distinct user

messages. On average, users used 11 words and 62.7 characters (less than half of the standard maximum of 160 characters) for on-topic posts, and only about half for off-topic and declined posts.

Did *DIS* facilitate discussions? Our data analysis shows no evidence of sustained discussion and only little evidence of conversations within the system. Although *DIS* currently does not support explicitly directing replies, we expected more users to address each other through the automatically generated usernames. In online forums or comment sections, users commonly respond directly to a previous comment. They do this even if threads are not explicitly supported. However, during this study only one message included a username. Even when including the number of messages that were loosely in relation to a previous post, there were only 12 occurrences (Table 1), 3 of them were on-topic, e.g.: "*More bike ways to make riding safer and separate from cars*" was later directly responded to with "*Agreed on the bike paths. They should have been included in the busway designs to run in parallel. Build bike tracks along the railway lines too.*" This begs the question how a more explicit support for targeted or threaded replies could be achieved without sacrificing simplicity? [4]

Civic discussions did occur amongst passive users who read the posts, similar to what was observed within the TexTales project [1]. Repeatedly, members of groups who knew each other would read posts aloud, agree or disagree and elaborate on the issue. Future iterations need to look into ways to further motivate and activate passive residents who clearly do have an opinion, but are deterred by the lack of evidence that their input counts. HCI design can close the feedback loop to some extent but this issue is mainly a political task.

ANALYSIS RO1: THE HYPOTHESIS

In light of the overarching hypothesis, it was crucial to explore during Stage III if the contributors are the type of residents who are already civically engaged and vocal within their community. Or, did the system's low barrier of entry provide a new opportunity for residents who otherwise do not usually have their say?

Three of the contributors were under 20, five in their 20s and one in his 50s; four were renting, four still lived with their parents, while the oldest participant lived on a boat (Table 2).

When asked about their emotional attachment to the community (how they would feel about negative changes happening where they live or work), three had no emotional attachment, three had some, and three were emotionally attached (cf. attach. Table 2).

Participants' previous civic engagement was low (cf. previous engagement Table 2). P7 was the only one who would consider himself civically engaged and up to date with local issues. Only P7 and P1 immediately remembered having contacted the council once before to provide feedback (F) via an online survey. In a follow up question, three more participants remembered having contacted the council once before, but only to lodge a complaint (C). Participants had contacted the council by either filling out an online form (P6 complaint, P7 survey), calling the hotline (P6 complaint), sending an email (P3, P8 complaint, P1 activism), writing a letter (P1 activism) and visiting a community event (P7).

	demo.			attach.				previous engagement							online presence		
	age	sex	resi.	none	some	high	civic eng.	web	form	phone	email	letter	events	stand	forums	private	Tools used
P1	50s	m	b	x				I	-	-	F	F	-	F	1	1	FB
P2	U20	m	wp		x			I	-	-	-	-	-	-	0	1	FB
P3	U20	f	wp			x		C	-	-	C	-	-	-	0	3	FB
P4	20s	f	R		x			-	-	-	-	-	-	-	2	0	FB,T
P5	U20	f	wp			x		-	-	-	-	-	-	-	0	2	FB
P6	20s	f	R			x		C	C	C	-	-	-	-	2	1	FB
P7	20s	m	R		x		x	I	F	-	-	-	I	F	0	0	B
P8	20s	m	wp	x				-	-	-	C	-	-	-	3	2	FB,T
P9	20s	m	R	x				-	-	-	-	-	-	-	n/a	n/a	n/a

wp: with parents
R: rent
b: boat

I: for information
C: to complain (noise, tree)
F: to provide feedback

0: never
1: rare
2: occasional
3: regular

FB: FaceBook
T: Twitter
B: Blog

Table 2: Overview of contributors' responses

Was the installation a success? The sample size of 9 participants is admittedly small to draw any conclusions towards the hypothesis past the anecdotal evidence collected. Further, 168 on-topic messages over 15 working days may not seem like much. However, examining the bigger picture of the test setting reveals a good first result.

First, the overall apathy towards local civic issues within the target audience was higher than anticipated, presenting a "tough crowd". E.g., out of the 32 interviewed non-users, only one had lodged a complaint once before and another one had filled out a survey. Although the majority claimed to have some attachment to their local community, they also seemed overwhelmed that they were being asked for their feedback in the first place. They often mentioned that they would rather leave these things to their parents or that they simply did not have any opinion, because they were never confronted to think about such civic issues. Further, their transient outlook contributed to their apathy: *"There is a good chance I am not going to be here [in the future], so couldn't be bothered"*. The apathy also reflected onto the council's "bright ideas" stand. The stand was mostly quiet, even when the foyer was full with students. Planners rarely had students to talk to and often needed to persuade them heavily.

Second, out of the nine participants who sent a thoughtful message about Brisbane to the screen, only the civically engaged P7 and P1 also talked to the planners. While two others could not talk to the planners because the stand was not occupied at the time, five others preferred to submit a useful, thoughtful post, which would have been lost otherwise: *"I didn't talk to the planners on site [...] I wouldn't have told them my opinion if it weren't for the screen installation"* (P6). They did not want to get involved in a face-to-face conversation; they simply preferred the less personal submission process. Further insight why contributors sent a message to the screen is discussed below.

Lastly, the contributors were not necessarily publicly vocal online users, i.e., they did not have a great willingness to share their views and opinions online. Four contributors (of 8 respondents) had never submitted a post on any *public* online forums or commented on news websites, blogs or YouTube. Only P8 claimed to actively use forums regularly (cf. online presence Table 2). So the contributors are quite different or at least much broader to the ones who are already vocal in presenting their views in the online arena.

Our aim here was to bring residents' ideas and feedback to light that are otherwise not heard. The interview data with contributors suggests that *DIS* was successful in doing so. In addition, a focus group study with urban planners [22] revealed that the data was useful and different to the data that they usually collect.

ANALYSIS RO 2A: USER ARCHETYPES

The evaluation, coding and grouping of the received messages (cf. Table 1) in combination with the field notes from the covert observations and the interview data, provided a picture of the different nuances of use, which led to the development of user archetypes. They are not mutually exclusive; one user can take on multiple roles. However, they may have different – contradicting or supporting – user needs. The following section presents the user archetypes and corresponding user needs from which design implications are drawn in the Analysis RO 2B section.

User Archetype: The Contributor

The Contributor considers the questions and maybe even previous posts of others, to type and send a well-articulated message about the topic (cf. thoughtful Table 1). This archetype was particularly relevant to this study's hypothesis and already discussed above. Below, we explore their perceived motivation, usability and accessibility of *DIS*:

Why does the Contributor contribute? 1. Public exposure: 7 (of 9) participants mentioned that they had a desire to make their opinion heard in public. They wanted their view to receive public exposure through the system: *"With this particular application, it's very engaging. You get feedback straight away. If you submit something, it comes up on the screen and you can see it. For me, it was an incentive to get my opinion on the screen. I'd assume that anybody who is going out to actually give feedback would want their feedback to pop-up"* (P4).

2. Low barrier of entry: It also became clear that this desire to make themselves heard was amplified by the low barrier of entry, just as the design intended: *"I took advantage of the convenience and that it was just there, otherwise I wouldn't have bothered"* (P6) or *"The screen didn't have what I wanted to say so it was kind of a spur of the moment, like 'yeah, I'll try that'"* (P3) were typical responses.

3. Curiosity: Four participants also mentioned curiosity and testing the technology (cf. user archetype: The Curious), particularly the near real-time aspect: e.g., *"I wanted to see how fast it would actually get on the screen or if it would go through some sort of filter"* (P4). Note that despite this ulterior motive, they chose to submit thoughtful posts, although they could have tested the system with simple, random messages as well. This raises the question of whether the system is sustainable for gaining feedback from the public or whether users may not use the system anymore once the novelty factor of the technology has worn off.

4. Inspiration by others: Another common theme amongst the participants was that the inspiration for what they sent to the screen came from reading previous posts: "*I did have a bit of a read first before sending in a message. Thought I might as well mention something and contribute to the many opinions*" (P8) or "*There was one post I agreed with and I wanted to elaborate on that further*" (P6). Even off-topic served as inspiration. P6 added that another reason for sending in thoughtful messages was also *"the fact that there were too many dodgy posts"*; two others mentioned similar reasons.

5. An inoffensive environment: Contributors unanimously agreed that they preferred a controlled, inoffensive environment. Furthermore, some also did not wish for a more "confrontational" discussion in public. P4 put it as follows: "*[In online forums] you usually get people with strong negative or strong positive opinions, so you are not getting anything in-between, you are not getting the average sample.*" She, like many others, welcomed the light-heartedness of the posts, to be able to just throw in their idea.

6. Quality control: Similarly to the point above, "quality control" through moderation was greatly appreciated by all, while for some it did not go far enough: "*I had mixed feelings because I liked the application but there were a lot of dodgy posts completely irrelevant to the question*" (P6). Participants agreed and accepted that quality control was necessary, while nobody complained about the process during the interviews.

7. More space? During the phone interviews, we asked contributors if SMS provided them with enough space to express what they wanted to say. Only one person would have written something more informative if the submission provided more space. All contributors had the feeling that they managed to get their point across, although some admitted that it was a bit of a challenge: *"With issues that you could talk about for a very long time it's hard to express it in a short message, but it's possible"*.

User needs: The process of identifying this user archetype was helpful for pinning down a set of corresponding user needs. They are the need for public exposure of their opinion; low barrier of entry; confirmation that their opinion has received exposure; inspiration from previous posters; an inoffensive environment; quality control. They do not need a more elaborate input channel.

User Archetypes: The Troll, The Clown, & The Social Player

The Troll likes sending obscene or otherwise unsuitable messages, often multiple times in a row, testing the moderators or the moderation process (cf. unsuitable Table 1). Figure 3 shows that the more SMSs one distinct user posted, the more likely the messages were declined (or off-topic). In one instance a user set up automated scripts to spam the system with the same message every 10 min. The Troll generally likes to stay undercover and only reveals their identity to close friends when sending messages from their personal device.

The Clown likes sending funny messages and wants to entertain others. The social environment mentioned above was also more conducive to fun messages, which were mostly off-topic, but not exclusively. 189 posts (out of 656) were tagged to have a fun element (cf. fun Table 1), 21 of them were also on-topic, such as: "*Put in a canal between gardens pt & st Lucia, make west end a student focused island*"; "*Super slides on skyscrapers*".

The Social Player, similar to the Clown, appropriates the screen for social or technological play, sending flirt or birthday messages, making fun of friends, or having a playful, public conversation with them via the screen (cf. personal & fun Table 1): "*Nathan has the most beautiful eyes in the world*"; "*Kristy if you read this I'm already up stairs waiting for our next class.*"

Specifically the immediacy and near real-time aspect in combination with the public nature of the platform provided a fun element. Frequently, participants were observed in eager anticipation for their message to appear. This was particularly noticeable in groups of friends, who would celebrate a successful submission high-fiving each other. On the other hand, users were also mildly disappointed if their message did not appear or had disappeared in the meantime. There are shy and extroverted Clowns or Social Players. The shy ones prefer to stay undercover similar to the Trolls, whereas the extroverted use their performance to draw the attention of bystanders.

Compared to our previous case studies, this study had a high percentage of declined (26%) and off-topic (49%) messages. E.g., running a university related topic within a university building featuring a less prominent screen only attracted 6% of declined posts (26% off-topic); running the same topic ("Share your bright idea") at a bus stop screen, which presented a more open, urban environment, less busy, and a more ambient placed screen, we received 4% declined posts (31% off-topic), but also at a much lower frequency (0.7 posts per day). The bus stop was located within a university campus, so the demographic of users was largely the same.

These numbers demonstrate how not only the *content*, but also the *location* and screen placement is directly causing an increase of Trolls, Clowns and Social Players within the same demographic (*people*). In this case study, the environment was more social, where students waited with large groups of friends. The group dynamics caused bored teenagers to dare each other, testing the system and the moderation process by sending in various inappropriate, or to motivate funny and flirtatious messages. The centrality of the public screen provided a bigger platform and hence more of an incentive for users who were not serious contributors towards the civic topic.

User needs: The user archetypes of the Troll, the Clown and the Social Player indicated a shared user need for a display that was positioned as a big, central platform offering instant gratification through the instantaneous display of the user's content posting.

Passive/Non-User Archetypes: The Interested & Shy Lurkers and the Uninterested Non-User

We observed two types of passive users: The Interested Lurker who reads the posts but does not feel the need to contribute, and the Shy Lurker who reads the posts while others are not looking, but does not want to be watched reading the posts. And then of course there were the Uninterested Non-users, who consciously ignored the public screen application.

Why did passive and non-users not contribute? The interviews carried out during the last few days of the installation provided an opportunity to learn insights towards this question. Note that some users did not want to admit having sent a message, although having been identified as a Clown or Social Player during observations. 20 respondents were under 20 years old, the others were in their 20s; 17 still lived with their parents, 13 were rental tenants, 2 did not answer.

Twenty-eight respondents gave the following reasons for not contributing to the screen: the cost[1] of sending an SMS (8), having nothing to say (5) or could not think of anything on the spot (5) (partially because they had never been asked about their opinion on such matters), not being bothered (4), not knowing how to use (2) or that they *could* use the system (2), not wanting to take the time to type a message (2), the topic being not interesting (1), their idea already being on the screen (1), and being opposed to short-text communication (1). Some participants gave multiple reasons. Nobody voiced any privacy concerns. Overall, these results point towards a good usability of the system, but accessibility still being hindered by the cost of SMS for some of this young demographic.

Initial reactions and effects: Only 3 (out of 30) did not like the application and preferred the TV news content that is usually featured on the screen. During observations, others were overheard not liking being asked a serious question during a time and at a location they consider for leisure: "*Cool app, and what do they do? They turn it into question time!*"

On a positive note, even the more apathetic towards civic issues sometimes found it interesting to read through the posts and ideas. The application proved to have potential to 'convert' the not so interested or to at least raise more awareness towards civic issues amongst them. Many participants also mentioned to be *"pleasantly surprised"* about the council's attempt to get their feedback through this fun medium, and *"greatly appreciated"* the council reaching out to them in that way.

Another positive side effect was in relation to participants from outside of Brisbane or residents who recently moved to Brisbane. They did not feel qualified enough to actively contribute a message. However, they appreciated the glimpse into the local issues of the city that the application provided. One self-proclaimed transient resident noted: "*You learn a lot from neighbours. If you move around a lot, that's how you get to know about things.*"

Overall, participants felt the system 'provided a better sense of community': 23 of 37 respondents agreed with this statement, whereas 7 did not know and 7 thought it did not. Furthermore, 20 felt 'more connected to the people around them', whereas 11 could not tell if they did and 6 said they did not feel more connected. These findings align with similar previous works [4, 5, 17, 18, 24].

Passive/non-user needs: There is a need for the screen to be seen by passersby who might not actively seek out local information but who could nevertheless benefit from the sense of community it engendered.

ANALYSIS RO 2B: DESIGN IMPLICATIONS

This section presents the design implications drawn from the user needs of the different user archetypes above.

Moderation

The moderation process did not only decline inappropriate posts, but also marked posts as on- or off-topic. This allowed giving preference to on-topic posts over off-topic posts on the screen. As mentioned in the system design, the algorithm selecting the array of messages being rotated around within the speech bubbles could be set in different ways.

During the first day of the study, off-topic posts appeared to remain on the screen for too long. Users who sent the off-topic message had left already and the messages did not seem to provide much value for people who came into the space afterwards. It also seemed to distract from the civic content. To counter this, and to emphasize and encourage more meaningful posts, the algorithm was changed so that off-topic posts would expire after 15min and replaced by the most recent on-topic posts. This allowed users to still have fun, but not take up valuable and limited screen real estate once they had their fun and left.

Some might argue that the heavy handed adherence to the designer's view of what the system was intended for is out of place, and an approach should be taken that allows users to modify the technology to meet their needs [14]. *DIS,*

[1] The SMS gateway provided a standard number, incurring standard costs. This was communicated via the footer of the screen and the T&Cs. Standard cost varies per mobile plan, but would be approx. 0.25 AUD.

however, was designed to serve a particular goal, maximizing useful comments from a young demographic to inform urban planning processes. If local governments are to adopt this system as an additional engagement tool, it must add value to them, aim to be efficient and encourage use of Contributors.

Contributors vs. Trolls

DIS attracts trolls and spam like any other public Internet forum. The need to control offensive and disruptive posts is more crucial for public screens due to their public nature. As shown above, the "quality control" also enhances the user experience of Contributors and passive users.

The interview data further suggests that a more liberal and open approach, resulting in an influx of off-topic and even declined messages displayed on the screen, could possibly discourage users to contribute something thoughtful, as they prefer an inoffensive, controlled environment. Under these circumstances, a more open design would be undemocratic as it further discourages an already underrepresented demographic from having a public voice about issues that affect the future of the city.

In this study, Trolls were not notified in any way. While a blacklist was implemented for repeat offenders, they were not told about it. They could be sent a warning and a link to the T&Cs through SMS or Twitter. During the study, we tried to remind users to not be offensive via red admin speech bubble saying "No offence! Be constructive! Terms & Conditions apply (see poster @ column near BCC display)", but this had little or no effect. Rules indicating a ban after x amount of offenses and sending out warnings could be more effective in locations where spam is a problem.

Contributors vs. Deliberation Goal

The primary aim of this study was to provide a platform for underrepresented young demographics to provide feedback to inform urban planning decisions. The secondary aim was to possibly encourage civic discussions, although a more explicit support to deliberate was not implemented in the initial design so not to compromise the primary goal. The study revealed that this secondary aim might contradict the Contributors' need of an inoffensive, moderate environment. Their reaction and acceptance towards possible heated discussions unfolding via this medium needs to be carefully considered when designing for deliberation.

Contributors and Lurkers vs. Clowns and Social Players

Not everybody finds off-topic/fun messages equally funny, which can reflect badly on the overall user experience for some. There are, however, several reasons to not categorically discount off-topic posts:

1. Off-topic posts can be a motivation or inspiration for Contributors to send a more meaningful message (cf. Contributors' user needs).

2. Off-topic messages can create a positive vibe in the area surrounding the screen, giving people something to smile about: Several times, a group of Clowns or Social Players had a public "conversation" over the screen, while others observed their play amused in the background. The application provided something for the outgoing type who likes to perform as well as the more voyeuristic non-user archetype, the Lurker, who prefers to read the posts and observe without actively participating or contributing. Creating a better sense of community and connectedness amongst residents this way are side effects of the system that could well be in the interest of a local government when installing urban screens.

3. The fun element of the application turned out to be an element, which drew a lot of users' attention to the screen, and eventually to the civic issue at hand.

Therefore, trade-offs must be carefully considered. From other deployments, we know that the distribution of these archetypes highly depends on the local setup, environment and sometimes even the time of the day. The more social the location and the more central the screen is positioned within that location, the higher the incentive for the Clown, Troll and Social Player to interact with the screen. Except for the Troll, future design iterations must aim at providing elements that encourages interaction of *all* of the above user types, but also incorporate trade-offs that encourage interaction towards its intended goal, in this study, the civic feedback about a local plan.

URBAN PLANNERS

In three 90-min focus groups sessions with 12 professional urban planners and architects, the on-topic posts collected during this study were discussed and analysed [22]. In summary, the planners appreciated the positivity of the posts and being able to ingest the short texted idea proposals quickly and easily. They further noted that this publicly brainstormed data was different ("*more thinking outside the box*") to data collected through conventional brainstorming activities, and be particularly useful during the visioning stage of an urban planning project, as well as to identify community issues and hotspots when post-evaluating planning projects.

CONCLUSIONS

Supporting serious discourse about the local urban environment is a great challenge in a world of nomadic lifestyles and information overload. This paper presents a new mechanism in using situated public screens and personal mobile devices to engage with young, new digital locals, an often underrepresented demographic in civic engagement initiatives.

Our study found that *DIS* taps into those residents who are 'borderline' engaged. Contributors were more engaged and showed more interest in local issues than the non-users we interviewed. The system does not overcome apathy, but it does trigger valuable thought processes in both the engaged and the apathetic, by raising general awareness through the public visibility of civic issues afforded by the display.

Overall, it validates previous works [1, 4, 12] about the key role that public screens and mobile devices can play in providing an accessible window and input channel into the digital, civic sphere for everyone on the spot.

Our target group widely appreciated the attempt of our local government partner to reach out and 'speak their language'.

We have shown the importance of providing design elements motivating a wide range of different user archetypes to interact with the screen, but also the trade-offs that need to be incorporated to not discourage the overall intended goal, to give young digital locals a voice in urban planning decisions.

We also discussed in what ways external factors, independent of the design of the system, such as the nature of the location where it is deployed, the positioning of the screen as well as the selection of the content influence not only the frequency of interactions with the screen, but also the quality of the interactions.

Further, we demonstrated that emphasizing SMS as the primary engagement channel was the right design decision at this point in time. This case study purposefully employed the simplest means to communicate with the screen in order to create low barriers of entry. Richer functionalities, e.g., allowing SMS users to set their own usernames, or other forms of personalization, would further complicate the interaction experience, which would deter from our outreach and engagement goals. However, that does not mean that such functionalities may not be added in environments where the system has been established and initial novelty has worn off.

FUTURE WORK

In the future, we want to incorporate features such as rating posts, creating new community topics or following an ongoing topic, into a smartphone application, which we envisage to be downloaded by residents who like to take a more active role in their local community. The public screen would then serve as a gateway to connect the less engaged with their community leaders in an attempt to draw them into a more civic role within their community. While the system would remain a local government initiated engagement tool, it would move towards a more collaboratively driven one with the community.

ACKNOWLEDGMENTS

This research was supported by the Australian Research Council (Linkage LP0776341), Brisbane City Council, the Queensland Department of Housing, RedTV and Optus Business. The author thanks Marcus Foth, Christine Satchell, Paul Roe, Mark Bilandzic and our study participants as well as the anonymous reviewers for their valuable comments.

REFERENCES

1. Ananny, M. and Strohecker, C. TexTales: Creating Interactive Forums with Urban Publics. In Foth, M. ed. Handbook of Research on Urban Informatics: The Practice and Promise of the Real-Time City, IGI Global, Hershey, PA, 2009.
2. Australian Communications and Media Authority. ACMA Communications Report 2006-2007, Australian Communications and Media Authority, Melbourne, Australia, 2008.
3. Brignull, H. and Rogers, Y., Enticing People to Interact with Large Public Displays in Public Spaces. In Proc. Interact 2003, IOS Press (2003).
4. Churchill, E. and Nelson, L., Interactive Community Bulletin Boards as Conversational Hubs and Sites for Playful Visual Repartee. In Proc. HICSS 2007, IEEE (2007).
5. Churchill, E., Nelson, L., Denoue, L., Helfman, J. and Murphy, P., Sharing Multimedia Content with Interactive Public Displays: A Case Study. In Proc. DIS 2004, ACM Press (2004).
6. Coleman, S. and Gotze, J. Bowling Together: Online Public Engagement in Policy Deliberation, Hansard Society, London, UK, 2001.
7. Goodman, E. Created by Everybody: Engaging Participation with Mobile Interfaces, User Centered Design Group, Intel Corporation, 2005.
8. Huang, E.M., Russell, D.M. and Sue, A.E., IM Here: Public Instant Messaging on Large, Shared Displays for Workgroup Interactions. In Proc. CHI 2004, ACM Press (2004).
9. International Association for Public Participation (IAP2). IAP2 Spectrum of Public Participation IAP2, 2007.
10. Jacobs, J. The Death and Life of Great American Cities. Random House, New York, NY, 1962.
11. Kavanaugh, A.L., Zin, T.T., Carroll, J.M., Schmitz, J., Manuel Perez-Quinones and Isenhour, P., When Opinion Leaders Blog: New Forms of Citizen Interaction. In Proc. dg.o 2006, ACM Press (2006).
12. Lane, G., Thelwall, S., Angus, A., Peckett, V. and West, N. Urban Tapestries - Public Authoring, Place and Mobility Proboscis - Social Tapestries, Proboscis, Southampton, UK, 2005.
13. Lévesque, M., Bélanger, L. and Lewis, J. P2p: Cityspeak's Reconfiguration of Public Media Space. Wi: Journal of the Mobile Digital Commons Network, 1, 1 (2006).
14. Marsden, G. Under Development Electronic Tablecloths and the Developing World. Interactions, 16, 2 (2009). 67-69.
15. Martin, K., Penn, A. and Gavin, L. Engaging with a Situated Display Via Picture Messaging. In CHI '06 Extended Abstracts on Human Factors in Computing Systems, ACM Press, New York, NY, 2006, 1079 - 1084.
16. Maunder, A.J., Marsden, G. and Harper, R., SnapAndGrab: Accessing and Sharing Contextual Multi-Media Content Using Bluetooth Enabled Camera Phones and Large Situated Displays. In Proc. CHI 2008, ACM Press (2008).
17. McCarthy, J.F., Congleton, B. and Harper, F.M., The Context, Content & Community Collage: Sharing Personal Digital Media in the Physical Workplace. In *Proc. CSCW 2008*, ACM Press (2008).
18. McCarthy, J.F., Farnham, S.D., Patel, Y., Ahuja, S., Norman, D., Hazlewood, W.R. and Lind, J., Supporting Community in Third Places with Situated Social Software. In Proc. C&T 2009, ACM Press (2009).
19. Morrison, A., Jacucci, G. and Peltonen, P. CityWall: Limitations of a Multi-Touch Environment. In Proc. PPD 2008, ACM Press (2008), 31-35.
20. Munson, S.A., Rosengren, E. and Resnick, P., Thanks and Tweets: Comparing Two Public Displays. In Proc. CSCW 2011, ACM Press (2011).
21. Schroeter, R. and Foth, M., Discussions in Space. In Proc. OZCHI 2009, ACM Press (2009).
22. Schroeter, R. and Houghton, K. Neo-Planning: Location-Based Social Media to Engage Australia's New Digital Locals. Australian Planner, 48, 3 (2011). 191-202.
23. Strauss, A. and Corbin, J. Basics of Qualitative Research: Grounded Theory Procedures and Techniques. Sage Publications, Newbury Park, CA, 1990.
24. Struppek, M. The Social Potential of Urban Screens. Visual Communication, 5, 2 (2006). 173-188.

Between Us and Them: Building Connectedness Within Civic Networks

Jennifer Stoll, Kirsten Foot[1], W. Keith Edwards

GVU Center and School of Interactive Computing
Georgia Institute of Technology, Atlanta, GA
jstoll@gatech.edu, keith@cc.gatech.edu

[1]Department of Communication
University of Washington, Seattle, WA
kfoot@u.washington.edu

ABSTRACT
Civic networks of community-based organizations face significant challenges in working together to combat issues facing their community (e.g., gang violence, sex trafficking). In our research, we examined how local organizations tried to build and maintain connectedness over time as a network to fight child sex trafficking. We sought to understand how technology supports the social processes of connectedness in this context. Based on our analysis of the field data from this case study, we identify three categories of activities for building and maintaining connectedness. We also find that while different technologies are suited towards supporting different aspects of connectedness, there may be gaps in how adequately social media tools support connectedness in civic networks.

Author Keywords
Interorganizational collaboration, civic networks

ACM Classification Keywords
K4.2. Social Issues: Miscellaneous

General Terms
Human Factors, Design

INTRODUCTION
In the face of large-scale social problems, e.g., gang violence, homelessness, or child sex trafficking, the combined efforts of government agencies and expert service organizations are often inadequate. Members of communities facing such issues must often self-organize, despite efforts by government and service providers to help combat these issues [3]; these community-based organizations often co-construct an information ecosystem that allows them to coordinate and share information [7]. In our work, we studied the appropriation of information and communication technologies (ICTs) in and between such organizations, focusing on a particular social location [12]: an umbrella organization that functions as a hub in building and coordinating a multi-organizational network to fight child-sex trafficking.

Our exploration of connectedness in civic networks builds on the work of [1, 2, 4, 10]; we summarize connectedness as *interdependence between organizations that is supported by processes of information sharing*. Prior research such as [1] explored the formation of connectedness among organizations, while other studies [c.f. 4] examined properties of organizations creating such ties. We build on this work by focusing on the appropriation of ICTs (specifically Facebook, Twitter, email, and a custom website) initiated by a hub organization created to support interorganizational connectedness. This paper contributes to CSCW by illuminating the social processes of ICT-mediated connections an under-studied context, i.e. a civic network, wherein the configuration of cyberinfrastructure emerges in situ between community-based organizations. By examining the ways that low-budget community-based organizations develop and structure connectedness via ICTs, we offer findings that complement prior work on interorganizational ICT use such as [2, 10], which tended to focus on large-scale, large-budget, bespoke systems or analyses of the human infrastructure of networks.

Through this case study, we identified three categories of social processes utilized in creating connections within the network, and which could be useful as a framework for future research. We also found that social media was primarily being used for the processes of *enabling and reinforcing connections*, but not for *raising basic awareness* to initiate connections. The significance of these findings is that the configuration of ICTs in this network seems to require a more other- or group-centric rather than an individual- or "ego-centric" orientation [9]. These findings point towards an opportunity for configuring technology to better support *groups of groups* rather than just individuals.

METHODS
To understand the social processes of ICT-mediated connectedness among community-based organizations, we conducted a field study of a civic network working to fight child sex trafficking in a U.S. metropolitan region. This network is coordinated by a nonprofit organization created

for the purpose of connecting or *bridging* the other existing organizations engaged in anti-child sex trafficking efforts. As in the network/s studied by [11], establishing such a "coordinating organization" was an explicit aim of several community-based organizations in our study, as they sought to fill gaps in their network and facilitate joint activity. They vested responsibility in this separate entity to coordinate information sharing to extend the network, establish best practices, and create information systems to support those practices.

The network we studied comprised over 100 organizations. About half the organizations were faith-based, the other half were organizations seeking to revitalize the local metropolitan region by assisting at-risk communities within it. The police and governmental agencies were not part of this community network, but about an eighth of the member organizations were affiliated with government agencies to help provide victim support.

During 2008-2011, we undertook observations of interorganizational meetings, conducting interviews with organizational members of this network. We were given access to emails and documents exchanged between members of the network and the bridging organization. We observed a range of meetings from seven "start-up" meetings where community organizations began the process of working together, six monthly meetings open to the public, and nine staff meetings of the bridging organization discussing their interactions with other organizations in the network. At these meetings, we recorded observations of information-sharing challenges, types of information shared, and names of individuals with whom the information was being shared. Following each meeting, we conducted interviews with individuals and groups; subjects included the entire staff of the bridging organization (four individuals) as well as representatives from a sample of organizations (n=21) from across the network.

We employed a general inductive approach in our data analysis as we sought an in-depth understanding of ICT appropriation for supporting ties in a multi-organizational network. To identify the themes of this characterization, we coded the data across artifacts as well as within individual documents to uncover themes about current practices in using ICTs for information sharing. We first labeled the notes for categories of sharing and ICT use, and then identified sub-themes among the categories and grouped the labels accordingly. Finally we grouped the sub-themes to identify the role of technology support for connectedness. Together we analyzed the ICT-mediated social processes that facilitated multi-organization connectedness and the ICTs appropriated in this case.

CASE STUDY: BUILDING CONNECTEDNESS

Prior work has demonstrated two types of connectedness in civic networks: transactions and social bonds [1]. Transactions are ties "involving exclusively the exchange of information and resources necessary to the pursuit of shared collective goals." In contrast, social bonds are deeper connections, often tied to identity or strong interpersonal interactions. Social bonds create tight clusters of interconnected organizations in a network while transaction ties tend to bridge between these tight clusters.

Connectedness in Civic Networks

Within the civic network we studied, both types of connectedness were evident. We identified three distinct social processes in which connectedness was instantiated:

Raising basic awareness through gathering and disseminating information about contact details, organizational goals, capabilities, and opportunities [13].

Enabling connections, through face-to-face meetings, updates, and encouragement to exchange basic awareness information in order to foster informal coordination [1, 11]. Through connection enabling processes, organizations may achieve a functional agreement to begin assessing the feasibility of working together towards a common goal.

Reinforcing connections, through follow-up meetings, joint events, and other opportunities involving multiple organizations in the network [1, 4]. These activities bring organizations together to engage in the actual work of coordinating to fight child sex trafficking jointly.

A range of ICTs were used by members in this civic network to support these three social processes for creating and sustaining connectedness—from cellphones, to email, to custom websites, to social media. Below we present findings from our field data analysis to illustrate the ways ICTs (specifically Twitter, Facebook, email, and a custom website) were appropriated to support the creation of both transaction ties and social bonds.

Raising Basic Awareness

A lack of *basic awareness* about other member organizations' activities and capabilities in anti-child sex trafficking efforts posed a challenge for some members of the network [13]. Such awareness is a necessary pre-condition for more complex relationships among organizations, including collaboration, cooperation, coordination, implementation, and evolution [5]. However, the organizations we studied were critically hindered in some of their efforts (e.g., legislative advocacy and petitioning where a high volume of participation is needed) due to a lack of awareness beyond their immediate social circle. That is, clusters of organizations were often in silos of awareness. Also lacking were persons with overlapping memberships in multiple circles who could act as bridges [6] between these silos.

This network's process of building greater awareness among its member organizations followed a trajectory that occurred over a span of 2 years. Initially, the organizational members we interviewed primarily relied on word-of-mouth for learning about the existence and activities of other organizations also fighting child sex trafficking.

Being aware of these silos, they began organizing start-up meetings to increase awareness and encourage interorganizational coordination. After introductions were made at these face-to-face start-up meetings, organizations then determined whether further connection would be fruitful, often resulting in follow-up meetings to facilitate the process of enabling these connections and to begin the process of reinforcing them. The organizations that were the most energetic in reaching out to others soon assimilated connections brought in by other organizations. Other organizations desiring to connect joined an email list created by those organizing the start-up meetings. The email list was forwarded to others who had not joined and became a primary tool for raising basic awareness.

During these meetings, organizational members would inquire about the status of current efforts as a whole. They often asked questions related to where the nexus of overall activity was in the fight against child sex trafficking, and "who was doing what" in terms of the overall flow of activities, and whether or how the actions of one organization could contribute to the overall efforts of the community. We believe a significant commonality underlying these questions is that they point to a need for what we call a *whole network perspective*—that is, a perspective informing basic awareness at the network-wide level rather than simply details about singular entities. Our analysis of the follow-up interview data of these organizations about this perspective indicated they were seeking a bird's eye view of the community, integrated with specific details about each member fighting child sex trafficking. Additionally, this bird's eye view needed to convey more than just membership but also *commitment* over time to specific aspects of the overall community effort e.g. prevention, advocacy, restoration, etc.

In an attempt to provide this perspective, the organizations we studied created a custom website (developed by the hub organization) listing the organizations as partners in the fight against child sex trafficking. This listing detailed organizations' contact information, and details of each organization's mission, capabilities and opportunities were aggregated and made available to members of the network via a password-protected directory on the group website. What we find interesting here is that Facebook and Twitter were not used at this time to obtain a whole network perspective. The time and expense invested by this organization in creating a custom website to help facilitate *other* awareness points toward a gap in solely using a combination of Facebook, Twitter, and email to support the basic awareness needed by a civic network.

Connection Enabling and Reinforcement

This specialized directory listing supplemented existing practices of member organizations in finding each other (i.e., through word-of-mouth, meetings, and email lists): member organizations used the directory to peruse other organizations and select ones to engage with in face-to-face meetings or joint events. Additionally, the website provided member organizations with a persistent visible representation of how connectedness in the network was maturing and solidifying, and prompted them to consider how it could be extended and strengthened further.

For example, one organization (P14) that focused on prevention had developed a strategy of providing weekend mentoring opportunities for at-risk youth in 2009. In 2010, P14 sought to expand its offerings by partnering with summer camps for these youth. P14 was part of the initial start-up group of organizations in the network. After working through the process of building their basic awareness by attending face-to-face meetings and joining the mailing list, P14 initiated a connection-enabling process for collaborating with another community organization to jointly offer summer camp for at-risk youth.

ICTs facilitated P14's efforts in several ways. First, the website directory listing of organizations willing to work together provided a foundation for P14 to initiate connection-enabling and reinforcing processes with any of the organizations listed. The initial process of creating a connection was completed such that when P14 was ready, it was able to immediately initiate meetings with potential partners. Through the custom website, P14 could message other organizations by posting opportunities for joint coordination activity, thus enabling a bi-directional means to foster connections. Additionally, organizations collaborating with P14 used Twitter and Facebook in efforts to strengthen connectedness by further broadcasting (retweeting) and responding to opportunities posted by P14. We note here that these tweets and Facebook postings did not reflect basic awareness-raising within the network. Instead, the content of the social media activity revealed the reiteration of collaboration opportunities that had been initially posted elsewhere, especially on the custom website, and which relied on connections formed earlier.

In another example of how the online directory listing was used, when this civic network stepped up efforts to encourage state senators to vote "yes" for a bill that would secure more protection for victims of child sex trafficking, the coordinating organizations encouraged everyone in the network to change their Facebook profile picture for individual and group pages to indicate support for this particular bill.

These two examples illustrate that while the custom website helped to support all three types of social processes for creating and sustaining connections within the network, social media only supported connection-enabling and reinforcing activities. That is, organizations in this network did not use Twitter and Facebook until basic awareness had already taken place, even though the functionality of these systems could have partially supported it. Based on our analysis of the data, we infer that these organizations preferred to attain a level of common agreement in terms of goals and coordination efforts before utilizing social media

ICTs. Once some level of agreement was reached, those in the network used social media tools to bring attention to information being distributed elsewhere in order to enable and reinforce connection rather than adopting these channels to continue to raise basic awareness.

DISCUSSION

In our case study, we examined a *group of groups* attempting to build connectedness by cobbling together a combination of ICTs built for individuals managing information sharing. Previous work on grassroots political campaigns identified forms of ICT-based miscommunication and communicative overload that can result from such cobbling together of ICTs [6]. Unsurprisingly, we observed similar mishaps, such as data fragmentation due to data storage in multiple "stand alone" applications, incomplete or redundant messaging as not everyone in the network used social media tools and each organization maintained different email lists. Also, the "noise" in these social media channels, especially Twitter, seemed to render the raising-basic-awareness process less effective than word-of-mouth, emails, meetings, or online directory listings.

However, in addition to the above issues, our data suggests an underlying gap between these cobbled technologies and the needs of this civic network. We believe this gap arises from email, Twitter, and Facebook being primarily oriented towards the needs of the *individual* user. That is, the features, functions and data visually represented by these tools are designed primarily to support connectedness among individuals, or between individuals and groups. Such ICTs are effectively "ego-centric" technologies [9], as they are geared toward the needs of individuals. The features and functions of these tools did not adequately inform the basic awareness that network members needed to establish connectedness, i.e., an overview of the entire network, meaningful categorizations of organizations within this specific network context, and a sense of the commitments of member organizations in the network.

To begin to address this gap, network members began to rely on a custom website that was explicitly designed *by* the bridging organization *for the network*. The coordinating group sought to enhance basic awareness within the network by increasing visibility. They did so by creating an online directory listing on a custom website. With this listing they formalized and publicized the *commitments to collaboration* that these community organizations had made. They also provided an overview of the network such that members could see the possibilities for coordinating activities. Consequently, this listing was used to instantiate and *make visible* these commitments to interorganizational collaboration. Connections represented in social media tools likely do not adequately convey a *comprehensive network overview* nor convey the *weight* of organizational commitment to the network over time. We infer these are the primary reasons why social media tools were not appropriated to support basic awareness in this network.

CONCLUSION

The findings we present in this paper indicate that there is a critical need for low-cost, more group-centric technologies for maintaining connectedness between community-based organizations over an extended period of time. Our work offers a lens for better understanding a context of an informal civic network where such connectedness needs to be supported as a first step in designing such technologies. This lens can help guide how more group-centric ICTs can be leveraged to create connectedness in civic networks. In future work, we plan to explore design approaches to supporting the processes of awareness-raising in this community-based context.

ACKNOWLEDGEMENT

This research was supported by the NSF under grant IIS-0915624.

REFERENCES

1. Baldassari, D., Diani, M. The Integrative Power of Civic Networks. AJS 113, 3:735-80, Nov. 2007.
2. Carroll, JM et al. Community Network 2.0: Visions, Participation, and Engagement in New Information Infrastructures, End-User Development LNCS, 2011, Volume 6654/2011, 270-275
3. Foot, K. & Toft, A. "Collaborating Against Human Trafficking," Conf on HT, UNL, Sept. 30-Oct. 2, 2010.
4. Gulati, J., Garguilo, M. Where do Interorganizational Networks Come From?, AJS 104, 5:1439-1493, 1999.
5. Hogue, T. Community-based collaboration: Community wellness multiplied. OR Cen. for Comm. Leadership, Oregon State University, 1993.
6. Kavanaugh, A. et al. Weak ties in networked communities. C&T (pp. 265-286) 2003. The Netherlands: Kluwer Academic Publishers.
7. Nardi, B. and O'Day, V. Information Ecologies. MIT Press, Cambridge, MA 1999.
8. Nielsen, R.K. The Labors of Internet-Assisted Activism: Overcommunication, miscommunication, and communicative overload, JITP, 6, 3:267-280, 2009.
9. Pederson, T. Egocentric Interaction. CHI Workshop: Quebec, CAN. April 22-27 2006.
10. Ribes, D., Finholt, T. Representing community: knowing users in the face of changing constituencies. CSCW 2008.
11. Shumate, M., & Lipp, J. Connective collective action online: An examination of the hyperlink network structure of an NGO issue network. Journal of Computer Mediated Communication, 14, 178-201, 2008.
12. Stinchcombe, A. Information and Organization. Berkeley and L.A.: University of California Press, 1990.
13. Stoll, J., Edwards, W.K., Mynatt, E.D., "Informal Interactions in a Nonprofit Network". CHI 2010.

Unfolding the Event Landscape on Twitter: Classification and Exploration of User Categories

Munmun De Choudhury*
Microsoft Research
munmund@microsoft.com

Nicholas Diakopoulos
Rutgers University
diakop@rutgers.edu

Mor Naaman
Rutgers University
mor@rutgers.edu

ABSTRACT
Social media platforms such as Twitter garner significant attention from very large audiences in response to real-world events. Automatically establishing *who* is participating in information production or conversation around events can improve event content consumption, help expose the stakeholders in the event and their varied interests, and even help steer subsequent coverage of an event by journalists. In this paper, we take initial steps towards building an automatic classifier for user types on Twitter, focusing on three core user categories that are reflective of the information production and consumption processes around events: organizations, journalists/media bloggers, and ordinary individuals. Exploration of the user categories on a range of events shows distinctive characteristics in terms of the proportion of each user type, as well as differences in the nature of content each shared around the events.

Author Keywords
Events; Social media; Twitter; User classification

ACM Classification Keywords
J.4 Computer Applications: Social And Behavioral Sciences

General Terms
Algorithms; Experimentation

INTRODUCTION
As a computer mediated communication channel, Twitter has become a powerful destination for people posting content around events. Whether those events be the marriage of royalty, the destruction due to a tornado, or the launch of a product, there is valuable information about these events to be gleaned by examining the content shared by thousands of individuals. In particular, the composition of communities posting content for events is of interest. This paper takes initial steps towards building an automatic classifier for user types on Twitter, differentiating between organizations, journalists/bloggers, and ordinary individuals. We then use those classifications to characterize a series of diverse events.

*This work was performed while the author was at Rutgers.

Such study of intrinsic differences in events and the types of participants and reactions they induce is interesting in its own right, to develop a theory of event-related information production, and can enable the next generation of event content exploration tools. Such tools will improve the understanding of the stakeholders in an event and their actions and interests, and even help steer subsequent coverage of an event by the mass media. Understanding event participation can also help estimate source credibility.

This work builds on that of Starbird et al. [7] and Vieweg et al. [8], that addressed the characterization of events by the types of Twitter users that posted messages about them. However, these studies rely on manual coding of users, and only examine events of one type (natural hazards). Other recent studies have considered characterizing users on Twitter outside the context of events. These efforts include using Twitter lists to identify elite users such as celebrities, bloggers, media, and organizations [9], classification of political affiliation [1], and classification of demographic attributes [3]. Other efforts have looked at characterizing events: e.g., the temporal signature of event messages as well as user participation breakdown [6, 4].

In this work, we classify users according to three primary categories: *organizations*, *journalists/media bloggers*, and *ordinary individuals*, that may participate in events in ways that exhibit different interaction, content, and usage patterns. For instance, organizations may coordinate rescue efforts for emergency events, ordinary individuals may have "eyewitness" information [8], and journalists may engage in synthesis and amplification as second hand information providers [7]. In this light, the contributions of this work include: (1) developing a robust automatic classifier for user types on Twitter, thus overcoming the limitations of manual coding efforts; and (2) extending the understanding of participation in Twitter activity around events by using our classifier to examine participation in a diverse range of events.

CLASSIFYING USER CATEGORIES ON TWITTER
As noted above, we focus on three user archetypes: organizations, journalists/bloggers, and ordinary users.

Organizations are entities associated with some social, political, or business goal and often have a Twitter account for the sake of marketing, public relations, or customer service. Organizations can be commercial (e.g. a marketing firm), or non-profit (e.g. an NGO on breast cancer awareness) and could include a company, brand, product, or charity.

Journalists/Media Bloggers include individuals who are associated with a mass media enterprise/news organization or who maintain a blog that reflects their professional interests on various local and global issues.

Ordinary Individuals are users likely to be on Twitter for a variety of reasons such as posting updates on their day-to-day life, expanding professional opportunities, maintaining contacts with their friends, or to discover relevant/useful content relating to their interests.

Other. This final category includes all users who do not satisfy the properties of any of the above three categories.

We note here that in certain cases, there could be Twitter users who belong to more than one category, or their category affiliation is ambiguous. For example, a user may be a low visibility journalist, not strictly associated with a media organization, making her Twitter behavior similar to both an ordinary individual and a journalist. For simplicity, in this paper we assume that each user can belong uniquely to *exactly one* category. Multi-category probabilistic assignments will be addressed in future research.

Classification Methodology. We use a standard machine learning framework to classify Twitter users into our categories. For the classification features, each user is represented as a vector of the following features, selected to capture the differences between categories:

- *Network/structural features* consist of the indegree (#followers) and outdegree (#friends) of a user.
- *Activity features* consist of the number of posts by a user until the time of the crawl and the number of posts they marked as favorites.
- *Interaction features* include the patterns of how a user engages with their Twitter "audience". The specific features are: the fraction of re-tweets among all the posts from a user, the fraction of replies directed to other users, the fraction of @-mentions of other users in a user's posts and the fraction of posts with URLs in them.
- *Named entities* capture the presence or absence of named entities in the content of the posts from a user (like a place name, or a company). The named entities are derived using the natural language toolkit OpenCalais.
- *Topic distribution* is the topical association of the history of a user, to a set of 18 broad themes from the IPTC Media Topic News Codes, again derived using OpenCalais.

Next we compared eight different classifiers to empirically determine the best suitable classification technique. We also compared to a baseline method that used the profile description of a user's Twitter account to infer categories. The baseline checked for the existence of terms specific to organizations (e.g. company, brand, charity) or journalists/media bloggers in the profile text. The best performing classifier was found to be k Nearest Neighbors with $k = 10$ (that also far outperformed the baseline by $\sim$30%). Due to limited space we report only on this classifier here.

TRAINING AND VALIDATION

We begin by describing our training model which we developed by gathering and labeling users from the Twitter public timeline, as well as collecting users from pre-existing labeled directories on Twellow and Muckrack.

We first gathered a random sample of 1,850 users from the Twitter public timeline during April 2011(http://twitter.com/public_timeline). The users from this source were categorized using *Amazon Mechanical Turk* (http://www.mturk.com). We set up the tasks so that they could only be performed by Turkers located in the U.S. with a more than 95% approval rating. Each Turker was presented with a Twitter user's screen name, linked to the user's Twitter profile page. We had each user's profile labeled by two Turkers (Scott's PI was moderate at 0.55) and then excluded exemplars where there was no agreement (16.4% of sample) to train our model on less ambiguous data.

On top of the timeline we also used the *Twellow* directory (http://www.twellow.com/) to collect a list of 1,532 organizations and the *Muckrack* directory (http://muckrack.com/) to collect a list of 1,490 self-identified journalists and media bloggers on Twitter.

Combining the three different sources above, we obtained a training dataset comprising 4,932 Twitter users, who are labeled into one of the four categories. For each labeled user in our training dataset, we used the Twitter API to collect the data required to compute the features described above. We used each user's 200 most recent Twitter status updates (through May 2011) to compute the named entities and topic distribution features.

Actual \ Predicted	Organizations	J/MB	OI	Other
Organizations	**1341**	240	24	6
J/MB	42	**1957**	19	5
OI	9	27	**1208**	11
Other	2	7	22	**12**

Table 1. Confusion matrix combined over all the five folds of cross validation on the training dataset.

We validated our training model using five-fold cross validation. The confusion matrix of classification is shown in Table 1. We note that our training model performs extremely well for "Journalists/Media bloggers" (J/MB) and "Ordinary Individuals" (OI). Table 2 further shows the balanced accuracy[1], precision, recall and F1 measure for the label predictions. We observe high values of the four metrics across the categories, which suggests that our training model is suitable to be used for categorizing users on Twitter. The poor performance for the 'Other' category can be explained by its lower number of users, as well as the fact that the category is loosely defined—comprising users who do not fit into the other categories.

TESTING ON EVENTS

Since our goal is to understand the user categories spanning different events on Twitter, we now describe the various

[1]Balanced accuracy curbs skewness in category sizes, and is given as the mean of sensitivity (true positive rate) and specificity (true negative rate).

Category	#users	Bal. acc.	Precision	Recall	F1
Org	1611	94.21%	0.96	0.82	0.89
J/MB	2023	92.41%	0.86	0.97	0.91
OI	1255	96.45%	0.94	0.96	0.95
Other	43	71.01%	0.42	0.27	0.33

Table 2. Balanced accuracy, precision, recall and F1 measure of the results of predicting user category labels using our classifier. Results are averaged across the five cross validation folds.

events used in this work, and the categorization of users in them using our classifier. We first collected data on a set of events from Twitter. For each event we manually identified keywords, and then used the Twitter streaming API to download a large sample of English-language tweets corresponding to the keywords that are (presumably) representative of the event's discussion on Twitter. Table 3 provides information about the number of posts and number of users in each event sample.

EVENT NAME	#POSTS	#USERS
Bonnaroo 2011	22,159	13,685
Search keywords: #bonnaroo		
Earth day 2011	587,750	359,131
Search keywords: earth day, #earthday		
2011 Egyptian Revolution	4,798,828	530,629
Search keywords: #egypt, egypt riots, egypt revolution		
Release of iPad 2	151,356	78,768
Search keywords: #ipad2		
Osama Bin Laden's death	3,258,319	1,656,967
Search keywords: #OBL, osama, osama bin laden		
Academy Awards 2011	854,154	293,601
Search keywords: #oscars		
Super Bowl XLV 2011	831,172	399,209
Search keywords: #superbowl2011, superbowl		
Wikileaks	72,448	26,143
Search keywords: #wikileaks, #cablegate, #assange		

Table 3. Description of the eight events used in this paper.

To construct our exploration dataset on each of the eight events, we randomly sampled 5,000 users from the set of posts for each event. For each such user, we collected the data required to construct the features used in the classifier. The previously discussed nearest neighbor classifier was then utilized to label each user (of the 5,000 users in each event) to a particular category. For validation, we generate ground truth labels for 100 random users per event using Mechanical Turk, as before. The results of comparing the user labels indicate that our classification technique yields high accuracy over all the events (88.73%, averaged over the three core categories); demonstrating that our training model is efficient in categorizing Twitter users over a diverse set of events.

EXPLORING USER CATEGORIES

Participatory Behavior of User Types

We show here how users of different categories participated in each of the eight events. Participation is evaluated using the relative representation of each category in the events, in terms of users (the proportion of the number of users in the category to the number of users captured in our test set), and in terms of content (the proportion of content posted by users of each particular category for the event). The results are shown in Figure 1, and discussed below. We wish to emphasize here that verification across a much larger set of events may be necessary for the purposes of generalization.

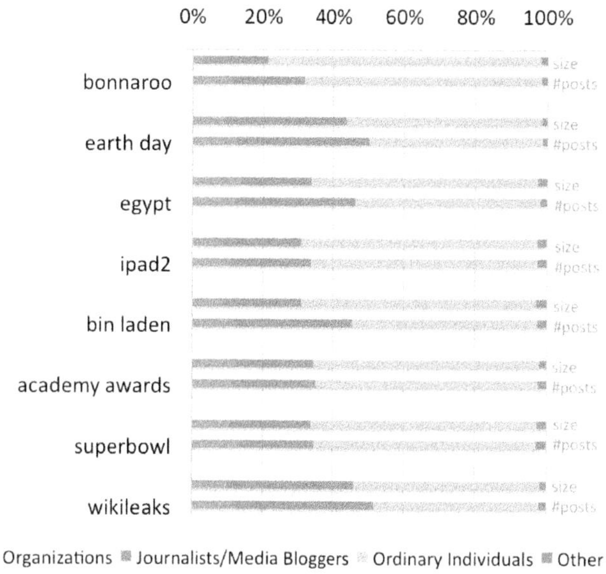

Figure 1. Distribution of sizes and posts from different user categories.

Figure 1 shows, perhaps unsurprisingly, that localized events such as Bonnaroo Music Festival are characterized by a large number of ordinary individuals that post a large proportion of the content. On the other hand, national events, such as Earth Day and the Wikileaks news event seem to involve a large proportion of organizations and journalists/media bloggers. Earth Day, for example, is more likely to involve organizations and journalists/bloggers spreading environmental awareness. Similarly, Wikileaks was an event of great interest to news organizations and political journalists/ media bloggers: consequently these categories seem to have posted a larger proportion of content for Wikileaks than their numbers predict. Events manifesting as 'breaking news', such as the Egyptian revolution and the death of Bin Laden appear to gather even more participation and attention, in terms of category size and disproportionate fraction of posts, from organizations and journalists. Planned events scheduled to happen at a fixed date and time or at a known location/set of locations (e.g. release of iPad 2, the Academy Awards and Superbowl XLV) appear to involve large participation from ordinary individuals, perhaps due to the fact that some of these events are nationally televised [6].

Content Characteristics of User Categories

The classification also allows us to examine the differences in terms of characteristics of content posted by different categories of users. Due to lack of space, we demonstrate this potential for only two of our events, a local event (Bonnaroo), and a mass-media news event (Wikileaks). For each event and user category, we report numbers that reflect the proportion of posts on the event having URLs, that are @-replies to other users, is a re-tweet, reflect an exclamatory sentiment (presence of the exclamation sign) and are questions. These five aspects of the posts are indicative of various types of content typically shared on Twitter.

The results are shown in Table 4. We observe that in these events, organizations have a relatively higher number of posts with URLs. For Bonnaroo, the organizations tend to be

Category	Frequent Keywords	Category-specific Keywords
	bonnaroo	
Organizations	festival, live, video, headline, news, tickets	#madness, #newfavoritesong, rock, videos
Journalists/Bloggers	you, festival, live, see, artist, listen	#partyplane, #coachella, fans, stars, volunteer
Ordinary Indv.	my, festival, going, live, we, excited, awesome	seeing, performing, bad, interested, haha, epic
	wikileaks	
Organizations	#cablegate, they, government, censorship, news	documents, statement, threat, report, classified
Journalists/Bloggers	why, #cablegate, who, secret, media, blog	#obama, secrecy, rumors, diplomats, president
Ordinary Indv.	assange, us, truth, my, secret, government	interpol, law, #iamwikileaks, information

Table 4. High frequency keywords (stopword eliminated, based on tf–idf computation) associated with different user categories and category-specific keywords corresponding to two events.

more 'interactive', as shown by the higher proportion of @-replies. Organizations and journalists appear to re-tweet more extensively in the Wikileaks dataset, perhaps propagating released information and news updates by re-tweeting. Ordinary individuals are characterized in these events by a low proportion of URLs in their posts, and a higher proportion of interactive posts that are @-replies to others.

In both events, organizations appear to pose very few questions ("?" column), whereas journalists/media bloggers and ordinary individuals exhibit the opposite behavior, perhaps indicating interactive behavior seeking feedback, and thoughts of others on the events. The expression of exclamations are also more frequent in the case of all categories for Bonnaroo, compared to Wikileaks, which provides evidence that there are inherent differences among events, and that user types respond differently in the context of different events.

Category	URL	@	RT	!	?
	bonnaroo				
Organizations	0.77	0.58	0.07	0.33	0.01
Journalists/Bloggers	0.52	0.48	0.16	0.28	0.13
Ordinary Individuals	0.37	0.56	0.13	0.19	0.11
	wikileaks				
Organizations	0.71	0.31	0.41	0.05	0.06
Journalists/Bloggers	0.63	0.39	0.37	0.05	0.09
Ordinary Individuals	0.63	0.52	0.29	0.08	0.09

Table 5. Different content types shared by user categories corresponding to two events. The columns are not mutually exclusive, i.e., a post with a '?' which is also an 'RT' is considered for both the columns.

In the final segment of our exploratory analysis on content characteristics of user categories, Table 5 shows high frequency keywords and keywords appearing more frequently in a particular category (left) compared to the rest (right). We chose to compare the same two events, Bonnaroo and Wikileaks. Again, there are differences in the content shared across the categories on the two events. Organizations tend to use words such as headline and news frequently, reflecting that there could be several news organizations reporting on the events. Journalists/bloggers tend to engage in more interactive behavior by using terms such as 'you' and by reflecting their interests with words like media and blog. Finally, for ordinary individuals we observe the presence of sentiment words (e.g., excited, awesome, bad) and heavy reference to themselves in the first person (e.g., my, us).

CONCLUSIONS AND FUTURE WORK

In this paper, we took initial steps towards categorizing the stakeholders of events on Twitter. We developed a classifier that automatically identified users whose behavior corresponded to three core categories: organizations, journalists/media bloggers and ordinary individuals. Exploration of events from Twitter provided several interesting insights. First, we showed that different events gather different degrees of participation (number of users from each category) and attention (proportion of posts from each category). Second, we demonstrated differences in the nature of the content that were shared by the categories on different events. In our examples, while organizations tend to frequently point to external information sources via URLs on their posts, ordinary individuals appeared to be more reflective of their personal experiences and sentiments on the events, and were observed to engage in greater interaction with others.

ACKNOWLEDGMENTS

This work was supported by a Google Research Award, by the National Science Foundation under award IIS-1017845 and by CRA award CIF-197.

REFERENCES

1. J. An, M. Cha, K. Gummadi, and J. Crowcroft. Media landscape in twitter: A world of new conventions and political diversity. In *Proc. ICWSM '11.*
2. M. De Choudhury, S. Counts, and M. Czerwinski. Identifying relevant social media content: Leveraging information diversity and user cognition. In *HT '11.*
3. D. Gayo-Avello. All liasons are dangerous when all your friends are known to us. In *Proc. HT '11.*
4. M. Naaman, H. Becker, and L. Gravano. Hip and trendy: Characterizing emerging trends on twitter. *JASIST*, 62(2):902–918, 2011.
5. M. Naaman, J. Boase, and C.-H. Lai. Is it really about me?: message content in social awareness streams. In *Proc. CSCW '10.*
6. D. A. Shamma, L. Kennedy, and E. F. Churchill. Conversational shadows: Describing live media events using short messages. In *Proc. ICWSM*, 2010.
7. K. Starbird, L. Palen, A. Hughes, S. Vieweg. Chatter on the red: What hazards threat reveals about the social life of microblogged information. In *Proc. CSCW '10.*
8. S. Vieweg, A. L. Hughes, K. Starbird, and L. Palen. Microblogging during two natural hazards events: What twitter may contribute to situational awareness. In *Proc. CHI*, 2010.
9. S. Wu, J. M. Hofman, W. A. Mason, and D. J. Watts. Who says what to whom on twitter. In *Proc. WWW '11.*

Fresh Faces in the Crowd: Turnover, Identity, and Commitment in Online Groups

Laura Dabbish[1], Rosta Farzan[1], Robert Kraut[1], and Tom Postmes[2]

[1]Human-Computer Interaction Institute
Carnegie Mellon University
5000 Forbes Ave., Pittsburgh, PA 15213
{dabbish, rfarzan, robert.kraut}@cs.cmu.edu

[2]Dept. of Social and Organizational Psychology
University of Groningen
Grote Kruisstraat 2/1, 9712 TS Groningen, NL
t.postmes@rug.nl

ABSTRACT
Turnover is commonplace in many online groups because of low barriers of entry and exit. In offline settings, turnover can have a negative impact because of reduced attachment to the group as an entity. However, in an online setting, turnover in terms of changes in the visible membership of a group may have a very different impact. Online only a limited amount of information about members and their activities is observable; in particular, it is easier to see the behavior of the subset of members who are active than the potentially larger set who are not. In this paper, we describe an experiment examining the influence of visible membership turnover on commitment to an online group. Our results suggest that increased turnover in an online group may increase social presence, creating perceptions of liveness, in turn leading to increased levels of participation in the group. However, this result holds primarily for groups with a common identity, suggesting that attention to behavior of others may be stronger when people share an identity with those others. Our results extend understandings of attachment in an online setting as well as theory about social tuning.

Author Keywords
Online groups; turnover; attachment; commitment; identity.

ACM Classification Keywords
H5.3. Information interfaces and presentation (e.g., HCI): Group and organization interfaces.

General Terms
Human Factors; Experimentation; Design.

INTRODUCTION
Online communities are blessed and cursed by low barriers to entry. Joining an online group can be as easy as clicking a button or writing a profile. Leaving is even easier. As a result, most social sites experience high turnover. Despite their popularity, sites such as Youtube, Myspace, Flickr, to name a few, have high churn in membership, with most visitors coming only once and leaving after a short interval. Even in successful online communities, such as the English Wikipedia with its 1.5 million editors, high turnover is the norm, with sixty percent of editors staying only a day [9].

Turnover in a group is a composite phenomenon: some group members enter while others leave. Entry and exit may have distinct effects on the people who remain. For example, people tend to leave organizations in clusters, dragging with them those who occupy similar network positions in the organization, although friends who remain in the organization become more satisfied after the leavers depart [8]. However in many online sites no one knows when others leave. Online, members have only limited visibility into others' behavior, based on impoverished cues of presence and activity [10]. When people depart an online group, unless they make a visible proclamation, it is sometimes hard for others to even notice. For example, in Flickr leavers do not take down their profiles and photo collections, and Wikipedia editors do not erase their user pages or edits. Therefore, high turnover in online groups – lots of joining with no visible signs of leaving – can be associated with larger perceived group size. Turnover associated with new members joining a group could signal growth and group prosperity, suggesting a possible positive impact overall.

In this research, we examined the influence of visible membership turnover and common group identity on member commitment and participation in an online group. We conducted an experiment manipulating the amount of turnover and the presence of a common group identity within online game groups inside of a Facebook application. Our results suggest that turnover has a positive influence on commitment and retention when a common identity is present. We consider the implications of this result for the design of online social settings and for theory about social tuning – the influence of personally relevant social behavior.

RELATED WORK

Previous work has examined antecedents to commitment in online organizations and turnover in offline organizations. We consider this work in relation to theory on social influence and social tuning effects.

Commitment and Turnover

Commitment to a group or organization can be defined as attachment to and willingness to stay in the group and exert effort on the group's behalf [11]. Turnover in an online group may influence commitment by changing the information members have about others' interest in participating in the group. This informational effect of turnover may depend on what aspect of turnover is most visible in an online group– that lots of people are present or that lots of people are leaving. This information may in turn influence a member's own behavior, and likelihood of staying or leaving in a group.

At a basic level, the mere presence of others is a powerful cue for behavior. If you believe that many people are performing a certain behavior, you want to join in [2, 12]. Turnover in the visible membership of an online group could serve to increase social proof that a group is an attractive place to be by creating a sense of liveness or the feeling there are many others present. In this way, social presence generated through turnover can be thought of as communicating group interest in the focal activity. This social presence may generate the feeling that lots of people are engaged in the group, increasing the attractiveness of the setting and its focal activities.

There is some evidence that this informational influence can lead individuals to stay in a group. Previous work on online community survival suggests that people stick around in communities that seem active, or have perceived critical mass [1, 10]. This is perhaps unsurprising, as literature on social influence and diffusion of innovation has long described that perception of critical mass (that lots of people are doing something) has a powerful influence on an individual's willingness to engage in a behavior [2, 12]. What is more surprising, perhaps, is that online, this perception is based primarily on the level of visible activity within a group. Raban et al.'s [10] analysis of online community survival found responsiveness and activity level, and not group size, were important indicators that a community would last.

Previous work on designing for attachment online has surprisingly found that large groups where individuals are salient, but do not share a common group identity, seem to generate sustained participation in the form of persistent membership and effort expended on the group's behalf [3]. This runs counter to theory on motivation and effort in collectives, where groups with many members can dampen individual efforts because of reduced sense of responsibility and perceived impact on the group as a whole [6]. Thus visible turnover in a large group may generate commitment because it increases the social presence of the group or the perception that others are interested in the group.

If visible member turnover increases social presence of an online setting, making it seem more popular and attractive, then we can expect that higher levels of turnover will in fact increase participation.

> ***Hypothesis 1***: *Increased levels of visible turnover in an online group will increase participation.*

Social Influence and Social Identity

As noted above, the mere observation of others acting is a powerful cue for people determining what they want to do [2, 4, 13]. Previous research on social tuning suggests this influence should be strongest when they have something in common with the referents and cognitively identify with them [4]. Cognitive identification with others can be fostered by a common social identity [3, 11]. Modeling influences are especially powerful when behavior referents are others in the same social category (e.g. similarity as in [4, 7, 13]). This previous work suggests that turnover that creates a feeling of social presence, liveliness and activity, should have strongest effects on behavior when group members have a common social identity.

> ***Hypothesis 2***: *The influence of turnover on participation will be strongest when there is a common social identity among members.*

METHOD

In order to test these hypotheses, we conducted an experiment in the context of a Facebook application for the game Tetris®. We chose Tetris® because it is typically a non-social, one player game; therefore we could attribute any influence of the experimental conditions to the nature of the manipulations rather than intrinsic properties of the game. In addition, because Tetris® is a popular game, we were able to recruit enough new participants. The experiment manipulated the surround of the game by placing participants into nominal game groups, thus inducing a social setting (see Figure 1).

Experimental Manipulations

In order to expose all players to the same representation of the group, participants were assigned to groups initially populated with fake players. As more real players arrived at the game, the fake players were replaced with real ones. In order to test the hypotheses, we varied turnover among visible members of the game groups, and whether or not these groups had a common social identity. The experiment was a 3 (turnover: low, medium and high) by 2 (social identity: team vs. no team) between-subjects design, with an additional non-social control condition to provide a baseline comparison.

Turnover

In the social conditions, players saw a leader board with pictures of themselves and six other people, refreshed with every new game they started. We manipulated the level of turnover in the game by assigning players to game groups of size 7, 17 or 49, which resulted in players seeing higher turnover in larger groups. In the low turnover condition, all seven team members (6 players plus the participant) were displayed at all times. In the medium (and high) turnover conditions, 6 of the 16 (48) other members of the group were displayed on the leaderboard, and the leaderboard was refreshed to show a random subset of the 16 (48) players after each game. The different player pools in each condition resulted in different rates of visual turnover in terms of number of unique faces seen by each player.

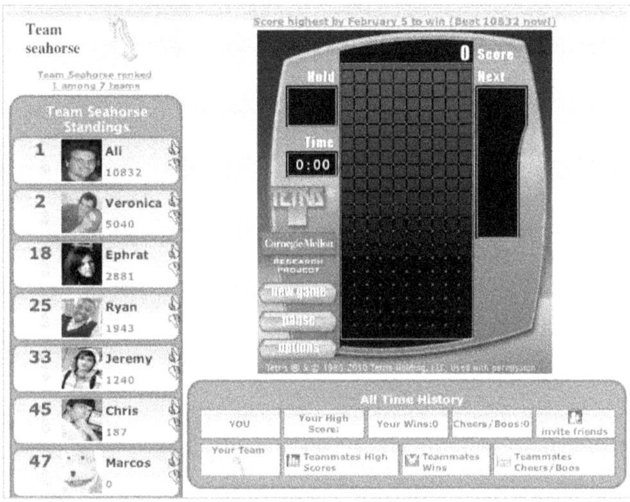

Figure 1. Game application in team, high turnover condition.

Social identity

We manipulated the presence of a common social identity at the group level by assigning participants to a team or non-team condition. In the team condition, upon entering the game, participants selected a team name and mascot animal for their group. The mascot was emblazoned on each team member's name placard in the leader board. In addition, their team was ranked out of the 7 total teams in the study (see Figure 1 for an image of the team condition). In the non-team condition, participants were assigned to groups with no team name or mascot. In both conditions the goal was to score the highest among the players in their group by the end of the challenge week.

Dependent Measures

In order to examine the influence of our experimental manipulations, we measured participant commitment in terms of effort expended and player retention. Effort was measured in terms of number of games played and player retention was measured in terms of days in the experiment.

RESULTS

A total of 1,941 participants joined the application between November 20th, 2011 and February, 15th, 2011. Three players were omitted from our analysis because they represented extreme outliers in number of games played. On average, players started 6.95 games (Std. Dev. = 32.53) and returned for 1.57 days (Std. Dev. = 2.48). For ease of interpretation, in this paper we only report an analysis comparing low and high turnover conditions by social identity conditions (2x2). Including the medium turnover condition does not change the substantive results.

Because the number of games played is count data and because some players loaded the application without ever starting a game, we analyzed the data using a zero-inflated negative binomial regression [5]. The model predicted the number of games started at the participant level as a function of turnover condition and presence of a team identity. For the inflation variable, we used a binary variable set to 1 if the player performed any actions (and zero otherwise). There was no main effect of turnover on the number of games played (IRR=0.77, SE-0.15, p=0.09). However, Figure 2 illustrates the significant interaction between turnover and team identity. Turnover almost doubled the number of games played when players had a common team identity (IRR=1.93, SE=.22, p<0.01), but had no effect with no team identity. This is consistent with our second hypothesis.

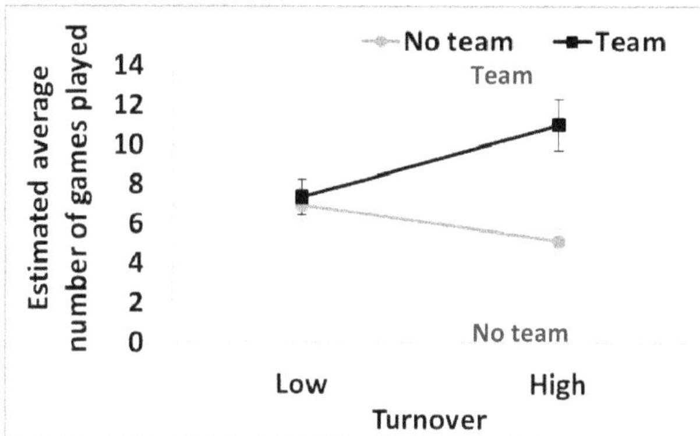

Figure 2. Turnover by identity interaction on games played.

In order to examine this result more closely, we decomposed the overall analysis to examine games per session and retention (i.e., days played). We defined a session as a continuous set of actions with fewer than 10 minutes of idle time between the actions. We calculated games per session by dividing the total number of games by the number of sessions for each player. In order to account for zero-inflation and skewness of data we used a Tweedie regression model with log link [14]. We found high turnover in conjunction with team identification increased the number of games play per session, consistent with our analysis for the overall number of games per player (Figure 3, Wald χ^2=10.38, df=2, p<0.01).

We next examined retention, meaning player likelihood of coming back to the game over different days. We ran a survival analysis to predict the number of potential players who would return on each day of the experiment, as a function of their experimental condition. We used a cox regression model and censored players who had joined the game only 15 days prior to end of the experiment (to account for the fact that they could have returned after our observation period). The results were consistent with the earlier analyses, showing that high levels of turnover under a common team identity increased survival rate, with players in that condition 30% less likely to drop out (Exp(B)=.70, SE=.064, $p<0.001$).

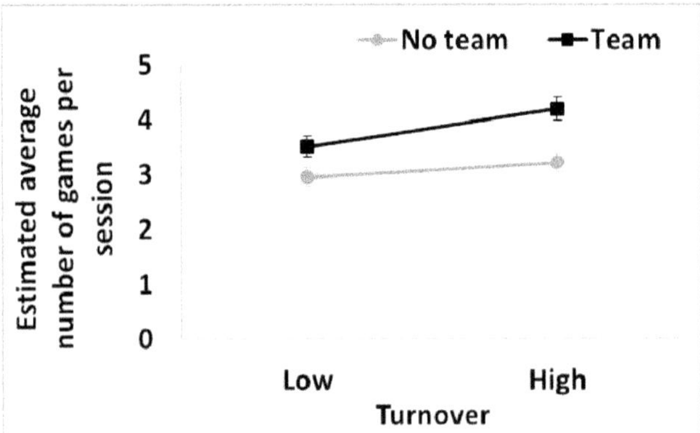

Figure 3. Turnover by identity interaction games per session.

DISCUSSION

Our results suggest turnover can lead to increased levels of commitment in an online community, counter to conventional wisdom and previous results in offline groups. Turnover in an online setting seems to generate social presence by creating a feeling that others are also participating, rather than influencing familiarity with particular players. This social presence has the strongest impact on behavior when players share a common team identity.

These findings complement and extend previous work on online community survival and commitment. We find that turnover highlighting member presence increases effort and participation, supporting previous work showing that activity level is central to sustaining participation and retaining members [1, 10]. However, our results show that it matters who is engaging in the activity. Mere social presence, in our setting, was insufficient to engender increased participation. A connection to these other members in the form of a common identity had to exist for players to be influenced by their behavior. This result suggests that even in an online setting, cognitive similarity can have a strong impact on behavior change and eventually community survival. Future work should examine whether these results generalize to other task settings where work is more interdependent (such as in Wikipedia) and whether these results persist in the face of pre-existing personal connections to other group members.

Our results may have important implications for designers of online communities often facing low modal participation rates. Visible turnover can encourage more participation by presenting a sign of life to other members when used in combination with a representation of common identity.

ACKNOWLEDGMENTS

This research is supported by the National Science Foundation under award #OCI-0943159. We thank The Tetris Company, LLC, Blue Planet Software, Inc. and Tetris Online, Inc. for use of the Tetris® game in our research. We also thank Henk Rogers, Alexey Pajitnov, Chris Nelson, Corey Facteau, Danny Han, and Gerilynn Okano for their assistance with this process. Finally we thank project members Marcos Ojeda and Meng Hu.

REFERENCES

1. Butler, B, S. Membership size, communication activity, and sustainability: The internal dynamics of networked social structures. *Information Systems Research 12*, 4 (2001), 346-362.
2. Cialdini, R. *Influence: The Psychology of Persuasion.* Collins, New York, NY, 1998.
3. Farzan, R., Dabbish, L., Kraut, R., & Postmes, T. Increasing commitment to online communities by designing for social presence. In *Proc. CSCW 2011,* ACM Press, (2011), 321-330.
4. Goldstein, N., Cialdini, R., & Griskevicius, V. A room with a viewpoint: Using social norms to motivate environmental conservation in hotels. *J. of Consumer Research 35* (2008), 472-482.
5. Hilbe, J.M. *Negative Binomial Regression.* Cambridge University Press, Cambridge, UK, 2007.
6. Karau, S.J. & Williams, K.D. Social loafing: A meta-analytic review and theoretical integration. *J. of Personality & Social Psychology 65*, 4 (1993), 681-704.
7. Kilduff, M. The interpersonal structure of decision making: A social comparison approach to organizational choice. *Organizational Behavior & Human Decision Processes 47*, 2(1990), 270-288.
8. Krackhardt, D., & Porter, L. W. When friends leave: A structural analysis of the relationship between turnover and stayers' attitudes. *Administrative Science Quarterly, 30* (1985), 242-261.
9. Panciera, K., Halfaker, A., & Terveen, L. Wikipedians are born, not made. In *Proc. GROUP 2009,* ACM Press (2009), 51-60.
10. Raban, D., Moldovan, M., & Jones, Q. An empirical study of critical mass and online community survival. In *Proc. CSCW 2010*, ACM Press, (2010), 71-80.
11. Ren, Y., Kraut, R., & Kiesler, S. Applying common identity and bond theory to the design of online communities. *Org. Studies, 28,* 3 (2007), 379-410.
12. Rogers, E.M. *Diffusion of Innovations.* Fourth Edition. The Free Press, New York, NY, 1995.
13. Shteynberg, G. A silent emergence of culture: The social tuning effect. *J. of Personality & Social Psychology 99*, 4 (2010), 683-689.
14. Tweedie, M.C.K. An index which distinguishes between some important exponential families. In J.K. Ghosh & J. Roy (Eds.), *Statistics: Applications and New Directions,* Indian Statistical Institute (1984), 579–604.

We Don't Need No Stinkin' Badges: Examining the Social Role of Badges in the Huffington Post

Julie Jones and Nathan Altadonna
Gaylord College of Journalism and Mass Communication
395 W. Lindsey, Norman, OK 73019
juliejones@ou.edu, nathan.altadonna@ou.edu

ABSTRACT
News sites commonly allow users to post comments under each article, but, until recently, did little more than allow these social spaces on their sites. The Huffington Post took a pro-active stance when they introduced badges that award users for the frequency of their posting behaviors. Both social role and network theories posit that groups create their own normative structures when left to grow organically. However, badges may be symbolic of hierarchical control since they are defined, determined, and awarded by the organization rather than from the group itself. This study is a first step in examining the relationship between badges and group behavior within threads. As active members of the group, badge owners may be serving the role of discussion catalysts [1]. If so, then threads started by badge owners should be longer than for non-badge owners. Preferential attachment posits that highly connected users are "richer" in the social network [2]. Thus, threads started by badge owners may draw in more badge owners to the discussion. If badges have no influence on thread characteristics, then what does? Findings suggest that badges at the thread start do not generate longer threads but rather the type of news story does. Furthermore, some of the most popular commenters were not badge owners despite the overwhelming number of fans they had attracted. This is a first attempt at understanding how parameters set by news organizations are accepted, or rejected, by online communities.

Author Keywords
Journalism, political discourse, comments, badges

ACM Classification Keywords
H.5.3 Group and Organizational Interfaces: Asynchronous interaction; H.4.3 Communication Applications

General Terms. Human Factors.

INTRODUCTION
One of the participatory tools news sites provide their audiences is the ability to post their own comments directly under a news story. Allowing their readers/viewers to comment upon, share amongst, and connect with individuals other than journalists introduces a new paradigm for news organizations – a social exchange within their property that is somewhat independent from their control. Because of this shift, news managers tend to approach social spaces tied to their news product somewhat nervously [3, 4]. This is not the case for the Huffington Post. From its beginnings, the HuffPost aspired to encourage salient political discourse on national issues [5]. In accordance with this pro-active stance, the site introduced badges to their site in 2010. Badges are awarded to commenters by parameters set by the organization rather than through the contributions recognized by the social group. The commenting community on the Huffington Post is an extremely active group who has, for five years, been left largely to its own growth. Badges may represent Huffington Post's goals in contrast to the social roles and values already established. This study is a first step in examining whether badges function as a social role and, thus, influence threads. We are specifically interested in relationship – or lack thereof – between the presence of a badge at the beginning of a thread to the length of the thread and to how other badge owners are drawn to the thread. If badges do not influence these two outcomes, then what does? To answer this question we identified the most active commenters to look for common attributes within the group.

SOCIAL ROLES, NETWORKS, AND NEWS PLATFORMS
Sociology has long recognized the self-organizing principles at play within the development of social groups and networks. Two strains of sociology inform this study – social roles (in the form of discussion catalysts) and network theory (in the form of preferential attachment).

Discussion catalysts as a social role
A social role is a pattern of behaviors characteristic of one or more people in a given context [6]. Social roles are developed from the interactions between group members

and, as such, have cultural meaning [7]. Since they are situational, roles are perceived and assessed differently in different contexts. Callero [8] calls this variance cultural evaluation (connotation of a role) and cultural endorsement (perceived legitimacy of a role). Research on computer-mediated communication has shown that the recurring interaction patterns within threads serve as artifacts that can be used to identify social roles [9]. For instance, consider the difference between two roles found in Usenet groups. Through the consistent pattern of their posting behaviors, Welser et al. [10] identified the role of answer person in technical support newsgroups and Himelboim et al. [1] identified discussion catalysts in political newsgroups. Answer people are active in responding to others but rarely start threads themselves. Discussion catalysts are active thread starters and receive significantly more replies than other authors. Thus, the answer person provides a quick bit of information - an answer to a question - and then moves on. Discussion catalysts, though, play the role of agenda setter by drawing in others to topics they introduce. Himelboim and colleagues suggested a few explanations for the existence of discussion catalysts including preferential attachment.

The "rich get richer" effect in network

Commonly referred to as the "rich get richer," preferential attachment is a function of networks as they grow [2]. As individuals enter social networks they tend to attach to others who are already highly connected within the group. Preferential attachment patterns have been found in the development of Flickr [12], Wikipedia entries [13], and social tagging online [14]. However, it is unclear as to whether preferential attachment occurs because of something about the person or the content they consistently bring to the group. For example, in examining features that drive comments in Digg, Hsu et al. found that a commenter's past history (how well their comments' were rated and replied to) and the features in the actual writing of comments (grammar, length, etc.) were better predictors of the community's overall preference than the person's time on site or frequency of posting [15].

Huffington Post and badges

Established in 2005, the Huffington Post built an active base of commenters that surpassed 3 million comments per month by 2010 [16]. The HuffPost encourages users to flag inappropriate content for review and employs about two-dozen editors who supervise the comments section. The first three badges the HuffPost introduced were: the *networker* badge based on a commenter's popularity among other HuffPost commenters, the *superuser* badge based on the amount HuffPost content the person shares outside of the platform, and the *community moderator* badge based on commenter's reliability in tagging inappropriate material [17]. Computer algorithms determine the first two badges; networker badges are awarded by how often a user is fanned and favorited (*f and f'd* in HuffPost terminology) while superusers earn their badge by the number of HuffPost stories they post to Facebook or send out to Twitter. Community moderator badges are earned by flagging at least 20 posts that the editors agree are uncivil. Once a moderator has flagged 100 posts as inappropriate they are given the power to remove posts without review from the editors. Users can earn a combination of badges.

Because badges are a new phenomenon within news sites, this exploratory study asked three sets of research questions:

1). First, what is the relationship between badges at the thread start and the thread length as well as the number of unique badges the thread attracts?

2). Since commenters can earn more than one badge, the next set of research questions focused on the possible influence of specific badges or combination of badges. What is the relationship between the type of badge(s) at the thread start and the thread length as well as the number of unique badges the thread attracts?

3). A third set of research questions investigated other possible influences on the character of the threads including the content of the story and the make-up of the popular commenters. What is the relationship between the type of story and the thread length as well as the number of unique badges? What common attributes, including badges, do the most popular commenters share?

METHODS

Operational definitions and variables

For this study, anything posted to the comments section was considered a *comment.* A *post* was an individual comment that never generated any response. *Threads* are posts that received at least one reply. *Replies* appear below the original post or the *thread start.*

Independent variables were the presence of a badge at the thread start, the type of badge (networker, moderator, or superuser or any combination of the three) at the thread start, and the type of news article the thread appeared under. Dependent variables were the length of the thread and the number of unique badge owners draw to the thread. Length of thread was merely the number of replies within a thread. Unique badge owners were defined as badge owners within a thread who were *not* the thread starter. Regardless of how often a badge owner replied within a thread, each unique badge owner was counted only once in a thread.

Three stories from the Huffington Post's coverage of the Tucson shootings were used for data collection. The three were chosen because they are different types of news stories. *Breaking news:* The HuffPost posted its first story the afternoon of the shootings on January 8, 2011. *Political controversy:* A story focused on Sarah Palin's comments on the shooting and her use of the term "blood libel." *General news:* A story about Congresswoman Gifford's rehabilitation progress once she arrived in Houston. All three were published in the first two weeks of the Tucson shootings coverage.

Sample

All comments (posts, thread starts, and replies) underneath the three articles were collected. This yielded nearly three thousand posts/threads (N=2933) that were hand counted by the authors. Data collected included type of story, the presence of badge(s) at the thread start, individual badge owners within the thread, and the length of the thread overall.

For the last set of research questions, a three-step process was used to identify the most popular commenters. First, the screen names of all thread starters who had generated threads with 4 or more replies were collected. These were ranked by the frequency of thread starts. Commenters who started three or more threads were selected and the fan data on their profile pages was collected. In this manner, we sought to identify not only those who were generating an-above-average number of replies, but also individuals who were active in posting popular threads.

Descriptive statistics

The 2933 posts/threads generated 7716 replies and attracted 3941 unique badge owners. Badge owners started 61% of posts/threads (n=1792). As with many distributions within social media platforms, length of thread and unique badges were highly skewed positive distributions commonly known as power law distributions; thread length ranged from 0 to 41 replies (M = 2.64, SD=4.53) and unique badge owners ranged from 0 to 21 (M=1.28, SD=2.31). A number of steps were taken to account for the skewed distributions. First, single posts and threads that received only one reply were dropped from the data resulting in a smaller sample (n=1159). Second, thread length and unique badges variables were log-transformed, a statistical procedure recommended for positively skewed distributions [17]. Both t-tests and ANOVA analyses used this transformed variable. Since log-transformed variables lack interpretive clarity, the results section uses the raw data coefficients to explain what these findings mean in practical terms, but the statistical significance tests used the log-transformed variables.

Results

The first set of research questions examined the relationship between badges present at the thread start to the length of the thread and the unique badges attracted to the thread. Threads where a badge was present at the start were longer (M=6.50, SD=5.64) than threads started without a badge (M=6.14, SD=4.81). However this relationship was not statistically significant, $t(1) = 0.69, p = n.s.$

Threads where a badge was present from the start drew only slightly more unique badge owners (M=3.29, SD=2.82) than threads started by non-badge owners (M=3.11, SD=3.32). The relationship was not significant, $t(1) = 0.28$, $p = n.s.$

The next set of research questions examined the relationship between the type of badge(s) present at the thread start to the thread length and number of unique badges. Since Huffington Post commenters can earn all three of the badges, there were 7 different combination of badges with no badge and the networker badge as the most frequent commenters to start a thread (n=430 and 339 respectively) followed by the networker-superuser (n=191), superuser (n=95), the networker-moderator (n=63), and users who had earned all three badges (n=37). Those who had only a community moderator badge had the lowest activity at the thread start (n=4).

Although the relationship between the type of badge and the thread length was not significant [$F(6, 1152)$=1.49, p = $n.s.$] a certain pattern did emerge. Moderators, who only accounted for 4 thread starts, produced the least replies. However, networker/moderators produced an average thread length of 7.32 or one more reply than the grand mean (see table 1). The relationship between the type of badge at the thread start and unique badge owners drawn to the thread was not significance [$F(6,1152)$=1.49, p=$n.s.$], but a similar pattern emerged. The networker-moderator thread starter drew roughly two more badge owners than moderators who had the lowest number of unique badges.

Type of badge at thread start	N	Mean Thread length	Mean Unique badge
No badge	430	6.11	3.10
Networker	339	6.68	3.36
Networker-superuser	191	6.17	2.96
Superuser	95	6.06	3.15
Networker-moderator	63	7.32	3.84
All three	37	6.78	3.95
Moderator	4	3.25	2.00
Total	1166	6.37	3.22

Table 1. Thread length & unique badge by type of badge

The next set of research questions examined the influence of the type of news story on thread length and unique badge owners. The breaking news article attracted 84% of the threads with two or more replies (n = 969) followed by the Palin story (n =136) and the general news story on Giffords (n =54). The type of article had a significant influence on the thread length [$F(2,1156)$=4.33, p<.05] but not on the number of unique badge owners in the thread [$F(2,1156)$=0.28, p=$n.s.$]. Interestingly, even though the general news story on Gifford's health received the least amount of attention, the threads under this story had, on average, the longest thread length (M=7.04) compared to the breaking news (M=6.50) or political news (M=5.04).

Lastly, we sought to find attributes common to the most popular thread starters. Thread starters' screen names for any thread longer than 4 replies were collected. This yielded 733 threads posted by 88 thread starters. Commenters were ranked by the accumulative number of replies in all of the threads they had started. Those with 30 or more were selected. This narrowed the list down to the top 21 thread starters who produced 104 threads that attracted a total of 1051 replies. To put these numbers in perspective, they accounted for nearly 9% (.089) of the threads and generated 14% (.142) of the replies from the sample of threads with two or more replies. Among this group, 12 were badges owners, 6 were not, and two had their profiles removed since they had posted. What was surprising, though, was the amount of fans between badge and non-badge owners; badge owners had, on the average, 715 fans. Non-badge owners, though, had an average of 1065 fans and three had a fan count in the thousands (n=1402, 1535, and 2423).

CONCLUSIONS

We examined whether badge owners may be serving as discussion catalysts for the Huffington Post commenting community and whether they, as active members, might be attracting more badge owners to their threads than non-badge owners. This study is salient since more news organizations are struggling with how to leverage commenting communities for their own goals. This approach is counter to social network theories that posit groups grow into their own normative structure. Hsu et al. and Himelboim et al. argue that it is the type of content and value certain individuals bring to the group that creates their role. Content, at least at the story level, did influence the length of threads with the general news story producing longer threads than for breaking news or political controversy.

This study also revealed two directions for future research; one focused on specific badge owners and one focused on the non-badge commenters. The moderator badge produced the least threads and attracted the fewest replies from other badge owners. This may be due to their "cop" role within the group. However, networkers-moderators drew in the longest average thread length and the second highest average of unique badge owners. This begs the question of whether the networker badge itself may play a discussion catalyst role or whether the networker-moderator combination has more value to the group.

Another question centers on the non-badge commenters. Given that 6 of the top 21 commenters were non-badge owners *yet* had accumulated thousands of fans, could some of the popular commenters be declining badges outright? In the end, the title of our paper, while meant to be somewhat humorous and attention grabbing may be true. The Huffington Post, established as a progressive and a forward thinking news platform centered on aggregating content and opinion, may have attracted the very kind of individuals who would be suspicious of a symbolic gestures introduced by a corporate structure. In the end, the Huffington Post may have attracted the type of person who most identifies as someone who does not need those "stinkin' badges."

REFERENCES

1. Himelboim, I., Gleave, E., and Smith, M. Discussion catalysts in online political discussions: Content importers and conversation starters. *Journal of Computer-Mediated Communication, 14*, 4, (2009), 771-789.
2. Barabási, A.-L., and Albert, R. Emergence of Scaling in Random Networks. *Science, 286*, 5439, (1999), 509-512.
3. Greer, J. and Yan, Y. New ways of connecting with readers: How community newspapers are using Facebook, Twitter and other tools to deliver the news. *Grassroots Editor, 51*, 3, (2010), 1-7.
4. Braun, J. and Gillespie, T. Hosting the public discourse, hosting the public. *Journalism Practice*, 5, 4 (2011), 383-398.
5. Lyons, D. (2010). Arianna's answer. *Newsweek, 156*, 5, (2010), 44.
6. Biddle, B. J. *Role Theory: Expectations, Identities and Behaviors*, 1979. New York: Academic Press.
7. Parsons, T. *The Social System*, 1951. Glencoe, IL: Free Press.
8. Callero, P. From role-playing to role-using: Understanding role as resource. *Social Psychology Quarterly, 57*, 3, (1994), 228-243.
9. Gleave, E., Welser, H. T., Lento, T. M. and Smith, M. A. A Conceptual and Operational Definition of 'Social Role' in Online Community. In *Proceedings of the 42nd Hawaii International Conference on System Sciences, 2009*. (Big Island, HI 5-8 Jan. 2009). HICSS '09
10. Welser, H.T., Gleave, E., Fisher, D., and Smith, M. Visualizing the Signatures of Social Roles in Online Discussion Groups. *Journal of Social Structure, 8*, 2, (2007), 1-32.
11. Capocci, A., Servedio, V. D. P., Colaiori, F., Buriol, L. S., Donato, D., Leonardi, S. and Caldarelli, G. Preferential attachment in the growth of social networks: The internet encyclopedia Wikipedia. *Physical Review E*, 74, 3 (2006), 036116.
12. Mislove, A., Koppula, H. S., Gummadi, K. P., Druschel, P. and Bhattacharjee, B. Growth of the flickr social network. In *Proc. on first workshop on online social networks* (WOSN '08). ACM Press (2008), 25-30.
13. Raban, D. R., Ronen, I. and Guy, I. Acting or reacting? Preferential attachment in a people-tagging system. *Journal of the American Society for Information Science and Technology*, 62, 4 2011), 738-747.
14. Huffington, A. Introducing HuffPost badges: Taking our community to the next level. *The Huffington Post*, (2010, April 29), n.p.
15. Hsu, C.-F., Khabiri, E. and Caverlee, J. Ranking Comments on the Social Web. In *Proceedings of the Computational Science and Engineering, 2009*. CSE '09. (Vancouver, BC, 29-31 Aug. 2009).
16. Spiers, E. A force of nature. *Forbes*, 2010. 187(7): p. 58.
17. Howell, D. C. *Statistical Methods for Psychology*, 2001. Belmont, CA: Thomson/Wadsworth

Lurking as Personal Trait or Situational Disposition? Lurking and Contributing in Enterprise Social Media

Michael Muller
IBM Research
One Rogers Street, Cambridge, MA, USA
michael_muller@us.ibm.com

ABSTRACT
We examine patterns of participation by employees who are members of multiple online communities in an enterprise communities service. Our analysis focuses on statistical patterns of contributing vs. "lurking." The majority of contributors (in one or more communities) were also lurkers (in one or more other communities). These results argue against hypotheses derived from common theories of participation and lurking. We propose that contributing and lurking are partially dependent on a *trait* (a person's overall engagement), modified by the individual's *disposition* toward a particular topic, work task or social group. Contributions include critique of theory, an analytic framework, and implications for design of community services.

Author Keywords
Lurking, enterprise, community-of-practice.

ACM Classification Keywords
H5.3. CSCW

INTRODUCTION
The theme of "lurkers" (people who read social media data, but do not directly contribute) has received renewed interest in CHI and CSCW. Characterizations of lurkers have varied from pro-social [1,7,9,11] to universal [6] to derogatory [4]. Essentialist theories of lurking considered lurking as a trait (summarized in [4]) or a relatively invariant attribute [8] of a person. Developmental theories treated lurking as a stage through which a person passes on the way to more active, visible contribution [2,9,10]. In this note, we examine hypotheses derived from these theories, in a new dataset in which each person may act as a lurker or a contributor in multiple online communities.

We explored lurking using a dataset of 8711 online communities from an enterprise "community service" in IBM. The service had been in operation since 24 April 2007.

During April 2010, we crawled the communities dataset, extracting all person and object data from the launch-date of each community until the crawl-date. Each community comprised a group of members, a group of organizers, and the members' and organizers' contributions.

Descriptive statistics appear in Table 1. All distributions were strongly asymmetric. Communities varied widely in size; in shared contributions; in duration of activity; and in percent of members making visible contributions. Of the 224,232 unique users, 62% were members of multiple communities. The social entities in the communities service supported diverse organizational groups, including teams, communities of practice, and other emergent structures. In general, membership was voluntary, although some employees were "encouraged" to join certain communities.

Unlike email-based discussions, the communities service was accessed via web pages on the company's intranet. Members were optionally notified of new entries, and a personalized summary page of the service showed recent activity in communities in which a person was a member.

A total of 22,949 people made at least one contribution in at least one community (10% of all users, analyzed on a *per-person* basis). Contributions tended to occur together in the most active communities. Many communities had very few contributions, resulting in a 0.64% contribution rate analyzed on a *per-community* basis (Table 1). Contributions took forms such as shared bookmarks, shared feeds, posts in a discussion forum, items in a shared to-do list, blog entries or comments, shared files, or new or revised wiki pages.

Definitions of "lurker" in the research literature have used criteria of zero contributions, or zero *recent* contributions, or fewer contributions than other users [6,11] (see [3] for

Ratio Measures	Min	Max	Median
Members/Community	1	14997	9
% Contributing Members/Cmy.	0	100%	0.64%
Communities/Member	1	184	2
Contrib/Memb (forums, blogs, etc.)	1	2473	3
Contrib/Cmy (forums, blogs, etc.)	1	2384	6
Duration of activity/Cmy (days)	1	1053	86

Table 1. Descriptive statistics of the 8711 communities.

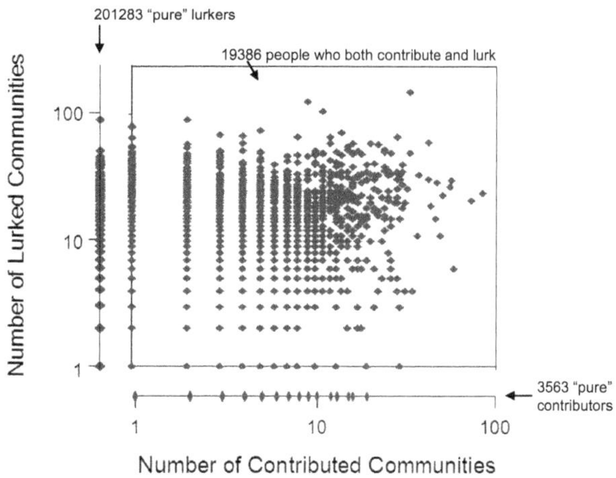

Figure 1. Scatterplot of 224,232 members of one or more communities, focusing on 19386 people who contribute in at least one community, and who lurk in at least one community.

review). We choose the first of these definitions – i.e., a lurker is a community member who has made zero visible contributions to the community. We assume that lurkers are using information from the community in their work outside of the social media, as shown in [3,6,11].

Because each individual can be a member of multiple communities, this dataset allows a new type of analysis of lurking and contributing, by comparing an individual's usage patterns across different communities. We can ask: *How consistent was each person's pattern of lurking or contributing from one community to another community?*

Lurking as personal trait. Under this theory, lurkers are a type of person – a "loafer," "freeloader," etc. [4]. The personal trait theory would predict that a particular user was *either* a contributor *or* a lurker across all her/his communities. In the related "born vs. made" analysis [8], early behavior in a community is predictive of subsequent behavior (i.e., lurkers are "born" that way, and thus their behavior can be predicted as a personal trait).

Engagement. Under this theory, both lurking and contributing are acts of engagement with the community (as implied in [7]). Some users engage to a greater degree, and some users engage to a lesser degree. This theory would predict that users who *contribute* to many communities should *lurk* in many communities; users who *contribute* in few communities should *lurk* in few communities.

Social learning trajectory. In this approach, lurking and contributing are seen as developmental stages of membership in a community (e.g., a community of practice) [2,9]. Lurking is seen as an early stage, in which a person learns about the community, and eventually develops enough understanding to begin to contribute. The member's contributions grow over time, as s/he develops deeper knowledge and reputation among the other members of the community [2]. This theory predicts that a lurker would grow into a contributor, and (crucially) that a contributor's visible actions in a community would increase over time.

METHOD

The analyses were limited by sparse lurking data. The community service records no view data (lurking data). We note that most internet community services also omit lurking data. Therefore, we cannot tell how often a person visits a community. We had hoped to use server logs and email records to estimate lurking, but these were unavailable due to company privacy policies. We use membership in a community as a potential indicator for viewing the contents of the community. We define a "lurker" as someone who has membership, but makes no contributions.

Because of these limitations, we reduced our representation of contributor data so that it matched the detail of lurking data. For our first two analyses, we counted the number of communities in which a member had contributed, and the number of communities in which s/he had lurked (i.e., had membership, but did not contribute any comments or resources). As stated above, among the 224,232 users, 22,949 people contributed in at least one community, and 220,669 people lurked in at least one community. 19,386 people fell into both categories – i.e., each of them lurked in at least one community, and contributed in at least one community.

RESULTS

Personal trait theory would predict that each user would be either a lurker or a contributor. Figure 1 shows a scatterplot, in which each person is located by the number of communities in which s/he is a contributor, and the number of communities in which s/he is a lurker.[1] According to personal trait theory, users should fall on the *external* axes of Figure 1 (either a "pure" lurker with zero contributing-communities, or a "pure" contributor, with zero lurking-communities). There should be no one who lurks in some communities and contributes in other communities. The observation that 19386 people (84% of the contributors) both lurk (in at least one community) *and* contribute (in at least one other community) argues against this hypothesis.

Engagement theory makes predictions that are nearly the opposite of personal trait theory. This theory argues that contributing and lurking are both forms of engagement, and that a person who engages in some communities by contributing, is also likely to engage in other communities by lurking. The number of contributing-communities and the number of lurking-communities should be correlated. This hypothesis was supported by the data in Figure 1 (Pearson

[1] For clarity, the axes of Figure 1 are logarithmic. Zero crossings cannot not appear on log axes, so we have represented the "pure" contributors (zero communities in which they lurk) and the "pure" lurkers (zero contributions) on separate axes, immediately external to the log-log plot.

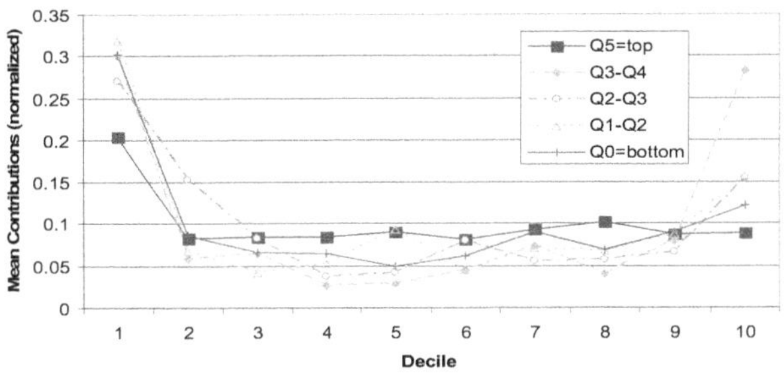

Figure 2. Contribution-timelines of five 100-person samples.

r=.375, Spearman rho=.352, both p<.01). However, Figure 1 also shows many users who do not fit this hypothesis.

Social learning theory predicts that a new member of a community will begin with relatively few contributions – perhaps initially with no contributions, as a lurker. Over time, the new member gains knowledge and confidence, and begins to contribute. Her/his contributions increase over time, as s/he developers competence and confidence.

To examine this hypothesis, we focused on the more detailed contribution data. We wanted to analyze the pattern of each person's contributions to each community in a common framework. Each contribution was a data object or revision that was shared with other members. Our measurement period began with the date of membership of the user in the community, and ended with the most recent contribution by the user to that community (range 0-1058 days, median=37 days, across all users' tenures in each of their communities). We divided each measurement period into ten equal intervals (deciles). The deciles provided a *temporal normalization*, allowing us to analyze the pattern of each member's contributions across all of the communities in which s/he was a member.

There was one problem with this approach: We had defined the end of the measurement period in terms of each member's most recent contribution. The tenth decile was therefore guaranteed to contain at least one contribution by each member – an overestimation for that decile. Therefore we omitted the member's most recent contribution to prevent this potential distortion.

The decile-based representation allowed us to analyze all of each member's contribution-timelines in a normalized format that could be compared and combined across communities, to allow us to characterize a person's pattern of contribution across multiple communities. Computing the contribution-timeline for each of 19386 members across as many as 184 communities was computationally prohibitive, so we made an ordering of the number of communities per member, and created five samples of 100 people each, equally-spaced across quartile-boundaries of the distribution of number-of-communities per member: i.e., 100 people with the largest number of communities ("Q5," at the top of the highest quartile), 100 people at each of the inter-quartile boundaries (Q4-Q3, Q3-Q2, and Q2-Q1), and 100 people with the smallest number of communities

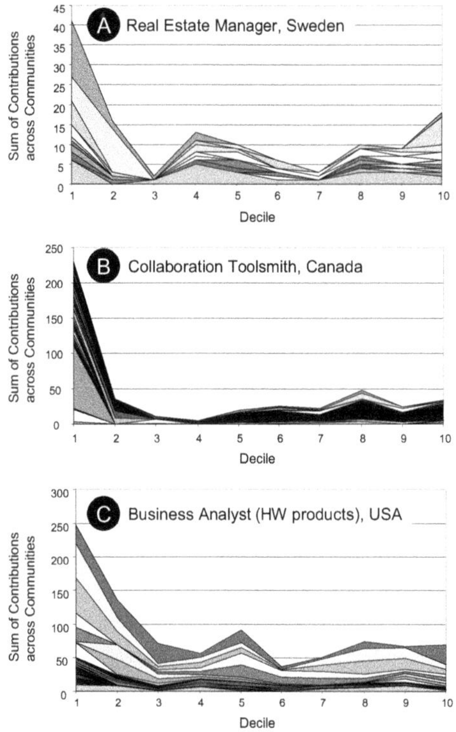

Figure 3. Decile contribution-timeline analyses. Each graph stacks the contributions for multiple timelines. The horizontal axis is a normalized timeline of contributions in deciles of each user's presence in the community (from date-of-membership to the day before the most-recent contribution). The vertical axis is sum of the number of contribution by that user in that community, in which each community has a different color.

("Q0"). A repeated measures ANOVA showed significant effects for deciles ($F_{(9,4455)}$=20.06, p<.001), for the five samples ($F_{(4,495)}$=86.06, p<.001), and for the interaction ($F_{(36,4455)}$=11.38, p<.001).

Figure 2 shows the contribution-timelines across the ten deciles, with one line for each of the five samples. Because the highest group (Q5) had 25 more contributions than the smallest group, we normalized the distribution for each timeline before plotting. The shape for each of the samples is roughly similar, except for one group in decile 10.

The pattern in the first nine deciles is the opposite of the prediction of the social learning hypothesis, with significantly *more* contributions *early* in the timeline. Similar patterns were found in [8].

The contribution-timeline representation allows to "stack" the communities for a user, resulting in the kinds of analyses in Figure 3 for three representative users. For the real estate manager of Figure 3A, the stacked timelines across 13 communities show roughly the same overall pattern as in Figure 2. The collaboration toolsmith of Figure 3B and the business analyst of Figure 3C show similar patterns across their 56 and 49 communities, respectively. These individual results are consistent with the statistical analysis, and provide little support for the social learning hypothesis.

DISCUSSION: LURKING AS DISPOSITION

The dataset provided data for each person in multiple online communities, allowing tests of three hypotheses of lurking and contributing derived from personal trait theory, engagement theory, and social learning theory. There was moderate support for the hypothesis from engagement theory, and little support for the other two theories.

We propose that each person's actions (i.e., lurking, contributing, or a combination) is driven in part by the person's overall engagement (i.e., a trait), but strongly modified by the person's attitude or disposition toward a topic, a group of colleagues, and/or individual or shared tasks. This view is a departure from the essentialism of earlier formulations [4], and from trajectory-oriented accounts of "delurking" [10] or "reader to leader" developmental models [9].

The next steps in this research programme will be to examine how members conceive of their levels of engagement, what use they make of community information *outside* of the communities service (e.g., [6,10], and particularly how they construct their dispositions to join, lurk, and/or contribute in our complex environment of multiple workplace communities – conceptually building on earlier investigations of single communities [7]. It seems likely that the nature of each type of community (team, community of practice, etc.) [5] will be crucial to determining the degree and type of contribution to be made, as will each member's role within those teams and communities [2]; these analyses are likely to test and extend the "born vs. made" predictive study of [8]. It will be interesting to compare the influences of individual traits, situated conditions, and social responsibilities, as they affect members' decisions to join, lurk, and contribute in communities and similar structures in organizations. These investigations will involve ethnographic work with members, as well as more formalized typologies of online groups (e.g., [5]).

CONCLUSION AND CONTRIBUTION

We tested hypotheses derived from three theories of lurking and contributing [4,9,10] in a complex dataset of many employees in multiple online communities, and we found only moderate support for one of those theories from the data. We proposed a more nuanced theory based on engagement, plus the individual's attitude or disposition, and we sketched a research programme to explore this theory.

In addition to theory implications, our work also provides a first look at a new contribution-timeline framework for analyzing complex ecologies in which multiple members join, lurk, and contribute in multiple communities. We anticipate re-using the contribution-timeline framework for analysis of individual communities and types of communities, extending the analysis in [5].

Finally, our work suggests the design of new features for online communities. Based in part on the roles analyses of [2,6], we argue against a binary distinction of lurkers vs. contributors [1,4,7]. Instead, we recommend a better understanding of distinct types of enterprise communities (e.g., [5]), and a set of user interface features, such as previews, and recommendation services, that support each member to choose an appropriate role in each community.

Community roles are likely to emerge from the needs of each community [2], and members should be in a position not only to *choose* an appropriate role, but also to *co-create* and *co-refine* roles with other members. These developments will inform enterprise community services, organizational development, and the application of participatory principles to enterprise community governance.

ACKNOWLEDGMENTS

I thank Kate Ehrlich, Jenny Preece, and Sadat Shami for comments.

REFERENCES

1. Antin, J., & Cheshire, C., 'Readers are not free-riders: Reading as a form of participation on Wikipedia,' *Proc. CSCW 2010.*
2. Bogdan, C., & Bowers, J., 'Tuning in: Challenging design for communities through a field study of radio amateurs,' *Proc C&T 2007.*
3. Cranefield, J., Yoong, P., & Huff, S., 'Beyond lurking: The invisible follower-feeder in online community ecosystem,' *Proc. PACIS 2011.*
4. Curien, N., Fauchart, E., Laffond, G. & Moreau, F., 'Online consumer communities: Escaping the tragedy of the digital commons.' In E. Brousseau (Ed)., *Internet and Digital Economics*. Cambridge U. Press, 2006.
5. Matthews, T., Whittaker, S., Moran, T., & Yuen, S., 'Collaboration personas: A new approach to designing workplace collaboration tools,' *Proc. CHI 2011.*
6. Muller, M., Shami, N.S., Millen, D.R., & Feinberg, J., 'We are all lurkers: Consuming behaviors among authors and readers in an enterprise file-sharing service,' *Proc GROUP 2010.*
7. Nonnecke, B., Andrews, A., & Preece, J., 'Non-public and public online community participation: Needs, attitudes, and behavior. *Elec. Com. Res. 6* (1), 7-20, 2006.
8. Panciera, K., Priedhorsky, R., Erickson, T., & Terveen, L., 'Lurking? Cyclopaths? A quantitative lifecycle analysis of user behavior in a geowiki,' *Proc CHI 2010.*
9. Preece, J. and Shneiderman, B., 'The reader-to-leader framework: Motivating technology-mediated social participation,' *AIS Trans HCI 1* (1), 13-32, 2009.
10. Rafaeli, S., Ravid, G., & Soroka, V., 'De-Lurking in virtual communities: A social communication network approach to measuring the effects of social and cultural capital.' *Proc. HICSS 2004.*
11. Takahashi, M., Fujimoto, M., & Yamasaki, N., 'The active lurker: Influence of an in-house online community on its outside environment.' *Proc GROUP 2003.*

Question Temporality: Identification and Uses

Aditya Pal, James Margatan, Joseph A. Konstan
Department of Computer Science & Engineering
University of Minnesota, Minneapolis, MN 55455, USA
{apal,james,konstan}@cs.umn.edu

ABSTRACT
In this paper, we introduce the concept of *question temporality* as a measure of the usefulness of the answers provided on the questions asked in the Question Answering sites (QA). We define question temporality based on when the answers provided on the questions would expire. We use classification methods to show that the question temporality can be assessed automatically. Our regression analysis highlights features that predict temporality of the questions. Our research can be instructive for interface designers to design temporality-aware interfaces and influence selection of questions and answers for display.

Author Keywords
Question Temporality, Question Answering Community, Social Q&A, Machine Classification

ACM Classification Keywords
H.3.1 Content Analysis and Indexing: General

General Terms
Experimentation; Human Factors

INTRODUCTION
In this paper, we introduce the concept of *question temporality* as a measure of the usefulness of the answers provided on the questions asked in the Question Answering sites (QA) and propose Machine Learning methods to automatically identify question temporality. We define a question's temporality as how soon the answers to that question are likely to expire or become obsolete. We illustrate this point using an example.

EXAMPLE 1. Consider the question-answer exchange presented in Figure 1, where a user is inquiring about the day and the date of occurrence of Thanksgiving. Even though the question asker has not specifically mentioned the year, it can be inferred that the asker is interested in knowing the date of Thanksgiving in the year 2007 based on the date the question was asked. The answer that was judged as the best answer

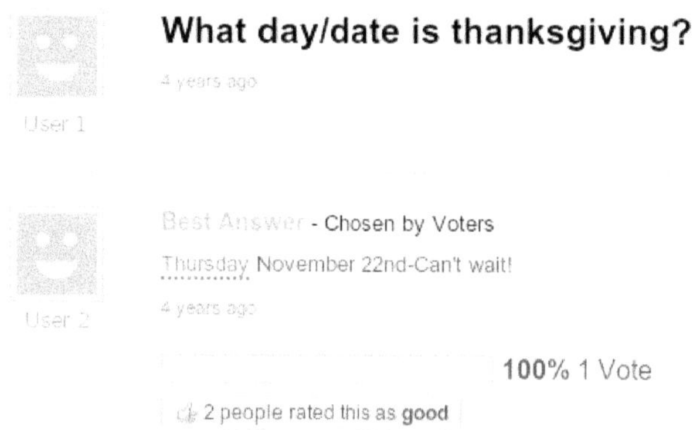

Figure 1. A question-answer thread taken from Yahoo Answers.

rightly points out that Thanksgiving would occur on November 22nd, *which was correct in 2007*. Even though the answer is labeled as the best answer, *it is no longer correct in the year 2011*. This is because the date of Thanksgiving changes every year. The question is temporal and its answers thus become outdated after some time, a few months in this case. We can envision scenarios in which the outdated information can lead to serious negative consequences when a person is acting on the advice provided on a question like - *whether a particular company's stock is overvalued, where to travel to see the next eclipse*, or *what hours a particular store is open*.

Applications
Identification of question temporality can improve the use of question-answering sites in several ways. First, it can help sites and search engines in weeding out outdated content. A major purpose of QA sites is to provide information that would not otherwise be available online. While internal mechanisms such as "best answer" awards can help identify whether the information provided was good at the time, temporality can help determine whether older answers are likely to have retained their value months or years later[1]. An understanding of how long a question's answers are likely to be valid could also enable different archiving strategies of question-answer threads [4].

Second, QA sites could better handle the phenomenon of duplicate question-asking if they were temporality-aware. When a user presents a question that has been asked and answered before, many QA sites treat this as a user error and

[1]It would also be useful to be able to identify the temporality of each answer to a question; while such work would be an interesting follow-on study, it is beyond the scope of this work.

proceed to present prior answers to the user. For many questions, this behavior may be correct, but for questions with short-lived answers, it provides an annoying and unwanted experience. Consider the real-world example of questions regarding immigration and visa rules. Old answers are almost always unsatisfactory and misleading due to frequent changes in visa rules. QA communities can benefit by automatically flagging old answers, requesting updated information, or providing tools to help the community do so.

Third, temporal analysis of questions could result in more useful lists of open and answered questions. Recent work by Kulkarni et al. [5] suggests that some web queries are also strongly influenced by time. As a result it is more appropriate to alter search result rankings based on time in order to present higher quality ranked lists. We draw a parallel in the QA domain where question presentation can be altered based on the temporal nature of the questions. For e.g. a question whose answer expires everyday (such as *How is the weather in Seattle?*) can be displayed on the main page more frequently than questions which have a longer life. Answers on some questions expire faster than others, e.g., *How is the weather in Seattle?* vs *When is Thanksgiving*? We don't propose to know the right strategy for factoring temporality into QA displays, but only by first establishing temporality can these interfaces be explored.

Finally, identification of question temporality can provide deeper insights into how questions can be altered to increase their longevity. Improving the usefulness of questions answered is a major goal of ours. Consider again the Thanksgiving example. The way this question has been posed, the answers are likely to expire within a year. If we modify the question slightly to read: *What day/date is Thanksgiving in the year 2007*?, correct answers never expire. The example highlights that a question's temporality can be altered by binding it with specific time reference; resulting in greater archivability (and potentially greater usefulness in documenting history). E.g. *Who won last Thursday on American Idol*?, can be improved automatically by adding date binding to read *Who won May 10, 2011 in American Idol*? We're not proposing simplistically adding time bindings to all questions (many would produce little value and simply be annoying to users), but for questions with potential long-term value, the approach seems promising.

Our Approach

We propose 4 temporal categories based on how soon the answers are likely to expire on any given question. These temporal categories range from short-duration (questions whose answers can expire within weeks) to permanent (questions whose answers never expire). To separate questions where temporality doesn't apply, we also propose an *other* category. We use the 5 category taxonomy to label a set of 100 questions taken randomly from Yahoo Answers. The 5-category taxonomy allows us the flexibility to group categories together depending on the objective of our classification. We then identified and extracted the key features that we thought would help in identifying their temporality. We use the extracted features to run Machine Learning models to show that the temporality of the questions can be estimated automatically with promising precision. We further run regression analysis to identify the features that are most effective in identifying question temporality.

QUESTION TEMPORALITY

We define *question temporality* as a measure of how long the answers provided on a question are expected to be valuable. The Thanksgiving example shows that the answers on it would be valid for up to a year, depending on when the question was asked. On the other hand consider the question: *Which is the largest country in the world?*. The answers for this question can be expected to be valid for several years, though likely not permanently. In contrast, answers to a question that asks about the weather of a certain place, e.g., *Is it raining in Seattle?*, are expected to expire within a few hours. The examples provided here are representative of the factual questions on actual QA sites.

Category 1: Permanent

The answers on these questions do not expire. Generally these questions directly or indirectly specify a specific time frame or they are permanent factual questions. A factual question can be of the kind *What is the chemical symbol for Gold?* In a time-specified frame question, the time frame can simply be a year, or a past dated event. E.g. *Who was the US president in 1957?*, *When did World War II happen?* We can modify our Thanksgiving example such that it can belong to this category by adding a time reference: *What day/date is Thanksgiving in year 2007?*

Category 2: Long-Duration

Long-duration questions are those whose answers do not change often. The answers are expected to change every few years or decades. Questions that fit this category are: *Which is the largest country in the world?*, *Which is the oldest mammal found by archaeologists?*, *How many planets are there in the solar system?*

Category 3: Medium-Duration

Answers to medium-duration questions are expected to become invalid within a few months to a few years. The Thanksgiving question presented above fits this category. Other examples of questions in this category are: *Who's the mayor of Washington DC?*, *What is the fastest CPU in the market to buy?*

Category 4: Short-Duration

Short-duration questions are those whose answers are expected to expire in less than few months. Some examples of questions that belong to this category are: *How is the weather in Seattle?*, *What is the most recent House episode?*

Additionally, we introduce *Category 0: Other* to cover all questions where temporality does not apply.

Category 0: Other

Questions that do not fit any other category such as non-factual questions, opinion questions, advice questions are put in this category. Questions such as *Do you like Brad Pitt?*,

What is better Coke or Pepsi? belong to this category. Additionally, future directed questions that are open for speculation belong to this category, e.g., *Who will be nominated as the best actress in Oscar 2012?*

With only 100 questions, most of our analysis could not make full use of our category set. Based on our goal of identifying questions where the answers are not likely to remain useful for long, we make a binary distinction between Categories 3 and 4 (short- and medium-duration temporal questions) and all the other categories. Most of our results report on our efforts to identify these Category 3 and 4 (strongly temporal) questions.

EXPERIMENTAL DESIGN

Dataset

We sampled 100 questions randomly from the main page of Yahoo Answers over a period of one week. The sampled questions contained 10.59 words on average and a total of 448 words. The word frequency distribution follows a power law [1], indicating that the selected dataset captures the characteristics that occur naturally in online social systems.

Survey Design

The first screen of the survey provided details of the 5 categories along with example questions as described above. Subsequent screens would show 100 questions[2] one by one and provide check box to select only of the above 5 categories. A user could also select a "not sure" button and move to the next question. The order in which the 100 questions were presented was also randomized.

Survey Takers

We asked Computer Science graduate and undergraduate students to take the survey. Overall 8 students took the survey. The inter-rater agreement between the raters was 0.22 (Fleiss kappa, error = 0.009 $p < 0.01$ with 95% CI). The agreement between the raters was not accidental and is considered to be satisfactory agreement. Moreover, when computed based on our binary classification (strongly temporal vs. not), inter-rater agreement is 0.88 which is very strong agreement (and which illustrates that most disagreement was over which category within high-temporal or not should be used).

Survey Results

We need a measure to combine the eight user ratings to compute the categories of the questions. The most commonly used strategy of taking the mean does not work since the ratings are categorical. As a result we consider the majority rating strategy: As per this strategy, we assign a category to the question based upon the majority votes (out of 8). We break the ties randomly (5/100 had 2-way ties and only 1 question had a 3-way tie). Figure 2 shows the frequency distribution of question' being assigned to each of the 5 categories. It shows that 47 question exhibit temporality and among those 47 questions, 17 are short-duration and medium-duration questions. It is these 17 strongly temporal questions that we attempt to identify automatically.

[2]We only showed the questions and not the answers provided on those questions.

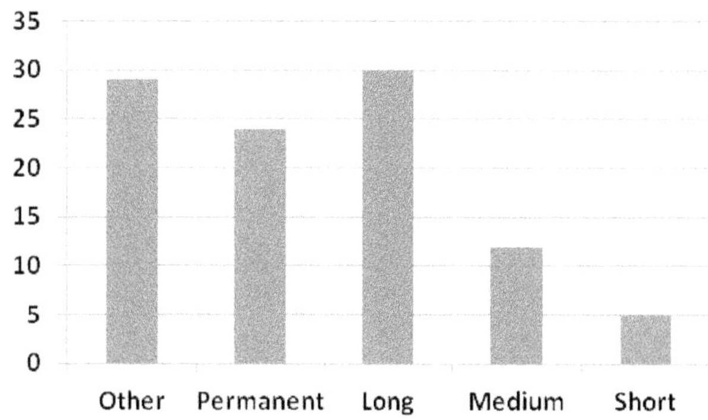

Figure 2. Frequency distribution of the questions per category.

CLASSIFICATION METHODOLOGY

We combine short- and medium-duration temporal questions as class 1 (17 questions) and all other questions as class 0 (83 questions). Note that the categories are combined as performing multi-way classification over a small dataset would not be effective. This binary separation enables us in answering the question: *Can we automatically separate questions which would likely expire "soon" from those more likely to remain valid for years or longer?*

Question Features

We consider a question as a vector of words (after removing stop words and special symbols like ?, !, *, etc). Then we computed the tf/idf score for the question vector, which were used as question features. Additionally, we considered several other features such as *Does the question reference a specific time (e.g. date, month)?*, *Is the referenced time fixed or relative (ago, after, before, today, tomorrow)?*, *Does it reference a date in past?*, *Does it reference a date in future?*, *Is the tense of question past tense?* These features along with the tf/idf scores were used to build a feature vector per question, which is then used for question classification.

Classification Method

We considered several state-of-art classification algorithms (such as Support Vector Machines, Decision Trees, Ada Boost, Naive Bayes, Gaussian discriminant Analysis). Ada Boost [3] which is an ensemble algorithm consistently performed better than other algorithms. We ran our experiments using 10-fold cross validation and report the aggregate accuracy over the 10 folds.

RESULTS

Identifying Strongly Temporal Questions

Table 1 shows the performance results of the model in identifying short- and medium-duration questions (class 1) from the rest of the questions. It shows that we can automatically

	Precision	*Recall*	*F1*
Class 1 (Category 3, 4)	0.70	0.41	0.52
Class 0 (Category 0, 1, 2)	0.89	0.96	0.92

Table 1. Performance of Ada Boost model in distinguishing strongly temporal questions from other types.

identify 41% of class 1 questions (7/17). It also signifies that of all the questions called out by the model as temporal, 70% are short- or medium-duration temporal. Overall the result shows promise for automatic detection of question temporality.

Identifying Features of Strongly Temporal Questions

We run ridge regression [6] using binary class as the output variable. The $R2$ of the fitted distribution is 0.83 which indicates that the extracted features provide a good linear fit over the ratings ($error = 0.2$). Table 2 shows features with the highest and lowest weights found using ridge regression. The highest weight features are indicators of question temporality and alternately the lowest weight features are indicators of the non-temporality of the questions. We can see that words such as what, who, current, etc or presence of a *relative time* indicates that a question is strongly temporal. Indeed we found short-duration temporal questions such as *What is the current weather/temperature in San Diego, CA?, How much has the price of gas gone up in the past 5 months?* containing these features.

On the other hand questions from our dataset such as *When was Super Bowl XLV played in 2011?, Who was the first US president to visit the Soviet Union?* indicate that indeed the features such as when, was, fixed time, etc are indicator of permanence of the questions. The words such as *likely* are indicator of opinion questions (e.g. *who is likely to be Vikings qb this upcoming NFL season?*) and the questions containing it are considered non-temporal (category 0).

These features and their corresponding weights can be used to automatically detect question temporality class. The regression analysis can be used along with classification model to detect temporal questions.

Type	Features
Class 1	what (0.12), who (0.07), current (0.08), recent (0.11), today (0.11), does (0.06), during (0.06), *Relative time* (0.11)
Class 0	when (−0.09), was (−0.09), worst (−0.06), which (−0.06), this (−0.04), likely (−0.06), *Fixed time* (−0.06), *Ordinal Number* (−0.07)

Table 2. Features (and their weights) that are most indicative of temporality or non-temporality of the questions.

RELATED WORK

Content temporality has been extensively studied in the context of web queries. Zhang et al. [7] analyzed query volume at Yahoo to detect time sensitive queries, *based on which queries are accompanied by year*, and proposed a ranking method for web results for the time sensitive queries. Dakka et al. [2] presented a framework for handling time sensitive queries and identifying the important time intervals that might be interesting for a given query. They ran their experiments on news articles to show that temporality aspect of a document is an important aspect during ranking of web results. Recently, Kulkarni et al. [5] considered query popularity over time to re-rank web results and understand the user intent while keeping in perspective the temporally evolving web pages. Our work compliments prior work in several ways. We posit that question temporality can be useful in ranking of QA data. We also show how questions can be slightly modified to change the question's temporality class. We demonstrate that question temporality can be automatically detected from simple features extracted from question text.

CONCLUSION

In this paper, we propose a novel concept of question temporality in QA communities. We argue that the detection of question temporality would benefit search engines and allows QA providers to explore interesting interface design choices towards providing better user experience. It also leads towards developing deeper insights into how questions can be altered to increase their longevity.

Our results show that question temporality can be satisfactorily detected automatically using question vocabulary and other simple features. Our results indicate that features such as *relative time* (e.g. today, tomorrow, ago, etc) or words such as what, who, etc can be used to successfully estimate the temporal questions. We propose using classification as well as regression models to build a confidence score about the temporality of the questions.

This paper focuses on introducing question temporality and showing that it can be estimated effectively. As part of future work, we would like to explore other features that could help improve the classification performance. We also aim at applying some of the ideas presented in this paper in a real world QA system and measuring the effectiveness of their application towards improving user interaction.

ACKNOWLEDGEMENT

We would like to thank the anonymous reviewers for providing their valuable feedback. This work was supported by the National Science Foundation, under grants IIS 08-08692 and 08-12148.

REFERENCES

1. Barabasi, A. L., and Albert, R. Emergence of scaling in random networks. *Science 286*, 5439 (1999), 509–512.
2. Dakka, W., Gravano, L., and Ipeirotis, P. G. Answering general time sensitive queries. In *CIKM* (2008), 1437–1438.
3. Freund, Y., and Schapire, R. E. A decision-theoretic generalization of on-line learning and an application to boosting. In *EuroCOLT*, vol. 904 of *Lecture Notes in Computer Science*, 23–37.
4. Harper, F. M., Moy, D., and Konstan, J. A. Facts or friends?: Distinguishing informational and conversational questions in social Q&A sites. In *CHI*, ACM (2009), 759–768.
5. Kulkarni, A., Teevan, J., Svore, K. M., and Dumais, S. T. Understanding temporal query dynamics. In *WSDM*, ACM (2011), 167–176.
6. Tychonoff, A. N. Solution of incorrectly formulated problems and the regularization method. In *Soviet Mathematics 4* (1963), 1035–1038.
7. Zhang, R., Chang, Y., Zheng, Z., Metzler, D., and yun Nie, J. Search engine adaptation by feedback control adjustment for time-sensitive query. In *HLT-NAACL*, ACL (2009), 165–168.

Bootstrapping Wikis: Developing Critical Mass in a Fledgling Community by Seeding Content

Jacob Solomon
Michigan State University
solomo93@msu.edu

Rick Wash
Michigan State University
wash@msu.edu

ABSTRACT
Online communities depend on content contributed by their members. However, new communities have not yet achieved critical mass and are vulnerable to inadequate contribution. To encourage contribution, many fledgling communities seed the site with data from 3rd parties. We study the effectiveness of such seeding by looking at how people react to different types of seeded content. We found that people make larger contributions when there is no seeded content. But when there is seeded content, users learn from that content and contribute similar types of content. Therefore, if websites prefer specific types of contributions, seeding that type of contribution can be a valuable way to elicit appropriate contributions.

Author Keywords
online contribution, bootstrapping, critical mass

ACM Classification Keywords
H.5.2 Information Interfaces and Presentation: Miscellaneous

General Terms
Human Factors

INTRODUCTION
System designers frequently seed content into newly created social media sites in an attempt to establish expectations and elicit participation. This seeded content presents the appearance of site activity for first-time visitors, and can be interpreted by visitors as the behavior of other community members. This is an attempt at *bootstrapping* participation on the site.

The perception of site activity by first-time visitors can establish expectations of the community's utility and the behavior which is afforded on the site. These expectations can then influence a user's motivation to contribute to the community. Motivations to contribute to online communities can be diverse and complex. Motivations can vary across dimensions of function or sociality [1]. They can also be related to expressions of values or ideology [6] or simply a desire to provide information [4]. If newcomers perceive the affordances or utility of a site to be incompatible with their motivations to contribute, the site could have difficulty in developing a critical mass of participation.

In this study, we hope to inform the design of online communities by examining the influence of bootstrapping on the behavior of contributors. We investigate how seeding content to a site can be used to influence user contributions. This influence may be the result of a perception on the part of the users that the existing content on a site is a representation of the behavior of other community members. The content on the site can serve as a model from which first-time users can learn. Social cognitive theory is the basis for this argument. Social cognitive theory asserts that people learn through the observation of models [2]. First-time users of a site can use the seeded content as a model for their own behavior.

It is important that the model of behavior provided through seeded content be congruent with the goals of the site. As an obvious example, seeding spam would be counter-productive to the goals of most sites. The behavior modeled in seeded content must be consistent with visitor's motivations to contribute. Inconsistencies in incentives and motivations for a particular behavior can be de-motivating [7]. Because there is considerable variance in motivation to contribute to online communities, it can be difficult to model behavior through seeded content which can reliably motivate first-time visitors to contribute.

For this reason, it is important to understand the contexts in which bootstrapping can effectively be used in congruence with the goals of an online community, as well as the contexts in which it is best avoided. Seeded content provides a model of behavior for first-time contributors. But which characteristics of contributions are detected by users as being the behavior of community members which can be modeled?

We have looked at the type of information which has been contributed as a marker of the behavior of community members. We have examined variance in information type across two dimensions. First, contributions vary in their subjectivity, ranging from factual to opinionated. Second, some contributions can provide structure to a community, such as new pages, headings, threads, or sections. The type of seeded content can be interpreted by newcomers as the behavior of existing community members, thus influencing newcomers' behavior.

RQ1. When users are given a behavioral model in the form of seeded content, will their contributions be different than if they are given no model?

Table 1. Specific Hypotheses

H1.1: Users in the blank group will contribute more structural information than users in the seeded groups.

H1.2: Users in the blank group will contribute less factual information than users in the seeded groups.

H1.3: Users in the blank group will contribute less opinionated information than users in the seeded groups.

H1.4: Users in the blank group will contribute less total information than users in the seeded groups.

H2.1: The percentage of sentences containing facts will be greatest for users in the factual group than for users in the opinion or structure groups.

H2.2: The percentage of sentences containing opinions will be greatest for users in the opinion group than for users in the factual or structure groups.

H2.3: The percentage of structural sentences will be greatest for users in the structural group than for users in the factual or opinion groups.

Since social cognitive theory explains that the behavioral models perceived by users will influence their behavior, it is important to understand what users will do when they have no such models. Because the blank wiki contains *no* structure, we hypothesize that the blank group will be compelled to add a greater percentage of structure than the seeded groups. However, we hypothesize that users will contribute more non-structural content, as well as more total content, when given a wiki seeded with content. Hypotheses 1.1–1.4 (in Table 1) operationalize this research question.

RQ2. Will users follow the model provided in seeded content by contributing the same type of information?

Answering this question is of value to designers who want to direct the behavior of contributors through bootstrapping. In contexts where certain types of information are more desirable to the goals of a site than other types of information, designers may consider bootstrapping so that contributors follow a carefully selected model of behavior. The extent to which users follow the model of behavior in contributing, as well as the strength and boundaries of this effect, is important in determining how to bootstrap. Likewise, a test of information type as a marker of the behavior of community members can help designers determine whether or not to vary information type in order to elicit the desired perceptions of behavior by first-time visitors. These questions have been examined in Hypotheses 2.1, 2.2, and 2.3.

DATA

Students in introductory communications courses were invited to participate in the study. Students were told that participation in the study would lead to the creation of a wiki which would be an open, community-generated resource for information about communications related courses at the university. Additionally, students who agreed to spend at least 20 minutes (in their own time outside of class) making contributions to this wiki and who would complete a survey about their contribution were offered a small amount of extra-credit in their course (approximately 1% of their final grade; all subjects received the same amount of credit regardless of contribution.). 96 students fulfilled this request. In this experimental stage of the study, a new wiki (using MediaWiki software) was created for each participant based on one of four randomly assigned templates (rather than taking all participants to the same wiki).

The *factual* template listed six courses along with strictly factual information taken from the university registrar's course descriptions (i.e. instructor name, number of credits, basic description). The *opinion* template listed the same courses, but included opinionated statements about the course. These statements were paraphrased (to best fit the experimental context) from actual course reviews on publicly available websites in which students share information about courses and instructors. The *blank* template gave only a title and no other information. The *structural* template listed some categories of classes as section headings (i.e. Advertising, Retailing etc.) and listed links to pages for a few courses. These pages were blank, and the structural template contained no other content.

After the experiment, the text contributed by participants was separated from template text and divided into sentences. Each contributed sentence was manually coded. A sentence was coded as *factual* if it contained any factual information and no opinionated information. An example of a factual sentence would be "The class had four tests." A sentence was coded as *opinion* if it contained opinionated information with no strictly factual information. "This class was boring." Some sentences were coded as containing *both* factual and opinionated information. "The class had two tests, but they were very easy." The amount of factual information contributed was measured as the percentage of sentences coded as *factual* or *both* from the entire contribution. Opinionated information was measured the same way, and *structural* information was the percentage of sentences that only provide structure (headings or new page links) to the wiki from the entire contribution.

METHODS

Two-tailed t-tests were used to compare the mean information ratio of the blank group to all other groups for H1.1, H1.2, and H1.3. Post-hoc OLS regression models were used to clarify the results and provide more precise comparisons between the blank group and each other group. The total number of sentences contributed was found to be a covariate with the type of information contributed and was included in these models. A two-tailed t-test was also used to compare the total amount of information contributed (total number of sentences) between the blank group and the non-blank groups (H1.4). OLS regression provided an additional test of this hypothesis.

OLS regression was used to test H2.1, H2.2, and H2.3. A model was built for each sub-hypothesis which regressed the experimental condition (structural, factual, or opinionated) and the total number of sentences contributed on the ratio of structural, factual, or opinionated information. In each model,

Table 2. T Test statistics for hypotheses tests of Hypotheses 1.1-1.4.

	# Sentences	Facts	Opinions	Structure
Blank	19.7	70%	38%	8%
Non-Blank	10.0	59%	17%	25%
Difference	9.7	11%	21%	-17%
P-Value	0.053	0.107	0.008	0.000

the base condition corresponded to the congruent dependent variable. This allows us to see most clearly how contributions differed between condition in which the type of information of the dependent variable was seeded, versus the conditions in which it was not seeded.

RESULTS

Table 2 describes the differences between the non-blank groups and the blank group, as well as the t-tests. H1.1 was disconfirmed. Contrary to our prediction, the non-blank groups added *more* structural information than the blank group. H1.2 was not confirmed. Participants in the blank group actually contributed a higher ratio of facts than participants in the non-blank groups. However the difference was not statistically significant. The regression analysis determined that only the structural group contributed less factual information than the blank group. H1.3 was disconfirmed. Participants in the blank group contributed a *higher* ratio of opinionated information than participants in the non-blank groups. The post-hoc OLS regression analysis revealed that each group with seeded content contributed less opinionated information than the blank group. H1.4 was disconfirmed, as participants in the blank group contributed *more* sentences than participants in the non-blank groups. The t-test approached significance, and the regression analysis determined that the difference between the blank group and each of the other groups was significant.

Table 3 shows the results related to RQ2. H2.1 was confirmed, as participants who saw factual information on the wiki added a greater percentage of factual information than participants who saw either structural or opinionated information. H2.2 was partially confirmed. Seeing opinionated information led participants to contribute more opinions than those who saw factual information. The opinion group also added more opinions than the structure group, but the difference was not significant. H2.3 was confirmed. Participants who saw only structural information contributed more structural information than those who saw factual or opinionated information.

DISCUSSION

RQ1. When users are given a behavioral model in the form of seeded content, will their contributions be different than if they are given no model?

Participants who were shown a blank wiki contributed far more than those who saw seeded content, suggesting that a blank wiki was more motivating to participants than seeded content. It could be that a blank slate gives users more freedom, which they took up. Self-determination theory [3] argues that autonomy is an important characteristic of intrinsic motivation, particularly in creative behavior [7]. The presence of seeded content and the cognition of social expectations may have inhibited users' perception that complete autonomy of contributions is afforded.

Table 3. OLS regressions for Hypotheses 2.1-2.3. Each column is a separate regression using either the Fact, Opinion, or Structure Ratio as the dependent variable. The empty level for the condition IV was used as the baseline in each regression and corresponds to the type of content that matches the DV.

	Fact Ratio		Opinion Ratio		Structure Ratio	
(Intercept)	70%	***	22%	***	45%	***
Factual			-14%	*	-27%	***
Opinion	-26%	***			-10%	
Structure	-33%	***	-10%			
# Sentences	+1.0%	**	+0.2%		-0.8%	*
R^2	0.29		0.07		0.22	

Signif. codes: 0 '***' 0.001 '**' 0.01 '*' 0.05 '.' 0.1 ' ' 1

Ling et al. [5] found that users contribute more when they feel their contributions are unique. A similar effect may have occurred in this study, as users contributing to a blank wiki may have been cognizant that their contributions will be salient and important, leading to greater motivation to contribute.

The stark contrast between the level of contribution in the blank group and contribution in the structure group is important to note. The structure template essentially offered participants a coloring book approach to editing, with blank sections and pages that needed filling. Like the blank template, there was no real content. Seeding a community with only structure could be harmful to eliciting contribution because it may detract from user's autonomy and provide an insufficient model from which expectations can be established. Since users in the blank group contributed very little structure, we conclude that users are likely least intrinsically motivated to add structure compared to other types of content.

The results of H1.1 and H1.2 can be explained by the significant portion of sentences in blank wikis which were coded as containing both factual and opinionated information. Users in the blank condition appeared more likely to add opinionated clauses to factual statements. For example, "This is a photography class that is pretty fun." The factual statement that the class is about photography is qualified with an opinion that it is fun. A post-hoc analysis using OLS regression revealed that the blank group had significantly more statements containing both fact and opinion (17% of all sentences) than any of the seeded groups. If separating factual information from opinionated information is an important goal for the design of a site, designers must consider ways to do this without demotivating users through structure.

RQ2. Will users follow the model provided in seeded content by contributing the same type of information?

The results of this study suggest that users do look at the nature of previously contributed information as a model for their own behavior on the site. There are several possible mechanisms which might explain this behavior. This may be an example of social cognition [2] whereby users learn about the functionality, utility, or expectations of a site by observing how others behave. The seeded content on the site may also have primed users to think about certain types of content when considering their own contributions. Regardless of the mechanism, the results suggest that seeding content at an early stage of development can direct future contributions.

The results suggest that the nature of seeded content must be carefully thought through and must be consistent with the goals of the community. A community which seeks to elicit specific types of contributions may benefit from bootstrapping. A community seeking diversity in contributions may find that goal inhibited by bootstrapping, and may prefer to provide users a blank slate for contribution. These results have application to communities at more mature stages of development as well. An established community which finds an imbalance in the types of contributions it receives may find that seeding content can lead to more balanced contribution. For example, a wiki with considerable information but lacking structure can seed some structure into the wiki and make those contributions salient. These data suggest that users would react to such contributions by increasing the ratio of structural contributions.

LIMITATIONS

As an experiment, this research falls between a true laboratory experiment (with high internal validity) and a true field experiment (with high external validity). Since the subjects did the experiment on their home computers, we cannot control the environment the subject is in and cannot ensure that subjects actually worked on the wiki for 20 minutes. It is possible that some subjects (such as those in the blank condition) spent less time reading than others, and therefore spend more time contributing. This is a possible explanation for the blank condition results. It is also possible that subjects were trying to do the minimum work to get the extra credit. However, since that should be true across conditions, this should not be a confound for the study. These issues, however, potentially limit the external validity of the study. We cannot be sure that extra credit motivates users in similar ways to whatever motivates contributions to wikis online. However, this principle of least effort would seem to apply to other types of motivations, whether it be to earn reputation or merely help a friend. People are not likely to do more than what is required to satisfy their motivation. So the differences between conditions do still suggest that bootstrapping can influence behavior. Also, the errors for the OLS models predicting structure ratio and opinion ratio were not normally distributed, violating an assumption of OLS regression making the significance of those models somewhat questionable.

CONCLUSION

Many new social media systems use bootstrapping — seeding the site with third party content — as a way to encourage users to contribute. We found that users tend to contribute more content, and more unstructured content, when they are given a blank slate. This suggests that bootstrapping is not always a positive. However, users tend to contribute content roughly similar to any seeded content. Bootstrapping can be used to direct user effort toward contributing specific types of content. Site designers should carefully consider the goals of the site when seeding content.

Future work can look for markers of behavior other than information type which provide models for newcomers. Some possibilities include the style of language, chronemic characteristics, the size of individual contributions, variations in the structure of contributions, and other characteristics. For example, the discussion surrounding a wiki article may be useful to newcomers by providing a model of behavior which encourages direct communication and collaboration. The extent to which these characteristics can motivate newcomers to contribute or direct their future behavior on a site can inform designers in how they can best bootstrap a fledgling site. Evaluating these characteristics would then be an important extension of the current work.

REFERENCES

1. M. Ames and M. Naaman. Why we tag: motivations for annotation in mobile and online media. In *Proceedings of the SIGCHI conference on Human factors in computing systems*, pages 971–980, San Jose, California, USA, 2007. ACM.
2. A. Bandura. *Social foundations of thought and action: a social cognitive theory*. Prentice-Hall series in social learning theory. Prentice-Hall, Englewood Cliffs, N.J., 1986. xiii, 617 p.
3. E. L. Deci and R. M. Ryan. *Intrinsic motivation and self-determination in human behavior*. Springer, Aug. 1985.
4. C. Lampe, R. Wash, A. Velasquez, and E. Ozkaya. Motivations to participate in online communities. In *Proceedings of the 28th international conference on Human factors in computing systems*, pages 1927–1936, Atlanta, Georgia, USA, 2010. ACM.
5. K. Ling, G. Beenen, P. Ludford, X. Wang, K. Chang, X. Lee, D. Cosley, D. Frankowski, L. Terveen, A. M. Rashid, P. Resnick, and R. Kraut. Using social psychology to motivate contributions to online communities. *Journal of Computer-Mediated Communication*, 10(4), 2005.
6. O. Nov. What motivates wikipedians? *Commun. ACM*, 50(11):60–64, 2007.
7. D. H. Pink. *Drive: the surprising truth about what motivates us*. Riverhead Books, New York, NY, 2009. 242 p.

Supporting Reflective Public Thought with ConsiderIt

Travis Kriplean[1], Jonathan Morgan[2], Deen Freelon[3], Alan Borning[1], Lance Bennett[3,4]
Computer Science[1], Human Centered Design & Eng.[2], Communication[3], Pol. Science[4]
University of Washington, Seattle

ABSTRACT
We present a novel platform for supporting public deliberation on difficult decisions. ConsiderIt guides people to reflect on tradeoffs and the perspectives of others by framing interactions around pro/con points that participants create, adopt, and share. ConsiderIt surfaces the most salient pros and cons overall, while also enabling users to drill down into the key points for different groups. We deployed ConsiderIt in a contentious U.S. state election, inviting residents to deliberate on nine ballot measures. We discuss ConsiderIt's affordances and limitations, enriched with empirical data from this deployment. We show that users often engaged in normatively desirable activities, such as crafting positions that recognize both pros and cons, as well as points written by people who do not agree with them.

Author Keywords
governance, deliberation, consideration, politics, reflection

ACM Classification Keywords
H.5.0 Information Interfaces and Presentation: General

General Terms
Design.

INTRODUCTION

> *My Way is to divide half a Sheet of Paper into two Columns, writing over the one Pro, and over the other Con. Then during three or four Days Consideration I put down under the different Heads short Hints of the different Motives that at different Times occur to me for or against the Measure... I find at length where the Ballance lies... And tho' the Weight of Reasons cannot be taken with the Precision of Algebraic Quantities, yet when each is thus considered separately and comparatively, and the whole lies before me, I think I can judge better, and am less likely to take a rash Step.* – Ben Franklin, inventor of modern pro/con list [5]

Franklin recognized the value of challenging himself to consider tradeoffs through *personal deliberation*. For decisions that involve many people, engaging others in *public deliberation* has further benefits, such as making better decisions, uncovering new solutions, and including diverse others in decisions [13, 20, 19]. Yet public deliberation is difficult. It is challenging for people to listen to perspectives that contradict their own; most people, at least in America, are averse to even engaging with those with whom they suspect of harboring different views [36]. The use of communication media reflect these tendencies, with people highly attracted to content that aligns with their prior beliefs, even those who do not actively avoid challenging content [18, 27, 28, 35]. The problem is reinforced by a lack of effective socialization in the skills and values associated with productive exchanges of ideas, particularly in public schools [38]. We find our capacity to publicly deliberate undercut by people framing issues as zero-sum games between opposing sides, with members of each side speaking past each other and missing opportunities to factor other perspectives into their thoughts.

We think we can do better. By building interfaces that subtly encourage people to consider issues and reflect on the diverse perspectives of others, we think we can help build public trust while improving upon our collective ability to take more effective action on problems such as financial reform and climate change. We offer a modest step in this direction with the ConsiderIt platform.

ConsiderIt builds from the basics of personal deliberation to foster more effective public deliberation. It focuses people on thinking through the tradeoffs of a proposed action, such as a ballot measure in an election, by inviting them to create a pro/con list. ConsiderIt augments this familiar activity by enabling users to not just author pro and con points, but to *include* into their own lists the points others have already contributed, and in turn share with others the points that they author. The considerations of others thus become raw material for one's own considerations. Complementing the pro/con lists, participants summarize their stance on an issue on a continuum of conviction, rather than a binary yes/no vote. The focus is on augmented personal deliberation, rather than direct discussion with others, thus potentially mitigating the activation of political identity and flaming.

ConsiderIt then repurposes these personal deliberations to offer an evolving guide to public thought. Here, ConsiderIt surfaces the most salient overall pro/con considerations based on how often they are included and whether they are included by people with different stances on the issue. ConsiderIt also enables drill down into the salient points for different segments of the population: *"What were those who strongly opposed this thinking???"* Users can thus gain insights into the considerations of people with different perspectives, rather than making assumptions based on caricatures. As we describe in our results, this can help users identify unexpected common

CSCW'12, February 11–15, 2012, Seattle, Washington, USA.

ground. We also contribute a pro/con ranking metric tailored to highlight points that resonate with a diverse public, to promote persuasive points while still encouraging a diversity of views, and to hopefully be resistant to strategic manipulation.

ConsiderIt is the result of a design process initiated with the high-level goal of supporting a community-written voters guide for Washington State in the contentious 2010 U.S. election. In this paper, we ground our system contribution by reporting on ConsiderIt's deployment in September 2010 as *The Living Voters Guide* (LVG). It attracted thousands of users and hundreds of contributors in the five weeks leading up to the election. This style of pragmatic inquiry reflects our philosophy for making progress on the broader, complex challenges of civic participation: deploy a novel system into a real situation and examine whether it has basic utility for people using it at their own discretion. From this vantage point, we can then describe the approach's particular affordances and limitations as they become apparent through use.

This paper thus presents generative social system research: (1) we have *created a new interactive approach* for supporting public deliberation that has successfully weathered a large field deployment; (2) we describe a design strategy that *may spark new ideas*; and (3) the deployment *identifies opportunities for future controlled experimentation.* Our field deployment complements hypothesis testing in a lab, gaining insight into the utility and affordances of a social system operating in a contested and often vitriolic domain. After discussing past approaches to supporting public deliberation and the theoretical underpinning of this work, we present ConsiderIt in detail. We then describe the LVG deployment, followed by an analysis of ConsiderIt's appropriation. We end with a discussion of challenges and future directions.

THEORY AND DESIGN FOR PUBLIC DELIBERATION

Any organized group must make tough decisions when setting policy and choosing how to allocate scarce resources. Traditionally, CSCW researchers have focused on small-group decision-making embedded in hierarchical organizations [29]. However, with the advent of social media, it is now possible to assemble larger publics to help deliberate, whether these constituents are citizens, customers, a student body or employees. The input can be merely consultative, as with Facebook's Site Governance initiative for gathering feedback on terms of service changes or U.S. President Obama's use of platforms for gathering ideas about implementing open governance. Or they can run deep in the DNA of the organization, such as in Wikipedia where contributors struggle to conduct distributed self-governance [6, 14, 21]. As we move outside hierarchical organizations, we believe we should expand our guiding theory to incorporate insights from political communication in order to more effectively design for these wider, more casual engagement efforts.

Deliberation is just one normative ideal of collective decision-making, and it is sometimes in conflict with others. Social scientists have begun to draw on political theory to juxtapose and measure these conflicting ideals [2, 8, 16, 48]. Freelon [16] maps out three such ideals and their associated behavioral indicators within online spaces. Aside from the deliberative style, liberal individualism [10] is an egocentric perspective celebrating self-expression over listening, manifesting in monologues and flaming. Liberal individualist behavior is prevalent online, occurring primarily in spaces that are ideologically heterogeneous, such as the free-for-all comment sections of Youtube and major newspapers, which both offer broad freedom of expression but are abrasive and low in responsiveness [31, 47]. Communitarianism [15, 46] emphasizes group identification with like-minded people in order to better organize against groups with whom they disagree. Evidence from studies of ideological fragmentation and selective exposure have demonstrated that communitarian behavior is exceedingly common both online and off, with most people choosing to engage material that aligns with their prior beliefs [18, 27, 28, 35]. And while some people do not go out of their way to avoid challenging material, they still must encounter it first, an activity that platforms like Facebook and Google Reader do not encourage.

While we respect the importance of these different ideals, most, if not all, broadly used communication interfaces implicitly or explicitly support these non-deliberative styles. Some scholars and practitioners have developed methods and tools in response to this deficit in deliberative support. However, these efforts have yielded tools and methods requiring a high level of investment from both administrators and users, which limits both their scope and sustainability. Numerous methods have been invented to approximate the deliberative ideal in face to face settings, such as deliberative polling and citizen juries [13]. Most systems work in this domain has tried to translate aspects of these multi-day, resource intensive deliberative efforts into online tools [24, 25, 34]. They tend to centralize control over the agenda and delimit acceptable contributions, such as by instituting Robert's Rules of Order [40, 41]. One well-explored class of high-investment deliberative system disciplines participants to break down their opinions according to argumentation schemas drawn from linguistic theory or elsewhere, and incorporate them into a graphical visualization of the issues, arguments, positions, and so forth (see [43, 44] for an overview). Grave challenges to this approach have been found in practice, such as difficulty in learning the formalized schemas, breaking up narratives into the required fine chunks, and agreeing on classifications [23, 42], often requiring trained facilitators to be successful [7].[1] These systems have their place, but it would be unrealistic to expect them to be used widely. Aside from the unsustainable level of commitment demanded, not everyone shares the deliberative ideal. Insisting on a deliberative style in a discretionary setting may simply lead to low participation.

Our position is that if we want to make progress on addressing collective problems, we should try to support deliberative styles of interaction in more casually used interfaces, and further, in a way that accommodates aspects of the other styles without undermining deliberation. If we can attract the attention of diverse communicators, the interface can gently nudge people toward deliberative behavior, such as weighing trade-offs and considering what other people are saying about the issue. We may thus be able to promote an environment where people are more likely to find common ground and less likely

[1] Recent work such as Cohere [44], Pathfinder [32] and Videolyzer [9] show promise by relaxing some of the constraints of the argumentation scheme.

to participate in flame wars. This is certainly a challenge, but Mackuen [33] has shown that the communicative styles that people adopt are context sensitive. And interface design can play a large role in shaping this context [37, 45]. For example, Park et al. demonstrated that displaying multiple articles about the same news event, divided into clusters that emphasize different aspects of the event, causes people to read more diverse news stories than a simple random list [37], even though most people appear to desire only news stories that back their own beliefs [35].

Therefore, while it is difficult to design interfaces for wide public use that subtly nudge people toward a deliberative style of communication, we believe it is possible. Our approach to this challenge has three parts. First, we try to encourage people to explicitly consider tradeoffs for the issue at hand. In ConsiderIt, this is primarily facilitated by the pro/con list, where an unbalanced list challenges users to reflect on whether they are missing something. Second, we encourage people to listen to and recognize what others have to say. In ConsiderIt, this is primarily facilitated by enabling users to adopt into their own pro/con lists points contributed by others. When users adopt a point, they are both using it to consider a tradeoff, and also listening to someone else. (Whether they are cognizant of this dual role is another issue.) Third, we aggregate and repurpose these explicit acts of considering tradeoffs and listening to others to help everyone better understand and explore facets of the issue being deliberated. In ConsiderIt, this is facilitated by providing a view over the deliberations that ranks the pros and cons based how often and by whom the points are adopted.

Few other systems are designed with a similar strategy. Reflect [30] modifies the comment sections of webpages to facilitate the establishment of common ground by adding a listening box next to every comment, where other users are encouraged to succinctly restate the points that the commenter is making. This is a nudge to listen to other users. Other readers can then read the original comment and the listeners' interpretations of what was being said, supporting broader understanding of the discussion. OpinionSpace [12] plots on a two-dimensional map the individual comments in a web forum, based on the commenters' responses to a short value-based questionnaire. By navigating this space, readers are better able to seek out a diversity of comments as well as prime themselves for engaging the perspective of someone with different values. When users interrogate an individual comment, they are prompted to rate comments for how much they agree with and respect it. The size of the comment's dot on the map then grows when people with different values than the speaker respect and/or agree with it, facilitating users in seeking out comments that resonate widely.[2]

SYSTEM DESCRIPTION

In Washington state, measures can be added to the ballot by the legislature or, with sufficient signatures, can be submitted directly by citizens. Some of the nine 2010 measures were hotly contested, particularly Initiative 1098 which would have instituted Washington's first-ever state income tax, taxing income over $200k (single) or $400k (joint), reducing property taxes by 20%, and increasing tax credits for businesses. Other measures were opaquely worded and confusing, such as two irreconcilable measures for privatizing the sale of liquor. Unfortunately, there were few places for citizens to actively work through the various arguments and claims being made by campaigns and pundits, or hear the considerations of "everyday" people. This provided an opportunity to facilitate reflective public thought. Six months prior to the election, we partnered with Seattle City Club, a nonpartisan civic organization, with the goal of supporting a community-written voters' guide on the ballot measures.

ConsiderIt is the result of the design process undertaken to realize the *Living Voters Guide*. ConsiderIt was designed and developed by the first author, with assistance from the second author and a graphic designer. The second author also developed usage scenarios and conducted an early paper prototyping user study. The rest of the project team participated in decisions about features and helped test the system. ConsiderIt is implemented in Ruby on Rails, with extensive use of the jQuery Javascript library for client-side interactions. It is available under the AGPL open source license.

While ConsiderIt is applicable beyond electoral deliberation, we ground our system description in the LVG. We describe it in two parts: (1) supporting personal deliberation by crafting a position; and (2) exploring aggregated positions to understand the considerations that resonated most with other users. In each section, we use two personas to introduce the functionality, followed by a description of the components not covered in the scenarios. The personas' actions are composites based on the behavioral traces of real users from the LVG deployment who were considering the income tax measure I-1098. The points the personas include and author are actual user-contributed points. We dramatize the personas' motives based on two of the aforementioned communication styles in order to illustrate how users with diverse motives might appropriate the LVG. Specifically, Jim is an undecided voter who wishes to carefully weigh his options, while Maria is an advocate working on behalf of her cause, engaging in behaviors associated with communitarianism.

ConsiderIt: Deliberation through position crafting

Last week, a couple of Jim's friends argued over I-1098. It wasn't clear to Jim where he stood. This morning, he came across a link to the LVG while loading the home page at the Seattle Public Library and decides to see if it can help him sort out his thoughts. When Jim arrives at the LVG, he clicks the icon for 1098. Jim reads the official summary description of 1098 at the top of the page, but does not follow the link to the full description because he doesn't want to get bogged down in legalistic language. Under the description is a slider asking Jim's initial opinion, from strongly support to strongly oppose. He plays with the slider for a few moments, but ends up leaving it at "Neutral". Next he comes across a chalkboard slate with "pro" and "con" columns. In the margins, he sees four pros and four cons written by others. One of the Con points is similar to one his buddy mentioned: *"The state legislature may expand the income tax to the middle class in two years."* Jim thinks this is important, so he

[2] MetaViz [4] is also closely aligned in spirit, though not design strategy. It seeks to trigger critical thinking in political blogs by computationally identifying and exposing the metaphors upon which discussants are drawing.

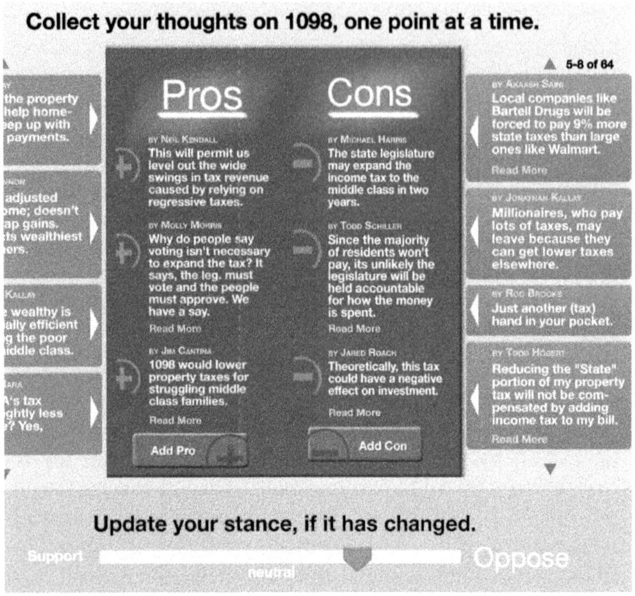

Figure 1. Jim's position on 1098. The "chalkboard" in the middle contains the user's pro/con list. On the sides, four pro and four con points written by others are shown. Clicking on the white arrow includes the respective point into the user's list. Not shown here is a neutral description of the issue being considered–it is above the pro/con list.

clicks the arrow on the Con point to include it into his own list. In the margin, another Con replaces the one he included. He cycles through several more sets of Con points, including two more. He then browses through the Pro points, including one. Then he notices a Pro point stating *"Why do people say voting isn't necessary to expand the tax? It says, the leg. must vote and the people must approve. We have a say."*. This contradicts the Con he included earlier. He has trouble reconciling these, although the full description of the Pro cites the relevant passage from the measure in the text, which makes him more dubious about his friend's argument. He removes his friend's point from his list. After reading through a dozen more points, Jim notices that one of the most important points that his other friend brought up is not represented. He decides to add it and clicks "Add pro": *"1098 would lower property taxes for struggling middle class families."* He includes a hyperlink to a *Times* editorial in the description of his point in case anyone is interested in reading more. As he scrolls down, he notices a second slider prompting him to update his stance if it has changed. Looking at his pro/con list (Figure 1), he thinks "am I still neutral?", then nudges the slider about a quarter way towards "Oppose" because he's still skeptical. He likes being able to convey his uncertainty, rather than simply saying yes or no, even if he ultimately has to vote. He clicks "Finish".

Maria volunteers for a campaign called "Yes on 1098." She has been spending part of her afternoon scouring the internet for discussions about I-1098 in order to make the case for it. She comes across the LVG and wants to make sure that the "Yes on 1098" perspective is being forcefully represented on the site. Maria reads that the LVG is a guide to the 2011 Washington state ballot initiatives written "by people like you". She knows from experience that sites like this often contain poor quality information or present a lopsided perspective. She wants to make sure that the arguments from the "Yes on 1098" campaign are properly and prominently represented, so she goes directly to the 1098 page. Maria already knows 1098 inside and out, so she breezes past the description and grabs the stance slider and moves it towards 'Support' as far as it will go. When she scrolls down to the Pro/Con list, she starts by cycling through the existing pro points, including many of them in her list. She then skims the Con points to see what her opponents are saying about 1098. She sees a couple that aren't completely out of line, but most are bogus. After some consideration she decides to include one Con point: *"Local companies will be forced to pay more state taxes than national companies like Wal-Mart."* If there's ONE thing about this bill that could be slightly tweaked, that's it. She sees one Con written by a guy named Lawrence that claims that 1098 will cause wealthy people to leave the state. "That's not right", so she writes a pro point to counter it: *"Bill Gates Sr. is one of the chief proponents of 1098, so despite what some people here are saying there's obviously some support for 1098 among the wealthy!"* Thus inspired, she goes on to create several more Pro points, ending each one with *"Vote Yes on 1098!"*

Additional details

The primary components of the position crafting page are two stance sliders and a pro/con list. After the description, users are asked to take a stance signaling their initial support for the issue. The pro/con list follows. Users can contribute their own pros and cons, providing a summary ($\leq$ 140 characters) and an optional long description ($\leq$ 500 characters). If a long description is provided, a "read more" link is displayed for the point, which expands on click to show the full description. Each pro or con displayed in the margin has a white arrow pointing toward the user's pro/con list. Clicking on the arrow includes the respective point in the user's list, and the included point is replaced by another point that has not already been displayed to the user. Every point a user authors while writing his or her personal pro/con list is made available for other users to include. A second slider after the pro/con list prompts users to reflect on whether their stances have changed over the course of creating their pro/con lists. The sliders are linked so that moving one also moves the other. Though having people state their stances before the pro/con exercise may cause opinion anchoring, we chose to include the two sliders for the simple reason that in early user tests, participants found moving the slider and seeing the "support" and "oppose" text grow and shrink to be very engaging and was thus a good UX hook. At the bottom of the page is a "Finish" button that submits the user's position and redirects them to the results browsing page.

ConsiderIt: Exploring the guide to public thought

Thus far we have described how ConsiderIt facilitates personal deliberation augmented by the considerations others are making. In this section, we describe the system components that helps users explore and make sense of emerging public thought arising from these personal deliberations.

Returning to our personas, after **Maria** submits her position, she starts browsing the guide (Figure 2). She clicks on the bar representing other strong 1098 supporters to make sure

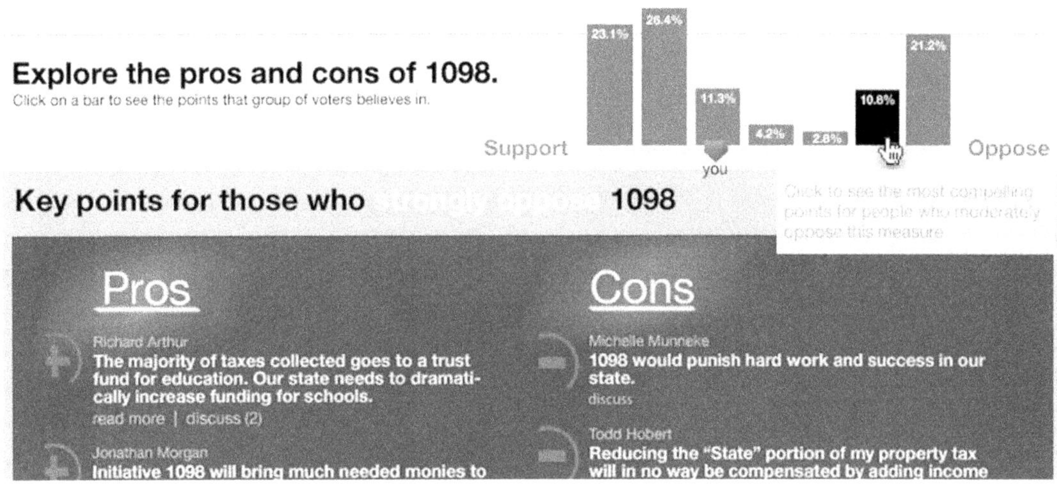

Figure 2. Browsing the guide. The current breakdown of support for a measure is shown in a bar graph to the upper right. The graph is interactive: clicking a bar changes the points shown in the pro/con list below the graph, revealing a ranked list of the most important points for those who took that particular stance. The initial list of pros and cons shown are the overall most salient. Not shown is a discussion forum below.

that all the basic points are there. They are. Then she clicks on the strong opposers bar to see what arguments the other side favors. She is surprised to see them admitting that 1098 would provide needed resources for social services, but otherwise rolls her eyes at the points they find persuasive. Regardless, maybe the social services consideration will provide a good starting point for dinner conversation when she goes to visit her conservative in-laws next weekend. She clicks a button that automatically leaves a post on Twitter telling her friends and followers to check out LVG page for 1098, noting that none of the Cons were convincing.

Jim submits his position and is taken to a page where he sees a bar graph of the support and opposition to 1098. After reviewing the top-ranked points, he clicks on each of the seven bars to make sure he has given supporters and opposers the chance to put their best arguments forward.

Additional details

The results page presents an evolving guide to the salient pro and con points. First, the stance histogram enables people to see the distribution of support. The seven bars are discrete stance groups (e.g., weak support), derived from the continuous slider values that users selected to represent their stances. Second, the results page has a ranked list of popular points, again shown on a chalkboard slate of pros and cons. The ranking metric is described later. The most innovative functionality is that the stance histogram is interactive; clicking on a bar updates the slate of pros and cons to show the most important points for the users who took that specific stance. The results page also contains a threaded discussion forum. Each thread can be pegged to specific pro or con point by clicking a "discuss" link for each point shown in the pro/con slate.

We developed PointRank to amplify the points that resonate widely while still allowing for new considerations to emerge. The ranking determines the ordering of the pro and con points shown on the margin of the pro/con list during position crafting and to identify the most important points to display on the results page. There are three terms in PointRank.

Persuasiveness: how well this point convinces people to include it. It is the ratio of users who included it to the number of users who viewed it.[3] Because new points always start with the maximum persuasiveness score (the author includes it and is the only viewer), this metric helps new points gain visibility and mitigates the preferential attachment (rich-get-richer) problem [22] in asynchronous voting systems. Moreover, Bailey & Horvitz found that users of an enterprise ideation system wanted the ranking to incorporate the ratio between views and votes [3].

Diverse appeal: measures the degree to which this point appeals to both supporters and opponents, in order to highlight points that might surface common ground, rather than divisive points. For each of our seven stance groups (from strong support to neutral to strong oppose), we calculate the persuasiveness of that point *for users who took that stance.* The diverse appeal measure gives the highest score to points where there is equal persuasiveness across all stance groups, i.e., given an inclusion of the point, there is equal likelihood that the includer has taken any of the seven possible stances. Entropy directly measures this quantity: the points with the most diverse appeal maximize entropy, while the most divisive points minimize it. To formalize the calculation, let I_s be the number of inclusions of the point by users taking stance s, and let U_s be the number of unique users who were served the point and took stance s. Let $\alpha_s = \frac{I_s}{U_s}$ be the persuasiveness of the point for stance group s. Then the probability of the inclusion of the point by a user taking stance s, assuming that there are n stance groups, is given by $p_s = \frac{\alpha_s}{\sum_{i=1}^{n} \alpha_i}$. Entropy is then $e = \sum_{i=1}^{n} -p_i \cdot \log_n p_i$.

Raw appeal: the number of people who included the point. The raw appeal metric helps account for the confidence we have in the ranking. We are far more confident in a five-star rating for a restaurant based on a thousand reviews rather than on only three.

[3] We logged all points a registered user was served while position crafting.

In our implementation, each of the three terms is normalized by calculating the respective point's percentile rank against the other pros or cons for the issue. The final score combines the three terms linearly with equal weighting, an arbitrary choice made because it is not immediately obvious what the "optimal" weights would be. Future experimentation should help refine this choice. To facilitate the drill-down functionality into the considerations of e.g. strong supporters, the diverse appeal term is dropped, and the popularity and persuasiveness terms are based on the actions of strong supporters. In the LVG, scores were updated hourly.

PointRank was also designed to help protect against covert strategic manipulation of the results. However, we believe that the LVG deployment did not sustain high enough traffic to attract the attention of campaigns that might execute such an attack. We therefore relegate our untested explanation of PointRank's resilience to a footnote.[4]

DEPLOYMENT DETAILS AND DATA

In the remainder of this paper, we present results from the LVG deployment of ConsiderIt. The LVG was launched on 9/21/2010 to a crowd of 150 at a Seattle City Club event. City Club seeded each ballot measure with one pro and con and led the outreach effort. Their nonpartisan reputation helped spread the word through liberal and conservative outlets statewide. We secured articles in the *Seattle Times* (9/27), *KIRO News* (10/5), the *UW Daily* (10/20), and the *Yakima Herald* (10/27), which drove most LVG traffic. Some websites linked to us from their homepage during the election season (e.g., the Seattle Public Libraries, public radio outlet KOUW). Furthermore, the LVG was used in several college and high school classes. Team members also reached out through email lists and social networking sites.

As an open deployment, we know little about the political attitudes of our self-selected population of users. On one hand, the *Seattle Times* drove the most traffic, and its comment sections are hyper-partisan. But perhaps only open-minded people followed the link. We cannot say, and we did not ask visitors to fill out a profile (to prevent the experience from feeling clinical). We can, however, provide some evidence in the form of metrics of use. Between 9/21 and 11/2, Google Analytics data shows LVG received 12,979 visits from 8,813 unique visitors. Ignoring the 6,082 sessions in which users visited only the homepage, users stayed an average of 10 minutes 39 seconds and visited 6.1 pages. Users from 134 Washington cities accessed the LVG (50.4% from Seattle). Traffic spiked on days of media coverage, but generally grew over time until election day (Figure 3). Many visitors opted to simply browse the guide, where they could see the pros and cons that others had already submitted.

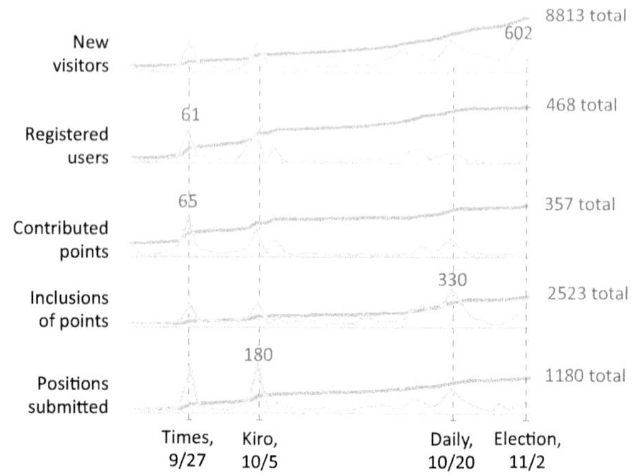

Figure 3. ***High-level trends.*** **In every plot, each line operates at different scales: the dark line gives a cumulative count and the light line is the daily count. Highest daily peek and final counts are labeled.**

Our results draw on the following data sources.

Activity traces. The timestamped activity traces captured in the database are our primary data source (Figure 3). A total of 468 people registered and submitted a position on at least one measure. 184 con and 160 pro points were written by 147 users. The maximum points contributed by one user was 10. 298 users included these points 2,687 times into 678 unique pro/con lists (503 pro/con lists were left empty). The number of points written per ballot measure was skewed ($\mu = 38.2$, median $= 29$, $[11, 113]$). All actions taken by any member of the project team are excluded from the dataset.

User study. On the last days leading up to the election, seven Seattle-area residents were recruited from Craigslist and offered a $20 Amazon giftcard for their participation in a lab study. Participants ranged in age from 18 to 47 ($\mu = 34.3$), all had some college experience, five were female, and they were racially diverse (two hispanic/latino, one asian pacific, two white, one black, and one multiracial). None had heard about the LVG. All but one had opinions about the ballot measures. The goal was (1) to get a sense of the perceived value of the LVG before the election had passed; (2) to learn how well users understood and valued the basic interaction mechanisms; and (3) to understand how participants reacted to the points others had submitted. Participants were not briefed about the nature of the site or our involvement in its development, and were free to interact with the site for a period of 35-40 minutes while thinking aloud. Though a researcher observed their activities and asked questions about their motivations, they were only prompted if they consistently bypassed some functionality. Audio and on-screen behavior were recorded. The first and second authors coded the data to identify aspects of the system that demonstrated ConsiderIt's limitations and affordances, or that revealed interesting tensions arising from the design. In our results, we refer to lab study participants as P1 through P7.

Survey. During registration, we asked users for permission

[4]What if a group opposing a measure instructs its members to visit a ConsiderIt application to distort the results? They have at least two options: (1) they could add a number of cons masquerading as pros and instruct their members to include them in their lists, thus crowding out legitimate pros; and/or (2) they could add a number of inane or offensive pros and instruct their members to include them in their lists, thus making the opposition look bad. However, PointRank mitigates these attacks. First, the diverse appeal metric makes it hard to increase a point's ranking without people who both support and oppose the measure including the point. One response is to instruct members to take a variety of stances, but that would act against their interest in showing overwhelming opposition to the measure. Second, the ability to click on a bar in the stance distribution enables people to see that the strong oppose group were the ones masquerading points or making inane or offensive points.

to administer a short post-election survey. 21.6% of the 250 willing users completed the survey. The average age was 42.5 ($\sigma = 17.1$), 50.3% male, overwhelmingly white, and high educational attainment (25% with postgraduate degrees). The questions were phrased as likert scale responses about their LVG experience. There may be a response bias: when we examined survey respondents' stances on two of the most ideologically polarized issues (1098 and 1053), we found that respondents exclusively took liberal stances (100%, 20/20), those who did not take the survey took mostly liberal stances (60%, 156/260), and the general election returns were 36% liberal stances on the two measures.[5] One dimension of bias in our population is thus clear: compared to the actual election returns, LVG users trended liberal; but our survey respondents were even more liberal than the LVG user population.

RESULTS

In this section, we synthesize data from our three sources to investigate how people appropriated the LVG. We start with our most important results, which quantify the extent to which users considered tradeoffs and engaged other users' points. This is followed by an analysis of survey data regarding the relative helpfulness of encountering points written by others. We then turn to data that helps us understand whether users actually shifted their opinions during their LVG experience. Finally, we draw on user study data to help provide an understanding about how users may have interpreted the considerations other voter segments were making.

Did the LVG encourage balanced consideration?

The power of pro/con lists is that they nudge the list creator to make sure they have thought about both sides of a decision. Despite this affordance, one might expect that few people participating in an open site during a contentious election would actually craft positions that acknowledge tradeoffs, given the partisan nature of our political discourse. However, **of the 678 positions that included at least one point, 41.4% of them included both a pro and a con.**[6] Discounting the 148 positions with only one point, the frequency increases to 53.0%. Moreover, in the 40 cases where users authored more than one point for a measure, 45.0% of them wrote at least one pro and con. Thus, nearly half of those who were motivated to write multiple points decided to write both supporting and opposing points. Without comparative data, we cannot say whether the pro/con list format caused people to consider both pros and cons more than they otherwise would have. We suspect that because an unbalanced list is visually salient, the nudge to explore and potentially include points that challenge one's stance is particularly strong when a user is looking at an unbalanced pro/con list, with the points that others have written beckoning in the margin. Future work should explore this in a more controlled setting.

Balanced consideration is not just about considering tradeoffs, but also about whose points are being considered. In

[5] A glitch in our survey caused us to lose the link to the actual user in the database for roughly half of survey participants, so this data only refers to those for whom we retained the link.

[6] We restrict our analysis to positions where users included at least one point (57.4%) because despite our efforts at making the inclusion functionality prominent, it was clear from our user study that some users had difficulty discovering it.

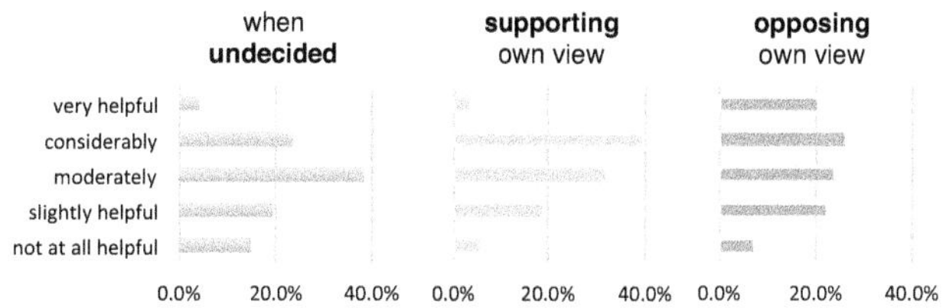

Figure 4. Helpfulness of reading points under different conditions, by fraction of survey respondents. Using pairwise 2-tailed Z-tests with $\alpha < .05$, we can reject the null hypothesis that the mean helpfulness of points is the same for those who are undecided vs. viewing opposing points, but not for those who are undecided vs. viewing supporting points ($p < 0.10$). There is no significant difference between the mean helpfulness of viewing supporting or opposing points.

ConsiderIt, a pro or con point may have been written by someone with a very different opinion on the issue. One might expect that few people would include points that were authored by people with whom they disagree. This is not the same as including both pros and cons: a given political stance can recognize both pros and cons for a given issue. For example, the recent bailout of the auto industry in the U.S. has distinct pros and cons for conservatives (preventing national security risk vs. state intervention) and liberals (saving local jobs vs. rescuing irresponsible corporations). In the LVG, **of the 599 positions where a user with a non-neutral stance included a point written by another user with a non-neutral stance, 33.7% included a point written by someone who took an opposing stance**. We suspect that the prevalence of users including points written by opposers has something to do with the pro/con list's structural nudge toward balance, as with including pros and cons. But another possibility is that ConsiderIt does not enable users to gain insight into a point author's political affiliation or stance on the issue beyond what they could infer from what the user wrote. In other words, *ConsiderIt does not provide group cues to activate political identity*. Social identity theory [39] would predict that had these cues been included, there may have been less diverse engagement because of internalized tendency to conform to a role (e.g., would someone with my political identity recognize a point written by the enemy?).

When was it useful to read others' points?

When we look at the inclusion metrics, we find that the stronger the stance that someone took, the less likely that person was to include both pros and cons (linear regression, $r^2 = .249$, $p < 10^{-12}$). Similarily, the stronger a stance, the less likely they are to include a point written by someone taking an opposite stance ($r^2 = .082$, $p < 10^{-5}$). But this does not imply that it was not helpful to read opposing points, or that it was useful to read supporting points. And it does not tell us whether undecideds actually found the points useful in establishing a position.

We turn to our survey to provide insight. We asked: (1) *"For issues you entered undecided on, how helpful was it to read the points others wrote?"* (2) *"If you were leaning in one direction, how helpful was it to read opposing points?"* (3) was the same as (2), except for supporting points. The results are shown in Figure 4. Viewing points was on average moderately helpful when undecided ($\mu = 2.83$, $\sigma = 1.08$). However, it was not as helpful on average relative to the helpfulness of viewing supporting or opposing points when already having formed some opinion. One interpretation is that those who were undecided may have been more likely to be stymied by not knowing what information to trust, whereas those who already had an opinion had a stronger basis to navigate amongst the subjective voices. Seeing opposing points was seen as the most helpful ($\mu = 3.30$, $\sigma = 1.23$), possibly because they serve as a check on one's own decision. As P5 stated, *"I would probably read the opposite opinions to see if they would help me clarify my own opinion. It's more helpful to me to read people who disagree with what I'm thinking."* The expressed utility of seeing opposing viewpoints is somewhat surprising given that the literature on selective exposure suggests that many people are challenge averse. Perhaps our survey respondents were a biased selection of diversity-seekers (to use Munson's term [35]). Interestingly, while there was no significant difference in the mean helpfulness of seeing supporting or opposing points, there was much greater variance for opposing points. This may reflect diversity in the normative preference for encountering difference (also found in a different context by [35]).

Did LVG participants shift their opinion on issues?

Despite users' proclivity to acknowledge tradeoffs, recognize points by opposition, and find reading points by others helpful, it still does not necessarily follow that the experience impacts users' opinion on the issue. This is difficult to examine, but a few sources of data together suggest that there was in fact an impact on opinion:

Stance slider changes. The stance sliders were instrumented to log any time the user manipulated them (starting midway through the deployment). Looking at the change between the last slider manipulation before and after users started including points into their pro/con list gives an indicator of the effect of pro/con list-building on opinion. In 36.7% of the positions, users only manipulated a slider before crafting their list, while 25.2% only did it afterwards. The remaining 38.3% manipulated a slider before and after creating a list. Of these, 47.4% shifted their opinion by least one stance group (e.g., from "strong" to "moderate" support), with 56.7% strengthening their stance, 30.0% moderating, and 13.3% flipping sides and strengthening (e.g., from "moderate support" to "strong oppose").

Position updates. A few users updated a position on multiple days (n=25). Of these, 36.7% strengthened their existing stances on the issue, 54.5% flipped sides, and 9.0% moderated their stances. 53.3% of these users also included at least one new point into their positions during the update, suggesting that they were not just updating their stances to reflect some external impact, such as talking to someone outside of the LVG who influenced their opinion.

Self-reported opinion changes. 46.3% of survey respondents claimed that they actually changed their stances on at least one measure while using the LVG, with 56.0% of these users saying that they switched from support to oppose or vice versa, 32.0% saying that they moderated their stances, and 12.0% saying that they strengthened their stances.

Although not unproblematic, this data together suggests that a sizable fraction of LVG users either strengthened or moderated their positions during or between their deliberations. Some even flipped their support.

What do participants look for in the considerations of others?

The system's most innovative functionality for exploring public thought is the ability to drill down into the most salient pros and cons for different stance groups by clicking on the bars of the histogram. This enables users to gain insight into the aggregated sentiment of people with whom they have different views, or to reflect on the sentiments of people who have taken a similar stance. As P4 remarked, *"It's interesting to be able to see a voting segment and [see what they value] and watch the points that slip off their mental map."* With this functionality, we hope to show people that there are other people with stances different than their own who are nevertheless "being reasonable" by explicitly recognizing the legitimacy of both pros and cons.

In an unfortunate oversight, we did not log every time that a user clicked a bar in the LVG, so we cannot report on user behavior in the deployment and must rely on user study data to gain insight into how this functionality may have been used. P3 provides an illustrative vignette. New to the state, P3 was unfamiliar with the measures. During the study, he used the LVG to form an opinion on one of the liquor sale measures. He found that the con points were actually prompting him the most to support the measure because he disagreed with what appeared to be the dominant con argument. After crafting his position, he started exploring the bar graph. *"If I was nervous about which side I'm taking, I can go to the strongly opposing, and they do give some cons there, so if I didn't see a con I liked earlier on the [position crafting page], these are the ones that people [who took a strong opposing stance] actually use"*. Thus, he could give each voting segment the chance to put their best case forward, supported by the drill-down functionality. While doing this, he noticed that one of the pros he found most convincing was listed highly in the salient points for those who strongly opposed the measure. This caused him to reconsider his stance: *"If the person who is... all the way on the oppose, still has the same opinion as you do on the pros, it makes it a whole lot stronger of a foundation for thought because even people who are fully against it are still agreeing on that pro with you. So that does make it a lot more of a valid point they're making [about opposing]."* This suggests that ConsiderIt might help people find common ground. P5 shows the converse, while exploring the bars: *"[there are] pros and cons, until you get all the way down to strong oppose where there aren't any pros at all, which is pretty unusual because even the people who are strongly supporting it have a few cons... I would probably be more swayed by uh, people who are a bit more open... I just find it a little bit strange that there's not a single pro on that."* Our data, however, is too sparse to claim that this affordance for evaluating how seriously to take different voter segments is likely to be discovered and exploited in the wild.

DISCUSSION

Here, we step back and examine some of the problematic aspects of ConsiderIt and what we believe are promising next steps. We first discuss the tension between trust and identity when users engage points written by strangers without an organizational affiliation. We then discuss aspects of point redundancy, including further techniques for encouraging users to factor other peoples' thoughts into their own opinions, and then scaling ConsiderIt-style deliberations though clustering and collaborative synthesis.

Whom and what do I trust?

Although statements of personal principle were common, preliminary analysis indicates that at least half of the points submitted to the LVG contained some kind of potentially verifiable statement of fact, such as references to numeric data, external information sources, the textual content of the measure, or specific predictions about potential outcomes of adoption or rejection. The feedback we received during the user study and in the survey all suggest that the biggest challenge users faced was evaluating the trustworthiness of these claims. This is a recurrent issue with nearly all "crowd" powered approaches [1, 26]. Making sense of claims seriously constrained the ultimate utility of the LVG as *an information resource*. We believe that an important future direction is to enable users to link information sources explicitly to individual points to allow fact checking. The platform providers can thus avoid accusation of strong-handed moderation [49] by not making a value judgment about the validity of the source—anyone could decide for him- or herself whether a link to a pundit's blog is a reliable source or not.

Tightly coupled with trust is identity. Almost immediately after raising the issue of trust, user study participants would comment that they wanted to know more about the point author. This is consistent with social translucence, which suggests that providing people with more information about other online users can help them make judgements about who and what to trust and how to engage [11]. Recall that it was not possible to learn more about point authors beyond their name. The obvious implication is to allow an author to flesh out a profile, and enable other users to explore the stances that a point author took in the LVG. But this would undermine our design decision to omit such information based on the hypothesis that the lack of information about political affiliation helps nudge people to consider the points of diverse others. The design implications we draw from social translucence [11] and social identity theory [39] thus appear to be in conflict here. Future research might examine the differences between versions of ConsiderIt that are identical except in their respective degrees of identity salience, to tease out the consequences of the tension between listening to diverse others and evaluating claims. This is important, as some researchers are creating interfaces that highlight ideological differences rather than downplay them [17]. We recommend that future ConsiderIt deployments enable people to fill out profile information so that users can get a sense of personality and life perspective, but steer clear of calling specific attention to political affiliations.

Self-expression, redundancy, and scale

Given that we are asking the "crowd" to generate pro/con considerations, one might expect a proliferation of duplicate points that make it difficult to identify unique considerations. While we have yet to complete an in-depth content analysis to identify the prevalence and nature of redundancy, we can see from the relationship between point additions and inclusions over time that **users self-regulated: 50% of all points were contributed by day 15, whereas it took until day 30 to reach 50% of all point inclusions** (Figure 3).

But we have found redundancy to be a more complex phenomena than it appears. First, "duplicate" points can add value by elaborating on an existing argument, reframing it in less (or more) inflammatory language to appeal to different audiences, or revising it for clarity. Second, there is a tension between expressiveness and redundancy: in a study of opinion influence in online discussion, Price et al. found that being in the presence of arguments only indirectly influenced post-discussion opinion by influencing the arguments that the respective participant chose to express themselves [39].

We draw an implication from this tension: if we provide more opportunities for users to put what other people are saying into their own words, participants may be more likely to incorporate the thoughts of others into their own opinions. We see two relevant extensions to ConsiderIt. First, when users include a point in their lists, ConsiderIt might prompt them to rephrase the point to their liking, starting from the original text. Second, taking a position might include the option of writing a summative position statement that weaves together the pros and cons to explain the user's stance.

While the ability to support self-expression through rephrasing might help reduce redundancy, further techniques are necessary if we are to scale ConsiderIt-style deliberation beyond what we attracted in the LVG. We see two broad steps in moving forward. The first step is to cluster points thematically via crowdsourcing or NLP, building a network of points linked by the semantic distance between them. This would allow us to better serve a diversity of points during position crafting, as well as enabling a range of recommendation opportunities, such as recommending a con point about the decision's impact on education after the user includes a pro point about education. Creating these similarity graphs is one step toward *synthetic deliberation*. In order to communicate at scale, we believe we will ultimately need to craft approaches in which users band together to express a larger point. For example, with clustered points, we could ask authors who have made very similar arguments to try to collaboratively merge their points. Or we could ask users to summarize clusters of points. Regardless, the design space around these synthetic mechanisms is vast and challenging; even wikis are confusing to many users. By first developing the core deliberative mechanisms of ConsiderIt, we feel we are in a better position now to extend them in potentially confusing but high value directions.

CONCLUSION

Our primary contribution is a novel technique that extends Franklin's pro/con technique for personal deliberation into the realm of public deliberation. ConsiderIt augments personal deliberation by enabling users to adopt points others have contributed, to contribute new points in turn, and to use the results of these personal deliberations to expose salient points. People can publicly deliberate and reflect on the thoughts of others without emphasizing direct discussion. Though we developed ConsiderIt for a regionally-focused election, ConsiderIt may be applicable for a wider range of organizations seeking to engage loosely organized publics of citizens, employees, and customers.

Our secondary contribution is to demonstrate ConsiderIt's utility for deliberation amongst the general public. We take the stance that a strong aggregate indicator of utility is a system's discretionary use in a real deployment. Users spent more than ten minutes on average at the LVG, many of them returning multiple times. Our claim about utility is simply that the nature of usage suggests our approach finds a sweet spot in a challenging design space, given that discretionary use by the general public has been an elusive target for deliberative systems. Beyond demonstrating discretionary use, we showed that LVG users often engaged in normatively desirable activities such as crafting positions that included both pros and cons and recognizing points written by people who do not agree with them. Still, there were some clear challenges for users, like the ability to decide what to trust.

Finally, we have highlighted opportunities for controlled experimentation to better understand the design decisions, such as whether the pro/con list structure itself actually nudges people to consider tradeoffs more than a simple list of considerations. More broadly, we designed ConsiderIt to provide extra support for deliberative communication, but tried to accommodate other communication styles, such as the communitarian and liberal individualist. Future research might help more precisely characterize the appeal of ConsiderIt to those adopting different communicative styles.

ACKNOWLEDGEMENTS

Thanks to our partners at Seattle City Club, Diane Douglas and Jessica Jones; Andrew Hamada and Michael Toomim for help with design; Sam Kaufman and Alena Benson for help with the user study; and Scott Bateman, Eric Baumer, Michael Bernstein, Amy Bruckman, Scott Golder, Kurt Luther, David McDonald, and three anonymous reviewers for feedback on the paper. This work is supported by NSF grant IIS 0966929.

REFERENCES

1. B. Adler et al. Assigning trust to wikipedia content. In *WikiSym*, 2008.
2. C. Anderson. Deliberative, agonistic, and algorithmic audiences. *Int. J. of Communication*, 5, 2011.
3. B. Bailey et al. A case study of a grassroots innovation pipeline within a large software company. In *CHI*, 2010.
4. E. Baumer et al. Fostering critical and creative thinking about metaphor in political blogs. In *CHI*, 2010.
5. Bell, W. and Labaree, L (eds). *Mr. Franklin: A Selection from His Personal Letters*. Yale University Press, 1954.
6. I. Beschastnikh et al. Wikipedian Self-Governance in Action. In *ICWSM*, 2008.
7. J. Conklin et al. 15 years on from gibis. In *HYPERTEXT*, 2001.
8. L. Dahlberg. Democracy via cyberspace. *New Media & Society*, 3(2), 2001.
9. N. Diakopoulos et al. Videolyzer: quality analysis of online informational video for bloggers and journalists. In *CHI*, 2009.
10. J. Dryzek. *Liberals, Critics, Contestations*. Oxford Press, 2002.
11. T. Erickson and W. A. Kellogg. Social translucence. *TOCHI*, 7(1), 2000.
12. S. Faridani et al. Opinion space: a scalable tool for browsing online comments. *CHI*, 2010.
13. J. Fishkin. Strategies of Public Consultation. *Integrated Assessment*, 6(2), 2006.
14. A. Forte et al. Increasing Decentralization in Wikipedia Governance. In *HICSS*, 2008.
15. N. Fraser. A Contribution to the Critique of Actually Existing Democracy. *Social Text*, (25/26), 1990.
16. D. Freelon. Analyzing online political discussion using three models of democratic communication. *New Media & Society*, 12(7), 2010.
17. M. Gamon et al. Using Blogs to Provide Context for News Articles. In *ICWSM*, 2008.
18. R. Garrett. Echo chambers online. *J. of CMC*, 14(2), 2009.
19. J. Gastil. *Political Communication and Deliberation*. Sage, 2008.
20. J. Habermas. *Structural Transformation of the Public Sphere*. MIT Press, 1991.
21. S. Hansen et al. Wikipedia and the possibility of rational discourse. *The Information Society*, 25(1), 2009.
22. B. Huberman. *The Laws of the Web*. MIT Press, 2001.
23. S. Isenmann et al. IBIS: a convincing concept . . . but a lousy instrument? In *DIS*, 1997.
24. S. Iyengar et al. Deliberative public opinion in presidential primaries. In *Voice and Citizenship Conference*, 2004.
25. N. Jankowski et al. *The Prospects for Political Renewal Through the Internet*, chapter Internet-based political discourse. 2002.
26. A. Kittur et al. Crowdsourcing user studies with Mechanical Turk. In *CHI*, 2008.
27. S. Knobloch-Westerwick et al. Looking the other way. *Comm. Research*, 36(3), 2009.
28. T. Kobayashi et al. Selective exposure in political web browsing. *Information, Communication & Society*, 12(6), 2009.
29. K. Kraemer et al. Computer-based systems for cooperative work and group decision making. *ACM Comput. Surv.*, 20, 1988.
30. T. Kriplean et al. Supporting Active Listening and Grounding on the Web through Restatement. In *CSCW Horizons*, 2011.
31. P. Lange. Commenting on comments. In *Society for Applied Anthropology*, 2007.
32. K. Luther et al. An online collaboration environment for citizen scientists. In *CHI*, 2009.
33. M. MacKuen et al. Resolute partisanship or reflective deliberation. *Am. J. of Pol. Sci.*, 54(2), 2010.
34. P. Muhlberger. The virtual agora project. *J. of Public Deliberation*, 1(1), 2005.
35. S. Munson et al. Presenting diverse political opinions. In *CHI*, 2010.
36. D. Mutz. *Hearing the Other Side*. Cambridge, 2006.
37. S. Park et al. Newscube: Delivering multiple aspects of news to mitigate media bias. In *CHI*, 2009.
38. W. Parker. *Teaching Democracy*. Columbia, 2003.
39. V. Price et al. Normative and informational influences in online political discussions. *Comm. Theory*, 1(16), 2006.
40. D. Schuler. *Online Deliberation: Design, Research, & Practice*, chapter Online civic deliberation with E-liberate. 2009.
41. B. Shanks et al. *Online Deliberation: Design, Research, & Practice*, chapter A module for parliamentary procedure. 2009.
42. F. Shipman et al. Formality considered harmful. *JCSCW*, 8(4), 1999.
43. S. Shum. *Visualizing Argumentation*. Springer, 2003.
44. S. Shum. Cohere: Towards web 2.0 argumentation. In *COMMA*, 2008.
45. A. Sukumaran et al. Normative influences on thoughtful online participation. In *CHI*, 2011.
46. C. Sunstein. *Republic.com 2.0*. Princeton Univ. Press, 2009.
47. M. Trice. *The Ethics of Emerging Media*, chapter How We Comment on Web Journalism. 2011.
48. K. Wahl-Jorgensen. Letters to the editor as a forum for public deliberation. *Crit. Stud. in Media Comm.*, 18(3), 2001.
49. S. Wright. Government-run Fora: Moderation, Censorship and the Shadow of Control. *Brit. J. of Politics and Int. Relations*, 8, 2006.

Barter - Mechanism Design for a Market Incented Wisdom Exchange

Dawei Shen
MIT Media Lab
Massachusetts Institute of Technology
dawei@mit.edu

Marshall Van Alstyne
MIT Center for Digital Business
School of Management
Boston University
marshall@mit.edu

Andrew Lippman
MIT Media Lab
Massachusetts Institute of Technology
lip@media.mit.edu

Hind Benbya
Montpellier Business School
Benbya@gmail.com

ABSTRACT
Information markets benefit the communities they serve by facilitating electronic distributed exchange and enhancing knowledge sharing, innovation, and productivity. This research explores innovative market mechanisms to build incentives while encouraging pro-social behavior. A key advantage of this study is a direct appeal to theories of information economics and macro policies to market design. We built and deployed a web-based software platform called Barter at several universities. Preliminary analysis of user data helps test information market effectiveness and illustrate effects of various market interventions. We present our design framework, demonstrate why such an architecture provides sustainable incentives, and list key findings learned in the process of system deployment.

Author Keywords
Knowledge markets; Information markets; Mechanism design; Organizational design; Incentive design; Information economics

ACM Classification Keywords
H.5.2 Information Interfaces and Presentation: Miscellaneous

General Terms
Design; Management.

INTRODUCTION
Knowledge and innovation represent significant organizational resources and directly affect organizational success and competitiveness. First-generation attempts to manage knowledge and support innovation relied mainly on centralized Knowledge Management Systems (KMS). Despite their potential, the top-down approach to both content elicitation and validation deployed in these systems has left a large community base with unsolved knowledge problems [2]. The emerging literature on open innovation and crowd-sourcing demonstrates the value of openness for innovation and problem solving[19]. But in addition to benefits, it highlights difficulties in motivating participation[13][11][1].We believe an important reason for participation failure is faulty incentive structures. Members of an organization lack the motivation to participate and share information, especially given their existing work commitments and reporting hierarchies. In other cases, the competitive culture of the organization discourages members from sharing knowledge; questions can be interpreted as a sign of weakness; or people believe information sharing implies giving up competitive advantage. These practical challenges motivate the research presented here.

The importance of incentive design goes beyond the scope of organizational knowledge management. Pervasive web and mobile platforms gather the "wisdom of crowds" [19]. Web 2.0 systems encourage self expression and promote collaboration [16]. "Peer production" refers to the aggregate work of a decentralized community [16]. A cookbook of community design properties has been proposed to facilitate "collective intelligence" [12]. The abundance and convenience of information create an unprecedented information ecology among human beings. A flurry of platforms have been invented to realize these crowdsourcing models, including social bookmarking (reddit.com), review/rating exchange (yelp.com, Amazon.com), Q & A (quora.com), and task completion (Mechanical Turk) to name a few. New systems appear constantly on the horizon.

These systems are predicated on incentives: users need to feel motivated to spend limited time and attention sharing knowledge with others. Success therefore depends on sustainable incentives. People contribute for a variety of reasons: altruism, building reputations, gaining expertise, fun, compensation, etc. Broadly speaking, these fall into "social incentives" and "material incentives." While many existing platforms rely heavily on social incentives, few explore material incentives. When they do, users may not perceive fair rewards in proportion to contribution. Fixed fees and managerial hierarchies employing top down centrally planned incentives, neglect the power of the crowd itself to determine appropriate rewards. As a result, market design has much to offer organizations whose earlier choices failed to deliver long-term effectiveness, fairness, and stability.

Our contribution is to apply economics and mechanism design to four problems: (1) Can we shift users from non-participants to participants? (2) Can we increase activity among those who do participate? (3) Can we cause information to be created? (4) Can we value this information? As a beta test, our description of Barter does not yet provide complete answers to all questions. Rather, we will show how to incorporate economics and mechanism design into system architecture for questions one and two. We then provide preliminary data to illustrate answers to questions three and four.

This paper is organized as follows. Section 2 develops our theoretical foundation. We then focus on applying this framework to designing an information market, covered in detail in Section 3 . Based on this design, Section 4 discusses software deployment. Section 5 provides lessons learned from analyzing user data. We conclude and point to future directions in Section 6 .

RESEARCH STRATEGY

There are many starting points for designing incentives. But, whether the levers are social or material, it helps to first ask which specific behaviors we wish to motivate. Designing an information market should depend on behaviors firms want to promote. As a starting point, we suggest desirable behaviors include (1) motivation to participate in the market. This is sometimes called "market thickness" as people need others with whom to trade [9]. (2) The market should motivate sharing and disclosure. As noted, there are many reasons why keeping information private can provide strategic advantage or why sharing might simply be too bothersome. (3) Design should also motivate efficient allocation of resources and attention. Time spent sharing gossip might be better spent sharing insights or even working solo. (4) Motivation should promote idea development even when others can free ride. (5) De-motivation caused by theft and fraud should be avoided. Thus design should include a measure of "market safety." (6) Finally, apart from individual motivation, design should enable regulation and motivate those responsible for running the system to do so for the benefit of the community.

These challenges inspire us to reconsider and compare how we human beings organize our production and wealth distribution in the real world: we have created a product-service economy with market forces that guide the allocation of resources and direct human power. The goal shifts away from design of an IT or a knowledge management system to design of a complete knowledge economy. The shift resembles the transition from a centrally planned system to one that is market based. One view characterizes this problem differently:

> "Managing an information economy within the firm can improve forecasting, innovation, and productivity. ... Markets cause resources to speak up and self-identify. Markets provide the framework to arbitrage the gap between problem and opportunity. To get these benefits, executives must bring market forces to bear within the firm. The rules, the rewards, and the running of internal markets differ from those of a hierarchy." [3, p. 67]

In our system, pivotal factors of such a decentralized economy include social factors such as status, reputation, and an ability to publicly acknowledge others members of the community. Economic factors include currency, a "Federal Reserve", prices, and transfer payments. Though stumbling occasionally, a well-established economy sustains its own growth, fairness, and efficiency.

Several branches of economic theory will provide a theoretical foundation for this research and guide the design of an information market. These include:

Economics of Information A classic problem of information asymmetry is motivating one party to disclose information another does not know. Another problem is trading information as a "commodity". When information is non-excludable with zero reproduction costs, how shall we design a market that accounts for these distortions and prevents market failure[5]?

Two-Sided Market Theory describes how to promote adoption of a technology standard and stimulate third-party development by subsidizing user/developer network effects. For knowledge management, this tells us how to get users to adopt a new system and how to subsidize content creation and content consumption so employees themselves add continuous value [17].

Price Theory describes how markets efficiently allocate resources across an entire economy using only private information. It also tells how markets supply missing goods. For knowledge management, this is critical in getting people to produce valuable knowledge for others but only when this is more valuable than what they are already doing. It can also tell us how to value intangibles [20, 10].

Quantity Theory of Money describes, as a special case of macroeconomics, how to manage a supply of value – money, credit, or points – to achieve economic vitality and growth by choosing expansionary or contractionary policies. For knowledge management, this shows how to stimulate and regulate trade volume in the firm's internal knowledge economy[8, 7].

Financial markets theory provides rules and guidelines for securitizing information products so they can be exchanged on a secondary market [14]. The theory also covers computerized market-making algorithms [6].

In addition to the economic theories listed above, several other research fields also play crucial roles in the design process of an information market and determine its overall success. For example, we apply Natural Language Processing (NLP) when necessary to compare, sort or index text content users create. Social network modeling and analysis helps understand the dynamics of social interactions and how information propagates through the network. Information presentation and visualization is particularly important when we design dashboards and gadgets to monitor or control global and personal economic activities. Another closely related area is user interface design, or more broadly, human-computer interaction (HCI), which determines the usability and user experiences of the software system.

SYSTEM ARCHITECTURE

This sections presents a detailed market framework and illustrates key concepts and design choices by using diagrams and screenshots from the software.

Overview of Barter

What is Barter? Broadly speaking, Barter creates an information economy inside an organization.

- Barter is a market-incented wisdom exchange, or simply speaking, an information market, designed for organizations and communities to maximize the creation, use, and sharing of information among members;
- Barter deploys multiple market sub-type to address different organizational challenges;
- Barter provides a mechanism to monitor and govern the economy, and apply macroeconomic policies to influence its operation;
- Barter can measure the value of information and provide long-term sustainable incentives to reward information contributors and encourage participation;
- Barter provides solutions to several problems that commonly happen to new IT platforms using innovative market-based approaches. Examples of these problems include early elicitation of participation, system abuse and fraud, system growth and self-improvement.

We find it helpful to compare Barter side-by-side with the U.S. economy to understand how different components of the platform operate, as shown in Table 1. It is worth emphasizing that fine-grained currency controls enable certain functions that are not feasible in our real-world economy, as explained in detail in subsequent subsections.

Design Principles of Barter

Barter is a market of a special type – an information market – where users exchange ideas the value of which are difficult to judge prior to disclosure. However, Barter first needs to adhere to general principles of market design, as summarized in Fig.1. These four principles should be satisfied in order to have almost any type of information market run stably and efficiently [9][18].

Next, when the exchanged goods in a market are information products, the following characteristics of information need to be carefully taken into consideration when designing Barter, as illustrated in Table 2. Otherwise, the market is prone to failure.

System Architecture

Before introducing how each individual market or module works on Barter, we first present the overall system architecture, as depicted in Fig.2.

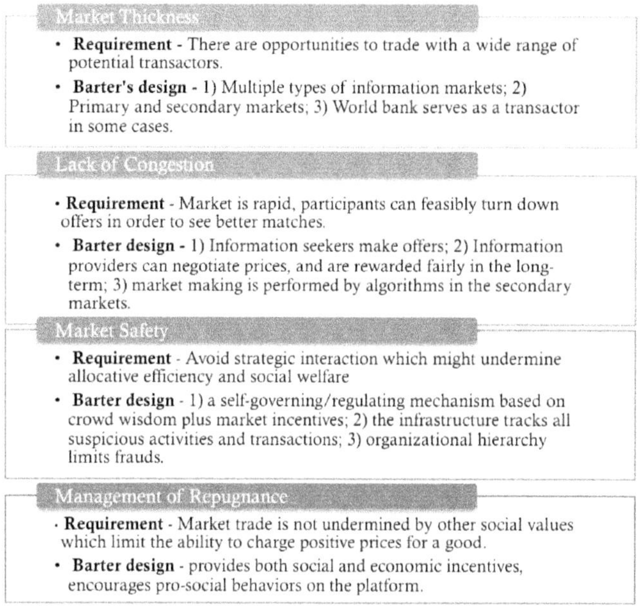

Figure 1. Market design principles implemented in Barter.

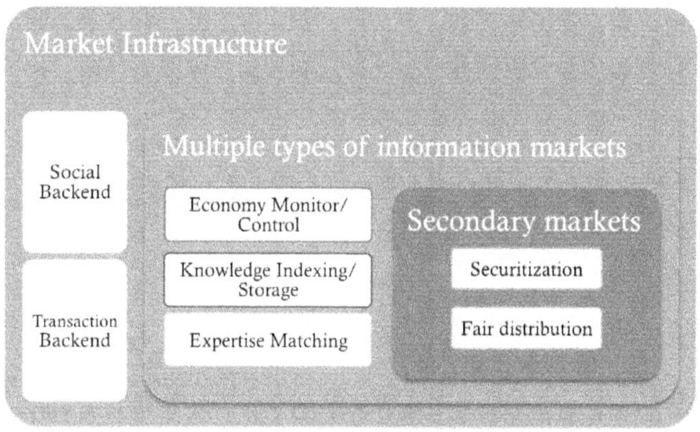

Figure 2. System architecture of the Barter market platform.

The infrastructure that underlies and supports Barter involves two critical modules: a social network backend and a transaction backend.

In the middle layer lies the core of the system - a suite of information markets of various types, designed to satisfy different organizational needs. Users on Barter perform most of their market activities through the suite of markets. Three important modules, 1) Economy Monitor/Control module, 2) Knowledge indexing/storage module, and 3) Expertise matching module, are designed and built as peripheral modules around the suite of markets, and are instrumental in managing information and maintaining the health of the economy.

On top of the system hierarchy is an interesting but powerful layer called secondary markets of information, also introduced in Table 1. It is built on top of two mechanisms - 1) information securitization and 2) fair distribution. Secondary information markets address some very significant challenges

Table 1. Comparison between U.S. economy and the Barter information economy

U.S. Economy	Barter Information Economy
Currency – U.S. $	Barter implements its own virtual currency system. A unit of currency is named a "Yuanbao". It is universally accepted and circulated inside Barter. Users can exchange "Yuanbao" for either knowledge or physical rewards. Advanced features include serialization and tracing.
Markets for products & services	Barter implements multiple markets types to meet various organizational needs. Markets include 1) Q&A, 2) document exchange, 3) ideas, 4) predictions, 5) services, 6) news, 7) auctions, 8) bug fixes, 9) fraud detection, etc. These are referred to as "primary information markets".
Federal Reserve Bank & monetary policies	Barter establishes an entity, dubbed the "World Bank" to track issuance and recall of currency. Dashboards help the "chief economist" monitor and understand the status of the economy. Another set of economic tools adjusts parameters of the economy to improve its operation and running.
Organizations versus Individuals	Users on Barter can form groups, and perform intra-group or inter-group market activities. More advanced group structures include "guilds", where users earn membership and "cliques" where membership is by permission.
Regulatory bodies	Barter also uses self-governing and self-regulating crowds that are rewarded for community activities such as policing members and cleaning content.
Securitization and secondary markets (Equity, Commodity, Bond markets, and Derivative markets)	On Barter, information products can also be securitized and traded on a secondary market. Securitization applies to multiple markets, such as the Q&A market, document exchange, and ideas. Trading increases market thickness, helps sort and organize information by its value, and improves information timeliness and quality by emphasizing ownership. Securitization gives people a share of the future value their ideas create, which alleviate the free-rider problem for idea generation stated in the research strategy (4).

Table 2. Challenges of Information Products and Barter's Solutions

Characteristics of Information Products	Barter's Design and Solutions
Information and innovation has spillover effects, and is non-excludable	1. The spillover effects should not be treated negatively in the context of organizational knowledge sharing and innovation creation. A more important issue is to reward information creators fairly; 2. We have devised algorithms to track information reuse, trace back contributors, and reward them fairly. 3. We encourage pro-social behaviors to reward information providers, such as tipping.
Information is costly to create and costless to replicate	1. The fair distribution mechanism guarantees that original information creators get continuously rewarded for providing valuable information; 2. A market-based approach for the detection of fraud and copyright infringement; 3. Several mechanisms are in place to protect information providers. For example, answerers in the Q&A market can choose to hide their answers until the question expires.
Evaluation of information requires accessing non-excludable information first	1. Rewards are offered by information seekers upfront, and are frozen by the World Bank to enforce payment and allocation. 2. Information seekers get penalized for ignoring to judge information quality and distribute rewards, and charged for extending the expiration time.

Figure 3. Types of information markets supported in Barter

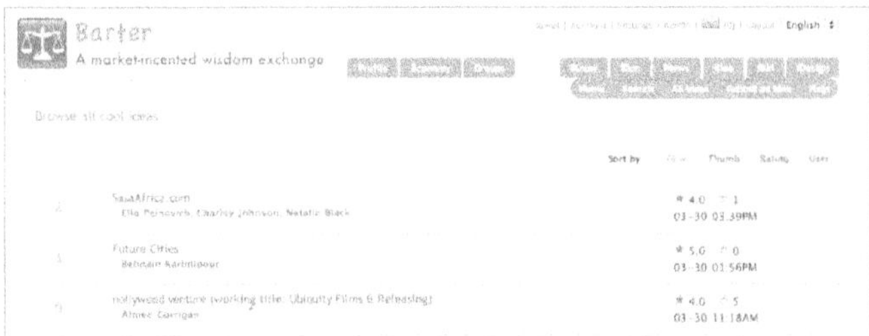

Figure 4. A Barter screen shot - A user is viewing ideas submitted to the iDea market; the tab bar at the top displays markets she can access.

such as the lack of incentives to spend or insufficient market liquidity.

In the following subsections, we first introduce the functions and mechanisms of different markets types, and then discuss each individual module in the system diagram.

Multiple Types of Information Markets

Various types of information markets are the primary interfaces to end-users. An organization deploys these markets (or a subset of them) to address different challenges. A list of different types of markets with their names and brief descriptions are illustrated in Fig.3. These markets are referred to as primary information markets, as opposed to "secondary markets" when we discuss about securitization and fair distribution in future.

Fig.4 displays a screen shot of the Barter platform. The tab bar on the top-right shows a list of information markets the user can access and participate in. Two dashboards selected from the "Global Economy" monitoring panel are shown in Fig.5, which illustrate the transaction volume categorized by market types, and transaction types.

Design Market

The purpose of the design market is to empower Barter to keep improving itself by having new features, bug fixes, and

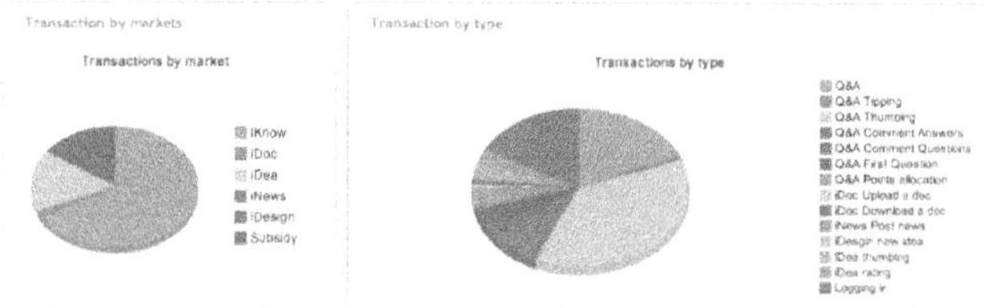

Figure 5. Two "global economy" dashboards displaying pie charts of total transaction volume by a) market types, and b) transaction types.

detecting market defects through the market mechanism itself. We also call it "design for self-design market".

The crowd of users collectively helps design the market and prioritizes tasks. When a user discovers a bug, a market loophole, or needs an extra feature, she can submit it to the iDesign market and offer a certain number of points as rewards to developers if her idea gets implemented. Other users can vote on the idea to change its priority. If they deeply like the idea and want the idea to be realized sooner, they can supplement more points to the pool of rewards.

Product Auction Market

iBid is an auction market where users can exchange their virtual currency for physical products or services they enjoy in real lives. Any user can post an item for sale and other users bid on the item using their "Yuanbao", as they do on eBay with real money. iBid provides a mechanism for users to acquire points when they run out of points, or cash out points for physical rewards. We need to emphasize two important roles the product auction market plays which are critical to the entire information market framework:

1. It provides the organization's management with an important tool to offer long-term sustainable monetary incentives to the platform. The auction market isolates the monetary incentives from unnecessary details of information creation;
2. It provides an important mechanism to take virtual currency out of circulation when the "chief economist" exerting contractionary monetary policies.

Fig.6 displays a screenshot of the product auction market. As seen from the list of products on sale, users are creative in choosing what products/services to sell.

Market Fraud and Fraud Market

A companion of any type of market is market fraud, which jeopardizes the market safety as highlighted above. Possible types of market fraud include

Money laundering For example, a user transfers points to another user by asking a simple question and allocating all points to the other user who just provides a naive answer. The goal is to 1) boost the user's expertise status for related tags, or 2) turn unearned points into earned points;

Market abuse Users leave garbage comments or information to earn system subsidies for certain activities;

Copyright infringement There are two possible cases - 1) upload copyrighted materials in the document exchange, or

Figure 6. A screen shot of the product auction market.

2) directly plagiarize other users' content and paste without acknowledgement.

All these types of market fraud were evident in our research deployment, where we did not deploy a governing and regulatory mechanism. To clean and prevent future market fraud, we have designed a market-based mechanism, i.e., the fraud market. Detection of market fraud is sourced to the crowd. When a user detects a potential fraud or inappropriate contents, she can red flag it. When flagged enough times, a case will be moved to the fraud market, where users can vote on whether the case actually involves a fraud. When the case is closed and a verdict is made, users who vote on the right side will be rewarded. The offender gets penalized so that she experiences both economic losses and social damages on reputation. Speaking in Information Economics terms, fraud market is another example of accurate signaling and screening, which echos our research strategy (5).

Other information markets

In this section, we briefly explain the roles and functions of the other major types of information markets.

Q&A Market (iKnow) is an information market that allows users to ask questions to the Barter community and reap a profit if their questions become popular. Each time a user asks a question, she needs to create an associated reward and an expiration date by which all answers must be received. When the question expires, the asker can review received answers and divide up reward funds based on the quality of the responses. The asker can also rate each answer so that users know the quality of provided answers. Other users can vote on answers, and if they find an answer really helpful, they can tip the answerer with extra funds.

Document exchange(iDoc) is an exchange that allows users to share documents with the Barter community. Other members of Barter can rate the documents, and pay a one-time fee in order to download or view what others have posted. When a user tries to post and share an important and original document, she can set the price of the download that each user must pay when accessing the document. If a document contains an idea which gives rise to other related contents on Barter, the original contributor receives a kickback for posting the original document.

News Market (iNews) is an information market that allows users to post articles, news, or announcements to the Barter community and reap a profit if their postings become popular. Members of the Barter community can vote on all submissions, and the popularity of a posting snowballs over time as top trending posts work their way to the iNews front page. When a user posts an article, news item, or personal anecdote, she needs to allocate for the posting an initial value (Budget) and a set number of points that are given to users who read her story (Points Per View, or PPV). It is helpful to think of PPV as an advertising cost paid for each user: when people read her story for the first time, the amount of points set as PPV is deducted from the user's Budget. When the Budget runs out, the post expires. A posting's Budget will increase if it would attract many users.

Idea Market (iDea) is a marketplace for innovation, and for matching solutions to problems. A user can either submit a standalone idea or submit one in response to another user's request. A member of an organization might have innovative ideas on the organization's operations, products or activities. She can submit her ideas on the idea market, get them examined, validated and improved by other members, and receive rewards when an idea gets promoted by senior management or even adopted.

The iDea market is used by two entrepreneurship courses at the authors' university as class tools for students to exchange venture ideas and do cross-evaluation.

All Q&A interactions, documents, news items, and ideas are tagged by both original information providers and the entire community as well, for knowledge indexing, searching and storage. Users get rewarded for cleaning or improving tags.

Backend & Peripheral Modules

Social Network Backend

Social features are instrumental in getting users attracted and engaged. On Barter, a user manages her profile and controls what information is accessible to other users. Users can establish friendship and form communities among themselves if they share similar interests or job functions.

The formed social graph constantly updates itself with new market activities. For instance, a user can make her question or document private by sharing it only with her friends network or within a particular group. Conversely, the system has the capability to tell a user who she interacts with most in the market so that a friendship link can be potentially established, users who share similar interests and interact more can form a group.

Fig.7 displays an interactive tool on Barter for social navigation with a user-centric view. Attributes of the visualization

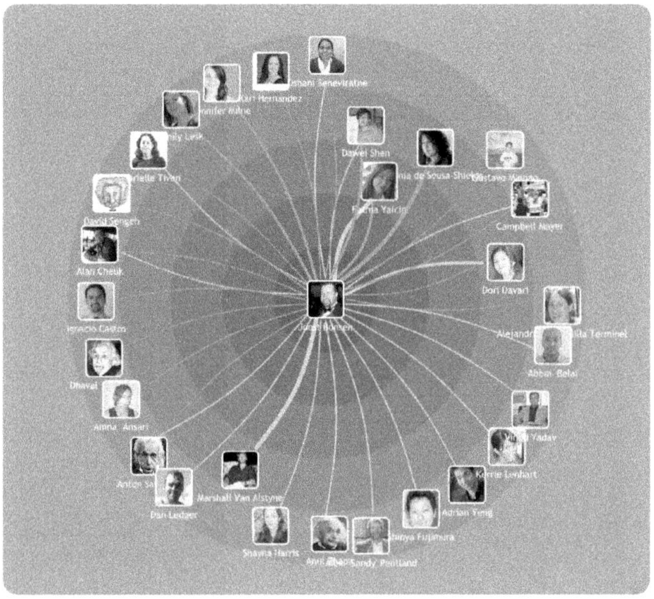

Figure 7. Social Navigation View.

are interpreted as follows: (a) Radius: frequency of interactions in the market; (b) Thickness of links: amount of points exchanged; (c) Color of links: inflow vs. outflow of points; (d) Popup list: past interactions in the market; (e) Buttons shown when a user's icon is clicked: ask the user a question or go to the target user's self-centric view.

When Barter is deployed as an internal market tool for an organization, organization hierarchy is implied in the social network in addition to user-formed connections. No user on such a socially bounded platform can act as an absolute stranger. Thus, we can expect that users exhibit socially responsible behaviors, which in turn reduces the risk of users gaming the system and sabotaging the market fairness.

Transaction Backend

Barter's transaction backend has two prominent features: 1) currency serialization, and 2) global bank accounts.

Each unit of currency has its own unique serial number, and has its assigned owner. Its creation and issuance is handled by a special entity in Barter called the "World Bank". The "World Bank" is treated as a special user, who also maintains a bank account. Transactions can occur either between two users, or between a user and the "World Bank". Any currency transferred from a user to the "World Bank" effectively jumps out of circulation, and reduces the global money supply. New currency is created when the "World Bank" needs to transfer currency to other users but without enough balance in the bank account.

The serialization of currency allows us to conveniently track the flow of currency in the economy such as currency's turnover rate and total supply. It also allows us to realize advanced currency controls such as the expiration of currency. Expiration of currency, when managed properly, is a mechanism to encourage user spending in the economy. It is also a revenue stream for the "World Bank" so that it has the budget to fund system subsidies. When transactions occur, the owner of corresponding currency units gets changed, and the expiration date gets reset according to predetermined rules.

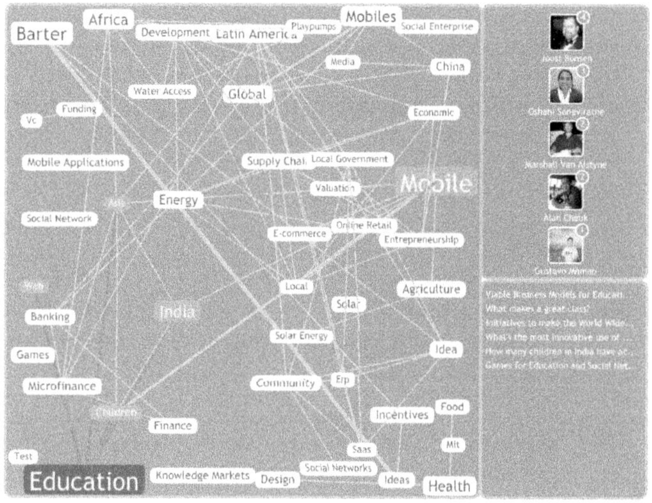

Figure 8. Expertise Tag Cloud and Expertise Matching.

Expertise matching

Barter keeps accumulating and mining historic data about a user's activities in the market, including questions she asks or answers, documents she shares and downloads, ideas she contributes or solicits, etc. "True" expertise tags are synthesized and displayed on the user's profile. Barter is able to accurately measure the value a user has created on a particular area (tag).

Fig.8 shows an interactive tool on Barter named "Expertise Cloud". On the left panel is a tag cloud that consists of the most popular tags in the system. Tags are positioned following a modified force-directed algorithm. Links between tags represent concurrence. Linked tags get highlighted when a tag is clicked. The top-right panel displays a list of experts for the clicked tag, sorted by scores, and the bottom-right panel displays a list of items in the market tagged by the clicked keyword. This is a visualization tool on Barter for exploring popular topics inside the organization and matching top experts to problem domains.

Here, Information Economics helps solve the disclosure problem as stated in our research strategy (2) . Barter helps knowledge suppliers "signal" their expertise via their earned expertise points. So they do know what they claim to know. Barter helps knowledge seekers "screen" for good content by helping filter on the highest rated content and the highest earning experts.

Discussion on Incentives/Motivation

Sustained participation in online communities and markets is driven by mixed and heterogeneous motives. They generally fall into three categories: (1) Social rewards include peer-recognition and professional reputation,(2) intellectual rewards include learning and problem-solving and (3) material rewards include virtual points, money and a variety of other benefits[3][4].

Users on Barter can spend their virtual currency either on information they need or on tangible rewards through the auction market. Barter adopts a floating-price mechanism. Information seekers raise offered rewards for critical issues that require more efforts to provide. Information owners choose whether to supply it given the current price, or directly negotiate with information seekers. The auction market provides an organization's management a layer to isolate material incentives from classifying and evaluating knowledge created inside the platform. Exchanges of all types of information products are denominated in virtual currency, the value of which is determined separately by market users through their activities in each market.

Instead of offering a one-time lump-sum reward, an organization can distribute material rewards through the auction market in a continuous and strategic way. Depending on several key economic indicators, such as user activities, price indexes and currency supplies, the "chief economist" of Barter can determine the density and value of the products posted in the auction market. While used to provide material incentives, the auction market is also an important mechanism to stimulate or stabilize the entire knowledge economy.

Applying multiple information markets provides users with plenty of knowledge products to trade and enhances market thickness. In the early stage of opening the platform, organizational management can seed the market by requesting information via these markets and pushing more rewards to the auction market. It is explicitly the seed and subsidize strategy of two-sided networks, which helps address the motivation problem listed as our research strategy (1).

METHODOLOGY: SYSTEM DEPLOYMENT & EXPERIMENTAL SETUP

Barter is a web-based software platform that realizes the information market designed in our research. New features are continuously developed and added to the platform. Barter has been deployed, or is being deployed, in a few different environments, primarily in university classrooms, including

- About 550 students at a french business school in a distance-learning program (French site);
- About 330 students/researchers from three U.S. universities used Barter as both class tools and daily knowledge sharing platforms (U.S. site);
- Two entrepreneurship classes at the authors' university used Barter - primarily the "iDea" market - for students to exchange venture ideas.

In these deployments, users started with certain number of points assigned to their bank accounts. We do not ask users to engage in any particular activity attentively. Barter simply serves as a day-to-day tool for students to exchange knowledge, share documents, contribute ideas, post news, etc., following the underlying market rules.

Incentive design, especially the translation of virtual points to meaningful rewards, is important to the deployment and

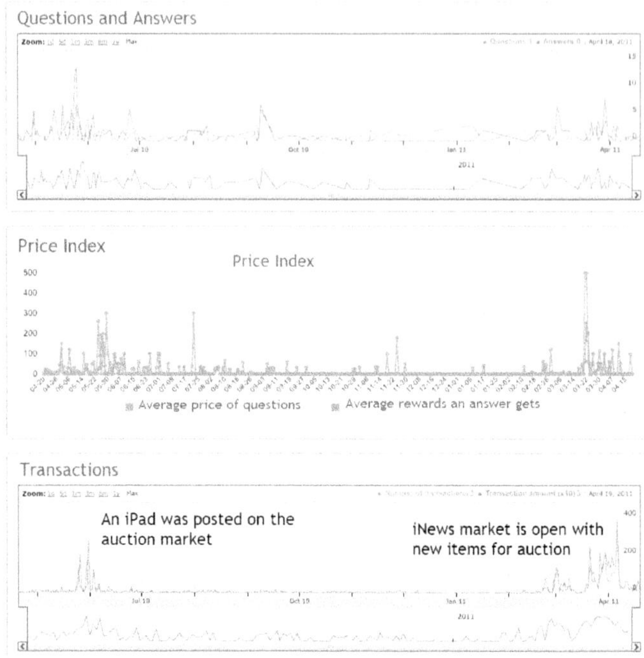

Figure 9. Economy monitoring dashboards that show time series of: 1) the number of question and answers (top), 2)Price Levels (middle), and 3) counts and volumes of market transactions on each day from 04/20/2010 to 04/16/2011. Jumps in activity and price levels occurred in June 2010 when we offered an iPad prize, and March-April 2011 when we launched the News market with material prizes.

experiment. The goal is to get users motivated and incentivized to participate. The auction market, "iBid", provides a mechanism for users to exchange earned points for rewards they care about. Meanwhile, we can use the auction market to measure the value of information in dollar terms for research purpose. We designed and decided upon an incentive structure, advertised it to users at the beginning of the deployment period. For example, We posted iTunes gift cards, small consumer products, and lunch opportunities with faculty members on the "iBid" market. For some classes, participation grades were associated with earned points. All user activities, transactions and market statistics have been captured by the system. Through the wide deployment of Barter, we are able to collect a rich dataset on market operations and user behaviors.

PRELIMINARY FINDINGS

Analysis of User Behavior & Market effects

1. Users are responsive to material incentives

Fig.9 shows several dashboards for monitoring the global economy for the past year (04/2010-04/2011) on the U.S. site - the number of questions and answers each day, the "price index" of the iKnow market, and the transaction volume as time series. The "chief economist" of Barter can use it to monitor several key economic indicators of the economy and decide if it is overheated or needs stimulation. For example, he can implement monetary policies following the Quantity Theory of Money, and it fits our research strategy (6).

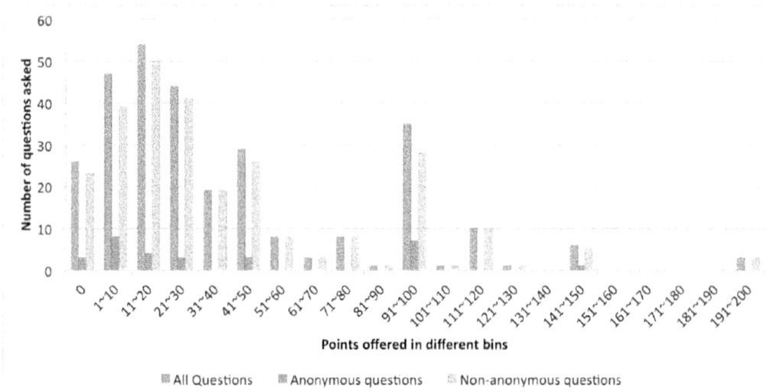

Figure 10. Number of questions asked categorized by the number of points offered - a) all questions; b) anonymous questions; c) non-anonymous questions.

It is evident from these curves that users do respond to material incentives. In mid-June 2010, we posted an iPad on the auction market, which greatly stimulated market activities (and market fraud too!). The number of transactions per day increased from 6.9 in April to 22.0 in May, when the iPad auction expired. It dropped back to 9.2 in June as fewer items were left in the auction market. The transaction volume increased from 337.0 points in April to 994.9 in May, and fell back to 160.3 in June. In March 2011, we released the iNews market to users and posted several valuable rewards on the auction market, which also stimulated the economy significantly.

2. Market forces are significant

A frequently asked question in the context of an information market is whether market forces are effective. The Q&A market (iKnow) was first implemented and used in the deployment. Thus, we analyze data collected from iKnow of the U.S. site to see whether offered points affect the quantity and quality of provided answers.

Fig.10 shows the number of questions asked on the U.S. site for each level of offered points - for all, anonymous, non-anonymous questions. Most questions were asked with around 25 points offered, while only a limited number of questions rewarded 100+ points.

Fig. 11 shows the average number of answers a question received for different levels of offered points. When the number of offered points is below 100, the average number of submitted answers received generally increase as the number of offered points arises. As the offered points exceed 100, the difficulty of the question increases more significantly, thus the number of submitted answers decreases sharply with offered points. There appears strong linearity for anonymous questions. As in [15], we use the average length of answers as a proxy for answer quality. It is evident from Fig.12 that the average length of answers keeps increasing as the offered points arises for a question, and when the offered points exceed 100, the increased difficulty thwarts good quality answers.

Both curves exhibit a reverse-U shape, and the local maximum is reached when the number of offered points are in the 90-110 range, for both the quantity and quality of answers. More interestingly, this is also where the curve in Fig.10 reaches a local peak value, which implies that users asked a significant number of questions within this price range.

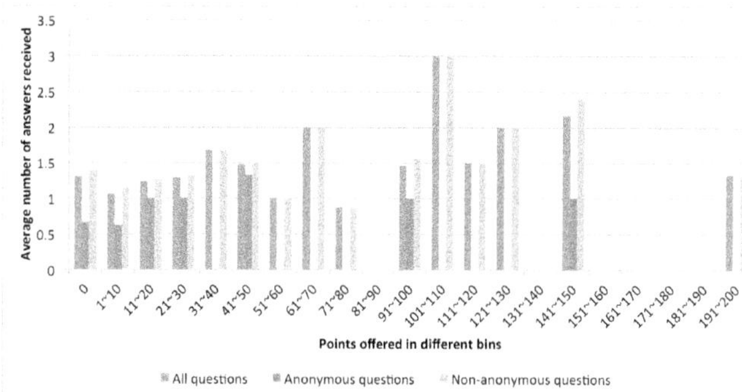

Figure 11. Average number of answers obtained, categorized by the number of points offered for questions - a) all questions; b) anonymous questions; c) non-anonymous questions.

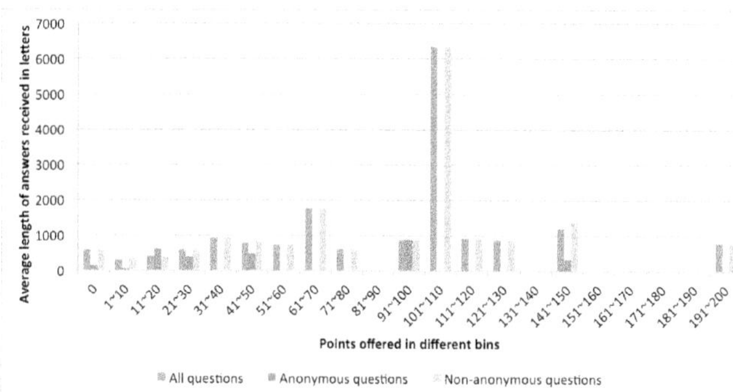

Figure 12. Average length of answers obtained, categorized by the number of points offered for questions - a) all questions; b) anonymous questions; c) non-anonymous questions.

Therefore, the price effects are prominent. Price Theory properly balances the marginal rates of substitution between using an expert's time to help others versus having him perform his own work, thus addresses the efficient allocation problem stated in our research strategy (3).

3. Cultural Differences

Different cultures can be cultivated in different communities. For example, on both the French site and the U.S. site, new users started with 2000 points. However, users on the French site offered much lower prices for their questions - 27.8 on average. In contrast, users on the U.S. site offered 63.96 on average. Users on the French site make their earnings mostly through "world bank" subsidies, instead of making earnings from other users by sharing knowledge and information. As clearly shown in Fig.5, the size of the pie "Q&A thumbing" is notably larger than "Q&A" itself. On the French site, users used the auction market much more actively, more than 96% of auction items were posted by users themselves, while on the U.S. site, over 90% of auction products were posted by researchers ourselves.

Evaluating information

Using virtual currency to exchange information following market rules, and exchanging virtual currency for material rewards through the auction market provide a mechanism to measure the value of information created on the platform. Using the U.S. site as an example, we select 11 product items of which we can easily learn the dollar values, such as a $10 itunes card or the ipad. Virtual rewards such as "Knight of Barter", or items with undefined $ value such as "A pingpong lesson" are not included.

After performing regression, we can obtain the approximate exchange rate between U.S. dollar and Barter's Yuanbao is $1 = 6.64(Yuanbao). During the 1-year period from 04.2010 to 04.2011, the total transaction volume happening in the Q&A market is 7476 Yuanbao - the sum of points offered and transacted for solved questions. Therefore, the value of information created in the Q&A market is $1126 denominated in U.S. dollars. This exceeds the value of what we spent to purchase the products and stimulate the knowledge economy, which was about $750. This doesn't include value created in other information markets such as the document and idea markets, and doesn't count other value created such as users' voting and tipping for helping sort and index information.

CONCLUSION

In this paper we present the design of an information market framework which is able to provide a long-term sustainable incentive structure to organization members to collaboratively share knowledge and create innovation. We have also introduced the software deployment and lessons learned from user activities. By applying innovative market mechanism design, we are able to address organizational challenges using a market mechanism efficiently. Our preliminary data analysis demonstrates that market forces are effective in incentivizing users to contribute information and engage in a new platform. Future research questions include:

- Which is more effective in getting users to contribute, social incentives or economic (market) incentives?
- Can an information market regulate and correct itself by using the same crowd-sourcing mechanism and market incentives, given the evidence of market abuse and fraud?
- Can securitization and a secondary market encourage user participation, increase market liquidity, and enhance the quality and validity of provided information?

We believe this is an interesting and promising research area that's worth more exploration. The learnings from the research will offer great insights into organizational design.

REFERENCES

1. Alavi, M., and Leidner, D. E. Review: Knowledge management and knowledge management systems: Conceptual foundations and research issues. *MIS Quarterly 25*, 1 (3 2001), 107–136.
2. Benbya, H. *Knowledge Management Systems Implementations: Lessons from the Silicon Valley. Oxford*. Chandos Publishing, 2008.
3. Benbya, H., and Alstyne, M. V. How to find answers within your company. *MIT Sloan Management Review* (1 2011).
4. Benbya, H., and Belbaly, N. Understanding developers' motives in open source projects: A multi-theoretical framework. *Communications of the Association for Information Systems 27*, 1 (2010), 589–610.
5. Brydon, M., and Vining, A. Understanding the failure of internal knowledge markets: A framework for diagnosis and improvement. *Information and Management 43*, 3 (12 2006), 964–974.
6. Chan, N. T., and Shelton, C. An electronic market-maker. Tech. rep., MIT, 2001.
7. Ernstberger, P. Linden dollar and virtual monetary policy. *SSRN* (2009).
8. Friedman, M. The quantity theory of money: A restatement. *reprinted in The Optimum Quantity of Money* (2005), 51–67.
9. Gans, J., and Stern, S. Is there a market for ideas? *Industrial and Corporate Change 19*, 3 (2010), 805.
10. Hirshleifer, J., Glazer, A., and Hirshleifer, D. *Price Theory and Applications: Decisions, Markets, and Information*. Cambridge University Press, 2005.
11. Horton, J., and Chilton, L. The labor economics of paid crowdsourcing. In *Proceedings of the 11th ACM conference on Electronic commerce*, ACM (2010), 209–218.
12. Malone, T., Laubacher, R., and Dellarocas, C. The collective intelligence genome. *MIT Sloan Management Review, Spring 51*, 3 (2010), 21–31.
13. McAfee, A. *Enterprise 2.0: New Collaborative Tools for Your Organization's Toughest Challenges*. Harvard Business School Press, 2009.
14. Mishkin, F. S., and Eakins, S. *Financial Markets and Institutions*, 6th ed. Addison Wesley, 2008.
15. Nam, K., Ackerman, M., and Adamic, L. Questions in, Knowledge iN?: a study of Naver's question answering community. In *Proceedings of the 27th international conference on Human factors in computing systems*, ACM (2009), 779–788.
16. O reilly, T. What is web 2.0? *Communications and Strategies 65* (2007), 17.
17. Parker, G., and Van Alstyne, M. Two-sided network effects: A theory of information product design. *Management Science* (2005), 1494–1504.
18. Roth, A. E. What have we learned from market design? *Economic Journal* (March 2008), 285–310.
19. Surowiecki, J. *The wisdom of crowds*. Doubleday Books, 2004.
20. Von Hayek, F. The use of knowledge in society. *American Economic Review 35*, 4 (1945), 519–530.

Puget Sound Off: Fostering Youth Civic Engagement through Citizen Journalism in a Local Community Context

Shelly D. Farnham
FUSE Labs
Microsoft Research
shellyfa@microsoft.com

David Keyes, Vicky Yuki
Dept. of Information Technology
City of Seattle
{david.keyes, vicky.yuki}@seattle.gov

Chris Tugwell
Technology Programs
Metrocenter YMCA
ctugwell@seattleymca.org

ABSTRACT
Social media technologies provide unique channels to empower youth to become more civically engaged. Puget Sound Off is an online blogging and networking site focused on helping youth connect, collaborate, and take action around local community issues. We performed an evaluation study seeking lessons learned from a real world deployment. We found that a core group of youth became highly engaged with Puget Sound Off, and that both usage and identification with the community was positively correlated with civic engagement. Youth reported an appreciation for the opportunity for meaningful discussion around issues that mattered to them. We found however that growth of Puget Sound Off was slow, in part due to the constraints of deploying to youth in a real world context with concerns about inappropriate use. We end with recommendations for fostering growth and civic engagement in related social media technologies.

Author Keywords
Youth, Internet, civic engagement, Puget Sound Off, PSO, blogging, blogs, citizen journalism, community action, civic efficacy, social participation

ACM Classification Keywords
H5.3. Information interfaces and presentation (e.g., HCI): Group and Organization Interfaces – *Asynchronous Interaction, synchronous interaction.*

INTRODUCTION
In the modern age of social media and user generated content millions of teens go online to connect with each other, share media, and play games. According to the Pew Internet and American Life Project [21] 74% of Americans and 94% of teens go online. 45% of boys and 55% of girls create original content, in the form of blogs and webpages, or personal media such as photos or videos. Around 65% use social networking sites such as Facebook, which now has over 500 million active users [8].

The rise of the Internet was predicted to have a positive effect on ***civic engagement*** [22] – those civic and political activities motived by a desire for social change either in local communities or national contexts. As noted by Bennett et al. "the Internet offers exciting possibilities for reconnecting young people with civic life [2, p. 1]." They argue that the more democratized nature of Web 2.0 technologies provides an avenue for a more participatory model of citizenship, with greater levels of peer-based information sharing and collective action. This opportunity for having an online civic voice is of particular importance to youth, who are historically disenfranchised in large scale, cultural conversations [22].

The blogosphere in particular has emerged as a prominent vehicle for the voices of heretofore disempowered voices seeking social change. Through blogs people are empowered to engage in ***citizen journalism*** [13] -- speaking in their own voices about issues that are important to them, and developing audiences outside the editorial control of mainstream media. In a recent survey report of the Pew Internet and American Life Project [18], it was found that 4% of online Americans write about a political or social issue in their own blogs, 8% in social networking sites, and 12% via comments. While powerful, the blogosphere is still dominated by adults, and the discourse of the prominent social media applications adopted by youth -- social networking sites -- tend to be focused on more lightweight, playful social interactions [9].

To address this issue in their local neighborhoods, in 2007 the City of Seattle [7] -- together with the Metrocenter YMCA [24] and the University of Washington's Center for Communications and Civic Engagement [5] -- started an initiative with the goal of creating a digital commons for youth to have their own voice. They hoped to develop an online venue for youth, designed by youth, that provided an environment for meaningful discussion that fostered civic engagement. In 2008 they launched Puget Sound Off [PSO], a web site that incorporates both blogging and social networking tools, oriented around social and political causes that mattered to local youth. See Figure 1.

In this paper, we present the results of a study assessing the impact of PSO and youth blogging on civic engagement through a combination of usage analysis, questionnaire results, and focus groups. An examination of the impact of PSO and its deployment in a real world context affords the opportunity for unique insights into the challenges of designing social media systems to have meaningful, real world impact on youth civic engagement.

Figure 1. PSO Home Screen, with call to "Connect! Collaborate! Take Action!"

RELATED WORK

Consistent with early hopes [22], there is some evidence that the Internet has had a democratizing impact on civic participation. Political bloggers were more likely to report the Internet helped them to become more involved in local issues [15], were more civically engaged, and had a higher sense of community collective efficacy. In reviewing hundreds of web sites in 2004, Bennett and Xenos [3] found that the youth web sphere had "come of age" with resources for political participation targeting youth. They characterized the more democratized, participatory model of Web 2.0 civic behaviors as *actualizing vs. dutiful* citizen engagement. In another survey of 264 web sites focused on youth civic engagement, Bennet et al. [2] found the sites that were online only (not associated with a more traditional offline organization, service, or activity) had much higher levels of *actualizing* features such as opportunities for sharing peer knowledge, training in participatory media such as blogging, joining peer groups or networks created by peers, and peer-generated calls to actions. While there is evidence that youth in the United States still have higher levels of political apathy, a telephone survey study [17] found that youth were also more involved in online civic activities than their elder counterparts, particularly for more local civic or political groups.

A recent report by the Pew Internet and American Life Project [22] found that both online and offline, political activity is positively correlated with socio-economic status, such that lower income corresponds with less online political activity, in part due to disparities in Internet access. Nonetheless, younger Americans are more likely than their elders to be participating online in political discourse. As they note, "there are hints that forms of civic engagement anchored in blogs and social networking sites could alter long-standing patterns that are based on socio-economic status [22, p. 5]".

While there is evidence for increased participation by diverse groups in political discourse online, and that online civic discourse is correlated with offline civic behaviors [6], it remains to be seen if online discourse actually mobilizes people toward *increased* levels of civic engagement. For example, a study of Taiwanese Internet users [6] found no evidence that participation in online political discourse promotes new real world civic behaviors.

In addition to increased civic engagement, we further look to the Internet to provide opportunities for civic learning that would translate into *effective* offline civic behaviors. Bennet et al. [2] outlined four civic learning goals that foster effective civic engagement: the **knowledge** necessary to be an effective citizen, the **skill to communicate** effectively, the ability to **join public groups or networks** that can emerge and organize around an issue, and the **skills to take action** in a public manner, including participating in voting, fundraising, running for office, or protests. Thus a key component toward effective civic engagement is the ability to join groups and networks that may engage in collective action. Online, communities require both networking features that enable everyday encounters and connections, and more group-based tools that facilitate community activism [12].

There have been few examples of real world studies examining the impact of specific communication technologies on civic collective efficacy. A notable exception is a case study [10] of the impact of video blogging on a rural community in Brazilia using semi-structured interviews. The study found clear examples that video blogging led to community empowerment, where participants were documenting topics with the goal of mobilizing the community to action. For example, one user blogged about the proper manner to dispose of waste, with a call to action to citizens and local government for proper trash disposal.

To aid in this line of research, Carroll et al. [4] developed a measure of community collective efficacy – beliefs that the shared capacities of the group may lead towards accomplishing joint outcomes. Through a questionnaire study they developed a model of Internet use and activism, illustrating that general Internet experience corresponded to the civic use of the Internet, which further corresponded to real world activism.

For this study, in addition to examining PSO usage, civic engagement, and the role of community collective efficacy, we were interested in exploring the role a sense of community -- a feeling of belonging and loyalty to a local community -- has on civic engagement and community efficacy. A recent study [19] illustrated that a place-based social networking tool could increase sense of community, loyalty, and participation in a community hub – a coffee shop. Similarly we expect a place-centric community technology may meaningfully impact civic behaviors through increased loyalty and attachment to the community.

PUGET SOUND OFF

The Puget Sound Off [20] website is a joint project of the City of Seattle [7], University of Washington's Center for Communication and Civic Engagement [5], and the Metrocenter YMCA [24]. In developing PSO, they adopted a participatory design approach. "The PSO website was created in Seattle, Washington by youth for youth. 18 Puget Sound area teens came together in the summer of 2007 to design it after gathering input from 180 teens [20]."

In the spirit of citizen journalism and a more bottom-up, peer-based, democratized approach to civic participation, the goal of PSO was to empower youth to express themselves, connect to local resources, discuss issues important to them, and engage with each other and policy makers in taking action [1]. In addition, PSO is a tool to help youth develop media literacy to achieve those skills that enable *effective* civic engagement: skills for knowledge, communication, joining groups and networks, and taking action. The primary message on the home page focuses explicitly on the transition from having a voice to taking action:

> *Take action! One voice makes a world of difference! It starts with one voice speaking out on an issue, then finding others to collaborate with and taking action. You can be that voice. You can get involved. You can make change happen. Puget Sound Off is the place to find your voice!* [20]

When users join, they create a profile, and through their profile can declare their school, neighborhood, and important causes. As members, they may post blog entries, comment on each other's blog entries, share photos, videos, events, polls, and so forth. On the home page, the content is structured according to primary cause categories (e.g., animal rights, education, and environment), and includes top blogs, top groups, most active members, and new members. See Figure 1. A take action image links to a page that guides members to specific actions, such as "contact the mayor" or "register to vote". A calendar provides lists of events that again help members transition from online participation to offline participation.

For the most part, users were recruited into PSO through partnerships with schools and a free summer program at the YMCA called Digital Connectors [24]. Youth are referred to the Digital Connectors program through the youth unemployment referral services if they have expressed an interest in improving their technical skills. The Digital Connectors program serves the purposes of a) training youth who care about their community to improve their technology and writing skills, b) seeding the PSO web site with content that sets the tone of conversation and c) recruiting further participation. An important goal in recruiting users and seeding initial content was to assure that a diversity of voices from various ethnic groups and neighborhoods were represented on the site.

In the following sections of this paper, we first provide an overview of PSO usage through the first two years of its deployment. We then examine the relationship between the use of PSO and civic engagement through a questionnaire. Finally we describe some of the lessons learned from two focus group discussions involving youth participating in the Metrocenter YMCA Digital Connectors summer program.

USAGE ANALYSIS

Over the course of its first 22 months use (through December of 2009, at which time we took a snap shot of usage statistics) 1125 unique accounts were created in PSO. Of those who reported gender, 45% were male, and 55% were female. About 45% reported their race in their profile, showing a very diverse ethnic background. See Figure 2. The average age was 22, however the majority of participants (62%) reported being under 18. 12 reported being 80-100 years old, suggesting participants were inflating or masking their age, introducing a bias to the average. Nonetheless, there are a number of adults in PSO, in the form of counselors, teachers, and technologists working on the system.

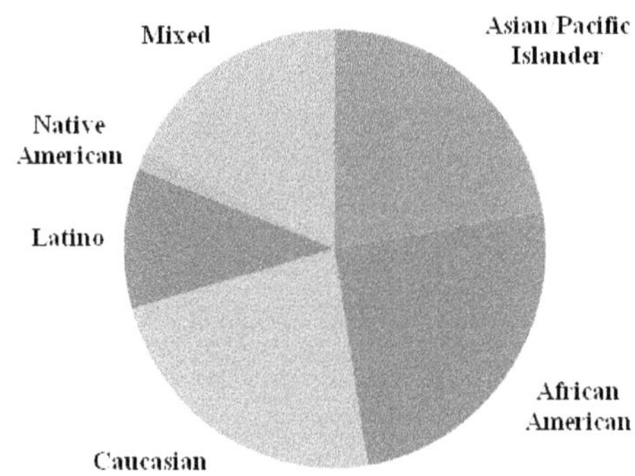

Figure 2. PSO has a very diverse population.

Through the first 22 months of use, a total of 624 blog entries were posted into the system, with 2234 comments. Many blog entries had long threads of comments, indicating that blog posts often served as instigators of conversation.

Contrary to expectations around social media, the growth of users in the system was linear, rather than exponential, over time. See Figure 3. This linear growth is probably because youth join the system as a part of youth educational programs, or as teachers introduce them to PSO in their classes. PSO does not aggressively promote participation using viral techniques common to social networks (e.g., tools for importing all your contacts from email). It should be noted however that the site has generated a reasonable number of non-registered user visits. Over the ten months leading up to the end of this study, during which Google

Analytics was enabled, the site receive a steady 148 visits a day, cumulating in 33,788 unique visitors from February through December of 2009. While steady, these traffic levels showed no or slow levels of growth.[1]

An important question is whether users tend to stay within the system after initial exploration, or tend to drop out. To address this question we examined how many days they stayed -- the time between when they joined the system, and their last log in date. 38% of users were one time users. However, of those who returned, the average length in days between first and last use was 101 days, with the proportionate life span (days in PSO/total days possible from start) being .31 (SD = .31). In other words, a sizeable proportion of users both returned to the site and became loyal members, participating over an extensive period of time.

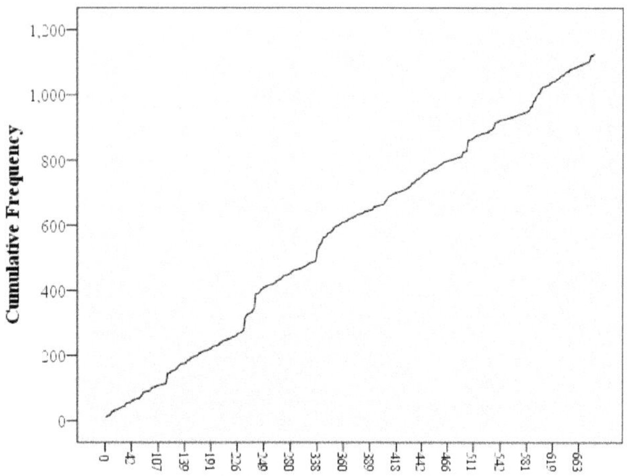

Figure 3. Growth of PSO users over time was linear.

Cause categories are a very important feature of PSO, orienting conversations around civic issues. When posting blog entries, members may select one or more predetermined cause categories for that post. The number of posts by cause category indicates that the topics of government and politics, social justice, and education inspire the most content and conversation. See Figure 4.

To further assess the civic content of the blog posts, we reviewed the last blog post of the 100 most recent posters, coding each one for whether it belonged to a cause category, and whether it had civic content. 53% were associated with a cause category, and 61% had civic content, including posts about civic issues in their schools, their neighborhoods, immigration, and local politics. Those blog posts without civic content were primarily personal posts, photos, or links to music. Of the 47% of the posts not associated with a cause category, many were associated with teen groups instead, such as Voices of Iraqi Youth and Black Achievers 2011 Senegal Trip. Many of the groups were created for specific teen programs (e.g., Youth Summit, The Leadership Project) or cause campaigns (e.g., Teens Against Distracted Driving), where it was clear teens were encouraged to post entries in PSO as an educational aspect of the program.

Of the blog posts reviewed, we found no evidence of inflammatory or antagonistic commentary, suggesting a strong norm for pro-social behavior. Three of the 100 posts inspired an in-depth conversation. For example, one person posted a "cyberbullying" question in a blog post asking the community members their feelings about the Seattle public schools' new policy giving school administrations the power to discipline students based on off-campus speech online. Eleven people responded, expressing very divergent views, which the original poster synthesized as the twelfth comment off the blog post.

The Teens against Distracted Driving group provides the best example of a conversation around blog entries leading to youth taking action. The group started by defining the problem (driving using a cell phone) and sharing statistics about distracted driving and accidents. They then decided to campaign to increase awareness in their schools and brainstormed methods for reaching fellow students. They took action by setting up tables in their schools and passing out bracelets to those who signed a commitment letter to not drive distracted.

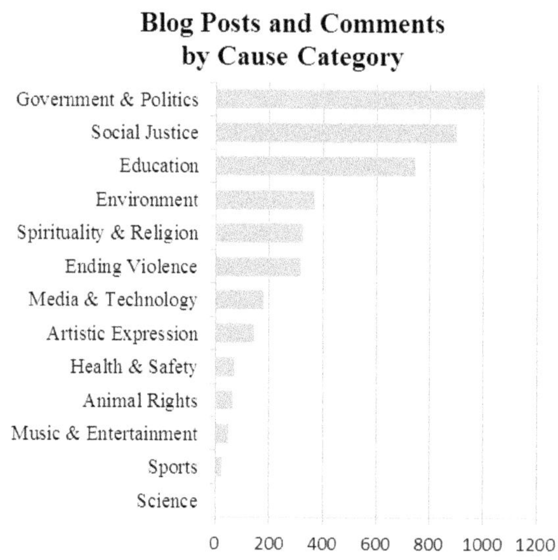

Figure 4. The number of blog posts plus comments by cause category, indicating conversational activity around causes.

QUESTIONNAIRE

We distributed a questionnaire to gain a deeper understanding of PSO usage, its impact on technology experience, and its impact on sense of community, civic engagement, and civic self-efficacy.

[1] We report usage through 2009 to correspond with the timing of our questionnaire and focus groups. However, at the time we write this paper in May of 2011, the unique visitors a day is 267 – indicating an ongoing slow and steady linear growth in traffic. Similarly, the number of blog posts has grown to 2287, with 6592 comments.

Procedure
We recruited PSO users to participate in a questionnaire both by posting an advertisement within PSO, and by sending an email invitation to all members. To add an incentive to complete the questionnaire, we entered each participant in a sweepstakes for a 50$ gift certificate.

Participants
Over two weeks a total of 26 participants completed the questionnaire, 56% male and 42% female, with an average age of 18. Five out of the 26 were over 18, and were removed from the analysis. 15% were Asian or Pacific Islander, 27% African American, 39% Caucasian, and 19% other or mixed. These numbers are more diverse than the City of Seattle population as a whole, which is about 70% Caucasian, 14% Asian, and 8% African American. When asked how long ago they had joined PSO, 11 participants indicated over a year ago, suggesting the questionnaire respondents tend to be more engaged users than the average. They had largely joined PSO through a group or a program (46%) such as the YMCA or the Urban Family Center. As noted earlier youth are often referred to these programs as a part of youth unemployment referral services. Some joined PSO through the recommendation of a friend (19%) and some joined through a school (19%). Two joined from an advertisement, and no one joined from Facebook or MySpace. Questionnaire participants were active Internet users, with 100% indicating they were online at least several times a week, and 62% indicating they were online several times a day.

Puget Sound Off Self-report Usage
When asked how often they used various PSO features, we found that reading blogs, browsing profiles, and browsing pages about causes were the most frequent behaviors, followed by adding comments to blog posts and writing blog posts. Clearly the blogs were a central feature of the system. See Figure 5.

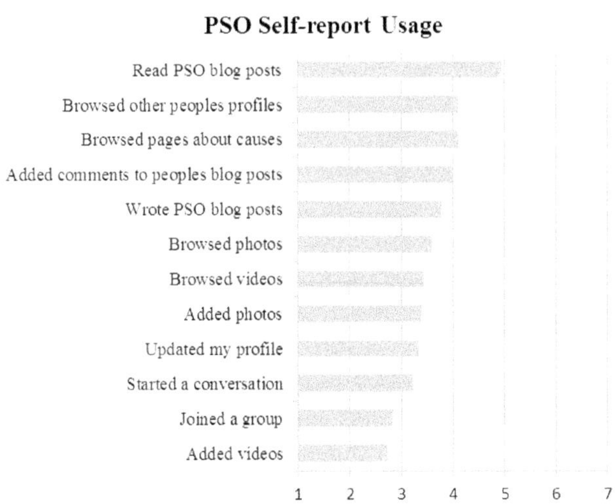

Figure 5. Self-report usage of various PSO features, where 1 = not at all, 7 = all the time.

We then then asked participants to indicate how much PSO helped them achieve any of a list of goals. As can be seen in Figure 6, the most highly rated goals achieved in PSO were having something to do that was positive, learning how to express themselves better, and having fun. See Figure 6.

It was considered very important when designing PSO and recruiting participants that it reflect the interests and diversity of the users and their communities. When asked specifically about these issues, respondents rated it fairly highly as reflecting their interests (M = 4.9, SD = 1.59), the interests of their community, (M = 5.0, SD = 1.78), and the diversity of their area (M = 4.7, SD = 1.76, where 1 = not at all and 7 = extremely so). For later use, we aggregated and averaged these items into one "PSO Reflects Community" measure.

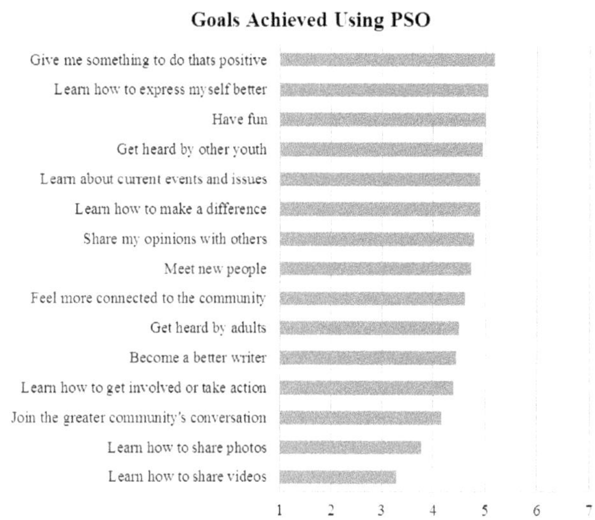

Figure 6. Extent to which PSO helped users achieve specific goals, where 1 = not at all and 7 = extremely so.

Puget Sound Off and Technology Experience
One of the primary goals in having youth use PSO was to give them an opportunity to develop their level of experience with Internet technology. To assess whether use of PSO had any impact, we first asked our respondents to indicate their overall level of experience with various technologies. See Figure 7. We then computed a general PSO usage score by averaging across types of usage.

To assess if PSO usage levels corresponded with general technology experience, we then measured the correlations between PSO usage and level of Internet experience. As can be seen in Table 1, PSO usage had a statistically significant impact on Internet experience levels in writing blogs, group emails, adding comments to blogs, making and sharing videos online, making and photos online, and text messaging. Given the correlational nature of this data, it should be noted an alternative explanation is that people with more Internet experience are more likely to use PSO from the start. To assess if this may be the case, we looked at the relationship between time since joining PSO and technology experience, and do find a trend that technology experience goes up with time since joining PSO, but this trend is not statistically significant.

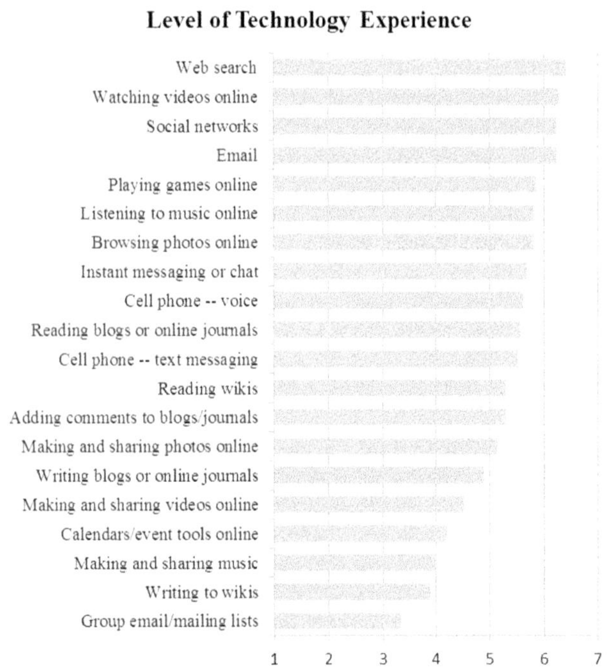

Figure 7. Self-reported technology experience, where 1 = none, never used and 7 = extremely experienced.

We asked participants several questions addressing whether they considered technology a viable tool for expressing their opinion and being heard. As can be seen in Table 2, users who had more general technology experience and PSO usage reported that the Internet was an effective tool for communicating opinions. Interestingly, PSO usage correlated much more highly with whether participants felt they had forums to be heard by local decision-makers, perhaps because of the local community nature of the web site and the fact that it is hosted by the City of Seattle.

Puget Sound Off and Civic Engagement

Another important goal of PSO was to provide a venue through which participants could become more engaged citizens, crossing the line from expressing their opinion on civic issues to taking action. To assess the relationship between PSO usage and civic engagement, we included a few measures.

Civic engagement. Civic engagement was measured using items from the Civic Engagement Questionnaire [16], a standard measure asking how often respondents had engaged in various civic activities such as *'Spending time participating in any community service or volunteer activity', 'taking part in a protest, march, or demonstration',* and *'playing a leadership role at school (such as student government or leadership in a club).'* Internet-related items were not included in this measure to assure it reflected civic behaviors outside of PSO usage.

PSO Usage and Technology Experience		
Type of Technology	r	p <
Writing blogs or online journals	**.69**	.003
Group email/mailing lists	**.62**	.007
Adding comments to blogs	**.59**	.012
Making and sharing videos online	**.54**	.024
Making and sharing photos online	**.53**	.030
Cell phone -- text messaging	**.49**	.047
Making and sharing music	.47	.055
Cell phone -- voice	.46	.065
Browsing photos online	.45	.072
Reading blogs or online journals	.45	.009
Listening to music online	.40	.110
Writing to wikis	.36	.102
Web search	.35	.173
Instant messaging or chat	.31	.230
Calendars/event tools online	.26	.322
Email	.26	.324
Social networks	.25	.342
Playing games online	.24	.361
Watching videos online	.22	.390
Reading wikis	.10	.740

Table 1. Correlations[2] between PSO usage and kinds of overall technology experience. Bolded items are statistically significant at $p < .05$ level, two-tailed.

Technology Attitudes Questions	Technology Experience	PSO Usage
What is the effectiveness of the Internet to communicate opinions?	**.59**	**.50**
What is the effectiveness of Internet to communicate with elected officials?	.25	.30
Do you have forums to express your opinion to other youth?	**.45**	**.48**
Do you have forums to be heard by local decision makers?	.39	**.64**
Do you like to participate in forums with diverse opinions?	**.59**	**.58**

Table 2. Correlations between technology usage and attitudes toward technology. Bolded items are statistically significant at $p < .05$, two-tailed.

[2] Correlations between .4 and .6 are considered moderate to large in size. Note the p values reflect a small sample size.

Civic competence. Civic competence, or the perceived ability to engage in civic action, was measured using items adapted [11] from the California Civic Index [14]. These items ask to what extent the respondent feels capable of accomplishing various tasks around a problem in their community, such as *'call someone on the phone that you had never met before to get their help with the problem'*, *'organize and run a meeting'*, and *'contact an elected official about the problem'*.

Civic self-efficacy. Civic self-efficacy, or the belief that one can make a difference civically, was measured using items adapted [11] from the California Civic Index [14], including *'I believe I can make a difference in my community'* and *'by working with others in the community I can help make things better'*.

Civic accountability. Civic accountability, or the sense of personal responsibility towards being involved, was measured using items from the California Civic Index scale [11, 14], including *'working on local problems/issues is important'*, and *'being actively involved in community issues is my responsibility.'*

Community efficacy. Community efficacy, or the belief that one's community has the ability to work to solve its own problems, was measured using items from the Community Collective Efficacy Scale [4], which included items such as *'as a community, we can handle mistakes and setbacks without getting discouraged'* and *'I am convinced that the people in my local community can improve the quality of life for the community, even when resources are limited or become scarce'*.

Sense of local community. We measured psychological sense of local community, or the feeling of connection, belonging and loyalty to a local community, using items from the psychological sense of community scale [23] adapted to refer to local community. We asked respondents to think about the local community that is important to them, and consider that community when answering these questions. Items included *'I feel loyal to the people in my local community'*, *'I really care about the fate of my local community'*, and *'I would work together with others on something to improve my local community'*.

For each measure, we averaged across items. We found that while respondents reported reasonably high levels on the more attitudinal measures (civic self-efficacy, community efficacy, or civic accountability) they reported lower levels on the more behavioral measures of civic engagement and civic competence. See Figure 8.

We then examined the correlation between a) these measures of civic engagement and civic efficacy, and b) levels of participation within PSO including writing blog posts, overall PSO usage, and the extent to which PSO reflected the interest and diversity of the respondent and his or her community. As can be seen from Table 3, writing blog posts and overall levels of PSO usage has a significant positive correlation with civic engagement. Thus the more users wrote blog posts and the more their overall PSO usage, the higher their levels of civic engagement.

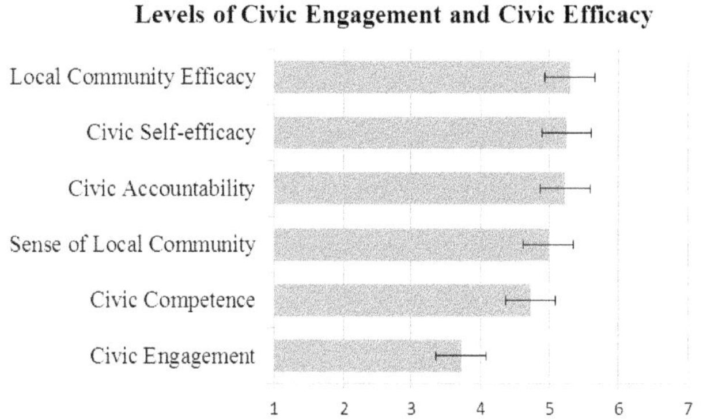

Figure 8. Psychological measures of civic efficacy and sense of community were higher than behavioral measures of civic competence and civic engagement, where 1 = not at all and 7 = extremely so.

Civic Engagement and Efficacy	Wrote PSO Blog Posts	Overall PSO Usage	PSO Reflects Community
Civic Self-efficacy	.29	.39	**.52**
Local Community Efficacy	.23	.38	**.65**
Civic Accountability	.21	.36	**.56**
Sense of Local Community	.08	.36	**.56**
Civic Competence	.39	.47	**.57**
Civic Engagement	**.56**	**.54**	.47

Table 3. Correlations between measures of civic engagement and PSO usage, where bolded items are statistically significant at $p < .05$, two-tailed.

Perhaps more interestingly, the extent to which respondents felt that PSO reflected their community had an even stronger relationship with these same measures. The more PSO reflected their community, the higher participants were on measures of civic efficacy and engagement. This suggests that identification with the PSO community is a mediator of the impact of PSO usage on civic engagement and efficacy. In other words, in order for a users' civic engagement to increase through use of PSO, they must identify with the PSO community. We further found that the measure of whether PSO reflected their community correlated with overall PSO usage ($r = .61$, $p < .05$), that accomplishing the goal of feeling more connected to the PSO community correlated with civic engagement ($r = .55$, $p < .05$) and that a general sense of local community correlated with civic engagement ($r = .52$, $p < .05$).

To provide a better overview of PSO usage and civic engagement, we split the respondents into two groups of high and low users to generate a bar graph. As can be seen from Figure 9, users who actively used PSO reported much higher levels of civic engagement.

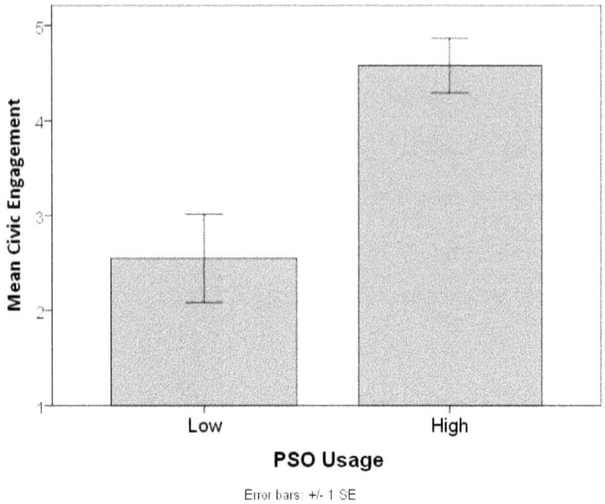

Figure 9. People with high PSO usage had much higher levels of civic engagement than people with low PSO usage, where 1 = not at all, 7 = extremely so.

Open-ended Responses

At the end of the questionnaire we provided respondents an opportunity to comment on what they liked about PSO, or what they disliked or would recommend changing.

Consistent with our usage analysis and questionnaire scale items, participants mentioned liking the opportunity to express themselves or be heard around topics that were important to them.

> *It really let me express myself and let me be heard.*

> *It's an outlet to address issues in the community and allows your voice to be heard.*

> *Being able to discuss topics that I was passionate about and having the modem [sic] to reach out to others about political issues.*

They did not care for posts that were off topic, and wanted to maintain the community's culture of conversation around issues that matter.

> *Because of the targeted outreach the past few months for PSO, a great deal of younger youth have been posting blogs on topics that aren't very serious and don't affect the community really. ... While we want all youth to have their voices heard, it should be taught what topics are appropriate- this isn't another Myspace or Facebook.*

> *If this is a civic engagement site then why are there posts about boyfriends and girlfriends, about what fieldtrips people just went on? The culture needs to go from pop culture/personal life to civic engagement and press the issues so that people actually start to take action.*

In addition to appreciating the more serious, civic topics of conversation, users indicated an appreciation for the opportunity to learn.

> *i like how some important people tell you what going on in you or close to your area.*

> *i am more informed about whats going on around my community and where to look for information's.*

Several participants mentioned the importance of connecting with similar others, particularly others their own age.

> *Being able to connect and interact with teens that are around my age, in my state, and where I live.*

> *Being able to say and discuss my opinions and get feedback from other people around my age.*

A few mentioned wanting better tools for inviting or adding friends or receiving updates, indicating a) an awareness that PSO was not leveraging some of the more viral features of many existing social networking systems, and b) a desire to have more people in the system. One person mentioned wanting less of a presence of adults.

And, a final comment from one of the teachers shows appreciation for its impact on his or her students.

> *PSO provides a badly needed service to teachers and students (from my perspective as a teacher). The writing that my students are doing has increased tenfold through the use of blogs and comments. PSO takes 'issues' far beyond the static pen and paper and allows my students to enter into a discussion of a particular subject and forces them to really think about their own values and ideas.*

FOCUS GROUPS

In August 2009, fourteen teens from the YMCA summer program participated in two focus group sessions. The goal of the focus groups was to provide further insight into how youth experienced PSO. For each focus group we asked a series of questions to assess if they understood and appreciated its core mission, how did their usage relate to their existing real world communities, and how would they recommend improving the user experience. Each focus group was transcribed and reviewed for emerging themes.

The focus group teens were a reasonably Internet savvy group, with 78% having Internet access at home, 71% having a Facebook account, and 71% going online at least several times a week.

Appreciating the Mission

In our discussion of the goals of PSO, the participants showed a clear understanding for the mission of PSO, and listed the mission as a primary reason for liking it.

On Myspace, people talk about a whole lot of nonsense, where here people talk about stuff that has meaning.

They appreciated this higher purpose relative to other networking sites, saying it was more productive, legitimate and authentic than MySpace or Facebook.

Relation to Real World Communities

We found through the questionnaire that the feeling of connection or identification with the PSO community meaningfully impacted levels of civic self-efficacy and engagement. During the focus group we asked participants whether they felt PSO reflected them and their communities. They reported a strong sense of belonging with the site membership, that it was comprised of people "like them" in their real world communities, and that the topics were fairly well representative of their communities' interests.

Blogger "Types" or Not

Participants indicated the biggest barrier to use was whether they were a blogging type of person, and that furthermore there was not enough of a sense of audience and conversation. The more active blog posters expressed a fair amount of frustration that they spend a lot of time on their blog posts, but then the posts would soon get lost as new blog posts came into the system. Active bloggers wanted more of sense of being read, of having an audience, and of having more active conversation.

Personal Networking vs. Serious, Educational Focus

Participants felt some tension between the mission of PSO and their desire for more casual socializing. An illustration of this tension between PSO's more educational goals and the more personal networking goals of its users was an adamant request for private messaging. Participants indicated the lack of private messaging was a primary reason for not recommending PSO to their friends. Yet, it was clear from the conversation they understood the reasoning for not including private messaging. They explained that if PSO became too much about personal, lightweight social interactions it may distract from its core mission and subsequently be blocked as inappropriate from use at their schools, as was MySpace and Facebook.

Age Split

The teens were very aware of two age levels within the system, preteen versus teenager. They recommended splitting content, profiles, and blogs based on this age difference, so the conversations were age-appropriate. Nonetheless, the older teens clearly appreciated the opportunity to speak to younger teens, to be a mentor and help them learn what to do or not to do in the community. In order for the older participants to retain this position as mentors, they felt the system should be segmented but not completely segregated by age group.

Overall, it was clear from the focus group discussion that participants were highly engaged by the system, appreciated the mission, had a strong sense of belonging, felt it reflected their community, and felt invested in its success. Much of the frustration expressed was in not having a sufficient feel for their audience or not having a large enough audience.

CONCLUSIONS

Puget Sound Off was designed to foster youth civic engagement by providing tools for youth to express themselves as citizen journalists in the context of their local communities. In order to evaluate PSO in its second year, we performed a combination of usage analysis, a questionnaire distributed to users, and focus groups.

Although growth has been slow, we found that many users were highly engaged by the system, feeling a sense of ownership and desire for its success. In discussing the site, participants showed strong appreciation for the *meaningful content* of the conversations, compared to MySpace of Facebook. Within PSO, blog posts were organized according to cause categories and groups in the users' communities, which successfully inspired conversation topics such as government and politics, social justice, and education. As a tool for increasing media literacy, we found that PSO usage correlated with higher levels of self-reported technology experience.

Most importantly, usage of PSO had a meaningful impact on our more behavioral measure of civic engagement, suggesting that engaging in online citizen journalism meaningful impacted their real world behaviors. We further found that the feeling that PSO reflected the interests of the participants and their communities had the strongest impact on levels of engagement and efficacy. This is consistent with Kim et al. [17], who found higher levels of online civic participation amongst youth in local groups -- presumably with whom they identify more than national groups. In other words, the success of PSO is only in part due to the increased literacy in media and the act of online citizen journalism – it is also because PSO provides a clear path from having a voice, to connecting to others in their local communities, to engaging in civic action.

Setting the right tone is of vital importance in any new community technology, and managing growth to adequately assure its continued focus can be challenging. Having created an environment with clear goals and expectations for topics of discussion, PSO is in a better position for expanding its audience. Its biggest challenge is how to increase opportunities for more voices to be heard, while retaining its ability to connect members to their local communities, and while still being considered appropriate for use in educational environments. One approach would be to include the viral features of social networks, while also further categorizing blog posts by neighborhoods. Other approaches would be to increase access to diverse groups by incorporating methods for posting content using the mobile phone, and increasing participation by enabling a limited number of private messages.

LIMITATIONS AND FUTURE RESEARCH DIRECTIONS

The correlational nature of our study creates some ambiguity around the causal relationship between PSO usage and levels of civic engagement. Nonetheless, the moderately strong correlation between PSO usage and civic behaviors, the high degree of civic content in the site, the participants' appreciation for its meaningful content, and the presence of constructive dialogue leading to taking action, converge on a picture of PSO meaningfully impacting civic engagement. Because of the large effect sizes we observed our small number of participants showed a significant impact. However, to perform more sophisticated analyses examining the relationships between technology usage, sense of community, and civic engagement, we will need a much larger number of study participants – again quite challenging in a local community site.

ACKNOWLEDGMENT

We thank the City of Seattle's Department of Information Technology, the Metrocenter YMCA of Seattle, and the participants for all their support in completing this study.

REFERENCES

1. Ballantine, A, Bennet, L., Freelon, D., McCaffrey, S., Norman, K., Parham, N., and Wells., C. *News 2009*, Volume 9. Center for Communication and Civic Engagement (2009).
2. Bennet, W. L., Wells, C., & Freelon, D. Communicating citizenship online: Models of civic learning in the youth web sphere. A Report from the Civic Learning Online Project (2009). Available online at: http://www.engagedyouth.org/blog/wp-content/uploads/2009/02/communicatingcitizeshiponlinecloreport.pdf
3. Bennet, L., & Xenos, M. Young voters and the web of politics 2004: The youth political web sphere comes of age. *CIRCLE Working Paper 42* (2005).
4. Carroll, J. M., Rosson, M.B., Zhou, J. Collective efficacy as a measure of community. In *Proc. CHI 2005*, ACM Press (2005), 1 -10.
5. Center of Communication and Civic Engagement. http://ccce.com.washington.edu/
6. Chen, D., & Lee, C. To reinforce or to mobilize? Tracing the impact of Internet use on civic engagement in Taiwan. In *Proc. ICEGOV 2008*, ACM Press (2008), 394-402.
7. City of Seattle. http://seattle.gov/
8. Facebook Statistics. http://www.facebook.com/press/info.php?statistics
9. Farnham, S. D. & Churchill, E. F. Faceted identity, faceted lives: Social and technical issues in being yourself online. In *Proc. CSCW 2011*, ACM Press (2011).
10. Figueiredo, M., & Camara, M. Empowering rural citizen journalism via Web 2.0 technologies. In *Proc. C&T* 2009. ACM Press (2009), 77-84.
11. Flanagan, C. A., Syvertsen, A. K., & Stout, M. D. Civic measurement models: Tapping adolescents' civic engagement. *Circle Working Paper 55*, CIRCLE (2007).
12. Foss, M., Choi, J., Bilandizic, M., Satchell, C. Collective and network sociality in an urban village. *Proc. Mintrek 2008*, ACM Press (2008), 178-183.
13. Glaser, M. Your Guide to Citizen Journalism. *Public Broadcasting Service*. Available at http://www.pbs.org/mediashift/2006/09/your-guide-to-citizen-journalism270.html (2006).
14. Kahne, J., Middaugh, E., & Schutjer-Mance, K. *California civic index* [Monograph]. New York: Carnegie Corporation and Annenberg Foundation, (2005).
15. Kavanaugh, A., Zin, T., Carroll, J., Schmitz, J., Perez-Quinones, M., Isenhour, P. When opinion leaders blog: New forms of citizen interaction. In *Proc. International Conference on Digital Government* (2006), 79 – 88.
16. Keeter, S., Zukin, C., Andolina, M., & Jenkins, K. The Civic and Political Health of the Nation: A Generational Report. College Park, MD: Center for Information and Research on Civic Learning and Engagement (2002).
17. Kim, B., Kavanaugh, A., Perez-Quinones, M. Toward a model of political participation among young adults: The role of local groups and ICT Use. *In Proc. ICEGOV 2007*, ACM Press (2007), 205-212.
18. Lenhart, A. Arafeh, S., Smith, A., MacGill, A., Writing, technology, and teens. *Pew Internet and American Life Project.* (2008).
19. McCarthy, J., Farnham, S., Patel, Y., Ahuja, S., Norman, D., Hazlewood, W., Lind, J. Supporting community in third places with situated social software. In *Proc. C&T, 2009*, ACM Press, (2009).
20. Puget Sound Off http://pugetsoundoff.org
21. Rainie, L. Internet, broadband, and cell phone statistics. *Pew Internet and American Life Project,* (2010).
22. Smith, A., Schlozman, L., Verba, S., Brady, H. The Internet and civic engagement. *Pew Internet and American Life Project,* (2009).
23. Wilkinson, Derek. The Multidimensional Nature of Social Cohesion: Psychological Sense of Community, Attraction, and Neighboring. *American Journal of Community Psychology, Vol. 40,* (2007), 214-229.
24. YMCA of Greater Seattle, Puget Sound Off Digital Connectors program. http://www.ysummer.org/program.cfm?rc=teens&pc=pugetSoundOff

What Do You Think? A Case Study of Benefit, Expectation, and Interaction in a Large Online Critique Community

Anbang Xu and Brian P. Bailey
Department of Computer Science
University of Illinois
Urbana, IL 61801
{xu26, bpbailey}@ illinois.edu

ABSTRACT

Critique is an indispensable part of creative work and many online communities have formed for this shared purpose. As design choices within the communities can impact the effectiveness of the critiques produced, it is important to study these communities and offer guidance for decisions. In this paper, we report the results of a case study exploring one large online community dedicated to critique in the domain of digital photography. We analyzed a large corpus of interaction data to understand the benefit of participation, the response dynamics, factors predicting critique ratings, and patterns of reciprocal interaction. Interviews with users were also conducted to uncover motives for participation and expectations of the critiques within the community. The results and insights gained from this work were distilled into recommendations for improving the design of systems that support community-based critique of creative artifacts.

Author Keywords

Critique; creativity; online community; reciprocity.

ACM Classification Keywords

H.5.3 [Information Interface and Presentation]: Group and Organization Interfaces – Evaluation/methodology.

General Terms

Design; Human Factors.

INTRODUCTION

Critique serves a central role in the evolution of a design concept and is a staple of design practice and education [13, 33]. A critique is traditionally performed in face-to-face settings where the designer communicates an artifact and its intent to peers and engages in reflective dialogue [33].

Due to the need for critique, many online communities have formed in the past decade with shared interest in critiquing creative work in domains such as photography [31], writing [11], and music [25]. The communities attract participation from novices to established professionals. In general, the communities offer interaction and incentive mechanisms for sharing creative work artifacts, encouraging critique of the artifacts, and building reputation. Design choices related to the interface and incentives can therefore impact at least the quantity, quality, and responsiveness of the critiques. For example, in the community we studied, site administrators have already tweaked the incentive structures and threshold for response length in order to promote effective critique.

These design choices could be informed by studies of Q&A [20, 21, 26], peer [32] and product review [29], and creative collaboration [3, 24] communities. However, it is not clear how well the results of these studies apply due to the unique nature of critique communities. For example, in a critique community, users share their own creative work artifacts rather than pose informational questions, the goal is to enhance individual content and creative skill rather than build shared outcomes or inform purchase decisions, and diversity of perspectives is valued more than "correctness."

In this paper, we report the results of a study exploring one large online critique community in the domain of digital photography (see Figure 1). Our study examined the benefit of participation (e.g., has the perception of skills improved), the response dynamics (e.g., the quantity, quality, and speed of critiques) and how they relate to expectations, factors predicting critique ratings, and reciprocal interactions. Our method consisted of analyzing a large corpus of interaction data and conducting semi-structured interviews with active members (N=12). The statistical analysis explored the content, ratings, and interactions of about 30K users, 500K photos, and 1M critiques spanning a six year period. The interviews were conducted first to help steer our statistical analysis and to uncover motives for participation and users' expectations of the critiques within the community.

Our study yielded several findings. First, we found that participating in a critique community can lead to favorable changes in the ratings of creative work but this depends on the quantity and quality of critiques received. Second, there are gaps between users' expectations and their experiences in terms of the quantity, quality, and timeliness of critiques. Finally, we found that reciprocity is an expected and welcome behavior and is most likely to occur between users with similar reputation scores. Overall, however, little direct reciprocity was observed in the community studied.

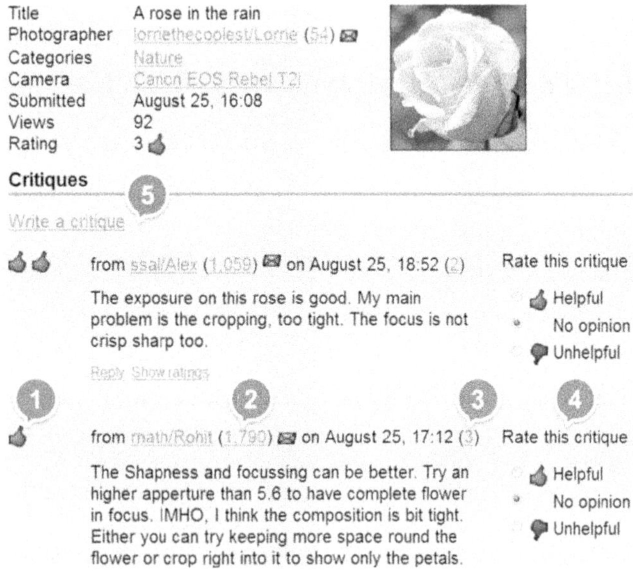

(a) The interface for viewing a photo, initiating a critique of the photo, and browsing or rating the existing critiques. The layout of the interface was compressed for the purpose of explanation.

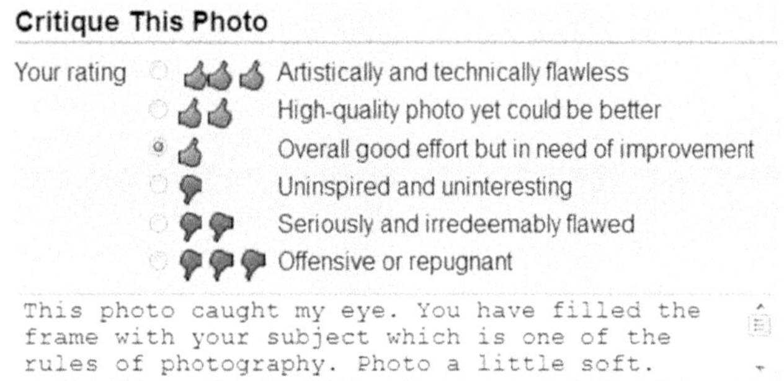

(b) The interface for writing a critique and rating the photo.

Figure 1. In (a) a photograph has received two critiques from the community. For each critique, the interface shows the user who wrote it, his reputation score (Callout 2), his rating of the photo (Callout 1), and the rating this critique has received from the community so far (Callout 3). After reading the critique, a user can rate it (Callout 4). If a user selects "write a critique" (Callout 5), the system responds with (b). In (b), the user rates the photo and writes the critique. Once submitted, it would appear with the other critiques of that photograph in (a).

The results and insights gained from this research were distilled into recommendations for improving the design of systems that support community-based critique of creative artifacts. The recommendations are most applicable to the domain studied (photography), but the issues discussed (e.g., promoting reciprocity and positive tone, organizing critiques, and structuring feedback) are relevant to many online critique communities irrespective of the domain.

RELATED WORK

We review the method of critique and its benefit for design and then situate our work within prior studies of Q&A, product review, and online creative communities.

Critique and Its Benefit for Design

Critique is a method for developing insights into a design artifact and illuminating the technical, cultural, and social values reflected in it [4]. In education, designers are taught structured procedures for conducting critique [14]. For example, a critique typically occurs as face-to-face dialogue where a designer describes the artifact, his intent and design choices while participants question and offer constructive advice about these elements. The outcome of a critique offers meaningful learning experiences for all participants, assists in the formation of mutually beneficial collaboration, and improves the teachability of the field [13].

In the CSCW community, Stevens et al. have demonstrated the benefits of end user critique for improving information technology artifacts [34, 38]. The authors created interfaces for end users to capture application usage situations and annotate the specific problem or need. The critiques are integrated and made available to the developers for review.

Studies of Q&A and Product Review

Critique can be loosely framed as Q&A (what do you think of this design?) and it shares similarities with reviews in product review sites. In [1], the authors studied many aspects of knowledge sharing behavior within Yahoo Q&A. The result most relevant to our work showed that reply length, number of answers and replier reputation were most predictive of answer quality. Similarly, Otterbacher showed how review submission time, reviewer reputation, product characteristics, and review content can predict community ratings of 'helpfulness' in Amazon.com product reviews [29]. Social network metrics have also been leveraged to help predict question quality [40] and question type [20] in Q&A. The analysis reported in this paper borrows from the analyses reported in these prior studies, for example, we include factors such as reputation scores, content attributes, and social metrics when trying to predict critique ratings.

However, our analysis is original because we also examine the benefit of participation from the ratings of artifacts over time and examine reciprocity. In addition, our approach is original in that we conducted interviews first to understand users' expectations of the community and compared them to actual experiences. Finally, we are exploring a type of online community that is unique relative to product review and Q&A. For example, in a critique community, users exchange feedback on each other's individual creative work.

Studies of Online Creative Communities

Researchers have studied other elements of online creative communities in which users collaborate on or share creative artifacts. For example, Luther et al. examined factors that contribute to successful collaboration in a large community of animators [24] while Sylvan uncovered predictors of project and social influence in a community formed around a visual programming environment [35]. In [3], the authors revealed the importance of feedback in online creative collaborations. Our research contributes to this corpus of prior work by studying a creative community from a unique perspective – *critique*. Critique can be framed as a form of communication with specific goals and learning how to give and accept constructive comments on creative artifacts.

CRITIQUE COMMUNITY STUDIED

We studied a large online community of users with a shared passion for digital photography; *PhotoSIG* [31]. In the community, users share photographs, critique each other's work, and try to improve their content and creative skills. The community attracts a diverse audience from amateurs to established professionals. Registration is required for participating and both free and paid memberships are offered. Free membership allows participation in all aspects of the community but the number of photographs is limited to one submission every three days. Paid membership increases this limit to three submissions every three days.

As shown in Figure 1, when a photo is shared with the community, any user other than the owner can write a critique and rate the photo, or rate the critiques posted by others. A photo is rated on a 6-point scale ranging from *three thumbs down* (-3) to *three thumbs up* (+3) without a neutral (0) rating. The total rating of a photo is the sum of the individual ratings. A critique can be rated as *helpful* (+1) or *unhelpful* (-1), with the default being *no opinion*, and the total rating of a critique is the sum of the individual ratings. As in [26], user activity is incentivized through a reputation system. A user's reputation is the sum of the ratings of the photos and critiques she submitted and is shown with her contributions. Extra points are awarded for behaviors deemed especially beneficial; e.g., being among the first three users to critique a new photograph.

We chose to study this community for three reasons. First, promoting critique has always been the mission and central design goal of this community, reflecting the importance of critique in design. Second, the community has a large, active user base, the rating methods are mature, and there is an open trace of interaction that can be analyzed. Finally, because the process of critique supported in this community is general, our results and implications should be of interest to similar communities in other design domains.

RESEARCH QUESTIONS AND METHODOLOGY

Our study was designed to understand critique within a large online community and centered on these questions:

- What are users' motives for participating in the online community and what benefits do they receive? How does participation (e.g. writing and receiving critiques) relate to the ratings of their creative artifacts, if at all?
- What are user expectations for receiving critiques online? For example, how many critiques do users want to receive, how quickly do they want to receive the critiques, and what makes an effective critique?
- What are the patterns of critique interaction? For example, what is the level of reciprocity and how important is reciprocity from the user's perspective?

These questions are not exhaustive, but rather intended to be a starting point for understanding the nature of online critique and identifying opportunities for improved interaction design that would foster more effective critique.

Our study used a mixed methods approach, consisting of quantitative analysis of interaction data and semi-structured interviews with users. Publicly available data was collected from the community using a custom extractor. We analyzed data from 2004 to 2009, as the community's rating system has been stable since 2004. Our analysis comprised 32,029 users, 526,561 photos, and 1,249,163 critiques. The data set includes ratings of each photo, critique content, ratings of each critique, reputation scores, and activity timestamps. Table 1 summarizes the data set. Our analysis examined relationships between users' photo ratings and participation in the community, differences between user expectations and experiences, and patterns of critique interaction.

To understand users' expectations of the community and help interpret the quantitative results, we conducted semi-structured interviews with twelve active users (two female) recruited via electronic postings in the community. Three were professional photographers while the others were

	Median	μ	σ	Range
Number of photos contributed per user	5	16.5	7.0	[0, 2090]
Photo ratings	3	4.2	4.8	[-8, 110]
Number of critiques received per photo	2	2.4	2.2	[0, 903]
Number of critiques written per user	6	50.5	275.7	[0, 26550]
Critique ratings	2	2.7	2.7	[-106, 117]
Critique word length	45	54.0	34.9	[1, 1956]
Reputation scores	27	174.6	866.2	[-53, 110,301]

Table 1. Descriptives of user activity in our data set.

Context and Motivation
Can you briefly describe a recent experience of either receiving or contributing a critique in the community? What was the effect of the critique?
What is your motivation for participating in this community? What is the benefit you hope to receive?
Writing, Receiving, and Reading Critiques
For what reasons do you critique photos posted in the community? How do you choose which photos to critique?
How often do you read the critiques of other users' photos? How does reading these critiques benefit you as a photographer?
How many critiques do you prefer when you submit a photo and how quickly do you want to receive the critiques?
How do you evaluate the quality of the critiques and how do you perceive the ratings assigned by others?
User Experience
What is your experience with having your photos and critiques rated by the community? How important are these ratings?
What do you believe are the main strengths and weaknesses of participating in the community?

Table 2. The main themes and a sample of the questions asked within each theme for the semi-structured interviews.

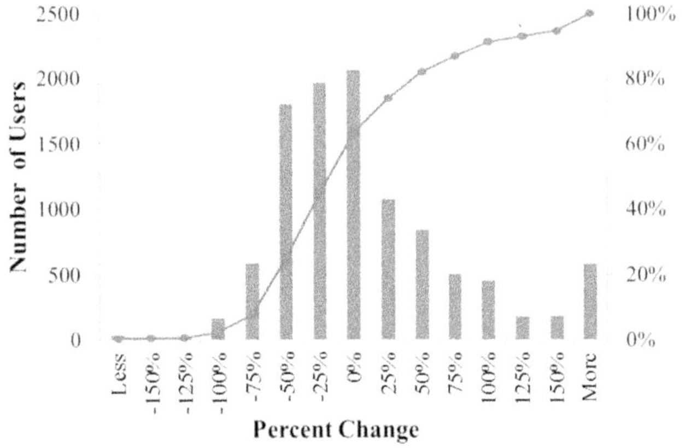

Figure 2. Distribution of percent change from a user's first 10% of submissions (avg.) to their most recent 10% (avg.).

amateurs. Their experience in the community ranged from 1 to 8 years and their reputation scores ranged from 250 to 5,600 points (all scores ranged from -53 to 110,301 points). The type of content contributed by the participants included nature, model, fine art, and architecture photographs.

Twelve prepared questions were asked during an interview, but additional questions were asked to pursue unexpected or interesting points raised by the participants. Table 2 shows the themes covered and a sample of the questions asked within each one. Interviews were conducted by phone (10) or instant messenger (2), whichever participants preferred. Interviews lasted between 60 and 90 min and remuneration was a $20 gift card. The phone interviews were recorded and transcribed and combined with the chat logs. Following [17], the data was coded to derive common responses.

BENEFIT OF ONLINE CRITIQUES

Users reported their main motivation for participating in the community is to gain diverse feedback on their creative work and to enhance their creative skills (11 users). This is unique relative to the motivations of fun and ideology that drive contributions for other types of user-generated content sites (e.g. Wikipedia) [28]. For example, one user was an amateur photographer who has actively participated in the community for two years. He reported that the largest benefit of participating is the opportunity to gain feedback:

> "*Wandering alone with my camera is relaxing and rejuvenating to me. Getting feedback on my work is icing on the cake. I enjoy feedback from other members. If I've looked over something, or if an image could be better, etc. Basically, it helps as I am not always as critical of my own work as I should be. Sometimes, I miss things; people point it out to me. It is a good driving force to keep going.*" [P5]

Other reported benefits include building and maintaining relationships with other photographers, establishing reputation in the field, and advertising photographic services (8 users). These benefits reaffirm findings from studies of other online communities [7, 9, 12, 22]. For example, another user was a professional photographer who runs an online photography school. His motives included not only honing his craft but also promoting his business:

	Coef.	SE	p	R^2
User's initial Photo Rating*	-0.343	0.084	<.001	0.30
Num. of Critiques Received*	0.170	0.058	<.001	0.45
Avg. Critique Rating*	0.154	0.042	<.001	0.51
Num. of Photos Submitted*	0.074	0.055	<.05	0.52
Num. of Critiques Submitted	0.046	0.045	0.304	0.52
Participation Time	-0.004	0.009	0.646	0.52

Table 3. Stepwise regression was applied to test how different variables of participation predict the change of a user's photo rating. Four of the six variables tested were significant. The coefficients are from the final model while the R^2 values are from each regression step. The model included the initial photo rating which is inversely associated with the change in photo rating. This may reflect a regression-to-the-mean effect.

> "*I am running an online photography school called...and I intentionally post some photos and critiques for exposure. If people like my work or my critiques, they would like to join my school.*" [P2]

Since the primary motivation for participating in the community is to improve photography skills, we examined the change in ratings of a user's photos from when they joined to their most recent contributions. We used the average photo rating within a given time window as a proxy for a user's photography skill. We computed the average rating of the first 10% and the most recent 10% of each user's photograph submissions. Only those users with a minimum of ten photos were considered (N=10,542) given our percent cutoffs, but analysis with other percent cutoffs yielded similar results. A t-test showed the average ratings of a users' photos improved from the first (μ = 3.8, σ= 2.6) to the most recent submissions (μ=18.5, σ = 40.7; p<.001).

Figure 2 shows the distribution of the percent change in the average rating from the first set to the most recent set of a user's photographs. Reflecting the prior result, the graph shows that a majority of users (56%) received the same or higher ratings for their photos over time, indicating that participation was helping to improve perceived skill. The figure also shows that a minority (44%) of users' ratings decreased. Though the true cause of this effect is unknown, it may be that the skill of some users was not progressing.

To gain further insight, a stepwise regression was applied to assess how different variables predict the change in photo ratings. Table 3 summarizes the independent variables considered and the regression results. The results show that receiving more critiques with higher ratings relates to an increase in photo rating, implying that the quantity and quality of critiques received has a positive correlation with the development of users' skills.

In contrast, the duration of participation did not show a measurable effect on the change in photo rating. And, interestingly, writing critiques of other user's work did not relate to the change in photo rating. This was somewhat surprising given that evaluating the work of others can build one's own design knowledge [4, 23, 32]. One explanation is that users are not effectively instructed on how to perform effective critique and therefore may not be gaining the full benefit of performing critical analysis.

USERS' EXPECTATIONS OF ONLINE CRITIQUES

We investigated users' expectations of online critiques, how their expectations align with actual experiences, and what design enhancements might close the gaps where they exist.

Quantity

There is a mismatch between the number of critiques a user wants to receive and the number s/he actually receives. In the interviews, we found that users want to receive at least four or five critiques for a photo (10 users), as they felt this offered the minimum feedback and perspective necessary for understanding how to move the work forward. The distribution of the number of critiques per photo is shown in Figure 3. While some photos receive many critiques, the vast majority (over 80%) receive less than four. The median number of critiques per photo is two. However, only a small percent (3.9%) receive no critique, which may be explained partly by the reputation incentive for contributing critiques of photos which have less than three critiques at the time.

To understand how it might be possible to encourage more critiques, we inquired about how users currently select photos to critique. From the interviews, users reported they typically select photos by browsing the area of the main page showing top-rated or recent photos. From this set, they look for photos matching personal interest or those submitted by a user with whom they had prior interactions. One solution for fostering more critiques is therefore to personalize this area of the main page, increasing the concentration of photos that may be of interest to the user. For example, filter or visually emphasize photos submitted by those with whom the user has an interaction history or photos matching an interest profile specified by the user. Another option is to expand the incentive for submitting the first critiques of a photo (e.g., raise the cutoff from three to six and increase the points awarded to the reputation score).

Content

Interviews revealed that users expect to receive constructive critiques which contain specific technical evaluation (e.g. related to composition, color, and depth-of-field) along with corresponding solutions, in order to facilitate the learning

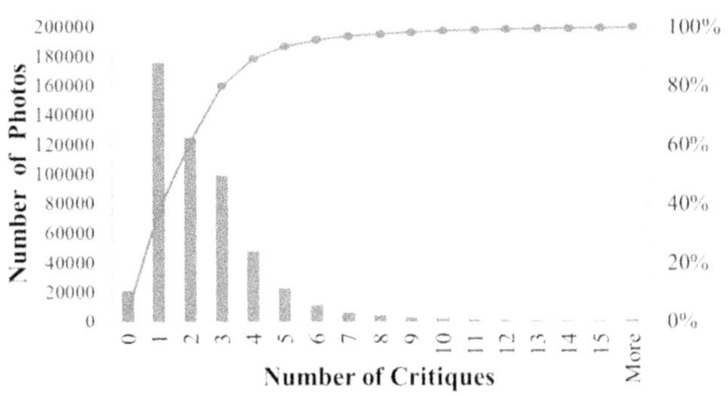

Figure 3. Distribution of photos receiving different numbers of critiques.

process (12 users). For example, a user said:

> "*Constructive criticism with solution is essentially the best criticism. This is a golden rule. If you want to tell me something wrong about my photo, tell me how I can fix it or how to make it different. Simply saying 'I like the photo' or 'I don't like the photo' either way it is worthless ... It didn't make me a better photographer.*" [P4]

More interestingly, several users preferred those critiquing their photos to not only tell them what to do but also "*show me how to do it*" (3 users). For example, a user reported that one user critiquing his photo would often revise his posted photo offline and send an email to show him the result:

> "*I even got some friends go into their emails and send me the picture to show me how to do It. I had that experience, which was really nice. This is pretty demanding of anybody's time. So I don't beg for it.*" [P7]

Though 'acting' on a photo was appreciated, the cost of acting on photos offline is high and disconnected from the online discussion. An enhancement would be to allow users to apply common technical operations such as crops and color balancing directly to a photo as part of the critique.

Critiques with positive expression can help users develop a sense of membership and further motivate them to engage in the community [8]. But new users may be not accustomed to follow this norm. As one user stated:

> "*If someone put a three or two thumbs down critique, I would like to read it to see what made this person be so aggressive. Most always they will have a small number (user reputation rating) beside their name. Like mine has the 21,000 (user reputation rating). Implying that they are beginner that also implying that they are newcomer to the community.*" [P1]

We therefore examined the relationship between reputation score and the percent of positive and negative emotion words written in a critique. This analysis was performed using Pennebaker's Linguistic Inquiry and Word Count (LIWC). LIWC counts the number of words in a source text that match the words within different linguistic categories. The positive category includes 406 words such as fantastic, love, and nice while the negative category contains 499 words such as hurt, ugly, and nasty [30]. A weak positive correlation ($r = 0.21$; $p<.001$) was found between reputation score and percent of positive emotion words, while a small negative correlation ($r = -0.10$; $p<.001$) was found between reputation score and the percent of negative emotion words. Users with higher reputation scores tend to use more positive words than users with lower scores. Similar to [8], system designers should therefore consider 'socializing' novices to help them understand how to write effective critiques consistent with the norms of the community.

Response Time

From the interviews, users want to receive most critiques within 24 hours after submitting a photo (9 users). Figure 4 shows that a photo accumulates about 60% of all its critiques in the first two hours. Although the majority of users were satisfied with the response time, several users

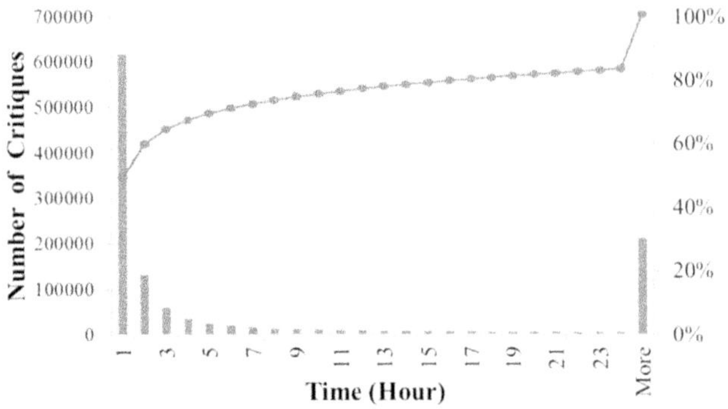

Figure 4. Distribution of the response time of the critiques.

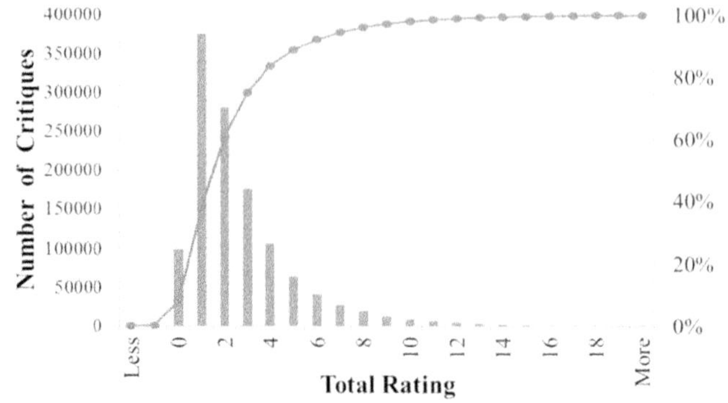

Figure 5. Distribution of the total ratings of critiques.

wanted to receive critiques sooner (3 users). These users often posted work-in-progress photos and they hoped to get "instant" critiques to help accelerate the working process:

> "*I expect to receive critiques in fifteen minutes. But sometimes I have to wait for five or six hours to get critiques. Most time I submit photos in the working progress. Especially the photos I have questions about. I post them to get feedback. Because if there is something fundamentally flaw in the photograph, then I can face that it does not work. Or there are small minor details I may miss. I can go back to correct them.*" [P10]

To meet these users' needs, a design enhancement might allow users to assign the label of "work-in-progress" to their photos to notify others that quick, high-level feedback would be appreciated. Other design alternatives to hasten response time include the use of reputation boosts, community guidelines, and active moderation [26].

Revisiting Critique

Several users reported that they often access prior critiques in order to engage in reflective learning or to reflect on their own experiences as a photographer (5 users). High-quality critiques may attract repeated access from users.

> "*I do occasionally revisit critiques. If I felt as if the person (the person's critiques) had an outstanding amount of knowledge, or something particularly worthwhile for me to concern myself with, I'll go back*" [P9]

However, the current interface does not offer mechanisms for organizing critiques based on different attributes (e.g. words of encouragement, technical suggestions, or social connections). Designing and including such interaction could better support users' reflective learning activities.

Who Makes the Critique

Users reported they prefer to receive critiques from those with similar or more experience than themselves (7 users):

> "*The person critiquing, unfortunately, does matter. If they're photographically novice, they'll be less prone to give me real technical advice. They don't have a lot of advice to impart... I treasure advice given to me by people who are better than I am.*" [P8]

This contrasts with [32] which found students in an intro programming course prefer to receive critiques of their code from those with *less* experience. One explanation may be that the students perceived they would receive a better rating if the critique was written by someone with less experience, whereas our users are mainly interested in improving their creative skill. Users also felt that critiques written by those familiar to them were easier to understand than critiques written by those unfamiliar (2 users):

> "*Sometimes it is more difficult to evaluate critiques from strangers. You don't have history and you don't have the same vocabulary.*" [P7]

Predicting Critique Quality

Users felt most critiques received were helpful to a degree, but only a small fraction offered deep insights into the work (8 users). This is reflected in the distribution of the total ratings of critiques shown in Figure 5. For example, the figure shows only a few critiques received very high total ratings while 92.2% of critiques received a rating of at least one. Among these critiques, 97.4% received only helpful ratings, 0.3% only unhelpful, and 2.3% received both. Users also felt that the score of a critique reflects the degree of community consensus around the statements made in it:

> "*Someone gives a good critique, but I may not like what they have to say. But if it's followed up by 10 more people agreeing with the critique, then I may tend to agree that they are correct.*" [P2]

To gain insight about what contributes to critique quality, we performed a linear regression of the critique score (total rating) with factors identified as relevant to quality. Our analysis uses critique score as a proxy for quality. From the interviews and prior work, we identified three categories of factors; content, critique context, and social attributes. For content, we counted the number of terms in the content that matched terms found in a comprehensive photographic dictionary, including crop, composition, lighting, exposure, and depth-of-field [18]. We also counted the number of positive and negative emotion words using the LIWC [30]. Response time, word length, and rating of the associated photo served as the contextual factors. For social attributes, we used the reputation score and social connectedness of the user writing the critique [35, 40]. Social connectedness was measured by the betweenness centrality of the critic's node in the directed graph where an edge in the graph is defined as a critique given from one user to another.

To increase robustness [29], 10K critiques with a total rating of at least ten were randomly selected from all of the

		Coef.	SE	p
Content Information	Technique	0.079	0.007	<.001
	Positive Emotion	0.229	0.019	<.001
	Negative emotion	-0.018	0.039	0.08
Contextual Information	Critique Length	0.438	0.016	<.001
	Response Time	-0.167	0.015	<.001
	Photo Rating	0.165	0.004	<.001
	Critic's Reputation	0.085	0.005	<.001
	Social Connectedness	0.043	0.006	<.001

Table 4. Linear regression results for predicting total critique rating. The model is significant (p<.001), with an R^2 of 0.51.

critiques for analysis. The factors considered and results of the regression are summarized in Table 4. Similar to [1, 29, 40], we found that message length, reputation score, and social connectedness are predictors of critique quality. In addition, we found that critiques posted earlier with more technical and positive emotion words receive higher scores.

Interestingly, critiques posted to a photo soon after it is submitted receive higher ratings than those posted later. One explanation is that, unlike product reviews [29], the community appreciates critiques more for their timeliness than for their content, especially for photos assumed to be work-in-progress. Almost all users (99.6%) rated others' critiques of their own work and a considerable portion (31.9%) of critique ratings were given by the owners of the corresponding photos. Another possible explanation is that later critiques offer fewer new insights relative to the earlier critiques and therefore receive lower ratings. Because of the small correlation between the critique response time and the *number* of individual ratings it received (r = 0.10; p< .001), it is unlikely that later critiques receiving fewer ratings accounts for the difference in the total critique rating.

CRITIQUE RECIPROCITY

Designers often rely upon one another for critiques, a form of *reciprocity* [2, 13]. This is enabled in the community studied by allowing users to both write and receive critiques. In fact, a few users reported that writing critiques was an effective way of scaffolding their participation. The distribution of Figure 6 shows that users may begin by submitting only photos or critiques but quickly become engaged in both activities. This motivated us to examine both direct and generalized reciprocity in the community.

Direct Reciprocity

Direct reciprocity refers to dyadic relations between users making critiques (see Figure 7a). From the interviews, most users reported making reciprocal critiques (11 users):

> "*It is a polite thing to do, if they critique your works it's nice that you do the same for them.*" [P11]

Reciprocal critiques can help build relationships. Many users reported that they have the experience of creating connections by critiquing each other's work (11 users):

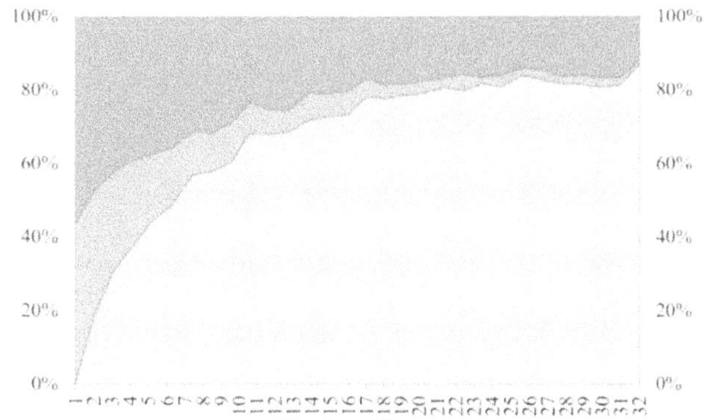

Figure 6. Percent of users who only write critiques, only receive critiques, or both, as a function of the number of items (critiques and photos) contributed.

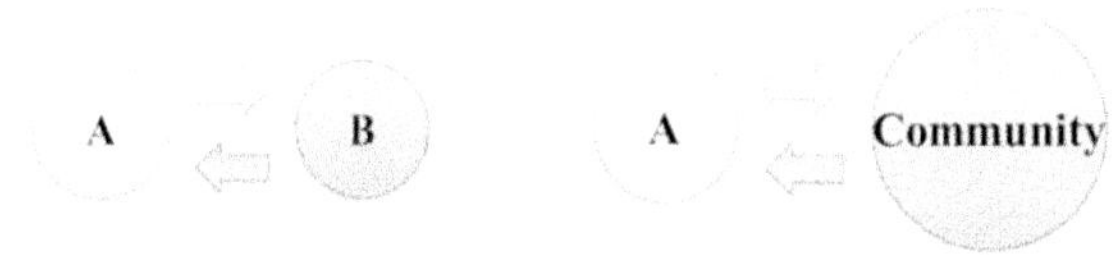

(a) Direct Reciprocity (b) Generalized Reciprocity

Figure 7. (a) User A critiques user B's photo, B then critiques A's photo; (b) User A critiques any photo in the community and someone else in the community critiques A's photo.

> "*Sometimes I critiqued somebody and they critiqued on mine. There is a part of it becomes an unspoken relationship. You say something to me and I say something back to you. And eventually we get on the track. We understand each other very well. I believe what happened it is the best when you recognize something in the work of somebody else that resonates with you that form the possibility of communication and mutual learning.*" [P6]

Users reported that they would pay special attention to the people they know and tend to give them more serious critiques (7 users):

> "*So many critiques become personal. That is with the people that your response to and for which there are some sort of mutual respect. You tend to spend more time and care in talking about their pictures and in reading or hearing from them about your own.*" [P12]

> "*It depends on who is on critique. If it is a good friend, I would be likely to give him/her an honest opinion. If I see something could be improved and some other techniques might be more successful, that kind of thing. Otherwise, you know, the critiques would be pretty light. For example, 'I like the photo', 'It gets the great color', and 'the subject is interesting' that kind of thing.*" [P3]

Surprisingly, however, only 18.1% of all critiques in the community are reciprocal and the degree of direct reciprocity[1] in the community is only 0.14, which is lower

[1] The degree of direct reciprocity in the community is calculated by the *link reciprocity* which considers both the ratio of the number of links pointing in both directions to the total number of links and the network density [15].

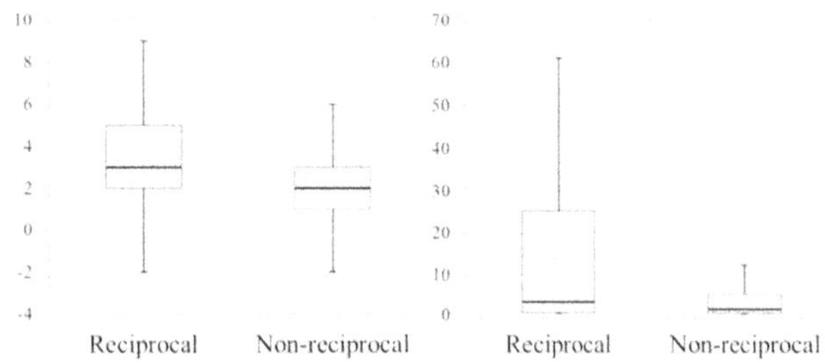

(a) Critique Rating (b) Response Time (Hour)

Figure 8. Comparison of rating and response time between reciprocal and non-reciprocal critiques. The data are skewed and therefore analyzed using the Mann-Whitney U test ($N_{recip.}$=1000, $N_{non-recip.}$=1000). (a) The median rating of reciprocal and non-reciprocal critiques is 3 and 2, respectively (*p*<.001); (b) the median response time for reciprocal and non -reciprocal critiques is 2.4h and 0.8h, respectively (*p*<.001).

than other social networks such as blogs (0.4), and email networks (0.231) [15]. The rating of reciprocal critiques was higher than the rating of non-reciprocal critiques (Figure 8); however, the response time of reciprocal critiques (median=2.4 h) is longer than that of non-reciprocal critiques (median=0.8 h). One possible explanation is that the community did not provide an immediate way for users to reciprocate. For example, users are not notified when those who have previously critiqued their work contribute a new photo. If a user wants to reciprocate, she must access her own critiques, identify the authors, and then visit the authors' photo sets. Additionally, there was no difference detected between reciprocal and non-reciprocal critiques in the photo rating carried by the critique. This indicates that users do not adjust their rating according to whether this is a reciprocal critique.

The relationship between direct reciprocity and reputation score is visualized in Figure 9. It shows that similarity in reputation score correlates with making reciprocal critiques. One user aptly explains this observed behavior:

> "*One can learn from someone closer in experience. When it's a wide gap, the learning curve is different. The expert gets tired of the same old questions and giving the same old answers. The novices or lesser knowledge have to have somewhere to start to ask the question. The closer the experience, the closer the communication.*" [P11]

This behavior reflects homophily [27], where increased similarity in users' experience increases the likelihood of communication and reciprocity.

Generalized Reciprocity

Generalized reciprocity (see Figure 7b) is an exchange among individuals without the expectation of immediate or specific returns but with the expectation that the benefit will balance out over time [2]. In the interviews, most users believed the community should balance the effort of writing critiques with the benefit of receiving critiques (11 users):

> "*It's basically the adage of "you get what you give." If you never make critiques, your popularity in the community should likely reflect this. This is how it works for about 99 percent of us, at least.*" [P8]

> "*I feel that on any photography site there should be a good family community where we all work and strive together to help each other learn.*" [P1]

Figure 9. A visualization of the aggregate pattern of reciprocal critiques in the community. About 30,000 users were sorted in descending order of their reputation scores and divided into 100 groups. Each node represents a group of 300 users. The larger size of a node represents users with higher reputation scores. Each edge indicates that more than ten reciprocal critiques were made in total between any two users in the groups. A majority of reciprocal critiques was made between users with similar reputation scores. Also, users with higher reputation were more active in making reciprocal critiques.

However, the correlation coefficient between the number of critiques a user writes and receives was only 0.19 (*p*<.001), where the number of photos contributed was used as the control variable. The weak correlation indicates that users often write more critiques than they receive and that a more balanced allocation would be welcome.

DESIGN IMPLICATIONS AND FUTURE WORK

From our analysis of critique behavior in this community, we have formulated recommendations for improving the design of critique communities in similar domains.

Foster direct and generalized reciprocity. The value of both forms of reciprocity was revealed in our interviews but little reciprocity was observed in the community overall. To catalyze direct reciprocity, one solution is to make visible the ongoing reciprocal relationships and current status, e.g., identify who has critiqued your work, number of critiques made, and how many times you have critiqued their work. Systems could be even more socially aware by suggesting photos to be critiqued based on factors such as similarity of expertise between users and their prior interaction history.

Expertise could be approximated using techniques found in [41] or, more crudely, using only the reputation score. Suggesting photos to be critiqued is similar to matching users with tasks that need to be performed [10], but the purpose would be to cultivate interpersonal relationships in addition to generating the critiques. To catalyze generalized reciprocity, one solution is to weigh the number of critiques and ratings of those critiques more favorably in the computation of reputation score. For those who often contribute critiques but receive few in return, another solution would be to give their work more exposure in the public areas of the site, e.g. display them on the main page longer, which may generate more critiques. A third solution would be to make visible the balance of critiques written vs. received for each user. This may cause others to adjust their decisions in regards to whose works they would critique.

Support 'acting' on the artifact being critiqued. In a critique, users often recommend applying various technical operators to the artifact, e.g., cropping or color balancing in photography. However, these operators are almost always described in words and it is up to the owner and community members to mentally simulate how these operations affect the artifact. To increase the communication effectiveness of a critique, one solution would be to allow an artifact to be directly edited as part of writing the critique. The edit operations could be captured, represented, and displayed with their written critique. This concept may look similar to the structured comment space created in [37], but the visual vocabulary of operators would be specific to photography or other design domain. In addition, when a user responds (replies) to an existing critique, the interface could allow the user to build on or modify the operators applied in the prior critique. This would simulate the face-to-face critique environment in which users can build on *each other's* ideas.

Structure feedback. Many users reported wanting their photos to be critiqued from multiple technical perspectives, such as composition, color, and depth-of-field, but there is no direct way of expressing this preference. An alternative design would be to allow the owner of an artifact to specify which technical perspectives they would like to receive feedback on and this information would be viewable in the interface for writing a critique. For example, the system can provide a comprehensive list of technical perspectives from which the owner can choose. As part of writing a critique, a user would have to select which of those elements are being addressed. This direction requires careful scrutiny because although specific requests for information can elicit greater community responsiveness [6], it may also increase the micro-costs of writing critiques and affect participation [5]. This opens an interesting research question about how to steer community responses towards the preferences of the owner of an artifact without compromising participation.

Manage variations and revisions. Users sometimes post variations of the same content in order to receive critiques and guide their design choices. We also found that users would revise or retake photos based on prior critiques and resubmit them. The problem is that they are unable to create associations between variations of the same content or revisions of their work; rather each item is viewed and managed as a separate artifact in the system.

Researchers have created interfaces for managing variations and alternatives (e.g. see [19]), but these interfaces target single-user applications rather than online communities. For the type of community we studied, variations could be supported by allowing a user to associate multiple artifacts as a 'variation set' indicating to the system these should be shown together when viewed and critiqued by others. For revisions, the system could allow a user to associate a new artifact with a prior version. When viewed, the associations could be navigated to see the evolution of the content and corresponding critiques. The benefit would be that a user could manage her design space more effectively and others could better understand the evolution of her work [36].

Organize and revisit critiques. Users may receive hundreds of critiques while participating in the community, yet there is no means for organizing the critiques based on the knowledge or insights contained. In order to enable more effective reuse of critiques, systems could allow users to create and apply their own personal or community-derived tags to the content of the critiques, create associations between critiques of different artifacts that make similar points, and aggregate parts of critiques that share the same tags to support review and reflection [16, 39].

Limitations. We analyzed interaction data within only one domain, digital photography, and it is unknown how our results apply to critique communities in other design domains such as writing or music. In addition, our inferences of what users expect from the community were based on a relatively small sample. We look forward to collecting data through surveys or other techniques that can provide new insight into user expectations and how these expectations might differ as a function of the perspective of the viewer (e.g., expert, peer, novice, or consumer).

CONCLUSION

Online communities offer a new approach for the critique of creative work, but there has been little research aimed at understanding online critique or how to improve it. In this research, we explored user behavior within a large online critique community in the domain of photography and conducted interviews with active members. We found that participation in the community can enhance the perception of creative work, but this effect depends on the quantity and quality of critiques received. We also found salient gaps between users' expectations and their actual experiences in the community and suggested design enhancements to close them. From an analysis of reciprocity, we found users with more similar reputation scores were more likely to critique each other's work, though little reciprocity was observed overall. The results were formulated into recommendations for improving the design of systems that support community-based critique of creative work.

ACKNOWLEDGEMENT

We thank Wai-Tat Fu, Joshua Hailpern, Vera Liao, and Andrew Harris for feedback on this work. This work was supported in part by the NSF under award no. IIS 06-43512.

REFERENCES

1. Adamic, L.A., Zhang, J., Bakshy, E., & Ackerman, M.S., Knowledge Sharing and Yahoo Answers: Everyone Knows Something. In *WWW*, (2008), 665-674.
2. Alexander, R.D. *The Biology of Moral Systems*. A. de Gruyter, Hawthorne, N.Y., 1987.
3. Aragon, C.R. and Williams, A., Collaborative creativity: a complex systems model with distributed affect. In *CHI*, (2011), 1875-1884.
4. Barrett, T. A Comparison of the Goals of Studio Professors Conducting Critiques and Art Education Goals for Teaching Criticism. *Studies in Art Education*, *30*, 1, (1988), 22-27.
5. Benkler, Y. *The Wealth of Networks: How Social Production Transforms Markets and Freedom*. Yale University, 2006.
6. Burke, M., Kraut, R.E., & Joyce, E. Membership Claims and Requests: Conversation-Level Newcomer Socialization Strategies in Online Groups. *Small Group Research*, *4*, 1, (2010), 4-40.
7. Butler, B., Sproull, L., Kiesler, S., & Kraut, R. Community Effort in Online Groups: Who Does the Work and Why? In *Leadership at a Distance*, Erlbaum Associates, 2001, 346-362.
8. Choi, B., Alexander, K., Kraut, R.E., & Levine, J.M., Socialization Tactics in Wikipedia and Their Effects. In *CSCW*, (2010), 107-116.
9. Cook, E., Teasley, S.D., & Ackerman, M.S., Contribution, Commercialization & Audience: Understanding Participation in an Online Creative Community. In *GROUP*, (2009), 41-50.
10. Cosley, D., Frankowski, D., Terveen, L., & Riedl, J., SuggestBot: Using Intelligent Task Routing to Help People Find Work in Wikipedia. In *IUI*, (2007), 32-41.
11. CritiqueCircle. http://www.critiquecircle.com/.
12. Diakopoulos, N. and Naaman, M., Towards Quality Discourse in Online News Comments. In *CSCW*, (2011), 133-142.
13. Dutton, T.A. Design and Studio Pedagogy. *Journal of Architectural Education*, *41*, 1, (1987), 16-25.
14. Feldman, E.B. *Varieties of Visual Experience; Art as Image and Idea*. H.N. Abrams, New York, 1972.
15. Garlaschelli, D. and Loffredo, M.I. Patterns of Link Reciprocity in Directed Networks. *Physical Review Letters*, *93*, 26, (2004).
16. Gilbert, E. and Karahalios, K., Understanding Deja Reviewers. In *CSCW*, (2010), 225-228.
17. Glaser, B. and Strauss, A. *The Discovery of Grounded Theory: Strategies for Qualitative Research*. Wiedenfeld and Nicholson, London, 1967.
18. Guy, N.K. *The Photographer's Dictionary: An A-Z of Technical Terms Explained*. Rotovision, 2008.
19. Hailpern, J., Hinterbichler, E., Leppert, C., Cook, D., & Bailey, B.P., TEAM STORM: Demonstrating an Interaction Model for Working with Multiple Ideas During Creative Group Work. In *C&C*, (2007), 193-202.
20. Harper, F.M., Moy, D., & Konstan, J.A., Facts or Friends? Distinguishing Informational and Conversational Questions in Social Q&A Sites. In *CHI*, (2009), 759-768.
21. Harper, F.M., Raban, D., Rafaeli, S., & Konstan, J.A., Predictors of Answer Quality in Online Q&A Sites. In *CHI*, (2008), 865-874.
22. Lampe, C., Wash, R., Velasquez, A., & Ozkaya, E., Motivations to Participate in Online Communities. In *CHI*, (2010), 1927-1936.
23. Lundstrom, K. and Baker, W. To Give Is Better Than to Receive: The Benefits of Peer Review to the Reviewer's Own Writing. *Journal of Second Language Writing*, *18*, 1, (2009), 30-43.
24. Luther, K., Caine, K., Ziegler, K., & Bruckman, A., Why It Works (When It Works): Success Factors in Online Creative Collaboration. In *GROUP*, (2010), 1-10.
25. MacJams. http://www.macjams.com/.
26. Mamykina, L., Manoim, B., Mittal, M., Hripcsak, G., & Hartmann, B., Design Lessons from the Fastest Q&A Site in the West. In *CHI*, (2011), 2857-2866.
27. McPherson, M., Smith-Lovin, L., & Cook, J.M. Birds of a Feather: Homophily in Social Networks. *Annual Review of Sociology*, *27*, (2001), 415-444.
28. Nov, O. What Motivates Wikipedians? *Commun. ACM*, *50*, 11, (2007), 60-64.
29. Otterbacher, J., Helpfulness' in online communities: a measure of message quality. In *CHI*, (2009), 955-964.
30. Pennebaker, J.W., Francis, M.E., & Booth, R.J. *Linguistic Inquiry and Word Count (LIWC): A Computer-based Text Analysis Program*.
31. PhotoSIG. http://www.photosig.com/.
32. Reily, K., Finnerty, P.L., & Terveen, L., Two peers are better than one: aggregating peer reviews for computing assignments is surprisingly accurate. In *GROUP*, (2009), 115-124.
33. Risatti, H. Art Criticism in Discipline-Based Art Education. *Journal of Aesthetic Education*, *21*, 2, (1987), 217-225.
34. Stevens, G. and Wiedenhöfer, T., CHIC - A pluggable solution for community help in context. In *NordiCHI*, (2006), 212-221.
35. Sylvan, E., Predicting Influence in an Online Community of Creators. In *CHI*, (2010), 1913-1916.
36. Tohidi, M., Buxton, W., Baecker, R., & Sellen, A., Getting the Right Design and the Design Right: Testing Many Is Better Than One. In *CHI*, (2006), 1243-1252.
37. Willett, W., Heer, J., Hellerstein, J., & Agrawala, M., CommentSpace: Structured Support for Collaborative Visual Analysis. In *CHI*, (2011), 3131-3140.
38. Wulf, V., Rohde, M., Pipek, V., & Stevens, G., Engaging with Practices: Design Case Studies as a Research Framework in CSCW. In *CSCW*, (2011), 505-512.
39. Yatani, K., Novati, M., Trusty, A., & Truong, K.N., Review Spotlight: A User Interface for Summarizing User-generated Reviews Using Adjective-Noun Word Pairs. In *CHI*, (2011), 1541-1550.
40. Yla R. Tausczik, J.W.P., Predicting the Perceived Quality of Online Mathematics Contributions from Users' Reputations. In *CHI*, (2011), 1885-1888.
41. Zhang, J., Ackerman, M.S., & Adamic, L., Expertise Networks in Online Communities: Structure and Algorithms. In *WWW*, (2007), 221-230.

Learning the Lingo? Gender, Prestige and Linguistic Adaptation in Review Communities

Libby Hemphill and Jahna Otterbacher*
Illinois Institute of Technology
3301 S Dearborn St, Chicago, IL 60616
{libby.hemphill, jahna.otterbacher}@iit.edu
*The authors contributed equally to this work.

ABSTRACT
Women and men communicate differently in both face-to-face and computer-mediated environments. We study linguistic patterns considered gendered in reviews contributed to the Internet Movie Database. IMDb has been described as a male-majority community, in which females contribute fewer reviews and enjoy less prestige than males. Analyzing reviews posted by prolific males and females, we hypothesize that females adjust their communication styles to be in sync with their male counterparts. We find evidence that while certain characteristics of "female language" persevere over time (e.g., frequent use of pronouns) others (e.g., hedging) decrease with time. Surprisingly, we also find that males often increase their use of "female" features. Our results indicate, that even when they resemble men's reviews linguistically, women's reviews still enjoy less prestige and smaller audiences.

Author Keywords
Gender; linguistic entrainment; online community; social voting.

ACM Classification Keywords
H5.3. Information interfaces and presentation (e.g., HCI): Asynchronous interaction, Web-based interaction.

General Terms
Human Factors.

INTRODUCTION
Much public discussion surrounds issues of gender and participation in online communities (OCs). For example, a March 2010 survey found that less than 15% of Wikipedia participants are women [11]. More recently, a *Room for Debate* session at NYTimes.com [34] questioned why, given that Wikipedia is meant to be the world's "free encyclopedia that anyone can edit," there is such a stark difference in participation between men and women. It is often claimed that men and women communicate and behave differently in their online interactions (e.g, [19,27,30]). Possible explanations for the Wikipedia findings included that women are too busy to contribute or that they are intimidated by the discourse [34]. Technological and social factors likely both contribute to the differences between genders in participation. We contribute to the literature on the social factors that influence participation by examining the differences between men and women's contributions to a popular review community, the Internet Movie Database (IMDb).

IMDb has been described as a male-majority community, in terms of participation and participant prestige. In a study of IMDb reviews of 250 all-time favorite movies, Otterbacher [27] reported a median utility score of 0.67 for male-authored reviews (i.e., two thirds of people who voted found these reviews useful), and a median of zero for females. Likewise, the contributions of males received more total votes. In short, females receive less attention than males and enjoy less prestige. Given that the default filter sorts on utility, females' reviews are effectively hidden, presenting users with a predominately male view.

Nonetheless, some women manage to be successful members of IMDb, participating actively and receiving high utility scores. Men and women communicate differently both in face-to-face and in computer-mediated settings, and our data concerning prolific participants reveals a number of differences in language use that the genders exhibit in their reviews. However, even when women resemble males linguistically, the utility of their reviews remains lower.

IMDb provides the opportunity to examine the interplay between technological features such as sorting, social aspects such as language use and gender, in the development of collaborative resources. Like Wikipedia, the reviews on IMDb are a shared resource created by many authors. While authors do not collaboratively write reviews, their behaviors can provide insights about OC engagement and participation. Earlier research demonstrated that it might not be necessary for people to engage in one-to-one communication, in order for them to feel affiliation toward the OC [5]. Our study contributes to the understanding of OCs and participation by identifying relationships between language use, gender, and the perceived value of authors' contributions.

CSCW'12, February 11–15, 2012, Seattle, Washington, USA.

PREVIOUS WORK

In mixed-gender communities, males typically enjoy more power and prestige than females [30]. At the IMDb, participants use plain text to present their views, making the language they use crucial – it is the vehicle through which others form an impression of them [22]. Here, we review findings related to gender, language and OCs.

Gender, power and online communities

In the early days of the Web, there was much anticipation for the creation of democratic, shared information spaces, in which all would get a chance to have their views heard. Years later, it has become apparent that this was an overly optimistic outlook. In the case of gender, Herring [19] claims that there is little evidence that online, power asymmetries differ from those in the offline world.

For instance, just as in face-to-face interactions, men tend to dominate conversations in online forums and are more likely to post aggressive messages. In contrast, female participants post fewer and shorter messages, are more polite, and write in a manner that aligns themselves with others [19]. Gefen and Ridings [16] explain that such differences have to do with how men and women use OCs. While women seek and offer social support (e.g., for problem solving), men seek to achieve and maintain status by showcasing their knowledge to others. Similar findings have been echoed in a variety of domains including e-commerce forums (e.g., [3]) and fan OCs (e.g., [7]).

At IMDb, participants do not comment on one another's postings, but rather, they vote as to whether or not reviews are useful. Therefore, there is less opportunity for harassment or direct criticism of others. However, males dominate the discourse by writing more, and longer, reviews. In addition, overall, males enjoy a more prestigious status, receiving higher utility scores and having their reviews prominently displayed by default.

Gender and language use

Men and women exhibit a number of differences in their language use behavior. Overall, women use more social styles while men use more broadcast styles. For instance, women tend to adapt a style that more directly engages their audiences ("rapport talk") while men tend to report information ("report talk") [33]. In written discourse, women use a more "outer-focused" style, in which they tend to acknowledge their perceived audience [4] and use far more pronouns [2]. Similarly, men are more likely to discuss objects, while women often discuss people [9]. In face-to-face conversation, women also exhibit more use of hedging phrases (e.g., "kind of," "sort of") [25].

Earlier work found similar differences between the style and content of IMDb reviews written by men and women [27]. Male reviewers often discussed the success of a movie and its special effects, while females wrote about characters and people. In terms of style, male-authored reviews were characteristically written in third person, while females more often wrote in the first person voice. However, the data set analyzed contained reviews written by a wide variety of reviewers, many of whom were not regular contributors. To contrast, we will analyze a set of reviews written by prolific participants at IMDb.

Language adaptation

Communication Accommodation Theory (CAT) provides a possible explanation as to how female reviewers might become more successful at IMDb. CAT holds that interlocutors adjust their linguistic patterns in order to be perceived as being more or less like their conversation partners [18]. This might result in social gains, such as fitting in with a desirable group (e.g., [12]).

While CAT was developed with face-to-face interaction in mind, such "linguistic entrainment" has been noted in computer-mediated contexts. Scissors and colleagues [31] studied pairs of participants playing a game, in which cooperation was required to win. During sessions, participants communicated only through text chat. Pairs with a high level of trust (i.e., who cooperated) exhibited more entrainment than low-trust pairs. Cassell and Tversky [8] studied an international community of young people and found evidence of both convergence and diverge in language patterns. One interesting finding was the increasing use of "we" and decreasing use of "I" over time, suggesting that participants increasingly identified with the community. With respect to gender, while initially, girls expressed emotion more often than boys, over time, girls decreased and boys increased their use of emotion words.

At IMDb, it might be that female reviewers, who want to their voices to be heard, recognize the need to adjust their communication style. In fact, Herring [20] described a "list effect." In her observations of two mixed-gender listserv discussions, she found that all participants posted in a male voice, implying that the voice of the majority had become normative. In such situations, it could be that female participants understand that the less personal, more objective "male" style is better received by others [32].

It is clear from existing research that men and male-marker language dominate online spaces [19,20]. What existing literature does not tell us is whether changes in language use correlate to an increase in the perceived value and visibility of women's contributions.

STUDY CONTEXT

At IMDb, gender is disclosed through a "male/female" review filter.[1] Participants communicate in an asynchronous and indirect manner, exchanging views by posting textual reviews and by rating movies on a scale of one to ten stars. Profile pages are simple, displaying the participant's contributions, an optional self-description and contact

[1] Though the terms "male" and "female" usually refer to one's sex, we use them interchangeably with the gender designations "man" and "woman," as done at IMDb.

	Measure(s)	Explanation
Complexity	-Word complexity: Character-to-word ratio -Sentence complexity: Word-to-sentence ratio	Some claim that women are often stronger writers than men (e.g., [14]). We use two basic measures of complexity used in automatic essay evaluation [15].
Hedging	Number of hedges, normalized by review length (words)	We use a list of 55 hedging phrases, updated from [24]. Examples include: "more or less," "sort of," "rather," "in a way," "basically."
Inner vs. outer-focused discourse	-Pronoun rate (#PNs / words) -Proportion of PNs that are first person	We compute reviewers' overall rate of pronoun use, as well as the proportion of pronouns used that are first person.
Vocabulary richness	Number of unique words / total words	Quantifies the diversity of words reviewers use. [27] reported that using a rich vocabulary is characteristic of female reviewers.

Table 1. Gendered language attributes studied.

information. Although IMDb collects gender information when the user registers, it is not explicitly noted on one's profile. When users display reviews for a movie, they may customize the display by various attributes (e.g., reviewer gender, prolific authors). The default filter is "Best," which orders reviews by utility (i.e., binary social votes collected on the question, "Was the above review useful to you?")

Data Set and Hypotheses

We began with a list of 250 top-rated movies. For each, we used the "male/female" filter. This returned all reviews written by participants who had disclosed their gender and allowed us to separate male-authored from female-authored reviews. This process resulted in a list of 21,012 unique reviewers. We found each reviewer's total contributions as listed on her profile, and then identified the most prolific 100 males and females. For each of these 200 participants, we obtained all reviews written (199,166 reviews in total).

Even among these prolific participants, males are much more active than are females, contributing a median of 1,187 total reviews to IMDb, versus only 183.5 for females[2]. In addition, the males write longer reviews than females, (a median of 249 words versus 223, respectively).

Our first hypothesis is that prolific female reviewers adapt their writing style over time. To this end, we studied attributes previously described as being gendered, detailed in Table 1. We focused on writing style, rather than on the content of reviews, to evaluate whether women change *how* they write, rather than what they write. We study changes in the six attributes, in the reviews that participants contribute over time. We identify trends for our prolific female reviewers, and compare them to those of prolific males.

H1: Prolific females write more like males over time.

We also compare the utility scores received by female reviewers, over the course of their tenure as IMDb participants. We expect that since they are learning how to write in a manner that appeals to the IMDb audience, that they will achieve more prestige with time.

H2: Prolific females improve their utility scores over time.

Defining Time

We define time in terms of the number of reviews written by a participant up to a given point (e.g., 10 reviews, 100 reviews), rather than in terms of absolute time (i.e., days since registration). We do this for two reasons. First, our hypothesis is that with repeated exposure to IMDb, a female will change her writing style. For us, writing a review represents an interaction with the community. The second is that participants in OCs might go through periods where they are inactive. Using the number of reviews written gives us a more consistent measure of the amount of active exposure to the community that participants have had.

Preece and Schneiderman [28] propose stages of participation in OCs. Their "reader-to-leader" framework explains how participants' initial activities might be limited, but that over time, they become more involved. In our data, this might be indicated by change in language use, signaling that a reviewer is assimilating and accepting the norms of the OC. To observe change over time, for each reviewer, we order her reviews chronologically, and then assign "dummy dates" (i.e., review orderings). It should be noted that since reviewers often write multiple reviews on a given day, dummy dates are not necessarily unique.

RESULTS: ALL REVIEWS WRITTEN

We used regression analysis to determine the impact of gender and the number of reviews written (i.e., dummy date) on reviews' utility and various features of the language within reviews. The results of our regressions are summarized in Table 2 and discussed below.

[2] A Wilcoxon rank-sum test for the difference between groups results in a p-value of approximately zero.

Variable	B	η^2	F	R^2	Variable	B	η^2	F	R^2
Hedging			373.08	.01	**Vocabulary richness**			1499.20	.02
# of Reviews	.00***	$.01^+$			# of Reviews	-.00***	$.02^+$		
Gender	.00***	.00			Gender	-.00*	.00		
Gender*Reviews	-.00***	.00			Gender*Reviews	-.00	.00		
First person pronoun use			1233.35	.02	**Word complexity**			2750.79	.04
# of Reviews	.00***	.00			# of Reviews	-.00***	$.03^+$		
Gender	.08***	$.02^+$			Gender	-.13***	$.01^+$		
Gender*Reviews	-.00***	.00			Gender*Reviews	-.00***	.00		
Aggregate pronoun use			2737.18	.04	**Sentence complexity**			588.79	.01
# of Reviews	.00***	.00			# of Reviews	-.00***	.00		
Gender	.01***	$.02^+$			Gender	-6.13***	$.01^+$		
Gender*Reviews	.00*	.00			Gender*Reviews	.00	.00		
Utility			253.10	.00					
# of Reviews	-.00***	.00							
Gender	-.06***	.00							
Gender*Reviews	-.00	.00							

Note. $N = 199{,}166$ $^*p < .05$. $^{**}p < .01$. $^{***}p < .001$. $^+$small effect size.

Table 2. Predictors of review utility and language differences (all reviews by all reviewers).

Using the CMOGRAM Stata module [29], we also plotted medians for each variable over time and display both scatterplots and lines-of-best-fit for males and females (see graphs in Table 3[3]). The graphs indicate positive trends for both genders on *aggregate pronoun use*, and negative trends for both genders on *vocabulary richness* and *word complexity*. For *hedging*, *first person pronoun use*, and *sentence complexity*, the direction of the usage trend differed between the genders. Finally, Figure 1 indicates a positive trend for both genders over time on review *utility*.

Even among prolific authors, some are much more active than others. The number of total reviews contributed by reviewers in our dataset ranged from only 106 (for the 100th most prolific female) to 8,167 (for the most prolific male). In addition, the most prolific female wrote a total of 2,061 reviews. Therefore, in the graphs of language features and review utility for all reviewers (i.e., Table 3 and Figure 1), the trend lines for females do not span the entire width of the graphs.

[3] In each plot, the x-axis represents numbers of reviews written, and the corresponding y-axis values represent the average medians over groups of 150 reviews. In order to make the distributions more visible, we removed axis markers and re-scaled each y-axis to make the axis intercept approximately the minimum for each value rather than 0.

Language Differences

Combined Model

All of our models showed both statistically significant and meaningful effects for reviews written, gender, and/or an interaction term. All those effect sizes are small, according to conventions established by Cohen [10] where an η^2 value of 0.01 constitutes a small effect, 0.06 a medium effect and 0.14 a large effect.

Reviews written

The number of reviews an individual had written (i.e., time) showed main effects on all our measures of language use. Of those six language differences, only *pronoun use*[4] and *hedging* increased significantly over time; the others decreased. We calculated effect size for each variable in each model as well, and these results indicate that while statistically significant, only *hedging*, *vocabulary richness,* and *word complexity* showed meaningful effects.

Gender

All language features showed a significant main effect for gender. In our data gender is coded as either 1 (female) or 0 (male), meaning that a negative coefficient indicates females used less of the given dependent variable than

[4] We use the term *pronoun use* to refer to both *aggregate pronoun use* and *first person pronoun use* at once.

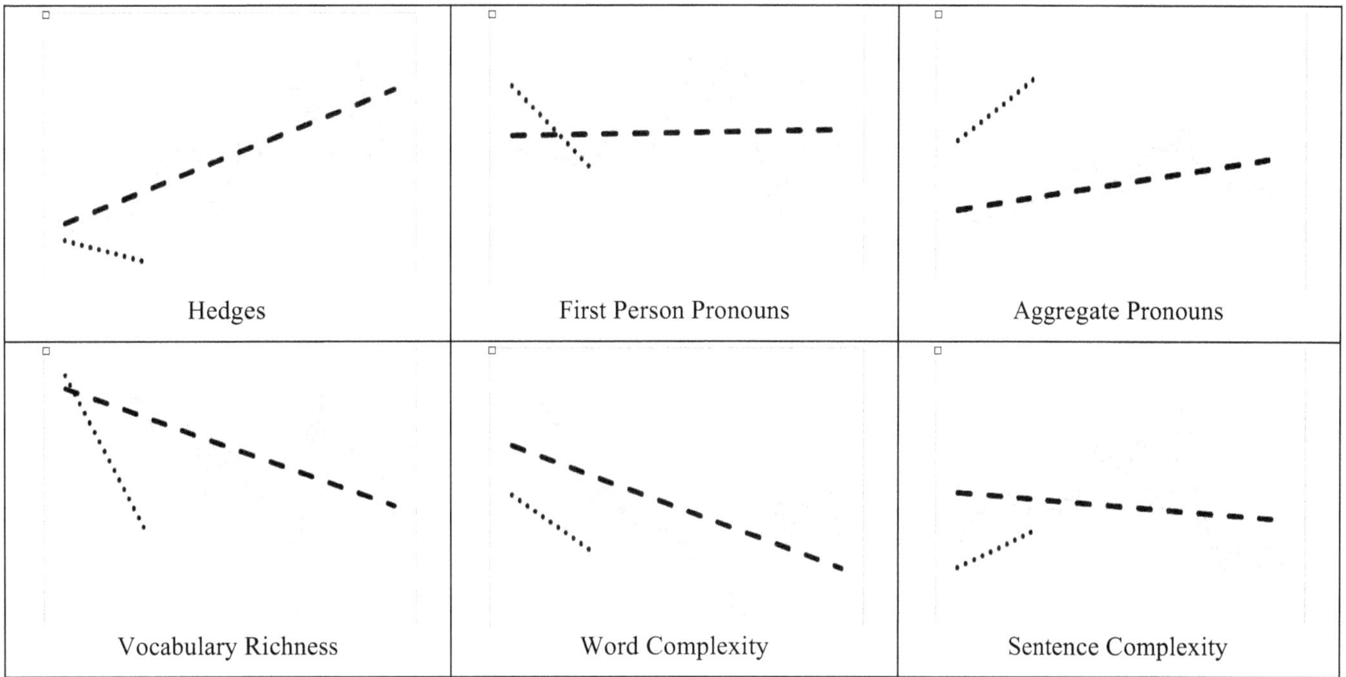

Table 3. Language use over time over all reviews and reviewers. Dotted lines represent females; dashed lines represent males.

males. Our results show that, in general, females exhibited more *hedging* and *pronoun use*, and less *vocabulary richness*, *word complexity*, and *sentence complexity*. Again, we calculated effect sizes for each variable in each model, and found that *pronoun use*, *word complexity*, and *sentence complexity* showed small meaningful differences. Therefore, it is clear that female reviewers, in general, exhibit a relatively outer-focused discourse, which is consistent with previous findings [2,4]. However, we did not find that females wrote with more complex word and sentence structures, nor that they used a richer vocabulary.

Rate of change

We included interaction terms in our regressions to compare the rates of change over time between the genders. Our results indicate females' changing rates of *hedging, pronoun use,* and *word complexity* use differed significantly from males' but that differences were not meaningful.

Utility

The results of our regression confirm Otterbacher's [27] findings and indicate that both the number of reviews written and gender had significant effects on *utility*. However, the effect sizes do not indicate meaningful effects for those statistics. Figure 1 shows the trend lines for males and females with respect to review utility. As mentioned, there is a positive trend for both. While the females appear to be increasing the utility of their reviews at a greater rate over time, they do not manage to catch up to the males (i.e., the female trend line never intersects that of the males).

RESULTS: REVIEWS WRITTEN DURING EARLY EXPOSURE

The regression results indicate significant effects for the number of reviews written on a variety of language use measures and utility, but the lack of measureable meaningful effects makes those results difficult to interpret. It might be that males and females do differ in their writing and utility over time but that those differences wash out by the time they've written thousands of reviews. Most reviewers don't write thousands of reviews though, so we examined the first 100 reviews posted by all reviewers to explore whether changes in language use or review utility appear early in a participant's exposure to the community.

For this limited dataset (the first 100 reviews written by each of the 200 reviewers), we used repeated measures ANOVA to determine the impacts of gender and the number of reviews written on reviews' utility and various features of the language within reviews early in a reviewer's tenure (see Table 4). We grouped the number of reviews into sets of 10 (e.g., reviews 1-10, 11-20) following Monk's [26] conventions for handling this kind of timed data. We labeled our effect sizes small, medium, and large according to Cohen's [10] recommendations where f values of .10, .25, and .40 indicate small, medium, and large effects, respectively. To illustrate these results, we use graphs of data about just two reviewers (see Table 5) – the most prolific male and the most prolific female.

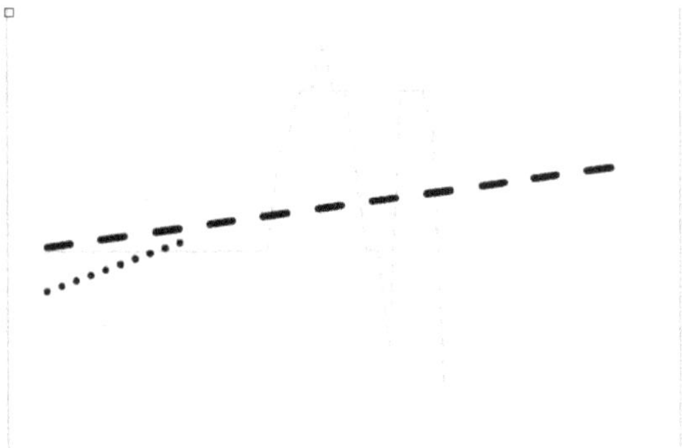

Figure 1. Review utility over time. Dotted line represents females; dashed line represents males.

Language Differences

The ANOVA indicated statistically significant differences in *first person pronoun use* and *vocabulary richness* over time; both effects were also meaningful. Our ANOVA results indicate main effects for gender in all language use variables except *vocabulary richness,* and our effect size analysis indicates that of those statistically significant results, *hedging*, *pronoun use,* and *word complexity* show meaningful differences. The ANOVA results indicate that the interaction between time and gender is not significant for any of the language use variables.

Utility

The ANOVA results indicate that the interaction of time and gender is significant for measures of *utility* and that the mean *utility* for female reviewers is lower than males' (M_f= .43 vs M_m = .49). In fact, at each interval, the males' mean *utility* is higher than the females', and the gap between them is larger after 100 reviews than after just 10 (M_m = .48, M_f= .47). Both gender and the interaction of gender and time showed meaningful effects on utility.

RESULTS: EXAMPLES FROM MOST PROLIFIC REVIEWERS

We now illustrate some of our analysis using data from the most prolific male and female. Table 5[5] shows aspects of language use (using means for each group of 10 reviews) over the first 100 reviews the most prolific author of each gender contributed. For each feature, except *vocabulary richness*, the intercept between the male's trend and female's trend occurs by 100 reviews, indicating that the major changes in writing style happen early on. Although the mean usage between the two reviewers often does not differ significantly, their patterns of use, especially in *hedging*, *pronoun use*, and *word complexity* differ remarkably.

Variable	F(df)	Cohen's *f*
Hedging		
Model	4.99(19)***	
Timebin	.18(9)	.009
Gender	76.19(1)***	.061+
Timebin#gender	0.89(9)	-
First person pronoun use		
Model	40.87(19)***	
Timebin	4.17(9)***	.037+
Gender	732.95(1)***	.191++
Timebin#gender	0.67(9)	-
Aggregate pronoun use		
Model	53.47(19)***	
Timebin	0.67(9)	-
Gender	996.63(1)***	.223++
Timebin#gender	1.46(9)	.014
Vocabulary richness		
Model	3.27(19)***	
Timebin	5.37(9)***	.044+
Gender	3.28(1)	.011
Timebin#gender	1.16(9)	.009
Word complexity		
Model	29.54(19)***	
Timebin	0.68(9)	-
Gender	544.78(1)***	.165++
Timebin#gender	1.16(9)	.008
Sentence complexity		
Model	13.07(19)***	
Timebin	0.75(9)	-
Gender	234.56(1)***	.108
Timebin#gender	0.77(9)	-
Utility		
Model	6.81 (19)***	
Timebin	1.42(9)	.014
Gender	92.39(1)***	.068+
Timebin#gender	2.70(9)**	.028+

Note. N = 20,000.

$^*p < .05$. $^{**}p < .01$. $^{***}p < .001$

+small effect size. ++medium effect size.

Table 4. Results of repeated-measures ANOVAs for each language use variable and review utility

These distributions for prolific reviewers indicate that the male exhibited a marked increase in *first person pronouns* before settling into a more consistent pattern of use. Also, he dramatically increased his use of *hedges*. Meanwhile, the female showed less variation in her *first person pronoun*

[5] Each x-axis represents numbers of reviews written, and the corresponding y-axis values represent the means over groups of 10 reviews. To ease visibility, we removed axis markers and re-scaled each y-axis to make the axis intercept approximately the minimum for each value rather than 0.

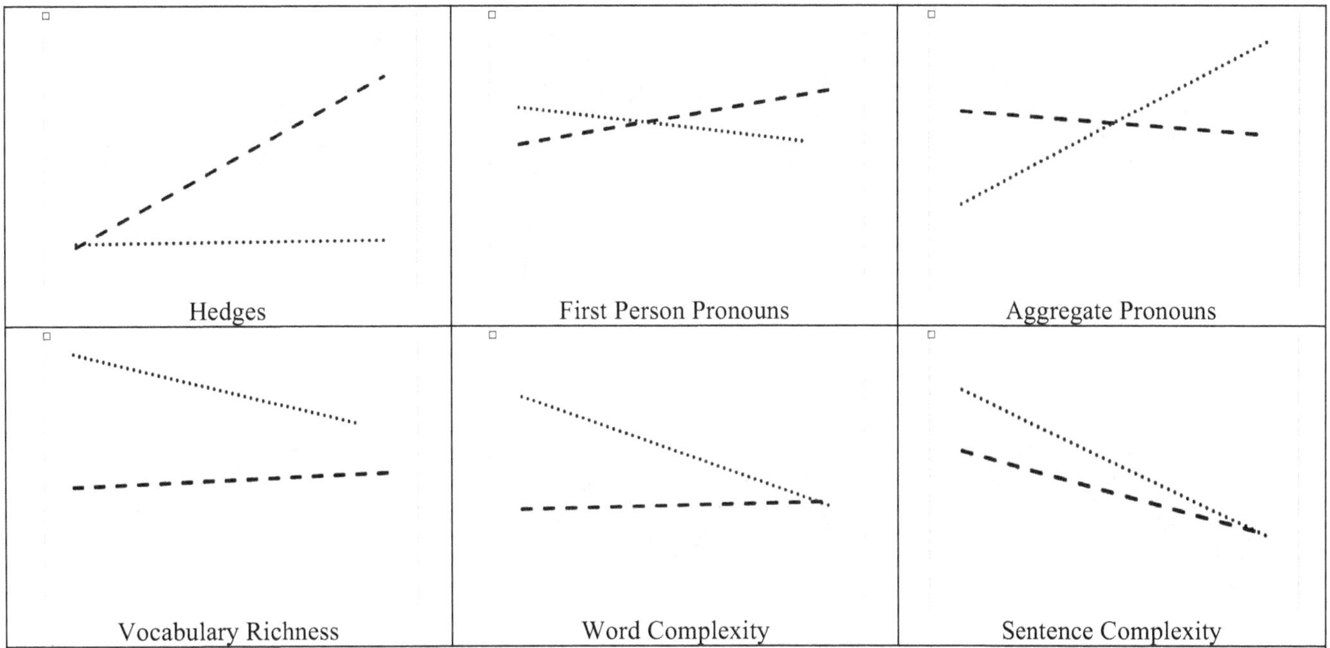

Table 5. Features of language use over first 100 reviews for the most prolific male (dashed line) and female (dotted line).

and *hedges* use, but also showed a decrease over time.

The two appear to converge on measures of language complexity – both *word* and *sentence complexity*. *Word complexity* differed meaningfully over time, indicating that the trends shown in their first 100 reviews likely continued – the female's likely decreased while the male's increased.

Next, we present a qualitative analysis of a set of reviews written by these prolific reviewers at four distinct points in time. In Tables 6 and 7, we show the opening sentences of the first review written, as well as the 25th, 50th and 200th. We also provide utility scores, in the second column.

Reviews by the male are shown in Table 6. Initially, he writes strictly in the third person, as evidenced by the first two reviews. In his first review, he simply provides a critique of the film. To contrast, in the second, while he still writes in a "reporting" voice, he describes the film's characters. By his 50th contribution, he has begun using first person pronouns to a limited extent. We also find one instance of hedging ("often"). Finally, by his 200th review, he is writing using an outward-focused discourse. In addition to expressing his feelings about the film, he interacts, using second person pronouns to address readers.

Table 7 shows the opening lines of four reviews by the female. We observe that she writes in third person in her first contribution. In contrast, her 25th review shows two markers of feminine language, namely one instance of hedging (i.e., "almost"), and one second person pronoun. Nonetheless, the voice used in the 25th review is not nearly as personal as the voice she uses in her 50th review. Here, she even apologizes to her readers for loving the film. We also observe extensive use of first person pronouns. Finally, in her 200th review, we find both singular and plural first person pronouns, as the writer interacts with her audience. In fact, she also references Hurricane Katrina, which touched all Americans, and discusses religion.

In summary, both the most prolific male and female move toward a more personal voice in their writing over time. The female explicitly uses more markers of feminine language overall. However, a change in writing style from a more reporting stance to a personal perspective is evident in both reviewers' styles.

DISCUSSION

Our data indicate support of our first hypothesis – that women write more like men over time. However, our second hypothesis – that women improve their utility scores – was not fully supported. In the first 100 reviews, females increased their scores. However, they never caught up to the males. Our findings are interesting for several reasons.

First, our results suggest that even without direct interaction, language convergence can occur. We saw evidence of linguistic convergence at IMDb that other researchers [8,20] found in more interactive OCs. Convergence has been interpreted as being positive (e.g., an indication that participants view themselves as part of the OC [8]), as well as negative (e.g., evidence that minority groups conform to majority norms [20]). That we find convergence indicates that even without direct interaction, collaborators can develop a common language.

That women reduced their use of some markers of female language is not surprising. Following Eckert [12] and Giles

Opening sentences of review		
1	15/18 (0.83)	The Apple (1980): Kudos to this German production by Golan/Globus. Who else could have conceived of a Scifi/Disco/Musical/Religious epic? Unlike Ed Wood's flicks (such as Plan 9, Glen or Glenda and Bride of the Monster), this movie proves that an embarrassingly silly and awful picture does NOT need to be made on a shoestring budget!
25	8/12 (0.67)	Tsuma Shimatsu (1967): This wonderful movie stars the great Toshiro Mifune as the leader of this family in feudal Japan. And, despite starring Mr. Mifune, it is NOT an Akira Kurasawa film! The patriarch, Mifune, is in a tough spot. His son has been ordered to divorce the wife he loves and marry another by his warlord.
50	2/2 (1)	Conte d'automne (1998): This was a little film with a simple plot and likable characters. In fact, Hollywood would learn a lot from films like this. It's not the dynamic plot, special effects or big name stars that **often** make a film exceptional, it's the writing and the acting! And this movie is written so lovingly and acted so honestly that **I** couldn't help but like it.
200	3/4 (0.75)	Laissez-passer (2002): This is a film directed by Bertrand Tavernier. **I** loved his film IT ALL STARTS TODAY, and **I** was quite impressed by this one as well. However, be forewarned that this film will not be for all tastes. If **you** are French or have a good knowledge of French cinema, then **you'll** no doubt enjoy this film.

Table 6. Examples of reviews by the most prolific male.

Opening sentences of review		
1	14/21 (0.67)	Leaving Las Vegas (1995): A big disappointment for what was touted as an incredible film. Incredibly bad. Very pretentious. It would be nice if just once someone would create a high profile role for a young woman that was not a prostitute.
25	4/5 (0.8)	Elvis (1979/I) (TV): This magnificently produced bio of Elvis Presley contains an eerie, **almost** frightening portrayal of Presley by Kurt Russell, who literally seems to be inhabited by Elvis' spirit. Physically, the movie is perfect in casting and location - **you** could see a freeze of any frame of this film and know it's about Elvis. All that being said, die-hard Elvis fans will be left frustrated by the movies' gaping holes and unnecessary inaccuracies, the biggest of which is that the film stops in 1970 when Elvis lived until 1977.
50	2/5 (0.4)	Phenomenon (1996): **Sorry** but **I** just loved it. **I** know for some it will be sentimental and trivial. It was on the slow side, a little too easygoing, but utterly charming with a terrific cast. The Robert Duvall role certainly did not need anyone of his caliber playing it, but it's always good to see him just the same. For the moment, it was just what **I** needed. If **you're** a man, don't bother.
200	3/4 (0.75)	Brigham Young (1940): This is a wonderful movie about the struggle of the Mormons and their final settlement in Salt Lake, Utah. The beginning and the ending are especially powerful, and the message is one **we** all have to be reminded of - God doesn't talk, but he communicates, if **we** would only listen. As **I** am writing this in the midst of the horrors going on in New Orleans and the surrounding area due to Katrina, **I** was especially moved by the Mormons having to leave everything behind and move on after Joseph Smith was assassinated.

Table 7. Examples of reviews by the most prolific female

et. al [18], we expected women to adjust their patterns. What we did not expect was to see a trend among males to adopt *more* feminine markers. Cassell and Tversky [8] reported males adjusting toward female style, but we expected a "list effect" here [19], since we knew that IMDb has a male majority. "List effect" was identified in listserv conversations in which all authors adopted the male voice. In contrast, we saw that men adjusted their language, especially by increasing hedging and pronoun use.

One possible explanation is that men are becoming more comfortable with their place in the OC over time. Rather than continuing to write with a detached voice, they begin to write in a socially engaging manner. This would be consistent with the observation that with increased involvement, one's personal identity (e.g., male, 28 years old) might influence behavior to a lesser extent than one's social identity (e.g., prolific reviewer of foreign films) [23]. We believe this is possible, even for participants who do not engage in repeated interaction with others, since participants often develop a personal connection to the OC as a whole (i.e., the site itself acts as a primary actor in the participant's social network [5]).

Likewise, female participants might not feel as attached to the OC, particularly if they do not feel that others value their contributions. Following [27], we observed higher utility scores for men. The gap between men and women was not as pronounced as in earlier work, but still matters. The implications of men having higher average utility, even if the gap isn't meaningful according to effect size calculations, is that men's reviews are more likely to be read than are women's. Because IMDb sorts its reviews according to utility by default, and users rarely read past the first page [1,17], women's reviews remain unseen, buried on later pages. As a result, female participants might adapt their writing patterns toward those of the majority.

Another surprising result is that in all language differences, the convergence between men and women's behavior occurs within the first 100 reviews. However, even though women's utility increases, it never catches up with men's, even after 2,000 reviews. The question remains – why are women's reviews consistently seen as being less "useful," even once they shift to the majority writing style? The apparent undervaluing of women's contributions may have broader impacts. For instance, women's contributions in other electronic media such as workplace email may be undervalued as well. The increased use of asynchronous communication in which contributions are addressed to a community rather than to an individual (e.g., Wikipedia, corporate knowledge management systems) implies the importance of the implications of the disparity in value and visibility awarded women's contributions.

LIMITATIONS

Our findings are subject to a few limitations with regard to the content and object of the reviews, and the authors' self-report of their genders. Differences in the content of reviews were not investigated in our study. However, Otterbacher [27] previously found that even when she controlled for aspects of reviews' content and stylistic features, reviewer gender and review utility were still highly correlated. We believe that several processes are at work beyond the differences in the way that men and women write, including the use of the social voting mechanism to order reviews, as well as the gender composition of the community and particularly of those who vote on review utility. Unfortunately, we cannot observe who votes for which reviews, but we suspect that just as male participants contribute more reviews than females, that they provide more social feedback as well.

We also do not investigate possible differences between various features of the movies being reviewed (e.g., genre, critics' rating, release date) that may impact reviewers' behavior. Aspects of the movie may influence how reviewers write about it – for instance, reviewers may adopt a different linguistic style for mainstream movies than for lesser-known films, or for romantic versus action films.

It is challenging to observe gender dynamics in OCs because participants often do not disclose their demographics. Even in communities in which it is customary to reveal one's identity, participants do not necessarily use their offline identities. They may have faceted identities, choosing to present certain personal characteristics in different situations [13], or they may adopt new identities. In fact, Bruckman [6] notes that many women use neutral or male identities (e.g., pseudonyms, avatars) to avoid unwanted attention from men, as well as outright harassment [21]. Accordingly, at IMDb, revealing one's gender is not mandatory. Our results rely on the assumption that users who provide their identity do so accurately.

CONCLUSION AND FUTURE WORK

Our results showed that even if women adopt language more like men's, their contributions might still go unnoticed. We identified a change in behavior over time, but only by asking authors could we really tell whether changes were made intentionally or even consciously. For instance, whether changes occur because a reviewer is trying to communicate more effectively, or wants to appeal to the voting masses is not clear.

Another possible reason for a change in language behavior might be that with time, reviewers' perception of their place in the OC might change. We would especially like to ask prolific reviewers if their *feelings* toward IMDb changed over time, as they contributed more reviews. Also, we would like to know to what extent, if any, the feedback on their reviews influenced these feelings.

IMDb reviews provide an accessible and rich data set for examining a number of questions about user-contributed content (UCC) and its authors. Our study reveals differences between the genders that impact what reviews other users see, and future work should explore other implications of differences in the style of UCC and the characteristics of its authors.

ACKNOWLEDGMENTS

We are grateful for the helpful, constructive feedback the AC and our anonymous reviewers provided.

REFERENCES

1. Adamic, L.A. and Huberman, B.A. The Web's hidden order. *Communications of the ACM 44,* 9 (2001), 55-59.
2. Argamon, S., Koppel, M., Fine, J. and Shimoni, A. R. Gender, genre, and writing style in formal written texts. *Text*, 23, August 2003.
3. Awad, N.F. and Ragowsky, A. Establishing trust in electronic commerce through online word of mouth: an examination across genders. *Journal of MIS 24,* 4 (2008), 101-121.
4. Biber, D. *Dimensions of Register Variation: a Cross-Linguistic Comparison.* Cambridge & New York: Cambridge University Press, 1995.
5. Brown, J., Broderick, A.J. and Lee, N. Word of mouth communication within online communities:

Conceptualizing the online social network. *Journal of Interactive Marketing 21, 3* (2007), 2-20.

6. Bruckman, A. Gender swapping on the Internet. In Ludlow, P. (Ed.), *High Noon on the Electronic Frontier: Conceptual Issues in Cyberspace.* Cambridge, MA USA: MIT Press, 1996.
7. Bury, R. *Cyberspaces of their Own: Female Fandoms Online.* Peter Lang Publishing, New York, NY USA, 2005.
8. Cassell, J. and Tversky, D. The language of online intercultural community formation in Junior Summit '98. *Journal of CMC 10,* 2 (2005).
9. Coates, J. *Women, Men and Language.* London: Longman, 1993.
10. Cohen, J. *Statistical Power Analysis for the Behavioral Sciences.* Hillsdale, NJ: Lawrence Erlbaum Associates, Inc., 1988.
11. Collaborative Creativity Group of the United Nations University. Wikipedia Survey – Overview of Results. http://www.wikipediasurvey.org/docs/Wikipedia_Overview_15March2010-FINAL.pdf (accessed May 13, 2011).
12. Eckert, P. *Jocks and Burnouts: Social Categories and Identity in the High School.* Teachers College Press, New York, NY, USA, 1989.
13. Farnam, S.D. and Churchill, E.F. Faceted identity, faceted lives: social and technical issues with being yourself online. *Proc. CSCW,* ACM Press (2011), 359-368.
14. Flynn, E.A. Composing as a woman. *College Composition and Communication 39*, 4 (1988).
15. Foltz, P.W., Laham, D., Landauer, T.K. Automated essay scoring: applications to educational technology. In *Proceedings of EdMedia* (1999).
16. Gefen, D. and Ridings, C.M. If you spoke as she does, sir, instead of the way you do: a sociolinguistics perspective of gender differences in virtual communities. *ACM SIGMIS Database 36,* 2 (2005), 78-92.
17. Gilbert, E. and Karahalios, K. Understanding déjà reviewers. *Proc. CSCW*, ACM Press (2010), 225-228.
18. Giles, H., Coupland, J., and Coupland, N. Accommodation theory: communication, context, and consequence. In Giles, H., Coupland, J. and Coupland, N. (Eds.), *Contexts of Accommodation. Developments in Applied Sociolinguistics.* Cambridge & New York: Cambridge University Press, 1991.
19. Herring, S. C. Gender and power in online communities. In Holmes, J. and Meyeroff, M. (eds.) *The Handbook of Language and Gender*, pp. 202-228. Oxford: Blackwell, 2003.
20. Herring, S.C. Posting in a different voice: gender and ethics in computer-mediated communication. In Ess, C. (Ed.) *Philosophical Perspectives on Computer-Mediated Communication.* Albany, NY: SUNY Press, 1996.
21. Herring, S.C. The rhetorical dynamics of gender harassment on-line. *The Information Society 15*, (1999), 151-167.
22. Jacobson, D. Impression formation in cyberspace: Online expectations and offline experiences in text-based virtual communities. *Journal of CMC 5,* 1 (1999).
23. Kim, H-W., Zheng, J.R. and Gupta, S. Examining knowledge contribution from the perspective of an online identity in blogging communities. *Computers in Human Behavior 27* (2011), 1760-1770.
24. Lakoff, G. Hedges: a studying meaning criteria and the logic of fuzzy concepts. *Journal of Philosophical Logic 2,* 4 (1973), 458-508.
25. Lakoff, R. Language and woman's place. *Language in Society* 2, (1973), 45-79.
26. Monk, T.H., Buysse, D.J., Reynolds III, C.F., Berga, S.L., Jarrett, D.B., Begley, A.E. and Kupfer, D.J. Circadian rhythms in human performance and mood under constant conditions. *Journal of Sleep Research* 6, (1997), 9-18.
27. Otterbacher, J. Inferring gender of movie reviewers: exploiting writing style, content and metadata. In *Proc. CIKM.* ACM Press (2010), 369-378.
28. Preece, J. and Schneiderman, B. The Reader-to leader framework: motivation technology-mediated social participation. *AIS Transactions on Human-Computer Interaction 1,* 1 (2009), 13-32.
29. Robert, C. CMOGRAM: Stata module to plot histogram-style conditional mean or median graphs, *Statistical Software Components*, Boston College Department of Economics (2010). http://econpapers.repec.org/software/bocbocode/s457162.htm (accessed November 19, 2011).
30. Savicki, V., Lingenfelter, D. and Kelley, M. Gender language style and group composition in Internet discussion groups. *Journal of CMC 2*, 3 (1996).
31. Scissors, L.E., Gill, A.J., and Gergle, D. Linguistic mimicry and trust in text-based CMC. *Proc. CSCW,* ACM Press (2008), 277-280.
32. Spender, D. *The Writing or the Sex, or, Why You Don't Have to Read Women's Writing to Know it's no Good.* New York, NY: Pergamon Press, 1989.
33. Tannen, D. *You Just Don't Understand.* New York, NY: Harper Collins Publishers, Inc, 1990.
34. Where Are the Women in Wikipedia? Room for Debate. http://www.nytimes.com/roomfordebate/2011/02/02/where-are-the-women-in-wikipedia (accessed November 19, 2011).

Your Space or Mine?: Community Management and User Participation in a Chinese Corporate Blogging Community

Qinying Liao[1] Yingxin Pan[1] Michelle X. Zhou[2] Tingting Gan[1]

[1]IBM Research China
Bldg. 19 Zhongguancun Software Park, Beijing, 100193
{liaoqy, panyingx, gantingt@cn.ibm.com}

[2]IBM Almaden Research Center
650 Harry Road, San Jose, CA 95120
mzhou@us.ibm.com

ABSTRACT
In this paper, we present a case study of MoCo Blogs, a publicly accessible, corporate blogging site, which is hosted by a large telecommunication company in China. We study the design and operation of the site from two aspects: (1) how community owners/administrators guide and coordinate blogger activities to meet the company's business goals; and (2) how participants respond to management guidance and act on their own incentives. Through the analysis of three data sources: 17-month activity logs with 1,046 bloggers and 10,291 blog entries, 4-month online participatory observation, and in-depth interviews, we present two key findings. First, we describe three key operational strategies employed by the site administrative team to encourage user contributions and manage content across the organizational boundaries. Second, we examine how these strategies directly influence user participation. Finally, we discuss the implications of our findings on an organization's roles in corporate social communities.

Author Keywords
Weblogs, blogging community, coordination, management, participation, China

ACM Classification Keywords
H5.m. Information interfaces and presentation (e.g., HCI): Miscellaneous.

General Terms
Human Factors; Design

1. INTRODUCTION
More and more enterprises have started to use social technologies, including wikis, blogs, and social networking services to better connect with their employees, customers, and business partners (e.g., [6, 8, 11]). While most of existing research focuses on studying participants' behavior in online communities (e.g., [2, 11, 12, 17], little work is on community management. Recent studies, however, have shown that management control is critical to the success of online communities in certain contexts (e.g., Chinese online communities [16] and corporate online communities [5]).

Our current work examines an organization's role in corporate online communities. Here, we present a case study of a corporate blogging site in China, where the participants' behavior is guided and managed to achieve the business goals of the organization. The blogging community in our study, MoCo Blogs, is created and hosted by a large telecommunication company in China. It is publicly accessible on the internet by MoCo employees as well as people outside the company. To guide and facilitate user participation, a dedicated group of MoCo employees manages the blogging site, including planning, editing, and promoting the site content. After a year of its formal launch, the site has attracted about 80,000 registered users with around 2,000 active bloggers. Nearly 70% of the active bloggers are MoCo employees.

To the best of our knowledge, our work is the first in examining the operations of a corporate blogging site with a mix of participants consisting of both employees and the public. As a result, our work offers three contributions. First, our work presents a comprehensive analysis on the design and operation of a unique corporate blogging community. Second, we provide valuable insights on fostering and maintaining a successful cross-organizational social platform that involves diverse participants. Third, our study opens a window to examining online communities in Chinese enterprises, which are less studied and understood.

The rest of the paper is organized as follows: we discuss related work before giving an overview of the MoCo Blogs community and its overall goals. We then examine the site's management operations and their impact on user participation. Finally, we discuss implications of our findings.

2. RELATED WORK
Compared to public blogging sites which have been studied extensively (e.g., [1, 7, 20, 21], corporate blogging sites are much less understood. Previous studies on 'corporate blogging' focus mainly on externally accessible blog sites main-

tained by an organization and used as the interface to the public. For example, Kelleher and Miller [13] find that external corporate blogs create "conversational human voice" and are better at managing public relations than traditional websites. Similarly, Ma and Zhang [17] study nine corporate blogging sites from the perspective of customer communication. They have identified three types of content and three types of management strategies from these sites.

In addition to examining external corporate blogging sites, there are also a number of studies on internal corporate blogging sites where the employees voice their opinions and share information behind the corporate firewall [12, 11, 24, 8]. A recent study is on IBM's internal blogging site, which identifies a set of its informational and social benefits, including network building and information sharing [12]. Similarly, Huh *et al.* discover that the main purposes for employees to blog internally are to share information and expertise, as well as to encourage discussions among the colleagues [11]. In their study on FeamCo's internal blogging site, Yardi *et al.* analyze the site's traffic patterns and readerships and find that the bloggers' perceived level of attention received has a great impact on their behavior and attitudes at workplace [24]. Efimova and Grudin conduct an extensive study on employee blogs in Microsoft [8]. They identify four categories of employee blogs based on where they are hosted and three work-related uses of such blogs.

Our work is also related to recent efforts on understanding cultural impact on social technologies [15, 16]. Although China has become one of the largest social markets on the Internet [4], little is known about the use of social technologies in enterprises in China. Our own recent study finds that there is a lack of motivation for Chinese employees to participate at the IBM internal blogging site, if it is not directly related to their work [15]. Chinese employees mainly blog about their personal or short-term team work, which receives limited readership and attention from the broader audience. On the other hand, another study of ours suggests that proper management could help foster online community development in China [16].

Compared to previous work on studying corporate blogging, our case study on the MoCo Blogs community is unique in several aspects. First, we focus on analyzing the interplay of community management and user participation. Second, the MoCo Blogs community is different from most corporate blogging sites as it involves a mix of participants from within and outside of the company. In particular, our study aims to answer the following questions:

- Why does the company host the blog site? What are the goals of the blogging community?
- How does the community owner coordinate participants' behavior to achieve the corporate goals?
- How do the users participate in the community? How do they respond to the community management?

3. STUDY OVERVIEW

We first provide an overview of the MoCo Blogs site, and then describe the data and methods used in our study.

3.1 MoCo Blogs

MoCo Blogs is created by MoCo Labs, the research institute of a large telecommunication company in China. MoCo develops and provides mobile communication services across the country. It has about 300,000 employees in more than 1,000 offices distributed over 31 provinces, covering almost every city and county in China. MoCo Blogs is a key component of the MoCo Labs Internet Portal, which is hosted by the company. The blogging site was initially tested internally in October 2007 and then launched to the public in January 2008. Both MoCo employees and people outside of the company can visit, register, and create their own blogs on MoCo Blogs. Figure 1 is the snapshot of the MoCo Blogs home page.

3.2 Data and Methods

We collected and used three sources of data to understand the operation and user activities on MoCo Blogs. First, in April 2009, we collected and analyzed 10,291 blog entries created by 1,046 bloggers. Second, two of the authors registered and created their own accounts on MoCo Blogs. Through their experience, we observed and studied the social interactions in this blogging community from March to July 2009. Furthermore, we conducted in-depth interviews with three MoCo Blogs administrators, the project manager, the editor, and a lead designer. Through the interviews, we learned the goals, usage, and management of MoCo Blogs.

4. GOALS AND AUDIENCE OF MOCO BLOGS

Based on our collected data, here we discuss in detail the goals of MoCo Blogs and its target audience. Since its inception, the goals of MoCo Blogs are two-fold: (1) providing an informal, external communication channel to the general public, and (2) fostering community building and knowledge sharing across organizational boundaries. To achieve these goals, MoCo Blogs target technical, business, and service staff of the company, as well as telecommunication domain experts outside of the company.

4.1 Goals of MoCo Blogs

Initially, MoCo Blogs was proposed to be the social platform for MoCo Lab employees to publicize their research externally. Here is how the project manager, Qiang, put it, "*Research is the engine for MoCo's innovation and the Internet Portal we developed for the Research division represents our external image. We wanted a platform to advertise our research work... But we believe a single voice from the official wouldn't be enough. We did not want the traditional things like the boring brochure, we wanted something...live.... Research is open and knowledge intensive and we don't think an official spokesperson could work out everything. So you shall build on the diverse experience*

Figure 1. Homepage of MoCo blogging site.

and expertise from people to achieve that goal." A blogging tool seems a perfect platform for achieving this goal, because it is simple enough for users to create their personal blogs to share their ideas. It also provides the possibility of interaction with others through commenting.

During its internal deployment, however, the team began to think about expanding the original scope to involve external experts. "*MoCo is a company that has a lot of influence on various parties in the telecommunication industry in China. In the long term, we want this platform to go beyond MoCo Labs to represent the whole company and become an influential community in the industry. Traditionally we were not this open, but that limited the company's development. And we realized that it is important to interact with other organizations in our ecosystem. This will finally stimulate the prosperity of the whole industry and in return grow ourselves.*" said Qiang. The goals of MoCo Blogs then became much clearer. First, it created a place for MoCo employees to share their views with the public on the business and technology trends of the company and the telecommunication industry. Second, it intended to attract external domain experts to share their outside-in perspectives and help develop the community for the entire industry. This initiative was well supported by MoCo's top management. The community developed quickly after its official launch and served multiple purposes: a MoCo's external communication portal, and a knowledge sharing portal for its employees and for the people in the industry.

4.2 Target Users and Community Incubation

Based on the goals of MoCo Blogs, the target users include approximately 100,000 business, technical, and service staff members from the MoCo headquarters to remote branch offices, as well as the external domain experts in telecommunication. To ensure the success of MoCo Blogs, MoCo Labs created a small, dedicated team to manage its users and the content produced by the community. The team included a project manager, a system administrator, a managing editor, and two part-time editors. Their first task was to advertise the blogging site and attract quality users.

The administrative team first solicited participation within the enterprise. *"We decided to first shoot for the internal market, then the external, and finally the whole industry. If our own employees find it interesting and useful, then people in other companies would be interested too. MoCo is the lead company in telecommunication in China and always gets attentions. I believe external users would come for at least two reasons. First, they want to get the latest information about what MoCo people are doing. Second, they come to develop and maintain connections with MoCo."* said the project manager.

The team recruited internal advocates mainly via emails. *"In the beginning, we broadcasted the internal pilot of MoCo Blogs through our OA system and emails. This yielded good results. Every time we sent out email advertisements, we got a good number of new registered users."*

By the time when we conducted our interviews in January 2009, MoCo Blogs already had 80,000 registered users, of which 70% were MoCo employee. The other 30% were external, including MoCo's suppliers, customers, people from consulting firms and universities, and independent industrial observers. In our interview, the project manager told us that their target ratio of internal versus external users was 20/80 in the long run. To achieve this goal, they maintained a list of external experts who had good visibility and big impact on the industry. These experts were invited to create their own spaces on MoCo Blogs. The project manager pointed out, *"For external users, our strategy is to attract and keep a good number of influential writers. ... I never doubt that after the community is built up, more and more people from other organizations in the industry would come themselves."* Most external experts accepted MoCo's invitation. While they contributed to MoCo Blogs, the site provided them with an extra channel to reach a wider audience, given MoCo's dominance in the industry.

Figure 2 shows the rapid growth of content at the MoCo blogging community. Just within a year, the monthly blog posts reached 1700 (the drop in January 2009 was due to the Chinese Spring Festival holidays). Below we describe how this development was achieved.

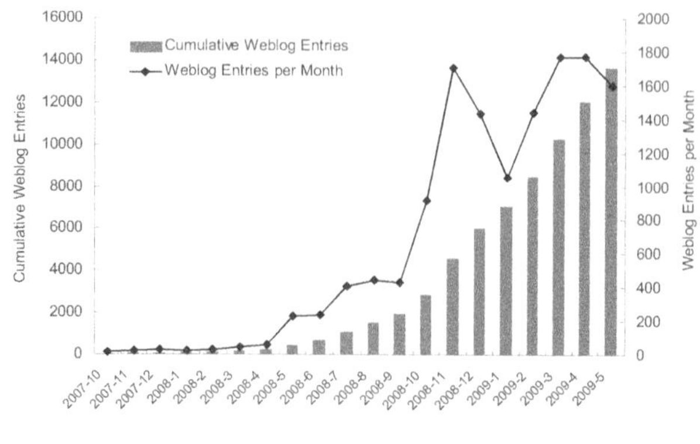

Figure 2. The blog entries by month.

5. COMMUNITY MANAGEMENT AND COORDINATION

To encourage and guide participation, the MoCo Blogs management team employed multiple strategies. Based on our log data analysis, participatory observation, and interviews, we have identified three key strategies: topic planning and guidance, editorial recommendations, and notable rewarding system.

5.1 Topic Planning and Guidance

Planning and coordinating the site's content is the key task of the MoCo Blogs administrative team. Aiming to become the industry's leading online community, MoCo Blogs focuses on featuring business and technology trends in telecommunication. Accordingly, the management team makes their own content development plan and provides guidance on the topics to be discussed at the site.

Content Planning

Content planning for the site is closely tied to MoCo's business. The planned topics include discussions on MoCo's key strategies, company-wide business events, and customer needs. For example, the management team made a content plan for the whole year of 2009 at the beginning of the year. *"We did this based on a general understanding of our business. For instance, what's gonna be hot in the year and what would be the key topics of our annual telecommunication summit. We also consider what our key customers expect us to deliver during the year."* said Min, the editor in chief. The plan identified 20 key topics for 2009 and specified the level of importance of each topic in each month of the year. Of these 20 topics, eight were on specific telecommunication technologies (e.g., "3G standards"). Another eight were related to MoCo's business operations (e.g., "3G marketing"). The remaining four topics were about the promotion and rewarding events designed by the management team to encourage the use of blogs, including "blogging competition" and "annual award event" (Section 5.3).

The plan was published on the MoCo Blogs' homepage and was also featured in the management team's blogs. While such a plan serves as a general guide to potential authors, it is the daily operation that ensures the execution of the plan and mediates the production of content at the site, which we'll examine in the next.

Content Coordination

During the plan execution, the management team made weekly adjustments to the plan according to the news and trends in the industry. They then communicated the identified topics to a core group of authors and encouraged them to contribute the content at the site. *"Currently we maintain a list of about 200 key users. They are all high quality contributors and have good impact on others in the community. Among these, about 40 are those we communicate on a weekly basis."* Min told us. These core users are categorized by their expertise areas and experiences. The team selected different bloggers to contact based on the topics and through various channels, including email, instant messenger, and even phone. *"We normally communicate with the selected potential authors twice a week. We first invite them to write an article on a certain topic, and we then send a reminder."*

Besides planning the topics and recruiting bloggers on specific topics, the management team also actively promoted selected blogs and recommended them to the community.

5.2 Editorial Recommendations

The management team employed several design elements to direct readers' attention and increase the visibility of selected authors. In turn, we believe these elements play a key role in motivating the participation in the community.

One design element is to direct the readers to certain articles featured on the homepage of MoCo Blogs, which serves as a gateway to the blogging community. As shown in Figure 1, the homepage of MoCo Blogs is complex. It aggregates not only the most recent posts, but also editor-recommended articles covering different topics. One segment of the page near the top is used to display a number of *headlines*, the most popular and important recent posts. Another large portion of the page displays *channeled news*, selected posts which are categorized into 6-8 channels. For example, channels shown in Figure 1 include “3G”, “Mobile Internet”, and “Cloud Computing”. These channels are organized manually by the editors and will change according to the content plan. On the right side of the page, it displays the ranking of top bloggers and top blog entries by the total number of visits and comments.

Another design element is the *daily newsletter*, which is called “Labs Today”. *Labs Today* features important updates of MoCo Blogs and is delivered through two channels daily: emailed to all subscribers to the website and posted in a blog hosted by the *Labs Today* editorial team. After the MoCo CEO and other senior leaders claimed that they were faithful readers of *Labs Today*, it became an effective way to stimulate blogger contributions to the community. *“This is especially significant to employees in branches in remote cities and counties. Normally there's no channel for them to voice their opinions to higher-level management in our headquarters. But Blogs provides an excellent platform for them to do so.”* [Qiang, Project Manager]

Incorporating selected user-generated content into the site's homepage and daily summaries required one full-time and two part-time designated editors. *“What you can see from the homepage and daily summaries are all done by our editors. We do not rely on automatic recommendation. Automatically recommending articles and authors by their popularity is good. But we care more about the content and use it to guide users to achieve the community's goals.”* [Qiang, Project Manager]

The yearly content plan is the start point for categorizing and selecting quality posts. *“The channels or the categories on the homepage are pre-defined according to our yearly content plan. Authors' tags help map their articles to each category. We then review and select what we want and put them on the homepage.”* [Min, editor-in-chief]

During March to April 2009, we observed the articles and authors appearing on the homepage and in *Labs Today* for 6 weeks. We identified several key characteristics of the management team's recommendation activities.

First, the editorial recommendation included contributions by a diverse set of authors. During the six weeks, 644 unique entries by 211 authors were recommended. Over 90% of these authors had never appeared in the “Bloggers Stars”. Moreover, 81 (38.4%) had one post featured, and another 45 (21.3%) were recommended twice. In contrast, only 17 (8.1%) authors had more than 10 posts recommended.

Second, the featured blogs were refreshed timely to keep the audience. For example, blog entries in headlines could stay as long as 6 days, with an average of 3.4 days (SD=1.3). Blog entries in channeled news are featured for 2.3 days on average (SD=.94). *Labs Today*, as its name dictates, is updated daily. Although the majority of the articles (72.7% in total) were recommended on the same day when they were posted, some entries were not recommended right away. For example, one article was recommended as a headline after 32 days when it first appeared. In another extreme case, one blog entry appeared in the channeled news after it was posted 221 days ago.

Moreover, certain articles were highlighted repeatedly through multiple channels. Among the total of 644 blog entries that appeared on the homepage and *Labs Today*, nearly 30% showed up in more than one place, e.g., headlines, channeled news, and *Labs Today*.

Overall, the site administration effort in selecting and promoting participants' contributions via multiple channels (e.g., the homepage and daily news) aims at achieving two goals. First, it helps attract and direct the audience's attention to the content that aligns with the goals of the community. Second, it also creates an environment for bloggers to compete for attention. This stimulates social engagement as well as guides the directions of topics.

5.3 Rewards

Besides rewarding contributions by promoting the visibility of authors and their posts in multiple channels, the site administrative team also developed two “formal” venues to reward and motivate user contributions: yearly awards and ad hoc honorable mentions.

Yearly Awards

MoCo Blogs Carnival is the biggest event held by the administrative team at the end of each year. The key purpose of the event is to acknowledge and reward outstanding bloggers. The evaluation criteria, as published in the management team's blog, include bloggers' contribution (quality and number of total posts) and popularity (readership and number of comments received). The management team first selects a short list of candidates based on the above criteria and the final winners are determined by the votes from an award committee and the site users. *“Although the number of bloggers who can receive our yearly awards is limited, it is not a competition.”* Qiang explained that acknowledging the participants' contributions is more important. *“Actually the Carnival is created to mainly thank our users. We set tens of awards to ensure a good coverage of bloggers. We also provide special rewards to new comers who have showed great potential in the community.”*

In the 2009 Carnival, 99 bloggers won the awards. The awards were in four categories: subject matter experts, innovation awards, top contributors of the year, and bloggers with great potentials. In the first category, 67 blogger were recognized as experts in 16 subject areas (e.g., mobile internet, 3G standards, cloud computing, and industrial policies). Among the 67 awardees, 17 (25%) were from the MoCo headquarters, 30 (45%) were from MoCo's remote branches, and 20 (30%) were external users. The second category was intended to acknowledge bloggers who brought innovative ideas to MoCo's business. Four MoCo employees from its remote branches won the awards. In the third category, two MoCo employees and one external user were rewarded for their outstanding contributions in the year. As for the last category, 25 were rewarded, including 19 MoCo employees and 6 external users.

Ad Hoc Honorable Mentions

Besides the formal yearly awards, the management team also hands out honorable mentions (stars) to posts that generate a big impact in the community.

For example, in one of their blog entries titled "Celebrate G. Chen for his influential article", the management team openly promoted an employee's post that received nearly 10,000 hits and over 100 replies in the community. As part of the promotion, it stated "*we'd like to cordially invite you to comment on the most recent news in telecommunication. We will feature your excellent contributions in our community and promote it on the Internet.*"

Another type of honorable mentions is to promote influential posts to other well-known media, e.g., the leading Internet portals in the country. "W*e have good collaboration with large Internet companies like Sohu and Tencent. We often recommend quality articles from our community to those websites.*" [Qiang, Project Manager] If the articles are accepted, the management team would broadcast the news in their blog and honor the authors.

So far, we have described three key strategies the MoCo Blogs administrative team has employed to manage and coordinate user activities according to their corporate goals. In particular, they devise a high-level, systematic content plan to guide the topics that are of importance to the company. Using editorial recommendations through three design elements, they direct the audience's attention and encourage contributions. Furthermore, they use two additional reward venues to award contributions. Next, we examine user participation in the community and the interplay between the strategies described here and user activities.

6. USER PRESENCE AND PARTICIPATION

We analyze the participants' behavior from three aspects: content production under guidance, reader attention management, and autonomous self-presence.

6.1 Content Production under Guidance

To understand how the site's content plan influenced blogger activities, we analyzed the logs collected during March to June 2009.

We sampled 1,491 articles posted during this period of time by randomly selecting a week from each month. As a result, we collected 367 articles for March, 420 for April, 404 for May, and 300 for June. We also recorded all the articles recommended on the homepage (headlines and channeled news) and in *Labs Today* during the same time frame. We then coded each article by the topics of participants' posts identified in the content plan. Based on the content plan, the topics fell in four categories by their level of importance: monthly focus (importance level 1), focuses in other months (importance level 2), regularly advocated topics (not monthly focus, importance level 3), and not planned topics (importance level 4). Three authors worked independently first and then jointly discussed the coding until consensus was reached.

Topics	Produced by participants (%)	Promoted by admins (%)
Monthly focus	12.2	22.8
Focuses of other months	24.0	33.2
Regular advocated topics	14.8	21.4
Not planned	49.0	22.6

Table 1. Content produced and promoted

We first looked at the types of articles produced by the community and found that nearly half (49%) of the content was *not* on the topics planned or advocated by the administrators. Among those fitting the content plan, about 12.2% were in accordance with the monthly focuses, 24% were the focuses of other months and 14.8% were regularly advocated topics. We then examined the articles promoted by the editors. On average, of the articles posted on MoCo Blogs during these four months, 30% were recommended by the editorial team either to appear on the homepage or in daily summaries. Interestingly, significant differences were found in the article types between the content produced and recommended (X^2=93.128, df=1, p=0.000). Among the promoted articles, about 22.8% exactly matched the monthly focuses, 33.2% were topics planned as focuses in other months, 21.4% were regularly advocated topics, and only 22.6% were not planned (Table 1).

To better understand the self-chosen topics, we took a closer look at the articles not in the content plan. They covered a diverse set of topics, including personal life stories (e.g. "My little beauty Joe"), entertainment, fun stuff (e.g. discussing TV series), news, and non-telecommunication related work interests (e.g., finance and investment). Only quality articles related to MoCo or telecommunication got recommended. Such articles mainly fell into three categories: situational hot industrial news (e.g., articles discussing mobile phone messaging spam after MoCo was blamed in a TV show); personal work experience sharing (e.g., articles by a manager in the headquarters talking about his experi-

	Headlines	Channeled news	LabsToday (newsletter)
Total # of articles	38	406	403
Days being visible	3.4	2.3	1.0
Days before visible	3.2	3.0	2.0
Avrg # of visits	1485	422	574
Avrg # of replies	20	4	6

Table 2. Comparing the three main design elements for coordinating attention (observation in 6 weeks)

ences visiting other offices); and news from remote offices (e.g., articles reporting new services released by the Guangzhou branch).

Moreover, we examined the 99 bloggers who received the yearly awards in 2009 to understand how reward processes affect user behavior. Our results showed that these users blogged more after being rewarded. On average, their monthly posts increased from 3 to 7 after receiving the yearly awards. On the other hand, the topics advocated by the management team also became better reflected in their posts. For example, Ma, an active external blogger, won the award of "champion blogger" for his large number of posts. His articles were mainly about the industrial news which fell in the 3rd level of importance. After rewarded, 17% of his posts (44 out of 264) were raised to importance level 1, and 42% (112/264) were at importance level 2.

In summary, our results indicated that bloggers' contributions were influenced by the content plan. However, the site administrative team also recommended topics that were not in the plan. To balance the goals of achieving community goals and encouraging user participation, community managers dynamically adjusted their strategies. This echoes our earlier analysis that the plan itself serves as a general guide while the daily operations are of the real power. Moreover, the official rewarding venues played an effective role in increasing both the quantity and quality of posts.

6.2 Reader Attention Management

To understand the effect of editorial recommendations in guiding readers' attention, we analyzed the daily changes of the visits and replies to the recommended blog entries through headlines, channeled news, and daily summaries (newsletters) compared to those not recommended. The results showed reliably greater readership to the articles featured by the editors (Figure 3). The average number of visits was 441 to the articles recommended, and only 109 to those not recommended. On average, each recommended articles had 4.22 replies, while those not recommended had only 0.34 each. We further compared the effects among different means of promotions, and found that headlines were the most influential way to guide user attention (Table 2). Figure 4 shows the daily increase of visits to the articles recommended through the three means. Since *Labs Today* proactively promoted articles by sending email notifications to all registered users and attracted attention from the high-level management team, we initially expected that it would be the most influential way for attracting attention. To our surprise, however, no evidence showed that it had any advantages over channeled news. On the contrary, daily visits to the articles in the headlines were found much higher than the other two. This indicated a combined effect of the length of stay, number of articles recommended each time, and the promotion channel. We suspect that articles on *Labs Today* are updated so quickly that the attraction of each entry could have been weakened.

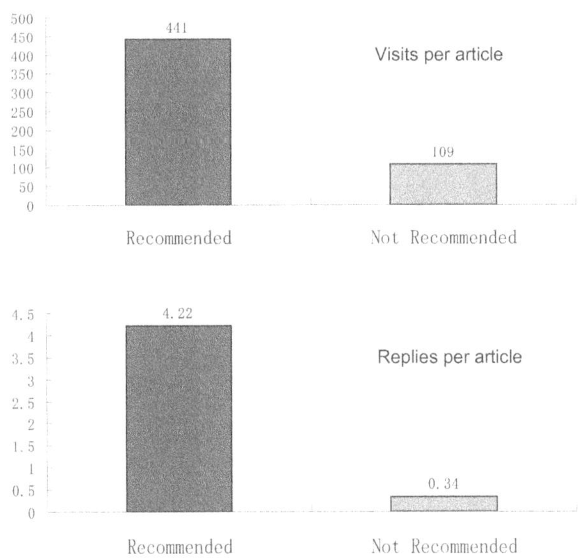

Figure 3. The effects of editorial recommendation on readership

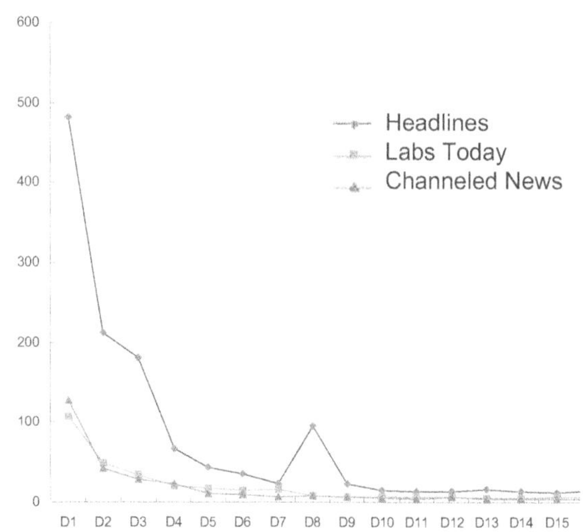

Figure 4. Daily visit increase to each article after promotion through different channels

6.3 Autonomous Self-Presence

So far we have analyzed the key strategies adopted by MoCo Blogs to encourage participation and coordinate contributions under corporate goals. We also examined their impact on user behavior. To acquire a better understanding on how community management is balanced against voluntary participation, we further looked at how users present themselves and maintain their own presence in the community. Our analysis identified key features that support participants' multi-faceted self-presence.

One of the features provided by MoCo Blogs is for users to manage their own identity. As the project manager put it, *"we do not set any hard rules for user identities. .... If we require people to post with their real names, we may limit what they feel comfortable to say."* An analysis on a random sample of 280 user profiles (166 from MoCo, 114 from others) revealed that not all users blog with their real identity. Of the 166 MoCo employees, 156 (93.98%) provided their real names[1] in their profile, one provided a fake name, and the other 4 were missing. As for the 114 non-employees, 92 (80.7%) provided their real names, another 4 provided their corporate names, 3 provided fake names, and the other 15 (13%) did not provide any name in their profile.

Another feature for self-presence is to build their own profiles. Our further analysis of the 280 user profiles revealed that bloggers' online identities were highly diverse. Three research members read through participants' self introduction in these profiles and examined them together. Six types of information were contained in these self-introductions: 1) personal background, including demographical (e.g. name, sex, age, region, etc.), educational and work information (e.g. affiliation, job role); 2) contact information. Some users left their email addresses, phone numbers, instant messenger accounts, and postal addresses in their self-introduction; 3) expertise and work interests. This could be as simple as "*I am familiar with software development*", "*I am interested in finance*", or as detailed as "*Specialized observer in the telecommunication industry. Have been observing and researching on Information Technology and telecommunication in China for a long time. Conducted deep analysis on the evolution, management and trends of communication. Familiar with 3G technologies and services. Good knowledge of the organization, operation and development of telecommunication industry.*" 4) personal hobbies/life interests; 5) corporate advertisement. Some provided introductions of their companies, and some even attached their logos and the website URLs; and 6) personalized expressions. Such expressions were diverse, including likes or dislikes, life attitudes, or even citations of proverbs or lines from users' favorite movies or simply fun stuff. For example, someone described himself as "*This man is so lazy that he doesn't wash dishes or cook meals. What he can have is only instant noodles.*"

[1] We could not really tell whether a name provided is actually the real name of the user. We coded a name as "real" when it appeared in the right format that a real-world identity could be.

Further comparison of the self-introductions provided by MoCo employees with those of external bloggers revealed interesting differences. MoCo employees expressed themselves in a more informal way and provided more information about their personal background and interests. In contrast, external bloggers from other organizations provided more information about their work experience, expertise areas, and the companies that they serve. As show in Figure 5, about 55% of the self-introduction by the 166 MoCo bloggers contained "personalized expressions", while only 22% external bloggers did so. On the contrary, about 13% bloggers outside MoCo advertised their companies in their profile, while only 2% MoCo employees provided company-related information in their profile.

Despite that the administrative team sought to attract more external bloggers (with the target proportion of 80%), the membership composition was dominated by MoCo employees during the time of our study. Surrounded by their own colleagues on MoCo Blogs, MoCo bloggers might have a better sense of community. External bloggers, however, may feel compelled to sell themselves, such as their expertise and their work organizations to the community. Second, for external users, providing more information on their work experiences could facilitate trust building when developing connections with other people in the community. In addition, since the site is publicly accessible, it may suggest that MoCo employees could only blog with non-confidential content. This could have brought a sense for them to be informal and encourages them to show more of their personal side in such an online community.

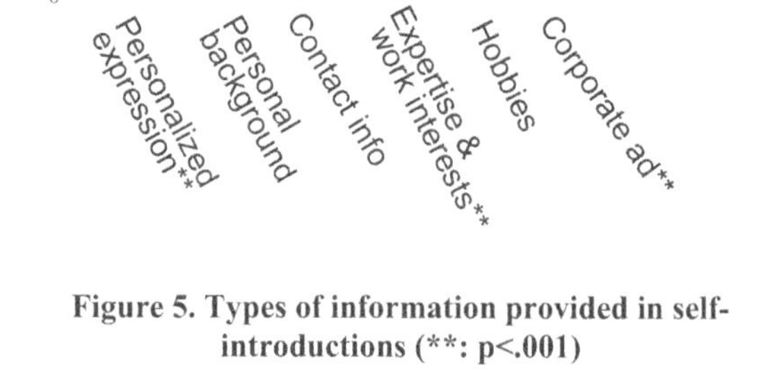

Figure 5. Types of information provided in self-introductions (: p<.001)**

7. DISCUSSIONS AND CONCLUSIONS

We have examined the dynamics between community goals and user participation in a corporate blogging community in China. We describe community administrators' strategies for managing a diverse group of members and coordinating user participation. We also study the interplay between community management and user activities. In our case, the community management is centralized and deliberate. This is mainly because that the community is hosted by and dominated by employees from a single enterprise. Moreover, the enterprise has the goals of the community in mind before starting it. Second, being publicly accessible with the mix of internal and external participants adds complexity to the community development. The success of the community requires substantial coordination among users to achieve its goals. Additionally, the Chinese cultural traditions that respect hierarchical power may have also contributed to the needs for management imperatives.

Previous research on online social communities has identified special features for encouraging participation, such as supporting for a range of different roles [20], tiered memberships [16], member selection [19], and setting community rules [20]. Our analysis suggests that a homepage with featured and categorized blog entries is an important design consideration for directing readers' attentions from a broad audience, as well as managing the authors' visibility by introducing the competitiveness in the community. In addition, direct promotion of community content through email updates with regular summaries is a good way for reaching people at the higher level of management. On the other side, it is important that members be made aware of such promotions. In return, this facilitates bloggers' reputation building, and stimulates and guides their contributions to the community. Our analysis also suggests that although community activeness and timely update of content are important to sustain participation, keeping content for a reasonable time period (e.g., 3 days) helps accumulating readership and interactions. Furthermore, formal reward venues are effective in motivating users.

Our study echoes earlier findings on the need for balancing management control and user autonomy in Chinese communities [16]. A group of designated editors/managers is the key to the success of maintaining a blogging community with a mix of users from different organizations. Here we briefly discuss the corporate roles that we have observed in developing and maintaining vibrant social communities, especially in China.

Host. The management team defines the goals of the community and guides the topics of discussion. Moreover, through invitations and frequent online or offline communications, the management team establishes personal connections with a core group of participants, which helps keep the livelihood of the community.

Broker. The management team mediates organizational goals and user participation. They deliver the planned topics and promote specific articles to authors and readers. By channeling user attention to a limited number of posts, the team effectively manages the visibility of participants in the community and guides the direction of content production.

Gatekeeper. The management team is also responsible for the appropriateness of the content in the community. Setting rules for posting and moderating the content is critical for maintaining the external image of the organization.

However, in our studies, we also observed the potential weaknesses from several aspects. The administrators' dashboard in our study allows the management team to delete unwanted postings that violate the blogging guidelines with predefined key words. For example, articles disclosing confidential information or discussing sensitive topics would be regarded inappropriate. A clear process for judging the appropriateness of a post is somehow lacking. As Qiang put it, *"We try to be equal and justified as much as possible. We delete unwanted posts. We promote quality and interesting articles, and those stimulating discussions. But we may make mistakes. For example, we once recommended an article which stirred strong debates on MoCo's business and made our bosses unhappy. And we once were complained by a third party company. We do by trial and error, and we learn."* [Qiang, Project Manager] Future research should further examine the boundaries for community management.

While the corporate goals are pushed into the community from top down, several special designs should be considered to stimulate social engagement from bottom up. Allowing dynamic self-presence leaves space for users with different interests to express themselves. Our study also reinforces that employee bloggers are incentive driven. Competing for attention is the major factor that encourages contribution. While user attention could be directed by nearly an infinite number of things on the Internet (e.g., [24]), we argue that the attention economy could be changed through a set of designs. In our case, author visibility to the audience and management recognitions serve as an effective means for managing user attention.

Our current work is merely a start to explore and examine corporate online communities. It leaves much room for future work. One topic could be an in-depth study on participants' feedback (e.g., collecting more qualitative data from participants to discuss the pros and cons of the management coordination on different users) to gain a deeper understanding of corporate blogging across organizations. The other may compare corporate communities hosted in different geographical regions and examine cultural impact on these communities.

ACKNOWLEDGMENTS

We thank our very helpful contacts at MoCo and all the participants who shared their experience with us. We would also like to thank our anonymous reviewers for their insightful feedback and comments, which helped us revise and improve the paper.

REFERENCES

1. Baumer, E., Sueyoshi, M., Tomlinson, B. Exploring the role of the reader in the activity of blogging. *Proc. CHI 2008*, ACM Press (2008)
2. Beenen, G., Ling, K., Wang, X., Chang, K., Frankowski, D., Resnick, P., Kraut, R..E. Using social psychology to motivate contributions to online communities. *Proc. CSCW 2004*. ACM Press (2004)
3. Cohen, W.M. and Levinthal, D.A.. Absorptive Capacity: A New Perspective on Learning and Innovation. *Administrative Science Quarterly*, 35, 128-152.
4. China Internet Network Information Center (CINIC). (2008), http://www.cnnic.net.cn/uploadfiles/pdf/2008/7/23/170516.pdf.
5. Chui, M., Miller, A., Roberts, R.P. Six ways to make Web 2.0 work, in *The McKinsey Quarterly*, Feb 2009
6. Danis, C. and Singer, D. A Wiki Instance in the Enterprise: Opportunities, Concerns and Reality. *Proc. CSCW 2008,* ACM Press (2008), 495-504
7. Du, S.H. and Wagner, C. Weblog success: Exploring the role of technology. *International Journal of Human-Computer Studies.* Academic Press (2006). Volume 64 Issue 9.
8. Efimova, L. and Grudin, J., Crossing Boundaries: A Case Study of Employee Blogging. *Proc. HICSS 2007,* IEEE Computer Society (2007)
9. Grudin, J. Enterprise Knowledge Management and Emerging Technologies. *Proc. HICSS 2006*, IEEE Computer Socienty (2006)
10. Hansen, M. Knowledge networks: Explaining effective knowledge sharing in multiunit companies. *Org. Science*, 13, (2002), 232-248.
11. Huh, J., Jones, L., Erickson, T., Kellogg, W.A., Bellamy, R.K.E., Thomas, J.C. BlogCentral: the role of internal blogs at work. *Ext. Abstracts CHI 2007*, ACM Press (2007)
12. Jackson, A., Yates. J., Orlikowski, W. Corporate blogging: Building community through persistent digital talk. *Proc. HICSS 2007*, IEEE Computer Society (2007)
13. Kelleher, T., and Miller, B. M. Organizational blogs and the human voice: Relational strategies and relational outcomes. *Journal of Computer Mediated Communication*, 11, 2, 2006
14. Kolari, P., Finin, T., Lyons, K., Yesha, Y., Yesha; Y., Perelgut, S., Hawking, J. On the Structure, Properties and Utility of Internal Corporate weblogs. *Proc. ICWSM 2007*, AAAI press (2007)
15. Liao, Q., Pan, S., Lai, J.C., Yang, C. Enterprise Blogging in a Global Context: Comparing Chinese and American Practices. *Pro. CSCW 2011,* ACM Press (2011)
16. Liao Q., Pan Y., Zhou X.M., Ma F. Chinese Online Communities: Balancing Management Control and Individual Autonomy. *Proc. CHI 2010,* ACM Press (2010)
17. Ludford, P.J., Cosley, D., Frankowski, D., Terveen, L. Think different: increasing online community participation using uniqueness and group dissimilarity. *Proc. CHI 2004.* ACM Press (2004)
18. Ma, S. and Zhang, Q. A Study on Content and Management Style of Corporate Blogs. *Proc. OCSC 2007*, Springer-Verlag, 116-123
19. Millen, D.R.and Patterson J.F. Stimulating Social Engagement in a Community Network. *Proc. CSCW 2002*, ACM Press (2002), 306-313
20. Nardi, B.A., Schiano, D.J., Gumbrecht, M. Blogging as social activity, or, would you let 900 million people read your diary?, *Proc. CSCW 2004*, ACM Press (2004)
21. Nardi, B.A., Schiano, D.J., Gumbrecht, M., Swartz, L.Why we blog, *Communications of the ACM*, v.47 n.12, December 2004
22. Preece, J. *Online Communities: Designing Usability, Supporting Sociability*. Chichester, UK ,Wiley, 2000.
23. Stoll, J., Edwards, W.K., Mynatt, E.D. Interorganizational Coordination and Awareness in a Nonprofit Ecosystem. *Proc. CSCW 2010*, ACM Press (2010), 51-60
24. Yardi, S., Golder, S.A., Brzozowski, M.J., Blogging at Work and the Corporate Attention Economy. *Proc. CHI 2009*, ACM Press (2009), 2071-2080

Socializing Volunteers in an Online Community: A Field Experiment

Rosta Farzan, Robert Kraut
Carnegie Mellon University
rfarzan,robert.kraut@cs.cmu.edu

Aditya Pal, Joseph Konstan
University of Minnesota
apal,konstan@cs.umn.edu

ABSTRACT
Although many off-line organizations give their employees training, mentorship, a cohort and other socialization experiences that improve their retention and productivity, online production communities rarely do this. This paper describes the planning, execution and evaluation of a socialization regime for an online technical support community. In a two-phase project, we first automatically identified from participants' early behavior, those with high potential to become core members. We then designed, delivered and experimentally evaluated socialization experiences intended to build commitment and competence among these potential core members. We were able to identify potential core members with high accuracy from only two weeks of behavior. A year later, those classified as potential core members participated in the community ten times more actively than those not identified. In an evaluation experiment, some potential core members were randomly assigned to receive socialization experiences, while others were not. A year later, those who had participated in the socialization regime contributed more answers in the community compared to those in the control condition. The socialization experiences, however, undercut their sense of connection to the community and the quality of their contributions. We discuss what was effective and what could be improved in designing socialization experiences for online groups.

Author Keywords
Online volunteer communities, Socialization, Experiment

ACM Classification Keywords
H.5.3 Information Interfaces and Presentation: Group and Organization Interfaces: Evaluation/methodology, Web-based interaction.

General Terms
Experimentation; Human Factors

INTRODUCTION
Volunteers are responsible for the user-generated content in most online communities, including videos on YouTube, code in open source communities, articles in Wikipedia and user support in both technical and health support groups. In these communities, a small fraction of the users generally provides a large proportion of the good content [16]. These members also do much of the administration and community building on the site [5]. Despite the importance of these core community members, neither site managers nor researchers understand how to select and develop a cadre of volunteers to take on these core roles.

Research on socialization in off-line organizations suggests that a well-designed regimen of socialization experiences can increase organizational members' commitment to the organization and their competence. Socialization is the process through which newcomers acquire the behaviors and attitudes essential to playing their roles in a group or an organization [17]. As organizational members become socialized, they move from the periphery of the organization towards the core [22]. Theories of organizational socialization describe institutionalized socialization practices that include socializing newcomers in a cohort, providing a clear sequence of stages through which members progress, providing training from experienced role models, and providing encouraging positive feedback, as well as constructive criticism [9]. The use of an institutional style of socialization by the organization is associated with more successful socialization outcomes: newcomers do their jobs better, are more satisfied with their jobs, become more committed to the organization, and leave the organization less often [20], [4].

Although evidence is strong that institutionalized socialization tactics are effective in developing commitment and appropriate behavior in conventional organizations, they are not common in online communities. Socialization processes in most online communities are informal and individualistic [19]. To thrive, online communities should incorporate processes for selecting and socializing committed members. One important step is to develop a process to identify newcomers who fit the community and will ultimately be valuable to it. Insuring a good fit between the newcomers and the community will lead to more positive outcomes for both newcomers and the community [11],[12],[10]. An efficient way to ensure good fit is to develop a screening mechanism. Often online communities employ a human evaluation process as the screen. For example, in many open-source software communities, volunteers must have offered code that meets quality standards before they gain committer status [13],[8]. However, human evaluation is by definition labor-intensive and time-consuming. Additionally, humans usually need long-term contribution data about a user to be able to make a reliable judgment. As a result, many potential core members may leave the community before being recognized.

This paper describes our experiences designing, implementing and evaluating socialization experiences in a question-and-answer community in which volunteers answer tax-related questions. The community recognizes users who contribute large numbers of high quality answers as "superusers". Superusers are selected through a manual human evaluation that takes into account individual users' contributions. The site contains more than 60,000 users and 83 superusers. Although anyone can answer questions on the site, 78% of answers judged as helpful by community readers are provided by the small group of superusers. Like many other online volunteer communities, this community faces the challenge of growing the number of committed users who contribute high quality responses. We use this community as an environment to explore practical ways that an online volunteer community can identify from their early behavior participants with potential to become core members, and to discover practical ways to socialize and train them so they are more competent and committed to the community. In a two-phase project, we first used machine learning to automatically identify from early behavior users with high potential to become core members. We then designed, delivered and experimentally validated socialization experiences to build commitment and competence among these potential core members. We discuss what was effective and what could be improved in designing socialization experiences for online groups.

IDENTIFYING POTENTIAL CORE MEMBERS

In the first phase of the project, we designed and implemented machine learning algorithms to automatically identify potential superusers. A complete description of the dataset we used, the classification algorithm, and its evaluation can be found in [18]. We used a dataset that included all of the observable behavior each user exhibited on the site from July 2006 to April 2009, including the text of their questions and answers, and meta-data such as time between posts and evaluations of their answers provided by other users. We reasoned that potential superusers should be highly motivated to help others, and they should have the required capability to answer questions correctly. We identified several possible indicators of motivation and ability. In this community users' motivation is reflected in quantity of contributions, frequency of contribution, and commitment towards the community. Ability of users is reflected in their domain knowledge, trustworthiness of their answers, and politeness and clarity in their responses. Table 1 below shows features we used to identify each indicator of motivation and ability.

We extracted motivation and ability features for the first two weeks of data per user to build the training dataset for machine learning. We used Support Vector Machine (SVM) and Decision Tree (DTree) learning models over these features to identify the potential superusers. The result of the evaluation of the algorithm shows that both motivation and ability factors have the same discriminating weight in classifying superusers. Information gain analysis shows that among all the features described in Table 1, number of answers, number of votes, number of best answers, frequency of login, average time elapsed between answers, and usage of pronoun I are the most informative features in distinguishing high potential users from low potential users.

Table 1. Features indicating users' motivation and ability

Quality	Indicator	Features
Motivation	Quantity	#of answers(+) # of questions(+)
	Frequncy	Average time elapsed between two answers(+)
	Commitment	# of logins(+) Time spent in the community(+)
Ability	Knowledge	# of best answers(+)
	Trustworthiness	# of votes on answers(+) # of positively voted answers(+) Ratio of answers with negative votes to positively voted answers(-)
	Politeness and Clarity	Language dimensions such as presence of typos(-), use of singular pronouns(-), use of negative terms(-)

† (+) and (-) signs represent the increasing or decreasing effect of each indicator on motivation or ability.

Since all the features in the algorithm are related to users' responses, including users with few posts or none does not affect the classification result. Therefore, we excluded users with fewer than ten responses from the dataset. That left 1,974 users in the dataset. Then we used our binary classifier on those 1,974 users to select potential superusers. The classifier classified all the users into one of two classes: potential superusers or not-superusers. Out of 1,974, 75 were classified as potential superusers based on data from their first two weeks in the community. Out of these 75, 40 were already recognized as superusers by community. That means, 53% (40/75) precision and 48% recall (40/83) for the algorithm. However, in terms of precision of the algorithm, the remaining 35 participants could have been misclassified as superusers by the algorithm (i.e., false positives) or could really have been potential superusers who were missed during the manual selection process. We conducted a formal human evaluation to further assess the effectiveness of the automatic classifier. We hypothesized that some of these 35 users were users with high potentials to become superusers. Human evaluation allowed us to examine this hypothesis. Employees whose job responsibilities included promoting people to superuser status evaluated a sample of users selected by the algorithm to be either high-potentials, medium-potentials, and low-potentials. For each category, we modified our classifier to return a ranked list of all 1,974 users instead of binary classifications. We then selected the top 35, middle 35 and bottom 35 to represent high, medium, and low potential superuser respectively. Twenty-five judges rated these 105 users. Each evaluator was presented with a list of 9-12 users from three categories in a random order. Each user was evaluated by two judges. The human judges had access to the full profile of each of those users on the site, which included all their responses in addition to statistics about their tenure, total number of responses provided, total number of positive and negative votes they received, and number of helpful responses provided. Human judges had access to similar information as the algorithm but the information was not limited to only two weeks of data.

Table 2 shows the confusion matrix, showing the agreement between the algorithm's assessments and the human judgments. The algorithm's extreme assessments in the high and low categories matched the human judgments very well (77% and 57% accuracy, where 33% is expected by chance). Human judged 57% of the algorithm-classified medium category as having high potential which suggests the algorithm is more conservative than the humans. Those in the medium category can potentially be trained to match superuser status.

Table 2. Agreement between the algorithm and the human judgments

		Human judgments		
		low	medium	High
Algorithm	Low	20	10	5
	Medium	9	8	18
	High	3	5	27

The results suggest that the identification of potential core members in this community from their early behavior can be done successfully with reasonably high accuracy. However, there is no ground truth for which of these people really had superuser potential. Therefore, it is impossible to assess the validity of the model without observing them in the subsequent tax season. Even though human judges might still be needed to vet the candidates, a preliminary sorting by the algorithm decreases the manual work significantly and can guard against judges failing to give serious consideration to high quality candidates.

LEADERSHIP CHALLENGE

The second phase of the project focused on the design and implementation of socialization practices to help the high-potential candidates build commitment and competence. Before we intervened, the site had no formal socialization process for new users. Newcomers were not aware of other newcomers and did not have methods by which they could communicate with others for support. Newcomers had to figure out on their own how to get started and how to make progress. They received very little feedback from the community, especially when they made mistakes. Additionally, identifying experts and communicating with them was a cumbersome and unnatural process on the site. Our goal was to discover practical ways of addressing these shortcomings to increase participants' motivation and abilities. As described earlier, prior research in organizational socialization, education and social psychology indicates that formal socialization is associated with positive outcomes. We developed Leadership Challenge incorporating elements of a formal socialization process that were compatible with an online production community in a low-cost and self-sustaining way – cohort-based socialization in which the newcomers were isolated from the surrounding community, sequenced training materials, and providing feedback. We did not include a formal mentoring program because of its likely expense.

Cohort based socialization

Newcomers to organizations are more likely to know what they should do, become more productive, are more satisfied and stay longer if they join the organization in a group with other newcomers and go through early socialization experiences with others in their cohort [4], [20]. Being part of a cohort helps newcomers share their experiences, collectively figure out the organization's values and work procedures, receive social support from their peers and build a longer term social support network. If training and other socialization experiences occur off the job, in an environment where consequential performance demands are minimized and fear of failure is reduced, they can practice job-related skills in a non-threatening way. This sequestered style of socialization improves their self-confidence and their job-related skills [4].

We implemented off-the-job socialization by conducting the Leadership Challenge between tax seasons, when newcomers could train on questions culled from the previous season. Answering these questions incorrectly would not put taxpayers at risk. We implemented cohort-based socialization by providing a discussion forum as a place for participants to interact with each other, compare their answers, and engage in group discussions. As described below, we attempted to stimulate discussion by requiring participants to grade others' answers in their training exercises. We populated the discussion forum with participants' answers and comments on these training exercises to stimulate interaction.

Goal setting and clear sequence of stages

Participants in the Leadership Challenge were given tax questions to answer and the answers of others to grade. Research on both goal-setting and socialization in organization suggests that providing people with clear goals and a defined sequence of stages to achieve as they move from the periphery to the core of an organization or community improves both role clarity and self-efficacy [4]. Providing clear goals can assist newcomers in figuring out what is expected from them, and achieving these goals can increase their sense of self-efficacy [9],[3]. Research in psychology and organizational behavior indicates that goals and goal-setting strongly motivate people, especially when the goals are specific and challenging [15]. A fixed time-table for advancing in the organization improves newcomers' role clarity [4].

We translated these ideas into the Leadership Challenge by giving targets for the number of questions they should answer and answers they should evaluate to advance through a sequence of pages in each of five functional areas of tax expertise (e.g., basic income, deductions and education). Participants could receive silver badges in each area for com-

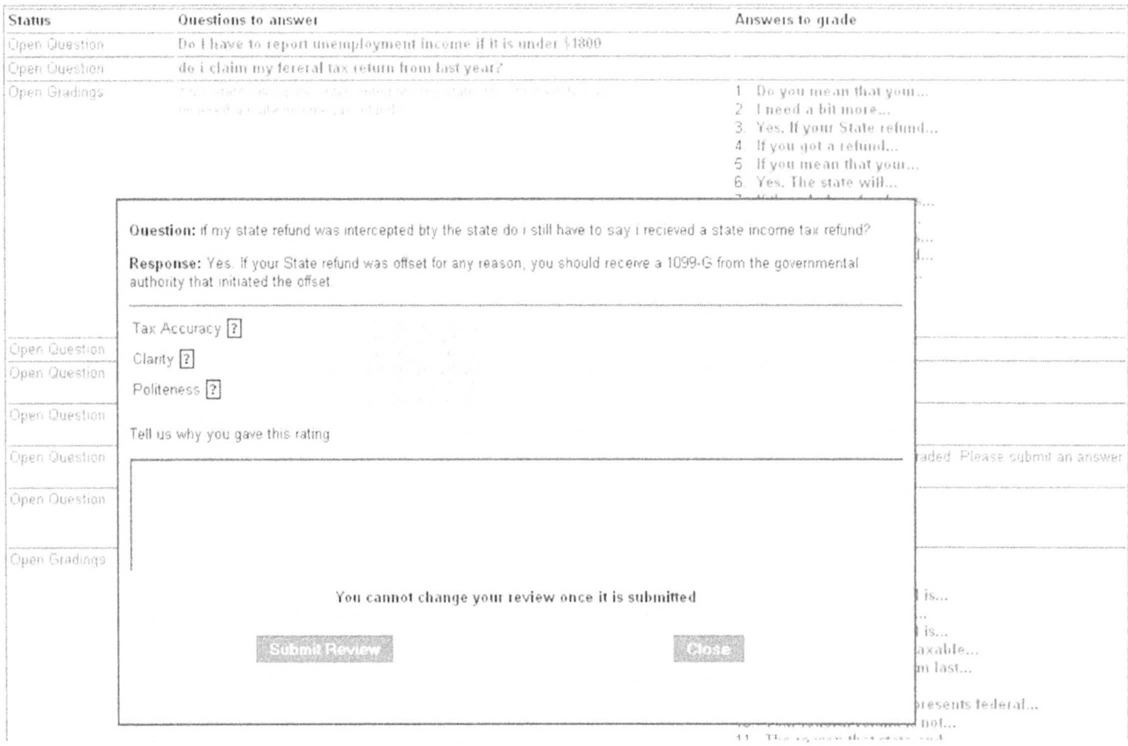

Figure 1. Interface for answering questions and grading

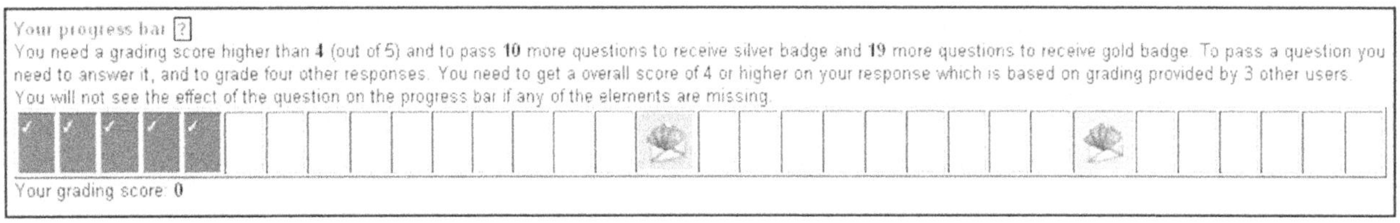

Figure 2. Progress Bar

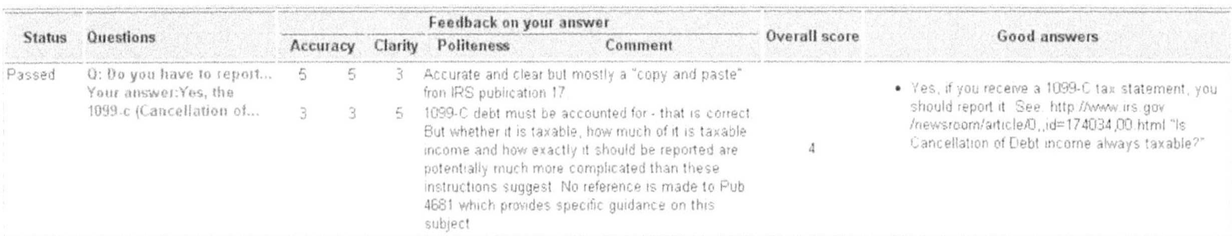

Figure 3. Interface for reviewing feedback from others

pleting 50% of questions correctly and gold badges for completing 80% of questions correctly. A question was considered complete if it received an overall score of greater than four out of five and if the participant graded at least two answers to the same question from others. The score was calculated as a weighted sum of peer reviewed scores on the three dimensions of accuracy, clarity, and politeness. A progress bar made the goal and their progress towards the goal salient (Figure 2).

To make the goals and the steps to achieve them more salient, we sent participants in the Challenge a personalized email reminder at the end of each week. Email reminders have been shown to be effective in encouraging contribution in online communities, especially when the messages are personalized [14], [7]. The reminders emphasized the amount of work the recipients had already done and highlighted what more they could do. A sample reminder is shown below.

```
Thanks for participating in the Leadership
Challenge. We would like to let you know new
questions are available on the site now.

Here is a summary of your activity over last week:

You responded to 8 questions and graded 2
responses of your peers. You have 12 more
questions to reply to and 18 more responses
to grade. According to scientific research,
answering questions, getting feedback from others
and evaluating others answers all help you become
more expert, by giving practice and offering
multiple points of view.

Login now ...
```

Training through worked examples

Educational research shows that providing learners with worked examples (i.e. the steps in a correct problem solution) fosters learning and stimulates deep understanding [2]. The paradigm of problem solving with worked examples originated in mathematics and physics. Worked examples typically consist of a statement describing the problem and an explanation of how to solve it, both meant to guide learners in solving similar problems [23]. Learning from worked examples is especially effective for beginners and for initial skill acquisition. According to the ACT-R cognitive theoretical framework, in the first stage of skill acquisition, learners refer to known examples and try to relate them to problems they are trying to solve [1]. This research from the educational domain suggests that learning from worked examples is a promising technique to help newcomers improve their domain knowledge.

We implemented these ideas in the Leadership Challenge by constructing a set of tax-related questions from an archive of questions asked in a prior tax season. The questions were vetted by a tax expert to be informative, potentially teaching those who answered them something new, interesting or non-obvious in a particular area. Every week ten new questions were offered for participants to answer. Once they answered a question, they could view all of the good answers from the archive (See Figure 1). A sample question and answer on regulations related to basic income is shown below.

My federal refund went DOWN when I entered in my second W2, why is that? My federal refund amount is decreasing the more W2s I enter, is that supposed to happen? If I don't owe taxes can I just enter in one and not the others to get a bigger refund?

```
No. You must enter all income received in 2009.
The reason your refund goes down after you enter
the 2nd W-2, is that your standard deduction and
exemption is subtraced from your 1st W-2 before
the tax is calculated...
```

Providing feedback

Research in peer-evaluation has shown that students learn from providing feedback to their peers and benefit from receiving feedback from others with similar experiences, especially when the review process is scaffolded, anonymous, and reciprocal [6]. Additionally, peer-reviewing can increase interaction among the newcomers and therefore improve their sense of community. After participants in the Leadership Challenge answered a question, they were required to grade answers submitted by other newcomers on three dimensions (accuracy, clarity, and politeness) and to complete a free-format comment justifying their evaluations (Figure 3).

FIELD EXPERIMENT

Often only a small percentage of people invited to an experiment actually participate in it. Since we required at least one control group for comparison, inviting only 75 high-potential users would have provided too few people to form the community. Additionally, the result of our human evaluation showed that more than half of users with medium potentials did exhibit superuser capabilities. Therefore, to increase the number of invitees, first, we relaxed our criteria of the minimum number of posts from ten to five and, second, we used our ranking algorithm to select all the users with medium or high potential to our experiment. This resulted in inviting 283 people.

Based on these criteria, we invited the 283 users to join the Leadership Challenge. The Challenge was run for six weeks in the off season, isolated from the live Tax Support Community site. All the users received the same invitation. To prevent selection biases, participants were randomly assigned to the control or experimental group only after they responded to the invitation. To create a critical mass of participants to interact with each other in the experimental condition, we assigned twice as many participants to the Leadership Challenge experimental condition as to the control condition. We used a randomized wait-list control experimental design, in which we promised the control group they could participate in the Leadership Challenge in the future. The experimental group received the treatment immediately after signing up and control group did not receive any treatment. The participants in both control and experimental group received a free copy of a tax software as compensation.

Data

At the end of the socialization period we conducted a survey to collect data about participants' evaluation of the Leadership Challenge along three dimensions - the extent to which participation in the Challenge influenced their tax knowledge, connection to the community and enjoyment. These questions were asked only of those in the Leadership Challenge (i.e. the experimental condition). The survey also included a scale measuring participants' future commitment to the Tax Support Community. This part of the survey was sent to both the control and the experimental group. Additionally, we collected participants' behavioral data[1] over the 2011 tax season to analyze the effect of the Leadership Challenge on participants' subsequent participation in the Tax Support Community. The behavioral data included a measure of quantity of participation (the number of questions that participants answers) and two on quality of participation (the total quality points they received for their answers, and the number of appreciations they received from other members of the community). Users can provide appreciations for answers they like by giving a "thank you" to the person answering a question. Users can accumulate points based on the feedback that others provide to their answers. Points are awarded such that each "thumbs up" awarded one point, each "helpful" tag awarded five points and each "solved" tag awarded 10 points. The points a member of the community earned were public information and were displayed whenever the member's moniker was displayed.

Of the 52 users who responded to the invitation, 16 were assigned to control group, and 36 to the experimental group. Thirteen of the 16 people in the control group filled out the survey, as did 24 of the 36 people in the experimental group.

In the next sections, we divide the results into three segments: accuracy of the automatic classification, a description of participants' behavior during the experiment and an evaluation of the effectiveness of the socialization intervention. We present the evaluation results in two subsections, because effectiveness changed from immediately following the interventions (when the interventions reduced participants' reported commitment to the community compared to those in the control condition) to a longer term follow-up (when the interventions increased the amount of participants' actual participation in the community compared to those in the control condition).

Accuracy of automatic selection

We invited 283 users to the Leadership Challenge based on the result of their leadership potential score from the automatic classifier, which measured how similar their early behavior on the site was to the early behavior of existing superusers. To test the predictive validity of the classification algorithm, we compared the 283 potential superusers' participation rates in the Tax Support Community in the 2011 tax season to participation of those not classified as potential superusers. The sample of non-selected users included 66,000 people. To address the imbalance in sample sizes, we compared the 283 potential superusers both to all 66,000 non-potential leaders and to a series of 1% random samples from the 66,000 population. The results of random sampling and complete datasets were similar. Here we report the results from comparing random sample with experimental data.

[1]The data does not include any personal information

Because participation rates are count data truncated at zero, we used negative binomial regression models to analyze them. The model included number of days since joining the community ("days"), number of answers in previous tax season (tax2010), and experimental condition as the independent variables. Experimental condition was coded as zero for those who were not selected by our algorithm, one for those who were selected but did not respond to our invitation, and two for those who were selected and responded to our Leadership Challenge invitation. The model predicted number of answers provided in the 2011 tax season. Results presented in Table 3 show that 283 users selected by the algorithm, whether they participated in the Leadership Challenge or not, participated at least 100 times more compared to those who were not selected. This result confirms the utility of the automatic classification in selecting those who demonstrated more potential. In addition, users who were selected and accepted the invitation to the Leadership Challenge contributed significantly more than those not selected. The algorithm was an accurate filter weeding out people with less motivation to contribute to the community.

Table 3. Estimated means of number of questions answered

condition		N	Mean	SE
Not selected		606	.01	.005
Selected		283	2.42	.181
	declined	231	1.13	.112
	accepted	52	8.67	1.440

† Covariates appearing in the model are fixed at the following values: tax2010=6.06 and days=934.50

Short-term evaluation of Leadership Challenge

General information about participants' behavior during the Challenge period is shown in Table 4. Their participation varied substantially. Some took the Challenge very seriously, logged in more than twice a week during the Challenge, answered more than 70% of available questions and provided good feedback to others. In contrast, others logged in only once to explore the Challenge. Similarly the quality of feedback on the Challenges varied significantly from very informative comments with references to relevant materials such as, "Wrong answer. The IRS Publication 17 states C. ... . If it is, you cannot deduct rental expenses that are more than your rental income for the unit. So, if you use your house for more than 14 days during the year and you decide to rent your house, you will need to check the yes box that used the house or dwelling unit more than 14 days. The conversion date is not the start of the tax year." In contrast, other feedback was perfunctory, consisting of only one word comments such as "ok", "clear", "correct."

Self-sustained community

We incorporated a peer-review process in the socialization practice for its learning benefit and its advantage in empowering the community as self-sustainable. However, as mentioned earlier, since the experiment was conducted in a small, isolated community, the number of participants was insufficient to make the community self-sustained. The problem may have been intensified by the amount of work required in a short period of time. Overall, participants provided 420

Table 4. Leadership Challenge Participation Descriptive Statistics

	Mean	Median	Min	Max	SD
Number of distinct days logged into the Challenge	5.42	3	1	17	5.2
Number of distinct sessions logged into the Challenge	8.83	3.5	1	40	11.9
Number of questions answered	16.21	7.5	0	107	25.1
Number of answered reviewed	16.67	1	0	116	29.5
Length of feedback in number of words	27.79	17.5	1	336	37.53

answers, but only 141 of them (34%) received at least two reviews from the community (Two reviews were the minimum needed to assure reasonable fairness in a peer evaluation process. In fact, the research on educational peer evaluation suggests a minimum of three reviews.) Of the 141 answers that were graded, 110 received a "correct" grade and counted towards winning a badge, but none of the participants received enough feedback to win any badges. We conducted a survival analysis to assess the effect of receiving feedback on users' survival. We calculated a feedback score for each participant as follows and classified participants into high- or low-feedback groups by a median split on the feedback score.

$$Feedback\ \ Score = \frac{Number\ \ of\ \ reviewed\ \ responses}{Total\ \ number\ \ of\ \ responses}$$

The result of a survival analysis shows that participants were significantly more likely to continue to answer questions when they received more feedback (See Figure 4). However, feedback did not seem to affect the number of days they logged into the Challenge (See Figure 5). This suggests that participants in the low-feedback group continued to log into the site to see if they received feedback on their submitted answers.

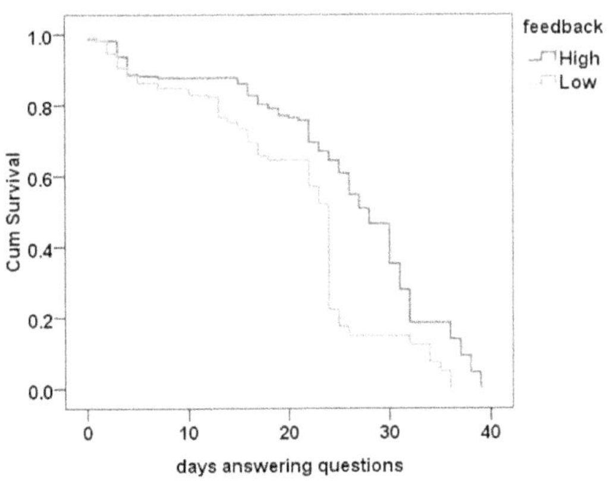

Figure 4. Effect of feedback on question-answering survival

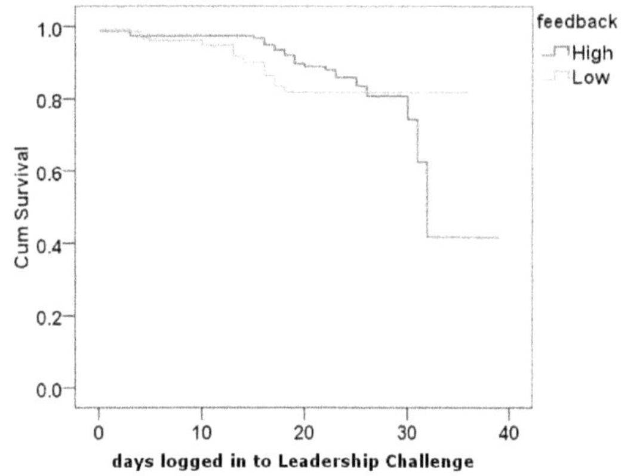

Figure 5. Effect of feedback on overall login survival

Effect of personalized reminders

As described earlier, we sent weekly personalized email reminders to participants who signed up for the Leadership Challenge. The data, presented in Figure 6, shows that each reminder caused a burst in the number of answers that participants produced and the size of this effect did not diminish with repeated reminders, at least over this six-week experiment. These results suggests the robust value of sending reminders to increase participation.

Subjective evaluations of the Leadership Challenge

We asked participants to evaluate the effectiveness of the Leadership Challenge in terms of how much it improved their tax knowledge, how much it helped them to learn about the community, and how satisfying the experiment was. Sample questions in each category are shown below. Answers were provided on 5-point Likert scales ranging from "Strongly disagree" to "Strongly agree."

We averaged the questions assessing each aspect of the Challenge into three reliable scales (Cronbach's $\alpha s > .67$, Table 5). While the overall opinion for all three categories was positive (Table 5), participants rated the value of the Challenge for increasing tax knowledge significantly higher than its value for learning about the community (Non-parametric test of related samples, $Z = -2.3, 2 - tailed\ p = .021$). Moreover, the correlation between the number of sessions they logged into the challenge and their evaluation of the challenge was negative ($\rho = -.404, p = .05$). This pattern suggests that the lack of activity in the site and the inadequate feedback participants provided each other led to dissatisfaction with the community.

```
Q1. Participating in the challenge sharpened my
tax knowledge

Q2. Participating in the challenge helped me
become more familiar with other users on the
community

Q3. Participating in the challenge was fun
```

Behaviorial evidence reveals that very little interaction hap-

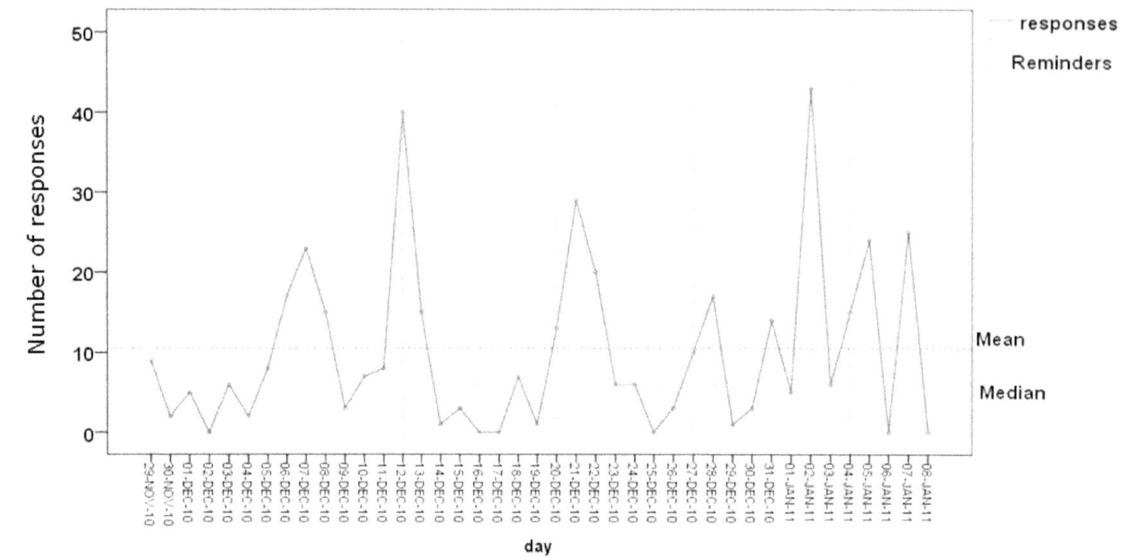

Figure 6. Effect of personalized reminders on number of users responding questions and total number of responses

pened among the participants. In particular, the discussion forum that was designed to support the cohort interaction was rarely used. Thus both attitude scales and behavioral evidence suggest that the experiment was not effective in promoting the feeling of the community. Participants found the training process helpful in learning about tax knowledge but not about the community.

Table 5. Participants' opinion about Leadership Challenge

	Mean	SD	Cronbach's α
Knowledge	3.62^{a}	.94	.87
Community	3.36^{b}	.81	.67
Satisfaction	$3.45^{a,b}$	1.09	.96

† Different superscript (a,b) indicate significant differences between values ($p<0.05$)

The survey also included four questions intended to measure participants' intentions to contribute to the community in the upcoming tax season (e.g. "I intend to participate in the community this tax season"). Answers to all four questions were interrelated (Cronbach's α = .91). We used the average answer to all four questions per users as a measure of commitment. Comparison of the participants' subjective opinion in the control and the experimental groups shows that the control group expressed a significantly greater desire to participate in the future (Mean commitment measure: 3.74 versus 2.92, independent samples t-test, T=3.04, p=.005), although behavioral data discussed below shows they participated less.

Long terms effects of participation in the Challenge

To objectively assess the effects of the Leadership Challenge, we examined behavioral data to compare the quantity and quality of participation in 2011 tax season for those in the experimental and control conditions. We used the number of answers provided as a measure of quantity and number of appreciations and number of points they received as measures of quality of answers. As shown in table 6, participants in the experimental condition answered more questions in the 2011 tax season than did those in the control condition, controlling for the number of answers provided in the previous year and number of days since they joined the community.

Table 6. Estimated Marginal Mean - Effect of socialization practice on quantity of contribution

condition	N	Mean	SE
Control	16	5.29	1.57
Experimental	36	9.99	1.76
p-value	.04		

† Covariates appearing in the model are fixed at the following values: tax2010=6.06 and days=934.50

Additionally, for the experimental group, we assessed how their participation during the Leadership Challenge itself predicted their follow-up participation during the 2011 tax season. Independent variables in the model are the number of questions users answered during the Challenge, the number of answers they reviewed, and the proportion of their answers that received reviews from others, controlling for participation in the previous tax season. Since the distribution of number of questions they answered and answers they reviewed was highly skewed, we converted these independent variables into binary variables using a median split. Again we used negative binomial regression to predict the number of questions they answered during the 2011 tax season.

The result shows that receiving feedback during the Challenge motivated more contribution in future. Those who had higher proportion of their answers reviewed in the Challenge, answered more questions during the 2011 tax season. A 10% increase in the proportion of reviewed answers resulted in a 45% increase in answering questions in 2011 tax season. (IRR=4.5, SE=.53, p=.004). Participants who were more active during the Challenge both in terms of number of questions they answered, and number of answers they reviewed, answered significantly more questions during the 2011 tax season. This is an expected result which can suggest that those were just more active users.

To assess the effect of the socialization intervention on the quality of contribution, we normalized the number of points and appreciations by dividing them by the number of answers for each participant. Since users who have zero answers cannot receive any points or appreciations, the distribution of our response variables are zero-inflated. To account for that, we used a regression model with Tweedie distribution with log link function [21]. In terms of number of appreciations, the difference is not significant but in terms of number of points during the 2011 tax season the control group received a higher number of points per answers as shown in Table 7.

Table 7. Estimated Marginal Mean - Effect of socialization practice on quality of contribution

		Control	Experimental
# of appreciations	Mean (SE)	.28 (.16)	.58 (.21)
		p-value.	.31
# of points	Mean (SE)	1.53 (.61)	.45 (.17)
		p-value.	.032

† Covariates appearing in the model are fixed at the following values: # of points per answer in 2010=1.09, # of appreciations per answer in 2010=.14

In summary our analysis shows that the socialization practices offered to the participants encouraged more contribution, especially when the participants received feedback during the training period. However, the socialization did not improve the quality of responses compared with the control group who did not receive any training.

DISCUSSION AND FUTURE WORK

This research shows that one can identify potential core members in an online community with high accuracy from only two weeks' worth of early behavior in the community. A year later, those categorized by our algorithms as potential core members participated in the community ten times more actively than those not identified. Approximately 20% of these potential core members who were offered socialization experiences agreed to participate in a six-week long program. Those assigned to participate in the socialization experiences increased their contributions to the community compared to comparable volunteers in the control group. A subset of them participated very actively, logging in to the Challenge site more than twice a week and answering more than 70% of the questions posed to them. These people expressed their satisfaction explicitly in the final survey: "Fun program. Wish I were able to spend more time with it but other priorities made that difficult". These factors suggest that a formal training program is possible in an online community like the one studied here.

However, the small number of participants in the experimental group meant that most of them got insufficient feedback when they answered questions or posted comments to the forum. As a result, participants probably became frustrated with the lack of interaction, especially those who were active on the Challenge and expected reciprocal feedback from the community; they were disappointed by both the amount and the quality of the feedback they received. Their frustration was reflected in the comments they provided in the exit survey. "I felt like I was the only one participating, so it was not very worthwhile. I stopped answering questions because no one else was offering feedback or answering other questions. ..." or "If you allow 'laymen' to grade the answers of tax professionals (and give [them] a failing grade), you should allow a dialog [so that the professional can] explain why the grader is wrong or misguided." Additionally, some participants complained that the amount of work expected of them in the Challenge period was too great.

The small size of the group receiving socialization, the design that isolated them from the community and our desire for the socialization experiences to be self-sustaining undoubtedly undercut their effectiveness. These limitations may explain why participants receiving the socialization experiences reported less commitment to the group the more they participated, although they participated more and the quality of their answers was worse than those from the control group. Although prior research on socialization suggests that socialization in a cohort isolated from the larger community should be beneficial, our experiment identified an important challenge. Without a critical mass of others actively participating, socialization in a cohort can undercut social experience. Incorporating the new cohort into the community and explicitly encouraging existing core members to mentor them might be a solution, providing more chances for newcomers to receive the feedback necessary to improve their domain and community knowledge. Bringing them into the live community might be especially important if too few newcomers join in any defined period.

The research presented here provides insight to designers of online communities on the effectiveness of identifying high potential contributors and coaching them to become more active members. Although formal socialization programs are frequent offline, they are rarely used in online communities. Our research shows that designers and managers of online communities can be more proactive in identifying and nurturing future core members. Even though not all aspects of the socialization experiences were successful, the research shows the promise of developing successful and self-sustaining socialization programs for growing the leadership in an online community. Future research should focus on additional ways to integrate more sustainable and effective socialization practices into online communities.

ACKNOWLEDGEMENTS

This work was funded by NSF grants 0812148 and 0808692. We would like to thank Howard Chen and Igor Podgorny from the Intuit Live Community for their assistance with this research.

REFERENCES

1. ANDERSON, J. R., FINCHA, J. M., AND S. DOUGLASS. The role of examples and rules in the acquisition of a cognitive skill. *Journal of Experimental Psychology: Learning, Memory, and Cognition 23* (1997), 932–945.
2. ATKINSON, R. K., DERRY, S. J., RENKL, A., AND WORTHAM, D. Learning from examples: Instructional principles from the worked examples research. *Review of Educational Research 70*, 2 (2000), 181–214.
3. BANDURA, A. Perceived self-efficacy in cognitive development and functioning. *Educational Psychologist 28*, 2 (1993), 117–148.
4. BAUER, T. N., BODNER, T., ERDOGAN, B., TRUXILLO, D. M., AND TUCKER, J. S. Newcomer adjustment during organizational socialization: A meta-analytic review of antecedents, outcomes, and methods. *Journal of Applied Psychology 92*, 3 (2007), 2707–2721.
5. BUTLER, B., SPROULL, L., KIESLER, S., AND KRAUT, R. Community effort in online groups: Who does the work and why? *Leadership at a distance 11* (2007), 171–194.
6. CHO, K., AND SCHUNN, C. D. Scaffolded writing and rewriting in the disipline: A web-based reciprocal peer review system. *Computers and Education 48*, 3 (2007), 409–426.
7. CHOI, B., ALEXANDER, K., KRAUT, R. E., AND LEVINE, J. M. Socialization tactics in wikipedia and their effects. In *Computer Supported Collaborative Work* (2010).
8. DUCHENEAUT, N. Socialization in an open source software community: A socio-technical analysis. In *Computer Supported Cooperative Work* (2005), vol. 14, pp. 323–368.
9. JONES, G. R. Socialization tactics, self-efficacy, and newcomers' adjustments to organizations. *Academy of Management 29*, 2 (1986), 262–279.
10. KRAUT, R. E., BURKE, M., AND RIEDL, J. Dealing with newcomers. In *In Evidence-based social design: Mining the social sciences to build online communities.*, R. E. Kraut and P. Resnick, Eds. MIT Press., Under contract.
11. KRISTOF, A. L. Person-organization fit: An integrative review of its conceptualizations, measurement, and implications. *Personnel Psychology 49*, 1 (1996), 1–49.
12. KRISTOF-BROWN, A. L., ZIMMERMAN, R. D., AND JOHNSON, E. C. Consequences of individuals' fit at work: A meta-analysis of person-job, person-organization, person-group, and person-supervisor fit. *Personnel Psychology 58*, 2 (2005), 281–320.
13. KROGH, G. V., SPAETH, S., AND LAKHANI, K. R. Community, joining, and specialization in open source software innovation: A case study. *Research Policy Special Issue On Open Source Software Development 32*, 7 (2003), 1217–1241.
14. LING, K., BEENEN, G., LUDFORD, P. J., WANG, X., CHANG, K., LI, X., COSLEY, D., FRANKOWSKI, D., TERVEEN, L., RASHID, A. M., RESNICK, P., AND KRAUT, R. E. Using social psychology to motivate contributions to online communities. *Journal of Computer Mediated Communication 10*, 4 (2005).
15. LOCKE, E. A., AND LATHAM, G. P. Building a practically useful theory of goal setting and task motivation. *American Psychologist 57* (2002), 705–717.
16. MOCKUS, A., FIELDING, R. T., AND HERBSLEB, J. D. Two case studies of open source software development: Apache and mozilla. *ACM Transactions on Software Engineering and Methodology 11*, 3 (2002), 309–346.
17. MORRISON, E. W. Newcomers' relationships: The role of social network ties during socialization. *Academy of Management Journal 45*, 6 (2002), 1149–1160.
18. PAL, A., FARZAN, R., KONSTAN, J. A., AND KRAUT, R. E. Early detection of potential epxerts in question answering communities. In *User Modeling, Adaptation, and Personalization (UMAP)* (2011), Springer.
19. PREECE, J., AND SHNEIDERMAN, B. The reader-to-leader framework: Motivating technology-mediated social participation. *AIS Transactions on Human-Computer Interaction 1*, 1 (2009), 13–23.
20. SAKS, A. M., UGGERSLEV, K. L., AND FASSINA, N. E. Socialization tactics and newcomer adjustment: A meta-analytic review and test of a model. *Journal of Vocational Behavior 70* (2007), 413–446.
21. TWEEDIE, M. C. K. An index which distinguishes between some important exponential families. *Statistics: applications and new directions* (1984), 579–604.
22. VAN MAANEN, J., AND SCHEIN, E. H. Toward of theory of organizational socialization. *Research in Organizational Behavior 1* (1979), 209–264.
23. VANLEHN, K. Cognitive skill acquisition. *Annual Review of Psychology 47* (1996), 513–539.

Diagnostic Work in Cloud Computing: Discussion Forums, Community and Troubleshooting

John Rooksby
School of Computer Science,
University of St Andrews, UK
jrnr@st-andrews.ac.uk

Ali Khajeh-Hosseini
Cloud Computing Co-Laboratory
University of St Andrews, UK
akh@cs.st-andrews.ac.uk

ABSTRACT
As systems scale, systems management often becomes partially reliant on web forums and other social media. This paper examines the use of web forums for diagnostic work in cloud computing. We argue that forums are not simply used to communicate information but that (with users attempting to negotiate and manage the attention of providers, forming coalitions, criticizing others, and framing problems in particular ways) forums are socially organised, value laden venues for information. We conclude that providers should focus not on improving communication, but more broadly on managing community.

Author Keywords
Infrastructure as a Service (IaaS), Conversation Analysis.

ACM Classification Keywords
K.4.3 Organizational Impacts: CSCW.

INTRODUCTION
The cloud computing paradigm sees computational resources (software, data storage, servers, etc.) accessed as a service rather than acquired as a product. IaaS (Infrastructure as a Service) is one model of cloud computing [1]. IaaS providers enable more or less anyone with a credit card to build and run a system on servers owned by and located with the provider. The idea is that if large providers supply computing services over the Internet on a commercial, pay-as-you-go basis, to a massive, self-service user-base, users will benefit from substantial cost savings, improved uptime, and extreme flexibility.

Using an IaaS provider involves developing and operating a system across organisational boundaries. Using a larger provider means the user may be just one of many thousands of others, which has implications for the way support can be provided. One convenient technology for providing support in this situation is the web forum. Forums provide a familiar, many-to-many line of communication, and simultaneously build a temporal, public archive of problems and solutions. This paper addresses how web forums are being used for identifying failures and planning remedial actions, for what Büscher et al [2] term "diagnostic work". The paper concludes that in order to improve user support, large providers need to focus not on "communication" with users but more broadly on how they encourage and manage the cooperative work of its "community".

DISCUSSION FORUMS IN CLOUD COMPUTING
Most IaaS providers maintain a discussion forum as a part of their support services. Smaller providers can rely on more direct contact if they wish, but the larger ones cannot. As the market in this area expands, reliance on this relatively cheap form of support is likely to increase.

This paper focuses on forums run by AWS[1] (Amazon Web Services), which is one of the larger and more mature IaaS (Infrastructure as a Service) providers. AWS provides free "basic support", giving access to discussion forums, to technical FAQs, and a dashboard detailing service availability. Paid "premium support" gives access to one-to-one web-based and telephone-based support. We have found premium support does not replace the forums, they are a first point of call, a hub for linking to other information, and enable user-user interaction. Discussion forums seem a convenient technology, both for provider and users. AWS currently provides twenty-one individual discussion forums. The two most popular forums, for Amazon EC2 (Elastic Compute Cloud) and Amazon S3 (Simple Storage Service), have tens of thousands of messages and millions of views.

The general design of the AWS forums is much like that of any other professional forum. Messages are organized into threads in order of posting. Their functionality, along with the 'house rules', both enable and constrain users in what they can do. However this does not in itself determine how people use the forums, it merely sets the stage for socially organized interaction.

[1]http://aws.amazon.com/ (Amazon, AWS, Amazon Web Services, Amazon S3 and Amazon EC2 are trademarks).

User1: **tons of 500 error messages** *Posted: 1:17 PM*

I am trying to upload a bundle and I keep getting 500 error messages like this one:

Failed to upload "/mnt/image.part.03": Server.InternalError(500): We encountered an internal error. Please try again.

ERROR: Failed to upload "/mnt/image.part.03": Server.InternalError(500): We encountered an internal error. Please try again.

Also I was trying to use S3Fox to delete things from my bucket and I get the same 500 error messages. This all usually works perfectly fine for me.

User2: **Re: tons of 500 error messages** *Posted: 2:28 PM*

Same here.

I've been unable to test my new image for the last 4 hours because of the same error.

This problem started yesterday for me, when I had to re-run the upload over 15 times before it would complete.

Well, it's Friday and there's no cloud. I might as well go to the beach early :)

User3: **Re: tons of 500 error messages** *Posted: 2:46 PM*

Having the same problem here. I expected to find more people complaining. It started this morning for me. Simple gets and deletes started throwing 500s almost consistently. Yesterday was fine.

John@AWS Re: tons of 500 error messages

Posted: 3:35PM

If you get a 500 response from Amazon S3, retry your request using exponential backoff between retries. With the EC2 command line tools, you can use the "--retry" argument to have the tools retry your request up to 5 times.

You can find more information about dealing with Amazon S3 errors in the documentation found here:

http://docs.amazonwebservices.com/AmazonS3/latest/ErrorBestPractices.html

If you continue to have problems after employing these measures, please provide the request ID (if available) and the bucket name for the failing request.

User2 Re: tons of 500 error messages *Posted: 4:58 PM*

Hi John,

this was using the api tool ec2-upload-bundle.

It seems it does not follow the ErrorBestPractices then.

I worked around the problem by no longer bundling amis.

Instead I started applying patches stored on s3, on top of a reference ami.

This has a faster turnaround time. Uses less traffic and is so far keeps me more productive than having my hands tied with bundle upload error.

Figure 1: Example thread (Anonymised and Formatted)

MUNDANE AND CATASTROPHIC FAILURE

In this paper we will focus on a mundane failure. Reason [4] argues that mundane failures are normal in complex systems, and that catastrophic failures usually involve unfortunate combinations and timings of familiar, ordinarily mundane factors. Catastrophic failures are certainly important to understand, but we argue 1) mundane failures are common and so important to understand in their own right, and 2) catastrophic failures are best understood with reference to mundane failures.

Catastrophic failure (of a kind) can and does happen in cloud computing. On the 21st April 2011, AWS suffered an outage in one of its data centers, taking around two days to resolve. In turn, a large number of systems built on AWS failed or were adversely affected. According to AWS[2] the failure was initiated by human error within the data center. AWS admitted that problems for users were then compounded by a lack of communication; users found it difficult to identify what was happening and what actions, if any, they should take. Studying the forums will not help in preventing future outages but does give insight into how information is shared and how lessons are learned by users. In response to the April 2011 outage, AWS has stated it is working on "improving communication". This is important, but through the lens of mundane failure we suggest there is a wider issue. How can the way knowledge is constructed and shared by providers and users of the forum be improved? We suggest the answer lies not just in "communication" but also more broadly in "community".

ANALYSIS OF A MUNDANE FAILURE

In this paper we draw from Antaki et al [3] to examine how posts to the AWS forums are socially organised. We will do so by focuing on the on-stage interactions; we will not try to explain what is going on behind the scenes at the provider's or users' workplaces. We focus on-stage because the forums are boundary objects situated between people who are unlikely to know each other and potentially have little shared interest except for the service itself. Antaki et al [3] have argued that the coherence and orderliness, and ultimately the meaningfulness and usefulness of a forum, must be achieved through the interactions that take place in writing on the forum itself, through how participants "make their messages achieve recognizable social and personal objectives while attending to the discursive perils" (such as rejection, criticism or silence).

Following Antaki et al [3], we will draw from ethnomethodology and conversation analysis to discuss a single thread from the AWS S3 forum (figure 1). We are

[2]Our comments are based on the official postmortem from Amazon http://aws.amazon.com/message/65648/

describing interactional not cumulative phenomena and so have chosen an example that gives relatively clear, concise demonstrations of phenomena we believe are salient. The example is slightly longer than many threads and relatively jargon-free, but is otherwise *in our experience* a run-of-the-mill thread. We have been visiting cloud forums (run by AWS and other providers) over a two-year period. Our analysis has involved three multi-disciplinary data sessions. The forums (including the example thread) are publically accessible and our findings reproducible.

Opening Message

The opening message in the example (lines 1-12) is entitled "*tons of 500 error messages*". This title serves as succinct problem statement. It is not designed to lure readers in (as might be a headline or advertisement) but written to make the message content unsurprising, to only attract the attention and time of those directly interested in the message content.

The message body describes how an error has started to occur (lines 2-3), illustrates this with copy and pastes of error output (lines 4-9), and is then backed up by describing another situation in which the same error has also started occurring (lines 10-12). This opening message, as is usual in any forum [3], is more than a factual problem statement. The problem is framed in three ways; it is said to be happening: a) repeatedly - "*I keep getting*" (line 2); b) in more than one context - "*Also I was trying to use S3Fox… and I get the same…*" (lines 10-11); and c) for something that has worked previously - "*this all usually works perfectly fine for me*" (line 12). Contextualizing the problem in these ways serves to justify its inclusion in the forum; it: a) gives a demonstration of competence; b) demonstrates the user has tried several possibilities before seeking help; and c) indicates the problem is most likely with AWS and not with the user's implementation. Ultimately the message is, in Antaki's terms [3] "accountable"; it is trying to solicit a particular account from the provider (an answer), gives the resources the author thinks are necessary for coming to that answer, and contextualizes the problem so as to avoid criticism and rejection.

Confirmations (and Challenges)

The second and third messages (lines 13-25) in the example thread are not answers but "me too" confirmations. Both messages state the same problem is happening and, as with the opening message, add contextual information that points to a particular diagnosis. Both refer to the fact that the problem is repeatedly encountered after multiple attempts: a) "*I had to re-run … over 15 times*" (lines 17-18); and b) "It [is] … *throwing 500s almost consistently*" (lines 23-25). Both also refer to the problem as being something that started at such-and-such a time: a) "*The problem started yesterday*" (line 17); b) "*It started this morning*" (line 23). Trying to identify consistencies is a method of externalising the problem, to locate it with the provider. The role of these confirmation messages is not to sympathise with the first author, but to help solicit a response from the provider. Confirmation messages serve to bring attention to a problem: they a) show it is not an individual, one-off problem; and b) bump the message to the top of the forum.

There is a hint of emotion in the second message. The comment about going "*to the beach early :)*" (line 20) is good humoured, playing down the urgency of the problem. We've noticed that when there are many confirmations the opposite often happens, they often become angrier in tone and start magnifying the importance of a problem.

Interestingly, the third message states "*I expected to find more people complaining*" (lines 22-23). This reveals how confirmation messages can serve to reinforce a user's suspicion that a problem lies with the provider. Because there are fewer than expected, the author now seems to doubt his/her initial suspicion.

Sometimes a message may challenge rather than confirm a previous one. These may directly dismiss a problem, or attempt to reframe it. Challenges serve as reprimands; they are a discursive peril, as discussed by Antaki et al [3].

Solution and Workaround

The example contains two answers. The first is from the provider. This answer begins by mentioning good behaviour in retrying requests: "*exponential backoff*" (line 29). This point is unsolicited; the provider is taking the opportunity to mention a good practice, one that helps them avoid getting swamped with retries. Next, the message points to documentation, leading readers away from the forum. The documentation itself actually contains very little extra information. The link serves not to provide extra details but as a strong indication that this problem is for the user to work out away from the forum. Finally, the alternative is to post information about a "*request ID … and bucket name*" (lines 38-39). This recognizes the possibility of a problem with the provider's service, but casts it as an individual rather than systemic issue. This answer closes down possibilities for appropriate responses. The user should a) go away and read the documentation, and b) failing that, give specific information to be used for a specific diagnostic act by the provider. User1 did their best to be a good customer, they pitched their problem in a respectful, meaningful way but the provider needs them to be a good customer on their particular terms: they want someone who checks the documents and then provides the information with which AWS can do the basic (and likely most effective) check.

The final response (to date) rejects the provider's answer and gives a workaround. User generated solutions and workarounds are common on these forums, but are often presented as a dis-preferred type of answer. User solutions contain not just information but typically a) criticize a perceived failure of the provider to follow the line of reasoning the user(s) have been taking in troubleshooting and then present a workaround; or b) where a workaround is offered in advance of an 'official' reply, it will be presented in a tentative manner, not closing down the possibility of an official response. As a rejection, the final message also touches on some of the emotional labour of diagnostic work: it employs an argumentative, almost angry tone.

FORUMS, COMMUNICATION AND COMMUNITY

In response to a catastrophic failure AWS have stated they will work to "improve communication". We believe the way this catastrophe was handled should be put in the context of how mundane, everyday failures are handled. This way the wider problem of fostering and managing *community* in cloud computing becomes visible.

Community is a word already used by AWS: their website links to the forums with the words "tap into the breadth of existing AWS community knowledge" and "engage with and learn from the AWS community." This study shows the term "community" is far from ironic. The term, however, does gloss over socially organized, interactional phenomena. Following Antaki et al [3], we have used a single example to illustrate how:

- Posts are matter of fact, but not statements of pure fact. They are written in what Antaki et al [3] call an "accountable" way (they are written to encourage certain next turns, while limiting the scope for others).
- Locating a problem (with provider or user) and deciding who holds responsibility for diagnosing and solving it can be negotiable and collaborative.
- Knowledge accumulates on the forum in a value-laden way. Hyperlinks are provided both as answers and for moving people away from discussion, and workarounds are presented as tentative.
- A 'good customer' for the provider is not just a polite one, but one who is able, without prompting and within a short message, to provide the information they need for carrying out their routine diagnostic procedures.
- Answers are oriented to a general audience (for example giving general points about good practice).
- Messages in the forums treat the attentions of the provider and other users as an extremely limited resource (correctly or otherwise).
- Interaction on the forum can draw upon and display emotion.
- The default assumption of the provider is that the problem lies with the user. Users form coalitions to dismiss this assumption (rightly or wrongly).

Büscher et al [2] point out that diagnostic work usually relies not on specialist technologies, but common, everyday ones. Because these technologies are relatively mature in design terms, the work done across them can often be overlooked. Discussion forums are one such technology. There may be limited design challenges, but the work done across them needs to be better managed. This paper makes a step towards that by unpacking aspects of this work.

SOCIOTECHNICAL APPROACHES TO FAILURE

The field of cloud computing has focused extensively on design for failure, but too often from an overly technical perspective. We argue that preventing, mitigating and recovering from failure is a socio-technical not technical problem. The April 2011 outage underscored this for us. The outage was initiated by human error in a data center, and compounded for users by a lack of communication. Subsequently, there was a debate on the forums and in the technical media about responsibility; some argued it was Amazon's fault that the systems built on AWS failed, others argued developers should have built their systems across multiple data centers. Irrespectively of where fault lies, an important point is that there are human, social and organizational issues at play. Dependability in cloud computing is a socio-technical, not purely technical problem. Addressing diagnostic work on the forums is just one small step into a much wider set of issues to which sociotechnical research can make useful contributions.

Some of the issues we have covered in this paper are familiar to CSCW. In particular there are some parallels here with studies of the use of forums in distributed software development (although in the case of cloud computing, the forum users are not working together on a project but are more self-interested, and relationships between users are likely to be more transient). Our ultimate intention with this work is not to describe some novel practice but to bring the knowledge and methods of CSCW to the development of cloud computing.

CONCLUSION

Diagnostic work across discussion forums relies not just on provider-user communication but on cooperative work between the provider and a community of users. If cloud computing is to become more reliant on discussion forums, we believe the social organization of this community needs to be understood and managed.

REFERENCES

1. Badger L, Grance T, Patt-Corner R, Voas J (2011) Cloud Computing Synopsis and Recommendations. National Institute of Standards and Technology, Special Publication 800-146.
2. Büscher M, O'Neill J, Rooksby J (2009) Designing for diagnosing. Journal of Computer Supported Cooperative Work, 18(2-3), 109-128.
3. Antaki, C., Ardévol, E., Núñez, F., and Vayreda, A. (2005) "For she who knows who she is:" Managing accountability in online forum messages. Journal of Computer-Mediated Communication, 11(1), article 6.
4. Reason, J. (2008) The Human Contribution. Farnham: Ashgate.

In Case You Missed It: Benefits of Attendee-Shared Annotations for Non-Attendees of Remote Meetings

Mukesh Nathan[1], Mercan Topkara[2], Jennifer Lai[2], Shimei Pan[2], Steven Wood[2], Jeff Boston[2], Loren Terveen[1]

[1]University of Minnesota
Minneapolis, MN, USA
{mukesh, terveen}@cs.umn.edu

[2]IBM T.J. Watson Research
Hawthorne, NY, USA
{mtopkara, jlai, shimei, woodsp, daddyb}@us.ibm.com

ABSTRACT

Corporate meetings are increasingly being held remotely using web technologies. With such remote meetings being recorded and made available after the fact, there is a pressing need for tools to access and utilize these recordings efficiently. Our work explores the utility of using annotations generated by meeting attendees to meet this need. We conducted a controlled lab study to evaluate the benefits of sharing annotations. Attendee-created annotations were shared with non-attendees to assist them on typical information retrieval tasks. Results indicate that (a) non-attendees given access to shared annotations performed about as well as attendees provided with their own and shared annotations, (b) non-attendees were more confident in their responses when they used shared annotations as access cues into the recording than when they directly skimmed the video, and (c) attendees utilized shared annotations more than their own, with similar success and confidence as using their own annotations.

Author Keywords

web-conferencing, video, indexing, meetings, recordings, annotations, tags, enterprise, collaboration

ACM Classification Keywords

H.5.3. Group & Organizational Interfaces: Computer Supported Cooperative Work

General Terms

Experimentation, Design

INTRODUCTION

Meetings are an important venue within the enterprise for information exchange, where the capture of important points, decisions and/or actions is often done informally and manually. With the rise in geographically dispersed teams, organizations are increasingly adopting technology to hold meetings remotely over the web. Commercial webconferencing products such as GoToMeeting and Webex [13] are being widely used by today's global companies to reduce travel and time costs. Many of these systems facilitate the automatic capture of information by recording remotely held meetings in their entirety and making them available for later viewing. Such systems can support people who did not attend the meeting but hope to catch up on what they missed. They create the possibility of using meeting recordings as archives of information.

As repositories of such recorded meetings grow, the value and utility of these stores will depend on providing tools that help users to quickly browse, find and retrieve elements of interest. Given the high time cost of viewing a recorded meeting in its entirety, there is a need for tools that assist efficient information retrieval. This is particularly true for people who missed a meeting, who frequently choose to learn about the proceedings from a colleague [1], rather than invest the time viewing its recording.

The capture of meetings has received a lot of attention in the research community over the last few decades. However, the majority of work has focused on supporting remote meetings by prototyping systems for the capture and access of these meetings [6, 19]. Many such systems not only record the meeting proceedings, but also capture associated artifacts such as user annotations made by attendees. Our work breaks new ground by being the first to systematically evaluate whether annotations created and shared by meeting attendees can assist non-attendees on information retrieval tasks. The Dogear system [14] showed how users could benefit from webpage bookmarks shared by others, creating a multiplicative effect of enterprise sharing. We examine whether people who miss meetings can benefit from using annotations shared by attendees as a tool to access video recordings of meetings.

Scope

Our long-term goal is to support distributed enterprise meetings – where attendees use a web conference along with a telephone bridge – such that attendees and non-attendees alike can easily discover and retrieve information from the recordings of meetings. As a first step, we focus on helping non-attendees retrieve information from a video recording of the meeting. We study a 1-to-N type meeting (in which a speaker has a discussion with a group) that is hosted in a meeting capture system deployed in a large enterprise. Those in attendance create time-stamped textual annotations during the meeting. These annotations are captured, synchronized with video and shared with those who missed the meeting as a possible aid for retrieving meeting-related information.

CSCW'12, February 11–15, 2012, Seattle, Washington, USA.

We present the results of a controlled lab study with 40 knowledge workers who used shared annotations to answer questions about the meeting after it had taken place. The study examined the following research questions:

RQ1. *Do annotations created and shared by attendees help non-attendees retrieve information from recordings?*

On the information retrieval tasks, we found that non-attendees with access to shared annotations performed (a) better than non-attendees without shared annotations, (b) about as well as attendees given shared annotations and their own annotations, and (c) about as well as attendees given only their own annotations.

RQ2. *To what extent are shared annotations utilized?*

We found that non-attendees (a) relied more on shared annotations as cues into the recording than skimming the video alone, (b) were about as successful using shared annotations or video skimming, and (c) were more confident in their answers when using shared annotations. For the same retrieval tasks, we found that attendees (a) utilized shared annotations more than their own, (b) were about as successful using shared or their own annotations, and (c) were about as confident in their answers using shared annotations or other retrieval methods.

The rest of the paper is organized as follows. We first present prior work related to meeting capture and review systems. We describe one such system using which our study was carried out. We then describe the design of a lab study to evaluate our research questions. Finally, we present the results of this study, discuss limitations of the study and conclude with a brief summary.

RELATED WORK

Meeting Capture and Review Systems

Creating systems to capture meeting-related information has received much attention over the past few decades. Such systems record meeting artifacts such as audio, video, slide images etc. and make them available post-hoc using a playback interface. Jabber [10], LiteMinutes [2], NotePals [3], and FiloChat [16] are just some systems from this rich line of research. Our current work was carried out in one such system (refer to 'Collaborative Recorded Meeting System' section). Unlike these systems, ours is a web-based collaborative service that focuses on supporting geographically distributed users to attend remote meetings and to browse meeting artifacts. Among past research systems, TeamSpace [6] is closest to ours. Our research focus is not on building such systems, but examining their ability to address meeting-specific retrieval needs of those who miss meetings.

Indexing Meeting Recordings

Prior research on meeting capture systems has highlighted two types of indices to support random access into recordings: *(1) Derived indices*, which are automatically calculated by the system, such as media stream analysis to detect slide transitions or sensors to detect who is in the room [4, 6, 10], and *(2) Explicit indices*, which are created by users, including digital bookmarks and personal annotations [8, 11]. Such explicit indices could be kept private to the creator, or shared with other meeting attendees as well as non-attendees. While users can create explicit indices as part of a regular meeting interaction process, the creation of derived indices often requires custom hardware or post-processing. Our current work builds on this body of research by evaluating the benefits of *explicit indices* to assist users in retrieving information discussed in meetings they missed.

Recording User Annotations

Our research builds on prior systems that co-index meeting recordings and user-created annotations [3]. In such systems, time-stamped annotations from different meeting attendees are combined and merged with a separately captured audio/video stream, thus making both the annotations and the media stream available for later playback. The Live Conference Dashboard (LCD) system [11] supports "live-tagging" during audio-only remote meetings in an enterprise setting. In a study, users preferred one-click tagging to other methods that allowed the tagging of meeting segments with multiple clicks (i.e. requiring both a start and an end point to the tag). We use this result in our work by allowing users to add tags with one-click. The LiteMinutes [2] system compiles meeting notes from different users into a single document that is correlated with the meeting recording. However, these studies mostly focus on implementation details of creating annotations during a meeting and their later access, without much empirical examination of the affordances they provide. Our work looks at advantages of having access to group annotations related to meeting recordings for retrieval tasks.

Retrieving Meeting Information Using Annotations

Kazman et al. evaluated the utility of keywords automatically extracted from a text transcript as *derived indices* into meeting recordings [10]. They found that having access to such keywords substantially improved the ability of meeting *attendees* to retrieve information from video recordings. Similarly, Banerjee et al. looked at the impact of automatic annotations *derived* from meeting structure on information retrieval [1]. In their user study, participants took less time to recall details of the meeting they *attended* when given annotations than when not given annotations. Our work complements this research by focusing on user annotations as *explicit indices* to assist *non-attendees*. We also examine the extent to which participants utilize shared annotations compared to other retrieval modalities.

The field of education is rich in studies that examine the benefits of having one's annotations available for review during retrieval tasks. Much of this research can also be applied to meetings, if we consider lectures to be a meeting of type 1-to-N. For example, a study of ChittyChatty [7], a system that supports the capture and access of notes during a lecture, showed that students were able to accurately recall information based on their personal notes indexed to the lecture audio. A review of the field noted that threefourths of such studies found positive effects of having access to one's own notes [7]. Kalnikaité and Whittaker showed a correlation of shared annotations with learning [8]. Students in a longitudinal study preferred accessing previously accessed annotations while re-

Figure 1. The Live-Annotations interface allows remote meeting participants to create annotations in real-time.

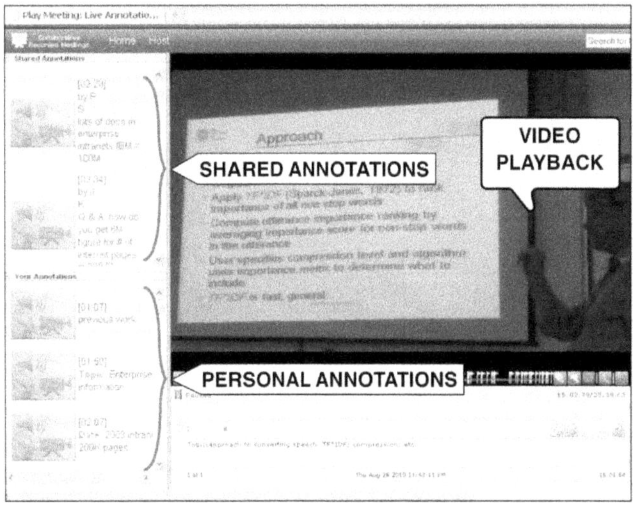

Figure 2. The Recorded-Meeting Playback interface. Clicking an annotation on the left starts playback from the point in the meeting video where it was created.

visiting lecture recordings. Our work extends this body of studies by reporting on a controlled lab study focused on examining the causal relation between shared annotations and performance on information retrieval tasks.

THE COLLABORATIVE RECORDED MEETING SYSTEM

The Collaborative Recorded Meeting (CRM) system is a research prototype that allows users to host and join web meetings, record them, and view previously recorded meetings in the form of videos. The CRM system has two primary modes of use: 1) during meeting interaction, where users can create text annotations while the meeting is being recorded, and 2) post-meeting interaction, where users can view the recording as well as annotations. The features relevant to this paper are the interface that allows for during-meeting annotations to be created (Figure 1) and the ability for users to view these annotations during playback (Figure 2). The remainder of the system is not relevant to this paper and can be seen in [15].

During a meeting users can create annotations that are timestamped and displayed at the bottom of the interface in a horizontal chronologically ordered list (Figure 1) as they are created. Only the users' own annotations are visible to them during the meeting. Users can mark annotations as private or public (shared), the default being public. Annotations shared by other attendees are not displayed during the meeting, but can be viewed after the meeting during playback. While one could imagine benefits in broadcasting all shared annotations in real-time as they are created, we decided for this initial version not to display them due to the distraction of seeing them come up while one tries to follow the meeting [11].

The CRM system automatically aligns user annotations on the meeting timeline and displays them in a side panel next to the video player (Figure 2). Clicking an annotation on the left causes the player to automatically seek to that point in the video and start playing from there.

USER STUDY

We carried out a controlled lab study (N=40) to evaluate the impact of annotations on retrieving information from a meeting recording.

Study Design

Users access meeting records as either (a) meeting *attendees* who later want to retrieve details based on information partially remembered, or (b) as *non-attendees* who are trying to discover information about a missed meeting [17]. Our study consisted of a between-subject, 2 by 2 design (see Table 1) where attendees and non-attendees were divided into 2 conditions, which differed by whether or not they had access to shared annotations during information retrieval tasks.

Participants

Forty people (32 males and 8 females) at a large corporate research lab responded to an email invitation. They were researchers or summer interns with a background in Computer Science. All the participants were fluent English speakers, and a majority (62%) regularly participated in remote meetings. Twenty participants were assigned to each of the two types of users (attendees or non-attendees) for a total of 40 participants. Within each of these user groups, participants were randomly assigned to either the *Shared* or *NoShared* conditions (see Table 1). They were given a lunch certificate for their participation.

Study Conditions

Participants in the *Attended-NoShared* condition only had access to their own annotations for retrieving meeting-related information. Those in the *Attended-Shared* condition had access to their own annotations, plus those created by 3 other attendees, during the retrieval task. These 3 users were randomly selected from the set of participants who created annotations. In a pilot study, users found that having access to 500+ annotations from all 20 meeting attendees was overwhelming. Scanning duplicate content in annotations was

	No Access to Shared Annotations	Had Access to Shared Annotations
Attendees	*Attended-NoShared* (own annotations) N=10	*Attended-Shared* (own annotations) N=10
Non-attendees	*Missed-NoShared* N=10	*Missed-Shared* N=10

Table 1. The conditions in the 2x2 between-subjects design

also frustrating. We observed that users could handle approximately 100 annotations comfortably. This led us to randomly pick 3 users (avg. of 27 annotations per user) whose annotations were shared. These 3 users were then assigned to the *Attended-NoShared* condition.

Participants in the *Missed-Shared* treatment were provided the annotations of the same 3 randomly selected users as *Attended-Shared* participants. Those in the *Missed-NoShared* treatment were not provided with any annotations during the information retrieval tasks.

Procedure

Wilcox et al [18] studied annotation capture and review behavior and found that information from previous meetings is often reviewed prior to the next meeting in order to revisit important details and refresh one's memory. In line with this finding, we designed the study with two phases: 1) a participation phase and 2) an information retrieval phase, spaced a week apart.

1) Participation Phase:

During this phase, only the 20 users assigned to the *Attended* conditions were asked to participate in a remote meeting. They were asked to make annotations using the Live-Annotations interface (Figure 1) during the meeting. Before starting the experiment, there was a short familiarization session where users created, edited and deleted annotations using the Live-Annotations interface. They were told that annotations could be shared, or not, with other meetings by marking them as 'private' or 'public' (the default was public). They were informed that while shared annotations are not broadcast in real-time with other attendees, they might be available to others after the meeting. Next, participants attended a meeting by viewing a video stream from a remote location. In order to ensure that all 20 participants in the *Attendee* conditions experienced the same meeting, the video stream was actually a recording. While they were told to assume the meeting was happening live, there was no telephone conference and they could not speak or ask questions.

The recording used as the remotely streamed meeting was chosen from a corporate database of real meeting recordings. In the selected recording, a researcher presents findings from experiments related to novel text summarization techniques. The talk is a traditional 1-to-N type meeting with a presenter speaking and using a slide deck. It is representative of a common meeting style in large corporations (e.g. technical talks, recurring meetings with an invited speaker). The meeting could be easily understood by users, as verified in a post-task survey, and did not require any additional context or knowledge in order to understand the topic being presented. The talk was edited down into a logical unit (introduction and results from 2 experiments) with duration of 25 minutes. None of the users had viewed the meeting recording previously, nor were familiar with the contents of the recording. The Participation Phase took less than an hour per user.

2) Information Retrieval Phase:

In this phase, all 40 participants were given a series of questions to answer based on information in the meeting recording. Participants in the *Missed* conditions were told that they had 'missed' the meeting but needed to attempt to answer the questions as best they could with the information available from the recording of the meeting. For users in the *Attended* conditions, the Information Retrieval Phase was conducted seven days after they attended the meeting. Participants in *Attended-Shared, Attended-NoShared* and *Missed-Shared* conditions were first given a tutorial to familiarize themselves with the Recorded-Meeting Playback interface (Figure 2). They practiced the use of random access into sections of the recording based on the selection of a specific annotation. Users were also showed how to search through the provided annotations. When they were familiar with the interface, they began the experiment proper. For users in the *Missed-NoShared* condition, no annotations were displayed.

Prior research has shown that users extract two main types of information from meeting recordings: gist or meeting overview, and specific *facts* [17]. Of the two types of information (gist vs. facts), we decided to focus on factual information since it can be more objectively evaluated. We asked all participants to answer 10 factual questions. The questions required them to extract facts from the meeting, as opposed to summarizing information distributed across the meeting. All questions required paying attention to the audio and video in the recording in order to answer them correctly. Questions were framed prior to the start of the study and were independent of annotations created in the Participation Phase. A pilot study was conducted to ensure the questions could be easily understood and were of comparable difficulty. The questions were not in a multiple choice format to prevent users from randomly guessing. An example question was: "The speaker demonstrates a software tool. Briefly describe what the tool allows users to do." The 10 questions were presented in random order. Participants were asked to answer them as quickly and accurately as possible. We imposed an upper bound of 30 minutes for the task. The Information Retrieval Phase took approximately 45 minutes per user.

Variables and Measures

The two independent variables in the study were *Meeting Attendance* {*Attended, Missed*} and *Access to Shared Annotations* {*Shared, NoShared*}.

The following measures were used:

Score: Two judges, blind to our research questions, created a key by viewing the meeting recording and generating target answers. The judges then combined their answers and specified keywords that needed to be present in each answer. Scores for each question ranged from 0 to 1 (in quarter point increments) depending on how much of the target answer participants mentioned. The judges scored the answers independently with disagreements being resolved by a third judge.

Time on Task: The question-answering interface automatically recorded the total time participants took to answer all questions, starting from the time they viewed the first question until they submitted an answer to the last question.

Retrieval Method: After each question, participants were asked to note the exact method they employed to answer the question. The options provided were: (1) *User Annotation* – Participants with access to annotations were instructed to indicate this option when the content of an annotation pointed them to a relevant segment in the video or in some cases, directly contained the answer[1]. Further, participants in the *Attended-Shared* condition also noted when they used their own annotations as opposed to a shared annotation. (2) *Video only* – In cases where participants answered questions purely by skimming through the video, they were instructed to select this option. (3) *Memory only* – This option was selected when users relied purely on their own memory, without having to use aids such as the video or annotations.

User Confidence: Participants indicated their confidence for each of their answers. A 3-point Likert scale with values 'very confident', 'somewhat confident' and 'not at all confident' was used.

CONTENT ANALYSIS OF LIVE MEETING ANNOTATIONS

During the Participation Phase of the study, 522 annotations were created by 20 users who were assigned to the two *Attended* conditions. On average, users entered 6 words per annotation. As noted by Kelkar et al. [11], annotations created during a meeting tend to be lengthy when compared to tags created on static data on the web. 30% of the annotations had more than 10 words, and 16 users added at least one annotation that had more than 10 words (e.g. "typical behaviors: with word excision, people are getting through the text quicker"). However, the majority of the annotations were not long. With short annotations, users created pointers to important parts of the meeting with keywords such as "fisheye", "graph", and "architecture". 48% of the annotations have less than 5 words. Here are some examples: "cool graphs", "user prefs", "demo time!", "excision - people miss stuff", "this technique is old".

The short annotations are very similar to the type of tags commonly seen in web tagging systems and are used as placeholders for rediscovering content. It seemed users in our study were creating 'bookmarks' into the meeting that could then be used to retrieve details if required. As one participant noted: *"I like to capture as much information in my tags so I don't need to view much of the video later"*. By contrast, notes created during a lecture are different in nature as they typically summarize or clarify the content being recorded, list questions and objections in mind, etc. [9]. In a survey, we asked participants to indicate whether their annotation behavior was influenced by the knowledge that the meeting recordings could be played back at the exact points where annotations were made. Participants strongly agreed with this view, providing credence to our notion of users being 'bookmarkers'.

[1] No distinction was made between using annotations only and using annotations to access video. The former occurred very infrequently. Users referred to the video even in cases where the annotation contained the answer. Post-task questioning revealed that users wanted to verify the annotation content by viewing the video.

We found the same content repeated in many annotations (e.g. 11 different users created an annotation with the term "fisheye"). Such repetition could be used to create a cluster or topic flow graph of the meeting. Repetition might be reduced if annotations were broadcast live among users as they are created, but as mentioned earlier we decided against it due to the additional cognitive load from the display of all shared annotations in real-time [11].

Another phenomenon we observed was that when several key concepts were mentioned back-to-back in the meeting, users were not able to capture all of them in their annotations. For example, at one point during the meeting the speaker introduces the term "strategic information processing", and within 1.5 seconds he introduces the concept of "golden triangle". Five users annotated "golden triangle", and three others recorded "strategic information processing". None of the users noted both in their annotations. This highlights the potential value of sharing during-meeting annotations where the speaker is not presenting in a structured educational lecture format that usually provides room for the students to digest terms that are being introduced.

The duration for entering free-form text annotations was on the average 17 seconds (max = 99 secs). We also observed that on average, users left 56 seconds between annotations and the minimum break was 1.2 seconds (max = 9 mins). These two data points suggest that it is important to provide users the ability to add quick, low-effort annotations during a meeting that will assist them in reviewing the details later.

RESULTS

We now discuss our findings from the Information Retrieval Phase of our study that evaluated participants answering factual questions based on the meeting. User performance on these tasks is summarized in Table 2.

Results of the retrieval tasks were first analyzed using a two-way ANOVA with *Score* as dependent variable, and *Attendance* {*Attended, Missed*} and *Access to Shared Annotations* {*Shared, NoShared*} as independent variables. A significant main effect for *Access to Shared Annotations* ($F_{1,36}$=16.66, $p<$ 0.001) was observed, indicating that participants with access to shared annotations scored higher, independent of meeting attendance.

There was also a main effect for *Attendance*, suggesting that participants performed better on the retrieval tasks when they attended the meeting ($F_{1,36}$=6, $p<$ 0.05). The interaction effect for *Shared Annotations* and *Attendance* was not significant, ($p>$ 0.1). A similar ANOVA with *Time on Task* as dependent variable found no significant results, ($p>$ 0.1). Hav-

Condition	Score [%]	Time [mins:secs]
Attended-NoShared	72 (±16)	22:05 (±4 : 43)
Attended-Shared	87 (±8)	22:23 (±4 : 42)
Missed-NoShared	63 (±9)	27:04 (±1 : 27)
Missed-Shared	78 (±11)	22:15 (±4 : 12)

Table 2. The performance (mean score and time on task) of users on retrieval tasks, along with standard deviations.

ing tested the main effects, we proceeded to answer our research questions.

RQ1. ***Do annotations created and shared by attendees help non-attendees retrieve information from recordings?***

We wanted to clearly understand the value annotations created by meeting attendees could provide people who missed the meeting. For this, we compared the *Missed-Shared* condition to the 3 other study conditions. (1) First, the performance of *Missed-Shared* users was compared with that of participants in the *Missed-NoShared* condition. This contrast served as a baseline. (2) Next, the *Missed-Shared* and *Attended-Shared* conditions were compared. This examined the advantage meeting attendance had during the retrieval tasks, keeping access to shared annotations constant. We wanted to see the extent to which providing annotations as retrieval aids could help compensate for having missed the meeting. (3) Finally, we wanted to see if access to annotations created by many users could provide non-attendees an edge over attendees who had access only to their own annotations. We explored this case by comparing the *Missed-Shared* and *Attended-NoShared* conditions.

Since there was a significant effect for *Access to Shared Annotations* on the *Score* for retrieval tasks, and not for *Time on Task*, we only compared the different conditions based on scores. The pair-wise comparisons were made using Tukey's HSD. We now discuss the results of the 3 comparisons as summarized in Table 3.

(1) ***Missed-Shared vs. Missed-NoShared***

H1: *Missed-Shared users will perform better than the Missed-NoShared users on questions about the meeting; Shared annotations act as semantic indices into the meeting recording and help users to quickly locate key ideas.*

Participants in the *Missed-NoShared* condition had no access to any annotations, while those in the *Missed-Shared* condition were provided with 67 annotations shared by attendees[2]. The results supported our prediction, with *Missed-Shared* participants performing significantly better than *Missed-NoShared* users. *Missed-Shared* users seemed to benefit on accuracy by having access to annotations made by attendees. They were able to effectively utilize shared annotations to answer the questions, while *Missed-NoShared* users had to rely only on skimming through the video to understand the structure of the meeting.

[2]Shared annotations directly contained answers to 2 of the 10 questions. In 6 cases, they had keywords pointing to the general region in the recording that contained the answer. It was up to participants to recognize and utilize them.

Comparison	diff	lower	upper	P adj
Missed-Shared vs. Missed-NoShared	1.45	0.05	2.85	0.04*
Missed-Shared vs. Attended-Shared	-0.95	-2.35	0.45	0.28
Missed-Shared vs. Attended-NoShared	0.60	-0.80	2.0	0.66

Table 3. Pair-wise comparisons of scores using Tukey's test. The lower and upper confidence limits are given. Difference in scores between the compared conditions along with the adjusted P values are shown. Significant differences are indicated using *.

The result that participants in the *Missed-Shared* condition performed better than those in *Missed-NoShared*, though seemingly intuitive, is non-trivial. They did so by relying heavily on shared annotations. Though attendees shared almost all annotations they created, this was more to do with the default setting and not an explicit desire to share. Contrary to past findings [12], our informal interviews with *Attendee* users revealed that they did not change their annotation content despite knowing their annotations may be shared. This meant that annotations were primarily created for the benefit of their author. The fact that the *Missed-Shared* users could utilize potentially esoteric shared annotations makes this result interesting. It highlights the value of sharing annotations: non-attendees can exploit annotations made by someone else to navigate to important parts of meeting recordings.

(2) ***Missed-Shared vs. Attended-Shared***

H2: *Attended-Shared users will perform better than Missed-Shared users; having attended the meeting, their own memory and personal annotations will prove useful for information retrieval purposes.*

Contrary to our prediction, we were surprised to see that there was no significant difference in scores for these treatments (see Table 3, row 2). Access to shared annotations alone seemed to be sufficient to perform comparably well on the retrieval tasks, irrespective of attendance. For *Attended-Shared* users, having their own personal annotations as well as memories of the meeting did not provide a statistically significant advantage for the purpose of retrieving *factual* information from the meeting recording. Having participated in the meeting, attendees were able to remember its general structure, as they indicated in the post-task interviews. However, the questions in the Information Retrieval Phase required extracting specific details from the audio/video recording, details that could have been hard to recall from memory. As one participant commented: *"For the most part I had forgotten details in the video from when I attended the first part of experiment. My comments reminded me of what I had seen."* We must point out that *Attended-Shared* users did not perform poorly. They did exceptionally well as shown by the high success rate (87%). It is just that non-attendees given shared annotations performed comparably well (78%).

(3) *Missed-Shared vs. Attended-NoShared*

H3: *Access to one's personalized annotations will help Attended-NoShared users outperform Missed-Shared users. Reasons mentioned in hypothesis H2 also apply.*

We found no significant difference between the scores of these two treatments, (see row 3 in Table 3). One would expect that participants who had attended the meeting earlier would have an advantage over those who missed the meeting. This was not the case in our study. On the other hand, the absolute scores for those who missed the meeting were better than the attendees (see Table 2).

Once again, we were surprised to see that *Missed-Shared* users performed nearly as well as participants who had attended the meeting. The *Missed-Shared* users had access to 67 shared annotations while *Attended-NoShared* only had their own (avg=27) annotations for assistance on retrieval tasks, besides their organic memory. This seemed to have leveled the playing field on retrieval tasks, as shared annotations seemed to help *Missed-Shared* participants to compensate for not having attended the meeting. We speculate that this could also be because of the factual nature of our questions. Attendees would possibly perform better on *gist* type questions that require an overall understanding of the meeting content. Nevertheless, these findings were intriguing and require further exploration in the future.

Having established that participants with access to shared annotations performed well on the retrieval tasks, despite having missed the meeting, we looked more closely at the groups that had access to shared annotations – *Attended-Shared* and *Missed-Shared* – to examine the extent to which shared annotations were actually used. What role did shared annotations play in the success of *Missed-Shared* participants? Why didn't personal annotations give *Attended-Shared* users an advantage over *Missed-Shared* users? We examine such questions in RQ2.

RQ2. ***To what extent are shared annotations utilized compared to other available retrieval methods? Can using shared annotations lead to more successful outcomes?***

During the Information Retrieval Phase, participants were asked to indicate whether they used 'video skimming' or 'annotations' to arrive at the answer, after answering each question. For each question, they also indicated their level of confidence in their answer. The usage of different retrieval methods, the success of using the different methods and user confidence in their answers are shown in Table 4 for *Missed-Shared* users. Table 5 shows similar values for *Attended-Shared* users.

(1) *Missed-Shared condition*

H4: *In the absence of personal memories from attendance or other any other aids, Missed-Shared subjects will rely more on shared annotations than video skimming to identify segments relevant to the retrieval tasks.*

Measure	Annot.	Video	t(9)	p
Retrieval Method Usage	90%	10%	10.96	0.00*
Success Rate	68%	47%	1.48	0.17
Confidence in Answers	70%	30%	2.28	0.04*

Table 4. Comparison of 'Annotations' and 'Video Skimming' alone as retrieval methods for *Missed-Shared* condition using paired *t*-tests. Success rates indicate % of answers with a score > 0.5 Confidence scores indicate the % of answers marked 'Very Confident' by users. Averages of usage, success and confidence are shown.

Usage: Our hypothesis was confirmed. Participants used shared annotations significantly more compared to video skimming to locate relevant information (see Table 4). In a survey, *Missed-Shared* participants were asked to rate the usefulness of having shared annotations available during the retrieval tasks on a 1-5 Likert scale. They unanimously indicated (avg. score=5) that having shared annotations helped them perform well on the tasks (*"shared annotations are super-useful"*) and that they would use a system with shared annotations if it was available.

We asked all participants about their general strategy to answer questions. For participants who had access to annotations, the most common approach to answering a question was to 1) 'search' for keywords/synonyms in the annotation content 2) 'browse' through the annotations if search failed 3) 'skim' through the video as a last option. Users tried to avoid viewing the video as far as possible. Annotations pointed to the general area in the recording where information potentially relevant to a question was. They then used their judgment to answer the question.

Success: There was no statistically significant difference in the success rates when participants used annotations created by someone else, or when they depended solely on their own ability to skim the video to answer a question. User feedback towards annotations was generally positive. Participants liked having access to annotations and were *"surprised by how useful annotations are for finding information in the video."*

Confidence: Participants were more confident in their answers when they used shared annotations than when they used the video alone. Clicking on and following annotations increased their chances of getting to the correct region in the video. More often than not, the region contained the information to be retrieved, as is evidenced by the high success rate using annotations. The video and annotation content reinforce each other, thereby instilling confidence.

(2) *Attended-Shared condition*

H5: *Meeting attendees will rely more on their own annotations than other methods to answer retrieval questions; they will understand the organization of their own annotations better. Further, we predicted that attendees would be more confident in answers using their own annotations, as these will trigger one's memory and instill confidence during retrieval tasks.*

Measure	Own Annot.	Shared Annot.	Video & Memory	F(2, 27)	p
Usage	18%	72%	10%	62.2	0.00*
Success	58%	89%	47%	3.15	0.04*
Confidence	72%	69%	45%	1.50	0.24

Table 5. *Attended-Shared* participant's usage of annotations (own and shared), video skimming and organic memory for retrieval. Success indicates % of answers with a score > 0.5 Confidence = % of answers marked as 'Very confident'. Each row shows results of a one-way ANOVA. Averages of usage, success and confidence are shown.

Usage: Our results showed a significant difference in retrieval method usage (see row 1 in Table 5). Follow up comparisons (using Tukey's HSD) showed a significant difference between shared annotation usage and video/memory alone ($p < 0.001$). Contrary to our prediction, *Attended-Shared* participants utilized shared annotations significantly more than their own ($p < 0.001$).

One reason for the high usage of shared annotations could be the sheer number of them available. All *Attended-Shared* users had access to 67 shared annotations as opposed to an average of 27 (std. dev=12) personal annotations. The playback interface clearly separated personal and shared annotations into separate sections (see Figure 2), so participants could easily restrict themselves to using their own annotations if they wanted to.

A common sentiment was that *"Finding something just using the video requires lengthy playback and that's a problem"*. This was something we hoped annotations would address by acting as indices into the video stream. When provided with both their own annotations from the meeting as well as annotations shared by other users, attendees did not favor their own annotations over those shared by others, as long as they helped reduce video playback.

On the post-task survey, participants indicated that shared annotations helped them on the retrieval tasks (avg. score =4.1 out of 5). In the case of 4 of the 10 *Attended-Shared* users, they rated the usefulness of their own annotations low and those of shared annotations high. These participants used shared annotations to answer 72% of the questions, and performed as well as other participants in their treatment condition (average score=85%). The utility of shared annotations was evident: *"Good thing I had access to shared comments because my comments were useless!"* Shared annotations made up for the inadequacies of personal notes. One user felt that sharing annotations even resulted in *"division of labor where lots of people commenting around the same video can provide benefit to everyone else."*

Success: We wanted to see if using annotations to answer questions lead to more successful outcomes for attendees. Results indicated a significant difference between success rates when using various retrieval methods (as seen in row 2 of Table 5). Post-test comparisons (using Tukey's HSD) showed a significant difference in success rate between using shared annotations and video/memory ($p < 0.05$). Most importantly, there was no significant difference in success when attendees used their own annotations or those shared by others. They were about as likely to get an answer correct, irrespective of whose annotations they used.

Confidence: There was no significant difference in confidence using any of the 3 retrieval methods (row 3 in Table 5). When using (shared or own) annotations to answer questions, participants were equally confident in their answers irrespective of the creator of the annotation. Subjective feedback from users shed some light on this unexpected outcome. Since users did not favor their own annotations over shared annotations while searching for answers, once they found success utilizing another user's annotations, they began to *"trust shared annotations"*. When shared annotation content was not clear, participants played the recording to confirm the intent of the annotation creator. This could be one reason for having the same confidence in their answers, using personal or shared annotations.

The results from RQ2 shed some light on why *Missed-Shared* users performed as well as *Attended-Shared* users, as per the results of RQ1. *Attended-Shared* users relied heavily on the 67 shared annotations. Their high success rate using others' annotations shows that shared annotations greatly helped in locating answers in the meeting recording. Since the same 67 annotations were shared with *Missed-Shared* users, they were able to reap similar benefits as *Attended-Shared* users.

The value of shared versus personal annotations is further highlighted by three observations:

(a) There was a significant difference between the score of *Attended-Shared* and *Attended-NoShared* users ($p < 0.05$, using Tukey's HSD).

(b) It was not always possible for attendees to capture all key events in their annotations 'live' during the meeting resulting in personal annotations missing details. This was seen in our Content Analysis as well as in feedback from *Attended* participants. Further, recent research has shown that users often expend effort recording information in annotations that may turn out to be irrelevant [7].

(c) Attendance did not seem to provide any clear advantage for the purposes of retrieving factual meeting-related information. With a one-week gap between the two study phases, utilizing annotations as memory cues could have become more challenging, as seen in [7]. Personal annotations may also turn out to be ineffective if users can no longer remember what they mean [16].

LIMITATIONS AND FUTURE WORK

Interacting During Remote Meetings

Our current study reports results from a single 1-to-N style meeting. While we believe that this type of meeting is representative of a large number of corporate remote meetings, it is a limitation of this work that users were not able to interact with the speaker or other attendees. In reality, there are a certain number of these types of presentations that are closed to question asking due to the large number of people on the call. In 'remote' meetings participants do not have the same level of attention as face-to-face meetings, since they are distracted by email and IM. While the setup of needing only to watch the meeting instead of directly engaging may differ from real life settings, we believe it sets the upper limit on annotation activity level. Also, having the annotation UI available gave users *"something to do"* and helped them *"stay focused"* as they commented. Different meeting styles could generate different levels of annotation activity and the gains of sharing attendee annotations will have to be examined across different meeting styles.

Handling Information Overload

Based on results from a pilot study we decided to share the public annotations of only 3 of 20 meeting attendees with others as shared annotations since otherwise the amount of duplicate annotations would be overwhelming. We envision that real world systems will use a combination of information filtering and interaction techniques to prevent information overload. More research would be needed to understand the best mechanism for presenting large numbers of annotation (e.g. greater than 100 annotations).

Real-time Sharing

As implemented, our system does not broadcast annotations as they are being generated. Few users mentioned that it would be useful to have such realtime exchange of annotations. They felt that it could inspire new annotations of their own as well as help them avoid repeating the same annotations as others. Broadcasting tweets around a shared hashtag at events is a comparable practice that people already indulge in today. However, viewing (redundant) shared annotations could lead to a processing overhead. The trade-offs involved would need to be examined more closely.

Annotation Browsing Interfaces

In many cases users had the information needed to answer a question available in the annotations (own and/or shared), but failed to find it. They either did not use the right keyword in their browser-search or skimming through all the annotations was not easy and they gave up. This points to the vital importance of presenting annotations in a way that favors effective browsing. For example, many shared annotations repeated the same information. Common items across all shared annotations could be extracted and made into a hyperlinked summary to present the important points in a meeting. Another approach would be to provide a better search interface tailored to during-meeting annotations that possibly contain repetitious information and typos.

Explicit vs. Derived Indices

Our results showed that user-generated annotations co-indexed with meeting recordings could be a useful information retrieval aid, especially for non-attendees. However, it remains to be seen how such *explicit* indices would fair against machine-generated *derived* indices. While retrieving verbatim facts from the recording via *derived* indices (e.g. text transcript) could be accomplished, we conjecture that the value of *explicit* indices will be in retrieval tasks that rely on interpretations of information shared in meetings.

CONCLUSIONS

We present the findings from a lab study (N=40) that examined the usefulness of sharing annotations created during a web conference meeting with those who missed it. The context for our research is enterprise meeting capture and review systems, which allow distributed knowledge workers to participate in and record meetings. These recordings are available to attendees as well as non-attendees with the need to retrieve specific information that might be hard to find using automatically created indices for meeting recordings (e.g. slide transitions). Our study evaluated the ability of non-attendees to retrieve information using shared annotations by measuring their performance on retrieval tasks, which consisted of a set of factual questions about a meeting. We wanted to see if having access to annotations could aid non-attendees to answer the factual questions.

Our results indicate that having access to shared annotations substantially improves the ability of non-attendees to retrieve relevant information. When provided with shared annotations, non-attendees performed better than those without access to such annotations. We found that non-attendees frequently used shared annotations over other retrieval methods, and were significantly more confident in their answers when doing so. This was true of attendee participants as well, who utilized annotations created by others more than their own, underlining the value of shared annotations. Most interestingly, we observed that non-attendees given access to shared annotations performed about as well as those who had attended the meeting. The main difference between attendees and non-attendees, as reported in [17] is that for attendees the retrieval process is one of assisted reconstruction, whereas non-attendees have no prior information available to structure their access. Our results indicate that shared annotations can partially address this disparity by acting as retrieval cues for non-attendees.

Shared annotations assist in augmenting individual memory, leading to what Engelbart called "Collective IQ" where a group can "leverage its collective memory, perception and experience into applicable knowledge"[5]. Storing participant annotations along with meeting recordings in organizational multimedia repositories can help build a knowledge base of semantic information. Such enhanced records can then prove beneficial to users across the organization, and not just those who participated in the meeting originally. In line with these ideals, our work shows how attendee-generated annotations can be valuable to non-attendees in distributed enterprise meeting systems. Sharing of annotations between attendees and non-attendees can address the need for relevant indices into meeting records such as those found in ever growing corporate meeting recordings repositories.

REFERENCES

1. Banerjee, S., Rose, C., and Rudnicky, A. The necessity of a meeting recording and playback system, and the benefit of topiclevel annotations to meeting browsing. In *Human-Computer Interaction - INTERACT 2005*. Springer Berlin / Heidelberg, 2005.

2. Chiu, P., Boreczky, J., Girgensohn, A., and Kimber, D.

Liteminutes: An internet-based system for multimedia meeting minutes. In *Proceedings of the 10th International Conference on World Wide Web*, WWW '01 (2001).

3. Davis, R. C., Landay, J. A., Chen, V., Huang, J., Lee, R. B., Li, F. C., Lin, J., Morrey, III, C. B., Schleimer, B., Price, M. N., and Schilit, B. N. Notepals: Lightweight note sharing by the ggroup, for the group. In *Proceedings of the SIGCHI Conference on Human Factors in Computing Systems*, CHI '99 (1999).
4. Ehlen, P., Purver, M., Niekrasz, J., Lee, K., and Peters, S. Meeting adjourned: Off-line learning interfaces for automatic meeting understanding. In *Proceedings of the 13th International Conference on Intelligent User Interfaces*, IUI '08 (2008).
5. Engelbart, D. C. Augmenting Human Intellect: A Conceptual Framework. Technical Report AFOSR-3233, SRI International, 1962.
6. Geyer, W., Richter, H., and Abowd, G. Towards a smarter meeting recordcapture and access of meetings revisited. *Multimedia Tools and Applications 27* (2005), 393–410.
7. Kalnikaité, V., and Whittaker, S. Software or wetware?: Discovering when and why people use digital prosthetic memory. In *Proceedings of the SIGCHI Conference on Human Factors in Computing Systems*, CHI '07 (2007).
8. Kalnikaité, V., and Whittaker, S. Social summarization: Does social feedback improve access to speech data? In *Proceedings of the 2008 ACM conference on Computer Supported Cooperative Work*, CSCW '08 (2008).
9. Kam, M., Wang, J., Iles, A., Tse, E., Chiu, J., Glaser, D., Tarshish, O., and Canny, J. Livenotes: A system for cooperative and augmented note-taking in lectures. In *Proceedings of the SIGCHI Conference on Human factors in Computing Systems*, CHI '05 (2005).
10. Kazman, R., Al-Halimi, R., Hunt, W., and Mantei, M. Four paradigms for indexing video conferences. *Multimedia, IEEE 3*, 1 (1996), 63 –73.
11. Kelkar, S., John, A., and Duncan Seligmann, D. Some observations on the "live" collaborative tagging of audio conferences in the enterprise. In *Proceedings of the 28th International Conference on Human Factors in Computing Systems*, CHI '10 (2010).
12. Marshall, C. C., and Brush, A. B. From personal to shared annotations. In *CHI '02 Extended Abstracts on Human Factors in Computing Systems*, CHI EA '02 (2002).
13. Meetings in america v: Meeting of the minds. mci whitepaper, 2003.
14. Millen, D. R., Feinberg, J., and Kerr, B. Dogear: Social bookmarking in the enterprise. In *Proceedings of the SIGCHI conference on Human Factors in Computing Systems*, CHI '06 (2006).
15. Topkara, M., Pan, S., Lai, J., Wood, S. P., and Boston, J. Tag Me While You Can: Making Online Recorded Meetings Shareable and Searchable. Research report, IBM, 2010.
16. Whittaker, S., Hyland, P., and Wiley, M. Filochat: Handwritten notes provide access to recorded conversations. In *Proceedings of the SIGCHI conference on Human Factors in Computing Systems: Celebrating Interdependence*, CHI '94 (1994).
17. Whittaker, S., Tucker, S., Swampillai, K., and Laban, R. Design and evaluation of systems to support interaction capture and retrieval. *Personal Ubiquitous Computing 12* (2008), 197–221.
18. Wilcox, L. D., Schilit, B. N., and Sawhney, N. Dynomite: A dynamically organized ink and audio notebook. In *Proceedings of the SIGCHI Conference on Human Factors in Computing Systems*, CHI '97 (1997).
19. Yankelovich, N., Walker, W., Roberts, P., Wessler, M., Kaplan, J., and Provino, J. Meeting central: Making distributed meetings more effective. In *Proceedings of the 2004 ACM Conference on Computer Supported Cooperative Work*, CSCW '04 (2004).

Markup as You Talk: Establishing Effective Memory Cues While Still Contributing to a Meeting

Vaiva Kalnikaitė
Interactables
Cambridge, UK
vaiva@interactables.com

Patrick Ehlen
AT&T
San Francisco, CA
patrick.ehlen@att.com

Steve Whittaker
University of California
Santa Cruz, CA
swhittak@ucsc.edu

ABSTRACT
Meeting participants can experience cognitive overload when they need both to verbally contribute to ongoing discussion while simultaneously creating notes to promote later recall of decisions made during the meeting. We designed two novel cuing tools to reduce the cognitive load associated with note-taking, thus improving verbal contributions in meetings. The tools combine real-time automatic speech recognition (ASR) with lightweight annotation to transform note-taking into a low overhead markup process. To create lightweight notes, users do not generate the notes' content themselves. Instead they simply highlight important phrases in a real-time ASR transcript (Highlighter tool), or press a button to indicate when they heard something important (Hotspots tool). We evaluated these markup tools against a traditional pen-and-paper baseline with 26 users. Hotspots was highly successful: compared with handwritten notes, it increased participants' conversational contributions and reduced their perception of overload in the meeting, while improving recall of the meeting two months later. Highlighter also improved recall without compromising conversational contributions, although users found it more demanding.

Author Keywords
Meetings, cognitive load, speech recognition, automated transcripts, summarization, note-taking, markup, memory cuing, recall.

ACM Classification Keywords
H5.m. Information interfaces and presentation (e.g., HCI): Miscellaneous.

General Terms
Experimentation; Human Factors.

INTRODUCTION
Meetings are a critical organizational practice and a key way that organizations generate knowledge and make decisions. Despite their prevalence, prior research has identified many meeting inefficiencies [23]. The result is not only frustration for participants, but reduced productivity for the organization.

Considering these well-documented problems, meetings have proved remarkably resistant to technological intervention. Over two decades of work have seen experiments with large displays to share notes about emerging discussions [1, 4, 25, 28], recording tools to capture key points [41, 46, 47], ubiquitous methods to support idea capture [9, 35], as well as more recent forays into automatic multimedia analysis [17, 33]. In general, however, these technologies are not widely deployed.

Here we examine one simple, but important, aspect of meeting behavior: note-taking. Much prior theoretical and empirical work indicates that meetings induce *cognitive overload*. They require participants to make constant trade-offs between two competing tasks: contributing to current discussion, and preparation for later recall [27, 30]. A participant's main focus should be to actively contribute to the meeting itself. On the other hand, they also need to record important information to aid future recall. Prior work shows they are dissatisfied with their attempts to do both [20, 26, 27, 28, 42].

We designed two novel markup tools to address overload. We wanted to promote post-meeting recall without diminishing a participant's ability to contribute effectively to the meeting. To increase meeting contribution, we wanted to minimize the cognitive overhead imposed by our note-taking tools. We aimed to do this by simplifying note-taking from a demanding process of selecting and recording important information to a lightweight markup process.

Many other projects have used automatic speech recognition (ASR) to create rich transcripts of meetings that can be browsed and searched after the event [13, 14, 21, 24, 33]. This has obvious intuitive benefits: written records are created automatically, thus reducing in-meeting cognitive load and allowing participants to contribute to the meeting without having to think about taking notes. Nevertheless, these approaches have not generally been successful [43]. This may be because complete recordings omit an important characteristic of notes. Effective notes are a *personal view of a critical subset* of the meeting. People want notes to be a short summary of critical personal points, rather than a complete record of all that was said [26, 42, 46, 47].

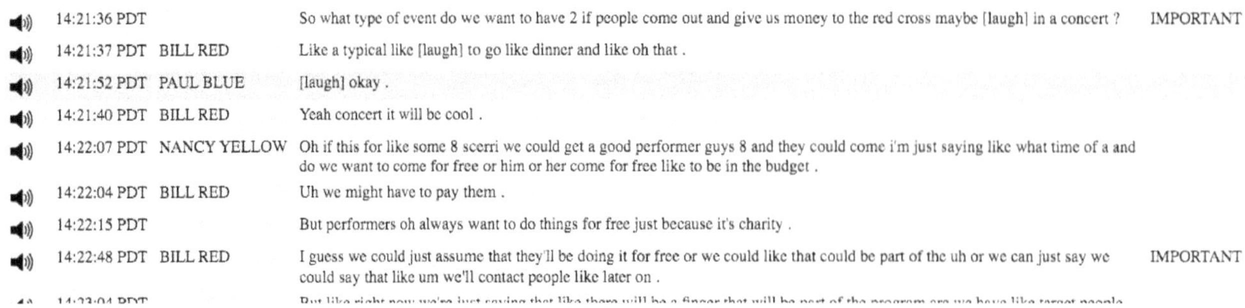

Fig 1. Highlighter post-meeting rich transcript. The transcript is generated using ASR. User selections are highlighted in yellow in the transcript, and marked as 'important'. Clicking on an utterance replays the underlying speech.

However very recent technical developments in real-time ASR [33, 39] have made it possible to develop new classes of lightweight note-taking applications. These can reduce cognitive load while allowing participants to note just those parts of the meeting that are personally relevant. Instead of 'recording everything,' these advances in ASR mean that participants can view an ASR transcript of the meeting *in real-time*, allowing them to select only parts that are of interest. Such ASR tools can therefore be lightweight. In contrast with manual note taking, users do not have to laboriously record specific content, like who said what to whom. Instead, they identify just those parts of the transcript that they think are critical for future recall, creating a personal summary of what was said.

Our first meeting markup tool, *Highlighter*, combines real-time ASR transcription with a pen-based highlighting tool. It allows users to view and mark up important parts of the transcript as it unfolds. It combines the ability to select personally important elements with the low cognitive overhead of automatic transcription.

However, it could be argued that Highlighter is still too cognitively demanding, as users have to follow the ASR transcript while participating in the meeting. Our second markup tool, *Hotspots,* simplifies note-taking even further. Like Highlighter, Hotspots allows selection of important elements of an ASR transcript. But with Hotspots, users do not view a potentially distracting transcript during the meeting. Instead they press a large button on the screen of an Internet tablet when something occurs that they want to make a note about. Pressing the button marks up points in the meeting transcript that can be accessed later.

Both Highlighter and Hotspots also provide UIs for post meeting review. In both cases, users view an ASR-generated transcript that is marked up with their personal selections and temporally indexed to the originating speech. The transcript markup differs for each tool. Highlighter depicts user-highlighted regions akin to using a highlighter pen on paper—showing user-defined highlighted regions marked up in yellow. To facilitate retrieval, clicking a highlight replays the speech indexed to the highlighted region (see Fig 1). With Hotspots, the user markup is indicated by a large red button beside the transcript text (see Fig 2). Clicking on the button replays the speech for a fixed region of one minute around the point when the index was created.

We evaluate these two new tools, comparing them with traditional pen-and-paper notes as baseline. We measure in-meeting effects on meeting *contribution* and post-meeting effects on *memory*, determining whether our tools do indeed reduce perceived cognitive load according to standard metrics. More specifically, we address the following questions concerning the benefits of ASR-based markup methods.

- *In-Meeting Contributions*: Do Highlighter and Hotspots allow people to *contribute more* to the meeting than when they use pen and paper?
- *Perceived Cognitive Overhead:* Do Highlighter and Hotspots reduce people's *perception* of cognitive overload compared with Manual Notes?
- *Post-Meeting Recall*: Are people able also to *remember* more about meeting content using the rich annotated records of Highlighter and Hotspots tools compared with pen and paper or unaided memory? And since these are novel technologies and ASR contains errors, we wanted to know how *confident* people were in the recall responses that they had generated.

There are three main contributions of this work. First, as far as we are aware, our tools are novel: ASR has not previously been deployed to support real-time markup to create personal notes. Second, our designs are motivated by prior theoretical and empirical work documenting problems of cognitive load in meetings that have not been tackled in this way before. Third, we measure in-meeting contributions and cognitive load as well as subsequent recall. Previous work has tended to focus on post-meeting recall rather than examining in-meeting effects.

RELATED WORK

Meeting systems have been the focus of much prior research. One important class of system focuses on support for personal note-taking that is used to access speech recordings. People take digital notes that are co-indexed to recorded speech to control playback. Filochat [41] combined an audio speech recorder with a PC tablet for taking handwritten notes to construct a meeting record. It

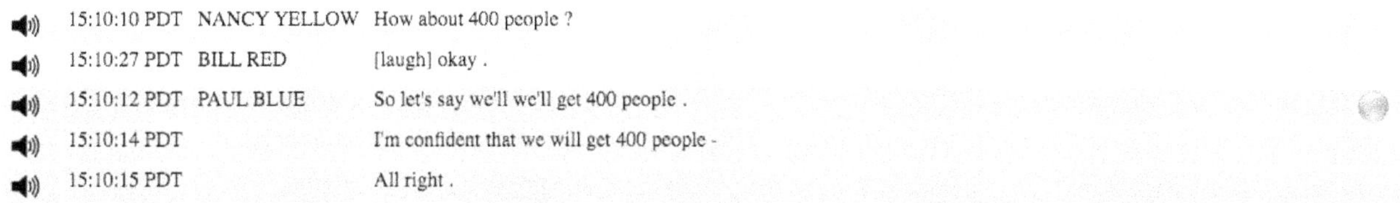

Fig 2. Hotspots post meeting UI: Transcript overlaid with hotspots showing a user selection of an important region. Clicking on the button plays back one minute of speech centered around the time when the button was pressed.

proved successful both in field and lab experiments, increasing the quality and timeliness of minutes produced after meetings. Participants were also better able to recall meeting content. Similar systems include Forget-me-not [13], Audio notebook [34] and PARC's salvaging application [26] that was successfully evaluated with patent lawyers. NotePals [11] extends this approach to allow multiple users to share notes. Dynomite [46] is a further extension: users can classify their notes into different types (e.g., 'todo', phone number, name, date, URL, etc.), allowing them to create different views onto their notes (e.g., all notes regarding 'todos' for the last month).

Other systems capture rich multimedia records of meetings. These records are subjected to visual or linguistic analysis, with browsers and search for access. The UI focus is on collaborative artifacts such as whiteboard notes, ASR transcripts or agenda items, rather than personal notes. Cutler et al.'s [9] meeting browser presents captured whiteboard images. The interface also contains a participant and whiteboard index, allowing users to jump to particular segments of the meeting. Two video components support a panoramic view and a close-up view of the current speaker. The browser also allows users to speed up playback, and to skip the contributions of selected participants. Lee et al.'s [24] system does not require a dedicated meeting room; instead, capture involves panoramic and speaker-based videos with microphones to record audio. A real-time interface allows meeting participants to examine audio and video during the meeting, as well as make notes. The system also provides an automatically produced ASR transcript of the meeting, and a set of automatically generated keyframes which can be used to navigate the meeting. Ranjan et al. [32], extend this approach using methods from television production to automatically control video views. The Ferret [40] and Jabber-2 [21] browsers also use the ASR transcript as the main UI focus along with video and speaker indices. Bett et. al. [3] also add textual meeting summaries to the transcript. TeamSpace [14] supports recording and reviewing meetings, organized around slides and an agenda.

Other work has explored browsers that allow users to access speech records of meetings in mobile contexts. Tucker and Whittaker [36] developed various ways of compressing meetings speech, including summarization, speed-up, and hybrid approaches that for example presented unimportant words much faster. Catchup [37] is a further application of this approach, presenting meeting latecomers with a spoken summary of the material they have missed.

Another approach is to augment the meeting browser with information extracted using machine learning and NLP tools. Ehlen et al. [12, 31] automatically extracted key semantic content such as action items and discussion topics from ASR transcripts of meeting discussions. User post-meeting actions on this content (e.g., correcting an action item text or clicking to add it to a to-do list) then served as implicit feedback to help retrain semantic extraction models.

Finally there is extensive work looking at note-taking in education. While note-taking is well documented to be a difficult process, several studies [20, 22, 30] show that it helps to focus attention, improving memory even when notes are not used at recall. Other studies show that the value of handwritten notes decays rapidly, aiding recall no better than unaided memory after one month [19].

NOTE-TAKING TOOLS

While this study uses *post-meeting browsers* to test recall, a key focus was on the *in-meeting* tools people used to initially record or index ideas, and whether these reduce cognitive load. We now describe the underlying tools and technologies in more depth.

CALO Meeting Assistant

The note-taking technologies used in this study were developed as part of the DARPA "Cognitive Assistant that Learns and Organizes—Meeting Assistant" (CALO-MA) program. The purpose of CALO-MA is to develop a personal assistant for meeting capture, transcription and annotation, based on real-time ASR of ordinary conversational speech that occurs during meetings [39]. Meeting participants each wear a headset connected to a Java VoIP client that transmits Speex-encoded audio to a central recognition server. Real-time speech recognition is achieved by acoustic and language models developed jointly by SRI and ICSI using SRI's Decipher recognizer, with a model trained specifically for recognition of open-domain, human-human meeting dialogue. This system produces a word error rate of 28.6%, reduced to 27.1% after unsupervised within-meeting-sequence adaptation for the CALO-MA project [39]. ASR results can be accessed via an XML-RPC protocol that provides transcriptions at a rate close to real-time, so results are returned across the network from 1-5 seconds after speech occurs, depending on the length of the utterance to be processed. Participants use these real-time ASR results in different ways, depending on the note-taking tool being used.

Highlighter

The in-meeting Highlighter tool (Fig. 1) runs as a browser-based application on an HP tablet PC running Windows Vista. Highlighter allows participants to manually annotate regions of importance in an automatically-generated ASR transcript. Text is dynamically displayed, time stamped, and color-coded for each participant. Participants use the tablet PC's pen to highlight noteworthy regions of the transcript during the meeting (Fig 3a), in exactly the way that someone might use a highlighter pen to identify critical parts of a paper text. For post meeting review, a web-based version of the system presents the ASR transcripts along with user markup highlights (see Fig 1). Selecting a markup highlight plays back the speech associated with the highlighted region.

Hotspots

The in-meeting *Hotspots* tool runs on a Nokia N810 Internet tablet. Unlike Highlighter, Hotspots does not show the real-time transcript during markup. Instead, the tablet displays a software button that can be pressed at any time during the meeting to create a temporal bookmark to indicate when something important was said. When the button is pressed, the application creates an index associated with a time-stamp. As with Highlighter, this is co-indexed to the ASR-generated transcript. For the post-meeting review tool, the hotspot markup appears alongside the ASR-generated utterance that was spoken when the button was pressed. Selecting the hotspot causes speech playback of a one-minute region around the point specified (see Fig 2).

Manual Notes

Our experimental control for Highlighter and Hotspots was "Manual Notes," a basic pen-and-paper-based note-taking method that uses a digital pen. We used a Nokia SU-27W Digital Pen with a 5"x7" Anoto dot paper notepad. Aside from being slightly thicker than an ordinary pen, these digital pens use real ink on real paper, and look and feel the same as an ordinary pad and paper (Fig 3b). Thus the user experience is effectively identical to traditional manual notes. However, the digital pen was tooled to stream pen stroke information over Bluetooth as it occurs, recording time-stamped handwriting stroke information for every note taken, to index notes against audio. Again, a web-based version of the system was used for post meeting review. In addition to reviewing regular manual notes, participants could exploit the time indexing feature by clicking on a note to hear exactly what was said when that note was taken. Co-indexing of notes and speech has been widely used elsewhere [1, 10, 13, 19, 26, 34, 46].

While we obviously expected participants to be familiar with Manual Notes, it reproduces the cognitive overhead of traditional notes. Unlike the ASR-based tools, users have to create and organize content relating to the important aspects of what is being said, potentially interfering with their ability to contribute to the meeting.

EXPERIMENTAL SET-UP

This study was divided into two different phases, a *meeting* phase and a post-meeting *recall* phase. During the meeting phase, participants held a series of three consecutive face-to-face meetings lasting roughly three hours in total. The recall phase involved each participant answering questionnaires on a website two months later. We discuss each phase in more detail below.

Method

Participants

A total of 26 participants aged 19-60 took part. There were 7 females and 19 males. All participants took part in the meeting phase, and 19 completed the recall phase. Many previous studies of meeting technologies have used students who may not be representative of target users, as they have limited work and meetings experience. To avoid this, participants were recruited via Craigslist, flyers, and word-of-mouth to find people with more extensive and varied work experience. Recruits were all native English speakers from varied work backgrounds, including nurses, teachers, charity workers, IT professionals, a taxi driver, and a managing director. All were employed and all had experience of everyday office work and meetings. They were randomly assigned to the different participant teams and received $30 for participation in the *meeting* phase and $10 for participation in the *recall* phase.

In total, there were 9 meetings with 3 participants in each meeting. One of these meetings had one no-show participant, forcing us to co-opt a local researcher. The data collected from the researcher were excluded from the results.

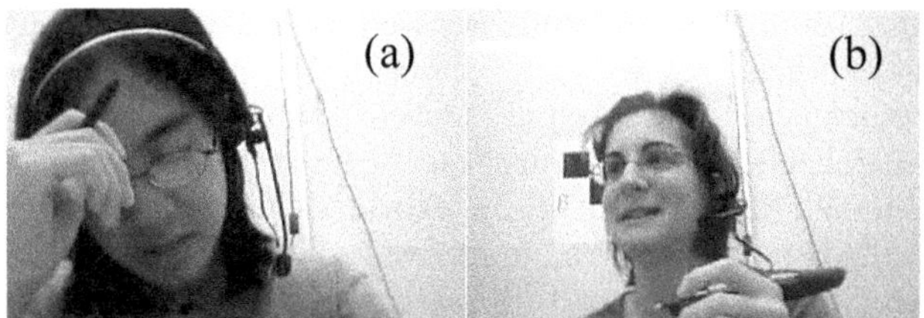

Fig 3. Study setup using: (a) the Highlighter tool to create marked up ASR transcripts; and (b) Nokia Digital Pen to create manual notes.

Meeting Phase

During the meeting phase, groups of 3 people came to our laboratory. For each group, we first described the experiment, and then ran brief hands-on tutorials to explain the note-taking technologies (Highlighter, Hotspots and Manual Notes) that participants would use during the meeting, allowing participants time to get familiar with them. The Highlighter tool in particular, with its real-time transcript, tended to provoke curiosity and a desire to play with the tool, so we allowed participants to thoroughly explore the system before the formal experiment started. After the tutorial, participants were asked if they felt confident with using the technologies, and all reported they did.

During each meeting, three participants sat around a medium-sized round table in a meeting room instrumented for meeting capture using the CALO-MA system. Each participant wore a boom-mic headset connected to an instance of the CALO VoIP client. Audio was streamed to a central server for subsequent speech analysis. The note-taking tools were placed in front of participants on the table, and could be moved about freely.

Participants were each given nametags with pseudonym names such as "Mr. Green," "Ms. Red," etc., and were asked to refer to each other by these names throughout the experiment in order to preserve anonymity. These names were associated with each media channel in the CALO-MA system, so the transcript would attribute utterances to the correct pseudonym.

Participants were told that they were a committee charged with the goal of planning a charity event. Participants were asked to make decisions about the charity cause, the location of the event, the date, the food and refreshments, the entertainment, the itinerary, and the budget. We deliberately left the details of these items open-ended to foster active participation, discussion, and decision-making. We did not assign participants particular roles, as we believed that was likely to be one of the first decisions they might come to on their own. Before the meeting phase, participants were told they would later be given a short memory test about their discussions.

In real-life, a single meeting seldom satisfies an entire work objective, and repeated meetings with interstitial independent work are the rule. To emulate this, we divided each experimental session into 3 submeetings, lasting 20-30 minutes each, separated by intervals when participants worked independently on project objectives. We chose a single session broken into separate submeetings rather than conducting submeetings on different days to avoid repeated scheduling with potential participant attrition.

We recorded the entire conversation in each submeeting. Between submeetings, participants had a 10-15 minute period to complete independent research to address action points decided in the previous submeeting. Each participant was given a workstation outside the meeting room, located far enough away from one another to discourage chatting or discussion of details before they began the next submeeting. Their independent research entailed searching for possible project resources using the Internet with all participants starting on a search page.

The participants could also send e-mail to the "Committee's assistant"—an experimenter observing the proceedings from another room—who would occasionally reply with constraints such as, "The committee would like you to keep the budget under $20,000" to ensure the decision-making process remained active. As we wanted participants to be undistracted, they could not access their mobile phones during the entire meeting phase.

We used a within-subjects design to minimize effects of individual differences, so each participant used each note-taking tool (Highlighter, Hotspots, Manual Notes) for one submeeting. Thus a participant using Highlighter in submeeting 1 might be given the Hotspot tool in submeeting 2, and Manual Notes in submeeting 3. The tools were also varied across participants so that in any given submeeting one participant would be using Hotspots, one using Highlighter and one using Manual Notes. They were also counterbalanced for order across participants. All participants were encouraged to take note of any information relevant to their project role. While we are aware that in some meeting contexts a dedicated scribe takes notes for an entire team, observational studies of note-taking behavior show that it is more common for all participants to take personal notes [42].

After each submeeting, participants were asked to complete the standard NASA TLX (Task Load Analysis) questionnaire [16] for the tool they used in the previous submeeting. This multi-dimensional rating process uses six 7-point subscales to measure mental demand, physical demand, temporal demand, performance, effort, and frustration, combined by weighted average to provide an overall workload score to assess workload in human-machine environments. At the end of the meeting phase, we also administered a final survey where we asked open-ended questions about the tools, specifically addressing their main advantages and disadvantages as well as what could be done to improve them.

Recall Phase

A note-taking tool is only effective if it helps people to recall or reconstruct important information at a future time. So an important aspect of this study was to test participants' post-meeting recall of details, using the notes provided by each tool. We compared this to Unaided Memory; i.e., without any notes.

To give ample time for forgetting to occur, based on prior work [19] we situated the recall phase 2 months after the meeting phase. Participant recall was tested by asking each person a total of 8 questions. For six of these questions people had access to a note-taking tool and the remaining two were answered from memory. Each participant was asked two factual questions about each submeeting they participated in. To help recall, they were provided with the tool they had used in the initial submeeting. Each person had used a different note-taking tool in each of the 3 submeetings, which meant that we were able to compare their recall using the post-meeting recall version of each tool. So for example, if a participant had taken notes with Highlighter in submeeting 1, when we tested their recall of submeeting 1, they were given the post-meeting recall version of Highlighter. We also included a final two Unaided Memory questions where we asked participants to remember meeting details without a tool. The order of the 6 tool-based questions and 2 Unaided Memory questions was counterbalanced across users. All tools were fully interactive, allowing participants to use notes to access underlying speech.

To generate the recall questions, three people listened to each of the submeetings and created factual questions based on the important decisions made during each submeeting. Example questions were: "What cause did you choose for your fundraiser?"; "What kind of entertainment did you decide on for this fundraiser?"; and, "How much money did you estimate you might make?" For each question we also generated model answers that were used to assess recall quality. We recorded binary accuracy (correct/incorrect decisions) for each question based on whether each participant's answer matched the model answers. On the rare occasions when the main judge felt uncertain about how to score a participant response it was discussed with another judge to reach consensus.

Prior work [7, 44] has shown that errorful ASR can undermine people's confidence in transcript-based tools. We therefore examined whether people were less confident in their ability to recall using our ASR tools compared with traditional Manual Notes or their own memory. After people had answered each recall question we asked them how confident they were about their answer. Ratings were generated on a 5-point scale.

RESULTS

We first report in-meeting results on spoken contributions and perceived cognitive load. Then we look at post-meeting cognitive effects on memory, and participants' confidence about their recall.

For statistical analysis, we used repeated measures ANOVAS. Before the analyses, we checked the sphericity of our data using Mauchly's test. Where the test is significant we apply Greenhouse-Geisser correction with post-hoc Bonferroni at .05.

In-Meeting Spoken Contributions

Each participant's primary goal was to contribute to the meeting. Our first question was whether the different note-taking tools affected meeting contributions. We assessed contributions by counting the number of words each person spoke in each of the submeetings. Number of words has been widely used to measure conversational contributions in the CMC literature [2, 5, 6]. It has been shown to correlate well with other contribution metrics such as turn frequency [5, 6].

Our expectation was that using Hotspots and Highlighter would reduce cognitive load, allowing participants to contribute more to the meeting. In contrast, we expected that Manual Notes would reduce contributions.

The results are shown in Fig 4. We conducted a one-way ANOVA using contribution as the dependent variable and Note-taking Tool as an independent variable. Our results show significant differences for contribution ($F_{(2,50)} = 115.2$, $p<0.0001$). From post-hoc Bonferroni tests we found that participants using Hotspots contributed more to meetings than those using Manual Notes ($p<0.04$). However, contrary to our expectations, there was no difference in contributions between people using Highlighter and those using Manual Notes ($p>0.5$). This contribution advantage of Hotspots over Manual Notes is consistent with our expectation that the single-button-press action of Hotspots reduces cognitive overhead compared with the effort required for taking Manual Notes. In contrast, Highlighter fared no better than Manual Notes, but was not worse.

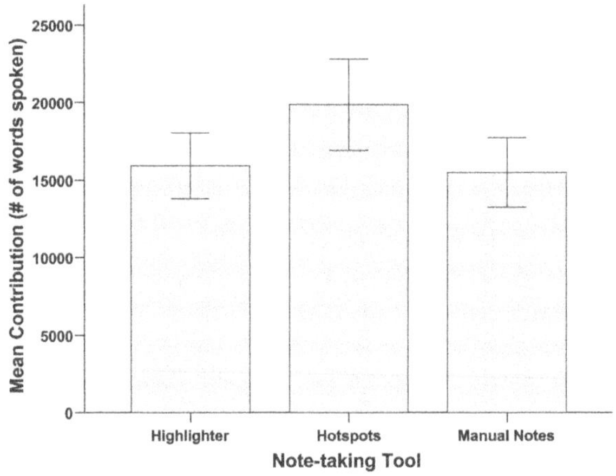

Fig 4. Mean meeting contribution for participants using each Note-taking tool. Hotspots increases contributions compared with Highlighter and Manual Notes.

In-Meeting Perceived Cognitive Effort

Hotspots increased users' contributions compared with Manual Notes and Highlighter. But is this because Hotspots reduces cognitive overhead associated with note-taking, allowing participants to participate more fully in the meeting? To answer this, we looked at the extent to which perceived cognitive overhead, as measured by the NASA TLX—matched participants' actual contribution levels. We expected that perceived effort would be reduced with our two ASR tools.

The results are shown in Fig 5. We again conducted a one-way ANOVA using the weighted average TLX score as dependent variable and Note-taking Tool as independent variable. There were significant differences among the TLX scores across all three tools used ($F_{(2,50)} = 22.5$, $p<0.0001$). As we expected, post-hoc Bonferroni tests indicated that Hotspots was perceived as less demanding than Manual Notes. However, Highlighter was perceived as *more* cognitively demanding than Hotspots ($p<0.0001$) and Manual Notes ($p<0.01$).

To better understand the cognitive load results, we analyzed participants' comments about the different tools. Consistent with prior research on note-taking [27, 30, 42], our participants thought that taking regular manual notes was both effortful and distracting: *"It takes more time and effort to make notes. It acts as a distracting force in a meeting."*

Consistent with both the contributions and perceived effort data, people thought Hotspots demanded little effort: *"Least interruptive in meeting, least work involved."*

Some participants were positive about Highlighter, feeling it reduced note-taking effort by automatically providing content for mark up: *"[I liked it] because it translated every single word and conversation so you can mark the most helpful thing that was said."*

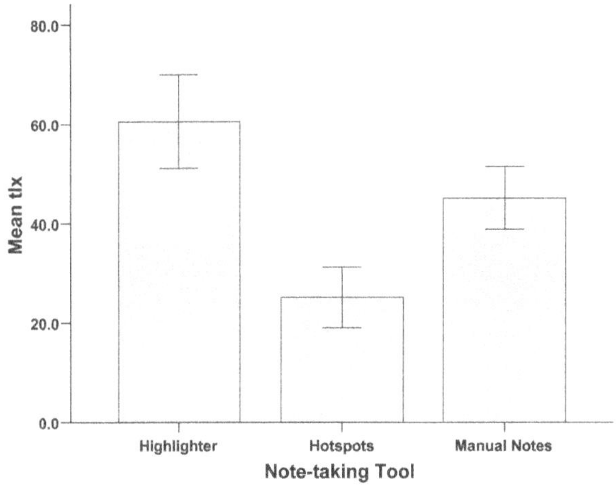

Fig 5. Perceived Cognitive Effort: Task Load Index (TLX) scores for each Note-taking tool. A higher score indicates greater cognitive effort. Perceived effort is greatest for Highlighter and least for Hotspots.

However, several other participants pointed out that Highlighter demanded additional effort: transcription lags in Highlighter increased the difficulty of identifying the relevant parts of the conversation for mark up. This problem was also exacerbated by ASR inaccuracies: *"The Highlighter took way too long to update and it was difficult finding the line of conversation that I wanted to highlight."*

These comments indicate that the advantage of Highlighter automatically generating content was partially offset by the effort needed to skim an errorful and laggy transcript to identify important regions for markup.

Overall, consistent with the contribution results, the perceived effort scores confirm that Hotspots is a cognitively lightweight annotation technique. Hotspots requires a single action to define a markup annotation, and eliminates much of the effort that goes into Manual Notes. In contrast, Highlighter, in its current form, seemed more complex. It requires users to skim the errorful transcript to identify regions of interest. Attempting to read an ASR transcript that is 1-5 seconds behind the ongoing conversation significantly increases perceived effort.

Post-Meeting Recall

So far we have seen the benefits of Hotspots in increasing meeting contributions, with Highlighter being equivalent to Manual Notes. But Highlighter and Hotspots were also intended to enhance recall compared with Manual Notes. Our next question was how well participants could *remember* details of the meeting after the event.

We examined recall of the set of factual questions generated for each meeting. Participants used the post-meeting web-based recall tools (Highlighter, Hotspots or Manual Notes) at retrieval. Each participant had initially used a different tool for capturing each submeeting, for example, using Manual Notes for one submeeting, Highlighter for the next, and Hotspots for the third. We tested recall for each submeeting, providing participants with the post-meeting version of the tool they used along with the notes they had generated during that submeeting. They therefore experienced 3 different recall tests: One for each submeeting, using the original tool they had been assigned during the meeting phase. We also test recall using Unaided Memory, with no tools provided. Our expectation was that recall would be better overall when people used the ASR markup tools (Highlighter or Hotspots) than with Manual Notes or Unaided Memory.

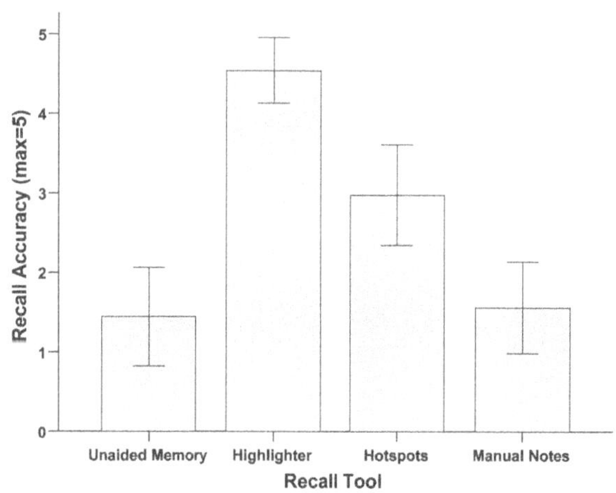

Fig 6. Mean Recall Accuracy using each Recall Tool and Unaided Memory. Recall is greater with Highlighter and Hotspots than with Unaided Memory and Manual Notes.

We conducted a one-way ANOVA using Recall Accuracy as the dependent variable and Recall Tool (Hotspots, Highlighter, Manual Notes, Unaided Memory) as the independent variable. There were significant differences in Recall Accuracy depending on Recall Tool ($F_{(3, 75)} = 31.9$, $p<0.0001$), as shown in Fig 6. Post-hoc Bonferroni tests showed that Highlighter helped to generate more accurate answers than Hotspots, Manual Notes and Unaided Memory ($p<0.001$). Hotspots was also significantly more accurate than both Manual Notes ($p<0.002$) and Unaided Memory ($p<0.001$). These results confirm our expectation that ASR-based tools would improve recall over manual notes and unaided memory.

Post-Meeting Confidence in Accuracy of Recall

Although people recalled significantly better using ASR-based tools compared with Manual Notes and Unaided Memory, our next question was, how confident were they about Recall Accuracy using these tools, given that ASR transcripts contained errors?

To assess people's confidence in recall accuracy, we conducted a one-way ANOVA with Confidence as the dependent variable and Recall Tool (Hotspots, Highlighter, Manual Notes) as independent variable. There was a significant difference in confidence based on recall tool ($F_{(2,50)} = 8.3$, $p<0.0001$), as shown in Fig 7. Bonferroni tests showed that people were less confident about recall accuracy with Hotspots than Manual Notes ($p<0.02$). However, there were no significant differences between Manual Notes and Highlighter ($p>0.9$). The greater confidence with Highlighter compared with Hotspots may occur because Highlighter forced people to process transcripts more carefully when generating in-meeting notes, allowing people to establish the transcript was good enough to aid recall. In contrast, Hotspots required no in-meeting transcript processing, possibly leading participants to be less confident that the button-press actions would serve as effective annotations into the meeting.

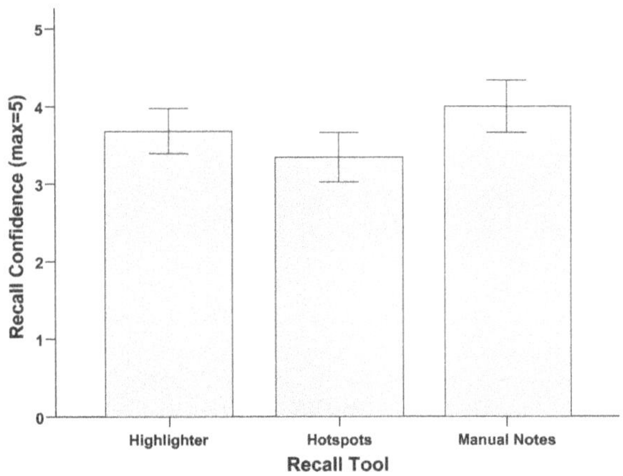

Fig 7. Mean Confidence score for each Recall Tool. People are less confident using Hotspots than Manual Notes.

Consistent with this lack of confidence, participants pointed out problems using the ASR transcript with Hotspots, noting that the transcript could be hard to interpret when ASR was poor: *"It's very difficult to read the text shown here, I can barely make anything out."* Despite this lack of confidence, recall performance was still better with Hotspots than with Manual Notes and Unaided Memory.

DISCUSSION AND CONCLUSIONS

Overall, these are highly positive results showing the clear utility of novel ASR-based markup tools in addressing the perennially tricky problem of note-taking in meetings. Prior theoretical and empirical work has repeatedly demonstrated that note-taking imposes a high cognitive load, and detracts from a participant's ability to contribute to meetings [27, 30]. However recent developments in real-time ASR allowed us to address such 'divided attention' by developing new lightweight note-taking tools. Both ASR tools support effective markup without compromising meeting contributions. For the primary task of contributing to the meeting, Hotspots increased contributions, while at the same time improving post-meeting recall compared with Manual Notes. Highlighter supported equivalent contributions as Manual Notes, and again improved post-meeting recall compared with Manual Notes.

Hotspots seemed to promote enhanced contribution by reducing in-meeting cognitive overload compared with Manual Notes (as assessed by TLX). Enhanced meeting contribution may result from Hotspots' very simple design: users simply hit a button when they hear something important. Its sheer simplicity may be crucial, because of the high cognitive demands of contributing to a meeting. In contrast, Highlighter increased perceived overload, possibly because people were focused on trying to identify regions of interest in the errorful ASR transcript, although this did not affect their contributions compared with Manual Notes.

Both Highlighter and Hotspots improved post-meeting recall compared with Manual Notes, demonstrating the benefits of the ASR transcript as a retrieval aid. However these benefits need to be tempered by the fact that transcript based methods seemed less efficient than Manual Notes or Unaided Memory, as it seemed to take participants longer to locate relevant material in the ASR transcript. In addition, despite having better actual recall with Hotspots, users were less confident about their answers than when using Manual Notes. In contrast, Highlighter elevated recall, but did not depress confidence compared with Manual Notes. Highlighter may preserve confidence because people are focused on the ASR transcript during in-meeting note-taking, allowing them to see that it provides a reasonable index into the speech recording. In contrast, with Hotspots they don't view the transcript during the meeting, possibly leading them to be unsure about its utility for recall.

These results are encouraging, especially for Hotspots, showing it to be a low-overhead tool that increased both in-meeting contributions as well as post-meeting recall. But for Highlighter, we should also ask whether its cognitive load issues are due to a nascent technology that is not quite ready for adoption. However with improved ASR models of human-human dialogue, faster processing and network speeds, and more user exposure to both speech recognition and tablet-based interaction, some of the load disadvantage may be ameliorated, or vanish altogether.

From a methodological perspective, this is the first study to directly measure in-meeting effects on contribution and cognitive load, as prior note-taking research has tended to focus only on post-meeting recall. Still, there are limitations to this work. We need to explore technological acceptability and generality with larger numbers of diverse users outside a lab context. In addition, this study lacks one potential comparison condition: simply providing participants with an ASR transcript post-meeting, with no in-meeting markup. This would have the putative benefit of low in-meeting overhead (as no annotation is required), but providing a rich recall record. While this could be an important control to run, we do not believe it would be more effective than Hotspots and Highlighter in promoting recall, as prior work has shown the importance of *active user annotation* for inducing recall. Users who actively take notes subsequently recall material better than those who have access to verbatim meeting recordings but who did not generate notes [20, 22].

Our work also has design implications. Several user comments concerned the benefits of capturing meeting content in their own words. This suggests a modified system that is a hybrid between traditional manual notes and our new markup techniques. A simple addition to our system would be to allow users to supplement the ASR transcript in real-time with their own short comments. These personal comments could be time-aligned as in prior systems [19, 26, 41, 46]. However we do not advocate full transcript editing as in [7] because this would dramatically increase cognitive overhead, and also because our data shows that imperfect ASR indexed transcripts are still an effective retrieval aid. A final modification might be to use machine learning techniques such as entity extraction to add actions or decisions to the evolving transcript [12, 31].

Finally, there may be extensions of this approach to other applications. There has been recent interest in collecting audio lifelogs, such as sound recordings of aspects of one's everyday life [11, 29]. There are clearly problems in retrieving such records, but techniques such as Hotspots may provide simple ways to access this data, by using a simple button to mark a significant event when it occurs. It might also be possible to extend our 'divided attention' theoretical approach to lifelogging, as lifeloggers persistently have to decide whether to remain 'in the moment' or distract themselves by annotating their lifelogs to promote future retrieval [18].

In conclusion, we demonstrated the utility of two novel ASR-based markup tools. These address well-documented problems in supporting both in-meeting contributions and subsequent recall. We demonstrated that very simple methods of annotation for ASR transcripts—particularly Hotspots—can promote increased recall, while also increasing people's ability to contribute to meetings. In future work we plan to explore other situations where minimal annotation might promote enhanced memory without compromising people's current practices.

ACKNOWLEDGMENTS

Thanks to Stanley Peters and members of the CSLI Computational Semantics Lab who assisted with experimental design and setup, including Jonathan Kass, Sharareh Noorbaloochi, Justin Stimatze and John Niekrasz. This material is based upon work supported by DARPA CALO (FA8750-07-D-0185, Delivery Order 0004) funding. Any opinions, findings, and conclusions or recommendations expressed in this material are those of the authors and do not necessarily reflect the views of DARPA. The work was also partially supported by EPSRC grant EP/G010714/1, EU FP-6 30008, and IST FP6- 033812.

REFERENCES

1. Abowd, G.D., "Classroom 2000: An experiment with the instrumentation of a living educational environment." IMB Systems Journal, 1999, 38 (4), 508-530.
2. Anderson, A., et al. Video data and video links in mediated communication: what do users value?. Int. J. Hum Comput. Stud. 2000, 52, 1, 165-187.
3. Bett, M., et al. "Multimodal meeting tracker." In Proc. of RIAO, 2000, 324-326.
4. Brotherton, J.A., et al. "Automated Capture, Integration, and Visualization of Multiple Media Streams" In Proc. of the IEEE IMCS 1998, 54.
5. Carletta, J., et al. The effects of multimedia communication technology on non-collocated teams: a case study. Ergonomics, 2000, 43(8), 1237-1251.
6. Clark, H. H. Using language. Cambridge: Cambridge University Press, 1996.
7. Burke, M., et al. "SCANMail: Error Correction in Voicemail Transcripts" In Proc. of CHI 2006, 339-348.
8. CHIL – http://www.limsi.fr/tlp/chil.html - retrieved Sept 2011.
9. Cutler, R. et al., "Distributed Meetings: a Meeting Capture and Broadcasting System." In Proc. of ACM Multimedia 2002, 503-512.
10. Davis, R.C. et al., "NotePals: Lightweight Note sharing by the Group, for the Group." In proc. CHI 1999, 338-345.
11. Dib, L., Petrelli, D., and Whittaker, S. "Sonic Souvenirs: Exploring the Paradoxes of Recorded Sound for Family Remembering." In Proc. of CSCW 2010, 391-400.
12. Ehlen, P., et al."Meeting Adjourned: Off-line Learning Interfaces for Automatic Meeting Understanding." In Proc. of IUI 2008, 276-284.

13. Lamming, M., and Flynn, M. "Forget-me-not Intimate Computing in Support of Human Memory." In Proc. of FRIEND 21, 1994, 125-128.
14. Geyer, W., et al. "A Team Collaboration Space Supporting Capture and Access of Virtual Meetings." In Proc. of GROUP 2001, 188-196.
15. Geyer, W., et al. "Making Multimedia Meeting Records More Meaningful", In Proc. ICME 2003, 2, 669-672.
16. Hart, S.G. and Staveland, L.E. "Development of NASA-TLX (Task Load Index): Results of empirical and theoretical research." In Human Mental Workload, 1988, 139-183.
17. Janin, A., et al., "The ICSI Meeting Project: Resources and Research." In Proc. ICASSP 2004, 537-541.
18. Kalnikaitė, V. and Whittaker, S. "Beyond being there? Evaluating Augmented Digital Records" In IJHCS 2010, 68 (10), 627-640.
19. Kalnikaitė, V. and Whittaker, S. "Software or Wetware? Discovering when and why people use digital prosthetic memory." In Proc. CHI 2007, 71-80.
20. Kalnikaitė, V. and Whittaker, S. "Cuing Digital Memory: How and Why Do Digital Notes Help Us Remember?" In Proc. British-HCI 2008, 153-161.
21. Kazman, R., et al. "Four Paradigms for Indexing Video Conferences." In Proc. of IEEE MultiMedia 1996, 63-73.
22. Kidd, A. The marks are on the knowledge worker. In Proc. CHI 1994, 212-220.
23. Kraut, R. "Applying social psychological theory to the problems of group work." In J. Carroll (Ed.) HCI Models, Theories and Frameworks, 2003, 325-356.
24. Lee, D., et al. "Portable Meeting Recorder." In Proc. of ACM Multimedia 2002, 493-502.
25. Mantei, M. "Capturing the capture concept: a case study in the design of computer-supported meeting environments." In Proc. of CSCW 1988, 257-270.
26. Moran, T.P. et al "I'll Get That Off the Audio: A Case Study of Salvaging Multimedia Meeting Records" In Proc. CHI 1997, 202-209.
27. Olive, T. "Working Memory in Writing: Empirical Evidence from the Dual-Task Techniques." In European Psychologist, 9 (1), 2004, 32-42.
28. Olson, J. S., et al. "How a group-editor changes the character of a design meeting as well as its outcome." In Proc. of CSCW 1992, 91-98.
29. Petrelli, D., Villar, N., Kalnikaitė, V., Dib, L. and Whittaker, S. "FM Radio: Family Interplay with Sonic Mementos." In Proc. of CHI 2010, 2371-2380.
30. Piolat, A., et al. "Cognitive effort in note taking. Applied Cognitive Psychology", 2004, 1-22.
31. Purver, M., Niekrasz, J. and Ehlen, P. "Automatic Annotation of Dialogue Structure from Simple User Interaction." In Proc. of MLMI, 2007, 48-59.
32. Ranjan, A., et al. "Improving Meeting Capture by Applying Television Production Principles with Audio and Motion Detection." In Proc. of CHI 2008, 227-236.
33. Renals, S., et al. "Recognition and interpretation of meetings: The AMI and AMIDA projects." In Proc. IEEE ASRU 2007, 238-247.
34. Stifelman, L., et al. "The Audio Notebook: Paper and Pen Interaction with Structured Speech." In Proc. of CHI 2001, 182-189.
35. Streitz , N.A., et al. "Roomware for Cooperative Buildings: Integrated Design of Architectural Spaces and Information Spaces." In Proc. of CoBuild 1998, 4-21.
36. Tucker, S. and Whittaker, S., "Time is of an Essence: an Evaluation of Temporal Compression Algorithms." In Proc. CHI 2006, 329-338.
37. Tucker, S., Bergman, O., Ramamoorthy, A., and Whittaker, S. "Catchup: a Useful Application of Time-travel in meetings." In Proc. CSCW 2010, 99-102.
38. Tur, G., & Stolcke, A. "Unsupervised Language Model Adaptation for Meeting Recognition." In Proc. IEEE ICASSP 2007, . 173-176.
39. Voss, L., Ehlen, P., et al. "The CALO Meeting Assistant." In Proc. NAACL-HLT 2007, 17-18.
40. Wellner P, et al. "Browsing recorded meetings with Ferret." In: Proc. of MLMI 2004, 12-21.
41. Whittaker, S., Hyland P., and Wiley, M. "Filochat: Handwritten notes provide access to recorded conversations." In Proc. CHI 1994, 271-277.
42. Whittaker, S., Laban, R., and Tucker, S. (2005). Analysing Meeting records: An Ethnographic Study and Technical Implications. In Lecture Notes in Computer Science 3869, Machine Learning for Multimodal Interaction, Springer, New York.
43. Whittaker, S., et al. "Design and Evaluation of Systems to Support Interaction Capture and Retrieval." In PUC 2008, 197-221.
44. Whittaker, S., et al. "SCANMail: A Voicemail Interface That Makes Speech Browsable, Readable and Searchable." In Proc. of CHI 2002, 275-282.
45. Whittaker, S. and Amento, B. "Semantic Speech Editing." In Proc. of CHI 2004, 527-534.
46. Wilcox, L.D., et al. "Dynomite: A Dynamically Organized Ink and Audio Notebook." In Proc. of CHI 1997, 186-193.
47. Yu, S., and Selker, T. "Who Said What When? Capturing the Important Moments of a Meeting". In Proc. of CHI 2010, pp 3283-3288.

SketchComm: A Tool to Support Rich and Flexible Asynchronous Communication of Early Design Ideas

Guang Li[1,2], Xiang Cao[1], Sergio Paolantonio[1], Feng Tian[2]

[1]Microsoft Research Asia
Beijing, China
{xiangc, sergiopa}@microsoft.com

[2]Institute of Software, Chinese Academy of Sciences
Beijing, China
{liguang, tf}@iel.iscas.ac.cn

ABSTRACT
When designers explain their early design ideas to others, they usually use face-to-face communication along with sketches. In practice, however, sometimes face-to-face meetings are not possible, and designers have to rely on asynchronous communication. Important contextual information that is available in face-to-face meetings often becomes missing in such asynchronous communications, which can lead to confusion and misunderstanding. To address this challenge, we present SketchComm: an enhanced tool to support rich and flexible asynchronous communication of early design ideas. The key of the system is to allow designers to capture and communicate important contextual information to the audience in addition to sketches. A user study with designers and audience demonstrated effectiveness of asynchronous early design communication using SketchComm.

Author Keywords
Design, asynchronous communication, tool.

ACM Classification Keywords
H5.m. Information interfaces and presentation (e.g., HCI): Miscellaneous.

General Terms
Design; Human Factors.

INTRODUCTION
Communicating designs to others and getting feedback is a key practice in the design profession. Especially in the beginning of a design process, when designers communicate their early design ideas to others, they usually use face-to-face communication along with hand-drawn sketches. Relatively little effort was needed to draw these sketches, saving considerable work that would otherwise be required if using sophisticated digital tools tailored for later-stage expression of concrete and/or finalized designs, such as Photoshop or 3D Studio. Indeed, the inherent "roughness" of such sketches matches the preliminary, non-specific, and incomplete nature of early design ideas, and serves as a reminder for the audience to focus their attention and feedback on the concept rather than details of the design. All this allowed designers to obtain feedback as early as possible in their design process, which proves to be essential to the design success [4].

However, the casualness and openness of these early sketches usually also means that they have to rely on the designer's personal presence to be understood. The rich contextual information available in face-to-face communication, both provided by the designer themselves and from the physical surroundings, nicely complements the sketches to deliver a holistic message. In practice, however, such face-to-face meetings (or even synchronous telecommunications such as audio/video conferences) are not always feasible due to various constraints such as conflicts of schedule, geographical distances, time differences, or the need to communicate to multiple audiences. In these situations, designers have to rely on asynchronous channels, e.g. sending their ideas through email in the form of digital sketches and/or written descriptions. However, when taken out of the context of face-to-face communication, sketch as a communication tool may become inadequate on its own, precisely because of the reasons that makes it powerful otherwise. The non-specificity and lack of details in early sketches now often leads to confusion and misunderstanding. As a result, designers often set aside asynchronous communication altogether and wait until an opportunity for face-to-face meeting (often too late for early feedback), or have to resort to later-stage design expression tools and lose all the merits of hand-drawn sketches.

To address this dilemma in asynchronous communication of early design ideas, we present SketchComm (Figure 1), a tool that preserves the light weight and flexibility of sketch, while completes the missing contextual information essential in face-to-face communication. This is achieved by allowing the designer to capture such rich information, such as multimodal remarks, real-world references, logical order etc., in ways as lightweight and flexible as drawing sketches themselves, and incorporate and transmit them together with the sketch over asynchronous channels. We conducted a three-stage user study with both designers and audience, demonstrating the effectiveness of SketchComm from both perspectives, as well as how SketchComm was creatively appropriated by users.

Figure 1. SketchComm being used by a designer.

RELATED WORK
As a classic category of Creativity Support Tools (CST), many researchers have created tools to support the work practice of designers. In particular, given the central role of sketching in design processes, it is not surprising that many systems involved digital sketches. Some of them looked at

sketching as a flexible input mechanism to create computer representations. Early examples can be dated back to SketchPad [22], a system to create engineering drawings with a light pen. More recently, the Electronic Cocktail Napkin [8] enables people to sketch design concepts and attempts to interpret drawing elements and configurations; and ILoveSketch [1] is a virtual sketchbook that directly supports the sketching of 3D curve models. Some systems go beyond static representations, e.g., SILK [14] and DENIM [15] both allow designers to create interactive user interface prototypes through digital sketching; and K-Sketch [6] supports novice animators in creating kinetic animations through simple sketching. Others have employed freehand sketching and gesturing as a lightweight way to annotate existing designs. For example, Boom Chameleon [24] allows viewing and annotating 3D designs by both touch gestures and voice. Space Pen [13] is a web-based system that allows participants in a design project to "walk-through" the work in 3D and annotate it with location-specific text comments or by drawing directly on the 3D model. We share the same basic rationale with these works in keeping sketching at the center of our tool to retain its light weight and flexibility, but focus on interpersonal communication rather than computer input. Researchers also created systems that aim at fluid design collaborations. For example, Design TeamMate [16] is a system in which individual workstations of designers are fluently integrated with an augmented tabletop and wall display, and Digital Scrapbook [23] is a web tool that automatically aggregates design students' online content for the tutor to oversee their design process. Pictionaire [10] is based on a large-sized interactive table, which supports design groups to integrate physical and digital artifacts using an overhead camera and projector for design meetings. However, so far there has not been research dedicated to asynchronous communication of early design ideas.

Some other domains that often require such enhanced asynchronous communication support include education and business collaboration. For example, MRAS [2] is a web-based system that supports annotation of multimedia lectures. Students can access the website to study, and make shared annotations to discuss. Similarly, Petkovic et al. [19] developed an asynchronous multimedia annotation platform for web-based biology education. MemTable [12] is an interactive tabletop that supports collaborative work, which can capture and asynchronously search and review past meetings during co-located meetings. These focused on communication around pre-generated or recorded information, rather than creative design ideas.

Also related are tools for active note taking, which share some similar attributes as the design sketching activity. In addition to commercial systems such as Microsoft OneNote [17], there exist several research prototypes. For example, InkSeine [11] is a tablet PC application that interleaves inking, searching, and content gathering. NiCEBook [3] is a prototype paper notebook, which supports taking, structuring and reusing notes in both the physical form and the digital representation. These focused on individual information work instead of communication.

One of the key features of our system was the capturing of real world content. Some creative systems also share the similar feature. This includes CopyCAD [7], a system that allows users to copy 2D shapes form arbitrary real world objects, and then modify them through sketching. The I/O brush [21] is a physical paintbrush with an embedded camera that can pick up color, texture, and motion from the physical environment and paint with them. TellTable [5] is a storytelling system that allows children to take photos of real world objects to create story elements, and use them to tell animated stories on an interactive table. In contrast, we focus on using content captured from the physical world to facilitate asynchronous communication, rather than as raw material for real-time creation.

Finally, some existing works focused on capturing and replaying the design activity. Design Amanuensis [9] is a tool to assist researchers to conduct think-aloud studies of design processes, by capturing the designer's spoken and drawing actions into a replayable and searchable document; Where Were We [18] supports instant video replay of recent events in design brainstorm sessions to facilitate the ongoing design activity; and XNETWORK [20] is an environment for computer network design which captures design discussions into the design artifact itself. These systems target at passively archiving the design activity itself for later reference, while we aim to support the designer to actively find relevant contextual information to capture in order to construct the design communication.

In comparison to these prior works, SketchComm targets at a unique yet common challenge, asynchronous communication of early design ideas, which has not been specifically tackled in the research field. Although SketchComm may indeed share some rationales or features with some of these systems, the contribution of our work is not necessarily in inventing individual interactions and features, but in a holistic solution and a seamless experience that are based on the understanding of and tailored for this particular activity.

CONTEXTUAL INFORMATION TO CAPTURE

Given the key of our tool is to capture contextual information to be transmitted with sketches, we first sought to identify some of these most common categories of information that are essential in face-to-face communication of design ideas, but missing in current asynchronous channels.

We obtained such information from three sources: informal interviews with four professional designers about how they currently communicate their early ideas face-to-face; observations of three early-stage design meetings in interdisciplinary teams; as well as the own professional experience of the authors (two of the authors were professionally trained as industrial designers themselves). By examining the common practices in face-to-face design communication obtained from these sources, and contrasting them with functionalities of current asynchronous communication channels, we identified the following categories of contextual information that are especially useful, which we propose to capture in our asynchronous design communication tool:

Multimodal Remarks

One of the most powerful attributes of face-to-face communication is that it is inherent multimodal. Although the communication of the design idea is usually centered around sketches, such static representation is constantly augmented by verbal explanations, iconic gestures, dynamic demonstrations, etc. These provide essential additional information for the audience to understand beyond what is conveyed in the sketches themselves. We sought to capture such freeform multimodal remarks from the designer.

Real-world References

A common way to facilitate early design communication, especially when explaining concrete artifacts, is to refer to physical objects in the surrounding. Such real-world references can be used to easily and vividly illustrate many attributes that are difficult to describe through abstract sketch or speech, such as shape, color, size, material, or even sound. In addition, designers often use physical objects as opportunistic props to demonstrate ideas. By enabling capturing such real-world references, we sought to enrich the vocabulary of the designers through our tool.

Thought Process and Logical Order

Often time understanding the thought process of reaching the design idea is as important as the resulting idea itself. Seeing the thought process allows the audience not to be overly caught in the specifics of the single design idea, but can better understand the rationale of the designer and provide feedback on a higher conceptual level. This is especially important in the early design stage, when the idea itself is often incomplete and open to redefinition. Equally important is the logical order in the idea representation for the audience to comprehend it, which is often not apparent due to the unstructured nature of early sketches, and relies on the designer to guide the audience through in face-to-face communication. In our tool we sought to provide lightweight mechanisms for designers to record the thought process and indicate the logical order to their audience.

Communication Context

Finally, the overall context of the communication session itself, such as topic, time, place, and participants, is not only useful for the audience to understand the bigger picture of the design project, but perhaps also importantly contextualize their memory of the idea and let them recall it more easily. This may be equally helpful for both the audience and the designers themselves. We sought to support capturing such communication context in a rich and flexible manner.

Obviously, this is not meant to be an exhaustive list of all contextual information available in typical face-to-face communication. What we aim for is to include functions to capture the most common categories of information, while keeping them as flexible as possible so that designers can creatively repurpose them to capture other information as they find useful to the communication.

SKETCHCOMM SYSTEM

Based on the above rationales, we created SketchComm, a software application running on a Windows 7 Tablet PC with both pen and multi-touch input, and connected to a webcam. SketchComm was designed through an iterative process, incorporating feedback from trial usage by real target users (designers and audience) at several stages of the development. In designing the system to capture the four categories of contextual information mentioned above, we maximized richness and flexibility in the expression, both of which later proved essential to the success of SketchComm.

SketchComm consists of two interaction modes: *Creation* mode (Figure 2a), in which the designer creates the content for communicating the design idea using a mixture of sketch and captured information; and *Review* mode (Figure 2b), in which the audience reviews the idea.

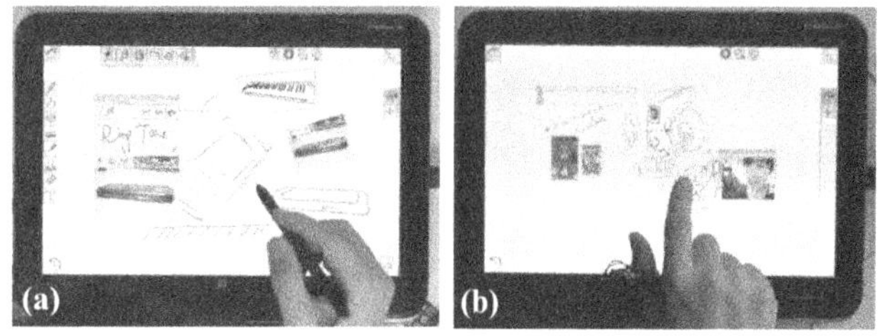

Figure 2. System Interface. (a) Creation Mode. (b)Review Mode.

Creation Mode

In the Creation mode, the designer is provided an infinite blank canvas that can be freely zoomed and moved using two-finger gestures. Interface buttons to trigger additional functions are laid out along the edges of the screen, which can be operated using either the pen or a finger. Similar to other freehand sketching applications, the designer can use the pen to sketch on the canvas with a variety of stroke colors and widths, as well as erase sketches with an eraser function. Additionally they may insert text boxes into the canvas, with which they can input text using a physical or software keyboard, or through onscreen handwriting recognition.

Capturing Media Content from the Real World

At the base of the system, SketchComm provides a generic set of functions to capture various types of media content from the real world. These can be used by the designer for various purposes described later.

Using the webcam and its built-in microphone, the designer can capture a photo, an audio clip, or a video clip of the real world (Figure 3a, b, c). The captured content then appears in the canvas, and can be freely manipulated using single- or multi-touch finger gestures (moving, rotating, scaling) to be positioned together with hand-drawn sketches. Dragging the content into the trashcan in the bottom right corner of the screen deletes it.

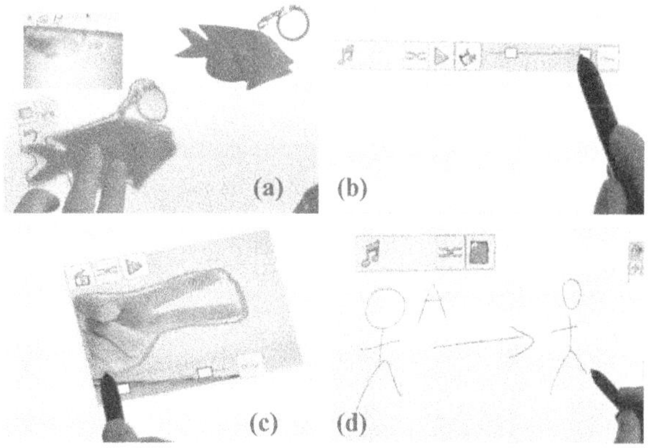

Figure 3. Captured media. (a) Photo. (bottom left: cropped photo; upper left: viewfinder; upper right: original physical object) (b) Audio clip (being trimmed). (c) Left: Video clip (being cropped). (d) Synchronizing sketch with audio.

Both photos and video clips can be cropped to arbitrary shapes using the pen so as to show only the region of interest; and both audio and video clips can be trimmed in time using a pair of slider knobs to keep only the segment of interest. The audio and video clips can then be played in place. In the case of capturing a photo or a video clip, a live on-screen viewfinder is displayed on the canvas to facilitate framing. Similar to captured content, the viewfinder can also be manipulated using finger gestures. These capturing functions allow the designer to easily make references to the real world or incorporate personal remarks.

A common practice of designers in face-to-face communication is to explain verbally in synchronization as they are sketching. This is a perfect example of multimodal communication. In our system, as the designer captures an audio or video clip, they may select the "link with sketch" option, so that they can sketch at the same time and have the sketch strokes recorded together with the clip (Figure 3d). When playing back the clip, the sketches are redrawn in synchronization, emulating the above practice in face-to-face settings.

Aside from directly capturing content from the real world, the designer may also insert media content from secondary sources. This includes image, audio, and video files from a local folder, or from a mobile phone through Bluetooth. The latter especially opens up the space for the designer to capture real world content anywhere and at any time, without being constrained to content near the tablet. In addition, the designer can open an embedded web browser within SketchComm, and capture an interesting portion of its content as a snapshot. This also matches today's common practice of designers searching for reference material online.

Borrowing Sketching Elements from the Real World

In addition to using captured media *along with* sketches, the designer may also sample attributes of the real world to be used *in* their sketching. This is made possible by the color picker and texture picker functions, which allow the designer to click any point on the screen to pick its color for sketching, or select any rectangle on the screen to pick the texture inside as the brush pattern for painting (Figure 4a). By picking either from a captured photo or directly from the live viewfinder, the designer can borrow the color and material of real world objects and apply them to sketches. In some sense this can be seen as a software incarnation of the I/O Brush [21], while our functions also provide the further flexibility to sample from purely virtual content such as web pages or existing sketches.

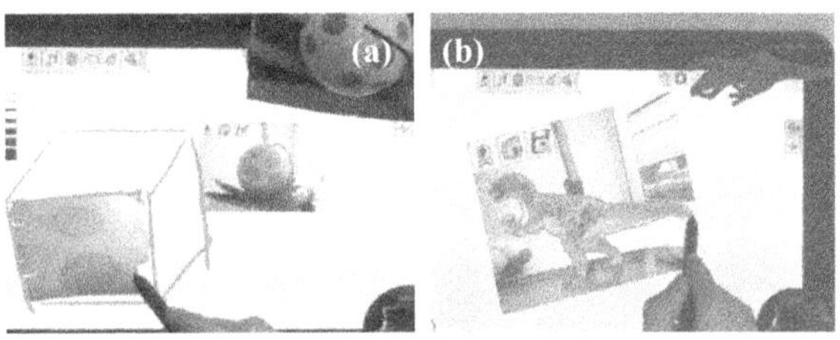

Figure 4. Borrowing sketching elements from physical objects (top right in photos) (a) Painting a texture. (b) Tracing a shape.

Another feature that comes "for free" is that the designer may also borrow the shape from a physical object by tracing over it (again either from a captured photo or from a live viewfinder) (Figure 4b). This allows the designer to more accurately depict certain objects when necessary, or simply to complement their freehand sketching skills.

Multimodal Annotations

Annotations are a common constituent in most hand-drawn design sketches. Designers use them to communicate additional information regarding specific component of the sketch, usually indicated by visual marks such as callouts and bubbles. With the ability to capture multimodal content, richer and more vivid annotations can be supported. Although it is possible to simply combine hand-drawn marks with captured media to indicate an annotation (e.g., placing an audio clip in a hand drawn callout bubble on the canvas), this solution soon becomes infeasible as the number of annotations increases. The canvas will soon be taken up by annotations, leading to visual clutter (caused by both the annotations themselves and callout marks), less space for the original sketch, and eventually confusions. This is a common challenge in paper sketches, and may be further aggravated in digital sketches given that multimodal annotations such as photos or videos often need to take up considerable screen space to be displayed.

In order to address this challenge, we provide an annotation mechanism that aims to be lightweight, flexible, unambiguous, and scalable. The designer can use a single finger to indicate a canvas region they want to annotate, by either circling the region of interest, or alternatively dwelling the finger on the screen when the region of interest is a single point. Once the system detects a circle or dwell, an annotation icon appears near the finger and follows the finger movement on the screen (Figure 5a). The designer can then move the finger to where they wish the annotation to appear. A rectangular annotation panel appears once the designer releases the finger. The annotation panel functions as a mini canvas. The designer can sketch in the panel, or drag any type of content (e.g., photos, audio/video clips) from the main canvas into it.

The annotation panel is connected to the annotated region, which is visualized as a translucent halo, through a curved line. Each annotation is automatically assigned a color code upon creation, reflected by the panel, the halo, and the connection line. The opacity of the halo is reversely proportional to its area, so that smaller annotated regions appear more prominent than larger ones, allowing them to be easily distinguishable in the case of nested annotated regions.

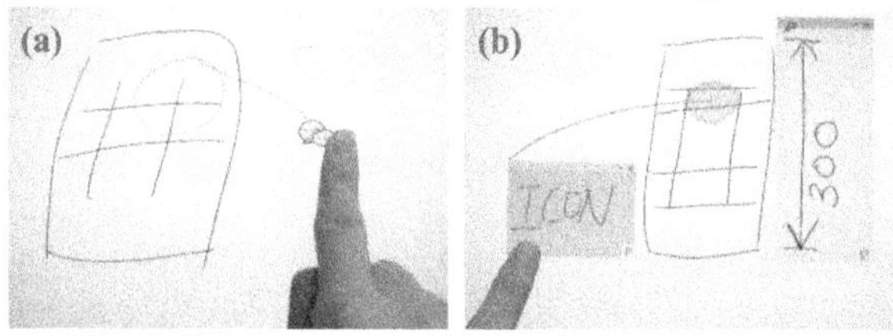

Figure 5. Annotations. (a) Creating an annotation. (b) Floating (left) and fixed annotations (right).

Depending on the designer's need, an annotation panel can be set to be floating or fixed (Figure 5b). A floating panel can be freely moved and resized using the finger, while a fixed panel remains static. The former is particularly useful when the designer needs to lay out multiple annotations or avoid occluding content on the canvas, and the latter is suited for annotations whose meaning is dependent on their positions, such as length markings.

Each annotation panel can be individually hidden or shown by tapping on the corresponding halo. The halo remains visible in either case as an indication of an existing annotation. This allows only showing annotations that the user is currently interested in, and avoids visual clutter. The user can also hide or show all annotations at once, so that they can choose to see content on the canvas only or have an overview of all annotations. Dragging an annotation into the trashcan deletes it.

Combining multimodal content both on the canvas and in annotations, the designer may describe their design idea in a much flexible and vivid way. The following example illustrates how this may be achieved (Figure 6). The designer wants to communicate his idea about a mobile phone design. He sketches the basic shape of the phone, and captures a photo of his face to be placed in the phone screen to illustrate a video call. He uses the texture picker to select a wooden texture from his desk and paint the bottom of the phone with it to illustrate a wooden shell. Around the sound wave icon near the phone, he adds an audio annotation, recording knocks on the desk as the ringtone. He adds another annotation around the charging socket on the phone, this time combining sketches and a cropped photo of a mango to show the idea of charging the phone using a fruit battery. Finally, he adds a video annotation around the entire phone, demonstrating his hand holding a real mobile phone and using different gestures to pick up and hang up the phone, along with his verbal explanation.

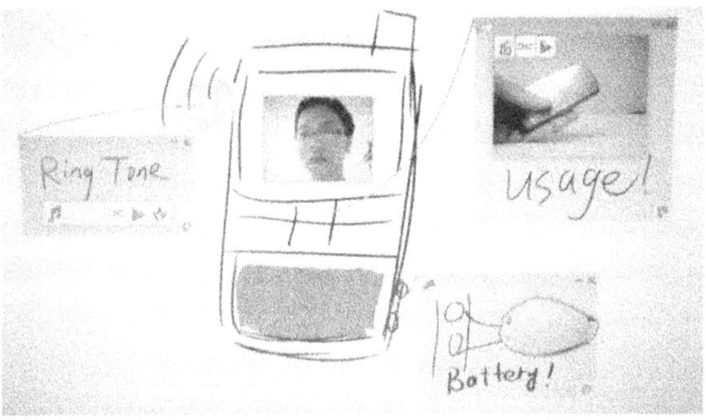

Figure 6. An example of multimodal content and annotations.

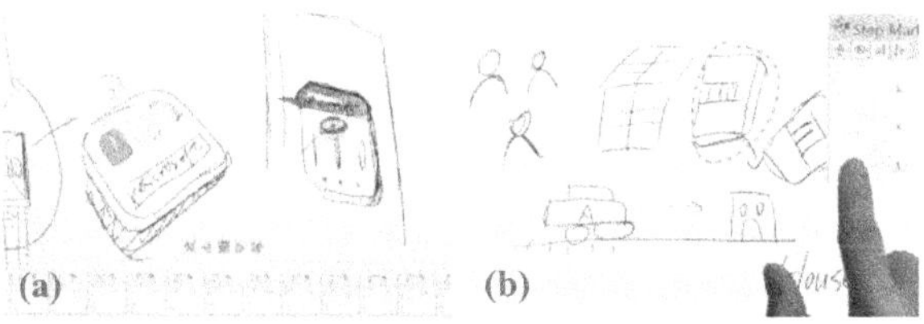

Figure 7. Captured thought process and logical order. (a) Timeline (bottom). (b) Step mark (dotted circle).

Recording Thought Process

To capture the thought process of the designer, the system automatically records a timeline of the entire interaction history, such as sketching, adding annotations, capturing content, canvas manipulation, etc. This allows others to review the process through which the designer has reached the final presentation. The timeline can be accessed through an interface button, and is represented by a series of canvas thumbnails (Figure 7a). It can be replayed at various speeds and in both directions, to be viewed in the main canvas area. The designer can also directly return to a specific point in the timeline, after which they can start further interaction from that point. In our current implementation this overwrites the rest of the timeline, whereas in the future we plan to offer the option of saving as a different version of the design idea to allow branching explorations.

One thing we should note here is that the system is capturing the thought process of generating the communication material, and not necessarily that of generating the design idea itself. However, in practice these two processes often overlap to some extent, and the former can often provide insights into the latter.

Indicating Logical Order

Due to the nature of early stage design communication, the communication material generated by the designer may often appear less planned and structured. In order for the designer to indicate a logical order after the material has been created, they can create "step marks" that highlight certain regions of the canvas (Figure 7b). This is done by selecting the "add step mark" button and then circling the region in question with a finger. The step marks panel on the right lists all step marks in the order of creation. Using the arrow buttons on the panel the user can display each step mark in the order indicated, or click a specific mark in the list to jump to that step.

The step marks act as a lightweight suggestive viewing path for the audience to guide understanding, yet is by no means binding. Different from the timeline which is an objective capturing of the creation process, the step marks convey the subjective understanding of the logical structure by the designer.

Capturing Communication Context

To convey the overall context of the communication session, the designer can open the "Communication Context" screen, which includes four fields: Topic, People, Time, and Location. Each field is simply a blank canvas in itself, and similarly the designer can fill it with a combination of sketch and captured content to convey the according communication context in a flexible and vivid way (Figure 8).

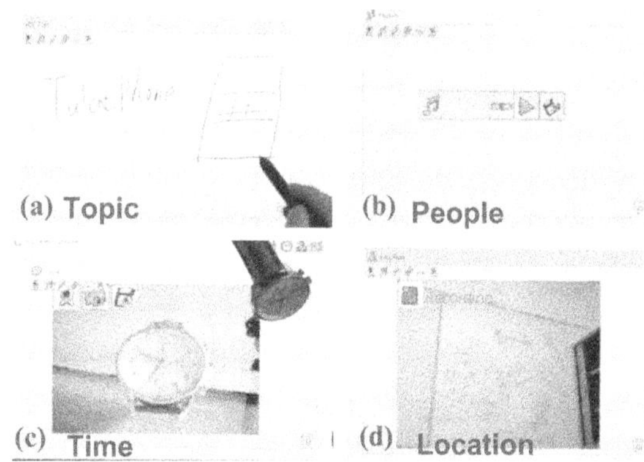

Figure 8. Captured communication context. (a) Topic (here represented by sketch). (b) People (here represented by an audio clip of their verbal greetings). (c) Time (here represented by a photo of a wristwatch. (d) Location (here represented by a video sweeping through the meeting room).

All the material created by the designer is stored in a project folder, which can be then transferred to the audience through file share or other channels. The audience can then open the project in the Review mode.

Review Mode

The Review mode is a read only mode of the application. It includes all viewing, navigating, and replaying functions as in the Creation mode, but does not allow adding or modifying content. This allows the audience to review the communication material created by the designer to understand the design idea being expressed.

Although our current system design targets at a one-way communication model with passive audience, one can also imagine the audience using the Creation mode to provide feedback or further develop on the idea, especially if the audience themselves are also designers. We will leave this scenario for future explorations.

USER STUDY METHOD

We conducted a user study in order to understand how effective SketchComm is in supporting asynchronous communication of early design ideas from both the designers and the audience perspective, as well as how the system is appropriated by the users to suit their needs.

Procedure

The study included both designers and viewers (to avoid confusion, from now on we use "viewer" to refer to the individual participants who reviewed the designers' ideas in our study, and "audience" to refer to this general user population). It consisted of three stages: the designer expressing the design idea using the tool; the viewer reviewing the idea through the tool and then describing their understanding and feedback; the designer evaluating the viewer's understanding and feedback.

All participants used the same HP TouchSmart 2 tablet PC for the study, saving the step of transferring the material between users.

Stage 1: Designer Expressing Ideas

Each designer was asked to express two design ideas, one using SketchComm, the other using an alternate tool (to be explained later). These ideas were generated by the designer to address two design problems of their choice from a list of five open-ended problems we provided:

(a) A design to remind people to get better nutrition;
(b) A design to urge office workers to do more exercise;
(c) A design to cheer people up when they are depressed;
(d) A design to keep people in closer contact with former classmates;
(e) A design to help people stick to their schedule.

These problems were chosen for their generalizability and familiarity to everybody, so that both the designers and the viewers can directly relate themselves to them. Given that SketchComm is targeted at the stage of communicating early design ideas, neither generating the idea itself (the stage before) nor communicating a complete design (the stage after), we decided to inform the designer of the design problems two hours before the study started. This allowed the designer to have some ideation and come to the study with an early idea, while not to the point of having a complete design. In particular, the designer was told not to pre-prepare any material for the communication.

When the designer came to the study, they were given a demonstration of the functionalities of SketchComm, after which they were asked to explore and familiarize with the tool using a simple example design problem. Then they used the tool to express the design idea they generated before the study.

Since SketchComm is addressing an activity that had not been supported by existing tools, it is in principle unnecessary and infeasible to include a baseline comparison. Nonetheless, in order to gain some insights on how and why SketchComm is effective, we decided to offer a variety of related alternative tools that might be reused for this purpose, from which the designer could choose one or a combination that they felt comparably most feasible to complete the same activity. These included OneNote (a freehand sketching and note taking tool with basic audio/video recording functions), PowerPoint and Word (often used for asynchronous communication between information workers), Photoshop (the most common visual design tool), and InkSeine [11] (a tool combining active note taking and in situ search and gathering). We should note again that none of these tools had been designed or widely adopted for asynchronous communication of early design ideas. Therefore the comparison with them in our study should not be taken as a rigorous experiment, but a conduit to better understand the usage of SketchComm. A tutorial was given to the designer for tools they were not already familiar with. After the designer made the choice, they followed the same procedure as with SketchComm to explore and familiarize with the alternate tool and then express the idea using it.

Stage 2: Viewer Reviewing Ideas

Each viewer reviewed two design ideas, one expressed using SketchComm (reviewed using the Review mode), one using the alternate tool chosen by the designer. These two ideas were from two different designers, to prevent the viewer from becoming overly familiar with a certain design style. The viewer followed a similar procedure as the designers did: For each idea, they were first demonstrated the functions of the respective tool, and then allowed to explore and familiarize with the tool with an example design idea created from a pilot study. They then reviewed the idea generated by the designer. Afterwards, they were asked to describe their understanding of the idea via two mutually complementary channels: a written form and a verbal description. The written form consisted of the following questions:

1. What is the idea about?
2. Who is it used by?
3. In what situation is it used?
4. How is it used?
5. What is its innovating/distinguishing feature?
6. What did I not understand about the idea?
7. Any comments or suggestions to the idea.

And the verbal description, which was video-recorded, allowed the viewer to describe the idea in spoken language and provide any feedback to the design as they wished.

In both Stage 1 and 2, the order of using SketchComm and the alternate tool was counterbalanced between participants, and they took a short break between the two.

Stage 3: Designer Evaluating Viewers' Understanding

Finally, the designer was presented the viewers' descriptions and feedback (written form and video recording of verbal description) for each of their ideas, and judged accordingly how well the viewers understood their ideas and how valuable the feedback was.

Participants

Eight people, aged 23-26, participated in the study, who were interns and contractor workers at the China office of an IT company. The design problems used in our study were unrelated to their work.

Designers

Four of the participants (1 female, 3 male) were professionally trained as industrial designers, and currently working on user experience design projects. They acted as the designers in the study (D1-D4). In terms of sketching skills, according to self report, one was proficient, two were average, and one was below average by designer standard. Two of them had experience sketching on a digital tablet. All were familiar with common computer-aided design tools. They all had collaborated with people from other disciplines, mostly with engineers, and in some cases with people from management and psychology backgrounds.

Viewers

All 8 participants acted as viewers. Besides the 4 designers mentioned above who doubled as viewers ("designer viewers", again D1-D4) for other designers' ideas, the other 4 viewers ("general viewers", G1-G4) were from other disciplines. This allowed us to observe the effectiveness of SketchComm for both audience who were designers themselves, and audience from a general background. Although in our case the 4 general viewers (2 female, 2 male) were all from a computer science education background, and currently working on research or development in computer technology, we considered them qualified as general viewers since the design ideas were not directly related to computers. Among the 4 general viewers, three had experience discussing with designers, and two directly collaborated with designers.

As a result, each design idea was reviewed by two viewers: one general viewer and one designer viewer. And in turn each designer evaluated understanding of their two ideas by four different viewers. The assignment of the ideas from the designers to the viewers was counterbalanced using a Latin Square.

On average, D1-D4 each spent 5 hours for the study (Stage 1: 2 hours; Stage 2: 1 hour; Stage 3: 2 hours), and G1-G4 each spent 1 hour (Stage 2).

Data Collection

We collected both qualitative and quantitative data during the study. As mentioned earlier, the fact that SketchComm was the first tool to specifically support this activity means that the rich behavior and subjective feedback from our participants would provide more insights than necessarily quantitative comparison with a different tool appropriated for this purpose. This was the rationale behind our relatively small participant pool but more extensive study process, so as to gain richer insights from each participant. Nonetheless, we collected quantitative ratings to compare the effectiveness of SketchComm with the alternate tool in order to ground and strengthen the qualitative findings. To reduce potential bias, it was clearly stated to the participants that SketchComm was a work-in-progress prototype, and we were looking for most objective feedback in order to improve it.

Quantitative Data

In order to evaluate how well the design idea was communicated from both perspectives, both the viewers and the designers were required to fill a rating form for each design idea they reviewed/created:

In Stage 2, the viewer filled the form after they finished reviewing each idea. The form consisted of the following dimensions in terms of the clarity of the communication, each to be given a rating on a 7-point scale, with 0 being the worst, and 6 the best:

VQ1: Clarity of the overall idea;
VQ2: Clarity of the target population;
VQ3: Clarity of the target situation;
VQ4: Clarity of the usage;
VQ5: Clarity of the innovating/distinguishing feature.

Similarly, in Stage 3, the designer filled the rating form after they were presented the viewer's description for each of their own ideas. The form consisted of the following dimensions, mainly in terms of how well the description matched the original idea, with one additional question DQ6 on the value of the viewer's feedback:

DQ1: Match of the overall idea;
DQ2: Match of the target population;
DQ3: Match of the target situation;
DQ4: Match of the usage;
DQ5: Match of the innovating/distinguishing feature;

DQ6: Value of the viewer's feedback.

Qualitative Data

At the end of each stage, we conducted a semi-structured interview with the participant, each with a slightly different focus. In Stage 1, we focused on the designer's general impression of SketchComm, how it met their need for expression, etc.; In Stage 2, we focused on how and why the viewer found the idea expression clear or confusing, their preference between different forms of expressions, etc.; and in Stage 3, the focus was on the designer's reflections on the feedback from the viewers. Where applicable we also asked them to compare to the experience using the alternate tool. In addition, we probed about some general questions, e.g., how they saw the value of communication in the early design stage.

We also actively observed and video-recorded the participants throughout the study, aiming to understand how SketchComm was used by them, and to identify creative usage of the system.

USER STUDY RESULTS

All participants finished the study as planned, resulting in 8 different design ideas, reviewed 16 times in total. Interestingly, all designers chose OneNote as the alternate tool, quoting InkSeine as being "overly informal" and other tools (PowerPoint, Word, Photoshop) as being too time-consuming for early ideas, whereas OneNote seemed the right compromise point for them. On the other hand, the set of functionalities of OneNote was most similar to paper sketches, therefore we may also consider its effectiveness for asynchronous communication to be somewhat representative of that of paper sketches, the most common apparatus used in face-to-face early design communication. Each idea took 30-45 minutes to express, and 10-15 minutes to review. This time frame was similar for both SketchComm and OneNote. Where the expression involved handwritings and voice recordings, they were mainly done in Chinese, with a few cases mixing with English. All the designers agreed that communicating their early design ideas to other was necessary for getting valuable feedback: "*the earlier we communicate, surely the better for my idea*" (D3).

We now report how SketchComm supported asynchronous communication of the design ideas in our study, comparing to OneNote where appropriate. As will be seen throughout this section, richness and flexibility in the expression, supported by the SketchComm capturing functionalities, were the two key contributing factors reflected in all its usage.

Style of Expression

When the designers communicated the ideas, they adopted distinct styles of expression using SketchComm and OneNote (see Figure 9 for examples). Unsurprisingly, with SketchComm the designers incorporated a rich mixture of multimedia content, both on the canvas together with the sketches, and as multimodal annotations. This resulted in a more vivid visual style in SketchComm. Comparatively, with OneNote the expression was mostly restricted to plain sketch and text (some handwritten and some typed). As apparent in Figure 9b, there was a heavy reliance on textual descriptions/annotations in OneNote (637 words in total for 4 ideas): "*With OneNote, I had to write a lot to express clearly*" (D3). The majority of the text (367 words, 57.6%) was detailing the usage of the design, often the most cumbersome to describe with text given its dynamic nature. The rest was spent on the overall description (152 words, 23.9%), target situation (72 words, 11.3%), and target population (46 words, 7.2%) respectively. In comparison, the use of text was largely alleviated in SketchComm (319 words in total for 4 ideas) by replacing them with multimodal content and annotation. In an extreme case, D2 wrote 176 words with her OneNote design, but did not include any text in her design with SketchComm. Instead, she used a single audio clip synchronized with sketch to explain the usage scenario. Where the designers did use text in SketchComm, the text can be similarly categorized into describing the usage of the design (130 words, 40.8%), overall description (109 words, 34.2%), target situation (80 words, 25.1%), but not target population (0 words, 0%). Compared to OneNote, these were considerably reduced in all categories except one (target situation). This exception could be explained that while other categories of information can be easily illustrated or acted out using nearby physical references, target situation by nature often involves a different physical environment that is difficult to directly refer to in the designer's physical context.

Another notable difference was the level of structure in the content. With OneNote the designers' sketches were usually organized in a clear linear structure, both visually and logically, which required a fair level of preplanning. In contrast, with SketchComm the sketches were usually freeform and did not follow an obvious visual structure. This evidenced a more ad hoc and casual expression process: "*Actually I did not think it over when I started drawing. I just thought as I drew, so my sketch is a bit messy.*" (D2) This was made possible largely thanks to the infinite canvas and the flexible annotation function, which made pre-budgeting of the screen real estate unnecessary for both sketch and annotations. As important were the step marks, which allowed the designer to apply a logical order to unstructured sketches *after* they have been drawn (a feature used by all the designers). Such flexibilities are particularly suited for early design ideas that are still in the process of forming.

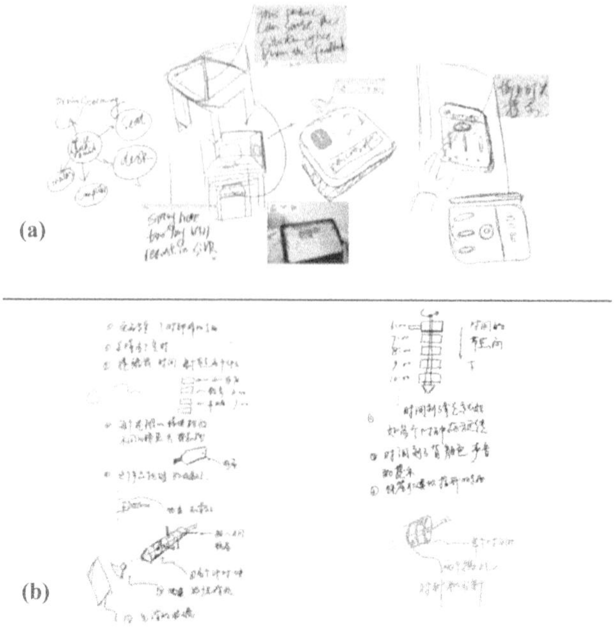

Figure 9. Examples of ideas expressed by participants using: (a) SketchComm. (b) OneNote.

Interestingly, both the reduced amount of text (thanks to richness in expression) and the unstructured nature of sketches (thanks to flexibility in expression) in SketchComm resemble hand-drawn sketches used in face-to-face communication (whereas the OneNote style represents more how paper sketches might be used asynchronously). This demonstrated how SketchComm helped converge the asynchronous communication experience towards the in person communication experience.

Effectiveness of Communication

We now examine the effectiveness of communication using both tools at two levels: understanding of the designer's idea, and the feedback generated by the viewers. The former indicated the information the viewer gained through the communication, and the latter indicated the reward that the designer gained through the communication.

Understanding the Idea

The ratings from both the viewers (VQ1-5) and the designers (DQ1-5) reflected how well the design ideas were understood by the viewers (Table 1). We see a general trend that SketchComm were rated higher than OneNote in all dimensions except one, suggesting that SketchComm facilitated the understanding better. In particular, the two overall ratings: Clarity of the overall idea (VQ1) and Match of the overall idea (DQ1), were highly correlated (r^2 = 0.843), showing a general agreement between the viewers and the designers on how well each idea was understood. The only exception (VQ4) where OneNote was on par with SketchComm regarded how the design should be used. As we reported previously, this was what the majority of the written notes in OneNote were focused on, in order to achieve a similar level of comprehensibleness as SketchComm. However this was at the cost of sacrificing clarity of other information. And even so, DQ4 revealed that the viewers' understandings of the usage through OneNote did not necessarily match with the designer's original idea as well as with SketchComm.

Category	Question	SketchComm		OneNote	
		Mean	Std dev	Mean	Std dev
Clarity of Expression	VQ 1 (Over-all idea)	4.75	0.463	4.375	0.744
	VQ2 (target population)	4.5	1.414	4.25	0.886
	VQ3 (target situation)	5.125	0.834	4.5	1.069
	VQ4 (usage)	4.25	1.035	4.25	1.488
	VQ5 (innovating/ distinguish-ing feature)	4.75	1.035	4.125	1.246
Match between viewer's description and original idea	DQ 1 (Over-all idea)	5.75	0.463	5.25	1.165
	DQ2 (target population)	5.875	0.353	5.5	0.535
	DQ3 (target situation)	5.625	0.518	5	1.414
	DQ4 (usage)	5.625	0.518	4.875	1.356
	DQ5 (innovating/ distinguish-ing feature)	5.25	0.707	5	1.069
Feedback from viewer	DQ6 (value of feedback)	5.75	0.463	5.25	1.165

Table 1. Ratings from participants.

We now look at places where the viewers found the idea unclear. Some of these were caused by the designers not having thought of or concretized certain aspects of the idea, which should not be considered a failure in communication, but rather opportunities for audience feedback. Others were specifically related to the communication channel. For example, with OneNote there were two instances where the viewer could not recognize the handwriting of the designer, which directly resulted in misunderstanding of the idea, and in one case failing to identify the innovating feature. A similar situation happened with SketchComm where the viewer could not recognize a handwritten annotation, however he was able to recover the information by listening to the linked audio clip. The rich multimodal remarks in SketchComm provided redundant information that helped enforce and disambiguate the communication, again similar to what happens in face-to-face communication.

Feedback Generated

Since the major motivation of communicating early design ideas is to get early feedback from the audience, the value of the feedback generated is also an important criterion for the effectiveness of the communication. As shown in Table 1 (DQ6), the designers felt the feedback from viewers using SketchComm to be more valuable than those using OneNote. This rating was grounded by more closely examining the feedback the viewers had given. Through the written form and video recording, 12 pieces of feedback in total were provided by viewers for the 4 ideas expressed using SketchComm, as opposed to 7 pieces for those using OneNote. The feedback mainly focused on the target situation, the usage, and the underlying mechanisms of the design idea. In addition to the quantity of feedback, SketchComm also resulted in better quality. For example, after watching the timeline and seeing the designer's thought process, G3 was able to provide a great deal of good feedback, far surpassing the designer's expectation for feedback from a general viewer.

Subjective Preference

When asked about preference between the two tools, 5 of the participants preferred SketchComm (D1, D3, G2, G3, G4), 1 preferred OneNote (D4), and 2 said they did not care which tool to use (D2, G1).

For designers who preferred SketchComm, they felt that it matched their practice and satisfied all their needs in early idea communication. The various capturing functions in SketchComm was said to result in less effort and less skills required from the designer, hence easier expression: "*I feel it is hard work to use OneNote to express my idea, since I need to write down a lot of things. Your system (SketchComm) is much better.*" (D3)

The flexibility in SketchComm was again emphasized on by the designers. As mentioned earlier, this flexibility meant the designers did not require preplanning in terms of visual structure or screen real estate. Furthermore, the flexibility in expression through the variety of modalities also resulted in high error tolerance: "*There is a trial-and-error process when you learn any new software. When I use SketchComm, although I do make mistakes, I can achieve what I want in whatever way.*" (D3)

The richness in expression was also highly appreciated, especially by the viewers. They saw this as being very effective in attracting the audience's interest. All the viewers felt that reviewing the idea through SketchComm was an enjoyable activity, while reviewing OneNote felt more an assigned task. Some general viewers even stated strong interest to use SketchComm to express their own ideas after the study.

Only one designer (D4) preferred OneNote because of its simplicity. He was a proficient sketcher and very comfortable with sketching with pencil and paper, thus he felt OneNote was sufficient for his need, particularly for the relatively simple design problems in our study. However he then added "*If I were to express a sophisticated idea or multiple solutions, I would use your tool (SketchComm)*", again testifying for its rich expressiveness.

Creative Usage

The participants actively used all the functionalities in SketchComm, in ways mostly consistent with our anticipations. However, we also observed many creative usages. Such creative re-appropriations of the functionalities were the best testimonial for the flexibility supported by SketchComm. Below are merely a few interesting examples:

The video capture function was often used in a 3rd person perspective to capture objects. One designer wanted to demonstrate usage of a phone she designed. Instead of looking for a real phone, she noticed the voice recorder used for our user study and picked it up for its similar appearance, then pointed the webcam to her hand to capture the demonstration (Figure 10a). This repurposing of physical objects as ad hoc mockups is also common in face-to-face communication. The same designer, however, when sketching to further explain the idea, pointed the webcam to capture her own face and talked as she sketched, creating a 2nd person perspective to allow the audience to feel as if they were communicating face-to-face (Figure 10b). And in another example, a designer asked the experimenter to help hold the webcam to shoot over his shoulder and capture his hand sketching on the tablet, resulting in a 1st person perspective to directly guide the audience's attention (Figure 10c).

Figure 10. Videos captured in different perspectives. (a) 3rd person view. (b) 2nd person view . (c) 1st person view.

Although SketchComm was designed for communication, it became clear that some designers were also using it to facilitate ideation. One designer had a rough idea of a hybrid device between a wristwatch and a mobile phone but was unsure what it should look like. So he wrote down these words on the canvas, and started using the embedded web browser to search for such images. As he saw more images his idea started to concretize, and finally he used a combination of these images along with handwriting, sketch, and audio to express his idea. This blurring between design ideation and design communication may point us to new opportunities to design tools that seamlessly support both.

Also interesting was the usage of the timeline. In addition to using it to follow the thought process of the designer, some viewers simply watched the timeline for fun: "*I find watching the timeline a very enjoyable experience, and would not mind how much time I have to spend on it*" (G3). Some general viewers learned about the user experience in the Creation mode that they were not aware of, simply by watching the timeline: "*It must be extremely convenient for the designers to use this*" (G2), or felt a more intimate connection with the designers' practice after watching: "*I always felt the designers can draw everything so well, but after watching..., I realize designers have to draw things step by step, too.*" (G2) On the other hand, the timeline was also creatively repurposed by the designers: after erasing and redrawing her sketches several times, D2 happened to replay the timeline and was excited to see her sketches became "animated". She decided that next time she would plan the timeline to purposely create animations.

CONCLUSION

We presented SketchComm, an asynchronous communication tool that allows designers to capture rich contextual information in addition to sketches for communication of early design ideas. Our user study demonstrated that SketchComm enhanced the effectiveness of such communication, enabled rich, flexible, and creative expression. Our work is a successful exploration in addressing a realistic challenge that has not yet been tackled before.

In the future, we plan to further improve SketchComm based on our findings. Most importantly, we would like to design for the audience to provide feedback through the tool, e.g. for iterative design and brainstorming scenarios. We are also interested in exploring specialized hardware designs for the camera and the tablet to enable a more comfortable and flexible capturing experience. Finally, we plan to explore how SketchComm might be appropriated and adapted to support other creative user groups beyond designers.

ACKNOWLEDGEMENTS

This work was conducted during the first author's internship at Microsoft Research Asia. We thank all study participants, anonymous reviewers, and supplementary support from the National Key Basic Research and Development Program of China under Grant No. 2009CB320804 and the National Natural Science Foundation of China under Grant No. U0735004, 61170182, 61100151.

REFERENCES

1. Bae, S, Balakrishnan, R, Singh, K. ILoveSketch: as-natural-as-possible sketching system for creating 3d curve models. *UIST*, (2009), 151-160.
2. Bargeron, D., Grudin, J., Gupta A., Sanocki E., Li, F., Leetiernan, S. Asynchronous collaboration around multimedia applied to on-demand education, *Journal of Management Info. Systems*, (2002), 18(4), p.117-145.
3. Brandl, P., Richter, C., Haller, M. NiCE-Book: supporting natural note taking. *CHI*, (2010), 599-608.
4. Buxton, B. Sketching user experiences. (2007), *Morgan Kaufmann publishers*.
5. Cao, X., Lindley, S.E., Helmes, J., Sellen, A. Telling the whole story: anticipation, inspiration and reputation in a field deployment of TellTable. *CSCW*, (2010), 251-260.
6. Davis, R.C., Colwell, B., Landay, J.A. K-sketch: a 'kinetic' sketch pad for novice animators. *CHI*, (2008),413-422.
7. Follmer, S. , Carr, D., Lovell, E., Ishii, H. CopyCAD: remixing physical objects with copy and paste from the real world. *UIST*, (2010), 381-382.
8. Gross, M.D., Do E.Y-L. Demonstrating the electronic cocktail napkin: a paper-like interface for early design. *CHI*, (1996),5 - 6
9. Gross, M.D. Do, E.Y-L., Johnson, B.R. The Design Amanuensis: an instrument for multimodal design capture. *CAAD Futures*, (2001). 1-13
10. Hartmann, B., Morris, M.R., Benko, H., Wilson, A.D. Pictionaire: supporting collaborative design work by integrating physical and digital artifacts. *CSCW*, (2010), 421-424.
11. Hinckley, K., Zhao, S., Sarin R., Baudisch P., Cutrell, E., Shilman, M., Tan, D. InkSeine: in situ search for active note taking. *CHI*, (2007), 251-260.
12. Hunter, S., Maes, P., Scott S., Kaufman H. MemTable: an integrated system for capture and recall of shared histories in group workspaces. *CHI*, (2011), 3305-3314.
13. Jung, T., Gross M.D., Do, E.Y. Sketching annotations in a 3D web environment. *CHI extended abstracts*, (2002), 618-619.
14. Landay, J. and Myers, B. Interactive sketching for the early stages of user interface design. *CHI*, (1995), 43-50.
15. Lin, J., Newman, M.W., Hong, J.I., Landay J.A. DENIM: an informal tool for early stage web site design. *CHI extended abstracts*, (2001),205-206.
16. Martens, J., Parthesius, F., Atasoy, B. Design TeamMate: a platform to support design activities of small teams. *AVI*, (2010), 119-126.
17. Microsoft Office OneNote: http://office.microsoft.com/en-us/onenote/.
18. Minneman, S.L., Harrison, S.R. Where were we: making and using near-synchronous pre-narrative video. *Multimedia*,(1993), 207-214
19. Petkovic, D., Lank, E., Ramirez, F. A., Raghavendra, S., Chen, F., Pathuri, S., Pekiner, C., Fergoso, J., Hsieh A., Marquez, A. Asynchronous multimedia annotations for web-based collaboration in biology education. *Storage and Retrieval Methods and Applications for Multimedia*, (2005), Vol. 5682, 108 -113.
20. Reeves, B., Shipman, F. Supporting communication between designers with artifact-centered evolving information spaces. *CSCW*, (1992), 394-401.
21. Ryokai, K., Marti, S., Ishii, H. I/O Brush: Drawing with everyday objects as ink. *CHI*, (2004), 303-310.
22. Sutherland, I.E. Sketchpad: a man-machine graphical communication system. *SHARE design automation workshop*, (1964), 6: 329-346.
23. Swan, L., Tanase, D., Taylor, A.S. Design's processional character. *DIS*, (2010), 65-74.
24. Tsang, M, Fitzmzurice, G.W., Kurtenbach, G., Khan, A, Buxton, B. Boom chameleon: Simultaneous capture of 3D viewpoint, voice and gesture annotations on a spatially-aware display. *UIST*, (2002), 111 - 120.

Contents and Contexts: Disclosure Perceptions on Facebook

Natalya N. Bazarova
Cornell University
318 Kennedy Hall, Ithaca, NY 14850
nnb8@cornell.edu
(607)255-7821

ABSTRACT
Social network sites (SNSs) provide new forms of communication, in which people routinely share personal information with a large audience. The goal of this research is to examine how a public context in which disclosures are revealed influences receivers' impressions of disclosure and a discloser on SNSs. The results of the original study reported in this paper indicate that publicly shared disclosures were perceived as less intimate and less appropriate than privately shared disclosures on Facebook, and perceptions of disclosure appropriateness mediated the effects of public/private contexts on social attraction for a discloser. The results inform research on social outcomes associated with SNS's use, as well as design considerations for privacy- and disclosure-related behaviors in social media.

Author Keywords
Social networking sites, Facebook, disclosure, privacy.

ACM Classification Keywords
H5.3 [Information Interfaces]: Group and Organization Interfaces; Web-based interaction; Computer-supported cooperative work.

INTRODUCTION
Social network sites have become increasingly popular for establishing and maintaining personal connections. Millions of SNS users share details about their private lives and get updates on their friends' lives on a regular basis. Personal information can be easily broadcasted to a whole network allowing users to share personal information (self-disclosure) with multiple people at once. This type of public sharing of private information can blur the boundaries between private and public, raising questions about how people make judgments about disclosure and construct intimacy on SNSs.

Understanding how social affordances affect disclosure interpretation on SNSs is important for several reasons. First, disclosure interpretation forms the basis for relational closeness and bonding [11]. Self-disclosure does not automatically lead to relational closeness and liking for a discloser, as assumed by early models of self-disclosure [5]. Instead, the effects of self-disclosure are contingent on how a receiver interprets self-disclosure, especially its intimacy and appropriateness. Whereas intimate messages generally facilitate relational closeness, their effects can backfire if these messages are considered inappropriate [4]. As people share personal information in order to develop and maintain relationships on SNSs [6], receivers' perceptions are important for understanding relational processes and outcomes. Although sharing a disclosure with the entire network reduces transaction costs for a sender [13], it may negatively impact how receivers view disclosure intimacy or appropriateness. This, in turn, can affect relational processes, such as social attraction for a sender. Indeed, recent research shows that different communication forms contained within a single SNS platform may be associated with different social capital and relational closeness processes [3], although the mechanisms underlying these differences have not yet been explored.

Second, understanding how people interpret disclosure interpretation may inform research on privacy and disclosure production on SNSs. According to communication privacy management theory (CPM), receivers become co-owners of information [8]. Whether receivers keep this information to themselves or pass it to third parties depends to a large extent on their perceptions of privacy rules around disclosure, including perceived disclosure intimacy. Although the CPM theory does not directly address how receivers assess disclosure intimacy, psychological research shows that compared to a discloser, receivers underestimate disclosure intimacy [10]. Social media contexts may further complicate disclosure intimacy interpretation because receivers' interpretation of disclosure intimacy may be affected by socio-technical affordances of media. Misreading disclosure intimacy may, in turn, lead to its inappropriate use, such as sharing private information outside of the network, which violates contextual integrity of private information [7].

Therefore, the goal of the present study is to examine how people interpret disclosure on SNSs. In particular, this study compares the effects of private messaging versus public wallposting on perceptions of disclosure intimacy and appropriateness, as well as social attraction for a discloser on Facebook.

DISCLOSURE PERCEPTION IN CONTEXT

Because people derive message meaning partly based on a disclosure context, disclosure interpretation cannot be reduced to only contents of disclosure, without regard to a conversational context of disclosure [1]. Furthermore, to understand contextual effects on disclosure perceptions, a context of disclosure has to be examined separately from the disclosure contents.

According to Prager (1995, p. 174), contextual factors can be classified according to a "continuum of immediacy or distance relative to the space-and-time of the interaction" [9]. The most basic contextual level is a disclosure situation, which includes the nature of occasion, the number of people involved in the interaction, and the degree of privacy. The next level is a relational context, which characterizes personal characteristics and relationships between individuals involved in the interaction; followed by a larger social group level, and an even broader socio-cultural system in which an interaction is embedded.

The current paper is concerned with the situational context, which most closely maps onto the distinctions associated with different interactional contexts on Facebook, such as private messaging and wallposts, because they differ in the number of people involved in the interaction and the degree of privacy. Specifically, whereas wallposts are public and visible to uninvolved third parities, private messaging is limited to only discloser and receiver.

First, let us consider the effects of a public versus private context on perceived disclosure intimacy. According to Schoeman's subjective intimacy framework [12], people decide whether information is intimate or private partly based on their assessment of what information holds for a discloser himself/herself. One way through which receivers decode the subjective value of information for a discloser is through a context in which it is revealed. "The information is to be regarded as special and thus only revealed in certain contexts – contexts in which the very giving of the information is valued as a special act" [12, p. 406]. In this way, a private context serves to "envalue personal experiences", regardless of their objective value [12, p. 406]. Consequently, a message received in a private context is likely to be interpreted as having a special meaning to a discloser. In contrast, indiscriminate sharing of a disclosure with a broad audience conceivably devalues its specialness and intimacy in the receiver's eyes because a discloser has chosen to share it with many others. Based on this rationale,

H1: Facebook disclosure shared publicly is perceived as less intimate than Facebook disclosure shared privately.

In addition to perceived intimacy, a context can also shape perceptions of disclosure appropriateness. Whereas revealing personal disclosures publicly on SNSs is becoming a more common social norm, studies of intimate disclosures in face-to-face interactions suggest that people tend to judge intimate disclosures as more appropriate in private than in public interactions because of the potential mismatch between a private content and a public context [4]. Based on this rationale, an interaction effect between public/private context and low/high message intimacy is proposed:

H2: Whereas low intimacy disclosures are perceived as equally appropriate in public and private Facebook contexts, high intimacy disclosures are perceived as less appropriate in public than private contexts.

Finally, how do perceptions of disclosure situated in public/private contexts affect impressions about a disclosure sender? According to information-processing theories of attraction, self-disclosure predicts social attraction for the sender if the receiver has positive beliefs about the sender as a result of his/her self-disclosure [5]. Although self-disclosure can increase liking for a sender directly, this relationship depends on the perceived disclosure appropriateness [4]. Thus, whereas public self-disclosure prompts less social attraction for the sender than private self-disclosure, this relationship should be mediated by perceived disclosure appropriateness.

H3: The relationship between Facebook public versus private contexts and social attraction for the sender is mediated by perceptions of perceived disclosure appropriateness.

METHOD

Participants

Two hundred and twenty participants (68.6% female) were recruited to participate in an experiment, in exchange for course extra credit. The mean participant age was 20 (*SD*=1.19). 60% of the participants were Caucasians, 24% were Asian, 6.5% were African Americans, 4.5% were Hispanics, and 5% identified themselves as others. Only 1.8% of the participants did not have a Facebook profile; 90% of the participants had a Facebook profile for 2 years and more.

Experimental Design

The hypotheses were tested with a 2x2x2 factorial design, with message intimacy (high, low), private-public disclosure context (Facebook private messaging vs. wallpost), and disclosure valence (positive vs. negative) to control for potential valence effects. A total of 4 different fictitious Facebook profiles were created for this study, with minimal bio information featured on the profiles (e.g., a place of residence, birth date, current occupation, and the number of friends). Each profile featured a unique disclosure message, with manipulations of message intimacy, valence, and context embedded in the profiles. The contents of each disclosure were modified to fit the disclosure intimacy and valence conditions. The messages were generated based on the analysis of disclosures that people commonly share on Facebook while controlling for their intimacy and valence levels. For example, "Just got back from spring break – it rained most of the time so I didn't have a chance to do any swimming" (low intimacy and negative valence); "Just got back from spring break – I had the chance to catch up on my favorite TV shows" (low intimacy and positive valence); "Just got back from spring break with an empty bank account. I'll have to work forever to make up for my mistakes" (high intimacy and negative valence); "Just got back from spring break – I'll always love the friends I spent the week with" (high intimacy and positive valence).

All the disclosures were pretested by a different group of judges (N=36) for how intimate and how personal the message was (*alpha*= .71) and for message valence, which yielded a significant difference between low and high intimacy messages, $F(1, 67)=101.90$, $p<.001$, and between positive and negative messages, $F(1, 67)=263.44$, $p<.001$.

The manipulation of the disclosure context included 2 conditions: a private Facebook message exchanged between two parties only and a Facebook wallpost exchanged between the same two parties, but visible to the entire network. Both the owner of the profiles and their "friend" were female. The experiment took place entirely online; participants viewed the profiles with the embedded disclosure intimacy/context/valence manipulations and answered questions about message intimacy and appropriateness after each of the profiles. Each profile was presented in all of the intimacy x context x valence conditions. The Latin Square experimental design was employed to randomly assign participants to the experimental conditions, with each participant viewing each of the disclosure message and profile exactly once.

Dependent Variables and Manipulation Check

The message intimacy scale consisted of four bipolar items measured on a 7-point scale: non-intimate/intimate, impersonal/personal, public/private, and superficial/in-depth, *alpha*=. 81, which were adapted from the message intimacy scale [2]. Message appropriateness was measured with four items: appropriate-inappropriate, suitable to the situation/unsuitable to the situation, out of place for this context/normal to share in this context, and improper/proper, *alpha*=. 85.

For each of the profile participants were asked a manipulation question to check whether they were able to distinguish private (i.e., seen only by the profile owner and her friend) from public disclosure conditions (i.e., seen by all of the profile owner's Facebook friends). Across all the responses, the private/public condition was misidentified in 8.1% of cases, which were excluded from the reported analyses.

RESULTS

The analyses were carried out with multilevel modeling that included disclosure intimacy, context, valence, and their interaction as fixed factors. Participants and profiles nested within participants were used as random factors to control for potential non-independence of residuals due to repeated observations from each participant and to parcel out the random effect of profile.

First, the analyses were run on the dependent variable of perceived disclosure intimacy. Disclosures in private context were considered more intimate than disclosures in public wallpostings, $F(1, 619)=219$, $p < .001$: $M_{private}=4.82$, $SE=.06$, and $M_{wallposting}=3.79$, $SE=.06$. This effect held across disclosure valence and intimacy levels, as none of the interactions emerged as significant: for valence and context, $F\ (1, 592)=.72$, $p=.40$, and for disclosure intimacy and context, $F\ (1, 619)=2.03$, $p=.16$. In addition, there were significant effects of disclosure valence, $F\ (1, 593)=6.24$, $p= .01$, and disclosure intimacy levels, $F(1, 215)=117$, $p< .001$. The results support H1 by showing that people perceive disclosure intimacy differently in private vs. public disclosure contexts on SNSs. Specifically, the same disclosure contents were evaluated as less intimate in public than private contexts, which was true for both high and low intimacy messages, as well as positive and negative messages.

H2 predicted the interaction between message intimacy and disclosure context such that the disclosure context would affect perceived appropriateness for high intimacy messages only. Consistent with the prediction, there was a significant interaction effect of disclosure intimacy and public/private context conditions, $F\ (1, 617)=31.98$, $p < .001$. High intimacy disclosures were evaluated as less appropriate in public than in private: $M_{public}=3.74$, $SE=.09$, and $M_{private}= 4.66$, $SE= .10$, $p < .001$; but no such difference emerged for low intimacy disclosures: $M_{public}=5.05$, $SE=.09$, and $M_{private}=5.13$, $SE=.09$, $p=.44$ (with higher numbers indicating greater appropriateness). In addition, all of the main effects were significant: for message valence, $F\ (1, 593)=34.85$, $p<.001$; for disclosure intimacy, $F(1, 217)=65.38$, $p<.001$; and for public/private context, $F(1, 617)=45.49$, $p<.001$. Thus, these results reveal that perceived disclosure appropriateness depends both on Facebook disclosure context and disclosure intimacy level.

The final analysis tested the proposed mediation effect of perceived disclosure appropriateness (H3) on the relationship between public/private context and social attraction for a sender. The results supported a full mediation effect. After regressing social attraction on both perceived appropriateness and public/private context, the effect of context ceased to be significant, $F\ (1, 631)= 1.58$, $p=.21$, while the effect of perceived appropriateness remained significant, $\beta= .29$, $SE= .02$, $t\ (805)= 13.00$, $p < .001$. Thus, judgments of disclosure appropriateness mediated between Facebook disclosure contexts and social attraction for a sender.

DISCUSSION

By giving access to large audiences and ability to easily control the audience of any given message, SNSs create new bases for making judgments about disclosure- and privacy-related behaviors. The results of this study show that people interpret disclosure intimacy and appropriateness differently in private than in public SNS contexts: Whereas private contexts heighten disclosure intimacy, public contexts appear to dampen it. Moreover, people judge high intimacy disclosures as less appropriate in public contexts, and perceived disclosure appropriateness mediated the effects of public/private contexts on social attraction for a discloser.

These findings contribute to understanding of relational processes and social capital building on SNSs. Research on social capital on SNSs is increasingly interested in how different uses of SNSs are associated with increase in social capital, such as social bonding and social bridging. For example, Burke et al. distinguished directed communication (e.g., private messaging, wallposts) from other uses of SNSs [3]. The results of the present study suggest the distinctions may go even further because directed *private* communication is not the same as directed *public* communication in terms of its effects on receivers' perceptions of disclosure, which can lead to different relational closeness and social bonding between partners. Future research needs to examine connections between disclosure perceptions and social capital processes on SNSs.

Future research also needs to examine how differences in disclosure perceptions relate to receivers' management of disclosure (e.g., tagging, sharing outside of the original context, gossiping). For example, are receivers more prone to distribute somebody's disclosure when it was received as a wallpost because they discount its intimacy? What are the effects of social affordances on sender-receiver differences in disclosure intimacy reading? Better understanding of disclosure perceptions on SNSs may suggest design solutions that ensure a more accurate reading of disclosure intimacy and other privacy rules between disclosers and receivers.

Limitations

Because the study has focused on the aspects of a situational context in influencing impressions about disclosure and the discloser, it used a third party reviewer of the messages. However, a relational context may also affect disclosure perceptions, such as knowing somebody on a personal level may influence how one interprets disclosure intimacy and appropriateness. Future research should offer attention to the effects of partners' familiarity and relational closeness on disclosure perceptions on SNSs.

CONCLUSION

The present work has examined the role of public/private contexts on disclosure perceptions on SNSs. Although disclosure is considered a means to intimacy and relational development, the present findings suggest that intimacy may be harder to attain through disclosures in public contexts because these disclosures are viewed as less intimate and less appropriate than disclosures in private contexts, which has implications for relational processes and privacy-related behaviors on SNSs.

ACKNOWLEDGMENTS

I wish to acknowledge Margaret Drislane, Jessie Taft, Jill Mendelsohn, David Rollins, Jennifer Herlihy, and Rachel Blady for their help in running the experiment and developing experimental stimuli, and Jeremy Birnholtz for his comments on the earlier version of this manuscript.

REFERENCES

1. Antaki, C., Barnes, R., & Leudar, I. (2005). Self-disclosure as a situated interactional practice. *British Journal of Social Psychology, 44,* 181-199.

2. Bonnesen, J. L., & Hummet, M. L. (2002). Painful self-disclosures of older adults in relation to aging stereotypes and perceived motivations. *Journal of Language and Social Psychology, 21,* 275-301.

3. Burke, M., Kraut, R., & Marlow, C. (2011). Social capital on Facebook: Differentiating uses and users. In *Proc. CHI 2011,* ACM Press (2011), 571-580.

4. Chaikin, A.L, & Derlega, V. J. (1974). Variables affecting the appropriateness of self-disclosure. *Journal of Consulting and Clinical Psychology, 42,* 588-593.

5. Collins, N. L., & Miller, L. C. (1994). Self-disclosure and liking: A meta-analytic review. *Psychological Bulletin, 116,* 457-475.

6. Ellison, N. B., Steinfield, C., & Lampe, C. (2007). The benefits of Facebook "friends": Exploring the relationship between college students' use of online social networks and social capital. *Journal of Computer-Mediated Communication, 12,* 1143-1168.

7. Nissenbaum, H. (2004). Privacy as contextual integrity. *Washington Law Review, 79,* 101-139.

8. Petronio, S. (2002). *Boundaries of privacy: Dialectics of disclosure.* Albany, NY: State University of New York Press.

9. Prager, K. J. (1995). *The psychology of intimacy.* New York: The Guilford Press.

10. Pronin, E., Fleming, J. J., & Steffel, M. (2008). Value revelations: Disclosure is in the eye of the beholder. *Journal of Personality and Social Psychology*, 95, 795-809

11. Reis, H. T., & Shaver, P. (1988). Intimacy as an interpersonal process. In S. Duck (Ed.), Handbook of personal relationships (pp. 367–389). Chichester, UK: Wiley & Sons.

12. Schoeman, F. (1984). *Philosophical dimensions of privacy.* Cambridge, UK: Cambridge University Press.

13. Tong, S., & Walther, J. B. (2011). Relational maintenance and CMC. In K. B. Wright and L. M. Webb (Eds.), *Computer-mediated communication in personal relationships* (pp. 98-118). New York: Peter Lang Publishing.

Technology-Mediated Contributions: Editing Behaviors Among New Wikipedians

Judd Antin†
Yahoo! Research
Santa Clara, CA 95054
jantin@yahoo-inc.com

Coye Cheshire
UC Berkeley – iSchool
Berkeley, CA 94720
coye@ischool.berkeley.edu

Oded Nov
Polytechnic Institute of NYU
Brooklyn, NY 11201
onov@poly.edu

ABSTRACT
The power-law distribution of participation characterizes a wide variety of technology-mediated social participation (TMSP) systems, and Wikipedia is no exception. A minority of active contributors does most of the work. While the existence of a core of highly active contributors is well documented, how those individuals came to be so active is less well understood. In this study we extend prior research on TMSP and Wikipedia by examining in detail the characteristics of the revisions that new contributors make. In particular we focus on new users who maintain a minimum level of sustained activity during their first six months. We use content analysis of individual revisions as well as other quantitative techniques to examine three research questions regarding the effect of early diversification of activity, nature vs. nurture, and associations with later administrative and organizational activity. We present analyses that address each of these questions, and conclude with implications for our understanding of the progression of participation on Wikipedia and other TMSP systems.

Author Keywords
Wikipedia, Wiki-work, Legitimate Peripheral participation.

ACM Classification Keywords
H5.m. Information interfaces and presentation (e.g., HCI): Miscellaneous.

General Terms
Human Factors

INTRODUCTION
Recent years have seen a substantial growth in the size and scope of technology-mediated social participation (TMSP) [24]. The success of a wide variety of collaborative efforts such as Wikipedia, open source software projects, Slashdot and others depends on sustained participation by volunteers [6,14,24]. As a result, in recent years HCI and CSCW researchers have studied the dynamics of online collective action, peer production [7], and TMSP.

Wikipedia, one of the web's top ten sites [2], is an unprecedented example of TMSP success in terms of scope and size. Prior research has explored the progression of Wikipedia editors' participation over time using a variety of methods. These studies have informed our understanding of how the participation evolves as individuals move from passive participation as readers, to peripheral, topic-specific editing, to more active and diverse forms of participation [1,8,22,24]. Yet our understanding of what substantive type of work (e.g. adding content, fixing typos, reorganizing text) editors do, as well as how contributors' patterns of work change over time, is limited.

In this study we examine the behaviors of new contributors in their first six months to address three research questions:

1. **Associations with early diversification**: how is early diversification into multiple editing activities associated with specific editing behaviors later?
2. **Nature vs. nurture**: to what degree are activity patterns determined at the point of account creation, and to what degree do they develop over time?
3. **Rank and file vs. administration**: What initial types of editing activities are associated with later organizational and administrative behaviors?

We address these questions by focusing on Wikipedia, which, for its size, scope, and prominence, provides an ideal setting to study questions concerning TMSP. Understanding how contributors' behavior evolves over time is important for theorizing about TMSP [15], and for improving the design and management of collaborative authoring systems and information sharing communities.

BACKGROUND & LITERATURE REVIEW
The evolution of individual participation in technology-mediated social participation venues has been studied from multiple theoretical lenses. The "Reader-to-Leader" framework [24] describes a funnel-like process in which social media are joined by new people who begin their career as readers or "lurkers", who at first do not contribute

†All authors contributed equally to this research. This research was made possible by a generous gift from the Hellman Family Research Fund at UC Berkeley.

directly. Some of these readers then become more active and make minor contributions, and some of these active participants go further and take on leadership and facilitative roles.

The specific nature of how individuals' technology mediated social participation evolves was studied from different perspectives and in different settings: for example, focusing on the role of new contributors' socialization, Lampe & Johnston [18] found that the behavior of new Slashdot users is affected by a combination of their viewing behavior, the moderation feedback they receive, and replies to their comments. In the context of open source software development, Ducheneaut [11] observed a process by which new contributors develop their identities as software craftsmen as they go through professional "rites of passage". In Wikipedia, Choi and colleagues [9] studied the effect of different socialization tactics on new participants in WikiProjects, a group within Wikipedia; they found that the general decline in the contribution of new members was slowed or reversed when they received welcome messages, assistance, and constructive criticism.

Another approach for studying newcomers' participation is legitimate peripheral participation (LPP) [19] which explains the process of learning and expanding into new (and often challenging) activities through less demanding tasks. For example, Bryant and colleagues [8] and Antin & Cheshire [3] describe the phases through which Wikipedia editors move from passive readers who learn about Wikipedia, to novice editors who focus on topic-specific activities, and finally to committed Wikipedians who take a broader community perspective and engage in administrative roles and responsibilities. This three-stage path does not describe the path of participation for all (or even most) Wikipedians, but instead describes a common path to the more committed roles.

Some Wikipedia studies examine the "nature vs. nurture" question: whether editors' behavior patterns are determined at the beginning of their participation, or if they change over time as a result of experience. Panciera and colleagues [22] compared the activity of highly active and less active Wikipedians over time, suggesting that editing patterns are formed early in one's career. They found that Wikipedians start their career in intense editing, and then tend to maintain a relatively lower but still high level of activity. While the findings support the "nature" side of the nature vs. nurture debate, more work is needed to both to characterize Wikipedians' activity in more detail, and extend findings to "rank and file" Wikipedians.

Studies of the progression of technology-mediated participation can also be framed by the types of work contributors do and the roles they take [23]. Recent research has explored Wikipedia contributors' distinct roles and editing behaviors. Kriplean and colleagues [16] divided editing activities into seven broad categories: editing work, social and community support actions, border patrol, administration, collaborative actions and disposition, meta-content work, and undifferentiated work. Each top-level category also contained multiple sub-categories of work. In particular, the editing work category included dimensions such as initiative (starting articles), major (substantial textual addition to an article), and classification (categorizing articles). Other studies have taken different approaches to categorizing editors' work. For example, Welser and colleagues [27] focus on editors' social roles and identify technical editors, substantive experts, vandal fighters, and social networkers as key editor roles in Wikipedia. Similarly, Liu & Ram [21] identify all-round editors, watchdogs, starters, content justifiers, copy editors, and cleaners as the roles that characterize Wikipedia editors. Cosley and colleagues [10] also focus on six Wikipedia tasks which they term stub, cleanup, merge, source, wikify, and expand. While addressing slightly different research questions, each of these classification schemes focuses primarily on high-level patterns of activity as well as substantive goals for Wikipedia, rather than on specific and detailed patterns of repeated activity.

Researchers have also examined the distribution of work into different namespaces as a way of understanding the types of work that Wikipedians do over time. Namespaces are a top-level classification of Wikipedia pages according to the type of content or interaction they contain. For example Viegas and colleagues examined important work that occurs through discussion on pages in the Talk namespace by classifying revisions in that space to understand the types of coordination work being done [26]. Similarly, Kittur and colleagues [13] examined the growth in coordination and conflict-resolution work done in namespaces other than the Main namespace where Wikipedia articles reside.

Overall, while there is substantial work on characterizing the activities of contributors in TMSP-based efforts, this work has focused on identifying social roles and broad work types on the one hand, and examining the activity changes of the most active contributors over time on the other. There is scant longitudinal evidence about the changes in the specific types of editing work that contributors do. Even less research has provided insights on the evolution of types of work over time or during contributors' first, formative experiences. In particular, we know very little about how the different types of activities new contributors engage in are associated with their overall trajectory of participation.

To address these gaps, we employ a multi-method and multi-metric approach to the analysis of editors' progression of Wiki-work over time. We use content analysis in combination with other types of quantitative analysis to more holistically study how much Wiki-work editors engage in, together with what types of Wiki-work they do and what effect it has on the Wikipedia body of knowledge.

Figure 1: Participants were recruited during a two month recruitment period. Revisions for each sampled Wikipedia editor were collected during the first month (T1) and during the sixth month (T2) after that particular editor's registration date.

We develop and extend two primary streams of Wikipedia research. Building on existing work which has identified and categorized social roles in Wikipedia [16,27], we first look for patterns of editing behavior based on the substantive types of revisions editors make to Wikipedia articles and the evolution of those patterns over an editor's first six months as a Wikipedian.

Second, we employ a definition of "active participation" that captures the experiences of new editors who maintain a minimal level of activity during their first few months. Much of the existing research on Wikipedia participation has largely focused on the most highly active contributors [8,22]. While some of this research involves the analysis of changes in participation patterns, we move away from focusing exclusively on users who make large numbers of contributions over extended periods of time. In contrast to prior approaches, we apply a definition of activity that underscores the importance of *minimal sustained activity* among new editors.

DATA SOURCES

As we describe above, our interest in this study is not only in examining the quantity of work that new editors do, but also in examining the substantive type(s) of work that they do during their first few months. Reflecting this multi-part focus, our analysis is based on three distinct sources of data.

First, following prior studies on Wikipedia editors' behavior, we examined the quantity of Wiki-work that individuals in our sample undertook during the study period. In addition to examining the overall number of revisions by user, we also examined the distribution of revisions between three Wikipedia namespaces. The "Main" namespace is Wikipedia's primary namespace, and contains primary article content. Each article in the Main namespace has an associated page in the "Talk" namespace, which is the space for discussion and organization on every Wikipedia article. Finally, the "Wikipedia" namespace contains pages used for higher-level organizational and administrative tasks.

Our second source of data was the amount of content that a user changes when making a revision. A user who makes fewer large revisions is arguably just as "active" as a user who makes a larger number of small revisions. In this study our measure of the amount of content changed in a revision is the Levenshtein distance [20]. Levenshtein distance (or simply "revision distance") is a common metric for capturing the similarity between two texts as an integer which represents the minimum number of characters that would need to be added, deleted, or changed to make the two texts identical. A large revision distance indicates that a revision has added, deleted, or changed a large amount of content. While other metrics would be appropriate for specific types of revisions (e.g. number of words added or deleted), Levenshtein distance is a common, standardized measure that is meaningful across all types of textual revisions.

In order to investigate the behavior of new Wikipedians, as well as how that behavior evolves over time, we must obtain a more nuanced and detailed view of the work that editors do. Therefore, our third source of data was the result of a content analysis and classification process [17] for *each individual revision* in our sample. There are many sub-categories of work within the broad scope of "article revisions" in the Main namespace. For example, as an article matures it may require addition and deletion of text, citations, copy editing, and reorganization. A single revision might be limited to one of these types of work or it might encompass multiple types. Our classification process focused on uncovering these specific types of editing work.

SAMPLE AND METHODS

We began the data gathering process by compiling a database of all new, valid Wikipedia accounts created during a two-month period between September 7th and November 7th, 2010. Deleted and banned accounts were

Variable	Revision Counts	
	T1	T2
Main namespace	34,106	25,004
User namespace	1,585	2,137
User Talk namespace	2,137	1,707
Talk namespace	1,602	2,175
Wikipedia namespace	118	372
Total	40,490	31,875

Table 1: N = 354; Complete counts of all revisions made by users in our sample, segmented by namespace.

not included in our sample. During the recruitment window 97,143 new accounts were created. For each account created during the recruitment window we sampled revisions from two distinct time periods, each defined on the basis of that individual account's creation date. We sampled each revision made during the first 30-day period after the account's creation date (hereafter referred to as "T1") as well as each revision made during the sixth 30-day period after the account's creation date (hereafter referred to as "T2").

Sampling revisions on the basis of each account's creation date ensured that we examined comparable time periods for each user. Figure 1 visually depicts the sampling procedure.

In order to draw meaningful insights about how new Wikipedians progress during their first six months, we required a sample of editors who were at least minimally active during that time. Many individuals who create a new Wikipedia account make only a few revisions, while a few complete a large number of revisions and continue to do so for a long time. Our focus, however, was on Wikipedia's "middle class," – editors who were not among the most highly active Wikipedians, but who nonetheless maintained, at minimum, a consistently moderate level of activity. Drawing from the definition which the Wikimedia Foundation itself uses to identify new editors, we adopted an informal definition of "moderate activity" as *at least ten revisions per 30-day period* [28].

Based on these criteria, we restricted our sample to only those editors who made at least ten revisions during the first 30-day period (T1) and at least ten revisions during the second 30-day period (T2). We found 354 new editors during the recruitment window who met these criteria.[2]

Table 1 describes the complete editing activity of all editors in our sample at T1 and T2. The primary focus of this study is on potential changes in the substantive types of article revisions that new Wikipedians complete. As a result, we selected only revisions to pages in the Main namespace for classification. Users in our sample made 34,106 revisions in the Main namespace at T1, and 25,004 revisions at T2. In order to reduce the total number of revisions for classification while also maintaining a representative sample of revisions, we randomly sampled 20% of revisions from each user's total at T1 as well as 20% from each user's total at T2. Following this procedure 11,834 revisions (6,939 revisions at T1 and 4,895 revisions at T2) were selected for classification. 197 revisions could not be coded because the content of the revision was unavailable via the Wikipedia API. The most common reason for missing revision data is that the revision in question was deleted from an article's revision history. A final sample of 11,637 revisions were sent for classification.

THE MECHANICAL TURK CLASSIFICATION TASK

To categorize the substantive nature of Wikipedia revisions we used the crowd-sourcing service Amazon Mechanical Turk (MTurk). MTurk is an online labor market in which requesters post small tasks (which typically take only a few seconds) that workers complete in exchange for a few cents compensation. We asked workers on MTurk to read a series of instructions about the classification task. We then displayed each revision in a before/after fashion, highlighting the sections and words which had been altered in each revision (see Figure 2). Finally, workers identified the substantive types of editing work within each revision.

We used the typology of Wiki-work developed by Kriplean and colleagues [16] as a basis for the task completed by MTurk workers. We began with the 10 work types that comprised Kriplean and colleagues' "Editing Work" category. We refined this typology through pilot testing and face validity agreement among the authors until we generated a comprehensive list of meaningful editorial work types that could be understood and identified by coders. The 10 revision types in our typology were: adding citations, adding content, changing Wiki markup, creating articles, deleting content, fixing typos, reorganizing text,

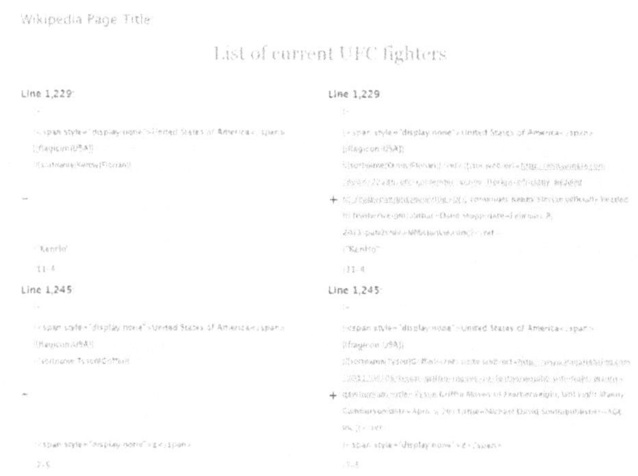

Figure 2: An example of the Mechanical Turk classification task. Changes are color coded and highlighted to indicate specific portions of text added, removed, or changed.

[2] Ten sampled accounts were removed from the final sample because they were bots (autonomous programs that do repetitive and organization tasks) or because they represented a class of "super-users" who, though, interesting, were not the primary focus of this study.

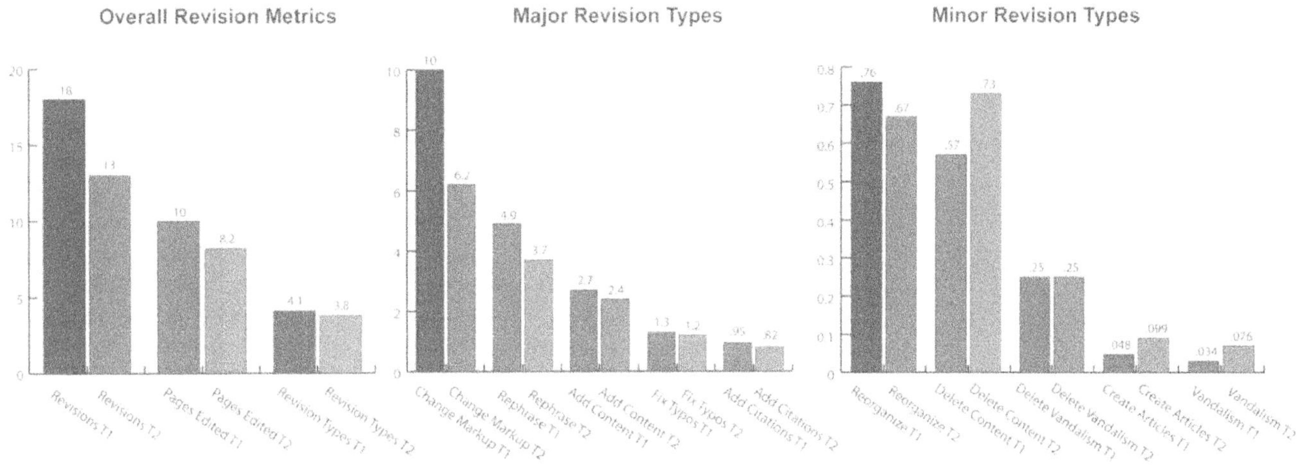

Figure 3: Average revisions per editor, categorized by overall revision metrics, major revision types, and minor revision types.

rephrasing existing text, vandalism, and deleting vandalism. In addition, "unsure" was an option for every revision if coders felt that the nature of the revision was ambiguous.

The classification tasks presented each revision to workers on MTurk and asked them to make judgments about which types of substantive work were represented by each revision. Since we could not assume that our coders would possess domain knowledge about Wikipedia, we provided comprehensive instructions and clarifying descriptions of the categories to make them as unambiguous and self-explanatory as possible. Coders were asked to select from among the final 11 categories (including an "unsure" option) in a "check all that apply" format.

Tetreault and colleagues showed that using MTurk for a similar content analysis task was both faster and more economical than using trained raters [25]. One key to harnessing MTurk workers as a substitute for dedicated coders is the use of "gold" questions. Gold questions are training questions for which the correct answer has been predetermined. As new MTurk workers begin work, gold questions are mixed in with non-gold questions. When MTurk workers provide incorrect responses to gold questions, they are provided with the correct answer and an explanation. A worker who answers too many gold questions incorrectly is prevented from completing further work and his responses are removed from the data set. In effect, then, gold questions constitute a basic training program for content coders. At the same time, MTurk provided us with a valuable diversity of perspective in our worker pool. We were able to gather judgments from multiple workers on each revision. The diverse nature of our workforce helped to mitigate the potential influence of biases and assumptions that could be more problematic if we had employed just a few full-time coders.

Over the course of approximately one week, 88 MTurk workers provided 36,796 judgments on 11,637 Wikipedia revisions. Traditional measures of inter-rater reliability with multiple coders (e.g. Fleiss Kappa) require that a fixed set of coders provide judgments on a shared set of tasks, and thus these measures are inappropriate for our data. However, as a means of validating the robustness of our dataset, we fit a cross-classified mixed-effects model in which coders and individual revisions were random effects. Model results indicated that the intra-class correlation for raters was greater than .9. Based on this strong result, we applied a minimal consensus model to determine a list of one or more substantive categories for each revision. If at least two-thirds of coders agreed on any given category for a revision, we applied that category to the revision. Following this model, coders were able to reach consensus on 97% of revisions (11,298).

Factor Analysis

In systems that support TMSP, activities often group together to form social roles. Prior work on Wikipedia [e.g., 8,18,24] has identified several roles on the basis of higher level activities. In this study we apply a similar logic to examine whether specific types of revision behavior might group together to form roles within the activity category of editing articles in Wikipedia's Main namespace.

To examine how revision types may group together, we conducted an exploratory factor analysis on revision counts at T1 and again on revision counts at T2. We used the principal axis (PA) factor analysis method as it does not rely on the assumption of multivariate normality. Table 2 describes the primary results of this analysis at T1 and T2. Several results are notable. First, at T1 we observe that the majority of editing activities loaded together on a single factor. The only exception was vandalism deletion, which loaded strongly onto a distinct factor. However, examining the results of the PA analysis at T2 reveals evidence of some role differentiation. Specifically, the editing activities concerned with major content handling (adding content, reorganizing sections of text, adding citations, and deleting content) loaded onto a single factor, while activities that might be classified as copy editing (rephrasing existing text

Variable	T1		T2	
	F1	F2	F1	F2
Rephrase Text	.76	–	–	.75
Change Markup	.76	–	.58	.50
Add Content	.70	–	.70	–
Reorganize	.64	–	.52	–
Fix Typos	.58	–	.58	.65
Add Citations	.57	–	.69	–
Delete Content	.55	–	.56	–
Delete Vandalism	–	.98	–	–
Add Vandalism	–	–	–	–
Create Article	–	–	–	–

Table 2: N = 354; Factor loadings less than .50 are suppressed. T1: TLI = .97, RMSR = .091, Cum. Var. = .53. T2: TLI = .98, RMSR = .01, Cum. Var. = .58.

and fixing typographical and grammatical errors) loaded onto a separate factor. This division of editing activity is suggested by prior research on Wikipedia [4].

Based on the results of the PA exploratory factor analysis, we combined related editing activities to form two latent factors for editing articles in the Main namespace. The first factor, which we term "Major Editing" included adding content, deleting content, reorganizing text, and adding citations (Cronbach's α = .79). The second factor, which we call "Copy Editing" consisted of rephrasing text and fixing typographical errors ($r(354) = .56, p < .001$).

We also created a third variable to capture organizational and administrative activities. This variable consists of the total number of revisions made to pages in the Talk and Wikipedia namespaces ($r(354) = .39, p < .001$).

Independent Variables

We use three types of independent variables in our analysis. First, we included several measures of overall editing behavior at T1: the number of unique pages to which a revision was made, the average revision distance of all revisions made, and a measure of the diversity of substantive revision types in which a user participated. Our diversity measure is an integer between 1 and 10, representing the number of unique, basic revision types an editor made (excluding the 'unsure' category). Second, we included the three latent factors described above: major editing, copy editing, and organizational/administrative activities. Finally, for some models we included revision counts of three infrequent but important types of revisions: article creation, adding vandalism, and deleting vandalism.

Dependent Variables

We examined eight outcome variables at T2 that correspond to our three research questions: RQ1 (revision diversity), RQ2 (major editing, copy editing, overall revision distance, article creation, vandalism deletion, vandalism creation), and RQ3 (administrative and organization activity).

RESULTS

To examine the research questions posed above we conducted a series of focused regression analyses. We employed negative binomial regression in order to appropriately model count-based data and account for over-dispersion. The complete results of all models are displayed in Table 3. Because we make multiple concurrent comparisons without specific hypotheses for each independent variable, we applied the conservative Bonferroni correction to adjust the family-wise error rate. Table 3 indicates corrected values for each research question (indicated by the corresponding numeral) that remain significant at $p \leq .10$ after the correction. Bonferroni corrected significance values are also reported in the text.

RQ1: Associations with Early Diversification

Before examining the potential influences of making many diverse types of revisions, it is useful to examine the prevalence of high or low diversity among our participants. Overall, participants in our sample were moderately diverse, but tended to narrow their focus towards fewer revision types between T1 and T2. The mean revision diversity at T1 was 4.08 (sd = 1.80) while the mean at T2 was 3.83 (sd = 2.22), and the decrease in diversity over time was significant ($t(353) = 2.01, p = .04$). Figure 4 illustrates the intersection of revision diversity and overall revision activity at T1 and T2. Examining the scatter plot, the lack of highly active but specialized participants in our sample is clear.

LPP suggests that a key element of socialization into communities of practice is experiencing many aspects of the ecosystem of activity surrounding that practice. To examine whether diversity of revision activity has this important association for new Wikipedia editors, we included our measure of revision diversity as an independent variable at T1 in all regression models. Results strongly support the notion that experience with a wider variety of revision types encourages increased participation over time. Higher revision diversity at T1 was strongly and significantly associated with greater revision diversity (β = .13, $p \leq .10$), greater major editing activity (β = .05, $p \leq .10$), greater administrative and organizational activity (β = .43, $p \leq .01$), greater vandalism deletion (β = .49, $p \leq .10$), and greater article creation (β = .40, $p \leq .10$) at T2. Revision diversity at T1 was not associated with copy editing at T2.

In addition to diversity of revision types, we also explored a second measure of diversity in our models: the number of distinct pages revised. Individual Wikipedia pages are likely to have distinct social dynamics and distinct communities of editors who pay attention to them. As a result, experience revising many different pages may be another key factor in socializing new participants. However, the pages revised variable was significant in only one model: it was a significant, positive predictor of increased revision distance at T2 (β = .02, $p \leq .01$).

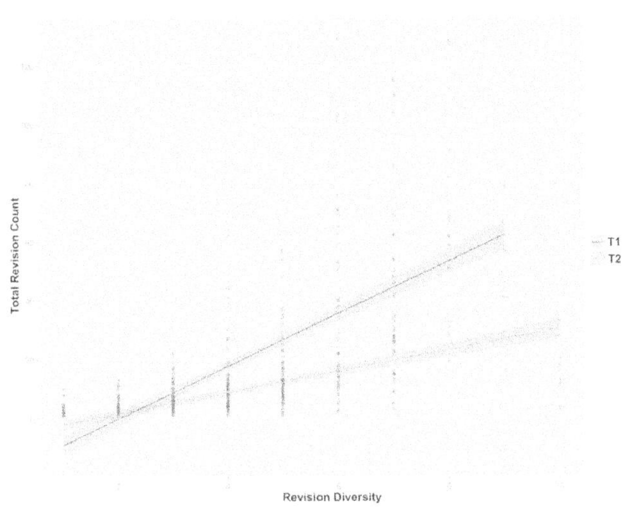

Figure 4: A scatter plot of revision diversity by total revision count at both T1 and T2.

RQ2: Nature vs. Nurture

Our goal in this analysis is to complement existing work on the nature vs. nurture question [22] with more detailed and specific data about the types of revisions that new Wikipedians tend to do. As a result, in each model a key relationship is between the dependent variable and its associated variable at T1. Our results suggest that, with the exception of revision diversity at T1 (as discussed above), the only reliable predictor of each activity at T2 is that same activity at T1. Revision diversity ($\beta = .05$, $p \leq .05$), major editing ($\beta = .13$, $p \leq .05$), copy editing ($\beta = .08$, $p \leq .01$), administrative and organizational activity ($\beta = .08$, $p \leq .01$), and vandalism deletion ($\beta = .55$, $p \leq .01$) at T1 were all significantly associated with their respective outcome variables at T2. There are several exceptions to this general pattern. First, creating an article at T1 was not a significant predictor of creating an article at T2. Second, none of the covariates we examined was a significant predictor of vandalism.

RQ3: Associations with Admin. and Organization Activity

Our final research question aims to identify the factors that may be associated with increased administrative and organizational activity over time. As we described above, a strong predictor of administrative and organizational activity at T2 is that same activity at T1 ($\beta = .08$, $p \leq .01$). However, a second strong predictor of administrative activity at T2 is higher revision diversity at T1 ($\beta = .43$, $p \leq .01$).

DISCUSSION

The primary goal of our research was to examine specific early contribution behaviors among new contributors and the progression of these activities over Wikipedians' first six months. While existing research on online collaboration, TMSP, and the socialization of new users provides an excellent foundation for understanding this progression, our study extends this literature in two important ways. First, we combine content analysis and other quantitative techniques to examine patterns of activity, roles, and the progression of participation at a detailed level. Secondly, we move away from a focus on the most active contributors, and instead examine those who maintain a minimum sustained level of activity over their first six months. First and foremost, our analysis allows us to make a general observation about the progression of new Wikipedians' participation over their first six months. Our results clearly show that the volume of most editing behaviors decreases over time, which is not surprising since we would expect most new contributors to experience a "honeymoon effect" – a short period of strong engagement and high output followed by a shift into smaller and sustainable quantities of work as the novelty of the work wanes [12]. The few contribution types that do appear to increase are the most infrequent activities (e.g., creating articles, deleting content, and vandalism). Given the very small numbers of such contribution types that take place during T1, the small mean increases that we observe are likely attributable to regression to the mean.

Working with our detailed dataset we also find clear evidence that addresses the three primary research questions mentioned above. Our first research question concerns the association between early diversification of editing activities and subsequent behaviors. Our analysis reveals that those who initially diversify their editing activities tend to do more advanced activities later, such as major editing activities, administrative and organizational activities, deleting vandalism, and creating new articles. These results are entirely consistent with the notion of LPP [19] as well as TMSP theories [24]. In this case, engaging in many different types of work is an example of Lave & Wenger's notion of peripheral, exploratory work. Furthermore, LPP suggests that engaging in different peripheral tasks provides hands-on experience with necessary aspects of the larger ecosystem of work, as well as the opportunity to observe the operation of core activities. Exploring different contribution types may provide new contributors with experience working with content and the chance to observe the types of more substantive revisions that other users make as they work. Engaging in this peripheral work [3,8] can also teach individuals about existing norms and conventions. The fact that these new contributors go on to do more work in general (and of no one type in particular) may be indicative of an increased level of comfort that comes from getting their hands dirty early on, but in relatively "safe" ways that allow for exploration and observation. It also underscores the importance of the initial induction period in which new contributors "dip their toes in" [24] and become more committed and active.

Independent Variables (T1)	Dependent Variables: Overall Outcomes at T2					Key Revision Outcomes at T2		
	Revision Diversity	Major Editing	Copy Editing	Admin. & Organization	Revision Distance	Create Article	Delete Vandalism	Add Vandalism
(Intercept)	.98 (.08)***	-.86 (.20)***	.21 (.18)	-.58 (.42)	5.25 (2.23)***	-4.35(.72)***	-3.77 (.78)***	-3.66 (.70)***
Revision Diversity	.05 (.02)^{**1,2}	.13 (.05)^{**1}	.04 (.05)	.43 (.12)^{***1,3}	.02 (.06)	.40(.17)^{*1}	.49 (.21)*	.21 (.17)
Pages Revised	.00 (.00)	.00 (.00)	.00 (.00)	-.00 (.01)	.02 (.00)***	.01 (.01)	-.00 (.02)	.00 (.01)
Revision Distance	.00 (.00)	-.00 (.00)	.00 (.00)	-.00 (.00)	.00 (.00)^{***1}	.00 (.00)	-.00 (.00)	.00 (.00)
Major Editing	.00 (.02)	.13 (.05)^{**2}	.02 (.06)	-.11 (.15)	-.02 (.08)	-.16 (.15)	-.21 (.25)	.02 (.16)
Copy Editing	.02 (.00)**	.01 (.02)	.08 (.02)^{***2}	-.04 (.05)	.02 (.02)	.02 (.05)	.01 (.08)	.03 (.05)
Admin. & Org.	.00 (.00)	.00 (.00)	.00 (.00)	.08 (.00)^{***2,3}	-.00 (.00)	.01 (.01)	.01 (.01)	.00 (.00)
Create Article	-	-	-	-1.18 (.68)†	-1.42 (.35)***	.38 (.57)	-1.17 (1.21)	-
Delete Vandalism	-	-		.00 (.05)	-.05 (.02)*	-1.63 (1.01)	.55 (.07)^{***2}	-
Add Vandalism	-	-	-	-	-	-	-	.13 (.88)
Dispersion	63.50	1.66	1.05	.14	.49	.78	.08	.64
Log Likelihood	-1448.92	-962.28	-1385.27	-1213.07	-4634.31	-209.64	-287.72	-179.69
Likelihood Ratio χ^2	61.01***	89.62***	77.06***	44.45***	52.58***	21.44**	20.44**	13.42†

Table 3: N = 354. Negative-binomial regression results, un-standardized coefficients, standard errors in parentheses. Superscript numerals indicate Bonferroni adjusted significance of $p \leq .10$ for the correspondingly numbered research question (family-wise corrections based on the number of comparisons in each research question). $^{***}p \leq .001$, $^{**}p \leq .01$, $^{*} \leq .05$, †$p \leq .10$

Our second research question concerns the nature vs. nurture debate: do individuals tend to start engaging in certain tasks from the very beginning, or do certain roles only emerge over time? We find that those who do more of the three major outcome types (major editing, copy editing and administrative/organizational activities) at T1 tend to do more of those activities at T2, controlling for other factors. These findings support and extend prior research arguing that "Wikipedians are born, not made" [22]. However, whereas prior research makes this claim on the basis of finding that highly active editors tend to be highly active from the start, we meaningfully extend that finding to include brand new editors who show a minimum amount of sustained activity over their first six months of participation.

Importantly, our results show that many contributors establish early patterns not only about *how much* editing work they to do but also *what types* of work they tend to do. This finding begins to fill an important gap in our knowledge about the progression of TMSP by illustrating that at least some contributors specialize in specific substantive types of activities, even as they tend to diversify among different activity types. Individual contributors may gravitate towards specific types of editing work which they feel are particularly important or enjoyable and continue to do so for a significant amount of time.

At the same time, however, our results suggest that a stark nature vs. nurture dichotomy is likely to be incomplete. We show that making a specific type of revision at T1 is highly predictive of making that type of revision at T2. However, we also show a modest but significant trend by which new Wikipedians narrow their focus towards a smaller number of revision types over time. We do not believe these results are in tension. On the contrary, they suggest that many contributors arrive with interest and expertise in specific activities, and that they carry that interest through their first six months of activity. However, many new contributors also appear to evolve through experience with the site over time. Again, LPP would predict just such an effect as new participants learn about the system and gravitate towards types of work which capture their interest or to which they are particularly well suited.

Our third and final research question deals with the types of early work that are associated with a later shift into more organizational and administrative activities. Prior research has illustrated the increasing importance of organizational work [5], making the question of what encourages such a shift extremely practical for the sustainability of TMSP-based efforts. Consistent with prior work, we find that individuals who are involved in organizational and administrative tasks from the very beginning tend to do more of these tasks later. Once again, however, the pivotal importance of revision diversity is evident. Participants who were initially more diverse in the types of revisions they tended to do made more revision to pages in the Talk and Wikipedia namespaces after six months. Trying one's hand at a variety of revision types seems to provide a level of perspective and holistic experience which may encourage users to get more involved in organizational and administrative activities (again, consistent with LPP as discussed above). This is also likely to constitute a virtuous cycle, in which initial experiences with administration and organization promote a diverse array of contribution, which in turn promotes attention to administrative and organizational needs.

LIMITATIONS OF METHODOLOGY

In this study, we use a large-scale content analysis technique to identify our participants' substantive editorial work. By leveraging the size and efficiency of inter-rater agreement across the mass of Mechanical Turk workers, we can reliably describe the content of individual revisions in a way that has never been done before at this scale. While prior research has validated the efficacy of using MTurk for large-scale content analysis [25], we are not aware of other research that has harnessed MTurk for classifying Wikipedia revisions. Additional research will be necessary to continue to establish the validity of the method in this context.

Although our classification is grounded in prior research and analysis, our results are necessarily limited by our own typology. The question of what belongs in the broad category of "editorial work" is clearly subjective and can (and should) be expanded beyond the ten fundamental revision types that we used here. Similarly, we only examine two data points (T1 and T2 in our analysis), which is a limited view of progressive activity over time. While this is an advancement over existing cross-sectional studies, future work would greatly benefit from the inclusion of more time points over a longer overall period.

FUTURE DIRECTIONS

The next steps for our method include (1) refining editorial work into a wider range of activities as discussed in the limitations above, (2) expanding our existing coding system to longer spans of revision activity, and (3) coupling our large-scale revision classification technique with longitudinal survey analysis of new Wikipedia editors. The findings in this paper are important in their own right, but they also serve as a proof of the usefulness and potential of our method of examining nuanced editing behaviors.

We also intend to iterate our typology to build greater consensus about how to classify Wikipedia revisions. In particular, we plan to work with members of the Wikipedia community to ensure that future typologies are inclusive and meaningful to both researchers and Wikipedians alike. In particular, one of the most exciting possibilities for our method is to use our growing database of coded edit types to train machine-learning algorithms to better detect revision types.

Finally, building on prior work in this domain [26], we will also expand beyond article revisions to include revisions to pages in the Main, Talk, and Wikipedia pages. For example, the use of discussion language that is interpreted as "building compromise" or "divisive" would be fascinating when combined with other Wikipedia behaviors and attitudes. Complex, nuanced types of social interaction such as these are perfectly suited to our consensus methodology using distributed human judgments on tens of thousands of revisions at a time.

IMPLICATIONS AND CONCLUSION

Our over-arching goal in this study was to contribute to the understanding of changes in TMSP among new contributors. We examined how Wikipedians progress in their participation over time as a suitable example of new user behavior. In particular, we place the focus on new Wikipedians not only because they are comparatively under-studied, but because they give us unique insight into the problems and questions that persist in many types of online communities and user-generated content sharing systems. What does it really mean to be *born* into a role instead of *learning* a role over time? Do new participants create accounts with existing motivations, goals, or preconceived ideas about what they plan to do? Alternatively, is there something about the initial, formative experiences with TMSP-based efforts that turn out to be influential for long-term behaviors?

Our focus on users who maintain a minimal sustained level of activity is very much in line with these questions. In some respects the ongoing success of Wikipedia and other TMSP systems rests on engaging this very group – those who have demonstrated a modest willingness to engage, but who have not yet committed themselves fully to the endeavor. By learning more about this key group, TMSP systems can better meet their needs in order to capture their work and knowledge and fan the flames of their interest in online participation.

In the ongoing battle to sustain TMSP-based efforts and improve its quality, this study also provides some guidance for how to treat new contributors. Our results reveal that there is no single path towards full participation which contributors regularly follow. Instead, contributors appears to attract new users who are, from the start, both specialists and jacks-of-all-trades, those who prefer to observe and dabble and those who dive right into the most core activities of adding and deleting content. Understanding the best ways to encourage additional participation, then, may be largely a function of understanding what type of editor an individual is inclined to be.

In our ongoing research we intend to combine an analytic method similar to the one we employed here with longitudinal surveys. Doing so will help us identify the attitudes and characteristics of contributors who gravitate towards one pattern of activity or another. In turn, we hope this information can be used to help TMSP-based efforts recruit and engage new participants and nurture them along their way. Furthermore, recognizing the potential path that a participant is on after only a month or two of activity could help TMSP-based efforts provide feedback to participants that encourages them to keep going and increase their contribution. Providing feedback that supports and validates the importance of choices that contributors are already making about their activities could be a useful tool for improving long-term engagement.

Understanding the dynamics of technology-mediated social participation is essential for ensuring the sustainability of large scale efforts such as Wikipedia or open source software. Combining multiple research methods, our study offers a first rigorous analysis of new contributors' trajectory, and as such provides an important step in the understanding of technology-mediated social participation.

REFERENCES

1. Adamic, L.A., Wei, X., Yang, J., Gerrish, S., Nam, K.K., and Clarkson, G.S. Individual focus and knowledge contribution. *First Monday 15*, 3-1 (2010).

2. Alexa.com. wikipedia.org - Traffic Details. 2011. http://alexa.com/siteinfo/wikipedia.org.
3. Antin, J. and Cheshire, C. Readers are not free-riders: reading as a form of participation on wikipedia. *Proceedings of the 2010 ACM conference on Computer supported cooperative work*, ACM (2010), 127-130.
4. Antin, J. My kind of people?: perceptions about wikipedia contributors and their motivations. *Proceedings of the 2011 annual conference on Human factors in computing systems*, ACM (2011), 3411–3420.
5. Arazy, O., Nov, O., Patterson, R., and Yeo, L. Information Quality in Wikipedia: The Effects of Group Composition and Task Conflict. *Journal of Management Information Systems 27*, 4 (2011), 71-98.
6. Bateman, P.J., Gray, P.H., and Butler, B.S. Research Note--The Impact of Community Commitment on Participation in Online Communities. *Information Systems Research*, (2010).
7. Benkler, Y. *The Wealth of Networks*. Yale University Press, New Haven, CT, 2006.
8. Bryant, S.L., Forte, A., and Bruckman, A. Becoming Wikipedian: transformation of participation in a collaborative online encyclopedia. *Proceedings of the 2005 international ACM SIGGROUP conference on Supporting group work*, ACM (2005), 1-10.
9. Choi, B., Alexander, K., Kraut, R.E., and Levine, J.M. Socialization tactics in wikipedia and their effects. *Proceedings of the 2010 ACM conference on Computer supported cooperative work - CSCW '10*, (2010), 107.
10. Cosley, D., Frankowski, D., Terveen, L., and Riedl, J. SuggestBot: using intelligent task routing to help people find work in wikipedia. *Proceedings of the 12th international conference on Intelligent user interfaces*, ACM (2007), 32–41.
11. Ducheneaut, N. Socialization in an Open Source Software Community: A Socio-Technical Analysis. *Computer Supported Cooperative Work (CSCW) 14*, 4 (2005), 323-368.
12. Helmreich, R.L., Sawin, L.L., and Carsrud, A.L. The honeymoon effect in job performance: Temporal increases in the predictive power of achievement motivation. *Journal of Applied Psychology 71*, 2 (1986), 185.
13. Kittur, A., Suh, B., Pendleton, B.A., and Chi, E.H. He says, she says: conflict and coordination in Wikipedia. *Proceedings of the SIGCHI conference on Human factors in computing systems*, ACM (2007), 453–462.
14. Koh, J., Kim, Y.-G., Butler, B., and Bock, G.-W. Encouraging participation in virtual communities. *Communications of the ACM 50*, 2 (2007), 68-73.
15. Kraut, R., Maher, M.L., Olson, J., Malone, T.W., Pirolli, P., and Thomas, J.C. Scientific Foundations: A Case for Technology-Mediated Social-Participation Theory. *Computer 43*, 11 (2010), 22–28.
16. Kriplean, T., Beschastnikh, I., and McDonald, D.W. Articulations of wikiwork: uncovering valued work in wikipedia through barnstars. *Proceedings of the 2008 ACM conference on Computer supported cooperative work*, ACM (2008), 47-56.
17. Krippendorff, K. *Content analysis: an introduction to its methodology*. SAGE, 2004.
18. Lampe, C. and Resnick, P. Slash(dot) and burn: distributed moderation in a large online conversation space. *Proceedings of the SIGCHI conference on Human factors in computing systems*, ACM (2004), 543-550.
19. Lave, J. and Wenger, E. *Situated Learning: Legitimate Peripheral Participation*. Cambridge University Press, Cambridge, UK, 1991.
20. Levenshtein, V.I. Binary codes capable of correcting deletions, insertions, and reversals. *Soviet Physics Doklady*, (1966), 707–710.
21. Liu, J. and Ram, S. Who Does What: Collaboration Patterns in the Wikipedia and Their Impact on Data Quality. *SSRN eLibrary*, .
22. Panciera, K., Halfaker, A., and Terveen, L. Wikipedians are born, not made: a study of power editors on Wikipedia. *Proceedings of the ACM 2009 international conference on Supporting group work*, ACM (2009), 51-60.
23. Pirolli, P., Preece, J., and Shneiderman, B. Cyberinfrastructure for Social Action on National Priorities. *Computer 43*, 11 (2010), 20-21.
24. Preece, J. and Shneiderman, B. The Reader-to-Leader Framework: Motivating Technology-Mediated Social Participation. *AIS Transactions on Human-Computer Interaction 1*, 1 (2009), 13-32.
25. Tetreault, J.R., Filatova, E., and Chodorow, M. Rethinking grammatical error annotation and evaluation with the Amazon Mechanical Turk. *Proceedings of the NAACL HLT 2010 Fifth Workshop on Innovative Use of NLP for Building Educational Applications*, (2010), 45–48.
26. Viegas, F., Wattenberg, M., and van Ham, F. Talk Before You Type: Coordination in Wikipedia. *Hawaii International Conference on System Sciences (HICSS)*, (2007), 78.
27. Welser, H.T., Cosley, D., Kossinets, G., et al. Finding social roles in Wikipedia. *Proceedings of the 2011 iConference*, (2011), 122–129.
28. Howie Fung, Wikimedia Foundation, Personal Communication, April 10, 2011.

Conflict, Confidence, or Criticism: An Empirical Examination of the Gender Gap in Wikipedia

Benjamin Collier
Tepper School of Business
Carnegie Mellon University
5000 Forbes Avenue
Pittsburgh, PA 15213
bcollier@cmu.edu

Julia Bear
Davidson Faculty of Industrial
Engineering and Management
The Technion - Israel Institute of Technology
Haifa, 32000, Israel
jbear@techunix.technion.ac.il

ABSTRACT

A recent survey of contributors to Wikipedia found that less than 15% of contributors are women. This gender contribution gap has received significant attention from both researchers and the media. A panel of researchers and practitioners has offered several insights and opinions as to why a gender gap exists in contributions despite gender anonymity online. The gender research literature suggests that the difference in contribution rates could be due to three factors: (1) the high levels of conflict in discussions, (2) dislike of critical environments, and (3) lack of confidence in editing other contributors' work.

This paper examines these hypotheses regarding the existence of the gender gap in contribution by using data from an international survey of 176,192 readers, contributors, and former contributors to Wikipedia, including measures of demographics, education, motivation, and participation. Implications for improving the design and culture of online communities to be more gender inclusive are discussed.

Author Keywords

Wikipedia; Online Communities; Gender; Production Communities; Survey; Empirical; Conflict; Confidence; Criticism

ACM Classification Keywords

H.5.3. [Information Interfaces and Presentation]: Group and Organization Interfaces – Web-based interaction, Collaborative computing, Computer-supported cooperative work

General Terms

Measurement

INTRODUCTION

A recent survey conducted by the United Nations University found a somewhat surprising result: less than 15% of contributors to Wikipedia are women [14]. Several studies of Wikipedia readership would suggest that the number of men and women reading Wikipedia is roughly equal: 56% of Wikipedia readers are men, according to a Pew Survey in 2010 [45]. In a text-only environment where gender cues are ostensibly removed and often not outwardly known, why is there such a staggering difference between the number of male and female contributors? The problem does not seem to be one of the overall community readership or awareness, but a problem of making the jump from readership to contribution.

In other online organizations such as open source software project, research has found a large number of male contributors relative to female contributors [30]. However, it is not entirely obvious that Wikipedia would naturally have this kind of a gender gap considering it is not a technical community. The goal of the Wikipedia is to make the world's knowledge available to everyone for free. Men and women both share this goal, and women have insight into the world's knowledge that men may not be fully representing in Wikipedia.

This paper seeks to delve deeper into the question of what is hindering women from transitioning from being readers to being contributors, and what may be causing female contributors to stop contributing. Drawing on theory from psychology and gender research, we hypothesize that gender differences in responses to conflict contribute to the dearth of female contributors. Similarly, research on confidence differences in expertise has demonstrated women may not assert their knowledge and expertise as worthy to contribute to the community. Previous research has shown differences in the style of collaboration with respect to giving and receiving criticism exist. We posit that this disparity contributes to gender differences in motivations for contributing. Teasing apart these gender differences with respect to conflict, confidence, and criticism would be difficult if not impossible with behavioral editing data. Using a sample from a large general user survey of Wikipedia allows us to dive into gender differences in perceptions and motivations of readers, contributors, and former contributors to get a more complete picture.

CONTRIBUTION

Exploring the underlying mechanisms that contribute to the gender contribution gap is important for three reasons.

First, any time a demographic is underrepresented in an organization it is imperative to ask what is causing the demographic to be shifted: personal preference, selection, retention, attraction, or discrimination. Only by understanding the root cause of the gender gap can interventions and organizational programs to recruit and retain female contributors to Wikipedia be designed. Sue Gardner, executive director of the Wikipedia Foundation, has made it a priority to have 25% female contributors by 2015. Having empirical insight as to the cause will aid in that campaign.

Second, the lack of women contributing to Wikipedia has arguably skewed the information found on the site, resulting in a male-dominated knowledge base in some parts of Wikipedia. Because Wikipedia has become widely used as a knowledge resource, with 42% of Americans turning to it for information online, the knowledge that this large portion of society receives should be representative of both men and women in our society [45]. For example, in Wikipedia biographies of females are more likely to be missing than biographies of males [32,33]. Additionally, media critics have pointed out some qualitative comparisons on traditionally female topics (fashion designers, Sex and the City) to male topics (The Sopranos, The Simpsons) suggest other topics besides biographies may be lacking due to the skew [8]. As Gardner states it: "everyone brings their crumb of information to the table, if they are not at the table, we don't benefit from their crumb" [8].

Third, recent research exploring what makes teams collectively intelligent (high performing across a variety of tasks) has shown that groups with a higher proportion of women outperform more male-dominated groups [44]. Women on average have a greater ability to read interpersonal cues and the motivations of others. If Wikipedia projects [47] and committees [48] within Wikipedia are lacking women, they are not living up to the full performance potential that having a higher proportion of women in the organization could bring.

HYPOTHESIS DEVELOPMENT

Recently the gender contribution gap was addressed in the media with a public discussion by gender researchers and industry experts in online organizations. This paper synthesizes writings from these experts paired with the gender research literature from the social sciences on gender differences to develop hypotheses as to what may be causing the gender contribution gap. Four empirically testable hypotheses were found from the research literature. Supporting quotes from those articles are found below, along with further development from theory on the psychological foundations of those hypotheses.

Conflict

Several authors suggested that the high level of conflict in the editing and writing process within Wikipedia contributes to the gender contribution gap. Referring to the high conflict culture in Wikipedia, Cassell writes that "rather than seeming like collaborations around the construction of knowledge, [talk pages] are full of descriptions of 'edit-warring' — where successive editors try to cancel each other's contributions out — and bitter, contentious arguments about the accuracy of conflicting points of view" [7]. Known as "the encyclopedia anyone can edit," Wikipedia may seem like an easy place to contribute knowledge, but in reality Cassell suggests that "to have one's words listened to on Wikipedia, often one must have to debate, defend, and insist that one's point of view is the only valid one" [7].

Strong evidence in the research literature on gender and conflict supports the claim that women tend to avoid conflict more than men [4,12,31,43]. Women tend to react to high conflict situations with greater levels of anxiety, increased cardiovascular activity, and stronger negative immune responses than men [17,23,40]. In developmental psychology, research suggests that boys and girls manage conflict in different ways: girls are more likely to accommodate and compromise while boys are more likely to react with hostility [36].

The heavy levels of conflict within Wikipedia may lead to a gender contribution gap for several reasons. From a cultural and societal view, "debate, contention, and vigorous defense of one's position are often still seen as a male stance" [7]. That is, there may be social pressure, often implicit, for female contributors to not engage in the conflict necessary to contribute to Wikipedia. The literature on gender differences in prescriptive stereotypes suggests that the expression of anger violates the prescriptive norm for feminine behavior, and women tend to be penalized for expressing anger to a greater extent than men [3]. In addition, research on gender stereotypes shows that when women assert themselves in a conflict situation, they are met with significant backlash [38,39]. A previous study on the gender contribution gap in an online email distribution list found that "whereas men tended to say that they found the 'slings and arrows' that list members posted 'entertaining' (as long as they weren't directed at them), women reported that the antagonistic exchanges made them want to unsubscribe from the list. One woman said it made her want to drop out of the field of linguistics" [18,19,20].

Previous research in negotiations has found that women tend to avoid negotiating and engaging in conflict, even at significant cost [1]. In some cases women will pay $1,353 to avoid negotiating the price of a car, and as much as 20%

of adult women say they never negotiate at all, even when they recognize the need to negotiate [1]. Since the Wikipedia model is largely based on considerable amount of conflict resolution, interpersonal debate, and negotiations to arrive at a single "neutral" point of view, gender differences in willingness to engage in these activities could have a significant impact on contribution.

The amount of conflict within Wikipedia may not even be due to many editors being contentious. As one author points out, the nature of Wikipedia is such that "the openness of such communities means that a minority of high-conflict members (including, for example, a misogynist or an internet troll) can have a disproportionate effect on the tone and dynamics of the community" [33].

Following from expert observations and previous empirical research, hypothesis 1 suggests the nature of conflict in Wikipedia in part leads to a gender contribution gap.

H1: *Female Wikipedia users are less likely to contribute to Wikipedia due to the high level of conflict involved in the editing, debating, and defending process.*

Confidence in Expertise

Experts suggested that gender differences in confidence in perceptions of personal expertise and the value of one's contribution contribute to the gender gap in Wikipedia. More specifically, authors argue that men on average have a stronger belief in their expertise on subjects and they are more motivated to assert their opinions (often as facts) to the rest of the world. Referring to previous research on this area, Herring writes that "men regularly post longer messages to online discussion forums than women do, and they rarely apologize for message length, even when they go on for 20 screens, whereas women apologize even for short messages. Some women may lack the confidence to contribute to Wikipedia or feel that it would be presumptuous of them to do so" [20]. Etzkowitz and Ranga agree with this take on gender differences in confidence and suggest that "women have often been reported to have much less self-confidence than men, which has a negative impact upon their drive to communicate their opinion to the wider world" [11].

Gender differences in confidence in personal expertise have been shown across disciplines and age groups and are most pronounced in fields such as math, problem solving, engineering, and science [6,21,22,27]. These findings hold across age and achievement groups, from the elementary school level [13] to junior high and high school [37] and undergraduate and graduate levels [10]. In a meta-analysis, gender differences in some areas were shown to be even greater in secondary and post-secondary students than for younger students [21].

The confidence differences, however, are not an indication of differences in actual ability and expertise. In some cases, even when females achieve as well or better than their male counterparts, they remain under-confident in their performance [13,46]. The confidence difference may not result from females being under-confident overall, but may be caused by males being overconfident even when incorrect [25]. For example, in one case data from achievement tests showed that girls are more likely to choose "I don't know" as an item response when they are unsure of the answer than boys, demonstrating male reluctance to admit when they do not know the answer [24].

It is worth pointing out that this hypothesis, like the others being suggested, is made with respect to population averages (general descriptive data) rather than prescriptive or deterministic outcomes. Of course, as Margolis writes, while "many women love to argue, debate, and write provocative books, there are still too many women who lack sufficient confidence to think that they are expert enough to define a subject" [26].

H2: *Female Wikipedia users are less likely to contribute to Wikipedia due to gender differences in confidence in expertise to contribute and lower confidence in the value of their contribution.*

Criticism of Others

While the process of being involved in improving Wikipedia is widely called "contributing", often the "contribution" involves deleting or modifying another editor's work rather than taking a blank article and producing an original body of knowledge. Similarly, while we often use the term "collaboration" in the sense that many people are collectively producing knowledge. More often in Wikipedia the collaboration process is not synchronous interpersonal collaboration, it is asynchronous individuals writing and editing articles with a technology to mediate and aggregate the output. A large part of contributing, then, is one person editing the work of others that he or she has never met, and competing (rather than collaborating) for one's words to cancel out the contributions of others.

Two major streams of literature in social science can speak to this phenomenon. The first theorizes that women prefer cooperative tasks over competitive tasks. As children, girls are more likely to select activities where there is no winner while boys select competitive games [5]. The theoretical reasons for these differences are investigated in several streams of research, but overall, theories range from an evolutionary base in which men simply enjoy competing more than women, to more nuanced reasons such as men's overconfidence in their ability to win, and a difference in how men and women receive and internalize feedback from winning or losing [28].

The second suggests that men and women respond differently to criticism. Specifically, experimental work has shown that men on average do not respond as much to either positive or negative feedback as women [34,35]. Women tend to respond to positive feedback by increasing their self esteem slightly, while men are relatively unaffected. When receiving criticism, women's self esteem is substantially decreased as a result, while that of men is again relatively unchanged [22,34].

It follows that gender differences in contribution may result because "a woman who wishes to share knowledge with others might not choose to be part of a forum where engaging in deleting others' words is key" [7]. Put differently, while women may be very interested in participation in "collaborations around the construction of knowledge", they are much less interested in the critical nature of the work in which "successive editors try to cancel each others' contributions out" [7].

H3: *Female contributors are less likely to contribute to Wikipedia because they prefer to share and collaborate rather than delete and change other's work.*

Discretionary Time

Lastly, one fairly simple explanation for the gender differences in contribution is that women may simply have less discretionary time to commit to contributing to Wikipedia. Women may be more involved in other volunteer and community activities, or family and personal responsibilities and not have as much discretionary time to be more involved. One expert suggests that "since women often have less time than their male counterparts, they may simply have chosen to contribute to other sites instead" [29].

Classic economic research examining human capital posits that one of the reasons for the pay gap between genders is that women take on more household responsibility, and thus have less time available to spend on market work than men [2]. Empirical research among dual career academic households, ostensibly a progressive sample of professionals, finds that among faculty members who are married with children, household labor is distributed in traditional roles, with wives doing substantially more domestic labor than their male counterparts [42].

H4: *Female contributors are less likely to contribute to Wikipedia because they have less discretionary time available to spend contributing.*

METHODOLOGY

The Wikimedia Foundation in collaboration with United Nations University – MERIT conducted the first worldwide general user survey of Wikipedia during the fall of 2008, from October 18th to November 12th. The survey went out to 22 language editions, including English, German, Spanish, French, and Russian, and included a total of 176,192 respondents including readers, occasional contributors, regular contributors, administrators, and bureaucrats. Survey items were developed based on previous research on open source software communities and with modifications and additions suggested by the Wikimedia community. Participants were solicited using a banner ad or page header on the top of Wikipedia sites. More details of the survey including tabulated data with an overview of results [15], quality perceptions [16], and age and gender differences [14] can be found at http://www.wikipediastudy.org.

Sample

For the purpose of this paper, the analysis will focus solely on the English version of the survey with 40,699 participants. Gender issues can be complicated to understand and compare when crossing cultural and language divides. While the English version may still cross many cultural boundaries, it does give us at least a common ground in the language to understand the readership and contribution patterns. Demographic information for the English participants is shown in Table 1. While only one survey was given, depending on the first question in which participants were asked "How do you interact with Wikipedia" the participants were given different questions. This was done because the motivational questions are different if the participant responded "I am a reader of Wikipedia, but I never edit any content", "I am an editor", or "I was a contributor but stopped contributing". That is, it does not make sense to ask a reader "Why do you contribute?", nor would it make sense to ask a current editor ""Why did you stop contributing?" The sample sizes (shown in Table 1) reflect sub-samples of respondents to the same survey, but are treated as separate samples since

	Total	Readers	Contributors	Ex-Contributors
N	40,699	22,170	18,573	557
Male	30,197	14,493	15,695	448
Age	26.59	25.88	26.99	30.88
Years of Education	14.12	13.82	14.68	14.74
Partner (Yes)	12,309	6,577	5,690	191
Children (Yes)	6,085	3,347	2,674	123
Employment				
Full Time	11,895	6,168	5,687	165
Part Time	2272	1,295	980	28
Student	19,577	11,102	8,622	165
Unemployed	2107	901	1192	58
Other	3,310	2,640	2,037	103

Table 1. English Version of Wikipedia Summary Statistics

for the purposes of this study they are responding to a different form of the survey.

Item Selection

Depending on whether the participant indicated they were a reader, contributor, former contributor, or indicated "no, I would not like to contribute more", they were asked different question stems with respect to their motivation.

The items were taken from the following responses to four questions, given to readers, contributors and former contributors:

Why don't you contribute to Wikipedia?

Why do you not want to be more active in Wikipedia?

Why do you contribute to Wikipedia?

Why did you stop contributing to Wikipedia?

In response to each of these, respondents were given a list of reasons to rate and the option to select "other." The "Why don't you contribute?" question had possible responses given as check boxes, and respondents were allowed to select as many as reasons as apply. Example responses include "I don't know how", "I would never interact on the internet", and "I am afraid of making a mistake and getting into trouble for it." The "Why do you not want to be more active in Wikipedia" question had responses that were rated from 1=I disagree fully to 5=I agree fully and respondents were allowed to rate each reason independently. Example responses include "I don't have time", "I don't feel comfortable editing other people's work", and "I am afraid of making a mistake and being criticized." The "Why do you contribute to Wikipedia?" question asked respondents to rate the top four reasons they contribute to Wikipedia, including "I do it for professional reasons", "I like the idea of sharing knowledge and want to contribute to it", and "I saw an error and wanted to fix it." The question "Why did you stop contributing to Wikipedia?" had the same response systems as the "Why don't you contribute?" with check boxes and the option to select as many as apply. Example responses include "I didn't have enough time to go on", "I became afraid of making a mistake and being yelled at", and "I didn't like the direction in which Wikipedia developed."

Items from the survey were selected to reflect the hypothesis being tested. Since readers, contributors, and former contributors were given different questions, in the analysis the same question may have two different coefficients (e.g. "I don't have time to contribute") if it were asked to participants regarding "Why don't you contribute?" or "Why don't you want to contribute more?"

Survey items matched with their stems are given in Table 2 using the numerical superscripts. Survey items matched with the hypothesis they are testing are shown in Table 2 along with the coefficients tested and statistical significance level.

Items for hypothesis 1 were selected to reflect the gender differences in (1) no longer contributing because of conflict with other editors, and (2) a dislike for having to defend one's work and being criticized or yelled at.

Items for hypothesis 2 were selected to reflect gender differences in confidence of one's own knowledge, expertise, information, or value of contribution. When asked "Why don't you contribute?" or "Why do you not want to be more active?" participants may have selected that they don't posses enough knowledge or expertise, they don't have enough information, or their edits would be reverted. Since we can assume from the population of readers that male and female readers have equal knowledge and information, these questions do not measure actual knowledge possessed but perceptions of knowledge possessed and confidence to assert that knowledge.

Items for hypothesis 3 were selected to reflect gender differences in (1) perceptions of editing other contributor's work and (2) preference for collaboration. If female users prefer not to edit others work, and prefer to collaborate more on tasks this would show support for hypothesis 3.

Items for hypothesis 4 were selected to reflect gender differences in perceived discretionary time to contribute to Wikipedia. Participants were given an option of lack of time as being a reason for (1) not contributing, (2) not wanting to be more active, and (3) no longer contributing to Wikipedia. All of these were included as items to support hypothesis 4.

ANALYSIS

The survey data were analyzed using each item as a dependent variable, being predicted from gender, age, years of education, whether the participant has a partner (binary yes or no), and whether the participant has children (yes or no). Descriptive data on all the independent variables are found in Table 1.

The question stem "Why do you not want to be more active in Wikipedia?" was asked on a scale from 1 (disagree fully) to 5 (agree fully), and is predicted using ordinary least squares. The question stem "Why do you contribute to Wikipedia?" allowed respondents to select the top 4 reasons they contribute and was coded as 4=most important reason and 1=fourth most important reason. Responses from this question were predicted using ordinary least squares. All other models were examined using a probit analysis, as each of the responses was either checked on the survey or unchecked (binary outcome).

RESULTS

Empirical results by survey item and hypothesis are shown in Table 2. The coefficient next to each item in Model 1 is the female coefficient from each model (probit or OLS) where 1=female and 0=male respondents. Model 1 represents the raw difference in responses between men and women. This raw difference is important because the difference in editing behaviors between men and women may be masked by other demographic and lifestyle differences. For example, if the sample happens to have a higher proportion of women with children than men with children, the effects would be confounded. Because of these types of possibilities, it is important to know both the raw difference and the controlled difference.

Hypothesis 1 examines the role of conflict in the gender contribution gap and is strongly supported from the survey data, having both large effect sizes and statistical significance. Controlling for other factors females were 26% more likely to select "I got into conflicts with other Wikipedia contributors" as a reason for no longer contributing. The coefficients for being afraid of being "criticized", "yelled at", and "getting into trouble" are all significant, and in the case of citing fear of being criticized women were 31% more likely to select it as a reason for not wanting to be more active in Wikipedia. These gender effect differences are stable in significance across raw and controlled outcomes.

Hypothesis 2 shows strong statistical significance and large effect sizes. Women are 43% more likely to select "I don't have enough knowledge or expertise" and 22% more likely to select "I don't have enough information" to contribute, despite presumably equal knowledge, expertise, and information between genders. Similarly women are 10% more likely to believe their edits are not valuable (they would be reverted or overwritten). When controlling for years of education and partner (both significant) the response rate to the item "I don't have enough knowledge or expertise to contribute" is reduced significantly, but still has a large effect at 43%.

Hypothesis 3 shows strong support, with women 34% more likely to select "I felt less and less comfortable editing other people's work" as their reason for no longer contributing. Similar findings suggest women are 23% more likely to select "I don't feel comfortable editing other people's work" as a reason for not wanting to be more active. Women also showed a small preference for collaboration and cooperation as a reason for contributing. Effects for this

	Model 1 Female Only	Model 2 Female with Controls
H1: Female Wikipedia users are less likely to contribute to Wikipedia due to the high level of conflict involved in the editing, debating, and defending process.		
I am afraid of making a mistake and being criticized[4].	0.366***	0.307***
I became afraid of making a mistake and being yelled at[3].	0.312**	0.249*
I am afraid of making a mistake and getting in trouble for it[1].	0.149***	0.126***
I got into conflicts with other Wikipedia contributors[3].	0.327**	0.264*
H1: SUPPORTED		
H2: Female Wikipedia users are less likely to contribute to Wikipedia due to a lower confidence in their expertise and lower confidence in the value of their contribution.		
I don't think I have enough knowledge or expertise to contribute[4].	0.524***	0.431***
It's a waste of time: my edits would be reverted or overwritten[1].	0.149**	0.104*
I don't think I have enough information to contribute[1].	0.219***	0.224***
H2: SUPPORTED		
H3: Female contributors are less likely to contribute to Wikipedia because they prefer to share and collaborate rather than delete and change other's work.		
I don't feel comfortable editing other people's work[1].	0.245***	0.232***
I felt less and less comfortable editing other people's work[3].	0.390***	0.339***
Because I like mass collaboration/cooperation[2].	0.035**	0.041***
H3: SUPPORTED		
H4: Female contributors are less likely to contribute to Wikipedia because they have less discretionary time available to spend contributing.		
I don't have time[1].	-0.084	0.065
I don't have time[4].	0.007	0.048
I didn't have time to go on[3].	-0.192*	-0.305**
H4: NOT SUPPORTED		

Model 1 coefficients represent the increased likelihood for females of selecting that survey item as a motivation.
Model 2 coefficients represent the increased likelihood for females of selecting that survey item as a motivation controlling for age, years of education, partner, and children.

[1]Respondents =Readers, [2]Respondents=Contributors, [3]Respondents=Former Contributors, [4]Respondents who indicated "No" to the question "Would you like to be more active in Wikipedia?"

* p < .05 ** p < .01 *** p < .001

Table 2. Hypotheses Items

hypothesis are stable across raw differences and controlled effects.

Hypothesis 4 was not supported, and in fact found that men are 19% more likely to select "I didn't have time to go on" as a reason for no longer contributing. The other two measures of perceptions of available time as a reason for non-contribution were not significantly different between genders. These differences were stable across the raw difference and controlled models.

Overall, the gender differences that relate most strongly to differences in contribution within Wikipedia are dislike of conflict, differences in confidence in one's knowledge, expertise, and information available, and differences in their collaboration approach, namely, women prefer to collaborate and cooperate rather than edit other people's work.

FOLLOWUP ANALYSIS

Previous research has shown that gender differences in confidence and avoidance of conflict may interact with age and education levels [21]. Similarly, research on gender and domestic labor has shown differences between men and women in special cases such as child-rearing; that is, women take on much more responsibility when they have children [42]. Further analysis was done using interaction terms for gender*age, gender*years of education, and gender*children. With the exception of a handful of models in which the effect sizes were negligible (<0.02) these interaction terms were all non-significant and did not materially affect the overall model.

Control variables did not have any systematic significant impact on the model outcomes. In most cases control variable effects were non-significant, while in others effects were small but statistically significant. In a small number of outcomes they were large and statistically significant, but not of theoretical interest. They are stated here for completeness. In H1, respondents that reported having children were 13% more likely to choose "I am afraid of making a mistake and being criticized" and were 29% less likely to stop contributing due to conflicts with other contributors. In H2, respondents with a partner were 19% less likely to select "I don't have enough knowledge or expertise" as a reason for not contributing. In the H3 model, no control variables that were significant had a meaningful effect size. In the H4 model, respondents with a partner were 20% more likely to select "I don't have time" as a reason for not contributing more, and 10% more likely to select the same response as a reason they don't contribute at all.

LIMITATIONS

Caution should be taken in interpreting a few aspects of this research. First, the data in this survey relies on self reported attitudes and beliefs and, especially in gender research, these behaviors and attitudes can be below the conscious surface. Second, this data sample is over-represented by contributors rather than readers and more active contributors than less active contributors. However, this limitation is mitigated to some extent by the inclusion of readers and ex-contributors who would not otherwise be in a sample of contributors only. There are only data for those who chose to respond to the survey. Those with good associations with Wikipedia may have been more apt to respond, resulting in a biased sample in that those who had negative experiences may be under represented in the sample. Third, while the survey items often speak closely to the gender difference hypotheses in motivational and experiential differences, the survey items were designed for more broad purposes and in some places do not contain items that would be present if the survey could be designed specifically to address the gender contribution gap in Wikipedia. Lastly, a handful of hypotheses from both gender research and the expert panel were not able to be tested from the available data; for example, one hypothesis from Oda suggested that trolling and other assaultive behaviors accounted for women not contributing to Wikipedia [29]. While this study sought to empirically test all the most relevant and theoretically grounded hypotheses as to what accounts for the gender gap in contribution, like any study this one is limited to a select few testable hypotheses.

DISCUSSION

This study found strong support for the hypothesis that the gender contribution gap is due in part to responses to conflict. While Wikipedia is the encyclopedia that anyone can edit, the process of doing so is not without interpersonal difficulty. Previous research has shown gender differences in the avoidance of conflict, however, these studies typically rely on experimental data rather than field data. This paper contributes to this stream of research on avoidance of conflict by both demonstrating that this phenomenon occurs even in computer-mediated environments in which gender is not salient, and that this effect impacts female engagement with the organization. In addition, it provides empirical field evidence to support this claim.

While confidence differences between genders with respect to math, sciences, engineering and technology have been explored in the fields of psychology and education, the findings from this paper extend this into the domain of online knowledge contributions. This striking finding that controlling for other factors women are 43% more likely to not contribute because they do not think they have enough knowledge or expertise informs both theory and practice.

Research on giving and receiving positive and negative feedback has demonstrated gender differences in affective outcomes (confidence and self esteem) but much less attention has been given on the impact giving and receiving feedback on withdraw from a task or an organization. This study shows that controlling for other factors women are

34% more likely to not contribute because of their comfort level in editing other's work. The impact of gender differences on giving criticism is understudied, and this paper takes a step in understanding the gender differences with respect to giving and receiving criticism can have on an organization that relies on continual improvement and the criticism from the crowd.

This study takes a stride forward in the research of online communities to better understand gender differences in the online experience. Even though interactions in cyberspace may be largely text based and anonymous, the gender gap in many areas still exists. The removal of explicit gender cues does not by itself create equal gender representation in an online community. As a research community and a design community examining socio-technical systems, understanding the gender differences in experiences of conflict, bolstering willingness to contribute knowledge, and aiding comfort levels in editing and criticizing other's work can be crucial to ensuring women are moving towards being better represented not only in Wikipedia, but in other communities such as software development, knowledge support systems, and online educational communities.

Designing online communities to have a more conducive environment for contributions from anyone makes the final product better for everyone. In the case of Wikipedia, it is not known the knowledge that is missing from the articles yet to be written and in the insights yet to be gained from the largely missing demographic of female contributors. Without empirical support to help understand the underlying "why" question of what is contributing to this problem, ineffective approaches to solving it may fall well short. Each of these findings of gender differences represents a solvable problem that online communities can begin to address to be more inclusive and welcoming to all potential contributors.

IMPLICATIONS FOR PRACTICE

Conflict

As Wikipedia becomes more mature and there are fewer articles that are "low hanging fruit" to edit [41], the editing behavior of existing articles is likely to become even more contentious and thus even more of a turn off for female contributors. Policies such as "Don't Bite the Newcomer" [49] are the in the right spirit, but perhaps have not penetrated the culture. Wikipedia culture can be very rules driven and one can very quickly find themselves being reverted and blasted on their user page for stepping over a rule you were unaware of. Wikipedia Administrators and editors should be encouraged to take it upon themselves to moderate conflict more carefully and with greater attention to human emotions. Other online communities can learn from these findings with respect to conflict as well. If a community tolerates a culture of conflict that males perceived to be simply "competitive" or witty and sarcastic, they are likely to find themselves losing the many benefits female contributors can bring to the table.

Confidence

Two key interventions could potentially narrow the gap in contributions due to differences in confidence: positive feedback and active invitations to contribute. One of the strongest boosters of confidence in expertise is positive feedback on performance. When women receive positive feedback they respond with a greater increase in self-confidence than men do [34]. Online communities should work to provide positive feedback when a contribution has an impact on the organization. For example, when contributors edit a page that later reaches a quality standard such as "Good" or "Featured", providing a badge or simply alerting them on their user page that their contribution was valued could boost confidence and the likelihood of future contributions.

While many contributors may not have the confidence in their expertise to jump write in editing an article, users have been found to respond to invitations and suggestions to participate [9]. Wikis and other contribution systems should include intelligent task routing and request systems to ask users for their participation in areas that the use may have the most confidence in editing. Confidence data could be mined by simple surveys of interest and expertise or past editing behavior.

Criticism

The empirical support finding gender differences in willingness to edit other's work and willingness to delete others contributions has implications for many wiki-based platforms, including Wikibooks, Wiki-news, and Wikiversity. Even though the premise of these communities is the acceptance of free and open knowledge, if these communities do not provide tools or systems that ameliorate women's dislike of editing others work they will likely find women underrepresented both in their communities and in the knowledge that goes into their output.

Women on average tend to prefer collaboration to competition and criticism. In Facebook and Twitter and other more social platforms we find women are heavily involved. However, Wikipedia and other knowledge repositories by their culture and policies proclaim to be a place that is not meant to be social. For example a previous policy at Wikipedia discouraged users from treating Wikipedia as a social space by proclaiming "Wikipedia is not MySpace" [50]. Design improvements to online contribution sites should allow for collaboration which involves social interaction rather than mutual criticism. For example, allowing for social or educational discussion of an article or subject would allow collaborators to first interact and get a sense of each other's interests and abilities and perhaps provide social motivation to collaborate together on article editing. Within the existing structure of Wikipedia, collaboration on WikiProjects [47] may encourage women to collaborate with other editors they have worked with in the past and foster a culture of collaboration rather than competition.

ACKNOWLEDGMENTS

We would like to thank Bob Kraut, Denise Rousseau, and Anita Woolley for feedback and assistance. This project was supported by NSF IIS-0963451 and NSF OC10943148.

REFERENCES

1. Babcock, L. and Laschever, S. *Women Don't Ask: Negotiation and the Gender Divide*. Princeton University Press, Princeton, NJ, 2003.
2. Becker, G.S. Human capital, effort, and the sexual division labor. *Journal of Labor Economics 3*, (1985), 533-538.
3. Brescoll, V.L. and Uhlmann, E.L. Can an angry woman get ahead? Status conferral, gender, and expression of emotion in the workplace. *Psychological Science 19*, 3 (2008), 268-275.
4. Brewer, N., Mitchell, P., and Weber, N. Gender Role, Organizational Status, and Conflict Management Styles. *International Journal of Conflict Management 13*, 1 (2002), 78-94.
5. Campbell, A. *A Mind of Her Own: The Evolutionary Psychology of Women*. Oxford University Press, Oxford, UK, 2002.
6. Campbell, N.D. and Hackett, G. The effects of mathematics task performance on math self-efficacy and task interest. *Journal of Vocational Behavior 28*, (1986), 149-162.
7. Cassell, J. Edit Wars Behind the Scenes. 2011. http://www.nytimes.com/roomfordebate/2011/02/02/where-are-the-women-in-wikipedia/a-culture-of-editing-wars.
8. Cohen, N. Define Gender Gap? Look Up Wikipedia's Contributor List. *New York Times*, 2011.
9. Cosley, D., Frankowski, D., Terveen, L., and Riedl, J. Suggestbot: Using intelligent task routing to help people find work in wikipedia. ACM Press (2007).
10. Dix, L.S. Women: Their underrepresentation and career differentials in science and engineering. *Proceedings of a workshop at the National Academy of Sciences*, National Academy Press (1987).
11. Etzkowitz, H. and Ranga, M. Nerd Avoidance. 2011. http://www.nytimes.com/roomfordebate/2011/02/02/where-are-the-women-in-wikipedia/wikipedia-nerd-avoidance.
12. Falbo, T. and Peplau, L.A. Power strategies in intimate relationships. *Journal of Personality and Social Psychology 38*, 4 (1980), 618-628.
13. Fennema, E.H. and Sherman, J.A. Sex-related differences in mathematics achievement and related factors: A further study. *Journal for Research in Mathematics Education 9*, (1978), 189-203.
14. Glott, R. and Ghosh, R. Analysis of Wikipedia Survey Data: Age and Gender Differences. 2010. http://www.wikipediasurvey.org.
15. Glott, R., Schmidt, P., and Ghosh, R. Wikipedia Survey – Overview of Results. 2010. http://www.wikipediasurvey.org.
16. Glott, R., Schmidt, P., and Ghosh, R. Analysis of Wikipedia Content: Quality of Wikipedia Content. 2010. http://www.wikipediasurvey.org.
17. Gottman, J.M. and Levenson, R.W. Marital processes predictive of later dissolution: Behavior, physiology, and health. *Journal of Personality and Social Psychology 63*, (1992), 221-233.
18. Herring, S. Gender and Participation in Computer-Mediated Linguistic Discourse. *Annual Meeitng of the Linguistic Society of America*, (1992).
19. Herring, S. Gender and Power in Online Communication. In J. Holmes and M. Meyeroff, eds., *The Handbook of Language and Gender*. Blackwell, Oxford, 2003.
20. Herring, S. A Difference of Communication Styles. 2011. http://www.nytimes.com/roomfordebate/2011/02/02/where-are-the-women-in-wikipedia/communication-styles-make-a-difference.
21. Hyde, J.S., Fennema, E., Ryan, M., Frost, L.A., and Hopp, C. Gender comparisons of mathematics attitudes and affect: A meta- analysis. *Psychology of Women Quarterly 14*, (1990), 299-324.
22. Johnson, J. Effects of successful female role models on young women's attitudes toward traditionally male careers. *Annual Conference of the Association for Educational Communications and Technology*, (1989).
23. Kiecolt-Glaser, J.K., Newton, T., Cacioppo, J.T., MacCallum, R.C., Glaser, R., and Malarkey, W.B. Marital conflict and endocrine function: Are men really more physiologically affected than women? *Journal of Consulting and Clinical Psychology 64*, 2 (1996), 324-332.
24. Linn, M.C. Meta-analysis of studies of gender differences: Implications and future directions. In J.S. Hyde and M.C. Linn, eds., *The psychology of gender: Advances through meta- analysis*. The Johns Hopkins University Press, Baltimore, 1986, 210-231.

25. Lundeberg, M. a, Fox, P.W., and Puncochar, J. Highly confident but wrong: Gender differences and similarities in confidence judgments. *Journal of Educational Psychology 86*, 1 (1994), 114-121.

26. Margolis, J. Hearing Women's Voices. 2011. http://www.nytimes.com/roomfordebate/2011/02/02/where-are-the-women-in-wikipedia/hearing-womens-voices.

27. Matyas, M.L. Science career interests, attitudes, abilities and anxiety among secondary school students: The ef- fects of gender, race/ethnicity and school type/location. *Annual Meeting of the National Association for Research in Science Teaching*, (1984).

28. Niederle, M. and Vesterlund, L. Do Women Shy Away From Competition? Do Men Compete Too Much? *The Quarterly Journal of Economics 122*, 3 (2007), 1067-1101.

29. Oda, T. Trolls and Other Nuisances. 2011. http://www.nytimes.com/roomfordebate/2011/02/02/where-are-the-women-in-wikipedia/trolls-and-other-nuisances.

30. Powell, W.E., Hunsinger, D.S., and Medlin, B.D. Gender Differences within the Open Source Community: An Exploratory Study. *Journal of Information Technology 21*, 4 (2010), 29-37.

31. Rahim, M.A. A measure of styles of handling interpersonal conflict. *The Academy of Management Journal 2*, (1983), 368-376.

32. Reagle, J. and Rhue, L. Gender Bias in Wikipedia and Britannica. *International Journal of Communications 5*, (2011), 1138-1158.

33. Reagle, J. 'Open' Doesn't Include Everyone. 2011. http://www.nytimes.com/roomfordebate/2011/02/02/where-are-the-women-in-wikipedia/open-doesnt-include-everyone.

34. Roberts, T.A. and Nolen-Hoeksema, S. Gender comparisons in responsiveness to others' evaluations in achievement settings. *Psychology of Women Quarterly 18*, (1994), 221-240.

35. Roberts, T.A. Gender and the influence of evaluations on self-assessments in achievement settings. *Psychological Bulletin 109*, (1991), 297-308.

36. Rose, A.J. and Asher, S.R. Children's goals and strategies in response to conflicts within a friendship. *Developmental Psychology 35*, (1999), 69-79.

37. Rosen, B.C. and Aneshel, C.S. Sex differences in educational-occupational expectation process. *Social Forces 57*, 1 (1978), 164-186.

38. Rudman, L.A. and Fairchild, K. Reactions to counterstereotypic behavior: The role of backlash in cultural stereotype maintenance. *Journal of Personality and Social Psychology 87*, 2 (2004), 157-176.

39. Rudman, L.A. Self-promotion as a risk factor for women: The costs and benefits of counterstereotypical impression management. *Journal of Personality and Social Psychology 74*, 3 (1988), 629-645.

40. Smith, T.W., Gallo, L.C., Goble, L., Ngu, L.Q., and Stark, K.A. Agency, communion, and cardiovascular reactivity during marital interaction. *Health Psychology 17*, 6 (1998), 537-545.

41. Suh, B., Convertino, G., Chi, E.H., and Pirolli, P. The Singularity is Not Near: Slowing Growth of Wikipedia. *WikiSym*, (2009).

42. Suitor, J.J., Mecom, D., and Feld, I.S. Gender, household labor, and scholarly productivity among university professors. *Gender Issues 19*, 4 (2001), 50-67.

43. Valentine, P.E.B. Management of conflict: Do nurses/women handle it differently. *Journal of Advanced Nursing 22*, 1 (1995), 142-149.

44. Woolley, A.W., Chabris, C.F., Pentland, A., Hashmi, N., and Malone, T.W. Evidence for a Collective Intelligence Factor in the Performance of Human Groups. *Science*, (2010), 686-688.

45. Zickurh, K. Wikipedia, past and present. Pew Internet & American Life Project. 2011. http://pewinternet.org/Reports/2011/Wikipedia.aspx.

46. Zukerman, H. Persistence and change in the careers of men and women scientists and engineers: A review of current research. In L.S. Dix, ed., *Women: Their underrepresentation and career differentials in science and engineering*. National Academy Press, Washington, DC, 1987, 123-156.

47. Wikipedia: WikiProjects. http://en.wikipedia.org/wiki/Wikipedia:WikiProject.

48. Wikipedia: Arbitration Committee. http://en.wikipedia.org/wiki/Wikipedia:Arbitration_Committee .

49. Please Do Not Bite Newcomers. http://en.wikipedia.org/wiki/Wikipedia:Please_do_not_bite_the_newcomers.

50. Wikipedia is Not MySpace. http://en.wikipedia.org/wiki/Wikipedia:NOT#MYSPACE.

What Do You Think? The Structuring of an Online Community as a Collective-Sensemaking Process

Yiftach Nagar
MIT Sloan School of Management, MIT Center for Collective Intelligence
100 Main St., Cambridge, MA 02142 USA
ynagar@mit.edu

ABSTRACT

I observe conversations that take place as Wikipedia members negotiate, construct, and interpret its policies. Logs of these conversations offer a rare – perhaps unparalleled – opportunity to track how individuals, as they try to make sense, engage others in social interacts that become a collective processes of sensemaking. I draw upon Weick's model of sensemaking as committed-interpretation, which I ground in a qualitative inquiry into policy discussion pages, in attempt to explain how structuration emerges as interpretations are negotiated, and then committed through conversation, and as they are reified in the policy. I argue that the wiki environment provides conditions that help commitments form, strengthen and diffuse, and that this, in turn, helps explain trends of stabilization observed in previous research. The proposed model may prove useful for understanding structurational processes in other large wiki communities, and potentially in other radically open organizations.

Author Keywords

Sensemaking, structuration, distributed cognition, social cognition, Wikipedia, organization studies, organization theory, committed-interpretation, collective-intelligence

ACM Classification Keywords

K.4.3 Organizational Impacts: *Computer-supported collaborative work*.. H.5.3 Information Interfaces and Presentation: Group and Organization Interfaces – *Web-based interaction*. J.4 Social and Behavioral Sciences: Psychology.

General Terms

Human Factors; Management; Theory

"A dominant question for scholars of organizing is: How do people produce and acquire a sense of order that allows them to coordinate their actions in ways that have mutual relevance?" [27]

"Wikipedia did not arise spontaneously, it arose through people interacting and, as a result of that interaction, finding ways that worked." Interviewee 3 (I3) [10]

INTRODUCTION

How groups, organizations, communities and societies form and change over time has been a key subject of inquiry in the social sciences. The structurational perspective [1, 21] posits organizational transformation as endemic to the practice of organizing, embedded in, and emergent from the situated daily practices of organizational members – *"an ongoing improvisation enacted by organizational actors trying to make sense of and act coherently in the world"* [21]. In this paper, my goal is to track such efforts of sensemaking by people in one social system, to learn about how these efforts lead to structuring of the organization.

The organization chosen as the site for this inquiry is Wikipedia, for a number of reasons. The first is opportunistic: studying real social settings, 'in the wild' often entails spending relatively long periods of time in the field, especially for researchers who are interested in collecting micro-level data. Also, ethnographers and other social scientists who pursue micro-level data, are bound to miss a lot of what is going on, as they are limited, physically, to being at certain times and places. The discussion archives of Wikipedia provide us unique access to vast amounts of verbatim conversations among its members. Because most interactions among Wikipedians are done online and remain documented, we get to glimpse into Wikipedia's communal and organizational stream of consciousness. Second, the shape of social interaction inside many organizations is changing as interpersonal communications are gradually shifting weight to textual interactions over social-software platforms. Wikipedia is one extreme example, as interaction among its members is almost entirely public. It therefore not only provides opportunity to study micro-level interactions among members of *an* organization, but rather, to do so in web-based organization that is radically open and distributed.

Assuming more organizations in the future will share at least some of these qualities [16, 17] (even if to lesser extent in comparison to Wikipedia), it is interesting to learn about how they might work, and to see whether, and to what extent, theories developed to explain more traditional organizations hold, and what assumptions might need revision. Finally, Wikipedia in itself has drawn focus of a diverse community of researchers, and this study can enhance our knowledge of some aspects of its work – specifically, to highlight some processes through which parts of its structure are formed and transformed.

I therefore set out to explore the ongoing process of sensemaking Wikipedians conduct as they discuss, negotiate, construct and change one of its policies. As detailed later, I took a grounded approach to this qualitative inquiry, while leaning on ideas from Karl Weick's work on sensemaking in organizations [26, 27] in interpreting and explaining the findings.

BACKGROUND

The Role and Importance of Wikipedia's policies

Wikipedia's success (as measured by several parameters, including popularity, engagement, and quality of its articles) has surprised many skeptics, and has been widely discussed. Wikipedia has organically developed a complex bureaucracy, which includes an organizational structure, organizational processes, and many formal "objects", including policies, guidelines etc. Several researchers point to the important part policies, rules, and guidelines play in Wikipedia's daily operation and their contribution to its success [e.g. 3, 5, 7, 11, 15, 20, 24].

Policies deal with a wide range of contexts – from matters of content, to rules of proper conduct, to discussion of enforcement and more [cf. 3]. Thus, they help Wikipedians make sense of complex situations and serve as references to legitimize action [3, 15].

Policies are not merely prescriptive of social behavior. Wikipedia's policies and guidelines (and all other components of the bureaucracy) are developed by the community in attempt to capture and institutionalize best practices. What is considered best practice is a matter of consensual view, and it is expected that any proposed change should usually be discussed in advance "to ensure that the change reflects consensus"[1]. Thus, policies and guidelines are also reflective of social practice [see also 10].

The accounts discussed above have helped us gain insight into the role of policies in regulating ongoing activity in Wikipedia. What has been less discussed, however, is the *process* by which the bureaucracy emerged, and specifically, how the policies are formed and transformed. Forte and Bruckman [10] dedicate parts of their discussion of Wikipedia's distributed governance structure to the process of policy creation, but the theoretical lens guiding their inquiry is a sociological one, drawing on theories of commons-based governance, and accordingly, their focus is the organizational environment and setting rather than the cognitive processes and micro-level interactions that lead to the social construction of the policy. Elaborating a case study of the creation of one of Wikipedia's policies, they carefully examine at the "thick tangle of circumstance" that set the stage for the process of creation of what started as a guideline, and later became a policy, and summarize: *"Eventually, after much off- and on-wiki discussion about the situation, a proposal page was started and the community began constructing what was initially a proposed guideline. Eventually, the page reached a form acceptable to most community members"*. What they leave unexplained, when they write "Eventually" (twice!), is exactly this "much of- and on-wiki discussion about the situation" and the social process of construction of the proposed guideline until it "reached a form acceptable to most community members".

In this paper I take a close look at the discussions among Wikipedians as they struggle to make sense of their social reality and reach consensus. I posit these discussions as a collective process of sensemaking, and, drawing on Weick's concept of ***committed interpretation*** [27], propose a model of how social structures within Wikipedia might emerge from this process. Before discussing the research, I briefly introduce some ideas about sensemaking in organizations.

Sensemaking and Committed Interpretation in Organizations

The study of sensemaking in organizations has produced tremendous amounts of work, which cannot be reviewed here. For the purposes of this paper, it is useful to highlight just a few points regarding sensemaking that will provide a substrate for discussion.

What is the study of sensemaking in organizations? The following points are drawn, adapted, and synthesized mainly from Weick [26], and, due to limits of scope, are brought here only in summary form[2]. Three – interrelated – key questions for researchers of sensemaking in organizations are the following: *"How are microstabilities produced in the midst of continuing change? How do people produce and acquire a sense of order that allows them to coordinate their actions in ways that have mutual relevance?"* [27], and, *"how are meanings and artifacts produced and reproduced in complex nets of collective action?"* [9, cited in 26]. Sensemaking has to do with

[1] http://en.wikipedia.org/wiki/Wikipedia_policies, accessed 2010-5-15

[2] Interested readers would find a much more subtle, elaborate and nuanced discussion in Weick [26]. The discussion in chapters 1, 2, 6 and 7 is especially insightful and related to the ideas discussed here.

interpretation, of course, but interpretation is just one component of sensemaking, which is also concerned with the construction of reality. Sensemaking is enactive of sensible environments. What this means is that as people try to make sense of reality, they do more than trying to cope with entities that already exist in the world and interpret them: in organizational life, as people act, they create materials and settings which then become constraints and opportunities in the environment they face.

Sensemaking can take many forms and work in many ways. In this paper I use one prototype of sensemaking in organizations – *Committed Interpretation* – that is offered by Weick [27] as a possible answer to the first question mentioned above (and, which, I believe, helps deal with the other two questions as well). In concise form, *"The concept of committed interpretation suggests that people become bound to interacts*[3] *rather than acts, that the form of interacts is itself committing, and that justifications of commitment tend to invoke social rather than solitary entities. These three seeds of social order enlarge and diffuse among people through enactment, imitation, proselytizing, and reification, thereby imposing order on confusion"* [27]. In the following sections I elaborate this concept, ground it in data collected from policy discussion pages, and show it can help us understand and explain the processes of structuring of Wikipedia, beyond what was offered in previous accounts.

TRACKING THE ONGOING PROCESSES OF POLICY STRUCTURING

Method

I focused my inquiry on Wikipedia's "Neutral Point of View" policy (NPOV), which is one of its core content policies (arguably, the most fundamental), and one which has drawn a lot of attention, discussion and action, as I detail below. In a nutshell, this policy states: "Articles mustn't *take* sides, but should *explain* the sides, fairly and without bias. This applies to both what you say and how you say it". As Reagle [22] points out, "…in the Wikipedia culture, the notion of 'neutrality' is not understood so much as an end result, but as a process"[4], and this policy details parts of this process.

The centrality and importance of NPOV to Wikipedia and its special constitutional status are captured in the following remark by Wikipedia's co-founder and de-facto leader, Jimmy Wales, excerpted from a talk he gave in 2005:

"So how do we do this? […] how does it work? So there [are] a few elements, mostly social policies and some elements of the software. So the biggest and the most important thing is our neutral point of view policy. This is something that I set down from the very beginning, as a core principle of the community that's completely not debatable." [25]

It is no wonder, therefore, that this policy is highly visible and serves as reference in many discussions. Ironically, what was proposed as a simple, "completely not debatable" core principle is highly discussed even today, a decade after the founding of Wikipedia. While the rate and intensity of the discussion varies, it is yet to reach an asymptote or level, and it may possibly continue indefinitely. According to WikiChecker (http://en.wikichecker.com), between April 2006 and May 2010, more than 800 people have participated in the online discussion of the NPOV policy page itself (i.e. in the associated "talk" page), and performed about 9500 edits of that page. Note that these discussions are assumed to revolve mainly around issues of framing the policy itself, whereas discussions of interpretation related to enforcement of the written policy are supposed to take place elsewhere (mainly over the Neutral point of view Noticeboard and in administrator discussions). The policy itself has been edited over 4,500 times between February 2002 and November 2011 (more than once a day, on average), by more than 1700 people.

I focused my attention on a period ranging from July 2005 to January 29, 2006 (NPOV discussion archives 004 – 014), as that period has produced profuse discussion (11 archives for a period of 7 months, out of 37 archives for the period 2004 – February 2010). I coded about one quarter of those 11 archives, and also sporadically sampled some NPOV discussion pages from earlier and later periods. I started with line-by-line coding [8] which was relatively open at first, and then gradually moved to coding larger fragments in a more focused manner. With the goal of tracking individual and collective acts of interpretation, sensemaking, intelligizing and construction, informed mainly by discussions of sensemaking (Weick) and structuration (Barley, Orlikowski, and others), I looked for expressions of surprise, puzzle, questions, clarifications, agreement and disagreement, divergence and reconciliation, and other expressions that related to sensemaking and interpretation. I augmented this by coding additional pages of the discussion around Wikipedia's "Five pillars" page[5], and have reviewed several other auxiliary materials including interviews with Jimmy Wales, correspondence of Larry Sanger (co-founder of Wikipedia and its first community discussion leader), and many other online

---

[3] An *interact* occurs when an action by Person A evokes a specific action in Person B. If B's response evokes a response in A, a double interact exists, and so on.

[4] While I agree with Reagle that this is the original intent of Wikipedia's founders and its core elite, based on my observations I believe that not all editors understand this difference, or accept it. This discrepancy is one source of fuel for the continued discussion of NPOV.

[5] This is a relatively new page, which is an attempt to create a higher level framework – a constitution of core principles out of which other rules are derived. This page's necessity, its status, and its content have all been subject to debate.

resources, and also used tools e.g. Wikidashboard [23], and Wikichecker, that helped me navigate Wikipedia and make sense of what I see.

Committed Interpretation in Wikipedia

In this section I present a thick description of the processes of sensemaking I have observed, grounding the discussion of 'committed interpretation' in the data.

Committing to Interacts

Sensemaking, as most action, is inherently a social phenomenon. As people try to make sense, they interact with others, whether those others are present in the moment, or imagined, because people know their actions and explicit interpretations will have to be understood, accepted, and implemented by others. Therefore, Weick argues, when people become bound to acts, those acts tend to be interacts rather than solitary acts. Further, in social settings, actions that are public, irrevocable, and volitional are harder to undo and disown, and therefore, create commitment. Therefore, Weick concludes, "interacts themselves generate their own conditions of commitment since each party's action is public, irrevocable, and volitional relative to the other party in the exchange" [27].

In Wikipedia's discussion pages, every act – and therefore, also, every interact - is indeed public, irrevocable (as the history of edits, including that of discussion pages, is kept), and of course, volitional. The Wiki environment, as a medium for interaction, therefore provides conditions that serve as catalysts for turning such interacts to commitments, because each party's action is visible not only to the other party in the specific exchange, but to anyone (both inside and outside the community), for an indefinite time.

Interaction over the discussion pages takes form in various rhetorical acts. The main form I have observed involves posing questions and proposing answers.

Posing Questions

I have identified several archetypes of questions that people ask, including informative questions, provocative question, etc. Notably, editors ask a lot of questions in attempt to make sense of others' views. I coded those as follows:

1. Asking clarification question

For example: *Causa, why do you say there is no need for an introductory sentence? If we have no sentence and no tag (and it's unlikely that any of the standard tags fit this page, so tagging in this case effectively means putting the introductory sentence into a box), then people coming to this page won't know what its purpose or status is. Why would we want to add to the mystery here? (That's not to say someone might not improve the introductory sentence we currently have.)*

<<Kotniski (talk) 08:56, 7 November 2009 (UTC)

As seen in that quotation, clarification questions are often asked not only to understand an issue about the policy itself, but rather, in order to understand *what someone else thinks* about that issue. In these cases, the question may sometimes be explicitly addressed to a specific person (e.g. "Causa, " above), but many other times it is clear from the discussion that a dialog or a conversation develops organically between two or more people as in this example:

I agree with John that a "re-shuffle" of relative importance of policies and guidelines, as originally proposed by TMoW, is probably not the best way forward (note that I propose some "precedence-reshuffle" every once and a while myself, but that's a very slow moving process, best you know that)

--Francis Schonken 21:17, 9 October 2005 (UTC)

Thing is, some POVs aren't worth including at all. But how to distinguish? As for NOR[6], i mean prove your point on the talk page (with ext sources) to see if it worth including. This is what i mean by having a reliable claim before its elevated from "justanother-claim" to another "POV". As John says, there are lots of editors which include any ol' claim to maintain NPOV. And once you decide to include, then by what degree and how? I feel a clarification/specification would clear up a lot. Okay so we kind of agree. But now what?

--The Minister of War 05:54, 10 October 2005 (UTC)

Again, in this excerpt we see that the user named "The Minister of War" is interested in knowing what his peers think. Thus, implicitly, he (she?) does not perceive the policy as a "fixed object" that is "out there". Rather, the policy is viewed as what he and his peers decide that it is - what they *make* of it. Asking "But now what?" is an attempt to elicit a proposition for action, and to continue the conversation, by which the interact will become a double interact, etc., and commitments will grow.

2. Asking about behavior, trying to understand the rules

Such questions are usually asked by people not sure what to do in various cases. Technically, the policy discussion pages are not the 'right' place to do this. However, since the bureaucracy is so overwhelming, some people are just not sure where they should channel their questions. These are not "total newbies" usually, since those are not very likely to reach the policy discussion pages. Thus, although not 'appropriate', discussions about policy use and enforcement sometimes blend into the discussion about the policy construction.

Here are two examples:

---

[6] Wikipedia's policy on "No original research".

I found some questionable pov elements from an article on John Milius and added a check pov template and removed the questionable elements. There has not been any response on the talk page nor any further revisions. Do i take down the check pov template? how long do i have to wait?

-Seasee 22:10, 21 Jun 2005 (UTC)

Some articles use terms like "God", "white people", "luck", "Jewishness", "fairies", "nobility" that people have invented to support various religious/superstitious or political programs. If I don't believe any of this stuff do I have a POV? Should I insert "so-called" or "alleged" in front of these terms?

24.64.166.191 06:03, 9 Jun 2005 (UTC)

All these types of questions demonstrate difficulties in interpreting the meaning of the policy. What people are actually doing by asking them, is trying to make sense, and their way to try and make sense is to engage others in conversation.

Engaging others in conversation is not the only way to try and make sense. One could, for example, read more. Obviously, some people may prefer to read more in order to try to make sense, while others prefer to ask. Even if more people prefer to try other methods first, eventually, there are at least some people who pose opinions and questions on the policy discussion page. This engagement of others in the hermeneutic process is how the personal act of trying to make sense of things first becomes an interact (by asking a question, and receiving answer); and then, the interact becomes committing – as the person either accepts the answer (the simple case), or resists, which may lead, through a longer process, to a change. Individual attempts to make sense thus become a collective process of sensemaking. Through this process, participants (both active and "passive", i.e. those who read the conversation of others) gain a better understanding of what others think/feel, and of other facets of their environment (temporary and tentative as those may be), and interpretations are created, negotiated, modified and committed. The policy, then, is the manifestation of these commitments.

3. Asking questions as a rhetorical technique

A different class of questions comes up, which are part-question, part-suggestion. When editors wish to propose a change in the policy, they sometimes do it by posing a question. This is done in the spirit of Wikipedia which strives to achieve consensus, and so, before actually being bold and introducing the change, they ask others for their opinion. For example:

There are places in the Wikipedia namespace where advice and guidelines are offered (as distinct from policy), and while a majority of Wikipedians may support this advice, there may be examples where a significant minority disagree (I have in mind inclusionist/deletionist type dichotomies). In such cases, should the NPOV policy be read as to force the inclusion of strong minority positions (e.g. ~20% support) into pages that discuss Wikipedian behavior (e.g. Offer voting guides). Dragons flight 20:47, Jun 19, 2005 (UTC)

Asserting by asking is another way of using questions as a rhetorical "trick". The person asks a seemingly technical question about something perfunctory and at the same time makes a statement by taking something as fact. For example, the following question:

Where would it be appropriate to add a blurb about quotation marks being used as a form of bias?

is seemingly technical - but at the same time also states that quotation marks are a form of bias.

Rhetorical questions and provocative questions are also occasionally posed, to promote or challenge an ideology or point of view. Sometimes, this can trigger further discussion, as in this case:

According to Wikipedia founder Jimbo Wales, NPOV is "absolute and non-negotiable". How is this different from religious dogma? It seems to me NPOV is taken to absurd extremes by some self-important administrators too enamored of their little barnstar award trinkets. Not to mention it is overly sanitizing the pedia to where even a sense of humor becomes verboten, hence the need for the new admin award category: the award of the NPOV Nazi

(unsigned, undated)

Well, you do have to give some creedence to this argument. Whenever anything is taken to be an absolute, it opens the door for a person to manipulate that to their own ends. Let me give you an example: the Salem Witch Trials. All someone had to do was describe someone as a witch, and then they could freely assualt that person with no consequences. Well, isn't it possible (indeed, likely) that someone might take this sacred cow, NPOV, and accuse someone else of being not NOPV simply for the ability to attack them or their ideas free of consequences? Surely, there must be safeguards to protect those who are the unortunate victims of this sort of manipulation. May I ask what provisions you have thought of to prvent NPOV from becoming a tool for witchhunters?

Dave (undated)

But note: even though rhetorical questions are not directly looking for information, a rhetorical act is one whose purpose is to persuade others. In that, rhetorical questions, too, are a mechanism by which people attempt to engage other minds, offer and seek interpretations, and pursue common grounds.

Proposing Answers

By answering questions posed on the discussion pages, I find that Wikipedians are doing several things, beyond the sharing of 'dry' information:

1. Offering interpretation.

Often (and especially when discussing such a term like NPOV, which is loaded with ambiguity and possible interpretations), questions are not simple informative questions, but are posing principle challenges of interpretation. Questions and answers serve as mechanism for a social process of hermeneutics. Questions of interpretation come up in the discussions of people who actually enforce the policy (which I do not discuss here), but I also found some traces of these discussions in the policy discussion pages. Indeed, it is often difficult, and perhaps impossible, to agree on a common interpretation. This difficulty is evident in the vibrant discussion of NPOV, as evident both in many of the actual answers I have observed and in the numbers that point turbulent editing of the policy, and which can also be inferred from the following note of Butler et al. [7]:

While the "Ignore all rules" policy itself is only sixteen words long, the page explaining what the policy means contains over 500 words, refers readers to seven other documents, has generated over 8,000 words of discussion, and has been changed over 100 times in less than a year.

In this context, it appears that the concept of *committed* interpretation should be preferred over that of *shared* interpretations, or *shared* meanings, as it alludes to the *satisficing* character of the activity of people [see also 26 in that regard]. Meanings and interpretations are never shared by all the people, all the time, under all circumstances. They are always only temporarily shared, never in whole, never by all. But while it is not always possible to have shared interpretations, it is still possible to find common ground even without them, by finding such interpretations to which people can commit. These may at least allow action to proceed.

Similar observations are made by Brennan as she discusses grounding in conversations:

"Understanding is not the same as agreement or uptake. When speakers and addressees have incompatible intentions, they might understand one another perfectly well but 'agree to disagree'" [4]

"Grounding Is Only as Precise as it needs to be [...] people in conversation do not try to get their hypotheses to converge perfectly-in fact, since neither party is omniscient, this is not even feasible. Instead, they try to reach a level of convergence that is sufficient for current purposes, satisficing in Simon's (1981) terms. "[ibid.4]

Thus, it should be clear that committed interpretations are only temporary points of stability in space-time, sensitive to change in circumstances. As circumstances change, commitments can be revisited, and broken.

2. Explaining and signaling to others what they think is the answer to the question.

Because NPOV deals with such fundamental issues that touch epistemological and even ontological issues and eventually boil down to *beliefs*, answers serve not only to express an opinion. By *signaling* I mean that, eventually, whether formally or not, Wikipedians do hold tallies of voices. Consensus is a key value in Wikipedia, but majority voices are counted more than minority voices (in fact this is a part of NPOV itself). If more people support an opinion - even in a policy - this opinion is more likely to be represented. I found this sort of signaling in another type of contribution to the discussion which is not technically an "answer" and which I coded as "Seconding input from another member" or "supporting proposition". Sometimes people would write things like "I agree" or "I agree with X" or similar. Indeed, at some point in time a norm of stating one's opinion in one word – "Agree" or "Oppose" (or similar words) – followed by further explanation, has emerged in policy discussion pages. By doing so, people clearly indicate their commitment to the proposed interpretations.

3. Explaining to themselves.

The mere act of writing helps people construct their arguments. By choosing to answer, people engage in a committing interact. It is easy to envision a case where a person would answer a question, and then be dragged, against her/his will into a longer dialog, and indeed such cases appear frequently in the discussion pages (with some comments expressing weariness and loss of patience). But once the conversation has started, it is not easy to disengage from it, at least not without 'losing face'. When it comes to persuasion, disengaging may have a price that is higher than that of not engaging in conversation in the first place, as it may be perceived as "admitting" to being wrong, or to accepting a certain opinion with which the editor does not really agree.

Thus, the entire discussion - questions and answers, may lead, eventually, to the forming of new interpretations that lead to changes to the policy, or, in other cases, serve to and re-enact the policy.

Invoking Policies to Justify Commitment

As mentioned above, policies and guidelines help Wikipedians make sense of complex situations and they are widely used by Wikipedians as references to legitimize action [3, 15]. For example, Burio et al. [6, reported in 14] mention that the "3-revert-rule" policy which was introduced in response to a growing number of "edit-wars" (recurring reverts by two sides arguing) has had an immediate effect of decreasing occurrences of those "double reverts". As one Wikipedia editor noted:

"The degree of success that one meets in dealing with conflicts (especially conflicts with experience[d] editors) often depends on the efficiency with which one can quote policy and precedent." [14]

These findings are in accord with the third part of the definition of committed interpretation, namely that *justifications of commitment tend to invoke social rather than solitary entities*. My data collection focused on policy discussion pages, where the discussion mainly concerns the *construction* of the policy, rather than its *use*, and therefore references to policies seem to appear somewhat less frequently, but they certainly do appear, as do references to other social entities such as Wikipedia's Arbitration Committee (ArbCom)[7].

Beschastnikh et al. [3], find significant growth in policy citations over time. They also find that enforcement (as manifested in policy citations) has diffused into the larger body of registered users, with the practice of policy citation increasingly becoming commonplace. Similarly, Butler et al. [7] and Forte et al. [12], note that over time making changes in the policies has become more difficult, and has slowed. Weick's conceptualization of the process of committed interpretation helps explain for these observed phenomena as well as it argues that what he recognizes as the "three seeds of social order" (namely: *that people become bound to interacts rather than acts, that the form of interacts is itself committing, and that justifications of commitment tend to invoke social rather than solitary entities*), "*enlarge and diffuse among people through enactment, imitation, proselytizing, and reification, thereby imposing order on confusion*". Invoking policies (and other parts of the bureaucracy) in the discussion as a means to justify commitment serves to reinforce them. As policies are enacted by administrators, and invoked as justifications in discussion, they become reified, and commitments grow. This creates a positive feedback loop, where enactment and reification of the policy feed each other.

As this "evolutionary" process makes changes to the policy rarer, editors redirect their efforts to creating and updating less formal parts of the bureaucracy, such as guidelines and essays [20].

The Seeds of Change

Weick asks how people produce and acquire a sense of order that allows them to coordinate their actions in ways that have mutual relevance. His answer is: by concrete communicative interaction in which people invoke macro structures to justify commitments. He concludes:

"Thus, social order is created continuously as people make commitments and develop valid, socially acceptable justifications for these commitments. Phrased in this way, individual sensemaking has the potential to be transformed into social structures and to maintain these structures. Commitment is one means by which social structure is realized. This proposal suggests a possible mechanism by which structuration (e.g., Barley, 1986; Giddens, 1984) actually works."

Indeed, the story I told so far, is mainly a story of regulation and creation of stability. But what about organizational change?

Structuration theory offers a dialectical, reciprocal account of social change, and has been adopted and adapted by organizational researchers to explain organizational change. It posits that social structures enable and constrain the actions of agents, and yet, do not determine their actions. Several notable works have tracked structuration processes following an external 'shock' such as the introduction of new technologies [1, 21], or new regulations [13] into an organization. Although in all these works change starts with an external shock, Orlikowski highlights the notion of change as an ongoing improvisation and quotes from March that "in its fundamental structure a theory of organizational change should not be remarkably different from a theory of ordinary action" [18, quoted in 21]. She further locates the beginning of the change process in the attempt of people to make sense of *a new situation*.

Obviously, when a big, external shock is introduced, it is not surprising that people try to make sense of it. But, excluding external shocks, what causes a new situation during 'ordinary action'? and how, exactly, are people attempting to make sense?

As seen in Wikipedia's policy discussion pages, collective-sensemaking can also start with a single person reviewing or reflecting previous understandings without any evident external trigger.

In Wikipedia, every newcomer may introduce an 'occasion' to discuss and negotiate meaning. This might be somewhat different in traditional organizations. There, if a newcomer does not understand something as s/he tries to make sense of 'what's going on' – the rules, the culture, the norms, s/he will likely ask a few people who are close (by rank, by geography, by departmental affiliation, by situated interaction). If that newcomer has other ideas, philosophies, and thoughts about values, and about how things should work, he/she might reserve those to him- or herself, so as not to lose status. If they are expressed, chances are they will not make a lot of 'waves', as this newcomer is not yet well connected. Therefore, chances that the existing order-of-things will be challenged are low. But newcomers to Wikipedia are slightly different. While status does play a role in Wikipedia, it probably has lesser implications on one's life overall, compared to member status in traditional organizations (where it can have significant effects people's social life and financial situation). And, importantly, whatever is said on the policy discussion page can be seen by the entire community. Thus, simply dismissing someone just because s/he is new, without reasoning, while perhaps possible, is more problematic.

[7] The ArbCom is "a panel of editors that imposes binding rulings with regard to disputes between other editors". See http://en.wikipedia.org/wiki/Arbitration_Committee_(English_Wikipedia)

So the process might just start with a new person who lacks knowledge about previous understandings, or an editor who decides to challenge the status quo. In either case, a change process may begin with just one small question, and an answer. What starts with a cognitive puzzle, turns into an act (asking a question), which really is already an attempted interact with others (who at first may be assumed, or imagined); which then turns into an interact when they answer, and may, to the extent the conversation evolves, become a seed of a structurational process. Observing the online discussions through a collective-sensemaking lens can therefore extend our understanding of how changes to the policy (and then, to the organization) originate and develop from individual attempts to make sense. Through conversation, cognitive efforts turn from individual to social, and commitments are formed and reified in the shape of policy text.

Citing March, Schulz, & Zhou [19], Butler et al. note that *"Because they are explicit and visible... written policies and rules are often sites of conflict" [ibid7]*. They further note that due to these characteristics (visibility, clear boundaries) written policies have greater potential as levers for stakeholders to affect the community, or in other words, to initiate change [ibid7]. Indeed, conflict is evident in many of Wikipedia's policy talk pages which I have reviewed. Yet the discussions I have read reflect different types of conflict – of interest, of world view and of interpretation. Therefore I find the following quote from Barley [2, brought in 21] more subtle and accurate in describing how policies can be sites in which, and around which, interpretation and negotiation take place:

> *". . . Because forms of action and interaction are always negotiated and confirmed as actors with different interests and interpretations encounter shifting events (. . .), slippage between institutional templates and the actualities of daily life is probable. In such slippage resides the possibility of social innovation. "*

I would even go further and say this: based on my observations so far, *tensions* between the "organizational templates", i.e. the policies, rules, guidelines and templates of Wikipedia and the "actualities of life" in Wikipedia are not only *probable*, but rather, *constantly present*. The case study of the creation of the "Biographies of Living Persons" policy, as depicted by Forte and Bruckman [10] provides an example of several such gaps and tensions that formed between Wikipedia's organizational templates and the actualities of life at a certain period. Accumulation of several such tensions was the trigger that drove efforts, acts and interacts of interpretation and sensemaking, which in that particular case initiated an organizational change in the form of the creation of a policy. In other cases, similar efforts often end in reinforcing existing structures.

CONCLUSION

Wikipedia's discussion pages provide a unique opportunity for micro-level organizational inquiry. These pages, powered by MediaWiki software, have two unique properties (when juxtaposed with discussions that take place in traditional organizations, or with private discussions in other online communication channels): One, they are publically visible, and two, they endure.

For organization members, not only do these pages facilitate conversation – they also accelerate the speed with which people can engage in it, the number of people who can take part in it, and its potential impact (both the immediate impact, and long-term one). For researchers, this allows unparalleled access to huge volumes of organizational discussion.

I was able to track how individual sensemaking efforts turn into interacts, using a mechanism of questions and answers over online discussion pages. People thus engage in a collective sensemaking process. I offer that a prototype of sensemaking - *committed interpretation* [27] can help us understand collective sensemaking processes in Wikipedia, and account for structurational activity that includes the construction of social structures; their ongoing transformation over time; and some trends of stabilization over time.

Interacts between people often become binding, and Wikipedia's discussion environment is especially conducive for creating social commitments, because participation in interaction is volitional, and because discussion pages remain publicly accessible.

While people do not always share meanings and interpretations, they can – and do – achieve temporary, partial interpretations that satisfice their needs, and to which they can commit. Those then become reified on the official policy page, and they stay so, so long as no challenger has managed to convince the majority of those who care that they need to be changed or removed.

This paper makes several contributions to the literatures of organizational studies, computer-supported-collaborative work, and Wikipedia.

To the literature of organizational science (in particular, sensemaking) it contributes an empirical account that grounds the idea of committed interpretation, which I believe to be the first that does so in a radically distributed, open, web-based organization. Weick notes that *"We already know that many current ideas about sensemaking assume vertical hierarchies (e.g. uncertainty is absorbed as communications flow upward). What we need to know is what happens to sensemaking when this assumption is replaced by the assumption that structuring unfolds laterally, more like the networks of conversation Winograd and Flores mentioned?"* [26].

At least in the case I have analyzed, the process model of committed interpretation seems to hold, and I found it helpful for understanding and explaining the phenomena. In fact, as discussed above, the wiki environment amplifies the publicity and irrevocability of volitional interacts, and thus intensifies the process of turning them to commitments. Therefore, it seems plausible that the model would hold for other wiki-based communities. As organizations gradually adopt social software platforms, widely-visible and virtually-permanently accessible communications are likely to become more prevalent, and there is reason therefore to believe that the model presented here will be useful for understanding them as well.

By tracking this collective sensemaking process, I was also able to offer how links are formed between individual and social cognitions, and provide empirical evidence of the way committed interpretation and collective sensemaking relate to structuration.

To the literature of Wikipedia in particular, and to CSCW in general, this paper contributes a sensemaking perspective on the processes of structuring of Wikipedia's bureaucracy, and a process model of regulation and change, based on the conceptual model of committed-interpretation. This modeling helps us propose explanation for structurational activity that includes several, seemingly unrelated phenomena, including the growth in policy citation counts over time [3], and the process of how social structures (e.g. policies) get enacted and changed within Wikipedia.

I believe this perspective of collective-sensemaking, and the concept of committed-interpretation should prove useful for studying structurational process in other related settings including heavily distributed organizations and online communities.

ACKNOWLEDGMENTS

My sincere thanks go to Susan Silbey, Lotte Bailyn and students in their doctoral seminars at MIT who provided constructive feedback in the early stages of this work; to the CSCW coordinator and three anonymous reviewers for detailed and constructive feedback on two earlier revisions of this paper; and to Rob Laubacher, Wanda Orlikowski and Stephanie Woerner for their valuable comments on the final draft. Any remaining flaws are, of course, due only to me. I am indebted to my advisor, Tom Malone for allowing and supporting my academic freedom. I am also grateful to MIT Sloan, the Duwayne J. Peterson, Jr. Fund, the MIT Center for Collective Intelligence and the U.S. Army Research Laboratory's Army Research Office (ARO) for financial support.

REFERENCES

1. Barley, S.R. Technology as an occasion for structuring: evidence from observations of CT scanners and the social order of radiology departments. *Administrative Science Quarterly*, *31* (1), 78-108.
2. Barley, S.R. Technology, Power, and the Social Organization of Work: Towards a Pragmatic Theory of Skilling and Deskilling. *Research in the Sociology of Organizations*, *6*, 33-80.
3. Beschastnikh, I., Kriplean, T. and McDonald, D.W., Wikipedian self-governance in action: Motivating the policy lens. in *International Conference on Weblogs and Social Media (ICWSM)*, (2008), AAAI.
4. Brennan, S.E. How Conversation Is Shaped by Visual and Spoken Evidence. in Trueswell, J.C. and Tanenhaus, M.K. eds. *Approaches to studying world-situated language use: Bridging the Language-as-Product and Language-as-Action traditions*, MIT Press, Cambridge, MA, 2005, 95-129.
5. Bryant, S.L., Forte, A. and Bruckman, A., Becoming Wikipedian: transformation of participation in a collaborative online encyclopedia. in *GROUP International Conference on Supporting Group Work*, (Sanibel Island, FL, USA, 2005), ACM, 1-10.
6. Buriol, L., Castillo, C., Donato, D., Leonardi, S. and Millozzi, S., Temporal evolution of the wikigraph. in *Web Intelligence Conference* (2006), IEEE CS Press, 45–51.
7. Butler, B., Joyce, E. and Pike, J., Don't look now, but we've created a bureaucracy: the nature and roles of policies and rules in wikipedia. in *Twenty-sixth annual SIGCHI conference on Human factors in computing systems (Session: Shared Authoring)*, (Florence, Italy, 2008), ACM, 1101-1110.
8. Charmaz, K. *Constructing Grounded Theory: A Practical Guide Through Qualitative Analysis*. Sage, 2006.
9. Czarniawska-Joerges, B. *Exploring Complex Organizations: A Cultural Perspective*. Sage Publications, Inc, 1992.
10. Forte, A. and Bruckman, A., Scaling consensus: increasing decentralization in Wikipedia governance. in *Hawaiian International Conference of Systems Sciences (HICSS)*, (Hawaii, 2008), IEEE Computer Society, 157.
11. Forte, A. and Bruckman, A., Why do people write for Wikipedia? Incentives to contribute to open. in *GROUP 05 workshop: Sustaining community: The role and design of incentive mechanisms in online systems.* , (Sanibel Island, FL, USA, 2005).
12. Forte, A., Larco, V. and Bruckman, A. Decentralization in Wikipedia Governance. *Journal of Management Information Systems*, *26* (1), 49-72.
13. Kellogg, K.C. Operating Room: Relational Spaces and Micro-Institutional Change in Surgery. *American Journal of Sociology*, *15* (3).
14. Kittur, A., Suh, B., Pendleton, B.A. and Chi, E.H., He says, she says: Conflict and coordination in Wikipedia. in *Twenty fifth SIGCHI conference on Human factors in computing systems (CHI '07)*, (2007), ACM, 453-462.

15. Kriplean, T., Beschastnikh, I., McDonald, D.W. and Golder, S.A., Community, consensus, coercion, control: cs* w or how policy mediates mass participation. in *Conference on Supporting Group Work*, (2007), ACM, 167-176.

16. Malone, T.W. *The Future of Work: How the New Order of Business Will Shape Your Organization, Your Management Style, and Your Life*. Harvard Business School Press, Boston, MA, 2004.

17. Malone, T.W., Laubacher, R. and Morton, M.S.S. *Inventing the Organizations of the 21st Century*. The MIT Press, 2003.

18. March, J.G. Footnotes to organizational change. *Administrative Science Quarterly*, *26* (4), 563-577.

19. March, J.G., Schulz, M. and Zhou, X. *The dynamics of rules: Change in written organizational codes*. Stanford Univ Presss, 2000.

20. Morgan, J.T. and Zachry, M., Negotiating with angry mastodons: the wikipedia policy environment as genre ecology. in *16th ACM international conference on Supporting group work (GROUP '10)*, (New York, NY, USA, 2010), ACM, 165-168.

21. Orlikowski, W.J. Improvising Organizational Transformation Over Time: A Situated Change Perspective. *Information Systems Research*, *7* (1), 63-92.

22. Reagle, J. Is the Wikipedia Neutral. 2005. Retrieved May 13, 2010, from http://reagle.org/joseph/2005/06/neutrality.html

23. Suh, B., Chi, E.H., Kittur, A. and Pendleton, B.A., Lifting the veil: improving accountability and social transparency in Wikipedia with wikidashboard. in *Twenty-sixth annual SIGCHI conference on Human factors in computing systems (CHI '08)*, (2008), ACM, 1037-1040.

24. Viégas, F., Wattenberg, M. and McKeon, M., The hidden order of Wikipedia. in *OCSC 2007 - Online Communities and Social Computing: second international conference, held as part of HCI International*, (Beijing, China, 2007), Springer, 445-454.

25. Wales, J. Jimmy Wales on the birth of Wikipedia. Video of talk at the TED conference, Monterey, CA, USA July, 2005. Retrieved May 17, 2010, from http://www.ted.com/talks/lang/eng/jimmy_wales_on_the_birth_of_wikipedia.html

26. Weick, K.E. *Sensemaking in organizations*. Sage, 1995.

27. Weick, K.E. Sensemaking in organizations: Small structures with large consequences. in Murnighan, J.K. ed. *Social psychology in organizations: Advances in theory and research*, Prentice Hall College Division, 1993, 10-37.

Classroom Wikipedia Participation Effects on Future Intentions to Contribute

Cliff Lampe
University of Michigan
4388 North Quad
Ann Arbor, MI 48109
cacl@umich.edu

Jonathan Obar, Elif Ozkaya, Paul Zube, Alcides Velasquez
409 CommArts Building
East Lansing, MI 48824
{obar, yilmaze2, zubepaul, velasq24}@msu.edu

ABSTRACT
One of the biggest challenges faced by social media sites like Wikipedia is how to motivate users to contribute content. Research continues to demonstrate that only a small percentage of users contribute to user-generated content sites. In this study we assess the results of a Wikimedia Foundation initiative, which had graduate and undergraduate students from 22 U.S. universities contribute content to Wikipedia articles as part of their coursework. 185 students were asked about their participation in the initiative and their intention to participate on Wikipedia in the future. Results suggest that intentions to continue contributing are influenced by the initial attitude towards the class, and the degree to which students perceived they were writing for a global audience.

Author Keywords
Wikipedia, CSCL, participation, efficacy

ACM Classification Keywords
H.5.3. Information interfaces and presentation (e.g., HCI): Group and Organization Interfaces.

General Terms
Human Factors; Measurement.

INTRODUCTION
In May 2010, with a $1.2 million grant from the Stanton Foundation [1], the Wikimedia Foundation launched the Wikipedia Public Policy Initiative (WPPI). The initiative has been an attempt to work with policy classes at American universities to increase the quantity and quality of Wikipedia's public policy-related articles, and to create more advocates of Wikipedia in the university community.

Given the reports of drop-offs in edits to most language versions of Wikipedia over the past several years [7, 11], one goal of this initiative has been to increase the propensity of university students to contribute original content to Wikipedia by making contributions part of their regular course activity. However, it is unclear if Wikipedia contribution tied to compulsory course assignments leads to either intention to participate in Wikipedia in the future, or actual contribution. Understanding students' perceptions of the Wikipedia course work is a necessary precursor to knowing whether initiatives like the WPPI can lead to increased participation in online collaborative projects like Wikipedia. We present results of a survey of 185 university students who participated in the initiative this past spring. We report on their impressions of the activity and intentions for future contributions.

CSCW'12, February 11–15, 2012, Seattle, Washington, USA.

LITERATURE REVIEW
As with many other user-generated content systems, a small percentage of users provide the majority of the content on Wikipedia [3, 9]. Given this phenomenon, combined with the decrease in new user edits identified above, there is a need by Wikipedia to find new ways to encourage user contributions. One method to broaden the base of Wikipedia editors is the use of classroom exercises to introduce potential contributors. Moy, Locke, Coppola, and McNeil [6] surveyed 540 chemistry students enrolled in courses to improve Wikipedia articles for classroom purposes. These students were asked to evaluate different information sources and classroom practices for accomplishing learning objectives. Wikipedia, as opposed to more traditional information sources, was ranked highest for communicating science to a general audience, identifying resources for building an argument, and for encouraging collaborative work. More broadly, Wikis as a general tool have been used in classrooms for strictly pedagogical purposes

Feedback from community-future contribution intention
Previous researchers have examined how to encourage users to participate in peer production sites like Wikipedia. Ling et al [5] used social science theories to encourage different types of contribution, finding it was difficult to closely match theories to design outcomes. Lampe and Johnston [4] looked at how feedback users receive on initial contributions affects continued contribution on the news site Slashdot. Priedhorsky et al [10] used prompts for familiarity and visually highlighting needed work in a

geographic wiki to increase participation, though this was for users who were already aware of the site.

Encouraging new participation on Wikipedia involves the combined issues of encouraging a potential contributor to submit their content, and learning how to make that contribution. Addressing these problems was one of the goals of the Wikipedia Public Policy Initiative.

WIKIPEDIA PUBLIC POLICY INITIATIVE (WPPI)

The Wikimedia Foundation (WMF) is the non-profit organization that operates Wikipedia, among other projects. After launching the WPPI in May 2010, WMF began working with 12 classes at 9 U.S. universities in the fall. The following spring, the numbers increased to 22 U.S. universities, 33 courses with more than 500 students participating in total. The WPPI is unique as it is "the first time the Wikimedia Foundation has launched a project designed to systematically increase the quality of articles in a particular topic area." [1] In addition to improving Wikipedia articles, the WPPI was also an attempt to train future Wikipedians and to create more advocates of Wikipedia in the university community.

With support from the Foundation's outreach team and local campus ambassadors (students and university staff trained to be liaisons between the WMF and the university), professors that had volunteered to take part in the Initiative replaced their course's traditional research assignments with the Wikipedia project. As the size, structure and content of each course varied, so too did the method for implementing the project. As students completed the individual Wikipedia contribution assignments designed by their professors, they were mentored by campus and online ambassadors. In addition, students received contribution mentoring from their professors, who were trained by WMF before the semester began.

One 94-student undergraduate class broke students into groups and required that work be completed outside of class-time; smaller graduate classes had students work individually and in-class. What all classes shared in common was the requirement that students research and contribute material to public-policy articles on Wikipedia.

METHODS

An online survey was made available on the SurveyGizmo website, and the link was distributed via email to professors, most of whom forwarded the link to their WPPI student participants. The survey was administrated over a period of 20 days beginning at April 25th, 2011. There were no material incentives for taking part in this study.

As some professors did not forward the link, 463 students out of approximately 600 participating in the WPPI (some graduate some undergraduate) received the survey request. A total of 185 participants completed an online survey about their impressions of the project, yielding a response rate of 40%. Participants ranged in age from 18 to 58 years old with an average age of 24.22 (s.d.= 6.35). Males comprised 53% of the participants, providing a relatively even distribution among participants. English as the first language was also collected to control for different levels of participation based on English language skills. Participants were primarily native English speakers (87%).

Measures

In addition to questions regarding their demographic backgrounds described above, participants were asked to evaluate their experience with the Wikipedia project. Preference for a more traditional course research assignment was measured as a "yes/no" item (Yes=23.8%, No=76.2%). The remaining variables; awareness of global visibility, social media exposure, and future Wikipedia contribution likelihood, were measured using multiple 5-item Likert questions. Each variable was constructed as an additive index and was reliable using Cronbach's alpha as the reliability metric (see Table 1).

Three open-ended follow up questions "Why did you answer yes/no to the previous question?", "What did you like about the Wikipedia project?" and "In terms of the Wikipedia project, what could have been done better?" were used to determine what course factors contributed to future Wikipedia contribution. These responses were analyzed by having two investigators review responses, developing a framework of response categories, and then aligning their interpretation of responses across categories.

QUANTITATIVE ANALYSIS OF SURVEY RESULTS

An ordinary least squares (OLS) regression, presented in Table 1, was performed in order to find the direction, size, and statistical significance of the effect of the independent and control variables on students' perceived likelihood of contributing in the future to Wikipedia.

	Stzd Beta coefficient	Sig.
Intercept		.027
Age	.229	.001
Male	.094	.141
English non-native speaker	-.188	.003
Level of engagement in class	.224	.002
Prefers traditional assignment	-.136	.043
Global visibility awareness α=0.78, mean=3.89, s.d.=0.74	.233	.001
Social media exposure α =0.74, mean=3.07, s.d.=0.90	.177	.010
R^2	.324	

Table 1: Influences on perceived likelihood of future contribution to Wikipedia (α =0.86, mean=3.19, s.d.=0.73)

The first three independent variables describe demographic characteristics of the population. Among those, participants who reported they were not native English speakers were less likely to believe they would contribute to the site in the future. Although participants were asked about the likelihood they would contribute to Wikipedia in the future, without mention of any language in particular, it is possible that respondents were primed to think about the specific articles they participated on for the class, which were all in English.

As the level of reported class engagement increased, the likelihood of perceived contribution to Wikipedia in the future increased as well. The magnitude of the effect of this variable is large compared to the rest of the variables. In this sense, it can be argued that the level of engagement in the class influences how likely it is that a student will intend to continue contributing to the site. In the same vein, whether students preferred a more traditional assignment in class instead of having the Wikipedia project as part of the course influenced their perceived likelihood of contributing to the site in the future. Those who did not prefer having this project as part of the class reported that they were less likely to contribute in the future, and this difference was statistically significant. Both the size and the direction of the effect of these two variables highlights the importance of identifying effective strategies that would make students more interested in the contents and activities planned in the courses.

Global visibility awareness, which measured the perception that the information they provided was open and accessible to a large audience on the Internet, is a factor that is associated with higher reported likelihood to contribute in the future. As the awareness that the information added to Wikipedia was visible to a global audience increased, the likelihood of contributing to Wikipedia increased as well.

We also included measures of social media use, which we operationalized as the reported frequency of reading and viewing the content of different social media applications. Results indicated that the exposure to social media sites increases the intentions to contribute to Wikipedia. Probably those students that are more exposed to other individuals posting different types of content to social media sites learn this specific kind of behavior, seeing it as a common norm among social media users, increasing their attitude towards contributing to these types of sites.

OPEN-ENDED RESPONSES TO SURVEY QUESTIONS

Of the 185 total participants, approximately 72% of them would **not** have preferred a more traditional class. The perceived benefits of participating in such a project among those that fell into this group can be grouped into several categories. First, some believed that this kind of class work provided them with the opportunity of having a novel experience that allowed them to work on their writings skills. As written by one of the respondents: "…it was important to try a different style of writing and accepting feedback". Responses suggested that using Wikipedia as a course project provided a greater degree of creativity in their writing style than they would have had otherwise. Having to think about a broader audience and receiving feedback from multiple sources demanded the use of more writing skills than writing "traditional essays" that would "have only be seen by the professor". Second, participants valued the learning opportunity related to technology use that engagement with Wikipedia provided. Several participants noted that in addition to learning course content, interacting with Wikipedia provided an opportunity to learn certain skills they otherwise might not have had an opportunity to learn in a course setting. Respondents highlighted the importance of learning about the online publishing and editing process in a "real" site; and familiarize themselves with all the work that takes place when contributing to a Wiki.

Two themes that emerged from the open-ended responses of participants that valued the course over a more traditional classroom experience, do have more direct implications for future Wikipedia participation: a global audience and interaction with non-class editors on Wikipedia. Participant responses suggested that those that enjoyed this format of class had a strong awareness of the global nature of Wikipedia and appreciated their role in it. Several responses touched on the theme of the importance of information being made publicly available, as opposed to instructor eyes only whom may have no specific interest in that topic. Making their assignment public, however, gave these participants a sense of doing something useful beyond their traditional course work fulfillment. Additionally, students were interested in the opportunity to receive feedback on their work from someone outside of the classroom context. Although some expressed concerns about negative feedback from other users outside of the class, generally participants valued the information provided by others. Participants enjoyed interacting with others in the perceived global Internet audience. The greater sense of purpose and social interactivity seem highly related to perceptions of future contributions to Wikipedia.

Among participants who did not prefer the Wikipedia pedagogical exercise, two themes of particular interest emerged. First, these participants had concerns about expertise. Citing hypothetical situations these participants expressed a commonly held concern about less knowledgeable others editing well-researched content. Whereas their "pro-course" counterparts enjoyed the open edit culture of Wikipedia, these participants saw such a structure as a potential threat to quality articles. A related theme, user control, was also expressed. These participants were uncomfortable with the concept that others could come in and change their work. Regardless of quality of work changes, these participants were simply uncomfortable with the lack of control over their content. Additionally, several participants struggled to understand the formatting structure and technical skills necessary to contribute to Wikipedia. While this was a component of the course, its relevance may have been muddied due to several competing course foci.

WIKIPEDIA PARTICIPATION POST-CLASS

Of the 615 students who edited Wikipedia as part of the WPPI, 25 had edited Wikipedia after their class ended. While this is a modest number, it's a much better conversion rate than usual for people who make one edit to the site. Panciera et al [8] show that rates of return for normal Wikipedia contributors is quite low, with only 0.0002% of users who make one edit becoming regular editors. With this ratio in mind, this exercise did seem to have fair conversion ate. Given that only a few months had passed between the class ending and the construction of this report, we don't know about long term patterns for those users, or whether other students decided after the summer to edit Wikipedia again. We also cannot track any contributions that might have been made anonymously.

DISCUSSION

In assessing whether class projects like the WPPI can be a method for introducing users to participation in complex peer production websites like Wikipedia, we see issues of audience, efficacy, and control affecting outcomes. We found that issues like language familiarity and technical efficacy affect how engaged students were with this type of exercise. Students needed to feel confident in their ability to participate to anticipate future participation. This finding is likely general for all potential contributors to Wikipedia.

Other users had mixed effects on intention to contribute in the future. Some students were motivated by the large potential audience for their work, while others worried that other contributors could overwrite their work. This discrepancy could be related to inherent factors in the student, differences in efficacy beliefs regarding their own capabilities to edit other users' work, or in different mental models for audiences vs. collaborators.

Course satisfaction was related to intention to contribute in the future, though as with all results, no causal claim can be made about this relationship. It could be that external factors like class size, effectiveness on the instructor, or level of the course can affect how effective this strategy is for encouraging future participation in sites like Wikipedia. Following the class, some students did continue to post to Wikipedia. These students had not been posting before, so for at least some students the classroom exercise did seem to lead to future Wikipedia participation.

This study depended largely on self-reports of behavior, which may differ from actual behavior. Future work in this vein should include a pre-post design to increase the ability to measure attitude change.

CONCLUSION

We found that future Wikipedia contribution can be encouraged through exposure in a classroom setting. Although some of the elements associated with future Wikipedia contribution may have been preexisting, these elements can be encouraged in a classroom environment. As Wikipedia and other Web technologies open to the general Internet public become incorporated into the educational experience, opportunities exist to encourage Internet community engagement, participation, and appreciation.

ACKNOWLEDGMENTS

We thank the Wikimedia Foundation for their efforts in including classrooms in the Wikipedia effort. This work was partially supported by NSF grant IIS-HCC-0812429.

REFERENCES

1. Wikimedia Foundation Public Policy Initiative. http://outreach.wikimedia.org/wiki/Public_Policy_Initiative, 2011.
2. Forte, A. and Bruckman, A. Citing, Writing and Participatory Media: Writing, Citing, and Participatory Media: Wikis as Learning Environments in the High School Classroom. *International Journal of Learning and Media.*, *1* (4).
3. Kittur, A., Suh, B., Pendleton, B.A. and Chi, E.H., He Says, She Says: Conflict and Coordination in Wikipedia. in *Human Factors in Computing Systems*, (San Jose, CA, 2007), ACM Press, 453-462.
4. Lampe, C. and Johnston, E., Follow the (Slash) dot: Effects of Feedback on New Members in an Online Community. in *Proc. GROUP '05*, (Sanibel Island, FL, 2005), ACM Press.
5. Ling, K., Beenen, G., Ludford, P., Wang, X., Chang, K., Li, X., Cosley, D., Frankowski, D., Terveen, L., Rashid, A.M., Resnick, P. and Kraut, R. Using social psychology to motivate contributions to online communities. *Journal of Computer-Mediated Communication*, *10* (4).
6. Moy, C.L., Locke, J.R., Coppola, B.P. and McNeil, A.H. Improving Science Education and Understanding through Editing Wikipedia. *Journal of Chemical Education*, *87* (11). 1159-1162.
7. Ortega, F. Wikipedia: A quantitative Analysis *GSyC/Libresoft*, Unversidad Rey Juan Carlos, Madrid, Spain, 2009.
8. Panciera, K., Halfaker, A. and Terveen, L. Wikipedians are born, not made: a study of power editors on Wikipedia *Proc. Group 09*, Sanibel Island, Florida, USA, 2009, 51-60.
9. Priedhorsky, R., Chen, J., Lam, S.K., Panciera, K., Terveen, L. and Riedl, J., Creating, destroying, and restoring value in wikipedia. in *Proc. Group 07*, (Sanibel Island, Florida, USA, 2007), ACM.
10. Priedhorsky, R., Masil, M. and Loren, T., Eliciting and Focusing Geographic Volunteer Work. in *2010 Conference on Computer Supported Cooperative Work*, (Savannah, GA, 2010), ACM Press.
11. Suh, B., Convertino, G., Chi, E.H. and Pirolli, P. The singularity is not near: slowing growth of Wikipedia *Proceedings of WikiSym 09*, ACM, Orlando, Florida, 2009.

Effectiveness of Shared Leadership in Online Communities

Haiyi Zhu, Robert Kraut, Aniket Kittur
Carnegie Mellon University
5000 Forbes Avenue, Pittsburgh, PA15213
{haiyiz, robert.kraut, nkittur}@cs.cmu.edu

ABSTRACT
Traditional research on leadership in online communities has consistently focused on the small set of people occupying leadership roles. In this paper, we use a model of shared leadership, which posits that leadership behaviors come from members at all levels, not simply from people in high-level leadership positions. Although every member can exhibit some leadership behavior, different types of leadership behavior performed by different types of leaders may not be equally effective. This paper investigates how distinct types of leadership behaviors (transactional, aversive, directive and person-focused) and the legitimacy of the people who deliver them (people in formal leadership positions or not) influence the contributions that other participants make in the context of Wikipedia. After using propensity score matching to control for potential pre-existing differences among those who were and were not targets of leadership behaviors, we found that 1) leadership behaviors performed by members at all levels significantly influenced other members' motivation; 2) transactional leadership and person-focused leadership were effective in motivating others to contribute more, whereas aversive leadership decreased other contributors' motivations; and 3) legitimate leaders were in general more influential than regular peer leaders. We discuss the theoretical and practical implication of our work.

Author Keywords
Shared leadership, online communities, Wikipedia, motivation

ACM Classification Keywords
H.5.3 [Information Interfaces and Presentation]: Group and Organization Interfaces – Collaborative computing, Computer-supported cooperative work, Web-based interaction; K.4.3 [Computers and Society]: Organizational Impacts – Computer supported collaborative work.

INTRODUCTION
Who are the leaders in online communities? Previous researchers tend to use traditional vertical leadership models [2,15] to explain leadership in online communities. They suggest that the leadership role is a specialized one. People who are appointed or elected to perform this role are designated as "leaders" [29, 6, 20]. According to this view, some of the responsibilities and functions associated with leadership cannot be shared too widely without jeopardizing the effectiveness of the group.

In contrast, we suggest a shared leadership framework to explain leadership in online communities. The shared leadership framework was originally proposed by researchers investigating offline leaderless groups such as self-managing teams, volunteer organizations and employee-managed companies [24, 23, 30]. They argue that leadership—involving persuading and influencing other people to pursue a common goal—emanates from members at all levels, not simply from elites in formal leadership roles. Any member of the group can exhibit some level of leadership at any time, and there is no clear distinction between leaders and followers. Members mutually influence each other on what tasks are to be done, how tasks should be done, and the way they relate to each other. Rather than leadership being invested in specialized roles, leadership is viewed as a shared influence process.

Although every member can enact some level of leadership behaviors, the shared leadership model does not assume the same effectiveness of leadership behaviors across individuals. This paper investigates how distinct types of leadership behaviors and the legitimacy of the people who deliver them (people in formal leadership positions or not) influence their effectiveness. Here, we operationalize the effectiveness of leadership in terms of the extent to which those exhibiting leadership behavior can motivate others to invest effort in the community and contribution to it.

In this article, we first review prior theorizing about types of leadership behaviors and leader legitimacy. Based on path-goal theory, we explain the process by which leaders influence others' motivation. We offer several hypotheses regarding the effectiveness of different types of leadership behavior and leaders. Subsequently, we describe our measurement and methods, present our results, and discuss research and design implications.

TYPES OF LEADERSHIP BEHAVIOR

Researchers investigating traditional vertical leadership have identified a range of effective leadership behaviors [2, 3, 30]. In a shared leadership context, these strategies continue to be relevant [23]. Rather than prejudge results with terms like "leader" and "follower", in the following sections we use the term "influencer" to indicate the influence exercisers and "targets" to indicate those they are trying to influence.

The distinction between task-based leadership behaviors (those dealing with task accomplishment) and person-based (those facilitating team interaction and development) is common in nearly every taxonomy of leadership behaviors. Similar dichotomies include initiating structure versus consideration in Ohio State's program on leadership research [12], task-oriented versus relationship-oriented behaviors in the University of Michigan research program [17], and task-focused versus person-focused behaviors in Burke et al's recent paper reviewing leadership behaviors [3]. We follow this general classification and then specifically differentiate three subcategories of task-based leadership behaviors, using Pearce and Sims's classification [23].

Task-based leadership

Transactional leadership

With transactional leadership, leadership behavior is considered a transaction or exchange between the influencer and the target. Transactional influencers provide praise and rewards or withhold punishment from targets who comply with role expectations. Representative transactional leadership behaviors include (1) providing personal rewards, (2) providing material rewards, (3) managing by exception (active), (4) managing by exception (passive) [23]. Sample questionnaire items measuring this type of leadership include 1) "X will recommend that I am compensated well if I perform well"; 2) "X gives me positive feedback or special recognition when I perform well"; 3) "X tracks mistakes"; 4) "X delays taking action until problems become serious".

Aversive leadership

In contrast to transactional leadership, aversive leadership uses intimidation and reprimands to decrease undesired behaviors from targets [23]. Sample questionnaire items measuring aversive leadership include 1) "X tries to influence me through threat and intimidation" and 2) "X lets me know about it when I perform poorly".

Directive leadership

Directive leadership emphasizes the need to provide direction to targets and specify their roles and responsibilities. Directive behaviors include 1) issuing instructions and commands and 2) assignment goals [23]. Sample questionnaire items measuring directive leadership include 1) "when it comes to work, X gives me instructions on how to carry it out" and 2) "X establishes the goals for my work".

Person-based leadership

In contrast to task-focused leadership behaviors, which directly focus on task accomplishment, person-based leadership behaviors emphasize the target as a person and personal relationships between the influencer and the target [3].

Consideration was first proposed as a type of person-based leadership behavior in 1950s in the Ohio State leadership research program [12]. Consideration is the degree to which an influencer acts in a friendly and supportive manner, showing concern for targets, helping them to develop, supporting group cohesion, and maintaining close social relationship with them [30]. In general, dyadic relationships characterized by consideration reflect two-way open communication, mutual respect and trust, and an emphasis on satisfying employees' needs. The concept of relationship-oriented leadership in the University of Michigan research on leadership [17] is similar.

Later, researchers developed and elaborated the concept of person-based leadership by proposing ideas such as transformational leadership, which highlights encouragement, inspiration and intellectual stimulation [4, 2, 23], and empowering leadership, which focuses on self-management skills and team work [23].

In general, person-focused leadership behaviors are friendly and supportive, aimed at maintaining close social relationships supporting group cohesion, and developing subordinates' self-confidence and skills.

LEADER LEGITIMACY

In addition to types of leadership behavior, our analyses examine the role of the influencer in the organization. Legitimate leaders are those who occupy formal leadership positions in an organization, volunteer community or other social system. The legitimacy stems from the selection process, whether they are appointed by supervisors, elected by the membership or appointed because they fulfilled more or less explicit criteria [30]. The specific procedures for selecting the leader are often based on tradition and the provisions of the organizations. Take two online communities as examples. In Newgrounds, a collective movie creation community, the role of project leader is typically assumed by the person who conceives the idea for the project [20], while in Wikipedia, administrators are appointed through a peer review and election procedure [26]. Deviations from the selection process that members consider legitimate will weaken the leader's legitimate power [30].

Their legitimacy gives these leaders the right to make requests within their leadership domain and increase the potency of these requests [30]. Legitimate leaders often have defined privileges, obligations and responsibilities. For example, administrators in Wikipedia have access to restricted technical features, such as protecting, restoring and moving pages [26].

HOW PEER LEADERS MOTIVATE OTHERS

"To be successful, online communities need the people who participate in them to contribute the resources on which the group's existence is built.... In almost every online community, there are important contributions not being made." [19]. For example, although Wikipedia is among the ten most visited sites in the world, two-thirds of assessed articles are categorized as low quality [19]. Furthermore, researchers have found a gradual decline in the growth of Wikipedia's active editor base in recent years [22]. The above suggest that promoting members' motivation to contribute is a crucial goal for online communities.

We use path-goal theory [11, 16, 30] to explain how peer leaders influence the motivation of other members in online communities. According to House [16, p. 324], *"the motivational function of the leader consists of increasing personal payoffs to subordinates for work-goal attainment and making the path to these payoffs easier to travel by clarifying it, reducing roadblocks and pitfalls, and increasing the opportunities for personal satisfaction en route."*, Path-goal theory borrows concepts particularly from expectancy value theory [14, 25] to explain how leadership behaviors affect targets' efforts. There are different versions of expectancy theories, but they all explain motivation as a rational choice process in which individuals decide how much effort to devote. According to the theory, in determining their level of effort, individuals consider the likelihood a given level of effort will lead to desirable outcomes (e.g. high pay, promotion, acceptance into a community, sense of achievement) and avoidance of undesirable outcomes (e.g. termination, rejection from the community, reprimands). The perceived probability of an outcome is its expectancy, and the perceived desirability of an outcome is its valence. If people believe that the outcomes are attractive (high valence) and the effort will result in the outcome (high expectancy), they will make the effort. Leadership behaviors have their effects primarily by modifying these perceptions and beliefs [30].

Task-focused leadership (transactional leadership, aversive leadership and directive leadership) have positive motivational effects to the extent that they reduce ambiguity and increase the expectation of successfully accomplishing tasks and goals.

Task-focused leadership also changes the valence of the outcomes. More specifically, transactional and aversive leadership behaviors change targets' motivation by changing their perception of the valence associated with their efforts— gaining rewards and avoiding punishments, respectively [16]. Transactional leadership is based on reward power, increasing the size of incentives for task success, whereas aversive leadership is based on coercive power [13]. Transactional and aversive leadership behaviors will influence targets' behavior only to the extent that the influencers control rewards that have positive valence for the target or punishments that have negative valence for the target, respectively. That is, to influence effort the influencer must control rewards that are contingent on hard work and punishments contingent on insufficient work, and the contingency must be clearly perceived by the targets.

In addition to these extrinsic rewards and punishments, aversive leadership behaviors may modify valence by decreasing the intrinsic attractiveness of the work. Previous research shows that aversive leadership tends to negatively impact subordinates' satisfaction in conventional organizations [9]. These negative effects on intrinsic motivation may be especially problematic in volunteer organizations where extrinsic motivators (e.g., money) are less powerful.

We predict that person-focused leadership should have a positive influence on members' effort, for a number of reasons. First, person-focused leadership behavior helps members build self-confidence and develop skills, which in turn influences their motivation by increasing their effort-performance expectation. In addition, person-focused leaders focus on interpersonal relationships, which will result in social support, friendliness among group members, increased cohesiveness, and team effort. These social outcomes have positive valence for most members [16]. Person-focused leadership should be especially effective in online communities because many peer production tasks (e.g., editing Wikipedia articles) often require cooperation and team spirit despite weak bonds between members, due to the distributed nature of the communities.

Legitimate leaders, who occupy formal leadership positions, are in general more powerful in influencing and motivating others' activities compared to peers who perform comparable leadership behaviors [8]. People in leadership roles are perceived to have the legitimate right to issue directions and distribute rewards and punishment. Because of past socialization experiences (e.g., with parents, teachers, religion), complying with legitimate requests from authorities is often intrinsically satisfying [13]. Furthermore, formal leaders are often perceived as central members of the social system and may induce a sense of connection and identification with the community, which in turns increases the positive valence of contributing to the community.

The following hypotheses summarize this reasoning.

Hypothesis 1. Shared leadership behaviors performed by members at all levels influence targets' motivation to contribute in online communities.

Hypothesis 2. Among task-focused leadership behaviors (transactional, aversive and directive), transactional leadership behaviors are most effective in promoting motivation; aversive leadership behaviors are least effective.

Hypothesis 3. Person-focused leadership behaviors will motivate members' contribution.

Hypothesis 4. Legitimate leaders are more powerful in influencing members' contribution than regular members.

STUDY PLATFORM

Wikipedia is the site of our empirical investigation. Wikipedia, formally launched in January 2001, is a free, web-based, collaborative, encyclopedia project and is the largest encyclopedia in the world. We used a complete download provided by the Wikimedia Foundation from Wikipedia's inception to January 2008 (approximately 182 million revisions). To handle this data volume, we used the Yahoo! M45 computing cluster running Hadoop and Pig.

MEASUREMENT

Measurement of leadership behaviors

We measured leadership behaviors as exchanged in the communication among Wikipedia editors by examining the messages editors left on each others' personal profile pages. We used machine learning techniques to automatically classify the messages into four categories of leadership behaviors: positive feedback, negative feedback, directive message, and social messages, which correspond respectively to transactional leadership, aversive leadership, directive leadership and person-based leadership. Messages could be assigned to multiple categories. Table 1 shows the sample messages sent by Wikipedia editors and their corresponding categorizations automatically generated by the machine learning tools.

We used machine learning models created by Zhu et al. [31]. They had two trained judges hand-tag 500 messages randomly selected from the Wikipedia corpus for the presence or absence of each of the four types of peer leadership behavior. Then they used support vector machine algorithms on 21 language pattern features to predict the human judgments. The machine learning models classified the four categories with high accuracy (89% on average). The agreement between the machine classifications and human judgments was moderate for negative feedback (Kappa = 0.48), but is very substantial or excellent for the other three categories (Kappa = 0.75, 0.71, 0.80) [31].

The most important features predicting each of the four types of leadership behavior are listed below [31].

- Transactional leadership: the frequency of the word "barnstar" (a barnstar is a type of virtual reward in Wikipedia) and the frequency of the phrases "thanks for" and "thank you for"
- Aversive leadership: the frequency of a set of strong negative words, including "block," "revert" and "remove";
- Directive leadership: the frequency of "you" followed by modal words such as "should," "could," "might," and the frequency of the word "please" followed by a verb;
- Person-based leadership: the frequency of greeting words and smiley emoticons.

Applying these classifications to 4 million messages sent between editors, Zhu et al. [31] found that a large proportion of leadership behaviors were performed by editors without formal leadership roles in Wikipedia. For example, non-administrators contributed 64% of directive leadership behaviors. In this paper we go beyond characterizing the types of leadership behaviors evinced in Wikipedia to examining the effects they have on their targets.

Measurement of leader legitimacy

We measure leader legitimacy by examining whether the leadership exerciser was an administrator or not. As discussed previously, administrators are formal leader-like roles in Wikipedia, selected by a rigorous peer review process and given special privileges, including protecting, deleting and restoring pages, moving pages over redirects, hiding and deleting page revisions and blocking malicious editors [26].

Measurement of the effectiveness of leader behavior

We measured the effectiveness of leadership behaviors by examining the extent to which they affected others' efforts. Particularly, we looked at changes in targets' editing before and after receiving leadership messages, depending on the types of leadership messages they received, and whether the leadership messages came from a legitimate leader or not.

Machine learning (ML) categories & Leadership type	Sample messages
ML category: Positive feedback **Leadership type:** Transactional leadership (Task-focused)	*"I award this barnstar[1] to XXX for your help and assistance in getting the WikiProject user warnings to the review phase, and to let you know your work has been appreciated."*
	"Thanks for all your work on the Survivor articles"
ML category: Negative feedback **Leadership type:** Aversive leadership (Task-focused)	*"If you continue in this manner you will be blocked from editing without further warning."*
	"...there is a concern that the rationale you have provided for using this image under "fair use" may be invalid. ... If it is determined that the image does not qualify under fair use, it will be deleted within a couple of days according to our criteria for speedy deletion."
ML category: Directive message **Leadership type:** Directive leadership (Task-focused)	*"Please read the instructions at... Using one of the templates at..., but remember that you must complete the template..."*
	"... one of these days do you think you could take some pictures at Mission Mill? I'd like to spruce up the article but it really needs some photos..."
ML category: Social message **Leadership type:** Person-focused leadership	*"Hi XX. Welcome to WikiProject XXX! I saw your name posted on the members list and wanted to welcome you... Anyway we are glad to have you. If I can help at all let me know :) ..."*
	"[[Image:Smiley.svg]] has smiled at you Smiles promote WikiLove and hopefully this one has made your day better... Happy editing"

Table 1. Sample messages sent by Wikipedia editors and their corresponding machine learning categories and leadership types.

ANALYSIS

The goal of this paper is to identify the effects of receiving different types of leadership messages from other Wikipedia editors on changes in recipients' editing behavior. In an analogy to a true experiment, we will compare the changes in editing behavior of those who received leadership messages (i.e., treated group) to those who do not receive messages (i.e., control group).

The sine qua non of a true experiment is random assignment of treatment to experimental units. Random assignment is the best way to assure that potential confounding variables, both measured and unmeasured, are on average equal among the treatment group and the control group [5].

Unfortunately, although Wikipedia has an enormous amount of archival data, these data are observational, and the receipt of a leadership message is not a true experimental treatment. The treatment here, as with most events in the real world, is endogenous in the sense that it is caused by other factors inside the system. In our data, the messages a recipient gets are partially a response to the recipient's previous behaviors. For example, the number of edits one person made in a previous week may cause others to send them messages in the following week. Similarly, editors who produce good edits may cause others to send them transactional leadership messages, while those who produce poor edits may cause others to send them aversive leadership messages in a subsequent week. Not controlling for confounding factors that influence both the treatment and the outcome can lead to biased estimates of the treatment effects.

To ameliorate the endogeneity problem, we use propensity score matching (PSM) to approximate randomization. PSM builds experimental and control groups by balancing the groups on potential confounding factors. PSM can effectively reduce the bias caused by these conditioning factors [10, 21]. However, because PSM balances only on measured variables, it cannot adequately control for all variables relevant to treatment. However, the results approximate a true experiment to the extent that one can reasonably presume that omitted variables are uncorrelated with the outcome.

Data preparation

We restricted the analysis to registered Wikipedia editors who had edited any Wikiproject page at least once, since this provided a basic filter against vandals and guaranteed that the editors had some experience in Wikipedia. The data were longitudinal, following the same editors across different weeks. For the analysis, we first defined whether an editor was active in a given week (the focal week) in terms of whether the editor made any edits during a five-week period (including the focal week, two weeks before, and two weeks after the focal week). Then we did an editor-week level analysis, restricted to the weeks in which the editor was active. The data comprised 31,676 unique editors, 2,053,405 editor-week observations and 1.6 million messages.

Dependent Variable

- *Contribution_change.* We measured editors' contributions towards Wikipedia articles through their revision count (i.e., number of edits). Edits are a direct measure of editors' effort, indicating the number of changes they made to articles during a period of time. Each edit indicates a set of editing actions, for example adding, changing, deleting or reverting text, references or illustrations, or communicating with other editors. The dependent measure was the log transformed edits in the week after the focal week minus the log transformed edits in the week prior to the focal week. Because the logarithm of zero is undefined, we added one before computing the logarithm.

$$contribution\_change = \ln(edits_{t+1} + 1) - \ln(edits_{t-1} + 1)$$

Independent Variable

- *Receive_msg.* This dummy variable[1] indicates whether the editor received any messages during the focal week. One indicates that the editor received at least one message, while zero indicates that the editor received no messages.
- *Transactional.* This dummy variable indicates whether in the focal week the editor received any message categorized as transactional (i.e., providing positive feedback). One indicates that the editor received at least one message with positive feedback, and zero indicates that the editor received no positive feedback. The following three variables are similar.
- *Aversive.* This dummy variable indicates whether the editor received any message categorized as negative feedback during the focal week.
- *Directive.* This dummy variable indicates whether the editor received any message categorized as directive during the focal week.
- *Person.* This dummy variable indicates whether the editor received any message categorized as social exchange during the focal week.
- *Admin.* This dummy variable indicates whether the editor received any messages from any administrator during the current week. One indicates that the editor received at least one message from an administrator, while zero indicates that the editor received no messages from any administrator.

We also examine the interaction between message type and legitimacy of leadership.

[1] For ease of interpretation, we use dummy variables to represent the independent variables. The results are substantively the same when using log transformed number of different types of messages as the independent variables.

- *Admin*Transactional*. This dummy variable indicates whether the editor received any messages categorized as positive feedback from any administrator during the focal week. One indicates that the editor received at least one positive message from an administrator, while zero indicates that the editor received none. The other three interactions were constructed similarly.
- *Admin*Aversive*. This dummy variable indicates whether the editor received any messages categorized as negative feedback from an administrator during the focal week.
- *Admin*Directive*. This dummy variable indicates whether the editor received any messages categorized as directive messages from an administrator during the focal week.
- *Admin*Person*. This dummy variable indicates whether the editor received any messages categorized as social messages from an administrator during the focal week.

Propensity Score Matching

For each editor who received messages, we selected a comparison editor who was most similar on confounding variables but did not receive messages. We used Propensity score matching (PSM) to pair editors. PSM involved three steps. First was to estimate the propensity score (i.e., the probability of receiving messages from others) from a set of conditioning variables. The variables used to predict receiving a message were the editors' prior activities (e.g., number of edits in previous week, number of messages received in previous week, tenure in Wikipedia). The rationale was that these factors might both cause other editors to communicate with them and also be correlated with subsequent changes in effort. Therefore, we chose six of the editors' previous activities listed below as conditioning variables.

In the second step, we matched each editor who received leadership messages in a particular week with another editor who did not receive a message, but who had the most similar propensity score based on six behavioral indicators. Propensity scores allow researchers to control for many variables simultaneously by matching on a single scalar variable. The variables with higher correlation with the treatment (also having higher risk to introduce bias) will be balanced better than the variables with lower correlation with the treatment. At the end of the second step, we tested whether the treatment group and control group were well matched in terms of the conditioning variables.

In the third step, we ran fixed effects regression analyses to estimate the effect of receiving messages, especially different types of leadership messages, on the treated groups and matched controls.

Step 1: Estimate propensity score

We first used logistic regression to estimate the probability of an editor receiving messages in a given week (t) based on the editor's previous activities. The estimated probability is the propensity score. The six predictors are listed below, and the results are shown in Table 2.

- $Edits_{t-1}$. The log of the number of edits done by the editor in the week before the focal week.
- $MsgReceived_{t-1}$. The log of the number of messages the editor received in the week before the focal week.
- $MsgSent_{t-1}$. The log of the number of messages the editor sent in the week before the focal week.
- $MsgReceived_{<t-1}$ The log of the total number of messages the editor received any time prior to the week before the focal week.
- $MsgSent_{<t-1}$ The log of the aggregate number of messages the editor sent any time prior to the week before the focal week.
- *Tenure*. The number of weeks between the editor's first edit and the focal week.

Receive Msg	Coef.	Std. Err.
Intercept	-2.8803**	.0046
$Edits_{t-1}$	.2906**	.0014
$MsgReceived_{t-1}$	.8926**	.0044
$MsgSent_{t-1}$	.1682**	.0039
$MsgReceived_{<t-1}$	.4730**	.0024
$MsgSent_{<t-1}$	-.0147**	.0018
Tenure	-.0062**	<.0001
Log likelihood	-828366.63	
Pseudo R2	0.2756	
Number of obs	2,053,405	

Table 2. Estimate the probability of receiving messages (propensity score) with logistic regression. ** indicates that p value is less than 0.0001

Number of obs	Full Matched	Treat 503,259 Treat 503,259		Ctrl 1,550,146 Ctrl 503,259		
Variable	Sample	Treat Mean	Ctrl Mean	% bias	Reduced bias
$Edits_{t-1}$	Full	3.33	1.44	109.8	
	Matched	3.33	3.36	-1.4	98.7
$MsgReceived_{t-1}$	Full	0.78	0.12	100.8	
	Matched	0.78	0.78	-0.7	99.3
$MsgSent_{t-1}$	Full	0.76	0.11	78.8	
	Matched	0.76	0.81	-5.8	92.6
$MsgReceived_{<t-1}$	Full	3.34	1.77	97.7	
	Matched	3.34	3.24	6.3	93.6
$MsgSent_{<t-1}$	Full	3.12	1.43	84.2	
	Matched	3.12	3.06	2.8	96.7
Tenure	Full	68.1	61.4	13.0	
	Matched	68.1	63.6	8.7	33.1
Dependent Var	Full	-0.055	-0.011		
Contri_change	Matched	-0.055	-0.606		

Table 3. Comparison between treatment editors who received messages in the focal week (treat) and control editors (ctrl) before and after propensity score matching (full versus matched).

Bias is defined as $100(\bar{x}_t - \bar{x}_c)/\sqrt{\{(S_t^2 + S_c^2)/2\}}$, where $\bar{x}_t$ and $\bar{x}_c$ are the sample means, S_t^2 and S_c^2 are the sample variances

Step 2: Matching based on propensity score

In this step, we matched editors who received messages during the focal week with non-recipients, based on the logit of the estimated propensity score. To do this we ordered the treated and control editors on their propensity scores and then for each treated subject selected a control editor with the closest propensity score within a maximum distance, called a caliper. We defined the caliper, the maximum distance, as 0.1. Following Rosenbaum and Rubin [21], we used the logit of the estimated propensity score to match because its distribution is generally approximately normal.

Table 3 reports the descriptive statistics (means, percentage of bias and the percentage reduction in the bias after matching), showing that the treatment group and the control group are balanced. The percentage of bias is the mean difference as a percentage of the average standard deviation: $100(\bar{x}_t - \bar{x}_c)/\sqrt{\{(S_t^2 + S_c^2)/2\}}$, where for each covariate $\bar{x}_t$ and $\bar{x}_c$ are the sample means in the treatment groups (editors who received messages in the given week) and control groups (editors who did not receive messages in the given week), respectively, and S_t^2 and S_c^2 are the corresponding sample variances [21].

Here are several points to note about Table 3. First, while editors who received or failed to receive messages differed substantially on all the conditioning variables before matching, they had similar means after matching. The reduction in bias was over 90% for five of the six conditioning variables. Secondly, we looked at the dependent variable—change in contributions—before and after matching. Prior research shows that editors decrease the amount they edit over time [6]. Without matching, one would be left with the erroneous conclusion that editors who received messages in a focal week were more likely to decrease their activities (-.055) than editors who did not receive messages (-.011). However, after controlling for previous activities with propensity score matching, one can see that receiving messages in the focal week slowed the general decline in contributions (-.055 versus -.606).

Step 3: Run the analysis

Using the matched sample, we then examined the effects of receiving messages on changes in contribution and how the effects interact with the types of leadership behaviors and the source. We used fixed effects linear regression to predict change in editors' contribution, with each treated-control pair as a group. Fixed effects allowed each pair a different intercept (pre-existing difference among pairs were embodied in the intercept); independent variables—the event of receiving messages and types of messages—determined the slope, which we assume was the same for all pairs (representing an average effect of receiving a certain type of message). Table 4 shows the descriptive statistics of the independent variables and the analysis results.

RESULTS

To understand Table 4, we first need to understand how to interpret the dependent variable *Contribution_change*. The dependent variable is the log transformed edits in the week after the focal week minus the log transformed edits in the week prior to the focal week. Therefore, the sign of dependent variable indicates whether the editor's editing increased (positive sign) or decreased (negative sign) surrounding the focal week. Furthermore, an increase of x in the dependent variable indicates that, holding the edits in the prior week constant by PSM, the edits in the subsequent week increased approximately x%.

First, model 1 in Table 4 shows that editors who received messages in a focal week subsequently edited more than those who did not. Note that the intercept is significantly negative, indicating that those who received no messages reduced their editing surrounding a focal week by 61%. However, receiving messages slowed this to a 6% decline

Dependent Variable	Descriptive Statistics		Model 1		Model 2		Model 3	
Contribution_change	Mean	Std.Dev.	Coef.	Std. Err.	Coef.	Std. Err.	Coef.	Std. Err.
Intercept			-.6059**	.0021	-.6059**	.0021	-.6059**	.0021
Receive_msg	.5000	.5000	0.5507**	.0030	.3326**	.0054	.2956**	.0060
Transactional	.1872	.3901			.1927**	.0067	.1615**	.0079
Aversive	.0646	.2458			-.1442**	.0098	-.1003**	.0115
Directive	.2884	.4530			.0859**	.0064	.0585**	.0072
Person-based	.2511	.4336			.2290**	.0061	.1698**	.0071
Admin	.2264	.4185					.1584**	.0086
AdminXTransactional	.0657	.2478					.0278 *	.0118
AdminXAversive	.0174	.1306					-.0945**	.0205
AdminXDirective	.1103	.3133					.0174	.0102
AdminXPerson	.1090	.3117					.0579**	.0103
Number of obs	1,006,518							
Number of groups	503,259							

Table 4. Regression predicting the effects of leadership behaviors on subsequent change in editors.
**** indicates that p value is less than 0.0001; * indicates that p value is less than 0.05**

(-61%+55%).

Secondly, model 2 demonstrates that different types of leadership behaviors differentially influenced subsequent motivation. (Hypotheses 1 to 3). The effects of messages that were not one of the four leadership types resulted in a 33% increase in edits in the subsequent week[2]. Among task-focused leadership behaviors, receiving transactional leadership messages (i.e., positive feedback) led to an additional 19% increase in subsequent edits. Directive behavior messages led to an addition 8.6% in subsequent edits. In contrast, aversive leadership messages (negative feedback) decreased members' contribution by 14%. We can also see that the influence of person-based leadership was substantial, increasing edits by 23%.

Thirdly, Model 3 demonstrates that messages sent by administrators were more influential than those sent by peers. Receiving a non-leadership message from an administrator increased edits by 15% compared to messages from non-administrators. Transactional messages sent by administrators increased editing an additional 2.8% compared to those sent by peers. Conversely, aversive messages sent by administrators decreased editing an additionally 9.5% compared to aversive messages sent by peers. Finally, person-based messages sent by administrators increased editing by 5.8% compared to those sent by peers.

DISCUSSION

Endogeneity

We used sophisticated matching procedures in the form of propensity score matching to control for endogeniety, in which something about the targets and their behavior induced others to send them leadership messages and was also associated with changes in their contribution from before to after receiving the messages. We built balanced experimental and control groups based on prior levels of activity (see Table 3). However, the validity threat associated with the propensity score matching procedures is omitted variable biases. It is possible that our experimental group and control group were unbalanced in some unmeasured variable. For example, we did not control for the quality of the work. It is likely that the editors who produced higher quality work than average were more likely to fall into the treatment group because their work attracted attention, and thus they were more likely to receive transactional leadership messages from others. (Conversely, editors who produced work of lower quality than average might have been more likely to receive aversive messages.) According to econometric theory, omitted variables are problematic only if they are correlated with the outcome of interest; otherwise the estimated effects of treatment will be unbiased [28]. Note that the outcome of our analysis is the *change* of the contribution from before to after receiving the messages, rather than the pure quantity of the contributions. Even though it is easy to speculate about potential omitted variables that can compromise matching, we were unable to identify pathways by which omitted variables—such as the quality of the work—would be responsible for the dramatic changes in editors' contributions in the week surrounding the receipt of leadership messages. There was no good reason for editors to suddenly increase or decrease their efforts solely because they were producing high or low quality wok. As long as we do not find omitted variables that substantially influenced both the receipt of leadership messages and the behavior change in the weeks surrounding the receipt, we believe that the analysis results shown in Table 4 capture the unbiased causal effect of leadership messages on the change in members' effort.

Natural experiment

Another way to deal with threats to validity associated with endogeneity is to identify external events that change the probability of receiving a treatment, but that cannot plausibly be attributed to the behavior of those receiving the treatment. For example, in the past researchers used natural experiments, such as arbitrary changes in laws, to examine how the threat of punishment influences the likelihood of obeying social norms, like obeying the speed limit or paying taxes [5]. We identified a similar natural experiment in Wikipedia, which changed the frequency with which aversive leadership messages were sent independent of the recipients' behavior.

Results described previously indicate that editors receiving aversive leadership messages decreased their editing. More than half of the messages categorized as aversive leadership were actually sent by a single editor who created a program

Disputed fair use rationale for Image: XXX.png

Thanks for uploading XXX.png. However, there is a concern that the rationale you have provided for using this image under "fair use" may be invalid. Please read the instructions at Non-free content carefully, then go to the image description page and clarify why you think the image qualifies for fair use. Using one of the templates at Fair use rationale guideline is an easy way to ensure that your image is in compliance with Wikipedia policy, but remember that you must complete the template. Do not simply insert a blank template on an image page. If it is determined that the image does not qualify under fair use, it will be deleted within a couple of days according to our criteria for speedy deletion. If you have any questions please ask them at the media copyright questions page. Thank you. – BetacommandBot (talk).

Figure 1. Template message about copyright issue sent by the editor Betacommand.

[2] Non-leadership messages include newsletters, notice of a Wikiproject-wide or Wikipedia-wide event, reports of the status of certain work, and discussions and arguments about certain issues, etc. The 33% increase in people's motivation and contributions can be explained by the fact that receiving messages from other members or from the whole community, even without any specific directions, criticisms or praise, can elicit a sense of belonging to and identification with the community [32].

he labeled Betacommandbot to automatically send messages warning other editors who uploaded pictures without proper fair use rationale. The sample template is shown in Figure 1. The editor used an aversive leadership style and tried to influence other contributors by threatening to remove their contributions[3]. From the time this automatic program was approved on May 2007 [27] until it was removed in March 2008, this editor sent out more than 150,000 warning messages affecting more than 40,000 distinct editors. Importantly, Betacommandbot's messages were sent to all past violators (even ones whose edits had been far in the past), thus controlling for issues such as the likelihood of receiving a message. Thus the Betacommandbot warning was a natural experiment, like a change in speeding laws, that was not induced by recipients' behavior.

According to Table 4, the editors receiving aversive messages decreased their contributions in the following week by 14%, on average. We conducted analyses to isolate the effects of receiving the Betacommandbot warning. We used two matching methods: 1) within-editor matching, in which we matched the work of each editor who received a Betacommandbot warning with the same editor's work before the Betacommandbot was created; 2) delay matching, in which we matched the work of editors who received the Betacommandbot warning during that week with others who had also uploaded images without copyright rationale but who did not receive the Betacommandbot warning during that week (although they would receive it in the future). Across these variations, editors who received the Betacommandbot warning decreased their editing more than 10%. The results provide additional evidence to support our main findings.

Elite and peer

The shared leadership model claims that leadership emanates from members from all levels rather than a few select individuals. Although each member can enact some level of leadership behaviors, it does not assume an equal distribution and the same effectiveness of leadership behaviors across individuals. Actually, administrators issue more leadership messages than do non-administrators on a per capita basis[31], and the messages they send have more impact on the targets' editing behavior in the week following the message compared to messages sent by non-administrators. The administrators, representing only 1.3% of those in the current sample, sent approximately forty percentage of the leadership messages. Moreover, both their task-oriented and person-oriented messages were more powerful than those of the non-administrators in changing others' rates of editing.

However, in the aggregate, leadership exercised by non-vertical leaders (i.e., regular editors) was very important. For example, the large numbers of non-administrators sent more than half of leadership messages [31]. Moreover, these leadership messages had substantial effects on others' editing. For example, their transactional leadership messages induced a 16% increase in others' editing in the week following their message, while their person-based behavior increases other members' efforts by 17%.

Implications

There are several important theoretical and practical implications from this research. First, shared leadership, which has heretofore been a relatively neglected area of research on online communities, seems to be an important force influencing the success of peer production communities. Even though members (especially those without formal leadership roles) might not perceive themselves as "leaders," they actually perform leadership actions which can substantially influence others' behaviors and thus significantly affect the continuous functioning of the communities.

Secondly, practitioners should consider how to encourage effective leadership behaviors and prevent ineffective leadership behaviors from members. Our research shows that the four leadership types—transactional, aversive, directive and person-based—are not equally beneficial. In particular, transactional and person-based leadership had the strongest effects, suggesting that interfaces and mechanisms that make it easier for editors to connect with, reward, and express their appreciation for each other may have the greatest benefits.

Aversive leadership is the least effective leadership style in terms of motivating members to work. People may argue that reducing the activity of harmful editors is a positive impact of aversive leadership. However, considering the fact that there is much work to be accomplished in Wikipedia and the recent downward trend of active editors, pure aversive leadership should be avoided. It is important to find ways to reduce low quality work while maintaining editors' motivation. Choi et al [7] showed that constructive criticism (i.e., gentle and sociable corrective feedback) exchanged between in-group members (Wikipedia editors in the same subgroups) increased, not decreased recipients' motivation. In future work, we plan to explore the effects of these nuanced variations of aversive leadership behaviors in terms of encouraging high-quality work and maintaining motivation.

CONCLUSION

This research introduced a framework of shared leadership to study the leadership process in online communities. We examined in particular how leadership types and leader legitimacy facilitate the effectiveness of shared leadership. We found that 1) leadership performed by members at all levels significantly influenced other members' motivation; 2) transactional leaders and person-focused leaders were effective in motivating others, whereas aversive leaders

[3] The warning message could also be considered (and categorized by machine learning models) as directive leadership, since it clarified instructions, though not person-based, since the messages used standardized templates.

decreased other contributors' motivations; 3) legitimate leaders were in general more influential than regular members.

ACKNOWLEDGEMENT

We thank the members of the Social Computing Group at Carnegie Mellon University for helpful feedback. We also thank Aya Betensky, Yarun Luon and Raechel Lee for editing help. This research was supported by NSF grants OCI-09-43148, IIS-0968484, IIS-1111124 and a grant from Carnegie Mellon's Center for the Future of the Work.

REFERENCES

1. Angrist, J.D., Krueger, A.V. (1999) Empirical strategies in labor economics. In Handbook of Labor Economics. Orley Ashenfelter and David Card, eds. Amsterdam: North Holland.
2. Bass, B. M. (1990) Bass & Stogdill's handbook of leadership: Theory, research, and managerial applications (3rd ed.). New York, NY, US: Free Press.
3. Burke, C. S, Stagl, K. C, Klein, C, Goodwin, G. F, Salas, E. (2006) What type of leadership behaviors are functional in teams? A meta-analysis The Leadership Quarterly,
4. Burns, J. M. (1978) Leadership. New York: Harper & Row.
5. Campbell, D.T., Stanley, J.C. (1963) Experimental and Quasi-experimental Designs for Research, Houghton Mifflin Company, Boston.
6. Cassell, J., Huffaker, D., Tversky, D. (2006) The Language of Online Leadership: Gender and Youth Engagement on the Internet. Developmental Psychology. Vol 42(3) May, 436-449.
7. Choi, B. R., Alexander, K., Kraut, R. E., & Levine, J. M. (2010). Socialization tactics in Wikipedia and their effects. In Proceedings of the 2010 ACM Conference on Computer-Supported Cooperative Work. New York: ACM Press.(CSCW'10)
8. Cialdini, R. B., and Goldstein, N. J. Social influence: Compliance and Conformity. Annual Review of Psychology, 55, 1 2004), 591-621.
9. Cox, J. F. (1994). The effects of superleadership training on leader behavior, subordinate self-leadership behavior and subordinate citizenship. Unpublished doctoral dissertation, University of Maryland, College Park.
10. D'Agostino, R.B., Jr. (1998). Tutorial in biostatistics: Propensity score methods for bias reduction in the comparison of a treatment to a non-randomized control group. Statistics in Medicine, 17, 2265-2281.
11. Evans, M.G.(1970) The effects of supervisory behavior on the path-goal relationship, Organizational Behavior and Human Performance, Volume 5, Issue 3, May 1970, Pages 277-298
12. Fleishman, E. A. (1953) The description of supervisory behavior. Journal of applied psychology
13. French, J., & Raven, B.H. (1959). The bases of social power. In D. Cartwright(Ed.), Studies of social power. Ann Arbor, MI: Institute for Social Research, pp. 150-167
14. Georgopoulos, Basil S.; Mahoney, Gerald M.; Jones, Nyle W., Jr. (1957) A path-goal approach to productivity. Journal of Applied Psychology, Vol 41(6), Dec 1957, 345-353.
15. Hogan, R., Curphy, G. J., & Hogan, J. (1994). What We Know About Leadership. American Psychologist, 49(6), 493-504.
16. House, R. J. (1971) A Path Goal Theory of Leader Effectiveness Administrative Science Quarterly Vol. 16, No. 3.
17. Katz, Daniel; Maccoby, Nathan; Morse, Nancy C. (1950). Productivity, supervision, and morale in an office situation. Part I. Oxford, England: Institute for Social Research.
18. Kittur, A., & Kraut, R. E. (2008). Harnessing the wisdom of crowds in Wikipedia: Quality through coordination. In CSCW'08: Proceedings of the ACM conference on computer-supported cooperative work. New York: ACM Press.
19. Kraut, R. E. & Resnick, P. (In press). Evidence-based social design: Mining the social sciences to build online communities. Cambridge, MA: MIT Press.
20. Luther, K and Bruckman, A. (2008). Leadership in online creative collaboration. In Proceedings of the 2008 ACM conference on Computer-Supported Cooperative Work (CSCW '08).
21. Rosenbaum, P. R., & Rubin, D. B. (1983). The central role of the propensity score in observational studies for causal effects. Biometrika, 70, 41-55.
22. Suh, B., Convertino, G., Chi, E. H.,and Pirolli, P. (2009). The singularity is not near: slowing growth of wikipedia. In WikiSym '09: Proceedings of the 5th International Symposium on Wikis and Open Collaboration, pages 1–10, New York, NY, USA. ACM
23. Pearce, C.L., and Sims H.P. (2002) Vertical Versus Shared Leadership as Predictors of the Effectiveness of Change Management Teams: An Examination of Aversive, Directive, Transactional, Transformational, and Empowering Leader Behaviors, Group Dynamics, 6(2).
24. Pearce, C.L., and Conger,J. A. (2003) Shared leadership: Reframing the hows and whys of leadership, Sage, Thousand Oaks.
25. Vroom, V.H. (1964) Work and motivation. Oxford, England: Wiley.
26. Wikipedia editors. http://en.wikipedia.org/wiki/Wikipedia:Administrators
27. Wikipedia editors http://en.wikipedia.org/wiki/Wikipedia:Bots/Requests_for_approval/BetacommandBot_Task_5
28. Wooldridge, J. M. (2003) Introductory econometrics, 2nd Ed. Mason, OH: South-Western.
29. Yoo, Y., & Alavi, M. (2004). Emergent leadership in virtual teams: what do emergent leaders do? Information and Organization, 14(1), 27-58.
30. Yukl, G. (1998) Leadership in Organizations
31. Zhu, H., Kraut, R.E., Wang, Y.C. and Kittur, A. (2011) Identifying shared leadership in Wikipedia. In Proceedings of the 2011 annual conference on Human factors in computing systems (CHI '11).
32. Zhu, H., Kraut, R.E., & Kittur, A. (in press) Organizing without formal organization: Group Identification, Goal Setting and Social Modeling in Directing Online Production. In Proceedings of the 2012 ACM conference on Computer-Supported Cooperative Work (CSCW '12).

Coordination and Beyond: Social Functions of Groups in Open Content Production

Andrea Forte
Drexel University
aforte@drexel.edu

Niki Kittur
Carnegie Mellon University
nkittur@cmu.org

Vanessa Larco
Playdom
vanessa@gatech.edu

Haiyi Zhu
Carnegie Mellon University
haiyiz@cs.cmu.edu

Amy Bruckman
Georgia Institute of Technology
asb@cc.gatech.edu

Robert E. Kraut
Carnegie Mellon University
robert.kraut@cs.cmu.edu

ABSTRACT
We report on a study of the English edition of Wikipedia in which we used a mixed methods approach to understand how nested organizational structures called WikiProjects support collaboration. We first conducted two rounds of interviews with a total of 20 Wikipedians to understand how WikiProjects function and what it's like to participate in them from the perspective of Wikipedia editors. We then used a quantitative approach to further explore interpretations that arose from the qualitative data. Our analysis of these data together demonstrates how WikiProjects not only help Wikipedians coordinate tasks and produce articles, but also support community members and small groups of editors in important ways such as: providing a place to find collaborators, socialize and network; protecting editors' work; and structuring opportunities to contribute.

Author Keywords
Open Content, Peer Production, Wikipedia, WikiProjects, Groupwork

ACM Classification Keywords
H.5.3 [Information Interfaces]: Group and Organization Interfaces – Collaborative computing, Computer-supported cooperative work, Web-based interaction

General Terms
Human Factors

INTRODUCTION: THE CHALLENGES OF OPEN CONTENT DEVELOPMENT
Organizing hundreds of thousands of volunteers in a single project is hard. Anyone who's collaborated on even a small group project like a conference paper knows that sharing a workbench can quickly become complicated. Eric Raymond's description of "a great babbling bazaar of differing agendas and approaches" that yields a seemingly miraculously stable community of developers has become the quintessential characterization of open source development [26]. Understanding the bazaar as a complex social space has kept researchers busy for over a decade: how do people organize themselves to accomplish feats like open source and open content? In this paper, we examine open content production in Wikipedia from the perspective that organizing volunteer collaborators involves more than getting people to pull in the same direction, it also involves supporting the well-being of workgroups and individuals.

One set of challenges for self-organizing communities involves meeting production goals by optimizing volunteers' efforts and allocating tasks. Volunteers need to know what needs to be done in order to align their interests and expertise with the needs of the community [5, 11, 15]. This is often referred to as the problem of coordination. Another set of challenges involves making the experience interesting, pleasant and beneficial to contributors to attract and sustain their participation. [18, 23, 25]. This is often addressed by speaking of motivation and incentives. Still another set of challenges involves supporting workgroups who assemble to accomplish a particular set of tasks, for example, through upkeep of morale and trust within a team [29]. Crowston et. al. integrate all of these perspectives in their review of literature on Free/Libre Open Source Software (FLOSS) development. We likewise integrate these perspectives with a focus on Wikipedia. In this paper, we examine the role of nested organizational structures in supporting these varied aspects of community health in Wikipedia by not only serving as a mechanism for orchestrating article production, but also by supporting sub-communities and individual community members.

RELATED WORK: WHAT'S GREAT ABOUT GROUPS?
Nested organizational structures are an important feature of large self-organizing communities [24]. Examples of nested structures include local chapters of large international organizations like the Red Cross or Wikimedia Foundation. Ostrom explains that such structures arise in self-organized resource regimes to

facilitate decentralized decision making; when organizations get big, nested structures allow people whose work is directly affected by decisions to continue playing a role in making them. Forte et al. identified WikiProjects as an example of Ostrom's "nested organizational structures" in Wikipedia [8]. WikiProjects are groups of editors who manage the production of Wikipedia articles related to specific topics and themes. Once a writing project becomes as large as Wikipedia, it becomes difficult to create policies and maintain social norms—particularly editorial conventions—that apply equally well to all the diverse areas of the site [8]. Setting editorial guidelines for writing about pharmacology topics requires different considerations than, for example, writing about marine life, Catholicism, sexuality, or Star Wars. Decentralization allows those with relevant expertise to make decisions about how to proceed with local affairs. We ask:

> Q. What are the mechanisms by which WikiProjects and their internal structures facilitate specialized work in Wikipedia?

Our analysis was influenced by Joseph McGrath's typology of group functions. This typology underscored the importance not only of production activities that target the tasks that need to be done, but also of activities that maintain the health of the group itself and support its individual members [20]. McGrath's typology juxtaposes three group functions with four modes of operation (Table 1). Jonathan Grudin has observed that the typology is useful for understanding computer-mediated group work because it can help researchers and designers not overlook important group functions: "A rational approach to supporting project activity is to ask 'what are these people trying to do and how can we help them?' Unfortunately, this leads to an exclusive focus on the Execution mode of the Production function: Performance" [9]. By focusing attention narrowly, designers and researchers run the risk of misapprehending failures and successes.

	Production	Group Well-Being	Member Support
Inception	Production demand and opportunity	Interaction demand and opportunity	Inclusion demand and opportunity
Problem-Solving	Technical problem-solving	Role network definition	Position and status attainments
Conflict Resolution	Policy resolution	Power and payoff distribution	Contribution and payoff distribution
Execution	Performance	Interaction	Participation

Table 1: McGrath's typology of group modes and functions (McGrath 1991)

Of course, production is an important aspect of group work and a number of studies have examined the ways that Wikipedians coordinate production tasks. For example, Kittur et. al. suggested that better task routing tools could help volunteers more efficiently direct their efforts [11]. Cosley et. al. developed an intelligence task routing tool for Wikipedia called SuggestBot [5]. Krieger et. al. followed up on this work by interviewing Wikipedians to understand how individuals in different roles manage tasks and, based on their findings, prototyped a tool called WikiTasks, to help facilitate better task coordination [15]. From this perspective, coordination is overhead that can be reduced to economize volunteer time. This is a rational response to Viegas et. al's findings in 2007 that an increasing proportion of editing activity was taking place on areas of the site dedicated to coordination activities, not on article composition itself [31].

Kriplean and Beschastnikh et. al. took a different approach to understanding coordination; they analyzed discussions to understand how policy is used to support coordination activities in Wikipedia [1, 16]. From their perspective, the work of coordination is critical to the process not only of producing content and arriving at consensus, but also provides opportunities for volunteers to interact, define roles and use power relationships, which are important features of group health. Kriplean et al. also examined mechanisms by which Wikipedia editors identify valued contributions through awarding one another barnstars [17]. Although it does not directly serve the goal of writing encyclopedia articles, awarding barnstars serves the function of member support. These perspectives are aligned with Grudin's observation that "non-production functions are not directly tied to a group's task, but in the long run they contribute to accomplishing it" [9].

In this study, our findings complement and build on the existing literature on Wikipedia and peer production by positioning WikiProjects as nested organizational structures engaged in all three of McGrath's functions, including not only production activities, but also maintaining the well-being of the group itself and supporting its members. McGrath characterizes groups as "complex, intact social systems that engage in multiple, interdependent functions, on multiple, concurrent projects, while partially nested within, and loosely coupled to, surrounding systems" [20]. This corresponds with our characterization of WikiProjects as nested organizational structures that exist to address specific needs within the broad goals of the English-language edition of Wikipedia.

METHODS AND PARTICIPANTS

Our work is based on the premise that social systems cannot be understood in isolation from the interpretations of the individuals who create those systems. We chose to begin with an interview-based approach to obtain a rich understanding of how members experienced WikiProject membership. We then followed up with a quantitative examination of editing activity on the site to understand how interviewees' perceptions might be made manifest in electronic trace data. This mixed methods approach reflects a phenomenological view of sociology, which suggests that social systems are reflexively constructed based on people's understanding of them [28, 32].

In our first round of interviews, we sought to understand governance in Wikipedia as a site-wide phenomenon. As such, we interviewed eleven individuals who had been involved in the site for many years, in many different capacities (See Tables 2 and 3 for roles and experiences of interviewees). Interviewees were recruited via public postings on mailing lists, by identifying some of the earliest posters on policy pages, and via snowball recruitment, in which participants recommend other informants. These interviews provided a rich description of organizational structures that had evolved in the community over time, such as the arbitration committee and WikiProjects. The theme of decentralization emerged in all of our interviewees' experiences and it became clear after several interviews that WikiProjects had become important organizational features of the site.

In our second round of interviews, we focused mainly on one WikiProject in order to understand them more deeply as local organizational structures. How do they work? What role do they play in supporting the goals of the community? How do they affect the experiences of members? We chose to focus on the WikiProject Military History because it is a particularly successful, long-standing project, has an active and prolific membership, and has a mature set of editorial guidelines. To recruit a strategic sample of interviewees, we posted messages on the WikiProject discussion page, identified the earliest contributors in the project, and again used snowball recruitment. Our nine follow-up interviews were with Wikipedia editors who were active in Military History, including founding members of the project, people who hold administrative positions in the project, and individuals who edit articles as part of the project without playing explicit leadership roles. In all, we interviewed 20 individuals, fifteen of whom were active in one WikiProject or another. All of these interviews were conducted on the phone or in person and recorded, with the exception of one interview, which was conducted via an exchange of emails.

Normally, research participants' identities are held in confidence and interview data are anonymized to protect interviewees' privacy. Questions about anonymity arise when participants have made significant contributions to a public project and desire credit [3]; moreover, public figures like Jimmy Wales are impossible to anonymize. With consent of participants and permission from our Institutional Review Board (IRB), we have identified Wales by name and use "light disguise" (Ibid.) for other Wikipedians.

Participant	Months Active	Approximate Edit Count
1	64	47,500
2	28	18,500
3	67	20,500
4	33	10,000
5	57	7,200
6	58	54,200
7	76	74,500
8	73	31,500
9	33	88,000
10	64	18,500
Jimmy Wales	88	3,800
12	54	14,000
13	68	1,500
14	22	300
15	3	few
16	11	unknown
17	26	12,000
18	8	unknown
19	53	5,000
20	36	57,500

Table 2: Participant editing activity in Wikipedia at time of interviews

Once the full set of interviews had been transcribed, they were iteratively examined to identify emergent themes using a grounded approach [30]. Initial affinity clusters of data were discussed by two researchers and examined by a third to assess the credibility of the interpretation. Successive iterations were completed by one researcher to compare and refine central concepts. McGrath's work provided a conceptual vocabulary or *sensitizing concepts* for analyses of qualitative data, but was not used as a theoretical proposition against which to "test" our data. Blumer describes the role of sensitizing concepts in qualitative work in contrast to definitive concepts: "definitive concepts provide prescriptions of what to see, sensitizing concepts merely suggest directions along which to look" [2]p. 7]. McGrath's theory sensitized us to ways that participation in Wikiprojects may address many different needs for individuals, groups and for the Wikipedia project as a whole.

The qualitative analysis was used to inform a series of targeted quantitative analyses that will be presented alongside qualitatively derived narratives throughout the next sections. The quantitative analyses are based on archival data from 379 projects from 2001 to 2008.

This mixed-methods approach has several benefits. Our qualitative data provides rich and grounded evidence of the importance of Wikipedians' activities in WikiProjects, but has limitations of generality and representativeness. Meanwhile, our quantitative data has the advantage of summarizing behavior on a large scale, but does not provide data on whether the activities so described are truly meaningful influences on members' behavior. By combining these approaches we provide converging evidence that has the advantage of both rich, meaningful interpretations as well as large-scale tests of representativeness and generality. Although the mixed-methods approach does not preclude alternative hypotheses, the convergence of approaches can help us be more confident that the phenomena we are studying are both real and widespread.

Wikimedia Foundation founder, Jimmy Wales
Arbitration Committee member/former member (6 participants)
Regular user / No special technical or social designations (5 participants)
Involved in Wikimedia Foundation (3 participants)
Developer of MediaWiki software (1 participant)
Involved in WikiProjects (15 participants)
Users with access privileges including: administrator, checkuser, oversight, bureaucrat, steward, developer (10 participants)

Table 3: Wikipedian roles represented among participants at time of interview

THE STORY OF WIKIPROJECT MILITARY HISTORY: A COMMUNITY WITHIN A COMMUNITY

In interviews, we found that scaling the community from fewer than 10 members in January 2001 to hundreds of thousands of editors in 2011 [34] involved the development of decentralized governance structures called WikiProjects:

> As [Wikipedia] gets larger it's kind of hard to know everyone who's there, so... people try and find new ways of dealing with issues when they don't know everything that's going on... WikiProjects are formed to kind of focus on articles in a particular area. And they can develop policies that just relate to their area. So it enables people to still work together within a small community even though Wikipedia itself is a really huge community. (I1)
>
> The fact that it's gotten so big, it's hard—people can't keep up to date with everything that happens anymore. So in a sense I think the growth of WikiProjects has been partly a reaction to that. In that, you know, you no longer feel part of a community of thousands and thousands of people. So people set up smaller communities. (I10)

WikiProjects as an idea appeared early in the history of Wikipedia but have become increasingly important features of the organization. Kittur et. al. showed that by late 2007, over 1% of edits on Wikipedia were made to WikiProject pages – note that these are not edits to articles that are within the scope of projects, but edits to the pages on which WikiProjects themselves are managed [13]. WikiProject Military History was one of the earliest projects. It was created in October of 2002 with the title of WikiProject Battles with the goal of standardizing all the battle articles on Wikipedia. "Specifically," remembers one of the earliest members, "we wanted to add an information box to those articles." (I13)

WikiProject Battles was a small, fairly quiet project for a few years. Then in mid-2005, one user adopted the practice of placing banners advertising the WikiProject on the talk pages of battle-related articles. This drew in more participants and the project quickly grew. In October of 2005, WikiProject Battles merged with WikiProject Wars to form WikiProject Military History. Starting in 2006, WikiProject Military History began electing members into the role of Coordinators:

> I think originally we started with a total of 3 [coordinators]... I think on the second election, there were 5, on the third election there were 7, on the fourth election there were 9. (I20)

Just as Wikipedia spawned nested structures to manage local interests as it scaled, Military History has created internal structures also. Task Forces are still smaller, less formal groups within the WikiProject that focus on a specific topic or effort—today, a goal such as the one WikiProject Battles started out with would be taken on by a Task Force. Task Forces benefit from the resources of their parent project and are still able to function as an independent group.

> They have task forces by eras—divided up into time eras, WW1 and WW2 and so on and so forth and then they also have special task forces that deal with weapons and weaponry and fortifications and those types of things. (I18)
>
> The Task Forces are pretty much autonomous, but they use the infrastructure that the central project has set up like review processes and templates and announcements. (I20)

WikiProject Military History has 1170 active members, 673 members who are no longer active (have not edited in three months), and 750 Featured Articles (these statistics are manually maintained at [33]). In his 2007 *Guide to Military History on the Internet*, Simon Fowler rated Wikipedia as the best general source for military research. Of the military pages, he said: "The results are largely accurate and generally free of bias." Wikipedians and knowledgable outsiders perceive Wikiproject Military History as a success.

FINDINGS: SUPPORT MECHANISMS THAT GO BEYOND PRODUCTION

Iterative coding of interview transcripts resulted in a set of categories that primarily describe dimensions of support that WikiProjects provide their membership as well as counterexamples of failure to provide support. Interviewees' descriptions of their WikiProjects experiences fell into four primary categories of *support mechanisms*: A) helping editors find expert collaborators, B) providing networking and socializing opportunities, C) structuring participation, and D) protecting editors' work. In the following sections, we will discuss how these perceived support mechanisms contribute to different modes of both production and non-production functions of groups. Support mechanisms do not map perfectly onto production or non-production functions, rather, they may support multiple modes and multiple functions. This discussion will be informed both by interviewees' experiences and by data collected in complementary, targeted quantitative analyses.

Getting Help, Finding Collaborators

One important support mechanism associated with WikiProject Military History is that it allows members to find help and expert collaborators when they need it. Instead of foundering alone with an article, writers of military history articles who need help know that there are interested experts to whom they can turn.

> The thing about Military History is that you could go there if you had a question and say "Does anyone know anything about-" and more often then not, you could find someone that knew about it. (I16)
>
> People can kind of specialize—in War Film, for example, there is a task force called War Film so people who have an expertise in this particular area can work on articles over there, of their expertise, while still being able to interact with people with other expertises [sic]. (I18)
>
> That's the thing about Wikipedia, is that the more involved you get in it, the more you realize the sort of back alleys, how it works... a more sophisticated user can direct you to resources like WikiProjects and Task Forces that can help you find other users to collaborate with. (I19)

In terms of the member support function of groups, finding skilled and interested parties with whom to collaborate appears to be an important part of sustaining individuals' interest in participating in WikiProjects.

An important characteristic of Military History that distinguishes it from other projects is its number of active editors. A critical mass of editors may be required for a project to "ignite" and become an engine for sustaining the participation of its membership:

> [WikiProject] Archeology is not organized and History is a bit organized, but it doesn't really work. And yeah therefore, I mainly work in Military History.
>
> *Interviewer:* When you said it doesn't really work, what does that mean?
>
> It's not a place you can go and get help if you have a problem. You want to improve an article, you want somebody to review an article and give you hints on what could be done better and for these issues you need at least a minimum number of active members. (I17)

While the above quote reflects the experience of a single interviewee, it suggests that without a certain number of people involved, a project may lose the critical mass it needs to maintain itself. Many projects have become inactive over the years as founders fail to engage new recruits or lose interest themselves. Here we apply a mixed-methods approach building on qualitative interview data to identify hypotheses that we can quantitatively measure as well.

In many online communities activity follows a power law function, in which a small number of communities are highly active but the vast majority have little to no activity. For example, out of the thousands of projects created in SourceForge, only 10% have more than three members [27]. Power law distributions have been shown to be a robust way to describe phenomena ranging from the network of Internet links to the growth of animal populations [7, 22]. In particular, truncated power laws (in which two different power laws are joined by a breakpoint) have been used to identify sub-processes that may affect how communities evolve [21, 35]. We hypothesize that if indeed there is a "critical mass" needed for a community to thrive, we should see it as a deviation from the standard power law distribution. In other words, we might expect a standard power law distribution for projects which have achieved a critical mass, but fewer projects than we would expect below that critical mass, as such projects would not survive for long (e.g., if newcomers decide to join other projects instead).

To answer this question, we examined the activity of each project as measured by the average number of edits to project pages per month (i.e., the pages where most of the coordination and discussion about the project itself happened, rather than the articles themselves). Figure 1 shows the resulting distribution. As is evident from the figure, this is not a standard power law distribution. There is no "long tail"; instead, there are many projects that have a moderate amount of activity, but very few projects with very low activity. This suggests that there may be forces at play that reduce the likelihood of low-activity projects, for example, if editors preferentially join higher-activity projects because of expectancy-value judgments as suggested by interviewees (e.g., expecting that the project will not provide them with significant benefits) or cognitive issues (e.g., being overloaded with choices such that the likelihood of seeing low-activity projects is low [7]). The "elbow" of the distribution appears to be around 5-10 edits/month, suggesting that even relatively low but consistent activity may be enough to keep a project alive.

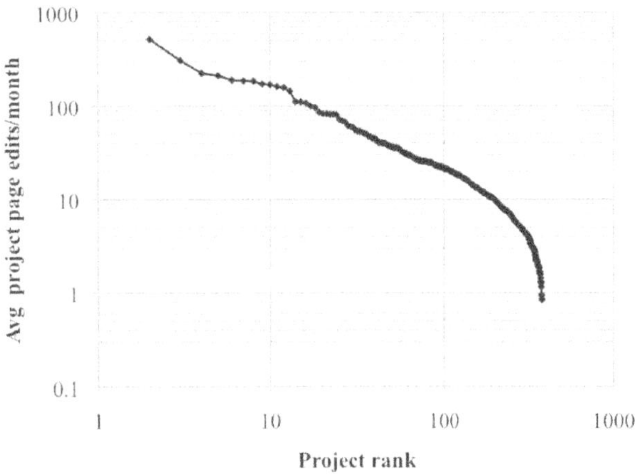

Figure 1: Distribution of project activity (avg edits per month) across a sample of 379 projects. MilHist is the leftmost (most active) project. (WikiProject Spam has been removed from this graph as an outlier, (~5000 edits/month) as it is used as a place to report spam.)

Networking and Social Opportunities

In addition to providing a place to find expert collaborators, WikiProject Military History creates a local work environment where editors get to know one another. Kollock observes that, in online communities, identity persistence and the ability to identify (and assess) past actions are critical factors in motivating collaboration and help members feel that their contributions will someday be reciprocated [14]. Working with people whom one knows, trusts, and whose strengths and weaknesses are known is a different experience than working with strangers who share a common goal. This sense of contribution and reciprocation is an aspect of member support.

> If somebody prominent in the Civil War area contacted me and said "Hey, I like your article, but here are some comments on improving it," I would whole heartedly be excited to get that sort of feedback, but when some anonymous person on the internet comes up with his advice to me on why he thinks it should be improved, I don't consider their advice to be any more valuable than my own. (I12)

It also helps resolve the group-support problem of role-network definition [20], for example by allowing the group to identify individuals who are able to fill important organizational roles.

> WikiProjects, these conglomeration of people, it is a point for networking, meeting a person in networks—you get to know an editor, for example by reviewing these articles and next time you have an article, you ask him for example to help on an article you want to improve—these projects do enhance the ability to form such networks. (I17)
>
> The cooperation with other coordinators and with other editors went very well and I quite liked it. (I6)

In WikiProject Military History, there are also explicit opportunities for members to have fun with the editing process. Organized events such as contests and awards have been touted as community-building activities [10] and help create a sense of group identity and promote group health.

> We have monthly newsletters that go out with things like project news and announcements, we have a number of award programs that we maintain to recognize editors that have done various useful things or have written good articles and so forth, we have announcement templates of a variety-some for individual task forces others for the project as a whole that editors can put on their user pages and keep track of everything that is going on and we have periodic special events or drives where there's some large task that we need to get accomplished so we actually go out and invite editors personally to come and participate. (I20)

Setting up these kinds of activities is precisely the kind of organizational "overhead" that happens on coordination pages of the site. Yet, we see that it is these activities that help create a sense of belonging and support the group and its members. One WikiProject Military History member noted that it was the level of coordination activities that kept him interested in participating in the project:

> I just kind of fell into the Military History group because they seemed to me to be the most organized group out there.
>
> *Interviewer:* And what made you feel that they were the most organized? What is it about them?
>
> Well they have that they are very active-if you go to their Wikiproject page they're (laughter)-they're very organized-you know with the style guides and writing articles-they have contests with the bronze star award and those kinds of things. (I18)

Moreover, working in smaller social groups affords opportunities for learning about how Wikipedia works from supportive peers. Learning is a social process that requires relationships with others, access to help, and models of good work [19]. In earlier work, we examined the processes by which newcomers to the community learned to be productive Wikipedians [4]. We found that participation in a WikiProject can provide important opportunities for new editors to learn how to contribute to Wikipedia successfully.

> I am just using these other articles to kind of get used to how to write articles and style guides and that kind of thing and I plan to, over the next few months, go over to WikiProject Systems, kind of full time… I used [Military History], having a learning place for me to learn what good article writing is all about. (I18)

> [In other WikiProjects] I can find certain people that are very passionate about some things, but there wasn't the same level of caring that there was [in Military History]… for me to go to computer networking and contribute, I wasn't going to be learning anything from that. (I16)

These qualitative findings suggest that active projects afford their members greater opportunities for meaningful interaction with other editors. To provide further evidence for this claim, we also examine members' interaction history upon joining a project. Figure 2 shows 30,189 editors' interaction activity before and after joining a project. Interaction activity is defined as total edits made to other editors' user talk pages or by other editors to their own user talk page; these data represent 1,386,100 interactions in total.

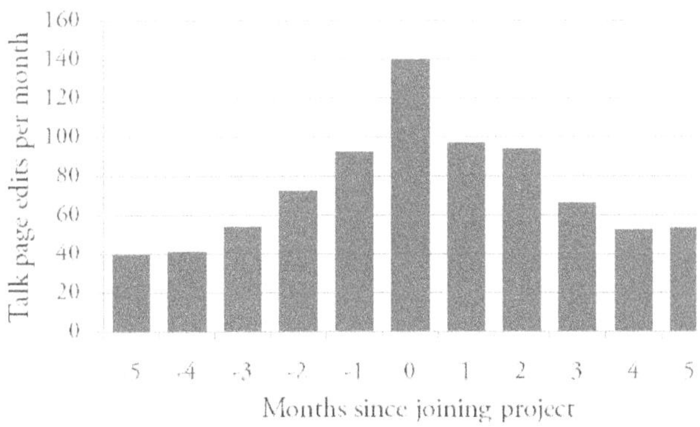

Figure 2: Average member interaction activity per month before and after joining a project

As can be seen from the figure, editors' interaction activity increases upon joining a project. After an initial peak of interaction activity when editors join a project, social activity ebbs off again; however, five months after joining, average interaction activity remains higher than before joining a project. The gradual rise before the peak and apparent drop of interaction activity following the peak can be attributed in part to the fact that in any given time period, some users join and others drop out of Wikipedia altogether. So although all editors are active at the time when they join a project (at the peak), some may have begun editing immediately before joining and others may have dropped out soon afterwards. Since interaction activity is still elevated 5 months after joining, it appears that joining a WikiProject has an effect on interaction activity, and could indicate an impact on overall editor retention. However, an alternative interpretation is that heightened commitment and interaction with other project members partially cause editors to join a project.

5.3 Structuring Participation

Contributing to a massive enterprise like Wikipedia can be a daunting experience. Where can one best contribute? What needs to be done? In an analysis of edit histories, Kittur and Kraut found that, upon joining a Wikiproject, members focused their editing activity on pages managed by that project [13]. In interviews, WikiProjects members described *how* projects influence their editing activities. In some cases, WikiProjects help structure members' participation explicitly by organizing to-do lists and task forces:

> Usually what [task forces] ask is for some people to commit to doing something, they get a goal, some task to do. (I19)

WikiProjects also structure participation in implicit ways, as a byproduct of content standardization. When there are models and standards to which editors aspire, bringing an article up to par involves addressing concrete deficiencies, not just "improving it" in an abstract sense. Systematically structuring content allows potential collaborators on an article to easily see what's missing and how they might contribute.

> If you go to just about any nation and look up something on Wikipedia, you will find a template that helps you to navigate between the different articles that are related. You know, if you go to the US Army page there will be this thing that has links to artillery, a timeline of US Military History. Well, they had that for the United States, the United Kingdom, Russia, but for smaller countries, that didn't exist, so I went in and did one for Argentina. (I19)

> I remember getting to the Music project's site. They have the templates and what they all mean. For instance, the little color of the info box signifies if it's like a band or a solo artist or a vocalist and then I was reading what each thing meant and I actually liked that part and I thought, you know maybe I should sign up for it. (I14)

Structuring the work so that many people can effectively contribute is critical to harnessing the power of the crowd for complex and interdependent tasks such as writing articles. For example, Kittur & Kraut [12] demonstrated how a small core of article leaders could implicitly structure an article in such a way that many peripheral contributors could make smaller but still useful contributions while avoiding some of the overhead of explicit coordination and communication. WikiProjects provide many of the same benefits of implicit coordination, but across a collection of articles rather than a single article. Interviewees' descriptions of these coordinating functions of WikiProjects suggest that structuring activities can have a motivating effect, whether through implicit mechanisms like content standardization or explicit calls to action. By structuring activities, WikiProjects engage both in group well-being and member support functions. McGrath notes that, in order to maintain their health as a unit, groups need to define networks and roles to establish who will do what, when, and with whom. In WikiProjects, volunteers self-select into these roles; supporting this process is an important aspect of maintaining group well-being. Furthermore, it provides member support for individuals who identify these opportunities for self-selected roles. Member support "includes both the self-selection side and the group assignment side of the practices and policies by which individuals attain positions or roles in the group" [20].

A further implication of WikiProjects structuring of participation is that, for a given activity, a small core of project members may be able to coordinate the activity of many others. To test this, we examined the benefits of increasing numbers of project members on predicting either coordination activity within the project or production activity on articles relevant to the project. We define coordination activity as edits to the project pages themselves, while production activity is defined as edits to articles the project has adopted (by adding a project template to the article). We examine activity from 379 projects over the course of 10,220 project-months, totaling 11 million project-relevant edits. For each type of activity (coordination/production) we run a fractional polynomial regression predicting activity based on the number of members in the project. Since the value of the number of members in a project is likely to be curvilinear, we also include a squared number of members term.

The results are shown in Figures 3 and 4 for coordination and production activity, respectively. These figures show predicted activity based on the number of members in the project. Interestingly, we see very different patterns for coordination and production activity. The convex function in Figure 3 shows that the first few editors drive most of the coordination activity, consistent with the hypothesis that a small core of leaders drives the structuring of project work. In contrast, Figure 4 shows a concave function for production work, with more members leading to even greater gains in article editing. Together, these results suggest that a small group of project members can provide much of the value in coordination activity, structuring the work so that very many editors can be involved in useful.

By structuring activities, coordination efforts make it clear how individuals can start contributing. Making it clear how to become part of the group is critical for a volunteer-based organization. It is important to note that coordination efforts do not necessarily amount to task assignment. In the FLOSS community, it has been found that self-assignment is the most common task assignment mechanism [6]. Making the choice to participate means that volunteers exchange their time and effort for the rewards of affiliation. In the next section, we examine one of the perceived payoffs of participating in a WikiProject.

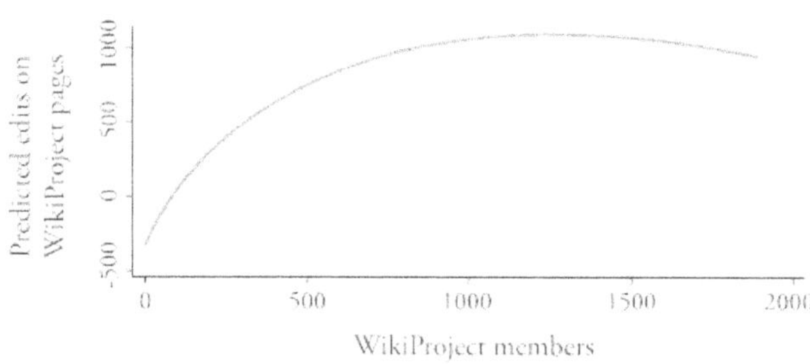

Figure 3: Predicted coordination-related activity (edits to project pages) versus number of project members.

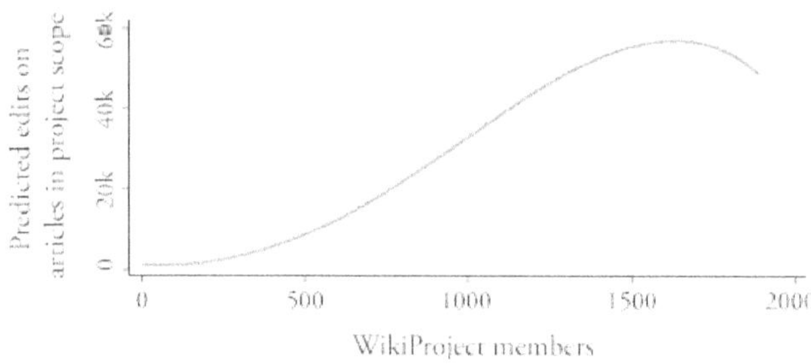

Figure 4: Predicted production-related activity (edits to project-related articles) versus number of project members.

5.4 Protecting and Valuing Editors' Work

Interviewees suggested that editing as a member of a group can be advantageous because, in the wilds of Wikipedia, it's nice to know that you have a supportive team protecting your work. Good work can get lost in the whirl of Wikipedia activity for many reasons, ranging from zealotry and vandalism to editors simply not knowing how to explain their efforts if challenged. When editing as part of a WikiProject, Wikipedians feel that their contributions have more staying power.

> If you are within the project, you are sort of a little safer. Like if you are just doing articles on your own, you are sort of like freelance, but it you are working with the Military History project than metaphorically it is like working in Chicago Tribune or something like that. Where you have the backing of all these people. (I14)
>
> I will enlist of the aid of other Wikipedia users to help me prevent some pernicious vandal or somebody… from screwing things up. (I12)

Aside from having allies in case of trouble, WikiProject members have a sense that their work will continue to be improved and is likely to lead to high quality content.

> I would start an article stub and then find someone to say "Hey, can you expand this?"... in many cases there are professional scholars that get involved and make it very scholarly, they're well written, well researched... I have seen them transform a lot of articles that way... some people will come in and clean it up and make it look neater and that's exactly what the project's designed to do. (I19)

The perception that one's work will be improved and maintained helps support members who invest their time and effort in the project. As in Wikipedia more broadly, WikiProject members also receive explicit rewards for their contributions to the group: "they have contests with the bronze star award and those kinds of things" (I18). Payoff is an important aspect of member support.

DISCUSSION & OPPORTUNITIES FOR FUTURE WORK

Developing an open content reference work requires retaining knowledgeable volunteers who are willing to learn and continuously improve a body of editorial guidelines and policies that ensure quality. We have demonstrated how local organizational structures help the Wikipedia community meet these goals by engaging in both production- and non-production-oriented member and group support functions.

McGrath's approach to understanding groups is a reaction to controlled, laboratory studies in which groups are asked to perform tasks by experimenters. In such contexts, anything that distracts groups from the completion of the given task implies a loss of efficiency and performance. McGrath's typology frees researchers from narrow assumptions about groups' and group members' goals and needs. Groups and their members do more than simply get jobs done; they set and revise goals, resolve disputes, bond, support one another, and may have multiple concurrent projects. In a volunteer-based project like Military History, with fluid membership that regularly waxes, wanes, subdivides, and regroups, all of the modes and functions seem to be experienced in an ongoing fashion by different members.

Although many interviewees described experiences with WikiProjects that supported their engagement with Wikipedia in different ways, editors' experiences vary. For example, some editors suggested that WikiProjects are important for the community:

> WikiProjects are good for Wikipedia because it helps keep editors motivated to write and edit. (I13)

and even indispensible:

> I probably would not have gotten involved [in Wikipedia] without the WikiProjects because they kind of set the standards for writing and they provide a forum, I guess, for experts to gather and put their work together. So yeah. The WikiProjects are critical to the whole Wikipedia thing. (I18)

One interviewee expressed indifference toward most of the support that projects provide, preferring to "freelance" and avoid the structure of the WikiProject, although he noted in his interview that he respects the advice of Military History editors:

> My name is not registered in the Project even though I am probably the most active person in that space... I have my own to-do list that is very very extensive and I don't need additional ideas where work is required (laughter) (I12).

Our analysis suggests that, for people who choose to get involved, WikiProjects provide many forms of member support that can help make editing Wikipedia an enjoyable experience. Our data suggest that Wikipedia editors who get involved in an active WikiProject experience some benefits that may affect their persistence as an editor. For example, interviewees describe benefits of project membership such as learning how to write well and conform to the standards of Wikipedia; however, we also found evidence that a "critical mass" of activity may be necessary to sustain the project and confer these benefits. The requisite kind and quantity of activity is an open question. We discovered that active Wikiproject members view opportunities to interact and socialize with editors who have similar interests as a benefit of editing in a Project and that they maintain slightly higher levels of social activity after joining a Project than before. Finally, WikiProject members observe that editing within a project gives them a strong sense that their work will persist and be improved.

Whether these perceived benefits of WikiProject affiliation have a lasting effect on the persistence of Wikipedia editors and the quality of their contributions poses an interesting question for further study. This work provides preliminary evidence that specialized workgroups play a critical role in peer production environments that go beyond coordination; they confer benefits in the form of member support that may encourage and sustain volunteer participation in the project as a whole.

ACKNOWLEDGEMENTS

NSF grants OCI-09-43148, IIS-0968484, IIS-1111124 and a grant from Carnegie Mellon's Center for the Future of the Work.

REFERENCES

1. Beschastnikh, I., Kriplean, T., and McDonald, D.W. Wikipedian Self-governance in Action: motivating the policy lens. in *Proc. International Conference on Weblogs and Social Media*. AAAI Press, 2008.

2. Blumer, H., What is wrong with social theory. *American Sociological Review*, *19*, 1, (1954), 3-10.
3. Bruckman, A., Studying the Amateur Artist: a perspective on disguising data collected in human subjects research on the internet. *Ethics and Information Technology*, *4*, 3, (2002), 217-231.
4. Bryant, S., Forte, A., and Bruckman, A. Becoming Wikipedian: transformation of participation in a collaborative online encyclopedia. in *Proc. Group:* 2005, 1-10.
5. Cosley, D., Frankowski, D., et al. SuggestBot: using intelligent task routing to help people find work in wikipedia. in *12th International Conference on Intelligent user interfaces*. ACM, 2007, 32-41.
6. Crowston, K., Wei K., L.Q., et al., Self-organization of teams in free/libre open source software development. *Information and Software Technology Journal: Special issue on Understanding the Social Side of Software Engineering*, *49*, 6, (2007), 564-575.
7. Dorogovtsev, S.N. and Mendes, J.F.F., Evolution of networks. *Advances in Physics*, *51*, 4, (2002), 1079–1187.
8. Forte, A., Larco, V., and Bruckman, A., Decentralization in Wikipedia Governance. *Journal of Management Information Systems*, *26*, 1, (2009), 49-72.
9. Grudin, J., McGrath and the Behavior of Groups (BOGS), in *HCI Remixed: Reflections on works that have influenced the HCI community*, T. Erickson and D.W. McDonald, Eds., MIT Press, Cambridge, 2008, 105-110.
10. Kim, A.J., *Community Building on the Web : Secret Strategies for Successful Online Communities* Peachpit Press, 2000.
11. Kittur, A., Suh, B., et al. He says, she says: Conflict and coordination in Wikipedia. in *Proc. CHI*, 2007, 453-462.
12. Kittur, A. and Kraut, R. Harnessing the wisdom of crowds in Wikipedia: quality through coordination. in *Proc. CSCW*, 2008, 37-46.
13. Kittur, A., Pendleton, B., and Kraut, R. Herding the cats: the influence of groups in coordinating peer production. in *Proc. WikiSym*. 2009.
14. Kollock, P. and Smith, M., The economies of online cooperation: gifts and public goods in cyberspace, in *Communities in Cyberspace*, M. Smith and P. Kollock, Eds., Routledge, New York, 1999,220-239.
15. Krieger, M., Stark, E., and Klemmer, S. Coordinating Tasks on the Commons: Designing for Personal Goals, Expertise and Serendipity. in *Proc. CHI*, 2009, 1485-1494.
16. Kriplean, T., Beschastnikh, I., et al. Community, Consensus, Coercion, Control: CS*W or how policy mediates mass participation. in *Proc. Group*, 2007.
17. Kriplean, T., Beschastnikh, I., and McDonald, D.W. Articulations of wikiwork: uncovering valued work in Wikipedia through barnstars. in *Proc. Computer Supported Cooperative Work (CSCW)*, 2008, 47-56.
18. Lampe, C., Wash, R., et al. Motivations to participate in online communities. *Proc. CHI*. 2010, 1927-1936.
19. Lave, J. and Wenger, E., *Situated Learning: legitimate peripheral participation* Cambridge University Press, Cambridge, 1991.
20. McGrath, J., Time, Interaction, and Performance (TIP): A Theory of Groups. *Small Group Research*, *22*, 2, (1991), 147-174.
21. Mossa, S., Barthélémy, M., et al., Truncation of power law behavior in "scale-free" network models due to information filtering. *Physical Review Letters*, *88*, 13, (2002).
22. Newman, M.E.J., Power laws, Pareto distributions and Zipf's law. *Contemporary Physics*, *46*, 5, (2005), 323–351.
23. Nov, O., What motivates Wikipedians? *Commun. ACM*, *50*, 11, (2007), 60-64.
24. Ostrom, E., Collective action and the evolution of the social norms. *Journal of Economic Perspectives*, *14*, 3, (2000), 137-158.
25. Panciera, K., Masli, M., and Terveen, L. 'How should I go from __ to __ without getting killed?' Motivation and Benefits in Open Collaboration. *International Symposium on Wikis and Open Collaboration*, 2011.
26. Raymond, E., *The Cathedral and the Bazaar: Musings on Linux and Open Source by an Accidental Revolutionary* O'Reilly & Associates, Sebastopol, CA, 2001.
27. Resnick, P., Konstan, J., et al., Starting New Online Communities, In *Building successful online communities: Evidence-based social design.* R.E. Kraut and P. Resnick, Eds., MIT Press,Cambridge, in press.
28. Schutz, A., *The Phenomenology of the Social World* Northwestern University Press, 1967.
29. Stewart, K.J. and Gosain, S., The Impact of Ideology on Effectiveness in Open Source Software Development Teams. *MIS Quarterly*, *30*, 2, (2006), 291-314.
30. Strauss, A. and Corbin, J., *Basics of Qualitative Research: techniques and procedures for developing grounded theory* Sage, London, 1998.
31. Viegas, F., Wattenberg, M., et al. Talk before you type: coordination in Wikipedia. in *Proc. Hawai'ian International Conference on System Sciences*, 2007.
32. Weber, M., *Basic Concepts in Sociology* Citadel Press, 1966.
33. Wikipedia. *WikiProject Military History Members*. http://en.wikipedia.org/wiki/Wikipedia:WikiProject_Military_history/Members.
34. Zachte, E. *WikiStats: Wikimedia Statistics.* [cited 06/03/2011]; http://stats.wikimedia.org/.
35. Zehavi, I., Weinberg, D.H., et al., On departures from a power law in the galaxy correlation function. *The Astrophysical Journal*, *608*, 1, Part 1, (2004), 16 - 24.

Do Editors or Articles Drive Collaboration? Multilevel Statistical Network Analysis of Wikipedia Coauthorship

Brian Keegan, Darren Gergle, Noshir Contractor
School of Communication, Northwestern University
2240 Campus Drive, Evanston, IL 60201
{bkeegan, dgergle, nosh}@northwestern.edu

ABSTRACT
Prior scholarship on Wikipedia's collaboration processes has examined the properties of either editors or articles, but not the interactions between both. We analyze the coauthorship network of Wikipedia articles about breaking news demanding intense coordination and compare the properties of these articles and the editors who contribute to them to articles about contemporary and historical events. Using p*/ERGM methods to test a multi-level, multi-theoretical model, we identify how editors' attributes and editing patterns interact with articles' attributes and authorship history. Editors' attributes like prior experience have a stronger influence on collaboration patterns, but article attributes also play significant roles. Finally, we discuss the implications our findings and methods have for understanding the socio-material duality of collective intelligence systems beyond Wikipedia.

Author Keywords
Wikipedia; collaboration; network analysis; coauthorship; exponential random graph model; ERGM; socio-material

ACM Classification Keywords
H.5.3 Theory and Models, Computer-Supported Cooperative Work

General Terms
Human Factors; Measurement; Theory

INTRODUCTION
"What makes Wikipedia work?" is a pervasive question in the literature on computer-supported cooperative work and social computing. The motivations of editors, design features of the community, affordances of peer production, and other latent social processes interact in complex ways at multiple levels to enable and sustain this massive collaboratively authored online encyclopedia.

Previous research makes clear that editors of Wikipedia articles fulfill distinct and diverse collaboration roles and different types of articles employ different forms of coordination [1, 2]. However, extant scholarship has not examined the interaction between these features: how do editors with particular skills self-organize around articles requiring different forms of collaboration?

To answer this question we examine a "boundary condition" for self-organization on Wikipedia. We compare the coauthorship of Wikipedia articles about current and breaking news events such as commercial airline disasters to topically similar articles about historical airline disasters. Articles about breaking news are coauthored under "high tempo" conditions which demand unique forms of coordination to manage interdependencies. We analyze the coauthorship networks of high and low tempo articles as well as the attributes of editors who contribute to them.

We review existing scholarship on the duality of Wikipedia as both user action embodied in artifacts and processes which support collaboration. Integrating this review, we develop a multi-theoretical, multi-level model describing how features of editors, articles, and interactions between both influence collaboration structure [3, 4]. Our findings suggest that while the features of articles and attributes of editors both influence structure, editors' experience more strongly governs the types of editors they collaborate with and the types of articles they work on. These findings have implications for how task demands intersect with user attributes to structure self-organizing collaborations.

We also make a methodological contribution by demonstrating how a class of statistical methods called p*/exponential random graph models (p*/ERGMs) enable multi-level network analysis. We specify statistical parameters which correspond to processes operating at each of the article and editor levels to disentangle which are more influential on collaboration structure. We discuss the implications p*/ERGM methods have for analyzing and comparing multi-level social interactions in other domains.

BACKGROUND
As is the case with many online communities, the majority of contributions to Wikipedia come from a fraction of the entire user base [5, 6]. Despite this disparity in effort, online communities like Wikipedia are able to escape traps

such as the tragedy of the commons and social loafing owing to members' uses and gratifications [7], diverse motivations [8], affordances of peer production [9], and design features of the community itself [10]. These approaches generally emphasize the agency of individuals to form and realize their own goals. In the context of Wikipedia, editors who are motivated to fulfill particular roles like copyediting or vandal fighting [1, 11], are socialized into sub-communities with like-minded collaborators [12], and recognize or revert the contributions of other editors [13].

Peer-production communities are oriented around producing and maintaining an artifact such as an operating system or encyclopedia article. Although these artifacts are the agglomeration of individual users' actions, artifacts like Wikipedia articles are embedded within socio-technical systems which imbue them with innate agency. This material agency enables them to operate outside of the control of any single person and emerges from the network of user and system interactions [14]. In the context of a Wikipedia article, content added or reverted by other editors, markup language interpreted into style formatting by the MediaWiki software, and page protections enforced by administrators are examples of articles "acting" on their "own" outside of any one user's direct control.

Coauthorship patterns on Wikipedia thus foreground the duality of persons and material artifacts [14-16]: collaborations occur around articles exhibiting particular features but articles also emerge from the contributions of editors with distinct traits. The material agency of articles such as topic, quality, age, or number of contributors influences the types of editors who are capable of making further contributions to an article. For example, a featured article about Barack Obama probably will not preserve contributions from newly-registered editors identifying with the Tea Party movement. However, the properties of editors also influence the types of articles they choose to edit and maintain. The human agency of these actors manifests in attributes such as varying expertise, editing experience, and roles. For example, a college freshman who uploads photos about soccer players will be unlikely to take up correcting formulae on general relativity. This suggests the features and attributes of *both* articles and editors influence the self-organization of collaboration on Wikipedia.

While scholars have articulated rationales for how and why collaboration and social action emerge from both internal human agency (what we refer to as editor-focused attributes) as well as external social foci (what we refer to as article-focused features), the interaction between these two approaches has not been studied. We review and identify themes from each of these literatures to motivate a statistical analysis which allows us to "decouple" this duality and model the individual influences as well as interactions between editor attributes, article features, structural pattern of editors' contributions to articles, and structural patterns of an article's contributions from editors. We advance CSCW scholarship by using a statistical approach that allows us to simultaneously examine how the features of articles, attributes of editors, and these network structures *all* influence the organizations of Wikipedia collaborations. While processes which occur at a single level of analysis (such as 1 and 2 below) certainly play a role, we expect the *interactions* between each of (1) an editor's attributes and his or her history of editing other articles, and (2) an article's features and its history of revisions from other editors, will provide a more complete account of self-organization on Wikipedia.

1. Editor based attributes. For example, do experienced editors contribute to more articles than non-experienced editors?
2. Article based features. For example, do breaking news articles involve more editors than traditional articles?
3. Editor-focused interactions with article features. For example, is an experienced editor more likely to contribute to breaking news articles if they previously contributed to *other breaking news articles* than a non-experienced editor?
4. Article-focused interactions with editor attributes. For example, are breaking news articles more likely to attract contributions from experienced editors if *other experienced editors* have also contributed than non-breaking news articles?

In the following sections we examine the prior literature that has typically focused either on article-focused features or editor-focused attributes and aim to consolidate this work using a multi-theoretical, multi-level modeling approach that allows us to describe how both features of articles, editors and the interactions between them influence the structure of collaborations on breaking news events about commercial airline disasters.

Article-focused: Task Coordination and Social Foci

The demands of coordinating coauthorship on Wikipedia articles vary substantially with the age of the article and the number of contributors to it [2, 17]. An additional dimension is the contemporary salience of an article. Like other forms of social media [18], current and breaking news events uniquely motivate editors to contribute to and collaborate in Wikipedia [19]. However, co-authoring an article about breaking news events like commercial airline disasters involves complex, time-sensitive, and highly interdependent tasks. In this section we review how the features of breaking news articles not only influence patterns of coauthorship, but how these article-focused features *interact* with the attributes of the editors who contribute to these articles.

Although prior research suggests the compounding coordination costs of many editors engaged in interdependent work will inhibit the development of high quality Wikipedia articles [2, 17], articles about breaking news complicate this assumption. On one hand, Wikipedia articles about breaking news events are often perceived to be exemplars of timeliness, breadth, and reliability in the immediate aftermath of an event like the Virginia Tech massacre [20]. On the other hand, the concentration of new editor activity is also densest while the article is less than 24 hours old and being intensively developed [19].

The popularity and quality of these articles in spite of these constraints poses a paradox in which "breaking articles" remain high quality in spite of the number of editors attempting to make simultaneous contributions with incomplete information and no centralized coordination. Examining the features of only articles or editors may present an incomplete picture and the novel coordination processes which enable these articles to be rapidly authored but also high quality likely emerge from the interactions between features of the article and attributes of its editors.

We argue these breaking news articles belong to a class of *high-tempo collaborations* characterized by non-routine and extremely urgent work, abrupt consequences, and intense attention. Coordination in these volatile environments demands high levels of heedful and interrelated action, knowledge integration, and information processing [21]. These "emergent response groups" are unique because group members have diverse motivations, mixed perspectives, varied resources to contribute, and substantial volition to come and go as they please. These factors contribute to unstable task definitions and the pursuit of potentially conflicting goals [22].

Members of these collaborations adapt by re-tailoring and sharing their particular expertise, emphasizing trust through action rather than credibility through expertise, and relying on narratives and knowledge artifacts to document actions taken [22]. What emerges from the on-going and repeated interactions between both editors and the article as they expand, update, copy edit, and fight vandals is not only the content of the article but also an artifact narrating prior actions and decisions.

Thus, an article feature such as being breaking or non-breaking is an important variable for modeling the collaboration patterns of editors. The salience of the topic and demands of coordinating interrelated tasks makes breaking news articles *foci* which actively bring people together and shapes their collective action much more than articles about historical events which do not demand high-tempo collaborations [23]. Therefore, we expect that articles about breaking news events may attract more editors than Wikipedia articles about non-breaking news events. Thus, we expect:

<u>H1</u>	Article attributes like salience will co-vary with number of editors. Breaking news articles will attract more editors than non-breaking articles.

There are latent tendencies for breaking news articles to receive many contributions (discussed above) or experienced editors to simply be prolific or engaged in many articles (discussed in the next section). However, considering the features of the article absent the attributes of the editors who contribute to it is necessarily incomplete. For example, the "sink or swim" coordination demands of a breaking news article or attempts to limit "dysfunction from diversity" [24] may predispose editors to only want to collaborate with other editors who exhibit similar characteristics or qualifications as themselves on a breaking news article. If other experienced editors are contributing this may be social proof about the collaboration and may attract other experienced editors. This would manifest as an article-focused homophily in which the attributes of the article result in similar kinds of editors collaborating [25].

<u>H2</u>	Article attributes like salience will co-vary with the types of editors who collaborate with each other. Experienced editors will co-author with other experienced editors on breaking news articles.

Editor-focused: Social Roles and Identity

An alternative rationale why collaborations around breaking news articles exhibit different processes of self-organization revolves around the attributes of the editors who contribute to these articles rather than the features of the articles themselves. Editor-focused attributes like experience can potentially explain why some editors contribute to more articles than others, but also how these editor attributes interact with article features and lead users to fulfill distinct roles contributing to particular types of articles.

Roles in social media manifest as behavioral regularities, structural position, social action, or self-identification. These roles form complex ecologies which are defined in relation to other roles such as substantive experts, technical editors, counter-vandalism, and community building [26]. Other typologies have identified the placeholders, completers, housekeepers, and shapers who contribute, integrate, and shape content on Wikipedia [27].

In general, roles are resources that enable individuals to adapt to new contexts by creating new structures as well as imitating behaviors that were previously successful [28]. Because dedicated Wikipedia editors have distinct but stable behavioral patterns [6], editors can be classified into distinct roles based on the distribution of their activity [1]. The patterning of interactions among editors inhabiting particular social roles across different breaking news article collaborations can potentially explain how breaking news articles are co-authored in spite of steep coordination costs.

Editors may have a particular interest in contributing to topical areas such as airliner disasters (the topic explored in this paper). Experienced editors in this domain may have deep expertise about the appropriate vocabulary and style for describing an accident or knowledge about relevant citations [12]. Thus, these editors' may be fulfilling "caretaker" roles in which they edit many articles while less experienced editors specialize on fewer articles.

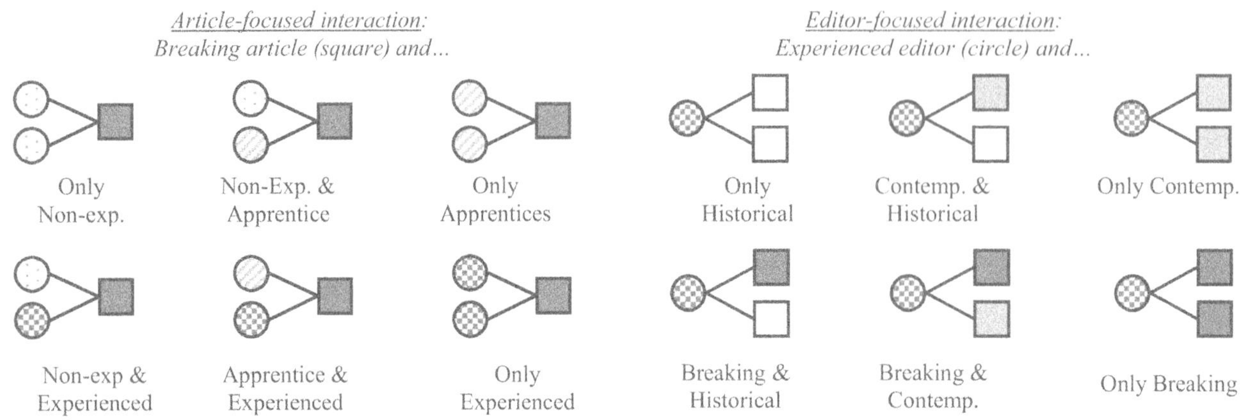

Figure 1: Visualization of p*/ERGM attribute interaction parameters that capture varying attributes of both the editors and the articles in Wikipedia. Dark-red circles are expert editors, medium-red circles are apprentice editors, and light-red circles are non-expert editors. Dark-blue squares are breaking articles, medium-blue squares are contemporaneous articles, and light-blue squares are historical articles.

H3	Editor attributes like experience will co-vary with the number of articles edited. Experienced editors contribute to more articles than other editors.

Again, considering the attributes of editors separately from the features of the articles they edit presents an incomplete account by divorcing the role editors play from the resources to which they contribute. Experienced editors may self-identify as "breaking news editors" who preferentially edit these articles out of novelty or immediate gratification of contributing to an in-demand information artifact. Experienced editors preferring to edit only breaking news articles would manifest as a pattern of editor-focused homophily in which the attributes of editors cause them to contribute to similar kinds of articles. Thus, we expect:

H4	Editor attributes like experience will co-vary with the types of articles they edit. Experienced editors will be more likely to contribute to similar types of articles than dissimilar types of articles.

Alternative Explanations for Collaboration Structure

In addition to the hypothesized explanations, we expect a variety of alternative processes could account for differences in collaboration structures between articles covering breaking, contemporary and historical events. We control for the influence of these factors by including them as parameters in the model in addition to our hypothesized variables of interest (breaking news article and editor experience).

Article features such as the severity of a catastrophe, proximity to developed countries, evaluated quality, and article length are also likely to influence collaboration patterns. For example, in our corpus of breaking news events centering on airline disasters we expect that the number of fatalities and survivors of an accident will be strongly correlated with the amount of attention an article receives from Wikipedia editors. Wikipedians also exhibit a "self-focus bias" in which geographic proximity influences why articles appear in one language but not another [29]. We expect that accidents occurring within or near developed countries will receive more attention from editors than accidents occurring in developing countries. Finally, a number of studies have identified that the number of editors, length of an article, and article quality are all correlated [30, 31]. We use both the article quality and article length as controls on the number of editors who contributed to the article.

Editor attributes such as tenure in the community and whether or not the editor is registered are also likely to influence the likelihood of editors making contributions to articles of various types. Editors who started editing earlier in Wikipedia's history likely have greater familiarity with best practices and may be more involved in editing many articles [12]. We also expect registered editors are both highly motivated and more committed to the community, both of which lead them to make more contributions than non-registered editors [10].

OUR APPROACH

Establishing which of the collaboration processes is most influential requires a model accounting for the simultaneous contribution of each of these processes. However, owing to the methodological limitations of common types of network analysis, studies often only examine one level of analysis which accounts for little of the overall variance in the network. Analyzing the effects of network parameters interacting at different levels of analysis allow us an integrated test of complimentary and competing theories of how network structure emerges [3, 4].

While descriptive approaches and regression analyses serve valuable purposes for answering particular research questions, these approaches are limited to analyzing the properties in a "snapshot" of a network. These kinds of analyses cannot explain the endogenous processes of how the network structures itself nor the simultaneous influence of exogenous actor-level attributes on the network structure.

Statistical models like p*/ERGMs extend the logic of multivariate logistic regression to relational data: the presence or absence of a binary tie in a network is an outcome variable predicted by a vector of independent variables called parameters. These parameters correspond to theoretically-motivated structural characteristics(s) we believe are more or less likely to occur in the distribution. Visualizations of these parameters are provided in Figure 1.

Because the likelihood that a network tie is present or absent in a network is not independently and identically distributed (IID) from other network ties' likelihoods, a statistical model must account for these dependencies [32]. In a p*/ERGM, parameters allow the models to reflect dependencies on both endogenous tendencies for ties to exist because of other local structures in the network (e.g., popular articles continue to attract more editor attention) as well as exogenous attribute covariates (e.g., experienced editors prefer to work with other experienced editors). These methods allow us to test hypotheses about the tendency for ties to form as a result of the properties of the sending node, receiving node, as well as the presence and properties of other local ties and nodes.

The model produces a set of parameter estimates whereby estimates of zero indicate the modeled effect does not alter the likelihood from random chance, a positive parameter suggests the effect increases the likelihood of a tie, and a negative parameter implies the effect decreases the likelihood of a tie. Significance is tested using a *t*-ratio and concluded to be significant when the absolute value of this ratio exceeds a critical t-value of 1.96. Details about the specification, estimation, and simulation of p*/ERGMs are beyond the scope of this paper but can be found in [32-35].

DATA, VARIABLES, AND METHODS

A variety of Wikipedia article genres like natural disasters, sporting events, and political scandals exhibit high tempo features which should require unique forms of coordination. We examine articles about commercial airline disasters for this study because these incidents occur with sufficient regularity to generate a large sample but are also "normal accidents" involving complex technology with prompt and serious consequences which make reliably notable events warranting coverage in Wikipedia.

Articles for the corpus were drawn from the "List of accidents and incidents involving commercial aircraft."[1] Our sample excludes hijackings and other instances of terrorism (such as the four flights involved in the September 11 attacks) because these incidents represent an archetype of catastrophe with distinct attention, salience, and causal attributions compared to "typical" accidents attributable to crew error, mechanical failure, or weather conditions. The resulting corpus includes 249 articles about commercial airline disasters which occurred since January 1990 and through December 2010.

Based on the list of articles identified above, we developed a tool to extract and stitch together XML revision histories for each article using Wikipedia's "Special:Export" function.[2] These data include revision-level data about the article name and ID, editor name and ID, timestamp, content, and comments. Registered users (n=6,462) identified by names and unregistered users (n=7,830) identified by IP addresses each have unique IDs. 14,292 unique user accounts made 58,500 revisions to this corpus between September 16, 2001 and May 24, 2011.

Each revision's article and editor ID were recorded as a duple representing an editor's modification of an article. Because p*/ERGMs estimate the binary presence or absence of a link rather than the weight or strength of a link, repeated editor-article duples were discarded creating a binary edgelist of 23,903 unique editor-article interactions. The edgelist was imported to the `statnet` statistical network analysis package in `R` for analysis using the `ergm` library [36]. The size of the resulting network required us to analyze the data on high-memory computing instances on Amazon Web Services' Elastic Cloud Compute (AWS EC2) infrastructure.

Bipartite Network Modeling

We conceptualize the Wikipedia revision data as a network consisting of a set of actors and a set of relationships among these actors. While traditional network analysis emphasizes unipartite or one-mode data where the relationships are between a single type of actor (i.e., people-to-people), two unique sets of actors actually exist in Wikipedia: editors and articles.

Because it is nonsensical for an article to edit another article or a user to edit another user, we structure our interaction data as a *bipartite graph* in which the nodes can be partitioned into exactly two mutually exclusive sets of actors such that ties only exist between sets and no ties exist within a set [37]. Thus, a link exists between an editor node, *E*, and an article node, *A*, if *E* made a contribution to *A*, but neither *E-E* nor *A-A* links can exist. This bipartite structure is alternatively referred to as a "two-mode" or "affiliation" network. A bipartite network is a natural approach for modeling collaboration because it explicitly models the duality of persons and groups: a link between the social actors as one level of analysis and the groups to which they belong as another [15]. We employ p*/ERGM parameters designed specifically for bipartite networks [34, 35].

Node Attribute Construction

A variety of article and editor variables were extracted from either the revision histories or article content to provide covariates for control, analysis, and modeling.

[1] http://en.wikipedia.org/wiki/List_of_accidents_and_incidents_involving_commercial_aircraft

[2] http://en.wikipedia.org/wiki/Special:Export

- **Article attributes** – The date of the incident and timestamp of the first edit to the article were recorded. Based upon the difference between these times and Wikipedia's creation in January 2001, three possible types of articles exist: *breaking articles* about events which are written within 72 hours of the incident (*n*=93), *contemporaneous articles* about events which happened while Wikipedia existed but were written well after the incident (*n*=50), and *historical articles* about events which predated Wikipedia's existence and are thus written well after the event (*n*=106).
- **Other article attributes** – The *word count* excluding markup syntax is recorded as a continuous variable. The modal *article quality* as evaluated by associated WikiProjects is coded as one of seven categorical attributes ranging from Stub to Featured Article-class.
- **Incident attributes** – The count of *fatalities* and *survivors* are recorded for each event as controls for the severity and thus salience of a particular incident. A dummy control variable for *OECD location* coded whether or not the crash occurred within or off the coast of one of the 34 developed member nations of the OECD.
- **Editor attributes** – The total number of revisions an editor made *within the corpus* over the 10 year span of time was recorded as an edit count. This count was binned into three categories to capture topical editing experience: 1 to 3 contributions (4 is the mean) was *unexperienced* (*n*=12,148), 4 to 42 contributions (mean plus one standard deviation) was an *apprentice* (*n*=1,992), and 43 or more contributions was *experienced* (*n*=152). Editors who had registered accounts (*n*=6,462) were dichotomized from non-registered users (*n*=7,830). Finally, editors were partitioned into three classes: *early contributors* who made their first contribution to the corpus before 2008 (*n*=5,366), *middle contributors* who made their first contribution to the corpus from 2008 to 2010 (*n*=6,224), and *late contributors* who made their first contribution to the corpus between 2010 and the present (*n*=2,702).

P*/ERGM CAPTURES MULTILEVEL INTERACTIONS

We specify one large p*/ERGM which includes single level main effects and structural tendencies (summarized on Table 1) as well as multi-level attribute interaction parameters (summarized on Table 2) to test our four hypotheses. This method reproduces similar "main effects" findings for the control variables as previous studies: the likelihood of editors revising an article increases with every additional fatality associated with the incident, incidents occurring in or near OECD nations, higher quality, longer word counts, early contributors, and registered users.

We also specify endogenous structural parameters which control for the latent tendency for links to be created by chance (*edges*), the network-level tendencies for articles or editors to become highly centralized (*article* and *editor degree distribution*), and the local-level tendencies for articles to accumulate multiple editors (*multi-editor article tendency*) as well as editors to contribute to multiple articles (*multi-article editor tendency*). The estimates for these parameters are listed in Table 1 as "structural tendencies."

Structural tendencies	
Edges	-2.626 (-217.0)***
Multi-editor article tendency	0.01321 (2.89)***
Multi-article editor tendency	0.08042 (36.9)***
Article degree distribution (α=2.5)	-4.476 (-16.8)***
Editor degree distribution (α=0.25)	4.616 (68.6)***
Article features	
Controls	
Fatalities	1.22E-03 (20.9)***
Survivors	1.61E-04 (1.40)
Location: OECD	0.145 (24.9)***
Quality – Start	0.158 (21.9)***
Quality – C	0.371 (56.1)***
Quality – B	0.366 (93.4)***
Quality – GA	0.309 (11.2)***
Quality – FA	0.127 (1.38)
Word Count	6.51E-05 (8.00)***
Main effects (Hypothesis 1)	
Temporal Type – Contemporaneous	-0.549 (-33.1)***
Temporal Type – Historical	-0.519 (-45.3)***
Editor attributes	
Controls	
Registered	0.700 (86.3)***
Cohort – Middle contributor	-0.137 (-6.87)***
Cohort – Late contributor	-0.154 (-3.45)***
Main effects (Hypothesis 3)	
Experience – Apprentice	-4.14 (-523.2)***
Experience – Experienced	-2.00 (-66.3)***

Table 1: "Main effect" p*/ERGM estimates (t-statistics). Estimates are net of parameters in Table 2. Cells are shaded green for positive & significant estimates and red for negative & significant estimates.
p = * < 0.001 < ** < 0.01 < * < 0.05**

The estimate for the negative *edges* parameter reflects the log-likelihood of a network tie appearing entirely by chance and serves as the "intercept term" reflecting the density of the network if no other effects were present. This can also be interpreted as the "cost" of creating a tie which other structural tendencies, factors, and interactions will need to overcome. The positive *multi-article* and *multi-editor* structural parameters respectively reflect the latent tendency for articles to accumulate editors and for editors to edit many articles. The negative *article degree distribution* reflects the tendency for articles to avoid long-tailed degree distributions while the positive *editor degree distribution* captures the tendency for editors to have a very skewed distribution. These findings suggest a tie is most likely to form between articles with few co-authors and editors who have also edited many other articles.

We find evidence for H1 that breaking news articles are more likely to attract editors than contemporaneous or historical articles. Both of these article types are less likely to have ties to other editors than breaking news articles.

Article-focused interactions (Hypothesis 2)			
	Breaking	*Contemp.*	*Historical*
Only Non-Experienced (P1)	-0.0109 (-2.37)*	-0.0101 (-15.5)***	-0.0086 (-1.90)
Non-Experienced & Apprentice (P2)	-0.0153 (-3.33)***	-0.00122 (-2.59)**	-0.01449 (-3.02)**
Only Apprentices (P3)	-0.00317 (-0.68)	-0.03674 (-16.9)***	0.00166 (0.39)
Non-Experienced & Experienced (P4)	-0.01588 (-3.46)***	-0.02601 (-17.5)***	-0.01590 (-20.7)***
Apprentice & Experienced (P5)	0.00613 (1.10)	0.02869 (28.02)***	0.00415 (0.64)
Only Experienced (P6)	-0.03552 (-19.9)***	0.00578 (0.85)	0.00090 (0.23)
Editor-focused interactions (Hypothesis 4)			
	Experienced	*Apprentice*	*Non-Exp.*
Only Breaking (P7)	0.00552 (1.63)	0.11540 (28.3)***	-6.027 (-135.9)***
Breaking & Contemp. (P8)	-0.06421 (-20.7)***	0.01308 (2.50)*	-5.977 (-52.7)***
Only Contemp.(P9)	0.04338 (3.98)***	0.23140 (13.0)***	-5.116 (-32.7)***
Breaking & Historical (P10)	-0.07691 (-25.7)***	-0.01577 (-4.22)***	-6.136 (-81.7)***
Contemp. & Historical (P11)	-0.05648 (-18.5)***	0.08355 (25.7)***	-5.517 (-54.8)***
Only Historical (P12)	0.00056 (0.12)	0.15120 (45.5)	-5.468 (-84.6)***

Table 2: Editor-article "interaction" p*/ERGM estimates (t-statistics) capturing the tendency for the row title to edit/be edited by the column title. Estimates are net of parameters in Table 1. Labels in parentheses next to attribute names are references for attribute interaction parameters.
p = * < 0.001 < ** < 0.01 < * < 0.05**

However, the p*/ERGM estimates testing H3 invert our expectation that experienced editors would be more likely to contribute to many articles than non-experienced editors. The negative estimates imply apprentice and experienced editors are much less likely than non-experienced editors to edit many articles. Experienced editors (within our corpus) make repeated contributions to a few articles (again only within our corpus) rather than a few contributions to many articles. This specialization points toward rejecting H3.

Modeling Attribute and Structural Interaction Effects

p*/ERGM methods stand out from traditional regression approaches in their ability to model the interactions between local editor-article authorship structure, editor attributes, and article features with parsimonious and statistically-valid parameters. We employ bipartite p*/ERGM parameters like those visualized in Figure 1 and use them to model the complex interactions between article features and editor attributes. These feature and attribute estimates are summarized in Table 2.

There are two broad classes of interactions reflecting the two possible explanations for editor-focused or article-focused processes to influence the collaboration structure. We use editor experience and article temporal type as the interacting attributes. "Article-focused interactions" capture the tendency for articles possessing a feature such as "breaking news article" to be edited by actors sharing similar or dissimilar attributes like experienced/apprentice/non-experienced editor. "Editor-focused interactions" capture the tendency for editors possessing an attribute like "experienced" to contribute articles sharing similar or dissimilar features like breaking/contemporary/historical article. Figure 1 visualizes six structural signatures for article-focused interactions with editor attributes on the left and six structural signatures for editor-focused interactions with article features on the right.

Within "Article-focused interactions", we observe a general tendency for significantly fewer interactions than would be expected by chance between non-experienced editors and apprentices (P2) and experienced editors (P4). Coauthorship among non-experienced editors (P1) is likewise rarer than random chance. Likewise, there appear to be strong disincentives for apprentice editors to work with each other (P3) on articles about contemporaneous incidents. Despite our expectation that experienced editors would fulfill crucial roles in high tempo collaborations around breaking news events by intensively collaborating together, after controlling for variables such as the severity of the event, experienced editors work together on high tempo collaborations significantly less often than we would expect by chance (P6). Nevertheless, the other findings support H2 that the coordination demands of an article influence the tendency of editors with similar or dissimilar levels of experience to work together.

Within "Editor-focused interactions", editors of all levels of experience are unlikely to contribute to both breaking and historical articles (P10). The lack of shared coauthorship on breaking and historical articles suggests these are very distinct sub-genres with limited interaction between each groups' editors. However, apprentice editors have a tendency to edit diverse combinations of articles above and beyond the latent tendencies for editors to edit many articles. This offsets the main effect for apprentice editors to be unlikely to contribute to articles in general as well as the lack of a bridging role by experienced editors.

Experienced editors contribute to contemporary articles (P9) at a rate much greater than chance and make contributions to different types of articles (P8, P10, P11) at rates much less (respectively) than expected by chance. Contrary to our expectations, the effects of experienced editors' sustained contributions to only breaking (P7) or historical articles (P12) are weak and non-significant. Highly experienced editors are instead characterized by deep and sustained involvement in a few articles rather than stewardship of many articles. Instead, it is the apprentice editors who appear to play a crucial role not only contributing to many articles but also acting as crucial brokers providing bridges within breaking (P7), contemporary (P9), and historical articles (P12) as well as between these article types (P8, P11). Again, these findings

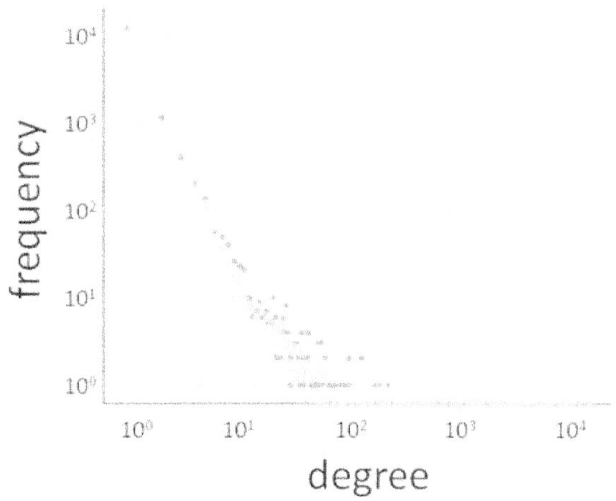

Figure 2: Degree distribution with mean values from 10,000 simulated networks based on estimated model (in yellow) compared against observed values (in blue).

support H4 that an editor's level of experience will influence the tendency for them to edit similar or dissimilar types of articles.

The magnitude of the coefficients for these editor-focused main effects and interaction parameters are generally larger than the article-focused parameters. This suggests the attributes and structural interactions focused on editors play a stronger role in explaining the presence and absence of links between editors and articles than the features and structures focused on articles. Thus, editor attributes are more influential on the self-organization of high tempo Wikipedia collaborations than the features of articles.

Confirming Goodness-of-fit by Simulation

The previous steps analyzed local-level processes but are these features sufficient to explain global network properties? We assess the model's goodness-of-fit by simulating other networks based on this model and use the resulting distribution of networks to compare the properties of these generated networks to the observed network [32]. Using the `ergm` package's "gof" function, we simulate a sample of 10,000 networks based on the p*/ERGM in Tables 1 and 2 and measure fit using the degree distribution. Figure 2 plots the observed values (in blue circles) and distribution of simulated values (in yellow boxes) for the combined degree distribution for both modes of the network. We observe a good-fitting model because the observed distributions are almost completely bounded by the distributions from simulated networks.

DISCUSSION

Adopting a socio-material approach which recognizes the agency of both articles and editors to influence the self-organization of collaboration requires analyzing the interactions between both articles and editors. We incorporated editor attributes and article features by modeling their interactions as a bipartite graph and using p*/ERGM methods. We expanded on previous approaches by not only analyzing processes occurring at different levels of analysis but also by modeling the interactions between these levels in addition to controlling for potentially confounding processes. p*/ERGM statistical models allowed us to disambiguate between the article-focused and editor-focused interactions by specifying a model which simultaneously incorporates each of these potentially confounding processes to assess the relative contribution of each to the network structure. This approach revealed new insights regarding how Wikipedia editors and articles self-organize in relation to one another.

Prior scholarship has either developed editor-focused accounts examining how editor attributes (e.g., experience) influence collaboration patterns [1, 26] or article-focused accounts of why some articles features (e.g., task coordination demands) lead to higher quality or more contributions [2, 17]. Our analysis is the first to simultaneously look at both levels of analysis to better understand the relationship each has on the self-organization of collaborations involving extreme coordination demands and varied editor experience. Our results suggest that editor experience and the features of articles in their contribution history have a stronger influence on the self-organization of the collaboration than article features like coordination demands and the attributes of editors who contribute to these articles. Our approach provides a more complete account of the processes which influence the structure of collaborations on Wikipedia than looking at the structure of network of just editors or articles.

Applying this approach to the paradox of how breaking news articles exhibit high quality despite steep coordination costs and varied editor experience, we unpacked how the attributes of editors have greater influence over this self-organization. These findings validated our hypotheses that not only are the coordination demands of articles matched with the number of editors who contribute to them (H1), but that coordination demands of certain article types also lead editors to seek or avoid other types of editors *depending on the type of editor* (H2).

However, as measured by both effect size and valence, the features of an article and its interactions with editor attributes play a secondary role in structuring the collaboration as compared to the attributes of editors and their interactions with article features. Although experienced editors exhibit a tendency toward concentrating their work in a few articles (H3), we found evidence that an editor's level of experience leads them to also work on or avoid certain articles *depending on the type of article* (H4).

While previous work examined how editors' varying level of expertise influenced how Wikipedia tools were used or other users were perceived and rewarded [12, 13], we demonstrate that editors' patterns of contributions are mediated through their own intrinsic attributes, the coordination demands of an article, the kinds of articles they have contributed to in the past, and the types of editors who also contributed to those articles. Unwinding these intricate dependencies is crucial for understanding the processes which contribute to the formation, maintenance, dissolution, and re-emergence of social and technological interactions in Wikipedia and other online communities and distributed organizations.

Implications

Wikipedia's coverage of breaking news events suggests that peer production systems are capable of operating far from conditions of stable task demands and community membership [19]. Our findings suggest that tasks which demand high tempo knowledge collaboration may benefit more from matching users to tasks based on their own experience level and history of contributions to similar tasks in the past rather than assembling a team solely by optimizing on the demands of the task or the experience of other members of a team. Recruiting members with diverse backgrounds and interests may increase group productivity [24], but our results suggest that special care should be paid to the particular configurations and combinations of interests rather than dimensionless indices of diversity.

Statistical models allow for a more parsimonious and theoretically-coupled representation of dense and complex network structures by capturing the local-level interaction tendencies as well as the emergent macro-level structure [35]. Moreover, complex dependencies in networks are difficult to make sense of with descriptive statistics, visualizations may not provide statistically valid inferences, and due to the differences in levels of analysis parameterizing and controlling for these complex dependencies is extremely difficult, if not impossible, with traditional OLS and even hierarchical regression (e.g., mixed model) techniques.

Like regression or other statistical approaches, p*/ERGM methods require specifying models with theoretically well-motivated parameters in addition to translating extant theoretical constructs into appropriate network parameters. Absent a theoretical rationale for model specification and appropriate controls, both types of models can recover spurious relationships. However, these approaches suggest scholars can pose more meaningful research questions about multi-level and multi-theoretical processes about self-organization in collective intelligence systems.

p*/ERGMs also allow comparative network analysis by examining the similarities of the processes which structure networks of very different size, scale, and context [38]. This analysis only looked at one particular sub-genre of articles about airline crashes, but it would be possible to estimate models for other topics with a breaking news component such as earthquakes, hurricanes, or sporting events. p*/ERGMs for each of these could be estimated and a meta-analysis performed to compare the collaboration practices across topics or even other collaboration systems.

Limitations and Future Work

p*/ERGM methods are computationally intensive and become even more so as both the complexity of the model and the number of nodes in the network increases. Although new "peta-scale" computational infrastructures may address these bottlenecks, for the time being extending p*/ERGM methods to very large networks containing tens of millions of nodes like the entire Twitter, Facebook, or Wikipedia graphs is impractical. However, well-motivated boundary specification and comparative analysis or sampling approaches combined with meta-analyses can make large-scale analysis more tractable [39].

The p*/ERGM we employed assumed the data was cross-sectional and thus omitted potential temporal dependencies such as a tendency for an editor to contribute *after* another editor contributes. Longitudinal models of network change and dynamics can also be specified [40]. Although, editors' social roles play a role in coordinating work, it may also be the case that articles can fulfill "roles" socializing editors into particular collaboration norms or introducing them to effective coordination practices. In light of the influence of these editor-focused attributes, future work should unpack how an editor's temporal "trajectory" of contributions influences the types of roles they fulfill across articles.

We encourage other researchers to adopt p*/ERGM methods to ask better questions about multi-level and multi-theoretical processes which influence communication patterns, knowledge sharing, and distributed collaboration in collective intelligence and other socio-technical systems.

ACKNOWLEDGMENTS

We would like to thank members of the CollabLab and SONIC groups for development assistance and feedback.

REFERENCES

1. Welser, H. T., Cosley, D., Kossinets, G., Lin, A., Dokshin, F., Gay, G. and Smith, M. Finding social roles in Wikipedia. In *Proc. iConference'11,* ACM (2011): 122-129.
2. Kittur, A., Lee, B. and Kraut, R. Coordination in collective intelligence: the role of team structure and task interdependence. In *Proc. CHI'09*, ACM (2009): 1495-1504
3. Contractor, N. S., Wasserman, S. and Faust, K. Testing multitheoretical, multilevel hypotheses about organizational networks. *Academy of Management Rev*, 31, 3 (2006), 681-703.
4. Monge, P. R. and Contractor, N. S. Theories of Communication Networks. Oxford U. Press, 2003.
5. Kittur, A., Chi, E., Pendleton, B. A., Suh, B. and Mytkowicz, T. Power of the Few vs. Wisdom of the Crowd: Wikipedia and the Rise of the Bourgeoisie. In *Proc. CHI'07,* ACM (2007).
6. Panciera, K., Halfaker, A. and Terveen, L. Wikipedians are born, not made: a study of power editors on Wikipedia. In *Proc. GROUP'09,* ACM (2009): 51-60.

7. Lampe, C., Wash, R., Velasquez, A. and Ozkaya, E. Motivations to participate in online communities. In *Proc. CHI'10*, ACM (2010): 1927-1936.
8. Rafaeli, S. and Ariel, Y. "Online motivational factors: Incentives for participation and contribution in Wikipedia." *Psychological Aspects of Cyberspace*. Cambridge U. Press, 2008.
9. Benkler, Y. *The wealth of networks: How social production transforms markets and freedom*. Yale U. Press, 2006.
10. Ren, Y., Kraut, R. and Kiesler, S. Applying common identity and bond theory to design of online communities. *Organization Studies*, 28, 3 (2007).
11. Geiger, R. S. and Ribes, D. The work of sustaining order in Wikipedia: the banning of a vandal. In *Proc. CSCW'10*, ACM (2010): 117-126.
12. Bryant, S. L., Forte, A. and Bruckman, A. Becoming Wikipedian: transformation of participation in a collaborative online encyclopedia. In *Proc. GROUP'05*, ACM (2005): 1-10.
13. Kriplean, T., Beschastnikh, I. and McDonald, D. W. Articulations of WikiWork: Uncovering Valued Work in Wikipedia through Barnstars. In *Proc. CSCW'08*, ACM (2008): 47-56.
14. Contractor, N., Monge, P. and Leonardi, P. M. Multidimensional Networks and the Dynamics of Sociomateriality: Bringing Technology Inside the Network. *Int'l Journal of Communication*, 5, (2011).
15. Breiger, R. L. The duality of persons and groups. *Social Forces*, 53, 2 (1974), 181-190.
16. Kane, G. C. and Alavi, M. Casting the net: A multimodal network perspective on user-system interactions. *Info. Sys. Research*, 19, 3 (2008), 253-272.
17. Kittur, A. and Kraut, R. E. Harnessing the wisdom of crowds in wikipedia: quality through coordination. In *Proc. CSCW'08*, ACM (2008): 37-46.
18. Palen, L. and Vieweg, S. The emergence of online widescale interaction in unexpected events: assistance, alliance & retreat. In *Proc. CSCW'08*, ACM (2008): 117-126.
19. Keegan, B., Gergle, D. and Contractor, N. Hot off the Wiki: Dynamics, Practices, and Structures in Wikipedia's Coverage of the Tohoku Catastrophes. In *Proc. WikiSym'11*, ACM (2011): 105-113.
20. Cohen, N. The Latest on Virginia Tech, From Wikipedia. *The New York Times* (2007).
21. Brown, S. and Eisenhardt, K. The art of continuous change: Linking complexity theory and time-paced evolution in relentlessly shifting organizations. *Administrative Science Quarterly*, 42, 1 (1997), 1-34.
22. Majchrzak, A., Jarvenpaa, S. and Hollingshead, A. Coordinating expertise among emergent groups responding to disasters. *Org. Science*, 18, 1 (2007).
23. Feld, S. L. The focused organization of social ties. *American J. of Sociology*, 86, 5 (1981), 1015-1035.
24. Chen, J., Ren, Y. and Riedl, J. The effects of diversity on group productivity and member withdrawal in online volunteer groups. In *Proc. CHI'10*, ACM (2010): 821-830.
25. McPherson, M., Smith-Lovin, L. and Cook, J. M. Birds of a feather: Homophily in social networks. *Annual Review of Sociology*, 27(2001), 415-444.
26. Gleave, E., Welser, H. T., Lento, T. M. and Smith, M. A. A conceptual and operational definition of 'social role' in online community. In *Proc. HICSS'09*, IEEE (2009): 1-11.
27. Yates, D., Wagner, C. and Majchrzak, A. Factors affecting shapers of organizational wikis. *J. of ASIST*, 61, 3 (2010), 543-554.
28. Baker, W. E. and Faulkner, R. R. Role as resource in the Hollywood film industry. *American J. of Sociology*, 97, 2 (1991), 279-309.
29. Hecht, B. and Gergle, D. On the localness of user-generated content. In *Proc. CSCW'10*, ACM (2010): 229-232.
30. Blumenstock, J. E. Size matters: word count as a measure of quality on Wikipedia. In *Proc. WWW'08*, ACM (2008): 1095-1096.
31. Hu, M., Lim, E. P., Sun, A., Lauw, H. W. and Vuong, B. Q. Measuring article quality in Wikipedia. In *Proc. CIKM'07*, ACM (2007): 243-252.
32. Robins, G., Pattison, P., Kalish, Y. and Lusher, D. An introduction to exponential random graph (p*) models for social networks. *Social Networks*, 29, 2 (2007), 173-191.
33. Robins, G., Snijders, T., Wang, P., Handcock, M. and Pattison, P. Recent developments in exponential random graph (p*) models for social networks. *Social Networks*, 29, 2 (2007), 192-215.
34. Faust, K. Centrality in affiliation networks. *Social Networks*, 19, 2 (1997), 157-191.
35. Wang, P., Sharpe, K., Robins, G. L. and Pattison, P. E. Exponential random graph (p*) models for affiliation networks. *Social Networks*, 31, 1 (2009), 12-25.
36. Handcock, M., Hunter, D., Butts, C., Goodreau, S. M. and Morris, M. statnet: Software Tools for the Representation, Visualization, Analysis and Simulation of Network Data. *J. of Stat. Software*, 24, 1 (2008).
37. Borgatti, S. P. and Everett, M. G. Network analysis of 2-mode data. *Social Networks*, 19, 3 (1997), 243-269.
38. Faust, K. and Skvoretz, J. Comparing networks across space and time, size and species. *Sociological Methodology*, 32, 1 (2002), 267-299.
39. Handcock, M. S. and Gile, K. J. Modeling social networks from sampled data. *Annals of Applied Statistics*, 4, 1 (2010), 5-25.
40. Snijders, T. A. B., Van de Bunt, G. G. and Steglich, C. E. G. Introduction to stochastic actor-based models for network dynamics. *Social Networks*, 32, 1 (2010), 44-60.

Learning from History: Predicting Reverted Work at the Word Level in Wikipedia

Jeffrey M. Rzeszotarski, Aniket Kittur
Human-Computer Interaction Institute
Carnegie Mellon Univerity
Pittsburgh, PA
{jeffrz, nkittur}@cs.cmu.edu

ABSTRACT
Wikipedia's remarkable success in aggregating millions of contributions can pose a challenge for current editors, whose hard work may be reverted unless they understand and follow established norms, policies, and decisions and avoid contentious or proscribed terms. We present a machine learning model for predicting whether a contribution will be reverted based on word level features. Unlike previous models relying on editor-level characteristics, our model can make accurate predictions based only on the words a contribution changes. A key advantage of the model is that it can provide feedback on not only whether a contribution is likely to be rejected, but also the particular words that are likely to be controversial, enabling new forms of intelligent interfaces and visualizations. We examine the performance of the model across a variety of Wikipedia articles.

Author Keywords
Wikipedia, Applied Machine Learning, Reverts

ACM Classification Keywords
H.5.3 [Information Interfaces and Presentation]: Group and Organization Interfaces.

INTRODUCTION
Wikipedia is one of the largest and most successful examples of online social production, gathering hundreds of millions of contributions into an encyclopedia of human knowledge that is among the top ten most accessed websites in the world. However, its very success in can pose an intimidating challenge to editors who may need to sift through hundreds or thousands of contributions to a page to avoid rekindling previous conflict, rehashing previous decisions, or violating agreed upon norms or policies. If they fail to do so, their work may be discarded or "reverted" with other editors undoing their work. This type of action can be discouraging and punitive, since an editor's contributions -- often made in good faith -- are discarded wholesale by the community. This may be especially true for newcomers, who have been reverted at increasingly high rates over the past years [11]; even for veteran users the experience of being reverted can be damaging to future participation [4,5].

Since every contribution is saved, in theory an editor could simply inspect the edit history for reverted contributions, vandalism, conflict, article conventions, and administrator caprices, all of which could be useful in avoiding future reverts. However, for many pages the article history is prohibitively large. In the case of contentious articles like *Abortion* and *Scientology*, there are over ten thousand edits, totaling hundreds of megabytes of text. Compared to the plain text of Jane Austen's *Pride and Prejudice*, the complete history of the *Abortion* article is roughly one thousand times larger, and a summary of word-by-word changes twenty times [2]. Few editors are likely to expend the effort of thoroughly learning a page's history in order to produce better edits.

However, this same history, processed appropriately, has the potential to help editors understand which contributions would be appropriate and valued. This paper describes a method of identifying edits likely to be rejected using machine learning on word level features in the edit history of an article. By learning from the past history of an article, the model not only identifies edits that are likely to be reverted, but also provides feedback at the word level. This word-specific information can enable new forms of page-specific visualization and feedback for newcomers and experienced editors alike.

STUDYING REVERTS
Reverts are employed by Wikipedians for a variety of reasons. Many reverts are used to quash vandalism, a constant problem in an open online encyclopedia. Researchers have developed means of identifying potential malicious edits, including examining macro scale features of edits, evaluating text case, vulgarity dictionaries, and user characteristics such as edit counts [1,8]. Vandals are often anonymous, and wipe entire pages or replace large swaths of text, as reflected by the features in vandal identification models [8]. These models do not examine the entire edit contents word-by-word, instead utilizing more general features about users and edit characteristics. Other

models do include words, but merge edits together [3]. In both cases, these methods can overlook valuable per-article vandalism behaviors, such as words that are vandalistic in one article context (the word "gay" used as a pejorative), but not in another (the word "gay" in an article about LGBT rights), that an article-level word model could discover.

Furthermore, we are interested in going beyond predicting simple vandalism to understanding differences in the perceived value of contributions. For example, reverts are also employed by Wikipedians as a part of inter-editor conflict [7]. Editors claim strong ownership over edits or articles, or guard pages based on their orthodoxy, resulting in 'revert wars' where cultural, historical, or other biases are repeatedly contributed and undone [5,7]. Much work has gone into visualizing and investigating this conflict using editor level features (such as the persistence of their edits or who they revert); however, these techniques do not provide editors with concrete feedback on improving their contributions [11]. While conflict is inevitable in a social space as rich as Wikipedia, newcomers may stumble into a warzone and never return. Word-by-word models could identify potential 'battlezone' words and help newcomers avoid them until they better understand the article's history.

Furthermore, many reverts are directed towards good faith edits, often made by newcomers, that are not perceived as valuable. This may be because they violate one of the many precepts contained in dozens of pages of Wikipedia policy, or per-article rules and conventions. For instance, the article on *Abortion* has a multiple-page discussion about editor conventions for the use of the terms "termination", "death", and "murder" in editing. Since such rules are held in pages-long discussion threads, the cost of understanding this level of nuance is high. Much like in a conflicted article, a word-by-word model could identify these word level conventions and warn newcomers or direct them to places to learn more.

MODELING ARTICLE HISTORIES

Our model operates on a per-article basis to gather features that are contextual to each Wikipedia page. This facilitates nuanced judgments based not only on general Wikipedia policy, but also article-specific conventions and conflicts. We use the contents of edits rather than user features since just as past vandals might make a good faith edit, a newcomer might make mistakes, and can be applied to contributions even by editors with no editing history.

To build a word-by-word model of reverting behavior for a given article on Wikipedia, we extract the edit history of the article using the Wikipedia API. These edit histories include full copies of each article for every edit made, editor comments, and usernames. Based on the number of edits, such histories range in size from several megabytes up to a gigabyte of plain text because complete copies are stored for every contribution. As a result, this process can be time consuming because the live Wikipedia API is not well adapted for dumping entire article histories.

Once we have a complete article history composed of many copies of the article evolving as editors make changes, we tokenize each contribution according to Wikipedia syntax into word level tokens. Since the Wikipedia servers store edits in code markup, our tokenizer checks for special cases such as references, links, tables, and images and counts such elements as 'words' as well. Once we have tokenized the complete article history, we conduct a text comparison (diff) of consecutive tokenized edits by temporarily converting each token into a unique Unicode character and performing a character level text comparison. This captures word level changes rather than character level ones. For example, a comparison of the phrase 'brown fox' -> 'brown foxes' is recorded as removing the word 'fox' and adding 'foxes' rather than inserting the letters 'es'. This procedure captures the region in which an editor is making changes over the long history of an article, providing a middle ground between sentence level diffs that may be too high level or letter-by-letter diffs that would focus on minutiae.

Once we have determined through text comparison how each editor changed the article in every edit, we convert their changes into datapoints. We count the number of times each word is added or removed as two separate features, leading to feature spaces that are on average three to ten thousand words in size. We also include comment length, the anonymity of the editor, and his or her edit count and time registered on Wikipedia. We identify reverted work using the same method as previous researchers [7,9,10] of MD5 hashing the contents of the page at each edit and looking for pages that hash the same, indicating a new edit has the same contents as a previous iteration of the page. We place the datapoints into two classes based on whether hashing shows that the changes have later been reverted.

CLASSIFYING WIKIPEDIA EDITS

To test the accuracy of our model and the quality of its feedback, we randomly sampled 150 articles from Wikipedia that each had over 1,000 contributions (well over 10,000 articles have at least this many edits). We chose 1,000 edits as a benchmark for a well established Wikipedia page that is not only likely to receive more future edits, but also is likely to have a varied and rich history. Our sample varied from as few as 1,114 edits to as high as 10,593 edits

Classifier	*Accuracy*	*F-Measure*	*Area Under ROC Curve*
Naïve Bayes	81.2% (SD 9.7%)	0.767 (SD 0.100)	0.659 (SD 0.118)
SMO Support Vector Machine	86.9% (SD 3.0%)	0.873 (SD 0.029)	0.802 (SD 0.056)
Random Decision Tree Forest	89.9% (SD 2.6%)	0.892 (SD 0.026)	0.880 (SD 0.052)

Table 1: Mean classifier accuracy, F-measure, and area under ROC curve evaluated using 150 randomly sampled Wikipedia articles under 10-fold crossvalidation

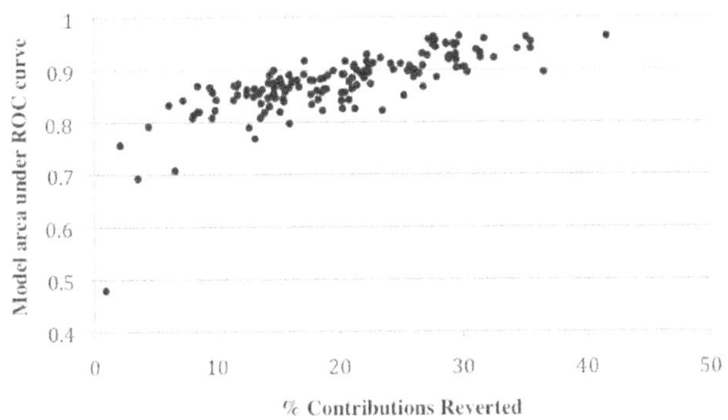

Figure 1: Proportion of edits that were reverted (x) in a given article versus the area under the ROC curve for its model (y).

(Mean 3,149 , SD 1,716), with as little as 11 reverted contributions and as many as 3,241 reverts (Mean 657, SD 496). Reverts comprised as little as 0.9% of article histories and as much as 41.6% (Mean 20.0%, SD 7.9%).

We used the Weka toolkit to construct and evaluate models on a per-article basis since each article represents a very different spectrum of editor behavior. We built and tested models using naïve Bayes classifiers (proven to work well on 'bag of words' models), support vector machines using sequential minimization optimization (able to deal with a large featureset), and decision tree forests (well adapted to highly unbalanced classes). We also used costs to even out the sometimes strongly unbalanced classes for the support vector model, and feature selection to limit the large number of extraneous words/features. We further limited the feature set by removing words/features that were shorter than 4 characters long. Overall, while naïve bayes models performed fairly, support vector machines and decision tree forests performed comparably well in a random test sample of 50 articles. Random decision tree forests proved to generate the best classifiers (Table 1), and were used to evaluate all 150 articles.

Using random decision tree forests under 10-fold cross validation, word level models of edits predicted which contributions were likely to be reverted with generally high accuracy, with a mean accuracy of 89.4% (SD 2.5%), an average F-measure of 0.886 (SD 0.026), and an average area under the ROC of 0.876 (SD 0.058). Several articles did not fare as well, but those primarily did not have a significant number of reverts. For instance, one article model, *RahXephon*, achieved a ROC area of only 0.69, but reverts only comprised 3.5% of its 1,693 edits. In general, fewer reverts corresponded significantly with areas under the ROC closer to 0.5 (an indicator of poor performance) ($F(149)=199.7$, $p<0.001$, Figure 1). We also investigated models on content with less than 100 edits such as the article on *Alkahest*, but were not able to predict reverts accurately, suggesting that this technique is limited to pages with a sizable number contributions. However, since such pages are more amenable to manual inspection, the need for a machine learning model is correspondingly lower.

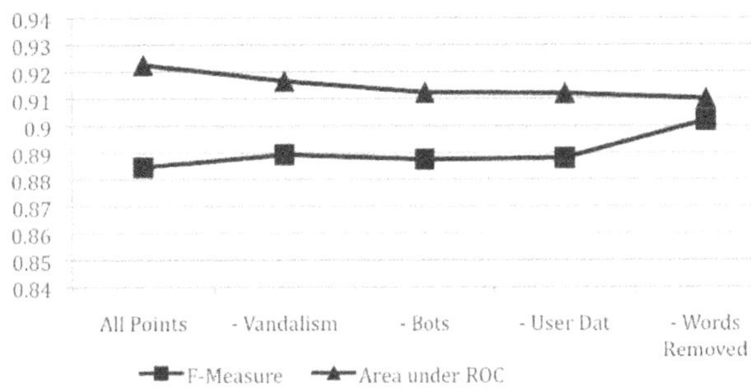

Figure 2: *Genetic Engineering* classification results as points/features are progressively removed

To explore the utility of different features we filtered out various points in the data. We filtered vandalism by checking for reverts with 'rvv' or 'vandal' included, and we filtered bots using the Wikipedia convention of the word 'bot' at the beginning or end of a user name. We also investigated eliminating features, including data about the user who made the edit, as well as limiting features to only words added (vs. removed). Using 10-fold cross-validation at each step, we investigated progressively eliminating features in the model using the *Genetic Engineering* article (see Figure 2). In the base case, the model showed high accuracy when including added and removed words, as well as vandalism, bots, and user data. Importantly, the model still obtained high accuracy when vandalistic edits and bots were filtered out, demonstrating its ability to identify meaningful value rather than just simple vandalism. Eliminating features for the words that a reverted edit removed, and only looking at words the edit contributed, the model still achieved high accuracy. We removed user data as well, limiting the model to knowledge of the user's anonymity, their comment length, and their contribution, with similar levels of accuracy. Finally, we cut the number of features in half by only examining words an editor added, still obtaining reasonable results. This suggests that word-level models may be robust across a variety of feature spaces.

IDENTIFYING WORD LEVEL CHARACTERISTICS

After verifying that the model accurately identified reverted edits, we extracted the individual normalized feature weights from a support vector classification model built out of the entire article history in order to examine word-by-word what edit characteristics lead to valued or discarded work. We coded a sample of various weight levels in the model.

We extracted the word feature weights from the *Genetic Engineering* SVM model, took a stratified sample of the words, and coded them based on Wikipedia policy and conventions (see Table 2). The features that were weighted highly towards reverted work (positive numbers) were generally those that violated policy or article conventions, had spelling errors, or had Wiki syntax errors. Neutral model weights could be construed as violating policy, but could also be employed otherwise. For example,

Word	Weight	Explanation
hello	2.00	"Hello" does not relate to the contents of the article
significant	0.09	"Significant" can be used with citations, such as, "The treatment showed a significant increase in mobility," or as a Wikipedia weasel word in "Significant numbers of researchers say genetic engineering is evil"
virus	-0.52	"Virus" is primarily neutral, used in sentences such as "The virus can be used as a vector..."

Table 1: Example Model Words, Weights, and Explanations for the *Genetic Engineering* article

"predicted" can be used in a useful phrase like "Mendel predicted", or in a phrase that violates Wikipedia 'weasel word' policies like "many scientists predicted". Low weighted (rarely reverted) words were often domain-specific to genetics. There were also many words that had no clear judgment for or against reverting throughout the weights, suggesting that there is a degree of noise in the data.

IMPLICATIONS FOR DESIGN

There are many potential design implications for the use of word level modeling of reverts. Foremost, we can immediately apply this classifier in the editing process to provide feedback to newcomers as they edit. The model could inform editors when their edit is likely to be reverted, enabling them to reflect on and revise their contribution to increase its perceived value. Coupled with heuristics that identify common reasons for being reverted, such as Wikipedia policy and discussion page mining, the feedback could be even more effective in improving both contribution quality and retention, as editors whose work is reverted are less likely to stick around [6].

The word-by-word model weights might also be used visually to show problem areas in the article, heatmapping sections that are suspect because they are more contentious. Word ratings between articles could be compared, showing the difference in editing conventions between articles. One could also calculate a set of weights for all Wikipedia pages combined, gathering information about general trends.

It is also possible that word level models might be applicable in other online settings, including online forums and reviews. There, content can be flagged as either offensive or of low value. There is potential for similar classifier models designed to help contributors write higher quality content.

CONCLUSION

Our research suggests that there is indeed a great amount of information encoded by discarded work on Wikipedia at the word level that could be useful for improving sensemaking and contribution. Using only the word-by-word changes made by editors discarding work, we were able to predict future discarded work, and characterize the nature of what types of words are reverted in an article, even when filtering out simple vandalism and bot edits. This suggests that there is great potential for future work using word level revert features to provide feedback for newcomers and experienced users about their edits.

ACKNOWLEDGMENTS

We thank the Carnegie Mellon Social Computing Lab for their support. This research was supported by NSF grants OCI-09-43148, IIS-0968484, IIS-1111124 and a grant from Carnegie Mellon's Center for the Future of Work.

REFERENCES

1. Adler, B., Alfaro, L. de, and Pye, I. Detecting Wikipedia Vandalism using WikiTrust. *Notebook Papers of CLEF*, 2010, 22–23.
2. Austen, J. Pride and Prejudice. *Project Gutenberg*, 1813
3. Druck, G., Miklau, G., and McCallum, A. Learning to predict the quality of contributions to wikipedia. *In Proc. AAAI Workshop on Wikipedia and Artificial Intelligence*, 2008, 7–12.
4. Ekstrand, M. and Riedl, J. rv you're dumb: identifying discarded work in Wiki article history. *In Proc. Symposium on Wikis and Open Collaboration*, 2009, 4.
5. Halfaker, A., Kittur, A., Kraut, R., and Riedl, J. A jury of your peers: quality, experience and ownership in Wikipedia. *In Proc. Symposium on Wikis and Open Collaboration*, 2009, 1–10.
6. Halfaker, A., Kittur, A., Riedl, J. Don't bite the newbies: Revertings effect on the quantity and quality of Wikipedia work. *In Proc. Symposium on Wikis and Open Collaboration*. 2011
7. Kittur, A., Suh, B., Pendleton, B.A., and Chi, E.H. He says, she says: Conflict and coordination in Wikipedia. *In Proc. SIGCHI conference on Human factors in computing systems*, 2007, 453–462.
8. Potthast, M., Stein, B., and Gerling, R. Automatic vandalism detection in Wikipedia. *Advances in Information Retrieval*, 2008, 663–668.
9. Priedhorsky, R., Chen, J., Lam, S.T.K., Panciera, K., Terveen, L., and Riedl, J. Creating, destroying, and restoring value in Wikipedia. *In Proc. CSCW*, 2007, 259–268.
10. Suh, B., Chi, E., Pendleton, B.A., and Kittur, A. Us vs. them: Understanding social dynamics in Wikipedia with revert graph visualizations. *In Proc. Visual Analytics Science and Technology*, 2007, 163–170.
11. Suh, B., Convertino, G., Chi, E., and Pirolli, P. The singularity is not near: slowing growth of Wikipedia. *In Proc. Symposium on Wikis and Open Collaboration* 2009, 1–10

Tweeting is Believing? Understanding Microblog Credibility Perceptions

Meredith Ringel Morris[1], Scott Counts[1], Asta Roseway[1], Aaron Hoff[1], Julia Schwarz[2]
[1]Microsoft Research, [2]Carnegie Mellon University
{merrie, counts, astar, aaronho}@microsoft.com, julenka@cs.cmu.edu

ABSTRACT

Twitter is now used to distribute substantive content such as breaking news, increasing the importance of assessing the *credibility* of tweets. As users increasingly access tweets through search, they have less information on which to base credibility judgments as compared to consuming content from direct social network connections. We present survey results regarding users' perceptions of tweet credibility. We find a disparity between features users consider relevant to credibility assessment and those currently revealed by search engines. We then conducted two experiments in which we systematically manipulated several features of tweets to assess their impact on credibility ratings. We show that users are poor judges of truthfulness based on content alone, and instead are influenced by heuristics such as user name when making credibility assessments. Based on these findings, we discuss strategies tweet authors can use to enhance their credibility with readers (and strategies astute readers should be aware of!). We propose design improvements for displaying social search results so as to better convey credibility.

Author Keywords

Twitter, Microblogging, Social Search, Credibility.

ACM Classification Keywords

H5.m. Information interfaces and presentation: *Misc.*

General Terms

Design, Experimentation.

INTRODUCTION

The popular microblogging service Twitter [twitter.com] lets users broadcast 140 character status messages known as *tweets*. Users currently assess tweets' credibility based on trust relationships with authors whose streams they elect to follow. However, consuming social media by *searching for a topic* rather than *following an author* is becoming increasingly prevalent. By June 2011, Twitter's search portal [search.twitter.com] was already servicing over 1.6 billion queries per day [35]. In addition to supporting explicit querying, Twitter also provides clickable "trending topic" terms, which launch searches for popular (and sometimes advertiser-promoted) keywords. General-purpose search engines have created separate portals specifically for searching public social streams, such as Bing Social Search [bing.com/social] and Google Real Time Search [google.com/realtime]. Google and Bing have also recently begun integrating social status updates directly into their main search results pages when appropriate [24, 33], enabling serendipitous encounters with socially-generated content.

Twitter acts not only as a social network, but as a news source [19]. Informing oneself about breaking news is a common motivation for searching public tweets [37], such as when seeking updates about local emergencies [39]. Unfortunately, social search tools amplify the audience not only of breaking news, but also of undesirable memes such as spam [36] and rumors [5]. Although some rumors, such as false reporting of celebrity deaths [5], are relatively harmless, increased reliance on social media for actionable news items (*Should I vote for candidate X? Should I donate to victims of disaster Y?*) makes credibility a nontrivial concern. Evidence of false tweets has recently been discovered in U.S. Senate campaigns [23], reporting of the Iranian election protests [8], and coverage of unfolding natural disasters such as the Chilean earthquake [22].

Factors influencing users' perceptions of the credibility of Web pages and earlier forms of social media (e.g., blogs and instant messaging) have been well-studied. Some influential factors for Web pages' credibility perception, like visual design [21], are not relevant to tweets, while others, like conflating search engine ranking with credibility [15], may apply. The relative importance of features may vary for this new medium, as well; for instance, author credentials [18] may take on heightened importance, given the social nature of tweets.

In this paper, we present an investigation of user perceptions of tweet credibility. We report the results of a survey about the features that impact users' assessments of tweet credibility. Our results indicate a discrepancy between features people rate as relevant to determining credibility and those that mainstream social search engines make available. Based on these findings, we conducted two controlled experiments to measure the impact of several tweet features (message topic, user name, and user image) on perceptions of message and author credibility. Our results indicate that tweet consumers have difficulty discerning truthfulness based on content alone, with message topic, user name, and user image all impacting judgments of tweets and authors to varying degrees regardless of the actual truthfulness of the item. Based on these findings, we discuss strategies tweet authors can use to enhance their credibility with readers, and manipulative strategies that wary social media consumers should be mindful of. We also offer ideas for redesigning tweet search result pages to better support credibility assessment.

RELATED WORK

The volume of activity on Twitter has increased at an extraordinary rate, to an average of 140 million tweets per day as of March 2011 [38] – this volume of information makes it increasingly impractical for users to monitor all messages from their network in order to identify the most relevant pieces of information. This has prompted researchers to develop novel interfaces and algorithms for filtering tweets, such as tools like Twahpic [28] or Eddi [1], which perform topic-based clustering and filtering, or algorithms for identifying Twitter authors with authority on specific topics [26]. Search-based access to tweets has become increasingly available through third-party search tools, including Google [24] and Bing [33], and researchers have begun to study how people use search to access microblog updates [7, 37]. Informing oneself about breaking news events is a common motivation for searching tweets [37], which is consistent with Twitter's increasing prominence as a news source [19].

Searching Twitter for news updates can provide users with real-time information not yet available in the mainstream media, such as when eyewitnesses' tweets provided the first information about a plane crash-landing in the Hudson River [20]. Unfortunately, the quality of news posted to Twitter is not uniform – spam [29, 23, 36], surreptitious advertising [14], false rumors [5, 8, 17, 22], and imposter accounts [25] are common occurrences. Users' ability to assess the *credibility* of tweets, therefore, has taken on increased importance. This paper presents both self-report and experimental data on the features that impact users' credibility assessments of tweets.

The credibility of information encountered online is a problem that has long perplexed educators and librarians, who have developed systems of heuristics for students to use when they encounter online content, such as assessing the accuracy, authority, objectivity, currency, and coverage of the material [18]. Researchers have studied factors influencing users' perceptions of Web page credibility [9, 10, 11, 15, 21], identifying many factors that contribute to this assessment including features of the Web page itself (e.g., visual design [21]), properties of the user (e.g., level of internet use [9]), and means of encountering the content (e.g., search engine ranking [15]). Fogg's Prominence-Interpretation theory [11] suggests that the impact that a Web page element has on perceived credibility depends on both its prominence (likelihood of being noticed) and interpretation (the meaning assigned to it). However, users are often forced to make credibility judgments about online content before having the opportunity to view a full web page – Schwarz and Morris [34] and Yamamoto and Tanaka [41] have proposed techniques for supplementing search results to support credibility assessment.

Like Web search results, tweets pose an example of a particularly challenging credibility-assessment scenario, due to their compact nature (a limit of 140 characters). The opportunity for customization of visual design, which is an important factor in the assessment of traditional Web pages' credibility, is quite limited, other than users' ability to select the avatar they use to represent themselves. While some researchers have studied the issue of credibility assessment for more social subsets of the Web, such as blogs [13, 30, 40], the issue of how users perceive the credibility of microblog updates is only just beginning to receive attention.

Schmierbach and Oeldorf-Hirsch [31] showed college students articles on the New York Times Web site as well as tweets from the official New York Times Twitter feed describing those same stories, and found that the students rated the news items less credible when reading the tweet than when viewing the website. While their finding indicates that users may have concerns about credibility when consuming tweets, it does not indicate what aspects of the tweets contribute to this impression; our research contributes findings to clarify this latter issue.

Pal et al. [27] did not examine credibility *per se*, but asked users to rate how "interesting" a tweet was and how "authoritative" its author was, manipulating whether or not they showed the author's user name. They found that authors who had more followers (and therefore presumably more recognized user names) received higher "interesting" ratings for their content when their user names were revealed. User names of organizations, rather than individuals, and those which were topically related to the tweet also received higher ratings than those which were not. User name style is one of several features we explore in this paper, though we focus on how this feature impacts credibility perceptions rather than content interestingness.

Some researchers have begun building systems to automatically or semi-automatically classify tweet credibility. Truthy [29] visually represents the diffusion of a Twitter meme; through crowdsourcing, these visualizations are inspected and flagged for potentially spam-like patterns. Castillo et al. [3] used Mechanical Turk to crowdsource judgments of tweet credibility, and used these judgments to train a machine learning system that rates the credibility of tweets on a particular topic. Our findings could enhance such automatic techniques by providing information about the features that end users rely on to make such judgments – such features could benefit automatic credibility classification by, for example, suggesting tweaks to feature weightings in machine learning approaches, or by helping determine what information to feature more (or less) prominently in crowdsourcing tasks.

SURVEY

To better understand the factors influencing users' perceptions of tweets' credibility, we conducted a survey. The following sub-sections discuss the methods used to design the survey, the question types, and the participants. We then report on our findings.

Survey Design

We started by conducting a pilot study in which we observed users thinking aloud while conducting a search on the search.twitter.com webpage. Five people, ranging in age from 17 – 49 years old, participated in the pilot. Participants had non-technical occupations (e.g., photographer, sales representative). Participants were familiar with Twitter and occasionally read tweets, but only one had an account.

Participants were given a task intended to simulate a realistic information need. Since all participants were residents of the state of Washington, they were instructed to search on Twitter's search engine for the name of a local candidate in the upcoming U.S. Senate election, in order to learn about his positions on the issues. Participants were instructed to "think aloud" while viewing the retrieved tweets. The experimenter prompted further think-aloud by asking questions about some of the tweets, such as whether participants thought certain tweets were from the candidate in question, from official news sources, etc.

The experimenter took notes on the features that participants mentioned paying attention to as they analyzed the Twitter search results. For example, participants often commented on the nature of the avatar associated with particular tweets, noting that a particular tweet seemed untrustworthy because the man in the photo "looks like a stalker," or that another seemed less official because the user's avatar was an "anime character." Participants attributed importance to user names, assuming that names that were linguistically similar to their search terms (e.g., "Dino Rossi HQ") were officially sanctioned. Repetition of similar content by multiple tweets increased participants' confidence in the veracity of a message. Some features were not explored by participants unless prompted by the experimenters, such as clicking URLs or clicking user names in order to view an author's Twitter homepage (which contains biographical information and that user's recent tweet history); when prompted to view these features, however, users noted their value – for example, one participant doubted the seemingly official nature of a particular tweet after noting the unprofessional visual design of the author's homepage.

The collection of 26 features discussed by these five pilot participants was used to design our survey. Respondents were presented with the list of features and asked to indicate whether they typically pay attention to each feature when reading tweets ("usually", "occasionally", "never"); the "never" option was split to allow the user to indicate that they never consider a feature but think they probably ought to, or that they never consider a feature and think there is no value in doing so. For each feature, respondents were also asked to assess how that feature impacts credibility on a five-point Likert scale ranging from "greatly decreases credibility" to "greatly increases credibility." The survey also asked users to indicate credibility concerns regarding various sources and topics of tweets, and gathered information about users' Twitter habits, social search habits, and demographic data. We asked only whether people pay attention to user images, but then broke out images into four types when asking about their impact on credibility.

Participants

Sampling a diverse array of Twitter users for our survey was a challenging goal, since directly purchasing advertising on Twitter was only an option for special "partner" companies as of late 2010 (the time when we distributed our survey) [32], with most advertising being conducted through tweets planted in popular accounts [14]. Advertising to our own Twitter followers was also undesirable, due to the drawbacks of snowball sampling techniques [2]. Consequently, in order to obtain a reasonably diverse sample of Twitter users for our survey, we advertised the survey in two venues: on an email list for social media users within Microsoft, and on a message board for alumni of Carnegie Mellon University. We received a total of 256 completed surveys, 101 from the corporate group and 155 from the alumni group. Reading tweets at least occasionally was a prerequisite for participation in the survey.

The Microsoft respondents ranged in age from 18 – 60 years old, with an average age of 32 years. 29% were female. 93.1% had a Twitter account, and all read tweets, with 91% reading them at least a few times a week, and 74% reading them at least once a day. All worked in the technology industry, albeit in a variety of job roles, including software development, marketing, legal, HR, and management.

The university alumni respondents ranged in age from 18 – 54 years old. 34% were female. 88% had a Twitter account, and all read tweets, with 91% reading them at least a few times a week, and 77% reading them at least once a day. Occupations varied. "Student" was the most common occupation (29.6%), but the majority of respondents had non-student professions such as administrative assistants, journalists, lawyers, architects, financial professionals, dentists, nurses, and customer relations specialists.

Responses to our survey from these two participant pools were similar in character, so we report their results jointly. The similarity of the two groups' results suggests the applicability of our findings beyond a single demographic. The reader should bear in mind that some demographics that consume tweets were not covered by our recruitment method, such as teenagers or adults without a college degree; such groups may have different perceptions of credibility, and studying their habits is left to future work.

Results

Here we establish that participants do encounter tweets through search and that this elicits greater concern for credibility than encountering tweets by those followed. We then describe the topic areas most pertinent to credibility concerns, and finally the extent to which participants reported using various tweet features when making credibility judgments.

Method of Encountering Tweets

In addition to reading tweets from users they followed, respondents consumed tweets by conducting searches on search.twitter.com (84%), clicking trending topics on the Twitter homepage (84%), searching for tweets using Bing's and Google's social search functionality (72%), or serendipitously encountering tweets mixed into the results of general Web searches (81%). While respondents place a great deal of trust in tweets from users they follow, tweets encountered through Twitter search ($\chi 2(2, N = 256) = 44.7$, $p < .001$) and general search engines ($\chi 2(2, N = 256) = 47.2$, $p < .001$) elicited concern (Figure 1).

Tweet Topic Type

Respondents were least concerned with credibility for celebrity news and gossip related tweets, and secondarily for movie and restaurant reviews. News, political, emergency, and consumer oriented tweets caused the greatest concern about credibility (Figure 2).

Tweet Features

Table 1 summarizes each feature's impact on credibility perceptions. Features associated with low credibility perceptions were the use of non-standard grammar and punctuation, not replacing the default account image, or using a cartoon or avatar as an account image. Following a large number of users was also associated with lower author credibility, especially when unbalanced in comparison to follower count – as one respondent articulated, "if someone is following significantly more people than they have following them, I mistrust them."

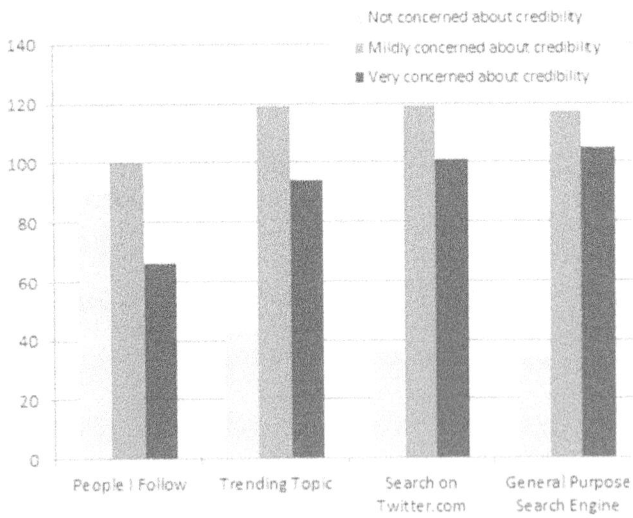

Figure 1. Histogram of respondents' credibility concern levels based on method of encountering a tweet. Tweets encountered through searching inspire greater credibility concerns than those encountered through following.

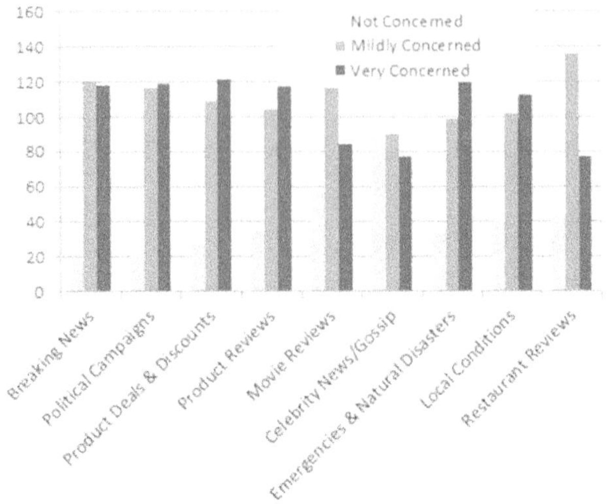

Figure 2: Histogram of credibility concerns for different types of content.

Features perceived as most enhancing a tweet's credibility generally concerned the author of the tweet. These included author *influence* (as measured by follower, retweet, and mention counts [1]), *topical expertise* (as established through a Twitter homepage bio, history of on-topic tweeting, pages outside of Twitter, or having a location relevant to the topic of the tweet), and *reputation* (whether an author is someone a user follows, has heard of, or who has an official Twitter account verification seal). Content-related features viewed as credibility-enhancing were containing a URL leading to a high-quality site, and the existence of other tweets conveying similar information.

Features respondents attend to also focused on author characteristics (whether the author is known or followed) and features immediately visible in the interface, especially properties of the tweet (e.g., is a retweet).

Discussion

Participants' responses indicated an awareness of the problem of tweet credibility, particularly for tweets not encountered through their following stream (Figure 1). Concern for credibility also varied across topic types (Figure 2). Participants were aware of features that differentially convey credibility, yet the features most attended to suggest that their ability to judge credibility in practice is largely limited to those features visible at-a-glance in current UIs (user picture, user name, and tweet content). Conversely, features that often are obscured in the user interface, such as the bio of a user, receive little attention despite their ability to impact credibility judgments. In the following section we experimentally examine the impact of the most salient features on credibility judgments of tweets and authors.

Feature	Credibility Impact	Attention Received
non-standard grammar/punctuation	2.71	1.46
default user image	2.87	n.a
cartoon/avatar as user image	3.22	n.a.
author is following many users	3.30	1.29
logo as user image	3.37	n.a.
contains shortened URL	3.39	1.89
customized Twitter homepage	3.41	1.22
author location near you	3.43	1.34
contains hashtags	3.48	2.05
contains a URL	3.50	1.91
author tweets frequently	3.52	1.68
contains complete URL	3.57	1.80
near top of search result list	3.58	1.66
posted recently	3.59	2.10
is a reply	3.61	2.09
author has many followers	3.65	1.56
author bio suggests topic expertise	3.66	1.60
is a retweet	3.66	2.17
username is related to topic	3.67	1.85
author location near topic	3.67	1.34
author often mentioned/retweeted	3.69	1.66
personal photo as user image	3.70	n.a.
many tweets w/ similar content	3.71	2.07
author often tweets on topic	3.74	1.96
account has verification seal	3.92	1.83
author is someone you've heard of	3.93	2.37
contains URL you clicked thru to	3.93	2.20
author is someone you follow	4.00	2.40
verified author topic expertise	4.04	1.84
is a RT from someone you trust	4.08	2.43
user image, generally	n.a.	1.75

Table 1. Mean ratings for tweet features' perceived credibility impact (5-point scale; higher = more credibility) and attention typically allotted (3-point scale; higher = more attention).

EXPERIMENTS

To better understand the impact of various tweet features on credibility perceptions, we conducted two online experiments in which we systematically altered several properties of tweets in order to measure their impact on readers' credibility assessments. We first describe our primary experiment and its results, followed by a description of a follow-up experiment we ran to explore an issue raised by our initial findings.

Method

To design a balanced experiment of a reasonable length (so as not to exhaust participants), we narrowed down the list of features examined in our earlier survey to a set of three. We selected the features to focus on in our experiment by choosing features that were self-reported as being highly influential on credibility perceptions in our survey, and that were currently and highly visible to end-users on Twitter.com and major search engines. Using these criteria, the three features we selected were *Message Topic*, *User Name*, and *User Image*.

Message Topic

Our survey participants indicated that their level of concern about credibility was affected by a message's topic; hence, we chose topic as a factor to manipulate in our experimental design. We included tweets on three different topics, each of which has been subject to false tweet phenomena: *politics*, *science*, and *entertainment*.

User Name

Survey participants indicated attributing credibility to user names, such as assuming that topically-relevant user names were associated with credible information. Additionally, survey participants expressed concerns about tweets containing non-standard grammar such as abbreviations commonly used in IM or text messaging, and other internet-age modifications to language. These factors led us to include three types of user name in our experiment: *traditional* (e.g., "Alex_Brown"), *internet* (e.g., "tenacious27"), and *topical* (e.g. "AllPolitics").

All user names were gender neutral. Traditional style user names were constructed by selecting first names from a list of popular gender-neutral baby names in the United States, and selecting last names from a list of common surnames in the United States. We verified that all user names were not actual registered Twitter account names, so that participants would not have prior assumptions about the quality of tweets from a particular author.

User Image

Survey participants indicated that a tweet author's account image (or "avatar") influenced their credibility perceptions, reporting that they attributed the most credibility to photos, followed by cartoons/icons, with the default image inspiring the least credibility. We therefore decided to include image type in our study design; we included five image types: *Male Photo*, *Female Photo*, *Topical Icon*, *Generic Icon*, and *Default*.

Male and female photos were chosen by taking photos from real users' twitter accounts, so as to achieve realistic photographic styles. Photos were obtained by using Twitter's search engine to search on stereotypically gendered topics (e.g., #nfl for men and #twilight for women). Photos from popular or celebrity accounts were not used. To avoid race- or age-based confounds in our results, we selected only headshot photos of Caucasians who appeared to be young adults (in their twenties or thirties).

Generic icon photos were also chosen from twitter accounts, to enhance realism of style. Topical icons were constructed using PowerPoint clip art, since many topical icons we encountered when searching twitter were associated with organizational accounts that may have been prominent enough to be familiar to study participants, and we did not want familiarity to be a confound. The "default" image used was the Twitter egg image that appears if a user does not upload his/her own image.

Tweet Content

We authored original tweets for the purposes of the experiment, in each of the three chosen topic areas. All tweets were in English, and were written with standard grammar, spelling, and punctuation. All tweets described a topically-relevant current event, followed by a URL. URLs were constructed to look like they were from the URL-shortening service bit.ly [bit.ly.com], a popular service that is frequently used to compress URLs so that they fit within the 140-character limit of tweets.

To validate that participants' credibility judgments were influenced by the features we manipulated (topic, user name, and/or user image) rather than the actual truth value of the tweet itself, we designed the tweets such that half described true news events and half described events that had never taken place, but were plausible. We pilot-tested these tweets on ten members of our organization to verify that they could not determine which were true or false.

Tweets were rendered using a .css stylesheet copied from Twitter.com and saved as image files, so that they looked as realistic as possible, but without clickable links (so that participants could not verify the credibility of a tweet by clicking on the fake bit.ly URL included with each). Figure 3 shows sample tweet stimuli created for our experiment.

Figure 3. Sample tweets constructed for our experiment. The five image types are (a) default, (b) topical icon, (c) generic icon, (d), male photo, and (e) female photo. Tweet (a) employs a *traditional* user name, (b) and (c) depict *internet* style names, and (d) and (e) feature *topical* names.

Study Design

Running a fully within subjects study design [message topic x user name x user image x truth value] would have required each participant to rate 90 (3 x 3 x 5 x 2) tweets, which we felt would be exhausting for participants. Instead, we made user image a between-subjects factor, resulting in 18 (3 x 3 x 2) tweets to be rated by each participant.

Hence, the set of 18 tweets consisted of six in each of the topic areas (politics, science, and entertainment). Within a topic area, there were two tweets of each user name style (traditional, internet, and topical), one of which was true and one of which was false. A given user saw these 18 tweets combined with one of the five user image types (with a different user image randomly combined with each tweet, except in the "default" image condition, where the the same image was used each time). No user ever saw the same user name, user image, or tweet more than one time; seeing only one tweet from a given author is similar to a Web search scenario (as opposed to a following scenario).

Participants completed the study online, in their Web browser. They were randomly assigned to one of the five user image conditions. The 18 tweets were shown to them one at a time, in a random order. Instructions reminded the participants that the links within tweets would not be clickable (ensured through the use of pre-rendering the tweets as images rather than using live HTML), and were instructed not to leave the current Web page or perform supplementary Web searches. Underneath each tweet, participants saw two 7-point Likert scales (from strongly disagree to strongly agree), asking them to rate whether "this tweet contains credible information" and whether "this author is credible." After rating all 18 tweets, participants took a survey that collected basic demographic information, as well as information about their use of Twitter.

Participants

Our online experiment was conducted during a one-week period in February 2011. It was advertised via email to 1,000 adult U.S. residents who had signed up through our organization's user study recruitment website. The recruitment email indicated that to be eligible for the study, participants had to know what tweets were and read them occasionally (familiarity with tweets was also re-verified through self-report on the post-study questionnaire). Entry into a drawing for an e-commerce gift certificate was offered as incentive for completing the study. 266 participants completed the study.

Random assignment to each of the five user image conditions resulted in approximately equal distribution of participants, with 54 participants seeing the *default* image, 52 seeing *generic icons*, 54 seeing *topical icons*, 51 seeing *female photos*, and 55 seeing *male photos*.

Participation was approximately gender-balanced, at 54% male and 46% female. 28% of participants were in the 18 – 24 age range, 28% were 25 – 34, 26% were 35 – 44, and the remaining 18% were 45 or older. Participants had a wide variety of occupations, including medical professionals, clergy, homemakers, students, web designers, personal fitness trainers, financial professionals, and sales.

49% of participants reported reading tweets at least once a day, with an additional 25% reading tweets at least a few times a week; the remaining 26% read tweets less

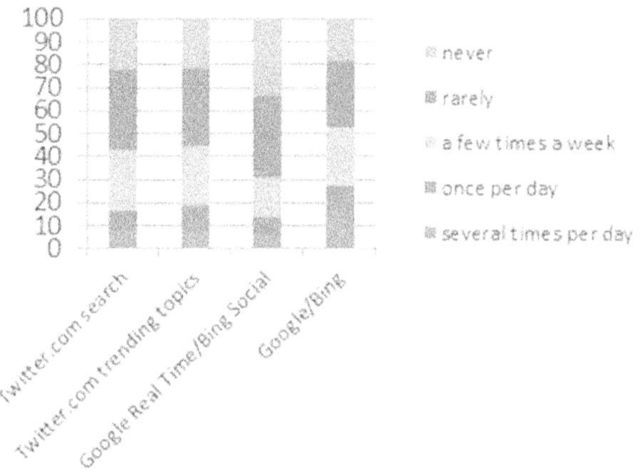

Figure 4. This figure shows the percent of respondents encountering tweets through different search mechanisms at different frequencies. About half of our experiment's participants reported encountering tweets through search (rather than following) at least a few times a week.

frequently. Participants read tweets both from people they followed (75% had Twitter accounts) and tweets they discovered using various search services. See Figure 4.

Participants who had Twitter accounts reported following a mean of 322 people (median = 30), and having a mean of 268 followers (median = 20). 44% of those with accounts reported authoring tweets at least a few times a week.

Results

Since participants' ratings of *tweet credibility* and *author credibility* were approximately normally distributed, ANOVA analyses were performed to test the impact of our experimental manipulations on credibility ratings, with follow-up pairwise t-tests when appropriate. Bonferroni corrections were used to mitigate the effect of multiple comparisons.

Tweet Credibility vs. Author Credibility vs. Truth

Participants provided two ratings for each tweet, one quantifying the credibility of the information conveyed by the tweet and one quantifying the credibility of the tweet's author, since our earlier survey results indicated that users' credibility perceptions are influenced by features of both the content and the author. We hypothesized that these concepts may not be independent of each other, since perceptions of an author may influence perceptions of their message (and vice-versa); indeed, our results indicate that participants' tweet credibility and author credibility ratings were highly correlated, with a Pearson correlation coefficient of $r = .85$ ($p < .001$). Average ratings for both tweet credibility (3.79) and author credibility (3.27) were slightly below the neutral point on our 7-point scale.

Averaging credibility scores on a per-tweet basis and comparing to the actual truth value for each tweet, we found only a moderate correlation between truth and tweet credibility rating ($r = .39$, p = .11) and between truth and author credibility rating ($r = .29$, p = .25). Neither of these correlations were statistically significant. This suggests that participants were generally unaware of the true truth value of the messages, and that their credibility judgments were mostly influenced by factors other than truthfulness.

Participants' prior experience using Twitter did not impact their ability to distinguish true from false tweets. Individual users' correlation coefficients for credibility ratings and truth value did not correlate significantly with users' Twitter account duration, frequency of reading or sending tweets, or follower/following counts. However, participants with more Twitter experience (those who reported authoring tweets at least a few times a week), gave higher tweet credibility ratings ($t(264) = 2.45$, $p = .01$) and author credibility ratings ($t(264) = 2.01$, $p < .05$) than those who had less experience, confirming prior findings that those with more experience with a given technology view it as a more credible information source [9]. We found no other interaction of demographics (age, gender, or Twitter experience) with any of our experimental manipulations.

Message Topic

Message topic influenced perceptions of tweet credibility ($F(2, 264) = 5.72$, $p = .003$), with science tweets receiving a higher mean tweet credibility rating (3.90) than those about either politics (3.74, $p = .001$) or entertainment (3.74, $p = .01$). Message topic had no statistically significant impact on perceptions of author credibility ($F(2,264) = 2.52$, $p = .08$).

User Name

Figure 5 shows how user name type impacted credibility ratings. User name type influenced perceptions of tweet credibility ($F(2, 264) = 23.36$, $p < .001$), with topical user names receiving a higher mean tweet credibility rating (3.99) than either traditional (3.69, $p < .001$) or internet (3.70, $p < .001$) name styles.

User name had an even more pronounced impact on perceptions of author credibility ($F(2, 264) = 62.64$, $p < .001$), with all pairwise differences significant at the $p < .001$ level. Topical user names inspired the highest mean

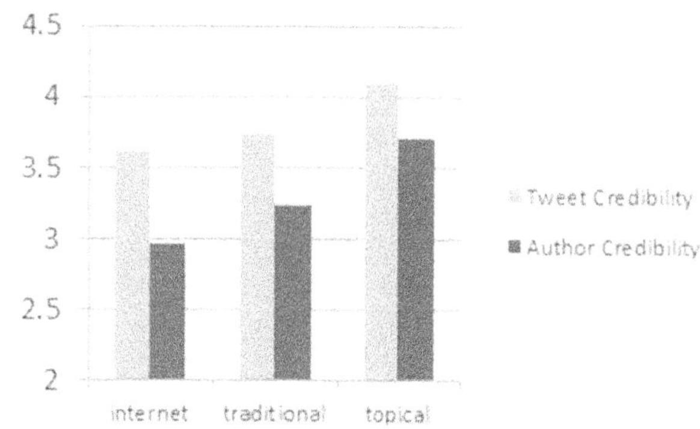

Figure 5. Users perceived topical user names as enhancing tweet credibility. Authors with topical names were considered more credible than those with traditional user names, who were in turn considered more credible than those with internet name styles.

credibility ratings (3.62), followed by traditional names (3.21), with internet style names inspiring the lowest credibility in the associated authors (2.97).

User Image

We found no significant impact of user image type on either tweet credibility ratings (F(4, 261) = .36, p = .84) or author credibility ratings (F(4, 261) = 1.17, p = .33).

Because our survey participants reported paying attention and assigning credibility value to user images, we were surprised to see little impact of image type on credibility perceptions in our experiment. We hypothesized that this lack of effect may have been due to the between-subjects nature of the user image feature (a study design selected so as to reduce the total number of tweets users would need to evaluate, thereby reducing fatigue). Specifically, seeing only a single image type may have made users ignore that factor (e.g., if everyone has the "default" image, it is not a noteworthy feature). Consequently, to further understand the impact of user image on credibility perceptions, we designed a follow-up experiment.

Follow-Up Experiment

The second study was similar to the first, except that each participant experienced two different image types (having each participant experience all five image types would have been impractical due to the large number of ratings that would be required from each user to achieve a balanced design). In order to enable us to study the relationships between each of our five user image types, participants were randomly assigned to one of ten study conditions, corresponding to the ten different possible pairings of our user image types.

We used the same 18 tweets and user names as in the first experiment. Recall that there were six tweets in each of the three topics (politics, science, and entertainment). Within each topic, there were two tweets for each user name style (traditional, internet, and topical). Each pair of tweets with a particular topic + user name style consisted of one true and one false tweet. Even though truth value had little impact in our original experiment, as a precaution we randomized the assignment of user image type with respect to truth value on a per-tweet and per-user basis. As before, all tweets were presented in a randomized order.

The follow-up experiment was conducted online during a one-week period in March 2011. It was advertised via email to a set of 1,000 adult U.S. residents that did not overlap with the set invited to participate in the original experiment. 296 people completed the study. 111 (37.5%) were women, 185 (62.5%) men. 77% of participants were aged between 25 and 54. Occupations ranged widely, including educators, retail workers, doctors, and writers. Participants followed 172 people on average (median = 44) and were followed by an average 263 people (median = 30).

Results

Use of the default Twitter icon significantly lowers ratings of content (t=2.41, p = .02) and marginally lowers ratings of authors (t=1.93, p = .06; Figure 6) in comparison to the other four image types. No other image types showed significant differences in comparison to one another. Examination of the relationship between content type and image type revealed that the default image pales most in comparison to topical, male, and female images. For instance, in the entertainment category, for ratings of authors, topical (t=2.93, p < .01), male (t=2.21, p = .03), and female (t=3.81, p < .001) images all generated significantly higher ratings than did the default Twitter icon.

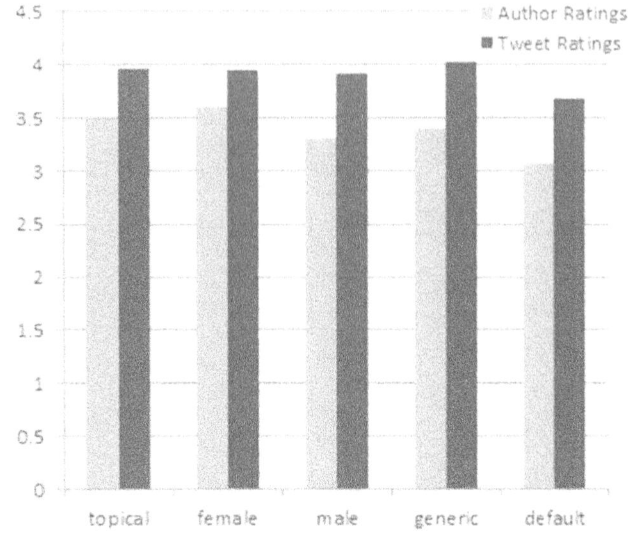

Figure 6. Histogram of respondents' credibility concern levels based on image type. The default Twitter image lowers credibility.

DISCUSSION

Our survey showed that users are concerned about the credibility of content when that content does not come from people the user follows (Figure 1). In contexts like search, users are thus forced to make credibility judgments based on available information, typically features of the immediate user interface (Table 1). Our survey results indicated features currently underutilized, such as the author bio and number of mentions received, that could help users judge tweet credibility.

It is sensible that traditional microblog interfaces hide some of these interface features because they aren't necessary when only consuming content from known authors. Without these established relationships, errors in determining credibility may be commonplace. Participants were poor at determining whether a tweet was true or false, regardless of experience with Twitter. In fact, those higher in previous Twitter usage rated both content and authors as more credible. This mirrors findings with internet use generally [9], and may be due to a difficulty in switching from the heavily practiced task of reading content from authors a person follows to the relatively novel task of reading content from unknown authors. Even topical expertise may not support reliable content validity assessments. We did find that for politics, those higher in self-reported expertise (by a median split) gave higher credibility ratings to the true political tweets ($t=3.67$, $p<.001$) and their authors ($t=2.00$, $p=.05$), yet these effects disappear for the science topic and for entertainment where those *low* in expertise actually gave slightly (though non-significantly) higher ratings to the true content.

In the absence of the ability to distinguish truthfulness from the content alone, people must use other cues. Given that Twitter users only spend 3 seconds reading any given tweet [6], users may be more likely to make systematic errors in judgment due to minimal "processing" time. Indeed, participants rated tweets about science significantly more credible than tweets on politics or entertainment, presumably because science is a more serious topic area than entertainment. Other types of systematic errors, such as gender stereotyping based on user image, did not appear to play a role. Although our survey respondents reported finding non-photographic user images less credible, our experiment found that in practice image choice (other than the detrimental default image) had little effect on credibility judgments. It is possible that image types we did not study (such as culturally diverse photographs) might create a larger effect.

The user name of the author showed a large effect, biasing judgment of both content and authors. Cha et al. [4] discuss the role of topically consistent content production in the accumulation of followers. We see a similar phenomenon reflected here in users incorporating the degree of topical similarity in an author's user name and tweets as another heuristic for determining credibility.

Implications

What are the implications of these difficulties in judging credibility and how can they be mitigated? Our experimental findings suggest that for individual users, in order to increase credibility in the eyes of readers, they should start by avoiding use of the default twitter icon. For user names, those who plan to tweet exclusively on a specific topic (an advisable strategy for building a large follower base [4]), should adopt a topically-aligned user name as those generated high levels of credibility. If the user does not want a topical username, she should choose a traditional user name rather than one that employs "internet" styled spelling.

Other advice for individual tweet authors stems from our survey findings. For instance, use of non-standard grammar damaged credibility more than any other factor in our survey. Thus, if credibility is a goal, users are encouraged to use standard grammar and spelling despite the space challenges of the short microblog format, though we note that in some user communities non-standard grammar may increase credibility. Maintaining a topical focus also increases credibility, as does geographic closeness between the author and tweet topic, so users tweeting on geographically-specific events should enable location-stamping on their mobile devices and/or update their bio to accurately identify location, which is often not done [16].

Tweet consumers should keep in mind that many of these metrics can be faked to varying extents. Selecting a topical username is trivial for a spam account. Manufacturing a high follower to following ratio or a high number of retweets is more difficult but not impossible. User interface changes that highlight harder to fake factors, such as showing any available relationship between a user's network and the content in question, should help. The Twitter website, for instance, highlights those in a user's network that have retweeted a selected item. Search interfaces could do something similar if the user were willing to provide her Twitter credentials. Generally speaking, consumers may also maintain awareness of subtle biases that affect judgment, such as science-oriented content being perceived as more credible.

In terms of interface design, we highlight the issue that users are dependent on what is prominent in the user interface when making credibility judgments [11]. To promote easier credibility assessment, we recommend that search engines for microblog updates make several UI changes. Firstly, author credentials should be accessible at a glance, since these add value and users rarely take the time to click through to them. Ideally this will include metrics that convey consistency (number of tweets on topic) and legitimization by other users (number of mentions or retweets), as well as details from the author's Twitter page (bio, location, follower/following counts). Second, for content assessment, metrics on number of retweets or number of times a link has been shared, along with who is retweeting and sharing, will provide consumers with context for assessing credibility. In our pilot and survey, seeing clusters of tweets that conveyed similar messages was reassuring to users; displaying such similar clusters runs counter to the current tendency for search engines to strive for high recall by showing a diverse array of retrieved items rather than many similar ones – exploring how to resolve this tension is an interesting area for future work.

CONCLUSION

Social media are increasingly being incorporated into general search engine results. Google and Bing both feature Twitter and Facebook in "social search" results. Twitter's own search was used by a significant percentage of our survey respondents. While a potentially valuable source for news and information, this transition removes a critical element of social media: that users are friends or followers of the content author. The result is that users must judge the credibility of content authored by people they do not know.

In this work, we examined key elements of the information interface for their impact on credibility judgments. We showed that users had difficulty determining the truthfulness of content and that their judgments were often based on heuristics (e.g., an item has been retweeted) and biased systematically (e.g., topically-related user names seen as more credible). In our discussion, we highlight pieces of information deemed helpful to credibility judgments that typically are buried in the interface. Many of these elements, such as an author's bio, may be minimally important when the reader knows the author but highlight critical interface changes needed to help users determine validity of content in social search contexts.

REFERENCES

1. Bernstein, M., Suh, B., Hong, L., Chen, J., Kairam, S., and Chi, E. Eddi: Interactive Topic-based Browsing of Social Status Streams. *UIST 2010*.
2. Bernstein, M., Ackerman, M, Chi, E., and Miller, R. The Trouble with Social Computing Systems Research. *alt.chi 2011*.
3. Castillo, C., Mendoza, M., and Poblete, B. Information Credibility on Twitter. *WWW 2011*.
4. Cha, M., Haddadi, H., Benevenuto, F., & Gummadi, K. Measuring User Influence in Twitter: The Million Follower Fallacy. *ICWSM 2010*.
5. Corcoran, M. Death by Cliff Plunge, With a Push From Twitter. *The New York Times*, July 10, 2009.
6. Counts, S. and Fisher, K. Taking it All In? Visual Attention in Microblog Consumption. *ICWSM 2011*.
7. Efron, M. Information Search and Retrieval in Microblogs. *Journal of the American Society for Information Science and Technology*, March 2011.
8. Esfandiari, G. The Twitter Devolution. *Foreign Policy*, June 7, 2010.
9. Flanagin, A.J. & Metzger, M.J. (2000). Perceptions of Internet Information Credibility. *Journalism & Mass Communication Quarterly*, 77(3), 515-540.
10. Fogg, B.J. Persuasive Technology: Using Computers to Change What We Think and Do. *Morgan Kaufmann*, 2002.
11. Fogg, B.J. Prominence-Interpretation Theory: Explaining How People Assess Credibility Online. *CHI 2003 Extended Abstracts*.
12. Fox, S., Zickuhr, K., & Smith, A. Twitter and Status Updating, Fall 2009. *Pew Internet &American Life Project*, Oct. 21, 2009.
13. Gamon, M., Basu, S., Belenko, D., Fisher, D., Hurst, M., & Konig, A.C. BLEWS: Using Blogs to Provide Context for News Articles. *ICWSM 2008*.
14. Grover, R. Ad.ly: The Art of Advertising on Twitter. *Businessweek*, January 6, 2011.
15. Hargittai, E., Fullerton, F., Menchen-Trevino, E., & Thomas, D. Trust Online: Young Adults' Evaluation of Web Content. *Int'l. Journal of Communication*, 2010.
16. Hecht, B., Hong, L., Suh, B., and Chi, E. Tweets from Justin Bieber's Heart: The Dynamics of the Location Field in User Profiles. *CHI 2011*.
17. Kanalley, C. Facebook Shutting Down Rumor Goes Viral: Site Said to be Ending March 15, 2011. *The Huffington Post*, January 9, 2011.
18. Kapoun, J. Teaching Undergrads WEB Evaluation: A Guide for Library Instruction. *C&RL News*, 1998.
19. Kwak, H., Lee, C., Park, H., & Moon, S. What is Twitter, a Social Network or News Media? *WWW 2010*.
20. Lamont, I. Plane Lands on the Hudson, and Twitter Documents it All. *Computerworld*, Jan. 15, 2009.
21. Lazar, J., Meiselwitz, G., & Feng, J. Understanding Web Credibility: A Synthesis of the Research Literature. *Foundations and Trends in Human-Computer Interaction*, 1(2), 2007, 139-202.
22. Mendoza, M., Poblete, B., & Castillo, C. Twitter Under Crisis: Can We Trust What We RT? *KDD 2010 Social Media Analytics Workshop*.
23. Mustafaraj, E. & Metaxas, P. From Obscurity to Prominence in Minutes: Political Speech and Real-Time Search. *Web Science 2010*.
24. Official Google Blog. An Update to Google Social Search. February 17, 2011.
25. Owens, S. How Celebrity Imposters Hurt Twitter's Credibility. *Mediashift*. February 20, 2009.
26. Pal, A. & Counts, S. Identifying Topical Authorities in Microblogs. *WSDM 2011*.
27. Pal, A. & Counts, S. What's in a @name? How Name Value Biases Judgment of Microblog Authors. *ICWSM 2011*.
28. Ramage, D., Dumais, S., and Liebling, D. Characterizing Microblogs with Topic Models. *ICWSM 2010*.
29. Ratkiewicz, J., Conover, M., Meiss, M., Goncalves, B., Patil, S., Flammini, A., and Menczer, F. Truthy: Mapping the Spread of Astroturf in Microblog Streams. *WWW 2011*.
30. Rubin, V.L. & Liddy, E.D. Assessing Credibility of Weblogs. *AAAI Spring Symposium*, 2006.
31. Schmierbach, M. and Oeldorf-Hirsch, A. A little bird told me, so I didn't believe it: Twitter, credibility, and issue perceptions. *Association for Education in Journalism and Mass Communication*, August 4, 2010.
32. Schroeder, S. Twitter Takes a Step Toward a Turn-Key Advertising Solution. *Mashable*, December 15, 2010.
33. Schwartz, B. Bing Adds Twitter Smart Answers. *Search Engine Land*, July 1, 2009.
34. Schwarz, J. and Morris, M.R. Augmenting Web Pages and Search Results to Support Credibility Assessment. *CHI 2011*.
35. Siegler, M.G. At 1.6 Billion Queries Per Day, Twitter Finally Aims To Make Search Personally Relevant. *TechCrunch*, June 1, 2011.
36. Sullivan, D. Twitter's Real Time Spam Problem. *Search Engine Land*, June 6, 2009.
37. Teevan, J., Ramage, D., & Morris, M.R. #TwitterSearch: A Comparison of Microblog Search and Web Search. *WSDM 2011*.
38. Twitter Blog. *blog.twitter.com*. "#numbers," March 14, 2011.
39. Vieweg, S., Hughes, A., Starbird, K., and Palen, L. Microblogging During Two Natural Hazards Events: What Twitter May Contribute to Situational Awareness. *CHI 2010*.
40. Weerkamp, W. and de Rijke, M. Credibility Improves Topical Blog Post Retreival. *ACL 2008*.
41. Yamamoto, Y. & Tanaka, K. Enhancing Credibility Judgment of Web Search Results. *CHI 2011*.

Social Transparency in Networked Information Exchange: A Framework and Research Question

H. Colleen Stuart[1], Laura Dabbish[1,2], Sara Kiesler[1], Peter Kinnaird[1], Ruogu Kang[1]
Human Computer Interaction Institute[1]
Heinz College[2]
Carnegie Mellon University
hcstuart@andrew.cmu.edu, dabbish@cmu.edu,
kiesler@cs.cmu.edu, kinnaird@cs.cmu.edu, ruogu1027@gmail.com

ABSTRACT
An emerging Internet trend is greater social transparency, such as the use of real names in social networking sites, feeds of friends' activities, traces of others' re-use of content, and visualizations of team interactions. Researchers lack a systematic way to conceptualize and evaluate social transparency. The purpose of this paper is to develop a framework for thinking about social transparency. This framework builds upon multiple streams of research, including prior work in CSCW on social translucence, awareness, and visual analytics, to describe three dimensions of online behavior that can be made transparent. Based on the framework, we consider the social inferences transparency supports and introduce a set of research questions about social transparency's implications for computer-supported collaborative work and information exchange.

ACM Classification Keywords
H5.m. Information interfaces and presentation (e.g., HCI): Miscellaneous.

General Terms
Human Factors

Author Keywords
Social transparency; information exchange; social translucence; awareness; visualizations; collaboration; innovation; theory

INTRODUCTION
More information than ever before is being revealed about content, people, and their interactions online. Internet applications make visible individual's identities and actions as they access and share information. Facebook tracks user activities, and allows search engines and advertisers access to that information [73]. Twitter explicitly supports attribution of retweets and embedding of Tweets within a webpage [54]. It is technically possible to make almost any action on a piece of information visible to users within or even across websites. Further, whereas early digital networks offered a comparatively impoverished social context for communication, today's information exchange may include text and audio conversations, faces, names, videos, and visualizations of social networks. Social transparency, which we define as the availability of social meta-data surrounding information exchange, is increasing at a rapid rate, and qualitatively changes the way we conduct work and interact with others online.

Only some aspects of social transparency have been conceptualized and studied in CSCW. Erickson and Kellogg [25] introduced the concept of social translucence and argued that making co-workers more visible, and letting them know when someone on the team acted on a joint project, would encourage participation and promote collaborative work. There also is a considerable history of research on awareness systems specific to a particular function, such as tracking the actions of a group on a shared artifact or the location of co-workers [1, 23, 32]. Advances in visual analytics have made online community activity more accessible as well. Suh et al. [74] and Viégas et al. [77] explored the benefits for Wikipedia projects of making edits and editors more understandable through visualizations.

Although this previous work illuminates the potential promise of increased levels of social transparency about co-worker actions for computer-supported collaborative work, we still lack a systematic way to conceptualize and evaluate social transparency. Technical advances are pushing the frontiers of social transparency beyond prior research frameworks and are starting to exceed some people's comfort levels. For example, the re-use of medical prescriptions in marketing led to a court challenge (e.g., U.S. Supreme Court, Sorrell v. IMS Health). Vigorous debates are being held on privacy, anonymity, and the use of personal identity data for communities and commerce (e.g., [47]).

The goals of this paper are fourfold: (1) we provide an overarching framework and consistent terminology for the concept of social transparency, showing how it extends from the basic model of information exchange. We build on previous work on social translucence and awareness, but capture a broader range of transparency in information exchange, including concepts already in use such as authentication, anonymity, and provenance. (2) We then consider the inferences made by users that social transparency supports and their second order implications. Inferences stem from the immediate effects of changes in technology, such as making it easier to share information. Second order effects are indirect, longer term, and sometimes hard to anticipate effects. We argue that social transparency designs are making information visible without careful thought to the social inferences these designs support and the second order effects[1] [72] of those inferences. We focus on effects critical for collaborative work, such as the quality of information shared, coordination and control. (3) We point to some of the tradeoffs that are, or will, arise as the result of increasing social transparency. (4) Finally, we identify future areas of research related to social transparency to encourage CSCW researchers to study how these changes will affect collaborative work and information exchange online.

INFORMATION EXCHANGE

A basic sender-receiver communication model, derived from information theory [67], can describe information exchange between two individuals. A source (or sender), "Bob," disseminates information to a receiver, "Alice," and obtains confirmation from Alice in the form of verbal and non-verbal feedback that she received and understood the message (Figure 1). Information, defined as "knowledge [that] can be transmitted without loss of integrity " ([41] p. 386), travels within a tunnel, whereby only Bob and Alice have access to the information, and know that the exchange occurred. Considerable research in communication, social psychology, and sociology has enriched this view of two-party exchanges, showing they are typically iterative and cooperative (e.g., [15]).

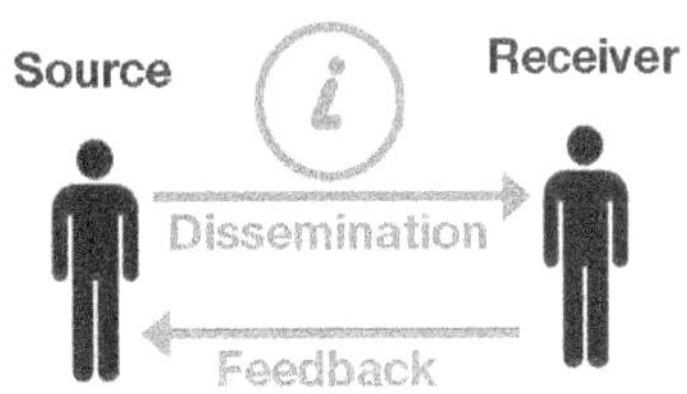

Figure 1. Dyadic information exchange

Today, dyadic information exchange is becoming less typical as people share their information on the Internet, purposely or not. Bob sends an email to Alice with copies to other people, posts comments in response to a blog, or posts a video of his family. Observers such as Lee, whom Bob may not even know, might get forwarded Bob's email or see his comments and video (Figure 2).[2]

The model in Figure 2 is as old as the Internet, but what is comparatively new is the increasing amount and quality of information that sources and receivers have about their information exchanges and the opportunity for observers like Lee to engage in these exchanges. Services within and across applications make visible three social dimensions of information exchange: the identities of those exchanging information—*identity transparency*, changes to content—*content transparency*, and actions taken during the interaction—*interaction transparency*.

IDENTITY TRANSPARENCY

Identity transparency refers to the visibility of the identity of the sender and/or receiver in an information exchange. For a source, identity transparency means information about the receiver is visible, whereas for the receiver, it means that information about the source is visible. Identity transparency also can be asymmetric; meaning only one party in the exchange has information about the identity of the other.

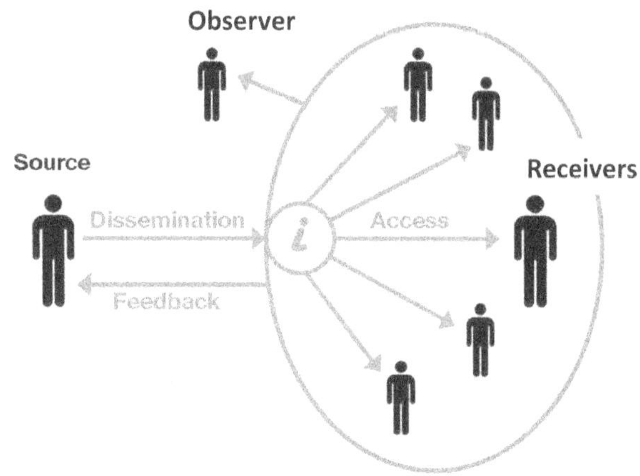

Figure 2. Networked information exchange: Multiple receivers access the same information and third parties can observe these actions on information.

Variations in Identity Transparency

Identity transparency overlaps with the security concept of message authenticity, which refers to the verifiability of the identity of a sender and/or receiver of a message. Where verifiability is typically all or none, however, identity transparency designs have many gradations and ranges from strong identity transparency, where much information about a person's real world identity is persistently available across applications and settings, to complete anonymity,

[1] Studies of email provide many historical examples of first and second order effects [72]. For instance, email made it easy for organizations to create virtual teams, a first-order effect. However, the huge rise in popularity of virtual teams led to second-order effects, such as team coordination challenges [21] and employee stress [2].

[2] Observers could be individuals, as in our example here, or organizations. See Wicker and Schrader [80] for an in-depth discussion on the implications of surveillance for commercial purposes.

where there is no persistent identifier of any kind. These variations in identity transparency influence social inferences about similarity, reputation, relative status, and perceived credibility of an information source.

	Anonymous	Alias	Real name
Sources	Take more risks; conform less		Take few risks; conform more
Receivers and Observers	Perceive source as less credible or judge credibility from group context		Perceive source as more credible

Figure 3. First order effects in the continuum of identity

Designs with strong identity transparency include a real name and/or information about source or receiver attributes, such as the person's demographic characteristics and membership in groups ("profiles"), acts as a signal or cue to a source's or receiver's trust in others and willingness to be accountable for what he says and does [53, 62]. Identity information about the source or receiver can support social inferences about how similar or dissimilar a user is to others involved in an exchange. The concept of homophily suggests that similarity perceptions can influence the likelihood of information exchange [52] in that we are attracted to and prefer to interact with those who are similar to us. In situations where identity is transparent sources should be more likely to initiate new information exchanges with receivers perceived to be similar (or have similar views) to themselves [45]; receivers should be more likely to accept information from sources who are similar than from sources who are dissimilar [3, 43]. Source attributes such as the designation "superuser" in TurboTax's Live Community and "barnstars" in Wikipedia, can also act as cues to social status, and increase the perceived credibility or the believability of a source and the information [53, 62].

Medium levels of identity transparency are created through designs that employ virtual identifiers such as unique user IDs and aliases allowing sources and receivers to be uniquely identified within an application and, if they choose, use the same identity across applications while avoiding using their real names or revealing demographic information about themselves. Virtual identifiers give sources control over their self-presentation in different communities [24], and receivers over contribution assessments within those communities. With repeated exposure and positive interactions, persistent aliases become more like real names in that they support trust, relationship development, and reputation building within sites and communities [61]. Persistent identifiers can also lead to reputational losses if people's interactions are negative (e.g., in the website Slashdot as described by Lampe and Resnick [44]).

Anonymity, the lowest level of identity transparency, makes it harder for sources and receivers to interpret one another's credibility, and can signal untrustworthy or suspicious information. Accordingly, anonymity seems to function best within communities or groups where almost everyone is anonymous. Sources and receivers develop norms of information exchange, and pay attention to the social context to interpret others' information [5, 17, 65]. Because anonymity reduces the personal risks associated with information sharing such as embarrassment, reputational losses, or social sanctions, anonymity in such communities and groups can facilitate the transmission of controversial, sensitive, critical, or novel information [38, 51].

To summarize, research suggests that different levels of identity transparency support different types of social inferences about sources and receivers. This research also suggests that sources and receivers change their behavior when we move along the continuum of weak versus strong identity transparency (Figure 3). When Bob uses his real name (or a persistent identity across many applications), he and his information are potentially more public, and he will likely take more care about the information he discloses or disseminates than when his identity is not known. Alice's trust in information from Bob will increase. Strong identity transparency therefore is likely to increase sources' sense of accountability and concern for how others perceive, value, and use their content online [38]. By contrast, when Bob is anonymous or uses a temporary alias, he will feel freer to say what he wishes, Alice is likely to take what he says less seriously, and she will need to look to the group context and norms to evaluate Bob's information.

Second Order Effects of Identity Transparency

We argue that increasing identity transparency of sources and receivers will have second order effects in collaborative groups and communities, as a result of the inferences it supports. In particular, increased perceived accountability will result in greater accuracy of information shared and used, while lowering creativity by reducing the amount of unique or novel information shared.

Information Accuracy

One plausible effect of identity transparency is an increase in the accuracy of information. Identity transparency should result in higher reputational accountability of sources and allow receivers to better evaluate the accuracy and usefulness of information from sources. In turn, the ability to evaluate information and its source should increase trust in information and information sharing. Research has shown that employees often fail to share or use information from their own organization that are held in repositories or databases because they are anonymous in the system. As sources, they do not know how others will use their information, and as receivers, they cannot evaluate the usefulness of the information or contact the source for more details [6, 7]. When sources and receivers are identified, potentially useful information is more usable. In one test of this idea, contributions to MovieLens, an online movie recommender system, were both greater in number and higher quality when contributors knew that their reviews would be checked by another MovieLens member [18]. This study began what could be a larger investigation into how online accountability, and designs for reinforcing it, affects the amount, accuracy, and usefulness of information that people create or disseminate to others within and across online communities. This research also could show how accountability changes, or fails to change, the psychology and detection of lying and false reporting online [59,79].

An open question concerns asymmetric identity transparency, when a source or receiver is identified but the other party is not. Figure 4 shows some examples of symmetric and asymmetric identity transparency, depending on whether the identity of the receiver and source are visible. The example of the downloaded paper will be familiar: Bob uploads his paper to his website. He will not know the identity of Alice, who downloads the paper and reads it. Applications such as Google Scholar offer post-publication citation services [10] and applications such as Turnitin.com offer plagiarism checking [22], but it is not as easy for Bob to know about Alice. Giving authors the ability to trace the identity of readers might be controversial, but would allow authors to have an early lead on potential collaborators or students, insight into the fields where they are having impact, and potential linkages to other relevant work.

Creativity

Within some communities and collaborations, an increase in accountability would lead to more conformity, a decline in risk taking, and less creativity. Because their identities are known, people in strongly transparent groups and communities are likely to work harder at being civil and doing what their group wants, but also increase their conformity to group ideas and norms. This consequence needs to be much better understood as it could affect the culture of creative collaborations. Suppose Alice, Bob, and Charles see that they have each accessed a particular paper; they may perceive they form a group [12]. As members of a group, they will be more likely to communicate with one another, and if they do, they will feel social pressure to adhere to each other's opinions. Members of a triad are less independent in their behavior than members of dyads [69,70]. Bob can be more confident that Charles will behave in a reasonably predictable and honorable way, because Bob and Alice can sanction Charles' inappropriate behavior. This increased sense of security for Bob and Alice, and civility of the group as whole, also comes with a cost to the individual group members—each will have to take more care with what he says.

Receiver's Perspective	Source's Perspective: Receiver Not Visible	Source's Perspective: Receiver Visible
Source Not Visible	*Symmetric* Anonymous public post	*Asymmetric* Company tracks product views
Source Visible	*Asymmetric* Downloaded paper	*Symmetric* Email between friends

Figure 4. Symmetry and asymmetry in identity transparency

The foregoing discussion suggests that there may always be defensible reasons within some communities to remove identity transparency, and to support anonymous information exchange for individuals and groups. The argument raises several research questions. First, what are the various situations in which communities and collaborations want anonymity? Researchers have investigated why some users choose not to actively contribute to online communities, which in turn hides their identity (e.g., lurkers [55, 56]). To our knowledge, however, there are no studies of when people prefer anonymity. Second, are there ways to assure anonymity for some parts of collaborative work (e.g., brainstorming) but maintain strong identity transparency for most of it? Google's Chrome browser incorporated a so-called "incognito mode," designed to remove traces of users' activity from their own machines [16]. Is it possible to design a similarly easy-to-use mode for controlling personal identification in groups? Tor and other similar proxy services provide anonymity today, but these solutions rely on third parties and are awkward for spontaneous work in collaborations. Researchers might consider the technical requirements for retrofitting such that anonymity (or lack thereof) is guaranteed for certain tasks.

CONTENT TRANSPARENCY

Content transparency refers to visibility of the origin and history of actions taken on information. For example, Wikipedia keeps a complete history of all the edits that have been made to every page. Viégas, Wattenberg, and Dave created the HistoryFlow visualization of editorial changes to improve the accessibility of these revision logs [77]. The history flow visualization uses edit timestamps in Wikipedia to construct a visual representation of the persistence of different pieces of text within a Wikipedia article. By making editorial changes more visible, the visualization increases individuals' ability to see how a document evolved over time as a result of many editors' actions on the content. Designs that incorporate content transparency can support inferences about others' activities (activity awareness) as well as inferences about the credibility of the content of a piece of information.

Variations in Content Transparency

One way systems can provide content transparency is using designs that make provenance information visible. Provenance refers to the origin or earliest known history of some artifact or content. When interface designs make provenance visible to sources and recipients, they both know where information originated. For instance, when Bob uploads his original essay to the web, then the parts of Bob's essay that Alice uses in her teaching lectures can be traced back to Bob. Provenance allows for checking plagiarism and the authenticity of data. A lack of provenance means that content has no clear ownership; hence it is easy to borrow, steal, repurpose, or fake.

Provenance can support inferences about others activities, leading to activity awareness, consciousness of other individuals' actions [23], because provenance is often determined by tracing back through prior actions on information. For example, Software developers become aware of others actions on code by looking at their commit logs [71]. Many researchers in CSCW have studied activity awareness but not usually because they are interested in determining the source or ownership of content. Instead, they have used the concept out of a larger concern for supporting coordination of collaborative work, especially distributed work [32, 66].

Revision control systems that require authentication, such as those commonly used in enterprise-scale software engineering, are a good example of content transparency used to support coordination. These systems provide detailed information about all changes to software. Engineers can make specific queries to see the changes. Visualizations of the system can help them create a mental model or narrative of the workflow [57].

Provenance can also support inferences about the characteristics of the individuals who have acted on the information over time. Visualizations of how people have edited or changed information over time not only aid coordination but also serve as an indicator of the expertise of those who created or changed information [40, 74, 77]. These visualizations can also support inferences about social structure within the set of individuals who have acted on the information, for instance, has anyone taken a leading role and are others following? Transparency of the development of content can reveal the roles of the individuals involved in its creation—what Gutwin, Greenberg, and Roseman referred to as structural awareness [33].

Second Order Effects of Content Transparency

Because content transparency lets people see what is happening to a project or a community issue, and when, where, and how sources and receivers have changed information, this meta-information can serve as a reminder for others to contribute or respond to the changes in content. We argue that these kinds of cues will produce broader second order effects.

Productivity

Activity awareness may drive productivity by reminding project members about interdependent projects, and through social facilitation processes. The reminding cues [36] that derive from strong content transparency should increase the productivity of collaborations and the self-corrective effects of crowd sourced information. Content transparency also can increase productivity through social facilitation processes; when sources know that their actions are visible, this awareness should prompt them to work harder. In one study, cashiers in a supermarket were more productive when they were watched by a highly productive peer [49].

Distributed teams are more likely than collocated teams to experience inattention to tasks, group conflict, neglect, and delays in their work [11, 19, 35]. We attribute some of the cause of these problems to weak content transparency, whereby members lack feedback and immediate knowledge of each others' activities, and fail to attend each others' progress [21]. Increased content transparency in the form of activity awareness can provide feedback as to whether the collaboration is proceeding as expected and keep collaborators on track, enhancing mutual knowledge and improving the accuracy of shared mental models [1, 23]. Documented work progress also provides collaborators with a common reference point for discussion, a shared understanding of the development of the project, what else needs to be done, and who might do it. For example, one IM prototype application shows activity in projects, with an icon indicating when any member of the project is changing a document [1, 23]. These kinds of cues may speed up content development by reducing lags between iterations of work, mitigating coordination problems, and reducing social loafing [37].

Stress

As with identity transparency, however, there are contexts in which strong content transparency is likely to have some negative consequences for collaborations and communities. Content transparency makes everyone's behavior more visible and therefore more open to being evaluated and second-guessed by others. Research on "evaluation apprehension" suggests that when people are worried about others' evaluations of their work, they sometimes make mistakes and learn less than when they are not watched (e.g., [75]).

Although there is much excitement about new visualizations supporting content transparency, it is not clear whether these designs can support detailed activity awareness without overloading and subsequently stressing users. Imagine that every project Bob is working on notifies him of Alice, Charles', Sam's (and many others') changes to content in each project. Are there upper boundaries to content transparency? Many visualizations of content changes provide people with vast meta-information about information. Examples of such visualizations include the history flow visualization mentioned above, and the code swarm visualization project [58]. Although these examples may excel for certain tasks, researchers have already identified a tension between visualizations of content changes and increased cognitive load from adding more resources to a person's desktop (see [75]).

In many cases, the volume of changes to pieces of shared information may far exceed the attentional capacity of individuals. For example, a study of awareness in software development suggested that engineers found the email messages generated to notify them of individual changes to code disruptive, and struggled to keep up with the information contained within often keeping changes private to avoid disturbing others [71]. Dashboards and feeds only partially alleviate these issues, and selecting the correct level of detail remains a challenge [76]. Notifications about changes to content can generate constant interruptions to ongoing tasks, known to be disruptive to productivity [50]. Also, transparency in collaborations might increase the stress that many people feel as they feel social pressures to keep up with multiple projects and collaborators [2]. Thus an important research question is at what level of detail does content transparency need to be to mitigate overload while supporting collaborative function? And how frequently should individuals attend to it, to avoid distraction while maintaining awareness?

INTERACTION TRANSPARENCY

When information is transmitted online, interface designs can make the details of an information exchange more or less visible to third parties. We define interaction transparency as the ability of a third party to observe an information exchange between a source and receiver, and (assuming symmetry) the knowledge that source and receiver have about the presence and identity of these third parties. This information supports social inferences about normative behavior as well as the social structure within a community or closed group. These inferences, when aggregated to the group level, may foster herding behavior, foster access to new information and influence creativity.

Variations in Interaction Transparency

Many Web applications track information access behavior and display it to one or more third parties (observers who did not create the content or access it). For example, if Alice publicly shares her photo on Flickr.com, the website indicates to Alice and anyone who visits the site how many times her photo has been viewed by others. Flickr allows users to designate friends as contacts and to track their activities in real time [46].

Interaction transparency supports social inferences about what constitutes acceptable behavior by sources, receivers, and third parties themselves. This happens because meta-information about third parties who opt to view an interaction can act as a source attribute. For example, if Charles and his friends watch Bob exchange content with Alice, the Bob-Alice interaction seems more important to Sally, another third party who sees that Charles and his friends have an interest in Bob's information. Generally, meta-information about people's behavior influences observers' interpretations of content and responses to sources (e.g., [4]). People tend to assume that others' behavior is usual, correct and worth following (see [13] for a review). Thus, guests at a hotel are more likely to reuse their towels when they are informed that most of the other guests at the hotel participate in the same environmental conservation program [30]. They are less likely to litter when they see a lonely piece of trash on the sidewalk than if there is no litter at all; the single piece of litter reminds them that most people are not littering [14]. Third parties who see others' information exchanges also are more open to learning from the information. For example, newcomers to an online community who observe exchanges among more senior members are more open to adopting community norms [42]. Interaction transparency may be beneficial to newcomers because they become acclimatized to the normative behaviors of the community [60].

Interaction transparency also conveys information about social structure to third parties. While knowledge of a social structure is an important resource (e.g., [8]), individuals are likely to make errors in their assessments of what that social structure looks like [39]. Having accurate information about others social relationships would allow individuals to make more accurate assessments of other's social capital and locate expertise within a network.

Third party meta-information also helps potential receivers filter through large amounts of information to bring the most valued content to the surface. When Kijiji, for example, lists the number of page views for each classified ad on that site (www.kijiji.com), and the New York Times lists its top articles based on recommendations and blog coverage, viewers get a sense of what is important to other users (www.nytimes.com). Suh et al. developed Wiki Dashboard to help users filter through Wikipedia articles [74].

Second Order Effects of Interaction Transparency

Interaction transparency reveals social information who is exchanging information with whom, who is dependent on whom for information, and which persons or groups are the primary conduits for information. We argue this information will have several second order effects.

Popularity and Herding

Interaction transparency increases people's knowledge about the popularity of information, sources, receivers, and third parties. Because popularity signals credibility, popular information and popular people have a huge advantage in gaining more popularity [64]. The result may be increased tendencies for herding behavior within communities and collaborations as interaction transparency increases.

Rating systems and public usage statistics exemplify information given to third parties about exchanges among sources and receivers. Someone coming to a site can see summary information at a glance about who has liked or disliked different content. Google HotPot and Stumbleupon curate content based on people's social connections [28]. Research suggests that this kind of rating information does cause herding behavior. In a study of music exchange markets, songs rated highly early in the rating process skyrocketed in popularity, irrespective of song quality [64]. Herding behavior could be expected to increase with more interaction transparency, and could affect the opinions and behavior of collaborations and communities.

Herding behavior is worrisome because it may reduce the variety of content that people access since they are being fed information that is consumed by others within their social network. Seeing what one's friends or coworkers are looking at could reduce access and use of new information, and increase segregation of information exchange based on ideology and group memberships [27].

New Information

Increased interaction transparency could make larger, more dispersed networks visible. For example, Microsoft Academic Search (academic.research.microsoft.com) is a visualization designed to display co-authorship networks that display, for instance, co-authors of co-authors. Making networks more visible could counteract the tendency for people to only interact within their own groups. It would show that social structure is not as rigid as might be assumed, and useful social capital [9]. Charles and Sue might be trustworthy and predictable collaborators but not the most useful contacts for each other in all situations. If Charles and Sue only share information with each other and their joint contacts, the information that Charles receives from Sue will tend to be redundant with the information he gets from his other existing contacts [31]. In short, we argue that revealing social networks could increase the uniqueness of information people seek and receive. This effect could have interesting implications for collaborative work and innovation.

Previous work has shown how attributes of a source influences the likelihood that new information is disseminated [63]. This previous work has not considered how interaction transparency will influence the spread and reuse of information. Reputation cues and collaboration networks should influence the information that users seek out and reuse. If a researcher learns though a revealed collaboration network about people who do similar work or have new ideas about similar topics, he might be more likely to seek out and reuse that content. Increased visibility would make a search for new information more efficient because users are pointed to individuals with similar interests who were previously unknown [34].

Interaction with Identity Transparency

Earlier, we noted that when receivers know the identity of sources, and this transparency is symmetric, sources may feel more accountable for their information and more careful about what they reveal. As well, knowing that third parties are observing them can make sources more cautious about their information exchange behavior, especially their use or reuse of sensitive information such as searches for health information. The influence of observers is especially influential in new, uncertain, or risky situations (e.g., [48]). Being observed may lead sources to alter the information they share such that it becomes more easily accessible to a broader audience, or they may omit certain content that would offend others or is proprietary or could be considered plagiarism. Third party transparency could affect the way receivers respond to information from sources. For example, receivers might confirm receipt of publically conveyed information more quickly than privately transmitted content, and provide more feedback, because they want to appear conscientious in the eyes of third parties or the broader community. These speculations have not been studied but are important to understanding the conditions under which interaction transparency increases or decreases innovation.

Privacy has received considerable attention in the CSCW research literature (e.g., [20, 29]). Perceived privacy violations can be caused by asymmetric identity and interaction transparency, as when a third party knows the identity and actions of sources or recipients but the reverse is not true [43]. Third parties could have codified, reused, or disseminated information about the sources or recipients without their knowledge or permission. Researchers have found that feedback regarding who is observing a user's activities (that is, creating symmetry) allays people's privacy concerns [43], where in other situations asymmetry might be desired by users [78]. However, we still lack sufficient information about the effects and tradeoffs involved in asymmetric interaction transparency. For instance, threats to privacy with asymmetric interaction transparency exist in countries with governments that block or censor websites, and even arrest people for their content. Often the rules are not clear and it is impossible to trace the existence or identity of third party observers or to make all parties anonymous. Shklovski and Kotamraju [68] describe how people in Kazakhstan and Russia self-censor their behavior and avoid anonymization services to avoid appearing suspicious. Their study suggests that cross-national and cross-culture research is needed to understand better the implications of asymmetry in interaction transparency.

Another important question regarding identity and interaction transparency is whether and how sources can stop the flow of meta-information about their content. The Internet makes it easy for recipients and third parties to archive content and meta-information without the source's knowledge. Once content is archived by another user, the source loses control over the lifespan of that content. Are there technical means to add tracking devices or automatic degradation of content over time? Just as a newspaper passed around on a rainy day will slowly fall apart, can the creator of content specify certain types of file accesses or modifications that would partially or fully corrupt the content?

Perhaps it is possible to design DRM solutions, accessible to individuals, to enhance innovation through attribution and tracking of content's reuse. Any transfer to a network-enabled machine could cause the data to "phone home." Systems like Vanish attempt to give the source control over the lifespan of data by supporting a data self-destruct date [26], but this solution has not yet been widely adopted. Researchers need to consider more fully the technical requirements and user impact of transparency control.

Table 1. Some Effects of Social Transparency

Dimension of Transparency	Transparency Components	First Order Effects Cited in Prior Research	Hypothesized Second Order Effects
Identity Transparency	Real names	**Accountability**: Names and virtual identifiers aid in developing a reputation [44,61]	↑ **Information Accuracy** More identifiably in a community or collaboration increases accountability, accuracy of information
	Virtual identifiers (e.g., IDs and aliases)	**Image maintenance**: Virtual identifiers provide control over people's self presentation [24]	↓**Creativity** More identifiably in a community or collaboration increases conformity
	Profile information (e.g., demographic, historic data)	**Trust**: Profile information increases credibility [53, 62] **Perceived similarity**: Profile information attracts similar others [45]	
	Anonymity	**Trust**: Anonymity applications are used to reduce risk [38] People use cues from the social context to judge sources and receivers [17,65]	
Content Transparency	Provenance and greater awareness of authorship	**Activity awareness:** Revision histories keep people in the loop (who is doing what) [74]	↑ **Productivity** Provenance and revision awareness increase productivity in collaborative projects
	Revealed revision history	**Credibility**: increases trustworthiness of content [40,74]	↑ **Attentional Demand** Provenance and revision awareness increase stress from collaborative work
Interaction Transparency	Evidence of third party access (e.g., link referral history)	**Social networks**: Reveals new connections between users [34] **Norms:** Reveals 'normal' behavior through popularity of content [64] **Self censorship:** Due to being in the public eye [48]	↑ **Herding** Revealed popularity multiplies the impact of popularity ↑ **Innovation** Revealing weak ties encourages access to new information and ideas
	Visualizations of social networks	**Network perception**: People don't perceive social networks accurately [39]	↓ **Privacy** Asymmetries in identity and interaction transparency increase privacy violations

CONCLUSION

Social transparency, the ability to observe and monitor the interactions of others within and across applications on the Internet is transforming the way we collaborate and share information online. Although the field of CSCW has conceptualized social translucence and awareness within a small group setting, we lack a framework for researching social transparency across a larger scale. In this paper, we have presented such a framework for analyzing social transparency on the Internet. This framework extends the notion of social translucence and activity awareness, and suggests new research on the effects and design of socially transparent collaborative work systems. A summary of the dimensions of social transparency, their related inferences and second order effects can be found in Table 1.

We argue that designers of social systems need to consider the inferences that transparency supports and its implications for broader social outcomes. In the offline world, cues about others behavior serve as powerful signals that inform our own activities. In the online setting, designs that incorporate social transparency are recreating many of the signals we rely on in our offline environment with potentially broader more far-reaching consequences. Informed by the existing research on social psychology, decision-making, and interaction in online communities, our framework suggests inferences individuals are likely to make based on social transparency cues. When aggregated across individuals, transparency related inferences in turn have implications for the social structures individuals are embedded in. We have considered here the influence of identity, content and interaction transparency on group and organizational-level outcomes such as information quality, creativity, productivity, stress, and herding (summarized in Table 1 above). The implications of social transparency for collaborative systems suggest a host of interesting research opportunities in CSCW. In particular, the second-order system level effects of social transparency are understudied. We insufficiently understand the social context for positive and negative effects of transparency--whether information quality will improve or creativity will decline, whether collaborations will be more effective or more stressful, and whether communities will attend too much to popular content or will be exposed to new content they might not otherwise have seen.

ACKNOWLEDGMENTS

This work was supported by a National Science Foundation grant, CNS-1040801.

REFERENCES

1. Bardram, J.E. and Hansen, T.R. The AWARE architecture: Supporting context-mediated social awareness in mobile cooperation. *CSCW 04*, (2004), 192-201.

2. Barley, S.R., Meyerson, D.E., and Grodal, S. E-mail as a source and symbol of stress. *Organization Science 22*, 4 (2010), 887-906.

3. Barnlund, D.C. and Harland, C. Propinquity and prestige as determinants of communication networks. *Sociometry 26*, 4 (1963), 467-479.

4. Bearden, W.O. and Etzel, M.J. Reference group influence on product and brand purchase decisions. *Journal of Consumer Research 9*, 2 (1982), 183-194.

5. Bernstein, M., Monroy-Hernandez, A., Harry, D., Andre, P., Panovich, K., and Vargas, G. 4chan and /b/: An analysis of anonymity and ephemerality in a large online community. *ICWSM*, Association for the Advancement of Artificial Intelligence (2011).

6. Boh, W. Mechanisms for sharing knowledge in project-based organizations. *Information and Organization 17*, 1 (2007), 27-58.

7. Boh, W.F. Reuse of knowledge assets from repositories: A mixed methods study. *Information & Management 45*, 6 (2008), 365-375.

8. Borgatti, S.P. and Halgin, D.S. On network theory. *Organization Science*, , 1-14.

9. Bourdieu, P. Le capital social: Notes provisoires. *Actes de la Recherche en Sciences Sociales 31*, (1980), 2-3.

10. Butler, D. Computing giants launch free science metrics. *Nature*, 2011. http://www.nature.com/news/2011/110802/full/476018a.html.

11. Cascio, W.F. Managing a virtual workplace. *Academy of Management Executive 14*, 3 (2000), 81-90.

12. Castano, E., Yzerbyt, V., Paladino, M.P., and Sacchi, S. I belong, therefore, I exist: Ingroup identification, ingroup entitativity, and ingroup bias. *Personality and Social Psychology Bulletin 28*, 2 (2002), 135-143.

13. Cialdini, R.B. and Goldstein, N.J. Social influence: Compliance and conformity. *Annual review of psychology 55*, 1974 (2004), 591-621.

14. Cialdini, R.B., Reno, R.R., and Kallgren, C.A. A focus theory of normative conduct: Recycling the concept of norms to reduce littering in public places. *Journal of Personality and Social Psychology 58*, 6 (1990), 1015-1026.

15. Clark, H.H. and Brennan, S.E. Grounding in communication. In L.B. Resnick, J.M. Levine and S.D. Teasley, eds., *Perspectives on socially shared cognition*. American Psychological Association, 1991, 127-149.

16. Clifford, S. Will Google's Chrome help or hurt advertisers? *The New York Times*, 2008. http://bits.blogs.nytimes.com/2008/09/03/will-googles-chrome-help-or-hurt-advertisers/?scp=6&sq=incognito chrome&st=cse.

17. Connolly, T., Jessup, L.M., and Valacich, J.S. Effects of anonymity and evaluative tone on idea generation in computer-mediated groups. *Management Science 36*, 6 (1990), 689-703.

18. Cosley, D., Frankowski, D., Kiesler, S., Terveen, L., and Riedl, J. How oversight improves member-maintained communities. *CHI 05*, (2005), 11.

19. Cramton, C.D. The mutual knowledge problem and its consequences for dispersed collaboration. *Organization Science 12*, 3 (2001), 346-371.

20. Cranor, L. Internet privacy, a public concern. *netWorker: The Craft of Network Computing June/July*, (1998), 13-18.

21. Cummings, J. Geography is alive and well in virtual teams. *Communications of the ACM 54*, (2011), 24-26.

22. Dahl, S. Turnitin(R): The student perspective on using plagiarism detection software. *Active Learning in Higher Education 8*, 2 (2007), 173-191.

23. Dourish, P. and Bellotti, V. Awareness and coordination in shared workspaces. *CSCW 92 3*, November (1992), 107-114.

24. Ellison, N., Heino, R., and Gibbs, J. *Managing Impressions Online: Self-Presentation Processes in the Online Dating Environment*. Blackwell Publishing Inc, 2006.

25. Erickson, T. and Kellogg, W.A. Social translucence: An approach to designing systems that support social processes. *CHI 00 7*, (2000), 59-83.

26. Geambasu, R., Kohno, T., Levy, A.A., and Levy, H.M. Vanish: Increasing data privacy with self-destructing data. *Usenix Security Symposium*, USENIX Association (2009), 299–316.

27. Gentzkow, M. and Shapiro, J.M. Ideological segregation online and offline. *NBER Working Paper w15916*, 10 (2010).

28. Gilbertson, S. Google Hotpot smartens up local search, but it's no Yelp killer. *Wired*, 2010. http://www.wired.com/epicenter/2010/11/google-hotpot-smartens-up-local-search-but-its-no-yelp-killer/.

29. Godefroid, P., Herbsleb, J., Jagadeesany, L., and Li, D. Ensuring privacy in presence awareness: An automated verification approach. *CSCW 2000*, (2000), 59-68.

30. Goldstein, N.J., Cialdini, R.B., and Griskevicius, V. A room with a viewpoint: Using social norms to motivate environmental conservation in hotels. *Journal of Consumer Research 35*, 3 (2008), 472-482.

31. Granovetter, M.S. The strength of weak ties. *American Journal of Sociology 78*, 6 (1973), 1360-1380.

32. Gutwin, C. and Greenberg, S. A descriptive framework of workspace awareness for real-time groupware. *CSCW 02 11*, 3 (2002), 411-446.

33. Gutwin, C., Greenberg, S., and Roseman, M. Workspace awareness in real-time distributed groupware: Framework, widgets, and evaluation. *CHI 96*, (1996), 281-298.

34. Guy, I., Jacovi, M., Perer, A., Ronen, I., and Uziel, E. Same places, same things, same people? Mining user similarity on social media. *CSCW 10*, (2010), 41-50.

35. Hinds, P.J. and Mortensen, M. Understanding conflict in geographically distributed teams: The moderating effects of shared identity, shared context, and spontaneous communication. *Organization Science 16*, 3 (2005), 290-307.

36. Hintzman, D.L. Research strategy in the study of memory: Fads, fallacies, and the search for the "coordinates of truth."*Perspectives on Psychological Science 6*, 3 (2011), 253-271.

37. Karau, S.J. and Williams, K.D. Social loafing: A meta-analytic review and theoretical integration. *Journal of Personality and Social Psychology 65*, 4 (1993), 681.

38. Kiesler, S. and Sproull, L. Group decision making and communication technology. *Organizational Behavior and Human Decision Processes 52*, 1 (1992), 96-123.

39. Kilduff, M. and Krackhardt, D. Bringing the individual back in: A structural analysis of the internal market for reputation in organizations. *Academy of Management Journal 37*, 1 (1994), 87–108.

40. Kittur, A., Suh, B., Chi, E.H., and Alto, P. Can you ever trust a Wiki? Impacting perceived trustworthiness in Wikipedia. *CSCW 08*, (2008), 7-10.

41. Kogut, B. and Zander, U. Knowledge of the firm, combinative capabilities, and the replication of technology. *Organization Science 3*, 3 (1992), 383-397.

42. Kraut, R.E., Burke, M., Riedl, J., and Resnick, P. Dealing with newcomers. In R.E. Kraut and P. Resnick, eds., *Evidence-based social design: Mining the social sciences to build online communities*. MIT Press.

43. Krishnamurthy, B., Naryshkin, K., and Wills, C. Privacy leakage vs. protection measures: The growing disconnect. *Web 2.0 Security and Privacy Workshop*, (2011).

44. Lampe, C. and Resnick, P. Slash (dot) and burn: Distributed moderation in a large online conversation space. *CHI 04*, (2004), 543–550.

45. Lampe, C., Ellison, N., and Steinfield, C. A familiar face(book): Profile elements as signals in an online social network. *CHI 07*, (2007), 435-444.

46. Lerman, K. and Jones, L. Social browsing on Flickr. *Proceedings of International Conference on Weblogs and Social Media*, arxiv.org (2006).

47. Madrigal, A. Why Facebook and Google's concept of 'real names' is revolutionary. *The Atlantic*, 2011. http://m.theatlantic.com/technology/archive/2011/08/why-facebook-and-googles-concept-of-real-names-is-revolutionary/243171.

48. Marwick, A.E. and boyd, D. I tweet honestly, I tweet passionately: Twitter users, context collapse, and the imagined audience. *New Media & Society 13*, 1 (2010), 114-133.

49. Mas, A. and Moretti, E. Peers at work. *American Economic Review 99*, 1 (2009), 112-145.

50. McFarlane, D. and Latorella, K. The scope and importance of human interruption in human-computer interaction design. *Human-Computer Interaction 17*, 1 (2002), 1-61.

51. McKenna, K.Y.A. and Bargh, J.A. Coming out in the age of the Internet: Identity "demarginalization" through virtual group participation. *Journal of Personality and Social Psychology 75*, 3 (1998), 681-694.

52. McPherson, M., Smith-Lovin, L., and Cook, J.M. Birds of a Feather: Homophily in Social Networks. *Annual Review of Sociology 27*, 1 (2001), 415-444.

53. Metzger, M.J., Flanagin, A.J., Eyal, K., Lemus, D.R., and McCann, R.M. Credibility for the 21st century: Integrating perspectives on source, message, and media credibility in the contemporary media environment. In *Communication Yearbook*. Lawrence Erlbaum, 2003, 293-335.

54. Nagarajan, M., Purohit, H., and Sheth, A. A qualitative examination of topical tweet and retweet practices. *AAAI Conference on Weblogs and Social Media*, (2010), 295-298.

55. Nonnecke, B., East, K.S., and Preece, J. Why lurkers lurk. *Americas Conference on Information Systems*, (2001), 1-10.

56. Nonnecke, B., Preece, J., and Andrews, D. What lurkers and posters think of each other. *Proceedings of the International Conference on System Sciences*, (2004), 1-9.

57. Ogawa, M. and Ma, K.-L. Code Swarm: A design study in organic software visualization. *IEEE Transactions on Visualization and Computer Graphics 15*, 6 (2009), 1097-1104.

58. Ogawa, M. and Ma, K.-L. code_swarm: A design study in organic software visualization. *IEEE Transactions on Visualization and Computer Graphics 15*, 6 (2009), 1097-1104.

59. Ott, M., Choi, Y., Cardie, C., and Hancock, J.T. Finding deceptive opinion spam by any stretch of the imagination. *Computational Linguistics*, (2011), 309-319.

60. Ren, Y., Kraut, R., and Kiesler, S. Encouraging commitment in online communities. In R. Kraut and P. Resnick, eds., *Evidence-based social design: Mining the social sciences to build online communities*. MIT Press, Cambridge, MA.

61. Resnick, P., Kuwabara, K., Zeckhauser, R., and Friedman, E. Reputation systems. *Communications of the ACM 43*, 12 (2000), 45-48.

62. Rieh, S.Y. and Danielson, D.R. Credibility: A multidisciplinary framework. *Annual Review of Information Science and Technology 41*, 1 (2007), 307-364.

63. Rogers, E. *Diffusion of innovations*. The Free Press, New York, 1995.

64. Salganik, M.J., Dodds, P.S., and Watts, D.J. Experimental study of inequality and unpredictability in an artificial cultural market. *Science 311*, 5762 (2006), 854-856.

65. Sassenberg, K. and Postmes, T. Cognitive and strategic processes in small groups: Effects of anonymity of the self and anonymity of the group on social influence. *British Journal of Social Psychology 41*, (2002), 463-80.

66. Scupelli, P., Kiesler, S., and Fussell, S.R. Project view IM: A tool for juggling multiple projects and teams. *CHI 05*, (2005), 1773.

67. Shannon, C.E. A mathematical theory of communication. *Bell System Technical Journal 27*, July 1928 (1948), 379-423.

68. Shklovski, I. and Kotamraju, N. Online contribution practices in countries that engage in Internet blocking and censorship. *CHI 11*, (2011), 1109-1118.

69. Simmel, G. Individual and society. In K. Wolff, ed., *The sociology of Georg Simmel*. Free Press, New York, 1950, 145-169.

70. Solano, C.H. and Dunnam, M. Two's company: Self-disclosure in triads versus dyads. *Social Psychology Quarterly 48*, 2 (1985), 183-187.

71. Souza, C.R.B. De, Redmiles, D., and Dourish, P. "Breaking the code", moving between private and public work in collaborative software development. *Proceedings of the International ACM SIGGROUP conference on Supporting group work*, ACM Press (2003), 105-114.

72. Sproull, L. and Kiesler, S. *Connections: New ways of working in the networked organization*. MIT Press, Cambridge, MA, 1992.

73. Steel, E. and Fowler, G. Facebook in privacy breach. *Wall Street Journal*, 2010. http://online.wsj.com/article/SB10001424052702304772804575558484075236968.html.

74. Suh, B., Chi, E.H., Kittur, A., and Pendleton, B.A. Lifting the veil: Improving accountability and social transparency in Wikipedia with wikidashboard. *CHI 08*, (2008), 1037-1040.

75. Thompson, L.F., Sebastianelli, J.D., and Murray, N.P. Monitoring online training behaviors: Awareness of electronic surveillance hinders e-learners. *Journal of Applied Social Psychology 39*, 9 (2009), 2191-2212.

76. Treude, C. and Storey, M.-A. Awareness 2.0: Staying aware of projects, developers and tasks using dashboards and feeds. *Work*, ACM (2010), 365-374.

77. Viégas, F.B., Wattenberg, M., and Dave, K. Studying cooperation and conflict between authors with history flow visualizations. *CHI 04 6*, (2004), 575-582.

78. Voida, A., Voida, S., Greenberg, S., and He, H.A. Asymmetry in media spaces. *CSCW 08*, (2008), 313-322.

79. Vrij, A., Granhag, P.A., and Porter, S. Pitfalls and opportunities in nonverbal and verbal lie detection. *Psychological Science in the Public Interest 11*, 3 (2011), 89-121.

80. Wicker, S., and Schrader, D. Privacy-aware design principles for information networks. *Proceedings of the IEE 99, 2* (2011), 330-350.

Friends, Romans, Countrymen: Lend me your URLs. Using Social Chatter to Personalize Web Search

Abhinay Nagpal **Sudheendra Hangal** **Rifat Reza Joyee** **Monica S. Lam**

Computer Science Department
Stanford University
{abhinay, hangal, joyee, lam}@cs.stanford.edu

ABSTRACT

People often find useful content on the web via social media. However, it is difficult for users to aggregate the information and recommendations embedded in a torrent of social feeds like email and Twitter. At the same time, the ever-growing size of the web and attempts to spam commercial search engines make it a challenge for users to get search results relevant to their unique background and interests. To address this problem, we propose ways to let users mine their own social chatter and extract people, pages and sites of potential interest. This information can be used to effectively personalize their web search results. Our approach has the benefits of generating personalized and socially curated results, removing web spam and preserving user privacy.

We have built a system called SLANT to automatically mine a user's email and Twitter feeds and populate four personalized search indices that are used to augment regular web search. We evaluated these indices with users and found that the small slice of the web indexed using social chatter can produce results that are equally or better liked by users compared to personalized search by a commercial search engine. We find that user satisfaction with search results can be improved by combining the best results from multiple indices.

Author Keywords

Web search, human curation, social networks, Twitter, email

ACM Classification Keywords

H.5.2 Information Interfaces and Presentation: Miscellaneous

INTRODUCTION

Web search is one of the most commonly used applications on the Internet. While it is a marvel that search engines like Google and Bing can quickly look up and rank hundreds of billions of pages in response to a query, we hypothesize that users can often get their answers from a relatively narrow and uniquely personal slice of the web. In this paper, we explore ways to automatically generate this slice, and thereby slant web search results towards sites of the user's interest. We show that a surprisingly small slice goes a long way towards satisfying the user's information needs.

In the early days of the Internet, users often created web pages with pointers to other pages that they liked. The original Yahoo directory is a prominent example. Algorithms like Pagerank were invented to take advantage of such curation and use the link structure of the web to rank search results [5]. However, the commercial importance of search engines has led to artificial manipulation of result rankings. A well-publicized example was J. C. Penney's success in influencing Google search to place its sites at the top for queries about a wide range of products [25].

In this context, there appears to be value in bringing back some elements of human curation to the search problem. Social recommendations are of particular value because friends often share common affiliation and interest. This fact is recognized by today's search engines, which are increasingly attempting to factor social information into search results.

Social Chatter as a Source of Curated Content

Our work is based on the observation that personalized and implicitly curated social recommendations of web content already exist in the user's personal communications (such as email) and social networks (such as Twitter). A key idea in this paper is to personalize search by *indexing only those domains mentioned in online chatter.* Many Internet users already use social media for exchanging pointers to web pages that are of interest and relevance to them. For example, Twitter is extensively used for sharing links; as of 2010, 25% of the approximately 90 million tweets per day contained links [24]. Similarly, users frequently recommend links to each other over email. We aim to let the user mine this ambient social chatter to infer sites that are likely to be relevant to her, and to use them while performing web search. Our approach of tapping into existing social chatter has the advantage of being useful for millions of online users who participate in social media (including email) and thereby allowing realistic studies.

Note that our approach is different from just searching the textual content in Twitter, email or the pages referenced therein because we use the *domains* referenced as the basis for creating a customized search index.

Four Types of Personalized Indices

In this paper, we describe a system called SLANT that incorporates four types of search indices that can *augment* (not replace) the results of a regular web search, which itself may be personalized by the search engine. The first three search indices in SLANT were designed based on links extracted from three sources of information: a user's personal email, his Twitter feed, and the topmost tweets on Twitter globally. The fourth index is based on pages that contain the names of user's friends. We layer these indices on top of a regular search engine like Google, in order to enable rapid experimentation.

We chose these indices for study as each one has different characteristics. Emails are personal, private and generally related directly to the user's online activities. On Twitter, messages are usually public and users tend to follow others they trust, whether or not they know them personally. The topmost tweets across all of Twitter capture socially curated, but non-personalized URLs. Results with friends names point to expertise or opinions of the user's friends on the query topic. As we describe later, a slightly intangible benefit of SLANT is that by adding color from their social network, search results can be made more entertaining than the uniform and somewhat monotonous results of a traditional search engine.

Implicit consumption of information

As suggested by the Shakespearean quote in this paper's title, there are multiple levels of social chatter around a user. The chatter may involve the user's inner social circles, outer social circles, friends of friends, people the user trusts but does not know personally, or members of a wider community. Each of these sources provides information valuable in different settings, though it is difficult for the user to process each nugget of information manually. Following too many sources takes too much time, while following too few represents a potential loss of opportunity.

Active Twitter users report being inundated with too much information, and are only able to "dip a toe" in the torrent of tweets [2] meaning that they rarely read everything in their stream. Similarly, many people may want to be on mailing lists related to their broader interests, but have no time to read even more email than they already get, and hence limit their subscriptions to lists of direct and current interest. SLANT's approach of funneling social chatter into a personal search engine benefits users by enabling them to indirectly consume streams of information they may otherwise have missed – not by reading them explicitly, but by capturing recommendations embedded in them. Even for messages they have already read, it is difficult for people to remember all the recommendations and links embedded in them, and it is therefore valuable to pipe them automatically into a personalized search engine. We envisage that such implicit consumption and total capture of social information will become commonplace in the future, resulting in users being able to follow more people on Twitter or subscribing to more mailing lists.

Privacy Considerations

Today's search engines collect detailed user information such as search history, location, profile, and social data in order to personalize web search. SLANT tackles some of the privacy issues inherent in this model by allowing the user to analyze her communications under her own control. Only the sites or terms of interest can be made part of the user's search index; even if this index is then given to a search engine, users have better privacy, since the search engine is not listening in on their detailed communications. A further benefit is that since only the user has access to all of his or her social data, the personalization can be relatively accurate and complete. In contrast, commercial search engines tap into social information only from specific sources of social media, based on commercial agreements between them and the source. For example, as of July 2011, Google has ended the commercial arrangement with Twitter that let a user's friends tweets appear in search results [27]. Similarly, Google has no visibility into a user's Facebook data.

Spam Elimination

An important benefit of using social media is the elimination of many kinds of spam and artificial gaming of search results. Users choose who to follow in Twitter; and while one can receive email spam, SLANT uses only messages in email folders that the user has chosen. The problem of spam filtering in email is also independent of link-indexing and search, and is addressed by an independent body of work.

Contributions

We now summarize the main contributions of this paper.

- *Socially curated search.* We propose improving the quality of search by extracting information from the users emails and Twitter feeds to create personalized search indices. We designed four types of search indices that can be useful: links in email, links in tweets, friends' names, and links from top tweets.
- *Evaluation of social and curated search.* Using an experimental system that we built, we perform an exploratory study to compare the efficacy of different kinds of curated search by asking users to evaluate the performance of each search index on queries from their organic search history.
- *Empirical results.* We report quantitative results from our study, and discuss examples that provide qualitative insight. Briefly, we discovered that the quality of results from the email and Twitter-based indices were rated slightly higher than personalized Google search. We attempt to provide insight into the types of queries that do well with different search indices. Further, we find that at least one of the different search indices is rated highly by users for most queries.

Interested readers can try out the SLANT research prototype which is publicly available at the URL: `http://mobisocial.stanford.edu/slant`.

RELATED WORK

Human curation

While automatic search algorithms currently play a large role in searching for information, there is much evidence that humans are also an important source of information. The success of social bookmarking services like del.icio.us and social news services like Digg is evidence of this fact. Social recommender systems also take advantage of human curation. For example, the zerozero88 system analyzes a user's tweets to recommend websites that may be of interest to her; however, it does not automatically use these sites for web search [8].

Search personalization

The closest related work to ours is by Teevan et al. who studied the modeling of user interests, built from both search-related information and documents and email the user has read and created [28]. They attempt to use this information to create a profile of the user and rehang the top 50 results returned by a search engine for each query. While their approach has better privacy guarantees than ours because it works purely on the client side, it cannot uncover results that may be buried deeper down in the search engine's ranking. It also does not utilize information embedded in social streams like Twitter. Another client-side solution that attempts to diversify results is due to Radlinski et al [23]; it does not utilize social data either. Luxenburger et al. studied personalization techniques for queries that are expected to benefit from prior history information and selectively applying personalization techniques [16]. They correctly point out that personalization does not always improve search quality.

Prior work indicates that users frequently have a need to re-find information that they have encountered previously [1]. Therefore it appears plausible that pages and sites encountered in social data in some form have a high chance of satisfying a user's information needs.

Commercial search engines

Commercial Search engines such as Google, Bing and Blekko have attempted to incorporate social elements into their search results. While the specific ranking algorithms are not publicly available, we summarize some of their features. Until recently, signed-in Google users who have connected their Google and Twitter accounts can see which of their Twitter followees have tweeted about a specific web page [7]. However, Google promoted the result only when the specific page in a search result has been tweeted (and not other pages on the site containing the page.) Bing has similar features, but is integrated with Facebook instead of Twitter, and therefore processes page "likes" on Facebook [17]. Blekko integrates with Facebook and allows users to specify a */likes* directive with search queries, which reports results from sites (not just pages) "liked" by their Facebook friends [4]. However, in our experience, Blekko's results tend to be noisy because when friends like any page on a very popular site, then all pages from that site are considered as endorsed by the friend, and tend to dominate search results.

All these search engines are limited to the information that the user allows them to access, and tend to be fragmented because different services access different parts of the user's social network that they can pick up. They also require full access to the user's social data, and none of them take advantage of links and other information embedded in email. In contrast, the SLANT approach not only gives users better control of their own data and privacy, but can also take advantage of multiple sources of chatter surrounding the user.

Social Q&A

There are several efforts to query social networks directly in response to an information need. Evans et al. analyze strategies used by users when looking up information from their social network [11]. They asked users to learn about topics that were hard to directly search for, and yet found that social searching, even when including Q&A sites such as Yahoo Answers and the ability to ask questions of their social network, did not perform as well as with traditional web search. Morris et al. study scenarios of when users directly pose a query to their social networks and compare them to traditional web search [20, 21]. Smith et al. propose using social context i.e., a user's friends and the communities to which the user belongs to improve search for social media [26].

Other systems like Aardvark [14] and Collabio [3] attempt to steer user questions towards a person who is qualified to address their information need. In contrast to these systems, SLANT combines the best of both worlds: automatic algorithms to harness the large pool of web content, and using social curation to select high quality information sources.

Collaborative searching

Search Together is a system that lets users collaborate in order to complete a specific task [18]. While links are exchanged between users, those links are used only for the duration of the task. Similarly, there has been much work in designing techniques to let groups work together on search tasks in a collaborative manner, whether or not they are co-located or working synchronously (e.g. [19]). In contrast, SLANT indirectly captures implicit and long-term collaboration, not focused on any specific task. Moreover, users are not even aware that they are "collaborating" with others; a link shared by a friend today may help improve a search result a year from now.

Personal data mining

Systems like Phlat [9] and Stuff I've seen [10] allow a user to browse and mine their personal data on a local computer including emails, documents and files, but have not been integrated with web search. Such mining can be exploited to improve the results of web search queries, without revealing all of the user's personal information to a service provider.

SOCIAL SEARCH INDICES

In this section, we describe four personalized search indices that we built in SLANT to exploit various kinds of social chatter. We developed these four indices by observing the results on our own search queries over time, and tuned them by deploying early test versions with ourselves and a few lead users. We performed informal user studies along the way which helped us refine the algorithms and improve precision and recall. We describe below how we extract links and other information from social data; in the next section, we will explain how these are weighted and used to create a personalized search index for the user.

Email links index

Email archives are very personal and capture a lot of information directly relevant and meaningful to the user. Email is widely used, with over 1.8 billion users worldwide [22]. Moreover, users routinely use email to send each other useful links, which constitutes an excellent form of curation. An additional advantage of email is that it is common for users to retain access to their email archives, spanning at least a few years, for their records. To create the index, we ask users to download a modified version of the MUSE program to their computer [13], login to one or more email accounts and specify email folders from which links are to be extracted. Typically, we recommend that users select their sent mail folders and any other folders which they think has high-quality information. We parse the body of email messages in the specified folders and extract links from each message.

Friends' names index

People are generally interested in their friends' opinions and experiences. For example, when selecting a movie to watch, people will take a close friend's positive recommendation over an expert movie critic's negative review. MUSE extracts names of email correspondents from the messages (after performing entity resolution to account for multiple email addresses or name spellings for the same person) and ranks them using communication volume as an approximate proxy for tie strength with that person. We use these names to perform query expansion – for each user query, we fork off multiple queries to the Google search engine by simply adding the name to the text of the query. For example, when a user with a friend named *John Riedl* searches for the term *Minneapolis*, a query of the form *Minneapolis +"John Riedl"* will be issued. We currently limit query expansion to the top 150 friend names in order to keep response times reasonable (in practice, this works out to a latency of about 1-5 seconds per query, which is tolerated by most users for experimental purposes). We score each link in the returned search result for each expanded query by simply accumulating the score for the user whose name was issued with the query. The results are assembled and ranked for the user, and presented using the same interface as normal Google search, including snippets. As we will describe later, users enjoy serendipitously discovering search results that involve their friends.

Users sometimes have friends with names like *Mike Smith* that are extremely common, and therefore lead to noisy search results. Our interface allows users to mark such search results with such noisy names so that future results with that friend's name are ranked below other results. We typically find that users encounter two or three friends with such names. Once the results with the names of these friends are demoted, the noise level is considerably reduced.

Twitter links index

To form the Twitter link index, users provide SLANT access via Oauth to their Twitter account. We extract all the links in tweets from accounts followed by the user. For each link, we check whether it belongs to one of about 90 URL shortening services like bit.ly, tinyurl, etc. If it does, the URL is replaced with the original URL pointed to by the shortened one.

As mentioned earlier, piping the links in a Twitter feed to a search index greatly expands the user's ability to follow more Twitter users, and implicitly consume an expanded tweet stream. We envisage that a user may have two categories of followees: one whose tweets he actually reads, and one whose tweets are implicitly consumed by feeding URLs into a search index. Our approach also works when the user is interested in a subset of topics about which a followee tweets. For example, if Alice is interested in restaurants, and follows Bob who is interested in restaurants as well as religion, Alice may import religious links tweeted by Bob in her search index. However, we expect that Alice will tend to perform queries relevant to her areas of interest, and therefore irrelevant links effectively get ignored.

TopTweets index

Twitter publishes a listing of top tweets that have caught the attention of many users based on retweeting and sharing patterns [29]. We create a search index based on these top tweets to understand the performance of content that, while being human-curated, is not personalized for individual users. These links also allow those users who do not have a Twitter account or who do not use it actively to experience the effect of human-curated search.

SEARCHING WITH SOCIAL INDICES

We implement the backend to the search indices in SLANT as a layer on top of the Google search engine, though other search engines with similar features could conceivably be used as well. When the user types in a search query, we perform the search using each of the four personalized search indices described above, along with regular Google search (which is personalized if the user is logged into Google.)

For searching sites with links extracted from Twitter and email, SLANT uses the Google custom search engine [12]. The custom search engine restricts search results to specified sites. Weights can be assigned for each site and up to 5,000 URL patterns can be specified, which turns out to be adequate for the users in all our experiments. The Google custom search engine is popular with publishers and is frequently used by them to offer a customized search service restricted to their own sites, using Google's search technology.

SLANT instantiates a new custom search engine and populates it with the domains containing these links. For example, a page like *http://example.com/123* would cause the domain *example.com* to be included in the search engine. We bias the weighting of a domain based on the frequency with which it appears in the extracted links. Weights for the

Figure 1. A screenshot of the interface used in our study. Results from the five different searches are shown side-by-side. From left to right: email-based, Twitter-based, personalized Google, friends names, and TopTweets. The user rates each set of results on a scale of 1 to 5. This screenshot shows the results when a user has issued the search query *310*. The results liked by the user for this query are highlighted in yellow.

Google custom search engines can be specified on on a scale of -1 to 1. We assign weights to domains based on two factors:

- A positive bias to reflect the popularity of the domain in the corpus. The bias scales linearly from 0.1 to 1 depending on the domain's number of occurrences in the corpus.
- A negative bias to prevent major websites such as aol.com and amazon.com from overshadowing the more personalized results. We implemented this negative bias after we found them dominating search results, defeating the purpose of personalization. This bias is applied to a domain if its rank is one of the top N sites on the Internet (in our experiments, N=100). It scales linearly from -0.1 for the N-th ranked site to -1 for the topmost site.

In summary, each user's index is represented by a weighted vector of domain names that appear in the corpus. The weight for domain i is

$$w_i = \begin{cases} 0.1 + 0.9 \times c_i/c_{\max} & \text{if } r_i > 100 \\ 0.9 \times c_i/c_{\max} - 0.9 \times (100 - r_i)/100 & \text{otherwise} \end{cases}$$

where

r_i is the rank of domain i in the Alexa rating,
c_i is the number of times domain i occurs in the user's corpus, and
$c_{\max} = \max_i c_i$.

User Interface

As an experimental interface, SLANT presents the user with a single query box, and when the user types in a query, it fetches results from all five search indices. The results are presented side by side (see Fig. 1). This interface is designed only for prototyping and evaluation purposes; in a real deployment, we envision other interfaces such as a browser sidebar that combines results from all the social search indices.

An Example

To give readers a flavor of how these search indices differ, Figure 1 shows the results of a query actually performed by one of our users: the term *310*. Personalized Google search returned results about area code 310 as the top link. However, the user has in mind the course ME310, colloquially referred to among his friends as 310. The results from the indices seeded from email and Twitter links capture the user's context better and return results related to the course. The people search index returns a page with the name of a friend who has attended this course in the past, and has it on his resume. The TopTweets index has Youtube as one of the domains, and videos from the ME310 course appear in its results. In this example, each of the four social search engines in SLANT was rated higher by the user than personalized Google search.

EXPERIMENTAL EVALUATION

To evaluate the different search indices we designed, we performed a user study with 7 subjects (2 female) in the age group 20-30, all students at our university and regular users of web search. We recruited users who self-reported themselves as having been active on Twitter for a period of at least 6 months, and to have access to an email account they had actively used for more than 1 year. On Twitter, our users followed a fairly typical assortment of friends, researchers, celebrities, journalists, university accounts, popular brands, etc.

To work around the limits imposed by the Twitter API and gather a sizeable corpus of tweets, we collected tweets over 4 rounds, at 7-10 day intervals for each user. For the email links index, users selected a subset of email folders (in addition to their sent email folders), which they judged to contain high-quality information. As mentioned earlier, this process is conducted entirely locally on users' own machines in order to assure them about privacy.

Users in our study had

- 5,397 to 11,398 emails over a couple of years,
- 807 to 1,442 unique domains in their email,
- 185 to 334 Twitter followees,
- 1,038 to 1,548 unique domains in their Twitter feed.

More details of these parameters are shown in Figure 2. The number of domains in each index is a few thousand, representing a tiny percentage of web sites that are actually present on the web and crawled by a search engine like Google.

	Min	Median	Max	Mean
Number of Twitter friends	185	262	334	260
Number of Email messages	5,397	7,618	11,398	7,847
Unique domains from Twitter	1,038	1,201	1,548	1,231
Unique domains in email	807	1,161	1,442	1,150

Figure 2. Statistics on the personal search indices

We conducted the experiment with each participant independently. All our participants used Google as their search engine by default. They were also generally logged in during their routine searches, except when using mobile devices. To lend ecological validity to our experiment, we asked them to look at their search history, (gathered by Google for signed-in users and available at `http://www.google.com/history`), and select about 10 queries to try out with SLANT. Users were thus trying out our search indices with queries they had already organically performed on their own.

Users were provided with the test interface shown in Fig. 1 and asked to enter their queries, while remaining signed in to Google. They were asked to carefully evaluate each set of search results (limited to the top 10 results), and rank the quality of each set of results on a scale of 1 to 5. Participants were not told which column corresponded to which search index, in order to elicit unbiased feedback. Typically, users spent about 60 minutes performing 8 to 9 queries and evaluating and rating the results from each search index. The whole process including the mining of email and Twitter took about 6 hours per user. In all, we gathered detailed information on 59 queries across our users.

We recorded all queries and ratings for analysis. We employed a think-aloud methodology and recorded qualitative user comments to gain additional insights. While we recognize that this process may somewhat alter user's normal behavior, we judged it necessary to obtain their qualitative comments; these comments provide valuable insight into the efficacy of each search index.[1]

For the TopTweets search index, we gathered links posted by the TopTweets account once a week, over 6 weeks. This ensured that the index had a sizeable corpus to work with; in all, it consisted of 1,073 domains.

[1]The supplemental materials in this paper include a spreadsheet listing all queries, along with their categorization, ratings and user comments on the results.

RESULTS

In this section, we present a quantitative analysis of the results of our user study. Our analysis of the results starts by testing the hypothesis that users tastes are very different, and that their search queries are satisfied by different sources. We then analyze how the different search indices in SLANT perform and classify queries to understand the relationships between query types and the evaluation results. Next, we evaluate whether the search indices provide different results and show evidence that combining these queries can produce superior results.

Similarity in Content of Social Chatter

Restricting search to domains mentioned in social chatter achieves two objectives: (1) the domains are human curated and (2) they are personalized. If most users are interested in the same set of the most popular sites, then there would be little need for personalization and we could just adopt a single human-curated index.

	User 2	User 3	User 4	User 5	User 6	User 7
User 1	0.16	0.05	0.09	0.05	0.14	0.12
User 2		0.12	0.03	0.07	0.13	0.11
User 3			0.18	0.10	0.06	0.08
User 4				0.03	0.12	0.08
User 5					0.04	0.07
User 6						0.13

Figure 3. Cosine similarity between weighted email indices of different users.

Fig. 3 shows the cosine similarity between the domain-weight vectors for the email indices of each pair of users. The vectors are normalized so all referenced domains have a positive weight while preserving the relative ordering with each other. The cosine similarity ranges from 0 to 1, with 0 indicating orthogonality and 1 indicating equivalence. As we can see, the similarity between users is fairly low. This is true despite the fact that our seven users, all being students at the same university, are more likely to have similar interests than people in the general population. This indicates that different users tend to have different sites in their social chatter and therefore personalization is likely to be highly beneficial.

Rating the Search Indices

We first summarize the ratings users gave to the different SLANT indices. Our baseline, personalized Google search, receives favorable ratings from most users, ranging from 2.9 to 4.1. We observe that both Twitter and email based indices obtained similar ratings. The Twitter-based search index rates between 3.2 to 4.1, while email-based search index rates between 3.3 and 4.1. For 4 out of 7 users, the email-based search was rated the best overall; compared to two for the Twitter-based index, and one for personalized Google search. This shows that social chatter based indices can match or outperform normal personalized search in terms of user satisfaction with results.

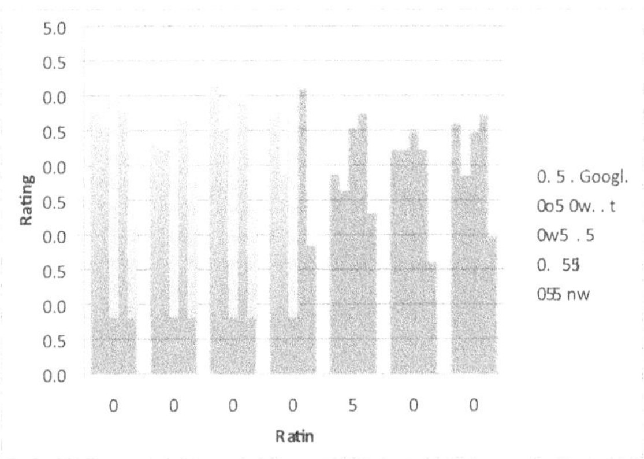

Figure 4. Average ratings of searches using different indices.

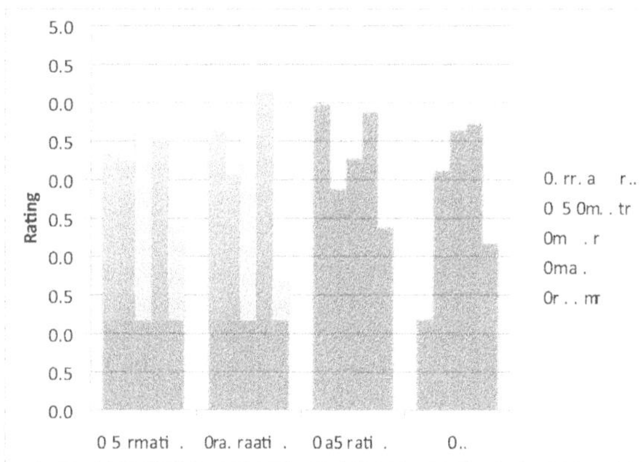

Figure 5. Average ratings across types of queries.

The search indices based on TopTweets and friends' names are not directly competitive with the other two personalized indices. The TopTweets index achieved ratings from 2.7 to 3.6 and friends names search ratings range from 1.6 to 2.8.

Categories of Queries

To gain better insight into the strengths and weaknesses of the search indices, we used Broder's web search taxonomy [6]. This taxonomy classifies queries into three categories: *informational*, where users are motivated to get more information about a subject; *transactional*, where users are interested in finding a site to perform a certain transaction, such as shop or download a file, and *navigational*, where users are looking for the URL of a specific site. Broder's analysis of query logs found that the distribution between informational, transactional, and navigational queries was 48%, 30%, and 20% respectively.

We manually classified the 59 query terms generated by our 7 users into one of these three categories. In some cases, if the categorization was somewhat ambiguous, we contacted the user and asked about his or her original intent. In these queries, the distribution between informational, transactional, and navigational queries is 56%, 27%, and 17% respectively, which is somewhat similar to the ratio reported by Broder.

Figure 5 shows the average ratings across the three types of queries as well as the overall average. The overall averages across Google, Twitter, and email are about the same: 3.5, 3.7, and 3.8, respectively. Looking at the results of the different categories, we observe the following:

- *Informational.* Personalized Google search fares slightly worse than both Twitter and email based indices in the informational category. Informational is the most important category, carrying over half of all the queries, but it is also the hardest to do well on.
- *Transactional.* Email is significantly better in the transactional category, with an average rating above 4.
- *Navigational.* Both Google and email are better than Twitter in this category.

Qualitative Analysis

Both the Twitter and email based search indices in SLANT index a tiny fraction of the world wide web. It is therefore surprising that their results are comparable to, or even better than, regular web search which indexes every one of the billions of web pages. In fact, before the study, several of our participants indicated skepticism about our personalized indices due to this reason. To understand why and how these indices work well, we now discuss some actual queries and comments from users.

Informational Queries

Examples of queries where personalized Google search performs best are *health hazards of clementine fruits* and names of famous personalities like athletes and political activists. In these cases, Google provides the general information sought by the user, such as a Wikipedia entry or a news page. For example, a search on *wikileaks* also earns Google the highest score because the user was happy to see the latest news about it.

Email has the most number of unique high scores in this category. A primary characteristic is that the user typed in just a word or two and was presented with information of specific interest. As we reported earlier, a user who searched for *"310"* was looking for a course numbered ME310 and this was captured in the user's email custom search. In this case, the user exclaimed *"Wow this needed so little typing"*. Similarly, a search for *iphone5* returned an article from the technology blog TechCrunch, a favorite of the user, and a search for the single word *"dock"* returned the Bower and Wilkins dock, related to the user's interest in audio docks.

The Twitter search also returns several unique high scores. For example, the search *Simpsons Monday joke* returns the exact joke that the user was looking for. Users also tended to like blogs and articles on the topics searched.

This suggests that these search indices have different

strengths. Google search tends to find general information for all queries. The Twitter links index returns results for what is trending, as well as interesting blogs and articles written by authors who the user is personally interested in. Finally, email contains a lot of links to domains of personal interest. We speculate that social chatter is useful for informational queries because users are often searching for information discussed in their conversations. An interesting effect we have observed is that SLANT results tend to be more personalized and colorful than with regular web search. One user remarked, *"I don't want results to be dull, like Wikipedia showing up on every query."* SLANT is also particularly useful for query terms that are commercially valuable and therefore likely to attract web spam.

Transactional Queries

SLANT's email-based index was clearly the best in the transactional category, and was rated 5 on half of the queries. We surmise that this is because email typically captures the user's personal context well. Email often includes personal information such as bank transactions, addresses, receipts, shopping information, etc. When users query for transactions related to a party they have already communicated with, this index is likely to generate good results. For example, a query like *lost cheque book* performed well with this index, without the user needing to specify details like the name of the associated bank. One user who searched for a query *disable unc check* related to compliance software was surprised to see a good result from a domain which had been emailed to him. Another user searched for *Russian roulette rihanna download* and remarked how she liked the result from a site she uses regularly.

Notably, Google search is rated the highest on all map and direction requests, particularly because it directly displays a map. It also provides the only 5-point rating on the query *matlab registry key*. Google is likely to perform well when looking for very specific information about a transaction. The Twitter-based index does better on queries like *Cauvery fishing camp* and *mac iso image mount*. It is likely that the human-curated links tweeted about these topics are of higher quality than the top Google links, and once again, avoid attracting spam.

Navigational Queries

Navigational queries are relatively unremarkable – we recorded almost no comments on the results relating to the top three indices. For these queries, all the Twitter ratings were between 2 and 4, while both Google and email score 5 on 40% of the queries. This is perhaps not surprising since Twitter is primarily used to share noteworthy news, and less for mundane matters.

Friends Names Index

Although the search index based on friends names performed poorly overall, it has turned up a number of unexpected and serendipitous results that delighted users. For example, one user searched for *parasailing san diego* and was amazed to find a Picasa photo album of a friend's visit to San Diego. Another searched for *Boston University* and discovered that a colleague of his was going there for his MBA. In yet another instance, a professor was looking up *Zigbee* and found that one of her students had written a paper on the topic, a fact she had not known. This kind of serendipitous finding, while rare, is remarkable. A topic for future work would be explore methods to improve the chances of this happening, and to estimate the quality of results from this index, so that they can be shown only if they are likely to surprise the user.

Query Length

It is well known that average search query length has been going up over the last decade [15], and that users need to formulate more precise queries to obtain accurate results. It is customary for users to iterate on queries when the results do not turn up answers they need. A couple of our users remarked how little typing was needed to get the results they wanted. Twitter and Email take advantage of the users' context to help disambiguate information, thus minimizing typing. The *310* query mentioned earlier in this paper is one such example. The ability to specify shorter queries is particularly useful when searching on mobile devices and other limited function input devices such as TV remotes, where typing is inconvenient.

Correlation Between Search Engines

Although the average ratings of the top three indices are quite similar, we observed that the ratings for each individual query vary quite widely. In addition, the qualitative results suggest that different searches perform well for different reasons. This leads us to ask if the domains present in the search indices and their weights are correlated to each other. The Pearson correlation coefficients between the ratings for each pair of search indices are shown in Figure 6. Except for a slight positive correlation between Google and TopTweets, there is very little correlation between any other pair of search indices. This lack of correlation suggests that the indices are complementary and it may be worthwhile to combine the results from different search indices.

	TopTweets	Twitter	Email	Friends
Pers. Google	0.21	0.05	-0.08	-0.08
TopTweets		0.13	-0.04	0.10
Twitter			-0.10	0.05
Email				0.08

Figure 6. Correlation between different search indices.

Combining results from multiple indices

Can we improve search by combining multiple customized searches? While investigating such a design is beyond the scope of this paper, our results can be used to compute the theoretical upper bound of a combined search with the maximum rating of its components. In our current study, each search returns ten results. A straightforward way of creating a combined engine is to simply return ten results from each search. Combining two searches will generate 20 results; combining three will generate 30. While it is preferable to return satisfactory results in the fewest number of search hits, further investigation of ways to combine the indices is desirable, given the likely increase in user satisfaction.

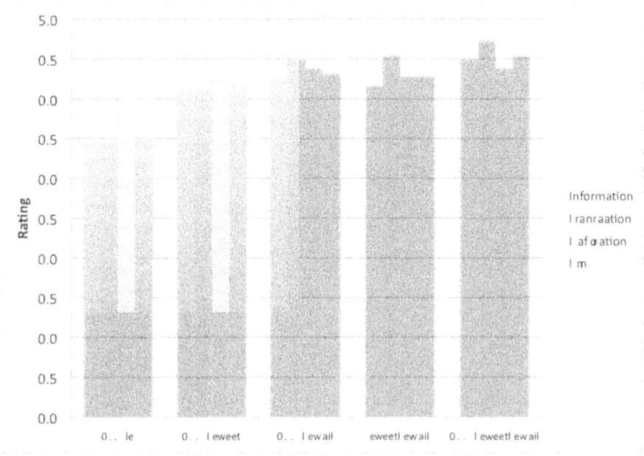

Figure 7. Combining the top performing search engines.

Figure 7 shows the possible ratings for four combinations, compared to the baseline of personalized Google search. Personalized Google obtains an average of about 3.5 for all categories, except for scoring a 4.0 average on the navigational category. Adding Twitter-based search boosts the average to above 4.1 in all categories; similarly, adding email-based search to Google boosts the average about 4.2, with transactional queries scoring a high 4.5 average. Interestingly, we can combine just Twitter and email-based results to achieve a similarly high rating. In other words, combining any two of the top three search engines will provide a significantly improved result, bumping up the average from 3.5 by 0.7 points. While users in our study are active on both email and Twitter, this result suggests that users who have a good corpus on only one of email or Twitter can benefit by adding their medium of choice to augment Google search.

Finally, we can combine results from all the top three engines. In this case, the average rating improves from 3.5 to 4.6. Specifically, out of the 59 queries, in 37 queries at least one index gets the highest possible score, in 20 queries the highest score awarded is 4 and in only 2 queries the highest score assigned to any index is a 3. With over 60% of the queries receiving the best possible score, combining the three customized searches can produce an exceptionally powerful search engine.

Summary

We now summarize the major findings from our evaluation.

1. The personalized SLANT indices have little similarity between individuals. This suggests that personalization is important.
2. Every one of the seven users found the quality of email and Twitter-based searches in SLANT similar to personalized Google, even though the results returned are very different, and from a small subset of domains.
3. Google is better at returning general results for terms and helping navigate to specific web sites when users type in its distinguishing characteristics. The Twitter-based index is better at returning trending topics and opinions, blogs and articles of interest to users. The email-based index, being personal, helps in disambiguating terms, thus minimizing the need for typing long queries and search refinement. Email-based search is useful for transactional queries because the domains that users routine interact with are often embedded in email.
4. Combining the best results from different search indices can significantly improve user satisfaction. Whereas Google only has an average rating of about 3.5, results from any pair of Google, Twitter-based, and email-based indices boosts the average rating above 4, and combining all three results could increase it further.
5. Although the friends names index generates generally poor results, it occasionally returns highly interesting results that surprise the user.

DISCUSSION

Our results are evidence of the somewhat surprising fact that custom search engines that index a tiny fraction of the entire world wide web can perform comparably with traditional search engines for general-purpose web search. Our form of social search could be implemented as a mostly client-side solution, with the search engine knowing only summary details such as the domains of interest to the user. While search engines have been personalizing search results for users, there is a sense of discomfort among users in giving out detailed information such as their email and clickthrough patterns to "Big Brother" portals. One of our users commented: *"I would not like to share my personal information with Google, or for that matter any company, as I always feel that it is a definite risk of loss of privacy. There could also be accidental information leak by a company with whom I might share my details, like Blippy accidentally leaked credit card information."*

In future, we envisage that users may see multifaceted search results. They can get authoritative and definitive results from a global search engine, along with the more personal and entertaining results from personal search engines that are automatically assembled from their social chatter.

Of course, social search indices also have limitations. We believe that the approach of generating socially curated results complements traditional search engines, but does not replace them. The quality of the indices in SLANT is dependent on the extent and quality of email archives, or links tweeted by the user's followees. One way of increasing and enriching the size of the corpus of the social indices would be to explore tweets from multiple levels within the network, such as a followee's followees, and assign trust and weights to the content generated by them.

CONCLUSIONS

We propose to leverage existing personal email archives and social media to improve the quality of web search. Social data is personalized, free of spam and can be analyzed directly by users on the client side, alleviating privacy concerns. Users can eventually employ all their social interactions and communications for the use of tools that aim to improve search.

User studies with SLANT reveal that search results derived from socially curated indices can be as good if not better than the results of commercial search engines, even when they use personalized search. We envision that combining results from these different indices will generate superior results that satisfy users for many types of queries.

ACKNOWLEDGMENTS

We thank Rakesh Ghiya for useful discussions, Diana MacLean and the anonymous reviewers for feedback on the paper, and all the users of SLANT. This research was funded in part by NSF POMI (Programmable Open Mobile Internet) 2020 Expedition Grant 0832820 and the Stanford MobiSocial Computing Laboratory.

REFERENCES

1. E. Adar, J. Teevan, and S. T. Dumais. Large scale analysis of web revisitation patterns. In *Proceedings of CHI '08*. ACM, 2008.
2. M. S. Bernstein, B. Suh, L. Hong, J. Chen, S. Kairam, and E. H. Chi. Eddi: interactive topic-based browsing of social status streams. In *Proceedings of UIST '10*. ACM, 2010.
3. M. S. Bernstein, D. Tan, G. Smith, M. Czerwinski, and E. Horvitz. Personalization via friendsourcing. *ACM TOCHI*, 17:6:1–6:28, May 2008.
4. Blekko. Friends make search better! `http://blekko.com/likes-info`, Retrieved Aug. 29, 2011.
5. S. Brin and L. Page. The anatomy of a large-scale hypertextual web search engine. In *Proceedings of WWW '98*. Elsevier, 1998.
6. A. Broder. A taxonomy of web search. *SIGIR Forum*, 36:3–10, September 2002.
7. M. Cassidy. An update to Google social search. *The Official Google Blog*, Feb. 17, 2011.
8. J. Chen, R. Nairn, L. Nelson, M. Bernstein, and E. Chi. Short and tweet: experiments on recommending content from information streams. In *Proceedings of CHI-2010*. ACM, 2010.
9. E. Cutrell, D. Robbins, S. Dumais, and R. Sarin. Fast, flexible filtering with phlat. In *Proceedings of CHI '06*. ACM, 2006.
10. S. Dumais, E. Cutrell, J. Cadiz, G. Jancke, R. Sarin, and D. C. Robbins. Stuff I've seen: a system for personal information retrieval and re-use. In *Proceedings of SIGIR '03*. ACM, 2003.
11. B. M. Evans, S. Kairam, and P. Pirolli. Do your friends make you smarter?: An analysis of social strategies in online information seeking. *Information Processing and Management*, 46(6):679 – 692, 2010.
12. Google. `http://google.com/cse`.
13. S. Hangal, M. S. Lam, and J. Heer. Muse: Reviving memories using email archives. In *Proceedings of UIST-2011*. ACM, 2011.
14. D. Horowitz and S. D. Kamvar. The anatomy of a large-scale social search engine. In *Proceedings of WWW '10*. ACM, 2010.
15. F. Lardinois. Hitwise: Search queries are getting longer. *ReadWriteWeb*, Feb. 24, 2009.
16. J. Luxenburger, S. Elbassuoni, and G. Weikum. Task-aware search personalization. In *Proceedings of SIGIR '08*. ACM, 2008.
17. Y. Mehdi. Facebook friends now fueling faster decisions on Bing. *Microsoft Bing Search Blog*, May 16, 2011.
18. M. R. Morris and E. Horvitz. Searchtogether: an interface for collaborative web search. In *Proceedings of UIST '07*. ACM, 2007.
19. M. R. Morris, J. Teevan, and S. Bush. Enhancing collaborative web search with personalization: groupization, smart splitting, and group hit-highlighting. In *Proceedings of CSCW '08*. ACM, 2008.
20. M. R. Morris, J. Teevan, and K. Panovich. A comparison of information seeking using search engines and social networks. In *Proceedings of ICWSM '10*. AAAI, 2010.
21. M. R. Morris, J. Teevan, and K. Panovich. What do people ask their social networks, and why? A survey study of status message Q&A behavior. In *Proceedings of CHI '10*. ACM, 2010.
22. The Radicati Group. Email Statistics Report, 2010-2014, 2010.
23. F. Radlinski and S. Dumais. Improving personalized web search using result diversification. In *Proceedings of SIGIR '06*. ACM, 2006.
24. L. Rao. Twitter Seeing 90 Million Tweets Per Day, 25 Percent Contain Links. *TechCrunch*, Sept. 14, 2010.
25. D. Segal. The dirty little secrets of search. *The New York Times*, Feb. 13, 2011.
26. M. Smith, V. Barash, L. Getoor, and H. W. Lauw. Leveraging social context for searching social media. In *Proceedings of the 2008 ACM workshop on Search in social media*. ACM, 2008.
27. D. Sullivan. As deal with Twitter expires, Google realtime search goes offline. *Search Engine Land*, Jul 4, 2011.
28. J. Teevan, S. T. Dumais, and E. Horvitz. Personalizing search via automated analysis of interests and activities. In *Proceedings of SIGIR '05*. ACM, 2005.
29. Twitter. `http://www.twitter.com/TopTweets`.

Who Gives A Tweet? Evaluating Microblog Content Value

Paul André[1,2], Michael S. Bernstein[3], Kurt Luther[4]

[1]Carnegie Mellon University
Pittsburgh, PA
paul.andre@cmu.edu

[2]Electronics &
Computer Science
Uni. Southampton, UK

[3]MIT CSAIL
Cambridge, MA
msbernst@mit.edu

[4]Georgia Institute
of Technology
luther@cc.gatech.edu

ABSTRACT

While microblog readers have a wide variety of reactions to the content they see, studies have tended to focus on extremes such as retweeting and unfollowing. To understand the broad continuum of reactions in-between, which are typically not shared publicly, we designed a website that collected the first large corpus of follower ratings on Twitter updates. Using our dataset of over 43,000 voluntary ratings, we find that nearly 36% of the rated tweets are worth reading, 25% are not, and 39% are middling. These results suggest that users tolerate a large amount of less-desired content in their feeds. We find that users value information sharing and random thoughts above me-oriented or presence updates. We also offer insight into evolving social norms, such as lack of context and misuse of @mentions and hashtags. We discuss implications for emerging practice and tool design.

ACM Classification Keywords

H5.m. Information interfaces and presentation (e.g., HCI).

General Terms

Design; Human Factors; Measurement

INTRODUCTION

Microblogging has been found to have broad value as a news and communication medium [3,6], but little is known about fine-grained content value. Existing studies focus on signals of positive or negative reactions like retweets [10] and unfollowing [5], but these signals capture only extreme reactions. Users' reactions to their feeds are often varied: items can bore, can spur interest, can be funny. However, there are no existing public signals for investigating users' more nuanced reactions at a large scale. If we could better understand what users do and do not value, and why, we could: 1) derive *design implications* for better tools or automatic filters, and 2) develop insight into *emerging norms and practice* to help users create and consume valued content.

This work contributes an analysis of microblog content from the reader's point of view, powered by a novel design for collecting large numbers of voluntary ratings. We developed a website that encourages Twitter users to give anonymous feedback to accounts they follow in exchange for feedback from their own followers and other users. Using our corpus of approximately 43,000 ratings, we ask: 1) *What* content do Twitter users value? For example, do users value personal updates while disliking opinions? We then ask: 2) *Why* are some tweets valued more than others?

Conventional wisdom exists around these questions, but to our knowledge this is the first work to rigorously examine whether the commonly held truths are accurate. Further, by collecting many ratings, we are able to quantify effect sizes. A better understanding of content value will allow us to improve the overall experience of microblogging.

BACKGROUND

Twitter content analysis has identified a number of different categories of user and message [9], which we use in our analysis to assess perceived value by category. Previous investigations of specific scenarios have identified positive evaluations related to retweeting [10] and search evaluation [4], especially for facts or useful links. Negative outcomes have been explored in the context of unfollowing, and have been linked to network structure and 'bursts' of (uninteresting) tweets [5]. Readers may also value content for mere social communication and awareness (the equivalent of saying 'hello' in the hallway [8]) rather than for any substantive content.

An analysis of tweets by visual attention [2] suggests that interfaces can direct users to high-value content, e.g., by highlighting infrequent authors. This prior work used interest judgments to conclude that there are no externally-visible markers like replies or retweets for many of the tweets that users found interesting. This paper extends previous work by gathering a large set of judgments that contain not just value but also *content* and *reason*.

DESIGN

To understand the perceived value of Twitter content, we needed a corpus of tweet ratings. We capitalized on Twitter users' curiosity of how others view them to build this corpus. We designed a web site, called *Who Gives a Tweet* (WGAT), that delivers anonymous feedback from followers and strangers in exchange for rating tweets.

After signing in to the website, users see a list of ten tweets that they must rate before receiving feedback on their own. This mechanism capitalizes on anticipated reciprocity: users are performing an action (that provides information to the site) in the hopes of receiving something they value (ratings). WGAT finds tweets to rate from Twitter accounts that the user follows, preferring accounts that have signed up for WGAT, and filtering out @replies. The user then rates each tweet as *Worth Reading*, *OK*, or *Not Worth Reading*. Users could also skip rating any tweet. Tweets are displayed with the corresponding author name and avatar to simulate the real-world experience of reading (and judging) a Twitter feed. Users may optionally explain why they chose that rating. We collected these details via checkboxes and a freetext response. The checkbox options were: *funny, exciting, useful, informative*, or, *arrogant, boring, depressing, mean*. These adjectives were adapted from previous work [1] and iterated with pilot studies.

METHOD

After Who Gives A Tweet launched, popular news sites like Mashable, TechCrunch, OneForty and CNN wrote about the site, and the link went viral. The subsequent spike in traffic provided us with a significant number of users and ratings from many different parts of the Twitter network. We base our analysis on this data from the period of 30 Dec 2010 to 17 Jan 2011. The dataset includes 43,738 tweet ratings from 1,443 users. These users rated the accounts they follow, an even broader population of 21,014 Twitter users. All analysis is drawn only from follower ratings.

Category Labeling

We gathered a sample of 4,220 ratings from users who rated at least ten tweets. For each tweet, we determined a content category using an adapted version of Naaman's [9] tweet categorization scheme, which includes categories like Me Now (current mood or activity), Presence Maintenance (e.g., "*Hullo twitter!*"), Self Promotion (e.g., sharing a blog post the author just published), and Information Sharing. We edited the typology by removing anecdote categories as they were very rare in both datasets. We also added a Conversation category to capture many discussion-oriented tweets that did not fit cleanly into the typology.

To apply content labels, we used the paid crowdsourcing service Crowdflower. Crowdflower provides a high-quality result by using questions with known answers (ground truth data) to discard the submissions of workers who do not substantially agree with the ground truth. The paper authors built a ground truth dataset by following Naaman's manual tagging scheme and gave the ground truth labels to Crowdflower along with the full set of tweets to label. Cohen's kappa between Crowdflower's labels and a held-out set of tweets labeled by the paper authors was 0.62: moderate to strong agreement. Experimentation indicated agreement would be as high as 0.81 if ground truth included multiple categories per tweet as Naaman did.

Sample Bias and Limitations

Given the naturalistic growth of the site and the technology-centric media attention, we began by investigating potential biases in our dataset. We compared our distribution of tweet categories to Naaman et al.'s random sample [9] and found two main differences: our dataset contained more Information Sharing tweets (49% vs 22%), and fewer Me Now tweets (10% vs 40%). This difference is likely attributable to the TechCrunch and Mashable demographic, and the inclusion of marketers and organizations in our dataset (unlike Naaman et al., who removed them).

Thus, our analysis should generalize to a population of information-sharing Twitter users, but may not apply evenly to all subpopulations on Twitter. For example, information sharing might be regarded more highly than in other samples. However, our sample is similar to previous analyses (e.g., [2, 4]), or broader than them due to viral spread, and it is orders of magnitude larger. We believe this sample is broad enough to draw valuable conclusions.

Regression Analysis

To examine the effect of tweet category on rating, we used an ordered logistic regression. Standard linear regression assumes that the outcome is ratio or interval. However, we did not believe that users' psychological distance between Not Worth Reading and Neutral was necessarily the same as the distance between Neutral and Worth Reading. For example, it is possible that the bar for tweets Not Worth Reading is lower than the bar for tweets Worth Reading. An ordered logistic regression is non-parametric and does not make this assumption, so we use it instead. We used content category as the predictor, holding out the Presence Maintenance category (the most disliked) as a baseline for the categorical dummy variables, and controlled for rater.

RESULTS

How Much of the Twitter Feed is Valued?

Followers described 36% of the rated tweets as Worth Reading (WR), thought that 25% were Not Worth Reading (NotWR), and remained neutral about the other 39%. Given that users *actively choose* to follow these accounts, it is striking that so few of the tweets are actively liked. On a per-user basis, we find that the average user finds 41% (sd=20%) of their rated tweets Worth Reading. This wide variation in quality suggests that the analyses to follow can have a large impact on the Twitter experience.

What Categories of Tweets are Valued?

It might be reasonable to assume that information sharing tweets are particularly valued, given Twitter's emphasis on real-time news. Or, it might be feasible that followers enjoy personal status updates, since they separate Twitter from other information sources like RSS feeds.

We investigated the impact of tweet category on rating using the tweets categorized by Crowdflower. Figure 1 summarizes category ratings. The results of our ordered logistic regression analysis are in Table 1. The odds ratios in the table can be interpreted as: *Question to Followers* had 2.83 times the odds as being rated Worth Reading instead of Neutral, in comparison to a *Presence Maintenance* tweet. Figure 1 illustrates these differences graphically. For example, Presence Maintenance tweets had a 45%

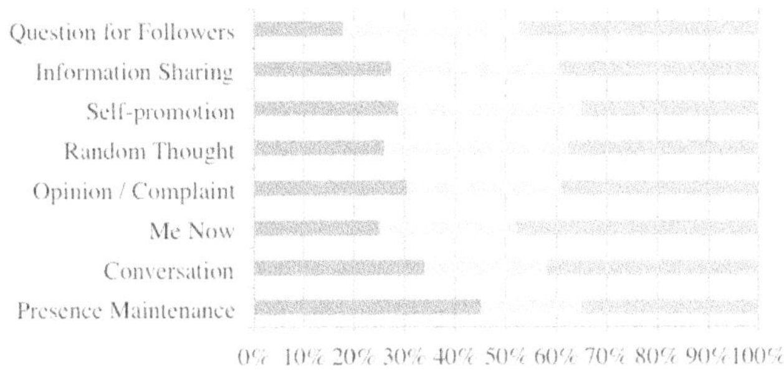

Figure 1. Ratings of a 4,220-tweet subset of our corpus. From left to right, the colors indicate percentages of Not Worth Reading, Neutral, and Worth Reading. (Ordered by Odds Ratio in Table 1.)

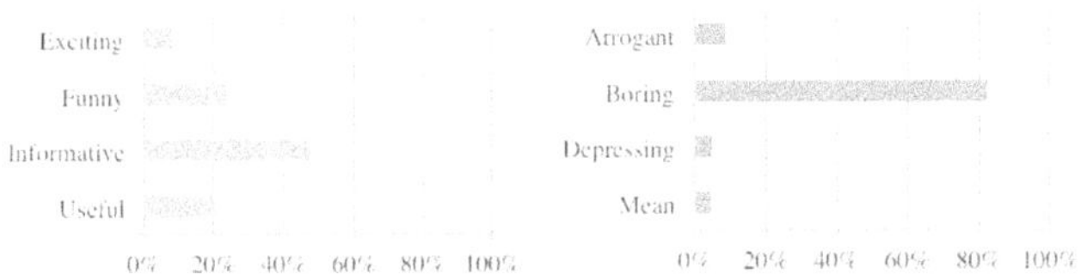

Figure 2. Based on 17,557 ratings from checkboxes, informative leads the reasons for liking a tweet, while boring dominates the reasons for disliking.

probability of being Not Worth Reading, compared to just 18% of Question to Followers tweets.

The three most strongly disliked categories were Presence Maintenance, Conversation, and Me Now (the tweeter's current status). For example, a Me Now tweet had just 22% chance of being Worth Reading. Odds of being Worth Reading (vs. Neutral) were just 1.89 times that of Presence Maintenance; z=1.94, p≈.05. One might reasonably expect followers to be interested in personal details. However, this does not seem to be the case. Analyzing the freetext responses to understand the reasons, we found many cases in which the follower was not interested by the tweeter's life details, e.g., *"sorry, but I don't care what people are eating", "too much personal info", "He moans about this ALL THE TIME. Seriously."* There is a special hatred reserved for Foursquare location check-ins: *"foursquare updates don't need to be shared on Twitter unless there's a relevant update to be made"*, or, more simply: *"4sq, ffs..."*

Presence Maintenance tweets (e.g., *"Hullo twitter!"*) were the most strongly disliked. These tweets had variously 1.5-2.5 times worse odds than any other category. Freeform text indicated that these pieces of phatic communication were generally considered contentless: *"I have one word for one word tweets: BORING"*, or *"useless."*

The most-liked categories were Questions to Followers, Information Sharing, and Self-Promotion (often sharing links that you created). To some extent, these results may reflect our sample bias of Twitterers. However, they also suggest that the Twitter ecosystem values learning about new content. For example, *"The headline arouses my curiosity"* or *"Wow. Didn't know that was happening. Thanks for informing me."* Questions to Followers were

Predictor	Odds Ratio	z value
Question to Followers	2.83	2.94*
Information Sharing	2.69	3.05*
Self-Promotion	2.69	2.61*
Random Thought	2.47	2.89*
Opinion / Complaint	2.05	1.93ˇ
Me Now	1.89	1.94ˇ
Conversation	1.57	1.26
Presence Maintenance	N/A	N/A

*Table 1. Odds ratios of the ordered logistic regression on rating. Presence Maintenance is the baseline condition. (e.g., Question to Followers had 2.83 times the odds as being rated Worth Reading instead of Neutral, in comparison to a Presence Maintenance tweet.) N=4220. *p<.01, ˇtrend p ≈ .05*

often liked either because the follower thought *"this is a good use of Twitter"* or because of an interest in the topic itself *"gives one pause to think about the question posted."*

Why are Tweets (Not) Valued by Followers?

The previous section covered *what* was valued about tweets; this section elaborates on *why*. This analysis uses our entire 43,738 tweet dataset as rated by followers. When WGAT users rated a tweet as worth reading (WR) or not (NotWR), they could also select reasons (*arrogant, boring, depressing, mean,* or *funny, exciting, useful, informative*), and enter free text. Of tweets rated WR, 67% were tagged with at least one reason; 38% of those NotWR had a reason.

Not Worth Reading: Being boring, repeating old news, cryptic, or using too many # and @ signs

Being boring is far more prevalent a problem than expected. It was the standout reason for rating NotWR, accounting for 82% of all explanations (Figure 2). Because Twitter emphasizes real-time information, tweeting old information led to Boring responses like *"Yes, I saw that first thing this morning"* or *"I've read this same tweet so many times."* Some users offered suggestions: *"since your followers read the [New York Times] too, reposting NYT URLs is tricky unless you add something."* Boredom is also associated with banal or prosaic tweets, leading to responses like *"and so what?"* or *"it's fine, but a bit obvious."*

Users often complained when the tweet did not share enough context to be understandable or worthwhile. Many updates linked to a photo or blog without any other explanation: *"just links are the worst thing in the world."* Local updates were a point of contention: *"don't live there, don't care."* Negative sentiments or complaints were not worth reading: *"Kinda negative :-((", "whining."*

Twitter-specific syntax was a common source of complaint, particularly the overuse of hashtags and @mentions: *"Too many tags – can hardly find the real content."* Users also disliked tweets mentioning someone rather than just @replying or Direct Messaging them: *"dm thanks for rts is better", "Twitter's fault; feels like listening in on a private conversation."* Sometimes the extra syntax was appreciated: *"If you dropped in a hashtag, I could save the search and find out the answer later."*

Our users also rated tweets by celebrities or organizations they followed. There was tension between expecting a professional insight, and getting personal ones: *"I unfollowed you for this tweet. I don't know you; I followed you b/c of your job."* News organizations should consider the tension between giving all the information in a tweet, and piquing a user's curiosity: *"Newsy, and all the news I want is here. Not much of a tease."*

Worth Reading: Information, humor, conciseness

Ratings revealed that our users primarily valued Twitter as an information medium. Tweets worth reading were often informative (48%) or funny (24%), as seen in Figure 2. These tags had very little overlap: a tweet was often one or the other, but not both. Information links were valued for novelty or an appealing description: *"interesting perspective on something I know nothing about", "makes you want to know more."* Humor was a successful way to share random thoughts or opinions especially: *"it's witty and snarky. worth the read."*

In keeping with Twitter's focus on short messages, followers appreciated conciseness: *"few words to say much, very clear."* A personal or human aspect was also appreciated: *"personal, honest and transparent."*

LIMITATIONS & FUTURE WORK

Our volunteer population was skewed towards technologists or "informers" [9]. Though our results provide insight into this user base, it will be important in future work to address all types of users and understand which results generalize, particularly whether there are different communities in Twitter with different value judgments.

We asked users to rate tweets, but not rate the person who tweeted. There may be a social obligation to follow people whose tweets are perhaps not personally valued. Long-term ratings of one's feed would enable detailed analysis on a per-user basis. An analysis of users *no longer* followed would provide another perspective on the value discussion, as would self-ratings on users' own tweets. We would also like to consider the effect of potentially unvalued tweets actually having a meta-level value in maintaining awareness and relationships.

DISCUSSION & CONCLUSION

Microblogging poses unique and unanswered questions of content value to its users. We designed a website to collect the first large corpus of follower ratings on Twitter updates. Using 43,000 volunteer ratings on tweets, we asked what is (or is not) valued, and why. We see two directions for utilizing these results. The first is in design implications to make the most of what is valued, or reduce or repurpose what is not. The second is in understanding accepted practice and value on Twitter, aiding users to create and consume more valued content.

Distribution. Our sample of Twitter users rated 36% of tweets as worth reading, 25% as not, and 39% as middling. The average user rated 41% (sd=20%) of tweets as worth reading. In a personally curated stream, it may be surprising that so few rated tweets were considered worth reading. These results highlight the need for better awareness and presentation of valued content.

Content. Information sharing, self-promotion (links to personally created content) and questions to followers were valued highly, while presence maintenance, conversational and 'me now' statuses were less valued.

Emerging Practices. Our analysis suggests: embed more context in tweets (and be less cryptic); add extra commentary, especially if retweeting a common news source; don't overuse hashtags and use direct messages (DMs) rather than @mentions if more appropriate; happy sentiments are valued and "whining" is disliked, and questions should use a unique hashtag so followers can keep track of the conversation.

Social media technologies present both new opportunities for connection, as well as new tensions and conflicts [7]. It is important to understand questions of value to aid in the production and consumption of valued content, and to shine a light on emerging norms. We contribute to an ongoing discussion of content value and changing attitudes to sharing and interaction, highlighting how we might design tools to reflect these attitudes, inform users of hard-to-gauge audience reaction and perception, while improving the overall experience of microblogging for all.

ACKNOWLEDGMENTS

We thank Robert Kraut, m.c. schraefel, Jaime Teevan, Ryen White, Sarita Yardi, and anonymous reviewers for helpful feedback on this and earlier versions of this paper.

REFERENCES

1. Barash, V., Duchenaut, N., Isaacs, E. & Bellotti, V. Faceplant: Impression (Mis)management in Facebook Status Updates. *Proc. ICWSM 2010.*
2. Counts, S., & Fisher, K. Taking It All In? Visual Attention in Microblog Consumption. *Proc. ICWSM 2011.*
3. Ehrlich, K. & Shami, S. Microblogging Inside and Outside the Workplace. *Proc. ICWSM 2010.*
4. Hurlock, J., & Wilson, M.L. Searching Twitter: Separating the Tweet from the Chaff. *Proc. ICWSM 2011.*
5. Kwak, H., Chun, H. & Moon, S. Fragile online relationship: a first look at unfollow dynamics in twitter. *Proc. CHI 2011.*
6. Kwak, H., Lee, C., Park, H., & Moon, S. What is Twitter, a Social Network or a News Media? *Proc. WWW 2010.*
7. Marwick, A. E. & boyd., d. Twitter Users, context collapse, and the imagined audience. *New Media & Society* 13(1), 2011.
8. Miller, V. New Media, Networking and Phatic Culture. *Convergence* 2008, 14:387.
9. Naaman, M., Boase, J. & Lai, C. Is it really about me? Message Content in Social Awareness Streams. *CSCW 2010.*
10. Suh, B., Hong, L., Pirolli, P. & Chi, E. H. Want to be Retweeted? Large Scale Analytics on Factors Impacting Retweet in Twitter Network. *Proc. SocialCom 2010.*

Prescriptive Persuasion and Open-Ended Social Awareness: Expanding the Design Space of Mobile Health

Eric P. S. Baumer[1,2], Sherri Jean Katz[1], Jill E. Freeman[1], Phil Adams[2], Amy L. Gonzales[4], JP Pollak[2], Daniela Retelny[2], Jeff Niederdeppe[1], Christine M. Olson[3], Geri K. Gay[1,2]
[1]Communication / [2]Information Science / [3]Nutritional Sciences, Cornell U || [4]R W Johnson, U of Penn
Information Science Department, 301 College Ave, Ithaca, NY 14850
{ericpsb, sjk237, jef34, pja22, alg49, jpp9, dr326, jdn56, cmo3, gkg1}@cornell.edu

ABSTRACT
Most mobile technology systems designed to encourage healthy decisions focus on prescriptive persuasion, telling the user either implicitly or explicitly what to do, as the primary means of improving health. However, other technically and socially viable options exist. Drawing on both relevant social theory and previous CSCW research, this paper suggests that *open-ended social awareness*, making users aware of both others' and their own decisions, may also serve as an effective central design principle for mobile health. To explore this approach, this paper presents analysis of qualitative data from two studies of such a system. Results suggest that open-endedness allowed users flexibility and freedom in defining what counts as health, and that the social aspects compounded both the positive and the occasionally negative impacts of this openness. The paper concludes with implications for the design and evaluation of research on mobile health technology, as well as suggestions for how future work can further explore the design space of mobile health beyond prescriptive persuasion.

Author Keywords
Mobile health, awareness, persuasion, user experience, reflective HCI.

ACM Classification Keywords
H5.m. Information interfaces and presentation (e.g., HCI): Miscellaneous.

General Terms
Human Factors; Design.

INTRODUCTION
"Health is a state of complete physical, mental, and social well-being and not merely the the absence of disease or infirmity." - WHO definition of "health" [42]

Issues of health, healthiness, and well-being have garnered significant attention from researchers in HCI, CSCW, Ubicomp, and related fields [2,6,7,18,31,33]. However, the best approach to designing technology that facilitates healthy living remains a somewhat open question. Thus far, most research in this space has focused on prescriptive persuasion and behavior change, encouraging users to be more physically active [7], to make healthier food choices [30], to get more restful and consistent sleep [40], to cultivate more stable emotional and social health [14], or to change some other health behavior. Indeed, a recent workshop [10] focused on using "persuasion, influence, nudge, and coercion" to effect general behavior change. This focus on prescriptive persuasion, we argue, unnecessarily constrains both the design space of technologies for health and the use of those technologies. Such designs often do little to account for differentiated users' needs or to encourage reflection on what being healthy means. This paper attempts to open up, and facilitate a conversation about, the design space of mobile health technologies. Prescriptive persuasion *per se* is neither necessarily harmful nor undesirable, but persuasion alone is not the only possible means of facilitating healthy behaviors.

Specifically, we suggest that *open-ended social awareness*, grounded both in social theories related to social awareness and previous CSCW research on awareness systems, may serve as one such means of expanding this design space. The term "social" here refers to awareness of the activities and decision of other users as well as the relationship of ones own activities to the group. Health decisions, like other decisions, are not made in a vacuum, and much recent work has demonstrated the value of social support for health [6,14,18]. "Open-ended" indicates that the system does not prescribe specific actions for users or focus on any one health activity (e.g., physical exercise, eating, sleep). Such open-endedness allows the user to define what counts as health (for better or worse), moving beyond the prescription of specific activities to support a user experience driven by user needs, emotions, and attitudes, which may thus be more conducive to a state of complete well-being.

This paper describes a system called VERA, which serves as one example of a health system that uses open-ended social awareness as a central design principle. We present qualitative results from two different deployments of this system, focusing on users' experiences to build an understanding of both the benefits and drawbacks of designing a health system around open-ended social awareness. These results also point to some broader implications for technology designed to support healthy living.

The contributions of this paper, then, are two-fold. First, we provide a theoretically-grounded argument for the value of open-ended social awareness as a central design principle for mobile health technologies. Second, we provide empirical qualitative evidence about the possible impact on user experience of designing such a system focused on open-ended social awareness. These contributions can facilitate further exploration of the design space of mobile health technologies.

CURRENT APPROACHES TO MOBILE HEALTH

In response to the prevalence of broad and diverse health issues, researchers and practitioners have developed numerous technology-based approaches to *health persuasion*, i.e., systems designed to assist users in making healthier choices [39]. It has been argued that, for a variety of reasons, mobile technology can be particularly effective toward this goal [10,11,21]. Using examples from the literature, this section summarizes the strategies commonly employed by such persuasive technologies, moving generally from most prescriptive to least prescriptive. While increasingly popular, the use of games for health [e.g., 19,25,32] is beyond the scope of this paper and not discussed here.

Prompting

Many persuasive systems seek to promote health by telling the user what to do via prompts, e.g., delivered to their mobile phone [13]. Prompts are an intervention that involves sending messages, reminders, or feedback to the user, and have been used for a variety of purposes [5]. For example, mDIET, an SMS-based system, encourages healthier food choices by sending messages tailored to the day of the week, the time of day, and a participants' eating behaviors [30]. In another project, the Computerized Automated Reminder Diabetes System (CARDS) used messages that reminded participants to check their blood glucose levels and reply with their results [20]. Text messaging has also been used to support smoking cessation, supplying users with personalized smoking advice, support, and distraction [35]. Although this prescriptive use of technology provides specific directions that have proven effective in some situations, such specificity can cause a "boomerang" effect of resistance to the message [3]. Furthermore, this top-down approach to health intervention may limit the engagement of users by constraining their participation in the system.

Feedback and Reward

Another common persuasive strategy is providing the user with various forms of feedback in response to the health-related choices. Feedback mechanisms usually directly link a user's behaviors with affirmation, condemnation, reward, or punishment, although the relative effectiveness of positive versus negative feedback is the subject of much debate [12]. A study of Time to Eat!, in which users' eating choices cause a virtual pet to become either happy or sad, found that both positive and negative feedback were necessary to promote healthier behavior [31]. On the other hand, a study of Fish'n'Steps, a system in which a user's fish in a shared virtual fishbowl grows in response to the number of steps s/he takes, found negative feedback off-putting [25]. Feedback also frequently includes reward, a fundamental extrinsic motivator [26]. For example, Ubifit Garden rewards users' physical activity by adding new flowers and creatures to their virtual gardens as new milestones are reached [7].

Tracking, Logging, and Diaries

While most tools incorporating persuasion involve explicitly telling the user what to do, others focus instead on tracking users' behavior. Previous studies have suggested that simply tracking one's behavior can help improve weight loss [2], physical activity [23], disease management [9,27], and other health outcomes. Some tools involve entirely manual input [14], some combine automatic tracking with user input [44], and some use entirely automatic tracking [7]. Many of these systems also provide some functionality that represents back to users traces or trends in their tracked activities. Thus, tracking and feedback are often closely coupled in practice.

Social Influence

Yet another strategy in promoting healthy behavior, one which we incorporate in VERA, is leveraging social influence. Among the various relevant theories, the most commonly employed is social cognitive theory [1], which, in part, describes how individuals model their behavior based on that of those around them. Designers often employ social influence to reinforce a specific shared goal or common perception of health. In persuasive health systems, this can often mean simply placing users into peer groups and providing them with tools to share, comment on, and discuss specific healthy behaviors, with the hope that such groupings will improve those behaviors. GE's Pic Healthy iPhone app [healthymagination.com] is a prime example, providing users with tools to share health choices with friends and leader boards to highlight the healthiest individuals. Other systems provide tools for users with similar health goals to communicate with and support one another. For example, EatWell uses voicemail to allow users to share their experiences of trying to find and enjoy healthier food in low-income communities [18]. Aurora, a mobile-phone based social support system for cancer patients, has been found to make users more comfortable sharing emotion and engaging in socially supportive behavior [14]. These and similar systems are not explicitly prescriptive, i.e., they do not tell the user specifically what to do, but they are in a sense implicitly prescriptive. Pic Healthy and EatWell both focus specifically on eating healthy food. EatWell, though, represents an important exception to the prescriptive trend, focusing on users' stories about and experiences of health. In this way, EatWell is similar to the VERA system in this paper, but VERA is not specifically focused on food.

Summary

The above categories of persuasive health strategies are neither mutually exclusive nor completely exhaustive. However, they do point toward a general trend of prescriptive persuasion, telling the user, either explicitly or implicitly what to do. For example, prompts give very specific directions. Feedback, reward, and tracking systems, while they may not include such explicit instruction, provide implicit guidance by focusing on, rewarding, or tracking one specific set of behaviors.

We suggest that there is an opportunity to expand the design space of health technologies beyond solely prescriptive persuasion, cf. [18,33]. Specifically, this paper argues that there is value in drawing on the long-standing CSCW tradition of research in awareness [37] in the design of mobile health technologies. While some research has examined the value of awareness [e.g., 6,14], we suggest that, specifically, *open-ended social awareness*, can serve as a useful central design concept for health systems. The following section summarizes both social theories relevant to awareness and systems designed to support awareness.

AWARENESS: THEORIES AND SYSTEMS

Often, research in CSCW focuses on awareness as "the tacit and seamless integration of ongoing cooperative activities" [37:290]. That is, it focuses on how individuals "pick up on what is going on around them and make practical sense of it" [37:291]. Generally, this meaning is applied in the context of shared work activity. This paper applies a similar perspective but focuses on social awareness [34], that is, an individual's knowledge of the activities of others in a group and the relation of her or his activities to that group. Our approach is grounded in two theoretical frameworks specifically related to open-ended social awareness: social cognitive theory and presentation of self.

As noted above, social cognitive theory [1], which describes how individuals model their behavior on that of those around them, has been useful in promoting healthy behavior. Modeling relates to specific features of the contextual environment, and social awareness of others is an important part of modeling [15]. Homophily, or the desire to connect with similar others, also plays a role in modeling; specifically, modeling is more likely to occur when viewing others perceived as similar to oneself [38]. Social cognitive theory has also been tied to greater participant agency [1] and relates to social facilitation theory, including notions of accountability [15,43]. Jacucci, Oulasvirta & Salovaara [22] tie social cognitive theory to the construction of social aspects of experience with respect to mobile media, noting the importance of active spectatorship.

Another theory that has been useful in promoting healthy behaviors is Goffman's [17] notion of presentation of self. This theory acknowledges that we are consciously aware of ourselves as social actors and frame our interactions accordingly. Put simply, we disclose some elements of self, while choosing not to disclose others. Research has related presentation of self to active forms of impression management and privacy in online environments [34] and to accountability [29]. Newman et al. [29] note how individuals use a specific set of strategies for impression management online. The relationship between the self and the group is also mediated by such factors as the composition of the group and the relative anonymity of group members; anonymity can lead to deindividuation [4], where users see the group not as a collection of individuals but as an undifferentiated whole. These theories informed the design of a new system, VERA, which both places users in a group and gives them great leeway in how exactly they choose to document and present health behaviors to the group.

SYSTEM DESIGN: VERA

In an effort to explore the design space of mobile health technologies, we developed VERA (Virtual Environments for Raised Awareness), a mobile phone application that allows a user to document health decisions and share them with other users. At the moment of making a health-related decision, the user opens the VERA app and takes a photo that in some way depicts their decision (Figure 1, left). Photos are used rather than text, audio, or video, as they afford both quick and expressive documentation. The system then prompts the user to identify whether they did or did not take the action depicted (e.g., the user might choose not to eat a piece of cake), rate the decision from -3 (most unhealthy) to +3 (most healthy), record their emotional response to the decision via PAM [32], and optionally enter a short caption (Figure 1, center). Once the user has completed her or his post, s/he is taken to a screen displaying recent photos posted by other users (Figure 1, right). This display also functions better with photos than with text, audio, or video. By tapping on a photo, the user sees a larger version along with information about who submitted it, when s/he sent it, and the caption s/he submitted. The post's health rating and their emotion are not visible. Here, the user can also leave a comment on the post. This design makes VERA most similar to previous mobile health systems that employ tracking and social influence [14,18], but its focus on open-ended social awareness draws on recent critiques of persuasive health [33]. VERA was developed natively for Android OS 2.x, with PHP and MySQL on the server side. It was later ported to Apple's iOS.

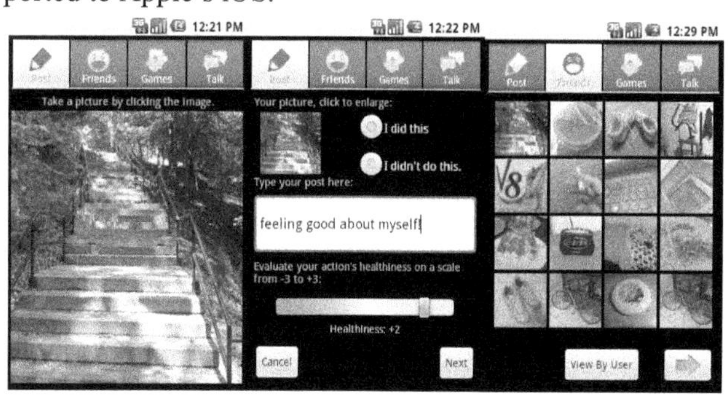

Figure 1: Screenshots of VERA taking a photo (left), posting details (center), and viewing others' photos (right).

While smartphones are becoming more prolific, they are not yet as common among many populations, such as low- and mixed-income users, as traditional cell phones. Therefore, we also developed an MMS-based version of VERA. With this version, users take a photo of a health decision and then send it as an MMS with text that includes the same types of information as described above. The social component of the MMS version is provided via a website, which allows similar capabilities as the social portion of the mobile application. While not providing identical functionality, this version enables a similar experience for those who choose not to or cannot afford to own a smartphone.

This design foregrounds open-ended social awareness and draws on theory in several ways. First, users are not explicitly required to document a specific type of health behavior, but can be encouraged to take photos of anything that they feel is related to health, including good and bad decisions, as well as both things they do and things they do not do. Second, presenting users with photos posted by others facilitates social modeling, accountability, and other aspects of social cognitive theory [1]. Third, selection of activities to photograph, and the ways in which photos are taken, facilitate users' self-presentation [17]. The flipside of our focus on social awareness is self-presentation; leveraging both Goffman and Bandura helps us understand and design for both sides of these social phenomena.

Methods: Two Sets of Deployments

VERA was deployed in two separate field studies. The first was part of a larger project, referred to here pseudonymously as mMoms (Mobile Mothers), that examines how technology can be used to support health among new mothers. Mothers with children under two years of age were recruited from an urban area in western New York via newspaper ads, library flyers, social media, and snowball sampling. A total of 45 participants were placed into groups of 7 to 11 participants and used MMS VERA on their own phones and computers for two weeks; some participants previously knew others in their group, but most were strangers. As part of the mMoms study, some participants were assigned to a condition where they received simple health tips via text message, e.g., "Increase the amount of brightly colored fruits and vegetables that you eat." These tips were not explicitly directly connected to participants' use of VERA, and we did not see major differences related to open-ended social awareness between these groups, so we include data from all participants in the analysis below. All participants completed a survey at the beginning of the study, and 36 participants returned a post survey. Phone interviews were completed with 29 participants. Each participant was compensated $50.

The second study focused on a wellness program for faculty and staff at Cornell University. Participants were recruited via two mailing lists: a general email list for all members of the wellness program (~4600), and a list specifically for individuals interested in weight loss (~125). We received a total of 44 interested participants from the general list (21 of whom were placed in a control group and are not reported on here) and 10 from the weight loss list. As with mMoms, a couple dyads or triads were previously acquainted, but most participants were strangers. For various reasons, a number of participants dropped out, leaving 16 in the general group and 8 in the weight loss group. Participants who owned an Android or iPhone installed VERA on their own phone; those who did not were lent a 3G MyTouch Slide for the duration of the study. Each of these participants used the VERA app for four weeks, completing a survey both before and after. All participants except two from the general list completed an interview during the third or fourth week of the deployment. Each participant was compensated $20 and entered in a drawing for a $250 Amazon.com gift card.

This paper focuses on the experiential ramifications of our system design; quantitative assessment of health outcomes is left to future work. We analyzed audio recordings of the 51 interviews across these two studies using the constant comparative method [16]. The audio recordings were divided among a team of researchers, each of whom listened to and analyzed the recordings for emergent themes. The researchers then conferred about these themes and compared them across different sets of interviews. The next section presents those themes that emerged across both of these studies and were relevant to our open-ended social awareness design approach.

RESULTS

This section focuses on how open-ended social awareness as a central design principle impacted users' experience of the VERA mobile health system. These qualitative results are organized around the two central aspects of our design: open-ended awareness and social awareness. The results from our two data sets mostly aligned, but we also note areas of disagreement. (HW) denotes participants from the Cornell health and wellness program and (M) denotes those from Mobile Mothers; participant names are pseudonyms.

Ramifications of Open-ended Awareness

What is Health? As mentioned above, for most users VERA's openness allowed participants to define health for themselves, both in terms of what is healthy or unhealthy, and in terms of what counts as health-related. For example, Melonie (M) described how "some people have to eat three meals a day, some people have to eat six smaller meals." Betty (M) described posting photos of her evening glass of wine, saying that she counted that as healthy. Similarly, "there were times where [Melonie (M)] would take a picture of, you know, Hershey kisses or something, because you do need to eat food like that sometimes." Some participants identified activities that had previously been viewed as frustrating or annoying and reframed them as healthy. For example, Val (M) posted a photo of herself chopping wood, explaining, "this is not a chore, [I need to] stop thinking of it as a chore, it's healthy." Kelly (HW) realized that "even little things throughout the day are still exercise, like walking the dog, is still being active, rather than just sitting on the couch." Sally (HW) contemplated the notion of healthy choices, saying, "A health choice is not just what do I eat, but do I take time to have fun, do I have things in my life that make me happy or make me smile."

There were, however, a few instances where our open-ended design led to some misalignments between how different participants defined health, as attested to by Tara (M). "You know what I seen [other people posted]? I seen some Dunkin Donuts, and it was something else in their pictures, but I know it was from Dunkin Donuts. Dunkin Donuts is not healthy.... They made it seem like it was good, but everybody knows, Dunkin Donuts is not good." This idea was supported by Jan's (HW) discussion on the different conceptualizations of health. She describes, "It's a good bet that if you said, 'You go girl' to someone who didn't eat the potato chips, there would be a common language, but if you say that to someone who is trying to gain weight, then they're going to be like, 'What?'" Whether or not Dunkin Donuts or potato chips are healthy for the particular individual, the openness of our system enabled differentiated definitions of health and encouraged participants to engage in reflective considerations of what health is, reflections that would not likely have occurred using a more prescriptive approach.

Despite intermittent misalignments, the openness ended up being seen as valuable for most participants. Ellen (M) described how her family was Greek Orthodox and had recently started Lent (a religious period preceding the holiday of Easter), which meant for them eating a mostly vegan diet. However, since she is nursing, she personally is deviating slightly from those dietary restrictions. Designing for this highly specific, cultural definition of health—mostly vegan during Lent but with key exceptions due to nursing—would be particularly difficult with a prescriptive approach, but the open-ended aspect of VERA allowed for this subtle flexibility. In another example, Sandra (M) considered posting images of steak or her breakfast of eggs, which are healthy for her because she is anemic, but she chose not to because they might be perceived by others as unhealthy. Even though Sandra ended up not posting these photos, the system helped promote this nuanced consideration of what is healthy. As Melonie (M) put it, "food isn't just food, it's the emotion, and it's being social, and it's family, and it's culture--I mean, it's everything." A prescriptive system design would likely have difficulty in accommodating for and allowing participants to enact such situated and varied definitions of health.

Flexibility, Selectivity, and Creativity: The open-ended aspect of the design afforded flexibility in terms of exactly what types of behaviors to post, but this flexibility was not universally embraced and, in some cases, caused confusion. Lynn (M) was not sure if she was "unnecessarily limiting it to food and exercise." Tara (M) was unsure why "everybody was putting how they was shoveling or how they was driving," as she did not understand what these activities had to do with the ostensible purpose of the system. At first, Carrie (HW) thought it "weird" that members of the group would post items such as dogs and cats, antibiotics, or their son's baseball games, but after seeing these types of posts frequently, she started to consider and subsequently include similar postings. After seeing such "pet posts," Kelly (HW) increasingly added pictures of her dog when she invited him to join her during exercise activities.

Another point of confusion was around the posting of decisions *not* to do something, or what has been called "negabehaviors" [36]. While potentially interesting, most participants did not include such negabehaviors. As Betty (M) explains, "I wouldn't have taken the time to think, oh, well I'm not going for a run, let me take a picture of my shoes and post it. It doesn't make any kind of logical sense to me to post something I'm not gonna do." As Jess (M) put it, "I was always just trying to take pictures of the healthy things I did; it didn't even cross my mind to think of the things I didn't do." Melonie (M) also expressed skepticism over the value of documenting the avoidance of unhealthy behaviors. "Sometimes it seemed kind of silly to take a picture of something you weren't doing.... You choose not to eat a million unhealthy things all day." These experiences align with the open-ended definition of health described above.

The openness of the system also enabled participants to be selective about what they chose to share. While participants overwhelmingly insisted they were honest with the system, many also revealed a preference to share healthier choices. Mindy (M) "took pains to include" the healthiest decisions she made. Melonie (M) said that she made an effort to take a photo of the healthy things she did. This selectivity also relates to presentation of self [17], discussed further below.

In addition to content flexibility, the flexibility of when to post was also important, especially for the Mobile Mothers, many of whom "buffered" their photos—taking pictures throughout the day and submitting them all in the evening when they had free time and when their children did not need their attention. This temporal flexibility afforded an additional benefit: reflection. As explained by Betty (M), "the days that I did send them all at once, I guess I always noticed a theme."

Finally, allowing participants to take their own photos and express their health decisions in their own ways ended up being a pivotal design feature in VERA that promoted a high level of creativity and novelty. Kendra (M) appreciated that VERA gave her "the opportunity to take pictures, to be a little more creative." Jan (HW) mentioned, "I saw people on there taking pictures of their tennis shoes and it was like, well how do I communicate my food in a more artsy way?" Ellen (M) described it as a "creative challenge." Chrissy (HW) described wanting to give things an artistic sense and incorporate photographic techniques such as perspective and colorful highlights. Although it may have contributed in part to some early confusion by users who favored more traditional posts, the opportunity for creative posting generally appealed to users and allowed for greater control over self-presentation (discussed further below).

Habits, Awareness, and Reflection: Many participants noted becoming more aware of, and consequentially more reflective about, their own health habits. As Melonie (M) put it, "I realized how much I eat the same foods.... I can't take a picture of yogurt every single day. I really need to increase the variety in my diet." Val (M) described how VERA "put it up in your face that you need to be healthy, you need to start doing this for yourself." Chrissy (HW) remarked that the social aspect, being aware of others' posts, allowed members to inspire each other to be healthier. For Regina (M), taking photos was key to making her "mindful of what [she] was eating." As she put it, "taking the pictures really made me pause, and really showed just how full that plate was." This notion of raised awareness emerged repeatedly throughout the interviews.

However, the openness of our design was again a double-edged sword. While it enabled participants to become more aware of their habits and routines, they were less interested in posting routine decisions. Mary (M) noted that "by the end it became kind of redundant" as "[she] got bored of posting the same things." Some participants therefore stopped posting habitual decisions, which is a concern, since some research has documented the link between health and regular habits [28]. Lisa (HW) suggested a future design that would enable users to post an icon for routinized behaviors and a photo for non-recurrent decisions. "So, I don't have to actually take a picture of breakfast every morning because it's the same, but when I do pass by the cookie jar and I want it, I have to take a picture."

Behavior Change: While VERA was designed to support healthy decisions, it was not intended as a means of effecting specific behavior change. As mentioned above, some of the mMoms participants received text messages with healthy tips, but these were not associated with their use of VERA. However, participants did describe some instances of changing their health behaviors. For example, participants described making such changes as choosing salad over a hamburger, water over soda, or adding fruit to breakfast. As Sandra (M) put it, "I knew I had to post anyway and it seemed like a better decision." Mindy (M) noted a shift during her use of the system. Initially, she would make a decision and then take a photo, but as she continued using VERA she found herself thinking about the need to take a healthy photo before making the decision, and she said using VERA steered her toward better decisions.

Such changes were not universal. Sally (HW) discussed VERA as a mechanism for change in her thoughts, but not her actions. She shares, "The application does not change what I do, but it changes what I think about what I do." Betty (M) describes an instance of recognizing the Chinese food she was about to eat was unhealthy but eating it and posting it, anyway. "When I was doing it," she explains, "I was like, wow, this is not good. I was conscious that it wasn't good but it didn't change that I did it." Ben (HW) explained, "I really don't think I've changed any dietary habits off of [VERA] because there are some people here that eat some really weird crap, and you know, I'm a more generic food kind of person."

Several participants mentioned maintaining their behavior changes. For example, Ellen (M) noted two weeks after the final survey that she "was still keeping up with a number of good habits that [she] started during the [study]." These general health impacts may have been due to the fact that all participants across both studies were drawn from populations that were already committed to making health improvements; results might differ with participants who did not have a prior commitment to health.

Summary: The open-ended design approach allowed users flexibility, control, and ownership over their health decisions, their health goals, and even the very definition of health. In some cases, this openness was detrimental, as it led to confusion over standards or expectations. However, it also enabled creativity in self-expression, and it promoted awareness of and reflection on patterns in health decisions.

Ramifications of Social Awareness

Social Interaction and Connection: Participants' social experiences with VERA predominantly revolved around the interactions that occurred while looking at and commenting on each others' posts. Val (M) describes how another user posted cheese and crackers with the caption "healthy snack for breastfeeding mom." Val saw this and felt more connected, thinking, "she does that, too." The make-up of the groups (i.e., new mothers with other new mothers, members of a health and wellness program in groups together) specifically fostered such homophily [1,38].

However, there were also instances where participants were unsure how to approach interacting with one another. Betty (M) explained this with respect to a photo of grapefruit: "I didn't really know what to say to that, like, awesome grapefruit?" Alexa (HW) described a similar experience upon seeing someone post a McDonald's Big Mac. "It's such an impersonal interaction already and I didn't feel comfortable saying, 'Dude, that sucks'."

Imitation and Influence: Many participants described how other participants' posts often influenced their decisions, both healthy and unhealthy, consistent with social cognitive theory [1]. For example, when Sheila (HW) saw that another user "got up and went to the gym in the morning," she said, "that really reminds me, I've got to start doing that again." Not all such instances were positive. Barb (M) saw another user posting that they had chosen not to eat a vanilla Oreo cookie, "but I was like, 'hmm, a vanilla Oreo, I haven't had one of those in a while,' so I picked them up." Instances of imitation happened not only in terms of the substance of health decisions but also in terms of the style of posts. The section above on creativity and flexibility described how many participants, when they saw other users posting photos of activities not traditionally related to health, began posting more creative photos themselves. Thus, we see that the social aspect of VERA compounded the benefits of the open-ended design.

Self-Presentation: As noted above, while many users included predominantly healthy photos, they also included photos that were unhealthy. Conscious of their status as social actors in the system [17], users did not want to present a completely positive picture of themselves, but rather an accurate picture. As Melonie (M) put it, "I would try to mix some bad choices in their too so I don't seem super virtuous, 'cause I'm not." Chrissy (HW) mentioned that she wanted to post unhealthy behaviors that were significant. She described that "Sitting in the car is not a remarkably 'bad behavior,' and I wanted to post things that really stuck out." Many participants described similar decisions, intentionally including photos of dessert, e.g., an ice cream cone.

A few participants were not particularly conscious of other users. As Ellen (M) said, "It kind of surprises me that other people were looking at my posts." This attitude resembles the "security through obscurity" some social media users feel [41]. However, this phenomenon's occurrence in VERA is somewhat surprising, as there is not a massive crowd within which to feel obscure. Some were conscious of other users but indifferent. "I didn't really care what they thought," said Tara (M), "'cause it's not like they know me or anything." However, participants who claimed not to care what others thought often shared examples of behaviors that indicated otherwise. For example, many of these participants were also those who avoided posting photos of the same thing so as not to be boring, or who described trying to make their posts more interesting and more creative. Although they denied it when directly asked, these participants' actions suggest that they did in fact take the presence of others into account when posting.

Many users, however, explicitly noted being keenly aware of others. Patty (HW) described crafting posts with her audience in mind; despite being "one-liners," she was quite cognizant that other people might read them and respond. Similarly, Chrissy (HW) "posted [her] horse because it was different and it would stand out" and be noticed. Vivian (HW), a semi-professional cyclist who follows a strict training regimen, was hesitant to post with a high level of specificity. "I don't want people to think that this is all a piece of cake for me to train 15 hours a week... It could have a negative impact." Others described similar difficulties, attributing them to the fact that most users did not previously know each other. Ultimately, Vivian chose to self-censor her posts to avoid such negative impacts on others, a choice which was based on her perception of her group.

Group Identity: Participants' impressions of other users in their group were of two types, either of other specific users (i.e., individual) or of the group as a whole (i.e., deindividuated) [4]. As noted above, the relative anonymity of a group can initially contribute to such deindividuation. Tara (M) describes how a series of posts from one user, with "everything all together..., helps you kind of build the picture of the person." Impressions of specific users often arose from photos that were either repeated or noteworthy. For example, the regular photos of running shoes posted by wellness participants such as Vivian and Ben became a point of conversation for other users. Sheila (HW) described getting to a point "where certain pictures were appealing... certain ones drew you to them, like the colorful ones and other ones it was like 'Ooh.'"

While participants did occasionally form distinct impressions of some other members of their group, many perceived their group entirely as a deindividuated whole. For example, Val (M) said that while posting pictures she was aware of her individuality, but while looking at others' pictures "you felt like a group, because then you saw everyone, what everyone was doing, and what they were taking pictures of." Many participants had a sense of what decisions were being made, but not of the distinct individuals making them. These experiences may have reinforced the feeling mentioned above where some users did not think about others viewing their posts. This deindividuation may also have been compounded when participants did not realize that they could see all the photos posted by a single individual user; this was a feature that participants commonly requested, despite the fact that the system provided a button to "View Posts by User." While the deindividuation may have prevented connecting to specific individuals, there was still a general "other" to which participants felt accountable.

Accountability and Who's Watching? As one might expect based on previous research connecting accountability to both social cognitive theory [15,43] and perception of self [29], participants indicated that sharing photos with others made them feel more accountable. Carrie (M) noted that "you think about it a little more when someone is watching... you're being more accountable." Chrissy (HW) built up a sense of competition with ambiguous others because she saw five sets of running shoes in one day. Kendra (M) said that "having to broadcast like the pizza box made [her] super aware... they don't know anything about me, but they still know what I'm eating." Jan (HW) suggests, "If you're in it by yourself, you're also not accountable to anyone."

For some participants, though, it was not abundantly clear exactly to whom "they" referred. In the cases described above, participants were clearly referencing other users. Others, such as Lynn (M), described being more accountable to the computer system itself, even though "VERA's not even a real person," than to anyone in her user group. Many participants, however, were keenly aware of the researchers conducting the study. In some cases, participants thought about these nebulous researchers when submitting their photos, particularly trying to make sure to do "what would help with the study" or that they were "giving us what we wanted." This awareness of and attention to the researchers raises both interesting and challenging questions for health technology research, discussed further below.

Summary: VERA's social aspect enabled it to leverage existing social processes, such as accountability and self-presentation, to facilitate healthy behaviors. In many cases, these accentuated the impacts of the system's openness. Social comparison and observation also played important roles, though users varied in whether they focused on other users as individuals, a deindividuated whole of users, the VERA system itself, or the researchers behind the system.

DISCUSSION

This paper is intended primarily as a means of expanding the design space of mobile health technologies to move beyond prescriptive persuasion. However, the findings presented here also offer an opportunity to reflect on the role that technology plays in defining, documenting, sharing, and assessing health behaviors.

VERA was designed intentionally to put the onus of health decision making on the user, from the point at which a behavior is deemed to be health related to the point at which a user decides to document a behavior and share it with others. This coupling of self-definition and self-reporting helps avoid problems where, e.g., a pedometer might not register exercise done on a gym's cardiovascular machine [6].

At the same time, such extreme openness can also lead to questionable assessments of healthiness. Most of the examples here, such as considering an occasional Hershey's kiss or a nightly glass of wine as healthy, were rather innocuous. However, it is possible that, say, the nightly glass of wine may expand to become a nightly bottle of wine; would the user still consider this activity healthy? Our results suggest that the social component of the system kept people slightly more accountable with regard to what is healthy. However, there is still a possibility for discrepancy between what medical and health professionals deem "healthy" and what users deem "healthy." On the one hand, VERA's openness does little to control for such discrepancies, which is a possible shortcoming of the system. On the other, we hope that this shortcoming is balanced by the fact that the data from such systems may provide "behind-the-scenes" access into perceptions of health, and the sociological processes by which those perceptions are formed, that can allow for greater accommodation of these varied definitions of health.

This issue of varying definitions and accuracy of health assessments raises a deeper underlying question: Did it work? Were participants healthier? On the one hand, this question is beyond the scope of the current paper. Our focus here is on user experience, i.e., "understanding use" [24], and we leave quantitative assessments of health outcomes to future work. On the other hand, our results call into question what exactly it means for a technological health intervention to "work." While some participants reported changing certain health behaviors, far more experienced greater health awareness. Users were not simply attending to specific behaviors pre-determined by health experts, but rather were empowered to make their own assessments of health.

The design principle of open-ended social awareness, then, is not meant to be yet another tool in the kit for health technology designers. Rather, it represents a reconceptualization of how technological health interventions are conceived, designed, implemented, and evaluated. With a few exceptions, e.g., [18,33], questions of "what is health?" and "who is empowered to define health?" are rarely interrogated deeply by current research in this area. Just as VERA was designed in part to promote consideration and discussion among users about how health is defined, we hope that this paper will promote similar discussion within the health technology community.

FUTURE WORK

While VERA represents one possible instantiation of the design principle of open-ended social awareness, there may be other ways to implement it. For example, this study used a convenience sample to form user groups, but there are many possible network formation methods. Future research should explore alternative implementations to help determine more specifically the ramifications of this principle.

The studies reported on here lasted either two or four weeks. Even in this short time period, we saw some evidence of user fatigue, in that participants began to lose motivation or became disinterested in repeatedly posting similar photos. Future work should examine whether or not users continue to use VERA or similar systems and, moreover, why or why not. Furthermore, are the benefits in terms of reflecting on the definition of health due largely to the novelty of the system, or would such reflection persist over longer time periods of system use?

Although the focus here is on health, we believe that this open-ended social awareness approach may be valuable in other contexts. For example, interest has recently increased in sustainable HCI, with much work focusing on persuasion and behavior change [8]. The reflection observed here may be particularly valuable in the area of sustainability. Since there is contention even among experts over what is sustainable, rather than tell users what to do, one might instead encourage users to consider what sustainability means.

Our results also showed that users were keenly aware of their status as participants in a research study, an awareness which impacted their use of the system. It may be possible, say, to make a system similar to VERA publicly available, allow users to create their own groups, and then ask them after they have used it whether they would participate in a study. While such an approach may be attractive, it raises numerous issues, not least of which being informed consent and the relationship between researcher and subject. Moreover, it sidesteps the primary issue raised here. If current understandings of health technologies come primarily from research studies, but the very status of being in a research study factors into participant behavior, we should perhaps be cautious about how the results of such studies are translated into more general prescriptions for more widely deployed technologies, policies, or health programs.

Finally, many of the themes described in the results—imitation, social interaction, defining what health means—relate to social norms, the rules that govern behavior and interactions in groups. As suggested above, the data collected during this study provide a unique opportunity for health researchers to examine how perceptions of health are formed and negotiated on an everyday basis. Future work should examine the content of photos, captions, and comments to understand better the formation and interpretation of norms in such systems and, perhaps, of health norms in general.

CONCLUSION

Despite abundant research on the use of mobile technologies to support health, work in this area has thus far been relatively constrained, with most work focusing exclusively on prescriptive persuasion. This paper expands the design space, examining the use of open-ended social awareness as a central design principle for mobile heath. The results show that the openness of the system allowed users to adapt and tailor it to their situated, contingent, everyday definitions of health. However, this same openness became a stumbling block for some, in that they occasionally experienced difficulty deciding what counted as a health oriented-decision. Both of these perceptions were amplified by the social aspects of the system; users' creativity in defining and representing health was inspired by the creativity shown by other users. However, concerns over what was healthy were also exacerbated by the social aspect when users saw posts from others that were either confusing or contradictory to their views of health.

This paper makes two primary contributions. First, it draws on previous theoretical and empirical work to expand the design space of mobile health technology, creating an opportunity for other, similar explorations [18]. Second, it uses empirical qualitative data to provide an understanding of how this design exploration impacts the user experience of health technologies. These contributions carry significance for the design of health systems, not only those that are open-ended or those that focus on social awareness, but more generally. The work presented here represents a viable and promising approach to designing technologies that can encourage and support "a state of complete physical, mental, and social well-being" [42].

ACKNOWLEDGMENTS

This research was supported by NIH Grant #HL-096760, NSF Grant #ISS-0910644, Cornell's Information Science and Communication Departments, and Google. Thanks to Meredith Graham, Kimberly Fluet, Vera Khovanskaya, Andrew Ehrlich, and Rebecca Robbins for helping with study logistics; and to the anonymous reviewers for helpful feedback and suggestions.

REFERENCES

1. Bandura, A. *Social foundations of thought and action.* Prentice-Hall, Inc, Englewood Cliffs, 1986.
2. Brown, B., Chetty, M., Grimes, A., and Harmon, E. Reflecting on Health: A system for students to monitor diet and exercise. *Proc CHI EA*, (2006), 1807-1812.
3. Byrne, S. and Hart, P.S. The Boomerang Effect: A Synthesis of Findings and a Preliminary Theoretical Framework. In C. Beck, ed., *Communication Yearkbook 33c.* Lawrence Erlbaum Assoc, Mawhaw, NJ, 2009, 3-37.
4. Cialdini, R.B. and Goldstein, N.J. Social influence: compliance and conformity. *Annual Rev of Psych 55*, 1974 (2004), 591-621.
5. Cole-Lewis, H. and Kershaw, T. Text Messaging as a Tool for Behavior Change in Disease Prevention and Management. *Epidemiologic Revs 32*, 1 (2010), 56-69.
6. Consolvo, S., Everitt, K., Smith, I., and Landay, J.A. Design requirements for technologies that encourage physical activity. *Proc CHI*, (2006), 457.
7. Consolvo, S., McDonald, D.W., Toscos, T., et al. Activity Sensing in the Wild : A Field Trial of UbiFit Garden. *Proc CHI*, (2008), 1797-1806.
8. DiSalvo, C., Sengers, P., and Brynjarsdóttir, H. Mapping the landscape of sustainable HCI. *Proc CHI* (2010), 1975-1984.
9. Eastwood, C.A., Travis, L., Morgenstern, T.T., and Donaho, E.K. Weight and Symptom Diary for Self-monitoring in Heart Failure Clinic Patient. *J of Cardiovascular Nursing 22*, 5 (2007), 382-389.
10. Eslambolchila, P., Wilson, M.L., Oakley, I., and Dey, A.K. PINC: Persuasion, Influence, Nudge, and Coercion through mobile devices. *Proc CHI EA*, (2011), 13-16.
11. Fogg, B.J. *Persuasive technology.* Morgan Kaufmann, San Francisco, 2003.
12. Fox, J. and Bailenson, J. Virtual Self-Modeling: The Effects of Vicarious Reinforcement and Identification on Exercise Behaviors. *Media Psych 12*, 1 (2009), 1-25.
13. Fry, J.P. and Neff, R. Periodic Prompts and Reminders in Health Promotion and Health Behavior Interventions: Systematic Review. *J Med Internet Res 11*, 2 (2009).
14. Gay, G.K. *Context-Aware Mobile Computing.* Morgan & Claypool, San Rafeal, CA, 2009.
15. Gay, G., Pollak, J., Adams, P., and Leonard, J.P. Pilot study of aurora, a social, mobile-phone-based emotion sharing and recording system. *J of diabetes sci and tech 5*, 2 (2011), 325-32.
16. Glaser, B.G. The Constant Comparative Method of Qualitative Analysis. *Social problems 12*, 4 (1965), 436–445.
17. Goffman, E. *The Presentation of Self in Everyday Life.* Doubleday, New York, 1959.

18. Grimes, A., Bednar, M., Bolter, J.D., and Grinter, R.E. EatWell: sharing nutrition-related memories in a low-income community. *Proc CSCW*, (2008), 87–96.

19. Grimes, A., Kantroo, V., and Grinter, R.E. Let's play!: mobile health games for adults. *Proc UbiComp*, (2010), 241–250.

20. Hanauer, D. a, Wentzell, K., Laffel, N., and Laffel, L.M. Computerized Automated Reminder Diabetes System (CARDS). *Diabetes tech & therapeutics 11*, 2 (2009), 99-106.

21. Intille, S.S. A new research challenge: persuasive technology to motivate healthy aging. *IEEE Trans on Info Tech in Biomedicine 8*, 3 (2004), 235-257.

22. Jacucci, G., Oulasvirta, A., and Salovaara, A. Active construction of experience through mobile media: a field study with implications for recording and sharing. *Pers and Ubi Comput 11*, 4 (2006), 215-234.

23. King, A.C., Ahn, D.K., Oliveira, B.M., Atienza, A. a, Castro, C.M., and Gardner, C.D. Promoting physical activity through hand-held computer technology. *Amer J of Prev Med 34*, 2 (2008), 138-42.

24. Klasnja, P., Consolvo, S., and Pratt, W. How to evaluate technologies for health behavior change in HCI research. *Proc CHI*, (2011), 3063–3072.

25. Lin, J.J., Mamykina, L., Lindtner, S., Delajoux, G., and Strub, H.B. Fish'n'Steps: Encouraging Physical Activity with an Interactive Computer Game. *Proc UbiComp*, (2006), 261-278.

26. Malone, T.W. and Lepper, M.R. Making learning fun: a taxonomy of intrinsic motivations for learning. In R.E. Snow and M.J. Farr, eds., *Aptitute, Learning and Instruction III.* Erlbaum, Hillsdale, NJ, 1987, 223-253.

27. Mattila, E., Pärkkä, J., Hermersdorf, M., et al. Mobile diary for wellness management--results on usage and usability in two user studies. *IEEE Trans on Info Tech in Biomedicine 12*, 4 (2008), 501-12.

28. Monk, T.H., Reynolds, C.F., Buysse, D.J., DeGrazia, J.M., and Kupfer, D.J. The Relationship Between Lifestyle Regularity and Subjective Sleep Quality. *Chronobiology International 20*, 1 (2003), 97-107.

29. Newman, M.W., Lauterbach, D., Munson, S.A., Resnick, P., and Morris, M.E. "It's not that I don't have problems, I'm just not putting them on Facebook": Challenges and Opportunities in Using Online Social Networks for Health. *Proc CSCW*, (2011), 341-350.

30. Patrick, K., Raab, F., Adams, M.A., et al. A Text Message-Based Intervention for Weight Loss: Randomized Controlled Trial. *J Med Internet Res 11*, 1 (2009).

31. Pollak, J.P., Adams, P., Gay, G., and Ave, C. PAM: A Photographic Affect Meter for Frequent, In Situ Measurement of Affect. *Proc CHI*, (2011), 725-734.

32. Pollak, J., Gay, G., Byrne, S., Wagner, E., Retelny, D., and Humphreys, L. It's Time to Eat! Using Mobile Games to Promote Healthy Eating. *IEEE Pervas Comput 9*, 3 (2010), 21-27.

33. Purpura, S., Schwanda, V., Williams, K., Stubler, W., and Sengers, P. Fit4life: the design of a persuasive technology promoting healthy behavior and ideal weight. *Proc CHI*, (2011), 423–432.

34. Raento, M. and Oulasvirta, A. Designing for privacy and self-presentation in social awareness. *Pers and Ubi Comput 12*, 7 (2008), 527-542.

35. Rodgers, A, Corbett, T., Bramley, D., et al. Do u smoke after txt? Results of a randomised trial of smoking cessation using mobile phone text messaging. *Tobacco control 14*, 4 (2005), 255-61.

36. Ross, J. and Tomlinson, B. Negabehaviors and Environmental Sustainability. *J of Sust Edu 2*, March (2011).

37. Schmidt, K. The problem with 'awareness'. *Computer Supported Cooperative Work 11*, 3 (2002), 285–298.

38. Slater, M.D. and Rouner, D. Entertainment-Education and Elaboration Likelihood. *Comm Theory 12*, 2 (2002), 173-191.

39. Suggs, L.S. A 10-year retrospective of research in new technologies for health communication. *J of Health Comm 11*, 1 (2006), 61-74.

40. Tahnk, J.L. 10 iPhone Apps for a Better Night's Sleep. *Mashable*, 2010. http://mashable.com/2010/06/25/iphone-better-sleep/.

41. Viégas, F. B. Bloggers' expectations of privacy and accountability: An initial survey. *JCMC 10*, 3 (2005).

42. World Health Organization. Preamble to the Constitution of the World Health Organization. 1946.

43. Zajonic, R.B. Social Facilitation. *Science 149*, 3681 (1965), 269-274.

44. Årsand, E., Varmedal, R., and Hartvigsen, G. Usability of a Mobile Self-Help Tool for People with Diabetes. *IEEE Conf on Autom Sci and Engr*, (2007), 863-868.

Briefing News Reporting with Mobile Assignments – Perceptions, Needs and Challenges

Heli Väätäjä
Tampere University of Technology
Korkeakoulunkatu 6, Tampere, Finland
heli.vaataja@tut.fi

Paul Egglestone
University of Central Lancashire
Preston, Lancashire, UK
pegglestone@uclan.ac.uk

ABSTRACT
Mobile handheld devices are an increasing part of everyday fieldwork of news professionals. Mobile assignments delivered to mobile journalists' smartphones are one potential future development step. We present findings on using mobile assignments from two exploratory user studies in which smartphones were used as news reporting tools. Mobile assignments were perceived as handy for fast reporting situations and simple stories but challenging in case of more complex tasks. Structured information content of assignments, process phase based information and supporting situation and activity awareness would support the work of both editorial staff and mobile journalists. The locationing of reporters for sending location-based assignments was found acceptable for coordinating the work although some privacy concerns were expressed. The findings provide new information on using mobile assignments in work where carrying out tasks involves creativity and the tasks may be complex, not strictly limited or they may not have clear completion criteria.

Author Keywords
News; journalist; smartphone; mobile; assignment; task; work; location; professional; crowdsourcing; privacy.

ACM Classification Keywords
H5.3. Computer-supported cooperative work.

General Terms
Design; Experimentation; Human Factors.

INTRODUCTION
Mobile devices and services are increasingly being adopted for keeping track of the mobile work force, coordinating work, enabling group cooperation and awareness, distributing tasks to workers and following up on the accomplished work in various fields of work [2,3, 24,22,23]. Mobile assignments, that is, tasks sent to mobile, handheld devices such as smartphones and tablets, are being taken into use in organizational settings such as home care, maintenance, and emergency response.

Due to economic pressure news industry is facing changes in how news are made. For example, the editorial staff numbers are reported to have fallen since 2007 by 27% in British news media industry [4], with an increase in subcontracting, freelancing and reader participation. Mobile and location-based assignments therefore seem one attractive alternative for coordinating news reporting work. Not only reporters employed in news organizations but also freelancers and reader reporters could be reached for carrying out tasks. As a new story to cover comes up, the closest available reporter could undertake the assignment. However, little is known about how mobile assignments fit to a professional mobile journalists' work, which can be characterized as creative, relying on professional's skill and autonomy and being a collective effort [6]. Furthermore, in news journalism the tasks to be carried out may not be strictly limited, or the completion criteria may not be clear at the time of creating the assignment. This is the case, for example, when reporting breaking news like catastrophes.

Mobile assignments change the current work practices, introducing challenges and needs related to the content of mobile assignments, news production processes and for mobile technology and services to be utilized. Professional reporters' own insight and experience as well as negotiation with the newsroom are traditionally important aspects of news making. Mobile assignments therefore not only change the current work processes, but also potentially change the roles and responsibilities of reporters and the editorial team in the newsroom as well as their workflows.

This paper explores reporters' perceptions and needs as well as emerging challenges on information content and assignment related processes when using mobile assignments for briefing news assignments to professionals. Furthermore, we address a possible future scenario on utilizing reporters' location information in organizing news reporting work. We present here the findings on mobile and location-based assignments from two field studies in which smartphones were used for making news. Reported two field studies are from a set of ten case studies related to professional news making with smartphones [29].

The paper is structured as follows. We first present the background of the study with a discussion on how mobile systems and assignments may change the current news making practices followed by a review of related work. Then the two user studies are introduced with findings on using mobile assignments and locationing in news reporting. We conclude with a discussion of the findings and the potential effect of the mobile information and communication technology (ICT) on work practices as well as proposals for future work.

BACKGROUND

The goal of our work was to support the development of a mobile service for mobile content co-creation and mobile work with a specific focus of our studies being in the context of news journalism. The first mobile service prototype was originally developed in 2007 at Nokia Research Center in close collaboration with journalists at Reuters for creating and delivering news stories.

During our first user studies in 2008 [12,27,29,30,31], newspapers were increasingly receiving user-generated content based on readers' own initiative. However, no mobile service clients existed for systematic requests for readers' content by a mobile phone, such as for example Tackable[1] today. In addition, indications from news organizations suggested that mobile assignments could be useful for professionals and freelancers. These needs motivated the development of an online and mobile production solution with an online assignment desk (dashboard) resembling the solution provided by kapost[2] and the Assignment Desk[3] plugin for WordPress. To support the mobile news content creation, mobile service client prototypes were developed which aimed to fit both crowdsourced news content creation and professional use. Mobile assignments and the usage of location information are currently implemented to a generic solution for mobile work processes for fieldworkers[4].

From traditional practice to mobile reporting

Traditional newsroom assignments are generally agreed at news conferences. The editorial angle, the duration or length of the story and its position in the running order or prominence in the paper is agreed by the editor. A resource is committed to cover the story in line with its scale and importance. In the case of a print story this may require a reporter and a photographer. A video or a mobile journalist working for a local paper will be expected to record audio and video. If the mobile journalist uses a mobile handset to record audio and video, it is likely they will also be expected to shoot still images and provide a copy in the field. Consequently, the assignment brief from the editorial team must be specific about what media is required.

A mobile journalist working with the small keyboard built into a smartphone will not easily or quickly be able to type a 400-word story. The story may be better compiled by a production journalist in the newsroom with access to a full size keyboard. However, she/he will require factual details and might prefer written quotes from interviewees along with captions that are spelled correctly in text form. This approach to the editorial workflow changes the nature of the assignment briefing breaking an assignment down into component parts. In addition, this workflow enables the newsroom to reflect the emerging story by quickly adding rich media (audio, video) elements as the story develops.

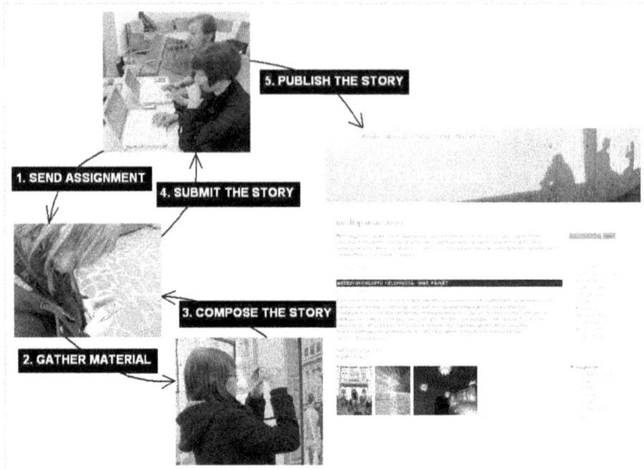

Figure 1. Simplified work process phases with mobile assignments from Study 1 [19].

Reporters using traditional methods for reporting stories do not generally 'drip feed' information to the newsroom in the manner that mobile journalism enables them to. The new process also opens the possibility for dialogue with the editorial team in the newsroom, who can respond to the information as it comes in and further refine the assignment brief by offering specific instructions to reporters. For example, after bringing together elements of a story in the newsroom, possibly from a number of reporters as well as readers, the team might assign a mobile journalist to shoot three 'vox pop' interviews as a reaction to an event. The editor could even go as far as sending the question to be asked of the interviewees to the reporter as part of the brief, knowing exactly where the video content will fit within the story once the reporter sends it back.

From within the editorial platform, the editorial team can evaluate the quality of the material sent by the reporter from the handset whilst they are in the field. The reporters can respond to requests from the newsroom and/or reshoot material or gather further information from contributors without leaving the scene. Consequently, the mobile assignment briefing of reporters differs fundamentally from the traditional practice partly because the mobile device and the reporter using it provide the editorial team with an open channel to direct the acquisition of content and to receive it from the field in a more interactive manner. This changes the role of the editorial team in the newsroom who can now be more directive if they so choose. It changes the role of the reporter, who may sometimes be responding to specific requests for particular media or interviews with contributors, and who may sometimes work proactively by

[1] http://www.tackable.com
[2] http://kapost.com
[3] http://openassignment.org
[4] http://www.newelo.com

feeding material to the newsroom more regularly. And with the evolution of these roles comes a change in the relationship between the reporter and the newsroom staff commissioning stories.

In this paper we focus primarily on the front-end of the mobile news reporting process (see Figure 1), concentrating on the issues related to mobile assignments. Our research covers the phases when creating and sending mobile assignments as well as when receiving and acting on a received assignment. In addition, we touch upon the needs when reporters have covered and submitted the story or material for the assignment.

RELATED WORK

Much of the HCI and CSCW research in the context of news reporting has concentrated on the work practices and organizing the editorial work, e.g., [10,13,11]. Mobile pocket-sized devices, like PDAs (personal digital assistants) or mobile phones, have in recent years received increasing attention [8,9,12,16,27,28,29,30,31].

Fagrell et al. [8] and Forsberg [9] studied PDAs with service prototypes for knowledge management in the first phases of reporting when transforming events into newsworthy stories. The aim is to provide mobile users with timely, contextual information related to the story they are covering. The provided information is related to the background information, such as previous reports on the topic, available expertise of others, and coordinating reporting with other reporters. In their solution, the worker creates him/herself a To Do item on the application, based on, for example, a phone call they receive, or after an editorial meeting. In our work the assignments are created by editors, producers or others responsible for coordinating the news production. Mobile assignments are then delivered to the mobile journalists' mobile devices, such as smartphones or tablets, via a mobile service. Our work, therefore, complements the work of Fagrell et al. and Forsberg by concentrating on the needs and challenges that arise especially for information delivered in the assignments and the related process when using mobile assignments for briefing news reporting.

Verburg et al. [26] studied the mobile virtual work of mobile customs employees, elevator service engineers, facility management and home care. They report the benefits of mobile virtual work to be, for example, increased efficiency experienced by employees and for organizations the possibility to track employees on the move and allocate unscheduled work better. Furthermore, Koponen et al. [16] report that the motivation to use mobile phones for writing text for news was the more efficient use of time and independence of time and place; "whenever inspiration hits".

A number of studies have been conducted on developing and evaluating context-aware and/or location-based services [8,24,22] for mobile field work. Our interest lies in reporters' perceptions on locationing, for example, when sending location-based assignments to the reporter closest to the scene of a newsworthy event. Previous studies on sharing location information show contradictory results on users' perceptions and concerns. For example, Consolvo et al. [5] report as the most important factors affecting willingness to disclose location information to be the identity of the requester, the reason for requesting and the precision of the request. In the study by Raento et al. [18] with two groups of office workers, users had no expressed concerns for automatic location disclosure when the revealed location was approximate on the level of the district and city. However, the organizational culture at the work place, trust and authority issues, as well as perceived benefits may influence results significantly in practice.

METHODOLOGY

We used a case study approach [32] to conduct two field studies where briefing news with mobile assignments and locationing were included as research themes. In both studies (Table 1), smartphones were used for delivering news briefings through mobile assignments, as well as for capturing, editing and delivering news content.

Setting. The field studies were conducted with postgraduate students of journalism and visual journalism within university course curricula. We used students as our sample because the system prototypes could not be integrated to the editorial systems with reasonable time and effort. Within their studies, students carry out practical news reporting tasks and publish real news stories with an editorial team and mobile reporters. Using the system in realistic, collaborative news reporting situations brings out usability issues, perceptions, and needs that usability tests in a laboratory [17] or heuristic evaluations [15] may not reveal.

The students' goal was to create, edit and deliver news content from the location of the news event with smartphones and an application dedicated for mobile news assignments and news content delivery. The researchers did not assign tasks to the participants. Instead, the reporting tasks were assigned within the course setting. The created news material was published in course-related online publications (Studies 1 and 2) and in a printed course-related newspaper (Study 2).

Participants. Most participants had extensive part and/or full-time work experience in the field of journalism (see Table 1). Work experience had been gained as freelancer work before or during the studies, working as a part-time or full-time, as internships and as summer traineeships.

Mobile devices and applications. The smartphones used in the field studies (see Table 1) were Nokia models N82 and N900 with multimedia capabilities. The iteratively developed mobile client application prototype versions used in the studies for mobile assignments and content delivery were fully functional prototypes developed at Nokia Research Center for Study 1 and at Newelo for Study 2.

Study	Nr of part.	Mobile Phone	Mobile client	Collected data (as hours or number of participants)	Research themes on mobile assignments	Participants (based on number of questionnaire respondents)	Other information
1 (Case 4, spring 2009)	8	Nokia N82 (Symbian): 2.4 inch display, numeric keypad, BT keyboard	MCC pre1	o (36 h), fc (8), q (8)	Information needs, locationing	Gender: female (7), male (1) Age: min-max=24-46 yrs, mean=30.4 yrs Work exp.: (part and full time).: min-max=1-25 yrs, mean=6.6 yrs	Students of visual journalism (photographers) used the mobile system on two pre-trial days and during one day in a media conference workshop demonstrating mobile journalism
2 (Case 10, fall 2010)	11	Nokia N900 (Maemo): 3.5 inch touch-screen display, full keyboard	N4F pre1	o (32 h), i (4), q (11)	Perceptions, needs, challenges and feasibility of assignments, locationing	Gender: female (6), male (5) Age: min-max=21-30 yrs, mean=25.0 yrs. Work exp. (part and full time).: min-max=1-27 months, mean=12.7 months	4 participants in Finland (students of visual journalism) used the mobile system over a period of one month; 7 participants in Great Britain for 5 days (6 print journalism students, 1 broadcast).
o = observation, i = interview, q = questionnaire, fc = focus group MCC pre1= MCC prerelease version 1, N4F pre1=Need4Feed client prerelease1							

Table 1. The conducted user studies addressing the usage of mobile assignments and locationing.

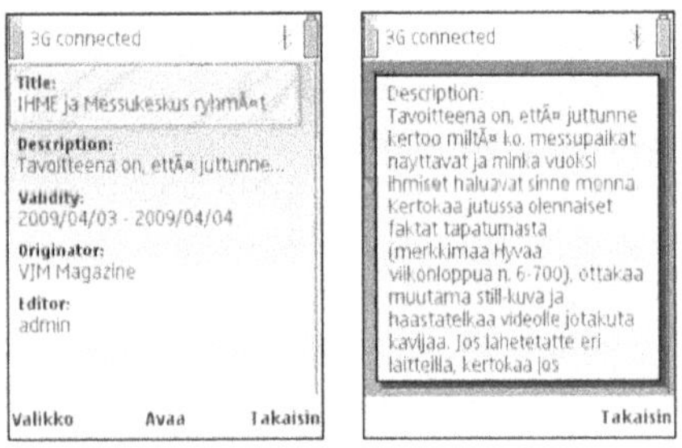

A) B)

Figure 2. Study 1: A) The main UI of the MCC mobile client and B) The task description field.

A)

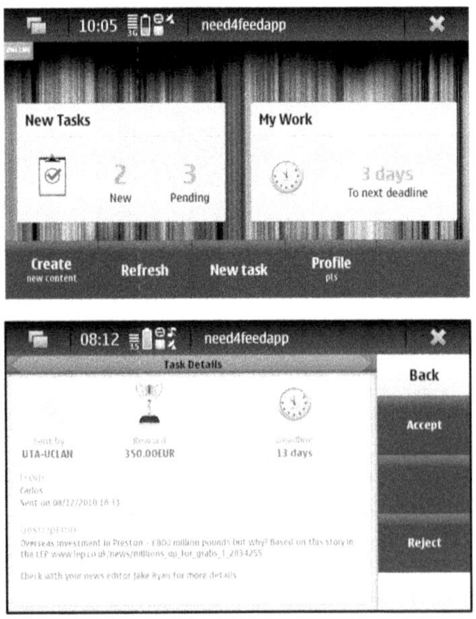

B)

Figure 3. Study 2: A) Opening UI of the Need4Feed mobile client and B) an opened assignment with details.

Both prototypes enabled the receiving of mobile assignments, accepting and rejecting them as well as replying to the assignment with news content (complete stories, photos, videos). The MCC prototype (Figure 2, Study 1) includes as assignment information fields "Title", "Description" of the assignment as a free text field, time for the "Validity" of the assignment, "Originator" for the publication and "Editor". The N4F prototype (Figure 3, Study 2) has as an opening interface an overview of the task situation. Main differences on information of the assignment compared to MCC prototype are "Reward" aimed for freelancers and crowdsourcing and "Deadline" indicating the time left to deadline. A major functional difference between versions is in the UI which is intended for touch screens in Study 2. In both studies, smartphones were used for the capturing and creating of news content (text, photos, video clips) either as the only devices used, or as one system among the others. Participants were free to use any other feature or functionality of the devices as well.

Data collection. The data collection methods varied depending on the study (see Table 1). In the first study, four researchers observed the participants on three days, whereas in the second study, one researcher observed selected participants on six days, during one day in Finland and five in Great Britain. The observations covered mobile system usage in field conditions as well as editorial work. At the end of Study 1, a focus group was held and a printed questionnaire was used to collect background information. In Study 2, four interviews were conducted in Finland and an online questionnaire was conducted with both Finnish and British students covering a wider range of themes related to perceptions on using mobile phones and services in news reporting. Privacy issues were not addressed directly by the researchers in the interviews and focus group, but they arose spontaneously in the participants' comments on locationing related themes.

Analysis. The hand-written field observation notes as well as audio recordings of the interviews and the focus group were transcribed. This data as well as data from the open-ended questions in the questionnaire were analysed by data-driven content analysis using open coding for emerging themes and grouping these under higher level categories. Closed ended questions from the questionnaire were analyzed by descriptive statistics.

RESULTS FROM STUDY 1

In the first study, two participants acted as editors of a mobile newsroom for an online publication, editing and publishing the material, and a producer (course leader) sent the mobile assignments to the reporters. The rest (six) were mobile reporters, who carried out the assignments in a mobile context. We present the findings on the editors' and reporters' needs in the mobile assignment process, as well as on locationing.

Needs in a mobile assignment process

Coordinating news reporting

Table 2 presents the information needs of the editorial staff and the willingness of the reporters towards sharing this information when sending mobile assignments to reporters. The reporters were willing to disclose information that could be used for profiling, but wanted to remain in control of their availability as well as of the locationing.

Editors' information needs	Reporter's willingness to share
Availability for carrying out assignments	Conditional: When on duty; As a freelancer when ready to undertake a job
Reporters' equipment	OK
Reporters' skills, special expertise or interests	OK
Location of reporter(s)	Conditional: Not all the time; In urgent reporting needs; When on duty and/or chooses to enable locationing; As a freelancer when ready to undertake a job; If the precision of the locationing can be approximate; In dangerous areas with safety risks.

Table 2. Information needs when assigning news reporting tasks.

The locationing of reporters raised primarily strong negative first reactions in the focus group participants, such as "*annoying*", or an expression of disgust, covering issues like "*feeling of being monitored*" or "*tracked*". As the participants continued the discussion, they mentioned specific cases or conditions in which they would allow the locationing, as exemplified in Table 2. The participants wanted to remain in control of the locationing and its precision, but some also mentioned that during working hours, the locationing of reporters would be acceptable, and sometimes even desirable for increasing the feeling of safety in dangerous areas. In addition, the participants expressed concerns indirectly, for example, related to losing freedom of how they spend their time.

Making sure that news material will be delivered

Traditionally, news reporting involves a high degree of planning, at the same time being prepared for rapid and unexpected changes to the plans. The participants emphasized that it is essential that the newsroom staff is aware of the current situation with the mobile assignments. The editors expressed that they felt unsure and nervous whether the reporters were going to carry out the assignments. In the study we found that the reporters read the assignment, but even though accepting and rejecting was enabled in the application, the reporters did not always remember to do it. The editors felt an urge to call or send a text message to make sure that the assignments were received and understood. Support was therefore needed for knowing whether the respondent(s) 1) has read the assignment, 2) has understood the assignment or needs clarification and 3) is going to carry out the assignment, especially if it is sent only to one or a few reporters.

In addition, the editors wished for information on 1) when to expect the story or the material, 2) whether there were significant problems in carrying out the assignment to negotiate the issues and 3) whether the story or material will be on time or delayed. This enables the editors to foresee changes in the publishing schedules, or a need for replacing the planned story with a new topic if needed, using photos from a photo agency or their own archives, for example, instead of the content that was planned.

Is someone else already covering the story?

One possible scenario is that the assignment could be delivered to a number of reporters, such as freelancers, to increase the possibility of someone undertaking the assignment, for example, in fast reporting situations. First, we found that the reporter would need to know whether he/she was the only one getting the assignment or whether it was sent to a number of reporters. The participants mentioned that their attitude towards the assignment is completely different if they know that they are the only receiver or if it is sent to a larger group for one to undertake. Second, if the assignment is sent to a number of reporters but intended for only one or a few to carry out the reporters need to get information if the assignment has been undertaken. Therefore, the mobile service should support delivering this information to others, as implemented in the study by Alt et al. [1], for example, in the case of mobile crowdsourcing.

Is further action by the reporter needed after submission?

The feedback provided by the MCC prototype when submitting news stories and media was found insufficient. The reporters wished for an automatic confirmation that the material was received by the editorial system. After the news story or material has been delivered by reporters, the editors may need to check some facts or details related to the stories from the reporters or ask for updates, or for more material. The reporters mentioned that they would need to know whether the assignment was completed as is or whether further action or information is needed. In most cases, the participants mentioned phone calls as the natural solution for this communication, but also chat, text messages (SMS) and email were mentioned which are already offered on most smartphones.

The newsroom needs to stay in control of news reporting

The MCC prototype enabled the creation of assignments from the mobile journalism client. The participants found creating news assignments with a mobile client as a possible scenario in the case of an urgent, newsworthy event. However, they seemed strict in their opinion that this is used to notify the editorial staff in the newsroom, which should remain in control of organizing news reporting and the delivering of assignments. For example, a reporter working in the field should not create a new assignment or delegate a reporting assignment he/she had received to a colleague. This was justified by the fact that the editorial team is responsible for coordinating the production. If assignments would be delegated between reporters, the newsroom could not stay up to date on the current situation, who is covering an assignment or a news topic, and take action if needed.

Reporters' needs for information in mobile assignments

The participants found the free text field of the prototype for assignment description to increase the possibility that important information is missing from the sent assignment. Similarly, structured information was mentioned to help reporters in using the assignment as a checklist in a mobile context. Identified needs for the information content are:

- The topic to be covered with (1) Basic information on the location (address), event/interviewee, (2) Background information such as links to information, old articles, etc;
- What kind of content is asked for (text, photos, video, audio), e.g. the (1) Length of text (e.g. nr of characters), (2) Number of photos and video clips, (3) Length of audio and video, and (4) desired quality or special requests for the media content;
- The reporting schedule and deadline(s), including information such as whether a fast report with certain material is wanted first and more material or updates later.

This information is similar to the information that reporters and freelancers in the current work process get and take along as notes when they leave to cover a story. However, when designing for a mobile phone's relatively small screen and for mobile usage situations, the design needs to have a clear and simple structure and provide the most important information preferably with one glance.

Reporter as an orchestrated "puppet"

Focus group discussion on mobile assignments and mobile reporting raised also a spontaneous and lively discussion on future work practices and the role of the professional reporter in case when news briefing would be mediated for example by phone or video calls and live streamed videos. Participants envisioned reporting scenarios ironically where the reporter would not use their own professional judgment and instinct in reporting. Instead, the reporter would ask the editorial staff should they take live video footage of the situation, what angles to capture and so forth. Participants spontaneously ideated a reporting situation on an accident scene, where people would be screaming in pain and the reporter would continuously ask for directions from the newsroom what to report and how. It appears that in this exaggerated future vision participants expressed their fears related to the effect of new technological solutions on their work. Technology would enable the newsroom to orchestrate the reporting more than reporters wished for and change the work practices and role of reporters fundamentally from a creative, skilled and relatively autonomous professional to a puppet that could in practice be anyone present at the scene of the happening.

RESULTS FROM STUDY 2

The second field study presented here was conducted in Finland and Great Britain (see Table 1). This study was used to complement and extend the previous findings with a new prototype version and to identify possible changes in the perceptions to support further development, with locationing as a special focus of the study. The Finnish participants (4) relied solely on mobile phones for the entire news reporting process. All their news reporting was based on news briefings sent as mobile assignments. The participants in Great Britain used the mobile phones as one device among their usual news reporting gear.

We first report the participants' general perceptions on mobile assignments. We continue with discussing the perceived benefits and disadvantages of mobile assignments, followed by a set of new information needs identified when using mobile news briefings. At the end of this section, we report the locationing related results.

Mobile assignments in general

The general perceptions of the respondents towards receiving mobile assignments on a mobile phone were assessed with sentence completion [21]. The respondents were asked to complete the sentence *"Receiving mobile assignments on a mobile phone is..."* with 1-3 endings. The responses (29) are presented in Table 3 and categorized into positive (11) and negative (18) perceptions. Four of the respondents completed only negative sentence completions, two only positive ones and the rest had both positive and negative sentence completions. The total number of negative perceptions is higher than of positive perceptions. Finns (4) created more positive completions than the British students (7), and considerably fewer negative completions. This may be due to the Finns relying solely on the smartphone-based solution, therefore getting more hands-on, real-life usage experiences. We discuss the results presented in Table 3 more closely in the following subsections, combined with the interview findings.

Benefits of using mobile assignments

The advantages of mobile assignments were described in the sentence completions to be related to quickness, as well as to ease-of-use and practicality (see Table 3). Some respondents (3/8) also found mobile assignments in general a good and important feature.

The interviewees mentioned as an advantage from the editors' viewpoint to be able to reach a reporter with mobile assignments instantaneously, independent of his/her whereabouts, needing no other equipment than a mobile phone. Furthermore, by being able to reach several reporters simultaneously, it is faster to find a person to undertake the assignment than by calling. Similarly to the first study, the mobile assignments were mentioned to be suitable as memory aids or notes, supporting mobile work. Compared to emails, the mobile client was also mentioned to be faster and more effective in finding assignment related information than browsing through the emails.

The interviewees perceived the usage of mobile assignments is especially suitable for catastrophe and accident journalism or similar fast news reporting situations. In addition, one of the interviewees described how mobile assignments remove the need to go the newsroom for news briefings:

"It is surely useful, at least in very fast news reporting work. And with small stories it is surely cost-effective that one can do the whole job, that one does not need to go back to the newsroom and the computer there, but you can do it all in a café and then go to the next news reporting gig. And you do not need to go and listen to the briefing at a certain location, and all this, at least for a fast pace it fits well." P-123

Drawbacks of using mobile assignments

The most commonly mentioned disadvantages in using mobile assignments based on the questionnaire answers were: 1) disturbing the process, 2) usage inefficient compared to a phone call which is traditionally used, 3) disrupting communication, and 4) seeing no clear benefit in using mobile assignments. One of the responses refers to the role and skills of the reporter in the changing work practice, by mentioning that assignments constrain the reporters's own instinct.

In addition, the interview and questionnaire results on development needs reflect our findings from Study 1 on the importance of clear and sufficient instructions. Missing or unclear information leads to a need for contact and communication. In addition, some participants perceived it to be faster and easier to call a person than to fill in a form online and follow up its completion. Overall, if the goal is to limit, minimize or even remove the need for communication, for example in the case of crowdsourcing, then the information and instructions given in assignments need to be paid attention to.

The participants also found the feasibility of mobile assignments to be related to the type of stories covered. As previously mentioned, small stories and fast news reporting situations were found to be suitable cases for getting news briefings in mobile assignments. However, larger feature stories were felt to not fit as a story type into the mobile assignment delivery. One interviewee explained:

"I feel it would not fit an extensive feature story like when one gets a given assignment from somewhere, so that the certain type of ideal..., and discussion, when in some kind of meeting it is discussed what will be in the story, when it is completely left out, then it does not fit like that, it does not correspond to what my experience is, how these big stories are done. When the assignment is sent, they do not have any idea of what I intend to do when it is not limited like that. Or the other way around, I do not have a slightest idea of what is really wanted." P-123

Perceptions	Categories	Sentence completions
Positive (11): Finland (6) GB (5)	Quickness (4)	Quick, instant, time saving, fast
	Easy, Simple, Practical (4)	Easy (2), simple, practical with basic stories
	Good, important (3)	A good idea, important, excellent feature
Negative (18): Finland (4) GB (14)	Disturbs process (4)	Hassle; not ideal; impossible for unexpected topics; sometimes full of technical problems
	Inefficient (3)	A waste of time; unnecessary extra layer of bureaucracy; most effective with a phone call
	Prevents or disrupts communication (5)	Easier to speak directly to be able to clarify aspects of story; difficult if one has questions and needs to discuss the assignment; most effective with a phone call; demanding in case of needing more information; possibility for misunderstanding
	Diminishes professional skill (1)	Constraining the reporter's own instincts
	Sentiment (2)	Impersonal, annoying
	No benefit (3)	Pointless, unnecessary, not giving clear benefit

Table 3. The results of sentence completion for *"Receiving mobile assignments on a mobile phone is…"*.

Reporters' needs for information in mobile assignments

As in the previous results, the participants emphasized the importance of a deadline as it gives the reporter an easy indication of *"...whether I have the possibility to undertake it"* (P-123). In addition, the participants found it useful to see the remaining time to the set deadline as provided. Further information needs found are:

- The intended usage context of the story/material, e.g. online, print, TV, radio/audio
- The type of the story– this can be described, for example, by (1) the intended department or category in the publication, or (2) using journalistic language and/or language of publications' staff, such as main/local news, column, first page, feature, short interview, premium, "grab by the sleeve" profile.
- The viewpoint or perspective to take to cover the story - for instance a lead, or whether it is up to the reporter to decide it
- What is wanted to be the object, target or angle of capturing photos or videos

Results corroborate and extend the results from the first study by showing that more contextual descriptions related to the intended usage and perspectives of reporting are needed in the assignment descriptions of professionals.

Locationing related results from the questionnaire

To study further the locationing related themes in mobile assignment processes, we included these themes both in the online questionnaire and the interviews.

Sharing location is risky, but not particularly worrying

To gain an assessment of the participants' perceptions on sharing location, we asked three questions. We followed the approach by Tsai et al. [25] for the general questions and scales. The following questions were asked:

- *How useful do you find sharing your location with others based on your mobile phone location?* (1=Not useful-7=Extremely useful) Md=2, M=1.91, SD=0.94
- *How concerned are you about sharing your location with others based on your mobile phone location?* (1=Not concerned-7=Extremely concerned) Md=5, M=4.36, SD=2.20
- *In general, what do you think about sharing your location with others based on your mobile phone location?* (1=Risk far outweighs the benefit,7=Benefit far outweighs the risk) Md=3, M=2.73, SD=1.35

In general, sharing one's location was not rated as useful, in addition to it being assessed as somewhat risky. The responses regarding concern about sharing location were more neutral, but also more dispersed. Furthermore, we asked whether the participants would want to stay in control when their mobile phone can be located in news production. Most respondents (8/11) wanted to stay in control of locationing, reflecting findings from earlier privacy studies.

Acceptability of locationing

We also asked for general perceptions on the locationing of the mobile phone with an open-ended question: *"In general, how do you feel about the locationing of your mobile phone?"* Six (6) respondents were negative towards locationing, whereas five (5) respondents were positive under specific conditions. The concerns mentioned in the responses were described as 1) Feeling uncomfortable or stressed about someone being able to know where one is, 2) Unnecessary monitoring, and 3) Invasion of privacy.

Locationing was mentioned in the answers to be acceptable for keeping track and organizing the workforce, proving the authenticity of the narrative from the scene, mapping a reporter online or on TV, or when covering something dangerous, in a life-threatening situation, when missing.

In the questionnaire, we asked with an open-ended question, *"Whom would you give a permission to locate your mobile phone?"* Five respondents mentioned *editor, producer or a* similar *senior figure*, one of these adding "*...if absolutely necessary as a freelancer*". In addition, the participants mentioned *a trusted colleague or fellow reporters* (3), *authorities* (3), *a friend* (1) and *no-one* (1).

Acceptable situations for locationing were asked with the open-ended question *"In what situations would you give permission to locate your mobile phone?"* The reasons mentioned were related to 1) foreseeable benefits in organizing work, for instance, to keep tab of the area to be covered or dividing an area between reporters, or for the reporters themselves, for instance to be directed to a story, and 2) protecting one's safety in a dangerous area. In addition, the participants mentioned acceptable situations, such as when on-call duty or when covering a story. The results are similar to the previous study, with potential tensions between privacy related issues, such as a feeling of being monitored and the possible foreseeable benefits.

Locationing reporters assessed as useful

To gain an understanding of the participants' perception of the usefulness of locationing, we asked them to rate three statements with a 7-point Likert scale (see Table 5). The first statement is from the point of view of the newsroom locationing the reporters in the field. Most respondents agreed at least to some extent with this statement. Similarly, most respondents agreed to some extent about the usefulness of locationing fellow reporters.

Statement – It would be useful...	Md	M	SD
..., if the newsroom could locate the reporters working in the field.	5	4.64	1.63
..., if the reporters could locate each other when working in the field.	5	4.55	1.51
..., if the reporters could locate their informants.	5	3.82	1.78

Table 4. Usefulness of locationing.

Locationing related results from the interviews

The benefits of locationing mentioned in the interviews were similar to the questionnaire answers and the results of Study 1. Location-based assignments were described as useful and handy to find the reporter closest to the scene of an event, as well as for finding out where reporters or freelancers are and using this information for coordinating news reporting. In addition, locationing was found useful in fieldwork for the locationing of a colleague working in the field to coordinate the work with them, such as meeting up when covering stories, or more generally sharing progress related information.

The interviewees seemed to consider whether locationing really is acceptable, but at the same time agreeing on possible benefits under certain conditions. One interviewee discussed how it depends on the country whether she would consider it safe and would trust to share one's location even in a professional context:

"...I do not know if it is a problem like, in conditions such as in Finland because this is a constitutional state... but since I have lived for quite a long time in Latin America, I would indeed not want that anyone could locate me since the risks there are much more substantial, or if one thinks about the political situation in [removed]. It would be really easy to locate certain reporters... it is not like your employer is... there are all these kind of hackers that can find out the information, then... it would work in Finland, but if one thinks in a bit wider context, then it is not good." P-124

The privacy related themes are otherwise similar to those found in the first study and in the questionnaire results of this study. The results therefore corroborate those findings.

DISCUSSION

In this section we discuss the themes and findings that emerged in the studies and point paths for future work.

Mobile systems and mobile assignments change work practices, including roles and responsibilities of both mobile journalists and newsroom staff. These changes on one hand provide new opportunities but on the other hand may appear as threats to the traditional role and responsibilities of the professional and his/her professional identity. These issues are not only driven by technology push, but also due to the organizational pull for enhanced performance. In our studies performance related impacts mentioned by participants were for example the diminished need to go to the newsroom for picking up assignment sheets as well as less need to participate editorial meetings. Being able to submit news content wirelessly from the field "anywhere, anytime" enables time savings for the journalist and makes news publishing faster. In addition, sharing of situational and activity related information enabled by locationing enhances not only coordination of work, but also knowledge sharing and collaboration of mobile reporters. There is a clear paradigm shift in news media industry due to changes in both consuming and producing news that drives towards new forms of production. These include outsourcing news content creation to freelancers and crowdsourcing or co-creating news with readers. ICT solutions need to support these needs (e.g. [28]).

New forms of mobile reporting are enabled by mobile technology and mobile assignments. In our studies participants compared the capabilities of the mobile systems and mobile assignments to traditional news making processes and how they fit into and can be used in these processes. The theme of "journalistic ideal" appears directly and indirectly in the perceptions of the participants. It is also related to their professional identity and role [7]. For example, in the first study participants perceived reporters passing assignments forward or creating new ones directly to colleagues as not acceptable. The possibilities of new work practices, for example with ad-hoc, mobile reporting and editorial teams, where the roles and responsibilities could be mixed and traditional teams could in fact vanish from existence were not mentioned by participants. As described in the Background section, reporting could at extreme shift to being more like material gathering at the scene of a happening and "drip-feeding" pieces to the newsroom where actual stories would be created from these pieces to emerging online stories.

Locationing is acceptable on agreed terms and if it does not threaten safety. Both the newsroom and the reporters in the field can benefit from locationing, not only when location-based news reporting assignments are used. The reporter may feel safer if he/she is tracked in a dangerous area. On the other hand, misuse of location information by outsiders may compromise the safety of the reporter as well as the anonymity of the informant in certain countries. As earlier studies suggest user initiated control for locationing and its preciseness is required. In addition, the consent and terms of when to allow locationing need to be agreed on.

Mobile assignments are suitable and cost-effective when briefing small, relatively simple stories and for fast reporting situations. However, they were perceived inefficient in communication compared to phone calls especially if further information or clarification is needed. It also seems that communicating the goals and perspectives of reporting are more challenging especially if the topic or story to be covered is large and can take multiple perspectives. If crowdsourcing, that is, using the audience as a means to carry out news reporting tasks, is considered to require similar activity, complexity and creativity [20] in carrying out complete assignments as with professionals, the needs and challenges regarding the mobile process and news briefings are likely to be similar to professionals. Structured information content and contextual information on the type of the story may be useful for them as well. However, at the moment the mobile assignments to reader reporters are in most cases relatively simple, usually asking for photos (see Tackable, and [28]). For crowdsourcing of complex and interdependent tasks in micro-task markets, such as MechanicalTurk, Kittur et al. [14] propose a solution called CrowdForge that enables task partitioning. They demonstrate successfully its use in two types of article writing: an encyclopedia article on New York city and in turning a scientific article into a popular press article. Further studies are needed in the case of crowdsourced news reporting on task complexity and needed creativity affecting task formulation and the ways to carry out news reporting tasks, as well as on the quality of contributions.

Limitations and future work. As the first limitation, the participants were students and the studies were carried out in university course settings. Although deadlines for reporting, for example, were set in addition to assigning news tasks to be carried out in realistic mobile news reporting situations, the real context of news reporting would reveal aspects that cannot be created in the current settings. Second, adopting the mobile and location-based assignments into use in a news organization and carrying out a longitudinal study would give firmer evidence on the perceptions, suitability and development needs. Future studies in the context of news journalism could address 1) freelancers and crowdsourcing as potential cases for mobile news assignments: in our studies, contract and rewarding related issues, for example, were not covered, 2) new emerging work practices and workflows with new mobile technologies, 3) impacts on roles and responsibilities of reporters and newsroom staff, 4) new types of news reporting and publishing enabled by mobile technology and 5) further studies on mobile assignments, that may require creativity, may not have clear completion criteria or criteria are situationally bounded.

CONCLUSIONS

We presented results from two user studies which explored the users' perceptions and needs as well as challenges when using mobile assignments in briefing news to cover. We found that mobile assignments sent to mobile phones were perceived as useful for small and simple assignments, whereas for more complex and larger themes they were found inefficient due to the lack of a possibility for discussing the topic. The information in the assignment description needs to be paid attention to in order to provide enough relevant information for the reporter to carry out the work and to take into account the mobility of the users and limitations for example in the size of the display for UI design. Both editors and reporters need process phase related information and updates on the phase, progress and further actions in the assignment and reporting process. Locationing was found somewhat acceptable, although privacy related concerns were expressed.

The findings of the study are applicable not only in a news reporting context, but in other fields of work where tasks may be complex, not strictly limited or completion may depend on situational issues. In addition, the results on, for example, process related issues may be applicable also to fields where "pro-ams" (professional amateurs) are carrying out assignments and participating in crowdsourcing, such as reader reporters in a news context [28].

ACKNOWLEDGMENTS

We thank Anssi Männistö and Timo Koskinen for co-operation in the studies and Tiina Koponen, Anni Uusitalo and Katja Suhonen for their assistance in Study 1. Special thanks to Kaisa Väänänen-Vainio-Mattila and Tiina Koponen for comments with the manuscript. This research was supported by Finnish Ministry of Education, Finnish Doctoral Program in User-Centered Information Technology (UCIT) and Nokia Research Center.

REFERENCES

1. Alt, F., Shirazi, A. S., Schmidt, A., Kramer, U., and Nawaz, Z. Location-based crowdsourding – Extending crowdsourcing to the real world. *Proc. NordiCHI2010*, ACM (2010), 13-22.
2. Bardram, J.E., and Hansen, T. Context-based workplace awareness. *CSCW, 19* (2010), 105-138.
3. Carroll, J. M., Rosson, M. B., Farooq, U., Xiao, L., Beyond Being Aware. *Information and Organization*, 19, 3, (2009), 162-185.
4. Chisholm, J. The Future is Yours: a survey of editors' attitudes. Society of Editors, retrieved 15 Nov 2011, http://www.societyofeditors.co.uk/userfiles/files/SoESurveyreport.pdf
5. Consolvo, S., Smith, I.E., Matthews, T., LaMarca, A. Tabert, J., Powledge, P. Location disclosure to social relations: Why, when, & what people want to share. *Proc. CHI 2005*, ACM (2005), 81-90.
6. Deuze, M. The professional identity of journalists in the context of convergence culture. *Observatorio (OBS*) J., 7* (2008), 103-117.
7. Dinka, D., Lundberg, J. Identity and role – A qualitative case study of co-operative scenario building. *Int. J. of Human Computer Studies, 64* (2006), 1049-1060.
8. Fagrell, H., Forsberg, K., Sanneblad, J FieldWise: a mobile knowledge management architecture. *Proc. CSCW '00*, ACM (2000), 211-220.
9. Forsberg, K. 1999. Navigating in the NewsSpace. *Proc. CSCWD99*, (1999) 329-336.
10. Helle, M. Disturbances and contradictions as tools for understanding the work in the newsroom. *Scandinavian Journal of Information Systems*, 12 (2000), 82-114.
11. Hössjer, A., and Severinson Eklundh, K. Making space for a new medium: On the use of electronic mail in a newspaper newsroom. *CSCW*, 18, 1 (2009), 1-46.
12. Jokela, T., Väätäjä, H., and Koponen, T. Mobile Journalist Toolkit: a field study on producing news articles with a mobile device. *Proc. MindTrek '09*. ACM Press (2009), 45-52.
13. Kensing, R., Simonsen, J., and Bødker, K. Participatory Design at a Radio Station. *CSCW*, (1998), 243-271.
14. Kittur, A., Smus, B., Khamkar, S., and Kraut, R.E.. CrowdForge: crowdsourcing complex work. *Proc. UIST '11*. ACM (2011), 43-52.
15. Kjeldskov, J., Graham, C., Pedell, S., Vetere, F., Howard, S., Balbo, S., Davies, J. Evaluating the usability of a mobile guide: the influence of location, participants and resources. *Behaviour & Information Technology, 24*, 1 (2005), 51-65.
16. Koponen, T. and Väätäjä, H. Early adopters' experiences of using mobile multimedia phones in news journalism. In *Proc. of ECCE 2009*. VTT, Finland (2009), 65-68.
17. Nielsen, C. M., Overgaard, M., Pedersen, M. B., Stage, J., Stenild, S. It's worth the hassle!: the added value of evaluating the usability of mobile systems in the field. *Proc. NordiCHI '06*, (2006) , 272-280.
18. Raento, M. and Oulasvirta, A. Designing for privacy and self-presentation in social awareness. *Personal and Ubiquitous Computing, 12*, 7 (2008), 527-542.
19. Sarjala, A. Supporting work processes of journalists: Design implications for mobile system development. MSc Thesis, May 2010. Tampere University of Technology. 112p.
20. Schenk, E. and Guittard, C., Towards a characterization of crowdsourcing practices, *J of Innovation Econ.*, 7, 1, (2011), 93-107.
21. Soley, L. C., and Smith, A.L. *Projective Methods for Social Science and Business Research*. The Southshore Press, (2008).
22. Sorensen, C., and Pica, D. Tales from the police: Rhythms of interaction with mobile technologies. *Information and Organization 15* (2005), 125-149.
23. Straus, S.G., Bikson, T.K., Balkovich, E., and Pane, J.F. Mobile Technology and Action Teams: Assessing Blackberry Use in Law Enforcement Units. *CSCW, 19*, (2010) 45-71.
24. Streefkerk, J.W., Van Ench-Bussemakers, M.P., and Neerincx, M.A. Field evaluation of a mobile location-based notification system for police officers, *Mobile HCI 2008*, ACM (2008).
25. Tsai, J., Kelley, P., Cranor, L., and Sadeh. N. Location-Sharing Technologies: Privacy Risks and Controls. *Proc. TPRC 2009* (2009).
26. Verburg, R.M., Testa, S., Hyrkkänen, U. and Johansson, N. Case Descriptions of Mobile Virtual Work in Practice. In Andriessen, J.H.E. and Vartiainen, M. (Ed.) *Mobile Virtual Work: A New Paradigm?* Springer (2006), 267-288.
27. Väätäjä, H., Männistö, A. A. Bottlenecks, usability issues and development needs in creating and delivering news videos with smart phones. *Proc. MoVid 2010* (2010) ACM, 45-50.
28. Väätäjä, H., Vainio, T., Sirkkunen, E., and Salo, K. Crowdsourced news reporting – Supporting news content creation with mobile phones. *Proc. MobileHCI 2011*, (2011) ACM, 435-444.
29. Väätäjä, H. Mobile work efficiency – Balancing between benefits, costs and sacrifices. To be published in International Journal of Mobile Human Computer Interaction (IJMHCI).
30. Väätäjä, H. User experience evaluation criteria for mobile news making technology – Findings from a case study. *Proc. OZCHI 2010, ACM, 152-159.*
31. Wigelius, H., and Väätäjä, H. Dimensions of Context Affecting User Experience in Mobile Work. In Proceedings of INTERACT 2009, part II, LNCS 5727, ACM (2008), 604-617.
32. Yin, R.K. 2003 *Case Study Research – Design and Methods*. 3rd ed. Sage Publications, USA.

Mixing Metaphors in Mobile Remote Presence

Leila Takayama
Willow Garage
68 Willow Road, Menlo Park, CA 94025
takayama@willowgarage.com

Janet Go
Autodesk
111 McInnis Parkway, San Rafael, CA 94903
janet.go@autodesk.com

ABSTRACT
Metaphors for making sense of new communication technologies are important for setting user expectations about appropriate use of the technologies. When users do not share a common metaphorical model for using these technologies, interpersonal communication breakdowns can occur. Through a set of three 8-week-long field deployments and one ongoing observation in-house, we conducted contextual inquiries around the uses of a relatively new communication technology, a mobile remote presence (MRP) system. We observed many nonhuman-like metaphors (e.g., orienting toward the system as a robot, an object) and human-like metaphors (e.g., a person, or a person with disabilities). These metaphors influence people's expectations about social norms in using the systems. We found that there is a serious risk of creating interpersonal conflict when the metaphors are mismatched between people (e.g., locals use nonhuman-like metaphors when remote pilots use human-like metaphors). We explore the implications for understanding remote pilots' rights and responsibilities and present design guidelines for MRP systems that support geographically distributed groups.

Author Keywords
Mobile remote presence; metaphor; source orientation.

ACM Classification Keywords
H.4.3. Communications Applications: Computer conferencing, teleconferencing, and videoconferencing.
H.5.3. Group and Organization Interfaces: Computer-supported cooperative work.

General Terms
Human Factors.

INTRODUCTION
Metaphors can (often unwittingly) influence the ways that we perceive and act [17]; we use metaphors to make sense of other domains (e.g., LIFE is a JOURNEY), drawing from basic source domains (e.g., journey) to make sense of target domains that are more difficult to conceptualize (e.g., life).

Similarly, we draw from basic source domains to figure out how we could and should use the new technology. This is the case with mobile remote presence (MRP) systems. As a relatively new technology, people have not yet formed a conceptual model for exactly what the MRP is, what it is not, and how they should use it. As such, people mix metaphors when encountering MRP systems. More critically, one interlocutor sometimes holds a mismatched metaphor from the other interlocutor, which is a potential source of interpersonal conflict.

Geographically distributed work teams already face more behavior and project management challenges than collocated and virtual teams [24]. In a study of collocated vs. distributed synchronous teamwork, Olson and Olson found that there are many factors that must align in order for communication technologies to improve distance work; they include sharing common ground, doing loosely coupled work, and having a culture of openness to collaboration and collaboration technologies [26]. Attaining this combination of factors is not easy. However, because we experienced the benefits of mobile remote presence in our own office, we chose to explore the possibility of supporting distributed work teams in other companies, too. We conducted an 8-week-long field trial at three different companies, along with an ongoing in-house observation of our own usage of the system.

The research questions in the current study and analysis are: How do people make sense of MRP systems in the workplace? How do the metaphors they use influence the

Figure 1. Remote pilot (in Boston, MA) talking with a local colleague (in Mountain View, CA) via an MRP system

ways that they interact through (and with) the MRP system? What are the underlying disagreements that cause interpersonal conflict when using MRP systems?

RELATED WORK

The most common question we hear when demonstrating our MRP systems is, "What is that?" Once they notice the live video feed of the remote person piloting the MRP system, they ask, "Who is that?" Knowing who (or what) we are communicating with is important. That is why "source orientation" is such a critical issue for human communication research.

Source Orientation

Source orientation refers to who (or what) a person believes is the source of the message. In the case of MRPs, people could orient toward the source of an utterance as being a "robot" talking, a person talking, or something else. People have a tendency to orient toward media (e.g., televisions, radios, and other communication tools) as if they were actual sources [28]. Furthermore, people orient toward the computer as if it were a source [34]; that is, people interact with the system as if it were a person in-the-moment, even though they do not reflectively believe that the system is a person [36]. Scholars such as Latour reflectively look upon nonhuman objects (e.g., doors [14] and speed bump [18]) as being actors, similar to humans.

Although many norms for how people interact with each other transfer to how people interact with computers, there are some differences in the degree to which these effects hold true. In human-robot interaction, there are individual differences in the ways that people orient toward robots (e.g., receptionist vs. informational kiosk [20]). Assertive people engage in more hostile power struggles when they believe they are interacting with a person as opposed to a computer [31]. This suggests that source orientation is affected by individual and contextual differences, which is explored in the current work.

Videoconferencing Systems

Aside from having remote mobility, MRP systems are similar to videoconferencing systems. As such, we examined the metaphors people use for talking and thinking about videoconferencing.

Videoconferencing Metaphor: Spaces

Spaces are a particularly powerful metaphor for setting videoconferencing user expectations about sharing a territory that spans across physical spaces. The Xerox PARC Media Spaces system connected the commons areas (i.e., shared workspaces) of labs in Oregon and California. Similarly, the EuroPARC RAVE system was networked throughout rooms in the EuroPARC building [12]. These researchers defined a media space as "an electronic setting in which groups of people can work together, even when they are not resident in the same place or present at the same time. In a media space, people can create real-time visual and acoustic environments that span physically separate areas" (p. 30) [4]. In the same vein, the CAVECAT (Computer Audio Video Enhanced Collaboration and Telepresence) was also conceptualized as a media space. It consisted of enhanced workstations that were connected via a digital-audio-video network, including a videoconferencing system for enabling small work teams to collaborate without leaving their offices [22].

Videoconferencing Metaphor: Windows

In contrast to the metaphor of being a space, other videoconferencing systems relied upon the metaphor of interacting through a window that separates two spaces. Most notably, the Bellcore VideoWindow system framed videoconferencing as interacting through a virtual window [11]: "imagine that you and your colleagues... are separated by a large sheet of glass that does not interfere with your ability to carry on a clear, two-way conversation" (p. 1). This system consisted of a very large video display and full-duplex audio connection between two geographically separate sites. The window metaphor also raised the saliency of transparency in the VideoWindow system.

This metaphor is carried on through similar projects such as the Xerox PARC and EuroPARC project, Portholes [9], which supported awareness across geographically distributed work groups. It provided images (updated every few minutes) of one or more sites. A lower bandwidth alternative was named "Peepholes," a system that created a virtual community of collaborators (from one's electronic address book) and provided activity/inactivity information about each of the collaborators [13]. Based on lessons learned from how people used the Cruiser system [5] to "ambush" colleagues (i.e., pounce upon them when they seem to be available enough to a conversation), the Peephole was built to enable awareness without requiring always-on video connections.

Videoconferencing Metaphor: Surrogates and Proxies

The most similar systems to the MRPs are ones that have actuated physical embodiments. These types of videoconferencing systems tend to rely upon the metaphor of being a surrogate or proxy. The Hydra, a small tabletop video conferencing system that each individual used to "take their place at the table" [6] set the stage for the notion of video surrogates. It was presented to users as a surrogate: "Don't think of the camera as a camera. Think of it as a surrogate eye. Likewise, don't think of the speaker as a speaker. Think of it as a surrogate mouth" (p. 8).

In this same line of thought, researchers have created many physical proxies that do not necessarily use video. Among these are the Surrogate motorized figurines and light patterns used to provide abstracted information such as the remote person's awareness and degree of interest [16]. More recent versions of these abstracted character figurines like the Cellular Squirrel [23].

This notion of a proxy is also visible in Microsoft Research's Embodied Social Proxy (ESP), a telepresence device that "represents the satellite coworker" in hub-and-satellite teams [39]; the ESP system sits on a rolling cart that can be pushed from location to location. Subsequent work has found that rotational control of the cameras is not as effective for increasing one's sense of social presence as being able to move the camera forward and backward [25].

Remote Mobility

The critical difference between prior work in remote video communication systems and the one presented in this study is that this system's motions are controlled by the remote operators, not the locals or the computer. The remote person is in control of what he looks like, where his cameras point, how loud his speakers are set, and where he goes. Thus, remote coworkers who use MRP systems can wander around the office, pounce on coworkers, engage in the hallway conversations, and participate in other informal communications that are critical to group work [42]. This difference breaks down the metaphors of spaces and windows. Being remotely controllable, the MRP systems are closer to the metaphors of surrogates and proxies.

Humanoid Robots

Android (e.g., Geminoid [30]) and humanoid robots (e.g., Wakamaru [25]) have also been used for supporting remote presence, using the metaphor of surrogates and proxies. While many of the same issues arise for humanoid robots as for the current system (e.g., identity mediation [33], movement increasing social presence [25]), there is one major difference. Unlike humanoid robots, the current MRP system uses the live video feed of the remote operator to represent the remote person; this enables anyone to operate the MRP system and look like oneself. The current MRP system is more likely to be perceived as an object or medium as opposed to an agentic robot because it is explicitly designed to project the remote operator's physical form (through live video) as opposed to only projecting the operator's voice and/or nonverbal behaviors.

Mobile Remote Presence Systems

Mobile remote presence (MRP) systems are not new. They have existed for over a decade in the form of UC Berkeley's Personal Roving Presence (PRoP) [27], HP Labs' BiReality [15], PEBBLES for hospitalized children [10], and other robotic telepresence systems in hospitals [40]. Commercially available MRP systems are being explored in the field, including the VGo and the Anybot QB [38]. From these studies and from observations of film-based physical avatars, researchers are generating design guidelines for such telepresence robots [8,29]. These telepresence robots take on many forms, not only as roughly human-scale systems; they also exist in tabletop forms (e.g., MeBot [1]).

Earlier research on this particular MRP system [19] was run in parallel with the current project. The current work was conducted by a separate and larger research team, started before and ended after the shorter-term study, included a larger set of companies, and used different empirical methods. The past work [19] focused upon interview, observation, and survey results gathered in parallel with this longer-term field study; the data sets remain separate.

SYSTEM

The MRP system used in this study was an Alpha prototype of a Texai remote presence system. It stands approximately 1.57 meters tall, consisting of a "head" that is supported by a metal stem on a motorized base. The "head" is a videoconferencing system with a color LCD screen, pan-tilt web camera, audio speakers, and a microphone. The motorized base has a remotely controllable active caster in the back with two passive wheels in the front; the base also has a polycarbonate bumper, a computer, and a large battery that lasts for approximately eight hours on each charge. Remote pilots control the MRP system via an Internet connection, video chat application, and web-based graphical user interface. See this MRP system in Figure 1.

Because we did not want to push any particular metaphor for understanding or using the system at the field sites, we framed the MRP system as a "system," not as a "robot." "Local" is the term we use to describe a person who is in the same physical location as the MRP system. "Remote pilot" is the term we use to describe the person who is remotely operating the MRP system.

FIELD STUDY

The current study presents a critical set of issues and breakdowns that were observed during the 8-week field study trials, focusing upon the metaphors that people seem to use when interacting through MRP systems and the breakdowns that occur when there is disagreement about those underlying metaphors. We conducted a contextual inquiry [3] to explore the ways that people would use and make sense of these MRP systems in the workplace. We recruited several companies that had hub-and-satellite work groups with the hub in the San Francisco Bay Area. See the other demographics for the sites in Table 1.

Field sites A-C participated in the following activities:

1. Intake interviews with remote pilot(s) up to 2 weeks before the MRP systems were delivered to the site
2. Contextual inquiry field observations on the day of MRP system delivery and every other week after that
3. Email, phone, or video chat interviews every other week before the field observations

Sites A and C also had ballot boxes left at their local sites, where local participants were invited to anonymously drop comments for the researchers.

Site	Dedicated Remote Pilots	Pilot Roles in Each Company	Distance From Local Site (Miles)	# of MRP Systems Available	Office Has Persistent Video Connection to Remote Site(s)?	Commonly Used Communication Tools
A	A1, A2	Executive, VP	50, 15	2	No	Email, Telepresence room, Skype
B	B1, B2	Software Developer, VP	>1200, >2900	1	Yes, but they turned it off	Internal Project Tracker, Skype
C	C1, C2, C3, C4	Project Director, Senior Engineers, System Admin	>2500, >800, >3000, >8000	2	Yes	Email, IRC
D	D1	Electrical Engineer	>2,000	5	No	Email, Skype, Phone

Table 1. Overview of MRP Field Study Participant Population and Communication Tool Usage.

Site D was different in that it was the company where the MRP prototype was originally created; this site had used the system for approximately 9 months longer than the other sites. While we did not conduct a formal field study at Site D, one of the coauthors works at this site is a full-time employee and has taken notes, videos, and pictures of events as they occurred in the workplace.

OBSERVED BREAKDOWNS

While our prior work discussed how MRP systems are used when interactions were working smoothly [19], this work focuses upon the common and major breakdowns we observed at the four field sites.

Hanging up

A common and problematic situation occurred across several sites: MRP systems would be found in the morning with dead batteries, sitting far away from their charging stations. This was typically caused by pilots thinking of the MRP system as a normal videoconferencing system that they simply "hang up" at the end of the conversation; however, MRP systems run on battery power so their batteries run out of charge if they are not parked in their charging stations at the end of the work day. At Site B, when one pilot did this, a frustrated local said to the MRP system, "You can't just turn off the robot in the middle of the floor!" Then, "Who's there? Wake up!" It was clear that the local felt a norm had been broken. Frustrated locals are not inclined to help move them back to their charging stations so some MRP systems were left with dead batteries for more than few days at a time.

Violating personal space

Problems often arose for pilots when locals broke the remote pilot's expectations about respecting "personal space" around the MRP system. Pilot C2 mentioned, "My boss hugged me. I don't know that he would have done that normally." Similarly, Pilot C3 was bothered when his local coworker was examining the base of the MRP system too closely; he exclaimed, "It's like you're looking up my skirt!" with an uneasy, but humorous tone. Similarly, Pilot C4 told the locals who were investigating the MRP, "Stay away from my buttons!" because they were pressing the volume control buttons on the MRP speakers. When a remote pilot feels like he *is* the MRP system, it becomes uncomfortable when locals behave differently than they would behave around a person.

Incapacitating

The most extreme breakdown occurred when a local shut down the MRP system that a pilot was trying to use to talk with her. Since she did not want to talk with Pilot D1 and felt that he was being disruptive, she simply hit the run-stop button on the MRP prototype base, which turned off the power supply to the motors. She reasoned that it was like hanging up the phone on someone. However, Pilot D1 felt that this was much worse than having someone hang up on him by phone. It felt to him like he had been incapacitated.

A theme that cut across these breakdowns was a mismatch between the ways that different pilots vs. locals thought about the MRP system. Because they seemed to be using different metaphors for making sense of the MRP systems, we chose to do a more focused analysis of those metaphors.

METAPHOR DATA ANALYSIS

To examine those metaphors people used to make sense of the MRP systems, we used the TAMS qualitative data analysis tool to sort our field notes and interviews, inductively coding them for contents such as (1) what metaphors people used for interacting with or talking about the MRP system, (2) how those metaphors were mixed over time and between people, and (3) the implications of using certain metaphors for understanding the rights and responsibilities of remote pilots. The metaphor categories used in the current analysis were inferred from the observations. We do not claim that these metaphors are consciously invoked when interacting with the MRP systems, but we do claim that people are (either explicitly or implicitly) using these metaphors to make sense of and use the MRP system.

Categorizing Metaphors

We inductively developed the categories of metaphors with the goal of identifying the metaphors that shed light upon problematic interactions observed in MRP usage. Behaviors and statements from participants that suggested the MRP system was a communication tool were categorized as "Communication Medium," e.g., using language about videoconferencing or calling in. Explicit mentions of the system as "robot" or references to science fiction notions of robots (e.g., "Rosie") were categorized as "Robot." The category of "Object" was used to tag behaviors and statements that referred to the MRP system as a thing, "it," or otherwise non-agentic entity. The last two categories of "People" and "People with Disabilities" were used to capture behaviors and statements that clearly referred to the system as a person (e.g., using pilots' names or behaving in socially appropriate ways in terms of how one would treat another person in the office, not objects).

RESULTS

First, we provide descriptions and examples of the metaphors people used to talk about and interact with the MRP system, along with potential sources of influence that might have encouraged the use of that metaphor. Second, we present the ways in which those metaphors are mixed and the sometimes negative consequences of mixing them. Third, we present the how the metaphor of MRP-as-person impacts issues of rights and responsibilities for MRP users.

The metaphors that people use for interacting with the MRP system changed over time, shifting from moment to moment, and varied widely between individuals.

Nonhuman-like Metaphors

Communication Medium

Technically, we consider the MRP system to be a communication medium. At Site B, a software engineer remarked to a colleague that this MRP system represented a logical step from Skype (online videoconferencing) to "Skype on wheels." At Site A, one local explained, "For me, with a bigger screen, it's more of a videoconference thing than a robot thing." When people used "robot in" as a verb, just as they might use the words "email", "phone" or "Skype" as verbs, it highlighted its role as a communication medium. They sometimes applied social norms from existing communication technologies to decide how to use the MRPs, e.g., "hanging up" the MRP as soon as the meeting ended. This presented the problem for locals, who then had to push the MRP system to the charging station.

Figure 2. Local participant showing us how he wants a remote control mute button for the MRP system

Robot

Despite our best efforts to refer to the MRP system as a "system," not a "robot," all of the field sites referred to the MRP system as a "robot" in the beginning. Both locals and remote pilots referred to the MRP system as a robot. When describing system breakdowns, a remote pilot from Site A explained, "My robot just got stuck." A local at this same site explained how this pilot would use the MRP system to be present in the office on the days when he telecommuted from the other office across the Bay: "So if ... there's a meeting, we would go to his office and the robot would roll up in his place." At Site B, one local wrapped up a project team meeting by asking, "Anything else? Anybody? Robot?" (in a somewhat humorous way) to see if anyone had final project issues to raise. A little more seriously, a different local bystander, who was annoyed by the disruption caused by the MRP told us, "What you need is a robot mute button," as he demonstrated a remote control button press. See Figure 2.

The use of "robot" extended beyond descriptions of the system, carrying over to greetings and verbs. At the end of one project meeting, one of the engineering team members said goodbye to Pilot C1 by calling out, "See ya, Rosie!" in reference to the Jetson family's robotic housekeeper.

Object

The most ambiguous form of reference to the MRP system was "it." Because we could not definitively categorize these references, we interpreted this as conceptualizing the MRP system as some kind of object. Whenever the MRP system was introduced into a new environment, the people who come to see it ask the inevitable question: How fast can it go? At Site C, a local asked Pilot C4, "Do you steer this thing?" while enacting driving with a car steering wheel.

For others, the MRP system was more like an unidentifiable object. Some locals were surprised by its presence, e.g., as Site A, "It just kind of snuck up on me and it was just kind of jarring, like, 'Oh my gosh! What is that? And why is it coming towards me?' [...] I was surprised there was this thing and then there was [Pilot A2] sort of in our conversation."

Even after many weeks of exposure to the MRP systems being used in the office, not everyone felt at ease with it. At Site C, one local bystander described it as, "It's big and loud and bangs into things like doors. It's also a distraction when it's moving around."[1] She did not seem to know who

---

[1] Sometimes the MRP system seemed too quiet because the ambient environment was noisy (e.g., computers humming, fans blowing, many people talking). Sometimes it seemed

was actually operating the MRP system and was not interested in finding out who it was.

Another common type of object metaphor was that of a container. Locals at Site C talked about having trouble with figuring out "who's in it that day" or who was "inhabiting" it. Remote pilots also used language to suggest this metaphor, reporting on conducting a job interview "inside of a tele-robot."

Consistent with the notion of the MRP being a mere object, we have observed people sitting on the MRP base like a chair and leaning on the MRP monitor like they lean on a porch railing. At Site B, we observed one local engaging in a very in-depth conversation with Pilot B2; the local was sitting in his desk chair, looking up at the MRP screen, and resting his feet upon the base of the MRP. See Figure 3. These are not typical interpersonal behaviors that one would see between collocated people in an office.

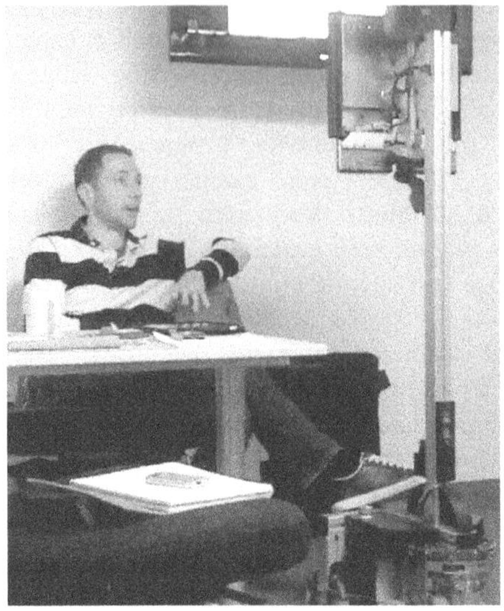

Figure 3. Remote pilot (in Colorado) talking with a local (in California), who is resting his foot on the MRP base

Human-like Metaphors

Person

Throughout the field studies, many people interacted with and talked about the remote pilots as if they were simply there. At Site A, one local participant described her interaction with a remote pilot this way: "When [Pilot A2] gets on the robot and goes around the building and stuff and we have a conversation, I argue with him and hand gesture. It's as if he's there. You know, the fact that the screen is that big, his face is almost kind of life size, maybe that adds to it, versus someone you're talking to on an iPhone or whatever. I treat him as if he's right there. I don't think I act any differently." Before anyone logs in, the MRP seems to be a robot, but someone logs in, the MRP seems to be a person.

The degree to which locals treated the MRP as a person was sometimes evident in how they observed social norms. Indeed, we often observed locals struggling with figuring out what was socially appropriate with the MRP. During a meeting at Site A, a local complained to Pilot A2 that he was too close and felt like Pilot A2 was staring at the back of his head; Pilot A2 then moved the MRP away. In another case, a local refrained from lowering the volume on the MRP speaker while the remote pilot was presenting to a group of visitors. The local reported, "There was an Ambassador training tour and the volume was scratchy. I had the idea in mind that maybe I should have stopped [Pilot A2] and play with the knobs, but I didn't do it..." In a voice conferencing setting, it is common for users to make adjustments to their speaker volume settings throughout a conversation. However, in a face-to-face conversational setting, it is less common to see people make adjustments to each other in the middle of a conversation (e.g., telling a group member to quiet down). This situation is an example of what happens when locals construe the MRP system as being something like a person.

too noisy because the ambient environment was quiet (e.g., single person office, mostly empty meeting room).

In other cases, participants not only treated the MRP as a person, but also specifically identified it a particular individual (i.e. the pilot). MRPs that were piloted by C1 and D1 were referred to by a combination of their name and "Bot" (as in "JohnBot" or "SmithBot"). In both cases, the pilots had been the only ones using an MRP for a period of time, and used it extensively.

Person with disabilities

The most surprising, yet common, metaphor was that the MRP system was like a person with disabilities.

Because the MRP system cannot open doors, Pilot C1 had difficulty with exiting the conference rooms at the end of meetings. He reported, "One meeting ended and I had to sit there to wait around to get help with opening the door. I don't know how to deal with that really." Locals at that office also reported feeling awkward about having to let the MRP system out of conference room. Similarly, as Site D, pilots have started to wander back and forth in front of office windows or to gently bump into the door a few times in order to "knock" so that locals will open doors for them.

At another time, network latency issues caused the video feed to update very slowly, making it difficult for Pilot C2 to move through the office (as he was visually impaired by the network latency). His local coworkers helped him navigate by telling him directions such as "turn to the left forty degrees" to turn a corner.

Pilots and locals continually referred to how MRP needed help because it "doesn't have arms," was visually impaired, or "died" in the middle of the hall. Pilot A1 suggested the MRP should display a sign when it lost a WiFi network connection; he compared it to a person wearing a "medical bracelet" so that paramedics know what to do if they find the person unconscious. The person with disabilities metaphor encompasses some of the limitations on what pilots would like to do with MRP, as well as how they relied on locals to help them.

Often in anticipation, locals adapted their behaviors to make up for the limitations of the MRP systems. For example, at Site A, one local drew a marketing diagram on the whiteboard much larger than normal just so that Pilot A1 could see it. Sometimes that same local would take high-resolution digital photographs of the whiteboards and email the photographs to Pilot A1 after the meeting adjourned. Many locals remarked at having to slow down their normal pace in order to walk with the MRP through the office. It was not uncommon to hear locals talking extra loudly so that MRP pilots could hear them better over the hum of office noises.

Mixing Metaphors

The metaphors people use for making sense of these MRP systems influence the ways that people form their beliefs about what is appropriate and inappropriate behavior for using these systems. We observed many instances of people mixing those metaphors between people and over time.

Mixing Metaphors Between People

As seen in the three examples of common breakdowns in interactions between people who use the MRP system, mixing metaphors can be quite harmful to interpersonal interactions in the office, especially when remote pilots vs. locals used mismatched nonhuman vs. human metaphors. In the "hanging up" example, pilots seemed to be thinking of the MRP system as a static communication medium, whereas locals did not agree. In the "violating personal space" example, pilots felt like the MRP system should be treated like a person, but the locals did not agree; pilots felt more like the MRP systems were more like people, but the locals experienced the MRP systems as objects that could be touched and handled. In the case of "incapacitating," the Pilot D1 experienced the MRP as an extension of himself, which is why it was so upsetting that the local had shut his MRP off; this local treated the MRP with more of a phone-like stance, finding it to be appropriate to shut it off just as one would hang up a phone.

Mixing Metaphors Over Time

Not all metaphor mixes work out so terribly. As one local at Site C said, "you can still walk with them…it," referring to his ability to walk and talk with the remote pilots as he could walk and talk with them whenever they visited in person. He corrected himself, saying "it," because he preferred to talk about the system as being an object, but found himself slipping into the language of a more person-like metaphor. Similarly, one local at Site C talked about how his perception of the MRP system changed over time. At first, he saw it and thought it was "so cool" that he got caught up in details like "how fast it can go," but later said that when he saw the MRP in the hallway, "it doesn't phase you [...] now it's just a person."

At Site A, one local participant described her transition from thinking of the MRP system as a robot to thinking of it as the remote person: "It's kind of funny and amazing when you see the person rolling up towards you. Just like, wow, there's [Pilot A1] or [Pilot A2] on the robot. But you feel like they're kind of there, present. And wanting to kind of include them because you feel like, you know, a lot of people don't know how to react to them at first." Although she referred to the MRP system as a robot, she had become accustomed to interacting with the remote people in a way that compelled her to help others learn how to interact with them as people, too.

Rights and Responsibilities

When Pilot D1 was shut down by a local, was that assault? Probably not, but the incident raised questions about what kinds of rights remote pilots could and should have. Along with rights come responsibilities.

Person-like metaphors encourage pilots to take more responsibility for the MRP system. When pilots felt like the MRP really was them (using the person metaphor), it had serious impacts upon how ashamed and embarrassed the remote pilots felt when the MRP system was not operating properly. As C1 noted, losing WiFi connectivity "gets kind of embarrassing because you end up being dead." He knew that it made more sense to blame the "network guys" who are supposed to maintain the WiFi network in the office, but he still felt that it was personally embarrassing (and mentioned it to us several times) even though he did not have much control over the situation. In this sense, remote pilots assumed responsibility for the faults of the MRP system.

Some locals took responsibility for helping the MRP to overcome technical glitches, similar to the ESP system Handlers [39]. This was most apparent at Site A, where one person was designated as the robot aide. He was always the first person the pilots called when the MRP systems were not functioning properly; he would immediately drop his current activity to troubleshoot the MRP system until it was back in working order. This may have been because the pilots were executives in the organization (as opposed to peers), but we observed similar behaviors (though less immediately responsive) at Sites C and D. This difference between sites suggests that the local Handlers are treating the MRP systems as if they were more people-like than machine-like.

Rights and responsibilities encompass much broader issues than simply who should be allowed to turn off MRP systems and who is to blame when MRP systems do not work. These issues become more complex by adding in bits of autonomy (e.g., [35]) and computer-generated behaviors (as in the Transformed Social Interaction paradigm [2]). As a social issue: If an obstacle avoidance system in the MRP makes a remote pilot drive straight down the middle of a narrow hallway, will the locals understand that the remote pilot did not intend to block their way? As a legal issue: If a semi-autonomously navigating MRP system bumps into a person or damages valuable furniture, who is to blame? The legal rights, responsibilities, and liability issues surrounding personal robotic systems in human environments are under active investigation (e.g., [7]). Autonomous robots already present challenges for existing legal systems (e.g.,[21,32]) and remotely-driven, semi-autonomous systems in human environments present an even more complex challenges.

DISCUSSION

Mixing Metaphors

The most problematic metaphor mixing seemed to take place between pilots and locals, using nonhuman-like and human-like metaphors. Unlike telephones and videoconferencing rooms, pilots have entirely different user experiences than locals. Pilots use their regular personal computers to do videoconferencing while using a typical point-and-click graphical user interface to move around. In contrast, locals encounter a very new, physically present entity that actively moves around in their office space.

The benefits for pilots tend to be more immediately obvious than for locals because pilots are typically isolated at satellite sites. Most of our field study pilots were quite frustrated with their existing solutions for communicating with the hubs (see Table 1), even if they had state-of-the-art solutions and were constantly connected. Thus, they were more patient and persistent with making the MRP systems work for their purposes, trying to be more present (as a person) at the hub site.

Contexts of Use

Although the current study does not include enough data to make conclusive claims about what aspects of what contextual variations influence MRP usage, we have formed several hypotheses about contexts of use.

Using the MRP system as a dedicated (one person to one MRP system) vs. shared resource influences how people conceptualize the system; dedicated MRP systems are more likely to get names like "JohnBot" than ones that are usable by more than one pilot. Similarly, the ESP system had dedicated pilots, which got names like "Virtual Fernando" [39], suggesting that having a dedicated system is more likely to be identified as the remote pilot himself.

The social status of the pilot within the organizational hierarchy is another potential influencer. The strength of that hierarchy likely matters, too. At Site A, locals seemed to feel more obligated and responsible for helping to keep the MRP systems up and running. When only the executives in an organization can pilot the MRP systems, we hypothesize that the MRP system inherits an executive status and becomes a symbol of organizational power, which can be intimidating for locals.

The current study produced at least three other data points against which to compare the creators of the prototype, Site D. Being a robotics company, Site D had a strong tendency to orient toward the MRP system as a "robot" at first, but that changed over the span of several weeks; in that sense, it was no different from the other sites. One major way that Site D was different from the others was that people at Site D more explicitly argued about what was proper vs. improper etiquette for interacting with MRP pilots. Although the conflicts were explicitly discussed, those debates did not seem to affect the shifting and mixing of metaphors in MRP usage.

Implications for Design

There are many minor design implications for this particular system that could be listed (e.g., monitor ambient noise levels and play appropriately quiet sounds so that locals are aware of the MRP's presence without being distracted by it). However, we chose to present two high-level design implications with suggestions for how to address the approach those design issues.

Relatively novel communication technologies should be introduced with a consistent metaphor if the system designers care about quickly reaching a coherent set of social norms. This has worked out reasonably well for previous metaphors of spaces and windows, but has not yet worked out for MRP systems. This does not mean that a single source domain must be used as a metaphor (i.e., the MRP system should not necessarily be treated like a person in every possible way). A plurality of metaphors would be fine as long as the locals and pilots come to a shared understanding of the system. Since most of the interpersonal and usability problems we observed came from mismatches in the metaphors between locals vs. pilots, our primary design guideline is to encourage shared metaphors for locals and pilots.

Taking the metaphor of "Person" too far can be dangerous in that it would be easy to set user expectations too high for the MRP system. If one chose the metaphor of "Person with Disabilities," then one might mark out MRP parking spots at meeting room tables, notify locals when the MRP system needs to be guided out of WiFi deadzones or back to a charging station (perhaps with something like medical bracelet instructions), and notify locals when the remote pilot is experiencing poor video quality by displaying a red band around the MRP system base (like a long cane). These kinds of elements can encourage locals to interact with the MRP pilots like people, but also encourage them to understand that the MRP systems have different abilities than other people around the office.

A second design guideline is to encourage locals to quickly move beyond the "object" and "robot" metaphors for MRP systems, encouraging more interpersonal interaction with

MRP systems in workplaces. Remote coworkers are not trying to operate machines in the office or to "be robots"; they are trying to be present, to communicate, and to get work done. The pilots in our study preferred to be treated with the same kind of respect that they would expect if they were at the site in person so it is safest to design for supporting metaphors of MRP systems being more like people (or people with disabilities) rather than objects that can be pushed around, muted, or shut down.

By highlighting the remote person, one can encourage locals to treat the remote pilots more like the other people around the office. Unlike android robots, this approach calls for the remote person to be the focus of attention instead of the local robot. One way to encourage more human-human interactions (as opposed to human-robot interactions) is to make the remote pilot's identity readily visible, e.g., using a high-fidelity audio and live video. If the system is being used in a shared office space, then it would also be helpful to make the remote pilot visible from all angles around the MRP system (e.g., [15]) so that bystanders are more likely to enter into conversations rather than see it as a big, loud thing that bangs into doors.

The ultimate design goal for MRP systems is to become invisible-in-use [37]. Pilot A2 said this most succinctly: "we know that we're really successful when the robot becomes invisible and it's just about the people there."

LIMITATIONS AND FUTURE WORK

As an exploratory field study, these findings are necessarily preliminary. We have formed more hypotheses than answered questions, but have identified potentially fruitful paths for future research. The generalizability of this work can be tested by comparison with other studies of other forms of MRP systems, in other environmental contexts, in other cultural contexts, and with other types of user groups.

Our follow-up studies are investigating the causal relationships between different design decisions and the ways that people interact with MRP systems. This field work points to other future research directions, including exploring the contextual influences upon the adoption and conceptual models that people form around MRP systems, considering the implications for the design of systems that are viewed as something like people with disabilities, and ways of designing for inherently asymmetrical user experiences [41] for remote pilots vs. locals.

CONCLUSIONS

The current study presents empirical data and results from four different companies that used MRP systems for workplace communication. By analyzing some common and serious breakdowns in MRP usage, we found that remote pilots vs. locals were orienting toward the MRP system in conflicting ways, using human-like vs. nonhuman-like metaphors. Mixing human-like vs. nonhuman-like metaphors is sometimes innocuous, but it can also cause interpersonal breakdowns, particularly when conflicting metaphors lead to conflicting beliefs about what kinds of behaviors are socially appropriate when using MRPs. It has been revealing to explore the rich set of metaphors that people use for making sense of new technologies. For the sake of smoother interpersonal interactions in work teams, we recommend that new communication technologies (such as MRP systems) be designed and introduced with consistent metaphors that encourage convergence upon a shared set of social norms.

ACKNOWLEDGMENTS

Thanks go to the Texai project team and the volunteers who tried out the Texai Alpha prototype. We thank Bianca Soto, Judee Humburg, Matti Hirpa, Helen Harris, and Parmita Dalal for their contributions as part of the field study team.

REFERENCES

1. Adalgeirsson, S.O. and Breazeal, C. MeBot: A robotic platform for socially embodied presence. *Proc. HRI 2010*, ACM Press (2010), 15–22.
2. Bailenson, J.N., Beall, A.C., Loomis, J., Blascovich, J., and Turk, M. Transformed Social Interaction. *Presence: Teleoperators and Virtual Environments*, (2004).
3. Beyer, H. and Holtzblatt, K. *Contextual Design: Defining Customer-Centered Systems*. Morgan Kaufmann, 1998.
4. Bly, S.A., Harrison, S.R., and Irwin, S. Media spaces: Bringing people together in a video, audio, and computing environment. *Communications of the ACM 36*, (1993), 28–46.
5. Brinck, T. and Gomez, L.M. A collaborative medium for the support of conversational props. *Proc CSCW 1992*, ACM Press (1992), 171–178.
6. Buxton, B. *Scientific Director's Report: Living in Augmented Reality, Ontario Telepresence Project Final Report*. Telecommunications Research Institute of Ontario, 1995.
7. Calo, M.R. Open Robotics. *Maryland Law Review 70*, 3 (2010).
8. Desai, M., Tsui, K.M., Yanco, H.A., and Uhlik, C. Essential features of telepresence robots. *Proc. TEPRA 2011*, (2011), 15-20.
9. Dourish, P. and Bly, S. Portholes: Supporting awareness in a distributed work group. *Proc. CHI 1992*, ACM Press (1992), 541–547.
10. Fels, D. I., Waalen, J. K., Zhai, Shumin, and Weiss, P. L. Telepresence under exceptional circumstances: Enriching the connection to school for sick children. *Proc. Interact*, (2001), 617-624.
11. Fish, R.S., Kraut, R.E., and Chalfonte, B.L. The VideoWindow system in informal communication. *Proc. CSCW 1990*, ACM Press (1990), 1–11.

12. Gaver, W., Moran, T., MacLean, A., et al. Realizing a video environment: EuroPARC's RAVE system. *Proc. CHI 1992*, ACM Press (1992), 27–35.
13. Greenberg, S. Peepholes: Low cost awareness of one's community. *Proc. CHI 1996*, ACM Press (1996), 206–207.
14. Johnson, S.C. Detecting agents. *Philosophical Transactions of the Royal Society B: Biological Sciences 358*, 1431 (2003), 549-559.
15. Jouppi, N.P., Iyer, S., Thomas, S., and Slayden, A. BiReality: Mutually-immersive telepresence. *Proc. ACM Multimedia 2004*, ACM Press (2004), 860–867.
16. Kuzuoka, H. and Greenberg, S. Mediating awareness and communication through digital but physical surrogates. *Ext. Abstracts CHI 1999*, ACM Press (1999), 11–12.
17. Lakoff, G. and Johnson, M. *Metaphors We Live By*. University of Chicago Press, 1980.
18. Latour, B. Where are the missing masses? The sociology of a few mundane artifacts. In *Shaping Technology / Building Society: Studies in Sociotechnical Change*. MIT Press, Cambridge, 1992, 225-258.
19. Lee, M.K. and Takayama, L. "Now, I have a body": Uses and social norms for mobile remote presence in the workplace. *CHI*, ACM Press (2011), 33–42.
20. Lee, M.K., Kiesler, S., and Forlizzi, J. Receptionist or information kiosk: How do people talk with a robot? *Proc. CSCW 2010*, ACM Press (2010), 31-40.
21. Lehman-Wilzig, S.N. Frankstein unbound: Towards a legal definition of artificial intelligence. *Futures*, (1981).
22. Mantei, M.M., Baecker, R.M., Sellen, A.J., Buxton, W.A.S., Milligan, T., and Wellman, B. Experiences in the use of a media space. *Proc. CHI 1991*, ACM Press (1991), 203–208.
23. Marti, S. and Schmandt, C. Physical embodiments for mobile communication agents. *Proc. UIST 2005*, ACM Press (2005), 231–240.
24. McDonough, E.F., Kahn, K.B., and Barczak, G. An investigation of the use of global, virtual, and colocated new product development teams. *Journal of Product Innovation Management 18*, 2 (2001), 110-120.
25. Nakanishi, H., Murakami, Y., Nogami, D., and Ishiguro, H. Minimum movement matters: Impact of robot-mounted cameras on social telepresence. *Proc. CSCW 2008*, ACM Press (2008), 303–312.
26. Olson, G.M. and Olson, J.S. Distance matters. *Human-Computer Interaction 15*, (2000), 139–178.
27. Paulos, E. and Canny, J. Social Tele-Embodiment: Understanding Presence. *Autonomous Robots 11*, (2001), 87–95.
28. Reeves, B. and Nass, C. *The Media Equation: How people treat computers, television, and new media like real people and places*. Cambridge University Press, 1996.
29. Riek, L.D. Realizing Hinokio: Candidate requirements for physical avatar systems. *Proc. HRI 2007*, ACM Press (2007), 303–308.
30. Sakamoto, D., Kanda, T., Ono, T., Ishiguro, H., and Hagita, N. Android as a telecommunication medium with a human-like presence. *Proc. HRI 2007*, ACM Press (2007), 193–200.
31. Schechtman, N. and Horowitz, L.M. Media inequality in conversation. *Proc. CHI 2003*, ACM Press, 281-288.
32. Solum, L.B. Legal personhood for artificial intelligences. *North Carolina Law Review 70*, (1992), 1231.
33. Straub, I., Nishio, S., and Ishiguro, H. Incorporated identity in interaction with a teleoperated robot: A case study. (2010), 119-124.
34. Sundar, S.S. and Nass, C. Source Orientation in Human-Computer Interaction. *Communication Research 27*, 6 (2000), 683 -703.
35. Takayama, L., Marder-Eppstein, E., Harris, H., and Beer, J. Assisted Driving of a Mobile Remote Presence System. *Proc. ICRA 2011*, (2011), 1883-1889.
36. Takayama, L. Perspectives on Agency: Interacting with and through personal robots. In M. Zacharias and J.V. Oliveira, eds., *Human-Computer Interaction: The Agency Perspective*. Springer, In Press.
37. Takayama, L. Toward Making Robots Invisible-in-use: An Exploration Into Invisible-in-use Tools and Agents. In *New Frontiers in Human-Robot Interaction*. John Benjamins, Amsterdam, NL, In Press.
38. Tsui, K.M., Desai, M., Yanco, H.A., and Uhlik, C. Exploring use cases for telepresence robots. *Proc. HRI 2011*, ACM Press (2011), 11–18.
39. Venolia, G., Tang, J., Cervantes, R., et al. Embodied social proxy: Mediating interpersonal connection in hub-and-satellite teams. *Proc. CHI 2010*, ACM Press (2010), 1049–1058.
40. Vespa, P. Robotic telepresence in the intensive care unit. *Critical Care 9*, 4, 319-320.
41. Voida, A., Voida, S., Greenberg, S., and He, H.A. Asymmetry in media spaces. *Proc. CSCW 2008*, ACM Press (2008), 313–322.
42. Whittaker, S., Frohlich, D., and Daly-Jones, O. Informal workplace communication: What is it like and how might we support it? *Proc. CHI 1994*, ACM Press (1994), 131–137.

HappyGo: A Field Trial of Local Group Buying

Huanglingzi Liu, Wei Wang, Dong Liu, Hao Wang, Nan Du
Nokia Research Center, Beijing
{linda.2.liu, wei.41.wang, dong.e.liu}@nokia.com hao.wang.iv@gmail.com dunanpersonal@gmail.com

ABSTRACT
Group buying is a business model where people with the same merchandise interests form a group and conduct the purchase together to achieve a discount. Third-party proxy websites negotiate with merchants for appealing deals and then provide them to end customers. We call it online group buying. Besides, there exists local group buying where the joiners, the initiator, and sometimes even the merchants are in the same local community. Such locality induces some interesting characteristics in group buying, which remain largely unexplored in the research community. This study attempts to reveal users' behaviors in group buying within the local context. We developed a mobile service called "HappyGo" that supports local group buying. We conducted a trial involving more than 300 users from a company office. From our findings, we believe that local group buying complements online group buying by creating a "local" economic circle while also providing users with social benefits.

Author Keywords
Group buying, mobile service, local community

ACM Classification Keywords
H5.m. Information interfaces and presentation (e.g., HCI): Miscellaneous.

INTRODUCTION
Group buying has been a fervent topic recently in both academic and industrial field. There are three types of participants in group buying: the merchant, the initiator, and the joiners. The initiator first negotiates with the merchant, promising to bring a certain number of customers in exchange for an appealing deal from the merchant. The initiator then distributes the information to gather a group of like-minded people and conduct the purchase. The joiners benefit from lower price which is unavailable to the individual buyer. The merchant benefits from bulk sale and word-of-mouth advertisement. Group buying can be initiated by one of the joiners to benefit others as well as oneself; as well as a professional proxy, who coordinates the group buying for a certain commission fee from the merchant, or the merchant itself as a marketing campaign.

Long before the Internet emerged group buying had already existed. At that time, information on deals was disseminated via word-of-mouth, so that limited group size could be reached. The joiners usually had strong ties among them such as relatives, friends, or colleagues. The initiator was a joiner itself of group buying who organized the activity for his/her own (as well as other joiners') benefit from the discount. We call this *offline* group buying since the entire process is conducted offline.

In the Internet era, group buying mostly involves the "daily deal," which is initiated by dedicated third-party proxy websites. They provide a limited number of appealing deals every day on their websites so that users can easily choose from them. Group buying is open to any user online. The joiner is insensitive to the location of the merchant and other joiners. We call this *online* group buying. Online group buying attracts many more joiners than offline group buying and thus usually has a better discount. On the other hand, joiners are usually total strangers. They have no information of each other except that they are interested in the same product. Their social interactions are therefore limited to the sharing of buying experiences such as comments and ratings, which are used to assist the buying activity. Explicit social benefits are hard to find in online group buying.

	Information dissemination	User base	Trust among joiners
Offline	Word of mouth	Small	High
Local	Internet	Medium	Medium
Online	Internet	Large	Low

Table 1. Comparison of offline, local, and online group buying

In this work, we study a less recognized type of group buying, *local* group buying, which already exists in many local communities (e.g., the same office building, apartment

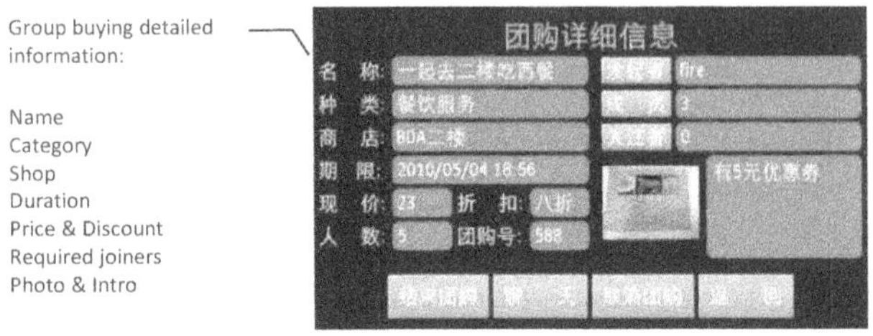

Figure 1. The UI for detailed group information and potential actions.

complex, etc.), and is weakly supported by the community online forums [5]. The initiator, the joiners, and sometimes the merchants, are from the same local community. Local group buying integrates online and offline group buying to some extent. We compare the three types of group buying in Table 1. Local group buying leverages Internet, which is the same as online group buying, to disseminate the information and gather joiners. But the purchase is conducted offline. It gathers considerably more joiners than offline group buying, but usually less than the number in online group buying. The joiners do not have strong ties as in offline group buying. But compared to online group buying, they perceive more trust towards other joiners because they may belong to the same affiliation or live close to each other. Such locality induces some interesting characteristics such as the role of the initiator and the social benefits for joiners, which remain largely unexplored in the research community.

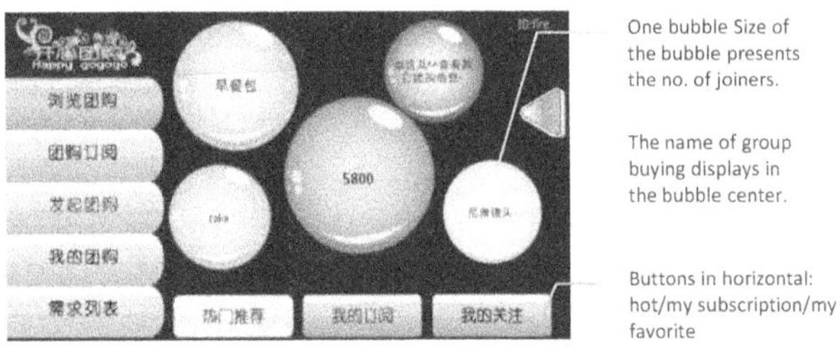

Figure 2. Browsing groups

In this paper, we attempt to reveal users' behaviors in group buying under the local context. Currently, local group buying is organized on community online forums, which are originally designed for user-generated posts. It does not well support group-buying-related actions such as group publishing, management, and statistics for initiators, and following, joining, and quitting for joiners. We thus developed a prototype system named "HappyGo" on the mobile devices to support local group buying. We believe HappyGo to be a better platform to support local group buying. First, it supports the aforementioned group-buying-related features. Second, HappyGo leverages the mobile devices to provide seamless communication (e.g., in-system chatting, SMS, and phone call) and faster information dissemination (e.g., real-time notifications when a new group matches users' shopping interests). Figs. 1 and 2 show the user interface (UI) of HappyGo.

We deployed HappyGo in a company campus in Beijing, China. During a one-month pilot test from May 2010 to June 2010, 318 users had tried out this service. We analyzed the activity log from the server after the trial, together with online questionnaire survey and focus group study. In order to compare with online group buying, we also crawled and analyzed more than 30,000 daily deals from hundreds of online group buying websites in a 3-month period.

We have two findings that distinguish local group buying from other forms of group buying: First, all three types of initiators (i.e., small merchants, proxies, and normal users) exist in HappyGo, which creates an economic circle to provide financial benefits to diverse types of users. Second, HappyGo is used as a group-buying-oriented social medium. Socializing itself could become one of the purposes for joiners to participate in group buying.

RELATED WORK

Group buying dates back to as early as 1860s in the form of "buying club" [1, 14], which is an appropriate offline group buying standard by our definition. This form remained largely unchanged until the Internet era. Mobshop, Mercata, Letsbuyit are pioneer online group buying websites that emerged at the end of the 20th century [8]. Most of them did not survive the burst of the Dot-com bubble. A few years later, the online group buying came back with greater success from websites such as Groupon [6] and Carrot-mob [2]. In the US, Groupon has over 35 million active users since its launch in 2008. In China, more than 5000 [4] daily deal websites exist at the time of this writing.

Most existing works on group buying study the theoretical business model and users' behavior. Chen et al. [3] investigates the motivation behind users' enthusiasm toward online group buying, including the dominant participant group, the most purchased items, and significant factors. Kauffman et al. [7] studied the relationship between the current group size and the purchasing decision of a potential buyer. They also found that more orders will be placed right before and after the price drop point and at the end of a trading period. Sheu et al. [10] have found that the past online shopping experience of a consumer would directly affect his/her decision-making. Surprisingly, the consumers who are willing to engage in a money-saving group buying are usually the ones with higher incomes.

Most of the above works are based on questionnaire survey and interviews, which lacks realistic context. We base our study on realistic data from a field trial and online group buying websites, with the hope to provide practical insights in this area.

Existing e-commerce websites, including online group buying websites, leverage social interactions to facilitate shopping. They encourage users to share their past shopping experience in the form of comments and ratings to help other users make shopping decisions [11, 13]. We found in our study that local group buying could be used as a social medium. Socializing could be one of the purposes for users to participate in group buying.

Few existing works study local group buying. Perhaps the most relevant reference is [12], where Tan *et al.* compares online and offline group buying in terms of users' technology readiness, social capital, merchandize category, reasons for group buying, etc. The authors conclude that online group buying is better in meeting shoppers' needs. We believe that local group buying complements online group buying by providing users with both financial and social benefits.

FINDINGS

Overview of Happy-Go Usage

As previously mentioned, 318 users participated in the field study according to the log data. 237 users joined or initiated group buying activities at least once. Among them, 52 users created 112 group buying activities. The average number of joiners per group was 7.6 (std. deviation 1.25), and the largest group had 77 joiners. 201 users had joined buying groups at least once. The other 81 users logged in to browse only. On average, a participant created 0.35 buying groups and joined 2.67 buying groups. Given the one-month period, we conclude that HappyGo had been actively used by the participants.

HappyGo is effectively used by three types of initiators for financial benefits

In offline group buying, most groups are initiated by one of the joiners, whereas proxy is the only type of initiator in online group buying. In HappyGo, we find all three types of initiators (i.e., merchant, proxy, and joiner).

There are three strawberry groups initiated by a user whose family owns a small strawberry plantation. He has sold strawberries to colleagues for several years. Before HappyGo, He sells to colleagues in nearby teams. He acknowledges that HappyGo helps increase the sales volume by a large margin. Another *merchant* initiator uses HappyGo to advertise her online shop. She says, "Actually I don't care how many people finally join the group … They noticed my online shop, that's good enough".

We observe that such merchants are mostly individual or family-owned small businesses. They serve for a small number of customers due to limited resources, and rely almost solely on word-of-mouth advertisement. Thus they usually target at returning customers from the same local community. Online group buying websites are not suitable for them as their capacities and visibilities are far below the requirement of those websites. HappyGo pools together the targeted customers of those small businesses, so as to attract them to initiate group buying in HappyGo. Another benefit is the saving of logistic cost as "I can finish all the transactions in one delivery as all the customers are in the same building", said by the initiator of the strawberry groups.

Proxy initiators also appear in HappyGo. The proxy is a normal HappyGo user who has a close relationship with a merchant. For example, one initiator organizes group buying on "Chinese dried dates" in HappyGo. The goods are provided by her roommate. This group successfully attracts 45 joiners. And the initiator receives monetary reward from her roommate afterwards. As usual, proxy is always motivated by the commission fee to explore possibilities to connect merchants with new customers. So it is not surprising to see proxy-initiated group buying in HappyGo.

Joiner-initiated groups are also common in HappyGo. For example, many users initiate lunch groups to enjoy a 25% discount from the company cafeteria if the group size reaches 4. Another user-initiated group conducts purchase in an online clothes store to enjoy the free shipping after the sales volume reaches a threshold.

We see many joiner-initiated groups in HappyGo for two reasons. From the joiners' perspective, they feel comfortable to join the groups initiated by other joiners. All participants share a common background, i.e., colleagues. It leads to a certain level of trust amongst users. From an initiators' perspective, they have some knowledge of other users in terms of the shopping interests because they share the same context. Taking group lunch as an example, almost everyone in the company prefers to have lunch within the office building due to limited break time at noon. Before a user initiates a lunch group, she knows there is a good chance to attract enough joiners. Such pre-knowledge reduces the perceived risk of the initiators to encourage more joiner-initiated groups.

We observed that, as an open platform, HappyGo attracts all three types of initiators to pursue financial benefits. It builds an economic circle in the community to benefit local merchants, proxies, and normal users.

HappyGo is used as group-buying-oriented social medium

In addition to financial benefits, joiners are also found to apply HappyGo for social benefits. We observed three patterns.

First, emotional communications among participants are observed in HappyGo. The joiners often express their feelings towards the initiators in the message board during the group buying session. For example, both compliments like: "You're so generous to help", and criticisms like "Just close the group if you are not serious …" are posted. It is a natural social interaction as the joiners know the initiator is a person. In online group buying, joiners perceive the initiator as a virtual entity so that such emotional expressions are rare.

Second, HappyGo is used by some joiners purely as a social platform. For example, someone proposes a group for "testing how many people know me in this building". The initiator asks others to join if they know him. Both the initiator and the joiners treat it as a fun experience.

Third, HappyGo offers a new opportunity for joiners to extend social networks. Merchandizes posted in HappyGo were categorized and compared with those in online group buying websites. While some categories like food and electronic devices appear frequently in both HappyGo and online group buying websites, we observe one category which is unique, and also the top category in HappyGo: *lunch together*. 37 groups for lunch together are created, which constitutes 1/3 of all groups. During the one-month trial period, at least one lunch together activity happens every working day.

Lunch together is a social activity for most people to exchange information and enhance social bonds. People usually have lunch with close friends and colleagues. People seldom *extend* their social network during lunch. However with HappyGo, offline social gatherings, like having lunch together, can be linked with group buying; since all joiners of a lunch together group share the same economic purpose (for a 25% discount at the company cafeteria), they now have a good "starting point" to meet new people. Many interviewees recognize lunch together helps them get to know new people and make new friends. "It's very natural to build a relationship with people working in the same company…" "We have a lot to discuss during lunch even we never know each other before…"

During the trial, we pose little limitation on how HappyGo can be used. The above observations suggest that group buying can be used as a social medium in the local context. *Socializing itself becomes the purpose*.

CONCLUSION

In this paper, we explore the characteristics of local group buying which has not been well recognized before. We developed a mobile service called "HappyGo" to support local group buying and deployed it in an office building for one month.

We have two findings that distinguish local group buying from other forms of group buying: First, all three types of initiators (i.e., small merchants, proxies, and normal users) exist in HappyGo, which creates an economic circle to provide financial benefits to diverse types of users. Second, HappyGo is used as a group-buying-oriented social medium, which provides users with social benefits in addition to economic values.

ACKNOWLEDGMENTS

We are deeply appreciative to the coordinator and other reviewers for their constructive comments. We also thank the other members of NRC Beijing on the HappyGo system development, and all the participants in the trial use.

REFERENCES

1. Bullock, Roy J., The Early History of The Great Atlantic & Pacific Tea Company. *Harvard Business Review* (3)11 (1933), 289-298
2. Carrot-Mob. http://en.wikipedia.org/wiki/Carrotmob
3. Chen, W.Y. and Wu, P.H., Factors affecting consumers' motivation in online group buyers, *Proc. of IEEE IIH-MSP* (2010), 708-711
4. GouTuan: A Chinese group buying navigation site. http://www.goutuan.net
5. Group buying board of a large community online forum. http://jc.hlgnet.com/
6. Groupon. http://www.groupon.com
7. Kauffman, Robert J., Bin Wang, New Buyers' Arrival Under Dynamic Pricing Market Microstructure: The case of Group-Buying Discounts on the Internet, *Proc. of the 34th Hawaii International Conference on System Sciences*(2001), 663-666
8. Kauffman, Robert J., and Bing Wang. Bid together, buy together: On the efficacy of group-buying business models in internet-based selling ,(2001) http://misrc.umn.edu/workingpapers/fullpapers/2001/0110_051601.pdf
9. Lin, Cheng-Hung, The Effects of Initiator's Trust and Perceived Risk on Online Group-Buying Behavior (2006), Available at http://en.scientificcommons.org/17901087
10. Sheu, Jyh-Jian, Yao-Wen Chang, and Ko-Tsung Chu, Applying decision tree data mining for online group buying consumers' behavior, *International Journal of Electronic Customer Relationship Management*, (2)2(2008), 140-157
11. S. Guo, M. Wang, J. Leskovec, The Role of Social Networks in Online Shopping: Information Passing, Price of Trust, and Consumer Choice, *Proc. of ACM EC* (2011), 157-166
12. Tan, W.K. and Tan, Y.J., Online or offline group buying? *Proc. of IEEE FSKD* (2010), 2853-2857
13. Y.A.Kim and J. Srivastava, Impact of Social Influence in E-Commerce Decision Making, *Proc. of ACM ICEC* (2007), 293-302
14. Y. Jia and Q. Wu, The differences between Groupon and other group-buying intermediaries: from transactional and relational coordination perspectives, Master thesis. http://www.iei.liu.se/program/smio/722a31/file-archive/1.273541/YijingJia_QiongshenWu_ThedifferencesbetweenGrouponandothergroup-buyingintermediariesfromtransactionalandrelationalcoordinationperspectives.pdf

Culturally Based Design: Embodying Trans-Surface Interaction in Rummy

Andruid Kerne[1], William A. Hamilton[1], Zachary O. Toups[1,2]
[1]Interface Ecology Lab | Department of Computer Science & Engineering
[2]Crisis Response Innovative Technologies Lab | Texas Center for Applied Technology / TEEX Disaster Preparedness & Response
Texas A&M University
{andruid, bill}@ecologylab.net, toupsz@tamu.edu

ABSTRACT

We present culturally based design (CBD), a new paradigm for designing embodied natural user interaction (NUI) with digital information by drawing on customary ways that people use physical objects. CBD coalesces experiences, practices, and embodied mental models of pre-digital activities as a basis for the design of interactive systems. We apply CBD to address *trans-surface interaction*, the manipulation of information artifacts from one device to another. We develop Trans-Surface Rummy, because the game involves highly dynamic combinations of turn taking and non-linear out of turn play, while transferring information artifacts to and from private and social surfaces. Through the CBD process, we create the *trans-surface wormhole*, an embodied interface technique. We investigate the trans-surface wormhole's efficacy and other aspects of culturally based design with young students, and with elderly members of our local bridge club. We derive implications for the design of trans-surface interaction, and more broadly, from the process of CBD. We initiate a research agenda for trans-surface interaction.

Author Keywords

design models, culture, natural user interaction, sensemaking, affordances, games, elderly, embodiment

ACM Classification Keywords

H.5.2 Information Interfaces & Presentation: Interaction styles, Theory and methods

General Terms

Design; Theory.

INTRODUCTION

We develop culturally based design (CBD), a new paradigm for designing embodied natural user interaction (NUI) with digital information by drawing on customary ways that people use physical objects. Abowd and Mynatt pose a research challenge for ubiquitous computing: to address our desire for natural interfaces that facilitate rich communication between humans and computation, support common forms of human expression, and leverage our implicit actions in the world [1]. To answer this ubicomp NUI challenge, CBD invokes the *engaged familiarity* that Heidegger uses to describe our everyday dealings in the world [11]. Through the implicit mandate of *in-order-to*, people manipulate equipment and materials that are *ready-to-hand* to perform activities and accomplish goals.

CBD draws engaged familiarity from pre-digital contexts into computing to define a design method for answering the ubicomp NUI challenge. A panoply of new technologies for NUI have become available, including but not limited to stylus, capacitive multi-touch (iPhone), FTIR [9], ZeroTouch [16], and Kinect. The design of new interaction paradigms lags. When new modalities of interactive computing are introduced, it can be hard for designers and engineers to know what to do with them. How can designers formulate new approaches? How does one design the "killer app"? How do we engage diverse populations, such as the elderly?

Many interactive systems are built to improve productivity on tasks [24]. To meet the ubicomp challenge, CBD inverts the task-centered design paradigm. Task-centered design is valuable for addressing needs and requirements. CBD alternatively seeks "interesting" human activities that can serve as the basis for deriving new NUI design ideas. The CBD process identifies activities to represent with NUI systems based on how people use culturally-based embodied mental models to function in them through ready-to-hand action. Criteria include engagement in rich embodied interaction, information exchange, communication, and expression. Interesting activities, for example card play, may even seem frivolous. CBD leverages underlying repositories of experience and practice, which people routinely access through engaged familiarity. By using NUI technologies to mimic ready-to-hand embodied practices, CBD carries the pre-digital world forward. The knowledge derived by building these systems has the potential to inform new interaction techniques.

Tabletops are common artifacts across cultures, differentiated by situated particularities of form, use, function, and custom. People put many things onto tables, enacting social, informational, and physical functions. A CBD approach seeks pre-digital tabletop activities to represent with NUI technologies, as a source of design ideas. Cards, while less universal, have been widely used on tabletops. Card play dates back to the 13th century in China and Japan, and the 14th in Europe, with subsequent practice in India, Russia, and North America, including among Native Americans [10]. Cultural functions include divination, gambling, and recreation. Card play is practiced across generations, making it a resonant cultural source for interaction design. Cards function as units of information, expression, and social interaction; they afford hiding and revealing information [22]. They are manipulated with and in hands, on and across tabletops. The present research investigates card play as a means for addressing the design of what we christen as *trans-surface interaction*, in which people manipulate information artifacts across devices as part of sensemaking, ideation, and play.

To instantiate CBD, and investigate the design space of trans-surface interaction, we develop and evaluate a system for collaborative card play, Trans-Surface Rummy. A tabletop iPad functions as a shared workspace. Handheld iPhones function as private information spaces. Through a user study in our local community bridge club, the CBD process draws us to formulate stealth education methods for teaching the elderly about technology.

We present cultural and cognitive framing and background for culturally based and trans-surface interaction design. We develop Trans-Surface Rummy, including the design of symmetric subspaces of the shared social surface, of a new, asymmetric trans-surface interaction technique, the wormhole, and of a private hand workspace. We develop a mixed methods evaluation, with college students and elderly card players, including a fluidity analysis methodology for validating the trans-surface wormhole design. We develop implications for trans-surface interaction design, and more broadly, for CBD.

BACKGROUND

We integrate prior work involving culture, embodied mental models, trans-surface interaction design, and stealth learning. We then provide a brief description of the game of Contract Rummy, focusing on aspects of game play that make it interesting as a target for culturally based design.

Culture

One side of Heidegger's engaged familiarity is rooted in culture. Kroeber and Kluckholn assembled concepts and definitions of culture, categorizing them as descriptive, historical, normative, and psychological [14]. Descriptive definitions address knowledge, beliefs, systems of thoughts, traditions, and customs. They include artifacts, technologies, and techniques. Historical definitions emphasize social heritage and tradition, the evolution of artifacts and processes, and everything that can be communicated. Normative concepts emphasize customs, traditions, attitudes, ideas, and symbols that constitute behavior patterns, forming a way of life. They include acquired or cultivated behavior, feeling, and thought. Psychological definitions are said to emphasize adjustment, such as the equipment and techniques by which people try to attain their ends, and standardized ideas, attitudes, and habits developed with respect to the satisfaction of human needs.

Geertz developed the concept of *situated knowledge*, implying that the layers of meaning that characterize what people know are deeply rooted in the particular places where they live, and concomitant people, relationships, roles, practices, artifacts, and experiences [6]. Suchman used the situated knowledge framework as the basis for the notion of situated action, fundamental for artificial intelligence, robotics, and context-aware HCI [26]. Star developed an ecological perspective on how computing infrastructures are situated in culture and practice [25]. Culturally embedded computing investigates how digital technology is situated in culture [23]. CBD inverts this paradigm, drawing on customary manipulations of non-digital technologies, and associated behavior patterns, processes, and movements, to design embodied interaction based on cultural practice.

Like other researchers, Thorensen uses specific situated contexts to drive integrated participatory action and research [27]. This is inherently valuable. As a methodology, CBD differs in its prescription to choose particular cultural practices to investigate specifically so knowledge situated therein can also contribute to human-centered computing in *other* contexts.

The 'workaday world' CSCW design paradigm prescribed the importance of going outside of formal work to wholly incorporate, "a melange of motivations, goals, practices, and social habits," including those, "not easily segmented into a series of tasks" [17]. This is kindred to the present approach, but its orientation nonetheless was based in work. *The present research emphasizes the need to investigate significant activities and artifacts from the full panoply of human experience, across our cultural gene/meme pool, as pre-digital instances of ready-to-hand knowledge that can inform NUI design solutions to the ubicomp challenge.* The rummy context serves as a culturally based source for designing trans-surface interaction. We choose the game Contract Rummy, because cards are transferred from private hands to and from a social tabletop through turn taking and more spontaneous interaction in which players override turns, and also because one author grew up playing it across generations of family and friends.

Embodied Mental Models

Heidegger's ready-to-hand is a phenomenological touchstone for embodiment. We connect affordance, mental models, and processes of cognitive restructuring to generally address CBD, and more specifically frame the rummy context, tabletops, cards, and trans-surface interaction. Cognitive restructuring processes are important, because they can play a significant role in ideation and the formation of mental models.

Another side of engaged familiarity connects cognition and action. We relate Gibson's concept of *affordance*, actionable properties of physical objects [7]. A person situated in an environment integrates embodied ready-to-hand knowledge with perceivable properties to manipulate actionable equipment and materials, i.e. affordances. CBD draws on cultural stores of knowledge that invoke "in-order-to" and thus inform ready-to-hand manipulation of equipment and materials, culturally situated as artifacts, through their perceived physical properties.

A key component of embodiment is how a human being is physically situated in a spatial environment. Kirsh analyzes ways in which people intelligently use space [13]. People use spatial arrangement to externalize the cognitive state of a

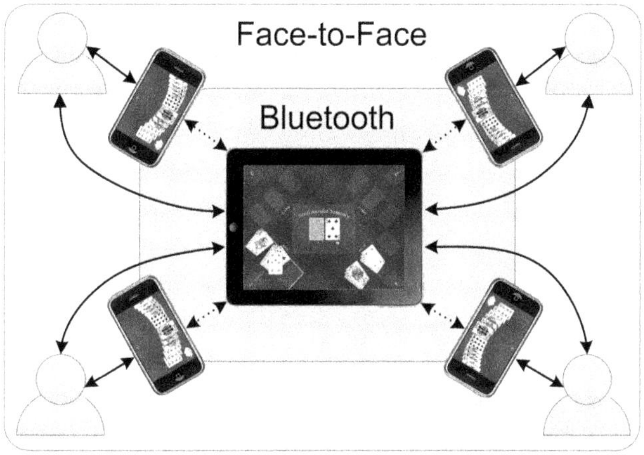

Figure 1. The game system incorporates private iPhone surfaces and a central social iPad surface. Dotted lines indicate digital communication. Solid lines represent touch and sight

task, assisting internal computation. Kirsh differentiates between informational and physical structuring by function: informational structuring serves the purpose of cueing cognitive events and processes inherent to a task; physical structuring constrains, to prevent specific actions. Restructuring occurs naturally to achieve both of these equally important functions, to externalize cognition during a task.

Glenberg shows that mental models are embodied by how they are experienced in situated contexts [8]. People combine affordances, knowledge, and goals through *meshing* processes. The affordances of an object are a function of the context in which they are perceived. How a person-as-body is situated with respect to affordances and larger environmental factors informs this process. As goals and the environment change, new possibilities for action, and associated mental models, emerge.

Cognitive restructuring, in which a problem space is transformed into a cognitive schema that supports the formation of solutions, is an important stage of sensemaking [21]. Embodied forms of physical information artifacts support restructuring by affording manipulations that represent schema transformations. Interaction designers can use restructuring strategies to inform design by mimicking and supporting them in digital designs. An important part of informationally structuring objects is to highlight and hide affordances to manage what information is readily perceived [13]. We investigate the affordances of physical and digital playing cards, with regard to support for informational structuring, cognitive restructuring, and mental model evolution.

Trans-Surface Interaction Design

An issue for trans-surface interaction is the design of mappings of affordances and feedback for moving objects across surfaces. In physical reality, an object moves continuously from one surface to another. In the digital medium, surfaces are inherently disconnected.

Prior techniques for trans-surface interaction were developed without a situated use context. In Rekimoto's seminal direct manipulation Pick-and-Drop technique, an information object, or state, is exchanged by using a stylus to touch one surface, picking up the information, and then touching another surface with the same stylus. [20]. Hinckley's stitching enables using a stylus to drag an object across tablets [12]. The present CBD approach defines the trans-surface interaction mappings of wormholes based on card playing practice.

Recent research seeks physical continuity between surfaces [2]. Computer vision was used to track interaction above surfaces; projection fills in the space between. These solutions are cumbersome and costly. We hypothesize that by simply designing transitions that contextually mimic physical transitions, without visual continuity, it is possible to economically achieve fluid trans-surface interaction.

Stealth Education & Engaging the Elderly

The CBD method brought us into card games, which emerged as a means for involving the elderly with new technologies, because cards are an old means of entertainment. Stealth education uses games as a means to teach, by making learning a by-product of engagement in game mechanics [3]. We pose a different form of stealth education, teaching how new technology works through culturally based interaction. Seniors bring their engaged familiarity with a cultural activity, card play, into their experience of technology. They are confident when cards are ready-to-hand; this confidence helps them forget any fear of technology.

Card play has been used as an activity context to expose elderly to touch-based games [4]. The game involved a single human playing against a computer agent. An analogy based on physical interactions with cards created intuitive interactions. The researchers found their game helped older, inexperienced users become acquainted with digital technology. The present research adds the social dimension, engaging co-located players in trans-surface interaction to play cards. Prior findings, that seniors prefer co-located interaction [5], coincide.

Leonardi et al. recently suggested that touch-based gestural interfaces are suitable for adoption by the elderly, as a result of their physical directness [15]. Like Turner [29], we find value in considering the role of familiarity in people's experiences of computing systems. We synthesize these findings, integrating Heidegger, to use engaged familiarity as a basis for designing trans-surface interaction. The activity's grounding in culture serves, for the elderly, as a gateway for gaining confidence. Researchers can build on the resulting skills and confidence to potentially engage the elderly in other activities, such as health monitoring, with the new technologies.

Contract Rummy

Contract Rummy[1] is an interesting context for trans-surface CBD because of its *game mechanics*, actions taken by players within the rules of the game [22]. These game mechanics involve highly dynamic combinations of turn taking and non-linear out of turn play, rapid transfer of cards between private and social surfaces, and iterative reorganization of the private hand to form strategy. These operations involve intensive social interaction, particularly at key junctures of play.

[1]The present system uses the rules for the rummy variant, Contract Rummy; by "rummy", we specifically mean Contract Rummy.

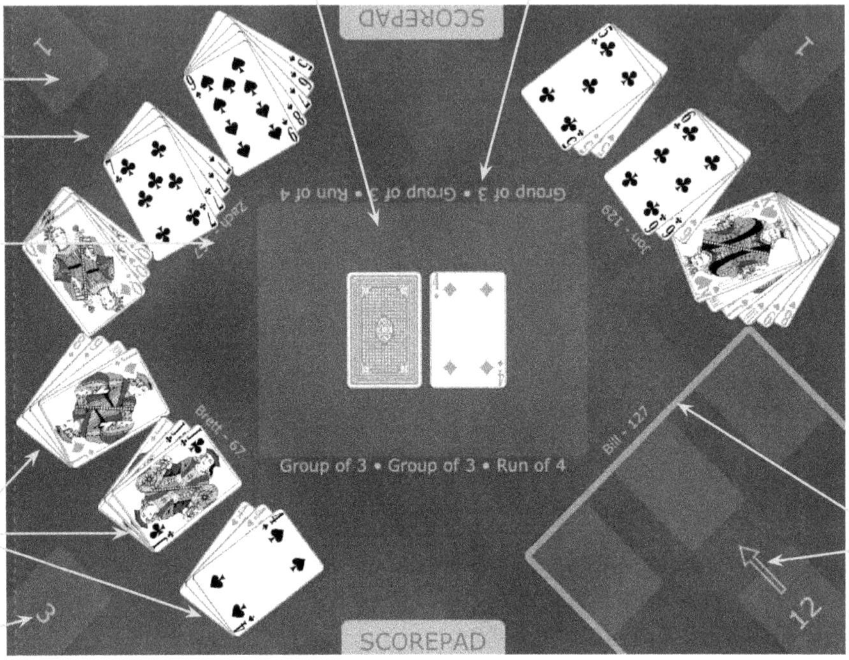

Figure 2. The social surface: a shared central space, and up to 4 symmetric individual player subspaces, at the corners. Each player subspace displays feedback, such as name, score, and cards remaining. When a player lays down, her melds are fanned out within her subspace.

Contract Rummy is played with two 54 playing card decks [19]. It requires players to construct *melds*: either a run or group. A *run* is consecutively ranked cards of the same suit (e.g. ♣4, ♣5, ♣6). A *group* is a set of same ranked cards (e.g. ♣3, ♠3, ◇3). A Joker can represent any card in a meld.

In play, a *round* consists of several turns. For each round, a *contract* specifies required melds. Undealt cards become the *stock*. A card initially drawn from the stock initiates the *discard pile*. Players take turns until one has no cards; players are penalized by points for their remaining cards. At the start of a turn, a player draws the top card from the discard or stock pile, attempting to privately construct contract melds. A player builds melds incrementally, over several turns, by informationally structuring cards in her hand.

When a player finishes her turn, she discards a card face up on the discard pile. In order to further remove cards from her hand, a player must 'lay down': building the melds set forth in the round's contract, then placing them on the table. As a player lays down, their melded cards become visible in the social space. On her turn, a player who previously laid down may 'lay off' cards by extending any existing public melds.

Contract Rummy play is characterized by unpredictable non-linear flows of control, involving Jokers and buying a card. The dynamic non-linear game mechanics necessitate mechanisms for fluid transfer of cards between surfaces. Some actions can be taken out-of-turn. These mechanics heighten social awareness and engagement. If a Joker is laid down, a player can substitute for it the card the Joker represents. This can occur rapidly, at any point during the game. Immediately following a discard, before the next player draws, any player can "buy" the top card from the discard pile. The buyer takes the top cards from the discard and stock piles as penalty for acting out-of-turn, placing both cards in her hand.

TRANS-SURFACE RUMMY

The Trans-Surface Rummy game system is constructed as a distributed network of mobile devices: an Apple iPad and 2–4 iPhones (Figure 1). The iPad serves as a common surface where social game information is presented and manipulated. Each iPhone serves as a private surface for the hand of an individual player.

Devices are connected by a Bluetooth Public Area Network. By communicating over Bluetooth, the system can operate in any environment, without need for an external network. The devices communicate via the open source Object Oriented Distributed Semantic Services (OODSS) framework [28]. OODSS facilitates serialization and distribution of information artifacts as message objects over the network.

We present the culturally based design of the social surface and the trans-surface wormhole information artifact transfer technique. We investigate the design of mechanisms for informationally structuring cards on the private surface.

Social Surface Design: Symmetric Subspaces

The social surface is composed of 4 individual player subspaces. These subspaces are situated symmetrically at the corners of the iPad, with the draw and discard piles at the center (Figure 2). Corner-based symmetry was chosen, in lieu of an asymmetric edge oriented layout, to create congruent player spaces around the iPad surface's 4:3 aspect ratio. Players lay down melds in their subspaces, affording easy view around the table. This structure is physically embodied, in that it situates each player and her private hand space with her social subspace, forming a basis for the trans-surface interaction design presented in the next section. An initialization dialog situates each player and their private surface iPhone at a particular corner subspace of the social surface.

Wormholes for Asymmetric Trans-Surface Interaction

Players transfer individual cards between private and social surfaces to execute core mechanics, such as discarding and drawing. We develop an interaction model for transfers based on the cultural practice of holding cards in a fan, and drawing and placing them when transferring to and from the table.

When playing card games that require managing many cards, common practice is for players to hold their hand in a fan. The player arranges cards in the fan to encode meaning and relationships. The physical shape of the fan affords transferring cards only in and out at the top (Figure 3). This embodied structure informs the design of trans-surface wormholes.

We design trans-surface interaction by mimicking pre-digital play. To move a card to the social surface, a player begins by *flicking* it through the top of the private surface, out of her hand. The card appears face down in the player's *trans-surface wormhole*, her corner region subspace of the social surface (see Figure 2). Spatial proximity embodies its connection with the private surface (hand). When a card reaches the wormhole face down from the private surface, the player must touch and move it across the social surface to play it where s/he wants, simultaneously revealing the previously private card. This technique is intended to be executed as one fluid transition, as with pre-digital cards. *Hypothesis: players will experience moving cards through the trans-surface wormhole as fluid, despite the lack of physical continuity.*

In reverse, from social to private, a player moves a card across the surface to her trans-surface wormhole. The card is sent to the player's private surface, animated as sliding in from above, into the hand. Embodied and culturally based design of the wormhole between social surface and private hand motivates our hypothesis that participants will fluidly engage its affordances and execute this interaction ready-to-hand.

The trans-surface wormhole hybridizes prior "wormhole" [32], and surface "stitching" [12] techniques, motivated by the mechanics of drawing and discarding playing cards. Unlike prior designs, source and destination spaces are asymmetric. The private surface's top edge is connected to a spatially oriented target GUI component on the social surface. The modeled interaction with physical cards is likewise asymmetric: the mechanics of inserting and removing a card out of a fan differ from placing a card on or picking up from a table.

Mental Models in the Private Hand

Each player builds a mental model about the cards in her hand, based on her goals in the context of the game. The mental model includes information about particular cards and their relationships to others in the player's hand, on the table, and in other players' hands. The player makes decisions based on this model to achieve goals.

In a traditional game, these relationships are embodied through the player's composition of cards in her hand. Typically, this composition is linear. The player arranges cards in ways that make relationships among them easier to perceive, embodying her understanding. Sometimes, we have observed more complex arrangement techniques (Figure 4).

Our private interface design affords recognizing and building potential melds. Players organize cards by moving them between two different spaces, each affording different manipulation interactions: a potential melds area of cards deemed essential to strategy, and an unmelded hand of other cards. Each space features mechanisms to help organize the cards.

Alas, the design breaks from the embodied affordances of how cards are organized pre-digitally. What is lost is the fluid flexibility afforded by composition of physical playing cards. In the evaluation, we will find that this flexibility is integral to sensemaking with playing cards.

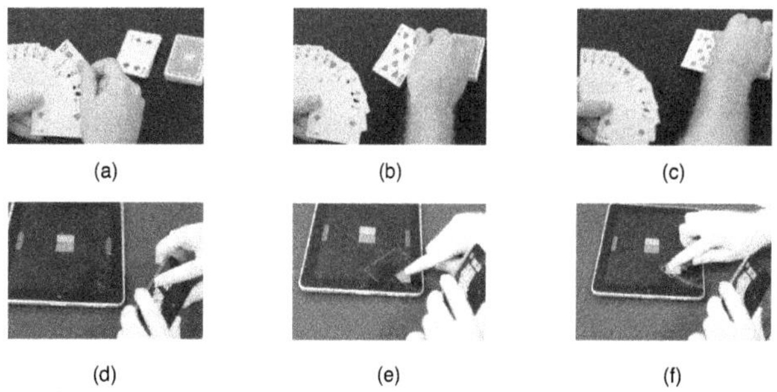

Figure 3. To transfer a physical card from to the table, the player begins by (a) selecting it and removing by upper edge from the fan of cards in the hand; (b) (with fluid transition) moving the card toward the table; and (c) placing the card on the table. Using the trans-surface wormhole technique: (d) selecting the card and sliding off the top of the phone; (e) transitioning to table to continue interaction; and (f) moving the card to the desired location on the social surface.

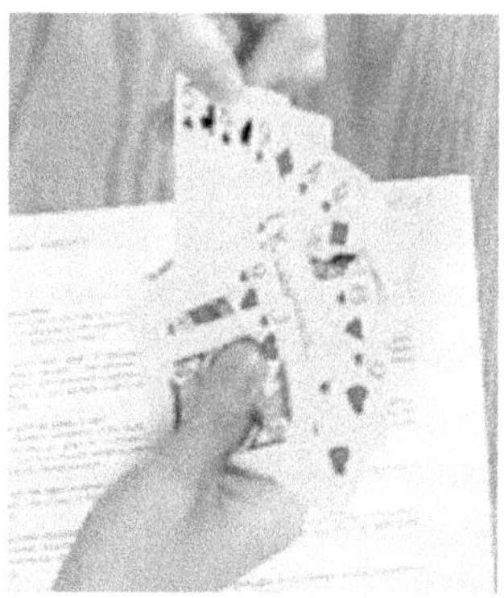

Figure 4. Participant informationally structuring their private hand with physical cards. In the bottom row of cards, the player has a complete run that she intends to play later in the game. In the upper row, the player holds several incomplete melds.

sort order button

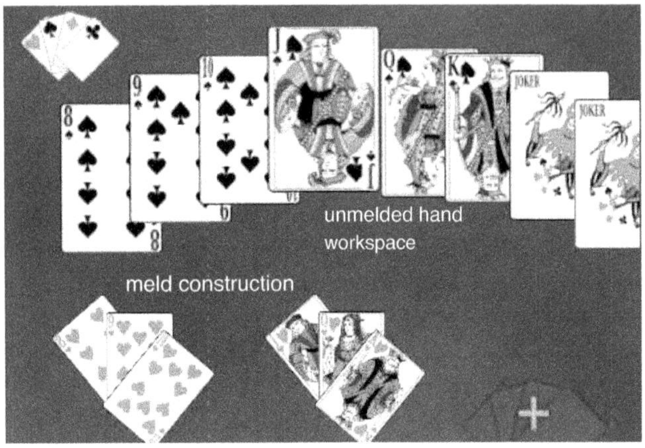

meld creation icon

Figure 5. Workspaces and controls within the private surface.

Meld Construction Workspace

The bottom of the private surface is reserved for the meld construction workspace (Figure 5, bottom). At any time, a player may construct up to four potential melds. When these melds satisfy the contract, she can play them during her turn, to lay down.

A player creates a new meld by dragging a card onto the meld creation icon. Construction continues by dragging cards into existing melds. Each potential meld is sorted automatically. Cards missing from runs are represented as gaps in the fan. A player enlarges a meld by tapping it, affording dragging cards back into the unmelded hand or directly to other melds.

When a player believes she has satisfied the contract, she specifies melds to send to the social space, toggling them using a swipe gesture. Once she has selected sufficient melds, the lay down button appears. When touched, melds are transferred from the private space to the social surface. Cards in unused melds remain in the player's hand.

Unmelded Hand Workspace

The private unmelded hand workspace stores other cards, serving as a tool for recognizing potential melds (upper half of Figure 5). Initially, all of a player's cards are here. To facilitate building and invoking mental models of strategy, this space sorts constituent cards in multiple configurations. A player toggles between sorting criteria by tapping the sort order button (upper-left in Figure 5): rank then suit, or suit then rank. These configurations afford recognition of potential groups or runs, respectively.

Users can also swipe across the unmelded hand workspace to select a focus card, which is displayed 10% larger. The focus card is displayed in the center, enabling the user to arrange fewer cards on one side of the focus, resulting in more space between them. This simulates how a player might adjust the spacing of physical cards in her hand.

EVALUATION

We conducted a continuous iterative design process of prototyping and formative user studies. Subsequently, we performed a summative user study, to evaluate the wormhole, interaction, and culturally based design in Trans-Surface Rummy. We observed participants playing Contract Rummy using the trans-surface system and pre-digital decks of cards. We observed a total of 24 participants, six groups of four. Participants were recruited as groups of friends or at least acquaintances. Fourteen players had previously played some variation of rummy. Eight participants were recruited from local bridge clubs. These participants had a mean an age of 73 (SD = 7.67). The remaining 16 were university students (mean age 22; SD = 1.90). Participants received 25 USD gift cards as compensation.

Participants played three rounds of rummy using pre-digital cards, and three rounds using the trans-surface system. This order of this independent variable was counterbalanced across groups. Each participant completed a pre- and post-questionnaire. They were video-recorded while playing (30 fps). Video records were analyzed to derive qualitative and quantitative data. Before playing, participants were read a script of the rules. They were invited to ask questions.

Fluidity Analysis Methodology

We devised a coding scheme to evaluate the design of the trans-surface wormhole technique. We coded the video, categorizing each occurrence of a player transferring a card from private to social surface, or in the physical condition from hand to table, as fluid or non-fluid. We characterize fluid transfers as those in which players smoothly transition from flick off the top of the private surface to moving their hand to the social surface to play the card. In other occurrences, participants hesitated for more than than 3 frames of video (100 ms), or moved their hand toward their body or face between flicking and starting to move their hand to the social surface. These two conditions were classified as non-fluid. We coded the physical condition in the same manner. Transfers that could not be seen in the video, were initiated by the proctor present at the study, failed to result in the card being transferred to the table, or did not result in the card being played on the social surface, were not counted.

There were 3 coders; each analyzed 4 groups. Each group was analyzed by 2 coders. From these codes we computed the percent of transfers that were executed fluidly for each player in each round. Inter-rater reliability was computed as the Pearson's Correlation Coefficient of fluidity ratings for each pair of coders (see Table 1). One participant is excluded from the results because it was unclear to coders if his interactions, in which he often used two hands, were fluid.

RESULTS

We use mixed methods to assess the efficacy of the culturally based design of the trans-surface interaction. We present qualitative and quantitative findings about the fluidity of trans-surface wormhole use. We compare results across the pre-digital and trans-surface conditions, young students versus

Coders	1&2	2&3	1&3	Mean
	0.81	0.85	0.87	0.84

Table 1. Coder pair inter-rater reliability scores.

the elderly, and with regard to early and later rounds of play. We present qualitative data regarding the design of the private hand interface for organizing player's cards, with regard to fluidity and embodied support for mental model formation. We report on the experiences of elderly participants, with regard to comfort, enjoyment, learning, and fluidity.

Trans-Surface Wormhole Fluidity

In the trans-surface and pre-digital conditions, we found on average 78% and 93% respectively of interactions were executed fluidly. A *t*-test indicated the difference was statistically significant ($p < 0.001$). In the trans-surface condition, we found a correlation of 0.38 ($p < 0.002$) between round number and the average percent of fluid transitions. In round one, 68% of transitions were executed fluidly versus 86% in round three. This indicates fast learning of the trans-surface wormhole technique as a fluid embodied trans-surface interaction.

In the trans-surface condition, elderly participants executed only 67% of interactions fluidly, while the younger student participants executed 82% fluidly, a significant difference ($p < 0.002$). No statistically significant difference based on age group was observed in the pre-digital condition.

Sometimes, in both the trans-surface and pre-digital conditions, non-fluid interactions occurred when players initiated a transfer and then had second thoughts. Participants left the card on the social surface while reconsidering. In other cases, participants preparing to swap a card for a Joker would transfer a card to the social surface, then wait until their turn, to make sure they didn't get stuck with the Joker's high value. In such instances, participants used the affordances of card playing media to ready actions to be executed in the future. The NUI trans-surface wormhole afforded this embodied cognition in a manner similar to the all-physical cards.

We observed how players experienced the trans-surface interaction. In one instance, an elderly player demonstrated to another player how to initiate a card transfer by swiping her finger in the air in an arc much larger than the screen. This shows how she perceived the interaction as extending off of the device and into the space between surfaces. While a majority of the participants activated card transfers with their index fingers, we also observed participants use a thumb to slide cards off the top of phone in a gesture mimicking how cards are drawn from a fan. This suggests that for these participants, prior play with physical cards influenced trans-surface experiences.

We also observed elderly participants, before becoming familiar with the interactions, tap cards, as if they were buttons, trying to draw or discard them. We expect this was due to previous experience with interfaces in which the primary mode of interaction was activating buttons. More direct manipulation was not a form of interaction that elderly participants expected from digital interfaces. In contrast, we observed younger participants attempt to flick cards, expecting that the interface incorporated inertial simulation. The contrast in kinds of attempts shows differences in familiar digital interaction between younger and elderly participants.

Flexibility of the Private Hand

Qualitative and quantitative data indicate that players put high value on flexibility in arranging their private hands. While they appreciated the digital system's capability to automatically sort cards in the unmelded hand, they wanted to be able to customize its ordering, beyond the constraints of sort-by-rank or by-suit. We observed participants dragging cards in the unmelded hand across the array trying to place them in a new location. which did not work. When asked about the disadvantages of the digital game, participants reported:

> "Cards could be organized by players' preference, but doesn't allow for multiple options on say, two melds, to be easily discernible."
> "Hard to arrange hands."
> "I wish I could have moved my cards around in my hand instead of making the groups at the bottom."

Participants were also asked in the post-questionnaire, via a semantic differential, how strongly they agreed with the statement: "I could organize my hand to help me consider options," for the forms of rummy (1 = strongly disagree; 5 = strongly agree). A Wilcoxon signed ranks test indicated a significant difference between responses for trans-surface and pre-digital forms of the game ($p < 0.05$). The average result was a 3.66 ($SD = 1.04$) for trans-surface and a 4.33 ($SD = 0.816$) for pre-digital, indicating that indeed participants found the flexible arrangement capability of tangible cards more supportive of embodied cognition.

Experiences of the Elderly

All 8 elderly participants reported lack of experience using the iDevices. When asked if they were more comfortable after the study, participants reported a mean value of 3.75 ($SD = 1.38$), 5 being strongly agree and 1 strongly disagree. Elderly participants reported they enjoyed playing the digital form of the game with a mean value of 4.25 ($SD = 0.886$). There was no significant difference with their reported enjoyment of playing with physical cards. Student participants reported more enjoyment in playing the trans-surface form ($p < 0.001$).

In round 1 of the digital condition, there was no significant difference between the fluidity of elderly and younger players. In round 3, the elderly executed 74% of transfers fluidly, while students executed 92% fluidly; the difference was significant ($p < 0.05$). This suggests that initially younger players were as likely to stumble in fluid execution of the trans-surface interaction as were elderly players, but in later rounds, perhaps due to reduced motor dexterity or learning ability, the elderly did not execute the interactions as fluidly.

Several of the elderly expressed interest in the iDevices during the study. One participant asked the proctor to clarify what the devices were. Another said that they thought it would be fun to play with their grandchildren. One remarked, "It is fun, but who is going to actually have all of these [indicating the iDevices]". Another participant jokingly asked in the post survey, "Do we get iPhones now?" The findings show that the relative foreignness of the embodied NUI technologies to the elderly, as situated by CBD, was neither a barrier to interest and motivation, nor, by and large, to use.

IMPLICATIONS: TRANS-SURFACE INTERACTION DESIGN

We distill implications for design of two levels. Before raising general implications of CBD, we begin with 3 implications for trans-surface interaction design between private surfaces and a social tabletop. Two are related to fluidity: one involves the efficacy of the trans-surface wormhole technique, which substitutes cultural for physical continuity; the other involves the importance of enabling flexible arrangement. A third implication involves using embodied properties of physical space as a basis for situating related digital information.

Substitute Cultural for Physical Continuity

Trans-surface interfaces can indexically reference the physical continuity of pre-digital cultural contexts. The data validate the trans-surface wormhole's efficacy for fluid trans-surface interaction. Participants quickly learned to execute trans-surface transfer of a playing card by flicking it off the iPhone and smoothly transitioning to interact with it on the tabletop. They were not bothered by the absence of physical playing cards' continuity; they did not mind the gap between surfaces. Most participants quickly discovered and executed the wormhole for trans-surface interaction without explanation. The initial effect was not affected by age group. However, younger participants learned to be almost perfect, while the elderly did not learn as quickly. Future research will investigate whether practice over a longer time frame mitigates this.

Substituting culturally based continuity for physical continuity is a valuable design principle. The increasing ubiquity of multi-surface environments means people will want to integrate their use by moving information and distributing control. Lack of physical continuity in digital interactions can be overcome through experientially based conceptual schemas derived from engaged familiarity. We have shown that in context, trans-surface interactions can be designed to activate embodied mental models of fluid interactions. Users execute resulting NUI in the same fluid manner as pre-digital practice. Thus, designers can support fluidity without relying on costly modalities such as vision-based tracking and intermediate projection.

Contexts of trans-surface interaction vary. Documents in a meeting are handled differently than playing cards. Sheets may be ripped off a notepad and handed directly to a co-worker or copies dispersed collaboratively around a table from a pile. Business cards and photographs are more like playing cards. Perhaps their similar physical affordances will enable transfer of these techniques to other activities. In construing implications, it is important to abstract playing cards as units of information. People have been working with cards, documents and other information artifacts for ages. This history of interaction experiences serves as a repository of knowledge that can be leveraged by designers to create intuitive and fluid trans-surface interactions.

Enable Flexible Arrangement of Information Artifacts

One of the great affordances of physical information artifacts is the flexibility with which we may arrange them to informationally structure our environments. One lesson learned is the integrality of this characteristic. The provided computational mechanisms to aid in human recognition of melds did not, for users, offset loss of flexibility. Flexibility enables more complex and meaningful informational structuring.

Flexibility is deeply embedded in the cultural understanding not only of playing cards, but of physical objects in general. Kirsch found that people manage the spatial arrangements of physical objects to categorize, and simplify choice, perception, and internal computation [13]. Not supporting fluid spatial arrangement of playing cards contradicted our participants' embodied mental models, and in doing so hindered their ability to make sense of and operate their hands.

Because we used CBD to contextualize our investigation of trans-surface interaction in card play, we were able to realize the importance of flexible arrangement. If we had simply begun with transferring documents or business cards, we might not have considered it. Part of the evolution of card play has been the culturally based development of techniques for managing and making sense of information artifacts. These techniques have been optimized. Thus, computational aids, such as automatic sorting and organizing, must be implemented with manual overrides, keeping the user in control.

Interaction designers must take care in understanding culturally based practice. Sometimes the affordances of new media warrant significant change from practice with original media. However, this must be measured against starving the formation of embodied mental models and associated affordances that form the basis of physical interaction in-order-to.

Embodied Properties of Physical Space

Personal regions of social space and flicking cards off the top of the phone were designed based on embodied properties of physical space. Corner-based symmetry was effective for structuring each individual's social subspace, referencing the embodied positioning of users and their private surfaces. This delineated individual sensemaking on the social surface, where others can watch. The positioning of the stock and discard piles in the center gives all users symmetric access.

Similarly, embodied spatial relationships inform users' processes of mental model formation, understanding that cards afford flicking from a private phone to the trans-surface wormhole on the shared social surface. Players hold a fan of physical cards in one hand, and use the other to draw from the top. Flicking from the surface's top recontextualizes this tradition. The mental model of the trans-surface wormhole depends on spatial orientation, and proximity of the user's body, hands, phone, and social subspace.

IMPLICATIONS: CULTURALLY BASED DESIGN

Having investigated trans-surface interaction design as an example of embodied culturally based design, we now consider implications of and for CBD, itself. We point out how CBD serves as a generative source of metaphors for interaction design. We present implications that result from contextualizing embodied interaction design in culture, and consider the importance of investigating transferability. We finish by assessing the potential for systems developed with the CBD method to support stealth teaching.

CBD: A Source of Design Metaphors

While CBD can provoke the creation of new interaction metaphors, it inverts the construct. In describing the original design process for the desktop metaphor at PARC, Liddle articulates that the goal of metaphors is not to imitate the physical world, but to provide abstractions to which users can relate [31]. The CBD method is, in fact, to directly imitate physical world activities with NUI technologies and systems, and to derive metaphors from resulting simulations. Answering Abowd and Mynatt's ubicomp NUI challenge [1], the goal, through this process, is to discover implicit actions that people are familiar with, ready-to-hand, and apply them to facilitate rich communication between humans and computation. CBD can result in the design of metaphors, like card flicking and waving. These abstractions result from processes that begin with direct imitation of physical world activities.

Context and Transferability

Design of digitally mediated interaction incorporates many techniques, including affordances, mappings, and feedback [18]. We designed the trans-surface wormhole technique from mental models of how cards move and are manipulated. Prior trans-surface interactions have been designed in more generic contexts [12]. While context-free empirically motivated interaction design may be fruitful, in a contextualized activity designers can rely on the cultural understanding of users to create expressive and efficient interactions.

Further, though CBD develops interaction in contextualized activities, we hypothesize that it will sometimes be possible to abstract CBD-derived techniques, that interactions derived from one cultural context will be transferable to others. When can users transfer functional understanding of an interaction technique beyond the original situated context to others? How can such mental model transfers be supported? Future research will investigate the *transferability hypothesis*.

Future work will explore how easily people learn to use trans-surface wormholes for exchanging business cards, web pages, and other information. What will be the impact of indexically referring to the context as a metaphor, as in, "Transfer the document from your phone to the tabletop as if it were a playing card?" We suspect that with familiar referents, such as playing cards, recontextualizing culturally based interactions will still activate embodied mental models. CBD shifts the focus to activating embodied mental models in order to contextualize activities that are at once partially physical, cognitive, and customary.

CBD Engenders Stealth Education

Non-technical populations, such as many elderly users, challenge interaction design [30]. Problems arise as a result of gaps in knowledge of commonly used interaction techniques among varying demographics. CBD addresses this by recontextualizing the experience-base of target populations.

Elderly participants were quickly able to play Trans-Surface Rummy. They leveraged their engaged familiarity to confidently manipulate digital cards ready-to-hand. Their experienced in-order-to mandate of playing cards trumped their fear of technology, resulting in excitement. As with other card play, they wanted to share this with friends and family.

CBD can provide a basis for stealth education tools that introduce new technologies to diverse populations, such as the elderly, by presenting embodied digital representations of cultural activities that evoke engaged familiarity. In the case of card play, players are not just familiar; they are aware of their own proficiency. This gives them the confidence to overcome uncertainty and engage with technology. The power of familiar activities as a cultural repository of knowledge, accessible for stealth education, should not be underestimated.

CONCLUSION

With the emerging advent of NUI technologies, developers and researchers seek to meet the ubicomp challenge by creating new intuitive interaction techniques. Cultural activities can serve as a source not only for new interaction metaphors, but further, for gestures, visual representations, and activity contexts. We have shown that CBD enables creating effective interactions that engage participants' embodied mental models. For example, they fluidly transferred information artifacts through the wormhole despite the physical discontinuity inherent in trans-surface interaction.

We as designers have much to learn from the information artifacts all around us. They are the product of cultural processes that have been influenced by generations of use and experience. It is important that we do not backtrack in our development of new interfaces for working with information artifacts. As our evaluation shows, flexibility is a critical affordance of physical information artifacts. Sensemaking systems should support people's natural skill of fluidly structuring artifacts informationally.

Designers can use CBD to cross barriers to reach non-technical populations. We focus on the application of culturally based digital experiences as a gateway for less technical populations to learn new technology. These experiences serve as an environment for inexperienced users to learn about and build confidence with unfamiliar technology.

We hypothesize that under some conditions, culturally based designs derived in one context will be effective in others. In future work we will explore to what extent and under what conditions we can initiate design in one context, and then recontextualize the results. This research must address questions of how to catalyze the activation of users' embodied mental models, and how readily will they be reactivated without stimuli from the original context.

The fluidity with which participants manipulate information artifacts through the private-social workspaces wormhole begins demonstration of embodiment's potential contribution. The sensing and display capabilities of popular devices enable a new NUI era, in which ready-to-hand surfaces, as equipment, recognize and respond to each other in a manner similar to how people do. Instead of people carrying around isolated blocks of computing, islands, we need to discover new methods that enable dynamic, synergetic forms of trans-surface interaction in-order-to expand the collective power of spontaneous gatherings of computers, displays, sensors, and people. Thus the present research initiates a research agenda of rich, responsive trans-surface interaction design.

We must embrace and draw from the deep and wide cultural repository of human experiences. Just as the gene pool spans diverse biological ecologies, from the Amazon to Siberia, and all between, so humanity possesses a rich pool of cultural experiences which can contribute fundamental resources to embodied interaction design. The transferability hypothesis leaves us wondering: what practices of what peoples have the potential to make what crucial contributions to the design of human-centered ubiquitous computing? We look forward to forging collaborations to explore this design space.

ACKNOWLEDGMENTS

Special thanks to the Brazos Valley and Star Bridge Clubs for welcoming our research. This material is based upon work supported by the NSF under grants IIS-0803854 and IIS-0747428. Any opinions, findings, and conclusions or recommendations expressed in this material are those of the authors and do not necessarily reflect the view of the NSF.

REFERENCES

1. Abowd, G., and Mynatt, E. Charting past, present, and future research in ubiquitous computing. *ACM Trans. Comput.-Hum. Interact. 7* (March 2000), 29–58.
2. Bader, T., Heck, A., and Beyerer, J. Lift-and-drop: Crossing boundaries in a multi-display environment by airlift. In *Proc. AVI* (2010), 139–146.
3. Falstein, N. Stealth education. *Game Developer 12*, 10 (November 2005), 40.
4. Gabrielli, S., Bellutti, S., Jameson, A., Leonardi, C., and Zancanaro, M. A single-user tabletop card game system for older persons: General lessons learned from an in-situ study. In *Proc. Tabletop* (2008), 85–88.
5. Gajadhar, B. J., Nap, H. H., and et al. Out of sight, out of mind: Co-player effects on seniors' player experience. In *Proc. Fun & Games* (2010), 74–83.
6. Geertz, C. *The Interpretation Of Cultures (Basic Books Classics)*. Basic Books, May 1977.
7. Gibson, J. J. *The ecological approach to visual perception*. Psychology Press, 1986.
8. Glenberg, A. Why mental models must be embodied. In *Mental Models in Discourse Processing and Reasoning*, G. Rickheit and H. C., Eds. Elsevier, 1999.
9. Han, J. Low-cost multi-touch sensing through frustrated total internal reflection. In *Proc. UIST* (2005), 115–118.
10. Hargrave, C. P. *A History of Playing Cards*. Dover, 1966.
11. Heidegger, M. *Being and Time*. Harpers, 1962.
12. Hinckley, K., Ramos, G., Guimbretiere, F., Baudisch, P., and Smith, M. Stitching: Pen gestures that span multiple displays. In *Proc. AVI* (2004), 23–31.
13. Kirsh, D. The intelligent use of space. *Artif. Intell. 73* (February 1995), 31–68.
14. Kroeber, A., and Kluckhohn, C. *Culture; a critical review of concepts and definitions*. Harvard University Peabody Museum, 1952.
15. Leonardi, C., Albertini, A., Pianesi, F., and Zancanaro, M. An exploratory study of a touch-based gestural interface for elderly. In *Proc. NordiCHI* (2010), 845–850.
16. Moeller, J., and Kerne, A. ZeroTouch: A zero-thickness optical multi-touch force field. In *Proc. CHI EA* (2011), 1165–1170.
17. Moran, T. P., and Anderson, R. J. The workaday world as a paradigm for CSCW design. In *Proc. CSCW* (1990), 381–393.
18. Norman, D. A. *The Design of Everyday Things*. Basic Books, September 2002.
19. Parlet, D. *The A–Z of Card Games*. Oxford University Press, New York, NY, USA, 2004.
20. Rekimoto, J. Pick-and-drop: A direct manipulation technique for multiple computer environments. In *Proc. UIST* (1997), 31–39.
21. Russell, D. M., Stefik, M. J., Pirolli, P., and Card, S. K. The cost structure of sensemaking. In *Proc. CHI* (1993), 269–276.
22. Salen, K., and Zimmerman, E. *Rules of Play: Game Design Fundamentals*. MIT Press, 2004.
23. Sengers, P., Kaye, J., Boehner, K., Fairbank, J., Gay, G., Medynskiy, Y., and Wyche, S. Culturally embedded computing. *IEEE Pervasive Comput. 3* (2004), 14–21.
24. Sharp, H., Rogers, Y., and Preece, J. *Interaction Design: Beyond Human Computer Interaction*. Wiley, 2007.
25. Star, S. L. The ethnography of infrastructure. *The American Behavioral Scientist 43*, 3 (1999), 377–391.
26. Suchman, L. A. *Plans and Situated Actions*, 2nd ed. Cambridge University Press, December 1987.
27. Thorensen, K. Principles in practice: Two cases of situated participatory design. In *Participatory design: principles and practices*, D. Schuler and A. Namioka, Eds. L. Erlbaum Associates, 1993.
28. Toups, Z. O., Kerne, A., and Webb, A. A lightweight object-oriented distributed services framework for engineering interactive applications. Tech. rep., Interface Ecology Lab, 2008. `http://ecologylab.net/techReports/oodss_TR_10_01.pdf`.
29. Turner, P., and de Walle, G. V. Familiarity as a basis of universal design. *Journal of Gerontechnology* (2006).
30. Whitcomb, G. R. Computer games for the elderly. In *Proc. CQL* (1990), 112–115.
31. Winograd, T. Design of the conceptual model: Interview with david liddle. In *Bringing Design to Software*. 1996.
32. Wu, M., and Balakrishnan, R. Multi-finger and whole hand gestural interaction techniques for multi-user tabletop displays. In *Proc. UIST* (2003), 193–202.

Evaluating the Effectiveness of Height Visualizations for Improving Gestural Communication at Distributed Tables

Aaron Genest and Carl Gutwin
Department of Computer Science
University of Saskatchewan
aaron.genest@usask.ca and carl.gutwin@usask.ca

ABSTRACT
In co-located collaboration, people use the space above the table for deictic gestures, and height is an important part of these gestures. However, when collaborators work at distributed tables, we know little about how to convey information about gesture height. A few visualizations have been proposed, but these have not been evaluated in detail. To better understand how remote embodiments can show gesture height, we developed several visualizations and evaluated them in three studies. First, we show that touch visualizations significantly improve people's accuracy in identifying the type and target of a gesture. Second, we show that visualizations of height above the table help to convey gesture qualities such as confidence, emphasis, and specificity. Third, we show that people quickly make use of height visualizations in realistic collaborative tasks, and that height-enhanced embodiments are strongly preferred. Our work illustrates several designs for effective visualization of height, and provides the first comprehensive evidence of the value of height information as a way to improve gestural communication in distributed tabletop groupware.

Author Keywords
Digital tables, deixis, gesture, gesture height, pointing

ACM Classification Keywords
H.5.3 Group and Organization Interfaces: CSCW.

General Terms
Human Factors, Design, Experimentation

INTRODUCTION
Gestural communication – particularly pointing as a deictic reference – is ubiquitous when people work together at tables in the real world. Pointing reduces the complexity of verbal communication by allowing people to easily indicate objects, areas, or paths through simple gestures [2]. When collaboration happens on distributed tables, however, it is much more difficult to remotely convey natural pointing gestures. Although digital embodiments can be employed (e.g., telepointers or video images), current techniques are inadequate for conveying the subtleties of deictic gesture.

CSCW 2012, February 11–15, 2012, Seattle, Washington, USA.

In particular, typical embodiments do not show the height of a gesture above the table. People use height for several things when they construct a pointing gesture: to make clear the target of the gesture (e.g., putting a finger on the object of interest); to indicate different types of gesture (e.g., indications of paths versus general areas); to show different qualities in the gesture (e.g., a high gesture might be used to indicate less specificity); or to indicate that the gesture points to a location that is out of reach or off the table [6]. Without a representation of gesture height, pointing-based gestural communication on distributed tables is prone to errors, misunderstandings, and interpretation difficulty.

Researchers in tabletop groupware have recognized some of these problems, and have suggested a few embodiment designs that show at least some aspects of height (e.g., [12,19]). However, these designs are primarily concerned with showing surface touches, rather than the full range of height above the table, and their effectiveness has not been evaluated in detail. In this paper, we investigate three questions that need to be answered in order to better understand the design of height visualizations:

- *Accuracy*: does height information improve people's ability to determine the type or target of a gesture?
- *Expressiveness*: can height visualizations reliably convey qualities such as specificity, confidence, and emphasis?
- *Usability*: can people make use of height visualizations in realistic work, and do they prefer these representations?

We answered these design questions with three studies. The first experiment showed that representing touch and hover significantly improve people's ability to determine both the target of the gesture and the type of gesture. The second study showed that people use height visualizations to interpret a gesture's specificity, confidence, and emphasis, and showed that these interpretations are consistent with the ways that people see real-world gestures. The third study looked at the ways that people use height representations in realistic collaboration, and showed that people quickly make use of the additional height information in their deictic gestures, that the height-augmented embodiments caused no new usability problems, and that the augmented versions were preferred by users.

This work makes two main contributions. First, we demonstrate several visualizations for showing key elements of gesture height, designs that refine and improve on previous solutions. Second, we provide a wide variety of evidence for the value of representing height in remote tabletop embodiments: we are the first to show that height visualizations can improve interpretation accuracy, can improve the expressiveness of remote gestures, and can be quickly learned and used in realistic collaboration. The design information and empirical evidence that this work provides can greatly help to improve the subtlety and precision of gestural communication on remote tables.

PREVIOUS WORK

Gestures and Deixis

Researchers have identified gestural interaction, specifically deixis or pointing gestures, as critical to the success of collaborative environments (e.g. [2,10,13]). It follows that distributed collaboration is hampered when users work in environments where they are unable to see the gestures made by remote collaborators. This can result in higher levels of frustration in communication and lower-quality results from collaboration [2]. Thus, supporting gestural communication between collaborators is an important goal for distributed groupware technologies. One way of providing support for gestures is through *embodiments* – representations of the participants in a distributed collaboration. There has been a great deal of work done on embodiments (e.g., [16,20,18]), but we are particularly interested in embodiments for distributed tables.

Remote Embodiments on Tables and Surfaces

Several systems have provided visual representations of remote users' arms and bodies, from early video-based tools such as VideoDraw [20], VideoWhiteBoard [21], and ClearBoard [11] to more recent tabletop and large-display groupware (e.g., [17,18]). Embodiments in these systems can be divided into two categories: abstract embodiments such as telepointers [9], which represent the user with lines and shapes, and realistic embodiments, which often employ video techniques (e.g., [21,19]). Each of these approaches has particular strengths and weaknesses [6]. Although realistic embodiments can be richer in their representation of natural deictic gestures, abstract embodiments are better able to indicate a specific touch point, or provide extra information such as additional visualizations, that are not available in 2D video (see Table 1). The question of whether video or artificial representations are best has received some attention, with some evidence for both sides: a study by Kirk *et al.* [14] found that realistic video of hands and arms was better than a representation of a stylus drawing tool; but several projects have also shown or implied that abstract visualizations are also useful [4,19].

In a comparison of abstract and realistic techniques, we [6] identified the height of a gesture as one component that video embodiments do not communicate well. This finding is supported by Fussel *et al.*, who found that lack of information about gesture height was a barrier to communication in collaborative environments [5]. These problems exist partly because of the 2D representation of a realistic embodiment, but there are also several practical problems in representing height with video – for example, higher gestures become much larger (since they get closer to a top-mounted camera), and higher gestures are much more likely to leave the camera's view frustum.

Table 1. Representational capabilities of abstract and realistic embodiments (adapted from [7]).

Component of Deictic Gesture	Abstract	Realistic
Differentiate similar gestures	No	Possible
Represent stroke gestures	Yes	No
Express full range of morphology	No	Possible
Represent height	Possible	No

We found that height differences were closely associated with variations in confidence, specificity, and emphasis. They also observed height used to indicate secondary references, to point at distant objects, and to mirror the real-world height variations of an object. They identified four important levels of height: on the surface, moving between on and just off the surface, hovering off the surface, and more than 5 cm above the surface [6].

Showing Gesture Height in Remote Embodiments

Previous work on embodiments has considered height in two ways: as an aspect of gestural communication, or as a way to provide feedthrough about others' actions.

Height in Existing Embodiment Techniques

One of the earliest video embodiments, VideoWhiteBoard, used real shadows cast on the display surface [21]. This had the side effect of showing diffusion in the shadows as people moved away from the surface, a cue that could be used by remote participants to better understand people's locations. Later implementations of the idea used digital rather than analogue shadows, and did not convey the same kind of distance information [1].

Distance information can also indicate intention to make a deictic gesture. Fraser *et al.* found that explicitly visualizing the approach of participants' pens toward a wallboard significantly improved coordination in a video-annotation task, and reduced conversational latency [4]. Both Fraser's work and VideoWhiteBoard are effective in showing heights or distances larger than 5cm, but neither of these projects explored a more complete design space for height.

Hilliges *et al.* [9] used the height from a surface as a method of providing more sophisticated interaction with 3D objects. They provided hand shadows as a feedback technique, inverted so as to appear smaller when hands were farther from the surface. As an interaction technique, distance from the surface can be mapped, as they suggest, to less engagement, and therefore less of a user footprint on the surface. We consider this in our designs, detailed below.

More recently, Tang *et al.* enhanced the VideoArms technique to show contact traces (called 'touch pearls')[19] when participants were touching the table surface, using an effect similar to telepointer traces [7]. They mention that proximity information was not well modeled in their design, despite the improvement provided by the traces; however, they note that the traces did provide a level of awareness not available through the original VideoArms design. No evaluation of the contact traces was carried out.

Height as Feedthrough

Height or distance from the surface can also provide information about user activity, since surface touches are often used to invoke commands in the system. Visualizations of height are therefore used to give feedback to the local user, and can also provide feedthrough to remote participants [3]. The visualizations generally show the difference between hover and touching states on touch or pen interfaces (e.g., with the C-Slate interface [12], or with Wigdor *et al*'s ripple visualizations [22]). Although work on feedthrough that incorporates height information provides valuable insight into embodiment design, this research has not investigated how including height affects communication in distributed collaborations.

DESIGNING AN ENHANCED EMBODIMENT

Our review of related work identified three important design factors in height representation for embodiments: the difference between touch and hover, the relative height of gestures above the surface, and the short-term history of movement. To better evaluate the usefulness of height in embodiments, we designed two components: one to represent surface touches and the short-term history of contact with the surface (contact traces) and one to represent the relative height of a gesture above the table.

Since height is difficult to see in video-based embodiments, our height visualizations are abstract rather than realistic; they could, however, be added to a video-based embodiment. There are also reasons for lower-fidelity or abstract embodiments to stand alone, such as situations of limited bandwidth or low computational power, or systems that support many collaborators. We anticipate that the designs below can be used in either context – as additions to high-fidelity, video-based embodiments or as components of high-efficiency, abstract embodiments.

Our designs build on previous work: traces and ripples are based on work by Tang [19] and by Wigdor [22], and the inspiration for our above-the-surface ellipses comes from work by Tang on VideoWhiteboard [21]. However, our designs are the first to comprehensively describe where gestures are situated in the space above the table.

Representing Touches on the Table

We designed embodiments to convey the location of a touch, and the recent history of contact with the table.

Showing Touch

The change in gesture height between just off the surface and touching is an important state change [6]. To emphasize this difference, we dual-encoded touch state using both shape and colour. When the gesture is above the surface we represent the user's pointer with an arrow (red and black for improved visibility on a variety of backgrounds). When a touch is detected, we add a crosshair shape under the arrow, and highlight the crosshair in green (see Figure 1). We used arrows and crosshairs instead of wider blob shapes (like those extracted from FTIR tables), since we were interested in comparing them to traditional telepointers. Differences in accuracy between the mouse arrow and a fingerprint-sized blob would be a confounding factor in evaluations.

Figure 1: Our table-touching designs, on the surface colour and shape change (left); above the surface, plain (centre); and combined with contact traces as ripples (right).

Showing the Touch Path with Contact Traces

Traces of interactions improve the interpretation of distributed gestures [19], and paths are common elements of gestures over tables [6], so we added a visualization of the path of a touch gesture (i.e., a contact trace).

We designed two variants of the trace visualization. The first showed contact traces in the form of ripples (Figure 2, top), based on the previous success of ripples as touch feedback [22]. The second version shows simple sketch lines along the path of the gesture (Figure 2, middle); this design more clearly indicates a path (ripples can occasionally be mistaken for a multiple point gesture). In this version, ripples are still shown at the point of initial and final contact with the table, which permitted tapping gestures and gestures that touched the surface at a single point to still show a contact trace.

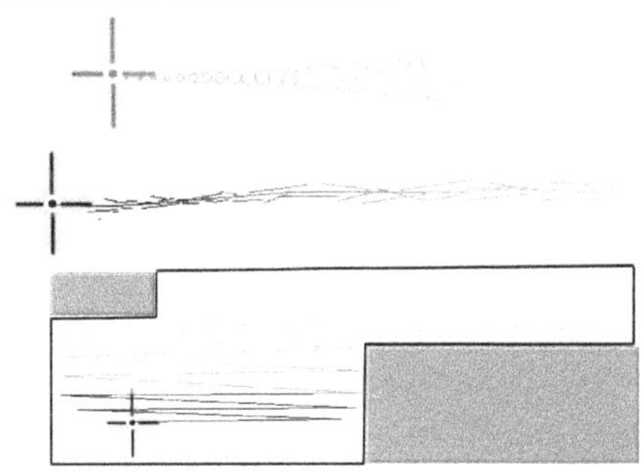

Figure 2. Top: ripple contact traces. Middle: line contact traces (slow movement with initial ripple at touch point). Bottom: line contact trace 'colouring in' an area.

The trace lines also showed the speed of the gesture: fast touching gestures resulted in straight and parallel sketch lines, and slower gestures showed lines that were slightly rotated and slightly further apart (Figure 2). This visualization was added since our early observations showed that people 'colour in' space with quick path gestures to indicate an area.

Representing Height Above the Table

Beyond the table surface, height is an ordinal variable. Although people use different layers in the above-the-table space, these differences are not uniform [6], so we represent height with a continuous visualization, but with added elements that allow people to make use of different layers.

The ordinal component of height above the surface is represented as an ellipse that increases in size and becomes more transparent as the gesture moves upwards (Figure 3). These visual cues are compatible with the idea that higher gestures are less specific [6] and that higher gestures might need to appear less engaged [9]. Our ellipse was multi-coloured, increasing its visibility on a variety of backgrounds (Figures 3 and 4). We also included a movement trace (to emphasize high-level path gestures) by fading out each ellipse after one second; the effect is one of a series of shapes left behind in the trail of the cursor.

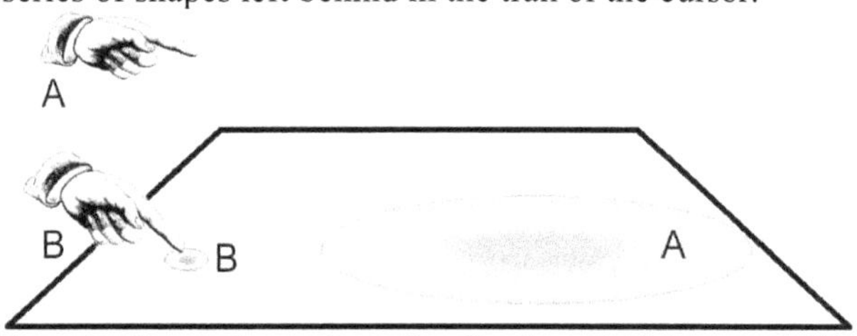

Figure 3: Above-the-surface visualization. A high gesture (A) with the large, transparent, ray-cast ellipsoid and a low gesture (B) with the small, solid, sphere.

Our design subtly reflected the change in height layer (between the 0-5cm layer and the above 5 cm layer) by changing from a perfect sphere (in the lower layer) to an increasingly narrow and long ellipse (in the higher layer) (see Figure 3). This visualization technique helps to show gestures that point to objects far away or off the table with a simulated ray-casting technique: as gestures move higher, the ellipse becomes narrower and longer, and the centroid of the ellipse moves away from the user (i.e., as a shadow would when cast from a light behind the user; see Figure 4). These effects were shown only when the gesture rose 5cm above the table surface.

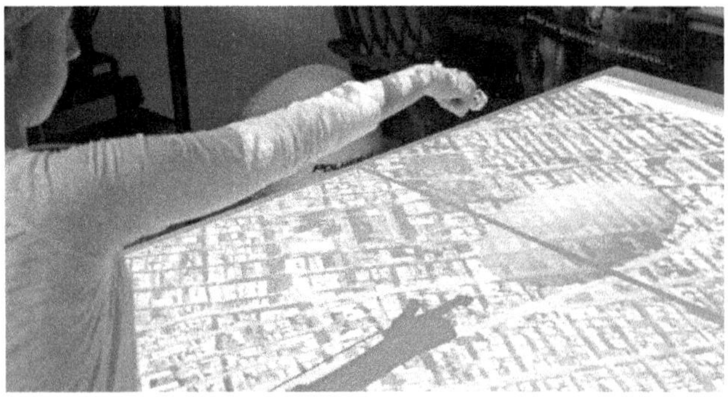

Figure 4: Simulated ray-casting with the ellipsoid embodiment. N.B., the shadow is an artifact of the overhead projection and is not part of the embodiment.

EVALUATION OF HEIGHT VISUALIZATIONS: 3 STUDIES

Although a few designs for touching and above-the-surface interaction been seen in prior work, there are no formal evaluations of the effectiveness of height visualizations for remote collaborators. We carried out three studies to assess three important design issues for height visualizations: *accuracy* (i.e., do they improve people's ability to determine the type or target of a gesture); *expressiveness* (i.e., can they convey the kinds of subjective qualities that are common in real-world gestures); and *usability* (i.e., can people make use of them in realistic work, and do they prefer them over basic representations).

The three studies are described below. The first two experiments are more controlled, and therefore investigate simple gestures – pointing at objects, paths, and areas. These gestures comprise a substantial proportion of simple deixis (i.e., many indicative gestures in the real world involve these simple actions), and are also components of more complex interactions (previous work has shown that complex gestures can be broken into smaller common components [13]). In the third study, participants carried out open-ended collaboration, and so the tasks and gestures were not constrained.

STUDY 1: INTERPRETATION ACCURACY

This study looked at the effects of touch and hover visualizations on observers' ability to identify the target of the pointing gesture (what was being pointed at), and on people's ability to identify the type of pointing gesture (i.e., whether the gesturer's intent was to point to an object, a path, or an area).

Height Visualizations and Tasks

We compared four of the visualizations described above in two tasks. Our visualizations (see Figures 1 and 2) were:

- *Arrow*: a red-outlined, standard arrow pointer (Fig. 1);
- *Touch*: a shape- and colour-changing pointer (Fig. 1);
- *Trace*: a red-outlined, standard arrow pointer (Fig. 1) with ripples as a contact trace (Fig. 2);
- *Touch+Trace*: a combination of Touch and Trace.

We used Arrow as a control condition because this representation provides the highest gesture specificity, and because arrows are a standard embodiment in groupware.

The visualizations were tested on two tasks, both of which used aerial photographs as background data. Participants were seated at a large table, on which was projected a satellite photograph of New York (see Figure 5). The image was selected on the basis of its high number of closely situated potential targets.

Task 1: identifying the target of the gesture. We pre-recorded twelve gestures that touched the surface of the table 3-5 times. Touches occurred at realistic targets (such as street intersections) and the appropriate point of each visualization was used for the touch (the tip of the Arrow representation, and the center of the Crosshair). After viewing the gesture (there was no accompanying speech), the participant used the mouse to click on each location where the gesture touched the surface. Participants were asked to be as accurate as possible (but were also aware that the task was timed). Participants could select the points in any order (our analysis used a best-fit technique that calculated the best possible accuracy value).

Figure 5: Gesture types used in Study 1: left (blue), a multiple points gesture; middle (red), a path gesture; right (green), a point gesture. An example of the background used in the studies.

Task 2: identifying the type of the gesture. We pre-recorded three kinds of gestures that can look similar [6], in order to determine whether height information helps people differentiate between them. The three types (see Figure 5) were *paths*, which indicated a straight or zigzagging path on the map; *single points*, which indicated single targets on the map; and *multiple points*, which indicated several points scattered across the map. Gestures were carried out at a variety of heights: paths could be on or above the table, and point gestures either touched the table or paused at each target in the gesture. Participants viewed 28 pre-recorded gestures (8 single-point, 8 multiple-point, 12 paths) in random order, and selected the type from a list.

Study Design and Procedure

The study used a within-participants design and RM-ANOVA to look for effects of visualization type on accuracy of target identification and type identification. Visualization were shown as a block (order balanced using a Latin square). Main tests used α=.05, and post-hoc comparisons used t-tests with the Bonferroni correction.

Participants completed a demographic survey and an orientation session that included previews of each visual condition. The type identification task was presented first, then the accuracy target location identification task. Sixteen participants (12 male, 4 female, 21-45 years old, mean 27.6) were recruited from a local university. Computer logs were used to track the participant's completion time, selected points for the accuracy task, and answers in the type-of-gesture task.

Study 1 Results

Accuracy in Identifying Target Locations

Since there were several targets in a gesture, and since participants were not required to specify the points in order, we calculated error using a best-fit technique that used the lowest overall error value (in pixels) for any possible mapping of participant selections to actual targets.

RM-ANOVA showed a main effect of visualization type on location accuracy ($F_{3,45}$=15.76, p<0.001). Figure 7 displays average error amount per target, and shows that participants were approximately 12 and 16 pixels closer to the targets with the two trace visualizations (Trace and Touch+Trace) than with the other techniques. Pairwise comparisons showed that both trace visualizations had significantly lower error amounts than Arrow and Touch (all p<0.01, no other differences found). RM-ANOVA of the completion-time data found no effects of visualization type ($F_{3,45}$=0.252, p<0.859).

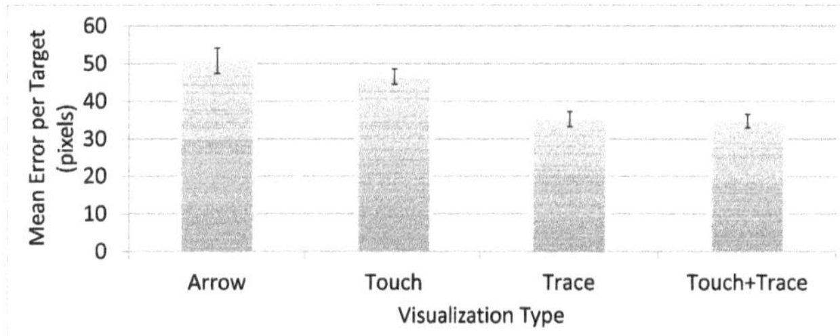

Figure 7: Error in pixels by visualization (accuracy task).

Accuracy of Gesture Type Identification

RM-ANOVA showed a main effect of visualization type on identification accuracy ($F_{3,45}$=154.85, p<0.001). As Figure 8 shows, all of the visualizations that represented touch (either with a visual state change or with a contact trace) had significantly lower error rates than the standard arrow (p<0.001 for all post-hoc pairwise comparisons involving the arrow; no other differences found). The differences were substantial: the nearly 50% error rate of the arrow cursor was reduced to less than 5% for all of the touch visualizations. This finding suggests that gesture identification is improved with any touch information, which helps to disambiguate between simple movement above the table (e.g., moving to the start position of the gesture) and the gesture itself.

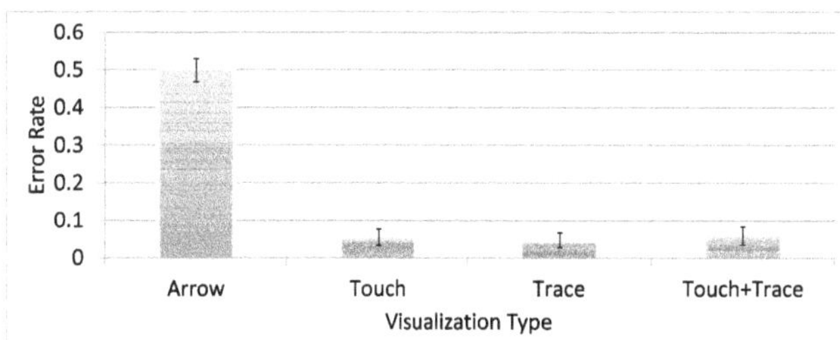

Figure 8: Error rate on the identification task

STUDY 2: EXPRESSIVENESS

The second study investigated the question of whether height visualization aids in conveying subjective qualities that are common in real-world gestures, such as the degree of confidence, specificity, and emphasis in the gesture. We explored this question in three parts. First, we looked at whether people interpret height information in a remote gesture as having an effect on the confidence, specificity, and emphasis of the gesture. Second, we looked at whether people associate visualizations of tapping with emphasis. Third, we looked at whether height information helps people to interpret gesture type. These explorations are motivated by prior work showing that in co-located situations, people do interpret gestures in these ways [6].

We considered two kinds of gesture height in the study: *global height*, indicating the overall height of the entire gesture above the table, and *local height variation*, which involved hand-bouncing or finger-tapping motions but did not change the global height of the gesture. We recorded gestures at three global heights: *high* (more than 20cm above the surface), *low* (between 5 and 20cm above the surface), and *surface* (in contact with the table). We recorded half of the gestures with local height variation within the global height (i.e., a tapping or waving movement that remained within the bounds of a specific global height), and half where the hand and fingers maintained a constant, global height (i.e., no tapping). Each gesture set (high, high with local variation, low, low with local variation, surface, and surface with local variation) included two kinds of path gestures, two kinds of point gestures, and two kinds of area gestures:

- Pointing gestures indicating a single target;
- Pointing gestures indicating multiple scattered points;
- A simple path between two points;
- Paths between multiple points;
- An area delineated with a contour gesture;
- An area that is 'coloured in' with the gesture.

Gesture height was shown using a combination of two designs described above: height above the table was shown using the ellipse and sphere visualizations (Figure 3), but the moment the gesture touched the table, the sphere disappeared and the line-based contact traces, state-change cursor and starting and ending ripples were used (Figure 2, middle). As discussed above, we used line-based traces rather than ripples because our design work suggested that lines are less likely to indicate multiple points to viewers.

Tasks, Design, and Procedure

The study used similar tasks to those described for the first experiment. Participants stated whether the gesture was a path, point, or area gesture, and also answered three questions related to gesture qualities: how *specific* was the gesture, how *emphatic* was the gesture, and how *confident* was the gesturer in making the gesture. These questions were answered on a seven-point scale. In addition, we included two distractor questions to reduce the chance of participants guessing the hypothesized link between height and specificity, confidence, and emphasis. These were: did the gesture indicate something off the edge of the table, and did the gesture indicate an out-of-reach object. Sixteen participants (11 male, 4 female, 19-33 years old, mean 23.9) were recruited from a local university. All watched several previews of the gesture visualizations.

The study used a within-participants design to examine the effects of two factors: the global height of the gesture, and the presence of local height variation in the gesture. These factors were fully crossed and contained either three or four trials for each of the gesture types (path, point, area). The difference in number results from the fact that some gestures would not realistically be used in some situations (e.g., hovering over an area works only above the surface). There were a total of 63 randomly-ordered trials.

Study 2 Results

We had two groups of data: participant measures of gesture qualities and an accuracy test. We examined the participant data to see how height variation (global and local) affected how participants interpreted gesture qualities.

Interpretation of Gesture Qualities: Global Height

All participants interpreted the ellipse height visualization as expected, inferring that lower height implied greater confidence, specificity, and emphasis. We performed an ANOVA to determine whether height visualizations at the three global heights led to differences in participant ratings of these three qualities. In all cases, the ANOVA showed a significant effect of height on the perceived level of the quality (confidence, $F_{2,30}$=24.84; specificity, $F_{2,30}$=30.27; emphasis, $F_{2,30}$=15.64; all p<0.001), see Fig. 9.

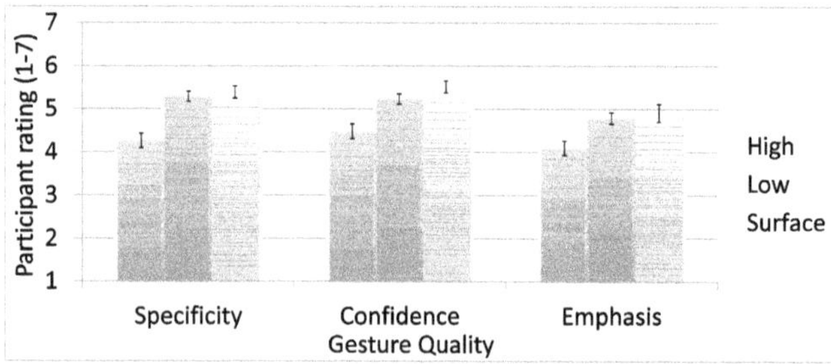

Figure 9: Interpretation of gesture qualities, by global height.

Interpretation of Gesture Qualities: Local Height Variation

RM-ANOVA also showed a main effect of local height variation on interpretation of qualities ($F_{1,15}$=6.39, p<0.001). As shown in Figure 10, people were more likely to interpret a gesture as emphatic if there was a bouncing or tapping motion in the gesture. There was also an interaction between global height and local height variation ($F_{2,30}$=4.68, p<0.001). Post hoc pairwise comparisons found significant differences between height variation and no height variation on specificity, emphasis, and confidence for globally high gestures (p<0.001), globally low gestures (p<0.01), but only on emphasis for gestures on the surface (p<0.01).

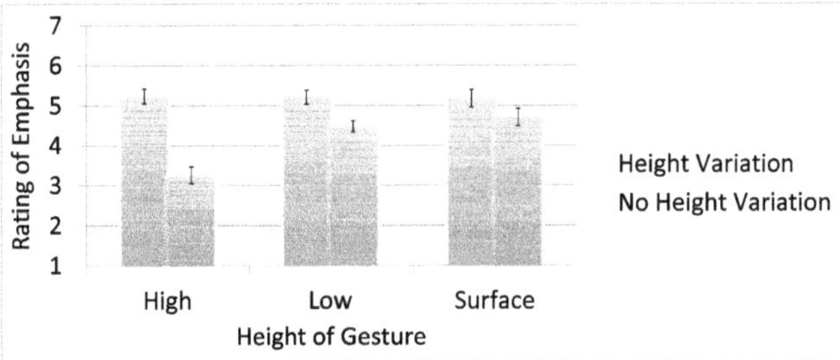

Figure 10: Interpretation of emphasis, by local height variations. Global heights are collapsed.

As the figure shows, when people saw only the global height, they were much more likely to reduce their estimation of emphasis with high gestures, but when there was local height variation, this information was consistently interpreted as implying that the gesture was emphatic. (Results were similar for specificity and confidence).

Accuracy of Identifying Gesture Type

RM-ANOVA showed a main effect of global height on interpretation accuracy ($F_{2,30}$=9.027, p<0.001). We investigated, post hoc, the high error rates we observed in some conditions. We discovered that the exceptional error rates were specific to particular gesture types: paths with points had high error rates above the surface and both multiple-point paths and area contours had high error rates on the surface. Participants largely misclassified the multiple-point paths and area contours surface gestures as path gestures, and both of these gesture types do share considerable information with paths. Part of this result is attributable to the complicated nature of gestures. The points-on-a-path gesture could also have been classified as a pointing gesture – participants interpreted it as a path on the surface and as pointing when in the air.

Despite these subtleties in measures of accuracy, Study 2 provides us with three clear findings. First, and most importantly, representations of gesture height allow people to interpret several subject qualities of a remote gesture. Second, the global height of a gesture is consistently interpreted as being inversely proportional to the gesture's emphasis, confidence, and specificity. Third, local height variations are consistently interpreted as increasing a gesture's emphasis, confidence, and specificity. Overall, these results show that visualization of a remote gesture's height can substantially increase gesture expressiveness.

STUDY 3: USABILITY IN REALISTIC COLLABORATION

The third study investigated the use of height-augmented embodiments in a realistic collaborative situation, and looked at three main issues:

- *Usage*: do people make use of the height visualization when making gestures, and for what do they use them?
- *Interpretation*: are gestures interpreted as intended, and do the visuals of the augmented embodiments cause any communication difficulty or confusion?
- *Preference*: do people prefer augmented embodiments over standard versions?

The study involved a realistic collaborative task between two participants: the *remote* participant was seated in one room at a (non-interactive) tabletop display, and the *local* participant was in another room at the table used in the earlier experiments. Local participants had a Polhemus Liberty 240/80 sensor attached to their primary pointing finger, which was used to capture the participant's gestures in 3D for display on the remote participant's table.

The height-augmented embodiment used in the study (and shown equally to both participants) were the same as those used for the second study (Figure 2, middle; Figure 3; Figure 4). The 'standard' embodiment was a standard arrow telepointer (Figure 1, middle). The background data on the tables was a satellite image of the participants' local city.

The remote participant was given a list of 22 questions about locations in the city (similar to those used by Kettebekov and Sharma [13]). The remote participant asked each question to the local participant, who responded by speaking and gesturing over the map. Participants were asked to continue discussing the question until both were satisfied that the answer was understood and correct.

The questions were selected to explore a wide range of open-ended interactions. Some questions involved areas that were familiar to one or both participants, and some questions were designed to involve unfamiliar areas of the city (e.g., safe boating areas or optimal pathways through neighbourhoods). Between questions, participants filled out a questionnaire which asked them to identify different qualities of the gestures that had been used in the exchange, and also asked how quickly they had achieved understanding, how well that understanding was achieved, and whether any locations had been out of reach or off the table. After each session, an interview was conducted to discuss the participants' experiences and to ask about preferences. We did not gather performance data since the nature of the tasks and the differences in familiarity with the locations led to high variance in completion times.

Half of the groups began with the height-enabled embodiment, and the other half with the telepointer. After 11 questions, they switched to the other visualization. Before each condition, participants were given as much time as needed to familiarize themselves with the embodiments. Eight pairs of participants were recruited from the local university (5 female, 11 male, ages 21-33, mean 24.4). Sessions were videotaped for later analysis.

Study 3 Results

Usage of height-augmented embodiments

Observations during sessions and during later video analysis showed that the local participant (the person constructing gestures) adapted quickly to the additional capabilities provided by the enhanced embodiment. All participants clearly understood what the remote participant would see of the visualization, and all participants showed evidence that some of their gestures were constructed to make use of the height visualization.

Indicating areas. Local participants regularly used the ellipse to indicate areas by hovering or moving slightly at a height that made the ellipse both an appropriate size for the target under discussion (e.g., Figure 13), and to indicate emphasis. For example, the following exchange occurred during discussion of shopping areas (LP: Local Participant):

LP: It's on this road. [*leaves hand on surface while tracing along road, scanning ahead to find target*]
LP: [*raises hand slightly to create ellipse*] And here's the mall. [*taps finger in the air, varying the size of the ellipse*]

Improved gesture visibility. When local participants constructed a path or contour gesture with the augmented embodiment, it was clear that they knew the other person would see the path (because of the contact traces). As a result, we observed no instances where the local participant repeated the gesture. When people constructed gestures with the plain telepointer, however, it was common for the participant to repeat the gesture several times, even without prompting from the remote participant.

Indicating out-of-reach targets. When tasks required the identification of far-away targets, local participants often used the augmented embodiment's simulated ray-casting ability (see Figure 13). The following exchanges illustrate the difference between the two embodiment conditions; participants were able to come to a shared understanding with much less effort using the augmented embodiment.

Telepointer condition:
LP: Somewhere up there... I can't reach very far but... [*stretches out of chair to reach as far as possible*]
RP: Yeah…
LP: [*sits down and retracts hand*] Up along the river.

Enhanced embodiment condition:
LP: Up along the river, in the middle, there. [*at limit of reach, raises hand to use raycasting, stays seated*]
RP: OK

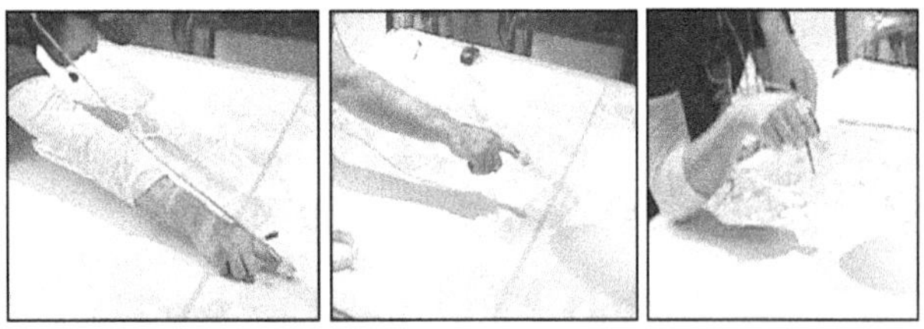

Figure 13: Left, reaching for a distant target in the plain condition; centre, reaching in the enhanced condition; right, hovering over an area in the enhanced condition.

Controlling specificity. Participants using the enhanced embodiment were clearly aware of the way that height was shown to the other person, and exercised much more control over gesture height than in the telepointer condition. For example, in several sessions, the local participant avoided touching the table unless they intended a high level of specificity. In the telepointer condition, however, participants were indiscriminate about the height of their gestures, since there was only one level of specificity in the embodiment. This did not cause a problem for the telepointer condition (although we wonder what would happen in mixed-presence settings), but indicates that participants made use of the additional expressive capabilities of the embodiment when these were available.

Interpretation of height-augmented embodiments

We analysed the video data looking for examples in which the additional visual information of the augmented embodiments caused clutter, confusion, or errors. In no cases did the extra information cause any noticeable problem, and nor did any participant report such problems in the post-session interview. We paid particular attention to issues of distraction and occlusion for the ellipse visualization, but the transparency of this effect appeared to successfully remove any difficulties for the participants.

It was also clear that remote participants made use of the features of the augmented embodiment in their interpretations. Evidence for the value of the visualizations came out in the interviews, where it was clear that remote participants understood the visual effects and wanted the local participant to make use of them. For example, one remote participant remarked, "I was hoping that she [the local participant] would use the difference between the ball [ellipsoid] and the pointer more than she did."

We note that gestures in this study were accompanied with speech, which likely limited interpretation problems (for either condition), in that accompanying speech could often be used to disambiguate a gesture. This indicates that (as expected) the information conveyed by height visualization may not be critical to the successful completion of the task; rather, the augmentations add subtlety and expressiveness to the overall interaction. (The fact that people did notice and appreciate these changes is shown in preference data).

Preferences and Participant Comments

When asked about their preferences after the session, 14 of the 16 participants stated that they preferred the height-augmented embodiments. In addition, remote participants universally preferred the height-augmented version. In one typical response a participant described the visualization as, "really nice, especially the trail left behind." The touch traces were appreciated by both participants: one remote participant said that the "pathways were a lot easier [to see]" with touch traces; a local user agreed, stating: "I liked the afterwards line. That was useful for generating paths." The two participants who preferred the plain telepointer were local participants, and both indicated that the plain telepointer was more familiar and therefore more desirable.

Other analyses

Analysis of the post-conversation questionnaires (using RM-ANOVA) found no significant differences between telepointer conditions (all $p>0.05$). We did not expect major differences in these measures because of the high variance introduced by the unconstrained task.

DISCUSSION

Our evaluations show three main results:

- Visualizing touch, hover, and contact traces significantly improved people's ability to interpret the type of gesture, and the targets of multi-point gestures;
- Visualizing height above the table allowed gestures to convey subjective qualities (e.g., specificity or emphasis), and these qualities were interpreted consistently;
- Touch, trace, and height visualizations were all easy to learn and use in realistic collaboration, and people made frequent use of the visualizations when gesturing.
- People strongly preferred the augmented embodiments.

Explanation and interpretation of main findings

Why height visualizations worked. There are three main reasons why the height-augmented embodiments were successful in our studies. First, and most obvious, there are several situations where useful and important information is encoded in a gesture's height – different types of gestures use different heights near the surface, specific actions such as tapping have characteristic height variations, and subjective qualities are strongly associated with height above the table. When height information is available in the embodiment, people get a richer representation of what is intended in a gesture. Although verbal communication can sometimes make up for gaps in this visual information (see below), augmented embodiments can allow distributed communication to be simpler and more subtle.

Second, our studies made it clear that remote embodiments on large tables and on complex workspaces are much less obvious and much less visible than real arms in co-located settings. This problem has been noted for other kinds of distributed groupware, but becomes more acute when tabletops are large (as in our studies). The lack of basic visibility makes it more difficult to determine when certain events (such as touching the table) occur, even with accompanying speech. The additional visual information of the augmented embodiments helped with this visibility problem – the change in representation when touching, the contact traces, and the ellipse all provided more noticeable representations that aided interpretation.

Contact traces were found to be particularly valuable in our studies, suggesting that it is difficult for observers to see and remember the details of a remote gesture. Traces of past activity have previously been shown to be valuable for other reasons (e.g., they are an 'awareness buffer' when attention is divided among several tasks [1,23]), but here we show that traces can also be useful when they are specific to a particular height – people in our studies knew that traces applied only to surface gestures. In future, we will explore the value of providing different traces at different heights, to determine whether we can obtain a broader benefit from this general approach.

Does talk remove the need for height information? Our third study showed that even when people used a simple telepointer, they were still able to carry out their tasks and come to an understanding, primarily through their verbal interaction. However, this does not mean that height visualizations are not valuable, for two reasons. First, there are many situations where verbal interaction is constrained – e.g., a gesture may be produced by a third person outside of the main conversation, participants may be trying to work on a task as quickly as possible, or a gesture may be intended as a side-channel communication. In these situations, height visualizations can allow people to convey more information than can be produced with telepointers.

Second, even when speech is available, the added information of the augmented embodiment can help to reduce communicative effort. For example, the tapping-in-the-air gesture made by a participant in the third study provided a clear indication of a location; if this were to be established through speech, the participant would have had to be more careful. It is almost always true that verbal interaction can suffice [15]; but the added capabilities of the augmented embodiment provide more possibilities for participants to make conversation simpler and faster.

Natural gestures and gesture languages. Although we intended to evaluate how successfully an embodiment can represent height to remote collaborators, it is almost impossible to fully duplicate natural gestures for remote participants, and so gesture visualizations will always be new visual languages rather than a representations of the gesture itself. In our third study, although we observed more natural pointing behaviour with our enhanced telepointer, we also saw new behaviours to take advantage of the facilities provided by the enhancements – for example, the use of the simulated raycasting to identify out-of-reach targets or the expanding ellipse to indicate areas. This raises the question of whether it is better to replicate the appearance of real-world gestures or to produce an artificial visual language that people will have to learn. Future work will explore whether hybrid embodiments (video plus abstract representations) can provide a middle ground in this regard.

Lessons for Designers and Future Work

Although more research needs to be done in this area, two main principles from our work can already be used by designers of tabletop embodiments. First, designers should consider representing height information in remote embodiments, since height can improve interpretation and accuracy, can allow gestures to express a much wider range of subjective qualities, and is strongly preferred by users. In the near future, height information will be simple to obtain (e.g., using depth-sensing cameras), making these changes a feasible option. Second, touch visualizations and traces are useful for a variety of tasks (involving both awareness and height issues), and should be easy to add to groupware systems since touch is already sensed on many tables.

Our work identified the role of height visualization as a stand-alone feature of embodiments, rather than as incorporated in already existing, high-fidelity, video-based embodiments. This has the added benefit of allowing our work to be used in high-efficiency, abstract embodiments for deployment where bandwidth or computational power are limited. In future work, we will examine how incorporating our height visualizations affects communication with both abstract embodiments and hybrid embodiments [6] (combined video and abstract visualizations). We are also curious to see if significant behavioural changes occur when just the contact traces and touching information are present in an embodiment, or whether the height visualization is also needed.

Finally, our work currently only applies to 2D display surfaces. There are a number of tabletop interaction designs that use false 3D or incorporate tangible components. We are interested to see how we can represent height when the display surface is no longer a uniform height.

Conclusion

The height of a pointing gesture above a table is an important part of collaborative communication. We evaluated how adding abstract height information to embodiments can improve the use and understanding of gestures in distributed collaboration. We found that embodiments can improve the accuracy of gesture and target identification, and that information about the height above the table allows users to consistently interpret subjective qualities of the gesture. Our evidence suggests that more information about the height of the gesture, both where it is and where it has been, can improve distributed communication and collaboration. We found that in realistic collaboration, users adapted quickly to the embodiments, and took advantage of the opportunities afforded by our designs when constructing their gestures; the augmented embodiments were strongly preferred. This work shows that height information can have important effects on the usability of distributed tabletop groupware.

REFERENCES

1. Apperley, M., McLeod, L., Masoodian, M., et al., Use of video shadow for small group interaction awareness on a large interactive display surface. *Proc. AUIC 2003, Volume 18*, 81–90.
2. Bekker, M., Olson, J., and Olson, G., Analysis of gestures in face-to-face design teams provides guidance for how to use groupware in design. *Proc. DIS 1995*, 157-166.
3. Dix, A., Finlay, J., Abowd, G., and Beale, R. *Human-Computer Interaction.* New York: Prentice Hall, 1993.
4. Fraser, M., McCarthy, M., Shaukat, M., and Smith, P. Seconds Matter: Improving Distributed Coordination by Tracking and Visualizing Display Trajectories. *Proc. CHI 2007*, 1303-1312.
5. Fussell, S., Setlock, L., Yang, J., Ou, J., Mauer, E., and Kramer, A., Gestures over video streams to support remote collaboration on physical tasks. *HCI, 19*, 3, 2004, 273–309.
6. Genest, A. and Gutwin, C., Characterizing Deixis over Surfaces to Improve Remote Embodiments. *Proc. ECSCW 2011*, in press. (*hci.usask.ca/publications/*).
7. Gutwin, C. and Penner, R. Improving interpretation of remote gestures with telepointer traces. *Proc. CSCW 2002*, 57-67.
8. Hayne, S., Pendergast, M., and Greenberg, S., Implementing gesturing with cursors in group support systems. *J.MIS, 10*, 3, 1993, 43–61.
9. Hilliges, O., Izadi, S., Wilson, A., Hodges, S., Garcia-Mendoza, A.,and Butz, A., Interactions in the air: adding further depth to interactive tabletops. *Proc. UIST 2009*, 139-148.
10. Hindmarsh, J. and Heath, C., Embodied reference: A study of deixis in workplace interaction. *J. Pragmatics, 32*, 12, 2000, 1855–1878.
11. Ishii, H., Kobayashi, M., ClearBoard: a seamless medium for shared drawing and conversation with eye contact. *Proc. CHI 2007*, 525-532.
12. Izadi, S., Agarwal, A., Criminisi, A., Winn, J., Blake, A., and Fitzgibbon, A., C-Slate: a multi-touch and object recognition system for remote collaboration using horizontal surfaces. *Tabletop 2007*, 3–10.
13. Kettebekov, S. and Sharma, R., Understanding gestures in multimodal human computer interaction. *J. AI Tools, 9*, 2, 2000, 205–223.
14. Kirk, D., Stanton Fraser, D., Comparing remote gesture technologies for supporting collaborative physical tasks. *Proc. CHI 2006*, 1191-1200.
15. Kirk, D., Rodden, T., and Stanton Fraser, D., Turn it this way: grounding collaborative action with remote gestures. *Proc. CHI 2007*, 1048-1058.
16. Li, J., Wessels, A., Alem, L., and Stitzlein, C., Exploring interface with representation of gesture for remote collaboration. *OZCHI 2007*, 179-182.
17. Ou, J., Chen, X., Fussell, S., Yang, J., DOVE: Drawing over video environment. *Proc. Multimedia*, 100–101.
18. Tang, A., Neustaedter, C., and Greenberg, S., Videoarms: embodiments for mixed presence groupware. *People and Computers 20*, 2007, 85-102.
19. Tang, A., Pahud, M., Inkpen, K., Benko, H., Tang, J., and Buxton, B., Three's company: understanding communication channels in three-way distributed collaboration. *Proc. CSCW 2010*, 271–280.
20. Tang, J., Minneman, S., VideoDraw: a video interface for collaborative drawing. *ToIS*, 9, 2, 1991, 170–184.
21. Tang, J., and Minneman, S., VideoWhiteboard: video shadows to support remote collaboration. *Proc. CHI 1991*, 315–322.
22. Wigdor, D., Williams, S., Cronin, M., et al., Ripples: utilizing per-contact visualizations to improve user interaction with touch displays. *Proc. UIST 2009*, 3-12.
23. Yamashita, N., Kaji, K., Kuzuoka, H., and Hirata, K., Improving visibility of remote gestures in distributed tabletop collaboration. *Proc. CSCW 2011*, 98-104.

A Comparison of Competitive and Cooperative Task Performance Using Spherical and Flat Displays

John Bolton, Kibum Kim and Roel Vertegaal
Human Media Lab
Queen's University
Kingston, Ontario, K7L 3N6 Canada
{bolton, kibum, roel}@cs.queensu.ca

ABSTRACT
While large flat vertical displays may facilitate persistent public sharing of work, they may do so at a cost of limited personal display space when everyone can see each other's activity. By contrast, new form factors, such as spherical displays, support sharing display space by limiting the user's view to at most one hemisphere. In this paper, we investigate how different interactive large display form factors can support differences in sharing of information during competitive and cooperative task conditions. We implemented three different large display types: spherical, flat, and a flat display with divider. Results show that task performance of the flat display with divider did not differ significantly from that of the spherical display. Additionally, we implemented and compared three peeking techniques that facilitated sharing of information. Results show participants peeked significantly more in competitive tasks than they did in cooperative tasks. Usage of peeking techniques between the spherical display and the flat display with divider were similar, and distinct from that of the flat display. Not surprisingly, results show that the affordance of easily glancing at a partner's work on the flat display provided a significant advantage in cooperative tasks.

Author Keywords
Spherical Displays, Organic User Interfaces, Collaboration, Shared Space.

ACM Classification Keywords
H5.m. Information interfaces and presentation (e.g., HCI): Miscellaneous.

General Terms
Design, Human Factors, Experimentation.

INTRODUCTION
Large interactive displays allow multiple collocated users to collaborate, share information and work in parallel. Large flat displays typically do not prevent co-workers from viewing each partner's work, unless a physical barrier is introduced between them. In both collaborative and competitive settings, users often need to be able to keep certain information private [3, 13, 16, 18]. The recent development of novel display form factors such as spherical displays [1, 2, 4, 12] offers new opportunities for designing sharing of display space, by presenting a natural visual barrier between users. While Benko [2] identifies spherical displays as a solution for single user scenarios that integrates both an interesting display form factor and input sensing, spherical displays also present a number of interesting properties that make them potentially suitable for cooperative as well as competitive tasks in multi-user conditions: (1) they increase the number of pixels on a display without compromising availability of personal physical space, by wrapping pixels around an optimal volume, (2) they offer more freedom in terms of users' physical body positions, with a smooth transition between shared and individual zones and (3) they enable curved data, such as satellite data images of the earth or panoramic visualizations to be mapped onto a volume without distortion.

Figure 1. Spherical multi-touch display used in the experiment

In particular, spherical displays physically limit a user's view to at most one hemisphere, and naturally provide users with their own personal territories, without restricting the amount of data displayed (see Figure 1). This lets users maintain their own display space while still allowing for collaboration using a single communal display. Because of its geometry, users of a spherical display may have an intuitive understanding of what information might be shared, and what information might be private. For example, information at the edge of a user's view is easily shared. On the other hand, due to the visibility constraints of a curved surface, opposite work areas are naturally separated from each other, thus reducing the potential for interference.

Another interesting characteristic of a spherical display is that it presents pixels around a central point, providing no set or single location for a user's workspace. Depending on the task, users can walk freely around a spherical display to select the location or part of the data they wish to work on. For example, if users plan to work in a tightly coupled fashion, they can choose to stand next to each other in front of the sphere. By contrast, if users require privacy, they can arrange themselves to segment the display into two opposite hemispheres. Users can potentially move freely between these various modalities, something that may be difficult to do with traditional flat displays.

The continuous nature of a spherical display requires different approaches to presenting information. Because information viewable to a user of a spherical display is determined by the user's location, availability of information is largely determined by sharing physical territory. This contrasts with flat displays where, in general, all information is viewable to all users from all locations at all times.

Spherical displays wrap an extraordinarily large number of pixels into a space much smaller than that of an equivalent flat display. For example, a 3' diameter spherical display has a surface area equivalent to a 10' diagonal flat display. Not only does this facilitate collocated collaboration in small spaces, it also means the available pixels in a user's display space are within easy reaching distance, while at the same time those pixels remain largely invisible to other users.

Although individual interactions on spherical displays have been examined [1, 2, 7, 10, 12, 15], to the best of our knowledge, it has not been shown whether a spherical display's unique natural affordances for individual work spaces allow for a true advantage in a group activity, when compared to a flat vertical display. In this paper, we present an empirical evaluation of a low-cost multi-touch spherical display, compared with flat display form factors in cooperative and competitive tasks. To allow viewing restrictions similar to those observed in a spherical screen in our flat display condition, we introduced a third condition in which a physical divider split the view of the flat display between two users. Throughout competitive and cooperative tasks, we observed how users would peek to view invisible information on the other side of the display, using a set of widgets designed for this purpose. Our hypothesis was that in terms of performance and peeking technique usage patterns, the flat display with divider would be more similar in characteristics to the spherical display than to the flat display condition.

This paper is structured as follows: in the next section, we describe related work. We then discuss the details of our experiment, display apparatus and three peeking widgets. Finally, we discuss our findings and conclusions.

RELATED WORK

In this section we explore existing work on the development of various hemispherical, spherical and large public displays and interaction techniques on each display.

Hemispherical Displays

Companje et al. [7] developed Globe4D, an interactive four-dimensional globe. The system consisted of a hemispherical display that can be freely rotated along all axes. The earth application on this display allowed users to rotate a globe while shifting time, allowing them to see the movements of continental drift. Globe4D could be physically rotated, with the projected image kept in sync. However, it did not feature any other touch interaction techniques. This system is an early example of an interactive hemispherical display. It made use of its unique form factor to allow interaction with information that is not well suited for traditional flat displays.

Spherical Displays

Grossman et al. [10] developed a 3D geometric model building application to demonstrate multi-finger gestural interaction on a spherical volumetric display. The user's fingers were tracked using a Vicon motion tracking system. This camera-based motion tracking system requires an external setup. Interaction techniques were designed to make use of the unique features of volumetric displays, specifically, the 360-degree nature of the viewing volume. Their set of interaction techniques consisted of *SurfaceBrowser* for file management, model transformations, and techniques to combine models to create scenes. *SurfaceBrowser* could be rotated by scrubbing the non-dominant hand's index finger along the display surface, bringing hidden objects into view. They made the observation that the 360-degree visibility of information when using a volumetric display makes it useful for exploring collaborative multi-user interaction. Due to the unique properties of a 360-degree display, the authors mentioned the need to examine considerations of how users share space. Additionally, it was found useful for the *SurfaceBrowser* to show information on the inner surface of the display, in effect, reducing it from a 3D volumetric display to a 2D hemispherical display.

Holman & Vertegaal [12] examined how a spherical display could be used to edit 3D NURBS (Non-uniform Rational Basis Spline) objects. Their display was projected upon using two external projectors. Multi-touch gestures were used to create curvilinear objects. Again, a Vicon motion capture system was used for tracking both the user's fingers and the display itself. This system was based on the metaphor of a pottery table, where the concept of spinning the display while using gestures such as poking or flattening allowed the manipulation of a 3D mesh. The non-dominant hand was used for context, while the dominant hand was used for manipulation and deformation. A set of four interaction techniques was developed for use with the sphere. These techniques were spinning, poking, pulling, and mashing. They were used in combinations to produce specific effects. For example, a pull while spinning the display resulted in an extrusion along the entire circumference of the Blobject. This was an early example of the implementation of multi-touch gestures on a fully spherical display.

Benko et al. [1] developed a multi-touch spherical display that did not require external motion tracking, based on a 24" diameter Magic Planet system. To evaluate the system, they implemented a set of interaction techniques and reported on user behavior within four applications; a simple photo and video browser, an omni-directional data viewer, a painting application, and a Pong game. Interaction techniques consisted of dragging, local rotation, and scaling. Additional techniques such as object auto-rotation, flicking with inertia, and a command to send objects to the opposite side of the sphere were designed specifically for cooperative purposes. During their observations, they found that data spanning the entire display was problematic with multiple users. Individual users could not see others touching the display and users often became confused when seeing the results of other users' interactions. As a consequence, users would compete for control of the display. They concluded that limiting the consequences of a user's action to a specific area might be necessary. Additionally, they found that users had no master position around the sphere, and instead picked a location at random. However, they found that a single user would not move extensively from their initial position during use. Their observations seem to indicate that a spherical display presenting, at most, one hemisphere to a user is an important design consideration. Users still chose a specific work area when using a spherical display. This indicates that implementing methods for viewing information on the non-visible hemisphere is an important consideration for applications on spherical displays. We implemented peeking interfaces on our system to allow users to view the information on the non-visible hemisphere.

Large Public Displays

Vogel & Balakrishnan [19] demonstrated an interactive large display supporting public and personal information, while allowing users to move seamlessly from implicit to explicit interactions. A framework of interaction phases was developed, consisting of ambient display, implicit interaction, subtle interaction, and personal interaction. During the personal interaction phase, direct touch was used to manipulate information items and provide additional detail. In this phase, the user's body helped occlude their personal information. Additionally, privacy gestures could be used to hide notifications and display elements, preventing the display from entering the personal interaction phase. Their observations indicated that privacy is an important consideration when designing interactive public large flat displays. They suggested that occlusion provided by a user's body was not sufficient when displaying sensitive information and that privacy design should be a major focus of production level displays.

Tsandilas & Balakrishnan [17] examined techniques for reducing spatial interference between users on shared displays. Four methods were considered, including object ownership, and split displays. With a shared screen, users had access to the entire display, but could only manipulate objects they owned. This allowed users to move freely around the display and control their own boundaries. However, this approach is dependent on the social situation. In some cases, a single user may try and control a disproportionately large area of the screen. Additionally, this does not take into account a user's desire for privacy. By contrast, a split display removed interaction conflicts between two users but limited users to an explicitly defined area. Spherical displays naturally provide a split screen method of interaction due to their visibility constraints. As a user's position is generally fixed around a spherical display, there are few disadvantages to restricting a user to an explicitly defined area.

EXPERIMENT DESIGN

Many previous studies in Computer Supported Cooperative Work (CSCW) show that when users can see where others are working, it becomes easier to establish common ground in cooperative tasks [8, 9, 14]. However, there are also complicated situations, particularly in competitive gaming, where participants may *not* wish to share all their information with each other but *still* need to check their partner's progress for strategic purposes. It is important to understand this fundamental tradeoff between sharing information, actively or passively, and preserving privacy as being juxtaposed. To better understand the effect of display form factors on this information sharing tradeoff in collocated tasks, we designed an experiment in which we investigated group activities in three single display groupware settings; a large spherical display, a large flat vertical display, and a large flat vertical display with divider.

As Benko et al. [1] pointed out, there are some characteristics of spherical displays that may make them suitable for shared tasks. Collaborators can, for example, stand opposite to each other, providing the potential for sharing of eye contact and facial expressions, if the sphere is small and low. To provide a leveled playing field, and to allow for comparative screen real estate with the large flat display conditions, we constructed a large spherical screen that allowed collaborators to only sense each partner's presence, but not to see each other's face. We also introduced a physical divider that split the flat display and used this as a baseline of our experiment, allowing for similar visibility, and thus privacy settings, as the spherical display.

In order to help participants access their partner's screen, which was not readily visible on the spherical and the flat with divider displays, we designed a number of peeking techniques. Those techniques allowed participants to easily browse their partner's workspace if necessary. Participants used three peeking techniques (i.e., button, windowing and scroll) as well as conversing with their partner or physically walking around the display to access their partner's work. Frequency of peeking techniques allowed us to measure the effects of visibility characteristics of different display conditions on group tasks.

Tradeoffs between preserving privacy and sharing a visual workspace may vary with respect to the privacy characteristics of the task. We therefore developed two different group scenarios: one cooperative and one competitive task setting. In the cooperative tasks, participants solved a puzzle together as a team. In competitive tasks, participants competed with their partners but also worked with them—the task was designed as a contest that still required the sharing of information. This cooperative and competitive task design enabled us to create collaboration styles where participants were required to maintain a balance of preserving their own work and sharing their partner's work actively or passively.

There has been some suggestion that spherical screens may be inherently more suited to 3D tasks, giving them an inherent advantage over flat panel displays [10]. To not positively bias the spherical condition, we decided to design our task using more common 2D graphics. Tasks included a mix of graphical object manipulation and text retrieval tasks common to most Graphical User Interfaces (GUIs). A second reason for using a graphical game was that it made it more difficult to verbally share information about the figures, thus encouraging participants to peek at each other's display instead.

We used a 3 x 4 x 2 within-subjects factorial design, with three factors: display type (3 levels consisting of spherical, flat, and flat with divider), peeking technique (4 levels consisting of button, windowing, scroll, and physical peeking), and collaboration style (2 levels consisting of cooperative and competitive). In the flat display condition, physical peeking required participants to simply turn their head. In the spherical and flat display with divider conditions, the participants walked around the display to view their partner's work. Each group of two participants completed the 24 tasks in a single two-hour session. To minimize any practice or carry-over effects, the order of the conditions was counterbalanced using a Latin square.

EXPERIMENT METHODOLOGY

We conducted a controlled laboratory experiment to compare the effects of display curvature and peeking techniques on cooperative and competitive collaboration

Figure 2. Large flat vertical display with divider used in the experiment.

styles. This section describes the apparatus and methodologies used to conduct our experiment.

Display Apparatus

The experiment was run on three different prototype displays; a spherical display, a large flat vertical display, and a large flat vertical display with divider.

Spherical Display

Our spherical display surface consisted of a 36" diameter hollow sphere made of acrylic, with a 19" hole cut in the bottom (see Figure 1). The acrylic was sandblasted to create a diffuser on the inside, allowing it to act as a projection surface. This also allowed it to act as a diffuse illumination surface for infrared light, which allowed multi-touch detection. The projector was mounted at the bottom of a base, an oil drum commonly known as a burning barrel, using a projector mount inside of the barrel. The projector was aimed upwards in order to project off an 18" hemispherical mirror mounted inside the top part of the sphere. This mirror projected light to the rest of the surface of the display. A custom Quartz Composer patch provided spherical distortion to the graphics so as to ensure graphics appeared undistorted after projection onto the sphere's surface. Infrared illuminators were pointed at the inside of the acrylic sphere and arranged to spread light evenly across the surface. Two SONY EyeToy cameras with wide-angle lenses were modified as infrared cameras. These were placed inside the sphere pointing towards each hemisphere. We used a diffuse illumination approach to register multi-touch points by the fingers on the surface of the sphere.

Large Flat Vertical Display

The large flat vertical display consisted of an 8' by 4' piece of 1/4" plexiglass mounted inside a wooden frame. Six 25mW infrared lasers with line generating lenses were mounted around this large piece of plexiglass, creating a plane of infrared light that was slightly elevated off the surface of the plexiglass. A large rear-projection screen was fastened to the back of the plexiglass to provide a diffuser. A SONY EyeToy camera with a custom lens that had been modified to allow it to sense infrared light was placed behind the plexiglass for touch detection.

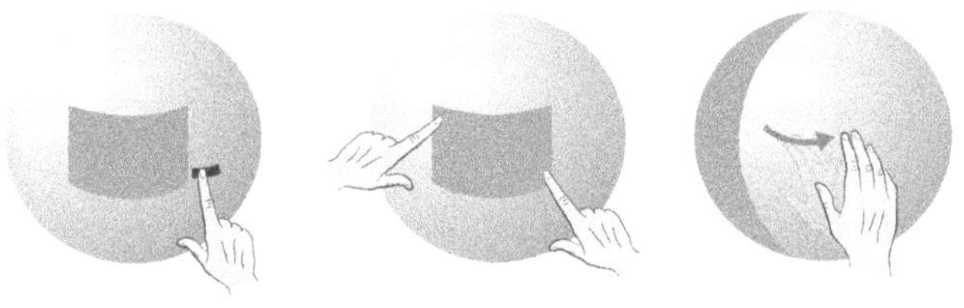

(a) Peek Button (b) Windowing (c) Scroll

Figure 3. Peeking techniques used in the experiment.

For the flat large vertical display with divider setting, we mounted a curtain as a divider in the middle of the large flat vertical display (see Figure 2). This blind was used to prevent participants from being able to observe each other's workspaces as well as each other's bodies, in one condition of the experiment.

Touch Detection on the Display

Touch detection was accomplished using the open source project Community Core Vision. An unmodified version was used for the flat screen hardware condition while a multi-cam version was used for the sphere. Care was taken that the final resolution of touches was identical in all display conditions.

Peeking Techniques

Participants were instructed that they would converse and physically walk around the display to see their partner's work but could also use peeking techniques as much as they pleased, in all display settings. We designed the following three peeking techniques to facilitate convenient access to a partner's workspace (Figure 3):

Peek Button.

A large button, labeled "PEEK", was placed to the right of the work area. When touched, this button opened a window showing the partner's workspace. The window was of fixed size, and covered the entire workspace. The window was removed by touching the "PEEK" button a second time.

Windowing

Here, participants used a bimanual pinch gesture to open a variable-size window into the partner's work area. Touches were used to form the top left and the bottom right corner of this window, allowing the participants to peek only at a portion of the partner's workspace.

Scroll

A scroll window was triggered when participants placed their hand flat onto the display surface. This scrolling window was of fixed vertical size, but brought more of the partner's workspace into view as the participants moved their hand horizontally away from left to right or to the opposite direction. This potentially allowed participants to view the entire workspace of the partner.

In all cases, changes were only visible to the participant performing the gesture, but the partner was informed of the peeking act by increasing a "Peeked" counter to the side of his workspace (see Figures 1 and 2). We expected that there would be a different preference for the chosen peeking techniques on each display and the frequencies of usage for each peeking technique might vary depending on the display form factor.

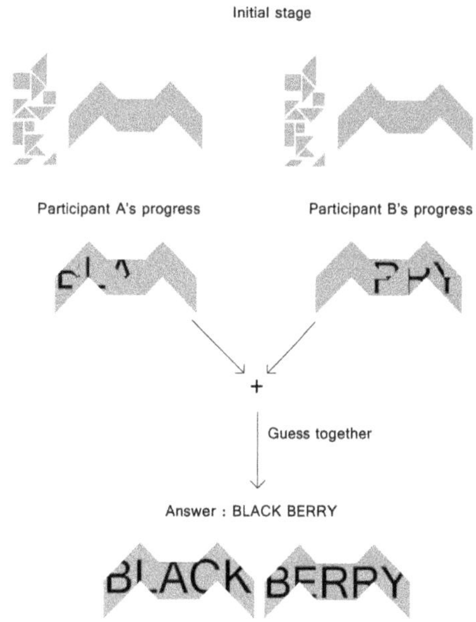

Figure 4. Tangram phrase guessing game (in cooperative condition).

Task

For our experimental task, we chose an electronic variant of the Tangram game, which is widely used to explore the creation and maintenance of common ground in CSCW and psycholinguistic literature [5, 16, 20]. The original Tangram game requires users to arrange a number of different geometric pieces into various shapes within a silhouette of the target shape provided. We modified this basic Tangram game by combining it with a phrase-guessing game in order to increase the need for peeking and communication between participants (Figure 4).

The goal of our modified Tangram game was to find a hidden two-word phrase inside the solution silhouette. When a participant moved a piece to the correct position on the Tangram silhouette, this piece revealed a portion of a word. Each participant received a different word, which together formed a phrase. Our Tangram phrase guessing game required participants to work individually as well as collaboratively to achieve the task goal. Participants would not need to assemble all pieces of the Tangram puzzle if they collaborated and guessed the phrase based on a partially solved puzzle. Both participants started with the same puzzle, displayed in different hemispheres on the spherical display or in a separate working area on the flat display. Participants were co-located in all conditions. They were able to use both hands to move pieces around their workspace. To ensure that any geometric distortion of the 2D graphical elements on a spherical screen would not negatively impact performance, all pieces were in the correct orientation, and did not require rotating the shape. When a piece was within 10 pixels of the correct location it would snap into place upon release of the piece.

During the game, participants were allowed to talk to each other as well as walk around to their partner's workspace to view his or her Tangram. In addition, they were allowed to use one of the three peeking techniques, based on the experiment conditions, to view what was on their partner's screen. This allowed us to investigate whether the peeking techniques were efficient and effective in use.

In the cooperative task, participants completed the Tangram game together as a team. They could share their partner's progress and help the partner move pieces or guess the solution. There were two components to completing a game: finding a word and finding a phrase. After a participant found a word, he or she was asked to click a button labeled "WORD". The round was complete when both participants had hit the "PHRASE" button and provided the correct solution (see Figures 1 and 2). This setup allowed us to measure both individual and combined task performance.

In the competitive task, the goal was to be the first to correctly guess the two-word phrase. Participants might monitor their partner's progress and take advantage of peeking to get a hint of how to assemble the pieces or in order to guess the phrase first. As with the cooperative condition, after a participant found a word, he or she was asked to click a button labeled "WORD". The winner was decided when one of the participants hit the "PHRASE" button and provided the correct solution by writing it on a note. The other participant continued work on the task until s/he was able to guess the phrase.

Participants

Fourteen groups of participants (mostly university students, 12 males and 16 females), all paid volunteers, worked in pairs to complete Tangrams in the three display conditions. Some partners knew each other and had previously worked together. The average age of the participants was 21.8 years, with a range between 18 and 36 years old. All participants reported some familiarity with multi-touch UIs.

Procedure

Before beginning the experiment, participants were asked to fill out a brief demographic survey as well as a consent form. They were then given written instructions for each task on a piece of paper.

Following this, participants underwent a training period for each display system. This allowed them to get a feel for the game and the different methods of viewing each partner's information. During the training session, participants were required to practice each peeking technique at least five times and were allowed to ask for any clarification. The training session took a total of 12 minutes of instruction on the game procedures in both cooperative and competitive conditions. Of this time, about 7 minutes was used to practice the different peeking techniques.

After the training session, participants were asked to complete the Tangram games on three different touch

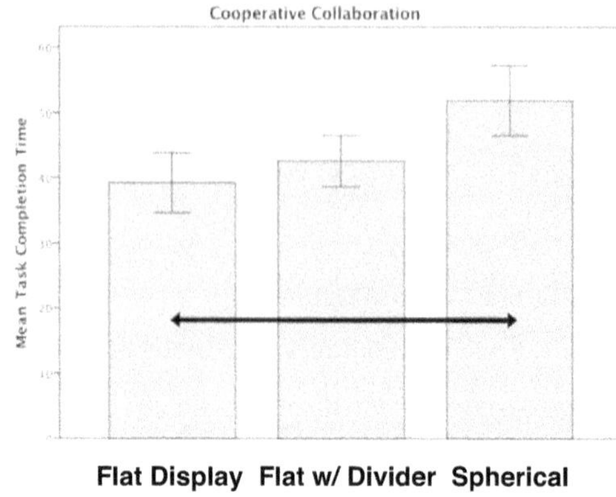

Figure 5. Task completion times in the cooperative tasks (arrow indicates significance between flat and spherical display).

screens: a spherical display, a large flat vertical display, and a large flat vertical display with divider. They proceeded to play 12 games in the cooperative condition and 12 games in the competitive condition. Participants were given a maximum of two minutes to guess the phrase. All conditions were presented in a counterbalanced order based on Latin squares.

To motivate efficient and accurate performance, the participants of the fastest team from all groups were rewarded with a $20 gift card for the cooperative condition. Additionally, the fastest individual participant of all groups in the competitive condition was rewarded with a $10 gift card.

After each display condition (i.e., spherical, flat, and flat with divider), participants were asked to finish the NASA task load index (NASA-TLX), which is a subjective, multi-dimensional assessment tool designed to obtain workload estimates from users. Finally, when participants completed all conditions, an experimenter conducted an interview with participants in order to collect general comments on their experience during the experiment. All experimental sessions were recorded on video to allow transcription of discussions between participants.

RESULTS

Results were calculated over 13 groups. Data from one group was discarded because they did not follow instructions and played the game cooperatively during the competitive condition. All results were analyzed using a within-subjects repeated measures analysis of variance (ANOVA), evaluated at an alpha level of .05.

Task Completion Time

Task completion time was defined as the slower of the two participants' time to the final phrase in the cooperative collaboration condition and as the faster of the two participants' time to the final phrase in the competitive collaboration condition. Our first analysis, which was a three-way ANOVA across collaboration styles, display types, and peeking techniques, showed a significant main effect of collaboration styles, but no significant effect for display types or peeking techniques: collaboration styles,

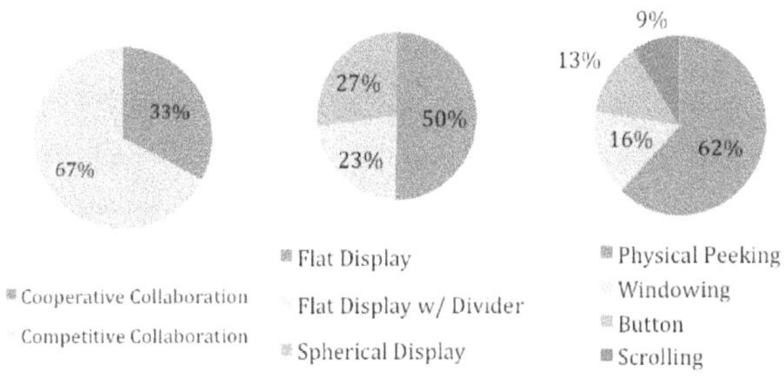

(a) by collaboration style (b) by display type (c) by peeking technique

Figure. 6 Frequency of peeking.

F(1,6)=18.62, *p<.01*; display types, *F*(2,12)=3.17, p=.08; and peeking techniques, *F*(3,18)=1.55, p=.24. Participants completed the task faster in a cooperative collaboration style than they did using a competitive collaboration style.

For our next analysis, we separated out the collaboration styles to see if they were affected differently by the form factor of the display. A two-way ANOVA showed a significant main effect of display types on performance in cooperative collaboration (*F*(2,13)=3.74, *p<.05*) but not in competitive collaboration (*F*(2,16)=2.99, p=.08). Post-hoc pairwise Bonferroni corrected comparisons of cooperative collaboration showed this difference to lie between the flat display and the spherical display (*p<.04*). It also showed there were no significant differences between the flat display with divider and the spherical display (see Fig. 5).

Peeking

To examine the effects of visibility of information, we analyzed how often the participants peeked during the experiments. Figure 6 shows the frequency of each peeking technique broken down by experiment factors. Results were analyzed by a within-subjects repeated measures ANOVA across collaboration styles, display types, and peeking techniques. There were significant main effects for all three factors (i.e., collaboration styles, display types and peeking techniques). Participants peeked more than twice as much in the competitive collaboration condition as they did in the cooperative collaboration condition (F(1,6)=34.51, *p<.001*). Participants also peeked almost twice as much on the flat display as they did on the spherical display or on the flat display with divider (F(2,26)=8.52, *p<.002*). Of the four different peeking techniques, physical peeking was preferred (F(3,39)=85.58, *p<.001*). It seems that the frequency of peeking was inversely proportional to the physical effort required—Turning the head in the flat display condition required less effort than traveling around the display in the spherical display or the flat display with divider conditions, resulting in more peeking using the flat display. Also, competitive conditions increased peeking and appeared to reduce conversation between the partners as compared to cooperative conditions.

Figure 7 shows the frequency of use of each peeking technique as a percentage of the total number of peeks per display type. There was a clear preference for physical peeking with the flat display. However, interestingly, participants used the software-based peeking techniques too on the flat display although they could easily see the partner's workspace by turning their head. This might be due to the novelty of these software-based peeking techniques, or because they wanted to peek without attracting any partner's attention. There was a slight preference for the windowing technique on the spherical display (26%) and on the flat display with divider (30%). The preference for the windowing peeking technique may indicate that participants tried to minimize the amount of their own workspace that was obscured.

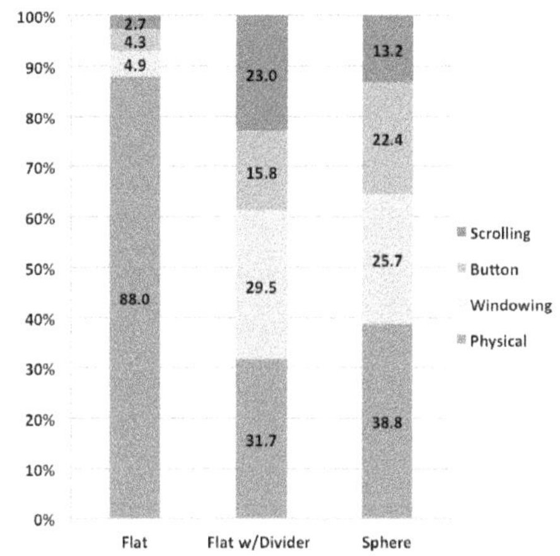

Figure 7. Peeking techniques preferences.

Physical Peeking

In addition, we isolated the case where participants were only allowed to physically peek. This means that none of the software peeking techniques (i.e., button, windowing, scrolling) were provided but participants could physically move around or turn their head to see their partner's workspace. This separate analysis of physical peeking helped us to understand participants' natural interaction with their partner in each display condition. Additionally, it allowed us to examine, in general, whether providing different peeking techniques changed participants' behavior in cooperative and competitive collaborations.

A two-way ANOVA showed significant main effects for display types and collaboration styles on the frequency of physical peeking (*F*(2,6)=10.86, *p=.010* for displays, *F*(1,3)=24.4, *p=.016* for styles) and the task completion time (*F*(2,22)=6.36, *p=.007* for displays, *F*(1,11)=8.04, *p=.016* for styles). Participants peeked less and completed tasks significantly faster in cooperative conditions (average 5.4 peeking counts, 44.2 seconds in task completion time, *p=.016*) than in competitive conditions (8.7 counts, 54.9 seconds).

A Bonferroni post-hoc test revealed that the time to complete the task was significantly faster on the flat display (42.1 seconds, *p=.008*) compared to the spherical display

	Spherical Display	Flat Display	Flat w/ Divider	
How physically demanding was the task?	6.50 (1.07)	4.42 (0.82)	5.73 (0.96)	*p=0.05*
How hurried or rushed was the pace of the task?	11.69 (1.19)	9.27 (1.39)	9.58 (1.33)	*p=0.02*
How hard did you have to work to accomplish your level of performance?	10.19 (0.79)	7.65 (1.01)	8.31 (0.99)	*p=0.01*

Table 1. Mean ratings (s.e.) for physical demand, temporal demand, and effort for each display condition. Lower scores are better.

(55.3 seconds). There were no statistically significant differences for task completion time between the flat display with divider (51.2 seconds) and the flat display (p=.23) or between the flat display with divider and the spherical display (p=.64). For the frequency of peeking, no statistical difference was found in pairwise comparisons of displays.

Overall, the result of physical peeking showed similar patterns to the cases of the software-based peeking techniques: (1) participants peeked less and completed tasks faster in cooperative collaboration than in competitive collaboration, and (2) peeked more on the flat display (14.1 times) than on the spherical display (3.9 times) or on the flat display with divider (3.1 times).

Subjective Preferences

In the post-experiment questionnaire, participants were asked to select which display they preferred. Six scales of the NASA TLX, *mental demand, physical demand, temporal demand, performance, effort,* and *frustration* were measured on a scale from 0-20 where 0 was a low and 20 was a high rating for that factor.

Table 1 shows the data summary for the mean of physical demand, temporal demand, and effort on each display. A Friedman test indicated that there were statistically significant differences in physical demand ($\chi^2(2)=6.000$, $p=0.050$), temporal demand ($\chi^2(2)=7.537$, $p=0.023$) and effort ($\chi^2(2)=8.521$, $p=0.014$) depending on the type of display.

Post-hoc analysis with Wilcoxon Signed-Rank Test was conducted with Bonferroni correction applied, resulting in the significance level set at p=0.017. For physical demand, there were no significant differences between the flat display with divider, and the spherical display or the flat display. However, there was a statistically significant reduction in physical demand in the flat display vs. the spherical display (Z=-2.551, *p=0.011*). For temporal demand, there were statistically significant reductions on the flat display (Z=-2.378, *p=0.017*) and the flat display with divider (Z=-2.641, *p=0.008*) versus the spherical display. However, there was no significant difference in temporal demand between the flat display and the flat display with divider. For effort, there were no significant differences between the flat display with divider, and the spherical display or the flat display. However, there was a statistically significant reduction in effort in the flat display vs. the spherical display (Z=-2.838, *p=0.005*).

OBSERVATIONS

We also observed differences in how participants interacted during each condition. In particular, we analyzed transcripts from our interviews and video footage, focusing on how participants collaborated.

Collaboration on the Flat Display

P1: "When we were trying to solve our puzzles together it was a lot easier when there was no screen in the way."

The ease with which participants viewed each partner's information on the flat display enabled both participants to be more aware of each other's context than on the spherical display or on the flat display with divider. Participants often conversed based on updates of their partner's work. This real-time monitoring of awareness information was not as straightforward with the non-flat display types.

Collaboration on the Spherical Display or on the Flat Display with Divider

P11: "Okay the two triangles are on the left side, the two big ones. The square is almost at the end of the G shape. My word is 'Roots'."

Similar to the spherical display, when using the flat display with divider, the context for participant's advice was not inherently visible. As a result, participants gave detailed instructions. In contrast to deictic references such as "this" or "that", which were more frequently observed in the flat display condition, participants *described* specific pieces, ensuring that the other partner could clearly understand their advice without having access to a view of the puzzle. In the above case, participant 11 was providing the correct location for two pieces. He made clear which pieces he was referring to by describing them and explaining where to move them. Following this, he provided his WORD to help the partner guess her WORD correctly and the PHRASE.

Verbal Communication

P12: "I found I was much more vocal, I suppose much more for communicating rather than just looking at his screen. We had a conversation while we worked collaboratively."

Although not always used by all groups, verbal communication was the predominant method of sharing information. Certain groups maintained a conversation while collaborating, constantly updating each other on the visible portions of their WORD, the correct position for various pieces, and guesses of what their WORD or the PHRASE might be. Some groups observed sharing strategies, which providing suggestions for which pieces to move into position upon starting the puzzle.

Peeking on Competitive and Cooperative Collaborations

P11: "When I'm collaborating I can just ask her but when I'm competing I can't ask her so I have to do it sneakily (i.e., peeking)."

During the competitive collaboration, participants were much more likely to use peeking techniques. As emphasized above, participants still wanted to view partner's information but were not willing to share information with their partner. The peeking techniques became a method of sneaking information during the competitive collaboration, in contrast to the sharing that was common during the cooperative collaboration.

P4: "I can see what she's doing and she can see what I'm doing and we don't necessarily have to communicate verbally."

Although verbal communication was a common method of sharing information between participants when collaborating, sometimes it was not necessary. By providing the partner with access to all information using peeking techniques, participants didn't feel a need to constantly update the partner verbally on progress, as a quick glance was sufficient for sharing the partner's work.

DISCUSSION

For the cooperative task condition, the flat display performed better than a spherical display or the flat display with divider. Participants completed cooperative tasks on the spherical display 32% slower than they did on the flat display. However, performance of the spherical display was not significantly different from that of the flat display with divider. As expected, easy sharing of information on the flat display was beneficial in the cooperative condition and, for this reason, participants could complete the tasks faster using the flat display than using the spherical display or the flat display with divider. As for the competitive task condition, contrary to expectations, display form factor had no significant effect on performance.

Although participants were provided with various peeking techniques to access the information on the partner's screen, we observed that participants were more likely to view their partner's information by turning their head or walking around. They used this physical peeking significantly more than all other methods of peeking. In the flat display condition, physical peeking tended to consist of head rotation, whereas in the other display conditions, physical peeking required the participant to walk around to the partner's side of the display to view what was on his/her screen, impacting performance. In the spherical display condition, participants took longer to walk around than in the flat display with divider condition.

Despite the fact that a participant could not see all the details on the partner's screen on the spherical display or on the flat display with divider, they could discuss what they were doing and where they were working, if necessary. This method of discussion seemed to be faster and relatively easier than using the software-based peeking techniques to view the other screen. Verbal conversations were the prevalent form of communication in all three display conditions. According to Clark's *principles of least collaborative effort* in language use, people apparently do not like to expend more effort than they need to get their addressees to understand them [6]. Such a principle helps account for the phenomenon of the prevalence of verbal communication offset use of the software-based peeking techniques in all three different display conditions.

In single display groupware, partitioning of workspace content and reduction of dominant behavior by one participant has often been achieved by establishing separated personal territories [16]. However, we found that the natural division of workspace on the spherical display and the flat display with divider did not eliminate dominant behavior. We observed several cases in which a participant who had completed his part of the puzzle moved to the partner's screen and took control of her Tangram pieces. This behavior was contrary to our expectations for the spherical display or the flat display with divider's ability to maintain privacy but it suggested an alternative method of tight collaboration.

When using the flat display, maintaining an awareness of the other participant was relatively easy, natural, spontaneous, and unforced [11]. Unfortunately, this awareness was much harder to maintain in the spherical display and the flat display with divider conditions, and as a result, it was often difficult to determine what the other participant was doing. Our peeking techniques on the spherical display and on the flat display with divider involved a kind of workspace awareness that was forced and punctuated rather than natural and smooth. The participants had less awareness about the other person's activities in those display conditions than they did with the flat display. There was no difference in performance between the spherical display and the flat display with divider, but significant differences with the flat display. It showed that collaboration on large displays was primarily affected by the affordance of awareness, and not the display shape itself.

In terms of task performance, we received mixed results: As we expected, participants could finish the task faster when they cooperated than when they competed, but surprisingly the display type did not significantly affect task performance. However, when analyzing the effects of the displays in detail, by separating cooperative and competitive tasks, we found that the flat display was superior to the spherical display in the cooperative task. This result reinforces the validity of previous CSCW studies in the effect of visual sharing in cooperative tasks [8, 9, 14]. On the other hand, we were not able to find that the spherical display's natural affordances for individual workspaces allowed for a true advantage in the competitive tasks, when compared to the flat display or the flat display with divider.

One limitation of this study is that we used 2D graphical data on a spherical screen and the task was confined to one factual task rather than a richer array of more complex collaboration in a real-world environment. If the task had required interacting with 3D graphical data and frequent translation between public and personal space, we might have obtained different results. Our prototype and initial user experiences were encouraging and a next step is to visualize and interact with 3D models within the display. We are currently working on interaction techniques for 3D objects on spherical and cylindrical volumetric displays [4].

CONCLUSIONS

In this paper, we investigated how different interactive large display form factors might naturally support differences in sharing of information during competitive and cooperative task conditions. We compared performance in a two-person Tangram game between three display conditions: a spherical, a flat display, as well as a flat display with a physical divider between participants. To explore different degrees of sharing, we implemented three peeking techniques that facilitated sharing information: a button, a windowing, and a scrolling technique. The flat display condition performed better than the spherical display condition in a cooperative task setting. However, performance of the spherical display was not significantly different from that of the flat display with divider. In competitive tasks, display type had no significant effect. On the other hand, display type affected both the quantity and mix of peeking techniques used. Usage of peeking techniques between the spherical display and the flat display with divider were similar, and distinct from that of the flat display. Participants peeked significantly more in competitive tasks than they did in cooperative task. Our experiment result suggested that the affordance for the awareness of a partner's workspace on the flat display might have a greater significant advantage in cooperative tasks, compared to the spherical display's natural affordance for private workspaces.

REFERENCES

1. Benko, H., Wilson, A. D., and Balakrishnan, R. Sphere: multi-touch interactions on a spherical display. In Proc. UIST, (2008), 77-86.
2. Benko, H. Beyond flat surface computing: challenges of depth-aware and curved interfaces. In Proc. MM, (2009), 935-944.
3. Birnholtz, J. P., Grossman, T., Mak, C., and Balakrishnan, R. An exploratory study of input configuration and group process in a negotiation task using a large display. In Proc. CHI, (2007), 91-100.
4. Bolton, J., Kim, K. and Vertegaal, R., SnowGlobe: A Spherical Fish-Tank VR Display. In Proc. CHI (2011), 1159-1164.
5. Clark, H. Using Language. Cambridge University Press, Cambridge, MA, USA, 1996.
6. Clark, H. and Brennan, S. Grounding in communication. In L.B. Resnick, J.M. Levine, & S.D. Teasley (Eds.). Perspectives on socially shared cognition. Washington: APA Books. 1991.
7. Companje, R., van Dijk, N., Hogenbirk, H., and Mast, D. Globe4D: time-traveling with an interactive four-dimensional globe. In Proc. SIGGRAPH. (2007), 26.
8. Fussell, S.R., Kraut, R.E., and Siegel, J. Coordination of Communication: Effects of Shared Visual Context on Collaborative Work. In Proc. CSCW, (2000), 21-30.
9. Gergle, D., Kraut, R. E., and Fussell, S. R. Action as language in a shared visual space. In Proc. CSCW, (2004), 487-496.
10. Grossman, T., Wigdor, D., and Balakrishnan, R. Multi-finger gestural interaction with 3d volumetric displays. In Proc. UIST, (2004), 61-70.
11. Gutwin, C. and Greenberg, S. A Descriptive Framework of Workspace Awareness for Real-Time Groupware. Journal of Computer Supported Cooperative Work 11, 3 (2002), 411-446.
12. Holman, D. and Vertegaal, R. Organic user interfaces: designing computers in any way, shape, or form. Communication of ACM 51, 6 (2008), 48-55.
13. Hudson, S. E. and Smith, I. Techniques for addressing fundamental privacy and disruption tradeoffs in awareness support systems. In Proc. CSCW, (1996), 248-257.
14. Kraut, R., Fussell, S., and Siegel, J. Visual Information as a conversational resource in collaborative physical tasks. Human-Computer Interaction 18, 1 (2003), 13-49.
15. Lin, J., Chen, Y., Ko, J., Kao, H., Chen, W., Tsai, T., Hsu, S., and Hung, Y. i-m-Tube: an interactive multi-resolution tubular display. In Proc. MM, (2009), 253-260.
16. Scott, S. D., Sheelagh, M., Carpendale, T., and Inkpen, K. M. Territoriality in collaborative tabletop workspaces. In Proc. CSCW, (2004), 294-303.
17. Tsandilas, T. and Balakrishnan, R. An Evaluation of Techniques for Reducing Spatial Interference in Single Display Groupware. In Proc. ECSCW, (2005), 225-245
18. Tse, E., Histon, J., Scott, S. D., and Greenberg, S. Avoiding interference: how people use spatial separation and partitioning in SDG workspaces. In Proc. CSCW, (2004), 252-261.
19. Vogel, D. and Balakrishnan, R. Interactive public ambient displays: transitioning from implicit to explicit, public to personal, interaction with multiple users. In Proc. UIST, (2004), 137-146.
20. Yamashita, N. and Ishida, T. Effects of Machine Translation on Collaborative Work. In Proc. CSCW(2006), 515–524.

A Model for the Design of Interactive Systems based on Activity Theory

Sebastian Döweling
SAP Research Darmstadt
Bleichstr. 8, 64283 Darmstadt, Germany
sebastian.doeweling@sap.com

Benedikt Schmidt
SAP Research Darmstadt
Bleichstr. 8, 64283 Darmstadt, Germany
benedikt.schmidt@sap.com

Andreas Göb
SAP Research Darmstadt
Bleichstr. 8, 64283 Darmstadt, Germany
andreas.goeb@sap.com

ABSTRACT
Activity theory has gained increasing popularity as a tool for the design of interactive systems. Its central idea is that user actions can only be fully understood when analyzed within the context of motive-driven activities. However, this context is currently only partially explicit in existing models; e.g. the well-known model by Engeström promotes social aspects of context, but does not make the physical and technical environment – relevant aspects for interactive systems design – explicit.

We present a model that incorporates the social, physical and technical context of activities. This model supports designers and developers in understanding users, their activities and the respective contexts, and allows deriving requirements for the design process directly from the model. We believe this will prove especially helpful when designing for novel devices and multi-user scenarios. We illustrate the practical use of our model with examples from two domains: composition of IT services and co-located collaborative modeling.

Author Keywords
Activity Theory; Systems Design; Context

ACM Classification Keywords
H.5.2 User Interfaces: Theory and methods

General Terms
Design; Human Factors; Theory

INTRODUCTION
In the last decade, the focus in personal computing has significantly shifted from desktop computers in office situations to new devices with different form factors, such as tablet computers or large interactive displays, which are used in a variety of ways, with different motives and in different contexts (e.g. the same mobile phone model could be used by a student to kill time with mobile gaming in spare hours, but also by a business consultant to check the latest version of a presentation before entering a meeting at a customer's site).

Yet, most contextual aspects are absent in traditional HCI models like the human-information processor [4]. Motivated by the criticism of the lack of context in these models (e.g. [2]), activity theory (AT) [23, 36] has been proposed as a framework for new methods, which overcome this limitation (e.g. [20, 22]). The use of AT is supported by the results of studies, which showed that people organize their work in terms of activities that are executed to meet some overall objective, often in collaboration with others (cf. [3]); moreover, AT has already been adopted as a design approach by a number of researchers (e.g. [2], [12] or [3]).

However, AT is often used rather as a set of guiding principles than as a model from which problems or requirements can be directly derived. Moreover, while AT "requires that the scope of analysis be extended from tasks to a meaningful context of a subject's interaction with the world" [20], this is currently only partially explicit in existing models.

First steps into the direction of making context explicit have been taken by Engeström [11], whose model promotes social aspects of context. This model, however, does not make the physical and technical environment explicit. While this may be acceptable when the focus is on the redesign of work processes on a rather high level of abstraction (where hard- and software can be treated as a unit subsumed under the tool concept of AT), it does not allow to make new challenges visible in the model that occur when novel hardware is used or integration with existing IT infrastructures is necessary.

Further on, while it was noted that activities shape the context for actions and operations [27], the way this actually happens has currently not been specified in an integrated model. This would however be necessary to integrate the findings of an AT-based analysis directly into commonly used design artifacts, e.g. wireframe models or conceptual sketches for new applications or interaction techniques.

In this paper, we propose a model that takes both the physical/technical and the human/social context explicitly into account and provides an integrated perspective on the different levels of analysis in AT. This model will allow designers and developers to identify potential conflicts between the individual elements and derive the respective requirements directly from the model.

The rest of this paper is structured as follows: First, we give a brief overview of AT. Then, we review related work, with a focus on context-of-use analysis and AT-based approaches. Subsequently, we present our approach, and illustrate how our model can be applied with two examples. We conclude with a discussion on design decisions and limitations of our approach, a summary of our contributions and a brief outlook on future work.

ACTIVITY THEORY

In this section, we briefly introduce the core concepts of activity theory (AT) and the basic model of tool-mediated interaction between subject and object, on which we build in the rest of the paper. A more comprehensive treatment can be found e.g. in the original works by Leontiev and Vygotsky [23, 36], as well as in newer introductory texts like [22] or [20]. Shorter introductions are also available in numerous publications on activity theory-informed designs, e.g. [12]. We also briefly touch the activity system model by Engeström, which introduced the idea of conflict analysis in the AT-model [11].

In AT the subject is seen as placed on a continuum between individual and collective, and is defined by possessing agency, which is understood as "the ability and the need to act" [20] – a need that focuses on objects, and is based on a *motive* [23]. An important feature of activity theory is, that the manipulations a subject carries out on an object are not seen as direct, but rather as mediated through *tools*, or more general *instruments*, and that thus "the object is seen and manipulated not 'as such' but within the limitations set by the instrument" [22]. Together with the aforementioned concepts, this is subsumed in Figure 1.

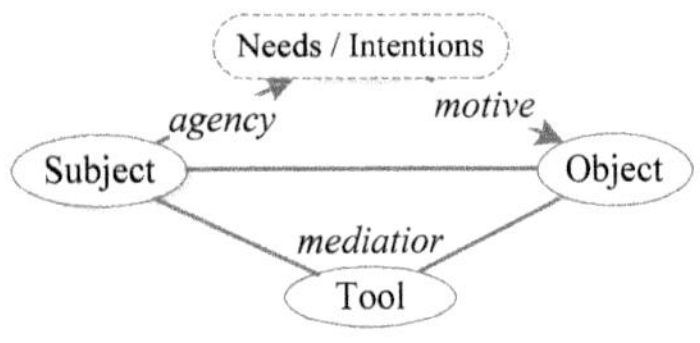

Figure 1: Standard model of activity theory (agency added).

The hierarchical structure of activity theory

Activities are not the only level of analysis foreseen by AT, but are rather seen as being composed of actions and operations. While activities are driven by motives, actions are conscious goal-directed processes executed to transform an object into the desired state. Given favorable circumstances, actions may become operations, which are intuitive interactions with the world that do not require much cognitive effort. The hierarchical structure of AT materializes some of these developmental aspects. Transitions between actions and operations are possible based on individual adaptation and contextual changes. Actions and operations for similar goals may exist in parallel and are selected based on the context and individual preferences. Notably, that implies that actions do not suddenly become operations when they are decomposed, but rather that they are equivalent solution procedures linked by processes of in- and externalization [20].

Engeström's activity system model

Among the various works based on AT, especially Engeström's model of AT has found wide adoption. In his work on learning activities [11], he extends the classical subject-tool-object triangle with additional elements derived from an integration of community/population perspective. He thus arrives at a combination of three "mediated" triangles: *rules* describe both implicit and explicit regulations of the interaction between a subject and the relevant community for an activity, "division of labor" describes how the community organizes work with and access to the relevant object (cf. elements in conflict analysis, Figure 2).

Among others, Engeström used this model for the re-design of work processes in hospitals, where he used it for a contradiction analysis between the respective elements (cf. Figure 2). Notably, the use of the model was not restricted to the analysts; it was a public artifact used to spawn discussion among the affected personnel of the hospital.

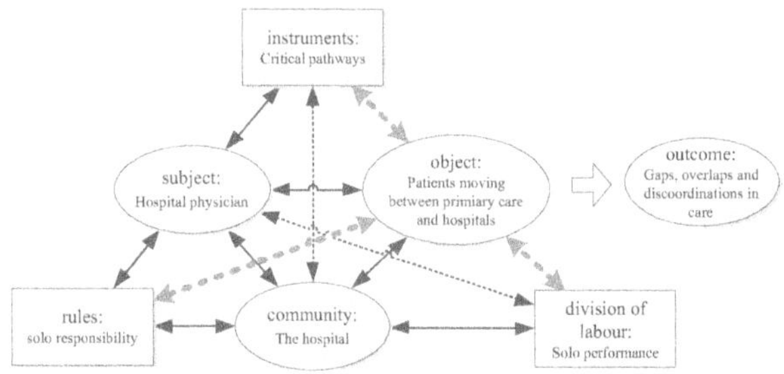

Figure 2: Example of Engeström's contradiction analysis (affected relations in bold red). Figure reproduced from [10].

Engeström's view of activity as object-oriented, collective, and culturally mediated [10] fits the requirements of analyses of organizations. There are, however, some subtle difficulties (discussed in more detail in section after the next) that prevent the immediate use of Engeström's model for other types of analysis, e.g. the dichotomy of subject and community, and the integration of collectives and the AT hierarchy.

RELATED WORK

While a large number of methods guide and support the design of interactive systems, for the review of related approaches we concentrate on two issues: first, existing work in the area of context-of-use analysis in general (orienting towards the human-centered design process as outlined by ISO 9241-210 [18]); and second, AT-based approaches that can help to understand the context-of-use.

Context-of-use analysis

The user-centered design process (ISO 9241-210) describes design cycles based on the transformation of 1) context-of-use details to 2) user and organizational requirements that are 3) transformed into system designs. The system's design is then 4) evaluated against the requirements, resulting in a new cycle or the successful finalization of the cycle.

The context-of-use is the foundation of the human-centered design process, with an important role in the requirement identification and the design evaluation context. The context-of-use consists of information about the user group, tasks, the technical environment, the physical environment and the organizational environment [24].

Existing methods focus on a structured collection of the required context-of-use information. Methods like discussions, interviews, surveys, diaries and field studies are used. Often context-of-use is captured by using artifacts like lists or tables. The methods collect single pieces of context information that are treated like atomic units without describing the relations that exist between them. Such a systemic relation is necessary. Context is not a static construct that consists of passive elements but a dynamic set of relations. As Schultze puts it, analysis should not only list what users do, but also needs to identify "what the doing does" [33].

The context-of-uses analysis for systems design in terms of activity theory describes the situatedness of an activity. One approach is given by [13], considering activities on a micro level (personal, independent activities), a meso (collective activities) and a macro (activities in large social contexts) level for past, present and future. For systems design, it is necessary to identify those context fragments that influence the system with respect to the introduction of new designs.

Approaches for context-of-use analysis based on AT

AT, with its understanding of context-embedded activities, provides a framework to describe systemic relations. Following this insight, different AT-based methods have been proposed that support the systems design process with respect to a context-of-use analysis.

Simple methods focus on the collection of data that conforms to AT. An example is the activity checklist to support ethnographic studies [19]. The list is used to support interview processes that are intended to identify relevant context elements.

Beyond the AT-conform collection of data, different methods use Engeström's model to create systemic relations. Neto et al. [28] combine the I* framework for organizational modeling and AT to address context-of-use analysis. Martins and Daltrini [25] use Engeström and decompose identified activities to actions and operations. Based on the creation of the systemic relations and the hierarchical decomposition of activities requirements are elicited. Korpela [21] uses concepts of activity theory to analyze information systems development as complex work practice based on activity networks. For Korpela the organizational perspective is in the focus: different involved stakeholders with different areas of expertise across organizational boundaries.

Other methods use Engeström's model and explicitly integrate the creation of conflicts in the designed model. Collins et al. [6] show the applicability of AT to capture data collected in interviews. They make a hierarchical use of Engeström's model to organize the findings of the interview and identify tensions and conflicts to derive design requirements. The Activity-Oriented Design Method (AODM) based on Engström's model [26] intends to support requirement elicitation based on a context-of-use analysis. The situation is modeled in Engeström's activity system and then decomposed to different sub-triangles that get analyzed.

Bardram describes activity analysis, a method of activity theory application that applies ethnographic field studies and an analysis of observations [3]. Activities within a setting are identified and, in a second step, patterns of these activities are analyzed.

Method assessment

The excerpt of design methods based on AT as well as a comparative study of AT-based design tools [29] show the trend to the application of Engeström's model. Especially the use of contradictions is an important mechanism that is used to identify requirements. E.g. AODM is a valuable extension of Engeström's model. The permutation of different sub-triangles of the activity system supports the identification of conflicts and contradictions.

Despite of the benefits of Engeström's model, there are different drawbacks. The roots of Engeström's model are in the analysis of organizational change [20]. Consequences are a focus on activity models with organizational mediators ("rules", "division of labor") that involve a community. Especially for the design of new systems other context factors are highly relevant. Examples are the physical and the technical environment.

Another limit of the reviewed systems is a lack of integration with respect to the hierarchical decomposition of activities. Only few methods make use of the hierarchical decomposition and if they use it, the decomposition is an additional method step that returns results that are not integrated in the activity system constructed with Engström's model.

Overall, we see a need for AT-based models for systems design that have a broad perspective on the context-of-use, explicitly integrating the technical and the physical environment. Such methods should reflect activities as hierarchical constructs and should, in particular, provide means to refine the context-of-use for an analysis of actions and operations during the process of decomposition.

A MODEL TO SUPPORT THE DESIGN OF INTERACTIVE SYSTEMS

We perceive the design of interactive systems as an exploration and analysis of the design space of possible solutions for a problem in a given context. Each design for a new solution introduced into this context, be it a tool or a new work process, can (and usually will) have consequences for other entities in the context, with effects differing, depending on the level of detail on which analysis and design of the new solution happen. This entails interactions between the newly introduced solution and other entities in the domain as well as interactions between different levels of analysis.

Support for a structured and integrated analysis of the effects of design decisions is currently not well supported by the reviewed AT-based systems design tools. Together with the initially outlined need to design for novel device contexts (e.g. smartphones, tablet computers, large interactive displays), the model we describe in this section has three major design goals:

- the generation of requirements for the design of interactive systems directly from the model,
- the explicit inclusion of the physical/technical and the human/social context into the model, and an
- integrated perspective on all levels of analysis in AT.

Beyond the general ideas of AT – in particular that a subject's actions can only be fully understood in context – our work is mainly inspired by the works of Engeström, especially his contradiction-based approach to the analysis of work with AT [10], and the work of Mwanza [26], who employed a systematic iteration through the subgraphs of Engeström's model to identify research questions.

Model overview

Each model instance is a fully connected hexagon (see Figure 3), in which we distinguish between mediating (rectangles) and non-mediating entities (ellipses). This distinction is largely identical to that of Engeström's model (we discuss the ways in which we deviate from his model separately in the next sub-section). A separate element is foreseen to represent the (intended) outcome of an activity (or action or operation respectively). Summing up, the seven elements in our model are ("(m)" = mediating entity):

- **Subject:** Individual or collective entities from the domain of interest that have agency
- **Object(s):** the material component of the entities towards which a subject directs its activities (, actions, or operations)
- **Outcome:** the state of entities or the information, which a subject seeks to produce through its activities (, actions, or operations)
- **Activity (, action, or operation) context**: material and social aspects of entities in the background that frame an activity (, action, or operation)
- **Rules (m)**: technical or social constraints imposed on the subject when pursuing an activity (, action, or operation)
- **Instruments (m)**: artifacts through which the subject perceives and/or modifies an object; reverse effects may include learning triggered by the application of an instrument to an object
- **Workflows (m)**: temporal patterns governing interaction between a subject and instruments, objects or entities from the activity's (, action's or operation's) context

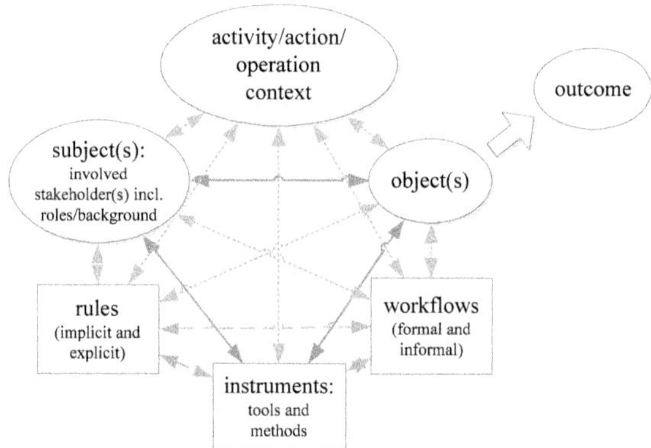

Figure 3: Our model is comprised of seven elements; the main difference to Engeström's model is the introduction of an explicit element representing the context of the activity/ action/ operation; relations have been derived from the original activity theory model (solid blue lines); Engeström's model (dotted green lines); or newly added to reflect changes to the model elements (dashed orange lines).

Differences to Engeström's activity system model

The elements in our model differ in three respects from those in that of Engeström's model (and those approaches that directly base on his model):

- We re-phrased *division of labor* as *workflows* to emphasize the inclusion of temporal aspects (e.g. access frequency to a system), even when the subject is actually only a single person.
- We introduced a new element called *activity context* (or action or operation context respectively), which describes the situation and the environment a user is in and acts in, i.e., for a start, the (physical or virtual) acts of other users in the immediate environment, but also material aspects of that environment (e.g. the layout of a meeting room or the type of device an application is installed on). With a view to the original model of activity theory, the *context*-element can be seen as an explicit representation of the idea that "the activity itself is the context" [27].
- We split up the "community" element in Engeström's model into those members actively participating in the analyzed subject-object-interaction and those involved in other interactions. The former have been merged into the subject-concept, which now explicitly incorporates collective subjects. This allows us to express situations in which a group of subjects shares a common goal, e.g.

software developers assembling in front of a whiteboard. Implicitly collective subjects are already present in existing works on activity theory, e.g. in [20] and [26].

The last aspect has further consequences for the semantics of the relations between elements in our model: first, in Engeström's model the "rules" element mediates the interaction between community and subject, yet our model sees it as a mediator between the subject and the activity context, essentially broadening its scope. We also perceive rules to be a mediator for interaction between subject and object, e.g. via user access rights; second, the "workflows" element can now describe both process coordination in the given context, but also the temporal patterns in which the subject accesses or manipulates the object of the activity.

While we also made the relations between rules, workflows and instruments explicit in our model, this does actually not mark a change to Engeström's model as "an activity is actually a systemic whole in the sense that all elements have a relationship to other elements, but all those connections have not been presented in the picture because of sake of clarity" [22].

Empirical grounding and conflict analysis

To use the described model for a concrete problem in a specific domain, it is necessary to specify the respective elements for each model instance. Similar to many AT researchers, we deem first-hand empirical research to be the optimal source for this specification, we also consider on literature reports of empirical research, (predictive) theories and practical experience/design knowledge as valid grounding. In addition, creative solutions may emerge from each of these methods of grounding.

Based on the element connections in the model, an analysis of the relations and interactions is possible, and conflicts and contradictions can be systematically identified. This analysis is not restricted to an "as-is" analysis of the status. One or more nodes can be filled with concepts for new solutions, e.g. tool designs, allowing a systematic analysis of the possible consequences of the change. Consequently a set of related models may be generated on each level of the activity, action and operation hierarchy that observe the presumed effects of design decisions or changes to other elements of the model. As such it is a powerful tool for the analysis of the effects of design decisions as well, especially based on an initial "as-is" analysis of the environment.

Multiple designs & design perspectives

Within the same domain, a set of model instances may exist that are horizontally or vertically connected. Horizontal connections stand for design space explorations on the same level of detail. This may be necessary because there are a number of designs (or design variants) to be evaluated. In a similar way, the system designer may decide to analyze with different design perspectives.

We foresee three of these perspectives: an instrument perspective (designing new tools or sign), a workflow perspective (proposing new ways of organizing actions) and a rule perspective (formulate new rules that govern interaction).

Subsequently each design can be explored in more detail by following the vertical connections. Vertical connections are the result of decomposing activities. Based on the possibility of our model to integrate the analysis on different levels of detail (see below), this decomposition can be repeated multiple times until the desired level of detail is reached.

Support for design on different levels of detail

Designing interactive systems requires specifications on multiple levels of detail, e.g. the design of landing pages, the layout of forms for data entry and the type of menu for a webpage. AT provides the perspective of activities and related actions or operations (e.g. for a web application on traditional desktop computers activities might be mapped to overview or landing pages, actions and operations may exist on the level of forms, menus and buttons).

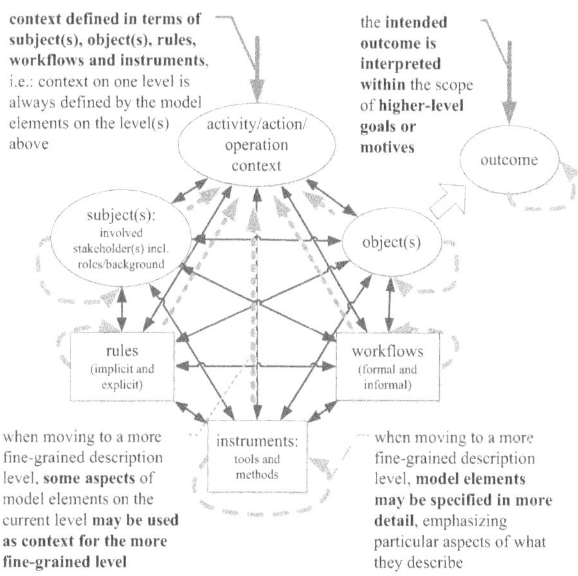

Figure 4: Integration of the different levels of analysis in AT is done by following a three steps approach when proceeding to a more fine-grained level of analysis: element refinement (green dashed arrows), context enrichment (orange dotted arrows) and context integration (blue solid arrows).

To support a holistic approach to the design of interactive systems, our model integrates the different levels of analysis via the newly introduced "context"-element. In particular, we propose a three-step algorithm when proceeding to a more fine-grained level of analysis (subsumed in Figure 4):

1. **Element refinement:** the individual elements are specified in more detail to reflect the appropriate

granularity for the analysis on the next level of analysis.

2. **Context enrichment**: the aspects/parts of the individual elements not directly involved in the interaction on the more fine-grained level are treated as background information (and background actions). They are thus carried over to the more fine-grained level for integration into the context element (this is particularly important to accommodate for the dual nature of computers and software, i.e. they may work as tools on a higher-level of abstraction, but also as a technical context/platform on a more fine-grained level).
3. **Context integration:** Context information carried over from the previous level of analysis is used to define the situation/background for the analysis on the current level. Also the objective/intended outcome is carried over to provide interpretation guidance to the intended outcome on the current level.

It should be noted that these steps will usually be applied multiple times for a transition between two levels, as higher-level interactions are commonly composed of multiple lower-level interactions (e.g. activities are composed of a larger number of actions or operations).

Using the model to identify requirements

To derive requirements directly from our model, we employ a method that builds upon the idea of using the AT model to detect conflicts between individual elements by Engeström [10] and that of systematic iteration through subgraphs of the model as proposed by Mwanza [26].

For a systematic identification of requirements for a new component that is part of a newly created (or re-designed) interactive system, empirical grounding and the decomposition of activities should be performed as described above. When the desired level of detail is reached, only two steps are necessary to generate requirements:

1. **Analyze possible permutations for conflicts**: treat four elements as fixed: subject, context, object, and a fourth depending on the initial choice of the design perspective (i.e. instrument, workflow or rule). Now iterate through the possible subgraphs (the graph itself is not considered) of the respective model and analyze for conflicts (as computer support would require extensive domain modeling, we assume this step to rely on the designers' assessment).
2. **Generate requirements from involved elements**: if a conflict occurred in the previous step, combine the elements to generate a requirement for a newly designed solution (e.g. a new software tool or functionality).

EXEMPLARY APPLICATIONS OF OUR MODEL

To illustrate how our model can be applied for the design of interactive systems in various contexts, we present two examples: composition of IT services and collaborative graphical modeling at a large touchscreen. While we did include some comments regarding the empirical grounding, the main purpose of this section is to provide more detail on the practical aspects of our contribution.

Composition of IT Services

Service-Based applications are a constituent part of many modern IT systems. One of the core principles of service-oriented architecture (SOA) is the composition of existing services to yield new functionality. Reuse as such is a well-established concept in software engineering and has been applied for many years, however merely for reasons of convenience and to increase development efficiency. In SOA, reuse via service composition is essential, especially in the context of cross-enterprise services [35].

Scenario

In order to facilitate efficient composition, services have to expose certain properties [14]. During service development, quality measures have to be taken in order to ensure the fulfillment of these properties. Of course, composition efficiency is only one out of many quality goals that are important when designing and implementing IT services. Most of the currently available quality models for software (e.g. the SQuaRE model [17]) share the approach of structuring quality along characteristics like maintainability, reliability or performance. However, this classification approach often lacks clear semantics regarding the relationship between super and sub-attributes. To overcome this, activity-based quality models were introduced [8]. These models describe software quality along activities that are conducted on or with a software system, leading to clear and intuitive decomposition semantics, which corresponds to the hierarchical nature of our model.

Design Perspective

From a systems design point of view, the investigation of possible problems can be used to improve tools involved in the customization process. We therefore take the instrument perspective when applying our model.

Empirical Grounding

The data that is necessary to fill the model elements is obtained in two ways. First, a literature review on SOA characteristics and their impact on product quality [35] provides the basic framework for the model. Second, industry experts are involved in applying the model, using their practical experience in order to provide information on specific parts, in particular the rules and workflow elements.

Model Application

In order to identify problems and derive quality requirements, first the activity to be analyzed has to be described in terms of our model. Second, several combinations of model elements are selected and considered conjointly. Subject, object and context are always selected; combinations of rules, tools and workflows are added optionally.

Figure 5 shows a problem identified using our approach. When creating a compound service, typical rules for the service integrator could be legal (there have to be license agreements in order to use the desired service), financial (the service must be available at acceptable charge in order to create a profitable compound service) or technical ones (the service interface has to match the available parameters and data formats). Using our model, we were able to deduce that the latter rule can be violated by services whose operations are not defined at a reasonable granularity. This observation further leads to the requirement that services should have adequately granular operations.

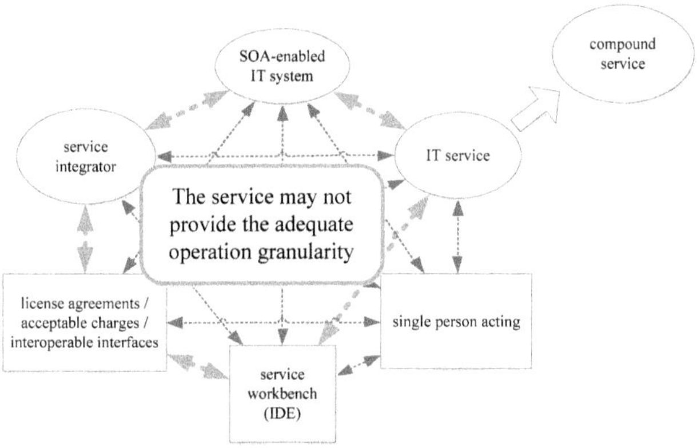

Figure 5: Example of a problem in the composition of IT services detected with our model

In a similar manner, a number of additional potential problems can be identified: A Service whose license is unclear, particularly restricted or incompatible with other licenses is hard to use for composition. Furthermore, the pricing model could be unfavorable for compositional use.

Generating Software Quality Models

Likewise, this procedure can be repeated for other common activities occurring during development, deployment, usage or maintenance of the SOA-based IT system, covering its whole life cycle. The resulting set of potential problems and derived quality requirements can be used to develop or enhance a corresponding software quality model [14]. Hence, our approach provides a theoretically well-founded and structured way to create activity-based quality models.

Collaborative graphical modeling

Scenario

Conceptual models, often in the form of diagrams, have many applications in modern enterprises. Among the most common types are arguably UML or UML-like diagrams used by software engineers and workflow or business processes diagrams used by system analysts. Building the respective models however is a complex task that requires both a thorough understanding of the domain as well as knowledge and practice in process design and visualization through formal modeling. This knowledge is commonly socially distributed, i.e. the input of multiple stakeholders with different backgrounds is required [31].

Current tools, however, fail to facilitate stakeholder involvement in the actual modeling process – as Rittgen recently noted, "the majority of the currently existing modeling tools are single-user tools. Strangely, this is even the fact for the ones that explicitly address group modeling" [31]. Moreover, even more advanced tools (e.g. COMA [30]) still rely on standard desktop computers – despite their limitations in displaying large data sets (cf. e.g. [1]) and their limited effectiveness for collaborative work; a few notable use electronic whiteboards (e.g. [5]) but focus rather on producing documentation quality diagrams than actual support of group interaction.

Recently, however, researchers have proposed the use of wall-size touchscreen displays for collaborative modeling [9]. Using these devices for collaborative model building will, however, require new tools that need to be tailored to the affordances and challenges of the devices.

Design Perspective

Using the example of interaction design for these new tools, the following section will illustrate the application of the analysis model described in this paper. Consequently the design perspective we adopt for the analysis is the instrument perspective. To illustrate, how analysis on more fine-grained levels of detail happens, the analysis will go through multiple steps of decomposition until a level suitable for support through interaction techniques for very large touchscreens is reached.

Empirical Grounding

For the empirical grounding of the analysis, we will largely orient towards existing literature on collaborative modeling, in particular the works of Rittgen [30], Rouwette [32] and those of Herrmann [15]. We can, however, also confirm the modeling actions found in their works from informal observation in a number of internal modeling sessions.

Model Application

The starting point, i.e. the activity under analysis, is the actual construction of a group model (cf. Figure 6a). While different motives for collaborative model building are possible, we assume the driving force is the need to understand the current situation of a company or government organization and the possible implications of strategies for the future (cf. e.g. [32]). This translates into the objective of building a shared mental model of the involved stakeholders, made explicit via a graphical representation.

Because more complex processes will likely require the input of multiple stakeholders, we assume that subgroups will be formed to work on specific aspects of the model (cf. e.g. [32]) and that these groups of users will interact in parallel. Furthermore, we assume that users will show respectful behavior towards their peers.

Pursuing this activity requires a number of actions to be executed, among them the use of divergent thinking techniques, e.g. brainstorming, to create an initial collection of model elements (cf. e.g. [15]), the discussion, or negation, of modification proposals for the model (cf. e.g. [31]) and, of course, actually performing modifications on a local part of the model. Each of these actions may happen multiple times and in parallel, when there are multiple sub-groups in the modeling session.

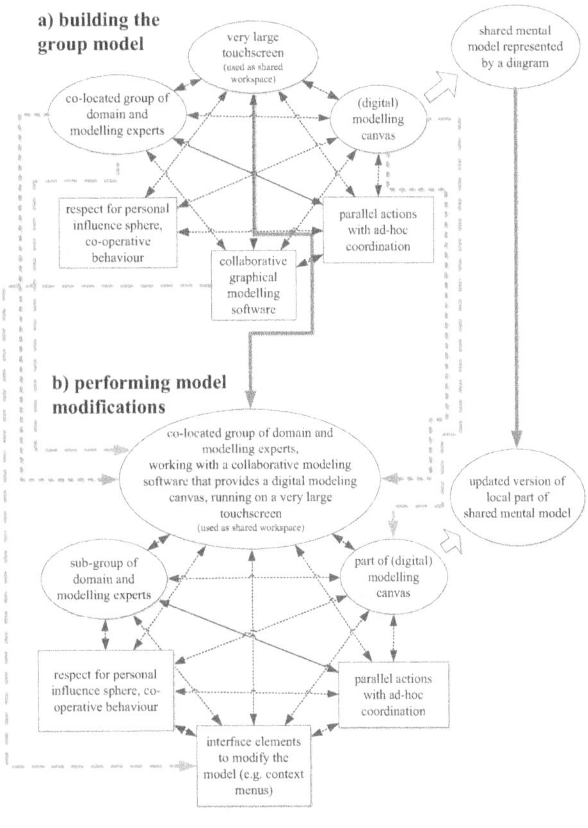

Figure 6: One problem detected by the analysis of the "access to nodes" operation as part of a "link nodes" action in order to update a local model in a collaborative modeling session.

For each of the identified actions, the three step procedure described in the model section has to be applied. Using the example of the "performing model modifications"-action, this means (cf. Figure 6b):

1. **Element refinement:** the "co-located group of domain and modeling experts" (subject element) is refined to the respective "sub-group of domain and modeling experts", the "collaborative graphical modeling software" (instrument element) to the "interface elements to modify the model (e.g. context menus)", and the "(digital) modeling canvas" (object element) to the respective "part of (digital) modeling canvas"
2. **Context integration:** the "very large touchscreen (used as shared workspace)" (context element) is carried over to the next level, the same applies to the "shared mental model represented by a diagram" (outcome element), which is however, specified in more detail, i.e. as an "updated version of local part of shared mental model"
3. **Context enrichment**: on the more fine-grained level of analysis, aspects of the subject element ("co-located group of domain and modeling experts"), the object element ("(digital) modeling canvas") and the instrument element ("collaborative graphical modeling software") become background to the action under analysis. Thus, the new context element integrates these aspects and now contains the "co-located group of domain and modeling experts, working with collaborative modeling software that provides a digital modeling canvas, running on a very large touchscreen (used as shared workspace)".

This procedure has to be repeated for the next two levels of detail to decompose the respective actions on the current level into more fine-grained ones; in the case of performing modifications on the model, these include creating, labeling, deleting or linking nodes. Assuming that linking happens by drawing an arrow from a source to a target node, this requires that users have access to both the source and the target node.

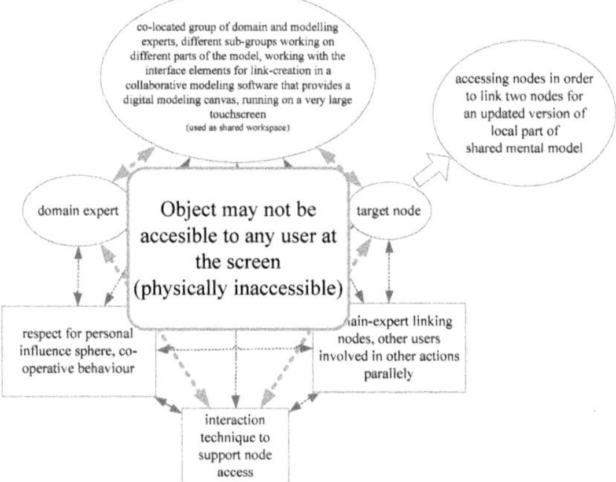

Figure 7: Conflict analysis for "accessing nodes" (example)

At this point, the conflict analysis outlined in the previous section can be used to identify potential conflicts that arise when users perform the linking action. The iteration through all subgraphs that contain subject, object, context and instrument (instrument perspective) reveals three potential conflicts (an example graph used for conflict detection is shown in Figure 7):

1. the display is very large and touch interaction is used (as indicated by the context element), thus nodes may simply be placed so distant on the screen hat they required physical movement to reach them (c.f. e.g. [7]).

2. multiple users occupy different areas on the screen (context element), thus conflicts with social protocols (rules element) may arise when one of the nodes of interest is located in the screen area right in front of another user (c.f. e.g. [34])
3. multiple users on the screen are interacting parallel and with different objectives (context element + workflow element), thus physical interference can occur when multiple users try to access nodes located near to each other on the touchscreen (cf. e.g. [16]),

To ensure efficient collaborative modeling, these problems need to be addressed with suitable interaction techniques.

DISCUSSION

The model is result of an iterative prototyping process that involved frequent tests of the applicability of the model to different types of system designs.

Design decisions

Although, our model is based on Engeström's activity system model, a number of significant changes have been made – among them the use of a collective subject. As a result, the community element from Engeström's model is split into subject and context, and rules are seen as mediators between subject and workspace rather than subject and community. This does however enable modeling of activities of groups consisting of multiple, equal actors, involved in ad hoc collaboration. Among others, this reflects the integration of semi-autonomous groups that are difficult to express in Engeström's organization-oriented model.

Open issues

AT with its perspective on human activity execution tackles a complex domain that is not accessible by formal methods. Terms like context, subject and tool are inherently fuzzy, not providing a precise one-for-all definition but require an understanding of the meaning for a domain. The proposed model demands the explicit identification of entities that realize the fuzzy terms.

As a result, entities for context, subject and instruments are required. Although the identification of the entities is a complex problem if a definition for the generic entity classes is required, the actual identification is simpler: an analysis of an explicit activity system generates entities that can be easily distributed among the different classes based on the systemic relations between the entities.

Another problem of AT is the representation of distributed systems that mediate between different subjects. Such activity systems require an extension of the model, e.g. the creation of two model instances that are interconnected.

CONCLUSION & OUTLOOK

In this paper, we have presented a model based on activity theory (AT), which supports the design of interactive systems. Contrary to existing AT-informed approaches, this model incorporates both the social, physical and technical context of activities, allowing system designers to handle both the technical possibilities and limitations of novel devices and new challenges that arise with ad-hoc collaborative interaction. Furthermore, the model integrates the different levels of activity theory analysis to allow design on all desired levels of detail.

Using a conflict-detection approach similar to the work of Engeström [11] and systematic iteration through possible subgraphs of the model (cf. [26]), this model allows designers to derive requirements directly from the model.

Preliminary results from interviews we conducted with requirements engineers and user interface designers show positive feedback on the context integration via our model. We also identified a need for integration with existing tools, e.g. personas or scenario descriptions. For future work, we will thus concentrate on a better understanding of these requirements for the use of our model by practitioners.

REFERENCES

1. Andersen, D.F. and Richardson, G.P. Scripts for group model building. *System Dynamics Review, 13*. 107-129.
2. Bannon, L.J. and Bodker, S. Beyond the Interface: Encountering Artifacts in Use. in Carroll, J.M. ed. *Designing Interaction: Psychology at the Human-Computer Interface*, Cambridge University Press, 1991, 227-253.
3. Bardram, J.E. and Doryab, A., Activity analysis: applying activity theory to analyze complex work in hospitals. in *CSCW '11: Proceedings of the ACM conference on Computer supported cooperative work*, (2011), ACM, 455-464.
4. Card, S.K., Moran, T.P. and Newell, A. *The Psychology of Human-Computer Interaction*. Lawrence Erlbaum Associates, 1983.
5. Chen, Q., Grundy, J. and Hosking, J. SUMLOW: early design-stage sketching of UML diagrams on an E-whiteboard. *Software: Practice and Experience, 38*. 961-994.
6. Collins, P., Shukla, S. and Redmiles, D. Activity theory and system design: A view from the trenches. *Computer Supported Cooperative Work (CSCW), 11*. 55-80.
7. Czerwinski, M., Robertson, G., Meyers, B., Smith, G., Robbins, D. and Tan, D., Large display research overview. in *CHI '06: Proceedings of the SIGCHI conference on Human factors in computing systems*, (2006), 69.
8. Deissenboeck, F., Wagner, S., Pizka, M., Teuchert, S. and Girard, J.-F., An Activity-Based Quality Model for Maintainability. in *ICSM '07: Proceeding of the IEEE International Conference on Software Maintenance*, (2007), 184-193.
9. Döweling, S. and Nolte, A., Closer to the Model – Collaborative Modeling with Wall-Size Interactive

Displays. in *MENSCH &COMPUTER '11: Workshop on "Anforderungen und Lösungen für die Nutzung interaktiver Displays im Kontext kollaborativer Arbeit"*, (2011).

10. Engeström, Y. Activity theory as a framework for analyzing and redesigning work. *Ergonomics, 43*. 960-974.
11. Engeström, Y. *Learning by Expanding: An Activity Theoretical Approach to Developmental Research*. Orienta-Konsultit Oy, 1987.
12. Fjeld, M., Lauche, K., Bichsel, M., Voorhorst, F., Krueger, H. and Rauterberg, M. Physical and virtual tools: Activity theory applied to the design of groupware. *Computer Supported Cooperative Work (CSCW), 11*. 153-180.
13. Gay, G. and Hembrooke, H. *Activity-centered design: An ecological approach to designing smart tools and usable systems*. MIT Press, 2004.
14. Goeb, A. and Lochmann, K., A Software Quality Model for SOA. in *WoSQ '11: International Workshop on Software Quality*, (2011).
15. Herrmann, T. and Nolte, A., The Integration of Collaborative Process Modeling and Electronic Brainstorming in Co-located Meetings. in *CRIWG '10: Proceedings of the Conference on Collaboration and Technology*, (2010), Springer, 145-160.
16. Hornecker, E., Marshall, P., Dalton, N.S. and Rogers, Y., Collaboration and interference: awareness with mice or touch input. in *CSCW '08: Proceedings of the ACM conference on Computer supported cooperative work*, (2008), ACM, 167-176.
17. ISO, J.S. ISO/IEC 25010:2011, Systems and software engineering - Systems and software Quality Requirements and Evaluation (SQuaRE) - System and software quality models, International Organization for Standardization, 2011.
18. ISO, T.S. ISO 9241-210, Ergonomics of System Interaction - Part 210: Human-centered design for interactive systems, International Organization for Standardization, 2010.
19. Kaptelinin, V. The Activity Checklist : A Tool for Representing the "Space" of Context. *Interactions, 6*. 27-39.
20. Kaptelinin, V. and Nardi, B.A. *Acting with technology - Activity Theory and Interaction Design*. MIT Press, 2006.
21. Korpela, M., Mursu, A. and Soriyan, H.A. Information Systems Development as an Activity. *Computer Supported Cooperative Work (CSCW), 11*. 111-128.
22. Kuutti, K. Activity theory as a potential framework for human-computer interaction research. in *Context and consciousness*, 1996, 17-44.
23. Leontev, A.N. *Activity, Consciousness, and Personality*. Prentice-Hall, 1978.
24. Maguire, M. Methods to support human-centred design. *International Journal of Human-Computer Studies, 55*. 587-634.
25. Martins, L.E.G. and Daltrini, B.M., Activity Theory: a Framework to Software Requirements Elicitation. in *WER '99: Workshop em Engenharia de Requisitos*, (1999), 30-44.
26. Mwanza, D., Where theory meets practice: A case for an Activity Theory based methodology to guide computer system design. in *INTERACT '01: Proceedings of the IFIP TC13 Conference on Human-Computer Interaction*, (2001).
27. Nardi, B.A. Studying context: A comparison of activity theory, situated action models, and distributed cognition. in Nardi, B.A. ed. *Context and consciousness*, MIT Press, 1996, 69-102.
28. Neto, G.C., Gomes, A.S., Castro, J. and Sampaio, S., Integrating activity theory and organizational modeling for context of use analysis. in *CLIHC '05: Proceedings of the Latin American conference on Human-computer interaction*, (2005), ACM, 301-306.
29. Quek, A. and Shah, H., A comparative survey of activity-based methods for information systems development. in *ICEIS '04: Proceedings of the International Conference on Enterprise Information Systems*, (2004), 221-232.
30. Rittgen, P., COMA: A tool for collaborative modeling. in *CEUR Workshop Proceedings No 344*, (2008), CEUR-WS.org, 61-64.
31. Rittgen, P. IT support in collaborative modelling of business processes - a comparative experiment. *International Journal of Organisational Design and Engineering, 1*. 98-108.
32. Rouwette, E.A.J.A. and Vennix, J.A.M. Group model building: A decision room approach. *Simulation & Gaming, 31*. 359-379.
33. Schultze, U. and Borland, R.J.J. Knowledge management technology and the reproduction of knowledge work practices. *The Journal of Strategic Information Systems, 9*. 193-212.
34. Scott, S.D., Carpendale, S. and Inkpen, K.M., Territoriality in collaborative tabletop workspaces. in *CSCW '04: Proceedings of the ACM conference on Computer supported cooperative work*, (2004), ACM, 294-303.
35. Voelz, D. and Goeb, A., What is Different in Quality Management for SOA? in *EDOC '10: Proceedings of the International IEEE EDOC Conference*, (2010).
36. Vygotsky, L.S. *Mind in Society: The Development of Higher Psychological Processes*. Harvard University Press, 1978.

"I'm Just Here to Play Games:" Social Dynamics and Sociability in an Online Game Site

Gregor McEwan[1], Carl Gutwin[1], Regan L. Mandryk[1], Lennart Nacke[2]

[1]Department of Computer Science, University of Saskatchewan 110 Science Place, Saskatoon, SK, S7N 5C9 {first.lastname}@usask.ca

[2]Faculty of Business and IT, University of Ontario Institute of Technology 2000 Simcoe St N, Oshawa, ON L1H 7K4 lennart.nacke@acm.org

ABSTRACT

There are many web sites that allow people to play board or card games against other human players. These sites offer tools and opportunities for social interaction, but little is known about how people really interact on these sites. To learn more about social dynamics on game sites, we analysed three months of log files from a large site to explore three themes: permanence (whether people formed a long-term association with the site); social interaction (in terms of shared activity and verbal communication); and formation of ties (whether people made contacts with others). Our analyses showed that while the site seems very social when we consider gameplay, the population was highly transient, and people talked very little. To explain these behaviours, we suggest that games and game-based activity should be considered as a legitimate form of human interaction. Our analysis provides new information and new ways of thinking about how game environments can be designed to support many kinds of sociability.

Author Keywords

Games, game sites, virtual social groups, sociability.

ACM Classification Keywords

H5.3. [Information interfaces and presentation]: *CSCW*

General Terms

Human Factors; Design; Measurement.

INTRODUCTION

The world-wide web has many game spaces where people meet to play parlor games (e.g. board or card games). Many of these sites are large and heavily used—for example, sites such as Yahoo Games, Pogo, and PlayOK host thousands of games at a time, and often have tens of thousands of players online at once. These large gathering places provide many opportunities for people to interact socially with others, both through shared activities and through verbal (usually chat-based) communication. The sites' persistence also provides opportunities for longer-term connections (e.g., people may play regularly with particular partners, form new friendships, or associate with subgroups).

Little is known, however, about social behaviour of people on these game sites. Previous work in CSCW has looked at other online communities (e.g., [3,6,15]), but game sites are a different type of gathering place than discussion forums, multi-user dungeons (MUDs), massively multiplayer online games (MMOGs) like World of Warcraft, or social virtual worlds (VWs) such as *There*. Game sites do not provide a persistent world (as with MUDs or MMOGs), but instead are based on playing individual short-duration games. In addition, interaction in parlor games is not driven by verbal communication, as it is in MUDs or social VWs (although games are certainly used as a setting for conversation in the real world). Understanding social dynamics in these kinds of online environments is important for designers to understand their user group and to inform decisions about providing social features in a site's interface.

To find out more about social behaviour among users of online game sites, we carried out an analysis of one large and popular site called PlayOK (www.playok.com). The site administrators provided us with logs detailing player activity and communication over a three-month period (totaling more than 400 million events); we also frequented the site, observed gameplay on a regular basis, and gathered responses from an on-line survey of 124 PlayOK players. Our primary analysis involved the activity logs, employing the 'social accounting' techniques that have been used in previous work [4,8]; observations and survey data were used to help interpret and fill out the log analyses.

Our study explored three themes that are frequently considered in work about online communities. These are: *permanence*, the idea that social groups benefit when people are long-term residents of a place (virtual or real) [2]; *social interaction*, which has been primarily considered in terms of verbal communication, but which can also include shared activity [7]; and *forming ties*, in which people meet others, associate, and make lasting connections (whether strong or weak) [7].

Our analyses show that PlayOK is quite different in terms of social behaviour depending on the questions being asked. When considering questions relating to playing games, people appear to be very social – for example, there are more than three million active members and more than 670,000 games played per day; many people (more than 10,000) play several games per day (more than 20), and people play much more frequently with a small group of opponents (on average, people play more than half of their games with only ten people).

In other analyses, PlayOK seems like a much less social place. Overall, people talk very little during games (72% of games have no chat messages, and 89% have three or fewer), and there is even less conversation outside of the games. Many interactions on PlayOK appear to be highly impersonal, with many one-time-only games; in addition, the interface automates much of the articulation work of the games, allowing people to play with no conversation. Last, the player population of PlayOK is highly transient – most people stay for only a few days, and only a small proportion of users stay active for more than a few months.

Although there are some exceptions to these findings (one person even met her future husband on PlayOK), the overall picture is one of a population whose only real contact with one another is through the games themselves. This poses a question that has not been widely considered previously in CSCW – how can an online gathering place survive for so long, and be so popular, with so few of the characteristics that are seen as vital to the health of a community?

This question leads us to consider the role of games as a social interaction mechanism. Our analyses suggest three ways in which games are interesting as social interaction, ideas that can help to explain how sites such as PlayOK succeed. First, play-based shared activity can be considered as a legitimate form of human interaction, where the social elements of the experience arise almost entirely from the game activity rather than from verbal communication. Second, the impersonal interactions that seem common in game sites (and that are facilitated by the games themselves) are still social connections that fill particular human needs, and that have parallels in a variety of real-world settings. Third, the 'unconnected interactions' of game sites like PlayOK are an opportunity and setting for people to engage in a pure kind of *sociability*, a surface-level but still-important part of human social engagement.

Although our investigation is preliminary, it seems clear that the kinds of interactions seen in PlayOK have as many benefits as potential drawbacks, and that game-based and activity-based interaction should be considered a legitimate type of social interaction. Our work shows the importance of considering a wider view of social interaction when designing for sociability in online game sites, and cautions that designers should not necessarily push towards more verbal communication or stronger personal connections.

RELATED WORK

We begin with an overview of virtual communities, then present studies of online games as virtual meeting spaces.

Virtual Communities

Research into real-world, place-based communities distinguishes between neighbourhoods and communities, similar to the distinction between space and place in the CSCW literature [10]. Communities are neighbourhoods that have a *sense of community*. A similar distinction can be made in the online world between virtual neighbourhoods and communities [2]. Considering whether a virtual community is a community according to classic definitions (e.g., Park's 1936 definition [18]) is beyond the scope of our paper, so we refer to previous analyses of this issue, such as those by Driskell and Lyon [7] or Wellman and Gulia [22].

In social psychology research a widely accepted definition of a real world sense of community is McMillan and Chavis's [14], which is composed of feelings of membership, feelings of influence, integration and fulfillment of needs, and shared emotional connection. Blanchard and Markus [2] have extended this work into the online world to define a *virtual sense of community*, which is composed of exchanging support, creating identities and making identifications, and production of trust.

However, a characteristic of these community analyses is that they are dependent on measuring the internal state of members through psychological measures (i.e., questionnaires) and/or content analysis of communication within the community. In contrast, we investigate a virtual community via large-scale log analyses. Our approach is closer to the archaeological style advocated by Jones [12], or the social metrics used by Ducheneaut et al. [8]. We explore sociality in the game site through simple cultural artifacts, such as counts of games and chat messages.

Games as Virtual Meeting Spaces

The game research literature has examples of different types of online games being used as virtual meeting spaces.

Initial studies of social interaction in MUDs followed shortly after the first MUD was developed in 1979 (see [6] for a brief history of MUDs and CSCW studies of MUDs). Although many studies of MUD-based interaction were based on 'social MUDs', a study of a 'combat MUD' – where the game was the primary focus – showed that players acted together to play the game, but had limited social involvement with one another [15].

Virtual worlds, such as Second Life, are not games according to most definitions; however, they do provide an interesting platform to study online social interactions. Brown and Bell [3] examined how play and sociability are expressed in *There*, a persistent virtual getaway that provided various games in its offering of activities. Their analysis shed light upon the practice of socializing through action in a VW, known as 'performing' a friendship.

There are many examples of MMOGs being studied for their support for social interaction. For example, an early study of Ultima Online used questionnaires to investigate social dynamics [13]. In the Daedalus project (nickyee.com/

daedalus), a series of studies investigated the psychology of MMO role-playing games (MMORPGs). Studies of the MMORPG World of Warcraft (WoW) [23] showed a prevalence of lively chats that go beyond just playing the game (70% chatted regularly about real life). Conversely, other work showed that some players prefer to play alone within a social milieu, meaning that other players provide an audience, and give a sense of social presence [9].

Researchers have moved beyond social dynamics to study how relationships can be formed or supported in MMOGs. Nardi and Harris [16] used ethnographic and interview techniques to investigate relationships in WoW. They show that guilds conform to the properties of communities and also discuss 'knots' – unique groups that form to complete a task of relatively short duration. Recent work has extended the concept of maintaining relationships in MMOGs by studying the concept of intimacy in WoW [17].

METHODOLOGY

Our results are based primarily upon analysis of three months of system logs from the online gaming site PlayOK. The logs contained events such as logins, games and chat messages (Table 1). We also participated on the server, in a variety of different game types, to get a feel for the player experience. Finally, we ran a small online survey to see how other players experienced PlayOK.

The Game Site: PlayOK

PlayOK was established in Poland in 2001 and has grown at a steady rate, with 5.2 million unique accounts as of June 2010 (accounts are removed after one year of inactivity). PlayOK is a web-based game site that offers 38 different turn-based games, including board games such as Chess and Backgammon, card games such as Hearts and Canasta, and other games such as Dominoes and Ludo. Three games are single player, and we removed these from our analysis. All other games are player-vs-player only. Free registration is required to play and the site is ad supported. The games are partitioned by language and region, so not all games are available to every person.

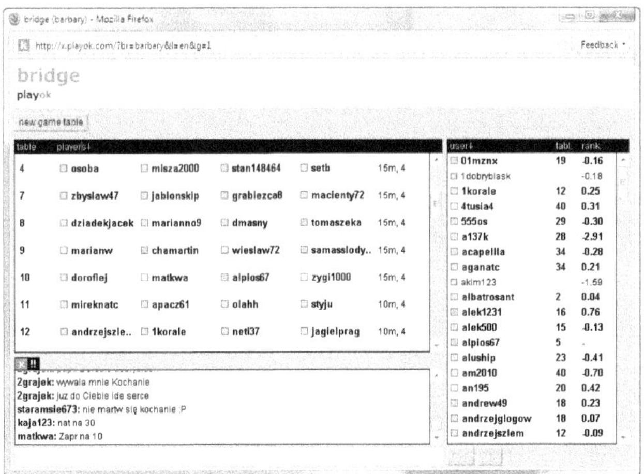

Figure 1: A bridge room: player list at right, table list at left, and room chat at bottom left.

After logging in and selecting a game type, the player is presented with a list of rooms. Selecting a room starts a java applet in a new window (Figure 1). In this window are a list of active game tables, a list of other people in the room, and a text chat. A game table is a virtual area for a single game, and each room can contain many game tables. Users can enter game tables currently in progress or create new tables.

Entering a game table opens a new window (Figure 2) with a view of the game, a list of people at the table, the names of the players (or empty places if the game is not full), and a chat area. If there is space at the game, and the game has not started, users can 'sit down' and become players.

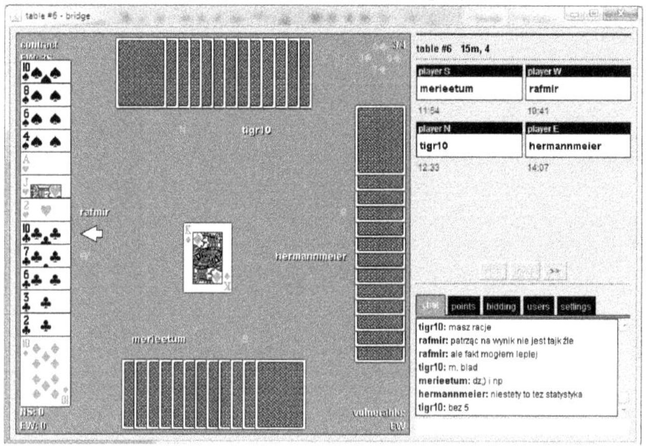

Figure 2: Bridge game table: player information at top right; chat area at bottom right.

Log Files

The PlayOK administrator made daily log files available to the authors. Our data covers 8 April 2010 to 8 July 2010 (91 days) and consists of ~12GB of compressed text files. Table 1 summarises the structure of the events recorded in the log files. Logging was started specifically for this study and the only historical data is a count of monthly unique logins since 2001 (not shown here).

Login	User ID, Language, Contacts (list of user IDs), Registration date, # people on the game type
Logout	User ID, Time logged in, # people in the game type
Room Chat	Sender ID,Room name
Table Chat	Sender ID, Room name + Table number
Private Chat	Sender ID, Receiver ID
Join Room	User ID, Room Name, # people in the room
Leave Room	User ID, Room Name, # people in the room
Join Table	User ID, Room name, Table number, # people at table
Leave Table	User ID, Room name, Table number, # people at table
Invite	Inviter ID, Invitee ID, Table number
Game Start	Room name, Table number, Player IDs (w/ rankings)
Game End	Room name, Table number

Table 1: Log events (all events include a timestamp)

Survey

We also deployed an online survey which was advertised in each game room for three days. We had 124 responses, 87% male, ages 18 to >50. Respondents represented 22 game types; the largest group were chess players (27%). Most (51%) had been playing on PlayOK for over 3 years. Almost 25% spent more than 12 hours per week on the site.

We note that the number of respondents in the survey is very small in comparison to the total population. Therefore we only use the survey responses for anecdotes of experience that cannot be found in the log data alone.

ANALYSES OF SOCIAL DYNAMICS IN PLAYOK

Our analyses looked at three themes frequently used to describe communities and social groups – permanence, social interaction, and formation of ties. Our goal was to take a broad initial look at how people behave in PlayOK, employing previously-used 'social accounting' techniques.

For each theme, we identify specific questions that can be answered through our log-based analyses. In some charts that accompany our analyses, we show a subset of games to reduce visual clutter. We selected ten representative game types for this subset: four board games (chess, reversi, gomoku, and backgammon), four card games (canasta, gin, bridge, and ludo), and two other games (blogpoly and dominoes). These games cover a range of values of games played, chat messages sent, and number of players (see Figure 3). The actual analyses, except where explicitly indicated, always take into account all games.

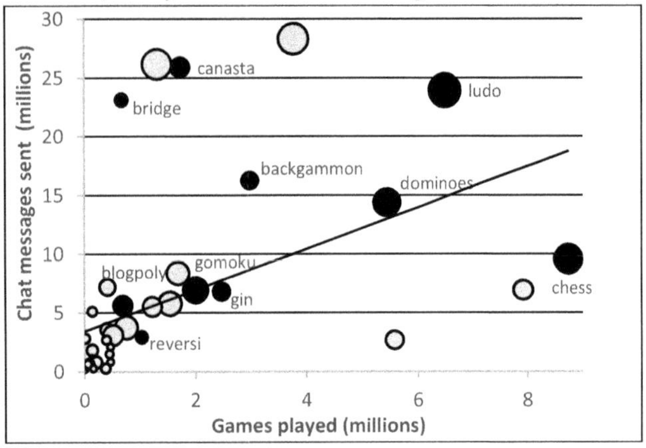

Figure 3: Game types by number of games and chat messages. Size shows population. Selected games are black and labelled.

Theme 1: Permanence

Because PlayOK does not have a persistent world like some on-line games, we explored the theme of permanence by looking at the degree to which people form a long-term association with the site – in real-world groups there is persistence of membership as people commit time to the group. We considered two specific questions: whether people remain in the PlayOK population for a long time; and whether people participate regularly.

How long do people stay active on PlayOK?

We used people's participation rates as an indicator of their degree of association. The logs told us each person's registration date, so we could examine participation rates for people of different 'PlayOK ages' (based on when they joined). Figure 4 shows numbers of active players during our logging period based on PlayOK age ("active" means logged in for more than 30sec at least once), and Figure 5 shows average activity levels. Both figures only record registrations before March 2010, to remove transients.

Figure 4 shows that the number of people who stay active on PlayOK declines steadily over time. However, there are a small number of people that still participate in the site after several years (including some who registered before January 2004, the first month that dates were recorded).

Figure 5 shows that average activity remains roughly equal regardless of registration date. This means that even older players still have significant activity on the site.

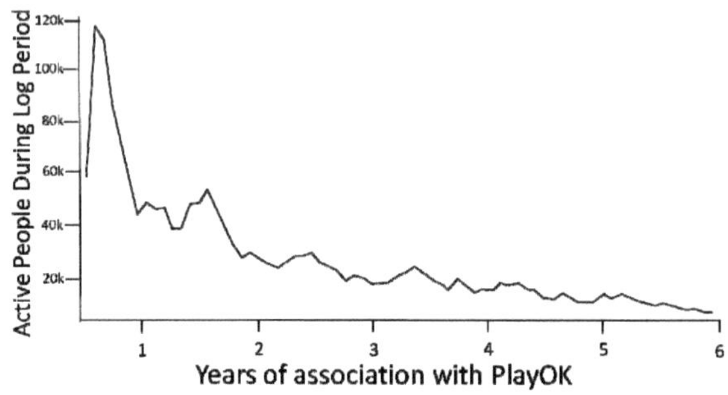

Figure 4: Numbers of people that showed activity during logging, by registration date since 2004.

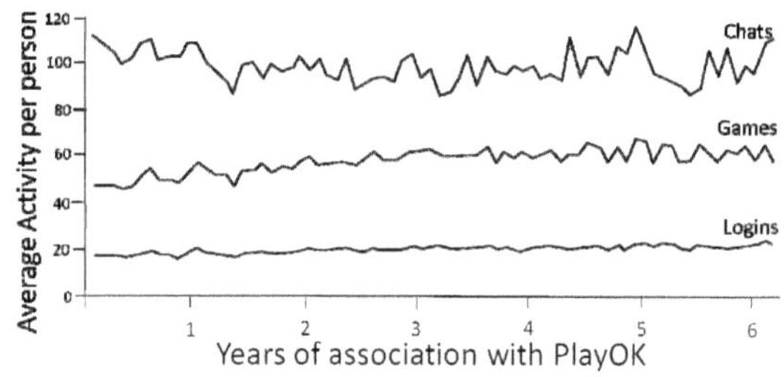

Figure 5: Average logins, games played, and chat messages sent during the login period, by registration date.

Do people participate regularly in PlayOK?

To investigate this question, we looked for two subgroups: stable players and transients. We defined stable players as those that had some activity every week, and transient players as those with all their activity within a three day window (not including people who could have been just starting their involvement with the site). Figure 6 shows proportions of stable and transient players.

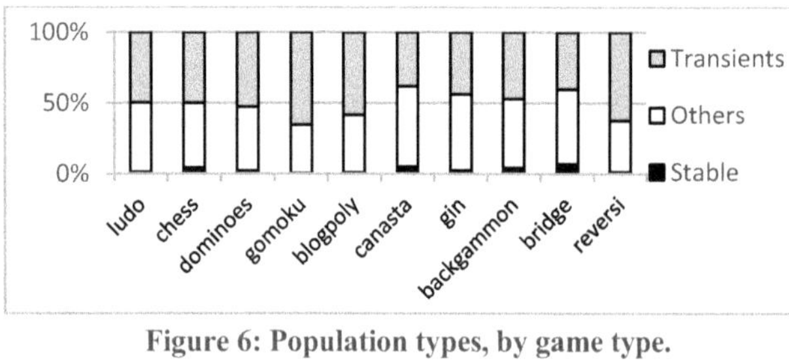

Figure 6: Population types, by game type.

The figure also shows a large proportion of 'other' people. This category covers a wide variety, such as irregular players, transients who participated a little longer than our threshold, or stable players who missed a week or two.

Our definitions are conservative and yet the proportion of transient players is very high. The smallest proportion of any game is 35% and for most games the majority of players are transient. This affects the establishment of behavioural norms, connections between people, support structures and other foundations of stable social groups.

Theme 2: Social Interaction

We carried out two investigations to look at people's social interaction in PlayOK: game interactions (doing things together), and verbal communication (talking together).

How much do people play together in PlayOK?

Real world social groups often do things together (e.g., a cycling club rides, a board game club plays games). The activity is an important part of social interaction, so we analysed how much people play games in PlayOK.

Figure 3 (above) gives a visual indication of the number of games, number of chat messages, and number of people in each game type. There were more than 60 million games played in three months. The game type with the most number of games was chess, which had approximately 8.7 million games during our logging period.

Figure 7 shows games per person for the three months of logging. There is a lot of variation: for example, more than 50,000 people played ten games, and more than 3,000 played 100 games. However, there is a large group that plays only a few games (e.g., transient players), and the largest group of people played only one game on average. In addition, there is variation by game type in the number of games played – Figure 8 shows some of the variability.

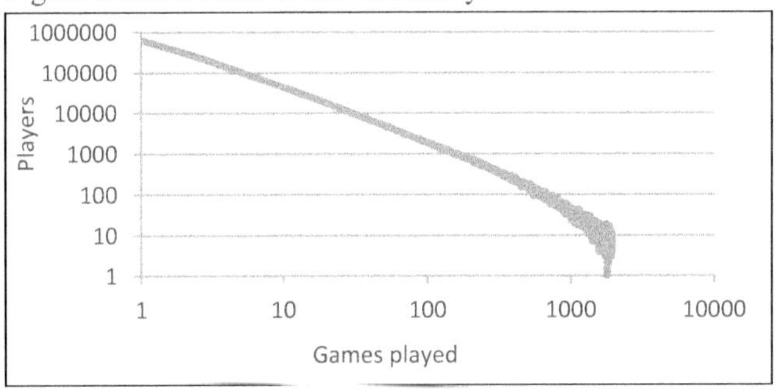

Figure 7: Histogram of games per player over the log period.

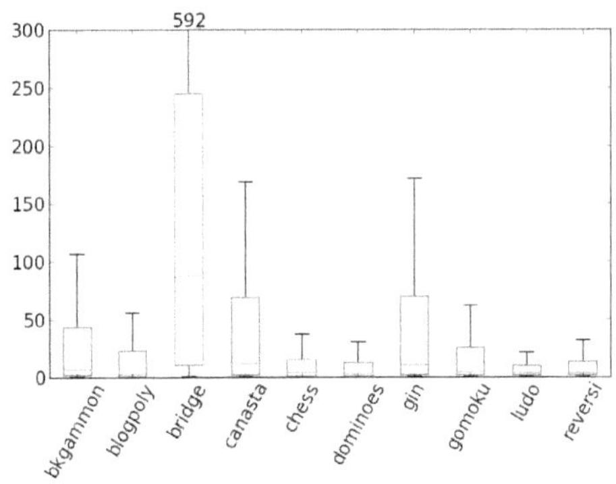

Figure 8: Games per person for sample game types. Whiskers show most extreme data less than 1.5*IQR fsrom the quartiles.

Verbal communication in PlayOK

A common characteristic of social groups is that when people get together, they talk. Verbal communication in PlayOK occurs through three types of text chat: room messages to everyone in a game room (Figure 1), table messages to the people at a single game table (Figure 2), and private messages to a particular person (not shown).

Although the total number of chat messages over our study period was large (Figure 3), this is an artefact of the large population of the site; our overall finding is that there is very little verbal communication on PlayOK. There was an average of 81 messages per person over the three-month period, less than one per day. In addition, 32% of the population did not talk at all during the log period.

On average, there were 3.2 messages sent per game (across all game types). There was wide variation in the amount of verbal communication in different games, with some card games having high numbers of messages per game (e.g., bridge: 28.8; or cribbage: 24.7), but with most games having very few messages. Overall, more than 72% of games were played without any chat messages at all. Figure 9 shows a partial histogram of messages in games. Our observations showed a distinct lack of several types of verbal interaction that one might expect in a social space: ordinary conversation, 'polite' communication such as greetings or departure messages, and the 'articulation conversations' normally seen at the start and end of a game (e.g., who will sit where, who will deal the cards, etc.).

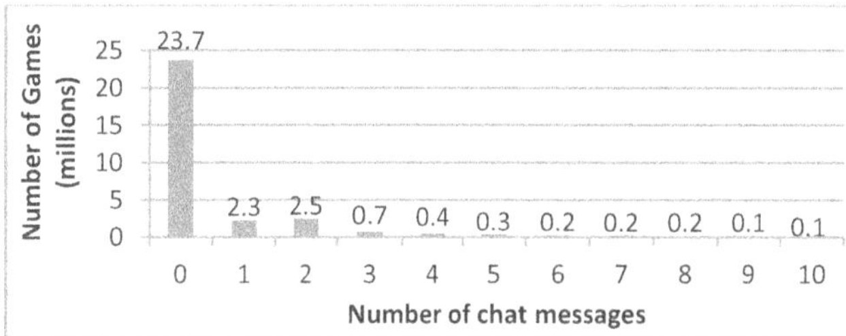

Figure 9: Histogram of number of chat messages per game.

Theme 3: Forming Ties

We looked at two questions to explore the ways that people can form ties and associations with others in PlayOK: how do people find opponents when they want to start a game; and do people play (or talk with) the same people over time.

How do people find opponents in PlayOK?

The primary interaction on PlayOK is playing games, and so we wanted to find out how the games were started, giving us insight into the beginnings of potential social ties.

There are four ways people can get together to start a game:

1. There is an established gaming relationship;
2. A conversation leads to a game;
3. One player invites another to a game;
4. A player creates a table and waits for opponents.

Our survey responses clearly establish that all of these strategies exist. One person reported only ever playing with the same group of friends (category 1). Another reported that he configures a table with specific settings, and waits for someone willing to play (category 4). Categories 1 and 2 are social while 3 and 4 rely solely on the interface.

We classified every game (skipping the first two weeks, since category 1 relies on historical information). The game was marked as category 1 if the players had played >2 games together previously. Otherwise, it was marked as category 2 if there were >2 messages exchanged in the last five minutes, or category 3 if there was an "Invite" within the last two minutes; everything else was marked as category 4. The thresholds were chosen to be favourable to the sociable categories (1 and 2).

Figure 10 shows the categories for our sample game types. Although most types have a substantial proportion of games played with previous opponents (see next analysis), the majority of games are started with no previous interaction between the players. For example, nearly 80% of backgammon games are category 4 (wait for opponents). These results show that the UI can act as a replacement for the extra-game interaction typically needed to start a game.

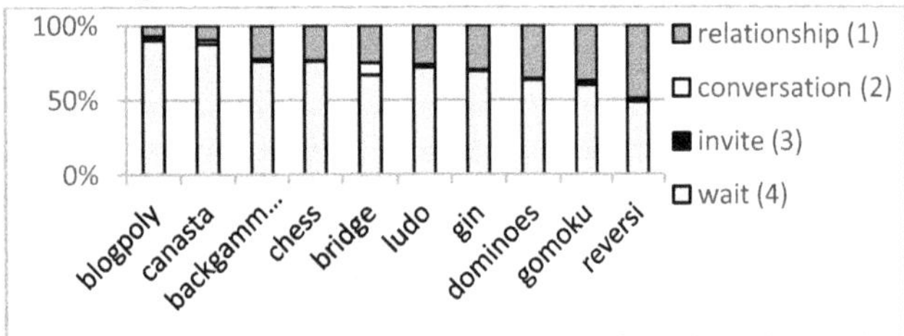

Figure 10: Different categories for starting games.

Do people play (or talk) more with a small group?

A common property of larger groups is that people associate more with a smaller subset of people. To look for group-forming behaviour in PlayOK, we looked at the amount people played with each opponent, at the time between repeated games with an opponent, and at the rate people added new opponents over the log period.

Frequency of playing against different opponents. Figure 11 shows the frequency of repeat games played against each player's top ten opponents. People do play against their most frequent opponents more often–the average frequency for the most likely opponent was 17.5%, whereas the mean across all opponents was 0.01%. This suggests that PlayOK players are maintaining small sets of favourite opponents with whom they spend most of their time. The favourite groups are small, however, and the graph quickly tails off.

A similar situation exists for chat partners (see Figure 12), showing that players are again maintaining sub-groups of partners, though once again the groups are small.

Recency effects. In real-world groups, people will often do something with a person a second time after meeting them (if the first encounter was positive). To look for this effect, we counted the number of games between repeated games with the same opponent. Figure 13 shows that there is a significant increase in likelihood that people will play the same person in their next game, but the likelihood drops off rapidly for later games. The increased likelihood of playing the next game with the same opponent can be partially explained by the convenience of already being at the game table, which makes it easy to start another game. Despite this, players' subgroups of favourite opponents and chat partners remain small.

Last, we examined the rate at which people played new opponents. People added new opponents at a near-linear rate throughout the three months; this implies that even though people play regularly with a small subset, they also consistently play with new and unknown partners. Overall, 65% of a player's opponents are seen for only one game.

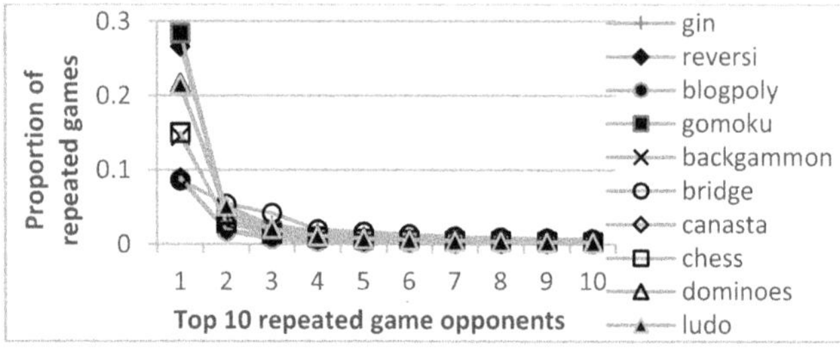

Figure 11: Mean opponent frequency by game.

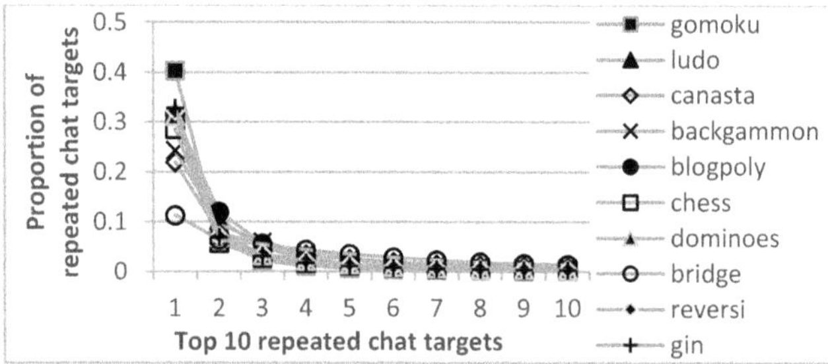

Figure 12: Mean repeated chat-partner frequency, by game.

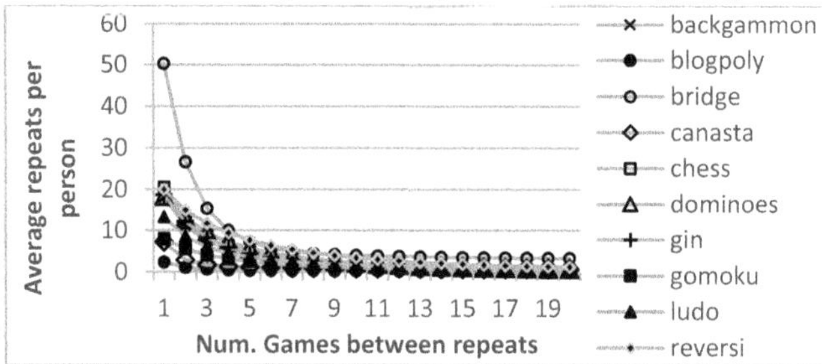

Figure 13: Repeated Opponents, by game.

DISCUSSION

Summary of Findings

Our analysis of PlayOK showed several main results that inform our investigation of the three themes.

Permanence: PlayOK has a highly transient population, with most people leaving very soon after joining; there is a general reduction in player numbers over time. However, a small number of players stay for long time periods.

Social interaction: shared activity is ubiquitous in PlayOK, with people playing numerous games with a variety of partners; however, verbal interaction is not common, with 72% of games occurring without any chat messages at all. In addition, the majority of games are started without any social history or interaction.

Forming ties: people do form some ties to other players, in that they play and chat more frequently with a small subset; however, they also often play with opponents outside this set – 65% of opponents are only seen once.

In the next sections we consider explanations for some of these results, and then turn to the questions of what the results mean for our understanding of sites like PlayOK, and whether there are potential benefits in a site where interactions are relatively impersonal and activity-based.

The Nature of Social Interaction in PlayOK

By most characterisations of communities or social groups, the PlayOK site is a failure – the people on the site don't talk to one another, don't stay long enough to make a commitment to the group, and only make a very small number of lasting connections with others. We begin by considering potential reasons for the lack of conversation.

No time for talk. In some games, the low message rate can be partially attributed to the speed of the game – many games in PlayOK are timed (e.g., chess or backgammon), and turns happen rapidly (on the order of seconds). In these situations, there is little time for typing chat messages.

Game moves as conversational turns. Many chat messages in PlayOK were not part of a clear verbal conversation, but comments on an action that had just occurred in the game. For example, a player in a Euchre game wrote "and yet there's no value in it", an odd statement given that this was the only chat message for several minutes. This comment followed the winning of a trick, and appears to be about taking a valueless trick. There may be other kinds of 'conversations' going on than those simply made up of chat messages. In particular, game actions could be viewed as conversational turns as much as they are game turns – much in the way of Clark's 'manifesting actions' [5]. These structures are not verbal utterances, but can play the role of an utterance, and can be responded to with a subsequent statement. In our example, taking a trick in Euchre is also a statement (i.e., "I am taking this trick"), providing context for subsequent statements (verbal or otherwise).

Game structures replace social conventions. The game interface provides mechanisms that render unnecessary certain kinds of conversations that are used in the real world to organize a game session. For example, the interfaces for games in PlayOK list the players and place them in locations at the game table, meaning that the players do not need to ask each other's names or talk about who will sit where. The interface also shows user profiles (e.g., country and rating) and game history, which frees players from having to use verbal communication to find out this information. In addition, the interface provides mechanisms for aspects of game control, such as inviting a player to join a game, or starting a game once players have joined. Our results show that the majority of games start with no social interaction at all and simply rely on the interface. Last, players' entry and departure from a game table are automatically indicated as system messages in the chat transcript; these messages may take the place of standard "hello" and "goodbye" conversations in real-world settings.

Language barriers. PlayOK was created in Poland and the user base is still predominantly European, spread across many countries. This results in a many languages being represented, and so playing the games could be viewed as the shared language. With no common spoken language, there is no possibility of verbal conversation.

Given the lack of conversation, it is of particular interest how this site has managed to succeed so well in terms of two more basic measures of health: PlayOK is doing very well in terms of both longevity (more than ten years) and population (over five million active members). We use our experiences with PlayOK and survey responses to explore possible explanations for its health.

In particular, we will explore the idea that the kinds of patterns seen in the PlayOK logs are legitimate forms of social interaction – even without extensive conversation, formation of subgroups, or long-term commitments. In this exploration, we consider three main ideas: first, that the interactions *within* the games on the site are a kind of social interaction; second, that the impersonal and anonymous interactions on PlayOK are legitimate social interactions that fill particular human needs, and that have parallels in a variety of real-world settings; and third, that the 'unconnected interactions' of game sites like PlayOK are a setting for *sociability*, a kind of interaction where personal issues and deeper implications are explicitly pushed away, and where the goal is to interact with other humans in an intentionally superficial, but explicitly social, fashion.

Actions in games as social interaction

Multiplayer games clearly involve interactions with other people – such as the moves in board games, or the bidding and trick-based play in card games. These interactions have not been widely considered in definitions of community or in analyses of social dynamics, but they are legitimate forms of human contact which create a shared experience through an (albeit stylized) form of human interaction.

There are two ways in which game actions stand as social interaction. First, as described above, actions in games are much like conversational turns – for example, each move in a chess game is like an utterance, and good players can read as much into a particular move as people do when they interpret a verbal utterance. If we consider games as providing people with a new language, we must reconsider the apparent dearth of conversation seen in our analysis, since 'speaking the language of the game' through play can represent a rich form of communicative interaction.

Second, the activity-based interactions of games can also be considered as a different kind of human social interaction, one based on the creation of an experience rather than one based on the establishment of shared knowledge, trust, or common bonds. The experience created by the game is, after all, a primary reason why people play – as noted by Stenros and Waern [20], gameplay as activity and as interactivity feature prominently in many classic definitions of games (such as those by Huizinga or Caillois, see [20] p. 3). Gameplay is an *enacted experience* – an experience that occurs only because it is created by the players themselves [20]. Recognizing the central role of this kind of experience gives legitimacy to the "I'm just here for the games" attitude evident in many of the survey responses – that is, the games are enough to make a complete experience, even without other types of social interaction such as talk or friendships. As Stenros and Waern state, "for players of a game, the purpose of playing is [...] *paratelic*: the activity of playing a game is not a means to an end but the end in itself" (p. 5). Thus, saying "I'm just here for the games" does not necessarily make players anti-social, but rather focuses on the created experience that the game enables.

Previous research into online game interactions has also noted this concept of gameplay as a surrogate for verbal interaction. In an ethnography of a combat MUD, Muramatsu and Ackerman [15] saw little traditional interaction and noted that non-game conversation was rare, but instead observed that players acted together to play the game through conflict and cooperation. Brown and Bell [3] call this type of activity "performing" a friendship in their study of the virtual world *There*. They argue that acting together around objects (called "social action") builds up a shared history of collective experiences. Ducheneaut et al. [8] also consider social activity in their analysis of an MMORPG and discuss the conflict between "instrumental" and "social" play present in many online games.

This type of social interaction *around* the game should be differentiated from social interaction *mediated* by the game [21]. In many situations a game is a means to an end, and a social end at that (e.g., getting together to play cards, where the game is really just an opportunity to be together with one's friends); however, the discussion above indicates that it is also valid to see the games themselves *as* the social activity, and therefore an authentic end in themselves.

Impersonal interaction

Player interactions in PlayOK are often anonymous and impersonal, and most players do not appear to make any lasting social connections with others on the site. Although impersonal interaction is sometimes seen as a sign of a failed community, there are real-world parallels suggesting that there may be more going on here than meets the eye.

Three examples of impersonal interaction in the real world can help to indicate some of the nuances. First, 'gay bathhouses' have existed for many years, where homosexual males go to obtain sex without emotional commitment or extensive social interaction [1,11]. These establishments have been the subject of much discussion, sometimes about the superficiality and lack of connection also seen in the game sites [11]; nevertheless, bathhouses are a lasting and successful part of many communities [1].

Second, there are activity-based groups that exist primarily for the shared activities they enable (e.g., a pick-up sports game facilitated by a recreational centre). Interactions between participants in these groups can be anonymous and highly impersonal. Although players in a pick-up sports game or on PlayOK may choose not to socialize with their team or opponents as part of the experience, these activity-based groups fill a role of providing a venue to perform shared activities without the need for social investment.

Third, there are situations where people make contact with others, but where the interactions are highly abstracted and where the participants have no interest in forming longer or deeper associations. One example is the amateur radio community, where people explore the airwaves and look for other stations to contact. These interactions are brief and impersonal (often limited to the exchange of station IDs), but are still an important part of this group's activities.

In addition to these physical-world examples, impersonal interaction has also been observed in virtual settings, for example Ducheneaut et al.'s [8] observations of healing and entertainment in the Star Wars Galaxies MMORPG.

The important thing about these examples is not to say that impersonal interactions are necessarily good or bad, but that they exist in real-world settings, and serve a variety of needs. Human-human interactions have a 'degree of anonymity' continuum, and the different points along this continuum are valuable for different purposes. In particular, both effort and risk on impersonal interactions are reduced – people in PlayOK can move quickly to the activity of the game, without worrying about whether they will 'get on' with their opponent. This idea that surface-level interactions have an important role leads to the idea of sociability.

Game sites as settings for sociability

In addition to being at least somewhat impersonal, game-based interactions are highly structured by the rules and environments of the games themselves. This kind of interaction can be thought of as a form of *sociability*, a concept described by the sociologist Georg Simmel [19], and later used to describe online environments such as MMOGs [8] and social VWs [3].

Simmel describes sociability as "association for its own sake" without the burdens that often accompany interactions in society. In sociable interactions, the deeper and more contentious aspects of human relationships are intentionally left out, and people interact in a formalized or rule-governed fashion that ensures that the interaction is successful and satisfactory for all participants. For example, the rules of 'polite conversation' ensure that settings such as a conference reception can proceed smoothly and safely for all parties – contentious issues such as religion or politics are left out of the discussions.

Although Simmel is interested in situations where conversation is the main mechanism for interaction (and this has been the primary application of the idea in previous

CSCW analyses [3,8]), sociability can also be considered in the setting of a game site, where game-based interaction largely replaces verbal communication, and where the rules of the interaction are formally constrained by the rules of the game. Although Simmel does not explicitly consider games, he touches on this connection in several ways. He calls sociability the "play-form of association" (p. 255) and suggests that it is an abstraction of other real-life interactions, making sociability a kind of practice for other situations and settings. This echoes the correspondence between games and real life – many games are abstracted representations of real-world activities. For example, board games such as chess are derived from the tactics of war; bidding games like bridge are abstract versions of negotiation and bargaining; and board games such as diplomacy simulate the development and maintenance of political alliances. As Simmel says, "And what joins art with play now appears in the likeness of both to sociability. From the realities of life play draws its great, essential themes: the chase and cunning; the proving of physical and mental powers, the contest and reliance on chance and the favor of forces which one cannot influence" (p.255).

Game environments can therefore be thought of as sociable settings where the distance between the activities and the real world is somewhat greater, and the 'play-form' is more concrete. This idea comes through again in Simmel's discussion of the importance of equality in sociability: these situations involve people "who give up so much of their objective content [...] that they are sociably equal, and every one of them can win sociability values for himself only under the condition that the others, interacting with him, can also win them" (p. 257). This sounds very much like the way that games ensure the equality of players, each of whom has an equal chance to win (although, it is clear that game environments are not as interested in equal *outcomes* as Simmel's sociable settings are).

Although researchers have considered sociability in other online environments, and even online game environments (e.g., [8]), the idea of games as a setting for a more extreme kind of sociability – with the activity-based interaction and formalized interaction boundaries that games provide – has not been considered previously. Although we do not argue that these environments provide all of the social interaction that a person needs, it seems clear that there are some deeper and more interesting characteristics in game sites than previously thought, and that game play can represent a different kind of interaction that should be considered further in future analyses.

Benefits of Impersonal and Activity-Based Interaction

There are several potential benefits to the kind of interaction and structure that is seen in a game site:

First, impersonal and anonymous interactions implies that as long as there are enough people in the environment, it is always possible to get the experience – that is, it doesn't any longer matter *who* is there, as long as *someone* is there. The large number of people on the site means that it is generally easy to find a person to play against; although less personal, the scale effects of the Internet greatly increase the interaction possibilities. For the same reason, longevity is also not important – the high turnover rate of a site like PlayOK is not a problem. The anonymity of the site may also allow people to test their abilities in a less risky fashion than in a real-world setting – for example, it may be easier to challenge a high-ranked player in an anonymous setting.

Second, the structures and rules imposed by games mean that each game provides its own 'language,' overcoming language and cultural barriers. As long as a person knows the rules of the game, she can play with anyone else. Given a situation where people share little linguistic or cultural common ground, the ability to rely on the game structure for organizing and regulating the interaction is critical.

Third, game sites support a wide range of interaction styles, from anonymous players through to groups of friends. This may be important as it provides a large player base so that even well-connected players can gracefully transition to anonymous play when their friends are not online. Although largely ignored during anonymous play, game sites also provide the communication tools needed to interact more personally with friends and acquaintances.

Fourth, the low barrier to entry in terms of time, effort, and emotional investment matches the general idea that the sites are primarily for fun. Similarly, the low cost of interaction afforded by the social actions in games played for fun means that the interaction is safe – there is little likelihood of social awkwardness, rudeness, giving or taking offense, or the raising of sensitive political or religious topics.

Fifth, the maintenance and recognition of social standing is still possible in a game site through the player rankings that are listed on the site. This idea that the large player population can be seen as an audience for a high ranking is similar to previous studies where people appreciated being in a large milieu (or showing off to that large audience) even though they did not interact with them [9].

Finally, there is a value to the players in challenging a human opponent. While PlayOK does not offer the ability to play against a computer opponent, it is easy to find single-player computerised versions elsewhere. Artificial intelligence opponents can play as well as advanced human players in most games. We speculate that playing against a human allows for more diverse play experiences, greater opportunities for learning and improvement in strategy, and potentially a greater feeling of accomplishment after a win. Although PlayOK does not provide player-vs-AI games, comparing to these types of games could offer further insight into the issues that we have raised here; we plan to investigate this in future work.

Implications for Design

One hypothesis that we considered in the early part of the project was whether the user interface of a site like PlayOK constrained possibilities for social interaction, and whether redesigning some of these tools could help to make the site more social. Although it does appear that the interface is somewhat awkward for social interaction, it does not seem likely given our other analyses that this is the main reason for the behaviours we observed. In fact, it may be counterproductive to improve the representations of people, or enhance the system's capabilities to better support communication; doing so might reduce the value of the site as an abstracted and sociable setting as described above. For example, providing an audio channel for verbal communication in every game might cause problems for sociability rather than benefiting social closeness.

Our analyses suggest the importance for these game sites of maintaining easy and anonymous entry, so that players can get in and play. However, supporting seamless transitions from anonymity to pseudonymity may also be important so that players can become more involved in the community in terms of their rank, profile, game history, and contacts.

CONCLUSION

We carried out a three-month log analysis of the PlayOK online game site to determine how people behave socially in this kind of environment. We organized our study around three themes: permanence, social interaction, and formation of ties. We found that while the site seems very social when we consider games played and subgroups of opponents, other analyses showed that the population was highly transient, and that people engaged in very little verbal communication. To explain how a game site can continue to be large and popular without some of the hallmarks of social groups, we explored the idea that games and game-based activity can take a larger role in our view of human interaction. We discussed three ways in which group behaviour in PlayOK can be seen as legitimate and valuable, including ideas about games as social interaction, the value of impersonal interaction, and game sites as settings for sociability. These ideas may prompt designers to think differently about the way that game environments can be designed in order to support a wide variety of social interactions and many kinds of sociability.

ACKNOWLEDGEMENTS

Funded by NSERC's Strategic Grants program, and the Networks of Centres of Excellence program (GRAND).

REFERENCES

1. Bérubé, A. The History of Gay Bathhouses. *Journal of Homosexuality 44*, 3 (2003), 33.
2. Blanchard, A., and Markus, M. The experienced "sense" of a virtual community. *SIGMIS Database,* 35, 1, 2004, 64-79.
3. Brown, B. and Bell, M. Play and Sociability in There: Lessons from Online Games for Collaborative Virtual Environments. In R. Schroeder and A. Axelsson, eds., *Avatars at Work and Play*. Springer, 2006, 227-245.
4. Bernheim Brush, A., Wang, X., Combs Turner, T., and Smith, M. Assessing differential usage of usenet social accounting meta-data. *Proc. CHI 2005*, 889–898.
5. Clark, H. *Using language*. Cambridge University Press, New York, 1996.
6. Dourish, P. Introduction: The state of play. *JCSCW,* 7, 1, 1998, 1–7.
7. Driskell, R. and Lyon, L. Are Virtual Communities True Communities? Examining the Environments and Elements of Community. *City & Community,* 1, 4, 2002, 373-390.
8. Ducheneaut, N., Moore, R., Nickell, E. Virtual "Third Places": A Case Study of Sociability in Massively Multiplayer Games. *JCSCW,* 16, 1-2, 2007, 129-166.
9. Ducheneaut, N., Yee, N., Nickell, E., Moore, R. "Alone together?": exploring the social dynamics of massively multiplayer online games. *Proc. CHI 2006*, 407–416.
10. Harrison, S. and Dourish, P. Re-place-ing space: the roles of place and space in collaborative systems. *Proc. CSCW 1996*, 67–76.
11. Haubrich, D., Myers, T., Calzavara, L., Ryder, K., and Medved, W. Gay and bisexual men's experiences of bathhouse culture and sex. *Culture, Health & Sexuality,* 6, 1, 2004, 19-29.
12. Jones, Q. Virtual Communities, Virtual Settlements & Cyber-Archaeology: A Theoretical Outline. *JCMC,* 3, 3, 2006.
13. Kolo, C. and Baur, T. Living a Virtual Life: Social Dynamics of Online Gaming. *Game Studies,* 4, 1, 2004, 1-31.
14. McMillan, D. and Chavis, D. Sense of community: A definition and theory. *J. Community. Psych.,* 14, 1, 1986, 6–23.
15. Muramatsu, J. and Ackerman, M. Computing, social activity, and entertainment: A field study of a game MUD. *JCSCW,* 7, 1, 1998, 87–122.
16. Nardi, B. and Harris, J. Strangers and friends: collaborative play in world of warcraft. *Proc. CSCW 2006*, 149–158.
17. Pace, T., Bardzell, S., and Bardzell, J. The rogue in the lovely black dress: intimacy in world of warcraft. *Proc. CHI 2010*, 233–242.
18. Park, R. Human Ecology. *Am. J. Soc. 17*, 1, 1936, 1-15.
19. Simmel, G. The sociology of sociability. *Am. J. Soc.,* 55, 3, 1949, 254–261.
20. Stenros, J. and Waern, A. Games as activity: Correcting the digital fallacy. In M. Evans, ed., *Videogame Studies: Concepts, Cultures and Communication*. Inter-Disciplinary Press, Oxford, 2011.
21. Stenros, J., Paavilainen, J., and Mäyrä, F. The many faces of sociability and social play in games. *Proc. MindTrek 2009*, 82–89.
22. Wellman, B. and Gulia, M. Virtual communities as communities. In M. Smith and P. Kollock, eds., *Communities in cyberspace*. 1999, 167–194.
23. Williams, D., Ducheneaut, N., Xiong, L., Zhang, Y., Yee, N., and Nickell, E. From Tree House to Barracks. *Games and Culture,* 1, 4 (2006), 338 -361.

Remix and Play: Lessons from Rule Variants in Texas Hold'em and Halo 2

Gifford Cheung
Information School
University of Washington
giffordc@uw.edu

Jeff Huang
Information School
University of Washington
cscw@jeffhuang.com

ABSTRACT

Players can change the rules of a multi-person game to experience a different gameplay mechanic, add thematic color, or fine-tune its balance. To better understand game variants, we use a grounded approach to analyze 62 variants for Texas Hold'em, a popular card game, and a follow-up case-study of 91 variants of Halo 2, a popular video game. We study their development and examine whether lessons from Texas Hold'em apply to a constrained system such as Halo 2. We discover video gamers' reliance on 'honor rules', rules dependent on the cooperative spirit of its players. We develop a theory of 'necessity' in rule adoption, showing players' sensitivity to the impact of one change on the whole game. In solving game-design problems, adjustments drawn from a set of 'canned' rule changes address common problems with familiar solutions. We find a complex interplay between who can play and what rules are chosen. Our findings have implications for game designers and for non-game variants.

Author Keywords

customization, poker, halo, game design, variants, honor rules

ACM Classification Keywords

H.5.3 Group and Organization Interfaces: Computer-supported cooperative work

General Terms

Human Factors, Design

PREFACE

One researcher recalls: During my childhood, I played the board game *Monopoly* with the following understanding: whoever landed on the "Free Parking" space would get the bonus money at the center of the board. During one game, I was surprised to find out that a new player did not know this rule. Smugly, I picked up the instructions to point it out; after reading and re-reading the rules for 20 minutes, I realized it was not there. To my surprise, Parker Brothers (the publisher) notes that this is a common 'house rule', a game variant but not part of the standard rules.

CSCW'12, February 11–15, 2012, Seattle, Washington, USA.

LET'S PLAY SOMETHING A LITTLE DIFFERENT

Changing the rules in a game produces a variant, allowing players to create a unique gaming experience that fits their playing style. Game variants and other customizations can extend a game's entertainment value when the players tire of the standard rules. Variants range from minor tweaks lasting a single game, to rules for specific contexts (i.e. '*House* rules'), to a complete overhaul of the gameplay mechanic. The rule change may be simple or complex, and its effects diverse: it may either be adopted as a popular variant or forgotten when the day ends; its impact on the game experience can be small or wide-ranging. For example, the rule of whether or not a dealer is required to hit on 17 in Blackjack can potentially double the casino's edge.

Variation may be developed through similar processes across different games and other collaborative customization contexts (such as software). The characteristics of variation inform designers and system builders about how to cater to their users. Additionally, a closer inspection of variants inform our understanding of appropriation and further the design of customizable systems. This study investigates:

- decision-making processes when players create a variant
- characteristics of rule changes
- relationships between system features and appropriation

Our study is exploratory and its scope is limited to two games: a card game and a video game. We selected the poker game Texas Hold'em and its variants to study (extending initial work [2]), and we picked the video game Halo 2 and its variants to study. Both are among the most popular games in their genre; these two cases provide a starting point for deriving insight into games in general. We conducted the first study on public descriptions of Texas Hold'em variants found online and analyzed the data using Grounded Theory [18]. Using the theory we derived, we conducted a case study on Halo 2 to explore the transferability of the theory and to focus on the challenges of variation in a software context.

In our analyses of both games, we describe how variant authors adopt a systematic perspective to evaluate how rule changes upset the balance of the original game. Rule changes disrupt and restore the games' equilibrium as part of a 'chain of necessity'. We discuss how this can be applied to understanding customization and supporting it.

What is a variant?

Merriam-Webster defines a variant as "a form differing slightly from a standard". Monopoly house rules are variants of standard Monopoly. Texas Hold'em has many twists to its basic formula, as do Halo and other video games. But what is a "slight" difference? Which of these variants on Halo, for instance, stands as a game in its own right? Pinning down the meaning of variation means engaging the thorny problem of ontology and essence. Others have pondered this problem under the name of 'genre'; for example, Jesper Juul wrests with categorizing the family of 3-match puzzle games [10]. Projects such as gameontology.com seek to broadly categorize games. In this study, we depend on the gaming culture to define variants by collecting game descriptions that are described as "variants of X". This approach exposes the perceived boundaries of a game and, by extension, the perceived essence of a game. Close scrutiny of "variants" promises to inform the creation of ontologies, design for appropriation, and the rhetoric of customization; the overlap between variation and these areas remain underexplored.

RELATED WORK

Variants are often mentioned in collections of games and game types to develop insights about games themselves or to make claims about larger sociological patterns. Parlett's collection of card games [14] is a thorough collection, but as a book written for players, it does not make many claims about variation except to say that card games are folk games, not established by any governing authority. Sutton-Smith's catalog of games [19] also reviews many games, but does so to create a theory of play rather than a theory of variation.

Studies of variation in individual games such as Iida et al. [9] examine the historical evolution of chess in seven variations. Using metrics to approximate conceptual features, they conclude that chess's variations have been refined to seek a balance between search-space complexity and entertainment impact. FlexibleRules [5] is a software framework that allows players to customize the rules in digital board games. They authors found that players enjoyed inventing and discussing new rules, and that they reported enjoying playing the custom game more than the standard game. Customization is often used to achieve different gameplay, but it can also be a solution to a social problem. In Xu et al. [23], players customized Halo 3 to make the game fair for inequally skilled players. Xu et al. explain that the players desired "a good social experience associated with the game".

Cheating [3], "bad play" [12], mischief [13], or griefplay [4] may seem like forms of variation. Mischievious players and griefers (disrupting the play of others) still play according to the rules of the game, but perhaps not in the spirit of the game. The variation can be of a social nature, breaking the rules of convention. Cheating, as Huizinga [7] points out, is meant to be hidden; the opposing players are led to believe that the rule-breaker is actually following the rules. Such malignant rule bending does not produce variation in play—it reinforces the importance of the original rules since the cheater purports to comply with the standard. When undisguised, rule-breaking represents a kind of playfulness with the rules that may lead the game's transformation [12]. Work such as Huizinga's lends us insight into actions that may produce game variations. However, not all variants arise from instances of cheating, malice, or even playful innovation.

In *digital* games, variation has been somewhat recognized by the examination of game "customizability" [15] and in the culture of co-optation by clever modification of the original code [16]. Players see customizability as a way of adding a proper level of difficulty and replayability, enhancing the entertainment value of replaying the game. Pinelle et al. uncover the primacy of customizability during the process of collecting heuristics from game reviews [15]. Modifications of existing games are of great interest to both industry and researchers in that 'mods' promise to extend the value of a commercial game [16] and foster creativity and learning [17]. However, variation need not be limited to complex reprogramming of the software. A layer of 'reconfiguration' is accessible to everyday variant authors who find effective ways to play new games without relying on programming skills. For example, Wright et al. [22] observe how *Counter-Strike* players cheat death by using a voting mechanism to communicate with their living teammates from the grave. Wright sees this as a creative response by players to overcome technical limitations established in the game.

We propose to explore variation in games as a core phenomenon rather than as a side-effect. To expose the rationales or processes behind rule changing, we start the investigation with the variants of a card game: Texas Hold'em.

TEXAS HOLD'EM

According to Parlett's ontology of card games [14], Texas Hold'em (or Hold'em, for short) is a popular *vying* game in which players vie with one another over who is holding the best cards. It is played in both living rooms and casinos, for fun and for profit. The breadth of the game's adoption in casual contexts implies that we are likely to find a large number of casual variations. The institutional presence of casinos establishes standards, providing an authoritative version against which we can compare casual variants.

In Texas Hold'em, players use money in the form of chips to back their claims to better cards throughout multiple rounds of betting. They make a round of bets each time cards are dealt or revealed, for a total of four rounds. In each round, every player must match or raise the bet amount if they wish to remain in contention for the chips. The players select from the mix of private and public cards to compose a 'hand'. Players are first dealt two private cards ('hole' cards), then three public cards are revealed, then an additional public card and a final public card enter play. Players who remain reveal their hands in a 'showdown' to determine the winner of the gambled chips. Sets of cards are generally ranked according to rarity; for example, five cards of the same suit (a 'flush') rank higher than two pairs (e.g. 4-4-J-J-8).

Methodology

The examination of Hold'em variants was conducted from a Naturalistic standpoint [11] using Grounded Theory [18]

Figure 1. Intermediary diagrammed memo during the axial coding phase focusing on the implications of bodies of associated rule changes.

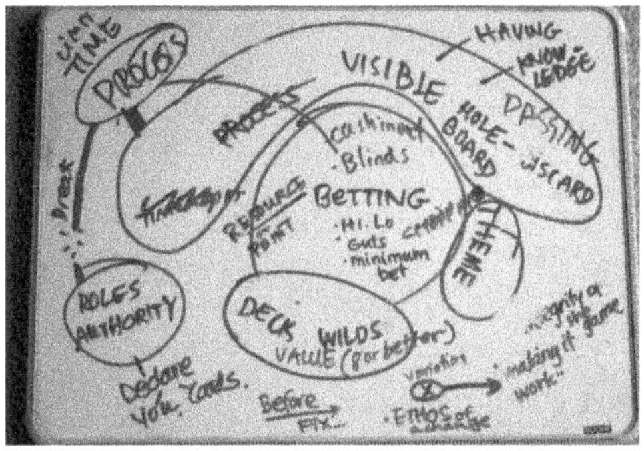

Figure 2. Cluster diagram of rule types for Texas Hold'em variants.

as a guide. Data sources were descriptions of Hold'em variants found on the Internet, taken from public websites, blog posts, forum posts, and comments (See Table 1 for a breakdown). We recorded the URL, an excerpt of the text, and descriptive notes from 83 reports of variations. There were 63 descriptions of variants, 15 comments on 'house rules', and 5 comments providing general advice about customizing games. The collections sites were general interest websites on poker, poker discussion forums, personal blogs, and general purpose informational sites (e.g. ehow.com). Theoretical sampling was used to collect data, prioritizing *variety* in sampling ([18], p.73). Here, the sampling strategy changes as 'theoretical saturation' is encountered. Saturation describes the condition where the theoretical insights that can be derived from gathering more data are so few that it is more profitable to turn collection efforts beyond the area in question, to either stop collecting (moving further into analysis) or to look for something different to collect. Analysis followed Strauss and Corbin's method of coding data, a progression from discovering instances and categories (open coding), relating those categories (axial coding, Figure 1), to review and refinement (selective coding) of the categories. The process alternated between diagramming and line-by-line micro-analysis ([18], Chp.5).

To collect data, we started with Web search queries for "Texas Hold'em Variants". When we encountered names of variants such as DOUBLE FLOP, OMAHA, and others, we also used those terms as queries until the diversity of variants reached saturation. As our model developed, following Theoretical Sampling, we returned to collection with theoretically informed queries, such as "is a horrible rule" in our search for spoiling rules. The conceptual completeness of our model (from the selective coding phase) indicated a sufficient level of saturation for us to stop data collection.

We recruited an outside auditor to validate our interpretations. From a fraction of the data (16 randomly selected excerpts) and our ontology of rule types, the auditor applied our categorization to the sample and kept a critical eye on the interpretive step between data and initial categories. From this feedback, we maintain that our theory does not make claims about why new rules are formed, only that it recognizes patterns in the rules and in the language used to describe rule variants. In our discussions, we recognized the difficulty of discerning the motivations for inventing rules from the kind of data we had collected, since the descriptions were typically written after the rules had been invented.

Variants

Clustering (by types of rule-changes, Figure 2) produced groups of paired changes; one type of rule was commonly associated with another type. We defined three clusters of associated sets of rule changes: variations on hole and community cards were typically accompanied with limits on what to play; unusual sets of community cards were accompanied by rules on dealing and revealing them; and, custom decks were accompanied by new rules on ranking hands.

Hole/Community ⇒ Play-limit Rules that increase the hole or community cards are accompanied by 'play-limit' rules on how many cards could be played. PINEAPPLE possesses new rules in which players receive three hole cards instead of two. As a consequence, PINEAPPLE limits the possible plays by requiring players to discard one of the three cards, sometimes before any public cards are revealed, sometimes after (in CRAZY PINEAPPLE). IRON CROSS grants players 5 hole cards and 5 board cards. Players are restricted to playing two hole cards, and the remaining 3 are taken from the board.

Community cards ⇒ dealing/reveal Unusual sets of community cards (such as IRON CROSS above) are accompanied by specific instruction on the manner of dealing (one at a time, all at once) and revealing (flipped over to be assessed and used).

Deck ⇒ Evaluation Custom decks lead to instructions about how to compare and evaluate hands. "MANILA is played with a strip deck of only 7-A (32 total cards). Because it is played with a strip deck, a flush beats a full house." (pokertips.com) The same rule is used in Spanish poker, which uses a stripped deck of 8-A.

Source Type	Variants
Poker websites (texasholdem-poker.com, etc.)	37
Online forums (pokerforums.org, cardschat.com, etc.)	25
General websites (ehow.com, googobits.com, etc.)	17
Blog (blogspot.com)	2

Table 1. The sources of data for variants in Texas Hold'em.

We reviewed these three associations and found a language of necessity (uses of the words, "because", "should", "must", etc...) and appeals to balance, fairness, fun, and other requirements. One rule flowed into the next, leading us to annotate them with directional arrows above. Our main interpretation of the clustered data is that, instead of clusters, these are *series* of rule changes. We call these series "chains of necessity" which we now introduce.

THE CHAIN OF NECESSITY

New Rule → Disrupted Nature → Necessity → Satisfying Rule

Texas Hold'em seems to exist in a state of proper equilibrium. Its basic rules facilitate a playing style that meets players' requirements for a fair, balanced, and engaging game of poker. The introduction of a new rule may upset the delicate balance of the game, ruining its fairness or making it predictable and uninteresting; thus one may adopt another new rule change to restore balance. This is an example of such causal reasoning in which a forum poster engages in a creative session of inventing a Hold'em variant:

> *all right, lets play hold'em wait lets play super hold'em, i'll deal everybody two extra cards well, lets see.... somehow this isn't fair. let's make it you have to use two out of your hand. i like that, lets call it super holdem* (SUPER HOLD'EM, pokerforums.org forums)

This variant author starts with an initial rule change: ("i'll deal everybody two extra cards"). However, this new rule disrupts the game, and the author is concerned that the game is now imbalanced ("lets see....somehow this isn't fair"). To resolve this, the author imposes an additional restriction ("let's make it you have to use two out of your hand"). He evaluates the new implications of this second rule and validates it ("i like that"). This pattern of justification exists throughout the variants: a new rule is introduced and the implications of the new rule create an incomplete game that requires a solution. The problem is resolved by introducing an additional rule which may cause a new disruption or produce a satisfying stasis to the game's condition.

The vocabulary within the data specifically exposes an implied necessity for new rules. Note the causal implication of this quote regarding PINATUBO POKER, a variant of MANILA: "*Because* Manila poker has five poker betting rounds, it does not play well at no limit or pot limit. This can be easily modified by eliminating the poker betting round between the second and third community cards." In this example, a new rule (playing no limit or pot limit) creates a poor game for MANILA ("does not play well"). This situation is remedied in PINATUBO POKER by adjusting the betting sequence. Thus we see a pattern where the variant creators perceive and employ a sense of cause and effect to explain further revisions to the original game.

The notion of necessity is accompanied by two concepts: optional rules and 'spoiling' rules. During our analysis, we found counterexamples of the claim that all rule changes could be linked to one driving need. In a game of *craziness*, we could not claim that all new rules must have a causal link back to *craziness*; instead optional rules supplemented the required ones. For example, a common option is to play a game *hi-lo*. To play hi-lo is to split the winnings between whoever has the highest ranking hand and whoever has the lowest ranking hand. The option of playing hi-lo is often tacked on at the end of the description. In the SUPER HOLD'EM example above, the variant author decided, as an after-thought, "....oh wait, lets throw in a hi-lo variation," implying that the variant is compatible with playing normally ('straight') or playing hi-lo. One can say that optional rule changes are considered as such when the implications of the rule change are believed to be inconsequential.

If satisfying rules and optional rules exist, the next step in selective coding is to project a third possibility. Are there rules that are the opposite of satisfying rules? These would be proposed rule changes that are rejected as incompatible with the desired nature of the game. After being sensitized to the possibility, we returned to the data seeking prohibitive language. One discovery is presented in Table 2.

This player at a casino found that if a player mistakenly bet too early, before another player had a chance to bet, the casino would still allow the game to continue. This person saw that players could abuse this rule to their own benefit: if a player intentionally bets out of turn, he can use this 'accident' as a way of influencing the choices of other players. From this person's perspective, this rule ruins the integrity of the game and should be removed. His rationale differs from that of the chain of necessity. Now, when a new rule disrupts the state of the game, the commenter's prescription is that this 'spoiling' rule should be removed rather than amended by another rule. That the casino ignores his request does not negate the rationale that he uses; the casino's refusal is a reminder of the subjective quality of this rule type. Rather than an objective assertion that certain rules are satisfying, optional, or spoiling, this ontology helps us understand and explain rule changes. The theory of necessity does not examine the correctness or persuasiveness of the argument.

In summary, satisfying, optional, and spoiling rules can be traced back to their relation to necessity in a game variant. Outside expectations such as fairness, craziness, and fun impose a need for new rules or the prohibition of others, and a new rule can provoke this need by creating a distinct change in the nature of the game. Sometimes rules can co-exist without any relation to necessity. Such optional rules imply that a game can have two variations: for example, a 'deck to evaluation' set can be played with the 'hi-lo' variation or without it. Lastly, the necessary imposition of new rules is accompanied by the necessary forbidding of other rules.

Canned Solutions

Continuing our analysis, we sought to explain why three clusters of common rule changes appeared in the dataset. This repeated phenomenon was notable for its pairing of two kinds of rule changes with causal language. The first rule in the pair disrupts the balance of the game (e.g. players receive more cards than normal, changing the expected odds);

Rule type	Texas Hold'em	Halo 2
Satisfying	"After all bets are placed, players turn their hole cards FACE UP on the table in front of them. The flop is then dealt face DOWN [...] My buddies and I made this up after a couple games of Pineapple, [...]. **We actually prefer it over Hold'em, much more suspense.**" (UPSIDE-DOWN PINEAPPLE)	"This gametype was **inspired by the raw scene in lord of the rings**, [...] wot u end up with is a seige, and the orcs hadicap means that to win they have to use thier greater numbers to good effect" (HELM'S DEEP, *a seige narrative*)
Optional	"This game is best straight without a high/low option with structured limits or no limit. **Optionally it can be a split pot game** where the winner of each of the two boards gets half the pot" (DOUBLE FLOP HOLD'EM)	"...being a big fan of the movies thought up some other aspects that would **make it more like the movie**. The people in the base should have either BRs or Snipers(arrows) and the secondary should swords(for inside the base)." (HELM'S DEEP)
Spoiling	"The most annoying one was they let raises out of turn stick [...] The raising out of turn was terrible and when I tried explaining it to the staff how people were taking advantage and how **it affects the integrity of the game**, they had no idea what I was talking about. (cardschat.com forums)	"Make sure you turn off Force Even Teams. As we learned the other night, **it ruins the respawning** if the teams are not even. I would consistently sit out for 45 seconds or more. Its not fun." (REINFORCEMENT CTF)

Table 2. Examples of different rule types in Texas Hold'em and Halo 2. Key phrases emphasizing the underlying motivation of the rule are bolded.

the second resolves the imbalance as a satisfying rule. These clusters were prominent, but did not encompass all the rule changes found. There were many rule changes that did not fit dual-paired clusters.

Also missing is an objective causal relationship between the two rule types. Consider the pattern that associates hole card variations with play limit rules (see above). Just because a player receives one or two additional cards does not mean that limits *must* be imposed on how many cards can be played; an equally balancing solution could be to change the ranking of hands. A careful analysis of how odds are changed by having one or two extra cards can allow players to rebalance the game without relying on a typical solution. Similarly, a game played with a stripped deck does not necessitate a re-ranking of hands as the discovered cluster suggests; other solutions exist.

Our interpretation of the nature of these clusters is that a *problem* and its *fix* reflect a 'canned solution': an easy to understand, off-the-shelf solution born of community norms. We anticipate that as communities play games and develop variations of those games, familiar patterns of rule changing will arise. Within such a community of practice, those who know many variations will recognize familiar solutions for common problems in (re)designing their game.

Summary and Next Steps

To solve needs, variant authors prescribe satisfying and optional rules and ward against spoiling rules. They employ 'canned solutions', a pattern of use that shows reliance on familiar solutions to solve common problems. These rules are evidence of a player's systematic perspective. The theory of necessity shows end-users' keen awareness of the ability of one small change to disrupt the balance of the game-system.

Beyond this card game, future inquiry can be directed toward other domains. We next examine this theory in a digital context, taking these insights from a traditional medium into a digital one. Digital games appear more difficult to customize than non-digital games; for example, video games currently feature automatic processes and discrete representations. These features deeply restrict the choices for variation as compared to a simple deck of cards, raising questions on the transferability of the theory of necessity and the quirks of game variants in digital media. To address these questions, we study variants for Bungie's Halo 2 next.

HALO 2

Halo 2 is a first-person shooting game on the Microsoft Xbox where players battle with plasma rifles, shotguns, and grenades. With over 8 million copies sold, Halo 2 is the best-selling Xbox game and can be played as a single-player campaign or a multi-player game (online, networked, or split-screen on the same device). In a typical multi-player match, players accumulate points for killing one another. When they die, players are revived ('respawn') in random places on the battlefield. The game ends when one player has scored a target number of kills (e.g. 25 kills in the *Slayer* game type).

We focus on customization in the multi-player aspect, in which one player (the host) can choose the type of game. Halo explicitly allows the host to create, play, and save different variants. Players can choose from seven built-in game types: Slayer, King of the Hill, Oddball, Juggernaut, Capture the Flag, Assault, and Territories. These game types feature programmed support for win conditions, respawn locations, count-down timers, game items, and territories. For example, *Capture the Flag* is a timed team game in which players try to steal an enemy flag and return it to their home base for points. Game logic is reconfigured to spawn team members on opposite sides of a map, to introduce a flag item for each team (spawned inside home territory), and to track the location of the flag to determine scoring. Players choose among different game types, each offering four to seven sub-variants for a total of thirty-eight built-in variants.

In addition to the predetermined types, players can fine-tune each variant as a "Custom Game Type" by adjusting the available weapons and armor, and the scoring and win condition (Figure 3). While the customization exhibits flexibility (technically, there are thousands of possible permutations), we have found that players still encounter limitations in how the software permits them to play.

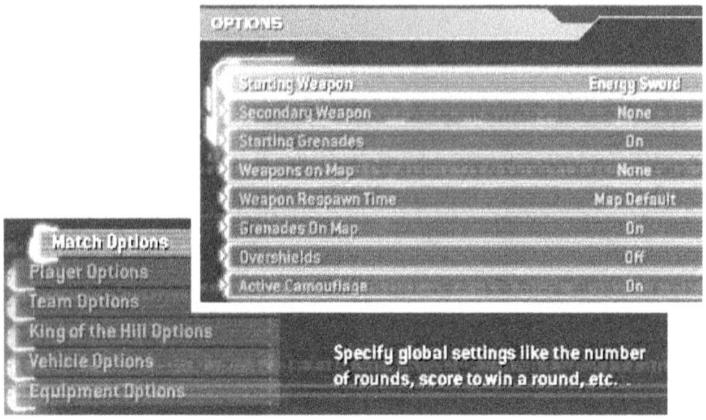

Figure 3. Customization categories for a Halo 2 custom game (top). Weapon and equipment options in a Halo 2 custom game (bottom).

Methodology

Our goal was to categorize rules in Halo 2 variants and to see when they were used to overcome challenges with the software. Unlike the Texas Hold'em analysis, we did not seek to produce new theory; instead, we started with the existing theory and a corpus of 91 variants of Halo 2. The data source is an online wiki page[1] where player-enthusiasts posted instructions for Halo 2 variants they have tried and enjoyed. Each variant consisted of the required game settings, rules (including 'honor rules' which we will describe later), and advice, along with occasional commentary by other players pertaining to each variant. 75 people publically contributed to the wiki at the time of retrieval. This number implies that a small community of players were engaged in the collection and curation of variants, rather than a collection of variants compiled by one enthusiast.

We analyzed these Halo variants via thematic analysis [1] by applying our existing categories and exploring sub-themes or overarching themes. The Hold'em analysis supplied two major constructs: (1) our theory of necessity and the three types of rule changes and (2) the finding that canned solutions exist within a community of players. To examine the design implications of working in a digital space, we subcategorized the canned solutions by the relationship between rules and technology, examining whether the new rules were socially- or digitally-mediated.

Variants

The writers of the Halo 2 variants from the data exhibited similar rhetorical strategies to those from Texas Hold'em. Some chose a theme and made rules to fit that theme: D-DAY, a reenactment of the World War II invasion at Normandy, specifyies a map with a beach and hills and weapons for each team. A canned solution is provided for the common problem of players spawning on the wrong side: *"There should be one designated non-fighter who gives rides back to the beach with a Warthog [*a 3 person vehicle*] for those who respawn behind it."* (D-DAY)

To illustrate a typical variant, we annotate excerpts from ZOMBIES, a variant so prevalent that Bungie Studios integrated it as a formal *Infection* game type in the next release of Halo. In *Zombies*, a smaller, weaker team with infinite lives assimilates members of the opposing team by killing them. Three people independently described this variant. An except from one such set of rules is:

> *"The object of the game is for the zombies to kill the non-zombies. When you are killed by a zombie, you have to change teams by pressing start and going to change teams, and change to the zombie team, [...] The catch is that the zombies can only use swords, they cannot use battle rifles!!"* —Searayman

Searayman describes two situations that depend on the players imposing the rules on themselves: players equipping the appropriate weapon depending on their team, and changing teams when a player dies as a human.

One player notices a problem on some maps where some weapons are too weak for the human team. While the weapons themselves are not weak in the standard Halo game, they do not fit the theme of ZOMBIES, which is that zombies should be easy to kill.

"Instead of pistols on map put Shotguns on map and Magnum/Sword start. This will help on levels like Midship were most of the pistols would end up being Plasma Pistols, Plasma vs Sword = Sword 99.9 percent win." —Tru3 SoLdi3r

One person identified spoiling rules and proposed a solution.

"No starting grenades or grenades on map (I originally had grenades, but zombies abused them...) No team damage (Again, I originally had team damage to force humans to be careful, but people over Xbox Live necessitated a change.)" —Bionic Pants

Several people suggest optional rules for weapons and maps:

Another version of this is 'Zombie Survival', basically its all normal zombie rules BUT there are no weapons on the map so you have to be careful with that ammo, I like playing this type of zombies on Zanzibar. —SF2006

"When I've played the game we usually spawn with swords and magnums, and allow shotguns on the map. In addition we turn off shields and the motion sensor." —Ven Rondua

Satisfying, Optional, and Spoiling Rules

Thematic analysis of the 91 variants exposed rules that could be categorized as satisfying. Similar to the cases in Texas Hold'em, rules were justified by their support of the theme of the game (e.g. ZOMBIES, BASKETBALL, BRAVEHEART), experiential qualities (e.g. chaos, fun, intensity), and balance. Because the source for these variants was a wiki, we were able to identify the contributors of the variants. The variant author would typically come up with satisfying rules for the variant, along with anecdotes of their experience playing the variant as encouragement for other players to try it. These satisfying rules captured the essence of the game and could be used to explain the variant to new players. Other people would comment in several ways: 1) noting

[1] http://h2.halowiki.net/p/Custom_Game_Types

that they had been playing the same variant and describing their own rules, 2) suggesting optional rules, or 3) identifying spoiling rules and providing canned solutions.

Variant authors did not always enumerate every setting for a customizable game. Many settings were excluded because they were considered 'optional'. Wiki entries often highlighted only the essential rule changes for their variant, the satisfying rules. Some variant authors emphasized that omitted settings were up to the host to choose. For example, GOLF prefaces its abbreviated rule list with, "the vital [*settings*] only, the rest is optional." Other players would often discuss different weapon settings or maps that enhanced the objective of the variant, as seen in the example in Table 2.

Spoiling rules were rare, but did appear in the data. REINFORCEMENT CTF is configured with a periodic respawn, meaning only one dead player can re-enter the arena per cycle. The experience is spoilt for players if a second respawn option is enabled ("Force Even Teams"). A dead player on a winning team will be unable to play until the losing team respawns enough players into the field. This complaint can be read in Table 2. Another spoiling situation appears in RUN LIKE HELL. This variant increases the power of weapons, raising the intensity of the game. However, the friendly fire option now becomes a more prominent problem, spoiling the game. The variant author suggests, "It is fricken insane with a lot of people, also you might want to shutoff team killing because between shotguns and grenades you accidently kill your own teamates a lot."

The three types of rules support the idea that players were concerned with a *systematic* understanding of the impact of rules on the overall game. Also, custom game entries in the wiki were often accompanied by descriptions of what to expect from the recommended game settings and tips on how to play well. Both types of entries show the game designers' careful consideration of the impact of individual settings on the game and the best practices for new players to follow in order to take full advantage of the new game settings.

Canned Solutions

The analysis revealed a number of 'canned solutions', commonly used rules that solved familiar problems. For example, a number of variants forbade combat (or as in the game FIGHT CLUB) permitted players to engage only in hand-to-hand combat. Players would ideally start the game without guns in hand. However, as it is impossible to configure the initial weapons loadout as empty, players arranged workarounds to this limitation. Three workarounds, or canned solutions, surfaced: decreeing that players must publically empty their ammo at the beginning of the game, exploiting a known game bug to have players drop their only weapon[2], or giving players weak initial weapons and not having any available to pick up in the game. These solutions appeared often in many variants or relied on expected common knowledge such as the game bug to drop weapons.

[2]An esoteric series of player actions will drop all weapons: charging a particular gun, picking up a grenade, and moving backwards.

Another common problem was the enforcement of the variant's rules when a player broke them, which could not be programmed as part of the customization. Canned solutions included: having everyone kill the rule-breaker, voting to eject the player from the game, assigning a player as an external referee to identify the rule-breaker for sanctioning, and watching post-game metrics such as awards or medals (if the game required no use of weapon, then any award for weapon skills would show that a player broke the rule).

Finally, spawn locations cannot be customized and three solutions surfaced: giving players immunity when they are walking to their designated locations, having one player take a 'cab driver' role to ferry players to the correct side of the map, or setting the game type to 'assault' or 'capture the flag' and ignoring the default objectives in those game types. Of these three, the immunity and the game type solutions appeared more than once, implying that players were familiar with them as known solutions. The 'cab driver' solution only appeared once in the data set. This uniqueness shows that viability and solution-popularity are different properties.

In addition to the themes surrounding the theory of necessity, we fixated on technology's role. Video games digitally encode the rules of the game and we sought to explore the challenges that players face when the medium of the game is limited. Halo 2 exhibits such limitations in its inability to start games without weapons or give the game host more control over respawn locations. We now highlight two subthemes regarding the limits of technology and strategies of variant authors: the right players and honor rules.

THE PROBLEM: PEOPLE OR SOFTWARE?

"No seriously, most people play this to practice splattering, and it ruins the whole game for everyone. If they don't get it, just tell them. If they still won't get off the rock, just end the game. If they can't play the right way, they shouldn't be playing at all." (TREMORS, a vehicle-based variant)

Unlike the Texas Hold'em variants, reports of custom games in Halo 2 regularly discuss how to manage uncooperative strangers. The Halo 2 data presents the opportunity to examine how players manipulate custom rules to produce the attitude necessary to successfully play a particular variant.

In the wiki text, the variant authors warned against several motivations for non-conformance: gaining an unfair advantage, boredom or lack of interest, ignorance of the rules, and playing a different game (see the above quote about splattering). The actions that non-conforming players used included rule-breaking and play that did not technically break prohibitive rules, but counteracted the expected goal of the game (e.g. delaying the game and ignoring expectations to cooperate with an arranged team).

The variant authors proposed diverse strategies. First, hosts could include the right people ("to make sure you have some trustworthy players. NO CHEATERS"). Second, players could threaten exclusion by limiting the lives of the players or booting them from an active game. Cheaters risked reprimands if discovered. To facilitate this, hosts employed methods of accountability by appointing referees or evaluating evidence. Third, hosts sometimes expected some players to break the rules and chose configuration options accordingly. For example, the variant author for BOOM BALL assumed that players might shoot their guns (breaking the 'no shooting' rule), so the starting weapons were weak pistols:

"The idea is that no one is to shoot weapons, only use grenades, however since not all people obey rules I choose the plasma pistol to limit the damage to kills etc." (BOOM BALL)

In summary, not only do the authors of the game variants tell players to choose their players wisely, they modify the rules of game itself to lessen the impact of spoilsports on the variant. These rules provide sanctions (killing and booting), accountability (observers and metrics), and compromise. This tension between adjusting the players or the rules is also reflected in Xu et al.'s study of sociability in Halo 3 [23], further supporting the recognition of complex ties between gameplay, configuration, and *who* comprises the roster.

Honor Rules

About one third of all the variants depended on the integrity of their players rather than the digital enforcement of behavior. Wiki authors described this system as honor rules. Here were a couple of examples:

- Players must all open a personal menu and choose a Severe Handicap setting, making players more vulnerable to damage (THE THING)
- No shooting vehicles or boarding them if you are playing as the "Mouse" (CAT AND MOUSE)

Honor rules in Halo 2 are rules not enforced by the software, but instead require that the players obey them or the variant would fail. Essentially, they are a type of satisfying rule that work around game customizations that one cannot implement in the software. They were unique to our analysis of Halo 2 variants and did not appear in Texas Hold'em variants. They depended on trusting the players to act appropriately in the spirit of the variant.

For example, the game variant DODGEBALL simulates the children's team sport using the 'Brute Shot' weapon to lob grenades at opposing teams from different sides of the map. Players treat the creek in the middle of the map as a line that they cannot cross. In the game, the players can technically cross this line since Halo does not know about the variant, but crossing it defeats the purpose of the game. Thus, the honor rule is that players should not cross the creek except to move back to the correct side after respawning.

While in DODGEBALL other players will notice when an honor rule is broken, in other variants breaking honor rules is easy to conceal; thus, following the rules truly depends on trust. Two variants had honor rules that were difficult to verify, and both emphasized the importance of playing with trusted people. In KING OF CRYSTAL, players have to be trusted to keep score for themselves, since only kills with a particular weapon were counted. In HIDE AND SEEK, the seeker must wait for a period before being able to move, so that the hiders had enough time to find a hiding spot. Our overall reading of the Halo 2 variants indicates that unverifiable honor rules are uncommon and that while the honor rules depend on trust, they are typically enforced by public disapproval of visible rule-breaking.

Honor rules may be successful because they are tied to social norms. First, 'Honor rule' implies that players are being called to adhere to a higher standard of behavior. Second, there are occasional references on the wiki page to a clan of players who promote a code of fair and courteous play[3]. These signals point to a dependence on cultural values (perhaps specific to Halo) to establish behaviors that would otherwise be an even greater challenge to enforce.

Honor rules are agreed-upon rules that enable hosts to create variants not fully represented by the software. While one may have thought that uninformed players or the anonymity of online multiplayer play may ruin a game, our findings suggest that there are ways to overcome those hurdles. Honor rules are one such framework.

DISCUSSION

The systematic perspective permeates the whole negotiated development of a variant. The Hold'em data reflects a common rhetoric seen in individual thought exercises (SUPER HOLD'EM), group ideas (UPSIDE-DOWN PINEAPPLE), polished variants, and critiques by players. We witnessed on the Halo 2 wiki that although the variant author dictates the satisfying rules, other people contribute to optional rules or identify spoiling rules and canned solutions. In the discussion of the ZOMBIES variant, the players would propose other rule changes, but also point out situations for spoilers and propose canned solutions to resolve them. When creating variants, the three types of rules play different roles, the most central being the first type: satisfying rules. We can now define a variant by claiming that satisfying rules solve problems and primarily shape the core game mechanic of the variant. Optional rules and advice about spoiling rules play supporting roles once the ethos is established.

Variants and Social Collaboration

In an offline game, players implicitly expect others to follow the rules; 'honor rules' are mostly an online phenomenon, since they are simply 'rules' in an offline context. However, we find one example of an 'honor rule' in a game of Foursquare among elementary school children, typically 3rd or 4th grade girls [6]. In this game, four players, each situated on a quadrant, hit a ball between their squares until one player is eliminated when they miss the ball. The player who has remained the longest is the 'King' who decides the rule variations for the next round. One popular variant is 'Rooie's rules', which comprises 'nice' rules such as "no slams", "no spins", and "no holds" but these are not enforced to accommodate younger players who may break them unintentionally. Therefore, Rooie's rules is essentially an honor rule to play nice, intended to prevent players from

[3] http://h2.halowiki.net/p/Code_of_Bob

intentionally eliminating others. When a group of 'rough' boys join the game, they slam or hold the ball, but the girls find it difficult to enforce violations, because 'niceness' depends on intent. When honor rules are broken in this offline game, the Foursquare rules do not instruct players to sanction the misbehaving player; the girls instead resort to social workarounds to keep the boys in line.

The foremost principle in an online game possessing honor rules is that they must be verifiable; otherwise, one can only play with those one trusts. Along with verifiabe rules, the game host should be able to reduce the potential damage caused by misbehaving players, by minimizing the effect of breaking the honor rule, removing the rule-breaker, or developing a workaround condition when it occurs (making it part of the variant). For example, in COPS N ROBBERS, if the cops become bored while guarding the jail cell, they are permitted to kill the prisoners. Or, in a hand-to-hand combat game like TROY, kills by ranged weapons are not allowed and players must immediately discharge their weapons upon initial spawning. However, if they happen to hit an opponent, then, "lucky you; if not, too bad!"

Appropriation, Customization, and Packaged Solutions

While the topic of appropriation and customization is not new to the CSCW community, we propose that the idea of variants provides a useful and new perspective on appropriation. Our findings on variants have been permeated with an emphasis on what might be called "packaging". First, variants themselves are packages, as they are designed to exist within a systematic equilibrium. As we have found, variant authors pay great attention to the completeness of a variant. The result is meant to be a playable, balanced, and complete package. Furthermore, we discovered canned solutions—packages of smaller scope. Game variants and canned solutions can be studied to reveal the values and design tendencies of a community of gamers.

Likewise, similar 'packaging' behavior can be explored in non-gaming communities of appropriation, such as behavior relating to open source patch files [21]. Customization of enterprise software does not appear to require the same systematic attention. Trigg and Bødker [20] find that software tailors lack systematic theories of the computer application. However, the existence of variants, forks, patches, and canned solutions suggests that end-users manage complex adjustments by bracketing problems and solutions into defined sub-systems of a different sort. These examples further illuminate how individualistic appropriation translates into a community resource.

Design Implications: Tackling 'Immutability'

So far, we have framed digital systems as 'rigid', supported by evidence of numerous strategies in the Halo 2 dataset where the software impedes the desired rule change. The cost of this 'rigidity' comes in the inefficiency of some of the solutions (e.g. relying on arcane sequences to drop weapons). Texas Hold'em's variants do not exhibit similar inefficiencies. What can be learned from this?

First, we find that 'rigidity' and 'flexibility' are best applied when measured against a set of rule changes. A vague assessment of 'rigidity' can be made concrete by scoping variant authors' expectations. Second, inefficient solutions are markers of 'rigidity', exposing desirable rule-changes. Finally, 'rigidity' favors neither digital nor analog configurations. Our interpretation of card games like Hold'em is that flexibility exists due to a well-developed match between the card medium and the players' desired set of rule-changes.

Canned solutions allow us to speculate on general solutions to common 'immutable' challenges in system design. A canned solution is familiar and well understood by the community of tailors. Researchers who look for canned solutions will discover the channels in which workarounds are transmitted, but they will also expose vetting processes and the community's design mindset. Thus, by investigating or supporting these social processes, perhaps by providing a catalogue and discussion area for canned solutions, unanticipated rigidities may be resolved more quickly by the community of users. And, treating solutions as packages will expedite their transmission.

The systematic perspective directs variant authors. To support this mindset, we suggest a quantitative approach. If the video games have an online connection, as most modern games now support, the setup, iteration, and outcome of each game variant can be recorded. This data can be exposed to the designers or analyzed automatically. To help create fun and balanced games, a game system may be able to anticipate imbalances and leverage historical data to offer canned solutions. The game system can propose adjustments for returning the game back to equilibrium by examining patterns of previous variant authors' rule changes. This use-case expands the application of game metrics beyond research [9] and industry [8] into the end-user's hands. In non-game systems, relevant real-time metrics can also inform customization activities. With access to aggregate metrics and proper information tools, users can pioneer new 'canned solutions' that fit their unique understanding of the system.

We observed two types of functionality that helped enforce honor rules: features for accountability and for sanctioning. Expanding these features would allow players to better enforce the rules they adopt. For example, a rich live feed of game events (*Player 1 has picked up a shotgun!*) enables players to keep each other accountable. Next, developers can make sanctioning options more versatile. Imposed timeouts and handicaps (*Player 2 may not pick up new weapons for 1 minute!*), allow players to continue the game despite rule-breaking. A variety of ways for players to monitor and sanction will make honor rules easier to enforce and perhaps provide software hooks for making some of those rules automatic. In similar collaborative contexts beyond gaming, we recommend a similar provision of accountability and sanctioning tools to accompany honor among strangers.

Limitations

We decided to study a large number of variants for two very different games rather than a few variants for a large number of games. This gives us deep insight into variants for these two particular games, but leaves us unable to generalize to games in general. Future work entails using alternate methodologies and studying more game types to allow us to validate our theories across different genres of games. Online sources provide a diverse and concrete product of variant authors' deliberations, along with discussion from other players for the particular variant. However, we can only infer why particular decisions are made in creating the variant since the variant author is unavailable to question.

CONCLUSIONS

The rules of the game have been changed. Not by the inventor of the game, but by its players. We have taken a grounded approach to analyze written reports of Texas Hold'em variants. Our analysis produced a theory we call 'the chain of necessity', in which the newly introduced rule requires additional changes until equilibrium is restored. Sometimes 'canned solutions' are adopted to address common problems in variations, such as too many cards in Hold'em. Our study of the Halo 2 video game exposed a similar process of variation development as well as the use of 'honor rules' to circumvent software limitations. In a customization system, both people and software factors determine which variants are possible. Variant authors are a kind of system designer. They are pragmatic, they bundle solutions in packages, and are flexible—ready to adjust the rules (or the roster).

Video game designers already provide customization options for players to expand the possibilities of the game; however, they cannot predict every variant that players may want to try. By taking a systematic view of game variants, designers may be able to create games that better support the creation of satisfactory variations. Perhaps records of past game variants can inform future variant authors of imbalances and useful canned solutions. Variant making is a community process involving game designers, players, and variant authors to enable more expansive gameplay in a single game.

Returning to the researcher's tale of Monopoly, he later found that *Free Parking* delays bankruptcy, resulting in tediously long games. This is a 'spoiling rule' for timeliness, but it was a fun rule and next time we play maybe we'll keep it.

ACKNOWLEDGMENTS

The authors thank Peyina Lin for her help auditing the coding, and Katherine Ye for editing earlier drafts of the paper.

REFERENCES

1. J. Aronson. A pragmatic view of thematic analysis. *The Qualitative Report*, 2(1), 1994.
2. G. K. Cheung. Customization for games: lessons from variants of texas hold'em. In *Proceedings of CHI Extended Abstracts*, pages 1849–1854, 2011.
3. M. Consalvo. *Cheating: gaining advantage in videogames*. MIT Press, 2007.
4. C. Foo and E. Koivisto. Grief play motivations. Nokia Research Center, 2004.
5. F. Frapolli, A. Malatras, and B. Hirsbrunner. Exploiting traditional gameplay characteristics to enhance digital board games. In *International Games Innovation Conference*, 2010.
6. L. Hughes. Beyond the rules of the game: Why are rooie rules nice? In K. Salen and E. Zimmerman, editors, *The game design reader: A rules of play anthology*, pages 504–516. MIT Press, 2006.
7. J. Huizinga. *Homo Ludens*. Beacon Press, 1938.
8. K. Hullett, N. Nagappan, E. Schuh, and J. Hopson. Data analytics for game development: Nier track. In *Proceeding of ICSE*, pages 940–943, 2011.
9. H. Iida, N. Takeshita, and J. Yoshimura. A metric for entertainment of boardgames: its implication for evolution of chess variants. In *Proceedings of IWEC*, pages 65–72. Kluwer, 2002.
10. J. Juul. Swap adjacent gems to make sets of three: A history of matching tile games. *Artifact Journal*, 2, 2007.
11. Y. Lincoln and E. Guba. *Naturalistic Inquiry*. Sage Publications, Inc., 1985.
12. D. Myers. What's good about bad play? In *Proceedings of the Australasian Conference on Interactive Entertainment*, pages 133–140, 2005.
13. B. Nardi and J. Harris. Strangers and friends: collaborative play in world of warcraft. In *Proceedings of CSCW*, pages 149–158, 2006.
14. D. Parlett. *The Penguin Book of Card Games*. The Penguin Group, 2008.
15. D. Pinelle, N. Wong, and T. Stach. Heuristic evaluation for games: usability principles for video game design. In *Proceedings of CHI*, pages 1453–1462, 2008.
16. O. Sotomaa. On modder labour, commodification of play, and mod competitions. *First Monday*, 12(9), 2007.
17. K. Squire. Open-ended video games: A model for developing learning for the interactive age. *The Ecology of Games: Connecting Youth, Games, and Learning*, pages 167–198, 2007.
18. A. Strauss and J. Corbin. *Basics of Qualitative Research*. Sage Publications, Inc., 1990.
19. B. Sutton-Smith. *The Ambiguity of Play*. Harvard University Press, 2001.
20. R. H. Trigg and S. Bødker. From implementation to design: tailoring and the emergence of systematization in cscw. In *Proceedings of CSCW*, pages 45–54, 1994.
21. P. Weißgerber, D. Neu, and S. Diehl. Small patches get in! In *Proceedings of MSR*, pages 67–76, 2008.
22. T. Wright, E. Boria, and P. Breidenbach. Creative player actions in fps online video games playing counter-strike. *Game Studies*, 2, 2002.
23. Y. Xu, X. Cao, A. Sellen, R. Herbrich, and T. Graepel. Sociable killers: understanding social relationships in an online first-person shooter game. In *Proceedings of CSCW*, pages 197–206, 2011.

Communication Channels and Awareness Cues in Collocated Collaborative Time-Critical Gaming

Victor Cheung, Y.-L. Betty Chang, Stacey D. Scott
Systems Design Engineering
University of Waterloo
200 University Ave W., Waterloo, ON, Canada
{victor.cheung, betty.chang, stacey.scott}@uwaterloo.ca

ABSTRACT
During collaborative gameplay players make use of various methods to become aware of the overall game status, develop strategies, and convey information to other players. Efficient and effective use of these methods is essential, especially during fast-paced time-critical collaborative games such as first-person shooters. This paper presents an observational study aimed to understand the communication channels and awareness cues used by players during gameplay to collaboratively achieve the game objectives. The study revealed that players utilize a variety of unconventional communication channels and awareness cues in both the physical and virtual environments to compensate for the inability to use commonly available collaborative human interaction mechanisms, such as eye gaze and gesturing, during gameplay. Players tended to use only auditory cues from their partner in the physical environment, while relying heavily on interacting with their partner *through* the virtual environment, using a variety of central and peripheral cues to maintain awareness during gameplay. Implications of these findings are discussed and recommendations for improving the quality of gameplay are provided.

Author Keywords
Collocated Gaming, Collaborative Gameplay, Console Games, Communication Channels, Awareness, Cues, Computer-Supported Cooperative Play (CSCP).

ACM Classification Keywords
H5.3. [**Information interfaces and presentation**]: Group and Organization Interfaces – *collaborative computing*.

General Terms
Human Factors; Design

INTRODUCTION
Even with the tremendous popularity of distributed gaming, evidenced by the 11.4 million subscribers to Blizzard Entertainment's online role-playing game World of Warcraft[1], collocated games—typically offered through gaming consoles such as Sony PlayStation3, Nintendo Wii and Microsoft Xbox360—continue to be popular among groups of family and friends. This gaming context can offer a more intimate social experience for those seeking face-to-face contact with others, while still offering an engaging gaming experience for the competitive gamer.

Collaborative games, where players work together in teams to achieve shared objectives in the game environment, are a common form of such console gaming. First-person shooter (FPS) and third-person shooter (TPS) games, a popular subset of these collaborative games that contributes more than 10% of video and computer game sales in United States [2], require players to work together to defeat a common enemy while navigating a complex virtual world. In FPS games, players see the virtual world through the eyes of their virtual avatar, while in TPS games players' avatars are visible on-screen from a nearby camera view.

The highly dynamic, time-critical nature of collaborative shooter games provides both a highly engaging gaming experience and a highly challenging teamwork environment that places heavy demands on effective and efficient communication and coordination among teammates. Given the rich verbal and non-verbal communication channels available to collocated collaborators [3, 22], this setting should, in theory, be well suited to supporting such heavy communication and collaboration demands. However, given the high cognitive and temporal demands of a shooter game itself, it is unclear whether sufficient opportunities exist during gameplay for players to take advantage of these rich communication channels. If not, then what, if any, tools are provided in common collocated shooter games to facilitate player communication and collaboration?

To investigate these issues, we conducted an observational study of two popular time-critical shooter games. The study

[1] "World of Warcraft Subscriber Base Currently at 11.4 Million", World of Warcraft News, curse.com, http://www.curse.com/articles/world-of-warcraft-news/956087.aspx [accessed June 1, 2011].

[2] "Essential Facts about the Computer and Video Game Industry 2010", http://www.theesa.com/facts/pdfs/ESA_Essential_Facts_2010.PDF [accessed on December 4, 2010].

revealed that the constant visual attention required by the game hindered players' use of typical face-to-face non-verbal communication behavior such as mutual eye contact and physical gestures. The potentially dire consequences (within the game) of removing their hands from the game controllers further hindered the use of physical gestures. Instead, players adapted their communication behaviors by communicating *through* the game, often using elaborate virtual gestures via their on-screen avatars. Though many players used this through-the-game communication strategy, participant interviews revealed a desire for stronger in-game support for such behavior. Players also reported dissatisfaction with the lack of support for physical gesturing, such as pointing, and suggested potential design improvements that may better support this behavior.

To provide context for the study, we first discuss related work and then overview player interaction in collaborative, time-critical shooter games. The study method is then described. Next, the study findings are presented, focused on the communication channels and awareness cues players used to facilitate their collaborative gameplay. Finally, design implications from these findings are discussed.

RELATED WORK

Collaborative Gaming

Much of the previous work that examines player interaction within collaborative gaming has focused on the multiplayer online gaming context [10, 16, 18, 19, 29]. Most of the communications supported in these distributed contexts aim to emulate practices found in a collocated environment beneficial to collaboration due to enhanced verbal and non-verbal communication [9, 23, 24]. This motivated us to look directly at communication in the collocated gaming context to understand whether the same communication mechanisms used in other collocated collaborative activities are employed or supported during collocated gameplay.

In the collocated context, Zagal et al. [31] investigated face-to-face communication in board game settings and proposed mechanisms that encourage collaboration, such as meaningful outcomes of the game. In a study of console gaming, El-Nasr et al. [5] evaluated cooperative games through predefined cooperative game design patterns, such as shared goals and interaction with the same objects. To understand the social aspect of gameplay, Voida and Greenberg [28] investigated how console gaming, specifically on the Nintendo Wii platform, served as a "computational meeting place for a diverse population of gamers" (p. 1562).

Voida et al. [27] proposed a taxonomy of console gaming practices that categorized player behaviors as individual- or group-oriented. They found that certain game elements supported such practices before, during, and after the actual gameplay. In our work, we focus specifically on the dynamics during gameplay. We also focus on these dynamics under time constraints, and by examining what, if any, influence this factor has on player interactions.

Another vital aspect of collaborative gaming is the ability of players to maintain awareness of gameplay status, including the status of their teammates. Sennersten et al. [21] investigated how visual cues directed visual attention and its effect on decision making in FPS gameplay. We extend this work by considering audio cues, which, when combined with visual cues, may provide improved awareness of the gameplay status. We also consider cues from both the game and the other player, and focus on their impact in decision making during collaborative gameplay.

Communication and Awareness in Other Contexts

There has also been significant research on communication and awareness in other virtual environments beyond gaming that provide insights and help focus this research. For example, studies have investigated collaborative tasks in other time-critical collocated environments, including trading [11], transit control [12], and ship navigation [15]. Most of these tasks are characterized by a clear division in task roles, unlike shooter games which require negotiation of task roles. Yet, all of these collaborative activities have strong interdependencies, and thus, require effective communication and awareness practices.

The time pressures in these environments offered little time for dedicated information transfer between colleagues. Instead, personnel adapted their working style to publicly display their activities to foster awareness, using two main practices. First, personnel made elaborate actions to gain attention of colleagues, for example, to "laugh or produce an exclamation and thereby encourage [a nearby colleague] to monitor [a phone] call more carefully" [12, p. 14]. Second, "outlouds" were used to make certain information available to nearby colleagues without addressing anyone specifically [11, 12]. Personnel also "organize[d] their conduct so that whilst engaged in one activity, they simultaneously monitor[ed] the conduct of others" [12, p. 10]. Thus, awareness was gained through an active process of displaying and monitoring activities. We found similar displaying and monitoring behaviour in our study, however, due to the need for sustained visual focus on the primary task display, players used a unique combination of monitor and display techniques that combined the use of outlouds in the physical world and visible actions in the virtual world.

Significant research has also been focused on promoting awareness in a shared virtual environment, primarily to support remote collaboration [6, 7, 14, 26]. As remote collaborators cannot view each other's displays, "awareness widgets" have been developed to provide information about the remote collaborator's activities [7, 13]. A study by Bolstad and Endsley [2] that examined the impact of awareness displays on team performance, found that showing a collaborator's full task display hindered task performance, while showing an abstracted view containing only essential task information improved task performance, especially in high workload situations. In a study focused on interruption mitigation, Dabbish and Kraut [4] found similar advantages of when providing remote collaborators with abstract awareness displays compared to full task displays; participants were able to time their interruptions appropriately in both conditions, but were distracted from their main task activity less with the abstract display. In shooter games, the partner's full display is available; however, our study found there were few opportunities for players to look at it; thus, these games also include abstracted partner status information within each player's own display. We discuss the impact of this abstracted information on gameplay.

COLLABORATIVE TIME-CRITICAL SHOOTER GAMING

When first introduced, the main objective of shooter games was for a single player to proceed through progressively harder game levels by eliminating enemies and solving puzzles. In current versions, players can now join forces and play the game together for a common objective, either in a distributed manner (using separate inter-connected gaming machines) or in a collocated manner (using the same gaming machine with separate controllers). To foster collaboration, game designers have included elements requiring players to work together in order to arrive at a favorable outcome. For example, a player can flank an enemy while his attention is drawn by another player, players can make use of different weapons to engage enemies at different ranges, or players can cover (or assist) another player who is busy performing a task. None of these scenarios would be possible without effective communication and awareness between players.

To distinguish from other games that contain elements of collaboration or time constraints, or involve shooting, we define collaborative, time-critical shooter gaming as games involving all of the following attributes:

- ***Collaboration between players.*** Players take the role of teammates instead of enemies. In order to fulfill the objectives of the game, players must collaborate with each other, either assisting each other with the same tasks or each working on their own specific tasks which combine to form an overall joint outcome.
- ***Time-critical decisions.*** Players must make apt decisions in a timely manner. Failure to do so will result in failure to accomplish the immediate game objective, or in most occasions, death of their avatars. Decisions include but are not limited to: where to go, what to do, when to do it, and how to do it.
- ***Shooting.*** In most parts of the gameplay players have to use their weapons to shoot targets. Although collaborative games without shooting exist, we focused on games with this feature because of their popularity and the intrinsic "shoot or be shot" time constraint.
- ***Avatar-centered perspective.*** The views that the players see are either from the eyes of (FPS) or from close behind (TPS) their respective avatars. In contrast, many other collaborative games, such as World of Warcraft, provide a birds-eye view, which results in different awareness requirements.

In the study, we focus on the collocated console gaming environment (e.g. Sony PlayStation3, Nintendo Wii and Microsoft Xbox360) for two reasons: 1) collocated gaming is rich in player interactions for collaborative purposes, by providing a platform for verbal, virtual and physical gestural communications; and 2) the majority of collocated collaborative games are available for these consoles rather than personal computers.

METHOD

An observational study on collocated collaborative shooter gaming was conducted in a laboratory setting. The study details are provided in the following sections.

Participants

Ten male participants, between 20-30 years old, participated in the study. Participants were recruited in pairs to ensure an existing comfort and familiarity between gaming partners. The study only included team sizes of two, because most collocated collaborative shooter games only support 2-person mode by splitting the screen into two equal portions. All participants had experience in playing shooter games, though not necessarily the games used in this study.

Equipment and setting

The study was conducted in a small university meeting room setting. Participants sat in a typical shoulder-to-shoulder collocated gameplay arrangement facing a large, projected display, which showed the split game screens of the two players, as shown in Figure 1. We chose this configuration as it was commonly found in a home environment where two players sit on a couch for the best viewing angles of a TV screen of considerable size. A digital video camera was positioned behind the players to capture both the on-screen game interactions and the physical and verbal interactions between players. The gaming console, a Microsoft Xbox360, the data projector, and a set of speakers were located on the table in front of participants.

Two shooter games, *Call of Duty: Modern Warfare 2* (FPS) (abbreviated as *Call of Duty*) and *Gears of War 2* (TPS)

Figure 1. The study setting, showing a pair of participants playing *Gears of War 2*.

were used in the study. These games were selected because of their representativeness in their respective shooter genres, their collaborative emphasis, and because both games can be played on the Xbox360 console platform, thus the same controllers could be used for both gameplay sessions. Also, both games had similar control configurations (e.g. the same buttons were used for aiming and shooting), and some game specific controls were taught on-screen.

Procedure

Each pair of participants was first greeted and welcomed by the researchers. They were then asked to read the study information sheet and complete a signed consent form. The pair was then asked to play each game for 20 minutes. For the *Call of Duty* game session, participants were instructed to play two to three cooperative (co-op) missions, which emphasize coordination and requires players to complete different, yet related, tasks most of the time. For the *Gears of War 2* game session, participants were instructed to play the campaign mission, which emphasizes cooperative navigation during which players complete similar tasks most of the time. The order of presentation of game title was counterbalanced to account for learning effects. After playing both games (40 minutes of total gameplay), each pair participated in a semi-structured interview, which focused on their gameplay experience and their previous experience in collaborative games.

In the remainder of this paper, we will use the prefix "P" followed by a number to refer to our participants and the prefix "G" followed by a number to refer to the groups.

Data collection

During the gameplay sessions, players' use of communication mechanisms was recorded in observer field notes. Players' interactions were also captured on digital video, including audio feed captured through a built-in microphone in the video camera. Field notes were also recorded during the participant interviews.

Data analysis

A qualitative data analysis was conducted on the collected data. The video recordings of gameplay sessions were first reviewed and any occurrences of players' collaborative and communicative behaviors were transcribed. The video recordings of the interviews were also reviewed, and discussions of players' collaborative activity during the game were transcribed.

Observations in the form of field notes and transcribed video data were organized to form an affinity diagram [1], which helps to synthesize qualitative data into emergent themes. A set of categories of communications channels and awareness cues that players utilized during gameplay emerged from the affinity diagramming process. These categories are summarized in Figure 2, and are described further in their respective Findings sections below. Relevant findings from the data are used to illustrate on how players utilized these communication channels and awareness cues during gameplay.

FINDINGS

The data analysis revealed that players not only made use of explicit communication channels to collaborate but also relied on implicit awareness of each other's gameplay status to adjust strategies "silently". Moreover, players made use of a combination of different communication channels to achieve one goal. This section presents our findings on how players utilized both the communication channels and awareness cues to collaborate in the gaming sessions.

Communication Channels

Communication channels are different ways for players to explicitly convey information. During the study, players utilized, to varying degrees, the following three different types of communication channels:

- ***Verbal communication.*** Players talk to each other directly to maintain mutual understanding, or to form strategies based on common ground [3]. This channel is typically available to both distributed and collocated players. However, participant interviews revealed that players tend to use this more frequently when collocated.
- ***Virtual gestures.*** Using movements of a player's avatar (visible on the partner's screen) to convey information. For example, a player can use their avatar's weapon to point to a certain item. Furthermore, collocated players can also demonstrate tactics or even special moves through their own screens.
- ***Physical gestures.*** Using physical body movements to illustrate intentions. For example, a player can point to an on-screen object with his finger. This channel is currently only available in collocated game setting, where players are physically together. While similar in purpose, this gestural channel is different from the commonly referred to face-to-face gestural channel [17] as players are shoulder-to-shoulder instead, with their main focus on the game screen in front of them.

The following sections further describe the use of these communication channels and illustrate them with examples from the study.

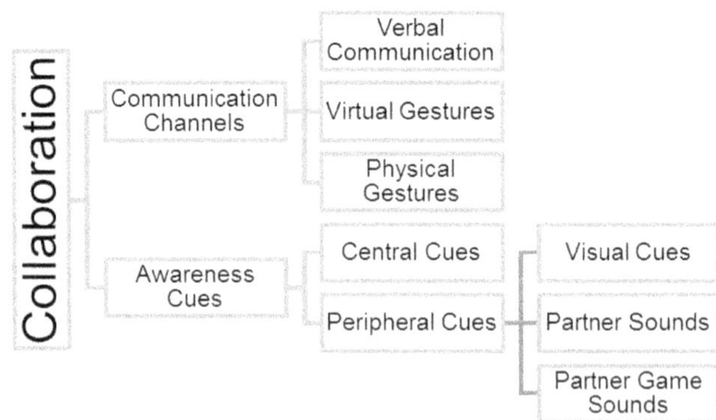

Figure 2. The categories of communication channels and awareness cues used by participants during gameplay.

Verbal communication

During gameplay, player used verbal communication to form strategies and to discuss useful and game related information. The data revealed that it was the most frequently used channel, and was used for a number of distinctive purposes, as described below.

Forming strategies. Players talked to each other to form strategies for reaching mission targets or performing better, in the form of a query or a proposal:

> G2, Call of Duty session:
> [Deciding which side along the road they should go]
> P4 [query]: We can go down the left, can we?
> P3 [answer to the query]: No…

> G3, Gears of War 2 session:
> [Split up and proceed to the next checkpoint]
> P5 [proposal, implicit agreement assumed]: You go up through that way. I will go through the right.

Each utterance tended to be short and quick, as expected from the fast pace of gameplay. There were also times when the recipient disagreed and suggested another strategy, typically leading to a short negotiation of strategy consisting of two to three verbal exchanges.

Announcing one's own status or actions. Players verbally announced their own status or actions that they thought would affect their partner:

> G1, Call of Duty session:
> [Entered an area under heavy attack]
> P1 [report status]: I just ran into a bad place.

> G1, Call of Duty session:
> P2 [report status]: I got him, but I'm nearly dead.

> G3, Call of Duty session:
> [Grenade would injure players when exploded]
> P5 [report action]: Thrown a grenade [in front of us]!

Unlike normal conversation, acknowledgements were rarely given to such announcements. We hypothesize this was due to the physical proximity of the players (thus reception was assumed) and the short-lived relevance of the status or actions. Announcing one's own status or actions often led to incidences of *forming strategies* or the other player *announcing their own actions*.

Announcing points of interest. Besides announcing status and actions, players made announcements of points of interest or activity they spotted:

> G4, Call of Duty session:
> P7 [enemy spotted]: That's a guy on the roof!

> G2, Call of Duty session:
> P4 [grenade spotted which would injure everyone nearby]: Oh crap! There's a grenade! There's a grenade!

> G3, Gears of War 2 session:
> P5 [item spotted which might be useful to partner]: There's an ammo box. Right here!

Verbal references to on-screen objects were often followed by or accompanied with a virtual gesture. When referring to an item, players often had to follow up with virtual gestures. We revisit this point in the following section.

Locating partner. Players also inquire about the location of one another's avatars in order to meet up or to help out. For example, when a player's avatar was down, the rescuing avatar had to stand nearby for reviving:

> G4, Call of Duty session:
> P8: where are you?
> P7: I'm crawling underneath you...

When a single response from the partner was not sufficient to clarify the location, players continued to talk to each other to guide and speed up the rendezvous. This led to the following type of verbal communication.

Guiding partner. Sometimes one player was stuck in a condition or location and required guidance from the other player. Typically the guiding player would describe landmarks in the game to direct the other player:

> G2, Gears of War 2 session:
> P4 [has reached a destination, and was waiting for his partner to meet up]: Look for this giant crashing thing coming down, just exploded.

> G4, Gears of War 2 session:
> P7 [has passed through a door and proceeding to another area of the game]: Hey, it's the door. You should also come this way.

In some cases when the avatars were close to each other, the guiding player simply said "Follow me!" and used his avatar to demonstrate the next step. This was an example of how verbal communication was used in conjunction with virtual gestures, and will be discussed below.

Virtual gestures

Similar to how gestures are used during other collaborative activities [25], virtual gestures were used by players to indicate objects, areas, and directions. In our study, these gestures were always accompanied by a brief verbal communication to provide context. However, unlike in typical collaborative work scenarios, the virtual gestures employed by players were mediated via avatars in a much more elaborate manner, typically through exaggerated movements and actions.

In most situations *virtual gestures* provided a faster means to convey information. For example, when P3 found the ammunition ("ammo") item being sought by P4, instead of describing its location, P3 shot at it using his weapon:

> G2, Gears of War 2 session:
> P3 [saw the ammo item at a corner]: [Found] one!

P4: Where?
P3 [while shooting at the ammo box]: Right here.

As shown in this example, the players seemed to already understand the virtual gestures from their previous gaming experience as they did not explain or discuss the virtual gestures. The verbal communication accompanied was for grabbing and directing the partner's attention.

Besides shooting, the data also revealed that players used their avatars in a playful way. In a scenario where both players were heading to a checkpoint, P1 appropriated the built-in rolling action in *Gears of War 2* to show the direction they should be heading. This action was primarily designed to make an avatar move faster into cover, but was used by P1 for way-pointing due to its overt appearance. In another scenario, P3 made his avatar move around in circles to grab the other player's attention and direct him to an item.

In general, *virtual gestures* were performed in an explicit and creative manner to attract attention more easily, in order to convey information as quickly as possible.

Physical gestures

Similar to virtual gestures, physical gestures were also typically used in combination with verbal communication. For example, in a scenario where P9 was helping P10 to navigate to his location, P9 used corresponding pointing hand gestures while speaking to P10:

G5, Gears of War 2 session:
P9 [moved one hand away from controller, leaving the avatar idle, and used the hand to point in the air]: Go through there, go through on the right, pass the…

However, we observed that physical gestures were infrequently used; in fact, only one incidence was observed in the study, and was limited to simple pointing gestures. This was not surprising since the shoulder-to-shoulder configuration of players directed their main focus to the shared screen. Thus, physical gestures required more effort to seize the other player's attention away from the screen. Participant interviews revealed that some players found the gameplay too fast and intense to use physical gestures to point at objects. Players also reported that they had got used to the controller and the posture, and they did not want to move (lifting their hands). During interviews some players reported a desire to point physically but felt hindered by the game interface. One player suggested having an action with which the avatar can direct a laser beam in the virtual world to point (similar to the connecting lines drawn between users' virtual embodiment and objects they manipulated in Hindmarsh et al.'s [14] collaborative virtual environment), while another suggested having a pointer on the physical controller to facilitate pointing in the physical world, similar to a laser pointer.

Awareness Cues

Players made use of various cues from both their central and peripheral attention to maintain awareness of the environment and of each other in the game, in order to adjust their collaborative strategies, without apparent use of the communication channels discussed above. Such awareness is described by Schmidt [20] as:

> "[actors] pick up what is going on around them and make practical sense of it… by observing or listening – so as to ascertain the state, progress, direction, etc. of these activities, … to determine exactly how one's own activities need to be adjusted to mesh with the unfolding work of the colleagues, and so forth." (p.291)

In our gaming context, *work* is the progress of the partner and *colleagues* are the players. The data analysis revealed the following two categories of awareness cues being used:

- ***Central Cues.*** Players make use of information presented to them in their center of attention in order to stay informed of their own and their partners' status. In our context, the central cues are presented through the players' own screen, indicating directions and player's health status.
- ***Peripheral Cues.*** Players gather information from their peripheral attention to stay aware of the partner's status. These cues are not restricted to functionality provided by the game, and they may include cues gathered from the visual channel, such as a glance at the partner's screen, as well as the audio channel such as game sounds directed to the partner or screaming sounds made by the partner.

The rest of this section discusses and provides examples of how players utilized these awareness cues during gameplay.

Central cues

Central cues are cues presented to the player in their center of focus, which is the player's own screen. Using these cues the player can keep track of their own status as well as gain clues about their partner's status, through map, arrow signs, appearance of partner's avatar, and environmental indicators.

In *Call of Duty*, a map of the surrounding area was shown

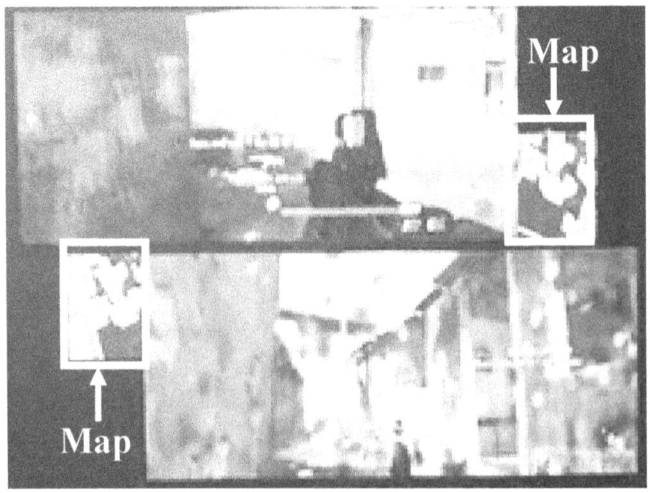

Figure 3. Partner's screen (lower) turned red when avatar was badly injured.

on the side of each player's game view displaying the layout of the area (see Figure 3), and locations of the players and their enemies. Players could locate each other and even find out which direction avatar was facing, which was helpful for them to form strategies and meet up.

Various arrow signs were present in both games for a number of purposes. For example, a small arrow was located on the edge of the screen providing a general idea of the relative location of the partner. A flashing cross would appear on the edge of the screen in the direction of the injured partner, if the partner was injured and required reviving. A special arrow near the center of the screen was used to show the direction from which the player was shot.

The appearance of the partner's avatar was used to both locate and keep a general sense of their well-being. Two typical uses of this visual cue were to find the injured partner who needed help and was lying on the ground, and to rendezvous. This awareness cue, however, was not always effective, even when a name tag was visible above each avatar's head as was the case in *Call of Duty* (name tags could be temporarily invoked in *Gears of War 2*). The data revealed several instances where a player was confused or even mis-recognized allies and enemies, as they "all look the same", according to some of the participants. Such confusion created instances of "friendly fire", and more importantly caused delay in reviving partners and eliminating enemies, thus undermining the process of collaboration. Embedding clearer identification information or making the difference in appearance more salient may reduce such confusion in the games.

Environmental indicators helped players stay aware of their avatars' surroundings. In one incident, a player saw the trajectory of bullets, and used that visual cue to extrapolate the location of the enemies.

The cues described above were frequently used by the players for maintaining awareness. Some of the cues, however, were sometimes coarse (arrow signs only showed a general direction) or even confusing (similar appearance of allies and enemies). Improvements could be made to better facilitate collaboration among the collocated players.

Peripheral cues

Peripheral cues are cues a player gathered from his peripheral attention area, which include visual cues, partner sounds, and game sounds directed to the partner.

Peripheral visual cues consisted of visual information a player gathered from the other player's screen. This awareness information is unique to the collocated gameplay context that provides split-screen interfaces. During the gameplay, these peripheral visual cues helped the player in the following ways:

- ***Verify grounding.*** By checking their partner's screen and noting the expected actions, a player could verify that they shared common grounding on their strategies. Deviation from expectation would lead to verbal communication to re-establish grounding. For example, when P3 and P4 had decided to snipe two nearby targets, P4 glanced at P3's screen to confirm that they were aiming at their corresponding target.
- ***Implicit strategy forming.*** By glancing at their partner's screen, a player could decide what to do without explicit communication. For example, P9 noticed his partner's split-screen (lower screen) was becoming red (see Figure 3), which indicated that the player had been shot and injured. He then took a safer approach to avoid getting shot while eliminating enemies, and looked for chances to revive his partner.

There were also times when the gameplay was too intense to spare any attention to the other player's screen, but the player could still use the sounds his partner made to become aware of their situation and to provide help when needed. Such sounds were often simple utterances like "ahhhh!" or "wow!".

Finally, sound effects from the game directed to the partner were also used by the player. For example, in *Call of Duty* a heavy heart-beating sound was played when an avatar was badly injured, which was also noticed by the player's partner. Conversely, the absence of such "danger" sound effects indicated that both avatars were healthy. Other sound effects such as enemies' shouting, shooting and even dogs' barking provide awareness of the partner. In a collocated setting, sound effects have the potential to cause confusion, as there are no separate "channels" to deliver player-specific sound. However, the study data did not reveal any incidents of players being confused by ambiguous sound effects. It was likely that players were able to combine these game sounds with other awareness cues to determine to which player the sound was directed. For example, when a player heard a barking sound, and saw from his screen that the dog was attacking his partner from behind, he then warned the unknowing partner.

DISCUSSION

In the above section, we reported and analyzed our observations on the use of communication channels and awareness cues during the gameplay sessions. In this section, we further elaborate on these findings and discuss their implications within the gaming context.

Game Design Hindered Use of Non-Verbal Communication

As reported above, the gaming environment under study placed players physically together and provided several channels for communication. As noted in previous literature [3, 22], such collocated settings typically provide a medium for rich social interaction on top of mere entertainment. This however does not ensure that players would be able to take full advantage of the physical proximity provided by the setting. In particular, our findings revealed that most players did not engage in interactions commonly found in a collocated environment, including mutual eye contact and physical gestures such as waving and physical contact to facilitate collaboration. Recall that only one instance of physical pointing was observed in the study. The study data revealed the following two reasons for the lack of non-verbal communication:

- ***Intensive fast-paced gameplay.*** Most of the time, players were required to pay constant attention to the main screen for combat or navigation purposes. Looking away and gazing at each other would introduce too high a risk of awareness or communication breakdowns.
- ***Lack of support for efficient physical gestures.*** Players also had to constantly maintain control of their avatars. Neither game provided any mechanisms for players to physically refer to points of interest of gameplay besides finger-pointing, which required them to remove their hands from the controllers. Again, this could have dire consequences within the game.

Such deviation from the typical face-to-face interaction suggested a special interaction model where players engaged in a shoulder-to-shoulder configuration.

Game-Mediated Shoulder-to-Shoulder Player Interaction

Given the absence of typical collocated interactions, players tended to compensate by adapting available game mechanisms for communication purposes, as well as using the collocated setting. Instead, players communicated "through the screen" when they had to refer to things in the game, by gaining the other player's attention in the virtual world using virtual gestures together with verbal communication. Here we discuss a number of the adaptations players made as highlighted in our findings.

Elaborate use of virtual gestures

Players used a variety of virtual gestures for referencing, instead of physical gestures which can be more expressive [30]. Performing a virtual gesture only requires a player to press buttons on the game controller without changing their current posture, and hence requires less effort than physical gestures in this context. It also does not require the receiving player to shift focus away from their own screen.

In addition, virtual gestures are more precise in referring to a virtual point of interest, as the screen is usually cluttered with various game items, and players are viewing the screen at different angles and from a considerable distance. To better convey such information, players tended to use virtual gestures in an elaborate manner, like running in circles around an item or rolling for way-pointing, as discussed above. This greater variety in virtual gestures is available in the virtual game world due to its higher degree of freedom, as compared to more conventional CSCW contexts, where virtual embodiments are often limited to telepointers [8] or abstract representations [14, 30].

Extensive use of the auditory channel

Players made extensive use of the auditory channel (verbal communication and peripheral cues) for collaborative purposes, instead of monitoring their partner's screen or the partner directly, which would divert them from their already occupied visual channel. Players talked constantly to form strategies, and to convey and discuss game-related information. This finding is consistent with Voida et al.'s [27] observation of players' use of conversation to construct a shared awareness of game-related information.

Moreover, the data showed that players were attentive to the short comments made by their partner, even though these comments were not directed to the player himself. For example, when a player heard a "woah" from their partner, they could infer that the partner's avatar was running into trouble, such as being shot or trapped.

On the other hand, the absence of face-to-face interaction limits acknowledgements to short verbal communications, or even no explicit acknowledgements, unlike in normal face-to-face communication where people may nod or provide other facial expressions. Thus, when verbal communications occurred, especially, announcing one's own status communications or when players simply made auditory reactions to the game, such as "wow" or "ahhh!", players tended to make more elaborative utterances to increase the chances of being noted by the partner. As discussed earlier, similar uses of "outlouds" also occur in other time-critical collocated collaborative contexts, such as control rooms, to facilitate collaboration [11, 12].

Partner's central cues as own peripheral cues

The games used in the study (as well as many other games in this genre) provided several central cues to the players to increase their awareness of their own status, such as the screen getting red and the heart-beating sound when injured, as described earlier. These central cues became available to all players in collocated settings via the split screens, and players treated some of the central cues for their partner as their own peripheral cues and used this information to maintain awareness of the overall game status. Such "peripheral monitoring" has also been observed in more conventional CSCW contexts where a person can infer colleague's status based on his/her observations of the surroundings [11, 12, 15]. However, their physical setups often include a combination of shared and personal displays, making some information only available to individuals. In collocated gaming, in contrast, everything the partner sees and hears is immediately accessible by the player, thus eliminating additional mechanism in providing partner's status information.

Moreover, due to the absence of one's partner's screen, detailed partner status information is commonly included in traditional distributed groupware to promote workspace awareness [7, 13], however, partner status information tends to be provided at a more abstract level in games to reduce distraction.

Promoting social interaction via split screens

Besides allowing players to stay aware of each other's gameplay status and adjust collaborative strategies accordingly, the availability of partner's screen appeared to promote players' social interaction. There were numerous occasions during the study, where players complimented or teased each other about their gaming activities. By noticing special visual effects on the shared screen, players were able to enjoy many "did you see that?" moments. In some instances, players even stopped what they were doing to watch the effects in their partner's screen.

In summary, it seems that, although collocated collaborative time-critical gaming occurs in an environment that typically supports rich non-verbal communication, the visual and physical demands of the game interface provide little opportunity for players to engage in such communication behavior. Instead, players rely on verbal and other auditory communication mechanisms, as well as tools within the game to visually communicate "through" the gaming interface, with behaviors such as virtual gestures. The following section suggests several possible design improvements that could be made within this gaming genre to better facilitate communication and awareness gathering among collocated players.

DESIGN IMPLICATIONS FOR COLLOCATED COLLABORATIVE TIME-CRITICAL GAMING

Given the shoulder-to-shoulder player interaction model and the corresponding adaptations made by the players to facilitate collaboration in the fast-paced gaming under study, several design implications were developed.

- ***Improved support for virtual gestures.*** The frequent and elaborate use of virtual gestures suggests better support for such actions. By providing players with the capability of performing virtual gestures more efficiently, and also more meaningfully, mutual understanding of game strategies and communication may be better achieved.
- ***Improved support for physical gestures.*** The time constraints of the game and physical configuration of players hindered the use of physical gestures such as pointing, though participant interviews revealed the desire to perform such actions during gameplay. This suggests a modified gaming interface that would enable physical gestures, in particular, pointing gestures. As one participant suggested, such support may be possible by incorporating laser pointer-type functionality into the game controller.
- ***Balanced use of game sounds.*** The extensive use of the verbal communication channel indicates the importance of this channel to support player collaboration. This suggests that sound effects from the game, while making the gameplay more realistic and engaging, should not overwhelm players' auditory attention in a manner that inhibits the players' ability to converse.
- ***Balanced use of visual cues.*** Players' use of both their own and their partner's central cues to maintain awareness of the overall gameplay indicates the need for game designers to take care in selecting the amount of visual cues presented to players throughout the game in order to avoid excessive visual distraction.

In summary, the shoulder-to-shoulder player interaction model led to heavy use of "in the game" communication, illustrated by frequent use of virtual gestures combined with verbal communication, and by passive information gathering, through the use of peripheral cues. Games that facilitate this would improve player collaboration and hence the overall gaming experience.

CONCLUSION AND FUTURE WORK

This paper presented an observational study focused on player interaction in collocated collaborative time-critical shooter games. The study revealed that players utilized a variety of communication channels and awareness cues to facilitate their collaboration during gameplay. Players used verbal communication, virtual gestures, and physical gestures to communicate. Verbal communication was used most frequently for strategy formation, information sharing, and status updates. It was also used in conjunction with virtual gestures to facilitate in-game referencing. Physical gestures were rarely used due to their high cost of use and their lower precision. Central and peripheral cues were used to maintain awareness of the game environment and partner status. Central cues came from their own screens, while peripheral cues came from their partner's screen, sounds made by their partner, and partner-directed game sounds.

These findings were then used to generate possible game enhancements aimed to better facilitate effective use of these communication channels and awareness cues, and ultimately to improve the collaborative gameplay process.

Though this study provides interesting and relevant results for game design, as true of any qualitative work, its scope and generalizability is necessarily limited by the particular population and incidents that were observed. Thus, further investigation of the reported communication channels and awareness cues in other player demographics is warranted to understand the effects of age, gender, and culture on their use.

Similarly, the collaborative games used in our study were limited to two players and in a typical "on the couch" configuration, investigation of games involving larger team sizes and other seating configurations is warranted to understand how the dynamics of communication and awareness are thus changed. Understanding how players manage peripheral cues in games with multiple partners would be of particular interest, as the multiplayer scenario introduces additional auditory and visual complexity, such as the additional complexity of determining the intended target of partner-directed game sounds.

In summary, collocated collaborative time-critical games are gaining popularity, and as these games become more sophisticated in content as well as gameplay styles, players can take full advantage of being collocated to complete the game and enjoy the gaming experience. In order to promote the social aspect of these collaborative games, and improve the overall experience, game designers should better facilitate the use of the communication channels and awareness cues reported in this paper.

REFERENCES

1. Beyer, H. & Holtzblatt, K. (1998). *Contextual design: defining customer-centered systems*. Morgan Kaufmann Publishers Inc., San Francisco, CA.
2. Bolstad, C.A. & Endsley, M.R. (2000). Shared displays and team performance. *Proc. of Human Performance, Situation Awareness and Automation Conference*.
3. Clark, H.H. & Brennan, S.E. (1993). Grounding in communication. Baecker, R.M. ed. *Readings in Groupware and Computer-Supported Cooperative Work: Assisting Human-Human Collaboration*, Morgan Kaufmann, Palo Alto, CA, 222-234.
4. Dabbish, L. & Kraut, R. (2004). Controlling interruptions: Awareness displays and social motivation for coordination. *Proc. of CSCW'04*, 182-191.
5. El-Nasr, M.S., Aghabeigi, B., Milam, D., Erfani, M., Lameman, B., Maygoli, H., Mah, S. (2010). Understanding and evaluating cooperative games. *Proc. of CHI'10*, 253-262.
6. Gutwin, C. & Greenberg, S. (1992). A descriptive framework of workspace awareness for real-time groupware. *Computer-Supported Cooperative Work, 11* (3), 411-445.
7. Gutwin, C., Greenberg, S., Roseman, M. (1996). Workspace awareness in real-time distributed groupware: framework, widgets, and evaluation. *Proc. of HCI'96; People and Computers XI*, 281-298.
8. Gutwin, C. & Penner, R., (2002). Improving interpretation of remote gestures with telepointer traces. *Proc. of CSCW'02*, 49-57.
9. Hall, E. (1966). *The Hidden Dimension*. Anchor Books.
10. Halloran, J., Fitzpatrick, G., Rogers, Y., Marshall, P., (2004). Does it matter if you don't know who's talking?: multiplayer gaming with voiceover IP. *Extended abstracts of CHI'04*, 1215-1218.
11. Heath, C., Jirotka, M., Luff, P., Hindmarch, J. (1994). Unpacking collaboration: the interactional organization of trading in a city dealing room. *Computer-Supported Cooperative Work, 3 (2)*, 147-165.
12. Heath, C. & Luff, P. (1992). Collaboration and control: crisis management and multimedia technology in london underground line control rooms. *Computer-Supported Cooperative Work, 1* (1), 69-92.
13. Hill, J. & Gutwin, C. (2003). Awareness support in a groupware widget toolkit. *Proc. of GROUP'03*, 258-267.
14. Hindmarsh, J., Fraser, M., Heath, C., Benford, S., Greenhalgh, C., (1998). Fragmented interaction: establishing mutual orientation in virtual environments. *Proc. of CSCW'98*, 217-226.
15. Hutchins, E. (1990). The technology of team navigation. in Galegher, J., Kraut, R.E. and Egido, C. eds. *Intellectual Teamwork: Social and technological foundations of cooperative work*, Lawrence Erlbaum Associates, Hillsdale, NJ, 191-220.
16. Mannine, T. (2002). Towards communicative, collaborative and constructive multi-player games. *Proc. of Computer Games and Digital Cultures 2002*, 155-169.
17. McNeill, D. (1992). *Hand and Mind: What Gestures Reveal about Thought*. The University of Chicago Press, Chicago, IL.
18. Nardi, B. & Harris, J. (2006). Strangers and friends: collaborative play in world of warcraft. *Proc. of CSCW'06*, 149-158.
19. Peña, J. & Hancock, J.T. (2006). An analysis of socioemotional and task communication in online multiplayer video games. *Communication Research, 33* (1), 92-109.
20. Schmidt, K. (2002). The problem of 'awareness': introductory remarks on 'awareness in CSCW'. *Computer-Supported Cooperative Work*, 11(3),285-298.
21. Sennersten, C.C. & Lindley, C.A., (2009). An investigation of visual attention in FPS computer gameplay. *Proc. of Games and Virtual Worlds for Serious Applications 2009*, 68-75.
22. Short, J., Williams, E., Christie, B. (1993). Visual communication and social interaction. in Baecker, R.M. ed. *Readings in Groupware and Computer-Supported Cooperative Work: Assisting Human-Human Collaboration*, Morgan Kaufmann: Palo Alto, 153-164.
23. Smith, R.B., O'Shea, T., O'Malley, C., Scanlon, E., Taylor, J. (1991). Preliminary experiments with a distributed, multi-media, problem solving environment. in *Studies in computer supported cooperative work*, North-Holland Publishing Co., 31-48.
24. Stewart, J., Bederson, B.B., Druin, A. (1999). Single display groupware: a model for co-present collaboration. *Proc. of CHI'99*, 286-293.
25. Tatar, D.G., Foster, G., Bobrow, D.G. (1991). Design for conversation: lessons from Cognoter. in *Computer-supported cooperative work and groupware*, Academic Press Ltd., 55-80.
26. Tuddenham, P. & Robinson, P. (2009). Territorial coordination and workspace awareness in remote tabletop collaboration. *Proc. of CHI'09*, 2139-2148.
27. Voida, A., Carpendale, S., Greenberg, S., (2010) The individual and the group in console gaming. *Proc. of CSCW'10*, 371-380.
28. Voida, A. & Greenberg, S. (2009). Wii all play: the console game as a computational meeting place. *Proc of CHI'09*, 1559-1568.
29. Wadley, G., Gibbs, M., Hew, K., Graham, C. (2003). Computer supported cooperative play, "Third Places" and online videogames. *Proc. of OzChi'03*, 238-241.
30. Wong, N. & Gutwin, C. (2010). Where are you pointing?: the accuracy of deictic pointing in CVEs. *Proc. of CHI'10*, 1029-1038.
31. Zagal, J.P., Rick, J., Hsi, I. (2006). Collaborative games: Lessons learned from board games. *Simulation & Gaming*, 37(1), 24-40.

Verbal Coordination in First Person Shooter Games

Anthony Tang[1,2] Jonathan Massey[2] Nelson Wong[3] Derek Reilly[4,2] W. Keith Edwards[2]

[1]University of Calgary
Computer Science
tonyt@ucalgary.ca

[2]Georgia Institute of Technology
GVU Center
{ragingpotato | keith}@cc.gatech.edu

[3]University of Saskatchewan
Computer Science
nelson.wong@usask.ca

[4]Dalhousie University
Computer Science
reilly@cs.dal.ca

ABSTRACT
We explore how expert First Person Shooter (FPS) players coordinate actions using a shared voice channel. Our findings emphasize the importance of the temporality and spatiality of these tactical verbal communications ("call-outs"). From here, we outline potential designs to mitigate problems in the production/interpretation of call-outs to better support coordination.

Author Keywords
First person shooter, FPS, CVE, coordination

ACM Classification Keywords
H5.m. Information interfaces and presentation (e.g., HCI): Miscellaneous.

General Terms
Human Factors.

INTRODUCTION
First-person shooter (FPS) games are fast-paced games that rely on quick, precise targeting and movement actions. Players each have their own view into a 3-dimensional world (Figure 1), navigating and scanning through the virtual world to quickly locate and disable avatars of the opposing team by shooting at them. FPSs are made more complex with team-based "objective" game variants where 4- to 8-player teams work together to achieve shared goals. For example, in "Sabotage" game variants, the offensive team moves to one or more well-known locations to "plant a bomb," while the other team works to defend those locations from the offensive team. In "Territory" game variants, teams try to capture control of certain well-known locations while defending locations from opponents.

These game variants require substantive team coordination under time constraints against an opposition. But because each player has his/her own viewport into the world, teams cannot make the shared, deictic references to objects or locations that we do in everyday life [1,5]: team members are rarely within sight, and have different visual perspectives on the situation. As a consequence, the shared voice channel becomes a principal point for contact, coordination and interaction [6]. Understanding how this

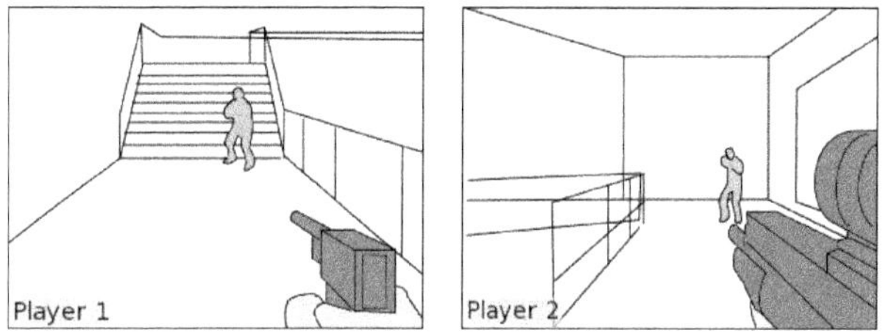

Figure 1. *Players have different views in a FPS game.*

coordination occurs may provide insight for building technologies to help real-life mobile teams such as fire-fighters who also rely on a shared verbal channel.

In this paper, we explore verbal communication strategies that expert FPS players employ to coordinate their actions. Our study focuses on audio/videotaped gameplay from local competitive FPS tournaments, informed by a survey of FPS expert players. An analysis of transcribed tactical verbal communications—termed *call-outs*—reveals several characteristics of verbal communication in FPS games: call-outs are brief, highly contextual (both spatially and temporally), encoded with game-state information, and can be difficult to produce when engaged in combat.

The main contribution of our work is a detailed characterization of voice-mediated coordination in FPSs. These insights detail how experts overcome coordination problems using a shared voice channel. These ideas lay the groundwork for novel tools to support coordination in FPS games, CVEs, and potentially real-life distributed mobile expert teams (e.g. firefighters) who rely on timely communication on a shared voice channel for coordination.

BACKGROUND
The principal challenge for FPS players is to build and maintain a shared understanding of the environment—the locations/intentions of fellow teammates, opposing players, and the state of the game. Early research exploring 3D collaborative virtual environments (predating most FPSs) foreshadowed many of the factors that impair coordination in 3D environments [1,5]: (1) narrow field of view; (2) inability to easily see others, and inability to understand what they can/cannot see; and (3) the inability to easily construct gestures to refer to objects in the environment. Moreover, the poor expressiveness of avatars, and the slow speed of text-based communication result in coordination problems [7]. Because FPS games necessitate rapid coordination, FPS players commonly use a voice channel [6]. In casual games, this voice channel is a medium for rich, social experiences for players [2,10], used for

			Halo	TF2	CS
Minutes collected			68:49	82:08	212:23
Call-out rate (phrases/min)			25.5	10.5	16.2
Call-out Codes	Intention (%)	Directive	28.4	23.6	23.7
		About self	27.5	20.4	38.7
		About enemy	12.7	32.5	13.7
		Question	5.9	5.1	3.2
		Confirmation	9.8	1.9	1.1
	Attributes (%)	Location: General	2.9	19.1	3.0
		Location: Specific	39.2	11.5	43.5
		Urgent: Temporal	13.7	7.6	11.3
		Urgent: Enemy	16.7	15.9	20.4
		Repeated	13.7	26.1	15.1

Table 1. *Summary of our audio coding analysis.*

Line	Time	Call-out	Convo	1 Intention	2 Location	3 Urgent	4 Repeat	5 By Dead
1	22:02	Where's that at?	●	Q	G			
2	22:03	I'm just prefiring	●	S				
3	22:08	Squiggy door, bomb is squiggy; get lower ramp go lower now	●	ED	S	T	*	*
4	22:12	I'm going	●	S				
5	22:15	Don't peek	●	D				*
6	22:16	<inaudible> red	●					
7	22:20	You got my <inaudible>	●					
8	22:20	Get lower	●	D	S			
9	22:21	Red, go up	●	D	S			
10	22:22	He's in headshot box	●	E		E		
11	22:23	I'm lower ramp	●	S	S			
12	22:23	Upper upper upper upper	●	E	S	T	*	*
13	22:28	'Nade the site, nade the site, nade the site right now	●	D	S	T	*	*
14	22:34	I'm going to go through their site	●	S	G			
15	22:39	There's one squiggy	●	E	S	E		
16	22:41	Up in three in outer -uhm- upper	●	E	S	E		*
17	22:47	There's four upper	●	E	S	E		
18	22:52	One in smoke	●	E	S	E		
19	22:58	Alright you gotta make a move, make a move	●	D			*	*

Intention: Directive/about Self/Enemy/Question/Confirm
Location: Specific/General
Urgency: Temporal/Enemy

Listing 1. *One minute coded transcript from one Counter-Strike session (some codes omitted for space). Location phrases highlighted.*

performative expression (taunting, support, accusations of cheating, etc.), and learning (teaching players new strategies, etc.).

Yet, what is the role of voice in tactical (i.e. moment-to-moment, low-level) coordination in FPS games? In competitive games, where players are focused specifically on winning, the character of the voice channel changes: rather than being used for socializing [10], experts use it for tactical teamwork [8] and implicit coordination [9]. Our research builds on this work, focusing on the subtle mechanics employed by expert players to overcome the problems identified by early CVE researchers.

STUDY

Our research goal was to understand how FPS players employ the verbal channel to coordinate activity. We first conducted a small formative online survey to sensitize us to issues pertinent to FPS coordination. Using these results, we coded transcribed audio and video recordings of team FPS sessions from two local competitive tournaments.

Because tactical communication is primarily characteristic of expert players [8], we chose three games (Halo 3, Team Fortress 2, and Counter-Strike) based on their use in professional video game leagues. While each game employs unique game mechanics and gameplay, they are all FPSs, and tournament play focuses on only a handful of maps, so experts have an intimate knowledge of the environments.

Participants. For the online survey, we collected 24 responses solicited from relevant online forums. These respondents aged 19-32, and all but one were male. At two independent competitive tournaments, we recruited 49 different players. These ranged in age from 18-40, and were almost all males (47 males, 2 females). We targeted competitive tournaments, and focused our analysis on the final stages of tournaments (the most successful teams).

Method. At the tournaments, we captured voice communications by attaching an audio recording client to voice servers being used by teams; in other cases, we used a physical audio splitter at one teammate's terminal, or put the audio recorder in front of the team. We videotaped gameplay where possible. In total, we collected approximately six hours of audio data (Table 1), along with some field notes and interview data.

Analysis. We inductively analyzed our transcribed audio data, coding each speech act using an iteratively developed coding scheme. This coding scheme was originally based on our field notes, and refined through the analysis process.

FINDINGS

Players are acutely aware of how timeliness and spatial context affect verbal communication in FPS. We briefly discuss these ideas with data from our coded transcripts. We then describe strategies that require coordination, showing how they are mediated by verbal communication.

Listing 1 is an excerpt that typifies much of the verbal communication in competitive FPS teams. Table 1 shows a summary of the data we collected, and some of our codes. Call-outs were generally coded with one of the "Intention" labels: *directives* were commands; *about self* were instances of verbal shadowing, where players reported on their own status [4]; *about enemy* were labels indicating when players reported on enemy status. We also coded call-outs with "Attribute" labels: *location* if the call-out contained a general (e.g. "left" or "right") or specific label (e.g. "sewer"); *urgent* if it was urgent regarding time or an enemy, and also *repeated* if it was repeating information.

Table 1 is suggestive of some patterns, namely that directives and awareness (about self/opposition) heavily dominate tactical communication. Of these classes, location plays a big role: 43.5% of directive call-outs have a location; 69.5% of call-outs about oneself or the opposition contain a location.

Verbal Communication in FPSs

As Listing 1 illustrates, "conversations" in the traditional sense (with explicit back-and-forth) are rare, or are brief. Instead, the vast majority of statements are declarative: referring to *specific locations* (code 2), and often addressed to the entire team. Players tend to listen to all call-outs to maintain awareness: "*[I am] always talking to [the] entire team, even when referring to a single player since his/her actions might have important change in gameplay. [P1]*"

Timing. Immediately striking is the *paucity of speech*—most call-outs are 8 words or fewer. This reflects the importance of timely communication, and the importance of crafting useful and meaningful call-outs under duress: "*[I am] Very specific when I'm not under pressure; otherwise I just blurt out the general area. [P2]*" *Temporal urgency* (code 3) becomes a prevailing theme, referring to important game states. Note how rapidly this information becomes stale: because the opposing team is also moving quickly, most information is out of date within a few short seconds.

Location. As indicated earlier, spatial location information is also important. In the vast majority of cases, experts used *named locations* rather than relative/general references to locations. For instance, in Line 3, the player not only indicates the current location ("squiggy"), but anticipates its location in the very near future ("lower ramp"). These named locations are how experts employ common references, as they provide all teammates information regardless of where they are in the environment. While some locations had well-known names, either from unusual/distinctive landmarks in the game or from "*hearing other people refer to them during games [P3]*", many players indicated, "*You just make them up, unless they have a label. [P4]*" Some players noted that external sources, such as screenshots and maps on forum posts, played a role in making names concrete for the entire community.

Production. It seemed generally difficult to produce interpretable/correct utterances for many players while under duress (navigating or engaged in combat): Listing 1 omits many such unintelligible call-outs, and Line 16 shows an example where the player hesitates and changes the information due to an incorrect call-out at the outset. Some players overcome this problem by performing *verbal shadowing* [4], where they call out their own actions as they are undertaken. In many games, "dead" players can continue to observe the game from the viewports of teammates who are still "alive" in the game. As illustrated in Listing 1, these eliminated players, freed from the responsibility of "playing," and become more involved in providing call-outs: Lines 3,5,12,13,16,19 (code 5) are examples of "dead" players contributing.

Understanding/Inference. Experts operate with a deep, shared understanding of the game environments (i.e. the maps) and game mechanics: this allows them to use short phrases, knowing that others will interpret those phrases in a rich, appropriate way. Line 13, for example, is a command (to "[throw grenades at] the site"); to an expert player, it reveals far more: first, the opponent is "planting the bomb"; second, that at least one fellow teammate is close enough to throw grenades onto the site; third, it is not clear whether there are other opponents nearby, hence the call for grenades. Accordingly, experts also understand what is to be perceived as out of the ordinary. In Line 1, the player is reacting to a nearby teammate shooting his gun, and asks, "Where are the enemies?" The other player responds (Line 2) that it is a pre-emptive shot.

Repetition. Repetition was fairly common (code 4)—in our sample, we found that many utterances were repeated (Table 1). Players provided several reasons for this redundancy: first, voice communication software might drop the first milliseconds, resulting in unintelligible speech; second, repetition is used to convey urgency, allowing players to emphasize important information, and third, repetition gave listeners "a second chance" to hear a call-out if they "missed it" the first time around.

Anticipation Ratio. As outlined by prior work, implicit coordination can be assessed by calculating the ratio of utterances with information "pushed" out *vs.* utterances with information requested ("pulled") (e.g. [9]). As evidenced by Listing 1, the vast majority of utterances are "pushes"—our expert players are anticipating necessary and/or useful information with the call-outs.

Coordination in FPSs

Within the context of the game, call-outs help coordinate team tactics. Although an exhaustive taxonomy of FPS tactics is beyond the scope of this paper, it is worth noting how verbal coordination supports some of these tactics.

Pairing involves two players working closely side-by-side. In TF2, this strategy was most often employed by "Heavies" (slower characters with powerful weapons) and "Medics" (weaker characters that can heal other characters). In these cases, there is a dual responsibility between the two characters to look out for one another, and it is understood that they are paired: relative location call-outs ("behind you") are extremely common, and are made with the partner's frame of reference.

Scouting is most common in TF2 with the "Scout" character, who is capable of moving very quickly through the map. The Scout is capable of "sighting" the opponent before quickly escaping. Players in this role will often run ahead of their team, scouting and calling out the locations and anticipated actions of opposing players. Players on the Scout's team monitor the verbal channel and ask questions if the call-outs do not make sense, or are in conflict with expectation.

Pushing/Falling back are strategies that require timed, coordinated movement of the entire team to be successful. Pushing means to simultaneously attack in tight formation as a large group to overwhelm the opponent; falling back is a strategy used when the team's forces are weak.

These strategies are generally very difficult to coordinate temporally and spatially without verbal call-outs.

DISCUSSION AND OPPORTUNITIES FOR DESIGN

As foreshadowed by the research in CVEs, FPS games present challenges to team coordination [1,5,6]: it is difficult to see where a teammate is, what they see, and to know what a teammate is referring to. Yet, survey participants reported having to evolve and learn strategies to overcome these problems: for instance, how to maintain an awareness of their surroundings (expert players frequently glance around themselves even as they move in a given direction), the names of specific locations, the contextual implications of certain utterances (e.g. Line 13 from Listing 1), and how to produce meaningful call-outs.

While this learning takes place in a specific game context, and well-known environments, these lessons open an interesting design space for supporting verbal coordination. We see three types of potential tools: supporting the *interpretation* of call-outs by others, supporting the *production* of useful call-outs; and enhancing *current* behaviours. While these tools may not be desirable from a game design perspective (i.e. fun), we take the view that exploring these designs (even as thought experiments) provides valuable insight into verbal coordination in other contexts.

Interpretation is hampered by an inability to identify the speaker, the location of the speaker (particularly if they are out of view), and to understand the context of the speaker (i.e. what s/he sees). Providing visualizations of this information in a quickly-understood manner would be useful: for example, a simple arrow to cue the player to the relative location of the speaker, or perhaps highlighting the speaker's avatar *through* the walls of the map altogether (i.e. so that the player would be able to judge the location/distance and orientation of the speaker). Alternately, the ability to quickly send an image of one's view to a teammate, or to quickly toggle between one's own view and a teammate's would help support interpretability of call-outs..

Similarly, players suggested enhancements that would help the *production* of call-outs. For example, in most Counter-Strike variations, the player's named location in the map is displayed prominently on the UI (many games do not have this): players can use these labels for a call-out. Further, an enhanced UI could also generate these call-outs, akin to verbal shadowing, on behalf of the player, indicate location, direction, enemy location, etc. These call-outs might include screen shots and text messages.

It may also be interesting to enhance *current* behaviours. For example, call-outs are often repeated multiple times so that if players miss the call-out the first time, they can hear it again. This is a crude way of approximating temporal persistence of information, something that can be emphasized by providing immediate transcriptions of call-outs in the UI. These transcriptions can fade over time, but provide the temporal permanence that repetition creates.

We also see potential for their application in ubiquitous technologies for real-life distributed mobile teams (e.g. firefighters), as members of these teams also have unique perspectives on the scene

CONCLUSION

Coordination is generally a tricky problem, as it involves building and acting on a shared mental model. This problem is exacerbated when people do not share the same view of the world (as in FPS games). In this paper, we demonstrated that expert players overcome these problems over the voice channel using nuanced, de-contextualized utterances (call-outs), communicated rapidly in short bursts, which are repeated for emphasis. These insights have implications for tools to support both the interpretation and production of call-outs in FPSs, and more generally for CVEs.

ACKNOWLEDGEMENTS

Thanks to GeorgiaTech GameFest and Atlanta LANFest. Huge thanks to reviewers for excellent feedback.

REFERENCES

1. Fraser, M., Benford, S., Hindmarsh, J., and Heath, C. Supporting awareness and interaction through collaborative virtual interfaces. *UIST* '99, 27-36.
2. Halloran, J. It's talk but not as we know it: using VoIP to communicate in war games. *IEEE Games & Virtual Worlds for Serious Applications '09*, 133-140.
3. Halloran, J., Rogers, Y., and Fitzpatrick, G. From text to talk: multiplayer games and voiceover IP. *Level Up '04*, 130-142.
4. Heath, C. & Luff, P. Collaborative activity and technological design: task coordination in London underground control rooms. *ECSCW '91*, 65-80.
5. Hindmarsh, J., Fraser, M., Heath, C., Benford, S., and Greenhalgh, C. Fragmented interaction: establishing mutual orientation in virtual environments. *CSCW '98*, 217-226.
6. Manninen, T. Virtual team interactions in networked multimedia games–case: "counter-strike" – multiplayer 3D action game. *Presence 2001*.
7. Moore, R. J., Gathman, E. C., Ducheneaut, N., and Nickell, E. Coordinating joint activity in avatar-mediated interaction. *CHI '07*, 21-30.
8. Rambusch, J., Jakobsson, P., and Pargman, D. Exploring e-sports: a case study of gameplay in counter-strike. *Proc DiGRA 2007*, 157-164.
9. Toups, Z. O., Kerne, A., Hamilton, W. A., and Shahzad, N. Zero-fidelity simulation of fire emergency response: improving team coordination learning. *CHI '11*, 1959-1968.
10. Wright, T., Breidenbach, P., and Boria, E. Creative player actions in FPS online video games - playing counter-strike. *Intl J of Comp. Game Res. 2* (2), 2002.

Infrastructural Experiences: An Empirical Study of an Online Arcade Game Platform in China

Qi Wang, Xianghua Ding, Tun Lu, Huanhuan Xia and Ning Gu
School of Computer Science
Fudan University
Shanghai 201203, China
{qi_wang, dingx, lutun, huanhuanxia, ninggu}@fudan.edu.cn

ABSTRACT
This paper discusses issues of infrastructure and user experiences based on an empirical study of the online gaming platform ArcOnline in China. ArcOnline has allowed millions of users to play and watch arcade games over the Internet. What the study of ArcOnline helps bring to the fore are the infrastructural aspects of user experiences, mainly because the high demand for responsiveness and resources of arcade gaming has made infrastructures visible. In this paper, we present our findings of how the experience of playing arcade games changes with different socio-technical infrastructures, the arcade room and the online environment, highlighting how the form of the infrastructure shapes experience and collaboration, as well as how new social infrastructures are emerging through the interplay between the game, the platform, the community and the media ecology. We end by discussing the importance of considering infrastructure in understanding and designing new media experiences.

Author Keywords
Arcade games; online games; video games; infrastructure; ArcOnline; new media.

ACM Classification Keywords
H5.m. Information interfaces and presentation (e.g., HCI): Miscellaneous.

General Terms
Design; Human Factors.

INTRODUCTION
Arcade games were extremely popular in China. In the early 90's, an influx of games rushed into arcade rooms: shooting games, action games, puzzle games, and fighting games. Then, arcade rooms, crowded with gamers cheering along with loud game music and the sound of button pressing, were everywhere in both the urban and rural areas of China. Arcade gaming reached its peak in the late 90s, as the fighting game series The King of Fighters (KOF) arrived in China, quickly became one of the most popular arcade games, and shaped China's entire post-80 generation.

In the turn of the 21st century, however, the rapid development of computing technologies as well as regulations from the government led to a quick decline of traditional arcade rooms [3]. They were then replaced by computer rooms, wangbas (cyber cafés), and family entertainment centers, followed by even more popular online role playing games such as World of Warcraft (WoW) and Lengend of Mir[1]. Now it has become hard to find arcade rooms outside of large metropolises such as Shanghai, Beijing, Guangzhou, Nanjing, and so forth. Old arcade game fans then turned to console emulators to recollect their childhood memories. Although there are some platforms available for online play, use of them has been limited due to poor technical performance and legitimacy issues such as skill transformability [24]. By and large in the past decade, arcade gamers could only compete with their computers or co-located friends.

As part of our effort to support real-time distributed collaboration, a group of researchers in our lab developed an online arcade gaming prototype called ArcOnline. In 2008, the system was opened to the public in order to draw real users to help test and improve our new technologies. During this process, a number of technical breakthroughs were made [27, 28]. To our surprise, since its introduction in 2008, the platform has become extremely popular, and attracted over millions of subscribers with thousands of users online every day.

The wide adoption of ArcOnline allows us to empirically explore questions of technology and sociality with real users. Specifically, how do users encounter and experience ArcOnline? How is online play similar to or different from offline play? What new practices emerge around the new platform? What a study of ArcOnline helps bring to the fore are an understanding of the important roles played by layerings of infrastructures in shaping gaming experiences. Not merely because arcade gaming has been transplanted onto a new technological infrastructure, but more importantly because the high demand for responsiveness and resources of the most popular arcade games has

[1]http://www.thelegendofmir.com

Figure 1. Screenshots of ArcOnline interfaces: From the top-left to the bottom-right, they are the game lobby interface, the replay panel, the game replay interface and the game play interface.(1) shows game rooms in the lobby with status, location, host, and latency information for each room; (2) is a panel shows a list of online users; (3) is a chatting window;(4) is current user's personal profile; (5) is a replay list with player IDs, time passed, and the number of spectators; (6) shows a replay game; (7) shows a game in play with information of players, current latency, current number of spectators and etc.

rendered layerings of infrastructures visible and turned them into an integral part of gaming experiences. In this paper, we will present the study, and report how online gaming experience is structured by existing socio-technical infrastructures as well as how new socio-technical infrastructures are emerging with the platform, gaming practices and other media ecologies. This is then followed by discussions and an extension of the perspective of infrastructure for new media research.

ArcOnline

ArcOnline is an emulator-based platform on which users can play arcade games over the Internet. To give an intuitive sense of what the platform looks like, screenshots of its user interfaces are shown in Figure 1.The top left illustrates its lobby interface where players can create a new room and wait for others to join or select a waiting room to join. They can also click "Replays" and select a game to watch. The replay panel (top-right) shows a list of most recent games along with the player IDs, the time passed, and the size of the audience. Screenshots of game replays and game plays are presented at the bottom of Figure 1. A chat window is also embedded at the bottom of all interfaces.

What really makes ArcOnline different, however, is a set of technical breakthroughs incorporated beneath its user interface. The first is the transparent synchronization mechanism by which gamers can port their favorite arcade games onto the platform without changing the source code. They simply need to obtain and insert the game ROMs into the assigned folder of the platform [27]. The second is the hybrid consistency control strategy employed to keep ongoing games in a consistent state for each player (For details, please refer to [28]). This hybrid approach helps to increase tolerance of network latency and improve the smoothness of play, which approximates an offline arcade machine. The last breakthrough is the spectator system that supports live watch over the Internet. Although a spectator system is not a new idea, to the best of our knowledge, ArcOnline is the first platform that has successfully addressed scalability issues using its P2P based architecture, which can support thousands of spectators watching games simultaneously. Spectators can easily join in or leave an ongoing game without interrupting gameplay or other spectators. Moreover, watching is also enhanced with live commentary services through YY Voice[2] - a software that supports group voice chat.

[2]http://www.yy.com

Infrastructure

Infrastructure is the substrate upon which applications and interactions rely. Some familiar infrastructures include electricity, railways and more recently, the Internet. While fundamentally important, infrastructure is usually taken for granted and stands invisibly in the background. Recently, however, it has changed from "a black box" into "an active topic" [19] to uncover the complex relationships embodied within infrastructures [2, 18], and to examine questions of how large scale systems can be developed and integrated into pre-existing infrastructures composed of already complex parts and interdependent artifacts [9, 15, 20].

While infrastructure has traditionally been approached from a sociopolitical perspective, our concern of infrastructure is an experiential one. This experiential treatment has received increasing attention in recent years mainly in the fields of pervasive and ubiquitous computing due to their direct reliance on infrastructures [5, 12]. In particular, we are inspired by Dourish and Bell's view of space as infrastructure [5]. In an exploration of the implications of pervasive and ubiquitous computing, they observe how our everyday encounter with space is structured by layerings of infrastructures - the infrastructures of streets, of transportation systems, and finally of pervasive computing technologies. As technological infrastructures are increasingly occupying the space in which we live, they are similarly loaded with social and cultural meanings, which not only shape user experiences but also allow users to encounter the world in new ways. In this paper, we will similarly explore the essential infrastructural aspects of user experiences of ArcOnline.

Based on conceptualizations of infrastructure developed in previous literatures, we emphasize here three important premises regarding infrastructure that are highly relevant to our discussions of experiences of ArcOnline.

First, infrastructure, while transparent and invisible by definition and by design, is "*a fundamentally relational concept*" [20], and remains visible to those who design and maintain it and when things malfunction. Therefore it is closely related to practice and use.

Second, it is shared, and importantly, possesses certain scope, reach, and distribution. As pointed out by Hanseth and Braa, "*Infrastructures differ from 'systems' in being a shared resource for a larger community rather than an organizational unit.*" [8]. With this reach, they further suggest that infrastructures cannot be designed or managed by a central hierarchical resource, but rather emerge and grow piece by piece.

Finally, it is heterogeneous, composed of both human and non-human elements. According to Hanseth and Lundberg, infrastructure is a perspective by which artifacts are intertwined with other social and non-technical elements [9]. Therefore infrastructures include not only material structures such as pipes, cables, and roads, but also orders, meetings, reports and other non-material foundations upon which cooperation and collaboration rest.

ArcOnline is based on the Internet, an infrastructure that is relatively obvious; however, not so apparent are additional layerings of infrastructures such as the home and other everyday spaces which the Internet permeates, the geographical infrastructure where the Internet is based, and other socio-economical relationships that are crystalized into the Internet. In what follows we will trace how these infrastructural elements become visible and integrated into user experiences around the platform.

Related Work of Online Gaming

Although computer gaming is an important site of CSCW investigations, infrastructure is not the explicit focus of such investigations. A great deal of work is put into Massively Multiplayer Online Role Playing Games (MMORPGs) such as WoW, and thus attention is mainly focused on social interactions within the virtual space [7, 13, 26]. Research of games built on pervasive computing technologies (e.g. mixed reality, mobile phones and physical games) is beginning to look beyond the virtual space, and exploring ways to combine both virtual and physical materiality into gaming experiences (e.g. [1, 4, 21]). At the same time, a number of researchers have also considered situated context in their investigations: for example, Sall and Grinter's study of physical games at home [16] and Lindtner's examination of WoW in China's wangba [11]. By looking beyond the interactions within the game itself, these studies have highlighted the situated nature of gaming experiences.

Su's study of Street Fighter IV is closest to ours in terms of game genre [24]. Based on a discourse analysis, Su illuminates how the hardcore players of the particularly competitive game work to assemble a range of Internet media in order to increase the legitimacy of fighting games. He also discusses how braggadocio, a central phenomenon in competitive games, has been translated and played out in the new digitally mediated world. His work uncovers many specifics and practices similar to our own findings (e.g. the importance of spectating and the lack of a live atmosphere online), some of which are implicitly related to infrastructural changes, although infrastructure itself is not his explicit focus.

METHODS

Our study is inherently exploratory. We started our investigation with minimal initial assumptions and expectations and very broad and general research questions. Through log analysis, participant observation, and semi-structured interviews, we attempted to collect the richest data possible. We additionally adopted a grounded and bottom-up approach to data analysis which allowed significant and common themes to emerge [22].

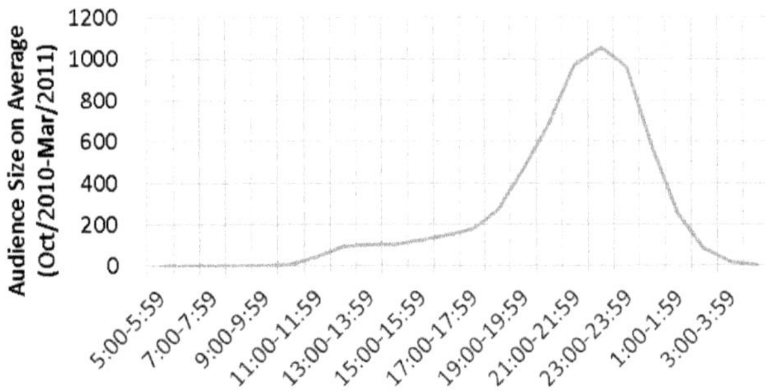

Figure 2. Audience distribution among time intervals

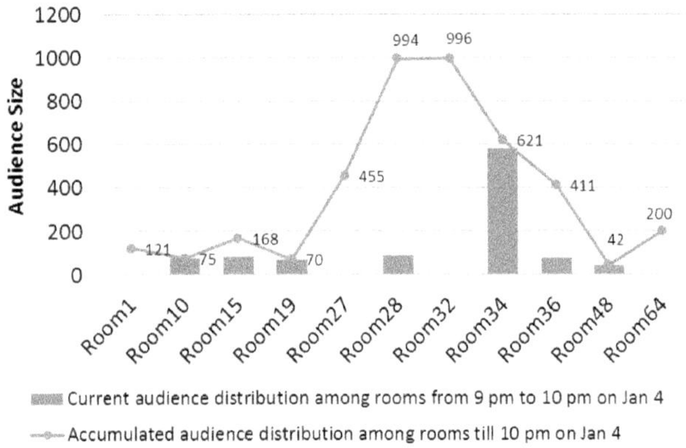

Figure 3. Audience distribution among rooms (4-Jan-2011)

We first obtained a system log and performed log analysis. The log contains six months of data (from Oct-2010 to Mar-2011) from ArcOnline's spectator system, including login and logout time and the replay rooms users enter and leave. Although it only records spectator behavior and contains information of hot rooms (rooms with over 20 audience members), it helps to confirm our observations of the prominence of the watching phenomenon and how games are watched on the platform.

The first and second authors, who are native Chinese speakers, also subscribed to ArcOnline and carried out participatory observation through the platform for about six months, from Dec-2010 to May-2011. We played and watched games, listened to commentaries, and read posts on game forums. In this way, we gained a direct experience about the playability, functionality and sociability of this platform, and also developed initial interview questions.

We then conducted semi-structured interviews. When recruiting informants, we tried to obtain a "holistic" view of the group, by including people with a variety of relations to the platform. Monoe, who voluntarily manages ArcOnline, introduced several informants with special communal roles (e.g. game commentators, celebrity players), and helped broadcast our recruitment criteria through YY. Ultimately, we interviewed 11 subjects in total (9 male and 2 female). Together, they represented a variety of occupations and diverse backgrounds including an ArcOnline designer, a national KOF'97 champion, two commentators, students, a company intern, a factory manager, and a cattle farm owner. All participants had played in the offline arcade room, and excepting the cattle farm owner and the two female gamers, all possessed over ten years of arcade gaming experience. They were all frequent users who logged into the platform almost every day to play and watch games. Their ages ranged from 24 to 30, which represented the post 1980 generation, and their arcade game expertise varied from S level [super star] to F level [newbie].

Our interview questions covered users' experience with old arcade rooms, their first encounter and everyday experience with ArcOnline, and the places and settings where they used the platform. We also asked them to recall concrete examples and specific details of relevant situations. Our interview with Monoe himself was face-to-face and lasted about 3 hours. All other interviews were conducted through YY, the same voice channel employed for live commentary. All of the conversations were audio recorded with the participants' permission, transcribed and translated. All informant names used in this paper are pseudonyms.

LOG ANALYSIS: CONCENTRATED WATCHING

The main finding from the log analysis is that watching is highly concentrated both temporally and spatially. Temporally, activity is mainly concentrated at night. As illustrated in Figure 2, 5am to 11am is the relative dead time, with little activity occurring. From there it gradually picks up, rapidly increases after 6pm, reaches its peak around 10pm and 11pm, and declines until 5am. We observed when there was an important game (one played by super stars for example), the size of the audience could explode into thousands in a short time. Spatially, audiences are highly concentrated into a few rooms. Figure 3 shows such a typical example: in the 9pm to 10pm window, only one out of over ten hot rooms attracted the majority of spectators, while over time, two rooms stood out as the most popular (game rooms with more than 20 audience members are logged).

The temporal pattern makes sense as it largely aligns with users' daily schedules: the majority of people have more free time at night for gaming. However, what does the spatial distribution mean? Its concentration suggests to us that the audience is far from a random collection of individuals but rather a structured group, which can be seen as a unit. In the section to follow, we will turn to the interview and participant observation data in order to understand how a range of infrastructures and media technologies affect gaming behavior and the community.

INFRASTRUCTURAL EXPERIENCES

With the development of ArcOnline and other computing technologies, arcade gaming has escaped the arcade room, spread into the corners of everyday life, and become subject to the regulations of new layerings of infrastructures which are not only technological but also physical, social, and geographical. Moreover, the demand of video games, their extreme sensitivity to speed and the employment of voice channels for commentary has also made these infrastructures visible to gamers themselves. What's more, new practices and structures are also emerging and have been established around the new infrastructures and the gaming cultures. In this section, we will discuss the infrastructured and infrastructuring aspects of experiences around ArcOnline.

Infrastructured Experiences

We will first illustrate how experiences are infrastructured technologically, socially, spatially, geographically and physically.

Technologically infrastructured

It is through the games' extreme demand for responsiveness and players' extreme sensitivity that the technological infrastructure is made visible. Fighting arcade games such as the most popular KOF series are very time sensitive, which means gamers must concentrate hard on the game and react quickly to defend themselves from the opponents or to launch an attack with perfect timing. Players who miss an opportunity and are caught by the opponent may lose the entire game. The introduction of combo moves makes mastering timing even more important. Combo moves are a chain of simple or special moves, which can strike opponents with more than 10 consecutive hits at a time. If players want to connect these moves successfully, they need to execute a series of joystick movements and button presses with precise timing. Consequently, gamers become highly sensitive to network delays and relevant infrastructural properties. When there is an unpredictable network latency, gamers will have to pause for a while to wait to receive remote inputs, which is vividly described in the Chinese word "ka" (卡). Monoe recalled how "ka" was a major issue preventing him from playing arcade games online before the arrival of ArcOnline, *"At that time I didn't play online fighting games, because its [VM] performance was really bad. When I was playing with my friends, the game always froze till both of us lost communication. It was unstable! Just like you were running but suddenly forced to stop. It was inevitable you would fall. Playing the game [online] was the same."* Therefore online arcade games and especially certain fighting games demand high computer and network support.

Now with ArcOnline, online play has become much more affordable, which at the same time has also rendered the new technological infrastructure visible, especially to some extremely sensitive top gamers. To mitigate the issue of "ka", local lag is applied into ArcOnline to temporarily store the local and remote inputs. Local lag is commonly used in real-time online games to relieve state divergence caused by network latency, and it should be chosen to balance the penalty to responsiveness [17]. ArcOnline's local lag was originally set to 100ms (According to [23], a player expects to see the effects of local inputs within 100ms.) by default and hidden from users. Surprisingly, however, we found that some expert gamers were able to discern the usage of this technique and openly discussed it on the forums. They were so sensitive that they could perceive the existence of a local lag even between 17ms and 34ms [28]. Thus, infrastructure is not *"a thing stripped of use"* [20], but is rather inherently dependent on it.

Indeed, the underlying technological infrastructure has become an integral part of gaming experiences. Through our interviews and from online forums, we found that people commonly talked about broad bandwidth, LAN, P2P, supplier networks, etc. Such aspects of underlying network infrastructure are supposed to be invisible to the end users, however, online arcade gaming has made them fully aware of them. For example, the issue of "ka" is especially salient when players are distributed in different supplier networks, and is reflected in a humorous saying popular among the game circle, "*The longest distance in the world is not from China to the USA, but from Telecom to Netcom* (They were two big network service suppliers in China)". As a matter of fact, finding an opponent with the right net speed, which amounts ideally to being in the same supplier network as well as geographically proximate, is critical to ensuring successful and pleasant play.

Socially and spatially infrastructured

Contrary to the common perception that the online world has escaped regulations from the offline and has become "virtual", we found that physical and social regulations are still very much in effect. It is simply relatively uniform arcade rooms have been replaced by new heterogeneous environments such as homes, dormitories, workplaces and cyber cafés. Compared to the online platform, the old arcade room was very loosely regulated and often depicted as a chaotic and noisy place full of rogues, fights, quarrels, and bullyings. Pero reported how it was largely ruled by physical strength, *"There were lots of rogues in arcade rooms who bullied younger kids, and fought for game machines. When someone beat him in the game, he would beat back physically in the real world with real forces."* We also spotted many similar bullying stories, which had been shared on the online forums. In fact, the public usually considers arcade rooms unhealthy and unsafe, which is the main reason that they were closed down by the government.

Moving games online was instrumental in relieving these often complained safety issues, and interestingly, created a much more accepting and welcoming environment for female gamers. Lele, one of our female informants, shared an experience of how standing out in arcade rooms led her to playing online, *"I used to go to some well-known arcade rooms to play. They were surprised to see me play KOF there because girls were rare in arcade rooms. Some friends told me not to play in arcade rooms anymore because it was unsafe and inappropriate for girls. Then I just turned to ArcOnline to play."* As confirmed by another girl informant, playing at home is much more acceptable, both to them and to their parents. However, as expected, safety comes at the cost of the live atmosphere, a crucial component of arcade game culture [24].

Indeed, the play ambience is radically transformed by the new physical and social infrastructures of the everyday environment, especially considering the "noisy" hype is an inherent component of the fun of arcade gaming [24]. Several informants reported that they now had to conform to the rules of their homes when playing. Suanxi described, *"I would manage to play with my friends when my parents were not around. If occasionally, my friends came to visit, and it was late already I would intentionally told them to play quietly and not to press too hard, and they would lower their voice to speak. The reason I enjoyed it so much the night of my brother's marriage was because we could play games as loud as we wanted, as it was noisy outside."* The use of YY Voice for live commentary has brought back the "noisy" atmosphere to some extent, while making contextual regulation even more notable at the same time. Ajian reported that he needed to get permission from his parents to commentate, *"Generally I would not comment a game after 11pm. If some important games were arranged at midnight, I would ask my parents for permission."* During our participant observation, we also noted that sometimes members were inquired to see whether it was OK for them to speak out through YY (e.g. at home) or they could only text (e.g. in wangbas, dorms or offices) to participate in discussions. Interestingly, audio commentary voices from YY are sometimes considered to be out of place for the home, especially when they have strong accents. Pero commented, *"To tell you the truth, I think some of the commentators' accents are too strong. So I would rather use an earphone when listening to them so that my wife won't think I am insane."* Thus there are collaborations and negotiations taking place at home around gameplay between players and non-players, which is similarly discussed by Sall and Grinter [16]. They also illustrate that noises or sounds as integral components of arcade gaming culture have made social infrastructures of the everyday environment visible.

Geographically and physically infrastructured

Infrastructure does not evolve in a vacuum, but instead on top of installed bases, and it inherits the "strengths and limitations of the base" [20]. The technological infrastructure for the arcade game is, similarly, built on top of other layers of infrastructures, including geographical structures, the demographical distribution of the country, dwelling structures, and so on. Some properties of these infrastructures have been folded and made invisible, while others penetrate through the technological infrastructure of gaming and are felt by gamers.

Overcoming geographical constraints is considered to be the main strength of ArcOnline, however this doesn't mean that geographical issues have gone away. Even though ArcOnline has greatly relieved this issue, we still found that it was sometimes problematic to connect with others over long distances. In fact, gamers can tell how close they are to each other just based on the smoothness of play, and they are thus inclined to play with those from the same geographical area whenever possible. Moreover, geo-demographical properties can also affect the social life surrounding the game and the platform, especially considering that it is a common practice for gamers who live close to each other to gather to socialize and deepen their relationships offline. For those who live in rural or border areas, however, geographical location has greatly affected opportunities to socialize with others in this way. Wolo, who lives in the borderland of China, was very vocal about this and reported that it was rare for him to run into other gamers and socialize beyond ArcOnline. Just as Olson & Olson argue that "distance matters" in distributed collaborations [14], we believe that distances and geographical structures still do and will continue to matter in computer mediated socializations, as the latter is after all inherently embedded in the former.

Besides geographical influences, properties of residential structures also have an impact on gaming experiences. With the online platform, one would expect that we now have unlimited resources for play, since computers are almost everywhere. However, unexpectedly, resource conflicts still exist, although now the conflict is no longer over game machines, but for limited underlying bandwidth and other shared technological infrastructural resources. Monoe's case illustrated such a situation, *"I rent a room with others. Their downloading slowed down the whole network speed."* Even in cyber cafés, a shared place dedicated to high speed Internet access, conflict can arise. As Wolo described, *"When you use a P2P software to download movies or something else, you will affect others even in a wangba with a 10 mega bandwidth."* In this way, living conditions sometimes impact where players choose to play these games [11].

Infrastructuring

Not only is gaming subject to the regulations of pre-existing infrastructures, but also that the platform and other technological services have attended to the infrastructuring process as they are integrated into the larger gaming practices and cultures. At the time of study, this platform has been adopted by millions of gamers, a new structured gaming circle has emerged, and new technological tools have been assembled to support gaming practices around it. In this section, we will trace and illustrate these new patterns and structures of community, their practices, and their use of technologies.

Reproducing meaningful experiences

Interestingly, we found that making infrastructures visible is not always problematic but often positively meaningful. For example, as mentioned, gamers can sometimes tell whether opponents are close by simply through the smoothness of play, and as a result, some have carried their interactions and relationships offline. Other anecdotes show that people can also easily feel whether they are in the same supplier network as their opponent. Although these are all very subtle processes, they remind us that infrastructural properties do not just manifest themselves through breakdowns or failures, but also through how well things work. The visibility of infrastructure is continuous, rather than an on/off switch.

More strikingly, far from simply experiencing the infrastructure passively, our informants also actively constructed meaningful experiences based on awareness of the infrastructure. For example, one commonly reported loss with the online platform is the live atmosphere [24] (Now, even in cyber cafés, which are public places, making loud noises is not allowed since it interferes with others using the Internet). But interestingly, we noted that our informants have found a way to work around it to reproduce desired experiences when they were affordable. In the case reported by Pero, *"We often put our laptops and PCs together, about 4 or 5 devices, to enhance the atmosphere of game play with ArcOnline. Sometimes we like watching top gamers' play together."* Suanxi provided another telling example, *"I have several computers at home, so I often invite my friends to my house and play KOF together. You know, playing in a local area network is always more enjoyable because of the 0 delay."* These "LAN parties" [10] illustrate that infrastructure is not just passively experienced but also actively leveraged to construct meaningful experiences.

"Match" oriented interactions and social structuring

"Match", used not to invoke a contest but rather comparability, turned out to be an important factor in regulating socializations surrounding arcade gaming. It is common for people to come to ArcOnline to meet and play not within their existing social relationships, but with strangers, a phenomenon described as "wild fight" (野战, yezhan) by the gaming circle. With thousands of unfamiliar others online every day, how would they decide whom to play with? It is in this respect that "match" becomes an important mechanism for online social interactions. In the chat window of the platform, we observed that substantial chat content is devoted to communication and coordination to find comparable players, e.g. "a scrub is waiting in Room X", "looking for a high level player", "a medium player coming to the Room X", and "looking for a keyboard player". Of course, "match" oriented social interaction is not a phenomenon unique to the online space. It existed in the offline arcade rooms as well. For example, Monoe recalled that sometimes when he was playing in an arcade room, 7 or 8 gamers just stood behind him watching him competing with the machine instead of standing up to play with him, because their skills were far below his. Nonetheless, in the computer-mediated world, besides skill-level, technological properties have also become part of match parameters, e.g. use of keyboards or joysticks.

"Match" oriented online social interaction is largely enforced by people's desire for skill advancement. Unlike some games that are designed with low learning curves for broader participation and for socializations among existing relationships, part of the charm of KOF-like fighting games is their professionalism [24], the high learning curve and the room for skill advancement. In extreme cases, having no comparable opponent could lead someone quitting the game entirely. Qinhe, one of the top players, is such a case: *"I won't spend much time on it anymore. Maybe it is hard for me to find a comparable opponent to play."* Ling described how her desire for advancement was the reason for her to seek comparable players, *"I can't get advanced if my opponent is not at my level. It won't work if they are above or below me."* Essentially, the true fun of fighting games comes not from the game itself or the technologies which support it, but from whom the game is played with. It is not necessary that you play with the people you know, but rather that you play with someone with corresponding skill and technological conditions.

In fact, the need for matching is so high that it has fundamentally shaped how people socialize with each other within the game. It is a typical practice for people to exchange contact information such as phone or QQ numbers once they meet a good match. As arcade rooms and goers are continually decreasing, it is especially important now to collect contacts as the chance to run into comparable players has become much smaller both offline and online. Monoe described to us how he made a conscious effort to collect gamers' phone numbers, so that he could call them to play arcade games together, instead of fighting with machines for a whole day. Although there are tens of thousands of gamers simultaneously playing on ArcOnline, numbers do not increase the chance to meet comparable players, as the chance to encounter a newbie also increases significantly. So it is also important for medium or advanced gamers to exchange QQ information if they encounter one online. Ling shared such a case: *"We could not find out who was better at that time because our scores were very close. We kept playing until both of us were tired, which lasted almost 10 hours. I remember I won him about 60 rounds and he won me nearly the same. After that we became friends and still kept in touch."* Gradually social relationships are created and maintained through QQ and phone contacts. At the same time, gaming circles also form as people gather around QQ groups devoted to arcade games. Taking ArcOnline users as an example, almost every gamer belongs to at least one group, and currently there are already hundreds of ArcOnline groups. These groups have helped to narrow the scope for match searching, and caused relevant social structures to manifest.

Because skill in fighting games correlates strongly with time of play, the gaming circle is also temporally structured. Unlike with RPG games, where a gamer can become a leader if he/she is rich enough to buy the top-level virtual equipment, in fighting games, time and skill are tightly coupled and the only way to reach a high level is through practice. As a result, the game circle is largely divided by the 10-year gap between those who started playing the game in the arcade and those who joined the game after the arrival of ArcOnline, or oldies and newbies as described in [24]. Indeed, it is hard for a newbie to bridge the gap. Lele has played KOF for one year, but she is still unwilling to attend a contest, "*Because they have over 10 year experience, it's a huge gap!*" Luckily, apprenticeship provides a way to penetrate this divide. Monoe, a master, and Ling, an apprentice, both commented on its effects:

Monoe: If a newbie takes me as his mentor, I'm pretty sure he will reach B level [above average] in three months.

Ling: I have to say it's really helpful to have a mentor. The expert gamers have their unique skills. My mentor once told me how to jump quickly to project a shadow on the ground. By following this tip, I was suddenly enlightened and mastered how to launch a combo of special moves.

Now with ArcOnline-like online platforms together with YY-like voice channels, it is common for apprenticeships to take place remotely. Just as shown in these quotes, apprenticeship is effective for learning, and provides a mechanism to break the boundary of game circles formed around skills and years of play.

Watching live and communal structuring

One of the distinct features of ArcOnline is its support for watching live gameplay. It is this feature that makes it possible for socializations to go beyond two players and involve hundreds and thousands of users simultaneously. In this section, we describe the structures and conventions emerging around watching live games. Before ArcOnline, people could also watch game videos from Youku, Tudou and other websites. However, almost all our informants commented that watching live through ArcOnline is incomparable, describing it as more "exciting". Lele reported that she is more motivated to watch live gameplay since it is still ongoing and the result is unknown: "*Sometimes I watched KOF videos on Youku, but I wasn't as excited as watching it on ArcOnline, because the result on Youku was there already. While on ArcOnline, I won't know which side will win till the last minute and I can cheer it up together with other thousands of audiences.*" Indeed, the watching live feature turns out to be a non-trivial attraction. As Monoe estimated, right after this feature became available in the late 2008, the number of registered users jumped up nearly 20%-30%.

Our log analysis has indicated a highly concentrated and synchronized online communal behavior, and our interviews further revealed relevant conditions and mechanisms for its production. Two types of events tend to become the center of communal focus. The first is periodical matches organized by a group of volunteers. The second is games played by well-known members of the community, a sort of "celebrity effect". The former is periodical and not on a daily basis, however, its capability to draw attention is impressive. We observed a burst of users coming online when an important match was coming up, and nearly half of them simply disappeared when it was over. Organized matches are usually broadcast through ArcOnline well in advance to draw people's attention, but how would people find interesting games to watch on a daily basis? Expectedly, social navigation [6] plays important roles in this regard. Those who are familiar with the community and well aware of the big names can choose based on player IDs, since games played by super stars are usually of high quality, and for others, audience size provides an important clue.

Further, other communication media are also leveraged to achieve communal synchronization - we call them tuning mechanisms. Like tuning a radio to listen to a program, gamers acquire game information from a range of technologies and services such as audio commentary or QQ groups. The use of YY Voice for audio commentary is especially powerful. Although YY Voice was originally employed to answer questions about ArcOnline, it was later turned into a channel for audio commentaries of exciting games by several volunteer commentators. For most, the commentary service is helpful for locating exciting games because usually only exciting games will be commentated upon. As an active member, Minjie reported, "*Although I only play KOF'98, I watch all series of KOF, because only top level gamers' game will be commentated.*" Several would simply leave the YY on in the background, and would gradually be drawn to it when hearing announcements or commentary. Suanxi works at home, and keeps YY Voice on every day. He commented that the audio channel made it much easier for him to find interesting games to watch, "*When I am working, I'd like to have my speaker on. If someone announces a game, I can immediately receive it and decide which one to watch. Anyway, I won't miss an exciting game, while before I had to search every room.*" It is important to note that audiences can also interact with commentators through YY as well, and commentators can answer their questions in real time. Thus, this is a two-way interaction through which the distance between the audience and the game is greatly reduced.

Besides YY Voice, people also get tuned into games through QQ group broadcasting. Our informants reported that if top gamers were going to play, gamers would usually announce it in the QQ group. Other times, people would just openly ask to get the game schedule. We also noticed that some top-level players were well connected with commentators and often notified them in advance if they planned to play. Then, a commentator would be arranged and game information will be announced.

DISCUSSIONS AND CONCLUSIONS

In previous sections, we've looked at the infrastructural aspects of gaming experiences. By definition, infrastructures, unlike objects, remain invisibly in the background. It is visible only to designers or people who maintain it, or when things malfunction. However, as shown in our study, infrastructure has become part of users' daily gaming experiences, not only at the moments when the platform fails but also at the moments when the connection is very good and when the play is smooth, as it may indicate geographical proximity or belonging to the same supplier network. It suggests that for ArcOnline-like new media applications, technological infrastructures present themselves not through a work/failure binary, but through a continuous spectrum of how well the system works.

More specifically, we can identify three characteristics of arcade gaming and culture that have helped infrastructure to manifest. First, the timing and response demand of some popular arcade games have rendered properties of the technological infrastructure visible. People are sensitive to the responsiveness of the play, and therefore they can tell whether they and their opponents belong to the same supplier network, or whether they are geographically proximate. This is especially true for masters or game professionals, who are so sensitive that they could perceive the existence of a local lag even between 17ms and 34ms.

Second, the sharing of infrastructural resources and their high demand lead to conflict issues and raise awareness of infrastructural properties. This is especially prominent in environments where people share space and access to the Internet, such as shared apartments, student dormitories, and wangbas. Our study found that conflicts were common in these settings and that they made gamers constantly aware of bandwidth, network connectivity and other infrastructural properties.

Finally, social infrastructures of everyday environments become visible and relevant through the dichotomy between the "noisy" culture of arcade gaming and the expectedly quiet everyday settings of homes and offices. ArcOnline inherits the reach and scope of the Internet, so game play is no longer confined in the relatively uniform and dedicated arcade room, but rather makes its way into the heterogeneous spaces of everyday environments and is mingled with other social activities and experiences. The loud and live atmosphere of arcade gaming culture is what people miss the most in the online environment. While the employment of YY voice channel brings it back in part, it also renders the conventions, rules and structures of the everyday settings apparent.

In addition, we have also demonstrated how new socio-technical structures emerge through the interplay between the game, the community, the platform, and other media technologies. Analysis from the log data suggests that it is not merely a collection of gamers who gather around the platform but rather a community with structure. Our qualitative analysis further elaborates upon its structural properties including skill rankings, celebrities, game circles, game conventions, communal focuses, and synchronized watching. Some of these are translated from the offline arcade rooms while others are transformed and enhanced by the online infrastructure and platform.

Therefore, technology and sociality have a complex relationship. On one hand, the emergence of these structures cannot be solely explained by the availability of ArcOnline or the new Internet infrastructure, as some of the online social practices are not created anew, but inherited from the offline gaming practices such as match based socialization, apprenticeship, contact maintenance, and so on. A diverse set of actors including arcade gaming culture, platform managers, star players, QQ, YY and the commentary service all work together for the evolution and structuring of online gaming practices and communities. On the other hand, the new technological infrastructure and the ArcOnline platform do play varied roles in supporting (e.g. the smoothness of online game comparable to that of offline), shifting (e.g. competing for gaming machines vs. competing for infrastructural resources), compromising (e.g. live atmosphere or safety), enhancing (e.g. broader exposure) and manifesting (e.g. relationships and circles manifested in QQ contacts and groups) these practices and relationships in the new online environment. The perspective of infrastructure provides one lens to unpack this complex relationship.

As more and more everyday collaborations are becoming Internet-mediated, and as more and more high demand and time sensitive new media applications (e.g. online TV, video conferencing, online Karaoke, etc.) emerge online, we believe the infrastructural perspective will become increasingly relevant. Just as infrastructure has already become a prominent feature in the research of pervasive or ubiquitous computing [5, 12, 25], similar infrastructural impacts will exist for new media applications as they leave their dedicated places and enter into other aspects of everyday life, demanding more and more underlying infrastructural resources. So upon examining new media applications, we shall not just see them as isolated artifacts, but instead consider them together with other technological, social, physical and geographical infrastructures. It is once again demonstrated that user experience is not just an issue of interface or even system, but rather involves the whole infrastructure that spans across distances and institutions. Simply put, new media experiences are more than just locally situated, but also globally infrastructured, and ArcOnline [3] provides us with a window into issues of infrastructure and new media experiences.

[3] The platform is only for testing purposes, and can be obtained through email requests. Some obsolete games are provided on the platform for free, and other games should be legally purchased by users from the relevant companies.

ACKNOWLEDGEMENTS

We would like to thank the development and management team of ArcOnline for the support. We also thank Norman M. Su, Silvia M. Lindtner and our anonymous reviewers for their helpful feedback, and Shirley Lu for correcting our English. This work was supported in part by the National Natural Science Foundation of China under Grant No. 60736020 and No. 60803118, and the Shanghai Leading Academic Discipline Project under Grant No. B114.

REFERENCES

1. Benford, S., Crabtree, A., Flintham, M., Drozd, A., Anastasi, R., Paxton, M., Tandavanitj, N., Adams, M. and Row-Farr, J. Can you see me now? *ACM Transactions on Computer-Human Interaction (TOCHI) 13*, 1 (2006), 100-133.
2. Bowker, G.C. The history of information infrastructures: The case of the international classification of diseases. *Information Processing and Management 32*, 1 (1996), 49-61.
3. Cao, Y. and Downing, J.D.H. The realities of virtual play: Video games and their industry in China. *Media, Culture & Society 30*, 4 (2008), 515-529.
4. Crabtree, A., Benford, S., Rodden, T., Greenhalgh, C., Flintham, M., Anastasi, R., Drozd, A., Adams, M., Row-Farr, J., Tandavanitj, N. and Steed, A. Orchestrating a mixed reality game 'on the ground'. *In Proc. CHI'04*, ACM Press (2004), 391-398.
5. Dourish, P. and Bell, G. The infrastructure of experience and the experience of infrastructure: Meaning and structure in everyday encounters with space. *Environment and Planning B: Planning and Design 34*, 3 (2007), 414-430.
6. Dourish, P. and Chalmers, M. Running out of space: Models of information navigation. Short paper presented at HCI'94 (1994).
7. Ducheneaut, N., Yee, N., Nickell, E. and Moore, R.J. "Alone together?": Exploring the social dynamics of massively multiplayer online games. *In Proc. CHI'06*, ACM Press (2006), 407-416.
8. Hanseth, O. and Braa, K. Technology as traitor: Emergent SAP infrastructure in a global organization. *In Proc. ICIS'98*, Association for Information Systems (1998), 188-196.
9. Hanseth, O. and Lundberg, N. Information Infrastructure in Use - An empirical study at a radiology department. *In Proc. IRIS 22* (1999), 407-424.
10. Jörissen, B. Virtual reality on the stage: Performing community at a LAN-party. P. Hernwall, E. ed. *Envision. The New Media Age and Everyday Life*, Stockholm University (2004), 23-40.
11. Lindtner, S., Nardi, B., Wang, Y., Mainwaring, S., Jing, H. and Liang, W. A hybrid cultural ecology: World of Warcraft in China. *In Proc. CSCW'08*, ACM Press (2008), 371-382.
12. Mainwaring, S.D., Chang, M.F. and Anderson, K. Infrastructures and their discontents: implications for ubicomp. *UbiComp 2004 (LNCS 3205)* (2004), 418-432.
13. Nardi, B. and Harris, J. Strangers and friends: Collaborative play in World of Warcraft. *In Proc. CSCW'06*, ACM Press (2006), 149-158.
14. Olson, G.M. and Olson, J.S. Distance matters. *Human-Computer Interaction 15*, 2 (2000), 139-178.
15. Pipek, V. and Wulf, V. Infrastructuring: Towards an integrated perspective on the design and use of information technology. *Journal of the Association for Information Systems 10*, 5 (2009), 447-473.
16. Sall, A. and Grinter, R.E. Let's get physical! In, out and around the gaming circle of physical gaming at home. *Computer Supported Cooperative Work (CSCW) 16*, 1-2 (2007), 199-229.
17. Savery, C., Graham, T.C. and Gutwin, C. The human factors of consistency maintenance in multiplayer computer games. *In Proc. Group'10*, ACM Press (2010), 187-196.
18. Star, S.L. The ethnography of infrastructure. *American Behavioral Scientist 43*, 3 (1999), 377-391.
19. Star, S.L. and Bowker, G.C. How to infrastructure. Lievrouw, L.A. and S, L. eds. *Handbook of New Media - Social Shaping and Consequences of ICTs*, SAGE Pub (2002), 151-162.
20. Star, S.L. and Ruhleder, K. Steps toward an ecology of infrastructure: Design and access for large information spaces. *Information Systems Research 7*, 1 (1996), 63-92.
21. Starner, T., Leibe, B., Singletary, B. and Pair, J. MIND-WARPING: Towards creating a compelling collaborative augmented reality game. *In Proc. IUI'00*, ACM Press (2000), 256-259.
22. Strauss, A.L. and Corbin, J. *Basics of qualitative research*. Sage Newbury Park, CA, 1990.
23. Stuckel, D. and Gutwin, C. The effects of local lag on tightly-coupled interaction in distributed groupware. *In Proc. CSCW'08*, ACM Press (2008), 447-456.
24. Su, N.M. Street fighter IV: Braggadocio off and on-line. *In Proc. CSCW'10*, ACM Press (2010), 361-370.
25. Williams, A., Anderson, K. and Dourish, P. Anchored mobilities: Mobile technology and transnational migration. *In Proc. DIS'08*, ACM Press (2008), 323-332.
26. Wong, N., Tang, A., Livingston, I., Gutwin, C. and Mandryk, R. Character sharing in World of Warcraft. *In Proc. ECSCW'09*, Springer London (2009), 343-362.
27. Zhao, S., Li, D., Gu, H., Shao, B. and Gu, N. An approach to sharing legacy tv/arcade games for real-time collaboration. *In Proc. ICDCS'09*, IEEE Press (2009), 165-172.
28. Zhao, S., Li, D., Lu, T. and Gu, N. Back to the future: A hybrid approach to transparent sharing of video games over the internet in real time. *In Proc. CSCW'11*, ACM Press (2011), 187-196.

Metaphors for Social Relationships in 3D Virtual Worlds

Gilly Leshed and Poppy Lauretta McLeod
Department of Communication
Cornell University
Ithaca, NY 14850 USA
gl87@cornell.edu, plm29@cornell.edu

ABSTRACT
A number of conceptual metaphors have been previously suggested for identity management, including, for example, theatre stage, onion layers, and identity segments. Based on an analysis of 30 in-depth interviews with Second Life residents, we examine the extent to which these metaphors can be used to explain experiences of social relationships in and across virtual and material worlds. The data suggest that these metaphors are relevant to social interactions in and across virtual and material environments: individuals perform on a stage to and with others, they gradually reveal layers of themselves, and they distinguish between segments of their identity in different social situations. At the same time, these metaphors do not explain all experiences, pointing to future research on virtual environments, social relationships, and identity management.

ACM Classification Keywords
H5.1. Information interfaces and presentation: Multimedia Information Systems: Artificial, augmented, and virtual realities

General terms
Human Factors, Theory

Author Keywords
Identity, social relationships, virtual worlds, Second Life, metaphor.

INTRODUCTION

> *My first partnership, I entered when I was two weeks in here, and we were married for 10 months, a very long time for here. In that time we grew to know each other very well and eventually she fell in love with me in RL. Problem is, she is a married woman with a family and we were to be a fantasy relationship, me a Dark elf, she a pixie. But the boundaries were blurred eventually, and it moved into RL, to the extent that we had to split to prevent further issues with her family. I did love her though. So, it is important, depending on the relationship, to keep very distinct and set boundaries. (Connor, May 2008)*

At this point in time, millions of people around the world regularly participate in 3D virtual worlds and games such as Second Life, The Sims, and World of Warcraft. As a result, new experiences are emerging for meeting and getting to know other people, becoming closer, and sometimes breaking apart. In this paper, we add to a growing body of literature in HCI and CSCW on social interactions in 3D virtual worlds [e.g., 7,11,26,28,42]. Specifically, we analyze how participation in 3D virtual worlds contributes to understanding issues of social relationships in multiple material and virtual worlds: when do relationships remain in one world and when do they cross over? Why and how do people keep these worlds separate or blur them together?

We use the term *material* rather than *real* world because as we learned from our data (and from others such as Turkle [38]), the virtual world is a legitimate part of reality for many users. Virtual and material worlds are ways to interact and engage with others in different contexts. In the material world an individual's physical body resides, and his or her brain processes the experiences, emotions, and knowledge gained through participation in the virtual environment with a virtual avatar. Our findings suggest that virtual and material worlds are ways to represent mutual sides, layers, pieces, or views of a person's *real* identity. As one of our interview participants eloquently said, *"we are all as real as the person at the keyboard."*

The primary contribution of this paper is an analysis of how well three classic metaphors of identity management—theatre stage, onion layers, and segmentation—developed before the advent of 3D virtual worlds, helps illuminate experiences of social relationships in and across virtual and material worlds. Our focus on social relationships was guided by considerable evidence in social psychology that identity management is inherently a social process: individuals define who they are through their interactions with others, and their perceptions of their own identity in turn help shape their social interactions and behaviors [33].

METAPHORS OF IDENTITY MANAGEMENT
It has long been recognized that metaphor has an important social scientific role in both individual cognition and in social relations. In 1980, Lakoff & Johnson argued that our "ordinary conceptual system, in terms of which we both think and act, is fundamentally metaphorical in nature" [17, p. 3], and the use of metaphor for system design is well-established in the HCI and CSCW literatures [e.g., 3,6,24,

29,38,41]. The explosion of social interactions as a primary Internet use, for example, through social media and virtual worlds, prompts attention to the metaphors that underlie conceptualizations about relationship development through these media. Examining the explanatory power of metaphors of social relationships will provide guidance for theoretical development and future research directions, as well as pragmatic issues related to system design.

Various metaphors of identity management have appeared in the literature, and many more are conceivable. Our intention is not to produce an exhaustive survey of such metaphors, but rather to focus on few that have received widespread attention in the social sciences as representative. The question of the applicability of pre-Internet metaphors to understanding identity and social relationships today is especially significant in 3D virtual worlds, with unique embodied experiences in immersive environments, unlike other technology-mediated settings. Through qualitative analysis of interview data on the ways in which people describe their social relationships in and across virtual and material environments, we ask, to what degree can these metaphors be generalized to experiences in this brave new world?

Theatre Stage

> *All the world's a stage, and all the men and women merely players*
>
> —*William Shakespeare, As You Like It*

Perhaps the most well-known metaphor of identity management comes from Goffman's *The Presentation of Self in Everyday Life* [14]. Goffman analogizes everyday social interactions to theatrical performances. An individual is like an actor performing on the stage of a theatre, with the other individuals in his or her social context acting as the audience watching the individual, and as co-actors in the drama. Individuals take on various roles, depending on the situation in which they are performing and the audience with which they are interacting. Through mundane, everyday interactions with others, they negotiate who they are: whether the audience is clapping or booing will shape their perceptions of self as well as future interactions with that audience. Through these social interactions, individuals develop patterns of actions in an attempt to establish a consistent positive impression others form of them.

Furthermore, each individual is not only a performer, but also the audience for other co-actors on the same stage. Thus the interaction between all individuals within that context is an n-dimensional negotiation process, in which all serve as performers and spectators, simultaneously shaping and being shaped by performances and responses to construct their self identities and social relationships.

For example, a bus driver and passengers perform to each other their identity roles: the driver drives the bus through a predefined route, greets passengers getting on and off the bus, and responds to questions about upcoming stops. The passengers get on and off the bus, greet the driver, pay with a card or cash, and find their seat.

Through the theatre stage metaphor, the development of social relationships can be seen as highly structured through the social norms that evolve as individuals consciously and unconsciously seek to achieve the goal of painting a positive picture of themselves. Goffman's metaphor of theatrical performance on a stage has been widely used to explain self identity and social interactions in online environments, including online dating sites [15], social networking sites [18,31,32], blogs [20], and online games [23].

Onion Layers

> *Life is like an onion; you peel it off one layer at a time, and sometimes you weep.*
>
> —*Carl Sandburg*

Altman & Taylor [1] conceptualized social penetration theory to characterize the ways in which individuals develop relationships with one another. One's identity is analogous to an onion, in which personality is conceived as a series of layers. The outer layers present biographical information, physical appearance and public behaviors, intermediate layers include attitudes and opinions about various issues, and at the core layers there are fears, hopes, and beliefs. Whereas external layers of an individual are open, common, and available to the public to interact with directly, internal layers are more intimate and private, such that individuals are less willing to engage in social exchange in these layers.

The onion metaphor analogizes the process of interpersonal relationship development to a pin penetrating through the onion layers. Individuals developing a relationship with each other reciprocally exchange information about themselves in a gradual, orderly, and linear manner, layer-by-layer, from the surface to the core. They continually estimate the rewards and costs of disclosing a deeper layer to others: becoming closer, open, and trustworthy but also exposing vulnerabilities to one another.

Going back to our bus driver, initially, the passengers may only know his name as indicated on his badge. Similarly, the bus driver only knows external details about the passengers: where they get on and off, what they wear, etc. Over time, the driver and regular passengers may start recognizing each other and exchange details about themselves. The bus driver may tell a passenger carrying a musical instrument about his own music activities with a local jazz band. After a while, the passenger learns about the driver's band upcoming performance and they talk about rehearsals and performances. The driver and passenger now know more about each other than at their initial encounter, through mutually sharing their experiences and passion for music.

Studies that have used social penetration theory as a basis for understanding the development of relationships in online environments have borrowed different aspects of the onion metaphor. Most common have been self-disclosure (deciding which layers to reveal) and reciprocity (mutually revealing deeper layers), in domains such as microblogging [27], online support groups [39], and online dating [13].

Segments

'Who are you?' said the Caterpillar.

This was not an encouraging opening for a conversation. Alice replied, rather shyly, 'I – I hardly know, Sir, just at present – at least I know who I was when I got up this morning, but I think I must have been changed several times since then.'

—Lewis Carroll, Alice in Wonderland

Tajfel's social identity theory [34] points to the idea that each individual manages not one single identity, but a number of distinct identities across the social contexts they take part in. An important aspect in an individual's self concept is derived from their perceived membership in various social groups, as opposed to their unique personal attributes. Culturally accepted norms of behavior associated with these social groups affect the ways in which their members interact with other individuals within and between these groups.

Segmented identity can be seen as various roles performed in different social contexts, and therefore complements the theatre metaphor. Similarly, the onion metaphor acknowledges the variety of categories such as family, work, religion, and hobbies in an individual's identity that can be penetrated deeper into core layers of one's identity. In other words, the segments metaphor is congruent with the previous two metaphors, illuminating the breadth, rather than the depth, in social interactions in various social contexts.

When roles are incompatible, such that it is difficult to meet the norms of multiple roles at the same time, individuals attempt to construct boundaries between the segments of their identity. As a result of this segmentation, one may develop relationships with others that do not cross between the different social contexts in which they operate. This is associated with a more complex identity structure [30]. Back to our bus driver, who is also a musician and a husband, his wife does not like it when he plays music with his band over the weekend instead of spending time with her. He therefore protects their intimate relationships by staying away from telling his wife about his music activities.

Farnham & Churchill examined the concept of segmented identity in the ways that people share information online, finding that segmenting is easier using email than in social networking sites [12]. Bargh et al. [2] and McKenna et al. [21] show how the Internet may allow individuals to express aspects of their identities ("the true self") that offline might be considered counter-normative. McLeod & Leshed [22], in analyzing identity management in virtual worlds, suggested a variation of the segments metaphor – a jigsaw puzzle wherein the pieces represent different segments of identity and together contain the whole picture. The deepening of online friendships can be compared to fitting the pieces of each other into a frame and seeing the images of each other become increasingly recognizable.

After describing three metaphors of identity management and how they may relate to the formation and maintenance of social relationships, we now turn to ask: given that these metaphors were established on an assumption that all (or most) interactions are face-to-face, to what extent can experiences of managing social relationships across material and virtual worlds be explained with these metaphors?

We examine this question in the context of Second Life: an online 3D virtual world in which users, called Residents, interact with the world and with others through avatars. Second Life was launched in 2003 by Linden Labs and as of Q4 2010, had over 750,000 residents spending more than 105 million hours in-world (see http://lindenlab.com/about). The variety of interactions available for Second Life residents includes interacting with other residents, playing games, building objects and environments through scripts, property management, shopping and selling, and exploring the world, among others. We believe that Second Life is particularly appropriate for the goal of this research, because it affords life-like experiences through its 3D embodied interactions (unlike online interactions such as forums) and its lack of game rules (unlike multiplayer games such as World of Warcraft).

SECOND LIFE INTERVIEW STUDY

Our analysis is based on data from in-depth interviews carried out in Second Life in the spring of 2008. Our methodological approach resonates with other studies in which the researchers participated in the virtual world with their own avatars [e.g., 4,7]. With our recruitment technique, we had no access to participants' material life name or other identifying information besides general demographics. We hoped that by giving participants control over the boundaries between their Second Life and material life identities in the interview they would be open with us about their experiences. For example, five participants talked about BDSM experiences, and we suspect they would not have shared this with us if interviews were held outside of Second Life.

Participants

Thirty Second Life residents were recruited and scheduled via a third-party Second Life market research company that specializes in Internet sampling and research. This company had access to participants' material life identifying information in order to compensate them for their participation, but this information was not shared with us.

Fifteen participants were female in their material life, and their material life age ranged from 21 to 68 years (median=35). According to quantcast.com, these distributions are roughly representative of Second Life users. All participants were US-based, and their Second Life age ranged from 3 months to almost 4 years (median=14 months).

Participants reported a range of activities that occupied their time in Second Life. A minority (n=5) described their time spent in Second Life as primarily work-related, such as managing property or working at a Second Life company. The rest described their primary activity as recreation, such as being with friends, shopping or going to parties, or a combination of recreation and work. Even for the few who spent most of their time in Second Life working, social relationships, professional or personal, were a central focus.

Interview Procedure

The researcher's avatar met with the participant's avatar at the set time at the entrance to a conference room in Second Life. The participant was invited to seat their avatar at a table inside the conference room and was given a Second Life notecard containing information about Informed Consent. Once the researcher's avatar received the participant's electronically signed consent form, the researcher conducted the interview via private instant messaging text.

The semi-structured interview included open-ended questions about how the participant sees and manages boundaries between Second Life (*SL*) and real life (we used the commonly used terms *real life* and *RL* in the interview rather than *material life*); how they make decisions about sharing different kinds of information about themselves in various situations; how and why they start, develop, maintain, and discontinue relationships; whether they know people in both worlds and the details of how and why this came about; and alternative avatars they use, what for, and how they are similar to or different from their current avatar. We ended the interview asking participants more general questions about how they spend their time in Second Life. Each question was followed with probing questions until we thought we received a full depiction of the participant's point of view. Interviews lasted approximately 90 minutes after which participants were given L$1500 (Second Life's currency, approximately $6 U.S.) for their participation.

Data Analysis

We saved the text of the interview conversations to files outside of Second Life, and gathered additional information about each participant from their Second Life profiles, voluntarily added by participants and publicly available to all Second Life residents.

To analyze the data, we carefully read the collected materials, marking parts that seem relevant to issues of identity management and social relationships. The metaphors were not part of the interview protocol design; rather, we wanted each participant to express freely his or her own perspectives. The idea to use these metaphors as a lens for analyzing and interpreting the data came from a combination of reading the literature and our initial examination of the transcripts. We therefore coded and organized the data according to the three metaphors, whether consistent with or conflicting any of them. This analysis was repeated iteratively until we exhausted the data.

In the analysis presented below we changed avatar names but kept gender identification. Given a relaxed norm in Second Life chat, we edited interview quotations to remove typos and other errors only enough to clarify meaning.

DIFFERENT LOCI OF RELATIONSHIP

We found that relationships participants discussed could be situated in three loci: relationships that are confined to the Second Life environment; relationships that start in Second Life and extend outside of Second Life; and material life relationships that sometimes extend to Second Life.

Within Second Life Primarily

Most participants described maintaining some boundaries between participating in Second Life and their material life. Robert, for example, describes his material life identity as being disabled, retired, and living an isolated ranch, in contrast to being a healthy and dominant person in Second Life's Gor community[1] who goes out dancing a lot. To maintain these boundaries, participants set limits on the information they disclose about their material life while interacting with others in Second Life, when they disclose it, and to whom. These boundaries play a role in that most relationships remained within the virtual world. That is, participants described their Second Life relationships as separate from the relationships they maintain with material life acquaintances, friends, and family:

> *It all depends on the person, I'm not going to tell someone I just met all my personal info, but I have known people here for over a year that know more about me than some of my family. I however would never meet someone from SL in RL or have any contact with them outside SL or other IM systems.* (Candace)

Candace's description illustrates the segmentation between her virtual and material life relationships. But on another level, from Candace's account transpires her view of her Second Life relationships as somehow deeper and more sincere than those in her material world.

What contributes to these differences? On the one hand, individuals reciprocate with each other in sharing personal information in order to develop and nurture meaningful relationships, as has also been observed in World of Warcraft [28]. But in order to maintain the boundaries between material life and Second Life, the kind of information that is disclosed is different. Shari says: *"I talk about my life in character-revealing ways, though not, I think in identity revealing ways."* That is, individuals share experiences, emotions, and who they are from the inside, as Connor says: *"my passions, likes and dislikes, food I like, hobbies,*

---

[1] A community based on the fantasy, science-fiction alternative world from the novels of John Norman. This community has a controversial reputation of sexual slavery and violence involved in the role-playing.

that sort of thing," while holding back information such as material life name, contact details, occupation, and age.

All participants reported that sharing personal experiences helps strengthen connections with others and happens naturally and gradually over time. Connor says: *"at some point a relationship becomes real; you dream about it you eat it you live it. Just like in RL. And the emotions are real. If someone makes you angry, it is RL anger, not avatar anger. We are all as real as the person at the keyboard."* This suggests that what begins as superficial staging of one's avatar for others' avatars over time internalizes to genuine, meaningful personal relationships. Indeed, 12 participants reported even getting married in Second Life, which involves paying Linden Labs a nominal fee for having official "partner" status listed on both avatars' profiles.

Participants reported that, as they get to know each other over time, they mutually and gradually exchange information about material life details such as their city, occupation, age, and marital status. Greta says: *"I have found that it is much easier to make friends and form strong bonds with people when you're willing to open up a bit... even if it's with something as trivial as rl age and marital status."* Participants acknowledged the value of sharing material life identity information in order to build trust and strengthen their relationships, as Gerome says, *"it can make you feel like a closer friend to somebody."*

This process by which participants described connecting with others through progressively exchanging deepening information, is in line with the central idea of the onion metaphor. Moreover, participants' accounts suggest some consistency in the pattern of what information is exchanged and in what order. It is this order, however, where the onion metaphor, as conceptualized by Altman & Taylor, breaks down. Our data suggest that the order of what are the external layers and what is on the inside seem to be altered when moving from face-to-face to the virtual world. In Second Life, external layers include avatar characteristics such as name, appearance, places encountered, and public profile details (a number of participants told us at the beginning of the interview that they looked at our profile, a common practice when meeting someone for the first time). Participants then described readily moving to layers of their personality and life stories that in material life relationships would be considered less accessible. And for many participants, at the deepest layers lie details that serve as external layers in the material world, such as age, name, and location. Although the metaphor of gradually revealing layers may hold well, the arrangement of the layers may not.

Furthermore, in some cases, even the gradual process of penetrating through deepening layers breaks down. Some reported revealing material life identity details early in the relationship, and few even offer such details in their public profile. Diane says that publicizing her city and occupation in her profile reminds others *"that there is a person behind the pixels."* This seems to contradict the onion metaphor, if material life identity details lie at internal layers in Second Life interactions. Our data suggest that one may wish to expose a deeper layer and become vulnerable as an expression of readiness to engage in developing friendships.

Alternative Avatars

23 of the 30 participants reported that they had more than one avatar, with 17 of them using 1-2 *alt avis* (alternative avatars), and the other six using 3 or more alt avis. Alt avis were often reserved for exploring different activities or communities such as BDSM, furries, unattractive physiques, and gender swap. Angela, for example, whose primary avatar is an outgoing, friendly female, has an alt avi that is *"male with a very bad comb over. He's not in the best of shape and likes to ogle women."* In line with the segments metaphor, alt avis therefore allowed participants to enact different aspects of their identity with different avatars in various social contexts.

Alt avis were often created to escape the social life in Second Life that could sometimes be overwhelming, because once logged in, your friends can see that you are online and want to contact you. Fiona's primary avatar is constantly *"bombarded with IM's as soon as she logs in and I wanted an alt so I could spend time in world without all the IM's."* Therefore, alt avis were often designated for non-social activities such as building and working, as Angela says: *"I don't want the alts to maintain friendships and stuff like that. They're usually used to get stuff done."* This is because maintaining social relationships is time consuming:

> *I created another avatar and used her for about a week - just because I sometimes felt overwhelmed by all the people I know in SL wanting to visit and chat. I thought she could be my explorer avatar and go running around the sims and go surfing and all the things I want to do that I have a hard time freeing myself up for in this Avatar's life. But...she kept meeting people too, so it seemed silly and pointless and she retired.* (Frances)

Participants often reported keeping their Second Life friends from knowing about their alt avis, segmenting their activities between their social and non-social avatars. This is also in line with the theatre metaphor, in which individuals attempt to control the boundaries between the front stage and the backstage. On the front stage they perform to their Second Life friends a positive, outgoing role with their primary avatar, keeping the non-social alt avi for backstage activities with no audience they feel a need to perform to.

In other cases, alt avis were reserved for specific social relationships. For example, Kira's primary avatar is a slave in Second Life's Gor community. She uses an alt avi for a more conventional intimate relationship outside the Gor community with *"one particular person when we both want to get away and not be bothered,"* keeping it secret from her primary avatar's Gor master. In such cases, the segmentation is not between a social and an asocial avatar, but between social selves, each reserved for separate social relationships. But despite this segmentation, Fiona explains about having 4 avatars, *"I honestly believe wherever you go there you are,"* and Greta says: *"I am my avatar... I don't pretend to be someone I'm not."* Ultimately, all the segments belong to one person, one identity.

From Second Life to Material Life

The exchange of material life information is not necessarily an indicator that a Second Life relationship will follow into the material life. For a number of our participants, the judicious choice of what material life information to share or not was actually a deliberate strategy for maintaining the boundary between the two worlds. For example, Angela discloses her material life full name because it is *"such a common American name that it would be tough to find me even if you wanted to,"* but Shari, a political activist in material life, never gives out her material life name because she is afraid to be *"googled."* In such cases, the segments of one's identity are carefully kept apart from each other despite some overlap in the information shared across them.

Sometimes however, providing enough material life details led participants to the point where they felt that they "knew" each other in material life as well as in Second Life. This kind of natural progression of allowing a Second Life relationship to breach the boundary was fairly common, and felt to many a comfortably inevitable step. Most of our participants (25 out of 30) said there was at least one person who they met in Second Life with whom they have mutually revealed material life contact information.

In a small number of cases, the extension of Second Life relationships into the material life was pragmatic. For example, Harry owns a Second Life sim through which he promotes his material life business, and he maintains transparency between the two in order to promote his business and to make a living. Deanna, who has a Second Life job, needs to be able to contact her colleagues outside of Second Life: *"we need alternate ways to reach each other. For example if there was a meeting and I didn't show in world someone might call to find out why."* In line with the theatre metaphor, the role played by these individuals involves constructing an image of a reliable person who does not hide behind the avatar. Such roles therefore call for extending the information they provide about themselves across the border between the virtual and material worlds.

In most cases, however, feelings of strong personal bonds motivated individuals to extend Second Life relationships to material life. In these cases, the onion metaphor is useful in explaining descriptions of reciprocal trust building processes, spending a lot of time together, and long conversations. Frances says: *"In all cases they are people that I met and knew for many months with whom I sensed a connection of some kind. In some cases, they were open with me about their lives, so I was more open about mine. Usually there was a slow revelation of facts and a building of trust."* Developing a relationship involves gradually peeling more and more layers over time until eventually individuals get to the core where their Second Life identity and material life identities converge.

People who became close enough to reveal their contact information outside of Second Life wanted to be able to talk to one another over the phone, see each other through a webcam, stay in touch through social networking sites and email, and sometimes meet in person. Kevyn, for example, found that one of his Second Life friends plays the same multi-player video game he did, and they exchanged information so they could find each other in the game and play together. John described his Second Life wife's upcoming visit and that they would also be meeting other mutual Second Life friends in the material world.

John's example illustrates a common finding that relationships that extended from the virtual to the material world were often more intimate than simple friendships, including romantic partnerships and Second Life family ties (e.g., siblings or children) [see also 28]. Angela, for example, says that her Second Life partner has her cellphone number and they talk occasionally: *"He went through a messy divorce last year and his family didn't approve of the divorce, so I helped talk him through some things."*

Not surprisingly, we also saw cases in which extending romantic relationships from Second Life to material life can be problematic. This was most often seen when the Second Life partner was married in material life to someone else:

> Kira: *I spend a lot of my time with him and we are the closest. And we will most likely meet in rl.*
>
> Researcher: *But you did not share addresses yet?*
>
> Kira: *addresses? hehe well he has not asked and I wont ask him for his because ... well, this is private and research. He is married in rl. I know the area he lives in. I know about his neighbors and I do have the address for his beach house. But i would never think to ask him about his primary home where he lives with his family.*

Through the lens of the segments metaphor, in all these cases the relationships reach a point where individuals feel that they want to include their relationship partner in other segments of their lives, to deepen and strengthen the bond with one another. Some even perceived marital status in the material world and in the virtual world as independent of each other. The virtual physicality of avatars' bodies assists in creating a sense of separation between all that happens in the virtual environment from that of the material. The segments are more than mere pieces of one's identity; they are compartments into which the carefully segmented parts of identity, with the respective social relationships, can be placed. The degree of permeability of the partitions between the compartments varies across people and over time. Moreover, the segments can sometimes collide.

At the same time, the segment metaphor has its limits. One important limitation is reflected in the perspective many participants shared, that all the segments belong to the same person. The life that the avatar leads in the virtual world –

the friendships or enemies made, the activities joined, the emotions felt – is also experienced by the material world person. Though technology provides an easy means to technically segment between the virtual and material worlds, those segments are no cleaner cut than are the segments that everyone constructs in everyday material life.

From Material Life to Second Life

Participants also told us about how some relationships extended from the material life to Second Life. The way this direction happened was different in nature than extending Second Life relationships to material life. Drew described how he tells everyone about his Second Life *"escapades,"* and his children and one close friend know that in Second Life he is a young gay male. However, they do not have Second Life accounts themselves: *"I try to convince people to try it out, but there is a lot of resistance in a lot of people."* In other words, whereas behind every avatar there is a person, the opposite is not true; very few people in every participant's material life are also Second Life residents.

This asymmetry was also illustrated in the consequences participants described of Second Life residents finding out their material identities in contrast to material life acquaintances finding out their Second Life avatar identities. Some participants feared potential stalkers or worse – murderers – hiding behind Second Life avatars, and this was one reason for the gradual and reciprocal trust building process before exchanging a key piece of material life contact information such as address or phone number. In the opposite direction, however, participants were mostly unconcerned about people in their material life finding out their avatar name and contacting them in Second Life. Participants said that many people outside of Second Life do not understand what Second Life is and its appeal or think it is a waste of time:

> Harry: *...so many have no clue about SL other than the sex stories they read about [...] They know I am involved but would not understand enough to have it make sense to tell them my name. I have told people that in SL I am 6'11" as compared to 5"4" in RL. They laugh. [...]*
>
> Researcher: *What do you perceive the consequences to be of people in your RL finding out your SL identity?*
>
> Harry: *Shock, distain, and confusion until they hear what I am doing here. Then they are amazed and impressed*
>
> Researcher: *What do you think leads them to the first set of reactions?*
>
> Harry: *I assume it is because the only things they have heard about SL are the horror stories.*

Our findings illustrate how people segment their lives and play different roles in the virtual and material worlds. Some participants used terms such as bizarre, insane, immoral, deviant, and sinful to describe how their participation in Second Life would be considered according to the social norms in their material life. In these cases, they chose to keep the social circles in their material life from knowing that they even participated in Second Life. In other cases, sometimes when family and friends saw them spending many hours at the computer and even watched them interacting in Second Life, they couldn't keep their Second Life interactions secret. Still, they often did not tell others in material life about the depth and significance of their Second Life experiences and interactions:

> *I would not reveal that I have a partner. I'm not sure how it might be perceived. I think it just might be best not advertised. I'm comfortable with it, but others might find it.... questionable. I'm having trouble finding the right word or words. I don't want to hurt anyone. I don't want anyone to think less of me.* (Thomas)

This separation between material life and Second Life is congruent with the segments metaphor. It is also in line with the theatre metaphor, in that on the material life stage individuals attempt to conceal some of their virtual life behaviors. For example, the material life audience may consider sexual activity in Second Life to be strange or objectionable. This may be a reason for individuals to attempt to control the boundaries between these two stages. For example, Candace, a stay-at-home mom, says she does not log on to Second Life when her husband is home.

Fourteen participants talked about material life relationships that extended to Second Life. These were often people who introduced the participants to Second Life, or that participants introduced them to Second Life. Sometimes, material life relationships were given a new form in Second Life. Irene describes her interactions with her best friend: *"we joined together in sl same time =) I think I found it first, told her about it, she said let's go in, so we registered. She and I live near each other in sl, shop together, hang out everyday in sl."* In other cases, these were material life partners, as in Walt's case whose material life wife is also his Second Life wife. Similar to friendships, romantic relationships can take new forms once they extend from the material to the virtual world:

> *My husband typically ends up dating my good friends... and becomes friends with my boyfriends... we have a unique relationship... very open minded. We don't believe in jealousy. We set up ground rules and follow them... one of which being no sl love ever makes it to rl. Email and IM's through yahoo are fine, but no meeting in rl and no phone calls...* (Greta)

In another case, Diane told us about her Second Life boyfriend and her material life husband: *"My hubby knows about the SL guy, and is ok with it. [...] He knows I would never leave him for anyone else."* She goes on to describe that she feels *"like being married to two men, good grief. Sounds odd, I know. But I love them both, each has his own place in my life."* The situation became *"very mixed up"* after Diane's husband joined Second Life, although they did not reveal that they are a material life couple. Once her Second Life boyfriend found this out, it became an issue, and they separated for a long time, but later secretly connected again, and Diane says: *"well, now things are just odd for us."*

These examples illustrate how relationships can be reshaped when shifting between the material and the virtual: people discover new ways to interact, and as a result find layers or aspects of themselves and of their partners they did not know of or did not have a chance to experience otherwise. Through the lens of the onion metaphor, layers can grow and change over time as people interact with one another and develop meaningful relationships across contexts. Similarly, from the perspective of the segments metaphor, when segments of their material and virtual lives come together or intersect, one's life experiences and social relationships can be positively enriched, or, as in Diane's case, become convoluted, confusing, and dysfunctional.

DISCUSSION

The three metaphoric lenses we used—theatre stage, onion layers, and segments—were developed in times when the ways of identity and relationship management that exist today were scarcely even conceived. It is not simply the reduced cues or new modalities of interactions that merit questioning the applicability of these metaphors. The ability to construct one or more bodies separate from the material body and the total immersion individuals experience as they socialize with others are unique characteristics of 3D virtual worlds that set these environments apart from other mediated contexts in which these metaphors have been previously applied. The foregoing analysis illustrated that these metaphors are nevertheless relevant to the mediated relationships in 3D virtual worlds – to a point.

Our data illustrate how the theatre metaphor can illuminate the ways in which individuals attempt to present themselves favorably in any specific context through choices they make in their interactions with others. For example, one may maintain a reputation of an outgoing, social personality with their primary Second Life avatar and keep alt avis for norm-violating activities. People conceal from others in their material world Second Life activities that may raise questions about their performance as a moral person in the material world. These performances are constantly negotiated and co-constructed with others they interact with in both the material and the virtual worlds.

But the theatre metaphor emphasizes that everything that is happening on stage is make-believe. If "all the world's a stage," and people are acting behind masks, then where is the true person, and where do true interactions and relationships happen? Boon & Sinclair [5] argue that "Second Life necessitates a commitment to the unreal" (p. 20), and that it is impossible ever to know through their avatar how authentic someone is. But to many of our participants, their interactions within Second Life are not less real than outside of Second Life. One interesting research question suggested here is what factors may be related to the extent to which people perceive virtual world experiences as "real." Factors related to the virtual environment [10,35], the individuals themselves [19,37], and the interaction between the two [9, 36,40] are all fruitful avenues for future research.

We also saw that the onion metaphor can explain many aspects of relationship development in Second Life, particularly in regard to the gradualness of personal information disclosure. But, the somewhat strict order of disclosure prescribed by social penetration theory for face-to-face contexts, where physical appearance and public behaviors serve as external layers and thoughts, feelings, and experiences lie beneath them, may not be so applicable. It is not just that in a virtual environment the onion is turned inside out, but instead, the very idea of layers nested within each other, along with the necessity to penetrate one before the next can be reached, is challenged.

We do not argue that the phenomenon of rapid disclosure of intimate information invalidates the onion metaphor within the context of relationships online. To the contrary, the onion metaphor helps highlight the circumstances under which the inner core can be laid bare, when new layers of avatar appearance and behaviors are available, and thus also calls further upon the theatre metaphor. This point is consistent with the analysis presented by Nach & Lejeune [25] suggesting that the vulnerability associated with loss of control over one's identity is an important challenge for Internet use in general, and for the process of relationships development in particular. Another important avenue for future research therefore would be to examine coping strategies for how people maintain control over their identity across contexts, and the factors related to those strategies.

Finally, the segments metaphor is evident through the division of material life and Second Life relationships, and within Second Life through the use of multiple avatars for different social purposes and aspects of the self. Interacting through virtual worlds provides more segmentation than was traditionally afforded, for example, in separating between one's family and work life. The usefulness of the segments metaphor is shown under circumstances in which segments are incompatible with each other or when they are brought together and then clash, for example, when separate romantic relationships in the material world and in Second Life are exposed to each other. This metaphor suggests that incorporating ideas developed about social identity complexity [30] would be a promising direction for future research on relationship development in virtual worlds.

Moreover, while all of the segments traditionally belong to one person, technically, more than one person can manipulate the same avatar (one participant, Irene, told us that she and her niece share an avatar; this was also described in [4]). The theatre metaphor applies here in thinking about different actors taking on the same role: although each actor uniquely interprets the role, there are qualities inherent to the role to be conveyed irrespective of the individual actor. The segmentation thus extends from not only the different parts of an individual's identity but also across different individuals. How well would the onion metaphor explain a situation of multiple occupants of a single persona when, each time one penetrates through the layers a different identity would be uncovered? Future research examining multiple individuals inhabiting a single avatar would make valuable contributions to theories of identity management and social relationships in virtual worlds.

Because each of the metaphors provided a different lens for examining our data, it is clear that there is not one single metaphor that best explains experiences of relationships in and across virtual and material worlds. A conceptual metaphor helps understand certain issues in concrete situations, but one needs to be cautious about what it marginalizes or when it distorts what we see. In such cases, turning to a different metaphor, combining metaphors, or updating a metaphor to hold in new situations not previously conceived may be needed. For example, combining the onion metaphor with the segments metaphor could clarify cases in which in different circumstances layers and their order may vary. In this new "onion garden metaphor," an individual grows a variety of onions, each with its own unique set of layers, but all nurtured from the same soil. Furthermore, the onions grow, mature, and sometimes eventually perish.

At the technical design level, our work highlights how system design might be ingrained with specific theoretical assumptions of how individuals should interact with and through the system. The endless choices of body shape, skin type, hairstyle, and clothing in Second Life are grounded in the theatre metaphor in that individuals should carefully choose the appearance they perform to others in the community. This capability, as well as the very idea of virtual avatars separate from the material body, also supports the segments metaphor, as individuals can construct avatars that are almost identical to or completely different from their material life physical appearance. We therefore encourage designers of systems that support social interactions to think deeply about the metaphors that underlie the systems they create: what they support, what they leave out, and how they are congruent with the goals of the system.

CONCLUSION

In this paper, we presented an analysis based on interviews with 30 Second Life residents about the ways in which they develop social relationships in Second Life and extend them between Second Life and their material life. We examined how well three conceptual metaphors—theatre stage, onion layers, and identity segments—could be used to explain our interview findings. We found that although these metaphors were developed well before 3D virtual worlds existed, to a large extent they are relevant to interactions in and across virtual and material environments: individuals in our study perform on a stage, choosing what to present to and with others; they gradually peel off and reveal layers of their identity to others; and they discriminate between segments of their identity in different social situations. Within these experiences, individuals meet others, bond with them, become closer, and sometimes break up.

We also found ways in which each of these metaphors ceases to explain our findings. This does not necessarily mean that a metaphor is useless. Instead, different metaphors can complement each other, be combined, or a specific metaphor could be updated for new situations that were not available when these metaphors were introduced.

Our contribution is twofold. First, we added to the growing body of literature in HCI and CSCW descriptions of individuals' experiences in managing identities and developing social relationships in 3D virtual worlds. Second, we examined the application of conceptual identity management metaphors to these experiences, pointing to strengths and weaknesses of these metaphors in explaining social relationships in and across virtual and material worlds.

ACKNOWLEDGMENTS

This research was supported in part by the Cornell Agricultural Experiment Station federal formula funds, Project No. NYC-131413 from Cooperative State Research, Education, and Extension Service, U.S. Department of Agriculture.

REFERENCES

1. Altman, I. & Taylor, D. 1973. *Social penetration: The development of interpersonal relationships*. New York: Holt, Rinehart and Winston.
2. Bargh, J.A., McKenna, K.Y.A. & Fitzsimons, G.M. 2002. Can you see the real me? Activation and expression of the "true self" on the Internet. *J. of Soc. Issues*, *58*, 33-48.
3. Blackwell, A.F. 2006. The reification of metaphor as a design tool. *ACM ToCHI, 13*, 490–530.
4. Boellstorff, T. 2008. *Coming of age in Second Life*. Princeton, NJ: Princeton University Press.
5. Boon, S. & Sinclair, C. 2009. A world I don't inhabit: Disquiet and identity in Second Life and Facebook. *Edu. Media Int.*, *46*, 99-110.
6. Brahnam, S., Karanikas, M. & Weaver, M. 2011. (Un)dressing the interface: Exposing the foundational HCI metaphor "computer is woman". *Interacting with Computers, 23*(5), 401-412.
7. Brown, B. & Bell, M. 2004. CSCW at play: *There* as a collaborative virtual environment. *Proc. CSCW'04*, 350-359.
8. Cheal, C. 2007. Second Life: Hype or hyperlearning? *On the Horizon*, *15*, 204-210.
9. Correa, T., Hinsley, A.W. & de Zúñiga, G. 2010. Who interacts on the Web? The intersection of users' personality and social media use. *Comp. in Human Beh.*, *26*, 247-253.
10. Demetrious, K. 2008. Secrecy and illusion: Second Life and the construction of unreality. *Australian J. of Comm.*, *35*(1), 1-13.

11. Ducheneaut, N., Yee, N., Nickell, E. & Moore, R.J. 2006. "Alone together?": exploring the social dynamics of massively multiplayer online games. *Proc. CHI'06*, 407-416.

12. Farnham, S. & Churchill, E. 2011. Faceted identity, faceted lives: social and technical issues with being yourself online. *Proc. CSCW'11*, 359-368.

13. Gibbs, J.L., Ellison, N.B. & Heino, R.D. 2006. Self-presentation in online personals: the role of anticipated future interaction, self-disclosure, and perceived success in Internet dating. *Comm. Research, 33*(2), 152-177.

14. Goffman, E. 1959. *The presentation of self in everyday life*. New York: Anchor Books.

15. Hancock, J.T., Toma, C. & Ellison, N. 2007. The truth about lying in online dating sites. *Proc. CHI'07*, 449-452.

16. IJzerman, H. & Semin, G.R. 2009. The thermometer of social relations: Mapping social proximity on temperature. *Psych. Science*, *20*, 1214-1220.

17. Lakoff, G. & Johnson, M. 1980. *Metaphors we live by*. Chicago, IL: University of Chicago Press.

18. Lampe, C., Ellison, N., & Steinfield, C. 2007. A familiar face(book): profile elements as signals in an online social network. *Proc. CHI'07*, 435-444.

19. Landers, R.N. & Lounsbury, J.W. 2006. An investigation of Big Five and narrow personality traits in relation to Internet usage. *Comp. in Human Beh.*, *22*, 283-293.

20. Mark, G. & Semaan, B. 2009. Expanding a country's borders during war: the Internet war diary. *Proc. IWIC'09*, 3-12.

21. McKenna, K.Y.A., Green, A.S. & Gleason, M.E.J. (2002). Relationship formation on the Internet: What's the big attraction? *J. of Soc. Issues*, *58*, 9-31.

22. McLeod, P.L. & Leshed, G. 2011. As long as they don't know where I live: information disclosure strategies for managing identity in Second Life. To appear in A. Peachy & M. Childs (Eds.). *Reinventing Ourselves: Contemporary Concepts of Identity in Virtual Worlds*. New York, NY: Springer.

23. Meredith, A., Griffiths, M. & Whitty, M. 2008. Identity in massively multiplayer online games: a qualitative pilot study. *Proc. iiWAS'08*, 543-546.

24. Meyer, I., Zaluski, V. & Mackintosh, K. 1997. Metaphorical Internet terms: A conceptual and structural analysis. *Terminology*, *4*, 1-33.

25. Nach, H. & Lejeune, A. 2010. Coping with information technology challenges to identity: A theoretical framework. *Comp. in Human Beh.*, *26*, 618-629.

26. Nardi, B. & Harris, J. 2006. Strangers and friends: collaborative play in World of Warcraft. *Proc. CSCW'06*, 149-158.

27. Oulasvirta, A., Lehtonen, E., Kurvinen, E. & Raento, M. 2010. Making the ordinary visible in microblogs, *Pers. and Ubi. Comp.*, *14*, 237-249.

28. Pace, T., Bardzell, S. & Bardzell, J. 2010. The rogue in the lovely black dress: intimacy in World of Warcraft. *Proc. CHI'10*, 233-242.

29. Palmquist, R.A. 1996. The search for an Internet metaphor: A comparison of literatures. *ASIS Annual Conference Proceedings*.

30. Roccas, S. & Brewer, M.B. 2002. Social identity complexity. *Pers. and Soc. Psych. Review*, *6*(2), 88-106.

31. Sas, C., Dix, A., Hart, J. & Su, R. 2009. Dramaturgical capitalization of positive emotions: the answer for Facebook success? *Proc. BCS-HCI'09*, 120-129.

32. Silfverberg, S., Liikkanen, L.A. & Lampinen, A. 2011. "I'll press play, but I won't listen": profile work in a music-focused social network service. *Proc. CSCW'11*, 207-216.

33. Stryker S., & Burke, P.J. 2000. The past, present, and future of an identity theory. *Soc. Psych. Quart.*, *63*(4), 284-297.

34. Tajfel, H. 1982. Social psychology of intergroup relations. *Ann. Review of Psych.*, *33*, 1-39.

35. Takatalo, J., Nyman, G. & Laaksonen, L. 2008. Components of human experience in virtual environments. *Comp. in Human Beh.*, *24*, 1-15.

36. Thatcher, A., Wretschko, G. & Fridjhon, P. 2008. Online flow experiences, problematic Internet use and Internet procrastination. *Comp. in Human Beh.*, *24*, 2236-2254.

37. Tosun, L.P. & Lajunen, T. 2010. Does Internet use reflect your personality? Relationship between Eysenck's personality dimensions and Internet use. *Comp. in Human Beh.*, *26*, 162-167.

38. Turkle, S. 1995. *Life on the screen: Identity in the age of the Internet*. New York, NY: Simon & Schuster.

39. VanLear, A.C., Sheehan, M., Withers, L.A. & Walker, R.A. 2005. AA online: the enactment of supportive Computer Mediated Communication. *Western J. of Comm.*, *69*(1), 5-26.

40. Webster, J., Trevino, L.K. & Ryan, L. 1993. The dimensionality and correlates of flow in human-computer interactions. *Comp. in Human Beh.*, *9*, 411-426.

41. Weller, H.G. & Hartson, H.R. 1992. Metaphors for the nature of human-computer interaction in an empowering environment: Interaction style influences the manner of human accomplishment. *Comp. in Human Beh.*, *8*, 313-333.

42. Yee, N., Ducheneaut, N., Nelson, L. & Likarish, P. 2011. Introverted elves & conscientious gnomes: the expression of personality in World of Warcraft. *Proc. CHI'11*, 753-762.

Come Meet Me at Ulduar: Progression Raiding in World of Warcraft

Jeffrey Bardzell
Indiana University
919 E Tenth St.
Bloomington, IN 47401
jbardzel@indiana.edu

Jeffrey Nichols
IBM Research
650 Harry Road San
Jose, CA 95120 USA
jwnichols@us.ibm.com

Tyler Pace
Indiana University
919 E Tenth St.
Bloomington, IN 47401
tympace@indiana.edu

Shaowen Bardzell
Indiana University
919 E Tenth St.
Bloomington, IN 47401
selu@indiana.edu

ABSTRACT
In spite of decades of research on virtual worlds, our understanding of one popular form of virtual world behavior—raiding—remains limited. Raiding is important because it entails intense, high-risk, and complex collaborative behaviors in computer-mediated environments. This paper contributes to CSCW literature by offering a longitudinal analysis of raiding behavior using system data manually collected from the game world itself, comparing two raiding teams as they worked through the same content. Supplemented with interviews and chat transcripts, this research sheds light on what actually happens during raids across four different temporal scales: seconds, hours, days, and months. It also distinguishes between behaviors that are imposed by the system design and those chosen by players. Finally, it derives two viable raiding styles from the data.

Author Keywords
HCI, World of Warcraft, raids, virtual teams, failure

ACM Classification Keywords
H5.m. Information interfaces and presentation: Miscellaneous.

General Terms
Design

INTRODUCTION
The rise of massively multiuser virtual environments, which had been building up since the 1990s with MUDs, MOOs, and EverQuest, hit a tipping point in the mid-2000s with World of Warcraft (WoW) and Second Life, which, at the height of their popularity, boasted over 24 million users between them. Research in anthropology, psychology, CSCW, education, HCI, and media studies has shed light on virtual world behavior, with implications for systems design, social psychology, virtual teams, pedagogy, and cultural theory. Such research has illuminated virtual world social behavior, from virtual rape [10] to the life and death of guilds [11]. Full-scale ethnographic research has presented studies of virtual community diaspora [25], of virtual personhood [4], and of WoW as a platform for cross-cultural aesthetic experience [23].

CSCW'12, February 11–15, 2012, Seattle, Washington, USA.

As researchers continue to shed light on the social behaviors and their meanings that unfold in virtual worlds, one form of social behavior continues to generate interest: end-game raiding. As large-scale, complex group activities that involve 10-40 people working together in real time to solve extreme problems, raids have clear implications for CSCW, in research areas such as knowledge gathering, software development, or military applications, especially where large virtual teams, fast time constraints, and/or a high risk of failure are prevalent. A concept critical to players' understanding of raiding is *progression*. For most players, the most basic definition of progression refers to how much high-end content guilds have worked through (i.e., how many raid bosses have been defeated).

The central goal of this project is to obtain a better understanding of raid progression, with particular emphases on how raid behavior and events shed light on player decision-making, leadership, failure, and multi-user interaction design. We offer two main contributions, based primarily on log data obtained from two raid teams in WoW over five months. First, we offer basic metrics of raiding in terms of time, human involvement, distribution of successes and failures, etc., providing a foundational understanding of *progression raiding behavior*. Second, we offer an analysis of the *management choices* two raiding teams made during the study within in distinct temporal structures.

BACKGROUND: RAIDING IN WOW
The raid is a type of large, complex, real-time activity common in many virtual gaming worlds. In WoW, they are available as 10- and 25-player challenges. In a raid, players typically enter a separate area of the game, called an "instance," and they take on a series of difficult challenges, usually involving combat against boss enemies. Success brings rewards: when beaten, raid bosses drop "loot"; in fact, they drop the most coveted items in the game, items that can *only* be acquired through raids. For any given win, only a small fraction of players will get useful loot. Additionally, raids are quite difficult; the majority of them result in the boss killing all of the raid team, called "wiping." When a team wipes, no one gets loot from that boss.

Success in raids is generally predicated on teams having sufficient resources to take on these elite challenges. Because of the difficulty of building sufficiently resourced teams, players usually group together across sessions. One mechanism to support persistent grouping is the "guild." As noted in earlier research [14, 30], guilds form around many aspects of the game, serving social as well as ludic needs. One major type of guild is the raid guild, which is a group of highly experienced players who take on the game's most difficult challenges. Not all raid guilds are the same: the most "hardcore" guilds raid 5-7 nights per week, are often highly regimented [30], and compete with other hardcore raid guilds on the server for first kills and other achievements, which are prioritized higher than social goals. Far more common is what Golub [16] refers to as "medium-core" raiding guilds, which blend both achievement and social goals. Medium-core raiding guilds generally try to raid 2-3 nights per week and prioritize fun and achievement equally. Because medium-core raiding guilds are far more typical than hardcore guilds, this study focuses on them.

Progression is the main aspiration of most raiding guilds. One of the most basic progression metrics raiding guilds use is whether they have cleared a raid's content before a new patch is released. *Content patches* are introduced by WoW designers about every 4-6 months. New content patches typically contain a new raiding instance with new rewards that are substantially better than anything previously available. For raid guilds that do not achieve clear content before a new patch, they typically move on to the new content and leave the old content behind.

RELATED WORK

The topic of user research in virtual worlds is hardly new to CSCW. Much of this work has come into CSCW collectively under the banner of "productive play." This body of work has done much to correct commonsense but highly problematic distinctions between work and play. CSCW research on virtual worlds has touched upon a number of key themes. This includes contributions that explicitly confront the work/play dichotomy already mentioned [5, 7, 33]. The exploration of virtual worlds for enterprise use is another area [7, 18]. Others [29, 30, 32] have explored the motivations and nature of enjoyment in virtual worlds to suggest design strategies for future virtual world collaborative applications. The significance of avatars as a particular kind of embodiment is another theme of this research [22, 34]. The multiplayer nature of virtual worlds also means that much of the research goes beyond the individual. Sociability, teams, grouping, and collaboration are a dominant sub-topic, including [3, 9, 11-15, 21, 24]. Some of the contributions focus on the nature of virtual worlds as spaces or ecologies, especially the particular ways that these spaces foster play, productivity, and collaboration [2, 6, 20]. Kahai et al. [19] emphasize that the medium or affordances of virtual worlds shape leadership and collaboration, proposing that researchers should "seek to understand leadership emergence during virtual team collaboration in virtual worlds." An underlying concern in all of this research is the extent to which virtual collaborative behavior is shaped or conditioned by technical systems, a concern also reflected in existing WoW research [e.g., 11, 23, 30].

Raiding in massively multiplayer games has also been researched previously [8, 16, 23]. These works ethnographically characterize the authors' experiences as members of a raid team. Common to all of this raid research, however, is that it relies on self-report, including the self-report of the researcher participating in the raids supported with interviews with fellow players. No published studies on raids, however, are based on data obtained from the game itself; neither are any raid studies based on the activities of more than one guild; nor has any of the raid research focused extensively on raid leadership. Several social networking studies, including [11, 14, 30] offer analyses of guilds, including raid guilds, using data derived from the game, but none of these focus specifically on raids or reveal much about actual raiding behavior. Williams et al. [30] account for this problem as follows: "a range of obstacles will confront any similar future work. Chief among these is securing access to the database of players and logs of player behavior." Blizzard notoriously does not collaborate with researchers, so access to their databases remains out of reach. In the present study, we present results based on longitudinal raid log data collected manually from two guilds. This data enables us to present the first analysis of raiding behavior from more than one guild, progressing through the same game content, based on data from the game itself.

METHODOLOGY

As with prior primarily quantitative WoW research [e.g., 11, 14, 30], the present study is informed on three levels. First, the authors of this study have been active participants in WoW for years, each logging hundreds of hours and participating in several guilds; three of the authors are guild leaders (of three different guilds on three different servers). Our research questions, data collection methods, and data analysis and interpretation are all profoundly shaped by this participation. The second level is system-generated combat log data manually harvested for this study; this data is our primary source of evidence. The third level is qualitative, involving follow-up interviews conducted with guild officers and study of chat logs.

We collected data about two medium-core raid teams' progress through the 25-person version of the most difficult raid zone at the time: "Ulduar." Released as part of content patch 3.1 in April 2009, Ulduar contains 14 bosses. The first raid attempt for each guild began on April 14, 2009. As of August 25, 2009, when we cut off data for the purposes of the study, neither guild had killed more than 12 of the 14 bosses. We codename the two raid teams "Judgment" and the "Titans." Officers from each of these raid teams are co-authors of this paper, and two authors were not in either raid team.

Data Collection

For each raid team, we manually collected combat logs and chat logs of the raids. *Combat logs* are system-generated text records that list every spell cast and weapon swing by every player in the raid group and every enemy they face; they are arguably the best source of behavioral data available in WoW. Combat logs are commonly collected by raiding guilds and fed into online analysis tools with the results made available in the raid guild's online forums. We collected a total of 65 combat logs, 31 from Titans and 34 from Judgment, each representing a single raid session.

Chat logs are text records of all the chat that appears in the chat channels in the game during the raid. This includes messages written by players, scripted event dialogue, and a variety of status messages generated by the game. The extent of the player-written messages depends on how heavily the guilds use VoIP applications; additionally, raid leaders often discuss planning issues in private chat channels before announcing their decision to the rest of the raid through a VoIP channel. In this paper, we use chat logs as a secondary source of data, focusing on the raid leader chat for qualitative results and game-generated messages that provide a clearer indicator for some events than the combat logs. We collected the same number of chat logs as combat logs, again, one for each session.

The final data source came from two interviews of guild officers who are not part of the research team. Interviews were conducted by researchers outside of the guilds in question. The two semi-structured interviews lasted approximately one hour each and included questions concerning the officers' impressions of the guild's progression, including achievements and failures, planning, and risk management. More informal follow-up interviews happened afterwards.

Data Extraction and Analysis

From the combat and chat logs of each raid, we extracted a summary of each raid as follows:

- How long it took for the raid to form from the start of invites to the first engagement with an enemy.
- How many bosses the raid fought.
- Which bosses the raid fought, and in what order.
- For each boss fight, how long the fight lasted and whether the team defeated the boss or wiped.

Combat and chat logs contain a great deal of data irrelevant to our analysis. The sheer scale of their content makes them hard to read manually: a 4-minute boss fight might entail 45,000 lines of text. To interpret the logs, we developed a parser to extract just the data important to the above questions into a structured format. Our parser is a combination of a modified freely available parser for combat logs [26] and our own chat log parser.

In the course of this work, we separated our data into two sets: the *complete raid data* from all sessions and all fights attempted during the study period; and a second set, which we nickname *Ulduar-25*, which includes only raids that met all the following criteria: Ulduar raid zone, 25-person parties, normal difficulty, bosses 1-12. We exclude data on bosses 13-14 because neither team ever defeated these during the study period. In the next section, we offer descriptive statistics from both variants of the data—complete and Ulduar-25—so readers understand both the overall scope of raiding in these teams and also what portion of the overall raiding was devoted to Ulduar-25. Later, where we explore managerial aspects of progression raid teams, we use only the Ulduar-25 data to facilitate comparison of the two teams, except where noted. Our analysis of the data was also informed by two of the authors, who attended every raid represented in the study. Their participation in the raids contributed to our interpretation of the system log data.

THE SCALE AND SCOPE OF RAIDING

The parsed combat logs reveal much regarding the scale and scope of these raid activities. In the following tables, we summarize several key descriptive statistics for the study, distinguishing between the complete and Ulduar-25 data sets. Table 1 summarizes several descriptive statistics regarding the time committed to raiding, by team.

	Titans	Judgment
Number of raid sessions	31	34
Avg. raid sessions/week	1.63	1.79
Avg. duration of sessions (h:mm)	3:55	3:13
Med. duration of sessions (h:mm)	4:04	3:19
Total time raiding (h:mm)	121:46	109:47

Table 1. Raid sessions and durations, by team (complete)

Both teams are quite similar on these measures of their overall level of commitment. Table 2 summarizes key descriptive statistics surrounding boss fight attempts for all raid sessions during the study period.

	Titans	Judgment
Total boss attempts (complete)	386	396
Total boss attempts (Uld-25)	302	355
Total boss wins (complete)	103	130
Total boss wins (Uld-25)	92	105
Win % (complete)	26.68%	32.83%
Win % (Uld-25)	30.46%	29.58%
% of total time in boss battles (complete)	23%	27%
Avg boss fights / hr of raiding (complete)	3.61	3.17
Avg boss fight duration (m:ss) (complete)	4:39	4:33

Table 2. Boss attempts and wins, by team

Again, the two teams are quite similar across these measures. That only roughly a quarter of the time spent raiding actually involved boss fights is a reminder that raiding is much more than boss fights: as with any collaboration, it is also a social event, with planning and preparation work, chatter, snack/bathroom breaks, etc. The data in Tables 1 and 2 offer empirical confirmation that these two guilds are "medium-core" guilds, comparable both in terms of time commitment and readiness for Ulduar content.

Table 3 summarizes raid participation in the two guilds. These numbers show who is in these raid teams (note, however, that this data tells us about characters, not human players). It is clear that the Titans have more team churn than Judgment: 50% more characters participated in at least one raid for the Titans than for Judgment. Additionally, the average number of raid sessions each character participated in for the Titans was half the average number of raid sessions for Judgment characters.

	Titans	Judgment
Num avatars raided at least once	121	80
Num raid leaders or assistants	15	14
Avg # raid sessions / avatar	5.99	12.06
Avg % of total raid sessions / avatar	24%	34%

Table 3. Avatar raid participation, by team (complete)

As these three tables show, raiding is a team activity that requires considerable commitment on the part of players. This commitment is immediately visible in the sheer number of hours they spend, but it is also visible in the patience they exhibit given the 70% failure rate.

FINDINGS: MANAGING PROGRESSION

Data from the combat logs exposes behavioral patterns that suggest player agency, i.e., player decisions that are not predetermined by the design of the game. In this section, we unpack this data by analyzing the raid data according to four temporal scales. In distinguishing among different temporal scales of progress trajectories, we are following in the footsteps of [27], whose analysis of collaboration in medical settings led them to understand the ways in which temporal scales are used to manage collaboration in hospitals. These temporal scales include individual patient illness trajectories (measured in days or weeks), nurse shift trajectories (measured in 12-hour units), and horizons (a "window of time" in which nurses optimize multitasking, measured in a few hours). As we reviewed our own data, we could see a similar set of progression trajectories taking place across four discrete temporal scales, as shown in Table 4.

Trajectory	Decisions Affect:	Time Scale
Raid zone	Team progress through a raid zone.	~4-6 mos
Raid zone lockout	The team's progress through a raid zone lockout (defined below).	~1 wk
Raid session	The team's progress within a single play session.	~3-4 hrs
Boss fight	The team's strategy and tactics during a single boss fight	~5 mins

Table 4. Summary of raid progression trajectories

These temporal trajectories are not simply passive structures in which play happens; instead, raid teams actively make decisions that affect how they progress within these trajectories. For example, choosing to be among the first five guilds server-wide to complete the Ulduar raid (i.e., defeat all bosses) is a decision at the level of the raid zone trajectory: it reflects players' intentions and commitments to one another over months. Deciding boss order within a raid zone, however, is typically done at either the raid zone lockout (explained below) or raid session trajectories. The decision to fight a boss in the corner as opposed to fighting it in a circular motion around the room is a decision at the level of the individual boss trajectory.

The Raid Zone Trajectory

The raid zone trajectory is the scope in which a raid team tracks its progress across the months spent within a given raid zone. Raid zone trajectories correlate with game patch releases, since each patch typically includes a new raid instance. Bosses in a raid zone such as Ulduar are mostly presented in a loose sequence; in other words, players have only limited choices about how they proceed through the zone. Players are well aware of this trajectory and celebrate their progress with respect to other raid guilds via popular community websites [17, 31]. To show progress, for each guild we identified two encounters for each boss: the date of the first attempt against each boss, and the date of the first kill of each boss. In addition to showing both the attempt and kill orders, this pairing of data offers evidence about the *duration* in between first attempt and first kill for each boss. The average number of days between first attempt and first kill for the whole raid zone for Judgment was 13 (median=11), and for Titans was 7 (median=5).

More telling than the overall zone averages for days between first attempt and first kill is the *distribution* of these ranges for the two guilds. Figure 1 charts the different raid zone trajectories of the two raid teams. For each team, Figure 1 displays the number of days it took to kill a raid zone boss for the first time after it had been engaged for the first time. Regression models were applied to the trajectory data for both Judgment [solid line; r^2 = .396, df = 1, p = .028] and Titans [dashed line; r^2 = .149, df =1, p =.216]. These models indicate that Judgment experienced a consistently increasing level of difficulty as the days required to first-kill early bosses were significantly lower than for later bosses. In contrast, the model for Titans reveals no such consistency in their progress. For Titans, the number of days required to kill a new boss was highly variable across all bosses leaving the Titans to experience inconsistent fluctuations in difficulty throughout the entire raid zone.

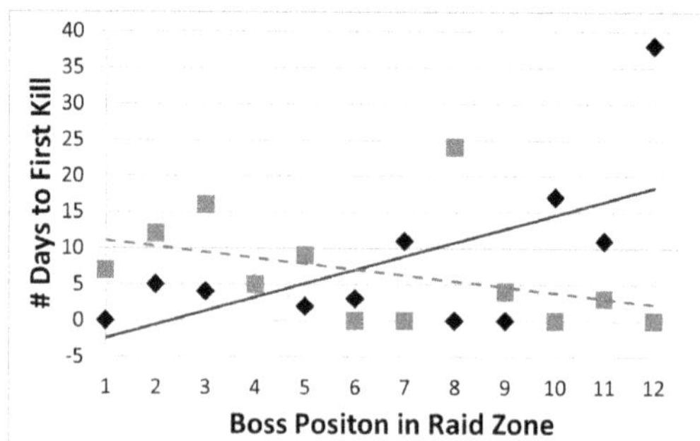

Figure 1. Days between boss first attempt and first kill, by guild [Judgment = Diamonds, Titans = Squares]

The difference in the guilds' numbers are not due to happenstance; they reflect the decisions of the raid leaders. Not visible in Figure 1 is the fact that in spite of the apparent chaos of the Titans, they killed the 12th boss for the first time in half the number of days Judgment needed to do the same. The reason is that whereas Judgment methodically progressed one boss at a time, the Titans tried and died and moved on to another—and the latter yielded faster results.

Other behavioral differences between the teams' raiding styles are visible in Figures 2 and 3. For each ~3 hour session during the study period, these figures chart the overall number of attempts (including successful and failed attempts, shown with black versus gray bars, respectively). Comparing them, we see that Judgment experienced considerably more wipes in the early part of the raid zone than Titans did. This suggests that Titans may have been more prepared for the zone wide challenges than Judgment. Figures 2 and 3 also chart two trends: overall attempts over time and overall wins over time. For both of the teams, the wins trended up: as the weeks passed, they defeated more bosses, which is not surprising since raid zone lockouts require repeated killing of earlier bosses to access later ones. More interestingly, the overall attempt trends differed: whereas Judgment's attempts trended down, Titans' trended upwards. Thus, over the course of the study, Judgment gradually won more and lost less, while Titans won more and lost more.

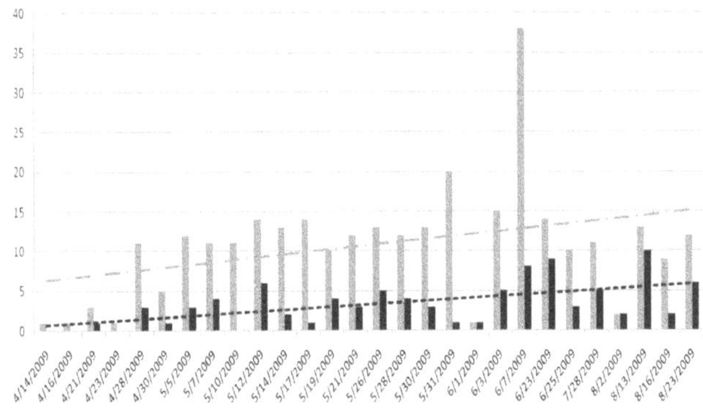

Figure 2. Attempts vs. wins over time, all bosses, by Titans

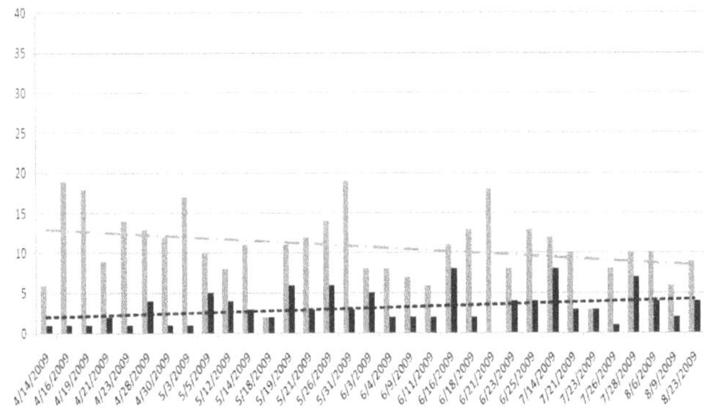

Figure 3. Attempts vs. wins over time, all bosses, by Judgment

The most common indicator of progress used by players is which boss their guild is on, e.g., 7 out of 14 bosses have been killed. On that measure, Titans is clearly superior to Judgment, since they progressed through the bosses more quickly. However, other metrics suggest that Judgment is doing better than Titans: Judgment's attempt/win ratio improves over time, while Titans' gets worse. Judgment's progress is more predictable and more closely aligns with the increasing difficulty over time curves found throughout WoW [11], while Titans' progress is much less predictable. In these numbers we begin to see evidence of a tendency of each guild, which reveals itself in our data across temporal trajectories: though both guilds are "middle-core," Judgment tends toward an incremental and methodical style, while Titans tend toward a tumultuous achievement style: we will return to this tendency more than once below.

The Raid Zone Lockout Trajectory

The *raid zone lockout* is a game mechanic that limits the duration of a raid instance to one week (Blizzard subsequently changed it), running Tuesday to Tuesday; this means that each Tuesday the instance "reset," and bosses that had been killed the prior week reappeared at full health. The lockout has two key implications: no bosses could be killed more than once per week (limiting the loot that could be won from the boss), and every Tuesday the guild had to start over on the first boss. Most medium-core raid teams hold several raiding sessions during each lockout period, including both Titans and Judgment, who aspired to 2-3 sessions per week, but as Table 1 shows, actually averaged 1.63 and 1.79, respectively.

Decisions that affect this trajectory include raid zone decisions (e.g., which raid zone to tackle), 10- versus 25-person teams, which bosses are emphasized, normal vs. heroic difficulty, and in what order to attack the bosses. What is at stake with these decisions? Both the scholarly [16, 23] and popular [1, 28] literature on raiding is universal in offering a two-sided answer to this question. First, defeating raid bosses for the first time, in Nardi's words, "were famously moments of performative ecstasy" [23]. Second, repeated failing has dangerous short- and long-term threats. Short-term threats are that raiders will quit a session or inexplicably go AFK (away from keyboard), a problem that repeatedly vexed officers throughout our game chat transcripts; one popular press book on raiding [1] devotes several pages to raid policies for managing AFK problems. Long-term problems include demoralization and social strife, both of which can lead to the dissolution of the raid guild itself; a guild officer for Judgment even offered a metric: if a raid is called off more than five times in a patch, "that's bad news, probably guild death."

With ecstasy as one outcome and guild dissolution the other, it's hard to imagine how the stakes could be higher for raiders. The winning formula, according to the literature, seems to be achieving a sufficient number of first kills while managing negativity during droughts [1]. Our officer interviews and chat transcripts suggested that some of these issues were decisions handled within a given session, rather than at the weekly planning level. However, we found that the system logs nonetheless shed light on how raid teams managed these issues week to week.

One way to compare teams is to see how they treat *farm status bosses*. Over time, bosses transition from achievement status to farm status. *Achievement status* refers to bosses that are difficult to defeat, and when they are defeated, raiders feel ecstatic. *Farm status* refers to bosses that the guild is confident it can defeat, and it takes on because they must in order to fight harder bosses in the dungeon, to win more loot that will improve the raid team statistically, or to give a safe boost to morale. The transition from achievement to farm status can be seen in log data. For example, Figure 4 shows attempts (gray bars) and wins (black bars) for Judgment against Kologarn, a boss positioned early in the raid zone. The first five weeks saw 16 attempts and 3 wins, while the next 8 weeks saw 9 attempts and 8 wins.

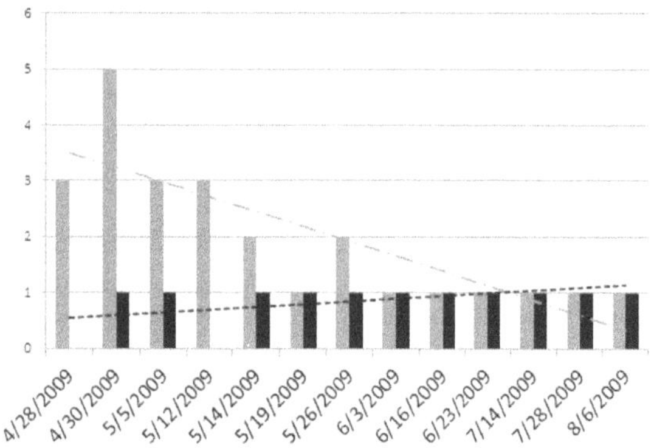

Figure 4. Attempts vs. successes against Kologarn, Judgment

In our officer interviews, we asked at what point they would consider a boss to be on farm status. Both independently replied with the same *farm status metric*: when a raid team has defeated a boss three times in a row in two or fewer tries each. Using their metric, we can say that Judgment converted Kologarn to farm status on May 26, 2009.

We then applied the officers' farm status metric to both raid teams on all 12 bosses included in the Ulduar-25 data set, with the results shown in Table 5. Because Titans defeated the twelfth boss in half the time Judgment did, we predicted that Titans would likewise convert these bosses to farm status sooner. Yet our data shows otherwise: Judgment made slightly more use of farm bosses, converting two more bosses to that status and winning seven more fights against bosses already on this status. In spite of that, as a proportion of all fights, the two guilds were quite similar: 38.0% of all Titans wins were on farm status bosses, while 39.0% of Judgment wins were on farm status bosses. One possible explanation for the similarity is that the design of the raid zone itself—especially the weekly resets forcing teams to start over—enforces a certain percentage of farm status wins on teams.

	Titans	Judgment
Num bosses on farm status	7	9
Num wins against farm status bosses	34	41
Farm status wins as % of all wins	38.0%	39.0%

Table 5. Use of farm status bosses as a resource, by team

The opposite of farm status is achievement status, and here the two guilds' respective approach to the 13th boss, Yogg Saron, is illuminating. Yogg data was excluded from the Ulduar-25 data set used for most of the present analyses for two reasons: neither team defeated this boss during the study period, which complicated statistical comparison to other bosses that they had defeated; and Titans' Yogg data was so different from the rest of the data set that it single-handedly distorted it. During the study period, Judgment took on Yogg (unsuccessfully) 2 times (0.5% of all their boss attempts during the study period). Titans took on Yogg 53 times, all wipes (14.9% of all attempts). Titans officers informed us after the study ended that they fought Yogg more than 200 times before they finally first-killed him, in what must have indeed been a "moment of performative ecstasy." Titans' persistence contrasted with Judgment's disinclination even to attempt him suggests that the guilds had different raiding priorities—and that Titans have a particularly high tolerance for failure for certain achievements.

We were able to identify several other measures of guild failure tolerance. We considered the highest number of consecutive wipes on any boss as an indicator of the length of droughts experienced while learning the mechanics of the fight. A related number is the overall average number of pre-kill wipes per boss as a measure of how long it typically takes a raid team to learn the boss mechanics and defeat the boss. We also considered the average number of wipes *after* the boss had been first defeated as an indicator of how well the guild team maintained its knowledge/skills against a given boss. Finally, we considered the number of times each guild wiped more times on a subsequent kill of a given boss than it did for the first kill. The results (which, once again, are from the more limited Ulduar-25 data set and exclude Yogg) are listed in Table 6.

	Titans	Judgment
Highest num consecutive wipes on any single boss (excl. Yogg)	21	30
Ave. num pre-kill wipes per boss, all bosses	8.10	12.75
Ave. num post-kill wipes per boss, all bosses	2.55	2.23
Num of times attempts for second kill > attempts for first kill	3	1

Table 6. Tolerating failure on a given boss, by team

The first two rows clearly show that Judgment took longer to master bosses for the first time than Titans did, a finding compatible with Titans' quicker first-kill pace through the raid zone. The second two rows tell a different story: Judgment was more likely to retain its gains than Titans, a finding consistent with the data suggesting that Judgment had more wins against farm status bosses. Another way of summarizing this is that the first kill was generally a more significant event for Judgment than for Titans, in the sense that it was harder for Judgment to achieve it and it also more strongly predicted smooth sailing afterwards.

System log data clearly does offer insight on how raid leaders managed the risk-reward ratio of progression raiding. It is compatible with existing literature in suggesting that first-kill is a key milestone in raiding, offering empirical evidence suggesting how difficult it is to achieve first-kill, for how many subsequent attempts a boss remains difficult, and when a boss finally becomes easy for the raid team. The log data also exposes one factor that prior research appears to have overlooked, which is the specific extent to which the game design itself forces raid teams to take on farm-status bosses. We speculate that this design was intentionally implemented to help raid teams manage the risk-reward ratio without absolutely pre-determining it.

The Raid Session Trajectory

The emotional highs and lows that dominate the felt experience of raiding occur predominantly within the ~3-hour raid session. Managing the team's success and emotions involves both practical decisions about which bosses to take on and when to give up, as well as communication skills to help the raid team emotionally cope with and also learn from failures. We saw evidence of such management in both our officer interviews and chat transcripts. The following chat transcript from Titans officers during a raid exemplifies this reasoning:

Officer_1: [should we do heroic or] easy mode FL [Flame Leviathan, first boss in Ulduar]?
Officer_1: get him down, go on to other bosses?
Officer_2: yeah, we really need to move forward on normal [mode] bosses and make up for our lackluster performance last week

In this next transcript excerpt, Judgment officers deal with negativity following a wipe:

Officer_1: lets not give too much focus to the negative stuff
Officer_1: it was only Player_1 [who was negative]
Officer_2: lets go over the genral strat[egy] again quickly... just to some ppl know what's expected
Officer_1: and we just way over-responded to it

One way to manage expectations is to preempt them. Titans' officers in our interviews reveal one such strategy: "We don't tell the guild what content we are going to raid. We try to trick them to get attendance to happen." Titans officers also have policies for managing failure: "if we're completely stuck for two hours, we go to a back-up boss." Our qualitative evidence confirms prior research indicating the intensity—good and bad—of raiding and that officers are quite sensitive to it.

	Titans	Judgment
Num sessions without a win	4/28 (14%)	1/33 (3%)
Num sessions last boss a win	8/31 (25.8%)	15/38 (39.5%)
Easier raid zone boss wins/attempts	10/16	22/27
Num of sessions with visits to easier raid zones	7	12
Final boss (Yogg) wins/attempts	0/53	0/2

Table 7. Measures of session success, by team

System logs shed light on some of the raid team behaviors that come about as a result of these issues. For example, our officers noted that ending a four-hour session on a failure hurt morale, and that two wins near the end of the session felt more successful than two wins near the beginning. A first-kill ending a session is obviously the best outcome of all. How raid teams prioritize the fights near the session end sheds light on leader predispositions to risk management. Table 7 shows how the two raid teams dealt with some of these issues.

This data tells a clear story: Judgment prioritized feel-good wins more than Titans did. More than that, the *positioning* of the wins within the session reveals each guild's priorities. Titans overall win percent for the study duration was 30%, and yet their final boss fight win percentage was 25.8%, below their overall average: we infer that Titans more often than not decided to throw caution to the wind and go for it, hoping for that elusive last-minute first-kill. Judgment, on the other hand, had an overall 29% win average, and yet their final fight was nearly 40% successful. Likewise, Titans' tolerance for nights without even a single win was higher by a factor of 14 than Judgment's. This data supports the hypothesis that Titans officers had more of a high risk, high reward disposition than Judgment officers.

We wanted to develop a more nuanced understanding of failure tolerance during raid sessions. Both the research and popular raiding literature and our officers all suggest that teams get into grooves, but that these grooves have limits, a phenomenon we refer to as the *flow state duration.* To get an empirical approximation of this duration, we combined two pieces of data. First is the highest number of consecutive failed attempts that have ever led to a success. The second is the longest number of minutes wiping in a boss fight (not including downtime between fights) that has led to a subsequent win. Each of these numbers suggests the outer limit a team can remain in a flow state on a single boss. Table 8 shows these numbers for our two teams.

	Titans	Judgment
Max number of unsuccessful attempts leading to eventual win (avg, all bosses)	4.6	6.6
Max amount of unsuccessful minutes leading to eventual win (avg all bosses)	31	41

Table 8. Flow state duration, by team

This data suggests that Judgment can stay in a flow state somewhat longer than Titans. Recalling that approximately 25% of all time is spent in actual boss fights, if we multiply Titans' 31 minutes by 4 (to estimate the total time spent in such sequences), we see that Titans almost exactly honored the two-hour policy specified by their officer in our interview, as cited earlier.

Setting outer limits on consecutive failure is not merely a matter of managing emotions, but it has productivity benefits. Once a guild falls out of a flow state, it begins to *backslide*, that is, to show a decrease in performance after many failed attempts on a single boss in one session. The Judgment officer also reported observing backslides and noted that these were often caused by a repeat problem that does not improve over multiple attempts. Given Titans' apparent higher tolerance for failure, Judgment's longer flow state might appear anomalous. One possible explanation for Judgment's lengthier flow states could be a difference in attitude towards failure during wipes. In our interviews, we asked both guilds' officers if they could recall sessions where they took on a boss many times without defeating it, and yet still felt that they had made progress. A Judgment officer replied that if a given boss has 3 phases, and over the course of the evening they survived into successive phases, or if they got boss health progressively lower, then that still felt like progress. A Titans officer, in contrast, replied, "Doesn't happen very often … [I] can't think of any raids where the boss didn't go down and it felt like progress was made." It is possible that Judgment had longer flow states because their progress criteria were more granular than Titans', though this is speculative.

Data at the raid session trajectory level exposes raid team behaviors that result from the leaders' dispositions with regard to managing risk and reward during the session. Our findings are compatible with prior literature on raiding, but they also add considerable detail in revealing how raid team dispositions translate into action, from feel-good strategies to the length in minutes of raid team flow states.

The Individual Boss Fight Trajectory

Boss fights last a matter of minutes, yet decisions made in this period obviously have an enormous impact on the guild's progress through raid zones. Much of the relevant data here pertains to low-level individual decision-making, such as should a healer cast a quick small heal or cast a slower more potent heal? Much of our data so far has suggested that raid teams generally have some room to make their own decisions and customize their gameplay experience to manage risk and reward in their own way. We wondered whether the boss fights themselves offered similar flexibility. We collected a number of descriptive statistics concerning specific boss fights, and they are presented in Table 9.

	Titans	Judgment
Num successful boss fights	92	105
Avg duration of successful boss fights (m:ss)	6:43	6:42
Standard deviation of successful fight durations	1:06	0:58
Num wipes	210	250
Avg duration of wipes (m:ss)	4:08	3:51
Standard deviation of wipe fight durations (m:ss)	2:00	2:16

Table 9. Durations of successful vs. failed boss fights, by team

Given the hundreds of boss fights between the two teams, spread across 12 different bosses and over three months, the average durations for both successes and failures is strikingly similar. The similarity of the two guilds' boss fight statistics suggests that these fights are deterministically designed. We infer that Blizzard has approximated the *attention span* of collaborators engaged in an intense computer-mediated collaborative activity to be around 7 minutes and designed their boss encounters to fit within this window.

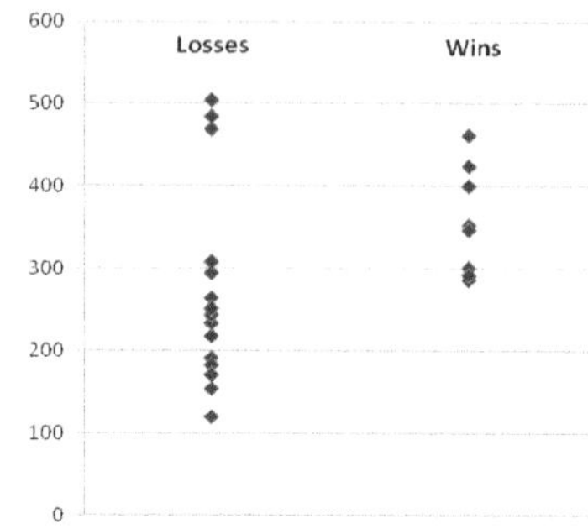

Figure 5. Scatterplot of loss vs. win durations in seconds, by Judgment on Hodir

To get a clearer picture of the timings of boss fights, we used scatterplots to show in seconds how long wins versus losses lasted per boss; Figure 5 shows a typical example. All the wins in this figure cluster around 390 seconds (6.5 minutes), while the losses cluster before or after this window. We infer that Blizzard designers use this window (400 seconds is a typical win duration for all the bosses) to help ensure that raid encounters are fun in at least three ways: 1) it introduces a sub-goal of surviving the fight long enough to get to the window, 2) it caps the fight length to prevent boredom and encourage failure, iteration, and learning, and 3) it discourages randomness in fight designs that could cause an otherwise well-executed attempt to suddenly end in failure. It should be noted that a few boss fights do not have a clear window of win. We do not believe that raid teams are explicitly aware of the window of win concept; however, our experiences suggest that some players may intuit it. It is not clear how raid teams might alter their management practices during a boss fight if they were explicitly aware of the window of win.

Data at the individual boss fight trajectory level suggests that raid teams have comparatively less ability to customize their experience or to differentiate themselves from one another during boss fights.

DISCUSSION

An ongoing question in our research was the extent to which raid teams can exercise agency, that is, make their own decisions in terms of how to raid, to manage their risks, and so forth. To the extent that this is possible, one expects to see some variation across teams. Our analyses of log data have shown many ways that raid teams, and in particular raid team leaders, can and do exercise such agency, with choices about which bosses to fight, how often and when in the sessions to insert feel-good wins, when to give up on a boss, etc. We have also found situations where raid teams have comparatively less room to differentiate themselves, primarily at the macro- and micro-levels. At the macro levels, overall failure rates, number of boss fights per hour, duration and number of raid sessions per week, and related statistics are quite similar: these seem to be defining qualities of a medium-core raiding guild. At the micro-level, we have seen that individual boss fights appear to unfold in highly scripted ways; here the game designers have exercised their power to create very specific kinds of interactive experiences.

It is the meso-level where medium-core raid teams differentiate themselves, where Blizzard steps back and provides broader latitude (though within broad limits, as we saw with the farm boss data). At the meso level team leaders make crucial decisions about how to manage failure, when to play it safe and when to go for it. Part of the pleasure of progression raiding is that later bosses are harder than earlier ones, so the guild itself must improve its own resources in order to take on new bosses. A raid team has two fundamental types of resource that it can improve: gear and skill. The acquisition of *gear*—in-game weapons, armor, and accessories—offers characters increasing statistical advantages, such as more damaging hits or stronger armor. Teams acquire better gear primarily by repeatedly defeating already vanquished bosses to farm their loot and distribute them throughout the team. The other basic type of resource is *player skill*, which includes an in-depth understanding of the statistically optimal sequence of actions, situational awareness, appropriate customization of game client UIs, the ability to quickly form good judgments about when and how to adjust tactics, etc. For all medium-core raid teams, progression entails improving both in-game gear and player skill. However, individual teams decide how to prioritize progress in these areas. The outcome of these decisions often constitutes what we consider to be *styles* of raid progression: farm progression versus achievement styles.

A *farm progression style* is embodied in decisions that prioritize taking on relatively easy bosses to ensure that the team has widely benefitted from a given boss's loot. This strategy offers strong statistical benefits, because players become well geared. It also offers social/team benefits, because all players get more opportunities to win valuable loot, increasing the pool of qualified raiders. Because of the improved in-game character gear, human play skill also can improve at a more leisurely pace. Using this style implies that achievements have lower priority, because much of the time spent raiding is taking on previously vanquished bosses. New boss progression may entail taking on only one new boss at a time. Goal setting in this style is arguably more methodical and conservative with immediate and achievable goals set before long term and higher risk goals.

An *achievement progression style* inverts the priorities. This style seeks to take down new bosses as soon as possible, even if earlier bosses have not yet been farmed. Character gear in this approach can start to languish, placing much higher demands on player skill, both individually and as a team; alternatively, gear can become stratified, as only core raiders ever receive the comparatively infrequent loot drops, creating gear inequities within guild, a situation described in [23]. Guilds acting in this style may get further into a raid instance quite quickly, but the gains in new loot are minimal because fewer easy bosses are killed. Maintaining gains may also be an issue: revisiting previously vanquished bosses is by no means an automatic win for these guilds, because they may not get practice on these bosses each week. Goal setting in this style reflects a higher tolerance for risk in favor of the higher potential returns of achieving more difficult goals.

Each of these styles represents possible ends of an emerging leadership/management spectrum, and raid teams have many options in between. And as we have already suggested, Judgment and Titans exemplify two different strategies reflecting fundamentally different predispositions about how to maximize the medium-core raiding experience for their teams: whereas Judgment leads toward a farm progression style, Titans leads toward an achievement style. These stylistic choices are evident in Judgment's prevalence for feel-good wins, higher use of farm bosses, and more systematic and predictable progress through the zone; and Titans' prevalence for achievement-before-all attitude, exemplified by their battles against Yogg, their lower reliance on farm status bosses, their comparatively chaotic kill order, and their patience for sessions without wins. From the perspective of socio-technical system design, both styles are acceptable, since both can be successful on their own terms. Indeed, the later history of the two guilds offers limited confirmation of this: more than two years and several raid zones, an expansion pack, and WoW competitor releases later, the core players of Titans and Judgment continue to raid together.

CONCLUSION

Progression raiding is a large-scale, complex social activity that places heavy demands on participants and evidently offers great rewards as well. Spanning hundreds of hours over months or years, a raid team's progression is slow and difficult. Previous research has provided a rich and compelling picture of raiding as a socio-technical experience. The present research has fleshed out this picture with new evidence of what medium-core raiding teams actually *do*, and how these behaviors relate to raid leadership decisions and constraints imposed by WoW's designers.

In particular, we identified a number of metrics, derived from system logs, that shed light on how raid team leaders are—or are not—able to customize their own play. We also saw that the behavioral decisions the metrics exposed, when viewed across different temporal trajectories, can be seen as constituting raiding styles, including farming versus achievement styles. This work sheds light on leadership aspects of virtual team collaboration in fast-paced, failure-prone socio-technical systems across different temporal trajectories.

REFERENCES

1. Andrews, S. *The Guild Leader's Handbook: Strategies and Guidance from a Battle-Scarred Veteran.* No Starch Press, San Francisco, 2010.
2. Bardzell, S. Enchanted Artifacts: Social Productivity and Identity in Virtual Material Ecologies. *Artifact, 2* (2). 123-136.

3. Bardzell, S., Bardzell, J., Pace, T. and Reed, K. Blissfully productive: grouping and cooperation in world of warcraft instance runs *Proceedings of the 2008 ACM conference on Computer supported cooperative work*, ACM, San Diego, CA, USA, 2008.
4. Boellstorff, T. *Coming of Age in Second Life: An Anthropologist Explores the Virtually Human. Princeton University Press, Princeton,* 2008.
5. Brown, B. and Barkhuus, L. Leisure and CSCW: Introduction to Special Edition. *Computer Supported Cooperative Work, 16* (1-2). 1-10.
6. Brown, B. and Bell, M. CSCW at play: 'There' as a collaborative virtual environment *Proceedings of the 2004 ACM conference on Computer supported cooperative work*, ACM, Chicago, Illinois, USA, 2004.
7. Cefkin, M., Stucky, S. and Ark, W. The grand diversion: Play, work, and virtual worlds. *Artifact, 2* (2). 108-115.
8. Chen, M. Communication, coordination, and camaraderie in World of Warcraft. *Games and Culture, 4*. 47-73.
9. Crabtree, A., Benford, S., Capra, M., Flintham, M., Drozd, A., Tandavanitj, N., Adams, M. and Farr, J.R. The Cooperative Work of Gaming: Orchestrating a Mobile SMS Game. *Computer Supported Cooperative Work, 16* (1-2). 167-198.
10. Dibbell, J. "A Rape in Cyberspace." *The Village Voice*. 21 Dec 1993
11. Ducheneaut, N., Yee, N., Nickell, E., & Moore, R.J. The life and death of online gaming communities: a look at guilds in world of warcraft. In *Proceedings of the SIGCHI conference on Human factors in computing systems (CHI '07)*. ACM, New York, 2007, 839-848.
12. Ducheneaut, N. and Moore, R.J. The social side of gaming: a study of interaction patterns in a massively multiplayer online game. In *Proceedings of the 2004 ACM conference on Computer supported cooperative work*, ACM, Chicago, Illinois, USA, 2004.
13. Ducheneaut, N., Moore, R.J. and Nickell, E. Virtual "Third Places": A Case Study of Sociability in Massively Multiplayer Games. *Computer Supported Cooperative Work, 16* (1-2). 129-166.
14. Ducheneaut, N., Yee, N., Nickell, E. and Moore, R.J. "Alone together?": exploring the social dynamics of massively multiplayer online games *Proceedings of the SIGCHI conference on Human Factors in computing systems*, ACM, Montreal, Quebec, Canada, 2006.
15. Ellis, J.B., Luther, K., Bessiere, K. and Kellogg, W.A. Games for virtual team building *Proceedings of the 7th ACM conference on Designing interactive systems*, ACM, Cape Town, South Africa, 2008.
16. Golub, A. Being in the World (of Warcraft): Raiding, Realism, and Knowledge Production in a Massively Multiplayer Online Game. *Anthropological Quarterly, 83* (1). 17-45.
17. GuildOx: WoW Guild Progress. http://www.guildox.com/go/g.asp.
18. Hansen, S., Berente, N., Pike, J. and Bateman, P.J. Productivity and Play in Organizations: Executive perspectives on the real-world organizational value of immersive virtual environments. *Artifact, 2* (2). 69-81.
19. Kahai, S., Carroll, E., and Jestice, R. Team Collaboration in Virtual Worlds. *DATABASE 38*, 4 (2007), 61-68.
20. Malaby, T.M. These great urbanist games: New Babylon and Second Life. *Artifact, 2* (2). 116-122.
21. Manninen, T., Virtual team interactions in networked multimedia games. in *In Proceedings of the 4th Annual International Workshop on Presence (PRESENCE 2001)*, (Philadelphia, PA, 2001).
22. Moore, R.J., Gathman, E.C.H., Ducheneaut, N. and Nickell, E. Coordinating joint activity in avatar-mediated interaction *Proceedings of the SIGCHI conference on Human factors in computing systems*, ACM, San Jose, California, USA, 2007.
23. Nardi, B. *My Life as a Night Elf Priest: An Anthropological Account of World of Warcraft*. University of Michigan Press, Ann Arbor, 2010.
24. Nardi, B. and Harris, J. Strangers and friends: collaborative play in world of warcraft *Proc. of CSCW'10*, ACM, Banff, Alberta, Canada, 2006.
25. Pearce, C. *Communities of Play: Emergent Cultures in Multiplayer Games and Virtual Worlds*. MIT Press, Cambridge, MA, 2009.
26. Racy. WowLogParser, 2010.
27. Reddy, M.C., Dourish, P. and Pratt, W. Temporality in Medical Work: Time also Matters. *Computer Supported Cooperative Work, 15* (1). 29-53.
28. Rezvani, J. *Guild Leadership: Lessons from the Virtual World*. Lulu, np, 2008.
29. Sweetser, P. and Wyeth, P. GameFlow: a model for evaluating player enjoyment in games. *Computer in Entertainment, 3* (3). 3-3.
30. Williams, D., Ducheneaut, N., Xiong, L., Zhang, Y., Yee, N. and Nickell, E. From Tree House to Barracks: The Social Life of Guilds in World of Warcraft *Games and Culture, 1* (4). 338-361.
31. WoWProgress: WoW Rankings and History. http://www.wowprogress.com/.
32. Yee, N. The demographics, motivations, and derived experiences of users of massively multi-user online graphical environments. *Presence, 15* (3). 309-329.
33. Yee, N. The labor of fun: How video games blur the boundaries of work and play. *Games and Culture, 1*. 68-71.
34. Yee, N., Ducheneaut, N., Nelson, L., and Likarish, P. Introverted elves & conscientious gnomes: The expression of personality in World of Warcraft. *Proc. of CHI2011*, 753-762.

Designing Online Games for Real-life Relationships: Examining QQ Farm in Intergenerational Play

Yong Ming Kow
UC Humanities Research Institute
University of California, Irvine
CA 92697
mail@kowym.com

Jing Wen
The State Key Lab of Software Engineering
Wuhan University, Wuhan
430072, China
jwen80@gmail.com

Yunan Chen
Department of Informatics
University of California, Irvine
CA 92697
yunanc@ics.uci.edu

ABSTRACT
Intergenerational players are online game players of different generations within an extended family. We investigated intergenerational play between older parents and their adult children in the popular Chinese social networking game QQ Farm. We identified game features that encourage intergenerational play. To do this, we conducted online observations and semi-structured interviews with nine pairs of Chinese parents and their adult children. The results of this study suggest that an online game for intergenerational play needs to consider a range of factors, including social and occupational responsibilities, gaming interests, and gaming expertise among extended family members. The data suggests that intergenerational online games may generally benefit from the following features: (1) low entry barrier, (2) appealing game theme, (3) online interactions that extend real-life relationships, (4) low time commitment, and (5) asynchronous play. We have also found features which may have unique appeal to Chinese intergenerational gamers.

Author Keywords
Intergenerational players, Online games, China, Social networking site.

ACM Classification Keywords
H.5.2 [User Interfaces]: User-centered design.

General Terms
Design.

INTRODUCTION
Intergenerational players are extended family members of different generations who engage in cooperative game play. Intergenerational players pose unique challenges to online game designers. In particular, social norms in the game players' real-life, e.g., parents as teachers and children as learners, may extend to online interactions, and designers of intergenerational games have to consider these issues [1,13].

CSCW'12, February 11–15, 2012, Seattle, Washington, USA.

Intergenerational games also have to appeal to all its players, although they may vary considerably in age, and possibly in computing skills [13]. Games that appeal to younger players may not appeal to older players [9]. Casual games are video games that are web-based or downloadable in small file sizes [9,10]. Researchers have found that players above forty enjoy these games more than the other game genres [9,10].

Online intergenerational game play is especially relevant in China where this research was conducted. In Chinese tradition, three consecutive generations often live together in the same household [11]. Nevertheless, with rapid economic development, many young adults in China are migrating to seek better jobs and life opportunities elsewhere [11]. New media, such as online games, present an opportunity to support extended family activities in the online environment [14].

In this study, we investigated game features that support intergenerational game play in the online game, QQ Farm. With 23 million daily players, QQ Farm is one of the most successful products of the Chinese Internet company, Tencent, Inc. Tencent developed QQ Farm in 2009 to run in QZone, Tencent's social networking site (SNS), which is similar to Facebook. We identified design features that encourage online game play between intergenerational family members. Some of these features have aligned with findings reported in the literature. In addition, we have also found other features, such as stealing of crops, which may have particular interest to Chinese players.

RELATED WORK
In 2005, the Entertainment Software Association (ESA) reported that 25% of video gamers are more than fifty years old [9,10]. The majority of these gamers preferred casual games [9,10] over fighting, racing, or sport games [12].

These older parents may adopt communication technologies, such as games, as a way to keep in touch with their children [5]. Due to the busier lifestyles of the adult children, games that require less attention from the users may better facilitate the communication needs between intergenerational members [5].

Intergenerational game design is also challenging because of how real-life relationships can influence online gaming practices [6,12]; intergenerational players often extend their existing family activities to the gaming environment [7,14]. In studies of play between grandparents and grandchildren, researchers observed that grandparents often perform teaching roles [1,5], while grandchildren act as learners [1], as happens in real-life situations.

Designing intergenerational online games for Chinese players may entail additional challenges. Golub and Lingley [4] describe the social perspective of Chinese parents towards online games:

> The allure of Internet games for children is like the poison of opium in China so many years ago; it doesn't discriminate between the poor and the rich, between those of high or low position. It doesn't matter if you're an unemployed worker, a wealthy businessman, or a Party cadre, the highest hopes of innumerable parents for their children's future may well be destroyed by Internet games.

Many Chinese parents vigorously disapprove of the idea of their children playing video games, let alone having the idea of playing them, themselves.

QQ FARM

QQ Farm is a popular online game in China and is widely played by both young working adults and their older parents. See Figure 1 showing two older parents discussing the game.

Figure 1 Two parents discussing QQ Farm

QQ Farm has a farm simulation theme, similar to the popular online game known as *Farmville* in the U.S. Nevertheless, features in the two games differ slightly. For example, QQ Farm allows players to steal other players' crops, a common children's game in rural China, whereas Farmville contains tractors which are more commonly seen in U.S. farms.

In QQ Farm, players act as farm owners and manage their own farms. Besides common farming activities such as cultivating, irrigating, and harvesting crops as real farmers do, players can visit farms owned by their SNS friends. In their friends' farm, players can perform limited actions—some helpful, others mischievous. Friends can help perform the weeding and the watering of plants. Friends can also steal matured crops, resulting in the victim losing part of his potential income. Each player has access to a personal message board telling him when his friends came to his farm and what his friends did. Each player can also personalize her farm, such as giving it a name.

METHODS

We performed semi-structured interviews with nine pairs of Chinese parents and their children between March 2010 and November 2010. Participants were recruited through the snowball sampling method. The parents were aged from 47 to 66 years old. The children were aged from 18 to 42 years old. In order to observe various online interactions affected by different real-life living arrangements, we examined four pairs of intergenerational players who lived together in the same households in China, or shared the same neighborhood; the other five pairs of participants lived apart, with the parents living in China and the children residing in the United States and elsewhere. All participants had at least six months of experience playing QQ Farm.

The semi-structured interviews pertained to experiences of intergenerational play in QQ Farm. Specifically, we asked: (1) How did you start playing the QQ Farm game? (2) How do you play the game in general? and (3) How do you play with your parent/child?

We interviewed all parents and children. Of the eighteen interviews, sixteen took place over the telephone, one was performed in-person, and one using instant messenger. All interviews were conducted in Chinese. Interviews were audio recorded and transcribed in Chinese, and then translated into English.

Three researchers independently conducted open coding of the transcripts to identify salient themes [3]. The initial themes and relationships were identified gradually in a manner of convergence. One researcher coded the rest of the data iteratively based on the initial themes. When all codes and memos were collected, the researchers grouped them in line with the categories or properties they represented.

KEY FINDINGS

We present five design features in QQ Farm that generally support and encourage intergenerational play. These key features are identified as factors that can be used in designing a wide range of online games for intergenerational play.

Low entry barrier

QQ Farm is easy to understand; and this feature appeals to novice gamers. The game rules are intuitive and mirror real-life activities. For example, the players' primary actions are to seed, fertilize, weed, water, harvest, and sell plants. This is easy for players to comprehend. *Liu*, a retired father, began to play QQ Farm when his daughter recommended it to him. He explains how he later became an avid player and even achieved a higher gaming level than his daughter.

> Last year my daughter invited me to play QQ Farm, so that I could kill time... Unexpectedly, this game is very simple to learn. Soon, I mastered all the techniques... In order to reach higher game level (game ranks), I set up five different game accounts so that I can gather more crops... now I am the top player in my friends list. (Liu, 61, China)

Intuitive operations and uncomplicated game rules can reduce barriers for novice players, which included many of those from the older generations we studied, encouraging their participation in online games.

Widely appealing game theme

Online gaming in China has become a controversial social issue, often being seen as a contest to parental authority and a hindrance to children's academic achievement [4]. However, we did not hear this rhetoric in our interviews. Rather, parents viewed QQ Farm's farming theme as appealing and viewed playing the game as a reasonable form of relaxation. *Zhang* is a proud mother of two children studying in American universities:

> My son and daughter have been hard-working students since they entered high school. Sometimes I can feel that they are tired and stressed by their studies... They needed other activities beyond burying themselves in books...I think that playing QQ farm could be viewed as an entertainment for them... (Zhang, 57, China)

Unlike other online games, QQ Farm has a good reputation among parents who believe that playing QQ Farm is a way to lighten up their life. Parents like Liu readily accepted QQ Farm when their children introduced it to them. Parents like Zhang are supportive of their children playing QQ Farm outside of their academic work as a form of relaxation. An appealing game theme makes parents more likely to play the game themselves and to encourage their children to do so.

Online interactions that extend real-life relationships

QQ Farm provides features that allow intergenerational players to convey messages of love, care, and concern for their gaming partners. *Peng*, a faculty member at a Chinese university, told us:

> My mother and father took great care of their own farms. To help them level quickly, my husband and I intentionally create opportunities for them to steal crops from our farms. And we have never stolen my parents' crops... My parents were so happy knowing what we have done for them. I have even bought a laptop for them [so that they have their own machine] to play QQ Farm. (Peng, 36, China)

Peng still lives with her parents, who help her take care of her child. Every member of Peng's household plays QQ Farm. For Peng's family, online games reinforce their values because family members behave online as they would in real-life, for example, gifting each other and giving a helping hand. The online interactions of QQ Farm reinforce Peng's family identity in the same way real-life family activities do. Online gaming activities have, in other words, become an online version of her family's real-life activities.

Low time commitment

Participants play QQ Farm in a way that does not affect their daily activities, such as their job. The game allows players to play as—and when—they want. QQ Farm also does not require players to play continuously for a long period of time in each gaming session. *Lee*, who is a father and a senior official of an institution in the city of Wuhan, China, told us the merits of this feature.

> Playing QQ Farm does not take up a big chunk of time. For example, some crops need two or three days to mature and harvest, so it is not necessary for me to attend to my farm in the meantime... on busy days, I usually logon to QQ farm one to two times a day. On other days, I logon three to five times a day. (Lee, 59, China)

This flexibility allows players to participate without affecting their real-life activities. In this sense, game play is inclusive of players with varying real-life commitments.

Asynchronous play

QQ Farm does not require players to logon at the same time. *Tong* is a Ph.D. student in the U.S. His story shows how he and his mother play QQ farm across different time zones.

> I helped my mother manage her farm when she is asleep in China... I have my mother's game account, so I can harvest her mature crops and even steal her friends' crops. In turn, when I was sleeping, my mother did the same things for me... that was why we leveled quicker than others, ha-ha... . (Tong, 29, U.S.)

Children like Tong can attend to their parents' farm when their parents are offline. As such, extended family members living in different time zones can participate in cooperative play, just as Tong and his mother helped each other level, without the need to logon at the same time.

Asynchronous play is important because intergenerational family members are becoming less likely to live together. They are also likely to have different social and occupational responsibilities. For players varying widely in localities and real-life responsibilities, asynchronous play allows them to cooperate in the same game without the need for them to be playing all at once.

DISCUSSION

Many of the features identified in our study have aligned with what have been reported in the prior literature, which included studies conducted in the U.S., Europe, and Australia [1,5,9,10,13]. These include a low entry barrier, a widely appealing game theme, online interactions that extend real-life relationships, low time commitment, and asynchronous play. The first three features are relevant to intergenerational play and the last two can be broadened to other casual game designs.

As previous studies have reported, parents feel motivated to adopt communication technologies that interest their children [5], and QQ Farm is used as a communication device for intergenerational family members to keep in touch. In addition, older gamers have been reported as having lower expertise in video gaming [13]. Some older gamers, like Liu, are attracted to QQ Farm because it is easy to learn. A gentle learning curve can help older gamers participate in game play (see [13]).

Intergenerational online games need to cater to players with heavy real-life commitments [5]. Playing QQ Farm also requires as little as a few minutes a day, which is ideal for busy players. For players, like Tong and his mother, who are located in different time zones, QQ Farm allows players to play asynchronously, accommodating each player's own real-life schedule. Older gamers, like Liu, are attracted to QQ Farm because it is easy to learn.

QQ Farm also contains features that seem to have evolved out of the Chinese gaming environment. One of these is "*stealing of crops*." Despite being seemingly unethical, crop stealing was seen by Peng's family as an act of care and concern. One possible explanation is that Chinese players see stealing crops in farming games as a form of social interaction [2]. Crop stealing among players with close-knit ties, such as family members or old friends, is seen by some players as a way of sending daily regards, a display of cordialness and intimacy with each other [2].

Considering that older Chinese parents were reported to distrust video games [4], our older interviewees were surprisingly receptive to QQ Farm. China has only freshly emerged from a rural society. The Chinese rural population only recently saw a reduction from 76% rural in 1985, to 56% in 2006 [8]. Thus, many Chinese individuals, feeling acquainted with the soil, and with rural experiences fresh in their memory, may identify better with the game's farming theme.

While the Chinese may have kept their affinity to notions of the soil due to many of them having actual experiences living on farms, the success of Farmville in the U.S. suggests that such affinity may be rooted culturally in other ways. Notably Farmville contains features, such as tractors, that reflect U.S. notions of farming not found in China. Thus, even when a farming theme appeals to a culture of players, what constitutes "farming" may differ in specific ways.

CONCLUSION

We have identified general features that support intergenerational online gaming. These design features include a low entry barrier, a widely appealing game theme, a low time commitment, online interactions that extend real-life relationships, and asynchronous play. At the same time, designers may consider paying attention to specific features, such as the stealing of crops, which are appealing to the Chinese gamers.

REFERENCES

1 Davis, H., Vetere, F., Gibbs, M., and Francis, P. Come Play with Me: Designing Technologies for Intergenerational Play. *UAIS, Online First* (2011).

2 Fan, X., Bi, S., Mo, S., and Yang, B. Social Interaction and Social Capital of Farming Games in Social Networking Sites. *chinaxwcb.com*, http://data.chinaxwcb.com/zgcb/shuzishidai/201102/7656.html (2011).

3 Glaser, B. G. and Strauss, A. L. *The discovery of grounded theory: Strategies for qualitative research.* Aldine de Gruyter, Hawthorne, NY, 1967.

4 Golub, A. and Lingley, K. "Just Like the Qing Empire" : Internet Addiction, MMOGs, and Moral Crisis in Contemporary China. *Games and Culture*, 3, 1 (2008).

5 Lindley, S. Shades of Lightweight: Supporting Cross-generational Communication through Home Messaging. *UAIS, Online First* (2011).

6 Lindtner, S., Nardi, B., Wang, Y., Mainwaring, S., Jing, H., and Liang, W. A Hybrid Cultural Ecology: World of Warcraft in China. In *Proc. CHI 2008* (2008).

7 Nardi, B. and Harris, J. Strangers and Friends: Collaborative Play in World of Warcraft. In *Proc. CSCW 2006* (2006), ACM Press.

8 NBS CHINA. *China's population, 1969-2006.* National Bureau of Statistics of China, Beijing, 2010.

9 Pearce, C. The Truth About Baby Boomer Gamers : A Study of Over-Forty Computer Game Players. *Games and Culture, 3: 142* (2008).

10 Schutter, B. Never Too Old to Play: The Appeal of Digital Games to an Older Audience. *Games and Culture, 6: 155* (2011).

11 Sheng, X. and Settles, B.H. Intergenerational Relationships and Elderly Care in China: A Global Perspective. *Current Sociology*, 54, 2 (2006).

12 Su, N. Street fighter IV: braggadocio off and on-line. In *Proc. CSCW 2010* (2010), ACM Press.

13 Voida, A. and Greenberg, S. Console Gaming Across Generations: Exploring Intergenerational Interactions in Collocated Console Gaming. *UAIS* (2011).

14 Wen, J., Kow, Y.M., and Chen, Y. Online Games and Family Ties: Influences of Social Networking Game on Family Relationship. In *Interact 2011* (2011).

Integrating Local and Remote Worlds Through Channel Blending

Ellen Isaacs, Peggy Szymanski, Yutaka Yamauchi, James Glasnapp and Kyohei Iwamoto*

Palo Alto Research Center (PARC)
3333 Coyote Hill Rd.
Palo Alto, CA 94304
{firstname.lastname}@parc.com

*Sony Corp.
1-7-1 Konan Minato-ku
Tokyo, 108-0075 Japan
kyohei.iwamoto@jp.sony.com

ABSTRACT

Recent advances in ubiquitous technology have greatly changed the way people stay connected. We conducted an in-depth video shadowing study to observe how close-knit groups use all the technology at their disposal to stay in touch and share their lives. We observed a pattern of related behaviors that we call *channel blending,* the integration of interactions and content over multiple channels into one coherent conversation, often including both local and remote participants. Channel blending is the opposite of multitasking in that it involves merging many lines of focus into one, rather than switching attention between them. We discuss ways technology could better support this emerging style of multichannel content-sharing and communication.

Author Keywords

Computer-mediated communication, mobile, ethnography, video shadowing, conversation analysis, channel blending.

ACM Classification Keywords: H.5.m. Information interfaces and presentations: Miscellaneous.

General Terms: Human Factors.

INTRODUCTION

The past five years or so have seen dramatic changes in the way people connect and share their experiences with others. People can now choose from a wide range of technology options when connecting remotely, and they can connect from almost anywhere any time. There are also more ways for people to capture their experiences and more options for sharing those experiences and other recorded content.

Not only are there more technology options, but the nature of content sharing and communication has also been changed by technology in the following fundamental ways:

- **Bite-sized content:** The content people share has become much smaller in that it takes less time to consume and often generate. People send one-sentence text updates rather than long emails, they share short video clips rather than full-length movies, and they share individual photos rather than a whole roll of film.
- **Ubiquitous content:** Content is available from almost anywhere through internet-enabled devices.
- **Proliferation of captured experiences:** People are capturing their experiences in many ways, not just taking photos and videos, but also using applications to track their sleep cycles, game-playing activity, and travel patterns, to name just a few.
- **Ubiquitous communication:** People can connect with each other from almost anywhere using a wide range of devices and media.

In this study, we set out to understand how these relatively recent changes in our communication and content-sharing technologies have affected the way people are staying connected and sharing their lives with those they care about. We did so not by looking at any one technology but instead by centering our investigation on groups of close contacts and video shadowing them to see how they enlisted different technologies (or not) to stay connected.

This study builds on the extensive body of research on the adoption and use of *individual* technologies by examining how and when people *integrate* and *combine* them to keep in touch. For example, studies of mobile text chat show that people use that technology to coordinate their activities, to arrange a time to talk later, and to chat [8, 16], and it can also be used to maintain a sense of "ambient virtual copresence" with others [10]. People also maintain this ongoing background awareness by sending each other photos through their phones [20], and by sharing status updates, photos, and links through social media [11, 15].

Studies of home video communication indicate that people use video conferencing both to support focused conversations and to maintain ongoing open connections that provide a similar sense of ambient co-presence [13, 14]. Although video is usually used for talking-heads style conversation, people also commonly use it to show each other things, such as a tour of their home or their children's activities. However, video also requires dedicated time, as people don't feel comfortable multitasking while video chatting. As a result, finding a time to video chat can be a challenge, especially for friends and family separated across time zones [3]. Social media addresses this problem by allowing people to check in asynchronously [11, 15].

People are starting to adopt mobile video to do a similar set of activities, specifically to keep in touch, coordinate, and show each other things, such as products in a shop [19]. However, the public nature of mobile video can cause socially awkward situations, since bystanders can easily overhear interactions and participants are more accountable to each other for their visual surroundings.

A common thread among these studies is that people use different technologies to stay aware of and connect with others, and they adapt their approach based on the strengths and constraints of each technology. What isn't well understood is how people combine them to achieve their goal of staying connected. In this study, we set out to learn: (a) How do people use and combine the myriad technologies available to stay connected, coordinate, and share their experiences? (b) How effectively are current technologies supporting people's needs? (c) How are people working around gaps in the patchwork of technologies to stay close to one another? By answering these questions, we can learn whether current technology is adequately supporting people's desire to stay connected and if not, how it may be improved.

We addressed these questions by conducting an in-depth video shadowing study in which we directly observed ten people in four close-knit groups as they went about their activities and connected with one another. For each group, we video recorded each member over the same period of time and micro-analyzed the interactions from each person's point of view. We captured interactions that varied among different dimensions, including cases when they were (a) physically together vs. separated by distance, (b) mobile vs. stationary, (c) sharing content vs. just talking, and (d) one-on-one vs. in groups.

Through a detailed analysis of these video recordings we saw a variety of ways that people's practices are changing as they adopt current technology. In particular, we saw how people are incorporating local people into their remote interactions and, conversely, bringing remote content into their face-to-face (F2F) conversations. We also saw how bite-sized, ubiquitous content is altering the way people tell each other the stories of their lives, and how people interact over a series of related interactions, both mediated and in person. By watching interactions as they unfolded over time, we noticed ways that technology is not adequately supporting these changing behavior patterns.

METHOD

To identify suitable participants for video shadowing, we recruited two- and three-person groups that considered themselves highly connected. Based on a screening survey and a logging study (not discussed here), we narrowed a set of 14 potential groups down to four that demonstrated they communicated with one another at least 1-3 times per day, used at least five communication technologies, were at least moderately mobile, and held a range of attitudes about technology, from enthusiastic to uninterested. The four groups consisted of two triads and two pairs, made up of eight women and two men, mostly in their 20s but ranging in age from 18 to 35. (The gender imbalance reflected the proportion of women and men who responded to our call for "groups of friends or family who like to stay in close contact.") All participants lived in the San Francisco Bay Area, except that one group included a member in Austin, Texas. Participants were paid $300.

Video shadowing consisted of separately recording each member of a group as they went about their activities during the same 5-6 hour period. Each researcher observed a different group member. Participants wore wireless microphones to ensure that we captured high-quality sound. When they used technology, we zoomed in on the screen to capture their mediated interactions as much as possible. During the shadowing we observed them in their homes, in their cars, and in many public places, including stores, restaurants, a farmer's market, a mall, and on the street. Despite our initial concerns about video recording in public, only once were we asked to stop recording, in a store, until we received management approval. Other researchers have avoided this method out of an understandable concern about the practicality of following and recording people all day [8, 10], but we were pleasantly surprised to find that it was relatively unproblematic and yielded very rich interactions.

To analyze the data, we used a Conversation Analysis (CA) approach in which interactions are analyzed turn by turn, taking the participant's point of view as the conversational interaction unfolds [12]. First, each researcher reviewed their video and selected segments they judged to be of interest to our research questions. Video clips usually lasted 1-5 minutes; longer interactions were divided into shorter segments. We then viewed these video clips as a group and did an initial assessment. Clips deemed to be of particular interest were transcribed in detail according to the standard format [23], including gestures, intonation, glances, etc. If the interaction involved other members of that group, we clipped the same segment from those videos and combined them to generate one "mosaic" video showing the interaction from everyone's point of view simultaneously. As a group, we then analyzed these merged video segments in more detail, repeatedly viewing them to ground our understanding of what was happening, using the transcripts as analytic aids. As we came to understand the videos, we sometimes went back to clip other segments that involved similar behaviors in another context, and in this way we built up collections of excerpts that demonstrated themes or patterns of action. (Isaacs & Szymanski [9] explains our method in greater detail.)

The CA method generates an in-depth understanding of the sort of behavior people take for granted, which makes it difficult to detect through self-report methods such as diary or probe studies, interviews, or experience sampling. It does not tell us how common these behaviors are, but it is useful in alerting us to patterns of action that may foretell interesting and subtle interactional shifts that may suggest opportunities for future technologies.

FINDINGS

During the video shadowing study, we recorded about 48 hours of the 10 participants' experiences. We clipped 83 interactions, transcribed 38 of them, and deeply analyzed 29 that best illustrated the patterns of interest. Our analysis revealed several ways that the basic changes in current technology discussed earlier (bite-sized content, ubiquitous content, proliferation of captured experiences, and ubiquitous communication) affected our participants' interactions, particularly when face-to-face. Further, we noted ways that technology is not adequately supporting these evolving interaction patterns.

The main theme that emerged from our data was the *integration* of interactions and content over multiple channels into *one coherent conversation*, often involving both local and remote participants. We call this phenomenon *channel blending*, where a channel indicates a means of connecting with a person or content (including face-to-face). Examples include cases where people: blended connections with both remote and local people into one interaction, interacted remotely with people over multiple channels, integrated data from multiple channels into local interactions, and switched channels when interacting with the same people over time.

Channel blending can be seen as the opposite of multitasking, which is the switching between multiple *unrelated* tasks or conversations conducted in parallel or in rapid succession, often across multiple media [4]. The challenge for multitaskers is in managing interruptions that divert attention from one task to another. In contrast, channel blending involves *combining* different activities into one interaction, and the challenge involves keeping people informed about content or communications from other channels so that everyone can maintain common ground. The following sections describe the ways our participants channel blended and discuss ways technology could better support this phenomenon.

Integrating local people into remote interactions

Perhaps the most compelling example of channel blending occurred when small groups attempted to carry on a synchronous interaction with both local and remote participants. This happened many times with a variety of technologies, and it generally involved one person playing the role of a "pivot person," integrating the contributions of local and remote participants. Since current technology doesn't support this configuration, it required skill and finesse to avoid breakdowns and pull off a satisfying interaction for all.

In many cases, the pivot person was focused on a remote conversation while a local person (or people) intermittently participated in the interaction. During phone and video interactions, the local parties could overhear the conversation, and with IM, texting, or email exchanges the pivot person read aloud the message being exchanged. The local people (who might have existed at both ends of the mediated connection) contributed to the interaction through the pivot person.

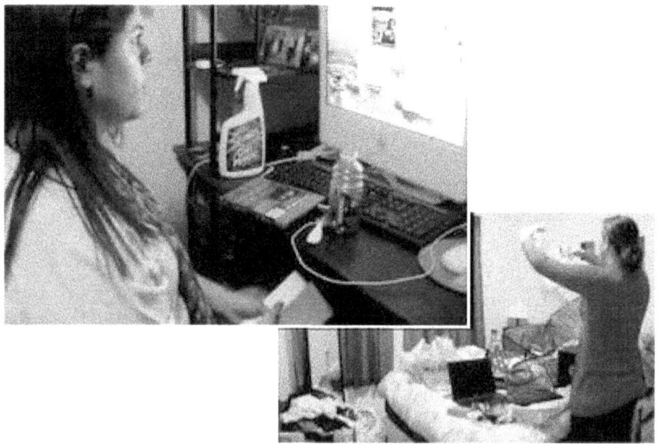

Fig 1. Anita (left) video chats with friends in her room as Cathy (right) eavesdrops while packing for a trip in her room.

One example of this situation occurred among two roommates in California (Anita and Cathy) and their friends in New York (Bo and John). Anita was in her room video-chatting with Bo and John, while Cathy was in the adjacent room packing for a business trip to Dublin. Cathy could hear the exchange, and during a topic transition she called out a question about whether to bring her pepper spray. This led to an exchange regarding movies involving danger in foreign cities, with Anita shuttling the comments back and forth between Cathy and the men. (We present transcripts in a simplified format. Square brackets in color indicate overlapping speech, and numbers in parentheses indicate pause lengths.)

Over video conference	**Calling between rooms**
	Cathy: Should I bring my pepper spray?
Anita: Cathy wants to know if she should bring her pepper spray	
Bo: Yes. Eh has she seen *Taken?*	
Anita: eh heh actually she hasn't seen *Taken*, I asked her and she said no	
John: Okay, that's good	
Bo: Has she seen *Hostile?*	
	Anita: Have you seen *Hostile,* Cathy?
	Cathy: No I I [refuse]
Anita: [she doesn't] like scary movies	
	Cathy: I refuse (0.4)
Bo: Is she gonna drink a lot of beer in Dublin?	
Anita: Wait, she can answer that.	
	Anita: Are you going to drink a lot of beer in Dublin?
	Cathy: Uuum, (0.2) probably.
Anita: Probably	

In this interaction, Anita acted as a pivot person, sometimes relaying the comments back and forth between the video participants and her roommate and sometimes answering on her behalf. A short while later, Anita conveyed Cathy's comments by simply incorporating them into her own, as

John wondered why Anita's upcoming business trip was to LA instead of a more exotic location.

John: Why don't *you* go abroad?
Anita: Yeaphhh
Cathy: I love when they ask you like that, like you have a choice
Anita: (laughing) I know, I don't really get a choice too much in the ma-, she's like 'I like how they ask you like you have a choice.' I don't really have too much of a choice,
Bo: What do you mean, I thought you could [pick a different program]
Cathy: ["Anita loves LA"] (as if quoting their bosses)
Anita: They're just like, "Anita loves LA, we should just put her there."

Cathy found John's question amusing, as it implies they have a choice about where they are sent on business, and Anita incorporated this reaction into her responses, first suggesting the comment came from Cathy ("*She's like*, 'I like how they ask you'") and then simply mimicking Cathy's personification of their bosses as if it were her own response. Anita thus showed great skill in blending the two separate channels to create a four-person interaction.

It's worth noting how Cathy moved in and out of the interaction during the video chat. She easily could have stopped packing and joined Anita in her room, but even when she called out she continued packing and made no gesture, or even glance, toward Anita's room. She clearly did not want to become a fully ratified member of the conversation but instead preferred to play a peripheral role.

We saw other configurations of this type of channel blending, and they weren't always handled as smoothly. In this excerpt, Lee and Alana were walking down the street as Lee spoke with Scott over the phone. Several times Alana interjected to make a suggestion or ask a question of Scott (through Lee), causing Lee to miss Scott's utterance and leading to breakdowns in the phone conversation. In one case, after Lee had just given Scott the combination to his locker (where he wanted him to return some sheet music), Scott confirmed the number just as Alana suggested another way to get the music.

Over phone call	**Walking side by side**
Scott: Four [forty-two (.) one eight three eight?]	
	Alana: [or you know what, he can bring it] when we do the gig, (0.2) the China gig
Lee: Uh huh, wait, what? (0.4) hello?	
Scott: What did you (0.2) hello? (0.4)	
Lee: Yeah, what's up?	
Scott: Four forty two, one eight three eight?	
Lee: Yeah. (0.2) Or you can just bring it on Friday at the China gig.	

In this case, Alana's comments during the locker combination confirmation sequence caused a breakdown, but Lee still managed to incorporate her suggestion into his next turn. In another example of this type of channel blending, Alana was instant messaging (IM) with Scott when Lee picked her up for dinner. She read aloud Scott's messages and then incorporated Lee's comments into her responses. Other cases involved different combinations of media, such as video chatting while using IM to consult with others as questions arose, and including local others while responding to email messages.

Other studies have also reported cases when overhearers became engaged in remote interactions through video and audio media spaces [5, 26], and through phone calls [21]. Some have also reported on troubles encountered when connecting remote and local spaces via home video conferences [14], mobile video calls [19], and mobile phone calls [21]. However, no one has highlighted this activity as a phenomenon in its own right and shown how it occurs over a variety of media, including text-based ones. The fact that we saw so many types of examples suggest that channel blending may be becoming more commonplace with the prevalence of mobile devices that allow people to connect from anywhere over multiple channels.

Technology implication: This finding indicates that there is a compelling opportunity to better support such small-group synchronous interactions among both local and remote participants. Even though there are many communication technologies available, none embraces the idea that when people connect remotely, they are often sharing a space with other parties who may also want to become engaged in the interaction. Instead, most such technology is designed to support one person at either end (phone calls, texting, IM, video chat) or many remote participants (social media, email). People adapt these technologies to incorporate local parties (to various degrees of success), suggesting that they would welcome a technology that explicitly supports multichannel sharing.

It is natural to assume that what's needed is something like a speakerphone that can provide a full connection to everyone in the conversation. But we saw how people don't necessarily want to become fully engaged in all the interactions around them, so the solution needs to take a subtler approach. Group membership is fluid, as people engage to different degrees at different times. Such a technology needs to let people vary their degree of participation over time and connect asynchronously, while letting distributed participants interpret and smoothly adjust to others' varying level of engagement. Some researchers have explored ways to support small, distributed groups where their level of participation varied over time [6, 24], but those did not incorporate local interactions.

Integrating remote content into local interactions

People also channel blended by integrating into their local interactions information from remote communications received through a mobile device. It was common for participants engaged in F2F interactions to check for updates in their text exchanges, Twitter feeds, status messages, emails, turn-based games, and so on. When they did, they frequently introduced into the local conversation information from these remote exchanges, again attempting to bridge their remote and local worlds. What often emerged with this type of interaction was an *episodic conversational style* in which a succession of unconnected or loosely related topics were each discussed for a short period. What fascinated us was how this F2F episodic conversation mirrored exactly the style of interactions people were simultaneously carrying on remotely with a multitude of others through their devices.

One example of this pattern occurred when Cathy and Anita went out to dinner. Both of them alternated their attention between their phones and each other, sometimes entering text while also in conversation. Figure 2 diagrams the 9 minute 16 second period after they sat down and before ordering. They briefly discussed 17 topics, 9 generated from mobile phone communications and 8 from the local environment, with long gaps in between. The longest topic was discussed for 1 min 20 secs and the shortest for 4 secs.

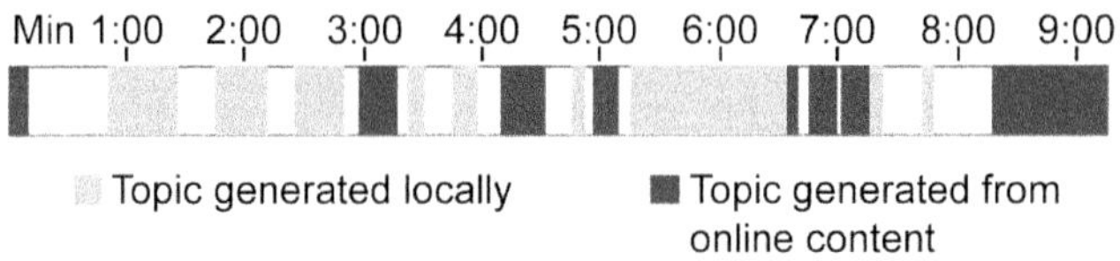

Figure 2. Duration of topics generated from local and online sources over a 9-minute period.

Examples of topics based on online content included Cathy's comment, *"Eric texted, 'Oh my God, are you being followed yet? What are you guys doing? Are people staring at you like you're a celebrity?'"* and Anita's report on the weather in New York, *"Arnold tweeted, he's like 'It's like Florida.' I wish it were, the weather's like blah here."* As for locally generated topics, Cathy asked about a work colleague, *"Didn't Evan look so upset when he came in this morning? Like did you notice that?"* and she complained about the slow service at the restaurant, *"I feel like they're ignoring us."* Each topic was discussed briefly and the discussion ended with minimal or no explicit closure. Often when Cathy or Anita responded to the tweet or text message, they read aloud their comment as they typed.

This interaction is notable for several reasons: First, their F2F conversation integrated multiple channels of remote interactions carried out on their phones, some synchronous (text messages) and some asynchronous (Twitter and FourSquare updates). Second, as noted, their conversation had the same episodic flavor as their online interactions. Third, neither of them gave any indication that this style of interaction, with its many gaps and lack of sustained shared focus, was problematic. They treated this multichannel style of interaction as normal.

This last point is interesting because it suggests how this activity again contrasts with multitasking. Adults and teens alike have reported that they consider it rude to carry on other activities while engaged in F2F or phone conversation – even though they sometimes do it themselves [1, 2, 21]. Yet in this case, the two treated it as unremarkable, likely because, as they simultaneously surfed their phones, they shared their finds with each other, thus turning their individual actions into a joint activity.

Technology implications: Although these two friends smoothly shared their remote interactions with each other, there may be ways to better support this activity. We might let remote members become aware of the local interaction or allow local people to easily join in the remote interactions through their own devices.

Integrating remote content into local interaction

When co-located, people also channel blended by sharing recorded content from multiple devices at the same time or in quick succession. It was interesting to us that these interactions usually followed the classic three-phase structure of storytelling [22], even though the stories were based on recorded content: (1) a *preface* in which someone introduces the story, foreshadows the expected the response (e.g. *"the funniest thing happened to me"*), and reserves a block of time to tell the story; (2) the *telling* where the story is told; and (3) the *response*, where people react (ideally by expressing the expected emotion) and discuss the story. It is common for others to follow up with stories of their own that share a common point or theme [22].

This pattern was nicely illustrated by the group of three musicians who got together with another friend (Jeff) for an evening of socializing. Rather than telling their own stories, they shared a steady stream of videos, music, and websites, displayed on their phones, a laptop, and a TV being used as a computer monitor. One of them would preface a "story" by introducing the content (e.g., "*Have you seen the dancing cockatoo?*"), then after searching for it they watched the video, which constituted the story. Then they responded with laughter or jokes, after which someone brought up another related video or song. This pattern of sharing a sequence of loosely related content can be seen as *episodic content sharing,* similar to our previous example except that the sharing is of pre-existing content rather than ongoing communications with others.

Because this type of content can be experienced in a short period of time and accessed from anywhere, people can now have this sort of media-sharing exchange of previously viewed content. They don't need to plan in advance what they want to share but instead can introduce media-based "stories" spontaneously based on the flow of conversation. In effect, they can create their own "collaboratively curated experience" on the fly.

It's worth noting that this pattern of sharing recorded content is different from earlier times when people got together to watch a two-hour movie – typically one that no one had seen previously. Here, people experienced a series of short videos or songs that were familiar to at least one of them. Indeed, this type of storytelling-through-media worked well as long as people were sharing content they had previously seen or heard. It became awkward as soon as they sought out new content. For example, when the musicians ran out of previously viewed content, they attempted to explore other music-related websites. This led to awkward interactions because the content was not always of interest or easily experienced together, especially when they landed on text-only web pages. At one point when Alana read aloud the highlights of a web page, Jeff teased her, saying, *"We have eyes,"* implying they could read for themselves, and the others rebuked him for being rude.

Another type of channel blending occurred during that same evening when they shared technology-based documentation of their lives rather than content produced by others. In one example, Alana showed the others a graph of her sleep cycle that had been recorded by a smartphone app. Upon establishing interest, Alana, who was seated between Lee and Scott on her right and Jeff on her left (see Figure 3), handed her phone to Lee, who remarked on how late she woke up. At the same time, she and Jeff interwove a related conversation in a style reminiscent of Anita and Cathy's dinner interaction. Then Scott responded by sharing his own sleep cycle on his phone, which he happened to have recorded with the same app.

Figure 3. Alana turns her phone toward Lee and Scott as Jeff looks on. Scott has just taken his phone out of his pocket.

Lee, Scott, and Alana	**Alana and Jeff**
Alana: (Turns toward Lee) Do you want to see my sleep cycle?	
Lee: Yes	
Alana: (Hands phone to Lee, Scott looks too)	
	Jeff: Oh, do you have that app
	Alana: Yeah
	Jeff: that wakes you up at an intelligent time?
	Alana: Yeah
(Scott takes out his iPhone, opens his sleep cycle app)	
Lee: [You woke up at ten?]	
	Jeff: Hjoo, that's like the only re- not the only re- that's [been the reason why] I [didn't want to buy] that app
	Alana: [It's not that great]

Alana: Yes, it was amazing
Lee: heh heh heh (Passes phone back to Alana)
Alana: It was the greatest thing ever. Actually I woke up at noon (0.2) to be- (turns phone toward Lee and Scott) I turned it off
Lee: heh heh
Alana: And then I was like, *screw this* (emphasizes by swiping phone down twice in sync with words)
Scott: (Shows his sleep cycle to Alana) I- I didn't sleep long enough last night for it to record, actually the past [two nights]
Lee: (Points to Scott's phone, takes out his phone) [What happened] did you like die for like three hours?
Scott: No this one, I had dropped my phone off the bed

What struck us about this interaction (beyond Alana's agility in managing the two related conversations) is how the technology was seamlessly introduced by both Alana and Scott as a way to "tell the story." Alana prefaced her story in the usual way by introducing the topic of her sleep cycle, but then she didn't tell a story at all but instead handed her phone to Lee, so the app *became* the story. The response came when Lee teased her about sleeping so late, which led her to elaborate on how she slept even later after she turned off the app. Then Scott followed up in the classic style by sharing his sleep cycle on his own device, which again became the story, leading to Lee's response joking about a flat portion of the graph that occurred when the phone fell off the bed.

The technology can become the story because it is a physical representation of a prior experience and because it is readily available at a moment's notice without any prior preparation. People have long used photographs to tell the story [7], but now it happens with many other forms of bite-sized captured experiences accessible from anywhere.

In contrast, we saw similar cases where the participants were remotely connected over multiple channels but were unable to achieve this seamless sharing across channels. In one particularly painful case, a pair of sisters (Drina and Clarisse) were on the phone and Drina told Clarisse how she had been Facebook "friended" by a grade school teacher who was the father of a boy she had had a crush on, Benny Bordick. Clarisse wanted to see the photo of Benny so Drina told her to look in the father's "Easter pictures" album on Facebook. As Clarisse struggled to find it, Drina got distracted by an IM from a friend and so provided little help to Clarisse, who eventually realized she couldn't see the photo because she wasn't friends with the father.

Over phone call	**Over Facebook chat**
Drina: Easter pictures.	
	Drina: (receives text message)
Drina: Go under Easter pictures.	
Clarisse: A- the album's called Easter pictures, right?	
Drina: Mmhmm (crooks phone into her neck, moves hands to keyboard)	

Clarisse: Yeah, I don't see it, it just says Rainbow and Profile pictures (Clicks on Rainbow album)
(6.0)
Drina: Ohh
Clarisse: I don't see it, let me look under Benny Bordi- what is his name? (Enters 'Benny Bord' into search field).
(4.0)
Clarisse: What does he go by, Ben? What's his real name?
Drina: (typing) Ah, I love
Drina: No it's not him. It's hi- it's a picture on his dad's thing
Drina: (typing) that song [Enter]
Clarisse: Let me see.
(3.0)
Clarisse: I guess cuz I'm not his friend maybe I can't- I mean
Drina: (typing) That should be his theme song [Enter]
Clarisse: yeah, I don't see any pictures.
(2.0)
Clarisse: But I can't believe he's in contact with you, that's good.
(4.0)
Drina: (Switches to another tab, enters search term.)
Drina: That's funny.

This painful struggle to share a simple photo contrasts sharply with the musicians' easy spontaneous sharing of their sleep cycles on different devices.

Technology implications: Through this last interaction we see how poorly technology supports channel blending. Even though the sisters had a real-time connection through their phones, their computers were unaware of it. Had they been face-to-face, Drina could have simply shown Clarisse the photo without running into permissions problems. If technology recognized that people carry on interactions over more than one channel, it could enable the sharing of content across them. Face-to-face interactions might also be improved by making it easier to share content with a group. In the first example, rather than passing around their phones to view them one at a time, perhaps the musicians could have projected the app onto the TV they were already using to display content for shared viewing.

Channel blending content over time

Norrick [18] discusses a variation on the practice of storytelling in which people tell each other the story of an experience they all participated in. He shows that people tell these "twice-told tales" to (a) foster group rapport, (b) ratify group membership, and (c) convey group values. We observed similar cases where participants re-told a shared "story" by re-experiencing together content they each had viewed separately. These shared re-experiences seemed to function in much the same way as twice-told tales, and they can be seen as channel blending over time.

In one example of this type, Alana and Lee were at dinner with another friend, Peter, who had previously emailed them a link to a recording by a 15-year-old violin prodigy (Sean) in which he played a difficult concerto but missed a few high notes in an amusing way. The concerto comes up in conversation, so Alana asks:

Alana: Do you guys want to listen to Sean's recording of it?
Peter: YES! (laughs)
Alana: (Picks up phone) Okay, okay, okay, okay, okay!
Peter: (laughing) Yes, I can listen to that as many times as hah hah hah
Alana: I listened to it yesterday

Since they had all listened to the recording earlier, they now shared the anticipation of the humor of the missed notes. Once Alana located the recording (more on this later), she played it, and as the bad notes approached they looked at each other smiling in anticipation. Once the squeaky notes played they all broke out in laughter as Alana tipped over from the waist and Lee put his head in his arms.

Alana: I love that, like "eeaawww" (mimicking the bad notes). Let's listen to that again.
(Laughing continues, she restarts the music just before blooper, and all laugh as music ends)
Alana: Baa, duuh huh, that's really good
Lee: That's so funny
Alana: That's so sad
Lee: He just like went up three octaves just in the middle of it. (Brings arm up as if holding violin) There's a note up so far there. (Peter and Lee laugh)
Peter: No, maybe not
Alana: (Mimicking the squeaky playing) dah, dah, dah dah dah dah dah
Lee: Ahhhh
Alana: It's sad.

Even though they had each listened to the recording many times on their own, they still wanted to listen to it again – twice in fact – so they could share the experience together. Perhaps this local re-experiencing of prior remotely-shared content played the same role as twice-told tales in that it fostered group rapport, ratified membership into the group of people who can appreciate the humor of the bad note, and conveyed their shared value of respecting the prodigy's skill even though he made a glaring mistake.

This example also shows an interesting way in which the technology affected the storytelling process. Using her phone, Alana initially had trouble locating the recording from Peter's email. While she waited for the email to load, Peter used the time to tell a story related to the clip: that a friend of Sean's played that concerto at Sean's wedding a few years later and re-enacted the very same mistakes from that recording. Peter explained, *"He like, like apparently listened to it over and over so he could get, like exactly the same mistakes."* After they laughed about this, Alana concluded that she couldn't find the clip, but Peter said she could get it from Sean's website. This led to a discussion about how impressed they were that Sean would make it publicly available, that he wasn't "traumatized" by it.

These topics were discussed *before* they listened to the clip together. In the standard sequence, this sort of discussion would occur in the response phase, *after* the telling. This reversal was caused by Alana's difficulty in locating and downloading the piece, which took about five minutes. As technologists, our instinct is to try to "fix" the problem by making it easier for her to find the clip, a good goal, but it's also worth noting that the delay allowed them to build up a rich context for the playing that enhanced their appreciation of it. Once they knew Sean's friends re-enacted his performance at his wedding, errors in tact, the replaying was even funnier.

Finally, we note that for about five minutes, Alana split her attention between the conversation and her phone as she searched for the music, but again her behavior was not treated as rude because it was in service of a joint activity.

Just as people wanted to share content multiple times with the same people, they also attempted to share the same content with different people as the opportunity arose. In one such case, Drina was listening to music on her laptop while on the phone with her other sister, Carmen. Carmen asked what the song was and after discussing it, she reciprocated by sharing her own song: *"You know what song I can't get out of my head?"* Once she got Drina's interest she looked for the song, but just as she found it Drina got another call and so disengaged before hearing the song. A short while later, Carmen was on the phone with her brother, who told her about his plan to buy a guitar for their other brother. She responded by saying, *"Teach him this song, bro,"* and played the same song. In a similar pattern, Lee played a recording of a Schubert cello quartet to Scott on his laptop, noting that he didn't like the composition's last two notes. Later, when the rest of the group arrived, he played it for everyone, looking for further agreement that the last two notes *"are so messed up."*

In these cases, the person had a recorded piece of content they wanted to share and they did so with multiple people over different channels as opportunities arose, both remotely and in person using mobile technology. We see these as cases of channel blending over time.

Technology implications: These examples indicate that technology could better support serial sharing across remote and local channels by keeping track of the content people have previously viewed or shared and making it easy to re-access, possibly via a different device. Since the topic of conversations is unpredictable and flows dynamically, it should be easy to re-find previously viewed content, even without saving or tagging the item in advance, without breaking the flow of conversation. The first interaction further suggests that asynchronous sharing of content can be less satisfying than real-time sharing, and so people may re-share the same content with the same people when they get together in person or establish a synchronous connection. Thus, we should make it easier to re-access content shared through other channels.

Channel blending interactions over time

When we think about storytelling or content sharing, we tend to think of it as happening in a single interaction in which the story is told and people respond in that same "session." Social media and email support asynchronous sharing, allowing one person to share at one point and others to express their response later. However, we saw cases where even synchronous sharing happened serially, that is across multiple sessions over different channels.

In one type of "serial sharing," people told the story of an experience over a series of interactions, perhaps starting the story in a phone call or text exchange and continuing it F2F. In one example, Clarisse went with a friend to a farmer's market at which she fell in love with chocolate mint plants. When she next spoke on the phone with her older sister Carmen, she enthused about it, (*"We got mint, oh my goodness!"*) explaining that she would try to grow it in a pot. Later when Carmen came over to visit, Clarisse showed her the mint and asked her to taste it, emphasizing how it tastes just like a real mint candy. (*"It feels like you're eating a mint, it feels like a mint!"*)

In this example the sharing is of a physical object rather than a recording, but we also saw cases where people carried out social acts serially. Invitations and subsequent coordination activities were especially likely to occur across multiple sessions and channels. In one example, Lee was instant messaging simultaneously but separately with Alana and a friend Peter, whom he was meeting for dinner. He invited Alana to join them, but she hedged in her reply.

Alana: i don't know if i want to come
Alana: …
Lee: you just want to sit in your room and be lame on film?
Lee: come come come
Lee: dinner's on me
Alana: OH HAYYY
Alana: well if you're paying
Alana: haha
Alana: just kidding
Alana: yeah I don't know
Lee: ok
Lee: ::hug::

Lee dropped the subject and they briefly discussed something else, and he updated Peter that Alana was "being flakey." A few minutes later, without ending the IM conversation, he called Alana while walking to his car, surprising her with the shift in media:

Alana: Lee
Lee: Hey
Alana: We're talking online!
Lee: uh, I'm outside, do you want to come to dinner or no?
Alana: (drawn out) Iiii dooon't knooow
Lee: I can come pick you up
[6 more turns]
Alana: Do you wanna walk? It's so nice
Lee: Okay, we can walk, do you wanna come?
Alana: Okay

After clarifying the reason for calling, Lee re-invoked the invitation, which Alana finally accepted. Here, the interaction took place over two sessions and two media. In other cases, the agreement to get together was only the beginning, as people then had a series of exchanges through different media to coordinate meeting up. Ling [16] characterized this phenomenon of micro-coordination in which people don't make firm plans but instead use texting and phone calls to coordinate as they converge. What was new for us was the large number of interactions that were carried out over multiple channels with multiple people as their plans changed and problems cropped up.

In one case, Drina made arrangements with her friend Brent to pick her up and drive to a coffee shop where they would meet up with another friend, Barton. Brent was more than an hour late, so they were delayed in meeting Barton. Drina's coordination effort with both friends involved a total of 18 interactions, 8 with Brent (5 phone calls, 2 phone text exchanges, and one Facebook post) and 10 with Barton (2 Facebook chats, 3 phone texts, and 5 phone calls).

Interestingly, 18 years ago, Whittaker, et. al [25] discussed intermittent interactions, noting that they mainly occurred F2F where people have many opportunities to run into each other. They stated, "the challenge for future technology is in supplying this type of information for geographically distributed groups." As technology developed, researchers noted cases when people carried on similar intermittent interactions over IM, or even across media by using IM to arrange a phone call [17]. Our examples show how technology has developed even further to support this activity. People are now continuing the same conversation across a wider variety of media (texting, voice calls, video calls, websites), sometimes crossing channels multiple times, and sometimes incorporating multiple people.

Technology implication: From the participants' point of view, these exchanges were part of one ongoing activity (telling a story, issuing an invitation, meeting up in person) even though they were carried out over time over multiple channels. Yet each technology treated them as a series of unrelated connections, with no history and no context. Each time the participants had to re-establish the status of their plans. Some of these interactions involved multiple people, again some local and some remote, who all needed to stay updated on the current state of the activity. Future technology could be designed so that context is maintained when people switch channels within a conversation, and support multiple participants who may participate over different channels to different degrees.

CONCLUSION

Together, these examples demonstrate a phenomenon we are calling channel blending, the fluid and coherent integration of interactions and content over multiple channels, often involving both local and remote participants. We also saw cases of people channel blending over time by carrying out one coherent interaction over a series of interactions using different media. We have shown that although it often involves the simultaneous use of multiple devices and communication streams, channel blending contrasts with multitasking in that people attempt to merge them into one shared activity, rather than switching between separate, unrelated activities.

To be clear, we do not claim that all these channel blending examples are newly discovered behavior. As noted, others have reported cases we are including in the notion of channel blending – conversations being conducted over multiple sessions [17, 25] or including people in the remote and local environment [5, 21, 26]. We are proposing that these instances are part of a larger phenomenon in which people attempt to blend their local and remote worlds into one coherent interaction when sharing content and experiences with friends through their devices. Further, these behaviors are becoming more varied, and possibly more common, because of the prevalence of ubiquitous devices and bite-sized content.

It is notable that we saw this activity among a generation that is touted as the ultimate multitaskers, people who think nothing of watching videos, doing homework, texting, checking status updates, and listening to music all at the same time [1, 2]. In light of our findings, it would be useful to study how often such people are in fact integrating those activities into a channel-blended interaction rather than simply switching among them as separate activities. We saw evidence that our participants didn't find it rude to focus on multiple channels when they were doing it in service of a shared activity. Perhaps at least some of the time, people are channel blending rather than multitasking, and therefore not inspiring others' frustration.

Our findings indicate that channel blending is not always easy to coordinate through current technology. It required great skill for a pivot person to smoothly integrate comments from both local and remote participants, and for people to monitor and smoothly introduce remote content into ongoing local conversations. People who were remotely connected over multiple channels had trouble sharing information across channels. It was difficult to re-access previously experienced content for re-sharing. Problems also occurred as people lost track of context when a conversation traveled across channels over time.

To address these difficulties, we might think differently when designing future communication and content-sharing technology:

- Rather than imagining people using a system alone, we should remember that people often use it in social settings with others who engage with them and the technology to different degrees over time. Rather than just connecting remote parties, we might find ways to integrate other co-present people who may be actively or passively engaged in the interaction.
- In addition to making it easier for people to access content from anywhere, we might find ways to facilitate the sharing of that content with others on another channel or device, whether co-located or

remote. Further, the response to a storytelling can become part of the story as it is retold a second and third time to others, perhaps through other channels.

- Rather than thinking of sharing as a one-time event, we can expect repeated sharings, sometimes with the same people and sometimes with others, remotely or F2F.
- Rather than thinking in terms of technology-based sessions, we might think about coherent social acts that may take place over time and across channels (including F2F), and allow people to build on the context created during the ongoing interaction.

We were able to detect channel blending by studying groups of people rather than one particular technology, and by directly observing each person carrying out their activities. The video recordings allowed us to review the interactions repeatedly until we understood them in all their richness. This method showed us that communication and content-sharing technology should be designed with the expectation that people share the stories of their lives over multiple interactions, using multiple devices and media, with different overlapping sets of people, as they converge and separate and come together once again.

ACKNOWLEDGMENTS

We are grateful to our study participants for giving us such open access to their lives. Erik Vinkhuyzen, Keiko Yabuki, Luke Plurkowski, and Victoria Bellotti contributed to the analysis, and Steve Whittaker and Kurt Partridge gave helpful comments on the paper. We greatly appreciate the extensive support provided by the extended Sony and PARC teams.

REFERENCES

1. Agosto, D. & Abbas, J. (2010) High School Seniors' Social Network and Other ICT Use Preferences and Concerns, *Proc. ASIST*, 47, 1-10.
2. Baron, N. (2008), Adjusting the Volume: Technology and Multitasking in Discourse Control, In Katz, J. (Ed) *Handbook of Mobile Communication Studies,* MIT Press.
3. Cao, X., Sellen, A., Brush, A., Kirk, D., Edge, D. & Ding, X. (2010) Understanding Family Communication Across Time Zones, *Proc. CSCW*, 155-158.
4. Czerwinski, M., Horvitz, E. & Wilhite, S. (2004), A Diary Study of Task Switching and Interruptions, *Proc CHI,* 175-182.
5. Dourish, P., Adler, A., Bellotti, V., & Henderson, A. (1996), Your Place or Mine? Learning from Long-Term Use of Audio-Video Communication, *CSCW,* 5: 33-62.
6. Erikson, T., Smith, D., Kellogg, W., Laff, M., Richards, J. & Bradner, E. (1999), Socially Translucent Systems: Social Proxies, Persistent Conversation, and the Design of "Babble," *Proc. CHI*, 72-79.
7. Frohlich, D., Kuchinsky, A., Pering, C., Don, A. & Ariss, S. (2002), Requirements for Photoware, *Proc. CSCW 2002*, 166-175.
8. Grinter, R. & Eldridge, M. (2003), Want2tlk?: Everyday Text Messaging, *Proc. CHI,* 441-448.
9. Isaacs, E. & Szymanski, P. (2012), Capturing Mobile Telepresence Through Logging and Video Shadowing: A Two-Phase Study Design, *Field Methods*, Sage: in press.
10. Ito, M. & Okabe, D. (2005), Technosocial Situations: Emergent Structurings of Mobile Email Use, in M. Ito, M. Matsuda, & D. Okabe (Eds.), Personal, Portable, Intimate: Mobile Phones in Japanese Life, 257-273.
11. Joinson, A. (2008) 'Looking At,' 'Looking up' or 'Keeping Up With' People? Motives and Uses of Facebook, *Proc CHI,* 1027-1036.
12. Jordan, B. & Henderson, A. (1995), Interaction Analysis: Foundations and Practice, *Journal of the Learning Sciences*, 4(1): 39-103.
13. Judge, T. & Neustaedter, C. (2010), Sharing Conversation and Sharing Life: Video Conferencing in the Home, *Proc. CHI*, 655-658.
14. Kirk, D., Sellen, A. & Cao, X. (2010) Home Video Communication: Mediating 'Closeness,' *Proc. CSCW*, 135-144.
15. Lampe, C., Ellison, N. & Steinfield, C. (2008) Changes in Use and Perception of Facebook, *Proc. CSCW,* 721-730.
16. Ling, R. and Yttri, B. (2002), Hyper-coordination via Mobile Phones in Norway, In Katz, J. & Aakhus, M. (eds.) *Perpetual Contact: Mobile Communication, Private Talk, Public Performance.* Cambridge University Press, 170-192.
17. Nardi, B., Whittaker, S. & Bradner, E. (2000), Interaction and Outeraction: Instant Messaging in Action, *Proc CSCW*, 79-88.
18. Norrick, N. (1997), Twice-told tales: Collaborative narration of familiar stories, *Language in Society,* 26, 199-220.
19. O'Hara, K, Black, A., & Lipson, M. (2006), Everyday Practices with Mobile Video Telephony, *Proc. CHI,* 871-880.
20. Okabe, D. (2004) Emergent Social Practices, Situations and Relations through Everyday Camera Phone Use, *Proc of Mobile Communication and Social Change*, Seoul, Korea.
21. Palen, L., Salzman, M. & Youngs, E. (2001), Discovery and Integration of Mobile Communications in Everyday Life, *Personal and Ubiquitous Computing,* 5:109-122.
22. Sacks, H. (1974), An Analysis of the Course of a Joke's Telling in Conversation, in R. Bauman, R. & J. Sherzer (Eds.), *Explorations in the Ethnography of Speaking,* 337-353.
23. Sacks, H. Schegloff, A. & Jefferson, G. (1974), A Simplest Systematics for the Organization of Turn-taking for Conversation. *Language, 50*, 696-735.
24. Viegas, F. & Donath, J. (1999), Chat Circles, *Proc. CHI*, 9-16.
25. Whittaker, S., Frohlich, D. & Daly-Jones, O. (1994) Informal Workplace Communication: What is It Like and How Might We Support It?, *Proc CHI* 94, 131-137.
26. Woodruff, A. & Aoki, P.M. (2004), Push-to-Talk Social Talk, *CSCW*, 13: 409-44.

Designing a Social Network to Support the Independence of Young Adults with Autism

Hwajung Hong, Jennifer G. Kim, Gregory D. Abowd, Rosa I. Arriaga
GVU Center
School of Interactive Computing
College of Computing, Georgia Tech
Atlanta, GA, USA

ABSTRACT

Independence is key to a successful transition to adulthood for individuals with autism. Social support is a crucial factor for achieving adaptive self-help life skills. In this paper we describe the results of a formative design exercise with young adults with autism and their caregivers to uncover opportunities for social networks to promote independence and facilitate coordination. We propose the concept of *SocialMirror*, a device connected to an online social network that allows the young adult to seek advice from a trusted and responsive network of family, friends and professionals. Focus group discussions reveal the potential for SocialMirror to increase motivation to learn everyday life skills among young adults with autism and to foster collaboration among a distributed care network. We present design considerations to leverage a small trusted network that balances quick response with safeguards for privacy and security of young adults with autism.

Author Keywords

Autism, independence, social network, collaborative care

ACM Classification Keywords

H.5.3 Group and Organization Interfaces: Collaborative computing, Computer-supported cooperative work

General Terms

Design, Human Factors

INTRODUCTION

The rise in the number of children diagnosed with autism began in the early 1990s. Since then, these individuals have transitioned from a protective school system to a much less protective adult world. [17]. Challenges in self-care, everyday life chores, and social communication adversely impact the attainment of independent functioning in adulthood. Several studies reveal that adults with autism, even those with higher intellectual abilities, rely heavily on their families' support in employment, living, and relationships [9,23]. The challenges of day-to-day functioning lead to higher dependency and create a formidable burden for caregivers [13]. We contend that appropriate social support is critical for independence of adults with autism [16] and decreasing the burden currently shouldered by primary caregivers [13].

Our research goal is to design a system to promote independence and facilitate collaboration around caregiving activities for adolescents and adults with autism. To this end, we created a concept called *SocialMirror,* a specialized online social network embedded into everyday life to support young adults with autism. In this paper, we describe the results of design exercises conducted with 12 young adults with autism and 16 caregivers actively involved in planning and supporting the transition to adulthood.

We propose two major CSCW contributions. First, we introduce a novel social networking concept for individuals with autism and their caregivers. Second, we provide empirically driven design implications for a system that helps individuals practice life skills in a social context by facilitating quick responses from a network of caregivers.

We begin by reviewing related work and discussing social and technological support for independent living. Next, we explain our overall design process, and present the design of SocialMirror along with usage scenarios. We describe the result of focus groups and highlight potential impacts and barriers to utilization of this social network by young adults with autism as well their caregivers. Finally, we conclude with considerations for leveraging a trusted network for balancing quick response while safeguarding the privacy and security of young adults with autism.

RELATED WORK

Autism and Independence Challenges

Young adults with autism face challenges in the area of organization, initiation, and generalization skills [3]. These challenges impact their communication, and social skills [16]. They also impede development of successful independent skills [10], increasing the need for adult prompting and continuous support [13]. For this reason few adults with autism live outside of their parent's home or are employed [9]. Even individuals who successfully transition to independent living still report that they often struggle with domestic tasks like cooking, taking medications, personal hygiene and other tasks [3,13].

The constant support that these individuals require also takes a toll on the relationship with their primary caregivers. Compared to parents whose child with autism lives away from home, parents who still have their child in the home report that the need to help with daily schedule management, child security, and constant prompts to perform everyday tasks contributes to their heightened stress level and negatively affects the quality of the relationship with their child [13, 23].

Prompting System for Independent Daily Tasks

Prompting systems have been used to assist individuals with cognitive disabilities in providing timely reminders of upcoming day-to-day tasks and completion of multiple step tasks [24]. For instance, a mobile prompting platform, MAPS (Memory Aiding Prompting System), provides directions from one location in a building to another and instructs individuals to attend to tasks on a minute-by-minute basis [2]. Similarly, self-operated prompting systems have also been used for individuals with autism to help them stay focused on specific tasks [15]. However, such technological interventions are still limited to giving individuals pre-programmed instructions. The real challenge is to provide personalized information tailored to the current situation the individual is facing.

Social Software for Supportive Activities

A growing number of studies highlight social software that supports a variety of community relationships in health [21] and wellness [6]. One study found that people were better able to cope with personal problems when they received on-line suggestions from a community of people [4]. Researchers have investigated the presence of supportive relationships online [20]. For example, websites, such as PatientsLikeMe [19], provide a social space for patients to update and share their status and ask for help. However, there are issues regarding a patients' uncertainty about what to post, and the workload in keeping their status updated [20]. To ease the coordination of this type of support, software has been developed that allows the individual and his or her social network to share their calendars [5] and wellness information [6]. Collectively, such social software facilitates on-demand support for the individual by harnessing the collective intelligence.

We propose that a similar opportunity exists to empower the autism community through social support. Individuals with autism have close-knit trusted networks that may include parents, siblings, relatives, friends on the autism spectrum, volunteers, residential staff, teachers, therapists, and other professionals. These care networks can play a key role in personal growth, acquisition of new skills, expanded social benefits, and access to community resources [13]. The Internet can be especially important for adults with autism with few formal supports, as online communities allow them to establish a collective informal support network. This may include both practical supports, such as job interview skills and emotional support, such as sharing of experiences and feelings [14]. Although this research acknowledges the benefits of both offline and online networks to support an individual, many concerns remain about building trusted relationships with anonymous groups for individuals on the spectrum [1].

RESEARCH CONTEXT AND METHODS

Our research employed a three-phase design process, summarized in Table 1. Our goal was to generate concrete design ideas for how technology would support the independence of individuals with autism from adolescence into adulthood.

The first phase involved three months of informal participant observation to better understand the needs of young adults with respect to performing everyday life skills in a social world [11]. Through a special invitation from a local autism center, three of the co-authors attended weekly social group meetings for adults (all over 25 years old) with high functioning forms of autism, or HFA, such as Asperger's Syndrome.[1] The purpose of this weekly social group was to allow individuals with autism and neurotypical volunteers to engage in fun social activities like bowling and trivia. This event not only enabled the individual with autism to socialize in a real but low stress environment, but also afforded us the opportunity to establish a rapport with the primary stakeholders of our design exercise. We gained valuable insights into a variety of everyday challenges that impede successful independent life.

Soon after meeting the adults, we began to imagine possible designs to mediate the challenges we observed. Initial ideas included building a mobile system that prompts pre-programmed instructions on how the individual should behave appropriately in response to a certain context such as time and location. We imagined such a system might be beneficial to the individuals, but remained uncertain about how the caregivers would react.

We conducted semi-structured interviews (Phase 2) with 13 caregivers to help us understand their concerns about the transition to adulthood and to discuss whether an imagined system could support their current practices and alleviate their concerns. The participants, recruited from the local autism research community, included high school teachers (n=8), a parent (n=1), a counselor (n=1), adult program coordinators (n=2), and a transition specialist (n=1). The preliminary results derived from these interviews motivated three design guidelines: (1) *motivate engagement in self-care activities,* (2) *embed advice in the context of the day's events, and* (3) *leverage a natural network of individuals and caregivers.*

[1] Though there is not a specific diagnostic definition for high functioning autism, or HFA, we use this label in this paper to represent individuals with autism who demonstrate the ability to communicate verbally.

A conceptual breakthrough came during the process of developing the guidelines. We realized that harnessing human intelligence to address the challenges faced by an individual would have a greater impact than relying on a single technology. This insight led us to speculate about the power of social networking, which could provide in-situ feedback to the individual by connecting him or her with a distributed network of qualified and available advisers.

We proposed a full-length mirror display as an initial embodiment of a social networking tool embedded in the natural environment. Dubbed the SocialMirror, this initial idea was intended to demonstrate the need to connect to advice on personal appearance and hygiene from within the home. We felt it is important to make this initial idea very concrete in order to further elicit reactions from potential stakeholders. We produced paper mockups, including screenshots of a social networking website and application, a simple prototype implemented with the Facebook API, and a concept video that presented various usage scenarios. We used these design mockups and the concept video in Phase 3 as the basis for a series of focus group studies with students, adults and caregivers.

Prior to the focus groups, we wanted to investigate whether our research procedures and questions were suitable for the participants. We conducted a pilot interview with a 26-year-old adult with HFA who moved away from home to go to college. Throughout the pilot study, we acknowledged structured interviews alone are not suitable for individuals with cognitive difficulties because they struggle with recalling and describing their experiences [24]. The modified procedure included introducing a set of pictures (Figure 1) that contained examples about real life problems to help the participants elaborate their own problems. We then showed the video mockup [8], to enable a discussion about how the participants would use such a system and in what contexts it would be useful.

After the pilot interview, we conducted focus group sessions with four groups of participants: The first group included three teachers and three students with HFA (mean age = 23) from a community school. The students currently lived with their guardians, but planned to live alone in the future. The second group was a mother and her son (age 27) with HFA who had successfully lived alone for two years, but recently returned to the family due to financial issues. The third group also was a mother and her son (age 35) with HFA who is living with a roommate on the autism spectrum. The fourth group involved a social skills coach and 6 young adults (mean age = 21.7) with HFA who meet regularly for a social evening out.

At the beginning of the session, individuals with autism and their caregivers were interviewed separately to minimize any potential influence of caregivers on the individuals with autism. We asked individuals what concerns they have for daily life, how they seek out a person to help them, and whom they would be most comfortable to ask.

Research Phase	Methods	Participants & Activities
Phase1	Participant Observation	• Participants: 11 adults with autism • Attended in social activities for adults with autism • Goal: Design inspiration
Phase2	Semi-structured Interview	• Participants: 13 caregivers • Discussed topic of barriers to independent life • Identified everyday challenges and strategies to cope with • Goal: Design refinement and documentation
Phase3	Homogenous Focus Group Interview Heterogeneous Focus Group Interview	• Participants: A pilot participant (A man with HFA) Group #1 (3 men with autism and 3 teachers) Group #2 (A man with HFA and his mother) Group #3 (A man with HFA and his mother) Group #4 (5 men and 1women with HFA and a coach) • Review and critique the SocialMirror concept • Discuss topic of concerns using social network • Goal: Design requirements and considerations

Table 1. Methods and Activities for each design phase.

Conversely, we asked caregivers about challenges to understanding the needs of individuals, ways to provide help, and potential people they would allow answering questions from the individuals with autism. Once this session was completed, the two groups of participants were brought together and shown an initial prototype and video of SocialMirror to elicit comments on how this specialized social networking service concept may or may not address their needs and concerns.

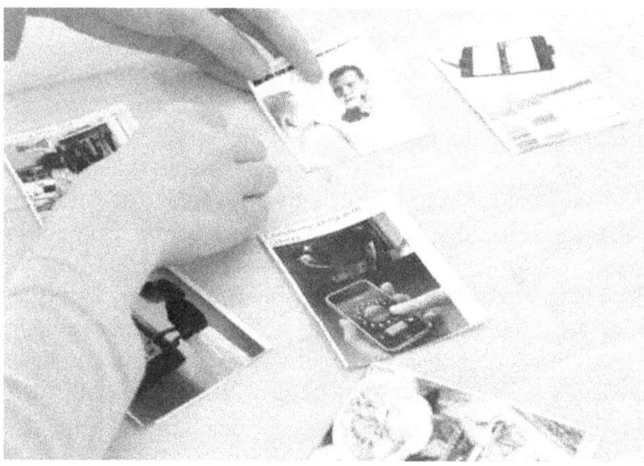

Figure 1. Life skills cards used in the focus group interviews before the introduction of SocialMirror.

All interviews were recorded and transcribed. Three researchers coded the data and the quotes presented in this paper are representative of broad themes of agreement grounded in our data [22]. We then iteratively clustered these codes into higher-level category groupings until we arrived at the themes that we will describe in the design guidelines and focus group results sections.

DESIGN GUIDELINES

The formative interviews with caregivers (Phase 2) yielded two results. First, we gained a better understanding of how assistance with transition works, what difficulties are inherent in current practices, and how the situation could be improved. Second, we identified guidelines to direct the design of technology for individuals and their caregivers seeking to help support independence in everyday living.

Motivate Engagement in Self-help Activities

Many caregivers reported challenges for individuals with autism in the initiation and motivation for performing everyday life skills, such as self-help activities (e.g., shaving, dressing, managing personal hygiene) or household chores. One participant (P1) is a father of a 23-year-old son with autism. He indicated that it is difficult for his son to notice and attend to the relevant aspects of himself and his environment: *"... He struggles with cleaning, and he's really not good at self-monitoring. He doesn't see a room and the level of dirtiness or disorganization that you and I might see. As a result, he ends up getting anxious and frustrated."* (P1)

Without external motivation, individuals with autism may not initiate self-care activities. Because the individuals with autism rarely know *whether* they have a problem with this area, direct prompting has been a dominant way to trigger self-help activities. One teacher explains: *"We have discussions about dirty and greasy hair... we go to the bathroom to see the mirror and I'd say this is not fine. Here, my hair is clean because I washed it this morning. Now, let's look at yours. See how it separates?"* (P4) However, caregivers pointed out this prompting at every single step would not be the ultimate solution because it may cause overreliance. Therefore, any support must help the individual identify what help he needs and initiate communication to seek help spontaneously.

Embed Advice in the Context of the Day's Events

Individuals with autism often have prepared scripts, or protocols, describing details of how to carry out an activity, but they often have difficulty understanding when to use that script. For example, caregivers stated that knowing *when* to do laundry is as important as knowing *how* to do laundry. For this reason, existing interventions that provide pre-made protocols, such as scripted to-do lists or visual cues for how to complete the activity, are not enough. Three teachers noted that individuals with autism have difficulty associating the protocol or visual cue with their ongoing activities.

Teachers and parents strive a great deal to integrate the protocols into the individual's daily routine so that the individual applies them to actual activities rather than simply having the directions available. *"Sitting in a computer terminal in isolation going through life and social skill programs, in my experience, does not give good results [...] skill training has to be a portion of the day."* (P3)

A notable example of the importance of the contextualization of skill training was shared calendar management. One of the high school teachers stated that each student in her school is required to have an electronic calendar that is shared with the teachers. The day's events appear on the calendar, allowing teachers to remind their students what they learned in school and to deliver adaptive advice when needed. Such schedule sharing can have a great impact on facilitating skill training by providing in-situ advice about what, when, and where the skill will be performed. For individuals with autism who may be resistant or unable to ask for help, a shared schedule provides a simple mechanism to facilitate intervention.

Leverage a Natural Network of Caregivers

Not surprisingly, our findings confirm that primary caregivers, usually parents, play a major role in orchestrating the transition from the family home to independent living. This centralized role raised concerns about overreliance or dependence on one-to-one support. A father described his son as inclined to rely on him too much, and to get extremely anxious if he was unavailable to answer questions over the phone: *"He has a tendency to call me too much to ask me for help coping with his problems"* (P1) For this father and other participants, being able to anticipate possible scenarios with other caregivers in advance of important events (e.g., job interviews) would be a good strategy to alleviate the anxiety felt when parents are unable to help immediately.

The natural formation of a supportive network benefits not only individuals with autism, by enabling on-demand support, but also benefits their caregivers by distributing caretaking responsibilities. Leveraging the existing network that provides support to the individual with autism, along with building up a wider trusted network, should be a primary consideration in developing a system to support transition to independence. A system that leverages the individual's social network provides caregivers with continued contact with the individual, but also a sustained communication channel with the other caregivers (e.g., residential staff).

In summary, we note that individuals with autism demand and desire independence, yet specific problems (e.g., little motivation for self-care) impede their ability to perform everyday life tasks successfully. Few interventions support individuals' ongoing activities. Even in cases where adults with autism manage to live in a semi-independent living facility, they often rely on repeated promptings and direct supervision to complete day-to-day activities. The design guidelines developed from our analysis led us to develop a system that supports individuals with autism in learning adaptive self-care skills through collaborative advice from a social network.

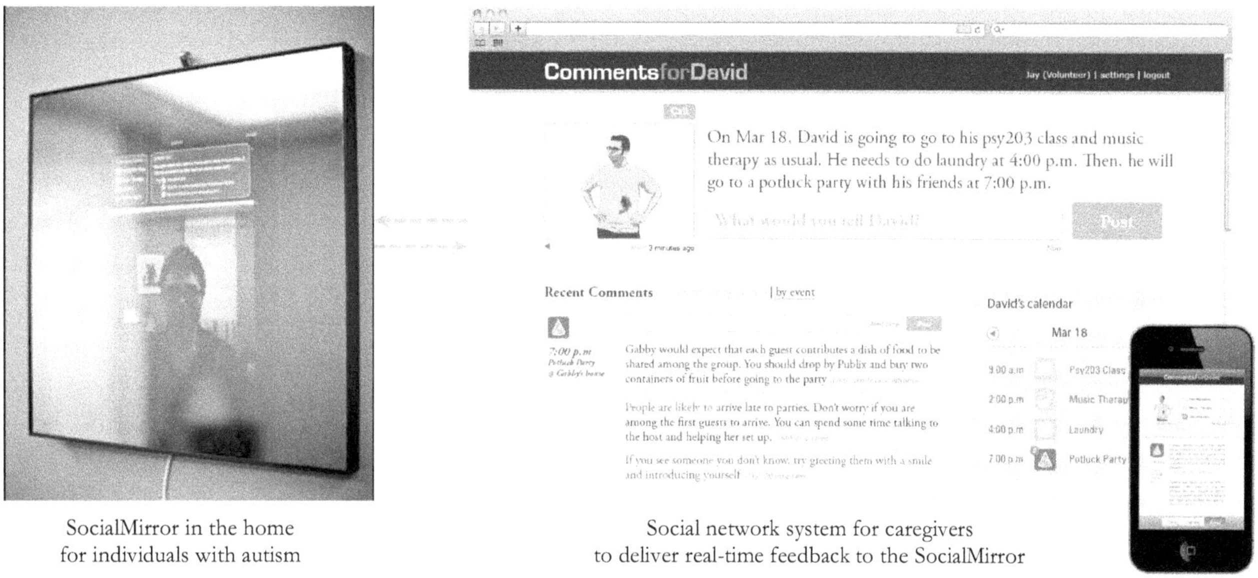

SocialMirror in the home for individuals with autism

Social network system for caregivers to deliver real-time feedback to the SocialMirror

Figure 2. SocialMirror deployed in home (left) and social network service as seen by a caregiver (right).

SOCIALMIRROR: SYSTEM DESIGN

Inspired by these three design guidelines, we developed a prototype, *SocialMirror*. Figure 2 provides an example of how we might embed a life skills support mechanism into everyday objects in the home. SocialMirror consists of two parts. First, an interactive display integrated into a mirror provides the opportunity to ask and receive advice with an attached day's calendar. Second, the system is connected to an online social network that sends questions to a trusted set of family, friends and professionals. At the beginning of each day or the night before, an individual with autism can see his calendar that indicates his day's events. He can take a picture of himself and send a question to his social network if he feels the need to ask for advice. For example, he might want to know if he is dressed appropriately for an upcoming event on his calendar. SocialMirror helps to contextualize the request to the rest of the network by attaching the picture, the question, and the day's calendar of events for all in the trusted network to see. When answers arrive from the support network, they are immediately reflected back to the individual. SocialMirror is also available as a webpage or a smartphone application, facilitating access to the support network at any time and from anywhere.

Mirror: A Natural Object for Asking and Getting Advice

The creation of a natural communication medium via an interactive display embedded in mirror provides a foundation for unobtrusive connection between young adults and their social network. The mirror is a display, and in fact its natural affordance could be made to sense when the individuals is in front of it and prompt them to seek advice on appearance or the day's activities. The networked SocialMirror allows them to be aware of their current status and helps them get feedback about their status from multiple caregivers. The feedback is also automatically replicated on the individual's 'portable mirror' (e.g., cell phone), in order to allow him or her to carry it around on-the-go (e.g., kitchen, school, or grocery store) and refer to it throughout the day.

Controlled Access: Safe and Trusted Network

While existing social technology often serves to form and maintain weak ties, the goal of our system is to extend pre-existing strong ties with intimate acquaintances, people whom the individual is able to trust such as family members, friends, and other professionals (e.g., teachers, counselors, job coaches, and transition specialists). This trusted network can also be expanded to include 'trusted strangers,' people who are willing to commit their time to help the individual in order to successfully distribute a main caregiver's workload and give the individual trustworthy feedback. One can imagine a trusted stranger as a close associate of one of the main caregivers (e.g. the mother's friend), or a trained professional or volunteer that is contracted for service by the individual or family.

We envision that primary caregivers will act as gatekeepers to ensure a safe environment for their children. Members of the extended social network are initially vetted by the caregivers. This process results in a reliable trusted network and ensures that the individual is aware of who the extended caregivers are in his or her social network.

Picture: Spontaneous Communication Medium

We use a picture taken by the individual as a communication medium between an individual and the trusted network. The picture is intended to let the individual easily initiate contact with their trusted network and explain the need for advice. Since individuals with autism often have difficulties initiating conversations [1], the simple picture-mediated interaction may allow them to initiate communication more easily without the need for a detailed verbal explanation.

Calendar: Day's Events with Visual Support

While existing calendars only show the time and the day's events in textual form, our calendar additionally includes representative imagery to illustrate the activity. Visual support is particularly beneficial to individuals with autism because it helps make abstract concepts concrete and capitalizes on their inherent visual learning strengths [7]. The representative images of each activity are classified into three categories: daily chores, official appointments, and social events. We differentiate these three event categories using different colors: green, yellow, and purple.

Contextualized comments on picture and calendar

To help the trusted network provide appropriate and contextualized instructions, the system allows members of the network to view upcoming events in the individual's calendar and the shared pictures that show his or her current status. By allowing multiple caregivers to provide comments on the shared schedule and picture, the system can facilitate communications among caregivers. The trusted network can give the following three types of comments.

On-demand Commenting: The trusted network gives feedback on the individual's queries or shared picture. This request implies that the individual requires feedback on his or her current situation as soon as possible, so a prompt reply is essential. When members of the trusted network get a notification that the individual has posted a request, they can add comments on the post. These comments are displayed right below the picture, so the individual can see the comments along with the related picture.

Allocated Commenting: Members of the trusted network can also assign relevant comments to a specific event on the calendar before the event takes place, and additionally specify the time when their comments are to be delivered to the individual (e.g., 10 minutes before the event). The individual is able to see the comments either by accessing the calendar or through the alert that is sent at the designated time.

Sub-Commenting: Even with a small number of people in the trusted network, the amount of comments provided may be overwhelming to the individual. Thus, the system contains a sub-commenting feature that aggregates multiple comments under a same topic. Under an original comment, multiple people in the network can provide more sophisticated advice. The main goal of this feature is to reduce the number of comments that the individual sees at any one time, and to allow the network to come to a consensus before a piece of advice is presented to the individual.

USAGE SCENARIOS

A video prototype of SocialMirror depicts three usage scenarios for David, a fictitious 22-year old with HFA [8]. Table 2 summarizes those scenarios. We implemented an initial prototype of SocialMirror that includes the hardware, a 7" tablet combined with a reflective panel (See Figure 2), and two essential social networking capabilities using the Facebook API, sending a picture to a group of registered people and receiving their comments.

Scenario1	Supporting self-care to stay neat and tidy.
Scenario2	Advice for acquiring better professional etiquette.
Scenario3	Learning subtle social rules in the moment.

Table 2. Usage scenarios in the video prototype.

FOCUS GROUP RESULTS

In summarizing the results of the focus groups, we describe reactions to the form factor of SocialMirror, how its blending of functional and social capabilities were received, and its potential for empowering a community of caregivers. We also sought to understand potential barriers to adoptions.

Form Factor Influence

SocialMirror is designed to stimulate spontaneous advice seeking by the individual with autism. It is meant to engage him or her in learning life skills and social norms suggested by others. The overall physical elements, such as the size of the display, the location of the mirror, and the interface itself, can all influence the willingness of the individual to initiate communication through the system. The form factor we suggested was a large mirror (head to waist) located in bedroom. An individual with HFA commented that SocialMirror might encourage spontaneous communication because it would be seen when they are most likely to require help: "*It would be nice to know whether I look fine. If not, what should I improve, like how can I look better, more appealing?*" (I1)

Beyond the physical form factor, the mirror is also a conceptual metaphor that affects the perceived usage. Our findings suggest that SocialMirror, through simple connection to a social network of advisers, serves as a tool to 'reflect' on the social norms and conventions that might seem opaque to many individuals with autism. A student with HFA said: *"For the longest time I wore socks with sandals, and I still have no problem doing it. But, if I have the mirror, I will stop doing it because people will start saying over the mirror, 'Hey, it's not okay, you have to stop.'"* (I5) We noticed that SocialMirror could be used to confirm the fact that a suggestion from a caregiver is supported by general social norms. A counselor noted: *"Now I can simply tell the student if you don't believe me go ask the mirror."* (C3)

Participants addressed the necessity of a portable version of SocialMirror, since opportunities to learn life skills arise in places beyond the bedroom where the mirror would be located. For instance, if an individual needed guidance with a recipe while preparing a meal, he or she could easily bring a portable version into the kitchen to interact with others while cooking. Participants also expressed a desire to use SocialMirror outside the home. A student said: *"I would use this in school or church to get social etiquette like what I should be saying to people."* (I2)

While most participants reacted favorably to the idea of a mirror as a simple querying channel, our results also indicate challenges for SocialMirror. For some passive students, the form factor would not in and of itself promote the desire to ask for help. Furthermore, just because the individual receives prompts or advice does not mean he will follow them. A man with HFA told us that: *"I don't like being forced to feel or to do something. I like to be relaxed and comfortable, and not being reminded constantly of all the million things I have to do is nice."* (I1) To encourage the individual to seek advice, encouragement both from the system itself (e.g., personalized help reminder) and from the social network (e.g., rewarding, offering help based on the individual's interests) may be required.

Blended Functional and Social Capabilities

Our participants resonated strongly with the concept of integrating pictures and calendars to give context to the feedback they receive. The focus group interviews revealed an interesting blend between the functionality of a calendar and the social aspect of a picture. This blending suggested two potential targets for increasing independence, elaborating problems and schedule structuring.

Supporting Elaboration of Problems

In our attempts to design a simple way to ask for help, we focused on the particular difficulty individuals with autism experience in dealing with new situations and verbalizing when they need help. One study participant noted that the ability to share a picture would enable him to explain the context of his problem without the complex information processing required when writing out a full explanation.

Caregivers also reported that the ability to 'see' the problem the individual is encountering by means of a picture would facilitate communication, allowing them to provide better support. One of the teacher in the first focus noted: *"I would feel better if I had a kid calling me because they don't know how to handle the situation, and if I can see the situation I am going to feel more useful to this kid. I also can make them take a picture to help me to understand the situation. It will help the individual to explain their current situation in detail."* (C2)

However, the picture-mediated inquiry may not be appropriate to an emergency situation due to the delay in communication. A feature that allows for synchronous communication was suggested: *"If there is a situation that they didn't know they have an exam at school, but unexpectedly after they get into the class room they realize that they have the exam. You may include the button like instant message or call for unexpected situations when they need immediate help."* (I5)

Structuring the Schedule

Participants were very excited to see a day calendar on the mirror since they already employ a calendar to help them stay on schedule. One individual always carried a small notebook to keep up with schedule updates. Also, teachers noted that their students were asked to set up an electronic calendar (e.g., Google calendar) that sends alerts to their mobile phone. A common problem that our participants stated was that it was difficult to deal with sudden changes to their daily plans. They expressed that being able to see the events for the day on SocialMirror would help them anticipate what would be going on for that day: *"I sometimes don't know about schedule details like few days or last minutes, so that would be very helpful for me to know what I expect in a [given] day."* (I2)

Another commonly cited challenge and opportunity for SocialMirror is in time estimation: *"I guess another challenge of mine would be accurately estimating time for each event."* (I5) Participants often found comfort in strict plans in detail including start, end and transition time. They recommended integrating an estimated "time per event" into SocialMirror's calendar. Beyond the day's scheduling, participants expressed that SocialMirror had the potential to alert them to anticipated challenges and skills to cope with the challenges for events in the future. Sharing the individual's calendar in advance would enable multiple members to think about issues that might arise in advance and provide adaptive prompts before the event starts.

Community Empowerment

Distribution of Labor

Parents and caregivers agreed on the value of a social network to distribute the labor associated with providing support to an individual. A counselor noted that an extended trusted network was desirable because an individual's needs become more complex as he or she assumes independence. She defined a term, "trust committee," as a collective stable group of supportive people who can provide advice. She also envisioned that the social networking system could allow the trust committee to have access to the individual who needs help at anytime and anywhere: *"If you can harness all the people that care about that individual, that seems to me really powerful. Everybody is tuned in at a given time."* (C3) She noted that a main primary caregiver does not need to be always available, but can still play a central role in monitoring the network and having the final say on any influential decision.

However, distribution of labor across multiple caregivers may result in blurring the obligation to respond: *"Sending [a query] to everyone at once can be tricky because people would be like, "Well, I would respond, but I'm busy. I bet one of his other friends will respond." And if they all say that, then no one ends up responding. It's the diffusion of responsibility."* (I1) Participants recognized such challenges for SocialMirror and converted them into potential new features, such as one where the queries can be targeted ahead of time (e.g., financial queries go to parents, homework queries go to teachers, queries about attire go to siblings or cousins).

Catalyzing Collaborative Helping Activities

The most commonly expressed benefit of distributed caregiving to the individuals themselves was that they could learn new skills and acquire new capabilities as a result of getting advice from multiple sources. A student noted that SocialMirror would help him be more flexible in dealing with a new unexpected situation: *"If there are multiple suggestions, I would go for a backup and see what the next best one was to deal with [a situation]."* (I2) Caregivers also saw that an additional benefit of SocialMirror is that their children would not be confined to receiving advice solely from them. A mother of a man with HFA (I5) pointed out, *"I think also it's better if he goes outside the parental network because – there are so many little things I saw that we do already. Now, if it came from somebody else, it might be so much better. So, this would be kind of different I'm thinking."* (C4)

Participants also noted that SocialMirror would become a powerful tool to connect the caregivers and facilitate communication between the various care domains (e.g., home, school, job). Typically, once a student learns a particular activity at school, a protocol describing the procedure is sent to the parents so that it can be practiced at home as well. This reporting procedure between caregivers could be easily transmitted through the social network.

Connectedness and Reciprocity

Our concept emphasizes features inherent in social networking — bridging, bonding, and maintaining relationships between an individual and strong ties (e.g., parents, siblings, or close friends) or weak ties (e.g., residential coordinators, counselors, neurotypical volunteers) [4]. However, at the outset it was not clear if the benefit of such social properties would hold for individuals with autism, who often lack the motivation to engage in social interaction. In contrast, all young adults that participated in the design exercise stated that they understood the value of communicating about life skills via an online community and were eager to get involved in a long-term study. This may have been related to their age and previous experiences with various social networking services (e.g. Twitter, Facebook, MySpace, SecondLife). Several participants stated they wanted to keep connected with their peers not just for feedback, but also for fun: *"Let's say if I got a haircut, I would share my haircut, 'look what I got on my haircut'... or I would share random ideas. It would be more for fun. "* (I6)

During the demonstration session, one participant suddenly took a picture with a hilarious facial expression. Teachers and students in the focus group session were laughing and talking about what he did. In this example, we found a side activity that we did not anticipate; that is, sharing an interesting moment and jokes could augment the main activity of 'asking for help,' making it a more casual and fun experience.

We also noticed that the participants themselves acknowledged the benefit of bridging weak ties with physical distances. A mother stated she would want to invite relatives who live in another state to join her son's SocialMirror network: *"It would be good way for him to stay in contact with his cousins and other family members, a couple of different folks that are not at home, or not where he's living [out of state]."* (C4)

The individuals with autism in our study anticipated the social reciprocity and emotional support they would attain through Social Mirror. One individual noted: *"I'll ask a friend like 'Hey, I'll do dinner today, you cook dinner tomorrow.' That's the social thing. Well, I guess I've asked for help communicating with others."* (I1) Many young adults in our study reported they would feel more attached to their peers and get more engaged in what peers suggested through such reciprocal activities.

Barriers to Utilizing Social Network

The participants engaged with the concept and quickly came up with situations where they could use the technology. However, we also identified concerns associated with using a social network. The potential challenges include safety and privacy, conflicting advice from multiple caregivers, and intensified tension between an individual and his or her parents.

Safety and Privacy

Participants expressed concern about being involved in bad incidents such as bullying and being taken advantage of in cyberspace: *"I think the area that would be of concern that I would have is the young adults, because they are very trusting. So the importance of who he entrusts that social network to and he could have a bad choice there."* (C4) This echoes other findings related to safety and privacy issues in computer-mediated communication for adults on the autism spectrum [1]. Although SocialMirror affords primary caregivers the gatekeeping authority to confirm network membership, participants still voiced their concerns. A teacher commented that SocialMirror could mislead the individuals with autism because they are very rule-driven and likely to interpret each comment too literally.

The individuals themselves also raised the issue of personal information disclosure. They noted that in asking advice from trusted friends, they might share details that reveal their personal information and lifestyles. Consequently, they were concerned that SocialMirror might become a surveillance camera that monitored their everyday activities: *"What if someone comes in and they can turn on your mirror or webpage and read all the messages, all the concerns you've had. That would be uncomfortable."* (I1) To address the privacy concern, this participant came up with the idea of controlling visibility based on the relationship: *"I will keep that [information] limited to my intimate family members, or my friends. I don't want everybody to know about my issues."* (I1)

Conflict of Ideas

As participants stated, the dynamics of members in the social network can broaden opportunities to get feedback from differing perspectives. However, it increases the potential for confusion if two or more pieces of advice are in conflict. One participant clearly suggested a way to reconcile such conflicts: *"Would it make sense to have certain people in certain categories for certain things?"* (C1) It is clear that management of conflicting advice needs serious consideration in a deployed system.

Tension between Young Adults and Parents

In the SocialMirror system, parents are expected to safeguard the social network by acting as the gatekeeper for membership in the network. However this role may intensify the tension between the parent and the child. An adult expressed a strong objection to having parents act as moderators: *"I'm completely opposed to giving someone else control in my social life."* (I1) The individual noted that simply offering help doesn't mean that the individual will accept it: *"I haven't been as receptive to help, because my parents will a lot of times offer to help, but I just don't want their help."* (I1) Furthermore, the participant noted that parental involvement in his social network would not produce independence. A teacher emphasized the importance of respecting the individuals' free will: *"You don't want to force or control people. You're supposed to educate and encourage."* (C2)

This reinforces the idea that creating the network must be the role of the individual and the primary caregiver's role is to support him in his decisions. In fact, parents in our study did not think they needed to have complete authority. Rather, they expressed that they would want to create the network together with their son or daughter to encourage them to think about strategies to deal with potential risks.

DISCUSSION

In summary, SocialMirror has a potential to both promote the independence of individuals with autism and to facilitate collaboration among their caregivers. The central features of the SocialMirror system include a natural form factor, blended functionality and sociability, and community empowerment leveraged by the distribution of labor associated with supporting an individual with autism. The concerns associated with a social network have been identified as safety and privacy, conflict of ideas between caregivers, and tension between the young adults and their parents. In this section, we present the design consideration for leveraging a trusted network that balances quick response with safeguards to ensure the privacy and security of the young adults with autism.

Scaffolded Network Building

Building a social network for young adults with autism and caregivers is not as straightforward as building a social support network for group coordination for the general public [20]. Previous research indicates that a deficit in understanding social rules leads to difficulty for individuals with autism in deciding whom to trust and how much personal detail to disclose in an online community [1]. A network vetted by a primary caregiver can ensure the safety of the individual, but such limiting of the network may decrease the possibility of getting quick responses. We address this dilemma by introducing a scaffolded network building model, which is initiated by a group of people living or working with adults with autism on a regular basis (e.g., family members, school counselors). We propose that these network members can then invite other trusted individuals, such as extended family members or teachers who work in other schools. With respect to individuals' autonomy and free will, the network-building mechanism allows the individual to choose whom to get advice from. To protect the individual from choosing potentially deviant people who request membership, a newly added member should be under review until a trusted member approves them.

Layering a Network by Classes of Queries

SocialMirror allows individuals to ask a community of family and friends for advice, instead of a single person who may feel obligated to help. However, there is a risk that the picture- and the calendar-sharing feature may encroach on the individual's privacy. Many participants reported concerns with disclosing too many personal details, and felt uncomfortable with everyone knowing the details of their struggles. However, they did express great interest in sharing sensitive queries with those they are close to. This suggests that there should be classes of queries and layers within the network, such that close advisors respond to intimate questions, while peers advise on less important issues. Applying a degree of sensitivity to the queries and assigning them to a member with the appropriate level of closeness would enable the use of a larger network without sacrificing privacy. Fine- or coarse-grained access could also be provided for network layering. Fine-grained access would allow a particular group to see all types of queries (e.g., all pictures and events) while preventing others from seeing certain pictures or events on the calendar (e.g., financial tasks could only be seen by people authorized to access the individual's checking account). Another approach is a layering mechanism in which closeness is based on the relationship and communication history between the individual and the member.

Internal Negotiation System

Our study has highlighted how the use of SocialMirror with a range of different stakeholders involved in the transitioning of adults with autism could generate social tensions. For instance, multiple caregivers could provide different or even conflicting solutions that may be confusing to the individual with autism. In general, a successful online community requires a system that reconciles the conflicts [18]. Kollok suggested the use of an internal negotiation system, which is a low-cost conflict resolution mechanism implemented by members of a community [12]. One possible way to facilitate the internal negotiation could be resource distribution and allocation. For instance, one or more members could assign themselves to a certain support category (e.g., cooking, cleaning, dressing up, or socializing). This would decrease the chances of getting overlapping or conflicting responses, while increasing the opportunity to get a response because of increased commitment, but lighter workload. Additionally, a 'committee' for each query area could have the authority to resolve conflicts before the comments are delivered to the individual.

In short, a scaffolded member recruitment mechanism, layered distribution of queries, and an internal negotiation system could be used in a supportive trusted social network. Such considerations are invaluable in mitigating the risks associated with safety and trust, conflicts in suggestions, and tension between the adults with autism and their caregivers. These strategies will ensure potential impact on long-term independence.

CONCLUSION

Our research was aimed at providing young adults with autism who are in transition to adulthood with a safe and responsive social network that allows them to get information and advice about their everyday life. Our study investigated the potential for the proposed SocialMirror system that promotes independence and facilitates collaboration among the social network. The identified implications for designing such a supportive network, including a scaffolded network-building mechanism, a network layered by the degree of query sensitivity, and an internal negotiation system, promise to generalize to other groups beyond individuals with autism. In so doing, independent living can become a reality for other segments of the population who require extended support.

ACKNOWLEDGMENTS

The authors would like to thank the adults who agreed to participate in the study, as well as everyone at the Emory Autism Center, Community School, and Brookwood High School.

REFERENCES

1. Burke, M., Kraut, R., and Williams, D. Social use of computer-mediated communication by adults on the autism spectrum. Proc. CSCW 2010, ACM, 425–434.
2. Carmien, S., Dawe, M., Fischer, G., Gorman, A., Kintsch, A., and Sullivan, J.F. Socio-technical environments supporting people with cognitive disabilities using public transportation. ACM Transactions on Computer-Human Interaction, (2005), 233-262.
3. Carnahan, C.R., Hume, I.K., Clarke, I.L., and Borders, I.C. Using Structured Work Systems to Promote Independence and Engagement for Students With ASD. Teaching Exceptional Children 41, 4 (2009), 6-14.
4. Ellison, N.B., Steinfield, C., and Lampe, C. The Benefits of Facebook "Friends:" Social Capital and College Students' Use of Online Social Network Sites. Journal of Computer-Mediated Communication 12, 4 (2007), 1143-1168.
5. Geyer, W., Dugan, C., Brownholtz, E., Masli, M., Daly, E., and Millen, D.R. An Open, Social Microcalendar for the Enterprise: Timely. Proc. CHI 2011, ACM. 247-256.
6. Grimes, A., Bednar, M., and Bolter, J. EatWell: sharing nutrition-related memories in a low-income community. Proc. CSCW 2008, ACM, 87-96.
7. Hayes, G.R., Hirano, S., Marcu, G., Monibi, M., Nguyen, D.H., and Yeganyan, M. Interactive visual supports for children with autism. Personal and Ubiquitous Computing 14, 7 (2010).
8. Hong, H., Kim, G.J., Abowd, G.D., Arriaga, R.I. SocialMirror: Motivate young adults with autism to practice life skills in a social world, CSCW 2012 Videos.
9. Howlin, P., Goode, S., Hutton, J., and Rutter, M. Adult outcome for children with autism. Journal of child psychology and psychiatry, and allied disciplines 45, 2 (2004), 212-229.
10. Hume, K., Loftin, R., and Lantz, J. Increasing independence in autism spectrum disorders: a review of three focused interventions. Journal of autism and developmental disorders 39, 9 (2009), 1329-1338.
11. Jorgensen, D.L. Participant observation: a methodology for human studies. SAGE, 1989.
12. Kollock, P. Design Principles for Online Communities. Proc. VRAIS 97.
13. Krauss, M.W., Seltzer, M.M., and Jacobson, H.T. Adults with autism living at home or in non-family settings: positive and negative aspects of residential status. Journal of intellectual disability research. 49, 2 (2005), 111-24.
14. Lester, J. Brigadoon: More about Brigadoon. 2005. http://braintalk.blogs.com/brigadoon/2005/01/more_about_brig.html.
15. Mechling, L.C. and Savidge, E.J. Using a Personal Digital Assistant to Increase Completion of Novel Tasks and Independent Transitioning by Students with Autism Spectrum Disorder. Journal of autism and developmental disorders, (2010), 687-704.
16. Muller, E., Schuler, A., and Yates, G.B. Social challenges and supports from the perspective of individuals with Asperger syndrome and other autism spectrum disabilities. Autism 12, 2 (2008), 173-190.
17. A Generation of Autism, Coming of Age. NYTimes, 2010. http://www.nytimes.com/ref/health/healthguide/esn-autism-reporters.html.
18. Ostrom, E. Governing the commons: the evolution of institutions for collective action. Cambridge University Press, 1990.
19. PatientsLikeMe. http://www.patientslikeme.com.
20. Skeels, M.M., Unruh, K.T., Powell, C., and Pratt, W. Catalyzing social support for breast cancer patients. Proc. CHI 2010, ACM, 173-182.
21. Smith, M.A. and Kollock, P. Communities in cyberspace. Psychology Press, 1999.
22. Strauss, A. and Corbin, J., Basics of Qualitative Research Techniques and Procedures for Developing Grounded Theory. Sage Publications, London, 1998
23. Taylor, J.L. and Seltzer, M.M. Employment and Post-Secondary Educational Activities for Young Adults with Autism Spectrum Disorders During the Transition to Adulthood. Journal of autism and developmental disorders 41, 5 (2011), 566-74.
24. Wu, M., Birnholtz, J., Richards, B., Baecker, R., and Massimi, M. Collaborating to remember: a distributed cognition account of families coping with memory impairments. Proc. CHI 2008, ACM, 825–834

Building for Social Translucence: A Domain Analysis and Prototype System

David W. McDonald
The Information School
University of Washington
dwmc@uw.edu

Stephanie Gokhman
Department of Communication
Cornell University
sbg94@cornell.edu

Mark Zachry
Human Centered Design & Engineering
University of Washington
zachry@uw.edu

ABSTRACT
The relationships and work that facilitate content creation in large online contributor system are not always visible. Social translucence is a stance toward the design of systems that allows users to better understand collaborative system participation through awareness of contributions and interactions. Like many socio-technical constructs, social translucence is not something that can be simply added after a system is built; it should be at the core of system design. In this paper, we conduct a domain analysis to understand the space of architectural support required to facilitate social translucence in systems. We describe an instantiation of those requirements as a system architecture that relies on data from Wikipedia and illustrate how translucence can be propagated to some basic visualizations which we have created for Wikipedia users. We close with some reflections on the state of social translucence research and some openings for this important design perspective.

Author Keywords
Social translucence, system architecture, wikipedia.

ACM Classification Keywords
H.5.3. Group and Organization Interfaces – Computer-supported cooperative work.

GENERAL TERMS
Human Factors; Design.

INTRODUCTION
Understanding and interpreting the behaviors of others in an online environment is hard. The cues and signals that we readily interpret in a face-to-face situation are not present or are at best attenuated. Lacking sufficient cues, users often misinterpret or misunderstand the actions and intentions of others. As the number of participants and the amount of interaction grows it becomes harder and harder for users to make sense of others' actions, much less their own place in the community and the health of the community at large.

Social translucence [13,14] is a socio-technical term to describe how systems can facilitate understanding with regard to the actions of people in online environments. Social translucence includes three key design attributes: (a) mutual awareness of activities, (b) contextual propagation of socially salient cues (visibility), and (c) accountability for one's actions. Through support for these three characteristics members in a community can better understand the types of activities that transpire, understand the norms of the community and the consequences for the actions that they may take.

Like many socio-technical constructs, social translucence is not something that can simply be pasted in or bolted on. Designing for social translucence begins at the level of software architecture. The underlying software architecture of a system facilitates the observation of different types of activities within the system, the communications among the processes of the system, and the data that is stored and retrieved — all at the behest of some user action.

This paper raises the broad question of the domain of social translucence and conceptualizes it across two dimensions; actions that a system facilitates and levels of interpretation enabled by those actions. We start with a review of some relevant literature in social translucence. We conduct a type of domain analysis to elaborate these two dimensions of social translucence. Through our analysis we show that there is a wider space of social translucence yet to explore. We describe a system architecture that relies on data from Wikipedia enabling a broader class of social translucence, and we illustrate its applicability with specific use cases implemented using our architecture. The paper closes with a discussion and some implications for our contributions.

SOCIAL TRANSLUCENCE IN SYSTEMS
Research to define and elaborate social translucence for systems derived from Babble [5, 12], a type of instant messaging system, and a subsequent version called Loops [16]. In these systems translucence was illustrated through a set of social proxies. A social proxy is a small visualization that represents activity or participation in some interactive online context [1]. For Loops and Babble,

social proxies represented various forms of group communication, such as participants in a chat room or an online lecture. Social proxies can represent other forms of activity such as participation in an online auction or individuals queuing up for a chat with an online technical support specialist [14]. In this way, social proxies are a form of social visualization.

The term social translucence and techniques that can be broadly construed as supporting social translucence have been applied to wikis, often in the case of Wikipedia. History Flow [10, 33, 34] visualizes the changes of wiki pages over time, which is directly related to the activities of the editors. One claim is that, through a History Flow visualization, a user can see an 'edit-war'. We point out that one actually sees a series of changes being removed and replaced. That this series of actions is an 'edit-war' is a social interpretation that is made by an observer who may know something special about the community for which History Flow is visualizing activity.

Wikipedia has seen the development of numerous social visualizations such as Chromograms [35], Revert Graph [22], WikiDashboard [30], WikiChanges [27], and Revision History [11]. Some of these were deployed in live or proxied versions of Wikipedia meant for user consumption [30], while others were stand alone or analytic visualizations designed mostly for research.

The majority of these prior visualizations are based on 'surface' data. Here we are defining 'surface' data as data that can be visualized without little addition transformation. That is, the action of an edit and who made an edit may be all that is necessary to create the visualization. There is no need to transform these surface actions into some other representation before a meaningful visualization can be created. The actions are likely to be meaningful in their own right. The idea that this is a good way to develop social translucence is supported by a short list of claims that Erickson proposed in later work [15].

A key exception to this is the Chromograms visualization [35]. This visualization processed revision comments, giving each comment a consistent hue, saturation and brightness based on the first three letters of the comment string. While this is not very deep, it moves one step beyond a surface representation that an edit happened or that an edit has a comment. Interestingly, this simple processing of comments demonstrated activity patterns like the systematic processing of article pages needing cleanup or categorization.

While much of the related work in social translucence as applied to wikis implicitly equates the need for visibility with a type of (often complex) social visualization, this is not a requirement of social translucence. Another of Erickson's claims is that the visualizations should be simple and open to interpretation [15]. This claim has had some support in at least two cases [13, 31]. This claim is the root of the distinction we drew above for History Flow between what is visualized and the potential interpretations of that visualization.

Social translucence has also appeared in the threads of research concerned with awareness and availability to interruption. In this thread, visualizations are one mechanism for providing awareness of patterns of work activity in order to gauge levels of availability [3]. Some systems like Lilsys [4], MyVine [18], and AvBox [31] went further to include a form of environment sensing, and often manifest this awareness through visualizations. These sensing applications often required more processing. That is, they relied on some type of inference engine operating on samples of the physical or virtual environment to determine what should be conveyed through the visualization.

Much of the systems work in social translucence focuses on the level of the interface through visualizations. Many of those visualizations are fundamentally stand-alone features that overlay an existing system. In many cases these visualizations are re-representing activity in the system that occurs at the surface. A few systems have relied on sensing and inference algorithms to infer that activity (or lack of activity) should be visualized.

We extend the existing work in social translucence by framing social translucence on two dimensions through a type of domain analysis. The analysis opens up a space of possible implementations. We begin exploring the space of implementations through an architectural extension to WikiMedia and illustrate some of that space through specific use cases. We first turn to our domain analysis.

SOCIAL TRANSLUCENCE: A DOMAIN ANALYSIS

A proper domain analysis would consider a full range of software that claims to support social translucence to understand the specific features and architectures that have enabled those systems. In the space of systems that claim to address social translucence, there is little work focused on the software architecture. Instead, most of the systems described exhibit social translucence through somewhat independent software features, many of which we have covered above.

As well, a strict domain analysis focuses on software and architectural aspects from a technical stance. Since social translucence is a socio-technical construct, taking either a purely technical or purely social stance would ignore the important interplay between social activity and the systems that facilitate that activity. In our domain analysis we consider both the prior technical systems and motivating examples of activity in contributor systems.

We draw our motivating examples from the range of activity that happens in wikis and specifically Wikipedia.

The keystone papers in social translucence often motivated their explanations with examples based on a chat or instant messaging (IM) system. Wikis share some of the properties of IM, but afford a potentially wider range of user activities — depending on the wiki.

The Domain of Social Translucence

While there has been work developing socially translucent visualizations, there has not been work to understand the broader space of social translucence. Our efforts to design an architecture that facilitates social translucence forced us to face this problem and attempt to analyze the space of social translucence. Taking a step back from the instantiations of social translucence that we see in the literature, there are two key aspects from the definition of social translucence that could influence an architecture that would support it: user action and contextual salience.

Much of the 'social' in social translucence is based on actions that are oriented toward others in an interactive context. In many collaborative systems those interactions are mediated by the system and can often be decomposed into discrete actions with the system that are later shared with some partner, either synchronously or asynchronously. At times a system might not even preserve strict temporal ordering among the sets of discrete actions taken by a distributed set of people.

Breaking down the notion of 'social' in this way is important to thinking through the range of actions that might form the basis for a socially translucent system. In short, from an architectural perspective, almost any action that a person might take with a system could be an opportunity for a mediated interaction. Thus, almost any action with the system is the basis for generating social translucence. Whether or not a system exposes that an action has happened is important for social translucence at an architectural level.

Contextual salience is another critical element of social translucence. The challenge architecturally is that a system implementation cannot possibly anticipate all of the salient contexts in which actions might be represented. Yet, in all systems, for an action to be possible in the system there must be some code that understands and implements the action whether it be a button press, a drag, a GET or POST request, or any myriad other types of actions. These actions are not simply for collecting, they form the frame for the users' continuing activity. A socially translucent system needs to account for this ongoing activity when presenting information to the user or taking actions.

Our domain analysis is framed by two dimensions; one related to types of user actions in collaborative systems, and a second describing the processing and interpretation done by the system. Loosely, the first dimension begins to layout the types of actions that we might want the system to know and reflect about individuals. The second dimension relates to the types of interpretations that the system could make. These system interpretations are not the same as those made by users. Instead they represent aspects of behavior that might be contextually propagated for users.

Action Dimension

The first dimension contains four categories of actions that we term Content, Interaction, Relation and Systemic. These categories are not arbitrary: they follow from the types of questions individuals want to answer about others' behaviors [8, 9, 10].

Content - Understanding and representing the contents of a user contribution is a key aspect of representing social translucence. Content covers a wide range of things such as text, pictures, sound, video as well as meta-data. The contribution of content is valuable in some contexts, but in many cases the architecture should represent an additional level of information, indicating what that content was about. Wikis tend to be content focused and in many wikis a change history makes every piece of content visible and inspectable. In Wikipedia, knowledge of the content can be used to infer attributes of possible future contributions and how they might be trusted [2].

Interaction - Collaborative systems are often about the types of interactions that individuals can have through the system. Exchange of messages are an obvious form of interaction, but user interaction can be mediated by systems in a number of more complex ways. The domain of social translucence should account for each user action that contributes to the interactions among users. Wikis have some properties that are similar to IM in that there are explicit places for conversation, even if they are not synchronous. In Wikipedia individual user pages and user talk pages are explicit locations for attempting interaction. But co-authoring and reverting edits have also been used to illustrate a type of mediated interaction between and among users [22, 32, 34]. Not all co-authoring or reverting actions are reciprocated. Indeed notions of what constitutes an interaction can vary as a function of the actions that individuals take and the social context in which those actions are taken.

Relation - Not all relations are a function of interactions. In collaborative systems users can articulate specific relations that might need to be represented as a form of social translucence. For example, the explicit 'friending' of one user, which may not be reciprocated, is an important action. Also, the act of tagging an item creates a relation between that item and other items that also carry that specific tag. Collecting, organizing and presenting relations among people and things are valuable for social translucence. Link or relation analysis has shown value for understanding web influence such as the use of PageRank and broadly in understanding social structure such as in the use of Social Network Analysis. Too often, a system reflects little of who

Structure	Structure is the higher level constructs like roles and norms that individuals can observe over time. Structures are made of sequences of Instances and Series. Since Social Translucence is a contextual entity, time periods necessary to observe structure are defined by the social context.			
Series	Series are comprised of Instances. However, a Series may include more than one type of Instance. Common series can be comprised of repetitive activities, such as a chat where individuals trade interaction Instances.			
Instance	Actions that contribute content, but not simply the fact of a contribution. A system can process the content to see what type it is, some meta data on the content, or what the content is.	A single action by one user oriented toward another user. An attempt to talk or post a reply is an attempt to interact by one user, but so is a "poke" or a barnstar award. An Instance of interaction does not have to be reciprocated.	Users create explicit relations through different actions. For example, "friending" is a single action that attempts to indiciate a relation. As well, tagging an item creates a relationship among the newly tagged item and all other items that are tagged the same.	Actions that change the status of users in the system or the state of the system. For example, login, banning, user permission granting, programming, or running a bot.
	Content	**Interaction**	**Relation**	**Systemic**

Table 1. Two dimensions of the social translucence domain analysis

created the relations nor anything about the context in which those relations were created.

Systemic - Systemic actions are those that change the state of the system and the status of users of the system. For example, many systems require a 'login' action, but not all of them represent that action publicly and make it available broadly. 'Login' is social in the sense that it moves a person from a social place of unknown outsider to a known or at least pseudoanonymous community member. In virtual worlds or 'space' based systems, the location of the user is often a systemic trait of a user. There are other systemic actions that are key to facilitating social translucence in a system. In Wikipedia the Request for Adminship (RfA) process engages the community in a review of candidate users to potentially grant additional permissions. This process has implications for the community, but the actual granting of permissions moves the user from one status to another. Status changes in the system are important for understanding what is happening socially in a complex collaborative system.

Levels of System Interpretation

The second dimension of our domain analysis consists of three levels of interpretation that a system might distill to represent actions that users take within the system. We define these three levels as *Instance*, *Series*, and *Structure*. Each level builds on one or more levels below it. The level of Instance is the basic level of representing that a user has taken some individual action. In the common example of a chat system, a *Systemic* Instance is that the person joined the chat, a *Content* Instance is the text of one contribution, an Instance of *Interaction* is **that** they contributed to the conversation without presenting the actual content, and a *Relation* Instance could be establishing a private conversation with one other member of the chat. These instance examples all have real world analogs for what we may see in public as a function of the translucency of a social setting (e.g., [20]).

Using a wiki-based example, a *Systemic* Instance is a status change, like being promoted to admin. A *Content* Instance is editing an article. An *Interaction* instance would be posting to a user talk page or an article talk page to try and engage in a conversational interaction. Lastly, in wikis, tagging and categorizing pages constitutes a *Relation* Instance activity.

At the second level, we define *Series* as repeated Instances, whether those instances are of a single type or a heterogeneous patterned set. Series are important because they reflect how individuals participate and act in consistent or patterned ways and how they take on key tasks within a complex collaboration. Series suggest behaviors and interactions that might be sustained. The meaning of a Series is open to interpretation. For example, one user might perform a Series by systematically vandalizing a set of wiki pages, or an admin might perform a series by moving through a set of administrative tasks such as sanctioning users. Series are an aggregation of Instances. For a system to identify Series it must maintain some large set of Instances for some period of time. Further, once a Series is recognized by the system, the knowledge that the Series has occurred needs to be made available and potentially stored. If Instances are stored for long periods of time, like in many wiki systems, then storing a Series may simply require the system to recognize that a Series has happened based on collected Instances.

Structure is our third level of meaning and interpretation. There are many ways that communities structure their social space. Expectations, normative behaviors, patterns of social interaction, and social roles are some of the types of structure that individuals in a community might observe.

We define a Structure as some combination of recognized Series and Instances over time. While Series do occur over time in the sense that the first Instance in a Series naturally comes before the last Instance in a Series, a Series would not necessarily let one recognize a Structure. Our notion of Structure specifically requires time before a Structure could be acknowledged, but we leave the specific notion of time open to interpretation and as a function of the social context in which social translucence would be conveyed. Similar to Series, we consider Structure to be composable over existing Series and Instances. We frame the proposition for our domain analysis by claiming that some combination of Series and Instance would be necessary for a Structure to be observed. Further, we open the question of how to make a Structure visible for interpretation by individuals in the community.

Our domain analysis opens up the possible implementation space of social translucence. Next we describe a software architecture that enables wider exploration of social translucence and illustrate some of that space through several social proxies.

RE:ARCH – AN ARCHITECTURE SUPPORTING SOCIAL TRANSLUCENCE FOR WIKIS

Our domain analysis raises architectural concerns that must be instantiated in some fashion in order to support social translucence. We have built an extension to Wikipedia that we call Re:Arch which allows us to explore how social translucence can be enabled at the architectural level. We implemented Re:Arch through proxying because we ultimately want to facilitate actual user interactions and we have no control over when or how new code is incorporated into the WikiMedia codebase. This approach is similar to other single use tools [23, 30].

The general architectural model we employ parallels the data centered architecture of many contributor systems. We describe Re:Arch as a type of loose blackboard architecture (see Figure 1). In software architecture, blackboards are a generic architectural style sometimes referred to as a "repository" or "data-centered" style. We call this a blackboard because this architectural style facilitates complex state sharing, while loosening the constraints of the formal blackboard system [29]. Initially "blackboard" defined a strict rule-based control structure [21], but modern adaptations allow for alternate control flows to influence the state of the data on the blackboard. We follow this architectural style as a complement to many types of contributor systems. Versions of our architecture could simplify the construction of a range of tools and visualizations that support social translucence.

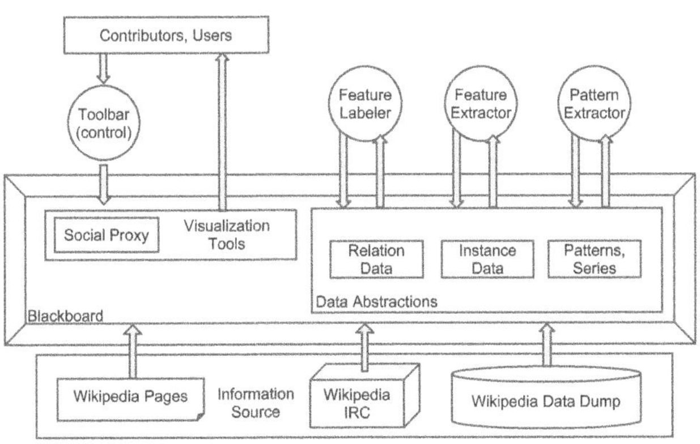

Figure 1. Re:Arch architecture diagram.

In addition to the core blackboard, Re:Arch includes visualization tools that allow user actions to alter the state of a blackboard: extracting data, designating patterns within the data, and posting this data in a new form.

Blackboard

The blackboard weaves together content, interaction, relations and system state. The blackboard has processes that inspect data from an information source, performs abstractions on this processed data and then utilizes this information to update the visualizations seen by the users. This information manifests itself within several different components that comprise the blackboard.

The blackboard provides a composable space in which each of these components can be manipulated by a contributor or user. Logically the blackboard enables users to see the entire state of the system at multiple layers; user, content, set of content, etc. A contributor can elicit meaningful information in their choice of context from separate but interrelated tools that are offered within the blackboard. These contexts are determined within the toolbar (or control) features of the architecture.

The data layer of Re:Arch instantiates key aspects from the domain analysis. A *feature extractor* reads Wikipedia pages, processes and extracts features from Wikipedia page dumps. The feature extractor can simply collect surface level features such as edits by given users, but it also processes the data to collect features that are not at the surface. In this way our Instance level subsumes what we previously defined as surface data. For example the feature extractor can collect headings, section contributions, template tags, links, and barnstars. The feature extractor implements much of what is needed at an *Instance* level.

Building from the feature extractor, the *feature labeler* annotates raw features in order to begin developing meaning from raw features. These labels are generated through a higher-level processing such as machine learning, crowdsourcing or human computation. The labeling is conducted in a contextually dependent way. One example is the awarding of barnstars on Wikipedia. Barnstars are small acknowledgments or achievements added to a user's talk page by another user. The feature extractor may identify a number of barnstars for a given user, and the feature labeler could label those barnstars with the type of work being acknowledged. It is up to user interpretation to determine whether the barnstars were awarded for negative or positive contributions. The feature labeler begins to address how interpretations can be presented that move from *Instance* to *Series* to *Structure* levels.

Building upon the feature extractor and labeler, the *pattern extractor* looks for patterns or chains of activity. Patterns could be mined for an individual user or for groups of users, such as WikiProject participants. The pattern extractor identifies and collects possible patterns from existing

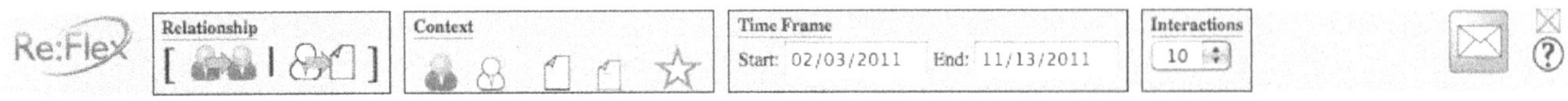

Figure 2. Re:Flex toolbar controls the composition of data sources and time window for the social proxy visualizations.

features or feature labels on the blackboard and posts them back. The pattern extractor is a direct instantiation of how Re:Arch identifies candidate *Series*. Identifying *Series* is valuable for users of the system and for understanding patterns of participation in open collaboration.

Re:Arch includes social proxies which rely on the visualization tools and data from the data layer. Our social proxies, much like those in the original conceptualization of social translucence, are not simply one visualization, but a range or set of possible visualizations. Social proxies can compose results from any information in the data layer of the blackboard.

Information Source

The system draws raw data from a number of sources to feed the blackboard. While our specific example draws on Wikipedia, the information source represents the logical connection between our architecture and potentially other user generated content systems that would want to implement social translucence.

The information source for Re:Arch is an aggregate itself of a number of Wikipedia data sources including Wikipedia Data Dumps, Wikipedia Special Pages and Wikipedia IRC Streams. The Wikipedia Data Dumps are the regular dumps of the entire edit history of Wikipedia from inception. This data set is cleaned and processed in order to populate our system's data abstraction layer. We can use the Special: page mechanism in Wikipedia to request specific updates, or make specific request from various Wikipedia tools.[1] Wikipedia also supports several Internet Relay Chat (IRC) channels where page changes are announced within the chat text. The architecture includes a process that listens to one or more channels and posts updates to the blackboard.

Toolbar as Control

A toolbar from the visualization toolkit facilitates a set of actions within this architecture. The toolbar provides the options to select data sources and present those sources in a number of different ways. The toolbar exists as a form that delivers specifications to the blackboard to pull meaningful information for the user. These specifications include: time window, types of data requested, and number of relations[2] to include in the visualization. In the following section we describe more about how the toolbar works, and give some examples of visualizations.

---

1. http://en.wikipedia.org/wiki/Wikipedia:Toolserver

2. This relation should not be confused with our analytic use of relation. The use here in the paper and in the toolbar is the general notion; a relationship between items.

RE:FLEX – INTERACTIONS AND VISUALIZATIONS

Re:Flex is a set of interface components built as part of Re:Arch. Re:Flex supports social translucence in Wikipedia by enabling editors to arrive at relatively complex understandings of other editors by visualizing interactions among editors or between editors and content. The system visualizes these Series that prior research has illustrated are meaningful to the Wikipedians (e.g., [6, 7, 9, 19, 22]).

For example a qualitative study by Bryant et al. [6] illustrated that newcomers to Wikipedia become part of the community through observing and modeling the behaviors of others in the community. This is not to dismiss the value of instruction, coaching, and sanctioning for shaping participants' behaviors, just that observation is a key aspect. This suggests that observing a Series maybe important to enabling newcomer participation.

Some quantitative work by Burke & Kraut [7] focused on the Request for Adminship (RfA) review process, wherein. regular Wikipedia editors who successfully complete the process are granted additional administrative capabilities. Their analysis resulted in a quantitative model of the user characteristics that account most for a positive outcome of the RfA process. While the model provides a score on how RfA candidates are judged, users are likely to want more than a composite score for a candidate — they may want to investigate that candidate in other ways.

In some initial work we did on the RfA process [9] reviewers wanted to know whether a candidate 'hung out with' the right kind of people on Wikipedia, and whether the candidate was participating in the right places. The subtlety is that for different reviewers what makes 'right' is open. Different reviewers value different 'right' people and different 'right' locations. This is reinforced by some exploratory design work of Kittur et al. [22] that investigated user revert graphs to visualize which users were in conflict with each other as a function of reverting each others' changes.

Re:Flex was developed to enable further exploration of social translucence as framed by our analysis (see Table 1). The current implementation is focused around supporting interpretations of Series. Little emphasis in this version was placed on visualizing Instance, and future work will focus on supporting the Structure level of interpretation.

The Re:Flex toolbar (Figure 2) floats over Wikipedia pages and offers users the opportunity to visually explore different kinds of relationships. While working in Wikipedia, users can turn on or off the toolbar, depending on the kind of work they are engaged in. When they want to know

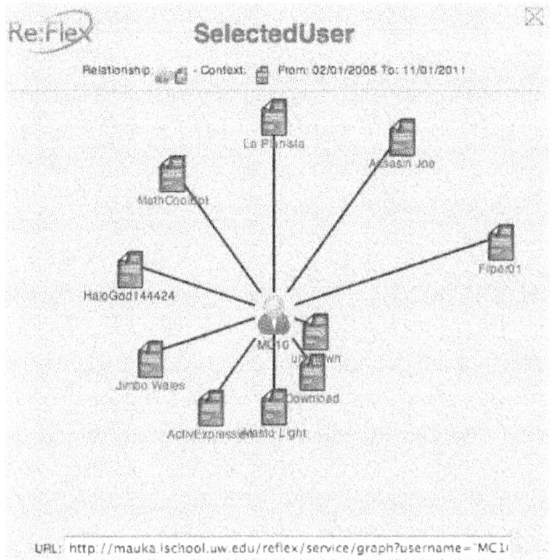

Figure 3. Example Re:Flex editor-article relation graph. Target (hovered) username presented in the middle, with top 10 edited articles placed by relative frequency on the edges.

something more about other editors, they can turn on Re:Flex and visually explore activities of another editor.

Use of the toolbar entails selecting the desired attributes of the target editor that will be included in the visualization. The set of visualizations that we describe allow the exploration of relationships between editors and relationships between editors and artifacts. These relationships are an example of taking Instance data (an edit) and transforming it to Series (a relation). The user may choose to expose editor-centric relations based on data from one or more of the four data contexts: article, article talk, user or user talk.

With one or more of these contexts selected, Re:Flex includes the relevant data in a visualization that is generated when the user hovers over an editor's username. The user has further control of what is exposed in the visualization by defining the date range of attributes to be included in the visualization and the number of top relationship entities to be visualized. For example, the user can select a target date range, say 3 months, for a given year, and specify the desired number of top interactions in any or all of the categories. Re:Flex will generate a visualization in a pop-up window located near a hovered editor's username. This visualization window persists until the user closes it or until the user navigates to another page. The user may generate several of these visualizations on a page, selecting the desired categories and hovering over different editor names to compare the visualizations.

Beyond these interaction categories, the Re:Flex toolbar also includes a feature for visualizing significant work and awards. This visualization is based on the barnstars or other significant recognition from the Wikipedia community. Unlike the other selections, this editor attribute cannot be combined with the other interaction categories. That is, when the recognition (star) icon is selected, the other interaction category icons are all deselected, and the user sees a visualization based on a hovered editor's barnstar acknowledgments. These are generated by processing the text of the barnstars that awarded to the target editor over the time period specified by the user. Details about how this awarding text is parsed, interpreted, and articulated to different categories of work is described elsewhere [26, 28].

The five types of visualizations that can be generated in this version of Re:Flex are motivated by use scenarios that we have identified from prior research with Wikipedians. These visualizations and the use scenario described below represent a small set of the possible ways that Re:Flex can support social translucence in contributor systems.

Re:Flex Example Scenarios

To illustrate how the Re:Flex system supports social translucence, we briefly point to one application scenario. We consider how Re:Flex enhances user understanding in the Request for Adminship (RfA) process in Wikipedia. The RfA process is a structured process wherein Wikipedia editors consider nominated members of their community for potential promotion to admin status [7]. Participants in this high-stakes process are encumbered with responsibility for making relatively sophisticated judgments about their peers, but provided with limited resources for doing so [9].

Consider Katie, an active Wikipedia editor. Katie stopped by her user page and saw a note from a friend saying that she should look at an ongoing RfA case. Katie has participated in an RfA review before. She believes in holistic evaluation of the candidate, to include edits to article pages, work with policy, removal of vandalism, and congenial interactions with other editors. In the past this has required that she plow through page after page of revision history. On the RfA page she sees a new tool, one that she has not seen before: Re:Flex. Since making article contributions is an important aspect to being a good Wikipedia editor, Katie selects article pages (document icon in Figure 2) as her initial exploration with the tool. She hovers over the candidate's username and a window pops-up showing the top five articles edited by that editor (Figure 3). These articles are good starting places for understanding how this individual contributes content.

But Katie also wants to understand with whom the candidate has interacted. She selects the user data source (user icon in Figure 2) and hovers over the username of the editor. A window pops-up (Figure 4) showing the relative relational strength between the candidate and the top five other editors with whom the candidate has interacted. Katie sees relationships rather than simply edit counts. These could be the key relationships that determine whether the RfA candidate interacts well with others and is worthy of adminship.

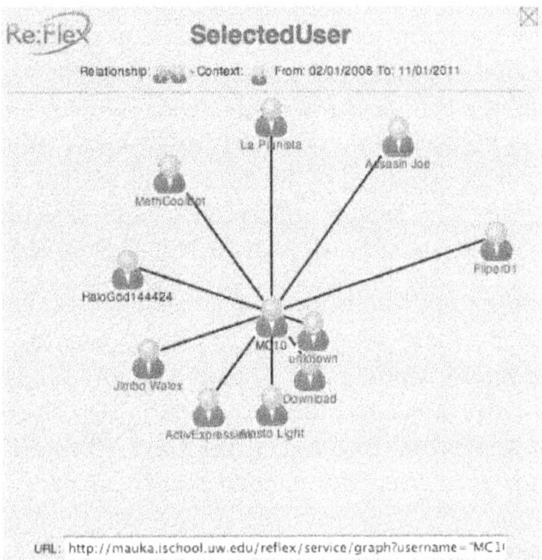

Figure 4. Example Re:Flex editor-editor relation graph. Target (hovered) username presented in the middle, with top 10 related editors spaced by relational strength.

Katie sees another option in Re:Flex, the work and award type of interaction (star icon in Figure 2). Katie clicks the star and hovers over the RfA candidate's username. A window opens containing a word cloud illustrating the relative weight of acknowledgements across seven broad categories of wikiwork; Administrative, Border Patrol, Collaborative Action, Editing, Meta-Content, Social and Community, and Miscellaneous (Figure 5). The word cloud conveys relative weight of types of work rather than a simple count of the barnstars or achievements. Based on the types of work, Katie can decide whether to explore one or more specific areas of Wikipedia edit history to better understand how this candidate contributes to Wikipedia.

RfA tools currently supported in Wikipedia are low level tools, mostly providing counts of content contributions often organized by namespace. Re:Flex addresses the relative paucity of information available to editors during this deliberative process by providing visualizations that go beyond just edit counts.

While RfA is illustrative of a formal Wikipedia process that might benefit from social translucence, there are many other, less structured places in Wikipedia where social translucence can be useful for the community, particularly, the desire among Wikipedians to know something more about the other editors they encounter. This desire is based, at least in part, on to the usefulness of understanding the intentions of others in order to react accordingly. Is this person serious? Is this person engaged in malicious behavior? Does this person need help or censure? Through Re:Flex, editors can develop some insight into other editors, discovering where another has contributed to the system.

DISCUSSION & IMPLICATIONS

Large-scale contributor systems present a special domain for considering social translucence. Applying our analytical framework for social translucence to these large-scale collaborative systems opens the space of socially translucent designs and implementations. Making visible the contextually salient work of users in these systems will enable a better understanding of each other's activities as well as facilitate productive work.

Based on our framing, it is not difficult to imagine redesigns of prominent sites to expose more of the users' contextual Interactions, Series, and Structure. We recognize that greater social translucence is not uniformly positive. For example, enabling more translucence in a social networking site would shift the nature of the system in a notable way. What if users' social searching and social browsing [25] were explicitly exposed? What if users' patterns of engaging in chat conversations about postings of others were made visible? Series and Structure insights like these could make social networking more socially translucent system, but might not complement existing uses and culture. Unlike a social networking site, contributor systems would generally benefit from greater social translucence. The point is that designers need to make informed decisions about where to use translucence. Our framework allows designers to make informed decisions about what activities to visualize at what interpretive levels.

The two-dimensional view of social translucence we have developed holds promise beyond providing heuristics for designing translucence into contributor systems. The definitional properties of the two dimensions — types of actions and the processing/interpretation done by the system — can also be operationalized as analytic categories for assessing the nature and prominence of social translucence in collaborative systems more generally. Categorizing the online systems that people use to work together on the web, for example, has proven to be difficult because such systems are varied in multiple ways [17].

Figure 5. Example Re:Flex award and recognition word cloud visualization. The word cloud displays the relative amount of recognition of an editor for a set of defined work types.

Given that all such systems share the fundamental characteristics of facilitating multi-participant interactions mediated by web-based tools, it would be possible to categorize this class of technology using our dimensions of social translucence. Such a structured classification of socio-collaborative systems would provide some reasoned order to the confusion of systems that are now labeled social networking sites.

Our contribution goes beyond just our intellectual framing of social translucence. Through Re:Arch and Re:Flex we provide a concrete instantiation of some properties derived from the framing. Re:Arch supports social translucence through the data on the underlying blackboard, through the processes that transform and label that data, and through the social proxy visualizations that we have designed.

Many of the prior system contributions that support social translucence are focused at the Instance layer, or individual actions with the underlying system. However, Instance based visualizations are only a small portion of the realm of social translucence. Building off the Re:Arch architecture with Re:Flex, we go beyond a single visual design toward validating the theoretical framework of social translucence at the Series level. Building Re:Flex on an architectural model designed to facilitate social translucence enables wider exploration of translucence at the interface.

The interaction category relationships present in the current Re:Flex prototype are relatively simple, based primarily on interaction counts. These were chosen because they align with existing Wikipedian practices and because few other tools address these needs. These visualizations suggest ways of exploring Series-based insights about others, but do not fully realize that interpretation layer of our analysis. We do not mean to imply that interpreting the existence of a relation based on Series is simple and solved.

In Re:Flex user-to-user relations can be requested of the blackboard in more than one way. A user-to-user relation is one way to visualize a Series of edits. But there are different ways to think about those individual edits. For example, the co-editing of an artifact is one way to recognize a potential user-to-user relation. But also, in the context of a user's page, which is a type of 'owned' artifact, a unidirectional edit might be sufficient to recognize a potential relation. Further, in that same context one might want to consider reciprocal edits, where users mutually edit each other's user pages. Yet further, the different mechanisms for considering the edit action might be combined — edit, co-edit, and/or reciprocal edit — to distinguish further ways of recognizing a potential user-to-user relation.

The award recognition visualization is built from more complex, Series-based observations about a given editor, thereby addressing a different aspect of our framework. The award recognition visualization relies on a multi-label machine classifier. Recognitions are then compiled over time as they are awarded. This feature based visualization is just an example and validating the utility of the visualization is future work.

Effective social translucence relies on mutual awareness of activities, contextual propagation of socially salient cues, and accountability for one's actions. Our analysis helps designers think more concretely about what activities are important to social translucence and how interpretive levels of those activities might provide contextual salience.

ACKNOWLEDGMENTS

We acknowledge the contributions of our collaborators, specifically Michael Gilbert, Casey Shey, Cheng Chuang, Alena Benson, and Siwei Kang for their work on Re:Flex. We thank the CSCW reviewers for an engaging discussion on our work and for the resulting improvements. We thank Wikipedia users for sharing their expertise and WikiMedia foundation for providing dumps of this valuable resource. This material is based on work supported by the National Science Foundation under Grant No. IIS-0811210. The opinions, findings, conclusions or recommendations expressed are those of the author(s) and do not necessarily reflect the views of the National Science Foundation.

REFERENCES

1. Ackerman, M.S. and Starr, B., Social Activity Indicators: Interface Components for CSCW Systems. *Proceedings of UIST'95*, 1995
2. Adler, B.T. and de Alfaro, L. A Content-Driven Reputation System for the Wikipedia. in *Proceedings of WWW 2007*. 261-270.
3. Begole, J., Tang, J.C., Smith, R.B. and Yankelovich, N., Work Rhythms: Analyzing Visualizations of Awareness Histories of Distributed Groups. *Proceedings of CSCW 2002*.
4. Begole, J., Matsakis, N.E. and Tang, J.C. Lilsys: Sensing Unavailability. *Proceedings of CSCW 2004*.
5. Bradner, E., W.A. Kellogg, and T. Erickson. The adoption and use of BABBLE: A field study of chat in the workplace. *Proceedings of ECSCW 1999*.
6. Bryant, S.L., Forte, A. and Bruckman, A., Becoming Wikipedian: Transformation of Participation in a Collaborative Online Encyclopedia. *Proceedings of GROUP 2005*. 2005.
7. Burke, M. and Kraut, R. Mopping Up: Modeling Wikipedia Promotion Decisions. *Proceedings of CSCW 2008*. 27-36.
8. Carley, K. M. A Dynamic Network Approach to the Assessment of Terrorist Groups and the Impact of Alternative Courses of Action. In *Visualizing Network Information*, Meeting Proceedings RTO-MP-IST-063 available at http://www.rto.nato.int/abstracts.aspx

9. Derthick, K., Tsao, P., Kriplean, T., Borning, A., M. Zachry, M., and McDonald, D. W. Collaborative Sensemaking during Admin Permission Granting in Wikipedia. *Proceedings HCI International*. 2011
10. Diaz, O. and Puente, G. Model-aware Wiki Analysis Tools: the Case of HistoryFlow. *Proceedings of WikiSym 2010.*
11. Ekstrand, M.D. and Riedl, J. rv you're dumb: Identifying Discarded Work in Wiki Article History. *Proceedings of WikiSym 2009.*
12. Erickson, T., Smith, D.N., Kellogg, W.A., Laff, M., Richards, J.T. and Bradner, E. Socially Translucent Systems: Social Proxies, Persistent Conversation, and the Design of "Babble". In *Proceedings of CHI'99.*
13. Erickson, T. and Kellog, W. A. Social Translucence: An Approach to Designing Systems that Support Social Processes. *ACM Transactions on Computer-Human Interaction*, 2000. 7(1).
14. Erickson, T., Halverson, C., Kellogg, W., Laff, M. and Wolf, T. Social Translucence: Designing Social Infrastructures that Make Collective Activity Visible. *Communications of the ACM*, 2002. 45(4).
15. Erickson, T., Designing Visualizations of Social Activity: Six Claims. *Proceedings of the CHI extended abstracts* (CHI'03), 2003.
16. Erickson, T., Kellogg, W. A., Laff, M., Sussman, J., Wolf, T. V., Halverson, C. A., and Edwards, D. A Persistent Chat Space for Workgroups: The Design, Evaluation and Deployment of Loops. *Proceedings of DIS 2006.*
17. Ferro, T., and M. Zachry. (2011). Networked Knowledge Workers on the Web: An Examination of US Trends, 2008-2010. *Handbook of Research on Business Social Networking: Organizational, Managerial, and Technological Dimensions*. Hershey, PA, USA: IGI Publishing.
18. Fogarty, J., Lai, J., and Christensen, J. Presence versus Availability: The Design and Evaluation of a Context-Aware Communication Client. *International Journal of Human-Computer Studies* (IJHCS), 2004, 61(3).
19. Forte, A. and Bruckman, A. Scaling Consensus: Increasing Decentralization in Wikipedia Governance. *Proceedings of HICSS-41,* 2008.
20. Goffman, E. *Behavior in Public Places*. Free Press, New York, NY, 1963.
21. Hayes-Roth, B. A blackboard architecture for control. *Artificial Intelligence*, 1985, 26, 251-321.
22. Kittur, A., Bongwon, S., Pendleton, B.A. and Chi, E. He Says, She Says: Conflict and Coordination in Wikipedia. *Proceedings of CHI 2007.*
23. Krieger, M., Stark, E. and Klemmer, S.R. Coordinating Tasks on the Commons: Designing for Personal Goals, Expertise and Serendipity. *Proceedings of CHI 2009*, 1485-1494.
24. Kriplean, T., Beschastnikh, I., and McDonald, D. W. Articulations of Wikiwork: Uncovering Valued Work in Wikipedia through Barnstars. *Proceedings of CSCW 2008.*
25. Lampe, C., Ellison, N. and Steinfield, C. A Face(book) in the Crowd: Social Searching vs. Social Browsing. *Proceedings of CSCW 2006.*
26. McDonald, D. W., Javanmardi, S. and Zachry, M. Finding Patterns in Behavioral Observations by Automatically Labeling Forms of Wikiwork in Barnstars. *Proceedings of WikiSym 2011.*
27. Nunes, S., C. Riberio, and G. David. WikiChanges - Exposing Wikipedia Revision Activity. *Proceedings of WikiSym 2008.*
28. Sajnani, H., Javanmardi,, S., McDonald, D.W. and Lopes, C. Multi-Label Classification of Short Text: A Study on Wikipedia Barnstars. in "Analyzing Microtext" Workshop at the Twenty-Fifth Conference on Artificial Intelligence (AAAI-11), 2011.
29. Shaw, M. and Garlan, D. *Software Architecture: Perspectives on an Emerging Discipline*, 1996. Prentice-Hall, Inc.
30. Suh, B., Chi, E., Kittur, A. and Pendleton, B.A. Lifting the Veil: Improving Accountability and Social Transparency in Wikipedia with WikiDashboard. *Proceeding of CHI 2008.*
31. Szostek, A.M., Karapanos, E., Eggen, B. and Holenderski, M. Understanding the Implications of Social Translucence for Systems Supporting Communication at Work. *Proceedings of CSCW 2008.*
32. Tang, L.V.-S., Biuk-Aghai, R.P. and Fong, S. A Method for Measuring Co-authorship Relationships in MediaWiki. *Proceedings of WikiSym 2008.*
33. Viégas, F., Wattenberg, M. and Dave, K. Studying Cooperation and Conflict between Authors with history flow Visualizations. *Proceedings of CHI 2004*, 575-582.
34. Viégas, F., Wattenberg, M., Kriss, J. and van Ham, F., Talk Before You Type: Coordination in Wikipedia. *Proceedings of HICSS-40*, 2007.
35. Wattenberg, M., F. Viégas, and K. Hollenbach, Visualizing Activity on Wikipedia with Chromograms, *Proceedings of Human-Computer Interaction – INTERACT* 2007.

Ubiquitous Collaborative Activity Virtual Environments

Aryabrata Basu
University of Georgia
basuarya@uga.edu

Andrew Raij
University of South Florida
raij@usf.edu

Kyle Johnsen
University of Georgia
kjohnsen@uga.edu

ABSTRACT

We introduce a new paradigm of collaborative computing called the Ubiquitous Collaborative Activity Virtual Environment (UCAVE). UCAVEs are portable immersive virtual environments that leverage mobile communication platforms, motion trackers and displays to facilitate ad-hoc virtual collaboration. We discuss design criteria and research challenges for UCAVEs, as well as a prototype hardware configuration that enables UCAVE interactions using modern smart phones and head mounted displays.

Author Keywords

Virtual environment, collaborative, mobile, ubiquitous, virtual reality, display

ACM Classification Keywords

H5.m. Information interfaces and presentation (*e.g.*, HCI): Miscellaneous.

General Terms

Human Factors; Design; Measurement; Experimentation.

INTRODUCTION

Collaborative virtual environments (CVEs) enable spatially distributed users to work together on shared tasks in a real-time artificial reality. While a variety of interfaces exist for CVEs, researchers have noted that immersive interfaces offer unique interaction affordances and potential benefits to collaborative work [9]. However, immersion is difficult to achieve in a widespread, practical manner. The "work to make it work" has been substantial; sufficient equipment has only been available in dedicated research and development laboratories, and these conditions limit widespread deployment [5, 9]. In this paper, we present the ubiquitous collaborative activity virtual environment (UCAVE) concept, which enables immersive virtual collaborations with minimal, portable infrastructure.

An immersive interface to a CVE most commonly includes technology for natural viewing of a virtual environment and control over an avatar embodiment. Examples include the immersive interfaces provided by the DiVE and Massive CVEs [4], such as head-mounted and spatially immersive displays with user body tracking for avatar control. This is in contrast to non-immersive interfaces, which typically employ fixed planar displays and indirect control schemes such as a keyboard, mouse and on-screen widgets.

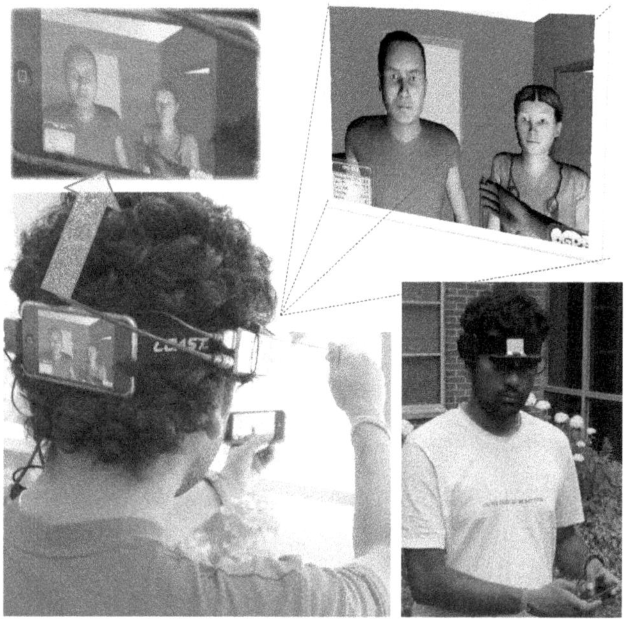

Figure 1 A user operating a UCAVE implementation inside and outside featuring a lightweight head-mounted display, smart phones and immersive 3D rendering.

While non-immersive interfaces are highly accessible to end-users and support a wide range of interactions, the viewing and control schemes are noted to be frustrating and perhaps misleading in some collaborative work situations [9]. For example, where an avatar is gazing is not necessarily where a user is gazing. Immersive interfaces are often suggested to counter such effects, where the user is directly controlling the avatar and seeing what others perceive the avatar to see [9, 10]. However, the practical reality of immersive interfaces includes high cost, visual quality tradeoffs, extensive setup, user encumbrance, and limited deployment possibilities.

The UCAVE concept presented here offers a vision that this reality is changing; that immersive interfaces to CVEs are possible and can be as useable, portable and inexpensive as non-immersive interfaces. The UCAVE aims to make an immersive interface a choice that is dictated by application requirements and not by logistical limitations.

UCAVE Applications

UCAVEs are targeted at different applications than those of traditional immersive CVEs. The targeted applications are more in-line with collaborative mobile applications, where an immersive CVE being quickly and easily available to users may be enticing.

There is a growing trend towards video conferencing on mobile devices. We believe that UCAVEs can add a new dimension to this application, particularly in the case of multi-party conferencing, where conversational gaze cues are misrepresented in video. When necessary, such as when it is important for conversational participants to share the same space, participants could switch into an immersive viewpoint via the UCAVE hardware. There would be a tradeoff of the loss of some facial expression, but gesture and gaze cues could be maintained. In addition, it is then possible to support concepts such as Transformed Social Interaction [2]. Studying such ad-hoc immersive encounters will also be of interest to social psychology researchers, where the UCAVE could scale the scope of experiments to dozens or even hundreds of users.

The mobility and convenience of the UCAVE also offers new opportunities for CVEs to be applied in locations outside of dedicated laboratories. For example, consider an architectural firm designing a new building. To use a traditional immersive CVE, each architect and client would need to have dedicated laboratory space. With the UCAVE, multiple users can participate in an immersive design review from the convenience of their own space, without the expensive, encumbering, and large equipment commonly found in immersive CVEs.

BACKGROUND

A set of important, interrelated events has occurred that has made the UCAVE vision possible, where it would have been unlikely before. First, there is a rather sudden ubiquity of mobile computational power and high-speed mobile communication. The Gartner group estimates that 468 million smart phones will be purchased in 2011 [8]. These ultra-portable computers are interconnected on networks capable of supporting CVEs, and have the computational power to render complex 3D environments, largely owing to the popularity of mobile 3D gaming. Second, head-mounted displays (*e.g.* Vuzix Wrap 920) have emerged to support large-screen viewing and privacy for consumers using such mobile systems. Such head-mounted displays have substantially lower field-of-view, but are lighter, oriented towards casual use, and are a small fraction of the cost of professional quality head-mounted displays. Finally, motion-control gaming devices have made motion-tracking devices inexpensive and ubiquitous. While largely based on inertial tracking, there are also consumer-level mechanical, electromagnetic and optical tracking systems available. These, coupled with the ubiquity of motion control sensors already in smart phones *form the hardware basis for portable immersive virtual reality systems and the UCAVE concept.*

That is not to say that the UCAVE is the first concept of a portable immersion system. Mobile augmented reality (AR) systems have existed for over a decade, using backpack-worn computers, head-mounted displays and tracked controllers [11]. The field is also moving towards smart phone platforms, which support augmented reality applications using built-in inertial sensors, global positioning systems, cameras, and displays [12]. However, collaborative AR systems have fundamentally different application domains and technical challenges than CVEs.

Collaborative AR applications are local collaborations, as the point of AR is to see virtual information fused with the real environment, while CVEs are targeted towards applications for geographically distributed users. Since users are geographically distributed, CVEs usually incorporate avatars for a number of reasons, including network bandwidth control and for a 3D user representation [3]. Thus, a fundamental challenge to CVEs is providing users with appropriate interfaces to manipulate his or her avatar and virtual objects. This can be accomplished through a variety of means, both direct and indirect.

In AR, the fundamental challenge is tracking the pose of the display to ensure consistent overlay of virtual information on the real world. However, this is not a requirement in a CVE. In fact, the lack of real world constraints is often a significant reason for using CVEs. In CVEs, physical space constraints do not limit the number of people that can take part in an interaction to the number that can comfortably fit in the real environment. CVEs also allow interactions not possible in the real world, such as two people simultaneously manipulating the same part of virtual space or viewing an object from the same location.

UCAVE BENEFITS

Hindmarsh *et al* raised a number of concerns pertaining to what would typically be called a non-immersive CVE interface (an ordinary keyboard, mouse, monitor configuration) [9]. These were:

- The horizontal field of view of the display was limited, causing difficulty observing spatial references of others while simultaneously observing the referenced object (source and target).
- Actions were not always reflected by user embodiments, which can also be extended to include both virtual actions and real world actions (*i.e.*. a user disengaging from the CVE interface)
- Navigation of the CVE was clumsy, owing to, amongst other things, the lack of an intuitive interface for navigation
- Parallel actions were not supported, such as moving an object and changing viewpoint simultaneously.

Hindmarsh et al suggested that an immersive interface (a tracked HMD with multiple tracked position sensors) could address these issues, but argued against an immersive interface because of logistical issues of cost, robustness, and setup difficulties [9].

The UCAVE aims to make the benefits of immersion accessible by reducing these logistical issues. *It should support immersive interaction, but not at the expense of user mobility or ease of use*. In other words, it should provide the expected affordances of a conventional immersive CVE interface: natural interactive viewpoint and avatar control, but be able to be carried around by the user and immediately deployed. While on its surface the principle is simple, immersion, mobility and ease of use are often conflicting, and thus design tradeoffs must be made.

UCAVE ARCHITECTURES AND PROTOTYPE

A general UCAVE architecture is shown in Figure 2. The smart phone (or similar handheld computing device) is the central core of the UCAVE architecture. Modern smart phones have a high-resolution display, a powerful system-on-chip (for interface, radio communication, graphics, and audio processing), and an array of sensors (*e.g.* touch-screen, accelerometers, gyroscopes, and magnetometers). The smart phone is connected to a head mounted audio-visual display. Additional body-worn sensors are incorporated as needed through personal area network technologies. When connected over a wide area network (*i.e.*. the Internet), remote users can join other UCAVEs, creating collaborative workspaces. Finally, at certain locations in the environment, external sensors may be available that provide additional capabilities to the user (*e.g.* a motion capture system).

A prototype of the UCAVE hardware has been constructed using only consumer level components. The hardware consists of a jailbroken Apple iPhone 4G (~\$599 USD), and a Vuzix Wrap920 Stereoscopic 640x480 (~\$299 USD) head-mounted display. The Vuzix Wrap920 has an iPhone connector that enables video to be transmitted from the iPhone and displayed on the HMD. Stereoscopic images are transmitted via side-by-side signaling. The Vuzix Wrap920 is powered by a small battery pack. To complete the UCAVE hardware, a stereo headset is employed for audio input and output.

As seen in Figure 1, the iPhone and the Vuzix HMD's display and battery components were assembled together into a single wireless head-mounted device, mounted by means of an elastic band, Velcro, and an iPhone case. This design has unique logistical properties. First, the entire device can be folded and placed in the user's pocket. The case allows the iPhone to be easily detached for other uses. Furthermore, mounting the iPhone removes the requirement that the user hold the iPhone. This relieves the user's hands for other activities and removes a wire from the configuration, making the design more compact. If desired, a second iPhone (or any device that has WiFi or Bluetooth communications, such as a Nintendo Wii Remote) can be employed as a hand-held interaction device.

Currently, we have demonstrated an immersive VE featuring avatars rendered with the open source Object-oriented Graphics Rendering Engine (OGRE). Immersive rendering is enabled through the built-in iPhone magneto-inertial orientation sensor. The simulation runs in real time, at 60 frames-per-second on the iPhone, with two 7000 polygon count avatars (with a skeletal and facial bone rig), and a 14000 polygon count virtual room.

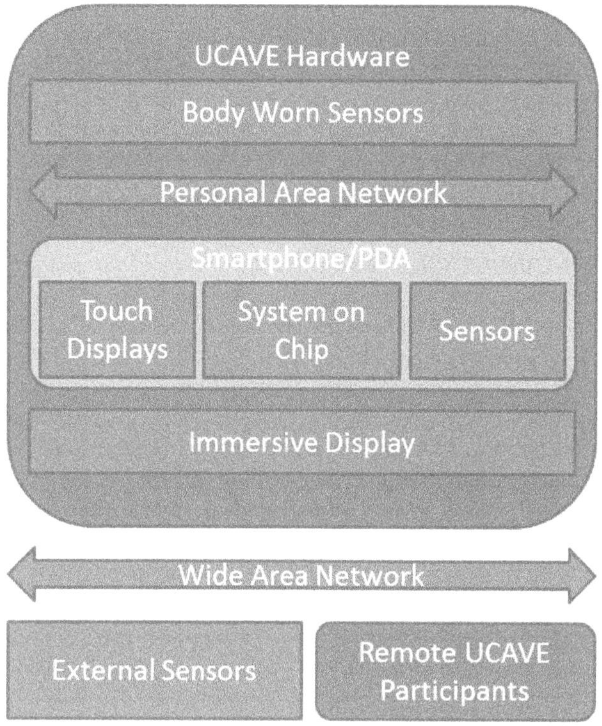

Figure 2 The UCAVE Architecture

User Immersion

For the prototype, we focused on providing a natural immersive viewpoint and natural avatar head and hand control. This is because gaze and hand gestures account for a substantial portion of non-verbal communication [1]. In a virtual reality laboratory, it would be possible to use motion capture techniques and tracking systems with fixed reference frames (optical, mechanical, electromagnetic, etc). While not strictly impossible with the UCAVE, it is useful to consider less encumbering and more practical approaches that would work in arbitrary environments and afford the user a greater degree of mobility.

To provide an immersive viewpoint, a source less head orientation estimation is conveniently obtained from the inertial sensors built into the head-mounted iPhone. To compensate for the iPhone being potentially tilted with respect to the face plane, calculation of an orientation offset is necessary at the start of an interaction. This calibration step can be completed by the user looking in a known direction and signaling the software. The head orientation computed for immersive rendering is directly used for the head orientation of the user's avatar as seen by other UCAVE users.

Avatar hand control has proven more challenging to support in accordance with the UCAVE design goals. The current design features two lightweight, head-mounted, mechanical position sensors taken from the MadCatz GameTrak motion control device. These sensors are inexpensive (\$75 USD) and offer excellent position tracking characteristics (1 cm accuracy, 1mm resolution, no jitter). From the tracked hand position, which is in the frame of reference of the user's head, the motion of the avatar's hand is derived through an inverse kinematics approach. The current limitation of this approach is that it does not provide as much range of motion as collaborative activities may demand (limited to approximately the field-of-view of the Vuzix display).

CHALLENGES AND LIMITATIONS

In contrast to spatially immersive displays, *e.g.* [6], head-mounted displays, such as the one shown in Figure 1, can be battery powered, lightweight, fit in a small pocket when not in use, and provide consistent visual quality from all viewing locations. While this makes head-mounted displays well suited to the UCAVE, the primary tradeoff is a relatively narrow horizontal field of view (~25-40 degrees, comparable to sitting three meters away from a two meter width television) provided by all but the most expensive head-mounted displays. A narrow field-of-view has many negative implications for CVEs, including lack of spatial awareness of other participants and lack of intuitive understanding of what is perceived by others [7]. However, users may compensate for the narrow field of view through sweeping head-rotations, and the UCAVE facilitates such actions by being lightweight and wireless. It should also be noted that aural immersion in the UCAVE can be complete, and this may be used to create spatial awareness of surroundings and others. Furthermore, without support for eye-tracking (currently difficult in head-mounted displays), a narrow field of view encourages the use of head motions to indicate attention [2].

The impromptu deployment possibilities of the UCAVE in the real world (*e.g.* in a crowded public space or in a natural outdoor setting) also raise important issues. First, supporting navigation about the VE is challenging. Unlike outdoor augmented reality systems, natural walking navigation is difficult, because users may bump into objects or people that are occluded by the head mounted display. As an alternative, techniques such as walking-in-place or using a smart phone touch screen as a joystick or pointing device could be used. Finally, as the technology matures, it will be possible to obtain an accurate 3D map of the real environment using vision sensors embedded in the smart phone. This 3D map could be used to implement collision avoidance algorithms or as the virtual environment itself.

CONCLUSIONS

The potential application space of widespread deployment of immersive collaboration technology is vast. Perhaps any CVE application that currently requires laboratory spaces could be extended to millions of people, and thousands of existing mobile applications could begin to leverage immersion. To enable this vision, we are currently preparing a practical prototype for study in the field. Our focus is on redesigning the tracking system to improve range of motion. Inertial and optical tracking approaches could improve range of motion and may not require custom modifications to the hardware. It is our belief that collaborative virtual reality "in the wild" offers exciting new challenges to the VR and CSCW communities and opportunities to develop novel applications free from the confinements of controlled laboratory spaces.

REFERENCES

1. Argyle, M. and M. Cook. *Gaze and Mutual Gaze*. (1976), xi, 210 pp.
2. Bailenson, J.N. and N. Yee. A longitudinal study of task performance, head movements, subjective report, simulator sickness, and transformed social interaction in collaborative virtual environments. *Presence: Teleoperators & Virtual Environments*, 15,6 (2006), pp. 699-716.
3. Benford, S., J. Bowers, L.E. Fahlén, C. Greenhalgh, and D. Snowdon. User embodiment in collaborative virtual environments. In *Proc. ACM Conference on Computer Human Interaction (SIGCHI)*. (1995), pp. 242-249.
4. Benford, S., C. Greenhalgh, T. Rodden, and J. Pycock. Collaborative Virtual Environments. *Communications of the ACM*, 44,7 (2001), pp. 79-85.
5. Bowers, J., J. O'Brien, and J. Pycock. *Practically accomplishing immersion: cooperation in and for virtual environments*. in *ACM Conference on Computer Supported Cooperative Work*. (1996), pp. 380-389.
6. Cruz-Neira, C., D.J. Sandin, and T. DeFanti. The design and implementation of the CAVE. In *Proc. ACM SIGGRAPH*. (1993), pp. 135-142.
7. Fraser, M., S. Benford, J. Hindmarsh, and C. Heath. *Supporting awareness and interaction through collaborative virtual interfaces*. in *ACM Symposium on User Interface Software and Technology*. (1999), pp. 27-36.
8. Gartner Group. *Forecast Analysis: Mobile Devices, Worldwide, 2008-2015, 1Q11 Update* (2011).
9. Hindmarsh, J., M. Fraser, C. Heath, S. Benford, and C. Greenhalgh. Object-focused interaction in collaborative virtual environments. *ACM Transactions on Computer-Human Interaction (TOCHI)*, 7,4 (2000), pp. 477-509.
10. Otto, O., D. Roberts, and R. Wolff. A review on effective closely-coupled collaboration using immersive CVE's. In *Proc. ACM International Conference on Virtual Reality Continuum and its Applications* (2006), pp. 145-154.
11. Piekarski, W. and B.H. Thomas. *Tinmith-Mobile Outdoor Augmented Reality Modelling Demonstration*. in *IEEE/ACM International Symposium on Mixed and Augmented Reality*. (2003), p. 317.
12. Reitmayr, G. and T. Drummond. Going out: robust model-based tracking for outdoor augmented reality. In *Proc. IEEE/ACM International Symposium on Mixed and Augmented Reality*. (2006), pp. 109-118.

Amateur Vision and Recreational Orientation: Creating Live Video Together

Arvid Engström[1] Mark Perry[2,1] Oskar Juhlin[1]
[1] MobileLife@Interactive Institute, Sweden
{oskarj, arvid.engstrom}@tii.se
[2] pandi, DISC, Brunel University, UK
mark.perry@brunel.ac.uk

ABSTRACT

We explore the use of a live video broadcast system by a group of amateur camera operators to film an event on networked cameraphones. Using an interaction analysis of physical interactions and orientations to the work of others, we examine their choice of camera angles and positions in their filming as they attempt to provide interesting visual content and a coherent narrative. Findings illustrate how users adapt their behaviour as co-ordination problems occur by drawing from a set of everyday visual practices ('amateur vision'). They also show how the specifically temporal aspect of live video requires extended attention on its production, and that this is at odds with the 'recreational orientation' of amateur film crews who simultaneously participate in events for their own enjoyment and film them on behalf of other viewers. Implications for the design of collaborative live broadcast media are made, focusing on approaches to interaction design that augment users' visual practices and allow users to look on behalf of others while experiencing places and events themselves.

Author Keywords

Collaboration, user-generated content, broadcast, live video, embodied interaction, leisure, amateur, professional

ACM Classification Keywords

H5.2. Information interfaces and presentation.

General Terms: Human Factors, Theory

INTRODUCTION

Recent years have seen a number of parallel trends in how video content is produced, distributed and consumed on the Internet. Enabled by high speed networks and advances in consumer video technology and smartphones, video now makes up over half of the traffic online, and is forecast to rise to 91% by 2014 [5]. A key component of this traffic flows from sites like YouTube, Vimeo and Facebook, largely powered by user-generated content. This content is evolving from single-user, single-clip uploads to *collaboratively produced* rich media (e.g Qwiki, Kaltura). It is also is increasingly offering the opportunity for *live* broadcast (Qik, Livestream, YouTube Live), and this has been applied in areas as diverse as live community and crowdsourced news broadcasts, sports TV and emergency management [6,8,14]. Alongside these developments, an emerging field of research addresses the interactional and experiential challenges of these new video formats [1,17,22,24]. As well as their impact on video consumption, these emerging technologies and platforms offer research challenges for the production of video media.

This paper adds to the research on video interaction by exploring issues in the production of video through these new technologies by presenting a field trial of a prototype system–the Instant Broadcasting System–that embodies a combination of *collaboration* and *liveness*. The IBS allows its operators to create user-generated content, namely broadcastable live video footage from multiple networked cameraphones. It represents a new genre of tools for collaborative video production among non-professional users. The issue of concern for us is that professional video production involves both technological and practical skills that are not easily transferred to amateurs, in addition to filming taking place in a very different organisational context. To explore this, we draw on a naturalistic field trial and describe some practical challenges that occur for users of the IBS. Focusing on the ways that amateur camera operators do 'looking together' to generate complementary video streams, their problems in applying their everyday visual practices to understanding camerawork ('amateur vision'), and their participatory immersion in events ('recreational orientation'), we then discuss implications for the design of technology for collaborative production and advanced user generated content.

One of the benefits of collaborative video production is that content can be captured on multiple devices, through their multiple perspectives on a topic, and these video streams can be edited live into a more visually interesting story. This obviates returning to the material at a later time to perform a secondary task of editing it *after* the event [16,24]. Live editing also has the advantage of immediacy, allowing content to be fed into broadcasts as events unfold, as well as giving multiple visual perspectives on an event to remote viewers. For professional broadcasters this is a key value, but it remains to be seen how such value can be realised for *amateur* productions. Much of the emphasis on non-professionally produced visual media in commercial applications and research has been on single camera productions and where the action is not live (such as YouTube). However, although collaboration could potentially support more advanced forms of broadcasting, collaborative work is rarely unproblematic, and our analysis indicates that multicamera video production is no different.

Looking at future directions for these trends in production practices online, the addition of advanced forms of collaboration has great potential for new forms of content [23]. However, alongside this we can expect familiar CSCW challenges, as previously professional practices and technology are transferred to wider user groups. We have already seen game-changing uses of *mass online collaboration* (most notably Wikipedia), but have yet to see successful examples of *live collaboration* as described in this paper. The live element of broadcast video, with no opportunity to re-edit content, adds another layer of complication to its production. At some point, as collaboration becomes more demanding, contributing to the best of one's ability (e.g as Wikipedia author) may not be enough to participate in a meaningful way in the new practices envisioned. Time-critical collaboration in live video may be close to that point. When designing future live media for group action, we need to understand these issues better, and our study offers insights into this topic.

Video in everyday life has received some attention in the research literature, most notably in Kirk *et al.* [16], which explores how video is produced, edited and consumed with existing devices. It makes evident how video production is an explicitly *social* process in all of these aspects of its use [see also 1,18,24], showing how its *end use* is a key driver in video production, be this to share 'in the moment' (typically on 'lightweight' devices, such as cameraphones) or for more meaningful events seen later on (on 'heavyweight' video recorders and used to create DVDs). In adding *collaboration* and *liveness*, live multicamera productions go beyond these everyday video practices; they are themselves social activities, with the added complexity of time-critical collaboration on a common visual product. But live video productions also support and enhance important qualities observed in Kirk's *et al.* work; they allow sharing in the moment and remove the need for cumbersome editing after the event.

The context of the user study presented in this paper is a music festival, and the video content created by the camera operators was broadcast onto public screens in front of a large audience between music sets. The role of the camera operators was to capture different and complimentary visual perspectives on the event on behalf of a vision mixer (the person assembling these multiple viewpoints into a narrative by selecting feeds to broadcast). Our study shows that the capture of multiple shot framings and angles is problematised by the ways that non-professional camera operators understand the production process, collaborate together, and rely on an ordinary understanding of visual media that is not well suited to filming.

While the familiar limitations of mobile networks and small format devices do feature to some extent as constraints on behaviour in the user study, detailed analysis shows that a focus on amateur collaborations that involve multi-camera filming brings new issues to the fore. These issues are different to those observed in the practices and problems faced by professional operators in live multi-camera broadcasts [cf. 7,21]. There is more to the difference between on the one hand video, and on the other text and photography, than the issue of technical literacy and skills. Live video production is an inherently time-based media, which requires a more extended attention to the production during the event than these other media. This requirement makes explicit a consideration of the different motivations between amateurs as media producers and professional media producers, what we term their "recreational orientation." We frame the issues observed with the amateur camera operators as a set of shared and embodied visual practices, and show how these have implications for the design of real-time video-based user-generated content.

MEDIATED LOOKING BY AMATEURS

Video technologies support a type of collaborative gaze in which camera users act as proxy viewers on behalf of someone else: the eventual viewer of broadcast content. You could call this type of camerawork 'mediated looking'. It involves looking editorially (making decisions on what to select for display), looking together as a team (in providing one of several complimentary camera perspectives), and looking on behalf of others (primarily the viewers, but also others in the production process, such as the person mixing the camera feeds). Obvious problems that might be faced by camera operators when they perform this mediated looking are, a) they may not look at what viewers are interested in, and b) where several camera operators are involved, they may not organise themselves in a way that provides an angle or position of camera gaze that complements the video streams provided by other camera operators. The latter is important for the person choosing which images to broadcast. These are problems faced by professional as well as amateur camera operators, but professional operators work within a community of practice that draws from a common understanding of the video production process, as well as organisational protocols, technical skills and knowledge that the amateur operators cannot exploit in their filming. Collaborative camerawork in a setting with limited means for communication relies on a shared set of expectations about how others in the team will act and make sense what of they are doing. Whereas professional operators have a rich set of knowledge and practices, amateurs must draw from other organizational resources. To complicate this, amateur camera operators may have other interests and concerns that impede their actions and interactions. We therefore turn to examine technologically mediated looking, and how non-professional users experience and make use of visual technologies.

The focus on *seeing* in research on collaborative systems has previously been on the ways in which people piece together visual observation and other resources to accomplish work. Seeing (and more broadly, awareness) is considered an important feature of work: it is important to look around to understand what is going on, where, and who is doing what. For example, the importance of supporting awareness, through making shared objects, such as flight strips [e.g. 20] visibly observable for team members has become a cornerstone of CSCW research. In this regard, there has been a focus on embodied interaction when sharing perspectives between collaborating participants, because of the ways that people are able to orient their bodily positions, gaze and manipulate objects, not just in order to do their individual tasks, but to make the nature of their ongoing work available to others.

Taking the point that amateur collaborative camerawork is not simply looking together, but working together to produce visual content, we turn to discuss this topic. How amateurs understand the way that work is visually made available to others is a topic of concern when non-professionals work together to create content. However, the terms 'professional' and 'amateur' are problematic, and views on amateur production tend to be skewed towards the notion of users' lack of expertise and knowledge. The distinction between them often focuses on skills and being a competent practitioner [cf. 15]. Thus professionals possess exclusive domain knowledge, while amateurs are seen either as inept, or having romantic qualities of authenticity. However, the wide dissemination of digital production technology has blurred these categories and brought a range of content that does not easily fit one or the other [4, 23]. Aspects other than skill may be as important, most notably for this paper, the amateur might have entirely different motives for doing a particular task than a professional. For professionals, performing the task is a source of income, whereas the amateur might be doing it primarily for a sense of belonging to a social group, or for their own enjoyment. For these reasons, we have used the term 'amateur' (in inverted commas), for lack of a better term, to denote practitioners with diverse skill sets and motivations, partly or entirely outside of traditional 'professional' categories.

If recreational enjoyment is a key motivation, then previous studies of enjoyment practices can be seen as resources for understanding this topic. For e.g., tourism often involves finding out what to do and where to do it, often in collaboration with others. In this regard, Brown and Chalmers [3] have shown how tourists balance the requirement of solving that task through a combination of techniques including the use of tools such as maps and guidebooks, but also through paying attention to making it as enjoyable as possible. The focus on enjoyment was, for example, visible in the way users perform scheduling in an ad hoc manner, and in the way that they prefer working on vague or crude resources, rather than detailed information; so for e.g. they might head out for areas with plenty of cafés rather than navigating to a specific shop, because of the likelihood of interesting encounters, rather than explicitly planning an efficient, goal-oriented excursion, but with the same overall intentions of going shopping.

Juhlin and Weilenmann [13] also show how users balance efficiency and enjoyment, but in a very different setting. Their studies of collaborative, non-professional deer hunting reveal how the recreational hunters' requirements for enjoying their day on the hunt and getting to their prey was organised into a rhythmic variation between concentration and relief, and between solitude and socialisation. Being an amateur, it appears, is not just about being inexpert, but is also managing a balancing act between enjoyment and action. To be an amateur camera operator is likely to be no different to these other domains, and of particular interest to UI designers, user actions performed on devices and the ways that they deploy devices may be as much to do with their engagement with the setting as it is with the task of camerawork.

THE INSTANT BROADCASTING SYSTEM PROTOTYPE

The Instant Broadcasting System (IBS) examined in this user study is composed of a *mobile client application* and a *server side application*. The channel between the two applications is provided by a mobile network, and in this study, operated over a private WLAN. The mobile client, Movino, is an open source application that captures a video stream from the built-in camera on a mobile telephone (Nokia N85, Symbian series 60), encodes it and streams it over TCP/IP [movino.org]. Originally conceived as a single-user application, we have further modified Movino to support communication between camera operators and a remote vision mixer. In terms of its interface, the Movino application shows camera feed, with the addition of a number indicating data connectivity, a red light indicating the camera is selected, and simple onscreen text messages.

Figure 1: Vision mixer interface to the IBS (part)

The server side application is a program that consists of an interface displaying windows of the incoming video streams (up to 5, see figure 1, bottom), and controls for mixing and other functionalities (not shown). In fig 1, three live cameras are ordered sequentially, with camera 3 currently selected to broadcast 'live' onto the Internet. The interface contains a 'live' window (top left, equivalent to a professional 'program' window) and 'preview' window (top right). Just visible at the bottom of fig 1, the interface also provided backchannel interaction from the mixer to the camera operators. This backchannel allowed the vision mixer (VM) operating it to send text messages to the camera operators, and to 'buzz' them with the vibration ringer on the cameraphones.

METHOD AND SETTING

Using empirical data of a team of amateur camera operators, we examined how they collaboratively created visual content for live broadcast using the Instant Broadcasting System. Data collection took place in Sweden during summer 2009 at a music festival. Two groups of camera operators were studied, one Swedish and one Dutch, aged 17-19. Both groups had previously undertaken a short introductory training course in video, photography and storytelling media production, so understood videocamera operation and live video mixing, although this was not at a sophisticated level. Both teams made a number of broadcasts using three cameras, typically of two standard formats: interview and action coverage. Camera operators were themselves filmed and screen captures were made of the vision mixer's monitors. We debriefed the participants immediately after filming, with a 30-minute group interview with camera operators and the vision mixer (VM); these were recorded and transcribed.

The field trial gave us a rich understanding of how the participants planned and performed the broadcasts. In the analysis that follows, we present material from both the debriefing discussions following filming, and on one filming episode by the Dutch team. The use of single data point, as in the latter case, is typical of interaction analysis [e.g. 10]. Whilst it may not cover the full breadth of behaviours, it allows us to examine–in depth–the impact of practices, technologies and contextual features that impact on social interaction and media production We recognise that it can be hard to generalise from a single case study, but this nevertheless stands as a perspicuous study [9]–one that focuses attention on features around important aspects of the collaborative production of amateur live video.

Before being issued with cameras, we gave the operators a 10 minute background introduction to the project. They met the VM, and were given basic instructions on using the cameraphones. They also received basic instructions on filming, i.e. to try to provide steady shots and provide footage that would complement that of the other operators, in camera angles and framing. Although relatively little training or instruction was given, this was not a technically complex or sophisticated system to operate. But as we shall show, using the system in collaborative filming proved to be a practical challenge for other reasons.

In the tables of data that follow, the first column shows the time from the start of video data collection. The second shows any visibly identifiable actions by the camera operators or significant relevant environmental events. The third column shows the current broadcast camera (identified as C1, 2 or 3), and if they occur, whether the camera has 'hung' and fails to broadcast while showing a still image displayed onscreen, or becomes active again; this is visible on our screen capture from the VM's computer and the public screens that are visible on the researcher's video recordings. Notably the camera operators can also tell that a camera feed has been dropped or hung by attending to the public displays or via their device's data connection icon.

In the textual explanations of the data (second column), 'forwards' and 'backwards' refer (respectively) to movement towards the front and rear of the basketball court. Simultaneously timed events are coupled within time boxes below to aid interpretation: they may, or may not, be connected in other ways. Arrows in the diagrams indicate paths and directions of movement. Finally, the 'ray' lines from the camera operators in the diagrams show the approximate perspectives as seen from the participants' cameras. Diagrams (figs 3 to 6), rather than photos, have been used because the camera operators and their visual orientations are extremely hard to ascertain from a static screenshot, and because these images are visually very dense, making annotations on the images hard to discern.

ANALYSIS

This case illustrates a situation where collaboration failed and as such, provides a critical point for drawing implications for design. It starts off by the camera operators providing a variety of shots to the VM, but these soon change to very similar camera angles. This sequence lasted around 5½ minutes. Prior to this broadcast, the Dutch team had filmed a ten-minute interview. For this, their second broadcast, they were asked to film an action sequence of their choice, without interviewing and focusing on camera angles and imagery. They selected a temporary basketball arena, around 20 metres directly in front of the stage and public screens (fig. 2).

Figure 2. Arena, starting positions of the camera operators (numbered) and public screen

The backchannel malfunctioned during this particular sequence, which hampered their communication with the VM pre-broadcast. This might seem to have been a serious issue for co-ordination, as the design of support of communication between the VM and the camera operator has been suggested as a critical aspect in designing multicamera systems for amateurs [21]. However, the text tool proved problematic in filming. During the debriefing sessions, the operators commented extensively on this, with

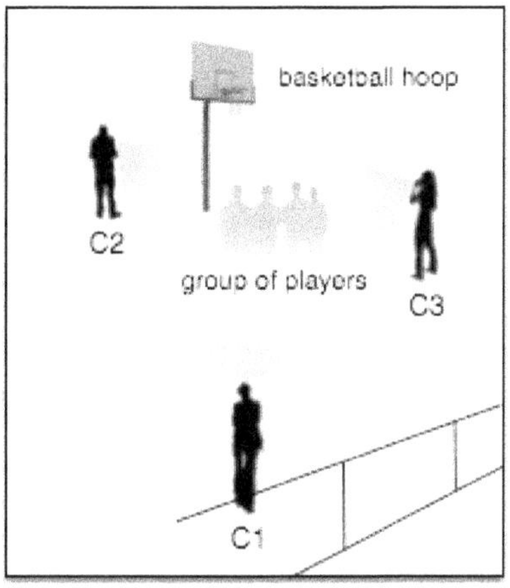

Figure 3. Setting, user positions and orientations prior to broadcast

comments such as *"In the beginning I got them, but when I was interviewing I didn't have really the time to check if she was messaging something"* being typical. Messaging also proved to be something of a distraction: *"You get a little more focused on what will come and a little less on what you're filming*. There was a broad consensus that the text backchannel was good for co-ordination up to the point of going live, but less useful while broadcasting. The iconic red *tally light*, meaning a camera is on air, was effective. Not relying on the text backchannel, the teams' organisation and camerawork was based on the on-going events around themselves, their orientation to the work of the other operators and to the live broadcast on the public screens. To support their collaboration with one another whilst filming, the camera operators were able to orient towards both the physical positions of the others (by attending to their spatial locations, bodily orientation and gaze) and what was currently being broadcast (through two large public screens either side of the stage area showing the live broadcast).

The participants had been in position for about 10 minutes, waiting for their broadcast to go live on the screens by the stage (see figs 2 and 3 for their relative positions and camera orientations). The transcriptions and discussion around the data is split into two phases to help structure the dense data. Although the observed action is continuous and there are no formal boundaries between stages, phases can be loosely considered to be composed as being topically distinct. In practice, the phases distinguish substantial spatial shifts of the participants around the arena, and segment the data into more easily referenced elements. In phase one, the camera operators remain largely in the same locations that they initially selected for their shots. Phase two begins with a rapid and extended movement by one of the camera operators, and involves the other camera operators attending to this reconfiguration in their formation. In the end all the three operators move around, adjusting their positions following intrusive movements from the others.

Phase one – Steady positions

Our analysis begins as the camera team of three took positions at the basketball court, awaiting their broadcast being shown on the public displays adjacent to the court (see figure 3). After having waited in place for over ten minutes, the live broadcast began with an inauspicious start: the selected camera (C3) showed a frozen image of the basketball game on the public displays. Indeed, screenshots from the VM show that all of the camera feeds were frozen. 11 seconds later, the cameras unfroze, and the mixer went on to alternate between two of the cameras. Over the next few minutes, the mixer broadcast all three cameras, but also had to manage the camera feeds occasionally freezing up. The camera operators largely kept to their original positions, only adjusting their viewpoints slightly, and attending to the resulting large public broadcast displays.

What we can observe in the data here is the VM initially working with poor broadcast footage, before settling into a sequence of paired shots from C2 and C3: long shots from behind the basket and close up shots of the players making the shots. During this period, it is visible from the data that C3 appears to be actively using the public screen as a feedback resource to check whether she is being broadcast. Indeed, in the debriefing interview all participants report that they do this to see who has been selected for broadcast.

The configuration of the camera operators in this phase provided multiple, complementary views of the game. Operators were dispersed over the site and not coming into shot or physically blocking each other's footage. We interpret this as that they were following the instructions they were given at the start of the event to shoot different angles and provide a mixture of close-up and overview footage. During this phase they step back and forwards, oscillating around a small area (see fig. 4, a). Their behaviour is similar to that of professional operators who take fixed camera positions and act according to operational conventions that guide them to frame particular topics and shot types [21]. We suggest that these micro-adjustments occur because they are searching for an acceptable shot within the instructions given. However, phase I ends with a marked change to this, led by the actions of C2.

Phase two – A Camera operator leaves his position

In this phase, we see a sudden disruption in the organisation of the camera operators, caused by C2 leaving his position. He circles the arena and eventually blocks another camera operator. The other camera operators both become aware of this disruption, and try to adapt to their unique spatial positions being usurped and their views of the action being blocked. The analysis and C2's own comments below provide alternative explanations for his experimentation with the organisational format of filming.

Figure 4: user movements in phase II

So, this phase starts

with C1 still selected, when C2 takes off, moving fast along **b** (fig 4), behind the basketball basket and towards C3's position. He pauses briefly, then moves further towards C3, circling behind, then around the other side of her. During all this time, C2 is not selected:

13.04	C2 begins to walk fast along **b** (see fig. 4)	
13.11	C2 circles behind basketball basket (see fig 4, along **c**), and stops	
13.12	C1 shifts position back along **a**	
13.14-13.28	C2 walks further down towards **c** (fig. 4) beside C3, then walks behind her (**d**, fig. 5)	C3 (@13.20)
13.25-13.40	C1 steps right 2 steps, then moves back against fence	
13.30	C3 glances quickly to her right	C3 hangs
13.33	C3 glances to her left (in direction of C2)	C1
13.37	C3 turns her head up and to her right at the basket	
13.38	C3 glances very quickly to right, then left towards direction of big screen	
13.40	C3 glances at C2 to her left again	C3

So above, we see C2 move around the basketball court to take up a position beside C3 to produce an almost identical perspective to her, and this is noticed: twice, C3 makes clearly visible glances towards C2 in his new position (13.30 and 13.40). The action sequence continues as C3 moves to avoid being hit by a basketball, but then continues to move away from her original position, passing C2 (ending at 13.44). C2 then moves again, stopping directly in front of C1. During all this time, C2 is not selected for another 16 seconds, and is only selected when the footage from the other cameras is unavailable for technical reasons. C1 then moves forward (**f**) and as she pauses, C3 begins her move to the rear of the court (**g**):

13.43-14.00	C3 jumps left to avoid being hit by ball, and continues to move to the back of the group of players and towards the rear of the court	C3 hangs (@13.45) C1@13.46 C1 hangs (@13.465)
13.44	C3 steps left and towards back of basketball court, filming the basket to her right	
13.48	C3 steps backwards	
13.49-13.53	C2 moves forward fast (see fig. 5, along **e**), stopping to block C1's view at 13.53 (C2 is several metres in front of C1, facing away from her)	C3@13.49 (v. poor image)
14.06		C2
14.12-14.22	C1 steps forward towards (**f**), stops at 14.22	C3@14.19
14.22	C3 edges towards the rear of the court (**g**)	C3 hangs

Perhaps the reason for the movement by C1 and C3 here is that during this time, cameras 1 and 3 lose their network connection and hang, and there is no reason for them to maintain a steady shots for broadcast, allowing them the freedom to move around before they come back online. Nevertheless the movement from C2 during phase II is odd, especially given the duplication of his perspective with C3 (starting at the end of phase I) and his physical blocking of C1's footage (13.53). The final part of the sequence is excluded for brevity. Then all three operators move around as they make adjustments to their positions following the changes imposed on them by the others, and they end up blocking two of the three shots provided to the VM.

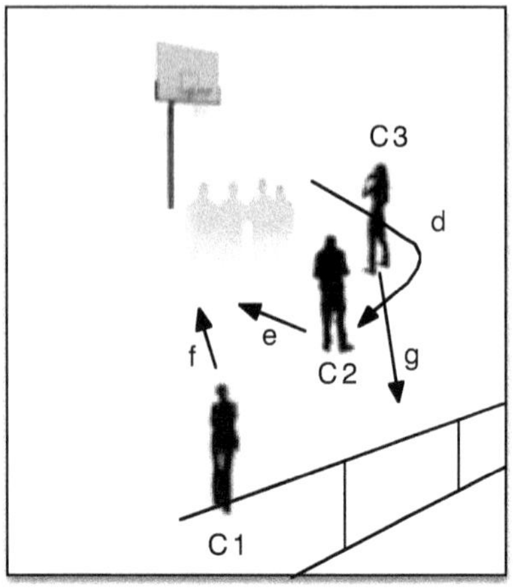

Figure 5: user movements in phase II

The most analytically interesting aspects of this phase consist of C2 moving off and C3's reaction to this duplication of her perspective and subsequently, C2's intrusion into her field of view. We can see from the data that C3 glances at C2 several times (13.33 and 13.40). She also glances towards the screen. Thus, she has a 'peripheral awareness' of what is going on (i.e. of C2's actions and the footage being broadcast). We therefore interpret her move (14.22) as a reaction to C2 moving into her area and thus providing a similar shot to her one. This interpretation is confirmed in the debriefing interview:

C3: I really wanted to zoom in on people. I started with that and then I looked around me and they were also close to the people and then I backed away and sat on the ground [...]
Interviewer: You were very close
C3: Yeah. I wanted to stay there but it was boring because they also came in very close. So I had to go away

Here, C3 wanted to provide a close up (or 'zoom in' as she refers to walking up towards people), but when she saw the other crew members, she moved away. Thus, her movement was motivated by the need to provide complementary and unique shots. The question we must ask here is what motivated C2 to impinge on the others' footage? Was it that he thought he was not providing the VM with interesting material? Looking at the actual broadcasts, although he had not been selected for 58 seconds when he began his move at 13.04, he had been selected three times already. That might tell us that he had another motivation than being receptive to the VM. Whatever the reason, we see C2 moving near to C3 to give the same shot angle, despite their initial instructions to provide complementary footage. The reasons for this are partially explained in the debriefing interview:

C2: Because nobody was making close-ups. Everybody went to the back
Interviewer: You said that nobody was making close-ups?
C3: I was standing in their faces!
C1: Ha ha she was
C2: and then you went back

Here, C2's first explanation is that he was trying to make a complementary shot to C3. C2 justifies this by inaccurately claiming that C3 was not making an appropriate close-up shot. It could be that he wanted to follow the filming instructions and act according to their initial setup, but then he did not think that C3 was delivering appropriate footage and tried to make up for her inadequate camera work, i.e. that he did not trust her to provide such material. Second, when challenged on this by C3 and C1 he explains why he started to move, by orienting to another principle of organising filming, that is, through an imperative for mobility in camerawork as the way to make a "picture", perhaps referring to the ways that professional camera operators use tracking shots:

C2: I think everybody must walk around. Then in order to [pause] moves like a picture [pause] if you not move. You must move. But not too much."

Although this reference to 'a picture' seems unclear (he is not a native English speaker), he goes on to describe that this references TV and film imagery. C2's explanation for leaving his initial position is both to back up another (in his opinion) failing camera operator, and to provide a new type of footage that is complimentary to footage from the other cameras. C2's explanation may be a *post hoc* rationalisation of his actions, but his justification provides us with insights into how he understands the role of camerawork, and when certain patterns of action become appropriate. We cannot discount the possibility that C2 gradually begins to follow other criteria in his filming that were not agreed upon beforehand or shared with the others and just starts to film as if he were on his own. Indeed, this is a strong possibility. In the following section, evidence emerges that C2 is not attending to the activities or positions of the other camera operators as he claimed.

What then is happening? There appears to be a contradiction between C2's organizational principles and individualistic behaviour, and this can be understood as a shift occurring over time. This is seen in that C2 shifts to another principle during filming, clearly not in understanding the others. This indicates that he is discarding his own footage over time and selecting a more preferable role–that of a moving camera. Thus, the sequence shows that he acts on individual preferences not shared by the others. So, it would appear that there are a number of organizational principles in camerawork that the participants reflexively orient towards. This does not mean that they always follow them, although where those rules are shared, the participants need to demonstrate that they are being attended to. This is exactly the point that we see in C2's explanations of his behaviour–he recognised that there were organisational principles that he had an obligation to orient to (in his interview explanations), yet this is very evidently not observed in the empirical data. This tension between teamwork and an individualistic perspective (i.e. as 'event vision') is a serious problem for camera teams and for future technology designers.

DISCUSSION AND IMPLICATIONS FOR DESIGN

The task of collaboratively producing a compound visual story out of a number of individual camera feeds is essentially the same whether it is done by a professional crew or a group of 'amateurs'; the topic of the story should be covered in a diversity of angles and sizes of framing, and made available to the VM who assembles the broadcast in real time. In this sense, the multicamera format dictates a practice that is essentially different from everyday forms of 'snapshot' video use observed in earlier work [16,18]. It would perhaps be beside the point to hold 'amateur' cameraphone teams, whose motivation may not be to produce high-end broadcasts, up to professional standards. But keeping professional organisational as a point of reference in how 'amateurs' go about managing this task, highlights some distinctive characteristics of collaborative production. Here, we discuss three of these: the roles of *sensemaking and organisational adaptation* around the perceived actions of others, the role of individual *visual practices* in social organisation, and *experiential tensions* arising during collaboration. We will show that these characteristics cannot simply be written off as lack of participant thought or effort, and discuss their implications for the design of future technology for collaborative production of live media for non-professional users.

1. Loose collaboration: shifting positions and roles

While professionals organise their camerawork in preset ways and rely on skilled workmanship to achieve this, 'amateurs' will usually be more loosely organised. In the broadcast situation examined here, we see how the team of three are able to quite comfortably emulate a basic camera setup after some brief instructions. But as time passes, it becomes clear that they do not have a clear or common idea of how to continue providing good footage and what organisational schemes to follow in their collaboration. Each individual's camerawork needs to dynamically adapt to what the other camera operators are doing, so that they each produce different angles and framing as their common topic changes over time. This is visible in the ways in which they check on the other operators and move in search for variation. This peripheral awareness–alternating between looking at the camera interface and a gaze taking in the other camera team members' actions–is an important resource in their collaboration. However, they do not only adapt the way they perform their roles. They also seem to shift role as part of this adaptation. C2 appears to simultaneously work with two organisational principles, in 1) backing up for another failing camera operator (as he describes it) and 2) that all of the operators should move constantly. It is clear from the video material and interviews that they were following several organisational principles. This coordination issue led them from initially filming multiple visual perspectives to providing similar viewpoints. Notably, there was no practical way to verbally communicate these principles during the ongoing filming.

A communication backchannel would appear to be a partial solution to this problem, but presents several challenges. An audio backchannel, as seen in professional systems, has the drawback of being unidirectional, as camera operators cannot reply to the VM verbally while filming. Indeed, text messages, as implemented in the IBS, quickly proved to be of limited use. Although not operational in the particular situation analysed here, the debriefing interviews also showed that while text messages were useful for pre-planning, they were too attentionally demanding for both senders and recipients for effective real-time interaction and organisational adaptation during broadcasts. Adding the ability for camera operators to speak over the backchannel would therefore seem inappropriate, and indeed might become cacophonous as the number of cameras scales up.

Design points: One of the obvious problems faced by the camera operators is that they have to be aware of intrusions into their own space, so that their shots are not physically blocked or that they share the same camera framing or perspective as the other users. For example, local proximity sensors (e.g. bluetooth) coupled with directional indicators (such an integrated compass) would allow the system to make its users aware of the presence of their collaborators encroaching into their space and filming in the same direction whist they were engaged in looking through the viewfinder. This could be similarly achieved with simple image processing on the server side. However, heavyweight technical approaches to co-ordinate camera positioning would seem unnecessary, as it is not easily possible to ascertain that similar perspectives are indeed shot duplications, moreover, the data shows that camera operators were at lest partially able to manage their own recovery from spatial intrusions by adjusting their positions and shot framings. It may be that simply making participants aware of such breakdowns would offer the possibility of socially organized resolution as the participants became aware of developing problems. Similarly, our video and interview data has shown that individual users' awareness of their own, and others', contribution to the production as a whole is important for effective collaboration. Support for such peripheral awareness could include a switch to view the broadcast program at any time. The camera's red 'tally light' proved to be instantly understandable and also served as a motivation to seek interesting content to film (although at the expense of adding a competitive edge to get 'the best' shot). This positive feedback could be extended to display total use of one's camera 'on air' over time and relative to other team members.

2. Ways of seeing: professional vs. amateur vision

While the work of the production team is to produce a coherent montage (i.e. create different footage that is cut together to form a continuous sequence) and the camera operators strive to do this, their lack of organisational skills and *individual* 'ways of seeing' appears to hinder their collaborative ability to practically achieve this. This is a special case of special case of organisational difficulty, and develops one of the issues around loose collaboration further: we call this *amateur vision*, because, in contrast to Goodwin's *professional vision*, the camera operators have no corresponding shared "socially organized perceptual framework(s)" [11: 616]. Each camera operator carries their own subjective interpretation of what categories of shot is interesting to view and what to highlight as relevant and meaningful when choosing what to film in combining their own footage with that of the others in their team [cf. 7]. We have deliberately not overtheorised 'amateur vision' as a conceptual contribution but a matter of practical concern for the participants. Our point is that the participants do not have the skills of seeing in a professional way for making video [cf. 21], and rely on skills drawn from their experience of other everyday activities. Thus, on his 'seeing' of the developing situation, C2's vernacular skills provide an imperative for mobility that is evidently inappropriate, in that it blocks the other camera operators' views, provides an unstable platform for filming and removes the opportunity to select shots from his original position. This can be seen in his interview data, when he describes how you must 'move like a picture'. It is not that team members are inexpert (they have many relevant and partially relevant skills), but that they visually analyse and orient to the setting as a resource for collaborative action using everyday sensemaking skills.

This is in clear contrast with the work of professional camera operators; the role of professional vision in video camerawork has been discussed by Macbeth, in what is described as 'the praxeology of seeing with a camera' ([19:152]. Given that the participants in this study have no encultured common practices or shared ways of seeing the visual landscape as a team, they must rely on their own existing visual practices, most likely drawn from, on the one hand, watching visual media, such as television, and on the other, producing visual media, such as photography or making home videos. In producing the footage, the production team (i.e. cameras and VM) are working to provide a sense of scenic intelligibility [12] in the reverse way to that of a viewer, who interprets the film "*much as we would understand the order and properties of the everyday social and natural world... Our understanding of a film text trades off our knowledge of the structures of everyday activity and practical reasoning"* [8:289].

Borrowing from Garfinkel [9:227], these observations act as an aid to our sluggish imagination, 'reflections through which the strangeness of an obstinately familiar world can be detected', and our findings uncover what now seems an obvious, yet important point. 'Amateur' crews *can have no* skilled or commonly-known-to-be-shared understandings of how to film beyond those they have discussed already, and they can have had no way to suddenly develop these in situ without further communication. We argue that the camera crew are drawing from a combination of vernacular visio-cultural practices (as competent members of a visually literate society) and their prior experience in viewing, filming and photography. Further, given their different experiences and the complexity of their task and setting, these are highly likely to be understood and enacted in a unique way by each individual. Hence, C2 surprised the other team members by apparently shifting to a different role during the broadcast. This role was not apparently arbitrary or constituting a lack of skill. But it was subjectively applied, uncalled for, and in conflict with the other team members' filming. Such individual practices may not facilitate the collaborative production of multicamera video, and herein lies a problem for design: how to develop methods of interaction that will allow camera teams to collaborate effectively in the absence of a shared, socially organized perceptual framework.

Design point: Non-professionals cannot rely on their training and encultured common understandings to change their practice as the unexpected happens. They may well be orienting to completely different notions about what to do and how the other participants will make sense of their own actions. Some micro-coordination can be done locally, but it is reasonable to expect that they should rely more on direction from the VM. To this end, this is a case where an audio backchannel could provide a practical addition for time-critical coordination by the VM. For a basic setup, or where the addition of headsets would be impractical, text communication could serve as a fallback. Such verbal interaction is also more sociable, thus offering a motivation for 'amateur' user involvement, and builds on existing conventions in co-ordinating online gaming.

3. Enjoyment: recreational orientation

The 'amateur' teams observed were doing this filming both for their own enjoyment and are also engaged in an enjoyable setting. So, whilst the collaborative effort of filming offers a reason for focusing on their task of creating video for remote broadcast, they were also oriented to, and engaged in, pleasurable aspects of the very event that they were filming. This leisure, or recreational orientation provides a conflicting set of attentional demands on them. Paradoxically, this personal enjoyment is the very reason for them being there so that they are able to do the filming. While it may seem to be a weakness for effective collaborative production and high production values, this recreational-orientation also offers valuable opportunities for collaborative video systems. First, when enjoying an event, users may be more motivated to record aspects of it for posterity or to show it to others. Second, they are likely to know what is interesting to broadcast–after all, this is why they are likely to be present at the event. Third, interesting leisure activities are likely to appeal to enough people to provide the likelihood of multiple camera users attending to offer different and complementary views of the event. This mix of motivation, topical expertise and critical mass are powerful tools to harness in collaborative video.

Furthermore, the role of the professional camera operator, as we have previously argued, is to look at something on behalf of someone else, i.e. the VM and the TV-audience. We argue that the 'amateurs' have another motivation in that they are looking on behalf of others while experiencing the event for themselves; combining the camera vision they adopt in their role when filming with an event vision. This dual motivation might explain C2's actions in moving around to both film similar angles and block the views of the other operators. That is, camera operators also look at the topic that they are filming as someone attending an event: the *camera vision* becomes confounded with the *event vision*, which implies strolling around and looking at events as an ordinary participant at the event or a tourist. Thus C2's concern for mobility may be as much a concern to please himself as to please those he is filming on behalf of. Moving around is a way to get a better view of the event for himself. So for the professionals, while looking with a camera is not quite the same as just looking [19], this may be a less relevant concern to amateur operators. Indeed, the way the participants describe the footage they were trying to produce, commenting on the action they were framing and using value words like "boring" and "interesting", suggests that the camera operators were experiencing the event in a relatively non-detached way while filming.

Design point: This recreational orientation that moves the focus of interest from the task (i.e. camera vision) to the recreational aspect of the activity (i.e. event vision) has wide implications for the user experience design of live media as it becomes more widely available. An 'amateur' production system should account for blending its users' event and camera vision. Thus the design of these productions should account not only for the users' visual focus of filming, but also for their actual engagement in the setting, whether it is an event as in this study, or other social situations or places that might be of interest to broadcast. This has been previously discussed with regard to other activities, such as tourism and hunting [3,13]. Given the pleasurable aspects of visiting places and events, the 'amateur' TV camera operator has to solve their task of filming and maintaining an awareness of the actions of other operators, in combination with event participation, and the devices' interface should reflect this. Designers therefore need to consider balancing the nature of the interaction away from requiring a high degree of concentrated attention to one in which they could segue into and out of collaborative filming. Such interfaces might support ad hoc planning and organisation, as this study points to a need for re-negotiating tasks and roles in 'amateur' settings. Thus, users filming an overview shot might request to replace close up camer operators when they were bored with their roles. What this requires is a communication system that is more a sophisticated than the vision mixer-oriented communication backchannel currently available on the IBS prototype. These extended functionalities could, for e.g. include unobtrusive signalling of an operator's level of engagement to all of the other team members, from full participation in the production to being on standby or even taking a break. Another way to support this would be to provide support for location or activity sharing, allowing users to check in to form ad hoc groups with friends or other people on location at an event, enabling low-effort social interaction and collaboration.

CONCLUSION

This paper aims to provide a new understanding of how live video can be produced as a group activity by non-professional users. Increasingly, advanced forms of internet-based user-driven production of video are emerging as part of a larger trend that puts traditional notions of the 'amateur' and 'professional' into question. The IBS, as a live video production suite that leverages collaboration among empowered 'amateur' users to produce live video broadcasts, has allowed us to explore this novel design space. The combination of collaborative production and live transmission shows promise for new forms of participatory media, but also presents some serious challenges. This paper unpacks some of the challenges that this genre of production tools brings; some are related to skills, but lack of training alone does not appear to account for all of the issues that need to be taken into account when adapting such tools for a broader user group.

Our analysis shows that it is extremely hard for users to manage their 'loose' collaboration effectively to create topically relevant and meaningful footage for potential live broadcast that is visually complimentary to footage from the other camera operators–even when they are able to see the other camera operators and the final broadcast output. To a large extent, professional operators use their knowledge of the roles of the other people that they are working with, allowing them to anticipate their colleagues' actions and to align their own footage appropriately with them [21]. 'Amateur' operators cannot draw on the same knowledge and practices. Users must therefore rely on, and draw from their practical, everyday experiences as a resource for co-ordinating their own actions. We call such non-professional visual practices 'amateur vision' in homage to Chuck Goodwin, as a corollary to his term 'professional vision'. Although 'amateurs' cannot have full access to the rich set of practices and production skills of professional camera operators, as competent members of society, it is possible that they can replicate at least some of this from their everyday experiences with image media. In essence, they may be able to reverse engineer aspects of the production process. Yet, as we have shown, the inferences that they can draw from this are not necessarily useful. What also emerges from the analysis is that while taking on the task of acting as "proxy viewers" for others, users' camerawork practices are not detached from their roles as participants; they combine being a member of a camera team with experiencing the event individually as it happens. This is important in understanding the motivation behind this rather advanced form of collaboratively-generated content, as well as for the user experience design of production tools for non-professional live media. Looking towards user orientation in the recreational aspects of the activities that their work is embedded in is likely to be of increasing relevance for systems in which media content is produced by non-professionals, although this will be likely to differ according to the setting and activity.

REFERENCES

1. Bentley, F.R. & Groble, M. (2009) TuVista: Meeting the multimedia needs of mobile sports fans. Proc. ACM MM'09 (Beijing, China, October 19-24), 471-480.
2. Bergstrand, F. & Landgren, J. (2009) Using live video for information sharing in emergency response work. Int. Jnl of Emergency Management, 6(3/4), 295-301.
3. Brown, B. & Chalmers, M. (2005) Tourism and mobile technology. Proc. European Conference on Computer Supported Cooperative Work (ECSCW'03, 14-18 September, Helsinki, Finland). Springer-Verlag, 335-354.
4. Burgess, J. & Green J. (2010) The entrepeneurial Vlogger: participatory culture beyond the professional-amateur divide. In The Youtube Reader (Eds. Snickars & Vonderau). Library of Sweden, Stockholm.
5. Cisco Systems Inc. (2010) Visual Networking Index. http://www.cisco.com/en/US/netsol/ns827/networking_solutions_sub_solution.html#~forecast
6. Davis, M. (2003) Editing out video editing. IEEE Multimedia, 10(2), 54-64.
7. Engström, A., Juhlin, O., Perry, M. & Broth, M. (2010). Temporal hybridity: mixing live video footage with instant replay in real time. Proc ACM CHI, 1495-1504.
8. Figueiredo, M., Prado, P., Câmara, M., & Albuquerque, A. (2009) Empowering rural citizen journalism via web 2.0 technologies. Proc. ACM C&T, 77-84.
9. Garfinkel, H. (1964) Studies of the Routine Grounds of Everyday Activities. Social problems, 11(3), 225-250.
10. de la Flor, G. Luff, P., Jirotka, M. et al. 2010. The Case of the Disappearing Ox: Seeing Through Digital Images to Analysis of Ancient Texts. Proc. ACM CHI, 473-482.
11. Goodwin, C. (1994) Professional Vision. American Anthropologist, 96(3), 606-633.
12. Jayyusi, L. (1988) Towards a socio-logic of the film text, Semiotica, 68(3-4), 271-296.
13. Juhlin, O. & Weilenmann, A. (2008) Hunting for fun: solitude and attentiveness in collaboration. Proc. ACM CSCW, 57-66.
14. Juhlin, O. Engström, A. & Reponen, E. (2010) Mobile broadcasting-the whats and hows of live video as a social medium. Proc Mobile HCI'10 (Lisbon, Portugal), 35-44.
15. Keen, A. (2007) The cult of the amateur: how today's internet is killing our culture. Doubleday: New York.
16. Kirk, D., Sellen, A., Harper, R., and Wood, K. (2007) Understanding videowork. Proc. ACM CHI, 61-70.
17. Lange, P. (2008) Publicly private and privately public: Social networking on Youtube. Jnl. of CMC, 13, 361-380
18. Lehmuskallio, A. & Sarvas, R. (2008) Snapshot video: everyday photographers taking short video-clips. Proc. NordiCHI '08 (Lund, Sweden, Oct. 20-22), 257-265.
19. Macbeth, D. (1999) Glances, trances, and their relevance for a visual sociology. In Jalbert (Ed.) Media studies: ethnomethodological approaches. UPA:Lanham, 135-170
20. MacKay, W. E. (1999) Is paper safer? The role of paper flight strips in air traffic control. ACM ToCHI 6(4) 311-340.
21. Perry, M., Juhlin, O., Esbjörnsson, M. & Engström, A. (2009) Lean collaboration through video gestures: co-ordinating the production of live televised sport. Proc. ACM CHI, 2279-2288.
22. Shamma, D.A., Bastea-Forte, M., Joubert, N., & Liu, Y. (2008) Enhancing online personal connections through the synchronized sharing of online video. Proc. ACM CHI Extended abstracts, 2931-2936.
23. Shirky, C. (2008) Here comes everybody: The power of organizing without organizations. Penguin Press: NY.
24. Vihavainen, S., Mate, S., et al. (2011) We want more: Human-computer collaboration in mobile social video remixing of music concerts. Proc. ACM CHI, 287-294.

Investigating Effects of Visual and Tactile Feedback on Spatial Coordination in Collaborative Handheld Systems

Koji Yatani[1,3], Darren Gergle[2], and Khai N. Truong[1]

[1] University of Toronto, Ontario, Canada
[2] Northwestern University, Illinois, USA
[3] Microsoft Research Asia, Beijing, China

{koji, khai}@dgp.toronto.edu, dgergle@northwestern.edu

ABSTRACT

Mobile and handheld devices have become platforms to support remote collaboration. But, their small form-factor may impact the effectiveness of the visual feedback channel often used to help users maintain an awareness of their partner's activities during synchronous collaborative tasks. We investigated how visual and tactile feedback affects collaboration on mobile devices, with emphasis on spatial coordination in a shared workspace. From two user studies, our results highlight different benefits of each feedback channel in collaborative handheld systems. Visual feedback can provide precise spatial information for collaborators, but degrades collaboration when the feedback is occluded, and sometimes can distract the user's attention. Spatial tactile feedback can reduce the overload of information in visual space and gently guides the user's attention to an area of interest. Our results also show that visual and tactile feedback can complement each other, and systems using both feedback channels can support better spatial coordination than systems using only one form of feedback.

Author Keywords

Visual feedback, tactile feedback, collaboration, spatial coordination, mobile/handheld devices, touch screen.

ACM Classification Keywords

H5.3. Group and Organization Interfaces: Computer-supported cooperative work; H5.2. User Interfaces: Haptic I/O.

General Terms

Human Factors

INTRODUCTION

Mobile and handheld devices are becoming commonplace as tools to support remote collaboration. People now use their mobile devices to coordinate and interact with others through email, instant messaging, and video conferencing. They use their mobile devices to communicate and collaborate in similar ways to those with desktop computers.

However, the physical form-factor of mobile devices can impact user collaboration. For instance, mobile devices offer a much smaller visual workspace in comparison to those available on desktop computers or tabletop displays. Furthermore, when the user interacts with a touch-screen interface, her hand can occlude much of the screen. As a result, the visual feedback often used in synchronous collaborative tasks to help users maintain awareness of their partner's activities [8] may impact collaboration differently on mobile devices.

We thus see many design opportunities for improving collaboration through mobile devices. This includes using different communication channels for providing feedback to collaborators such as vibrotactile feedback: Tactile feedback using vibration motors spatially arranged in a device can be used to convey spatial information [19, 22] (we refer to this as *spatial tactile feedback*). This can be used to improve the expressiveness of tactile feedback on a given device. Furthermore, tactile feedback can be used to design more accessible user interfaces, particularly for visually impaired users who may not be able to access the visual feedback channel entirely. Understanding the effects of tactile feedback on collaboration can contribute to better design of collaborative systems for visually impaired users as well as sighted users.

We investigate how different feedback channels can affect collaboration on mobile devices. We are specifically interested in spatial coordination in a visual workspace [8], an important aspect of collaboration. Such collaboration can happen when users are sharing screen views and discussing the content within them. To measure the effectiveness of feedback for supporting spatial coordination, we built a collaborative game played by two users on mobile touch-screen devices, and we observed how users played the game with and without receiving visual or tactile feedback about their remote game partner's action.

Through two user studies, we gain an understanding of the different benefits of each feedback channel and also demonstrate better performance through the combination of visual and spatial tactile feedback for spatial coordination in collaborative handheld systems. Visual feedback can provide precise spatial information about a collaborator's action, but degrades collaboration when feedback is occluded and sometimes can distract the user's attention. Spatial tactile feedback may not be appropriate for conveying precise spatial information; however, it can reduce the overload of visual information in the workspace and can gently guide a user's attention to an area of interest. Furthermore, visual and spatial tactile feedback can complement each other, and systems using both feedback channels can offer better spatial coordination support than systems using only one form of feedback.

RELATED WORK

Vibrotactile feedback has been widely used to provide tactile sensations on touch-screen devices. Active Click was perhaps the first demonstration of vibrotactile feedback on touch-screen devices [7]. Poupyrev *et al.* later brought this idea to mobile devices, and extended it by using different vibration patterns to increase the expressiveness of tactile feedback [17]. Yatani and Truong employed multiple vibration motors on the backside of mobile touch-screen devices to convey semantic information about the object which the user is touching [22]. These vibrotactile feedback systems are useful for a variety of tasks, such as item selection in a linear list [17], text entry [10], and eyes-free interaction [22].

These systems primarily provide the user with feedback about her own interactions on a mobile device. But, in this work, we focus on the use of tactile feedback for offering information about another user's interaction on a remote device to support collaboration between users.

Collaborative Systems with Tactile/Haptic Feedback

The use of tactile and haptic feedback has been explored in inter-personal communication systems, such as HandJive [6] and InTouch [1]. HandJive consists of two joystick-like devices enhanced by haptic feedback [6]. One person's movement on the device is propagated onto another device as an orthogonal movement (*e.g.*, when a user moves a HandJive device forward, the partner will feel horizontal movement from the device). InTouch [1] is a device with three cylindrical rollers, and the rotational velocity of each roller is synchronized with the paired device. Thus, remote users can feel each other's interaction with the rollers over a distance. Oakley *et al.* implemented several haptic effects for supporting communication in tasks with a collaborative editor using the PHANTOM device [14]. For example, one user can produce haptic feedback (called *haptic gestures*) on the other user's device to guide her to a specific point of the screen. They found that the participants frequently used haptic gestures to communicate with each other about the region of interest within the shared visual workspace or objects they wanted to discuss.

Tactile feedback is accessible to visually impaired users, and thus collaborative systems with tactile feedback often extend to this population. Plimmer *et al.* [18] developed McSig, a system to support visually impaired users in learning how to write letters through collaboration with a sighted user. Through a PHANTOM device held by a visually impaired user, the system haptically reproduces the trajectory of a letter written by a sighted user on a Tablet PC. Their user study showed that visually impaired users

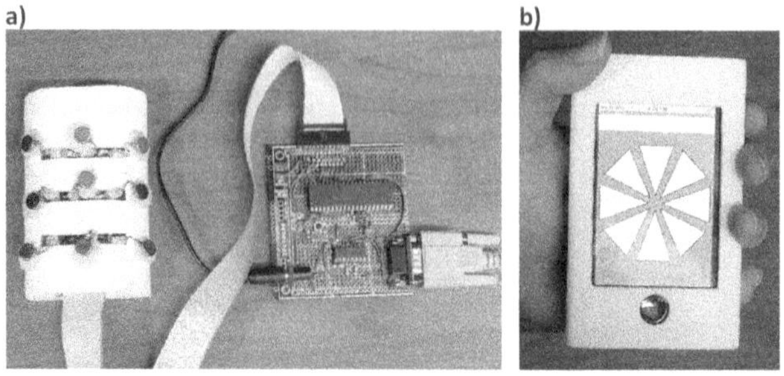

Figure 1. The mobile touch-screen device used in this study: a) the backside of the mobile device and the hardware to control the nine vibration motors embedded in the mobile device; b) the front side of the mobile device.

could successfully learn how to write some alphabets. Pielot *et al.* [16] built a belt-like device with multiple vibration motors and studied the effects of using it to provide tactile feedback of where fellow teammates are located in a 3D multiplayer game. Their user study revealed that users could sense the other players' locations, but did not show clear evidence on whether collaboration between the players was improved through their tactile system.

Communication Strategies Supported by Tactile Feedback

Research has focused on the use of a haptic or tactile channel for communication and collaboration as well. Chang *et al.* [4] investigated the effect of vibrotactile feedback on remote voice communication. In their ComTouch system, they explored the use of vibrotactile feedback as a supplemental communication channel for voice communication. Their user study revealed that the participants used tactile communication for five purposes: emphasizing a voice message, turn-taking, duplicating a tactile message, responding "yes" or "no," and conveying integer numbers. Brown *et al.* [2] explored how couples would develop communication protocols with their mobile audio-tactile messaging system called Shake2Talk. They identified four purposes for audio-tactile messages: coordinating events and calls, maintaining awareness, sharing the fun, and expressing affection. Chan *et al.* [3] examined the effects of haptic icons on turn-taking in collaborative tasks; specifically participants were instructed to solve puzzles while communicating through tactile feedback. They found that vibrotactile feedback can be useful to communicate some messages, particularly urgent requests in a visually-demanding situation.

Collaborative systems with tactile feedback can enable visually impaired users and sighted users to collaborate. McGookin and Brewster [13] explored the use of a collaborative tactile system to allow visually impaired users to explore a bar graph collaboratively. Through a user study with pairs of visually impaired users, they found that haptic feedback was useful for one user to guide the other user to the point of interest effectively. However, collaborative systems for visually impaired users are still in the early stage, and understanding the effects of different types of feedback including tactile feedback could be useful for

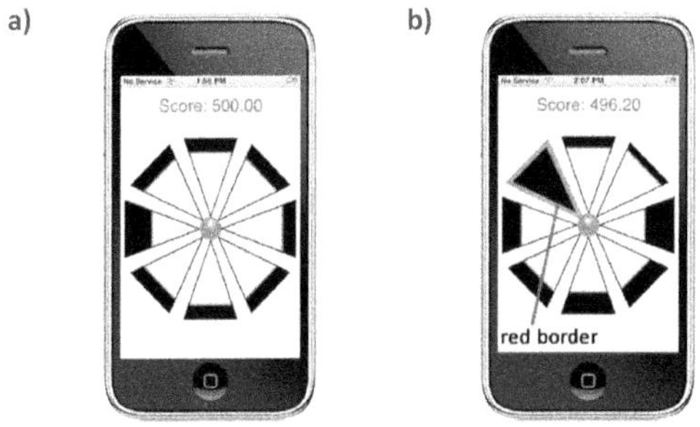

Figure 2. Screenshots of the game: a) The screen contains eight wedges, and they fill with the black color from the outside edge toward the center; b) When a wedge becomes completely filled, the system shows the red highlight and the players start to lose points.

designing collaborative systems for visually impaired users as well as sighted users.

Our work focuses on how tactile feedback can support spatial coordination in collaborative tasks. Spatial coordination is an important aspect of interaction between users to successfully accomplish collaborative tasks [5], but it has not been studied deeply in the context of tactile feedback. This paper contributes to the design of tactile feedback for collaborative systems.

SYSTEM

Hardware

We developed a spatial tactile feedback system for mobile touch-screen devices similar to the SemFeel device [22] (an iPhone in our system; Figure 1). We developed a special sleeve to embed the vibration motors in the backside of a mobile touch-screen device. The vibration motors are aligned in the 3×3 grid with 2 cm of separation. We determined this placement to satisfy a psychological limitation that it is hard to distinguish two distinct vibration sources with a gap smaller than 1 cm [15, 20]. It also offers eight different vibration points needed in the game design explained in the next section.

Game Design

The goal of the system is to measure the effectiveness of feedback on spatial coordination between remote users. We decided to build a game involving an abstracted spatial coordination task which can happen on mobile devices (*e.g.*, tapping the same region of the screen). This abstraction allows us to examine the effects of different feedback channels, while minimizing the effects of outside factors which could affect spatial coordination between users. At the same time, it maintains the generalizability of the study results to systems needing tightly-coupled spatial coordination in the workspace (*e.g.*, a collaborative drawing application or a system supporting visually impaired users in developing their motor skills to perform gestures or handwriting [18]).

Figure 2 shows screenshots of the game used in our study. The game screen is shared on the two mobile touch-screen devices when users play the game. Each screen shows eight interactive wedges and the score. The pair initially starts the game with 500 points. When the game starts, the system gradually fills a wedge (with black pixels) from the outside edge towards the center. The game fills each wedge at a different rate. When a wedge becomes completely filled, the system highlights that wedge with a red border, and the pair starts to lose points. One point is deducted for each completely filled wedge per second, and players do not have any way to gain points.

Success in this game depends on effective spatial coordination between the players. The objective of this game from the player's perspective is to keep as high a score as possible, given five minutes of play. To prevent a wedge from becoming completely filled, both must touch the same wedge, and at least one of them must perform a scrubbing gesture on that wedge. The game calculates the amount of black pixels to remove based on the length of the user's scrubbing gesture. The system ignores all scrubbing gestures when both game partners are not touching the same wedge. In this manner, the game requires frequent, tightly-coupled coordination between the players.

The game always provides the user with feedback about whether the touch screen has registered her touch by highlighting the selected wedge with a green border. Additionally, the game uses visual or tactile feedback to inform the user which wedge their game partner touches.

Visual Feedback

Figure 3a and 3b show how our system provides visual feedback. When one player touches a wedge, that wedge is highlighted by a blue border on the game partner's screen (Figure 3a). When both players touch the same wedge, its border color turns orange on both devices (Figure 3b).

Tactile Feedback

Figure 3c and 3d show how our system provides tactile feedback. When one player touches a wedge, the game partner's device activates the vibration motor associated with that wedge to generate a localized discontinuous vibration by turning it on/off every 200 msec (Figure 3c). When both players touch the same wedge, both devices generate continuous vibration with the motor associated with the contacted wedge (Figure 3d). The motor positioned at the center was not used in this study.

System Architecture

The mobile devices connect to a server machine through wireless communication, and they report all contact events to this server. The server computes how fast each wedge gets filled based on the predefined game pattern. When the players are scrubbing the same wedge, it also computes how much of the fill needs to be removed. This information is sent to each mobile device, which renders the game screen. When visual or tactile feedback is enabled, the server also sends each device the information about which wedge the game partner is touching. The mobile device then provides visual or tactile feedback as we described above.

STUDY1: EFFECTS OF EACH FEEDBACK TYPE

We conducted a laboratory study to examine how visual and tactile feedback individually affects spatial coordination on mobile devices.

Conditions

We designed three feedback conditions: *No feedback* (the system did not provide any visual or tactile feedback about the game partner); *Visual feedback* (Figure 3a and 3b); and *Tactile feedback* (Figure 3c and 3d). For each type of feedback, we also controlled the availability of the audio channel which allowed the participants to talk with each other: *Audio* (the audio channel was provided and the participants could talk with each other); and *NoAudio* (the audio channel was disabled). Table 1 shows the five conditions we studied. We excluded the condition of *No feedback* without the audio channel because it does not allow the participants to communicate in any way and they would not be able to collaborate strategically. Our main interest was to understand the effects of feedback on audio-enabled conditions as we were motivated by collaborative scenarios we can see frequently; however, this inclusion of audio-disabled conditions allows us to understand how well visual or tactile feedback could convey spatial information by comparing against the *Audio-only* condition.

The study was a within-subject design where each pair received exposure to all experimental levels, and presentation order of the system feedback was counter-balanced across the participant pairs. The order of the audio channel availability was fixed to *Audio* followed by *NoAudio* within *Visual* and *Tactile feedback* conditions. All of the conditions used a predefined script which specified changes in the rate at which the game would fill each wedge. Although the same script was used, the game rotated the script randomly for each condition. In this manner, we controlled the difficulty of the game to be the same across all conditions.

Procedure

Twenty-four participants were recruited in teams of two persons. Upon arrival to the laboratory, they were given an explanation about the system and the game. After this explanation, we separated the participants from each pair into different rooms. We gave each participant a device to use during the study as well as a microphone and speaker so that they could communicate with each other during the experiment. We asked each participant to wear a head-band with a mounted Web camera (Figure 4). We adjusted this Web camera so that it could record all interactions that each participant performed on the mobile devices. Participants then had a practice session to become comfortable with the system before starting the experiment.

		Feedback		
		No	Visual	Tactile
Audio Channel	Yes	*Audio-only*	*Visual-Audio*	*Tactile-Audio*
	No	(N/A)	*Visual-NoAudio*	*Tactile-NoAudio*

Table 1. The five conditions studied in the first user study.

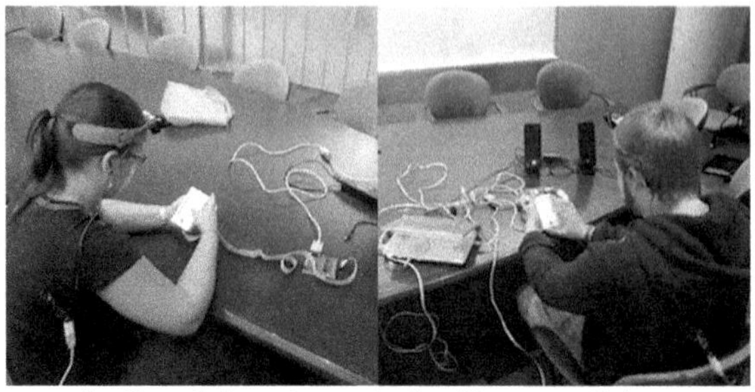

Figure 4. Our laboratory study. Two participants were brought to different rooms. In the audio-enabled conditions, participants were allowed to talk with each other through microphones.

All touch events generated by each user were recorded. The state of all wedges and the point score were logged every 100 msec. The system also audio-recorded all conversations and stored videos recorded by the Web cameras attached to their head-bands for analysis. At the end of the experiment, we conducted a short semi-structured interview to explore the difficulties with collaborating in each condition and their reasons.

Participants

We recruited 12 pairs of participants (PA1–PA12) between the ages of 18 to 39 with a variety of backgrounds (such as students, teachers, engineers, and business persons) for this study. Three of the pairs were both male, one of them was both female, and the rest consisted of one male and one female. All the pairs knew each other before participating in this study. The study lasted approximately 70 minutes. Each participant was compensated with $30 after the study.

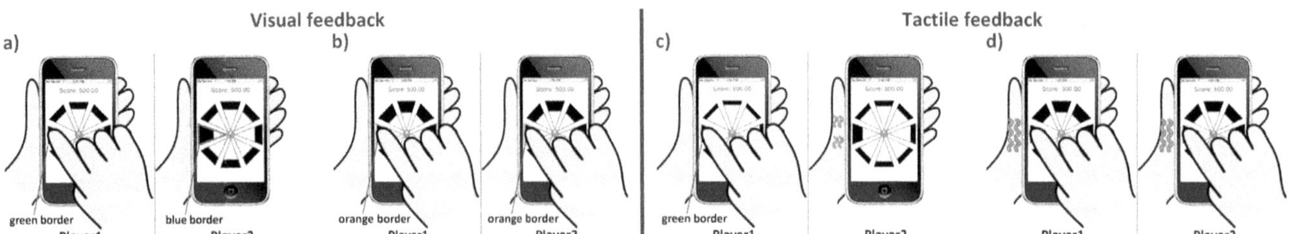

Figure 3. Screenshots of the game with visual and tactile feedback: a) When one of the players touches a wedge, it is highlighted with green, and the system also provides the blue highlight on the contacted wedge (in this example, the left wedge) in the game partner's screen; b) When both of the players touch the same wedge, the highlight turns orange; c) When one of the players touches a wedge, it is highlighted with green, and the system provides discontinuous vibration from the vibration motor associated with the contacted wedge; d) When both of the players touch the same wedge, the vibration becomes continuous.

Theme	Examples
Targeting	"Seven", "Go to top"
Confirmation	(in response to *Targeting* or *Planning*) "OK", "Yeah"
Clarification	(in response to *Targeting* or *Planning*) "What?", "One?"
Strategy switching	(Changing play strategies) "Go counter-clockwise", "Go this direction"
Awareness	"I'm doing it", "Where are you?", "keep going"
Planning	"Seven, nine, and one,"
Prompting (the next move)	(after swiping) "OK, go ahead"

Table 2. Coding scheme.

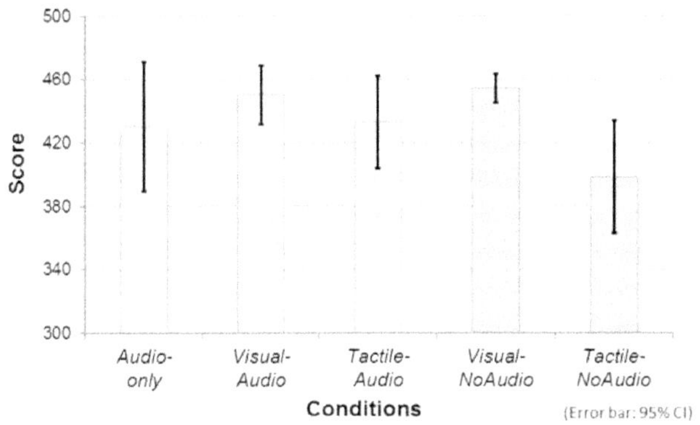

Figure 5. The average scores for the conditions tested in the first user study

Utterance Analysis

All the conversations that the participants had during the experiment were transcribed with timestamps as faithfully as possible. The authors conducted open coding of the quotes to identify seven themes pertaining to coordination, and developed the coding scheme as shown in Table 2. One of the authors and another coder independently categorized the recorded utterances along the scheme; they achieved high inter-rater reliability for every theme (higher than 95% agreement and 0.8 Cohen's kappa).

STUDY1 RESULTS

Score

All pairs played the game for the full five minutes in each condition. Therefore, we were able to remove playing time from our analysis and focus on the performance scores. Figure 5 shows the average score for each condition. Mauchly's test did not reveal a violation of sphericity and therefore permits the direct interpretation of the ANOVA F-test results. A one-way repeated-measure ANOVA revealed a significant difference in the scores by condition ($F_{(4,44)}$=.88, p<.05). Tukey's HSD revealed that scores for the two visual conditions (*Visual-Audio* and *Visual-NoAudio*) were significantly higher than the *Tactile-NoAudio* condition (p<.05). The other conditions were not found to be significantly different.

In addition to the performance scores, it is telling to examine the communication processes that take place in the different feedback conditions, and understand their influence on performance. By doing so, we gain insight into

Theme	*Audio-only*	*Visual-Audio*	*Tactile-Audio*
Targeting	**78.4** (16.0)	**37.8** (37.1)	**55.4** (36.0)
Confirmation	**12.2** (12.1)	**11.3** (12.5)	**14.0**(15.2)
Clarification	**1.4** (1.6)	**0.7** (0.8)	**0.7** (0.9)
Strategy switching	**2.1** (1.8)	**1.6** (1.8)	**1.3** (2.3)
Awareness	**3.3** (4.9)	**2.6** (2.3)	**2.5** (2.7)
Planning	**3.4** (5.6)	**1.8** (4.6)	**2.2** (6.3)
Prompting	**0.8** (0.9)	**2.4** (5.1)	**0.7** (1.4)
Total	**101.5** (24.0)	**58.3** (54.6)	**77.1** (54.0)

Table 3. The average number and standard deviation of utterances for the three audio-available conditions.

the type of coordinating information that each feedback mechanism provides. We classified the types of spoken content using the coding scheme described in Table 2 and the results are shown in Table 3 which reports the average number of utterances by content type for the three audio-enabled conditions.

To examine how these contribution types affected the game score in each condition, we used a random effects linear regression model where *Condition*, *Content Theme*[1], and the *Condition* × *Content Theme* interactions were included as independent variables. Because the pairs participated in all conditions, observations were not independent and were therefore modeled as a random effect. The resulting model fit was moderate (R^2=.64, $Adj\text{-}R^2$=.40).

This model controls for the types of utterances that were generated in addition to the feedback provided by the condition, and describes their influence on game score. Controlling for language, we see a significant effect of *Condition* ($F_{(2,19.19)}$=3.72, p<.05) where performance increased from *Audio-only* to *Tactile-Audio* to *Visual-Audio*. Of the content types examined, there is a main effect of *Targeting* content ($F_{(1,21)}$=8.37, p<.01), controlling for condition. Higher level interactions revealed significant interaction effects of *Condition* and the number of *Targeting* utterances ($F_{(2,19.96)}$=4.63, p<.05) and *Condition* and the number of *Prompting* utterances ($F_{(2,20.32)}$=4.22, p<.05). The other main effects and interaction effects were not found to be significant at the 95% confidence level.

Further examination of the interaction effects revealed that an increase in the production of *Targeting* utterances helped to improved game score in the *Audio-only* condition, but did not provide a similar improvement on *Visual-Audio* and *Tactile-Audio*. In other words, when the pairs did not have visual or tactile feedback, they had to compensate by increasing their production of spatial information regarding the targets. We also found that the increase of *Prompting* utterances was associated with a lower score in the *Tactile-Audio* condition, but such effects were not found in the other conditions.

[1] To avoid multicollinearity, we first examined the correlations among the possible independent variables, and chose those which were not strongly correlated with each other. As a result, our variables for *Content Themes* were the utterance counts of *Targeting*, *Clarification*, *Planning*, *Prompting*, along with their interaction terms with *Condition*.

Strategies

We analyzed the naming schema that the participants used for specifying the wedges on the screen. Understanding their naming schema is important because they are a part of the participants' strategies for effective coordination. We observed the three following naming schema:

- *Index*: Language using numbers the participants agreed on. For instance, "one" meant the top wedge, "three" meant the right wedge, and "five" meant the bottom wedge.
- *Clock*: Language based on the clock metaphor. For example, "twelve o'clock" meant the top wedge, and "six o'clock" meant the bottom wedge. The use of numbers is similar to *Index*, but the wedges that the numbers correspond with here differ from *Index*.
- *Direction*: Language based on the direction or orientation. "North" or "top" meant the top wedge, and "south" or "bottom" meant the bottom wedge.

PA10-1	Time [sec]	PA10-2
"Nine."  Moving to the left wedge.	46	 "Seven." Moving to the bottom-left wedge.
"What are you doing?"  Scrubbing the left wedge, but nothing occurred.	48	 Touching the bottom-left wedge.
 Scrubbing the left wedge.	49	 "Seven, seven." Holding the bottom-left wedge.
"OK."  Moving to the bottom-left wedge.	50	 Holding the bottom-left wedge.
 Scrubbing the bottom-left wedge.	51	 Holding the bottom-left wedge.

Figure 6. Collaboration observed in the *Audio-only* condition. This pair mis-communicated about moving to the next target. PA10-1 then explicitly asked where PA10-2 was holding and re-coordinated the position.

We observed that for most of the pairs, one participant would typically assume the responsibility of deciding the target and the other person would follow her. However, the participants often stop using this strategy when many wedges become almost completely filled. Both participants would then actively communicate about the next target. In terms of scrubbing, one person (who generally decides the target) would touch and continue to press the target while the other player scrubbed that wedge.

Collaboration in the Audio-only Condition

Participants used targeting utterances in the *Audio-only* condition most frequently as shown in Table 3. Because the system did not provide users with any feedback about their game partner's action, participants often failed to figure out their game partner's location. There were different reasons for this. For example, both players may specify different wedges as the next target, and then fail to recognize the need to negotiate or clarify which wedge both should touch (*i.e.,* once a participant expresses the next wedge she will target, she assumes the partner will follow her verbal instruction even though both in the pair spoke at the same time). Figure 6 illustrates a case in which both players

PA7-1	Time [sec]	PA7-2
 Moving to the top-left wedge. The bottom-right wedge is occluded.	119	 Moving to the bottom-right wedge.
 Noticing visual feedback and moving to the bottom-right wedge.	121	 Moving to the top-right based on visual feedback.
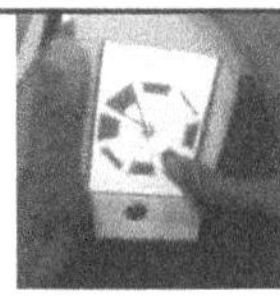 Noticing that PA7-2 had moved to the top-left wedge.	123	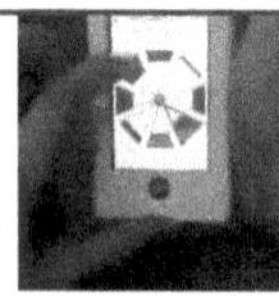 Scrubbing the top-left wedge, but producing no effect.
"Five"  Explicitly mentioning the target.	124	 Following PA7-1 after his instruction.

Figure 7. Collaboration observed in the *Visual-Audio* condition. While PA7-1 moved to the top-left wedge, PA7-2 moved to the bottom-left. But PA07-1 did not notice PA7-2's move because the visual feedback was occluded by his thumb. This caused another mis-coordination, and PA7-1 had to tell PA7-2 to come to the bottom-right wedge.

specified two different wedges as the next target, but did not make any clarification because both were focused on their own targets. This resulted in the pair falling out of synch and required explicit re-coordination.

Participants sometimes slipped and specified a wrong target, which led them to touch different wedges. In the post-experimental interview, one participant explained that the *Audio-only* condition was difficult because of possible slips in how to refer to the wedges.

> *"Probably the most difficult condition was audio-only... I keep getting confused by 'top-right' or 'top-left'."* [PA3-1]

Although participants performed well in the *Audio-only* condition, some participants commented that explicit audio communication increased the workload involved with playing the game compared to the other conditions. As shown in Table 3, this condition forced the participants to use more utterances. Although most of the utterances we observed were short, participants felt that frequent conversations often prevented them from collaborating efficiently in this tightly-coupled coordination task.

Collaboration in the Visual Conditions

We observed that the participants generally used fewer utterances in the *Visual-Audio* condition than the *Audio-only* condition. The participants mostly made utterances for targeting and confirmation in the *Audio-only* condition and the game provided visual feedback of where the game partner was touching on the screen; thus, they did not need to perform explicit coordination using voice in some cases.

In both *Visual* conditions, the participant's hand sometimes occluded a large portion of the screen, and the participants often failed to spot the visual feedback indicating which wedge their partner was touching. Figure 7 shows one of the instances in which the occlusion impeded collaboration. While PA7-1 moved to the top-left wedge, PA7-2 moved to the bottom right wedge. However, PA7-1 did not notice the game partner's move because the bottom-right wedge was occluded by the thumb. PA7-1 then noticed the visual feedback, and tried to follow the partner. But PA7-2 also noticed that PA7-1 was on the top-left wedge, and tried to follow him. As a result, another mis-coordination happened, and P7-1 had to specify the target verbally.

Collaboration in the Tactile Conditions

Similar to the *Visual* conditions, participants generally used fewer utterances compared to the *Audio-only* condition. The tactile feedback helped the participants identify which wedge their game partner was touching. Some participants, particularly those who had small hands, commented that they often had difficulty correctly identifying the location of the vibration; however, participants liked having a separate channel for knowing their game partner's location.

We found that the participants generally were able to use spatial tactile feedback to communicate a location with their partner and often did not need to confirm it explicitly. Figure 8 shows a common interaction that we observed in the *Tactile-NoAudio* condition. After this pair finished scrubbing the bottom wedge, PA3-1 moved to the bottom-right wedge whereas PA3-2 moved to the top-right wedge. PA3-2 immediately noticed the discontinuous vibration coming from the bottom-right. This caused PA3-2 to defer his location; PA3-2 then moved to PA3-1's location, and scrubbed the bottom-right wedge. Because PA3-1 was able to perceive that PA3-2's previous location through the tactile communication channel, after they finished the bottom-right wedge, they moved to the top-right wedge, which was PA3-2's previous intended target.

STUDY1 SUMMARY

We found that a system with visual feedback generally supports coordination better than one with tactile feedback or without any feedback. Our analysis also revealed that the

PA3-1	Time [sec]	PA3-2
	158	
Moving to the bottom-right wedge.		Moving to the top-right wedge.
	159	
Scrubbing the bottom-right wedge, but the tactile feedback happened at the top-right.		Scrubbing the top-right wedge, but P2 noticed the tactile feedback coming from the bottom-right.
	160	
Still scrubbing the bottom-right wedge.		Moving to the bottom-right wedge.
	161	
Scrubbing the bottom-right wedge. The black filling started to disappear.		Holding the bottom-right wedge.
	163	
Moving to the top-right wedge which P2 was touching before.		Moving to the top-right wedge.

Figure 8. Collaboration observed in the *Tactile-NoAudio* condition. This pair made different moves initially, but PA3-2 followed PA3-1 based on the tactile feedback. After the bottom-right wedge, both participants moved to the top-right wedge which PA3-2 wanted to work on before.

number of *Targeting* utterances affect game performance only in the *Audio-only* condition. The results imply that an additional feedback channel, either visual or tactile feedback, could help the participants perform spatial coordination without explicit audio communication.

The results also highlight different benefits of visual and tactile feedback, and suggest that these two feedback channels could complement each other well: visual feedback is beneficial to provide precise spatial information, and tactile feedback can address occlusion issues. We thus decided to conduct another user study to measure performance when users have both feedback channels.

STUDY2: EFFECTS OF COMBINED FEEDBACK

This user study focused on comparing user collaboration with a system combining both visual and tactile feedback against systems using either feedback channel. We used the same system and experimental procedure as the first user study. We included three audio-enabled feedback conditions: *Visual*, *Tactile*, and *Visual+Tactile*. We excluded any audio-disabled conditions because the results above already indicate that the audio channel has a substantial impact on the game performance. The presentation order of the conditions was counter-balanced across participant pairs. We recruited another twelve pairs of participants for this study (PB1–PB12). Their demographics were similar to the ones in our first user study. This study took 50 minutes on average, and each participant was compensated with $30 after the study.

STUDY2 RESULTS

Figure 9 shows the game scores across the three feedback conditions. Unpaired Welch's t-tests did not show any significant difference in the scores of *Visual* and *Tactile* between our first and second study ($t_{(21.0)}$=0.81, p>.05 for *Visual*; and $t_{(19.4)}$=0.28, p>.05 for *Tactile*). This implies that the scores in the second user study were comparable to the ones in our first study. A Mauchly's test of sphericity did not reveal a violation; thus, we once again report the results of the ANOVA F-tests. A one-way repeated-measure ANOVA revealed a significant difference in the scores by condition ($F_{(2,22)}$=6.01, p<.01). Tukey's HSD revealed that the scores in *Visual+Tactile* were significantly higher than the scores in *Visual* and *Tactile* conditions (p's <.05).

Similar to the first study, we examined the communication processes that took place to better understand the coordinating role of each feedback condition. We used the same coding scheme presented in Table 2 and the average numbers of utterances by content type for the second study are shown in Table 4. We then compared differences in the number of utterances between the first and second study. As a result, unpaired Welch's t-tests did not show any significant difference in the scores of *Visual* and *Tactile* between our first and second study ($t_{(16.1)}$=1.79, p>.05 for *Visual*; and $t_{(17.6)}$=0.80, p>.05 for *Tactile*).

We analyzed the data using the same random effects linear regression model described in the first study with one

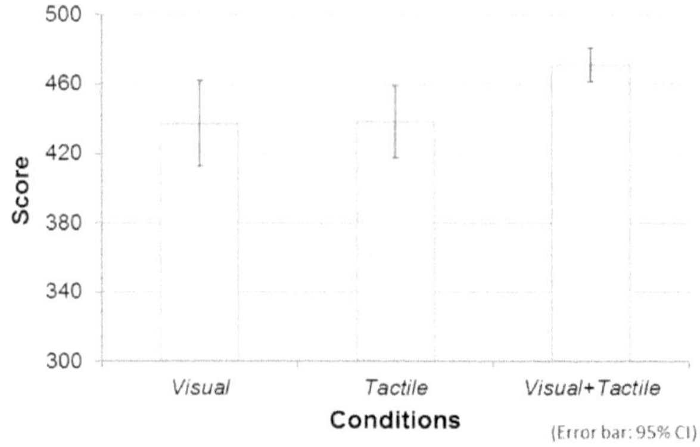

Figure 9. The average scores for the conditions tested in the second user study.

Theme	*Visual*	*Tactile*	*Visual+Tactile*
Targeting	**72.4** (26.0)	**77.3** (30.0)	**86.4** (12.2)
Confirmation	**10.5** (9.9)	**7.5** (6.0)	**5.8** (3.8)
Clarification	**0.9** (1.3)	**1.6** (2.0)	**1.8** (2.3)
Strategy switching	**1.8** (2.2)	**1.0** (1.6)	**0.9** (1.4)
Awareness	**4.3** (4.9)	**2.1** (2.6)	**1.6** (2.0)
Planning	**1.0** (1.2)	**1.7** (2.3)	**1.6** (2.1)
Prompting	**0.4** (1.1)	**0.5** (1.0)	**0.1** (0.3)
Total	**91.3** (27.0)	**91.8** (31.0)	**98.3** (11.0)

Table 4. The average number and standard deviation of

exception being that interactions were removed from the model due to the fact that there were no significant higher order interactions. The resulting model fit was relatively high (R^2=.70, $Adj\text{-}R^2$=.63).

Controlling for language, we still see a significant effect of *Condition* ($F_{(2, 21.37)}$=4.93, p<.05) where performance for the *Visual+Tactile* condition was better than both the *Visual* and *Tactile* conditions. Of the content types examined, there is a positive main effect of *Targeting* content whereby increases in the use of targeting comments was associated with higher scores ($F_{(1,26.33)}$=14.03, p<.01), controlling for condition. The other main effects and interaction effects were not found to be significant at the 95% confidence level.

While these findings suggest a link between the content of the discussions and the performance of the pairs, we found no evidence of differentiated influence of various discourse strategies in the conditions examined in the second study. This suggests that there may not be a difference in the need for additional information across the visual and tactile channels. Alternatively, it could be that our discourse coding scheme was not sensitive to the coordinating differences that are afforded by the visual and tactile channels; thus, we further analyzed the transcripts for evidence of differential use.

Most participants agreed that visual feedback was easy to understand and showed the location of a game partner accurately. But four pairs explicitly mentioned that occlusion by hands was a problem. In contrast, participants expressed different opinions on tactile feedback and used it in different ways. Four pairs mentioned that they needed more effort in associating tactile feedback to a particular wedge than visual feedback. However, tactile feedback could subtly guide a player's attention to the area of interest as one of the participants commented:

> *"The good thing [about vibration] for me was it was a more subconscious cue; wasn't something I had to pay attention to. But with color, I've got to pay attention to where the color is going, I had to process it. But vibration subconsciously pulled attention to the area."* [PB2-2]

Two pairs commented that tactile feedback offered a separate channel to maintain awareness about a game partner without disrupting the visual information space.

> *"The vibration is a much better safety net than visual. I think because I could feel that or maybe because so much was happening on the screen already. Tactile touch didn't add something extra on the screen... Changing colors was just a distraction, versus vibration wasn't another visual distraction."* [PB10-1]

Participants overall liked the *Visual+Tactile* condition, and often preferred it over the other conditions. One participant explained to us that she used tactile feedback as a redundant cue to ensure that she and her partner were contacting the same wedge.

> *"Vibration is confirmation of if you are doing the right thing. I'm hearing where to go, and vibration confirms me that we are going to the same spot."* [PB2-1]

STUDY2 SUMMARY

Our second user study revealed that a system using both visual and tactile feedback outperformed systems using only either type of feedback when verbal communication is available. Its qualitative results also support the notion that visual and tactile feedback can complement each other to support users' spatial coordination.

DISCUSSIONS

The results show that the occlusion caused by the participant's hand often impeded smooth collaboration in the *Visual* conditions. Occlusion is a well-known problem in touch-screen devices. To address this issue, Vogel and Balakrishnan demonstrated an interface which changes the locations of the objects depending on the position of the hand or arm over the screen [21]. This technique could solve some occlusion problems we observed in our user studies. But, rearranging the objects might introduce additional complexity on spatial coordination. For example, an object on the right side in one person's device might appear at a different location in the partner's device with an occlusion-aware interface. Tactile feedback can directly mitigate some occlusion problems, and provide awareness for coordination particularly when the visual components are complex (*e.g.*, online network multiplayer games).

The system had delays in tactile feedback during our experiments due to our hardware and system limitations. Gergle *et al.* studied the effects of delays in visual feedback for collaborative tasks [9]. They found that in rapidly changing dynamic environments, delays on the order of 200ms can cause performance deficits in visual piece arrangement tasks. Jay *et al.* conducted a study examining the effects of delay in haptic and visual feedback on collaborative tasks which require strict spatial and temporal coordination [12]. Their task was to move two cursors towards the target in a graphical user interface while maintaining the relative distance of the cursors within a threshold. Their results show that even a very small delay (25 msec in tactile feedback, and 50 msec in visual feedback) can impact the collaboration when strict spatial and temporal coordination is necessary.

The tasks studied in our experiment include higher temporal demand (*i.e.*, the system fills wedges constantly) than those in Gergle *et al.*'s study; thus, even a small delay might have caused a significant impact. This may be one reason why *Tactile-NoAudio* was the weakest condition in terms of the performance score because participants were unable to explicitly coordinate through the audio channel to compensate the delay in tactile feedback. However, as Jay *et al.* discussed in [12], supporting strict spatial and temporal coordination is challenging in both visual and tactile feedback, and thus future research is necessary on how to overcome the delay on the feedback.

We had the limited output resolution of spatial tactile feedback. Israr and Poupyrev have developed a method to create virtual vibration points where no physical vibration motors exist [11]. With their algorithm, a system would have an improved output resolution, enabling the design of combined feedback channel to support more precise spatial coordination. Our results, which highlight the different advantages for each type of feedback and benefits for combined feedback in spatial coordination, can inform the designs of collaborative handheld systems with higher output resolution than our system.

LIMITATIONS

There are several limitations in our study that should be considered. First, we abstracted spatial coordination tasks into a game that required participants to perform frequent spatial coordination. As a result, we were able to perform an in-depth analysis of spatial coordination processes. While the game provides a controlled environment for doing this, it is unclear the extent to which these processes will translate to more contextualized everyday interactions. In addition, there are different types of spatial coordination from what we studied, such as avoiding the same object or location. Our results suggest that the combination of visual and spatial tactile feedback can enhance the user's awareness about her collaborator's actions, and could help collaboration for other spatial coordination tasks. But, we note that the results may require careful interpretation when applied to more natural spatial coordination tasks. As such, this game may not relate directly to any specific application, and researchers should carefully consider the role that spatial coordination plays in their given task environment.

Second, the mapping of spatial tactile feedback between vibration locations and wedges is one-to-one in our game design. When this mapping becomes one-to-many, the user would need visual cues to correctly identify the precise location which both users are targeting. Spatial tactile feedback may not be beneficial in this case, but our results suggest that it can still help the user focus her attention towards a part of the workspace, and can reduce visual distraction. This can be important when the users' workspace shows a great deal of visual information.

CONCLUSIONS AND FUTURE WORK

We investigated how visual and tactile feedback affects synchronous collaborative tasks, in particular spatial coordination tasks, on mobile devices. Our results highlight the following findings in the context of collaborative handheld systems:

- Visual feedback can provide precise spatial information about collaborators, but can hamper collaboration when it is occluded and sometimes distracts the user's attention.
- Spatial tactile feedback can provide spatial information about collaborators as well, but improvements are necessary to convey precise spatial information. It can reduce the overload of information in visual space and can gently guide the user's attention to an area of interest.
- Visual and spatial tactile feedback can complement each other, and systems with both feedback channels can offer better spatial coordination support than systems using only one form of feedback.

Our results also imply that spatial tactile feedback could be used to support collaboration with visually impaired users. For example, sighted users can demonstrate to visually impaired users how to interact with interfaces on a mobile touch-screen device. The interaction will be conveyed through tactile feedback, and visually impaired users will be able to feel how to interact with a device remotely.

REFERENCES

1. Brave, S., Ishii, H., Dahley, A. Tangible interfaces for remote collaboration and communication. In *Proc. of CSCW,* ACM Press (1998), 169-178.
2. Brown, L. M., Sellen, A., Krishna, R., Harper, R. Exploring the potential of audio-tactile messaging for remote interpersonal communication. In *Proc. of CHI,* ACM Press (2009), 1527-1530.
3. Chan, A., MacLean, K., McGrenere, J. Designing haptic icons to support collaborative turn-taking. *Int. J. Human-Computer Studies 66*, (2008), 333-355.
4. Chang, A., O'Modhrain, S., Jacob, R., Gunther, E., Ishii, H. ComTouch: design of a vibrotactile communication device. In *Proc. of DIS*, ACM Press (2002), 312-320.
5. Dourish, P., Bellotti, V. Awareness and coordination in shared workspaces. In *Proc. of CSCW*, ACM Press (1992), 107-114.
6. Fogg, B., Cutler, L. D., Arnold, P., Eisbach, C. HandJive: a device for interpersonal haptic entertainment. In *Proc. of CHI*, ACM Press (1998), 57-64.
7. Fukumoto, M., Sugimura, T. Active click: tactile feed-back for touch panels. In *Extended Abstracts of CHI*, ACM Press (2001), 121-122.
8. Gergle, D., Kraut, R.E., Fussell, S.R. Language efficiency and visual technology: minimizing collaborative effort with visual information. *Journal of Language and Social Psychology 23*, 4 (2004), 491-517.
9. Gergle, D., Kraut, R.E., Fussell, S.R. The impact of delayed visual feedback on collaborative performance. In *Proc. of CHI*, ACM Press (2006), 1303-1312.
10. Hoggan, E., Brewster, S.A., Johnston, J. Investigating the effectiveness of tactile feedback for mobile touchscreens. In *Proc. of CHI*, ACM Press (2008), 2019-2028.
11. Israr, A., Poupyrev, I. Tactile Brush: Drawing on Skin with a Tactile Grid Display. In *Proc. of CHI*, ACM Press (2011), 1573-1582.
12. Jay, C., Glencross, M., Hubbold, R. Modeling the effects of delayed haptic and visual feedback in a collaborative virtual environment. *ACM Trans. Comput.-Hum. Interact. 14,* 2 (2007), 8.
13. McGookin, D., Brewster, S. An initial investigation into non-visual computer supported collaboration. In *Extended Abstracts of CHI*, ACM Press (2007), 2573-2578.
14. Oakley, I., Brewster, S., Gray, P. Can you feel the force? An investigation of haptic collaboration in shared editors. In *Proc. of EuroHaptics*, EuroHaptics Society (2001).
15. Palmer, C. I., Gardner, E. P. Simulation of motion of the skin IV responses of pacinian corpuscle afferents innervating the primate hand to stripe patterns on the optacon. *J. Neurophysiol. 64*, 1, (1990), 236-247.
16. Pielot, M., Krull, O., Boll, S. Where is my team? Supporting situation awareness with tactile displays. In *Proc. of CHI*, ACM Press (2010), 1705-1714.
17. Poupyrev, I., Maruyama, S., Rekimoto, J. Ambient touch: designing tactile interfaces for handheld devices. In *Proc. of UIST*, ACM Press (2002), 51-60.
18. Plimmer, B., Crossan, A., Brewster, S. A., Blagojevic, R. Multimodal collaborative handwriting training for visually impaired people. In Proc. of *CHI*, ACM Press (2008), 393-402.
19. Sahami, A., Holleis, P., Schmidt, A., Hakkila, J. Rich Tactile Output on Mobile Devices. In *Proc. of AmI*, Springer (2008), 210-221.
20. Stark, R., Carlstedt, T., Hallin, R. G., Risling, M. Distribution of human pacinian corpuscles in the hand. *J. Hand Surg. Eur. 23B*, 3, (1998), 370-372.
21. Vogel, D., Balakrishnan, R. Occlusion-aware interfaces. In *Proc. of CHI*, ACM Press (2010), 263-272.
22. Yatani, K., Truong, K., N. SemFeel: A user interface with semantic tactile feedback for mobile touch-screen devices. In *Proc. of UIST*, ACM Press (2009), 111-120.

PicoTales: Collaborative Authoring of Animated Stories using Handheld Projectors

Simon Robinson,[1] Elina Vartiainen,[1] Matt Jones,[1] Gary Marsden[2]

[1] Future Interaction Technology Lab
Swansea University, SA2 8PP, UK
{ s.n.w.robinson, e.vartiainen, matt.jones } @swan.ac.uk

[2] Dept. of Computer Science
University of Cape Town
Cape Town, South Africa
gaz@cs.uct.ac.za

ABSTRACT

In this article we describe a novel approach to collaborative video authoring using handheld projectors. *PicoTales* are created by sketching story elements on a projector+phone prototype, and then animated by moving the projected image. Movements are captured using motion sensor data, rather than visual or other tracking methods, allowing interaction and story creation anywhere. We describe in detail the design and development of our prototype device, and also address issues in position estimation and element tracking. An experiment was conducted to evaluate the prototype, demonstrating its accuracy and usability for ad-hoc creation of story videos. The potential of the system for story authoring is shown via a further experiment looking at the quality of the animated story videos produced. We conclude by considering possible future developments of the concept, and highlighting the benefits of our design for collaborative story capture.

Author Keywords

Mobile projection, story authoring, collaboration.

ACM Classification Keywords

H.5.2: Input devices and strategies; Interaction styles.

General Terms

Design, Experimentation, Human Factors.

INTRODUCTION

People like to create stories together. They may do this while co-located, sitting around a dinner table, for instance, reliving and embellishing a shared experience. They can also now do this in an asynchronous and dispersed fashion, by creating and then adding to a thread of comments and media in a social networking service.

Previous work has considered system support for capturing and authoring stories collaboratively. Much work, for instance, has considered the important role such interactions can play in education (e.g., [14]) or to aid community enhancement in developing regions (e.g., [15]).

Technologically, the platforms proposed have included web and desktops [4]; shared surfaces [9] and mobiles [14]. Unlike the conventional single user mouse and keyboard arrangements, shared surfaces such as TellTable [9] allow more than one person to engage in the process at the same time. This is achieved both directly, by support for multiple person touches and indirectly by groups gathering round and commenting on each others' efforts. These tabletop approaches, though, have the disadvantage of being fixed to particular locations. Mobile approaches, such as Mobile Stories [14] provide portability, enabling situated storytelling as well as the convenience of usage anywhere. Mobile devices have the further benefit of being particularly suited to developing world contexts where there is sparse access to other forms of computing technology [22]. The relatively small screens, though, bring both potential usability issues and may limit the forms of expression. Furthermore, the types of bystander participation seen with tabletop approaches are not possible.

Our work demonstrates a new platform for combining the benefits of larger shared surfaces with those of mobiles. This systems orientated paper, then, shows how pico-projectors and mobile sensors can provide for collaborative authoring.

Handheld pico-projectors are an important emerging technology. Now widely available, these portable large displays could potentially be included as a standard component of mobile devices in the near future, bringing many possibilities for interaction beyond small device screens. In particular, their high mobility shows huge potential for collaboration.

Naturally, previous research has looked at how these devices might be used and developed as public displays [29], or for group interaction [7]. Here, however, we are interested in the use of projections as *input*. Rather than using projection to display pre-constructed content, in our research we investigate how these devices might help groups author stories together for later retelling and reuse. We imagine people not just viewing existing stories using pre-compiled content, but also animating projected sketches to create interactive narratives that can then be retold and relived later. Consider the following scenario, which illustrates the approach.

Ajala is a health worker in a rural Indian village. Today she is with a group of young women villagers who are going to help author a story about the importance of giving babies clean water. She gives the storytelling devices to two of the villagers – Nisha and Prapti – and they point the projectors onto the wall in the community centre. Ajala asks the ladies what places in the village have good water – "the well," they reply. Nisha sketches a well on her device's touch screen and it is immediately displayed on the wall for all to see. Meanwhile, Prapti draws a woman carrying a water jug on her head; "make the jug bigger!" shout several of the ladies; the others laugh. Prapti moves the drawing of the woman towards the well and Nisha adds an arrow to show that water should come from it. Prapti moves the lady away from the well and Nisha erases her sketch, replacing it with a picture of baby. As Prapti moves the lady towards the baby, Nisha finishes her sketch by adding a smile to the baby's face. Later, Ajala sends the animated story to her PC and adds subtitles in two local languages. In the weeks to come, health team-members download it to mobile devices to show this village's story to many other discussion groups.

We have constructed a prototype that aims to support this group work by recording projected sketches into jointly-authored video stories – *PicoTales*. Participants use a mobile interface to draw simple story elements, then animate by pointing and moving the projected image. These sketches are saved by the system, then rendered into animated videos with no further interaction required by the users. The digital packages of content can, however, be edited if necessary. No visual tracking system is required – we take a sensor-based approach, aiming to allow story creation anywhere.

The contribution of this paper, then, is to introduce and demonstrate the notion of mobile projection as input for the spontaneous capture of animated video stories. We have had to innovate on infrastructure-free calibration and tracking to provide a robust platform for the system's applications. This paper describes the system and studies evaluating the accuracy of the tracking and the effectiveness of this lightweight platform in terms of the quality of the stories created.

BACKGROUND

The question we consider in this paper is whether we can support collaborative authoring of stories through the combination of pico-projectors and mobiles with motion sensors. As already noted, the work is motivated by previous collaborative authoring studies in various contexts. Our design was further inspired by research on the use of projections for engaging interactions. A key aspect of the platform is the lightweight, sensor based tracking employed. All the technology can be carried in the hand – we do not, for instance, have to deploy arrays of cameras in the environment to capture users' interactions. We review this work below, highlighting the points of departure evident in our contribution.

Motivating Collaborative Authoring

Much of the previous research into collaborative authoring has focused on technologies for children. KidPad [13], for example, extended existing sketching software to create a mouse-based storytelling environment that intuitively zoomed and panned children's creations. Stanton et al. [26] built upon this to allow multiple mice to be used simultaneously to encourage groups of children to collaborate in drawing story sketches. Cao et al. [9] investigated multitouch table-based collaborative storytelling with sketching and image capture. Two separate modes allowed children to first create story elements, and then use these to narrate the story.

More recently, Fails et al. [14] have investigated how these collaborative storytelling approaches might work on mobile devices. Their mobile system allows children to create book-like stories that draw from text, pictures and audio, using two phones held together to view the content. Balabanović et al. [2] describe *StoryTrack*, an early digital photo storytelling device that allowed recording of sequences of photos with associated voice annotations. Later work has investigated this type of interaction on mobile phones. Ah Kun and Marsden [1] created a synchronised mobile photo sharing and storytelling application. Each phone user can view and annotate shared photos, and interactions can either be turn-by-turn or completely ad-hoc. Related research has investigated how these technologies might be used to help record stories in developing world contexts. Bidwell et al. [5] created a mobile storytelling device aimed at enabling communities in rural Africa to record and share stories with audio and photos. Their findings highlighted the importance of collaboration in authoring, despite not explicitly supporting this behaviour.

In contrast to these mouse-, table-, phone- or touch screen-based collaborative approaches, our projector-based prototype focuses on real-time recording of story sketches. Like other collaborative sketching tools (e.g., [30]) we aim to support and promote quick, spontaneous sharing of users' ideas, as opposed to final polished narratives. Similar table-based storytelling systems can provide an attractive focus point for group story creation, but are as a result restricted to this single location. In our design we aim to allow story sketching anywhere, allowing the storytellers to choose both the place and the size of the surface they use for their creation.

Projection

Projection has been used in play and ad-hoc storytelling throughout history [32]. From digital shadow puppets [35] to torch-based exploration [16], researchers and artists have worked to develop digital versions of these interactions. Previous research has investigated the use of both lasers [19] and flashlights to interact with static projected content [21], to play games [8] or to control a projected display [10]. Commercial projector storytelling systems are also available,[1] showing story images while children follow along in a book.

Other researchers have investigated how projections might be used to interact and play with physical objects. Sugimoto et al. [28] used handheld projectors to guide a robot, finding that the system enhanced engagement and supported storytelling. Games are also a common theme for pico projection – Löchtefeld et al. [18] describe *LittleProjectedPlanet*, an augmented

[1] *Magic Storytime Theatre* – Tomy (2007)

reality game that uses real-world objects as levels on which projected balls can bounce and roll. In our design we focus on story capture without the need for visual tracking of the storytelling surface. In other designs, stories based around interaction with real-world objects must be replayed from the same viewpoint, or captured on video. PicoTales are standalone, and can be replayed at a later time based on the recorded movements of the projector.

Projector Tracking

Projector-based pointing interaction has previously been investigated (e.g., [3]), including multi-user variants (e.g., [7]), but has usually focused on peephole-type displays [20], or shadow pointing to the projected image to interact [11]. The majority of these systems have made use of visual-based device tracking methods, primarily due to their higher accuracy. Some previous systems (e.g., [3]) use cameras on the projection device but do not discuss tracking accuracy; others (e.g., [6]) use commercial image-based tracking systems with high (up to millimetre-level) precision, but substantial cost.[2] These previous methods either require infrastructure to be placed in the environment [7], or have limitations with respect to the distance that participants can stand from each other and the projection surface [25]. In our prototype we use a sensor-based approach, sacrificing pinpoint accuracy for the ability to project and interact spontaneously in any location – our aim is to be both affordable and portable. As a result, in evaluating our system a key question is the extent to which our low fidelity sensor-based design might impact on the value of the system for creating stories that can be later shared.

Previous sensor-based projection tracking designs have used fixed positions [12], or made assumptions about the user's arm position [23]. Willis et al. [33] used motion sensor input for pointing-based games, incorporating an ultrasonic distance sensor, though this was used only for evaluating users' pointing behaviour. While motion sensors are common on current mobile devices, long range distance sensors are unfortunately not currently included. More recently Willis et al. [34] have developed a camera-based approach, using a customised camera+projector with infrared fiducial markers for tracking. Their approach is an alternative to the sensor-based tracking we demonstrate, but it requires new devices and also does not allow tracking of projections outside the view of the device's camera. To allow for a potential implementation on current devices, in our design we use a novel projector-based position and movement estimation procedure that predicts where users are located relative to each other and to the projection surface.

Strachan and Murray-Smith [27] found sensor data to be sufficient for this type of pointing-based interaction even in high-uncertainty scenarios. In a similar approach to ours, Lee and Keh [17] used sensor data for simple position calibration, but at fixed distances from a wall, unlike in our prototype. Lee and Keh also noted the importance of accounting for shifts in users' arms as they move the device. In our design, a one-time calibration step when first using the device aims to measure this arm shift, and improve tracking accuracy as a result.

[2]Vicon Bonita (vicon.com), for example; $10,000 upwards

Figure 1. The PicoTales prototype. Each user holds their phone in-hand, sketching on the device's screen and moving it to animate their projected story. Movements are recorded by the attached sensor pack.

Figure 2. The simple phone-based sketching interface for drawing PicoTales. Users touch the screen to draw, selecting one of the coloured squares to use that colour, or × to erase the current sketch.

The entire display (including the interface elements) is projected, but only the sketch is shown in the resulting story animation.

PICOTALES PROTOTYPE

Our PicoTales prototype allows groups of people to draw and project simple sketches to author their stories. Projected story elements and interactions are automatically composed into a video animation of the action. Rather than using an integrated projector phone, we chose to combine three separate components, as current all-in-one models lack sufficient battery life and the sensors required for our approach. The prototype setup consists of a Nokia 5800 mobile phone, firmly attached to an Optoma PK101 projector and a SHAKE SK6 sensor pack [31]. Figure 1 shows the device configuration. A Python application on the phone provides the simple user interface. Story videos are created by a separate PC at present, to allow easier viewing of the resulting stories, though this step could be incorporated into the phone client in future versions. Our prototypes connect wirelessly to the story PC, streaming live accelerometer and magnetometer data, and receiving commands when user actions are required.

Authoring Stories

Each story participant holds one of our prototypes in-hand, with several participants able to take part in each story – we have tested with up to three simultaneous users. Each time participants create a PicoTale they are prompted to perform a lightweight distance estimation step before they begin. This allows the system to calculate their positions relative to each other, and their distance from the projection surface (see next Section for technical details). The phone then displays the interface shown in Fig. 2, and starts recording the story from this point onwards until users exit the application.

Participants draw on the phone's screen to tell their story, pointing the projected sketch to interact with other participants' drawings, and moving it to animate. While users sketch and move the phone, realtime sensor data is recorded to track

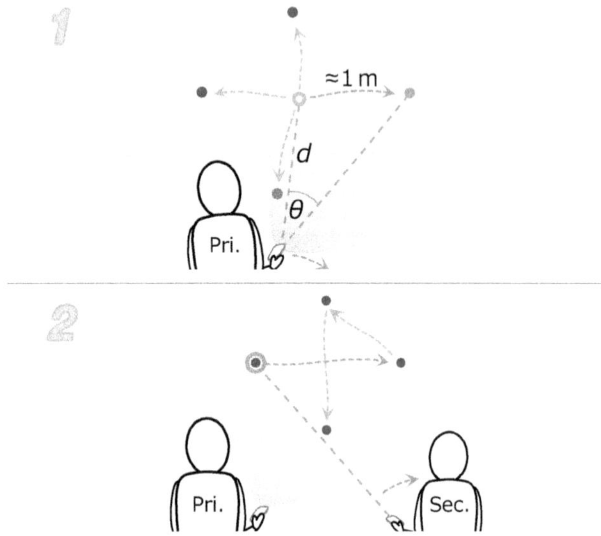

Figure 3. Estimating participants' positions. Step 1: The first (primary) participant initially points straight ahead at the projection surface, then estimates 1 m above, below, left and right of this point. Step 2: Other (secondary) participants join the session by pointing to each of four markers projected by the first.

where they are pointing to on the projection surface. All of the movements and sketches are recorded in the resulting story video. Currently only the visual story elements are recorded – we imagine users narrating as they animate, but we do not yet record the audio in the current implementation.

When participants finish their story, a separate PC creates the PicoTale. The logged sensor data is analysed to calculate the position each participant was standing during the story, and to track where they pointed while projecting each sketched story element. This is then brought together into an XML version of the story, containing the sketch data and all the timings, positions, and zoom levels required to show the elements in the positions they were projected. This PicoTale can then be played back immediately on-screen, or exported as a video.

Our current prototype only supports viewing of the PicoTale, but because we record both sketches and their positions, we plan future versions that allow later editing and reshaping of the animation. At first, users could retell the story with the same visual content, but just as the narrative evolves over time, so too could the visual elements of the PicoTale.

TECHNICAL CHALLENGES

In order to allow story creation on any surface, rather than just in places with visual tracking capabilities (e.g., [6]), we take a motion sensor-based approach to user and device position tracking. Although less precise than visual methods, this approach offers benefits that we believe outweigh its inaccuracies – we allow story creation anywhere, and record the actual sketches that users create, rather than a video.

Tracking

Sensor-based tracking gives only the orientation of a device, rather than its position in 3D space. As a result, a person animating their story elements by pivoting the phone around its axis could point to the same positions as another who moves their whole arm to animate, but the resulting sensor data would not reflect the extent of their movements. We address this issue with an approach similar to the calibration procedures often used for touch screens, by using the results from a one-time calibration step to scale the real-time sensor data that is recorded while users project. Provided that story participants are consistent in their pointing method (rotation or translation), this approach allows us to more accurately track the positions that they point to on the surface.

Effective tracking also requires knowledge of the distance of the projection surface from the user, because the angle at which they hold the device, and thus the position of their sketch on the surface, is dependent on its position. For example, consider pointing to an object on a wall from 0.5 m, then moving back and pointing to the same object from 2.0 m. In both cases the target object is the same, but the amount of movement required is considerably different. To address this, a short calibration step before each story authoring session estimates the surface distance via simple trigonometry.

Position Estimation

When using the PicoTales application for the first time, people are prompted to measure and stand 1 m away from a wall. The device then guides them through a calibration procedure – pointing straight ahead and then estimating 1 m to the left and right, then 1 m above and below the original point – see Fig. 3, part 1. Because the distance from the projection surface is known to be 1 m, we can calculate the actual distance they moved the device: $d_1 = 1 \times \tan\theta_1$. Future distance estimations do not require the user to measure 1 m from the surface; only the four 1 m estimates are required. We can then estimate the distance from the surface: $d_2 = d_1 \div \tan\theta_2$.

When only one person is telling a story, it is sufficient to know the distance of the surface to accurately track their pointing. For more than one participant, we must also discover their positions relative to each other. When additional (secondary) participants use the PicoTales application, their positions are estimated by pointing to four markers projected by the first (primary) participant. The primary participant points straight ahead while the others point to each marker in turn when highlighted – see Fig. 3, part 2. This procedure gives four estimates of secondary participants' relative positions. Currently we use these estimates to calculate relative positions and heights between users – in our prototype we assume that all participants stand at the same distance from the wall.

In total the distance estimation procedure takes around 14 seconds for two participants (average 9 s primary, 5 s secondary, based on data from our experiment).

EVALUATION

We evaluated the PicoTales prototype in two experiments, studying both technical and story authoring aspects. The first investigated the reliability and limitations of our sensor-based position estimation and tracking methods. The second study focused on authoring, and the value of the system for sharing.

STUDY 1: POSITION & TRACKING

Because our approach is technically very different to visual-based approaches, it is essential to test its accuracy for creating story videos that closely portray the animations users create. Our research questions were:

Position Estimation: Can our position estimation methods reliably determine where users are standing relative to the projection surface?

Tracking: Can sensor-based pointing tracking accurately predict where story elements are projected?

Tasks and Measures

Task 1: Position Estimation

To assess the real-world technical limitations of our positioning method it is important to measure its accuracy from a range of surface distances and user positions. We studied three separate distances and four separate secondary participant positions, allowing us to quantify position estimation accuracy from a range of distances and projection angles that represent the approximate usable range of the projector.

At the start of the task, the height at which each participant naturally holds the device is measured in order to be able to compare the position at which the projector is actually held with the estimates given by the system. One participant (P1 hereafter) then performs the primary position estimation procedure while standing at position D_3 on Row 1 (see Fig. 4), pointing straight ahead on Wall 1, then 1 m left, right, above and below this point. P1 then moves to position D_1 and Participant 2 (P2 hereafter) performs the secondary position estimation procedure from positions D_2–D_5, pointing to each of the markers projected by P1 while P1 remains at position D_1. P1 then repeats the primary position estimation procedure, and then stands at position D_5 while P2 repeats the secondary position estimation from positions D_4–D_1. This procedure is repeated on rows 2 and 3. Following this, the entire task is repeated with participants' roles reversed i.e., P2 moves to D_3 to complete the primary estimation procedure, with P1 now following the secondary estimation procedure.

In total, then, after each participant has completed the task in both primary and secondary roles, this task measures six primary and 24 secondary position estimates per person. Because participants are standing at known positions we are able to compare the estimated position with their actual position and measure the accuracy of our estimation procedure.

Task 2: Tracking

Each participant stands in turn at position T_1 (see Fig. 4), and points a projected circle to each of 15 tracking points on Wall 2. Points are labelled on Wall 2 in three rows of five markers at 0.1 m, 1.1 m and 2.1 m above the ground, on an evenly-spaced grid 1 m apart. The points are aligned so that the centre marker on each row of five is directly in front of the participant, with two either side on each of the three rows. The centre point is highlighted, and the remaining points are numbered 1–14. The markers are on a separate wall to that used for the position estimation task to avoid influencing 1 m estimates in that task.

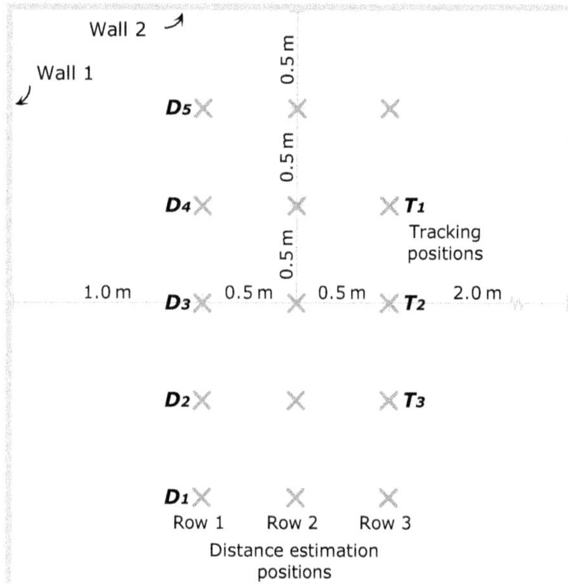

Figure 4. Participant locations and surfaces used for the study, viewed from above as marked on the floor of the user study lab. Position estimation took place from all 15 evenly-spaced positions (D_1–D_5 on rows 1–3), projecting onto Wall 1. Tracking tasks used positions T_1–T_3, projecting onto Wall 2. Story authoring took place from positions D_3 and T_2, again projecting onto Wall 2.

Participants complete this task individually, pointing first to the centre point, then to a random tracking point as instructed by the device, then back to the centre point. This procedure is repeated for each point at each of the three positions T_1–T_3. This task, then, measures 42 pointing estimates for each participant, allowing analysis of the differences between the system's estimated pointing positions and the actual (known) positions pointed to by participants for each point.

Procedure

16 participants (8M; 8F) aged from 18 to 65 were recruited to take part in a lab study. Two were left-handed, the remainder were right-handed. Ten participants were students, six were members of university staff. There were ten study sessions in total: four of the participants attended individually, completing the position estimation and tracking tasks; 12 participants took part in pairs. Participants had not met prior to the study.

Two researchers managed the study, with one observing participants' behaviours and the second guiding participants through the tasks. Study sessions took place in late afternoon (between 3:30pm and 5:30pm) due to the lighting constraints of the projectors, with sessions ranging in length from 30–90 minutes depending on participants' approach to each task.

At the start of each session each participant was met by the researchers, and introduced to the system and its purpose. Participants were then guided through an ethically-reviewed informed consent process, and given a short demonstration of using the system to create a sketched story. The resulting PicoTale was then replayed to the participants to highlight how the system might be used to record projected content.

Following this demonstration participants were led through the position estimation and tracking tasks. Participants were encouraged to try to be accurate when pointing, but asked to not spend a large amount of time being excessively precise – although the study is clearly evaluating the system in a controlled environment, we were keen to investigate its accuracy in likely real-world conditions, rather than just the best possible use case. To ensure we were able to compare position estimations with the actual location of the user, participants were asked to, when standing in each position, align themselves so that their hand holding the device was positioned over the appropriate position marker (rather than their feet). For participants who took part alone, the markers required for the secondary position estimation procedure were displayed by a projector held by one of the researchers.

Finally, a short interview took place to gather opinions about the system, its usability and suggested usage scenarios. After the study each participant was thanked for their time and rewarded with a bookstore voucher as a token of our appreciation.

Results and Analysis

Six primary and 24 secondary position estimates were gathered for each participant from each of the angles and positions shown in Fig. 4. Most needed some guidance from the researcher as to where they needed to stand for each position estimation step, but all completed the remainder of the task unaided. Many different approaches to the task were seen, including a large variation in 1 m estimations that was very clear from observation alone. For example, one participant approached this task by holding out their (non-device) hand to their side and lining up the projector beam with this in order to estimate the 1 m distance – an interesting approach that could help improve the accuracy of their distance estimation. There were also many different methods for pointing the projector – for example, two of the participants moved their whole body, several moved their arm only, and others instead rotated their wrist to direct the projection.

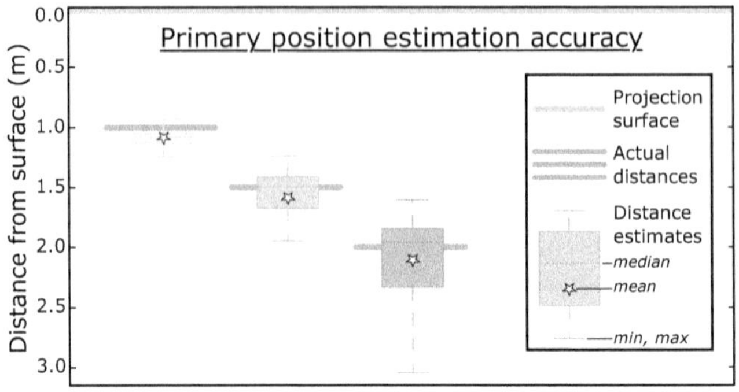

Figure 5. Primary position estimation accuracy. Estimations are more accurate when participants are closer to the projection surface.

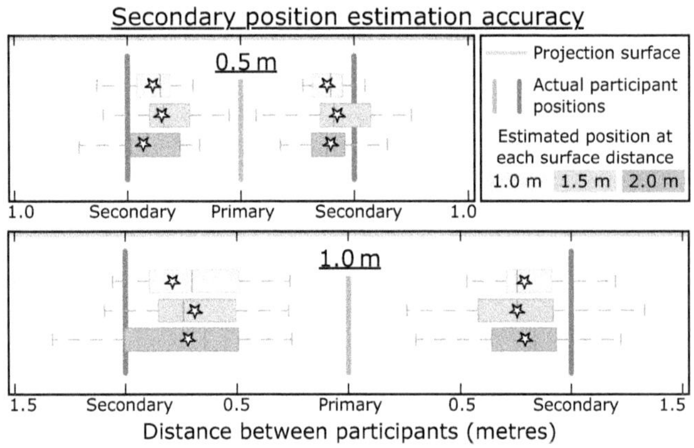

Figure 6. Secondary position estimation accuracy with participants standing 0.5 m (top) and 1.0 m (bottom) away from each other. During the task, secondary participants completed the procedure while standing both to the left and to the right of the primary participant – their actual position in each case is shown as a blue vertical line. The position of the primary participant is indicated by the red vertical line. Box plots show the positions estimated by the system when both participants were standing at 1.0 m, 1.5 m and 2 m from the surface. Estimations are more accurate when participants are closer to each other and to the surface.

Position Estimation

Turning first to the primary position estimation results, estimating distances from the projection surface. Figure 5 shows the distance estimates for all 16 participants combined, comparing the known position with that given by the system. Distance estimation is more accurate at 1 m from the surface, with a mean estimate of 1.08 m (sd: 0.07 m), increasing to 1.60 m (sd: 0.28 m) at 1.5 m, and 2.11 m (sd: 0.40 m) at 2 m from the wall. As previously noted, participants often made inaccurate and highly variable guesses of 1 m. However, as our results indicate, errors in distance estimation that would be caused by this variance have been mitigated by the one-time initial step we use to calibrate participants' 1 m estimation accuracy.

Turning now to the secondary position estimation results, estimating participants' positions relative to each other. Estimates are far more accurate when participants are closer together, tending to diverge when participants are positioned further away from each other. Figure 6 shows the range of position estimations for each distance from the projection surface and at 0.5 m and 1.0 m distances between the users, combined over all 16 participants. At these distances the estimates are within 0.25 m of the known positions (0.5 m: 0.40 m (sd: 0.15 m); 1.0 m: 0.75 m (sd: 0.33 m)). However, as participants moved further away from each other to 1.5 m and 2.0 m (not shown above), the deviation in estimations increases (mean: 1.22 m; sd: 0.75 m and mean: 1.84 m; sd: 0.88 m respectively).

Tracking

Forty-two tracking estimates were recorded per participant. There were 28 errors where participants misread the instruction and subsequently pointed to an incorrect marker. We removed these outliers, leaving a total of 644 estimates.

Table 1 shows the distance errors between the positions estimated by the system and the actual positions the participants were pointing to for each of the markers in the grid when standing at 1.0 m and 1.5 m from the wall. For points in columns 2–4 the tracking of participants' pointing is more accurate than those further away, where the position estimation varies more widely, and is clearly less accurate. This result

	Tracking points grid – participant at 1.0 m from the wall				
Row \ Col	1	2	3	4	5
1	0.97 (0.4)	0.33 (0.2)	0.23 (0.1)	0.35 (0.1)	1.39 (0.3)
2	0.77 (0.3)	0.30 (0.2)	–	0.35 (0.3)	0.75 (0.8)
3	1.15 (0.3)	0.82 (0.2)	0.69 (0.3)	0.63 (0.4)	1.40 (0.7)

	Tracking points grid – participant at 1.5 m from the wall				
Row \ Col	1	2	3	4	5
1	0.72 (0.4)	0.35 (0.2)	0.46 (0.1)	0.39 (0.1)	1.30 (0.4)
2	0.93 (0.6)	0.31 (0.2)	–	0.32 (0.2)	0.72 (0.5)
3	1.06 (0.4)	0.72 (0.5)	0.89 (0.3)	0.69 (0.4)	2.01 (1.2)

Table 1. Tracking accuracy, showing the mean absolute distance (metres (s.d.)) between the known point that the participant pointed to, and the estimate given by the system, at 1.0 m and 1.5 m from the wall. '–' represents the central point of the grid. Closer points (those within 1 m either side of the centre of the grid) are tracked more accurately than those further away. Tracking is less accurate at greater distances.

echoes that of the position estimation task, with relatively accurate position estimation possible up to around 1.5 m, and deviation rapidly increasing beyond this. Interestingly, in this task, points positioned lower on the wall have been less accurately tracked in all cases, suggesting perhaps that angling the device precisely towards a point near to the ground was more challenging than pointing to those markers placed higher.

STUDY 2: STORY AUTHORING

Our second investigation focused on the story authoring aspect of the system, looking at whether the prototype resonates with the people that use it, and at how effective the resulting videos are at telling the story to others. Our research questions were:

Story Authoring: What are participants' reactions to the concept, and how do they use it to animate stories?

Story Comprehension: To what extent can people other than the creators understand the stories from the videos generated?

Method

Twelve of the participants who took part in our first study in pairs also authored stories together, giving six story videos in total. Participants were not given time to prepare a narrative, just asked to animate a story together, about any subject they wished. When story authoring finished, the resulting PicoTale was shown to them on a separate PC, and they were asked to think aloud while a researcher noted their comments.

Following methods used by others (e.g., [24]), we conducted a separate story comprehension study in order to evaluate the potential of the system's animated videos for storytelling. 79 participants (39M; 40F) aged from 18 to 65 were recruited to complete a web-based questionnaire to assess each of the videos. Each person was sent a unique login code for the study website and could complete the questionnaire at their convenience. 55 participants were students, 24 were members of university staff; none had participated in the first study.

Participants were asked five questions about each video, rating the extent to which the video was understandable; whether the video was a useful representation of the story; if the entities in the conversation appeared in the video; whether there were meaningful interactions between sketched elements; and, the extent to which the low resolution of the sketches reduced their understanding of the story. Each question asked participants to rate the video on a Likert-type scale from 1 ('not at all') to 7 ('to a great extent'). After the study participants were rewarded with a gift voucher as a token of appreciation.

To maintain the anonymity of the original participants, we transcribed the conversations that took place during the story authoring sessions, and added these as subtitles to the original videos. Conversations were presented in subtitles exactly as they took place – we did not remove non-narrative elements or edit to improve comprehension. As a result, each story was shown as it might be represented if it had been created by real users rather than during an experiment.

Results and Analysis

The six pairs of participants who created story videos were enthusiastic about using the system to create animations, with most commenting that storytelling was fun and enjoyable. All 79 story comprehension participants rated the videos on each scale, and most gave further comments about the concept's potential and its usefulness for storytelling.

Story Authoring

Two distinct approaches were observed during story authoring. Two of the PicoTales were very much pre-planned, with participants choosing a familiar nursery rhyme and then animating the story as required. The eight remaining participants created animations more spontaneously by beginning to draw characters first, and then deciding what storyline to act out as the story progressed. All participants took time to negotiate with each other to agree on who would create each element, then collaborated to move the elements into place and animate interactions between them. Even when the storyline to animate was planned beforehand, all stories were told as part of a conversation rather than pre-agreed dialogues – participants interleaved the narration with their discussion about how to progress the storyline via their sketches.

All participants drew at least one sketch each, but three of the pairs sketched and erased several times to draw up to eight different story elements per person. The three remaining pairs drew only one story element per person. All participants edited or added to their sketches several times after initially projecting, however. Participants tended to draw, then animate briefly before adding more detail and reusing the same element in another part of the storyline. Most participants looked at the projected image ahead while sketching, rather than looking down at the device's screen.

The PicoTales generated were between 1 and 5½ minutes in length (average 2:48 minutes; sd: 1:45). The two stories that were pre-arranged were the shortest, and also involved only one sketched character per person. Participants in these stories spent most of their time sketching the characters, and then only briefly animated the nursery rhyme that they had chosen.

Several participants, including those who had pre-arranged a storyline, stated that they thought that they would have been able to author a more interesting story if they had had more time to plan beforehand: *"it was good, except for that fact*

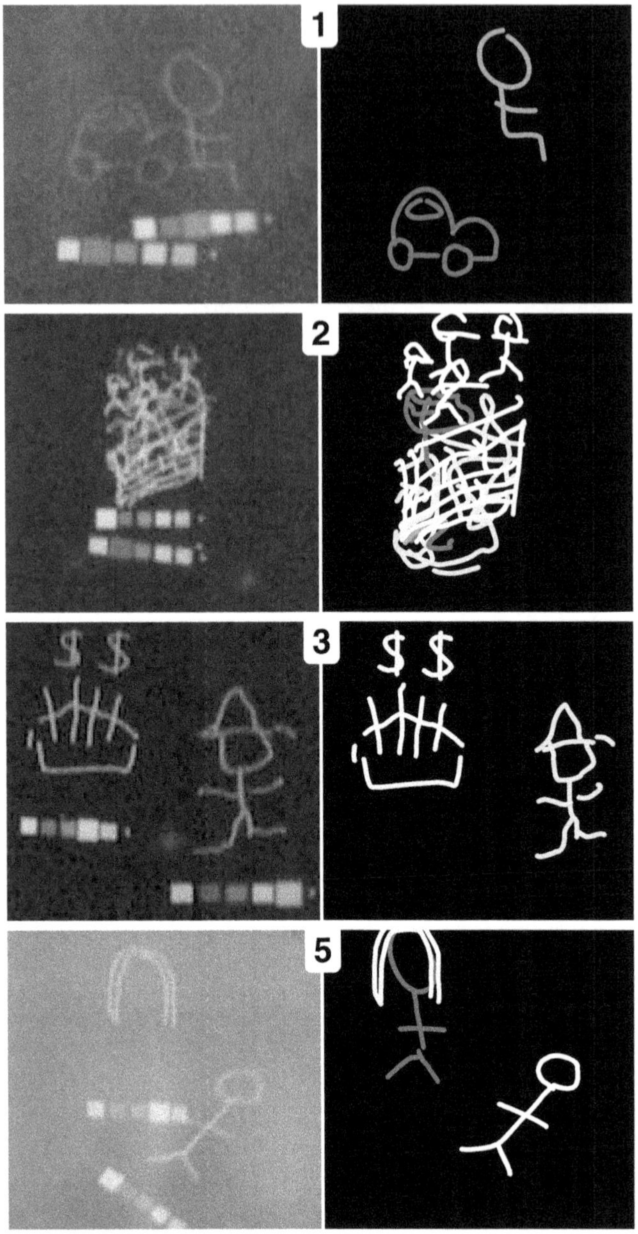

Figure 7. Representative frames from a selection of the stories authored by participants. In each case, a frame from the video of the actual projected story is shown on the left, and the system's rendering at the corresponding time is shown to the right. Numbers correspond to those in Table 2. Interface elements are projected, but are not shown in the PicoTale. Some participants (video 2, for example) spent a long time sketching; others found simpler elements to be more effective.

that we didn't really have a story" and *"if we'd had more time to decide what to draw, it would have been easier."* Clearly the restrictive environment of the study has affected some participants' story authoring experiences.

Others appreciated the simple interface – one participant said: *"the simplicity is actually quite a good thing, because it takes away the focus on the technology rather than the story that's being generated."* Some participants commented that they would like to be able to draw more than one character at a time, however. Rather than just sketching and erasing, these users would have preferred a more complex drawing interface that could re-load previous sketches or other content.

To what extent	Average rating for each video (s.d.)					
	1	2	3	4	5	6
...did you understand the story in this video?	4.8 (1.7)	3.9 (1.9)	5.2 (1.4)	4.4 (1.5)	5.4 (1.6)	4.6 (1.8)
...was the animation a useful representation of the story described in the subtitles?	4.5 (1.5)	2.3 (1.3)	4.5 (1.7)	4.1 (1.5)	4.0 (1.6)	4.5 (1.7)
...did the entities described in the conversation appear in the video?	5.2 (1.3)	3.7 (1.8)	5.1 (1.3)	4.9 (1.3)	4.6 (1.4)	5.0 (1.5)
...could you perceive meaningful interactions between the sketched elements in the video?	4.2 (1.5)	2.7 (1.4)	4.5 (1.6)	4.0 (1.5)	4.2 (1.7)	4.2 (1.6)
...did the low resolution of the sketches reduce your understanding of the video?	2.8 (1.7)	3.9 (2.1)	3.2 (1.6)	3.5 (1.7)	3.2 (1.8)	2.9 (1.6)

Table 2. Video ratings, showing the mean and standard deviation of each rating given for each video. Participants answered each question on a Likert-type scale from 1 ('not at all') to 7 ('to a great extent').

Figure 7 shows four examples of the actual projected content (left), compared in each case to the PicoTale animation at the corresponding time (right). Story authors liked watching their animation when it was replayed to them. Participants appreciated the value of the system for authoring, but noted that movement accuracy could be improved. Horizontal movement was usually more accurate than vertical, with comments such as *"overall the drawing was fine but the positioning was slightly off; [the positioning] is accurate around 70-80% of the time – close but not exact"* and *"the likeness is obviously spot on [...] they're going in the right directions, but [vertically] they're not quite in unison."*

Many suggested uses were noted for the system beyond story authoring, including several typical pico projector applications: mobile business uses and slideshow annotation, for example. More novel suggestions included helping with language learning by demonstration, developing world education support, and annotating (and animating) everyday objects. One participant commented that using the system was *"not practical, but fun [...] like a game"*, while another felt that it was a *"new way of interacting."*

Story Comprehension

Table 2 shows the ratings for each video averaged over the 79 participants who completed the story comprehension study. Ratings show that viewers were able to understand the videos and that, in most cases, the animation was a useful representation of the story. Despite the original participants having no training and limited sketching tool capabilities, they have been able to use the PicoTales system to author meaningful stories that can be understood by others who have had no experience with the system.

Viewers were able to recognise the elements described in the narrative from the sketches they saw in the video. Despite positioning inaccuracies caused by our lower-resolution tracking, the viewers could also perceive meaningful interactions between story elements.

When the quality and comprehensibility of the drawings are better, the ratings given have improved. Lower quality sketches have led to lower ratings for videos, despite the presence of subtitles. Comparing the snapshots in Fig. 7 for video 2 with those of video 3, for example, shows a clear difference in sketch legibility. This has been reflected in the ratings for video 2, which was consistently rated lower. This video told a simple pre-arranged nursery rhyme, the storyline of which is likely to have been familiar to most viewers. However, video 2 was also rated as less understandable than video 5, which told another familiar nursery rhyme. Both stories were narrated in the conversation in addition to the sketches, but video 5 has been rated as more understandable, with more meaningful interactions between sketches. The sketched elements in the stories have helped viewers to follow along and understand the narratives.

CONCLUSIONS

In this paper we have demonstrated and evaluated a novel pico projector-based story authoring tool. We believe this is the first example of using pico projectors to interactively author and record content by tracking device movements.

Participants in our experiment were able to author stories together despite having had no previous experience with the system, and not knowing that they would have to create stories before using the prototype. The stories that were created were understandable by other people later. Participants in our experiment enjoyed using the prototype, and were able to successfully author animated PicoTales. People liked the notion of using a projector for authoring.

We have provided this interaction using sensor-based tracking rather than the more constrained visual methods that have often been used previously. Clearly the tradeoff of our method is that the fidelity of the tracking is lower, but we believe that this is offset by our higher flexibility, lower cost and no requirement for nonstandard hardware. We are also able to remove restrictions in the positions that people can stand relative to each other and the surface they are projecting onto, by estimating these in a short calibration procedure before story authoring begins.

Following our initial study we have incorporated feedback from participants into the system's design, and have added several requested features. Our system now allows users to select between projecting sketches, images already on the phone, or photos taken with the device's front camera. Each of these story elements is projected and tracked as before, and appears in the resulting video. This addition allows story authors to include people or objects directly in the narrative – rather than sketching a figure, for example, they can take a photo of themselves and insert it in the PicoTale.

Impact of the Approach

In this research we have investigated the limitations of the PicoTales prototype, and shown its ability to support the creation of animated stories that are understandable after the event. However, we have not studied the impact of the approach on people's storytelling behaviour.

In our story authoring study we saw that people were able to create PicoTales with very little preparation. However, future implementations of the technology will need to consider how the spontaneous and unplanned usage we aimed for affects the way that people actually recall and tell their stories. We have since added facilities for including pre-loaded content, but other extensions might have to allow for slower and more considered reflection, rather than impromptu narratives.

Furthermore, stories have clearly been told and retold throughout history without any advanced technology. We have shown that the stories created by our prototype were understandable when viewed later, but did not investigate whether emotional impact or memorability were actually improved by augmenting storytelling with digital imagery. Future uses of such story authoring tools might focus less on sketching of stories, and more on ways to use the tools to support people's narratives.

Future Work

In our initial prototype we have shown how some of the key issues in tracking and position estimation can be addressed, allowing people to author stories that are understandable by others. Our current position estimation method can accurately estimate distances and relative user positions at smaller distances; at greater distances the level of precision is lower. Tracking of where users point the device is accurate to a similar extent. Our current approach, therefore, provides a quick way to allow story authoring via projector tracking and distance estimation without the overheads and location restrictions of visual or other methods. Our future work will explore potential improvements to both technological and story authoring elements of the system.

One exciting potential use for the system lies in the developing world. In their work on digital storytelling in Africa, Bidwell and Retmaier et al. [5] noticed how stories were recounted collaboratively: storytellers would speak in rapid succession, each adding their part to the narrative. The downfall of the digital storytelling system that was created was that it ran on a single handset, making it impossible to capture a collaborative story. Still relying only on individual handsets, the integration of the system we have created allows these shared stories to be authored and shared in a more natural way. Furthermore, the lack of light in most dwellings in Africa (there is little mains electricity in much of the continent) means that pico projectors are ideally suited to the environment – bright projections are not required, so current technology would be suitable.

ACKNOWLEDGEMENTS

This research was partly funded by EPSRC project EP/J000604/1. Elina Vartiainen is supported by the Wihuri Foundation.

REFERENCES

1. Ah Kun, L. and Marsden, G. Co-present photo sharing on mobile devices. In *Proc. MobileHCI '07*, ACM (2007), 277–284.

2. Balabanović, M., Chu, L. and Wolff, G. Storytelling with digital photographs. In *Proc. CHI '00*, ACM (2000), 564–571.
3. Beardsley, P., Baar, J. van, Raskar, R. and Forlines, C. Interaction using a handheld projector. *IEEE Computer Graphics and Applications* 25.1 (2005), 39–43.
4. Bers, M. and Best, M. Rural connected communities: a project in online collaborative journalism. In *Proc. CSCL '99*, ISLS (1999), 41–46.
5. Bidwell, N., Reitmaier, T., Marsden, G. and Hansen, S. Designing with mobile digital storytelling in rural Africa. In *Proc. CHI '10*, ACM (2010), 1593–1602.
6. Cao, X. Handheld Projector Interaction. PhD thesis. University of Toronto, 2009.
7. Cao, X., Forlines, C. and Balakrishnan, R. Multi-user interaction using handheld projectors. In *Proc. UIST '07*, ACM (2007), 43–52.
8. Cao, X., Massimi, M. and Balakrishnan, R. Flashlight jigsaw: an exploratory study of an ad-hoc multi-player game on public displays. In *Proc. CSCW '08*, ACM (2008), 77–86.
9. Cao, X., Lindley, S., Helmes, J. and Sellen, A. Telling the whole story: anticipation, inspiration and reputation in a field deployment of TellTable. In *Proc. CSCW '10*, ACM (2010), 251–260.
10. Chatting, D. and Sutton, J. Visible imagination: projected play. In *Proc. HCI '09*, BCS (2009), 405–409.
11. Cowan, L. and Li, K. ShadowPuppets: supporting collocated interaction with mobile projector phones using hand shadows. In *Proc. CHI '11*, ACM (2011), 2707–2716.
12. Dao, V., Hosoi, K. and Sugimoto, M. A semi-automatic realtime calibration technique for a handheld projector. In *Proc. VRST '07*, ACM (2007), 43–46.
13. Druin, A., Stewart, J., Proft, D., Bederson, B. and Hollan, J. KidPad: a design collaboration between children, technologists, and educators. In *Proc. CHI '97*, ACM (1997), 463–470.
14. Fails, J., Druin, A. and Guha, M. Mobile collaboration: collaboratively reading and creating children's stories on mobile devices. In *Proc. IDC '10*, ACM (2010), 20–29.
15. Frohlich, D., Rachovides, D., Riga, K., Bhat, R., Frank, M., Edirisinghe, E., Wickramanayaka, D., Jones, M. and Harwood, W. StoryBank: mobile digital storytelling in a development context. In *Proc. CHI '09*, ACM (2009), 1761–1770.
16. Ghali, A., Benford, S., Bayoumi, S., Green, J. and Pridmore, T. Visually tracked flashlights as interaction devices. In *Proc. Interact '03*, IOS (2003), 487–494.
17. Lee, G. and Keh, Y. A novel interface and application using synchronized multi projector phones. In *MP² Workshop at CHI '11*, 2011.
18. Löchtefeld, M., Schöning, J., Rohs, M. and Krüger, A. LittleProjectedPlanet: an augmented reality game for camera projector phones. In *MIRW Workshop at MobileHCI '09*, 2009.
19. Olsen Jr., D. and Nielsen, T. Laser pointer interaction. In *Proc. CHI '01*, ACM (2001), 17–22.
20. Rapp, S., Michelitsch, G., Osen, M., Williams, J., Barbisch, M., Bohan, R., Valsan, Z. and Emele, M. Spotlight navigation: interaction with a handheld projection device. In *Pervasive '04 Videos*, 2004.
21. Reeves, S., Pridmore, T., Crabtree, A., Green, J., Benford, S. and O'Malley, C. The spatial character of sensor technology. In *Proc. DIS '06*, ACM (2006), 31–40.
22. Reitmaier, T., Bidwell, N. and Marsden, G. Field testing mobile digital storytelling software in rural Kenya. In *Proc. MobileHCI '10*, ACM (2010), 283–286.
23. Robinson, S. and Jones, M. HaptiProjection: multimodal mobile information discovery. In *Ubiprojection Workshop at Pervasive '10*, 2010.
24. Sharmin, M., Bailey, B., Coats, C. and Hamilton, K. Understanding knowledge management practices for early design activity and its implications for reuse. In *Proc. CHI '09*, ACM (2009), 2367–2376.
25. Shilkrot, R., Hunter, S. and Maes, P. PoCoMo: projected collaboration using mobile devices. In *Proc. MobileHCI '11*, ACM (2011), 333–336.
26. Stanton, D., Neale, H. and Bayon, V. Interfaces to support children's co-present collaboration: multiple mice and tangible technologies. In *Proc. CSCL '02*, ISLS (2002), 342–351.
27. Strachan, S. and Murray-Smith, R. Bearing-based selection in mobile spatial interaction. *Personal and Ubiquitous Computing* 13.4 (2009), 265–280.
28. Sugimoto, M., Ito, T., Nguyen, T. and Inagaki, S. GENTORO: a system for supporting children's storytelling using handheld projectors and a robot. In *Proc. IDC '09*, ACM (2009), 214–217.
29. Virolainen, A., Åkerman, P. and Häkkilä, J. Burn-to-share: content sharing with mobile projectors. In *Proc. MUM '10*, ACM (2010), 18:1–18:4.
30. Weibel, N., Cowan, L., Pina, L., Griswold, W. and Hollan, J. Enabling social interactions through real-time sketch-based communication. In *Proc. UIST '10 Demos*, ACM (2010), 405–406.
31. Williamson, J., Murray-Smith, R. and Hughes, S. Shoogle: excitatory multimodal interaction on mobile devices. In *Proc. CHI '07*, ACM (2007), 121–124.
32. Willis, K. A pre-history of handheld projector-based interaction. *Personal and Ubiquitous Computing* (Online First; 21st April 2011), 1–11.
33. Willis, K., Poupyrev, I. and Shiratori, T. MotionBeam: a metaphor for character interaction with handheld projectors. In *Proc. CHI '11*, ACM (2011), 1031–1040.
34. Willis, K., Poupyrev, I., Hudson, S. and Mahler, M. SideBySide: ad-hoc multi-user interaction with handheld projectors. In *Proc. UIST '11*, ACM (2011), 431–440.
35. Worthington, P. *Shadow Monsters*. Interaction Design, Royal College of Art. 2005.

Collaborative Museums: An Approach to Co-Design

Heloisa Moura
Pontifical Catholic University of Rio de Janeiro
R.M.S.Vicente 225, Rio de Janeiro, Brazil
moura@id.iit.edu

Debora Cardador
Pontifical Catholic University of Rio de Janeiro
dcosta@inf.puc-rio.br

Katia Vega
Pontifical Catholic University of Rio de Janeiro
kvega@inf.puc-rio.br

Wallace Ugulino
Pontifical Catholic University of Rio de Janeiro
wugulino@inf.puc-rio.br

Marcos Barbato
Be! Interactive
barbato@be-interactive.com.br

Hugo Fuks
Pontifical Catholic University of Rio de Janeiro
R.M.S.Vicente 225, Rio de Janeiro, Brazil
hugo@inf.puc-rio.br
+55 21 81117109

ABSTRACT
This paper describes a systemic approach to co-design of collaborative museums, using ethnography, co-creation workshops and fast prototyping, amongst other Social Science and Human Centered Design methods. Focused on the creation of immersive and collaborative museum experiences, it provides a rationale for involving carefully selected multidisciplinary teams and users in the entire design cycle, and presents a process that supports this task, from research to development, pointing its value and limitations. In order to bring the discussion into context and exemplify the use of a group of methods that can support collaborative design, it introduces the case of a Brazilian Planetarium and Science Museum.

Author Keywords
Co-creation, ethnography; prototyping; museums.

ACM Classification Keywords
J4. Social and Behavioral Sciences.

General Terms
Design; Human Factors; Experimentation.

INTRODUCTION
The evolution of group systems research to an increasingly co-creative focus is changing the roles of designers and computer scientists. According to this approach, users' involvement start as early as the project begins, that is, much before the formulation of any conception of the system to be developed. And users' role changes from that of an observed subject or source of information, to that of a collaborative creator, working together with a multidisciplinary team of professionals bringing varied points of view, including designers and computer scientists.

Converging knowledge and methods from various fields, including Anthropology, Sociology, Psychology, Software Engineering, and User-Centered Design, amongst others, it is possible to take a systemic approach to co-design, while assuring user involvement, as well as the participation of professionals of various fields, from research to brainstorming, prototyping, development and implementation. As a result, more relevant technology systems can be proposed, which, at the same time, can add value to people in the real world and meet the business goals of sponsoring institutions in sustainable ways – socially, economically, environmentally and institutionally.

Focusing on collaborative museums, this article takes a human-centered, participatory approach to design and development of systems that support groups, social interaction and collaboration, presenting the case of a Brazilian Planetarium and Science Museum to demonstrate a process that uses ethnography, co-creation workshops, and fast iterative prototyping. The challenge was to co-create ideas that could transform the current space, exhibits, artifacts, interfaces and services into something exciting and engaging. Such as described in the words of a ten years old boy at one of the workshops, "I want to come here [at the Planetarium] and feel that I am an astronaut [...], travelling through space, exploring the planets, stars and black holes."

COLLABORATIVE MUSEUMS
Modern museums, as educational and recreational institutions, have systematically focused on enhancing the visitor's experience and understanding of exhibitions. Supported by ever more complex technologies – such as Mixed Presence Groupware, socialware, Virtual Reality,

Augmented environments, smart devices and simulators [1, 2] – they have introduced a wide range of new experiential possibilities for museums, such as visual and sensorial interactions, serious games, collaborative learning, edutainment, sociability and celebratory encounters [3, 4].

Museums like the Boston Museum of Sciences in the United States, for instance, enable visitors to turn into a curious group of explorers who, through social interaction and collaboration, discovers exhibit wonders [5]. Through a game called Mystery at the Museum, students and their parents work as a team of experts to solve fictitious crimes at the museum space. Teammates gather clues as they collaborate through communication and knowledge exchange, using location aware pocket computers.

Another example is the Lunar Surface Navigation System, at the Modern Industrial Science Museum in Japan, which connects co-located collaborators with a combination of tabletop Augmented Reality and virtual environment [6]. Children play the role of astronauts, while parents or teachers act as the mission commanders, who give instructions regarding exploration activities based on real lunar exploration episodes reported by NASA.

Designing systems such as those, and making them truthfully meaningful and intuitive to visitors of various demographic backgrounds is a challenge. Human-centered design [8], together with participatory methods [9, 10], offers a systemic path towards this goal, starting with the contextual understanding of the actual people that visit, work and interact with the particular museum context. Through a process of co-creation, involving people of varied backgrounds, it moves from ethnographic research to design criteria, and to relevant concepts that can respond to the identified problems and opportunities. Next, it prototypes and tests these ideas quickly, cheaply and iteratively, while interacting with those who will use the solutions, in order to continuously learn from them through the development and implementation phases. As a consequence, relevant and innovative solutions can emerge.

A HUMAN-CENTERED PARTICIPATORY APPROACH

Through a partnership between the Pontifical Catholic University of Rio de Janeiro and the Planetarium and Science Museum of Rio de Janeiro City, a research project was initiated, aiming to renovate the museum space and exhibits, combining cross reality systems and enabling groupware and socialware. For the purposes of this study, a human-centered participatory approach was taken to the design of collaborative museums, as illustrated on Figure 1. The process started with ethnographic research, and led to co-creation workshops and prototyping sessions.

The ethnography started with the study of the referred museum staff – including astronomers, market and administration personnel, architects, visitor guides and support workers, amongst others. And it was followed by

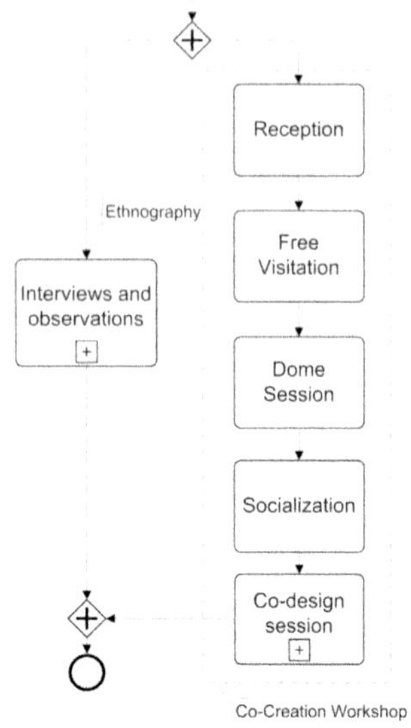

Figure 1. Ethnography and co-creation workshops used to design a collaborative museum.

the study of different types of visitors, in order to identify: patterns of behavior, relevant narratives, areas of interest, human needs and motivations. The protocol included in-depth contextual interviews and shadowing observations, documented through video, photos and notes. During the interviews, focus was given to mapping the different experiences of the referred museum in contrast to other entertainment venues, and collecting vivid stories.

Through bottom-up clustering [11], the collected data was analyzed and synthesized, in order to identify findings, guiding criteria, recurrent themes, and stakeholders' extreme user and group profiles – including variables such as number of visits, group size, content knowledge and technological expertise. And, from the documentation material of the interviews and observations, relevant narratives and behaviors were highlighted.

Using shared boards and socialware to facilitate the collaborative process, these items were then clustered, leading to patterns, correlations, and recurrences, as illustrated on Figure 2, as well as to insights and design criteria, seen on Figure 3. For instance, to: activate imagination before museum visit; provide tour options according to profile; support authorship; make the museum experience tangible; and attend to special needs.

As a result, problems related to the museum experience cycle, and spaces of opportunity for new solutions to emerge were mapped. A few examples of these emergent areas are: connection prior to visit, personalized tours, intergenerational edutainment, inclusive exhibits, easy-to-use technologies and tangible memories.

Importantly, the workshop gathered a selected group of participants with diverse profiles and demographics, including: children, teenagers, private and public school teachers, designers, computer scientists, and astronomers.

Narrative 15: *"Once you come to the dome session, you never forget it [...] You feel immersed in the sky projection. It is impactful [...]"*

Narrative 19: *"What I like most is the environment. [...] It's an immersive space."*

Narrative 20: *"If someone's bedroom was shaped like a dome and had a super lamp that could project the stars, then (s)he wouldn't need to come to the museum. Otherwise, this place is uncomparable."*

Observation 56: Children were impressed (and expressed it by exclamation) at the beginning of the dome session.

Finding 3: Immersive experiences stir emotions (which must be addressed).

Figure 2. One of the findings of the ethnographic study and its relation with selected narratives and observation.

Such variety was a purposeful choice, since it is considered a condition for the co-creation of groupware solutions [12] that can appeal to the various visitor and worker profiles, and fit the contextual dynamics of the museum.

The workshop started with the participants' free visitation to the museum, and a planetarium dome session, while their behaviors and narratives were shadowed and documented. The following co-design session began with an activity journal, which was individually filled by each participant, inquiring about topics such as daily routine, entertainment history, extreme cultural experiences, sources of information, past visits and view of the future of museums.

Next, participants worked in pairs and exchanged journals. After reading and analyzing what the other one wrote and asking probing questions, they presented their findings to the entire group. During the presentation, the participants profiles were represented on poster size graphs; relevant narratives were documented on a white board; and emerging guiding criteria were synthesized to the group on posters. These criteria were, then, discussed with participants, leading to refinement and new additions.

Based on the reviewed criteria, a brainstorming session was initiated, where each sentence guided the ideation of innumerous solutions by the participants. These ideas were written down on note size papers and handed to the moderator, who read them aloud to the whole group. In response, the participants wrote down complementary ideas or new concepts inspired by them. In 20 minutes, the 14 participants generated 81 relevant ideas, including: museum-school portal, 2nd Life Planetarium, online check-in, tour guide totem, iPad museum navigator, Augmented Reality space mission, planet hunt collaborative game, space wiki, visitor foot prints, and outdoor exhibits.

After the ideation session, the resultant ideas were grouped according to guiding criteria, as partially demonstrated on Figure 3, using cloud format, where the font size of each word or expression represents the number of correspondent ideas that were created. According to the participants' point of view, the top criteria were: 'Create an immersive experience', with 26 correlated ideas, 'Provide interactivity', with 18, and 'Provide specific tours according to visitors' interests, with 15. In addition, these ideas were classified according to subjacent theme.

Following the workshop, selected participants – including

Connect the Planetarium to the WWW

Create an immersive experience

Provide Interactivity

Provide specific tours by visitors interests

Simulate astronomy themes

Support entertainment in external area

Support role playing

Figure 3. Sample guiding criteria formatted according to the number of related ideas gathered in the brainstorming session.

architects, computer scientists and designers – were invited for a prototyping session. The method used was Blank Model Prototyping [13], which requires the participation of potential users, and design and technology professionals. Blank Model Prototyping is a rapid role-playing technique that uses readily available art and craft materials to construct rough physical representations of a technological concept, according to a predetermined scenario. The method was used with the intent to collect potential user impressions and detailed ideas about a new technological solution for collaborative museums.

During the prototyping session, participants read and discussed the idea cards and guiding criteria poster in order to select one or a combination of concepts, or even find inspiration for creating a new one. Next, they were asked to prototype their ideas, evolving the original concept and rationale into a systemic solution, or providing guidelines and design specifications.

The participants chose 'To create an immersive experience' as the main guiding criteria. And, as a result, they prototyped a trip to different planet environments – which could be shared on different social networks through pictures and short movies. The 'Provide interactivity' criteria was also addressed as they created a spacecraft to travel through a panel equipped with a multitouch device, in which visitors could interact with each other for the purpose of planning a trip and learning about the planets.

The prototype took into account the use of group and socialware to support interaction amongst visitors. For that purpose, they designed their interfaces within the rooms, and some of their functionalities – like identification cards with QR codes for social network sharing, and touch screen interfaces for selecting planets – shown on Figure 4.

Finally, the participants tested their prototype, reflected upon the results and re-designed the solution accordingly. The session was concluded with a discussion and presentation of the prototype, using the designed objects as a support for dramatizing a scenario that illustrated the simulation rooms.

Some of the lessons learned were: a) computer scientists should join social researchers in the ethnographic study and personally learn visitors points of view, leading to a shift in perception about the user and, consequently, more human centered technological solutions; b) workshop participants need prior time to be immersed in the ethnography findings to make optimal use of the material; c) group composition

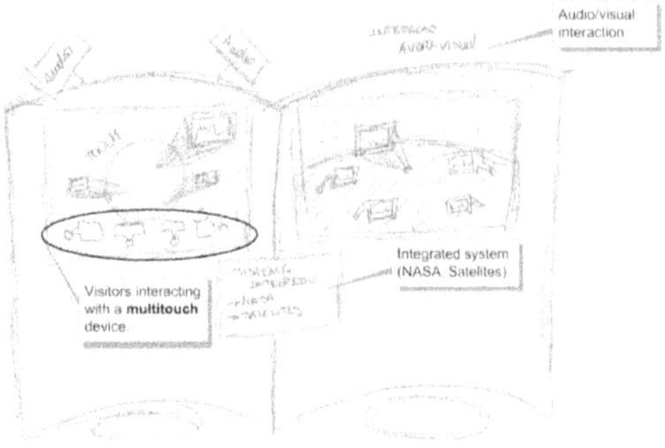

Figure 4. A multitouch device representation.

within co-creation workshops should consider complementary profiles, so that each can have an equal voice; d) Blank Model Prototyping sessions, in order to be successful, need careful selection of extreme users and important players, such as museum personnel, besides the typical computer scientists and designers – otherwise the solutions might easily fail to keep on track with the various identified needs of visitors and institution; e) building simple prototypes and testing them in real contexts leads to fast learning about users mental models, which helps to quickly refine and detail groupware interfaces, as well as review functionalities and requirements; and f) developing twin prototypes in the physical and virtual worlds leads to different but complimentary findings about collaboration, such as behavioral and motivational.

CONCLUSION

In the present research, the use of a human centered and participatory approach to design supported the fast generation and prototyping of numerous meaningful ideas for mixed presence collaboration and social interaction in the context of a Brazilian Planetarium and Science Museum. The involvement of multidisciplinary teams on different phases of the project and careful selection of varied user profiles – from ethnography to fast prototyping – helped bringing different points of views to the design cycle, resulting on the co-creation of group and socialware solutions that can potentially appeal to various visitor profiles, and fit the contextual dynamics of the museum.

A systemic process of co-design was adopted, starting with ethnography and followed by structured analysis and synthesis of research data. The resultant insights and design criteria helped mapping user profile polarities, problems with the museum experience and spaces of opportunity for new solutions to emerge. Based on these findings, co-creation workshops and Blank Model Prototyping sessions were conducted, leading to numerous innovative exhibits, artifacts, interfaces and services that can support collaboration and social interaction.

ACKNOWLEDGMENTS

Wallace Ugulino (142916/2010-2), Katia Vega (140859/2010-1), Debora Cardador (141520/2010-8) are recipients of individual grants awarded by CNPq. Heloisa Moura is the recipient of an individual post-doc grant awarded by FAPERJ (E-26/100.613/2008). And Hugo Fuks is the recipient of individual grants awarded by CNPq (302230/2008-4), FAPERJ/CNE (E-26/102777/2008) and UBILIFE FAPERJ/ADT1-190.116/2010. This work was partially financed by FAPERJ/INC&T (E-26/170028/2008) and CNPq/INCT (557.128/2009-9).

REFERENCES

1. Tang, A.; Neustaedter, C. & Greenberg, S. Embodiments for Mixed Presence Groupware. Research Report 2004-769-34, Department of Computer Science, University of Calgary, Alberta (2004).
2. Stahl, G. Group cognition: Computer support for building collaborative knowledge. Cambridge: MIT Press (2006).
3. Cosley, D.; Baxter, J.; Lee, S.; Alson, B.; Nomura, S.; Adams, P.; Sarabu, C.; & Gay, G. A Tag in the hand: Supporting semantic, social, and spatial navigation in museums. CHI, Boston (2009).
4. Vom Lehn, D., Heath, C. and Hindmarsh, J. Re-thinking interactivity. Rethinking technologies in museums. Limerick, June (2005).
5. Cabrera, J.; Frutos, H.; Stoica, A.; Avouris, N.; Dimitriadis, Y.; Fiotakis, G. & Liveri, K.. Mystery in the museum: collaborative learning activities using handheld devices. In Proc. 7th Mobile HCI, Salzburg, vol. 111. ACM Press, N. York, pp. 315-318 (2005).
6. Asai, K.; Sugimoto, Y.; Billinghurst, M. Exhibition of lunar surface navigation system facilitating collaboration between children and parents in science museum. In Proc. 9th ACM SIGGRAPH, Seoul, pp. 119-124 (2010).
7. Barthelmess, P.; Kaiser, E.; Lunsford, R.; McGee, D.; Cohen, P.; Oviatt, S. Human-centered collaborative interaction. In Proc. 1st ACM HCM, California, pp. 1-8 (2006).
8. Kensing, F.; Simonsen, J.; Bodker, K. MUST: A Method for Participatory Design. In J. Blomberg, F. Kensing and E. Dykstra-Erickson (Eds.): Proc. 4th PDC, November, Palo Alto, pp. 129-140 (1996).
9. Taxen, G. Introducing Participatory Design in museums. In Proc. 8th PDC. Toronto, Canada (2004).
10. Geertz, C. Thick Description: Toward an Interpretive Theory of Culture. In The Interpretation of Cultures: Selected Essays. N. York: Basic Books, pp. 3-30 (1973).
11. Glaser, B.; Strauss, A. The Discovery of Grounded Theory: Strategies for Qualitative Research. N. York: Aldine Publishing Company (1967).
12. Pimentel, M.; Fuks, H.; Lucena, C.J.P. Mediated Chat Development Process: Avoiding Chat Confusion on Educational Debates, Proc. CSCL, June, Taipei, ISBN 0805857826, pp. 499-503 (2005).
13. Arnowitz, J.; Arent, M.; Berger, N. Effective Prototyping for Software Makers, Morgan Kaufmann, Elsevier, Inc. (2007).

People in Books: Using a FlashCam to Become Part of an Interactive Book for Connected Reading

Sean Follmer[1], Rafael Ballagas[2], Hayes Raffle[3], Mirjana Spasojevic[2], Hiroshi Ishii[1]

[1]Tangible Media Group
MIT Media Lab
77 Massachusetts Ave.
Cambridge, MA 02139, USA
{sean, ishii}@media.mit.edu

[2]Nokia Research Center
955 Page Mill Road #200
Palo Alto, CA 94304
{tico.ballagas, mirjana.spasojevic}
@nokia.com

[3]Google
1600 Amphitheatre Parkway
Mountain View, CA 94043
hraffle@gmail.com

ABSTRACT

We introduce People in Books with FlashCam technology, a system that supports children and long-distance family members to act as characters in children's storybooks while they read stories together over a distance. By segmenting the video chat streams of the child and remote family member from their background surroundings, we create the illusion that the child and adult reader are immersed among the storybook illustrations. The illusion of inhabiting a shared story environment helps remote family members feel a sense of togetherness and encourages active reading behaviors for children ages three to five. People In Books is designed to fit into families' traditional reading practices, such as reading ebooks on couches or in bed via netbook or tablet computers. To accommodate this goal we implemented FlashCam, a computationally cost effective and physically small background subtraction system for mobile devices that allows users to move locations and change lighting conditions while they engage in background-subtracted video communications. A lab evaluation compared People in Books with a conventional remote reading application. Results show that People in Books motivates parents and children to be more performative readers and encourages open-ended play beyond the story, while creating a strong sense of togetherness.

Author Keywords

Reading, children, literacy, video conferencing, background subtraction, family communication

ACM Classification Keywords

H5.3. Information interfaces and presentation (e.g., HCI): Group and Organization Interfaces: Synchronous Interfaces

General Terms

Human Factors; Design.

INTRODUCTION

Today's families are increasingly diasporic, and are turning to the Internet to help bridge distances and maintain ties [15]. Cheap long distance phone calls and free video conferencing have made it easier for adults to keep in contact with other adult family members. However, communication with children remains quite difficult both over phone and over videoconference for a number of reasons [2].

One problem the community has identified in engaging children in teleconferencing or phone calls, especially those under the age of five, is the implicit assumption that the best way to support relationships is through conversation. However, young children – even in person – are not yet the best conversationalists, and co-located family members often engage children through activities such as play, games and reading [3].

A number of recent systems have demonstrated that better communication and long-term relationships with children can be achieved by structuring video conferencing interfaces around shared activities, such as structured play [12, 30], unstructured play [29, 13, 30], and reading books [2, 12, 30]. Central to all of these systems is the idea of

Figure 1. A sketch of proposed mobile tablets running the People In Books software. Here a Child and Remote family member play on a boat together.

Figure 2. A screenshot of a child and parent playing in the trees of *Where the Wild Things* are using the People In Books System.

playfulness as a means for engagement in distant communication. Our work builds on these ideas and presents a novel implementation of a shared reading experience that invites remote parties to become part of the story alongside characters in the book.

Interactive electronic children's books have been gaining popularity with the rise of affordable mobile devices and tablet computers coupled with an easy distribution system for books and applications. However many of these commercial offerings focus on interactive features that enable the 'pass-back effect' [8] where the parents pass there device to the child as a way to keep them occupied, thus removing the need for adult participation. Although this certainly has its time and place, we wanted to create interactive books that could harness adults as teachers, mentors, and play partners for children. We wanted to focus on the social interactivity of reading, the experience and activity of shared reading beyond the printed word. Parents can pretend to be different characters and read out loud with different voices, they can ask children questions to engage them in the story, they can even change the story completely, highlighting parts they know their children like [19, 32]. Likewise the child plays an important part in the interactivity of the book, in that the story often lives in their imagination rather than on the pages. Children who act out stories are able to better understand the books [11, 22]. Parents or family members can do a better job of estimating the zone of proximal development for a child than computer software [27].

In our work we aim to focus on encouraging character voices, play acting, and play beyond the written words in the book. Our goal was to create interactive book reading that could bring humans back into the loop. But instead of merely putting books online, we wanted to explore how to use technology to give even more freedom to parents and children to be part of the stories. In the People in Books system, background subtracted live video of children and family members are placed into the storybook setting along with the characters of the book, encouraging play (Figure 2). We intend this design to help break down barriers of distance and separation implicit in the GUI window metaphor. Instead of seeing each other in their real world distant locations, children and remote family members can both go together into the world of the story. We hypothesize that orienting geographically separate video streams in a shared virtual story environment can create a stronger sense of togetherness than traditional video conferencing approaches. We assume that visual togetherness will support a feeling of emotional togetherness, and that the stories can help structure families' shared play in the imaginary environments.

We previously introduced an early version of the People in Books concept as part of a series of four exploratory design concepts for shared activities over video conferencing [12]. Following that formative work, this paper demonstrates an evolved design with a novel high-fidelity technical implementation that works towards our vision of creating a mobile tablet based device that fits in with existing reading practices, see Figure 1. Although we have still not reached the final implementation, we have developed robust active background subtraction cameras that allow for movement and a stable video conferencing pipeline to transmit alpha encoded video. This enables us to more holistically study how families engage around the fantasy world of the book, and we present laboratory results that compare the system to traditional distance-reading tools.

RELATED WORK

Our work contributes to research in interactive books, video conferencing, and shared activities for Family Communication. Books have been explored as both a foundation and inspiration for interactive systems over the years. The XFR group explored how digital interactive paper books could immerse users in the spaces and experiences afforded by stories [14]. Listen Reader explored how users' orientations to books might change, and also inspired a category of talking children's books which have been popular in the marketplace for the past decade.

The growth of video technologies in mobile touch devices points to a need for children's video chat applications. Classic video experiments in CSCW inform the needs of children and family. ClearBoard explored the importance of eye gaze and facial awareness in shared video activities like drawing, painting, or the arts [17]. Mediaspaces [1] gives insight into roles of presence over a distance, and work such as Exertion Interfaces shows how non-conversational activities like sports and playfulness can support a sense of togetherness over a distance [20].

Work in the role of always-on video in the family environment [18, 16] forecasts children's emerging use of video to play with peers over a distance [29, 30]. Communication toys such as dollhouses [13] may also scaffold children to play together over a distance, rather than "conversing" in manners traditional for video chat.

Games and stories can help structure and scaffold interactions between children and remote adult family members. Our research builds directly on formative experiments in remote Video Play [12], and connected reading. Family Story Play [3] and StoryVisit [23] showed that systems for shared book reading can increase video chat times 5-7x over ordinary video chat, and can engage children as young as 3 years old in a sense of connectedness with distant adults. Those systems used a pedagogical agent to help children and adults engage in book content. Our work builds on the concept of "connected reading" for family togetherness, with our approach exploring how the books themselves might support more immersive experiences if children and adults can imagine being part of the story worlds created by the children's books' authors.

Our concept of play with books is informed by research in child development [4], insights into children's pretend play [22, 7] and pre-literacy activities like dialogic reading [11, 19, 32].

PEOPLE IN BOOKS

The People in Books prototype was developed to support reading and open-ended play with young children ages 3 to 5 years old and remote family members. The design focuses on supporting dialogic reading practices that involve children and adults beyond the printed words and illustrations to provide a more interactive experience. Readers can act out parts and ask questions to engage children in a richer reading experience. In addition we focused on minimizing the feeling of distance between the two remote parties. We attempted to address these two issues through inserting segmented video feeds of the remote users into the storybooks. Video segmentation allows for full-body gestures and poses of users to be captured and inserted into the illustrations, allowing for more performative reading. The system was designed through an iterative design process, and motivated by our prior experience with designing video conferencing applications for children and distant family members [12].

From our prior experiences designing interactive video conferencing systems for children we established these design goals for the People in Books system.

1. Create a sense of togetherness through shared context
2. Encourage active and performative reading
3. Allow for play beyond the printed words in the book
4. Fit into existing reading rituals

System Description

A simple UI minimizes distractions from the reading experience. The users are presented with a storybook, which takes up the full horizontal screen. Video of the users is segmented and composited into the illustrations of the book as live video avatars. The locations, sizes, and rotation of the live video avatars are modified for each page such that the images of users are placed into contextual locations in the illustrations and scaled appropriately to match the scale of other characters in the book. Foreground elements such as rocks, other characters or other props are used to obscure the bottom half of the user's live video avatars to create the illusion that their full body is in the illustration as opposed to a floating head or torso.

Layers of foreground and background elements can be grouped programmatically and animated along with the video layers to create the sense of movement. For example the live video avatars of two users are placed on a boat, and the boat is animated to sail along the sea, see Figure 3.

Interaction with mouse cursors is minimized. Users can change pages by clicking on the sides of the pages, and the segmented video of users is moved according to the page index. Beyond changing pages the only interaction is through video, where parents and children can move around and act as different characters.

Figure 3. An animation of a boat sailing moves both parent, child and book characters with it.

Designing Content for People in Books

Content for People in Books has to be selected and manually modified. Each page has to be manually segmented into foreground and background layers, and the location, scale and rotation for each live video avatar must be encoded for each page.

Not every storybook works well as a People in Books story. Through early prototyping with a number of different children's story books, we found that important qualities were a location based story, fairly consistent sizing of characters and many different locations. Although these are not hard and fast rules, our most successful stories had these qualities. Currently, we use existing storybooks and modify them to fit into the People in Books format. However in the future we hope to develop custom storybooks for the People in Books format that could be tailored to maximize the strengths of the People in Books system.

Technical Implementation

Our interaction design focused heavily on designing this reading experience around families' existing reading practices. For many families that often means in bed or on the couch with parent and children close together and book held between them.

We designed the technology so that it could be easily ported to mobile devices running on Linux. Our eventual goal is to make this system in a tablet form factor, so physical size and computational limits were of high concern.

Figure 4. FlashCam Pipeline: Top Left, unlit image of user. Bottom Left, IR Flash illuminates user. Top Right, Subtracted and threshold mask derived from difference of two previous images. Bottom Right, unlit image of user matted.

FlashCam: Active background subtraction

We chose background subtraction, over other methods such as face tracking, as a means for inserting users into illustration because of it's flexibility to capture full body poses or arbitrary objects. But because parents and children are holding the laptop or tablet running People in Books, our segmentation method needed to be robust enough to work while the device was in motion. In addition children and parents are very close to the book interface and often move closer to inspect pictures more carefully, so the system needed to work at close distances.

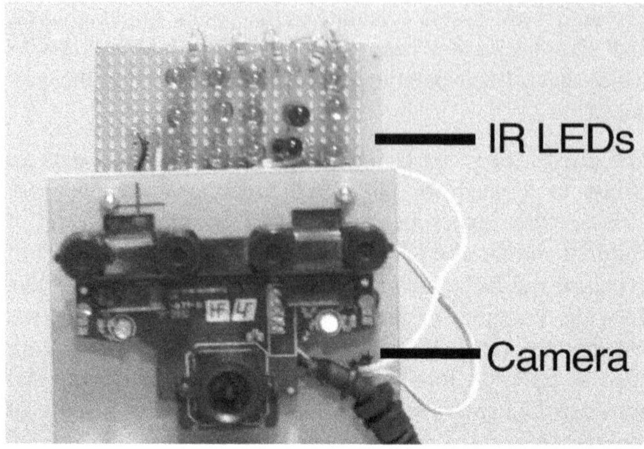

Figure 5. FlashCam prototype hardware. Above: IR LEDs which flash on every other frame. Bellow: modified PS3 camera.

Existing techniques for foreground/background separation often rely on a background model, where the background is known and image elements that differ are considered foreground. These techniques often require the camera not to move. There are other adaptive approaches that relearn the background, however these systems cannot operate robustly while in motion or when the changes are abrupt. Other systems rely on machine learning, which can be very robust but are difficult to implement and computationally intensive and cannot run on many mobile devices [31].

Another approach is active background subtraction, where some sort of structured light is added into the environment to make it much easier to determine background and foreground. We chose to implement a simple active background subtraction camera, that uses flashing IR lights to help segment the video which we call FlashCam [6, 25]. Although similar flash camera techniques have been developed before, they have not been applied to mobile devices or for video conferencing. We believe that because FlashCam is small, inexpensive, computationally cheap and robust to changes in orientation it makes a great candidate for mobile devices.

An array of IR LEDs are placed close to the lens of a camera. A small microcontroller listens to the trigger sync signal and flashes the LEDs on for one frame and off for the next. Our implementation uses a modified Sony PS3 Camera, see Figure 5. The computer software compares the pairs of images, and looks for areas that are brighter in the flash frame than the frame without flash, and labels those areas as foreground, see Figure 4. We use an adaptive threshold based on the amount of brightness in the flash frame, as the differences between the two images are changed slightly based on the amount of sunlight in the frame, which contains IR light. The camera system does not work in full sunlight as the IR LEDs are completely washed out.

The background subtraction algorithm was written in C as a Gstreamer plugin, allowing us to feed the background

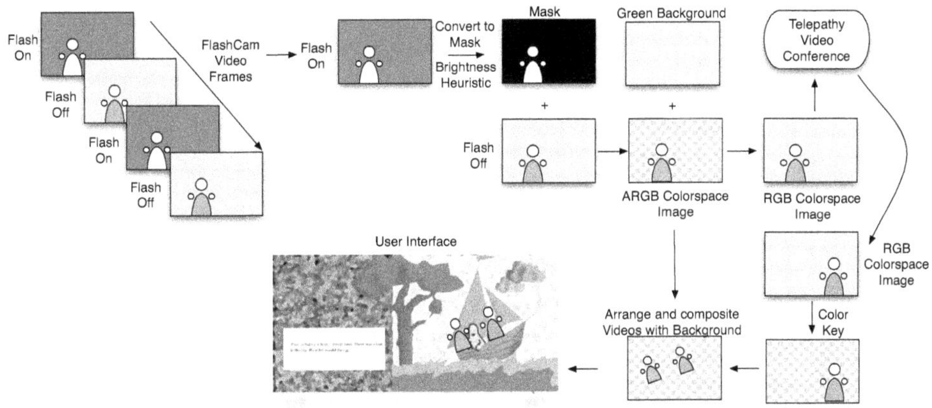

Figure 6. Video Conferencing Pipeline. FlashCam Segmented video is sent both to onscreen graphics and matted with green background and transmitted over Telepathy Video Conference. On the remote side the video is Chroma Keyed out and sent to on screen graphics.

subtracted video easily into our video conferencing pipeline.

Video Conferencing Pipeline

The video conferencing functionality for this prototype is built using the Telepathy-Farsight[1] open source software stack. The stack leverages the open source Gstreamer[2] multimedia library for video processing and codec support. In our video conferencing client implementation, we leverage the XMPP and Jabber protocols to stay compatible with a range of open videoconference client implementations including the Nokia N900 phone and Google's browser-based video chat client.

Our design requires the transmission of alpha matted video (e.g. ARGB color space). However, most video conferencing clients use H.264 video codec implementations that do not support color spaces with an alpha channel. In order to send alpha matted video easily over existing video channels and protocols we chose to add a green background and later chroma key out the background once received, see Figure 6.

Front End User Interface

The front-end user interface was implemented using Qt Quick[3] with QML. Our prototype ran on laptops running Ubuntu 9.10. Using Qt Quick allowed us to easily animate parts of the book to bring the book to life.

USER STUDY

To evaluate the People in Books system's influence on engagement, dialogic reading and feelings of togetherness, we chose to compare it to a more traditional shared book reading experience. We created a prototype control system based on a commercial shared reading product, Readeo.com. The control system, shown in Figure 7, has two equal sized video windows above the book content to view the local and remote video feeds.

We chose to evaluate the system in a controlled lab based study to allow for in-depth qualitative analysis on the use of People in Books for reading at a distance, to highlight differences in reading practices between the two systems, and to provide feedback into our design process for later iterations.

Methodology

We recruited 12 families with children aged three to five years old (5F, 12M), and their parents (11F,3M) to use both the People in Books system and our control reading system. Seven of the families had a parent and a child present, and three families had one parent and two children present, and two families had two parents and two children present. Ten families reported using video conferencing previously with their children, four of those ten families monthly used video conferencing, and two families of those ten reported weekly use. Predominately the prior video conferencing with children was with grandparents or other close relatives. None of the families had previously read a book over video conferencing with a service like Readeo or by sharing the images of a paper book through traditional video conferencing.

Each session with a family was split in to two parts, a People In Books session and a control session, with a short break between. Two Books were used to evaluate the system, *Where the Wild Things Are* by Maurice Sendak and *We're Going on a Bear Hunt* by Michael Rosen and Helen Oxenbury. The order of the sessions was counter balanced, as were the books, resulting in four conditions. Participant families were randomly assigned one of the conditions.

The children and parents were separated into two rooms, except for 5 sessions when a single room with a wall

Figure 7. The control system remote reading interface.

[1] http://telepathy.freedesktop.org/wiki/

[2] http://gstreamer.freedesktop.org/

[3] http://qt.nokia.com/qtquick/

divider was used. Parents and children could see each other's video feeds on the screen and hear each others voices through a polycom speaker phone system. To enable easy set up for the multiple conditions we chose to forgo the network infrastructure and instead build a lab only prototype. This prototype consisted of one laptop with its screen mirrored on another monitor. Long VGA and USB cables connected the monitor and FlashCam of the parent's system to the main laptop computer. Children used the 15.4inch laptop screen and sat on a couch, where as parents in the adjacent room sat at a desk and viewed the same content on a 23 inch LCD monitor. We chose this set up to mirror how we thought the systems would be used by people in their homes, with distant relatives, remote parents, or grandparents using the system on a desktop computer and children using a smaller mobile device that could be used where reading normally happens, such as on the couch or in bed. Both the parents and the children were able to use a mouse to control the book interface.

The sessions were screen captured and an additional video camera was used to capture the children's movement in the room (Figure 8).

Following the session, parents filled out a questionnaire and were then interviewed, to help us understand how the systems differed from traditional video conferencing, how the systems differed from normal reading, how the two systems differed, and any other information they wished to provide.

After all evaluations were conducted we analyzed the recorded sessions for qualitative evidence of participants exhibiting a sense of togetherness, examples of dialogic reading, extended play beyond the book, and engagement.

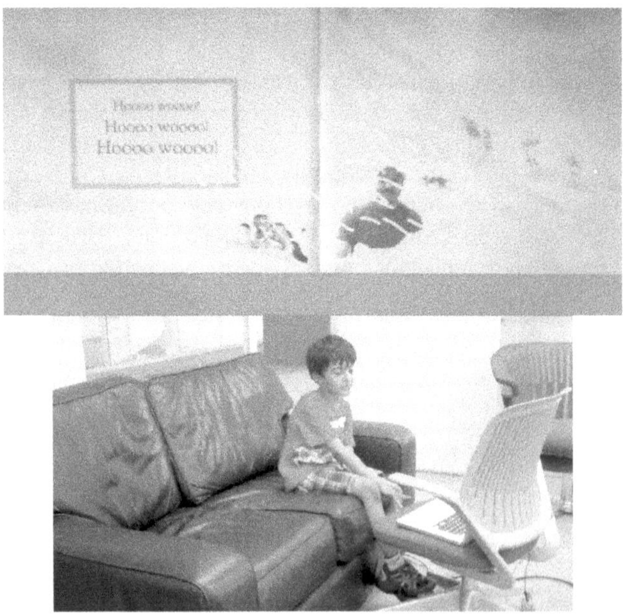

Figure 8. Above a screen recording of a study session where a father and son use People in Books to read *We're Going on a Bear Hunt*. Bellow, a secondary camera captures children's actions in the room for later analysis. The Child rests the laptop running People in Books on a Chair.

Findings

Closeness to remote participants

In many of the studies we observed a lot of evidence of children and parents expressing a sense of togetherness through dialog and through their actions. For example closeness was conveyed to console children who were scared by certain sections of the books. One child in a scary part of the story said, "I can see a monster! Mama, Are you still next to me?," and once they were next to each other in the next page layout "Now I am next to you, Mama." The mother responded "I'm going to protect you [from the monsters]" and the child said "Thank you mama!" [F4]. In this case it seemed as though the spatial proximity of the images of the children and parents affected their sense of togetherness.

Parents and children would also try to touch each other inside the People in Books session. In one example a mother reached out to touch the child's video she said "I'm touching your head" [F2]. We also saw children and parents preforming compassionate gestures, for example hugging and kissing each other's video inside the People in Books system. For example the son in session 4 leaned towards his mother's video and gave his mother a kiss, which was followed by a audible "Aww" from the mother [F4]. However, younger children also tried to touch or interact with the remote participants video outside of the system, often by touching the screen, which the remote parents could not see. This type of touching the screen was prevalent both with People in Books and the control system.

Often in the People in Books system participants would refer more to locations where participants were, such as "You are over by the monster" [F2]. And there was also a higher incidence of children and parents describing that they were at a location together. "Are we in Max's [the character from the book] room?" [F4]. Or "We are in the river" or "We are on a boat". The language used by parents and children seemed to highlight more of a shared, proximal experience. In the control system there wasn't as much evidence of this "closeness," instead children seemed to focus on the fact that they could see their parent. "I can see you," a daughter proclaimed to her father [F7].

Closeness to characters

Beyond feeling close to their long distance reading partners, parents and children using the People in Books system often expressed a sense of closeness to characters that their images were proximal to in the People in Books system. While reading *Going on a Bear Hunt* a child remarked, "This is the scary part... He's right behind you, papa," his father replied "Yes that's why we have to go home!" [F10]. The child was referring to the large bear that was next to the image of his father. This expression of fear or pretend fear, was very common when there were scary characters around in both books. "I can feel the monsters!" a child exclaims while reading *Where the Wild Things Are* using the People in Books system [F4].

We also saw a great deal more interaction with the other characters using the People in Books system. "I'm cuddling with Max", a child proclaims as they both mime cuddle with the illustrated character Max. The mom then grabs past Max to her son explaining, "I can feel you."[F4]. Another mother tickled the Monster's toes as a child laughed [F2]. Parents and children would also try to communicate with some of the characters. One child tried to tell the character Max, "Look, Max, there's food on your table" as his mother in the video pointed towards the food to show Max [F4].

Play Acting In the Story

In addition to interacting with characters in the book we also saw a great deal more play acting inside the People In Books System than the control system. Particularly there was more play referring to the different settings or locations in the book. *We're Going on a Bear Hunt* features many out door locations, such as rivers, grassy fields, muddy ponds or forests. By placing the video of the children and parents inside these locations they were more likely to pretend play that they were in these locations.

For example one father and son reading *Going on a Bear Hunt* with People in Books were on the river page. "See, if you want to go to the other side you have to swim." As they turn the page to the river the child says "I'm going to swim, swim, swim swim" as he lies on the couch and pretends to swim [F10]. There were other sorts of these activities such as pretending to run, jump, or play in the mud.

Parents also remarked that they felt like People in Books brought out "more acting for parents and children" [F9]. Some parents explained that it was a more theatrical experience; "I would use more dramatic facial expressions" [F5].

However, People in Books seemed to limit the amount that children pretended to be other characters. Children even made this explicit, for example one Mother asked "Should I say Max [the character in the book] or Ciallas [the child's name]." The child replied quickly and forcefully "Max!" [F7]. But with the control system parents and children were more likely to mimic the other characters' visible actions.

There were also certain words that triggered action in both systems. For example words pertaining to particular actions, like "growl," "show their terrible claws," or "roar" tended to be acted out in both our system and the control.

Play Beyond the Story

After they had finished the story a number of participants continued to play with the People in Books system. Often families would try to find their favorite page and then play in that page. "I like the one where you are upside down" the mother says as the child flips the pages back to that one and they continue to play and dance [F1].

	Video Conferencing	Control System	People in Books
Mean	4.45	4.91	5.54
Standard Deviation	1.33	0.93	1.42

Table 1. Results from post-test questionnaire asking participants to rate their sense of togetherness with their children while using three different interfaces. The parents rated them on a 7 point Likert scale with 1 being distant and 7 if they felt like they were in the same room.

Another common observed play act beyond reading that People in Books seemed to encourage were hiding games. Because of People in Book's foreground elements there are objects to hide behind, and a large number of children ended up hiding. Parents would say things like "Where did you go?" and then children would respond "I'm Hiding" and that would begin a game for them where the child would kneel down or move out of the frame, and then come back again [F4]. That family played hide and seek on a single page for more than one minute.

Engagement

As previously reported [2] parents often said in post test interviews and questionnaires that they had a hard time keeping children engaged with traditional video conferencing. "[While talking to] grandparents the kids get bored [with] Skype quickly, so this would certainly help with that" [F7]. All but two families thought this was an improvement over normal Skyping for keeping children's attention while video conferencing.

Most of the parents after the session responded that children were more engaged with the People in Books system compared to the control system. "[People in Books] holds the kids interest more" responded one mother [F9]. A number of parents thought children were more engaged with People in Books, even if they didn't prefer the system [F5, F6, F7]. However reading times for both systems tended to be similar. For *Where the Wild Things Are*, the average reading time with People in Books was 7 minutes 33 Seconds, and for the control system the average was 5 minutes 32 seconds. But for *Going on a Bear Hunt* the average reading time for People in Books was shorter than the control system and none of the results were statistically significant.

Problems with Field of View

Parents reported having problems seeing the children while using People in Books more than the control system. One parent explained that she had "less sense of what is going on in the room with people in books" [F5]. It was very clear to parents when using the control system if the child was in the field of view or not, but because of background subtraction and foreground elements in People in Books it was often hard for them to know if the child was out of view, hiding, or that the system was not working.

DISCUSSION

Increasing a sense of togetherness

Our qualitative data points to more active engagement with book content using People in Books. While we assumed this would correlate to a "sense of togetherness," these findings are not statistically correlated with post-survey data in which adults reported their "sense of togetherness" using both of our test systems, as well as previous experiences with Skype (Table 1).

However, many of the children of the families who said they didn't feel closer using People in Books tended to stay outside of the field of view of the FlashCAM. Although this certainly represents a shortcoming with the system, there may be ways to change this behavior through technological solutions. Wider field of view cameras in addition to larger video placement could go a long way towards helping this. Some of the parents in post test interviews complained saying that they only saw their children as "small heads" [F6] probably because the children sat further away from the camera or because they were outside the region of the background subtraction. Other research reiterates the importance of framing on emotional connections over video conferencing [21], so finding ways to get around these issues with the People in Books system is important.

Changes in reading practices

For parents reading to young children, often the words on the page are not the most important part of the experience in terms of learning. Research in dialogic reading [32] highlights the importance of tying the events back to experiences in children's life, asking children to answer questions about the story, and creating an engaging reading experience by using character voices or other types of more theatrical reading styles. On the whole parents who were practicing good dialogic reading with their children tended to do so in both sessions. In some cases we did see dramatic changes in reading styles, such as drastically increased dialogic reading when using the People in Books as opposed to the control system, but most of the readers who did not practice dialogic reading heavily in one system did not in the other. However, People in Books increased participants' dramatic presentation of the story and allowed for more open play pertaining to aspects of the stories. This is an important improvement that could impact how children learn to read [22]. In addition, to achieve a goal of making reading and learning a fun and enjoyable experience for children, it is important to engage parents in the experience because parental engagement in learning early on has great affects on the child's educational performance later in life [4].

Beyond the type of reading used by parents we could also see a change in the way children responded to the stories. Children using People in Books on average seemed to show a higher level of empathy for the characters in the stories. They often pretended to be scared, or excited, when the other characters in the story were more often than in the control case. This could be because they felt as though they were physically in the same situation, because their visual representation was. Parents and children also exhibited a larger shift from referring to the collective characters in the book as "They" to "We," than in the control case. This could also have had an effect on the level of empathy the children experienced.

However, there were some changes in reading practices with People in Books compared to the control system that may not be desirable. We noticed a lot more use of the mouse cursor in the control system to highlight important words or for parents to point out characters that were referred to. Parents also noticed this trend. "I Found it was hard to read as I normally do, asking kids to point or touch body parts as we read about them...ears, eyes, etc" [F6]. This may be because parents were more busy acting as embodied characters in the stories and have to split their attention between acting, reading and pointing. Further study should address how being an embodied character as opposed to a traditional reader changes reading practices.

This is also related to the issues of acting like characters vs. acting with characters. People In Books seemed to lessen the prevalence of acting as or mimicking other characters in the book, which was observed to a greater degree the control systems. Instead, while using People in Books, children and parents focused on being their own embodied characters in the story who were going along with them too. This could have effects on children's development of empathy, an important social skill that is helped by early reading practices. But children often shared similar emotions with the characters because they seemed to be more involved in the book's story. By seeing their image proximal to the scary monsters and animals that the characters were close to, they seemed to express similar fear to the characters.

In addition, many parents have different types of reading styles and maintain different levels of control, and People in Books clearly catered to some of those styles more than others. Some parents did not encourage their children to act like characters from the stories. One parent told child a child who was acting like a dog in the story, "You don't have to act like the characters. Sit down" [F6]. The mother later explained "If I wanted to do some tricky things then I would use People in Books" but that for normal reading it did not meet her expectations. [F6]

Two parents explained that People in Books seemed like a lot more work. Particularly they found difficult the fact that there were large meta issues while reading with People in Books (for example "why are we in the story?"), and some parents felt they had to explain the context to the children. "[People in Books] makes it more work to focus on the story, because you also have to comment on your own physical presence in its illustration" [F2].

Fitting in with Existing Reading Rituals

Although we designed the People in Books system to be flexible and portable enough for families to use the system where they normally read, the playful nature of the system may be a poor match for many parents' use of stories as a "calming ritual" [F7] before beditme. Because People in Books gives children the ability to see themselves as characters in the book and encourages them to act like characters in the book it tended to create a very high energy reading session. One parent explained, "really when you read you want them to calm down, settle down. So then you don't want to do things to get them more excited [F7]." However, parents did say that there were times during the day time when reading with People in Books could work especially well. A number of participants even suggested using People in Books on their own at home without a long distance partner. It seems that there are many different types and styles of reading for young children. Instead of designing one system for all types, designers should more closely choose aspects of reading to design for, such as time of day, number of participants, learning goals and attention spans. Just as there are different kinds of books, there can be different kinds of book reading applications.

FUTURE WORK

The positive results from our in lab user study have shown the potential for children and remote parents to read as characters inside of story books. The findings from our lab evaluation suggest a number of areas in which immersive ebook experiences could be improved.

A number of parents were concerned with the lack of vision of peripheral areas when viewing the background subtracted video of their child. Children would often move in and out of the view of the camera, however remote parents tended to stay inside the view of the camera at all times. We suggest presenting the remote participants with both the People in Books interface as the children sees it, but also with the raw video feed of the child to better understand what is going on. Similarly parents responded better when children's images were much larger in the story. A feature to allow users to zoom in on certain areas of the book with video images in them may help alleviate these problems.

We would also like to explore allowing users to interact with content in the book in a more direct way. Currently the books pages are fixed except for animated layers that run continuously. The outline of users silhouettes could be used to interact with on screen elements, for example if it is raining or snowing, particles could be simulated around the users to make it feel more immersive. Further investigation should help to find an acceptable level of interaction that still makes the experience feel like reading a "book."

The user evaluation presented here only covers a single session and the impact of novelty is still unanswered, although no users had used either People in Books or the control system previously. We plan to conduct longitudinal studies using smaller tablet based computers in users homes with remote family members to better understand how systems like People in Books are used, how they fit in with existing practices, and how they change reading behavior. Our robust video conferencing pipeline and active-background subtraction FlashCam will help support these longer studies.

Beyond tablet based systems we would like to explore other form factors or settings for the People in Books system. The living room, equipped with a large television screen and a depth camera like the XBox Kinect, could provide an interesting space for this kind of remote play. Instead of being limited to fixed positions in books, you could move around a 3D book scene by moving around in the room, while being tracked by the Kinect. We would like to explore how this design would influence full body interaction, as the current system focuses more on upper body movement. In addition larger settings like connecting two preschool classrooms for shared reading could be an exciting new area to explore. Different classes could take turns preforming and observing, or they could collaborate together.

CONCLUSION

People in Books introduces a new type of reading that involves and integrates remote readers' video chat streams directly into children's story book illustrations, supporting children and adults to play alongside the story characters. Being together in the story world allows children and distant family members to read books together in a way that goes beyond traditional videoconference, and beyond traditional reading. Reading with People in Books is a more active experience; we have shown that for many families it can promote more theatrical reading and encourage other pre-literacy activities, helping families move towards certain dialogic and educational reading practices. By making traditional video conferencing and reading more interactive, where parents and children can still be creative and imaginative, we have shown that children's book illustrations can provide a playful shared point of entry for young children and their long-distance reading partners to become connected with one another.

ACKNOWLEDGEMENTS

We would like to thank Hiroshi Horii for his advice and sketching skills, as well as the rest of the IDEAS team at Nokia Research Center and the Tangible Media Group.

REFERENCES

1. Agamanolis, S., Westner, A. and Bove, V. M., ``Reflection of Presence: Toward More Natural and Responsive Telecollaboration," Proc. SPIE Multimedia Networks, 3228A, 1997.

2. Ames, M., Go, J., Kaye, J. 'J.', Spasojevic, M. "Making love in the network closet: the benefits and work of family videochat." Proc. CSCW 2010, 145-154.
3. Ballagas, R., Raffle, H., Go, J., Revelle, G., Kaye, J., Ames, A., Horii, H., Mori, K., and Spasojevic, M. "Story time for the 21st century." IEEE Pervasive Computing, 9:28–36, 2010.
4. Barnard, W. M. Parent involvement in elementary school and educational attainment, Children and Youth Services Review, Volume 26, Issue 1, Promoting Well Being in Children and Youth: Findings from the Chicago Longitudinal Study, January 2004, Pages 39-6
5. Bly, S., Harrison, S.R., Irwin, S. Media spaces: bringing people together in a video, audio, and computing environment, Communications of the ACM, v.36 n.1, p.28-46, Jan. 1993.
6. R. M. Bolle, J. H. Connell, N. Haas, R. Mohan, and G. Taubin. Object imaging system. U. S. Patent 5,631,976, 1994.
7. J. Cassell and K. Ryokai. Making Space for Voice: Technologies to Support Children's Fantasy and Storytelling
8. Chiong, C., and Shuler, C. Learning: Is there an app for that? http://www.joanganzcooneycenter.org/Reports-27.html
9. DeVincenzi, A., Yao, L., Ishii, H., and Raskar, R. 2011. Kinected conference: augmenting video imaging with calibrated depth and audio. In Proceedings of the ACM CSCW '11. ACM, New York, NY, USA, 621-624.
10. Fails, J., Druin, A., Bederson, B., Weeks, A., and Rose, A. A child's mobile digital library: Collaboration, community, and change. In Mobile technology for children: designing for interaction and learning. Morgan Kaufmann, 2009
11. Fisch, S. M., Shulman, J., Ackerman, A., Levin, G. "Reading between the pixels: Parent-child interaction while reading online storybooks." Early Education and Development, 13(4), 435-451, 2002.
12. Follmer, S. Raffle, H., Go, J., Ballagas, R., and Ishii, H. 2010. Video play: playful interactions in video conferencing for long-distance families with young children. In Proceedings IDC '10. ACM, New York, NY, USA, 49-58.
13. Freed, N., Burleson, W., Raffle, H., Ballagas, R., Newman, N. "User interfaces for tangible characters: can children connect remotely through toy perspectives?" Proc. IDC 2010, 69-78.
14. Harrison, S., Minneman, S., Back, M., Balsamo, A., Chow, M., Gold, R., Gorbet, M., Mac Donald, D., Ehrlich, K., Henderson, A., Design: the what of XFR: eXperiments in the future of reading, interactions, v.8 n.3, p.21-30, May/June 2001
15. Hiller, H., and Franz, T. New ties, old ties and lost ties: the use of the internet in diaspora. New Media & Society 6, 6 (2004).
16. Hutchinson, H., Mackay, W., Westerlund, B. , Bederson, B., Druin, A., Plaisant, C., Beaudouin-Lafon, M. , Conversy, S., Evans, H., Hansen, H., Roussel, N., Eiderbäck, B., Technology probes: inspiring design for and with families, Proceedings of the SIGCHI 2003.
17. Ishii, H., Kobayashi, M., Arita, K. Iterative design of seamless collaboration media, Communications of the ACM, v.37 n.8, p.83-97, Aug. 1994
18. Judge, T. K. and Neustaedter, C. Sharing conversation and sharing life: video conferencing in the home. Proc. CHI 2010.
19. Mol, Bus, de Jong & Smeets (2008). "Added Value of Dialogic Parent-Child Book Readings: A Meta-Analysis," Early Education & Development, 19(1), 7--26.
20. Mueller, F., Agamanolis, S., and Picard, R. Exertion interfaces: sports over a distance for social bonding and fun, Proceedings of the SIGCHI 2003.
21. Nguyen, D. and Canny, J. 2009. More than face-to-face: empathy effects of video framing. In Proc. CHI '09. ACM.
22. Page, A. Children's Story Comprehension as a Result of Storytelling and Story Dramatization: A Study of the Child as Spectator and as Participant. Diss. University of Massachusetts, Amherst, 1983.
23. Raffle, H., Revelle, G., Mori, K., Ballagas, R., Buza, K., Horii, H., Kaye, J., Cook, K., Freed, N., Go, J., and Spasojevic, M. Hello, Is Grandma There? StoryVisit: Family Video Chat and Connected E-Books. ACM CHI 2011.
24. Sherman, L., Druin, A., Montemayor, J., Farber, A., Platner, M., Simms, S., Porteous, J., Alborzi, H., Best, J., Hammer, J. Kruskal, A., Matthews, J., Rhodes, E., Cosans, C., and Lal, A. 2001. StoryKit: tools for children to build room-sized interactive experiences. In Extended Abstracts of CHI EA '01.
25. Sun, J., Li, Y., Kang, S. and Shum, H. 2006. Flash matting. ACM Trans. Graph. 25, 3 (July 2006)
26. Vutborg, R., Pedell, S., and Vetere, F. 2010. Family storytelling for grandparents and grandchildren living apart. In Proceedings of the 6th NordiCHI '10 531-540.
27. Vygotsky, L. S. (1978). Mind in Society. Cambridge: Harvard University Press.
28. Whitehurst, G. J., Falco, F. L., Lonigan, C. J., Fischel, J. E., DeBaryshe, B. D., et al. (1988). "Accelerating language development through picture book reading." Developmental Psychology, 24(4), 552-559.
29. Yarosh, S, Inkpen, K.M., Brush, A.J. "Video playdate: toward free play across distance." Proc. CHI 2010, 1251-1260.
30. Yarosh, S. Cuzzort, S. Müller, H., Abowd, G.D. "Developing a media space for remote synchronous parent-child interaction" Proc. IDC 2009, 97-105.
31. Pei Yin, Antonio Criminisi, John Winn, and Irfan Essa, Bilayer Segmentation of Webcam Videos Using Tree-based Classifiers, inTrans. Pattern Analysis and Machine Intelligence (PAMI), IEEE, 2010
32. Zevenbergen, A.A. & Whitehurst, G.J. (2003). "Dialogic reading: A shared picture book reading intervention for preschoolers." In A. van Kleek, S.A. Stahl and E.B. Bauer (Eds.), On reading books to children: Parents and teachers. Mahwah, NJ: Lawrence Erlbaum Associates, pp. 177-20

A Study of Multilingual Social Tagging of Art Images: Cultural Bridges and Diversity

Irene Eleta
College of Information Studies
University of Maryland
College Park, MD 20742
ieleta@umd.edu

Jennifer Golbeck
Human-Computer Interaction Lab
College of Information Studies
University of Maryland
College Park, MD 20742
golbeck@cs.umd.edu

ABSTRACT
The goal of this study is to compare social tagging patterns in two languages in image collections of art, while seeking exploitable strengths for the application of multilingual social tagging in digital libraries and museums. Crowdsourcing the annotation of digital image collections of artworks to different language communities has the potential to bridge language borders and reach wider audiences. This mixed methods study is based on a collection of digital images of paintings for which tags in Spanish and English were collected. The results show that the level of agreement in the vocabulary describing an image does not change significantly when adding a second language, but different cultural perspectives can be found for certain images when comparing less frequent tags across languages. Understanding and comparing tagging behaviors across languages is necessary for the design of user interfaces that support diversity and encourage sharing of perspectives about the artwork images.

Author Keywords
multilingual, social tagging, image annotation, digital image collections, art images, culture, image search, metadata

ACM Classification Keywords
H.5.3 Group and Organization interfaces: computer-supported cooperative work

General Terms
Human Factors; Languages

INTRODUCTION
Digital image collections are becoming available for the general public in growing numbers thanks to the digitization and dissemination efforts of many cultural heritage institutions around the world, such as the Library of Congress, the British Museum, the Prado Museum, and the Louvre, to cite a few well-known examples. While digital image collections have the potential to reach global audiences, their volume poses many challenges for indexing, access and use.

These collections are accessed by the public through text queries, which requires images to be annotated with metadata. Traditional metadata is normally created by catalogers and typically includes the creator name, the title, institution, etc. This approach presents two problems: the increasing volume of digital collections makes annotation by catalogers infeasible, and image search is only effective for users who know the creator or title. New approaches have appeared to overcome this challenge, such as the study of user-centered indexing, automatic annotation and social tagging.

One advantage of social tagging is that the user does not need training to participate in the system; also, it facilitates browsing, information discovery and unanticipated uses [12]. Social tags reflect to some extent the vocabulary of the users and, if well harnessed, they could improve the accessibility of the images. In particular, social tags act as index terms that could be used for ranking images in retrieval systems, filtering the search of the user, suggesting terms for query expansion, recommending similar images, and clustering images to facilitate browsing [14].

However, there are drawbacks to a heavy reliance on social tags. For example, the social tagging environment has to stimulate participation to diminish the problem of sparse social tags in parts of the collection [16]. Furthermore, the absence of standards leads to noise, such as spelling variants, misspellings, and the use of languages that the system does not support [8].

This observation highlights the challenge that a multilingual Internet poses: the language barrier in digital libraries and museums is more present than ever due to the language diversity of Internet users. Also, collections are composed of images of art originating from different cultures whose peoples might want to access using their own language, but often those images are annotated only in the languages of the institutions that display them abroad.

Instead of considering social tags in a diversity of languages as "noise", as is frequent practice, a good design would leverage them for enriching the access paths to the images while bridging borders online. If we are able to translate tags from

CSCW'12, February 11–15, 2012, Seattle, Washington, USA.

one language to another or to enable the input of tags in multiple languages through localized user interfaces, it may enrich the annotations available for each image and diminish the problem of sparse tags. For instance, the annotation of images could be crowdsourced to different language communities (where members of the public conduct similar tasks than traditional workers [15]).

Once we have social tags in multiple languages, they could enable multilingual search (i.e. the search functionality supports more than one language) and cross-lingual search with the help of machine translation, where the user is able to find images annotated in a language different from the language of her query.

Furthermore, social tagging could add the value of different cultural interpretations, which would be more accentuated when engaging different language communities and in various countries. Understanding and comparing tagging behaviors across languages is necessary for the design of user interfaces that support diversity and encourage sharing of perspectives for the construction of the context and meaning of artworks.

We will use the term *multilingual social tagging* in this work to refer to the multilingual and collective quality of the annotations in the collection or an image, and not to the language skills of the individual annotators.

In this study we used a mixed methods approach to answer the research questions below; the tags were analyzed primarily with a quantitative method and then the results were complemented with a qualitative analysis.

RQ1: How similar are the tags provided by different language communities when tagging images of art?

RQ2: Does the agreement between language communities when tagging images depend on the type of painting?

RQ3: Are the popular tags in one language the same as the popular tags in the other?

RQ4: Do tags reflect cultural differences in the interpretations of the paintings?

We used a collection of 33 images of paintings for which tags in Spanish and English were collected. We analyzed these social tags to measure the agreement between speakers of the same language and speakers of two different languages; then we compared tags and tag categories to draw conclusions about tagging behaviors across languages.

This paper is organized as follows: first, we will discuss the related work from diverse fields; secondly, we will outline the method and instrument design; finally, we will present the results, followed by an analysis of the findings and future work.

BACKGROUND AND RELATED WORK

The study of patterns in social tagging has an important role in promoting useful applications in information access and discovery. Golder and Huberman [5], among others, observed that the social tags stabilize in fix proportions in the long run instead of growing chaotically. Often, the vocabulary for a resource resembles a power law or an inverse-logistic distribution [16, 14]; in both cases there is a small group of social tags that are very frequent, and a *Long Tail* of diverse tags that are less frequent. The frequent tags are called *Power Tags* and reflect the statistical consensus of the community on the terms that best describe the resource [14].

Many authors warn about the low discriminatory power in information retrieval that some frequent tags have and recommend to pay attention to more specific and helpful tags hidden in the Long Tail [14]. Building tools for social knowledge construction requires understanding and harnessing the statistical consensus, together with the diversity and specificity of the Long Tail. To achieve this, some degree of natural language processing is needed: in the context of tagging in art museums, Klavans et al. [9] showed how computational linguistic processing, morphological and semantic analysis using tag categorization could help reduce the noise in tag sets and impact tag clustering.

The caveat is that the individual tagging behavior is affected by the functionalities of the system [10], therefore the study of tagging patterns should take into account the design of social tagging systems and vice versa. In this regard, the taxonomy of tagging systems introduced in [11], distinguishes differences in tag aggregation (allowing repetition of tags or not for a given resource), resource connectivity, social connectivity and tag support, among others. Focusing on tag support, they identified three models: (1) *blind tagging*, where the user does not see other people's tags, (2) *viewable tagging*, where the user can see the tags already assigned for a resource by the community, and (3) *suggestive tagging*, where the system suggests tags to the user [11]. These design decisions are not petty because "existing tags directly influence the categorization of the document, which in turn influences the selection of tags" [4].

Multilingual social tagging has been studied in Flickr [6], and in the context of educational resources online in Europe [18, 19, 20]. Gonzalo et al. [6] experimented with cross-lingual search of images that were tagged in a language different from the language of the participants and reported, among other findings, that users did not think about languages in the first place, which hindered their search effectiveness.

Searching for images tagged in a foreign language is a difficult task and multilingual tagging might be the direction to start improving; Vourikari and Koper [19] provided evidence that 23% of resource discoveries across national borders happened through the multilingual tag cloud and 5% from the lists of "travel-well" tags (with spelling similarities across languages). Another project, the image search engine *PanImages*, uses both automatic and crowdsourced translation of index terms of images through a multilingual version of Google's *Image Labeler* for cross-lingual image retrieval [3]. They envision *PanImages* could be used for the translation of social tags in a variety of content sharing sites.

Multilingual tagging could have important applications in digital libraries and museums. The *steve.museum* project[1], a collaboration of several American Museums of Art, has explored the use of social tags in English for digital images of artworks with the hope of improving access to the museums' collections and engaging the general public [17, 14]. In this project, museum professionals concluded that 77% of the social tags could be potentially useful as index terms for the images of art objects [17]. Also, they tested different tagging environments, similar to the tagging support models described in [11], using an experimental collection of artwork images. The results suggest that users echo to some extent the curator's metadata they see, while they tend not to duplicate other people's tags when they are shown, and this reduces the number of tags they enter [17]. Finally, in [2] they wonder "how this new sort of engagement with museum objects might help ... draw contributors who bring a multi-cultural perspective to looking at our works of art".

The next step in utilizing social tags is embracing language diversity to make information accessible for the world's population.

METHOD AND INSTRUMENT DESIGN

This study used a mixed methods approach. We followed a concurrent embedded strategy, where both qualitative data (social tags) and quantitative data (participant profile characteristics) were gathered; then the data was analyzed primarily with a quantitative method to answer research questions 1 and 2 and, additionally, with a qualitative method to answer research questions 3 and 4.

Instrument design

First, we created a website to collect social tags for images of paintings (figure 1). The interface directed the participants in a sequence: from a consent form and a brief questionnaire of five profiling questions (for ensuring comparability) to successive images with a text box for tagging. There was an English and a Spanish version of the interface.

The participants could not see other people's tags, the title of the work, or any other metadata about the painting (except for the museum name and accession number in compliance with the requirements of the institutions). The text box next to the image allowed the participants to enter tags that were either single or multiple words. These design decisions had the purpose of encouraging individual creativity and preventing users from being influenced by any external information. This interface design is similar to the *steve.museum* environment where participants could only see the image with no metadata or tags [17] and fits into the blind tagging model in [11].

The images appeared in random order to compensate for any cognitive associations. There was a maximum of 10 images shown in each session and participants could skip images without tagging them. We conducted a pilot test with 14 participants, 7 speakers of each language, for checking the questionnaire, appropriateness of image size and duration.

[1] `http://www.steve.museum/`

Figure 1. Screenshot of the tagging interface adapted from the *steve.museum* blind tagging environment. Image represents "Still Life with Pink Fish" by Georges Braque (Indianapolis Museum of Art).

We selected 33 images of paintings from the *steve.museum* collection. First, we selected two-dimensional works of art, excluding tapestry works. Second, we classified the paintings represented in the images in five broad categories explained below, after consulting a museum professional. Finally, we selected a variety of themes within the five initial categories, adapted from the themes in the National Gallery of Art and other galleries. The final experimental collection comprises:

- non-western paintings (5),
- western representational paintings with no abstraction and a biblical theme (5),
- western representational paintings with no abstraction and a non-biblical theme (i.e. landscape, still life, human figure)—called "realistic" in tables and figures—(9),
- western representational paintings with some degree of abstraction (i.e. post-impressionist, cubist)—called "slightly abstract" in tables and figures—(9),
- western non-representational paintings—also called "abstract" in some tables and figures—(5).

Data collection

We decided to minimize the effects of language variety both in English and Spanish for simplification of the analysis. With this precaution in mind, we selected communities in Spain for the Spanish language data collection and in the U.S. for the English version. The choice of countries and languages has been influenced by the origin of resources and sponsorship.

The dissemination strategy consisted of sending an invitation to participate to specifically identified communities that included a link to the English or Spanish language version of the experiment as appropriate. The invitation included a request for further dissemination to speakers of the same language within the social network. The communities were: the iSchool of the University of Maryland (U.S.), the Ontology Engineering group in the Universidad Politécnica de Madrid (Spain), alumni of Universidad Autónoma de Madrid (Spain) and Universidad Complutense de Madrid (Spain). Because the purpose was to obtain a vocabulary sample different from

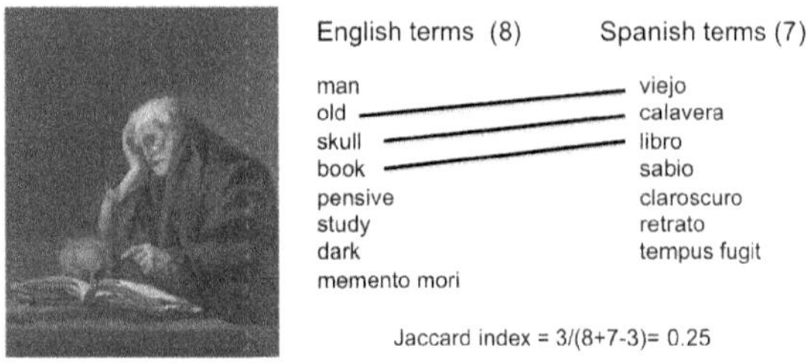

Figure 2. Quantifying term set similarity across languages with symmetric Jaccard index. English terms are shown on the left and Spanish terms on the right. Lines indicate correspondences between English to Spanish terms. Image: Heraclitus (or Saint Jerome) by Hendrick ter Brugghen (Cleveland Museum of Art).

the curators' terminology, we intentionally avoided art-related communities and the invitation explained that knowledge of art was not needed for the experiment.

Processing of social tags

Once social tags were gathered in both languages, we quantified how much taggers agreed in the vocabulary for describing an image. However, this required some pre-processing. The processing steps used are as follows: automatic tokenization using spaces between words, application of a stop word list, automatic normalization to lower case, computer-aided spelling correction, manual normalization (explained below), and manual union of tokens that form compound words.

The manual normalization consisted of reducing plural forms to singular, adopting one spelling when several were possible, and in Spanish female adjectives were transformed into the neutral form (masculine). We allowed verb derivations because they were scarce. The compound words included: geographic named entities, like "Middle East", "Puerto Rico", "United States"; Latin phrases (*memento mori*); and compounds with a single word translation in the other language, for instance, palm tree (*palmera*), rocking chair (*mecedora*), *pavo real* (peacock).

Quantification and similarity values

After obtaining the list of terms in both languages, we created a list of lexical correspondences. The lead author is a trained professional translator and created this list manually. When a term in one language had a translation in the other language, both the original term and the translation were assigned the same index number. This resulted in a list of lexical correspondences with 700 index numbers. Thanks to the normalized terms and the lexical correspondences, it was possible to calculate the similarity between English and Spanish term sets for each image.

Our next step was to compute similarity of term sets between two different languages and within the same language to determine the statistical consensus. We used both the symmetric Jaccard Index and cosine similarity measures in this analysis. The symmetric Jaccard index, as used by Olson and Wolfram [13] for studying non-expert indexers agreement, has the advantage of being a proportion, which facilitates interpretation and comparison. To measure the cross-language similarity, we used the symmetric Jaccard index:

$$SJI = \frac{A \cap B}{A \cup B} \tag{1}$$

In equation 1, A represents the set of terms in English for an image and B, the set of terms in Spanish for the same image. This index gives the proportion of similarity from 0 to 1. Figure 2 illustrates the process for quantifying term set similarity with the SJI.

Unfortunately, when the size of the term sets is very unbalanced for a particular painting (i.e. one participant was very prolific), it biases the index negatively because the denominator becomes disproportionately large.

Alternatively, the cosine similarity is used in the Information Retrieval classic vector model to compute similarity between documents. In this model, documents are represented as k-dimensional vectors, where k denotes the size of the vocabulary of the corpus [1]. This similarity metric is better suited to comparing term sets of varying sizes for the same image.

In this experiment, the terms issued by a participant for a specific image constituted a document. The term sets (documents) were represented as k-dimensional vectors. Each dimension in this vector represented the frequency (TF) of the corresponding term for the current image. The list of lexical correspondences introduced earlier represented the corpus and enabled the comparison of term sets across languages, because equivalent terms in different languages were associated to the same dimension of the vector.

Unlike the Jaccard proportions, comparing cosine similarity values across painting types does not provide information on the relative difference between the values for two types. To overcome this drawback, we computed the monolingual similarity for the English and Spanish subsets to serve as baselines for the comparison.

The monolingual similarity was calculated for each image following a partition strategy of the data sample similar to the cross-validation method, as illustrated in figure 3.

First, the participants that tagged the painting were separated in two groups of approximately equal size. Second, vector A representing the terms of the first group was computed by summing their TF-vectors for the given image. Vector B was computed analogously for the second group. The cosine similarity between A and B was then computed. This process was repeated for each possible combination of groups, and the mean of all cosine similarity values was finally obtained.

After calculating the English and Spanish baselines, we followed a similar procedure for quantifying the cross-language similarity for each image. To ensure compatibility with the baselines it was necessary to counterbalance the larger number of participants when considering both languages simul-

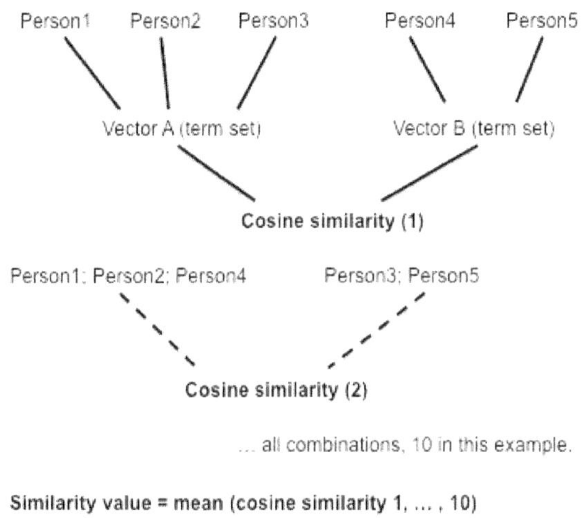

Figure 3. Quantifying monolingual cosine similarity with a partition strategy of the data sample similar to the cross-validation method. Users who tagged a specific image were put in groups, their tags were put into sets for that group, and the cosine similarity between sets was computed. We repeated this for all combinations of two evenly split groups, and averaged the cosine similarities over all permutations.

taneously. We did this by limiting the number of participants in each language contributing to vectors A and B.

Each subsequent comparison considered every possible combination of half of the American participants (to create vector A) with half of the Spanish participants (to create vector B). This resulted in vectors A and B receiving contributions from the same number of participants they received to compute their monolingual counterparts. Figure 4 illustrates the procedure for calculating the cross-language similarity with this method.

Qualitative analysis of tags

We divided the qualitative analysis in three parts. First, we categorized the processed terms. The categorization method was based on a faceted matrix used in [9] to categorize tags applied to images of paintings and was adapted from the frameworks and studies of Panofsky, Shatford Layne, Armitage and Enser. The matrix in figure 5 combines Panofsky's three levels of interpretation of paintings with Shatford Layne's four categories to account for the subject matter (topic depicted). Additionally, it includes "visual elements" and an "uncategorized' option, which in this work will be used to account for all non-subject related terms, such as creator names, nationality, styles, techniques, etc. The categorization of terms will provide a broad picture on the semantics of tags applied to images of artworks.

The second part of the qualitative analysis consisted in comparing the Power Tags in English and Spanish for every image, to ascertain if they could be translations. This analysis required previous preparation of the data in a table. The table displayed the most popular (processed) terms for each image in English and Spanish; we defined "popular" as those terms with frequency greater than one, in other words, more than one participant used the same term to tag a particular

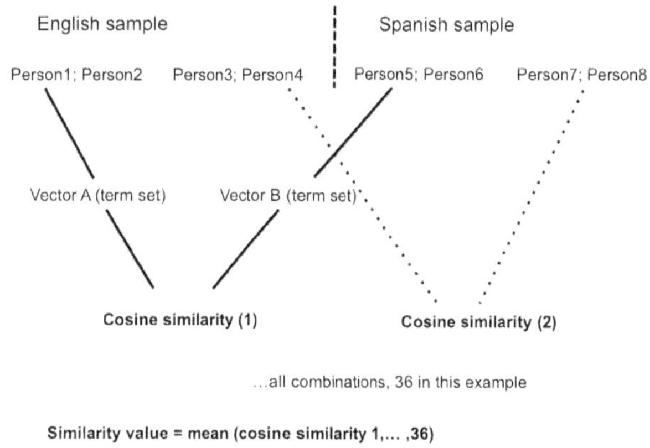

Figure 4. Quantifying cross-language cosine similarity with a partition strategy of the data sample similar to the cross-validation method. The approach is similar to the monolingual technique described in figure 3 except that English and Spanish taggers were kept separate.

	Generic	Specific	Interpretation
Person or thing	woman, elephant	Mary, chemist	[Mythical beings] Dragon, angel
Action, or state	sewing, death, war	[specific event] WWII	[emotions, abstract ideas] sorrow, fear
Place	city, forest	India	paradise
Time	Spring, night	Renaissance	*Memento mori*
Visual elements	[shapes, colors] square, red, colorful		
Non-subject matter	[author, style, nationality, uncategorized]		

Figure 5. Matrix with categories of index terms for artwork images and examples, based on the works of Panofsky, Shatford Layne, Armitage and Enser, Klavans et al.

image. To determine the popularity, the terms for each image were ordered by frequency. The table also included the English terms that matched an exact translation in the Spanish term set for an image, and the type of art. This display facilitated the comparison for detecting the consensus in vocabulary across languages and for validating the results of the categorization.

The third part of the qualitative analysis focused on the differences between English and Spanish in the descriptions and interpretations of images. For this purpose, we classified the raw social tags in broad themes that emerged while comparing the tag sets for each painting and language. Some example themes are: religious names and objects, negative or positive emotions, historical references, mentions of body parts in nudes, etc.

	English	Spanish
Have university degree	92.8%	83.3%
Under 40 years	67.8%	61.1%
Online everyday	96.4%	91.6%
Interested in art	64.3%	61.1%
Not so interested in art	28.6%	33.3%

Table 1. Participant profile

	English	Spanish
One-word tags	83.57%	84.63%
Two-word tags	15.01%	13.07%
Multi-word tags	1.42%	2.30%

Table 2. Classification of social tags by number of words.

RESULTS

Description of the samples: participants and social tags

The participants of the study were 28 native English speakers from the United States and 36 Spanish speakers from Spain. While collecting the data, we observed that Spanish participants were using far fewer tags; on average, Spanish speakers were assigning half the number of tags to each image as their American counterparts. Because the quantitative analysis required tag samples of comparable size, we recruited additional Spanish-speaking subjects, hence the higher number of participants from Spain. Table 1 summarizes the profile of participants in both samples.

At least three English language participants and three Spanish language participants tagged each image; the maximum number of participants per image was nine for both languages. Sometimes, the number of participants varied in each language for the same image. The mean number of American participants per image was 4.18, versus 5.22 for Spanish participants.

The total number of tags in English—including repetitions and before processing—was 773, while the number of tags in Spanish was 566. Table 2 shows the distribution of tags by number of words. For this analysis, articles, conjunctions and prepositions were not counted.

After processing the tags, the number of unique terms obtained in English was 486, and in Spanish, 375. The average number of terms participants assigned to a painting in English was 6.78, with an overall range between 1 and 21; and in Spanish the average was 3.41, with an overall range between 1 and 15.

Quantitative results: similarity values across languages

We used the symmetric Jaccard index for comparing the proportion of consensus in the vocabulary across languages and painting types.

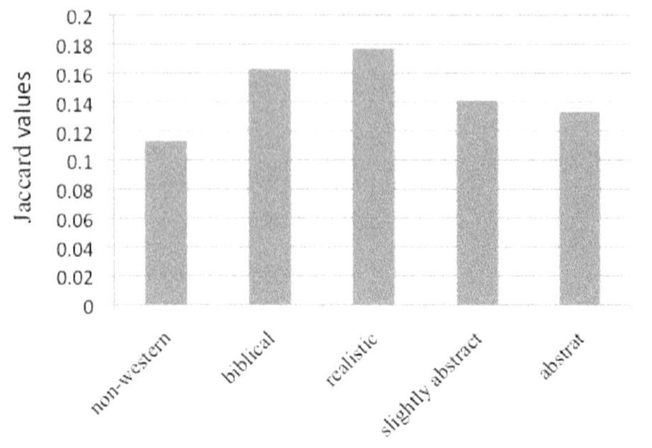

Figure 6. Cross-language similarity (consensus) with symmetric Jaccard index.

(a) Comparison of cosine similarity values across language samples.

Sample	Mean	Std. deviation
English only	0.3262	0.1701
Spanish only	0.3117	0.1722
Cross-language	0.2990	0.1063

(b) P values for pairs of samples using Wilcoxon signed ranks test.

Sample pairs	P value
Spanish—English	0.936
Cross-language—English	0.714
Cross-language—Spanish	0.893

Table 3. The cosine similarity values across language samples do not change significantly.

Figure 6 displays the mean Jaccard similarity between the vocabulary in English and Spanish for each type of painting. Although biblical and other realistic themes seem to facilitate greater consensus in the vocabulary across languages, the number of paintings was not enough to obtain statistically significant results.

The cosine similarity, used to represent the level of consensus in the vocabulary across language samples, did not change significantly between the cross-language sample of terms and the monolingual English and Spanish baselines, as shown in table 3.

Results of the qualitative analysis

Figure 7 summarizes the categories of terms most frequently used by the participants and their proportion within each sample. The most frequent category was "general person or thing", followed by "visual elements", which was especially frequent in the non-representational type of paintings, and by "non-subject matter" (i.e. painter names, nationalities and styles). Interestingly, the category "emotions and

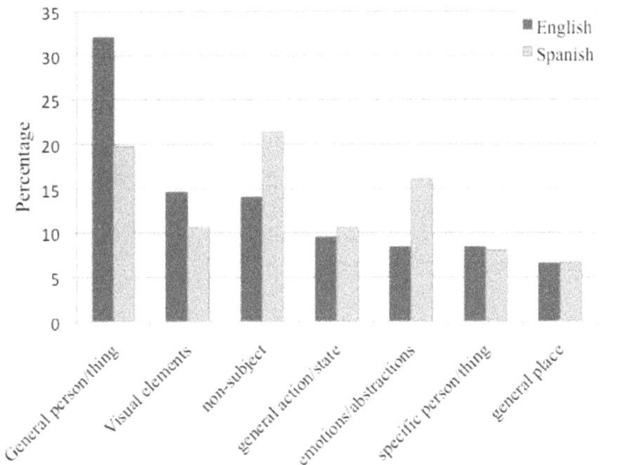

Figure 7. Percentage of most popular categories of terms in English and Spanish.

abstract ideas" was very popular; for instance, terms such as *tranquility*, *fear*, *religion*, and *justice* were in this category. Other popular categories were "general action or state", "specific person or thing" (i.e. biblical names), and "general place".

Regarding the similarity of Power Tags across languages, we found that often (in 45% of images), the most popular term in one language was an exact translation of the most popular term in the other. Also, in 36.36% of images, the most popular term in one language matched an exact translation among the second or subsequent most popular terms in the other. In line with the categorization results, these frequent terms that favored consensus across languages fell in the categories "general person or thing" (*elephant*, *woman*), "visual elements" (*color*, *green*, *blue*), "non-subject matter" (*abstract*), "specific persons or things" (*peacock*, *Jesus*). Despite "emotions and abstract ideas" being a popular category, the frequent terms were rarely found in it.

When focusing on the differences between English and Spanish tags, we noticed that a few paintings concentrated richer cultural references in one of the language samples. For instance, the painting "The Cotton Pickers" by American painter Winslow Homer, shown in figure 8(a), inspired culturally and historically charged tags in English such as "African American", "slavery", "south" or "southern", "racism", "Civil War", "imperialism". On the other hand, Spanish tags only included "esclavitud" (slavery) and related tags like "explotación" (exploitation) and "resignación" (resignation). Cross-language consensus tags for this painting were: "cotton picking", "cotton field", "young women" and "slavery".

Another example of richer interpretations in one of the language samples was the biblical painting "Christ and the Virgin in the House of Nazareth", by Spanish 17th century painter Zurbarán. The work displays an idealized young Jesus with long hair and a long dress sitting with the Virgin. As illustrated in figure 8(b), a popular English tag used to describe the scene was "two women". In this set, only the English tag "crown of thorns", which is a visible object on

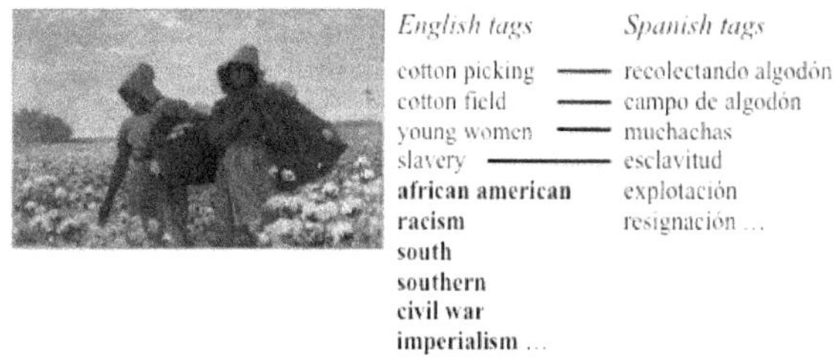

(a) *The Cotton Pickers*, by Winslow Homer (Los Angeles County Museum of Art). Both groups used tags that described the general content of the image (cotton picking, young women, slavery), but the image inspired a greater number of culturally charged tags among American participants.

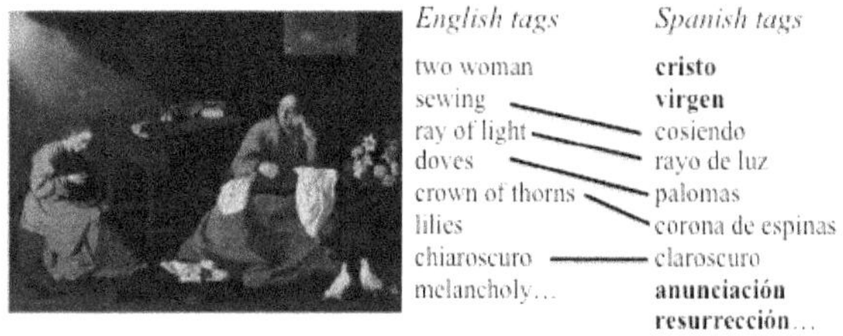

(b) *Christ and the Virgin in the House at Nazareth*, by Zurbarán (The Cleveland Museum of Art), favored a richer set of religious tags among Spanish participants.

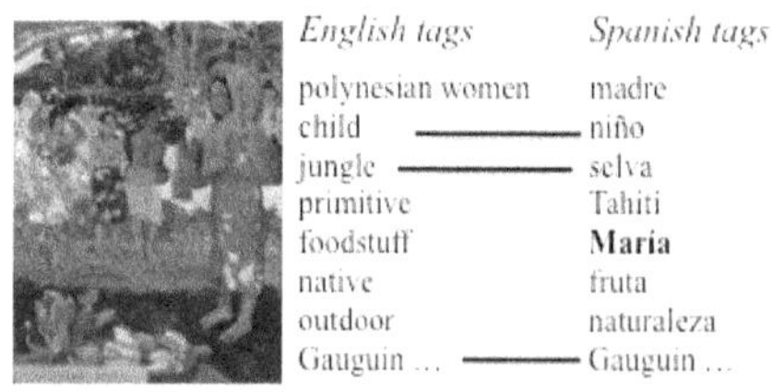

(c) *Ia Orana Maria (Hail Mary)*, by Gauguin (The Metropolitan Museum of Art). The tag maría in Spanish evokes Virgin Mary, but this tag was not used by any English taggers.

Figure 8. Images of paintings that inspired richer cultural interpretations in one of the language samples. The tags shown are only a selection from the original dataset for illustration purposes.

the knees of Jesus, uncovered a possible religious interpretation of this apparently domestic scene. However, the Spanish tags "cristo" (Christ), "virgen" (Virgin), "corona de espinas" (crown of thorns), together with more interpretative tags such as "anunciación" (annunciation) and "resurrección" (resurrection), provided a rich religious interpretation to the painting.

Similarly, the painting "Ia Orana Maria (Hail Mary)" by French painter Gauguin, displaying a Polynesian woman with a child on her shoulders, did not inspire religious tags among the English-speaking participants (i.e. Polynesian woman, child, jungle, primitive). By contrast, the Spanish tag "maría" in figure 8(c) suggested a religious interpretation.

ANALYSIS OF FINDINGS AND FUTURE WORK

The use of multilingual social tags for image access (and for access of other digital objects) requires a multidisciplinary approach, which includes human-computer interaction (HCI), information retrieval (IR), natural language processing (NLP), studying tagging processes, tag distributions, and semantic analysis of tags.

One unexpected finding uncovered that American participants used in average twice as many terms for tagging an image as the Spanish participants (6.78 vs. 3.41). Unfortunately, the reasons for this difference remain unclear. In [14], Peters surveyed various social tagging studies and remarked that the average tag allocation frequency varies with the system and type of resource: from 2.79 tags in *Flickr* pictures to 4.22 in *Connotea* bibliographic references.

Related to the study of tag distributions (RQ1), the level of consensus in the vocabulary did not change significantly when adding a second language; and this consensus was relatively small, which is consistent with the findings of related studies [5, 16]. This means that there is a small group of frequently used tags—called Power Tags—that reflect the consensus of the community. Future research could explore if the consensus level correlates with the distance between cultures and languages in the tagging community. For instance, if instead of Spanish we add Chinese tags for the same paintings, would that impact the level of consensus?

To answer RQ3 and complement the quantitative analysis, we compared the Power Tags in English and Spanish and found that they were often exact translations. This could be exploited as crowdsourced translation of index terms for the images. For example, frequent English tags for the image of the painting The Cotton Pickers in figure 8(a) were: "cotton picking", "cotton field", "young women", "slavery"; all of these tags had a match in the Spanish tag set for the same image. The agreement in the vocabulary between English speakers and Spanish speakers is useful for obtaining human translations of index terms that could enable multilingual retrieval of images (i.e. the search functionality supports more than one language). Previously, NLP would be necessary for tag normalization, disambiguation, and recognition of words that are translations [9, 14].

In response to RQ2 about tag distribution across panting types, it was reasonable to expect that western representational paintings would be the types that facilitated greater consensus in the vocabulary, while abstract and non-western paintings would show lower consensus. Unfortunately, the number of paintings in each type was not enough to obtain statistically significant results. One finding that supports the idea of representational paintings boosting vocabulary consensus comes from the categorization of tags: participants tended to name recognizable objects and people depicted in the images of representational paintings, which increased the number of Power Tags. Then, we could expect that as the abstraction of the painting increases, the chances of agreement in what the painting depicts are lower.

The popularity of the category "general person or thing" is consistent with the findings in [9], where they only included images of representational paintings; also, the surprisingly high proportion of tags that express "emotions and abstract ideas" is confirmed in [9]. Power Tags were scarce in "emotions and abstract ideas", which implies that the variety of perceptions and interpretations lie mostly in this category; these interpretative tags open the door for other forms of access that facilitate discovery or "serendipity", beyond traditional search [14]. In the case of non-representational paintings, the "visual elements" category was more popular, together with the tag "abstract". In summary, "users may need access to images based on such primitive features such as color, texture or shape, or access to images based on abstract concepts and symbolic imaginery" [7].

Of particular interest are places where there are cultural differences when aggregating tags from two language communities for an image. As observed in this study, if there is a popular word in one language not found in the other, this is a good indicator of a possible cultural difference (relevant to RQ4). In these cases, translation of tags in one language may be used to provide additional cultural understanding for users in another language. For example, when Spanish speakers attribute religious themes to an image that is not identified as religious by English speakers, the translated Spanish tags may help English speakers recognize these higher-level themes in the image.

The multilingual tags found in the Long Tail of terms describing an image, which are tags with low frequency and no correspondence in other languages used to describe the same image, could facilitate the discovery of images across languages with the help of automatic translation and IR methods. For instance, if a user types the keyword "peace", the system could display on the results page all the images that are tagged with the word "peace" and, additionally, the images tagged in Spanish with "paz", showing the translation when needed. Alternatively, the user could browse tag clouds in her language to access the images and, for example, she might select the tag "peace", which would direct to a cluster of images created with semantic analysis, using all the translations of "peace" available in the index of tags [9, 14, 18].

As explained in the introduction, the applications of social tags are manifold: filtering the search of the user, suggesting terms for query expansion, recommending similar images, and clustering images to facilitate browsing [14], to name a few. All of them would benefit from a greater number of tags. Supporting multiple languages, while adding complexity, could help solve the problem of sparse tags described in [16].

But, how should we handle this mixing and mingling of languages? From an HCI perspective, Vourikari [18] found that multilingual tag clouds can be distracting for some users. Therefore, digital libraries and museums should consider having separate language versions of their website and tagging environment, like in this study, while using multilingual social tags in the back-end for indexing and retrieval. This separation helps the processing of tags and eliminates the language identification problem encountered by Vourikari et al. [20].

Apart from the relatively small sample of images and participants, the limitations of this study derive from the simplification strategies. Processing the social tags into terms relied on the assumption of compositional meaning, while deeper semantic analysis could be used for conflating synonyms, reducing ambiguity, or accounting for the similarities of terms in the same semantic family, which also impacts the translation process.

For future work, increasing the collection and the number of participants, in addition to including more languages and a cross-cultural approach, would enable greater generalization. Other improvements might come from exploring semantic analysis with ontologies, and including tag bundling functions on the interface [14]. Finally, in relation to the design of tagging environments, we recommend expanding the work in [17] to study the impact of showing social tags and metadata in tagging behavior, term frequency distributions, Power Tags and, by extension, in the methods for translating social tags.

CONCLUSION

The increasing volume of digital image collections poses many challenges for indexing and searching. These collections are accessed by the public through text queries, which requires images to be annotated. In this context, the language barrier is more present than ever due to the language diversity of Internet users. Social tagging is a promising approach because it has the advantages of a user-oriented vocabulary for indexing images, which might improve access and discovery. Additionally, social tagging provides the possibility of adding multiple languages in an inexpensive way by crowdsourcing the annotation work to diverse language communities.

The goal of this study is to compare social tagging patterns in two languages in image collections of art, while seeking exploitable strengths for the application of multilingual social tagging in digital libraries and museums. We used a collection of 33 digital images of paintings for which tags in Spanish and English were collected. Following a mixed methods design, we analyzed these social tags to study the similarity of term sets used across languages and painting types.

The results revealed that the level of consensus in the vocabulary did not change significantly when adding a second language, and this consensus was relatively small, which is consistent with the findings of related studies. We compared the Power Tags—frequent tags that reflect the statistical consensus of the community—in both languages and found that they were often exact translations, which could be exploited as crowdsourced translation of index terms. In the cases where tags reflect cultural differences, automatic translation could facilitate discovery of images across language barriers and additional cultural understanding.

Another result showed that the tags in the category "general person or thing", mostly related to representational paintings, facilitated consensus in the vocabulary, while the category "emotions and abstract ideas" showed great vocabulary divergence.

Multilingual social tagging of images, and of digital objects, could enable access for a linguistically and culturally diverse population. At the same time, multilingual tagging could enrich the meaning of digital objects with different perspectives and cultural backgrounds. In particular, when artworks have cultural significance for one group, social tags could provide a new context for viewers of other cultures. The challenge lies in designing user interfaces that support diversity while adapting to locality, and in building systems that process multilingual tags in meaningful ways for retrieval, clustering and browsing.

AKNOWLEDGEMENTS

Thanks to Dr. Judith Klavans for her guidance on this research, and to the enthusiastic participants of the experiment. This research was possible thanks to a Fulbright scholarship, and it was sponsored, in part, with funding LG-30-08-0117-08 from the Institute for Museum and Library Services to the University of Maryland "T3: Text, Tagging and Trust to Improve Image Access for Museums and Libraries" and by the Army Research Laboratory under Cooperative Agreement Number W911NF-09-2-0053. The views and conclusions contained in this document are those of the authors and should not be interpreted as representing the official policies, either expressed or implied, of the Army Research Laboratory or the U.S. Government. The U.S. Government is authorized to reproduce and distribute reprints for Government purposes notwithstanding any copyright notation here on.

REFERENCES

1. R. Baeza-Yates and B. Ribeiro-Neto. *Modern Information Retrieval: The Concepts and Technology behind Search*. ACM Press Books. Addison-Wesley Professional, London, 2nd ed. edition, 2011.

2. S. Chun, R. Cherry, D. Hiwiller, J. Trant, and B. Wyman. Steve.museum: An Ongoing Experiment in Social Tagging, Folksonomy, and Museums. In J. Trant and Bearman D., editors, *Proceedings of Museums and the Web 2006*, Albuquerque, 2006. Archives & Museum Informatics.

3. S. M. Colowick. Multilingual search with PanImages, Mar. 2008.

4. W.-T. Fu. The microstructures of social tagging. In *Proceedings of the ACM 2008 conference on Computer supported cooperative work - CSCW '08*, pages 229–238, New York, New York, USA, Nov. 2008. ACM Press.

5. S. A. Golder and B. Huberman. Usage patterns of collaborative tagging systems. *Journal of Information Science*, 32(2):198–208, Apr. 2006.

6. J. Gonzalo, V. Peinado, P. Clough, and J. Karlgren. Overview of iCLEF 2009: Exploring Search Behaviour in a Multilingual Folksonomy environment. 2009.

7. A. Goodrum and A. Spink. Image searching on the Excite Web search engine. *Information Processing & Management*, 37(2):295–311, 2001.

8. M. Guy and E. Tonkin. Tidying up Tags?, 2006.
9. J. Klavans, R. Guerra, R. LaPlante, R. Stein, and E. Bachta. Beyond Flickr: Not all image tagging is created equal. In *AAAI 2011 Workshop: Language-Action Tools for Cognitive Artificial Agents*, San Francisco, 2011.
10. C. S. Lee, D. H.-L. Goh, K. Razikin, and A. Y. Chua. Tagging, Sharing and the Influence of Personal Experience. *Journal of Digital Information*, 10(1), Feb. 2009.
11. C. Marlow, M. Naaman, D. Boyd, and M. Davis. HT06, tagging paper, taxonomy, Flickr, academic article, to read. In *Proceedings of the seventeenth conference on Hypertext and hypermedia - HYPERTEXT '06*, pages 31–40, New York, New York, USA, Aug. 2006. ACM Press.
12. A. Mathes. Folksonomies - Cooperative Classification and Communication through Shared Metadata, 2004.
13. H. A. Olson and D. Wolfram. Syntagmatic relationships and indexing consistency on a larger scale. *Journal of Documentation*, 64(4):602–615, 2008.
14. I. Peters. *Folksonomies. Indexing and Retrieval in Web 2.0.* Knowledge and Information. De Gruyter, Berlin, 2009.
15. A. J. Quinn and B. B. Bederson. Human computation. In *Proceedings of the 2011 annual conference on Human factors in computing systems - CHI '11*, pages 1403–1412, New York, New York, USA, May 2011. ACM Press.
16. B. Sigurbjörnsson and R. van Zwol. Flickr tag recommendation based on collective knowledge. In *Proceeding of the 17th international conference on World Wide Web - WWW '08*, pages 327–336, New York, New York, USA, Apr. 2008. ACM Press.
17. J. Trant. Tagging, Folksonomy and Art Museums: Results of steve.museums research. Technical report, `http://conference.archimuse.com/jtrants/stevemuseum_research_report_available`, 2009.
18. R. Vuorikari. Can social information retrieval enhance the discovery and reuse of digital educational content? In *Proceedings of the 2007 ACM conference on Recommender systems - RecSys '07*, pages 207–210, New York, New York, USA, Oct. 2007. ACM Press.
19. R. Vuorikari and R. Koper. Evidence of Cross-boundary Use and Reuse of Digital Educational Resources. *International Journal of Emerging Technologies in Learning iJET*, 4(4):51–56, 2009.
20. R. Vuorikari, X. Ochoa, and E. Duval. Analysis of User Behavior on Multilingual Tagging of Learning Resources. In *Proceedings of the 1st Workshop on Social Information Retrieval for Technology Enhanced Learning, SIRTEL07*, pages 6–17, 2007.

Bodies in Critique: A Technological Intervention in the Dance Production Process

Erin A. Carroll
HCILab
University of North Carolina
at Charlotte
e.carroll@uncc.edu

Danielle Lottridge
Department of Communication
Stanford University
lottridg@stanford.edu

Celine Latulipe
HCILab
University of North Carolina
at Charlotte
clatulip@uncc.edu

Vikash Singh
HCILab
University of North Carolina
at Charlotte
vsingh7@uncc.edu

Melissa Word
Department of Dance
University of North Carolina
at Charlotte
melissa.word@gmail.com

ABSTRACT
The dance production process is strongly influenced within the physical rehearsal space by social context factors and dynamics, such as intimacy of bodies, gender distribution, and the hierarchy of choreographers and dancers. Introducing online tools for asynchronous collaboration can change the traditional dance production process and impact the social dynamics of the group. We developed and deployed the Choreographer's Notebook, a web-based, collaborative, multi-modal annotation tool used in the creative process of making dance. We collected usage logs and choreographer reflections on the use of this tool, along with conducting interviews and focus groups, from the interdisciplinary perspectives of both technologists and choreographers involved in the project. We describe the socio-technical impacts of the Choreographer's Notebook based on the results of its usage in three dance productions. We analyze these case studies through various contextual lenses and provide a visualization of how the choreographic correction process evolved.

Author Keywords
socio-technical principles, collaborative software, dance

ACM Classification Keywords
H.5.3 Information Interfaces and Presentation: Group and Organization Interfaces: Web-based interaction

General Terms
Human Factors

INTRODUCTION
Dance making is a social, embodied, creative process. The environment in which choreography emerges impacts the outcomes of the process in a variety of intricate ways. Just as the set of tools available determines the possible design space for any artist, the available resources and context in which dance is produced are major determining factors in its character and quality. The dance production process and the dance rehearsal studio have been and remain predominantly non-digital environments. Studio time provides critical support elements such as sprung marley floors, mirrored walls, ballet barres, and a floor-to-ceiling cyclorama. These are the 'technologies' of conventional dance practice. But studio time is a very limited and often expensive resource (in a poorly financed domain) and the best use of such space is to dance. Thus the interaction between choreographers and dancers has been predominantly synchronous, face-to-face within the rehearsal space, emphasizing physicality and movement. There has been little utility in the process for time spent sitting at a computer. Our collaboration in dance has led us to believe that dancers and choreographers have been less likely in the past to engage in extended computer interaction, favoring a more active and embodied life in general. However, with computing devices becoming increasingly pervasive in all aspects of life, dancers and choreographers are now using digital devices regularly.

Our goal is to enable dancers and choreographers to use technology to review, reflect, and comment on their current dance productions. As part of ongoing interdisciplinary research, we observed numerous occasions where dancers and choreographers would sit in a circle on the dance floor studio, communicating about aspects of the dance. We were curious about this practice, as we noted that a significant amount of studio time was spent in discussion rather than movement, which does not appear to be an effective use of dance studio resources. Our goal was to provide a means of communication and reflection about dance to occur outside of the studio, mediated through digital technology, which may free up more time in the studio for actual dancing. To this end, we developed and deployed the Choreographer's Notebook (ChoNo), a web-based, collaborative, multi-modal annotation tool used in the creative process of making dance.

Within the physical rehearsal space, the dance production process is strongly influenced by social context factors and dynamics, such as intimacy of bodies, gender distribution, and the hierarchy of choreographers and dancers. Introducing online tools for asynchronous collaboration can augment, enhance, and change the traditional dance production process. Socio-technical theory indicates that introducing a new technology will surely interact with existing social dynamics and practices [15]. Thus, the social context of dance making will influence how the tool is used, and the tool may in turn impact the social dynamics inside and outside the studio.

We previously introduced ChoNo from a technological perspective, where we described the development of the tool and how it differs from other video annotation systems [12]. In this current paper, we explore the socio-technical factors that shaped how ChoNo was used and how its usage impacted the social dynamics and other aspects of the dance production process. This paper contributes insights gained from using socio-technical lenses to analyze the emergent uses (and non-use) of ChoNo over three case studies of unique dance productions. The case studies are supported by domain perspective analysis from one of our principle users: a dancer and choreographer who used ChoNo in both roles, offering valuable understanding from both perspectives.

RELATED WORK

CSCW focuses on how human beings interact in and with various systems in the world [1], and a socio-technical perspective reveals how social systems and technology are treated together [15]. These perspectives provide insight into complex systems that require functioning software and hardware but also require supportive interactions with people that occur in particular places for diverse activities that exist within social contexts. Socio-technical phenomena are often identified in the context of in-depth field observations and challenge hidden assumptions about how people interact with technology. A rich viewing of the complex landscape of actors has been called 'interaction ecologies.' Suchman et al. used the ecology metaphor when proposing the necessary conditions for successful and innovative design: that new technology must work within an existing framework of situated technologies [14]. Nardi at al. described the information ecology of an intensive care unit, including relevant people (doctors, nurses, etc.), machines (monitors, probes, etc.), and information (medical data and instructions). Each of these sources influences the handling of patients [11]. Luff et al. used the term 'fractured ecologies' to describe design problems in communication technology [8]. We use socio-technical perspectives to better understand how our system is used in the world, which may then provide opportunities or necessities for improvement and change.

We draw from two core socio-technical principles relevant to this research: Trist's socio-technical systems approach [15] and Dourish's embodied interaction [3]. We also include five socio-technical perspectives identified as relevant to design [7]: situated action [13], peripheral awareness [4], routines and rhythms [2], co-adaptive systems [10], and distributed cognition [5]. Lottridge and Mackay caution that these five phenomena are not exclusive but provide actionable results. We discuss these five phenomena first.

Situated action describes human action as an emergent, spontaneous response to diverse aspects of any given situation at any given moment [13]. For example, you may have a plan for crossing a river on a canoe, however the actual steering does not resemble the plan; instead it is made of moment-to-moment behaviors that are responsive to the current location, waves, fatigue, etc. Heath and Luff's work on the London Underground control room brought to light the use of *peripheral awareness* in workgroups [4]. The operators' work was tightly integrated through constant awareness of the other's activities: through extra words uttered to the self, placement of artifacts to be within the visual range, and body language. The operators would conduct 'private' activities with subtle 'public' demonstrations so that co-located others could be kept aware of actions without prying in private space. Heath and Luff argued for HCI with seamless movement from private to public residuals of activities[4].

Rhythms and routines describe semi-predictable routines and respond to environmental rhythms, such as habits on weekdays versus weekends. Crabtree and Rodden studied how family members and activities shaped the use of mail in the home and found predictable patterns and actions [2]. For example, whoever comes home first brings the mail inside to a particular location, leaving an envelope addressed to a child at his/her 'place' at the dining table. *Co-adaptation* emphasizes how users adapt their behavior to meet the demands of technology, and they adapt the technology to their needs, sometimes in unforeseen ways that were unpredicted by the original designers [9, 10]. For example, email users redefined the basic email filter to create context-specific groups of rules that could be run at any time. The concept of *distributed cognition* applies the models of cognition beyond the confines of the physical skull to include groups of people, artifacts, places, and culture. Hutchins studied the coordinated work of Navy personnel engaged in navigation tasks [5]. He found that different members of the group understood and took responsibility for separate parts of the tasks. Artifacts were essential to the coordination of work, and members interacted with artifacts in different ways based on background and experience.

Embodied interaction changes the emphasis of study from abstract ideas and representations that may exist only theoretically to people's actions and phenomena occurring in the world. Embodied interaction goes further in highlighting the role of the body in those interactions. Dourish's work explains how interaction is physically and socially embodied and that ontology arises out of embodied activity [3]. Dourish calls upon the concept of phenomenology to support the emphasis of enquiry. One way to discuss systems in this light is with Heidegger's notion of ready-to-hand (for example, while interacting with windows using a mouse – the mouse is not

Figure 1. A screenshot of the Choreographer's Notebook, and the video loaded inside the tool is from a dance rehearsal. The pins above the timeline represent timestamps where comments have been added by the choreographer to give the dancers corrections.

consciously part of the activity) and present-at-hand (for example, when the mouse arrives at the edge of the mousepad and must be focused upon to be brought back to the center to continue the scrolling and selection activities).

Trist provides a wider perspective on socio-technical systems, focusing on the context of hierarchical production settings, the types of impacts of technological changes, and the output from the workers [15]. Trist's perspective was strongly influenced by his situated action research studies of social impacts on work brought about by technological changes that occurred in mining operations in the UK and Europe during the 1940s and 1950s. In fact, we adopted Trist's paradigm of Action Research in our work. Our interest in developing a tool to support choreography arises from years of interacting with dancers and choreographers through our project. Our team collaboratively designed interactive visualizations for dance productions; we were intimately involved as participants in the production process. The idea for an online dance annotation tool emerged from our observations of a lack of fit between the resources or 'technology' available and the needs of the participants. In particular, the technology was the dance studio: a specialized setting with sprung floors, mirrored walls, etc. We observed this studio being used like a boardroom with the dancers and choreographer sitting on the floor, engaged in discussions about what needs to be changed and improved from the last rehearsal. The dancers and choreographer need the studio resources to dance and explore movement, yet were unable to take full advantage of their time in the studio for movement purposes. Our goal was to introduce a new communication channel into the dance production process, which would exist outside of the studio, thus opening up more studio time for dancing and movement exploration

When introducing a new technology into an intricate creative process, we must be sensitive to unanticipated consequences. Dourish advocates: "the ability to develop systems that resonate with, rather than restrict, (or worse, refute) the social organization of action" [3]. Our goal was to apply socio-technical principles to not only better understand how the tool was used by dancers and choreographers but to also improve the tool and gain more awareness of the social organization of dance and the production process of making dance. This knowledge is intended to inform the development of features that resonate with and support the complexities of the dance production process.

CASE STUDIES OF CHOREOGRAPHER'S NOTEBOOK

The Choreographer's Notebook, or ChoNo, is a web-based, multi-modal annotation tool designed specifically for the dance community (Figure 1). It allows choreographers and dancers to collaborate with each other throughout the dance production process by creating temporal annotations that are associated with moments in dance rehearsal videos. The first version of the tool supported several types of annotation formats, including text and digital ink. Video annotations were also implemented, but were not deployed at the time of the case studies presented here. ChoNo provides visual, temporal indexing of annotations and rich navigational controls.

ChoNo has been used extensively by choreographers and dancers in the development of three full dance productions. All three dance pieces were modern dances, blending modern American dance with contemporary ballet. Each production lasted several months, and there were many variations across dance productions: from the number of dancers and choreographers involved to the length of each dance to how the choreography was developed (i.e. restaged versus new material). In this section, we describe how ChoNo was incorporated into the dance rehearsal process for three different productions. This is followed by a first-person analysis of ChoNo usage by Melissa Word, a dancer and choreographer who used ChoNo in both roles.

Figure 2. "An Instance Of...", Fall 2010

Figure 3. "In The Company Of Women", Fall 2010

Case Study 1: *An Instance Of...*
An Instance Of... was a 3 minute dance piece performed in Fall 2010. The movement material and concept for this piece was a collaborative effort between 3 dancers and 1 choreographer. The overall structure of the piece was (largely) developed during a summer 2010 dance/technology workshop for the Dance.Draw project [6]. While the choreography was developed, the choreographer filmed and uploaded each rehearsal to document the progress of the dance and edits that were made throughout the process. At this time, there was no immediate idea for when or in what capacity the dance would be performed; however, the material was recorded and uploaded to ChoNo so that it could be viewed and studied at any time. The development process of this dance needed to accommodate disparate dancer schedules that often prohibited all members from working in the studio together every rehearsal. For this reason, ChoNo's organized catalog of videos from previous rehearsals gave dancers and choreographers the ability to stay informed of choreographic changes that occurred while absent. When this dance was selected for the fall dance concert, ChoNo was used as a tool for memory refreshment between the formal dance rehearsals and for cleaning and refining movement.

Case Study 2: *In the Company of Women*
In The Company Of Women (Figure 3) was performed in Fall 2010 by 5 women as a re-staging of work originally choreographed and performed in 1993. The rehearsal director for this production was a member of the original choreographic team that created and performed this 22 minute work. This production was well suited for ChoNo, as the goal was not to generate new material but to embody previously created choreography in the most precise and efficient manner.

In this production, each rehearsal was filmed and uploaded to ChoNo to study and gage the progress that each dancer made in learning the nuances of the movement. The unfolding rehearsal process revealed three markedly different approaches to using ChoNo in order to support the needs of re-staging a dance. In the initial re-staging phase, the dancers studied video footage of the original cast to understand the broad structure of movement. While this was mostly done using DVDs, ChoNo was also used. This transitioned into the intermediate phase in which dancers compared their understanding of the movement to their ideal goal. To this end, dancers rehearsed their parts in real-time while projecting the original video footage behind them on a floor-to-ceiling cyclorama. This was then filmed and uploaded to ChoNo and used as a comparative study to clearly see the discrepancies between the original footage and the live dancer. The third phase primarily consisted of cleaning and detailing the fully learned and embodied movement of the re-staged dance. At this phase, the choreographer accessed ChoNo to post detailed commentary for individual coaching purposes. Used in this capacity, ChoNo provided the opportunity for both the choreographer and the dancers to spend as much time as they desired in improving the individual performance of dancers and the quality of the piece as a whole.

Figure 4. "The Angled Angels Assembly", Spring 2011

Case Study 3: *The Angled Angels Assembly*
The Angled Angels Assembly was performed in Spring 2011 as part of the Dance.Draw project [6] by 7 dancers and was about 13 minutes long. The creation process was a highly intensive workload, as it involved 2 choreographers. The main objective was to deeply explore how to create a highly integrated meeting point between projected visualizations and moving bodies in the space. Because of the need for communication between the dancers, dance makers, and technologists, it was imperative for this production to redesign the conventional rehearsal space. This meant that the time and attention traditionally devoted to creating, editing, and cleaning dance material would no longer be an exclusive exchange between dancer and choreographer but would be an environment to give equal collaborative weight to the technologists. In the new working environment, ChoNo was a resource for choreographers to film and review rehearsals during the creation period of this production. ChoNo provided a mutual space for the choreographers to process and synthesize what happened in each rehearsal; which due to the multiple parties involved, was often a chaotic and sensorily overwhelming process. Rehearsals were recorded weekly, and video was typically recorded with a Flip Cam and uploaded to Chono by one of the choreographers.

The Choreographer's Perspective

In this section, we offer the direct writing from a choreographer and dancer, which describes personal and social issues surrounding the video recording of bodies. As this section explores a deeply personal topic, we felt that it was best expressed from a choreographer and dancer's perspective, in her own voice. Melissa Word is an artistic researcher and choreographer for the project, who recently graduated with a BA in Dance. She has worked as dancer, choreographer, sound designer, and production assistant on our project. As one of two dance specialists on the team, she is intimately acquainted with the implications of bringing technology into the conventional dance rehearsal and performance space. She has closely observed the effects that technology has had on the psychological, emotional, and social norms of the dancers and choreographers involved in project productions. The following commentary illustrates these effects and how they altered her initial assumptions of what ChoNo might do to the traditional rehearsal model.

An early concern that I (and Choreographer Sybil Huskey) had with using ChoNo, was the proviso that each rehearsal must be filmed in order to create a running catalog of uploaded video footage. While this is a simple and seemingly harmless task, the act of recording dancers working in the creative process for every rehearsal, and then requiring they view this footage, is highly deviant from the traditional rehearsal model. There was an additional concern that this might be potentially destructive to a comfortable learning environment. This is the case for several reasons.

There is an inherent dichotomy within the psychology of dancers. Performers possess an innate confidence and excitement at the notion of being watched by an observer. Conversely, dancers as performers use their bodies alone as their tool of expression, understanding that audience gaze is the primary means of experiencing their performance. This concept alone dramatically shapes the psychology of dancers by setting an unspoken precedent that the way a dancer looks, while still and in motion, is of utmost importance. The extensive attention and emphasis placed on the body often breeds feelings of self-consciousness and a skewed body image among dancers. Furthermore, as the field of dance performance is overwhelmingly dominated by females, dancers face the additional pressure to be hyper critical of their bodies under the influence of a media-driven, consumerist culture that idolizes the feminine ideal through unattainable fabrications of beauty.

Initially, I was apprehensive about introducing a video camera into the rehearsal process, where these emotions and personal dynamics are already well-entrenched. I was concerned that a permanent record of every move, every mistake, and every physical and verbal exchange that occurred between dancers and choreographer might disturb the creative working environment in which body language and tone of voice serve to mitigate the potentially negative effects on the dancer mentality. I was further concerned with what might result from asking dancers to watch this video footage of themselves on a regular basis. In fully understanding the context of dancers as their worst, most obsessive critic, I wondered if it would be possible to ask dancers to objectively watch footage of themselves and glean corrections, either given by a choreographer or through personal assessment, without superimposing their own ego. There is a natural disconnect that exists between the kinesthetic feedback that a dancer has while moving and the visual feedback a dancer gets from watching a two-dimensional representation of that movement. Given this, I wondered if a dancer could remove the lens of personal body image issues to see the bigger picture of how he/she fits into the overall design of the work.

In working with ChoNo in multiple productions, both as a dancer and choreographer, my initial concerns about the psycho-social effects on dancers were greatly assuaged. When I worked as a dancer I found that the fixed obligation to watch video of myself after every rehearsal for a specific, task-based purpose, forced me to get over myself, so to speak, and sequester my ego for the common good of bettering the work. This is done by reading, understanding, and embodying corrections specific to the dancer's interpretation of choreography, and is given by an external source, the choreographer. Additionally, I realized that video, for all the apprehension it elicits, can be an invaluable tool for bettering the technique and performance of the individual. This is done through self-obtained feedback once the dancer learns to view video objectively. I observed through my long term use of ChoNo that this learning curve is facilitated by the task-based nature of the program. ChoNo does not ask dancers to watch video of themselves exclusively, as this obligation alone would likely unfold into a negative situation with self-loathing dancers. Instead, ChoNo asks dancers to watch themselves with annotated constructive corrections and reinforcements. This ultimately results in the opportunity, proportionate to a dancer's investment in ChoNo, to exponentially improve oneself as a dancer and contribute to the rate of improvement of the performance as a whole.

ANALYSIS

Socio-technical principles call for recognition of the complex web of elements that influence how ChoNo is incorporated in the dance production process. As described earlier, new technology is introduced into an existing 'ecology' of technologies which influence how the new technology is used. Dancers and choreographers embody actions and make meaning based on their own perspectives and interactions with the systems, their peers, and the world. The socio-technical principles sensitized us to examine how choreographers and dancers interpreted and experienced the technology and the dance making process, instead of trying to identify facts and measuring changes. In this section, we discuss the technological context, the social context, and the activity context, describing notable uses of ChoNo in relation to those social-technical elements. Our insights were derived from analysis of focus groups with dancers, interviews with choreographers, observations during rehearsals, and team reflection.

Technological Context

Dance rehearsals happen in the dance studio, and as previously mentioned, the dance studio is the most critical technology for dance with its sprung floors and mirrored walls. Prior to ChoNo, when the choreographer of our project wanted to review rehearsal video, this process involved dancers watching videos in the dance studio and taking notes. Sometimes the choreographer would give dancers a DVD, but other times, an analog video camera and TV were used in studio to review. After the introduction of ChoNo, this video review process was seldom used.

ChoNo is situated within an existing set of communication channels, such as email and texting. The technology to support ChoNo consisted of computer hardware to access the web application, video cameras to record rehearsals, and video software (such as iMovie) to compress and export recorded videos to the appropriate format. ChoNo was primarily accessed through laptops and personal computers from different locations, such as campus, home, and in the dance studio during some rehearsals. When used during rehearsals, projectors were used by the choreographer within the dance studio. Our experience taught us that this complex interconnected web of technology can break down at unexpected points. For example, we encouraged the choreographers to film their own rehearsals to investigate how this role might be shared and changed. When the resolution of the video was very high, this caused slow uploads and downloads that compromised the reliability of the entire system.

ChoNo in the Dance Studio

We anticipated that ChoNo would be primarily used remotely, as a form of asynchronous communication between choreographers and dancers. As the socio-technical principles of *situated action* and *co-adaptation* suggest, other behaviors emerged. We examine these unanticipated actions for embodied goals and needs, and we reflect on how choreographers chose to take advantage of the resources available. In the rehearsal space, the choreographer chose to spend time projecting ChoNo and going through the annotated comments in more detail with the dancers, allowing for discussion and clarification. It is clear that the choreographers understand the benefits of a physical rehearsal space. When the choreographic clarifications occur in a physical space, they can be quickly followed by physical practice. Dancers use peripheral vision of other dancers in the same space, performing similar or timed movements to learn the choreography. This attention to temporal proximity and physical embodiment was highly valued, as these tasks could have been offloaded to be outside the studio in a different form.

This use of ChoNo impacted the behavior of dancers. At each rehearsal, there were generally 2-3 out of the 6 dancers that brought their laptop to the dance studio. They voluntarily brought them for two reasons: to catch up if they had not reviewed all the comments on ChoNo and to use as a resource for reviewing and practicing movement when the choreographer was busy. This was surprising as dancers had not brought laptops to rehearsals in the past.

Projecting ChoNo During Dance

Because *In the Company of Women* was a re-staged performance, dancers had the opportunity to learn the material from video of the original dance. We observed a *situated action* that made extremely effective use of ChoNo in the rehearsal space: the choreographer projected the video of the original dance production behind the dancers as they learned the movements (Figure 1). Dancers used *peripheral awareness* in the physical space to keep in synchronicity with the projected dancers in the video. On a few occasions, the videographer filmed the dancers as they danced in front of the original video and then uploaded that video to ChoNo. Dancers said that this was useful, and one dancer noted:

> [They showed] the video of the original dancers on the back while we danced it, and then we could watch it on the Choreographer's Notebook. I found that helpful because then I could watch both at the same time, and I could see if I was late at a certain part, or learning it – it helped me learn my part and clean at the same time.

Technology Failure

On a few occasions, dancers had trouble accessing videos on ChoNo. The choreographer then opted to send comments to the dancers via email. The notes sent via email were extremely detailed because there was no video available to provide context. One interpretation is that the choreographer had become comfortable with entering text-based corrections and communicating with dancers asynchronously. She appeared to simply switch from ChoNo to another form of computer-mediated communication (CMC). Another lens of interpretation is the new *rhythm* for provision of feedback. ChoNo offloaded some of the in-person feedback given during rehearsal to outside of rehearsal. Choreographers and dancers were then accustomed to transmitting feedback in between rehearsals. Waiting until the next rehearsal would interrupt this new rhythm. During focus groups, dancers voiced that they felt the choreography was proceeding slowly, which can be interpreted as getting used to this new accelerated speed of development. Prior to ChoNo, the use of CMC for corrections would be rare. This choreographer reported that she relied on the ability to inform dancers of corrections online and expected dancers to internalize these corrections before the next rehearsal. These expectations are part of a very strong social context of use.

Social Context

Social context factors are relevant to all aspects of living and working, and they are manifested in particular ways within dance making. There is a hierarchy between dancers and the choreographer, and this hierarchy is embodied in how communication and action is executed and perceived. The historical power structure remains intact today. The choreographer is the artistic director, and he or she tells the dancers what to do: gives corrections, manages rehearsal times, and generally makes all decisions related to the dance production. Through years of experiences, dancers and choreographers experience their roles and the cultural norms that define appropriate behavior between peers and between dancers and choreographers. Phenomenology and *embodied interaction* sensitized us to observing and enquiring about the experiences of the social effects of the introduction of ChoNo. With ChoNo, new social actors entered the scene, for example, a videographer often filmed the dance rehearsals. While a formal videographer was not used in our project, this role was generally held by a technologist or the choreographer. Dancers reported that they felt the technologists were kind and polite but that they also felt observed.

Workload Impacts

Similar to Trist's review of the introduction of technology into various workplaces, it seemed likely that ChoNo would increase the workload associated with the dance production. We anticipated that the choreographers would utilize the ability to provide corrections offline and expect the dancers to come to the rehearsal with the corrections embodied. We also predicted that the dancers and choreographers may resent the extra time demanded by this new work. The choreographers did find the provision of corrections useful, and they sometimes found that entering comments was time consuming. It is noteworthy that the team never imposed demands in terms of how much time should be spent entering comments. One interpretation is that the nature of ChoNo and the project itself, created an unspoken imperative to use ChoNo to the fullest; ChoNo was always available for analyzing the videos instant by instant, and providing careful corrections to the dancers. From the dancer's perspective, there was a mix of appreciation for the ways in which ChoNo changed the process. While dancers agreed that using ChoNo required more time, there was positive feedback from *In the Company of Women*:

> To have the opportunity that someone was coming to film us every other day, that was kind of a luxury... for it to be so accessible. There was probably one or two times where I felt like, 'Oh no, I didn't do my homework' ... because it was something I wanted to be doing once I knew it was there.

There was some negative feedback from *Angled Angels*. During this production, large file sizes caused some reliability issues. Further, this choreography required a large floor space to rehearse, and dancers were unable to embody corrections discovered online. The dancers felt upset that they did not meet the expectations of their choreographers.

Video Recordings

There were many subtle, yet important, social dynamics at play in the rehearsal space: dancers have reservations about watching themselves on video, and having a videographer physically present in the rehearsal space changed their locus of awareness. In the first two case studies, a member of our technology team attended the rehearsals to capture the video. This person was typically male, entering a world that consisted exclusively of female dancers and choreographers in the 3 productions we described. Having an extra body in the rehearsal space who is observing initially made some dancers self-conscious. The dancers eventually became accustomed to this person, but it did change the nature of this intimate environment.

The dancers noted that the presence of the observer and the camera caused them to step up their performance. One interpretation is that the record of this run-through would be permanently available on ChoNo, another is that the videographer is viewed as an audience member in that dancers are stimulated to have more awareness of their performance. Another factor is that the technology increased the formality of the run-through, perhaps even heightening expectations for quality. The choreographers using ChoNo noted that this increase in dancer effort was critically valuable and led to higher quality performance.

Hierachies

Through the focus groups, interviews and observations, we became more sensitive to the power hierarchies in the conventional dance production process, in which the choreographer is in charge and giving most of the directions and corrections. Through ChoNo, we observed this hierarchy reified the ways in which the system was used. ChoNo was designed to be flexible and open-ended to allow for *co-adaptation*: it had one interface for all users; and it provided identical interfaces and functions for dancers and choreographers. The dancers and choreographers *could have* commented the same amount, yet we noted that almost all comments were made by the choreographers, and the comments posted by dancers were typically questions. Dancers explained that while in the physical rehearsal space they might advise or correct each other occasionally and would sometimes work together on movement in pairs or small groups, but they did not feel comfortable correcting one another through ChoNo. The permanence of the comments overemphasized them. There was a greater chance of misinterpretation because of the lack of physical body language available to provide context and softness. It should be noted that the dancers were never explicitly encouraged to comment on each others movements or form. In fact, social action (or the intentional lack of action) seemed to solidify these roles. These clear patterns of use suggest that different interfaces for dancers and choreographers might be appropriate.

Activity Context

The use of ChoNo for several kinds of activities were anticipated, such as for learning new choreographic material; self-corrections, in which dancers watched the rehearsal videos and noted issues about their own dancing that needed to be addressed; and cleaning/detailing, in which the choreographers made notes about corrections and rehearsal. ChoNo usage was greatly influenced by the phase of the production; we observed patterns based on *rhythms and routines* [2]. The early phase of production primarily consisted of creative editing. In the middle-phase, creative editing tapers off as choreographic decisions are made and the amount of cleaning-related comments and corrections grow. During the final phase of production, the choreographer uses ChoNo for positive feedback. This last usage switch is influenced by the timing and social dynamics of the production phase. In terms of timing, corrections require effort from dancers to internalize and embody through muscle memory. During production week, there is no more time to internalize more corrections. It is not useful or constructive to receive corrections when they cannot be internalized. It may even be frustrating to dancers to receive more corrections when they cannot embody them, as then they perceive their performances as imperfect and flawed. Moreover, *rhythms and routines* suggest that people develop patterns in space and time concerning their use of a new tool or technology. In these case studies, dancers and choreographers reported that they developed habits in how they accessed ChoNo, rooted in relation to other timed routines, such as entering comments during breakfast, launching ChoNo along with Facebook, and reviewing ChoNo before the Friday rehearsal.

Creative Editing

While the choreography was already developed for all three productions prior to using ChoNo, we observed that the choreographers used the tool to make creative decisions that impacted the dance production. The following comment exemplifies creative edits made during *An Instance Of...*

> [Dancer1], what happens if you come in between [Dancer2] and [Dancer3]? Looks like you really have to work to get upstage.

ChoNo provided a different representation of the dance for dancers/choreographers to consider and reflect on. Having a synchronous and embodied conversation with the ChoNo video as a shared artifact enabled the group to discuss ideas and create shared understanding through immediate feedback in terms of gestures and tone of voice.

Positive Feedback

In addition to providing critiques, choreographers used ChoNo to provide positive feedback to the dancers. This occurred later in the production process, when a dance became more polished, and also when a dancer made noticeable improvements. As performance week approached, the choreographer would transition from cleaning to providing positive reinforcement, such as:

> Very good job dancers. You should feel very confident in your performances since your work is more consistent with each performance. (From *In the Company of Women*)

The choreographer directed specific comments towards dancers that improved movements that were previously identified as needing more work "[Dancer], That promenade was much stronger. Good!" While comments like this were more frequent near performance week, this type of feedback also occurred earlier in the process.

Cleaning/Correction and Learning

ChoNo was designed as a tool for cleaning and detailing movements, and this is how it was often used. Because *In the Company of Women* was a re-staged dance production, it was important to precisely embody the previous choreography. The choreographer considered ChoNo extremely valuable in the success of this production because it allowed cleaning to occur outside of rehearsals. This was beneficial because the dance production cycle was very short, yet there was 22 minutes of choreography to learn. Some examples of cleaning from *In the Company of Women* include:

> Relax neck so head comes into chest before roll and then really register that position with the leg extended in the back.

> Remember to keep the feelings of weight in your arms as you lift them up, maybe go a bit slower too.

Dancers primarily used ChoNo in order to access feedback that the choreographer left for them. Typically, this involved logging into ChoNo, watching the rehearsal video, and reading comments that were applicable to them. Most dancers did not make comments in response to the feedback. In the focus group, one dancer explained, "When it came to the corrections myself, I feel like I didn't make notes on [ChoNo] very often. I just kind of internalized what I saw needed to be fixed," and other dancers agreed with this explanation.

ChoNo was also used for learning choreography. In *An Instance Of...* there was a gap in time from when the choreography was developed to when rehearsals began, and there were also different dancers involved. As a result, ChoNo was used to learn the choreography for the first time, or in the case of some dancers, to re-learn the material. Since *In the Company of Women* was a re-staged performance, dancers learned this choreography by watching a video of the original production. Most of the learning for this production took place outside of ChoNo by watching it on DVD. Using these alternative technologies in the 'ecology of technology of ChoNo' made sense for a few reasons: the 22 minute long dance was a large file that took a long time to load in ChoNo, thus it was faster and easier to use the familiar technology of DVD players. In the focus group, dancers also explained that ChoNo lacked necessary features, such as full screen and slow motion, in order to learn the material. Many of these features have been since added to ChoNo.

Correction Process

ChoNo was intended to move some of the rehearsal discussion outside of the dance studio to online communication. We visualized the changes in Figure 5, based on distributed cognition models [5]. The visualization was co-created with the choreographers. First, a subset of authors proposed a draft of the visualization, which was shared with the choreographers to discuss and alter to better reflect their perspective and embodied reality. Not only did the choreographers adjust the visualization in terms of how knowledge flowed through people and technology, they modified the language to more accurately match their own lexicon and terms.

From a distributed cognition perspective, ChoNo acted as an external archive. The interaction changed based on who accessed ChoNo and where it was accessed: dancers and choreographers embodied different roles for inputting or learning from the system, and tasks changed whether they were accessing it at home (personal use) or in the studio (group viewing to support shared understanding).

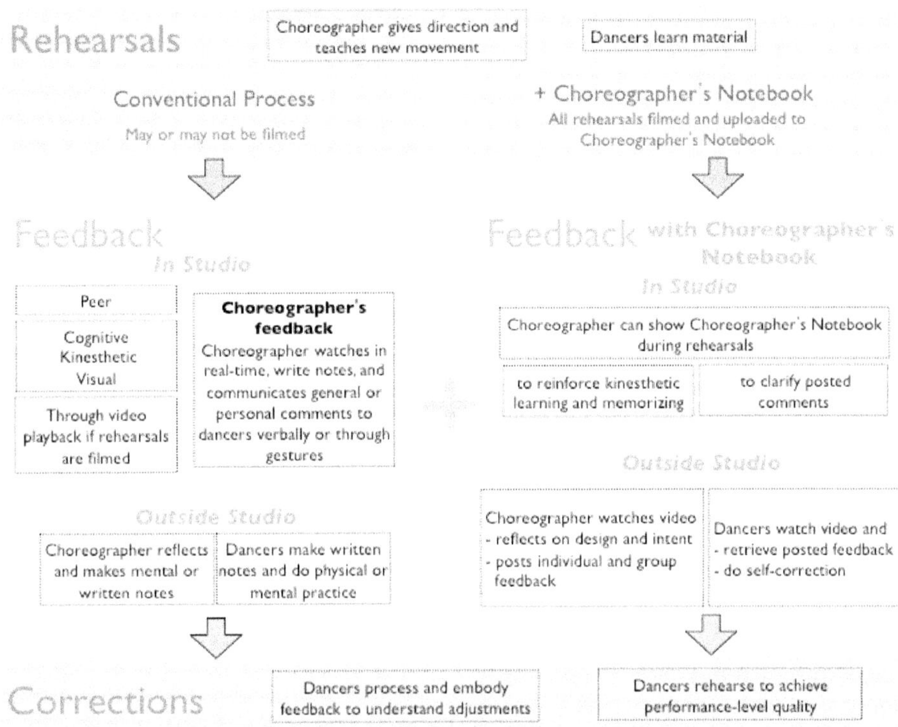

Figure 5. We visualize the conventional rehearsal process (left) and show how it evolved when ChoNo is introduced (left + right).

In a conventional rehearsal process, most activities related to dance correction and creative editing take place inside the dance studio. Dancers learn new material based on the directions of the choreographer. Choreographers may film the rehearsal but generally opt not to make any video recordings available to dancers. Instead, they prefer to watch the dancers in real-time, while making notes in a notebook. Comments, both general and personal, are communicated to the dancers. Inside the studio, dancers receive various forms of feedback from the choreographer and from their peers: cognitive and kinesthetic feedback from the way their body responds to their movements; visual feedback from their peripheral vision watching themselves in the mirrored wall; and often visual feedback from watching peers by their side. When rehearsal is over, the choreographer and dancers leave the studio. Outside the studio, the choreographer reflects and makes mental or written notes for the next scheduled rehearsal. The dancers practice, either physically or mentally, and they go over any written notes taken during the last rehearsal. Dancers use all of these feedback sources to understand the necessary adjustments to refine their movement.

The introduction of ChoNo in the rehearsal process provides another representation of feedback to the choreographer and the dancers. In the studio, the dancers often end the rehearsal with a full run-through of the material that has been learned so far. This material is filmed, and the video is uploaded to ChoNo. Outside the studio, the choreographer watches the recorded rehearsal video and posts comments directed to individuals or groups of dancers. The availability of the rehearsal video helps the choreographer to reflect on the overall design and intent of the piece. Dancers watch the rehearsal video and retrieve comments posted by the choreographer. Although it is not possible to practice the corrected movements in the absence of the marley floor, dancers make mental notes about the corrected movements, visualize these movements, and come prepared for the next rehearsal as much as possible, given practice space and embodiment constraints. During the next rehearsal, the choreographer can show ChoNo in the studio to clarify the posted comments.

The use of ChoNo in the rehearsal process adds an additional layer of feedback to the existing conventional rehearsal process: video and annotated comments. These representations benefit choreographers by making choreographic cleaning and creative editing available outside of the studio. The process of making rehearsal videos and commentary encourages the dancers to be more prepared for rehearsals. One of our choreographers described ChoNo as providing dancers with the "personal attention and coaching as if it was a solo." She further explained that she doesn't have enough studio time to give individual coaching in real-time to each dancer, especially when there are 6 dancers in one piece. Through ChoNo, individual coaching is more efficient: it can take place outside of the studio, while she is "sitting in her jammies with her coffee."

DISCUSSION AND CONCLUSION

In this research, we used socio-technical principles as lenses to examine how socio-technical elements influenced the usage of ChoNo and its effects on 3 full productions. The analysis of our case studies, focus groups and choreographic commentaries revealed insights across modes of use, unexpected uses, workload impacts, and social dynamics. The theme of psycho-social adjustment was explored from the personal perspective of a dancer-choreographer on the project. Her perspective provided observations, perceptions, and reflections of the rich psycho-social landscape of the dancers' experiences with ChoNo – personal issues that are often hidden and difficult to discuss. The insights from this analysis led to the development of a visualization of how the choreographic correction process changed with ChoNo.

The socio-technical principles allowed us to attend to different aspects of the system interaction, which we may not have been sensitive to otherwise. In Trist's work, examining traditional material production settings, the output was a separate entity from the workers. We have seen that performance settings are distinctly different. There is no technological intervention that would render the workers in a performance (the dancers, actors, or musicians) obsolete, or even lead to minimizing their roles. The output in dance and theater performance are the bodies, voices, movements of these workers, and cannot be decoupled from them: *they* are the output. Similarly, the supervisors in this context (choreographers or theater directors) are the creative force behind the output. Thus, the concern is not so much about minimizing or over-specifying an individual's role. Rather, the bigger concern introduced by ChoNo is workload, since like so many other forms of CMC, it blurs the lines between work and home life, allowing work to bleed out of the studio and into the outside life of the dancer and choreographer. Performance work can always be improved: there is no obvious stopping point ahead of opening night, and so the provision of this type of technology amplifies the demands of the work.

Analysis of ChoNo using socio-technical lenses led to a number of design changes. First, to better match the social environment of the dance production process in which choreographers soften dancer corrections with tone of voice and body language, we have implemented audio and video commenting modalities. To better match the activity of choreographic learning, we have added slow-motion playback, as well as looping handles that allow dancers to specify a segment of video to repeatedly loop over. To address the strong roles that we observed in the usage of ChoNo, we are working towards implementing a role-based access system that would provide different functionality to dancers and choreographers.

Complex systems of technologies, people, places, activities, and social contexts shaped how Choreographer's Notebook was used within 3 full dance productions. We investigated these systems through a set of socio-technical perspectives to better understand how the use of a novel tool plays out within the intricate, creative act of producing dance. Through this process of analysis, we gained a deeper understanding of the dynamics between these diverse socio-technical elements. We offer insights into these systems and processes, to foster the thoughtful development of useful and effective tools that support dance productions.

ACKNOWLEDGMENTS

This work was funded by the NSF CreativeIT (#IIS-0855882). We thank the dancers, choreographers, and other collaborators who have participated in Dance.Draw.

REFERENCES

1. L. J. Bannon and K. Schmidt. CSCW: Four characters in search of a context. In *Proceedings of CSCW '89*, pages 3–16, 1989.
2. A. Crabtree and T. Roddin. Domestic routines and design for the home. *Computer Supported Cooperative Work*, 13(2), 2004.
3. P. Dourish. *Where the Action Is: The Foundations of Embodied Interaction*. MIT Press, Cambridge, MA, USA, 2004.
4. C. Heath and P. Luff. Collaboration and control: Crisis management and multimedia technology in London Underground Line Control Rooms. *Computer Supported Cooperative Work*, 13(1):24–48, 1992.
5. E. Hutchins. *Cognition in the wild*. MIT Press, Cambridge, USA, 1995.
6. C. Latulipe, E. A. Carroll, and D. Lottridge. Evaluating Longitudinal Projects Combining Technology with Temporal Arts. In *Proceedings of ACM CHI '11*, pages 1835–1844. ACM Press, May 2011.
7. D. Lottridge and W. Mackay. Generative walkthroughs: Support for creative redesign. In *Proceedings of Creativity & Cognition '09*, 2009.
8. P. Luff, C. Heath, H. Kuzuoka, J. Hindmarsh, K. Yamazaki, and S. Ovama. Fractured ecologies: Creating environments for collaboration. *Human-Computer Interaction*, 18:51–84, 2003.
9. W. Mackay. Responding to cognitive overload: Co-adaptation between users and technology. *Intellectica*, 30(1), 2000.
10. W. Mackay. The interactive thread: Exploring methods for multi-disciplinary design. *Proceedings of DIS '04*, pages 103–112, 2004.
11. B. A. Nardi and V. L. O'Day. *Information Ecologies: Using Technology with Heart*. MIT Press, Cambridge, USA, 1999.
12. V. Singh, C. Latulipe, E. Carroll, and D. Lotridge. The choreographer's notebook - a video annotation system for dancers and choreographers. In *Proceedings of ACM Creativity & Cognition 2011*, pages 197–206, 2011.
13. L. Suchman. *Plans and Situated Actions: The Problem of Human-Machine Communication*. Cambridge University Press, Cambridge, UK, 1987.
14. L. Suchman, J. Blomberg, J. Orr, and R. Trigg. Reconstructing technologies as social practice. *American Behavioral Scientist on Analyzing Virtual Societies: New Directions in Methodology*, 43(3):392–408, 1999.
15. E. L. Trist. *Perspectives on Organizational Design*, chapter The evolution of socio-technical systems, pages 19–75. Wiley, New York, NY, 1981.

SynTag: A Web-based Platform for Labeling Real-time Video

Yen-Chia Hsu **Tay-Sheng Jeng** **Yang-Ting Shen** **Po-Chun Chen**
Interactive Architecture Laboratory, Department of Architecture,
National Cheng Kung University, Tainan, Taiwan
{N76994017, tsjeng, N78941044, PA6984029}@mail.ncku.edu.tw
+886-6-275-7575 ext. 54158

ABSTRACT
Real-time video streaming has been widely used in multimedia learning environments. As production of online videos is increasing exponentially, it is becoming more difficult for users to reach relevant content. In this paper, we propose SynTag, a web-based platform that enables users to label three types of tags—*Good*, *Question*, and *Disagree*—and to make comments synchronously and asynchronously with visualization of time-stamp video previews on an interactive timeline. SynTag generates real-time thumbnails by using real-time tags for presenters to receive instant feedback and for other users to retrieve presentation videos. In a pilot study, we found our users' tagging behaviors significantly different when they were in lecture events or discussion events. We envision that enabling users to apply tags in real-time will help reduce the complexity of classification of videos.

Author Keywords
Timeline Visualization; Collaborative Tagging.

ACM Classification Keywords
D.0 **[Software]**: General; J.4 **[Computer Applications]**: Sociology; H.5.1 **[Multimedia Information Systems]**: Video; H.5.2 **[User Interfaces]**: Graphical user interfaces, Interaction styles, Screen design, User-centered design; H.3.1 **[Content Analysis and Indexing]**: Indexing methods; H.3.3 **[Information Search and Retrieval]**: Information filtering, Relevance feedback, Retrieval models; H.3.5 **[Online Information Services]**

General Terms
Algorithms; Design; Experimentation; Human Factors.

MOTIVATION
Many learning environments record videos, but they lack efficient tools to record the interactions. The traditional education process tends to give students knowledge but not to encourage them to express their feedbacks, especially those which are implicit. This leads to information loss. Even if the feedbacks can be stored, most environments do not establish the relationships between audience feedbacks and the video. Even if presentations can be recorded properly, the current environments still lack an appropriate user interface for visualizing results. As a result, the retrieval process is complicated and time-consuming. People may need to spend tremendous time searching through videos aimlessly.

This paper focuses on the problem of how to reduce the complexity of indexing video content by labeling video presentations in real time through a web-based platform in today's multimedia learning environments.

Related Work
Some studies have addressed reducing the complexity of video classification by automatically or semi-automatically tagging the content in videos [1, 2]. However, SynTag uses collaborative tags as metadata which are designed to assist users with locating specific instances in a given resource [3]. Social tags yield an effective retrieval process, whereas automatically generated metadata do not [4]. As Marlow et al. [5] indicate, users attempt to express their opinions through the tags.

Similar research on video- or audio-sharing systems has allowed users to make real-time tags manually [6, 7]. The EVA system [8] lets users assign collaborative tags to video key frames to enable efficient retrieval. Unlike these systems, SynTag provides instant feedback to the presenter through a thumbnail. The visualization of tags makes it easier for presenters to track audience feedback instantly. SynTag also provides timeline visualization for archived timestamps and displays the density of tags inside timestamps. Timelines connote a story rather than simply a logical collection [9].

METHOD

The SynTag System
In this paper, we propose a software named SynTag (ialab.tw/legenddolphin/TagDisplay16/TagDisplay16.html), written in Flex and AmCharts (www.amcharts.com). It can record and broadcast videos, alternate between two cameras,

sort events, and visualize tagging results in timestamps. SynTag has three significant functions:

1. Collaborative Synchronous Tagging Scenario

In this scenario, users can react to the presentation by expressing their feedback in real time. SynTag allows three types of tags—*Good*, *Question*, and *Disagree*—allowing users to express positive, neutral, or negative feedback. We use only three simple tag types because we do not want listeners to be distracted while making tags. If listeners want to give more feedback, they can make comments. SynTag can parse comments and checks whether hyperlinks are included (e.g., http://www.google.com) by regular expressions. If so, SynTag immediately adds hyperlink nodes on the "hyperlink" curve. Listeners can click on a node and link to the hyperlink in a new browser window.

Figure 1. The screenshots of the tagging scenario's interface. Lecturing service (left) records videos and can alternate between two cameras. Listeners use broadcasting service (right) to watch live video and make tags.

2. Chronological Sorting Algorithm and Instant Feedback

SynTag first stores the information from tags in an array. The event title and description are stored in tag[0] and tag[1]. While tagging, SynTag stores the tags' properties, which include video ID, user ID, the time a tag was posted, the type of tag, and the tag content in tag[i+1], tag[i+2], tag[i+3], tag[i+4], and tag[i+5]. The variable *i* represents the last index of the tag array.

Second, SynTag evaluates the tag counter. If the difference between the current tagging time and the previous one is less than 10 seconds, SynTag adds a 1 to the tag counter for the type of tag node on the thumbnail. Otherwise, SynTag updates the last tagging time to the current one, resets the associated tag counter, adds 1 to the counter, and creates a new tag node on the thumbnail to provide instant feedback to the presenter.

3. Timeline Visualization

Finally, SynTag archives the results of collaborative labeling on a timeline to enable video retrieval (Figure 2, left). The color of timestamps represents the density of tags inside the timestamp. The darker the timestamp, the denser the tags inside. The timeline shows the information in timestamps when a user rolls the mouse cursor over the timeline. When users click on a timestamp, SynTag shows the content (Figure 2, right). Users can retrieve the presentation video by using the real-time tagging thumbnail inside timestamps below the video frame. For example, a user would like to watch the video segment at second 33 because he finds that there are many "Disagree" tags at that point. He can click the time node at second 33 on the thumbnail, and SynTag will adjust the video time bar to play the video segment at that point. Users can quickly watch the video segment without searching the entire video. SynTag also offers an asynchronous tagging scenario.

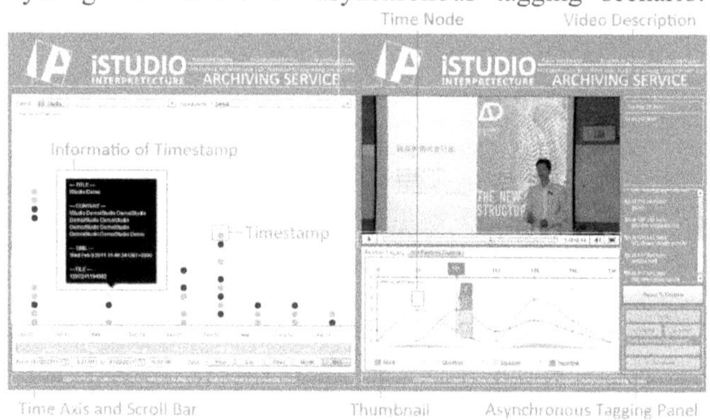

Figure 2. The screenshots of the interface of the archiving service. The timeline (left) shows all events in chronological order. The timestamp (right) shows the representation of the event and enables retrieval.

Participants

Two different types of participants are included in this study: presenters and listeners. Presenters are professors who hold lectures or students, alumni, and scholars who work in the design field. Listeners are presenters, teachers, students, and remote audiences anywhere in the world who are interested in the presentation.

Procedure

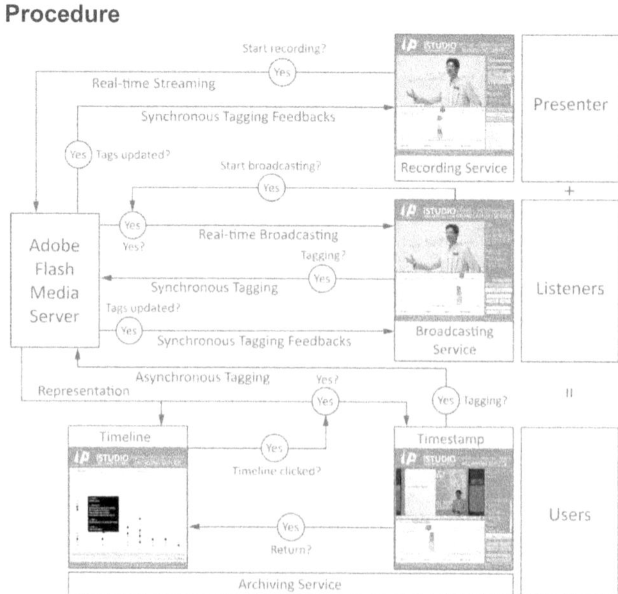

Figure 3. The procedure of SynTag.

Before beginning the recording, we asked 10 listeners willing to use SynTag to join the pilot study. The presenter then set up cameras and links to the lecturing service, entered information, and started recording. SynTag streams videos to the server for broadcasting. Listeners linked to the broadcasting service, started watching the live video, and expressed their feedback through SynTag.

During the recording, SynTag ran the sorting algorithm to add nodes to the tag curve on the thumbnail in real time. The presenter could monitor the thumbnail and respond to listeners' instant feedback, for example, by adjusting the speed of his presentation.

After the presentation, anyone could link to the archiving service and apply tags asynchronously or retrieve particular video segments by clicking time nodes on the thumbnail to adjust the video time bar.

Analysis

We recorded 51 videos from January 26 to March 31, 2011. Of these videos, 4 were lectures, 3 were discussions, and others were demonstrations and tests. In this pilot study, we collected 7 recordings of lectures and discussions. The videos are analyzed by three steps:

1. In Table 1, we classify event types and calculate the scale and total time of the event, the numbers of tags, and the effective peaks as shown in Figure 4 on the thumbnail visualization for video content indexes with the number of tags exceeding 70% of the number of people using SynTag.

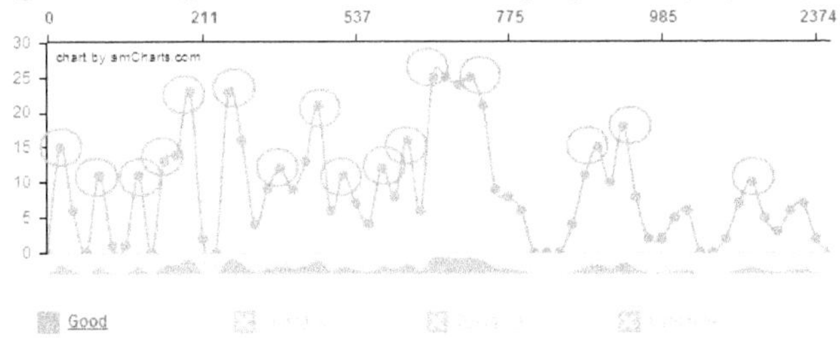

Figure 4. The circles indicate effective peaks.

2. In Table 2, we calculated the percentage of associated number of tags and the effective peaks in different events.

	Type	Description	Date	Scale	Presenter	Listener	Total number of			Tags/ min
							Time(min)	Tags	Effective Peaks	
A	Disc.	lab meeting	Mar 2	S	graduates	graduates	19.90	214	8	10.75
B		lab meeting	Mar 2	S	graduates	graduates	68.03	768	29	11.30
C		TED Tainan	Mar 29	M	students	students	177.77	366	12	2.06
D	Lect.	design lecture	Mar 1	S	teacher	sophomore	24.57	207	4	8.42
E		design lecture	Mar 10	M	alumni	sophomore	30.82	136	4	4.41
F		official speech	Mar 25	L	professor	citizens	20.24	279	10	13.78
G		official speech	Mar 25	L	professor	citizens	40.96	590	16	14.40
Average							54.61	365.71	11.86	6.70

Table 1. The properties of events. Ten listeners used SynTag in each event. *Lect.* and *Disc.* in type column represent lecture and discussion. *S*, *M*, and *L* scales represent approximately 15-20, 30-35, and 60-70 persons, respectively.

	Type	% of associated number of tags				% of associated number of effective peaks			
		Good	Que.+Dis.	Question	Disagree	Good	Que.+Dis.	Question	Disagree
A	Disc.	43.93	52.34	52.34	0.00	50.00	50.00	50.00	0.00
B		46.74	50.00	50.00	0.00	48.28	51.72	51.72	0.00
C		46.45	48.90	19.67	29.23	41.67	58.33	25.00	33.33
D	Lect.	85.50	6.28	6.28	0.00	75.00	25.00	25.00	0.00
E		74.26	5.15	5.15	0.00	100.00	0.00	0.00	0.00
F		71.68	13.26	11.83	1.43	90.00	10.00	10.00	0.00
G		91.53	3.56	1.02	2.54	100.00	0.00	0.00	0.00

Table 2. The analysis of different types of tags. *Que.+Dis.* on the top row represents combined Question and Disagree tags.

3. In Table 3, we calculated the p value (two-tailed) of two event types (lecture and discussion) by using student's t test.

Tag	% of associated number of tags	% of associated number of effective peaks
Good	0.001518531	0.001707755
Que.+Dis.	1.61673E-05	0.001707755

Table 3. The p value (two-tailed) of lecture events and discussion events in student's t test.

RESULTS

First, we found our users' tagging behaviors during lectures to be significantly different from those during discussions (the p values in student's t test in Table 3 being less than 0.05). As shown in Table 2, listeners applied more *Question* and *Disagree* tags during discussions while they tended to apply *Good* tags more during lectures. The differences between the percentages of *Good* tags and combined *Question* and *Disagree* tags during discussion events are much less than the differences during lecture events. This differentiates the characteristics of discussions and lectures.

Second, the values in the right-most column in Table 1 indicate that listeners using SynTag expressed feedback by making 6.70 tags per minute on average. We found that those people using SynTag were more willing to tag in large lectures and small discussions than in small lectures and medium discussions.

DISCUSSION AND FUTURE WORK

First, some presenters said that it may cause pressure for them to receive instant feedback through SynTag. However, we think it important for presenters to receive instant feedback from listeners and to respond by adjusting the content, the speaking speed, and manner of illustrating ideas, thereby improving the quality of a presentation.

Second, some listeners said that SynTag in some degree causes distraction at the live site because users tag by clicking buttons. The problem with the tagging methods could be improved by applying tangible interactions or pattern recognition, such as scanning spaces with webcams.

Third, SynTag is currently constrained in terms of the type of tags and tagging methods. An interpreter that can parse data from sensor networks and analyze human activities in specific spaces will be needed to augment the ability of SynTag. By applying the interpreter, SynTag would have the potential to assign videos attributes, classifying them in several sets and defining the relationships between them, thus making the retrieval process more efficient.

CONCLUSION

SynTag externalizes listeners' feedback through collaborative tagging (6.70 tags per minute on average), represents the presentation process in an algorithm, provides instant feedback to the presenter, and makes the retrieval process easier through viewing thumbnails and timelines. By applying users' real-time tags, SynTag can identify discussions and lectures (p values < 0.05 in Table 3), thereby reducing the complexity of video classification.

ACKNOWLEDGMENTS

This work was supported by the TOUCH Center and Taiwan National Science Council grant No. NSC100-2221-E-006-224.

REFERENCES

1. Bartolini, I., Patella, M., & Romani, C. (2010). Shiatsu: Semantic-based hierarchical automatic tagging of videos by segmentation using cuts. *Proceedings of the Third International Workshop on Automated Information Extraction in Media Production* (pp. 57–62).
2. Ballan, L., Bertini, M., Bimbo, A. D., Meoni, M., & Serra, G. (2010). Tag suggestion and localization in user-generated videos based on social knowledge categories and subject descriptors. *Proceedings of the Second ACM SIGMM Workshop on Social Media.*
3. Hill, J. R., & Hannafin, M. J. (2001). Teaching and learning in digital environments: The resurgence of resource-based learning. *Educational Technology Research and Development, 49*(3), 37–52.
4. Melenhorst, M., Grootveld, M., Setten, M. van, & Veenstra, M. (2008). Tag-based information retrieval of video content. *Proceedings of the First International Conference on Designing Interactive User Experiences for TV and Video* (pp. 31–40). ACM. Retrieved April 1, 2011, in press. CHI 2002, ACM Press (2002), 1-8.
5. Marlow, C., Naaman, M., Davis, M., & Hall, S. (2006). HT06, tagging paper, taxonomy, Flickr, academic article, to read. *Proceedings of the Seventeenth Conference on Hypertext and Hypermedia* (pp. 31-39).
6. Renduchintala, A., Kelkar, S., John, A., & Seligmann, D. D. (2007). Designing for persistent audio conversations in the enterprise. *Proceedings of the 2007 Conference on Designing for User Experiences.*
7. Topkara, M., Pan, S., Lai, J., Wood, S. P., Boston, J., & Heights, Y. (2010). Tag me while you can: Making online recorded meetings. Science, 25038.
8. Volkmer, T., Smith, J. R., & Natsev, A. P. (2005). A web-based system for collaborative annotation of large image and video collections: An evaluation and user study. *Proceedings of the Thirteenth Annual ACM International Conference on Multimedia* (pp. 892–901).
9. Moraveji, N., Ahmad, S., Kita, C., Chen, F., & Kamvar, S. (2011). Weblines : Enabling the Social Transfer of Web Search Expertise using User-Generated Short-form Timeline. CSCL 2011.

Author Index

www.ingramcontent.com/pod-product-compliance
Ingram Content Group UK Ltd.
Pitfield, Milton Keynes, MK11 3LW, UK
UKHW051420290926
15471UKWH00009B/1702

9 781450 319362